PANORAMA

Introducción a la lengua española

FOURTH EDITION

José A. Blanco

Philip Redwine Donley, Late
Austin Community College

VISTA
HIGHER LEARNING

Boston, Massachusetts

The cover of **PANORAMA, Fourth Edition,** features *Elogio del Horizonte* (In Praise of the Horizon) by the Spanish artist Eduardo Chillida Juantegui. The abstract sculpture overlooks the sea from the northern city of Gijón, in Spain. This is one of many places in the Spanish-speaking world that you will learn about in **PANORAMA.**

Publisher: José A. Blanco

Managing Editors: Deborah Coffey (Print), Paola Ríos Schaaf (Technology)

Senior Consulting Editor: Armando Brito

Project Manager: Lauren Krolick (Technology)

Editors: Darío González (Technology), Egle Gutiérrez (Technology), Carolina Zapata

Production and Design Director: Marta Kimball

Cover Design: Susan Prentiss

Design and Production Team: Manuela Arango, María Eugenia Castaño, Oscar Diez, Paula Díez, Mauricio Henao, Jhoany Jiménez, Sónia Teixeira, Lilliana Uribe, Andrés F. Vanegas García, Nick Ventullo

Student Text ISBN: 978-1-61767-705-2

Instructor's Annotated Edition ISBN: 978-1-61767-709-0

1 2 3 4 5 6 7 8 9 TC 16 15 14 13 12 11

Printed in Canada

Instructor's Annotated Edition

Table of Contents

The Vista Higher Learning Story
Your Specialized Foreign Language Publisher

Independent, specialized, and privately owned, Vista Higher Learning was founded in 2000 with one mission: to raise the teaching and learning of world languages to a higher level. This mission is based on the following beliefs:

- It is essential to prepare students for a world in which learning another language is a necessity, not a luxury.
- Language learning should be fun and rewarding, and all students should have the tools necessary for achieving success.
- Students who experience success learning a language will be more likely to continue their language studies both inside and outside the classroom.

With this in mind, we decided to take a fresh look at all aspects of language instructional materials. Because we are specialized, we dedicate 100 percent of our resources to this goal and base every decision on how well it supports language learning.

That is where you come in. Since our founding in 2000, we have relied on the continuous and invaluable feedback from language instructors and students nationwide. This partnership has proved to be the cornerstone of our success by allowing us to constantly improve our programs to meet your instructional needs.

The result? Programs that make language learning exciting, relevant, and effective through:

- an unprecedented access to resources
- a wide variety of contemporary, authentic materials
- the integration of text, technology, and media, and
- a bold and engaging textbook design

By focusing on our singular passion, we let you focus on yours.

The Vista Higher Learning Team

VISTA
HIGHER LEARNING

31 St. James Avenue Boston, MA 02116-4104 TOLLFREE: 800-618-7375
TELEPHONE: 617-426-4910 FAX: 617-426-5209 www.vistahigherlearning.com

Getting to Know PANORAMA

Now in its Fourth Edition, **PANORAMA** is better than ever. Its fresh, student-friendly approach to introductory Spanish makes both teaching and learning easier, more enjoyable, and more successful. The pedagogical approach of **PANORAMA** continues to be communicative. It presents vocabulary and grammar as tools for effective personalized communication as it develops students' listening, reading, writing, and speaking skills. Moreover, because cultural knowledge is an integral part of both language learning and successful communication, **PANORAMA** introduces students to all of the countries in the Spanish-speaking world and the everyday lives of Spanish speakers.

 PANORAMA offers features that make it truly different from other textbooks based on these same principles. Here are a few of our distinguishing features:

- **PANORAMA** and its parent textbook, **VISTAS,** were the first textbooks to integrate a dramatic video into the student text to model target structures. The hugely successful original **Fotonovela** has been replaced with an exciting, brand-new video for the Fourth Edition. It has the same goal as the original: to motivate and inspire the next generation of Spanish students.

- **PANORAMA** and **VISTAS** were also the first introductory college Spanish textbooks to incorporate graphic design—page layout, use of colors, typefaces, and other graphic elements—as an integral part of the learning process. To enhance learning and make navigation easy, lesson sections are color-coded and appear either completely on one page or on spreads of two facing pages. The textbook pages themselves are also visually dramatic.

- **PANORAMA** offers student sidebars with on-the-spot linguistic, cultural, and language-learning information, as well as **recursos** boxes with on-page correlations of student supplements, increasing students' comfort level and saving them time.

- **PANORAMA** provides a unique four-part practice sequence for virtually every grammar point. It moves from form-focused **¡Inténtalo!** exercises to directed, yet meaningful, **Práctica** exercises to communicative, interactive **Comunicación** activities, and lastly to cumulative, open-ended **Síntesis** activities.

- **PANORAMA** also offers two cultural videos, **Flash cultura** and **Panorama cultural,** as well as authentic TV clips and new short films in **En pantalla.**

- The **PANORAMA** Supersite now offers even more support for both students and instructors, with an intuitive, user-friendly interface and tools to simplify and enhance course management, gradebook, and reporting. Students can access all of the program's multimedia components, select activities from the textbook with auto-grading, plus additional Web activities; instructors can access a powerful course management system as well as all the instructor resources. For more information on the Supersite, turn to page xxv.

Before you delve into the remainder of the front matter in your Instructor's Annotated Edition (pages IAE-6 – IAE-16) and to learn about the **NEW!** features in the Fourth Edition, familiarize yourself with the following pages of the Student Text front matter: page iii (To the Student), pages xii–xxiv (**PANORAMA** At-A-Glance), page xxv (Supersite), pages xxvi–xxviii (Video Programs), and pages xxix–xxx (Icons and Ancillaries).

Getting to Know Your Instructor's Annotated Edition

PANORAMA, Fourth Edition, offers you the most thoroughly developed Instructor's Annotated Edition ever written for introductory college Spanish. The IAE features reduced student text pages, overprinted with answers, and a wealth of teaching resources in the side and bottom panels. The annotations complement and support varied teaching styles, extending the already rich content of the student textbook and reducing the time you spend on class preparation and course management.

This section is designed as a quick orientation to the principal types of instructor annotations you will find in the **PANORAMA 4/e** IAE. As you familiarize yourself with them, it is important to keep in mind that the annotations are merely suggestions. Any Spanish questions, or simulated instructor-student exchanges are not meant to be prescriptive. You are encouraged to view these suggested "scripts" as flexible points of departure that will help you achieve your instructional goals.

NEW! Icons

For your ease of use, the suggestions in the side and bottom panels have been labeled with **NEW!** icons if they elicit one of the modes of communication.

- →👤← **Interpretive communication** (Input) These exercises target students' reading or listening skills by assessing comprehension of something they have read or heard.

- ←👤→ **Presentational communication** (Output) These suggested contexts require students to produce a written or verbal presentation in Spanish.

- 👤↔👤 **Interpersonal communication** (Two-way) These suggestions provide students with opportunities to speak Spanish in simulated real-life contexts or in personalized communication with others.

For a teaching tip to be labeled with one of these icons, the activity must require students not only to work with Spanish at discourse level (meaning at least three sentences or exchanges) but also to maintain the context, focus, or topic throughout the activity. As with the activities in the student text, many of the teaching options require more than one mode of communication; in these cases the mode that is best represented in the "product" of the activity is the one that is reflected in the icon. For example, if students are asked to talk to a classmate (interpersonal) and write a summary of the conversation (presentational), the written summary is the product, and the icon will therefore reflect the presentational mode of communication.

On the Lesson Opener Pages

- **Lesson Goals** A list of the lexical, grammatical, and socio-cultural goals of the lesson, including language-learning strategies and skill-building techniques

- **A primera vista** Questions related to the photograph for jump-starting the lesson

- **Instructional Resources** A correlation to all student and instructor supplements available to reinforce the lesson

In the Side Panels

- **Section Goals** A list of the goals of the corresponding section

- **Instructional Resources** A correlation to student and instructor ancillaries

- **Teaching Tips** Suggestions for recycling language, leading into the corresponding section, working with materials, and carrying out specific activities

- **Expansion** Expansions and variations for the activities in the student textbook
- **Script** Transcripts of the audio and video recordings
- **Possible Conversation** Answers based on known vocabulary, grammar, and language functions that students might produce
- **Video Recap** Questions to help students recall the events of the previous lesson's **Fotonovela** episode
- **Video Synopsis** A summary of each lesson's **Fotonovela** episode
- **Expresiones útiles** Suggestions for introducing upcoming **Estructura** grammar points incorporated into the **Fotonovela** episode
- **Estrategia** Suggestions for working with the reading, writing, and listening strategies presented in the **Lectura, Escritura,** and **Escuchar** sections, respectively
- **Tema** Ideas for presenting and expanding the writing assignment topic in **Escritura**
- **El país en cifras** Additional information expanding on the data presented for each Spanish-speaking country featured in the **Panorama** sections
- **¡Increíble pero cierto!** Curious facts about a lesser-known aspect of the country featured in the **Panorama** sections
- **Section-specific Annotations** Suggestions for presenting, expanding, varying, and reinforcing individual instructional elements, including the sidebars in the student text (**¡Atención!, Ayuda, Nota cultural,** etc.)
- **Successful Language Learning** Strategies to enhance students' language-learning experience
- **The Affective Dimension** Suggestions for reducing students' language-learning anxieties

In the *Teaching Options* Boxes

- **Extra Practice, Pairs, Small Groups,** and **Large Groups** Additional activities intended to supplement those in the student textbook
- **Game** Games that practice the language of the section and/or recycle previously learned language
- **TPR** Total Physical Response activities that engage students physically in learning Spanish
- **Variación léxica** Extra information related to the **Variación léxica** boxes in **Contextos,** terms that come up in **Lectura,** and terms from the Spanish-speaking countries featured in **Panorama**
- **Worth Noting** More detailed information about an interesting aspect of the history, geography, culture, or people of the Spanish-speaking countries in **Panorama**
- **Heritage Speakers** Suggestions and activities tailored to heritage speakers, who in many colleges and universities are enrolled in the same introductory courses as non-heritage speakers
- **Video** Techniques and activities for using the **PANORAMA** video program
- **Evaluation** Rubrics for grading students' work in **Escritura**

> The **PANORAMA** Supersite provides additional instructor materials for each lesson. Visit **vhlcentral.com** for extra activities, supplemental vocabulary, assessment materials, and more!

General Teaching Considerations

Orienting Students to the Student Textbook

Because **PANORAMA 4/e** treats graphic design as an integral part of students' language-learning experience, you may want to take a few minutes to orient students to the student textbook. Have them flip through one lesson, and point out that all lessons are organized exactly the same way. Also point out how the major sections of each lesson are color-coded for easy navigation: red for **Contextos**, purple for **Fotonovela**, orange for **Cultura**, blue for **Estructura**, green for **Adelante**, and gold for **Vocabulario**. Let them know that, because of these design elements, they can be confident that they will always know "where they are" in their textbook.

Emphasize that sections are self-contained, occupying either a full page or a spread of two facing pages, thereby eliminating "bad breaks" and the need to flip back and forth to do activities or to work with explanatory material. Finally, call students' attention to the use of color to highlight key information in elements such as charts, diagrams, word lists, and activity models, titles, and sidebars.

Flexible Lesson Organization

PANORAMA 4/e uses a flexible lesson organization designed to accommodate diverse teaching styles, institutions, and instructional goals. For example, you can begin with the lesson opener page and progress sequentially through a lesson. If you do not want to devote class time to grammar, you can assign the **Estructura** explanations for outside study, freeing up class time for other purposes like developing oral communication skills; building listening, reading, or writing skills; learning more about the Spanish-speaking world; or working with the video program. You might decide to work extensively with the **Cultura** and **Adelante** sections in order to focus on students' reading, writing, and listening skills and their knowledge of the Spanish-speaking world. Or, you might prefer to use these sections periodically in response to your students' interests, as the opportunity arises. If you plan on using the **PANORAMA** Testing Program, however, be aware that the quizzes, tests, and exams check language presented in **Contextos**, **Estructura**, and the **Expresiones útiles** boxes on the **Fotonovela** spread.

Identifying Active Vocabulary

All words and expressions taught in the illustrations and **Más vocabulario** lists in **Contextos** are considered active, testable vocabulary. Any items in the **Variación léxica** or **Así se dice** boxes, however, are intended for receptive learning and are presented for enrichment only. The words and expressions in the **Expresiones útiles** boxes in **Fotonovela**, as well as words in charts, word lists, **¡Atención!** sidebars, and sample sentences in **Estructura** are also part of the active vocabulary. At the end of each lesson, **Vocabulario** provides a convenient one-page summary of the items students should know and that may appear on tests and exams. Point this out to students and tell them that an easy way to study from **Vocabulario** is to cover up the Spanish half of each section, leaving only the English equivalents exposed. They can then quiz themselves on the Spanish items. To focus on the English equivalents of the Spanish entries, they simply reverse this process.

Taking into Account the Affective Dimension

While many factors contribute to the quality and success of learning experiences, two factors are particularly germane to language learning. One is students' beliefs about how language is learned; the other is language-learning anxiety.

As studies show and experienced instructors know, students often come to modern language courses either with a lack of knowledge about how to approach language learning or with mistaken notions about how to do so. For example, many students believe that making mistakes when speaking the target language must be avoided because doing so will lead to permanent errors. Others are convinced that learning another language is like learning any other academic subject. In other words, they believe that success is guaranteed, provided they attend class regularly, learn the assigned vocabulary words and grammar rules, and study for exams. In fact, in a study of college-level beginning language learners in the United States, over one-third of the participants thought that they could become fluent if they studied the language for only one hour a day for two years or less. Mistaken and unrealistic beliefs such as these can cause frustration and ultimately demotivation, thereby significantly undermining students' ability to have a successful language-learning experience.

Another factor that can negatively impact students' language-learning experience is language-learning anxiety. As Professor Elaine K. Horwitz of The University of Texas at Austin and Senior Consulting Editor of **PANORAMA 1/e** wrote, "Surveys indicate that up to one-third of American foreign language students feel moderately to highly anxious about studying another language. Physical symptoms of foreign language anxiety can include heart-pounding or palpitations, sweating, trembling, fast breathing, and general feelings of unease." The late Dr. Philip Redwine Donley, **PANORAMA** co-author and author of articles on language-learning anxiety, spoke with many students who reported feeling nervous or apprehensive in their classes. They mentioned freezing when called on by their instructors or going inexplicably blank when taking tests. Some so dreaded their classes that they skipped them or dropped the course.

PANORAMA contains several features aimed at reducing students' language anxiety and supporting successful language-learning. Its highly structured, visually dramatic design was conceived as a learning tool to make students feel comfortable with the content and confident about navigating the lessons. The Instructor's Annotated Edition includes *Affective Dimension* annotations with suggestions for managing and/or reducing language-learning anxieties, as well as *Successful Language Learning* annotations with learning strategies for enhancing students' learning experiences. In addition, the student text provides a wealth of helpful sidebars that assist students by making relevant connections with new information or reminding them of previously learned concepts.

Student Sidebars

¡Atención!	Provides active, testable information about the vocabulary or grammar point
Ayuda	Offers specific grammar and vocabulary reminders related to a particular activity or suggests pertinent language-learning strategies
Consulta	References related material introduced in previous or upcoming lessons
¡Lengua viva!	Presents relevant information on everyday language use
Nota cultural	Provides a wide range of cultural information relevant to the topic of an activity or section

General Suggestions for Using the NEW! PANORAMA *Fotonovela* Video

PANORAMA, Fourth Edition, features a brand-new **Fotonovela**. The instructional design surrounding it, however, remains true to the original program. The **Fotonovela** section in each lesson of the student textbook and the **PANORAMA** Fotonovela Video were created as interlocking pieces. All photos in this section are images from the corresponding video module, while the printed conversations are abbreviated versions of the video module's dramatic segment. Both the **Fotonovela** conversations and their expanded video versions represent comprehensible input at the discourse level; they were purposely written to use language from the corresponding lesson's **Contextos** and **Estructura** sections. Thus, as of **Lección 2**, they recycle known language, preview grammar points students will study later in the lesson, and, in keeping with the concept of "i + 1," contain a small amount of unknown language.

You can use the **Fotonovela** Video and corresponding textbook section in many ways. For instance, you can use the **Fotonovela** spread as an advance organizer, presenting it before showing the video module. You can also show the video module first. You can even use **Fotonovela** as a stand-alone, video-independent section. You might decide to show all video modules in class or to assign them solely for viewing outside of the classroom. You could begin by showing the first one or two episodes in class so students gain familiarity with the characters, storyline, style, and **Resumen** sections. After that, you could work in class only with the **Fotonovela** pages and have students view the remaining episodes outside of class. For each episode, there are **¿Qué pasó?** activities in the **Fotonovela** section of the corresponding textbook lesson and video activities in the Video Manual section of the **PANORAMA 4/e** Workbook/Video Manual and on the Supersite.

You might also want to use the **Fotonovela** Video in class when working with **Estructura**. You could play parts of the dramatic episode that demonstrate the grammar point you are teaching or show selected scenes that review old grammar points and ask students to identify them. In class, you could play the parts of the **Resumen** section that exemplify individual grammar points as you progress through each **Estructura** section. You could also wait until you complete an **Estructura** section and review it by showing the corresponding **Resumen** section in its entirety.

No matter which approach you choose, students have ample materials to support viewing the video independently and processing it in a meaningful way. We hope you and your students will continue to find the **Fotonovela** Video and corresponding materials to be an engaging and effective tool for language-learning.

For more information on the new **Fotonovela** Video, see pages xxvi—xxvii.

General Suggestions for Using the *Panorama cultural* and *Flash cultura* Videos

The **Panorama cultural** video contains documentary and travelogue footage of each country featured in the lesson's **Panorama** section. The **Flash cultura** video expands on an aspect of the lesson theme in the format of a news broadcast. Like the conversations in the **Fotonovela** video, these video segments deliver comprehensible input. Each was written to make the most of the vocabulary and grammar students learned in the corresponding and previous lessons, while still providing a controlled amount of unknown language.

Activities for the **Flash cultura** and **Panorama cultural** videos are located in the Video Manual section of the **PANORAMA 4/e** Workbook/Video Manual and on the Supersite. They follow a process approach of pre-viewing, while-viewing, and post-viewing and use a variety of formats to prepare students for watching the video segments, to focus them while watching, and to check comprehension after they have watched the footage.

When showing the videos in class, you might also want to implement a process approach. You could start with an activity that prepares students for the video segment by taking advantage of what they learned in previous lessons. This could be followed by an activity that students do while you play certain parts or all of the video segment. The final activity, done in the same class period or in the next one as warm-up, could recap what students saw and heard and expand on the video segment's topic. The following suggestions for working with the **Flash cultura** video in class can be carried out as described or expanded upon in any number of ways.

Before viewing

- After students have practiced the lesson's vocabulary and grammar and worked through the **Cultura** section of the student textbook, mention the video segment's title and ask them to guess what the segment might be about.

- Have pairs make a list of the lesson vocabulary they expect to hear in the video segment.

- Read the class a list of true/false or multiple-choice questions about the video. Students must use what they learned in the **Cultura** section to guess the answers. Confirm their guesses after watching the segment.

While viewing

- Show the video segment with the audio turned off and ask students to use lesson vocabulary and structures to describe what is happening. Have them confirm their guesses by showing the segment again with the audio on.

- Have students refer to the list of words they brainstormed before viewing the video and put a check mark in front of any words they actually see in the segment.

- First, have students simply watch the video. Then, show it again and ask students to take notes on what they see and hear. Finally, have them compare their notes in pairs or groups for confirmation.

- Download the segment's Videoscript from the Supersite and create cloze paragraphs by omitting words and expressions related to the lesson theme. Distribute the scripts and have pairs or groups complete the sentences.

After viewing

- Have students say what aspects of the cultural information presented in their textbook appear in the video segment.

- Ask groups to write a brief summary of the content of the video segment. Have them exchange papers with another group for peer editing.

- Ask students to discuss any aspects of the featured country and topic of which they were unaware before watching. Encourage them to explain why they did not expect those aspects to be true of the country in question.

- Have students pick one characteristic about the country and topic that they learned from watching the video segment. Have them research additional information about that topic and write a brief composition that expands on it.

For more information on the complete **PANORAMA** video program, see pages xxvi–xxviii of the Student Text.

PANORAMA and the *Standards for Foreign Language Learning*

The *ACTFL Proficiency Guidelines* were first published in 1982 and, ever since, that document and its subsequent revisions have influenced the teaching of modern languages in the United States. **PANORAMA** and its parent book, **VISTAS,** were written with the concerns and philosophy of the *ACTFL Proficiency Guidelines* in mind, incorporating a proficiency-oriented approach from its planning stages.

The pedagogy of **PANORAMA** and **VISTAS** was also informed from its inception by the *Standards for Foreign Language Learning in the 21st Century*. First published in 1996 under the auspices of the National Standards in Foreign Language Education Project, the Standards are organized into five goal areas, often called the Five Cs: Communication, Cultures, Connections, Comparisons, and Communities.

Since **PANORAMA** takes a communicative approach to the teaching and learning of Spanish, the Communication goal is central to the student text. For example, the diverse formats used in **Comunicación** and **Síntesis** activities—pair work, small group work, class circulation, information gap, task-based, and so forth—engage students in communicative exchanges, providing and obtaining information, and expressing feelings and emotions. New to the Fourth Edition, icons in the Instructor's Annotated Edition now also clearly signal annotations that meet this Communication goal.

The Cultures goal is most evident in the lessons' **Cultura** sections, **Nota cultural** student sidebars, and **En pantalla, Flash cultura,** and **Panorama** sections, but **PANORAMA** also weaves culture into virtually every page, exposing students to the multiple facets of practices, products, and perspectives of the Spanish-speaking world. In keeping with the Connections goal, students can connect with other disciplines such as geography, history, fine arts, and science in the **Panorama** section; they can acquire information and recognize distinctive cultural viewpoints in the non-literary and literary texts of the **Lectura** sections. The **Estructura** sections, with their clear explanations and special *Compare & Contrast* features, reflect the Comparisons goal. Students can work toward the Connections and Communities goal when they do the **Cultura** and **Panorama** sections' **Conexión Internet** activities, as well as the activities and information on the **PANORAMA** Supersite. In addition, special Standards icons appear on the student text pages of your IAE to call out sections that have a particularly strong relationship with the Standards. These are a few examples of how **PANORAMA** was written with the Standards firmly in mind, but you will find many more as you work with the textbook and its ancillaries.

COURSE PLANNING

PANORAMA was developed with an eye to flexibility and ease of use in a wide variety of course configurations. The program can be used in courses taught on a semester or quarter system, and in courses that complete the book in two or three semesters. Here are some sample course plans that illustrate how to use **PANORAMA** in a variety of academic situations. Visit the **PANORAMA** Supersite (vhlcentral.com) for more course planning tips and detailed suggestions. You should, of course, feel free to organize your courses in the way that best suits your students' needs and your instructional objectives.

Two-Semester System

This chart illustrates how **PANORAMA** can be completed in a two-semester course. This division of material allows the present and the present progressive, including reflexive verbs, and the preterite tense to be presented in the first semester; the second semester focuses on the imperfect tense, the subjunctive, and the perfect tenses, as well as the future and the conditional.

Semester 1	Semester 2
Lecciones 1–7	Lecciones 8–15

Three-Semester System

This chart shows how **PANORAMA** can be used in a three-semester course. The lessons are equally divided among the three semesters, allowing students to absorb the material at a steady pace.

Semester 1	Semester 2	Semester 3
Lecciones 1–5	Lecciones 6–10	Lecciones 11–15

Quarter System

This chart shows one way to configure the **PANORAMA** materials in three balanced segments for use in the quarter system, allowing ample time for learning and review in each quarter.

First Quarter	Second Quarter	Third Quarter
Lecciones 1–5	Lecciones 6–10	Lecciones 11–15

LESSON PLANNING

PANORAMA has been carefully planned to meet your instructional needs, whether you teach on a semester or quarter system and whether you plan to use the textbook for two or three semesters or over three quarters. Vocabulary presentations and grammar topics have been methodically designed for maximum instructional flexibility.

The lesson plan presented here is not prescriptive. You should feel free to present lesson materials as you see fit, tailoring them to your own teaching preferences and to your students' learning styles. You may, for example, want to allow extra time for concepts students find challenging. You may want to allot less time to topics they comprehend without difficulty, or to group topics together when making assignments. Based on your students' needs, you may want to omit certain topics or activities altogether. If you have fewer than five contact hours per week each semester or are on a quarter system, you will find the **PANORAMA** program very flexible: simply pick and choose from its array of instructional resources and sequence them in the way that makes the most sense for your program.

The following lesson plan for **Lección 1** illustrates how **PANORAMA 4/e** can be used in a two-semester program with five contact hours per week. It deals with order of presentation rather than specific instructional techniques and suggestions because those are provided in the **IAE** annotations.

Sample Lesson Plan for *Lección 1*

Day 1

1. Introduce yourself and present the course syllabus.
2. Present the **Lección 1** objectives.
3. Preview the **Contextos** section; present the **Contextos** vocabulary.
4. Work through the **Práctica** activities with the class; have students read over the **Comunicación** activities for the next class.
5. Preview the **Fotonovela** and **Expresiones útiles**.
6. Have students read through the **Fotonovela** and prepare the first **¿Qué pasó?** activity for the next class.

Day 2

1. Review **Contextos** vocabulary; have the class do the **Comunicación** activities.
2. Present the **Fotonovela** and **Expresiones útiles**.
3. Do the first **¿Qué pasó?** activity with the class.
4. Have students do the next three **¿Qué pasó?** activities.
5. Preview the **Pronunciación** section and **Estructura 1.1**.
6. Have students read **Estructura 1.1** and prepare the **¡Inténtalo!** and **Práctica** activities for the next class.
7. Have students read **En detalle** in **Cultura** and prepare the first activity for the next class.

Day 3

1. Review the **Expresiones útiles**.
2. Do the first **Cultura** activity with the class.
3. Present the remaining **Cultura** features and have students do the activities.
4. Present **Estructura 1.1**.
5. Work through the **¡Inténtalo!** and **Práctica** activities with the class.

6. Have students do the **Comunicación** activity in class.
7. Preview **Estructura 1.2**.
8. Have students read **Estructura 1.2** and prepare the **¡Inténtalo!** and **Práctica** activities for the next class.

Day 4

1. Review **Estructura 1.1**.
2. Present **Estructura 1.2** and work through the **¡Inténtalo!** and **Práctica** activities.
3. Have students do the **Comunicación** activities during class.
4. Preview **Estructura 1.3**.
5. Have students read **Estructura 1.3** and prepare the **¡Inténtalo!** and **Práctica** activities for the next class.

Day 5

1. Review **Estructura 1.2**.
2. Present **Estructura 1.3** and work through the **¡Inténtalo!** and **Práctica** activities.
3. Have students do the **Comunicación** activities during class.
4. Preview **Estructura 1.4**.
5. Have students read **Estructura 1.4** and prepare the **¡Inténtalo!** and **Práctica** activities for the next class.

Day 6

1. Quickly review **Estructura 1.3**.
2. Present **Estructura 1.4** and work through the **¡Inténtalo!** and **Práctica** activities.
3. Have students do the **Comunicación** activities and the **Síntesis** activity.
4. Assign material from the **Adelante** section as desired for integrated practice and review.

Day 7

1. Go over assigned material from the **Adelante** section.
2. Review **Lección 1** with the class.
3. Have students prepare the **Recapitulación** activities on the Supersite.
4. Go over any remaining questions to review for the test.

Day 8

1. Administer one of the six **Pruebas** for **Lección 1**.
2. Preview the **Lección 2** objectives.
3. Have students read the **Contextos** section and prepare the **Práctica** activities for the next class.

For more examples on how to use **PANORAMA** in different course configurations, see the lesson plan templates on the **PANORAMA 4/e** Supersite (**vhlcentral.com**).

PANORAMA

Introducción a la lengua española

FOURTH EDITION

José A. Blanco

Philip Redwine Donley, Late
Austin Community College

VISTA
HIGHER LEARNING

Boston, Massachusetts

The cover of **PANORAMA, Fourth Edition,** features *Elogio del Horizonte* (In Praise of the Horizon) by the Spanish artist Eduardo Chillida Juantegui. The abstract sculpture overlooks the sea from the northern city of Gijón, in Spain. This is one of many places in the Spanish-speaking world that you will learn about in **PANORAMA**.

Publisher: José A. Blanco

Managing Editors: Deborah Coffey (Print), Paola Ríos Schaaf (Technology)

Senior Consulting Editor: Armando Brito

Project Manager: Lauren Krolick (Technology)

Editors: Darío González (Technology), Egle Gutiérrez (Technology), Carolina Zapata

Production and Design Director: Marta Kimball

Cover Design: Susan Prentiss

Design and Production Team: Manuela Arango, María Eugenia Castaño, Oscar Diez, Paula Díez, Mauricio Henao, Jhoany Jiménez, Sónia Teixeira, Lilliana Uribe, Andrés F. Vanegas García, Nick Ventullo

Student Text ISBN: 978-1-61767-705-2

Instructor's Annotated Edition ISBN: 978-1-61767-709-0

Library of Congress Control Number: 2011937592

1 2 3 4 5 6 7 8 9 TC 16 15 14 13 12 11

TO THE STUDENT

To Vista Higher Learning's great pride, **PANORAMA** and **VISTAS**, the parent text from which **PANORAMA** is derived, became the best-selling new introductory college Spanish program in more than a decade in its first edition, and its success has only grown over time. It is now our pleasure to welcome you to **PANORAMA**, **Fourth Edition**, your gateway to the Spanish language and to the vibrant cultures of the Spanish-speaking world.

A direct result of extensive reviews and ongoing input from students and instructors, **PANORAMA 4/e** includes both the highly successful, ground-breaking features of the original program, plus many exciting new elements designed to keep **PANORAMA** the most student-friendly program available. Here are just some of the features you will encounter:

Original, hallmark features

- A unique, easy-to-navigate design built around color-coded sections that appear either completely on one page or on spreads of two facing pages

- Integration of an appealing video, up-front in each lesson of the student text

- Practical, high-frequency vocabulary in meaningful contexts

- Clear, comprehensive grammar explanations with high-impact graphics and other special features that make structures easier to learn and use

- Ample guided practice to make you comfortable with the vocabulary and grammar you are learning and to give you a solid foundation for communication

- An emphasis on communicative interactions with a classmate, small groups, the full class, and your instructor

- A process approach to the development of reading, writing, and listening skills

- Coverage of the entire Spanish-speaking world and integration of everyday culture

- Unprecedented learning support through on-the-spot student sidebars and on-page correlations to the print and technology ancillaries for each lesson section

- A complete set of print and technology ancillaries to help you learn Spanish

NEW! to the Fourth Edition

- A dynamic new **Fotonovela** video that presents language and culture in an engaging context

- An improved **En pantalla** section in Lessons 3, 6, 9, 12, and 15, featuring a TV clip and an authentic short film each time

- **VText**, the online, interactive textbook

- New content and features on the **PANORAMA** Supersite, including audio-synced readings, video-related activities, extended grammar diagnostics, audio record-submit activities, a powerful bilingual dictionary, and much more, all designed to help you learn

PANORAMA 4/e has fifteen lessons, each of which is organized exactly the same way. To familiarize yourself with the organization of the text, as well as its original and new features, turn to page xii and take the **at-a-glance** tour.

table of contents

	contextos	fotonovela

cultura	estructura	adelante

table of contents

	contexts	fotonovela

cultura	estructura	adelante

table of contents

	contextos	fotonovela

cultura	estructura	adelante

table of contents

	contexts	fotonovela

cultura	estructura	adelante

Lesson Openers
outline the content and features of each lesson.

Communicative Goals

You will learn how to:
- Talk about your family and friends
- Describe people and things
- Express possession

La familia

3

contextos

pages 70–73
- The family
- Identifying people
- Professions and occupations

fotonovela

pages 74–77
The Díaz family spends Sunday afternoon in Xochimilco. Marissa meets the extended family and answers questions about her own family. The group has a picnic and takes a boat ride through the canals.

cultura

pages 78–79
- Surnames and families in the Spanish-speaking world
- Spain's Royal Family

estructura

pages 80–97
- Descriptive adjectives
- Possessive adjectives
- Present tense of -er and -ir verbs
- Present tense of tener and venir
- Recapitulación

adelante

pages 98–105
Lectura: A brief article about families
Escritura: A letter to a friend
Escuchar: A conversation between friends
En pantalla: Anuncio y cortometraje
Panorama: Ecuador

A PRIMERA VISTA
- ¿Cuántos chicos hay en la foto?
- ¿Hay una mujer a la izquierda? ¿Y a la derecha?
- ¿Hay una cosa en la mano de la mujer?
- ¿Conversan ellos? ¿Trabajan? ¿Viajan?
- ¿Están lejos de su casa?

A primera vista activities jump-start the lessons, allowing you to use the Spanish you know to talk about the photos.

Communicative goals highlight the real-life tasks you will be able to carry out in Spanish by the end of each lesson.

Contextos
presents vocabulary in meaningful contexts.

Más vocabulario boxes call out other important theme-related vocabulary in easy-to-reference Spanish-English lists.

Illustrations High-frequency vocabulary is introduced through expansive, full-color illustrations.

Práctica This section always begins with two listening exercises and continues with activities that practice the new vocabulary in meaningful contexts.

Variación léxica presents alternate words and expressions used throughout the Spanish-speaking world.

Recursos The icons in the **Recursos** boxes let you know exactly which print and technology ancillaries you can use to reinforce and expand on every section of every lesson.

Comunicación activities allow you to use the vocabulary creatively in interactions with a partner, a small group, or the entire class.

Fotonovela
follows the adventures of a group of
students living and traveling in Mexico.

Personajes The photo-based conversations take place among a cast of recurring characters—a Mexican family with two college-age children, and their group of friends.

Fotonovela Video Updated for the Fourth Edition, the **NEW!** video episodes that correspond to this section are available for viewing online. For more information on the **Fotonovela** Video, turn to page xxvi.

Conversations Taken from the **NEW! Fotonovela**, the conversations reinforce vocabulary from **Contextos**. They also preview structures from the upcoming **Estructura** section in context *and* in a comprehensible way.

Icons signal activities by type (pair, group, audio, info gap) and let you know which activities can be completed online. For a legend explaining all icons used in the student text, see page xxix.

Expresiones útiles These expressions organize new, active structures by language function so you can focus on using them for real-life, practical purposes.

Pronunciación & Ortografía
present the rules of Spanish pronunciation and spelling.

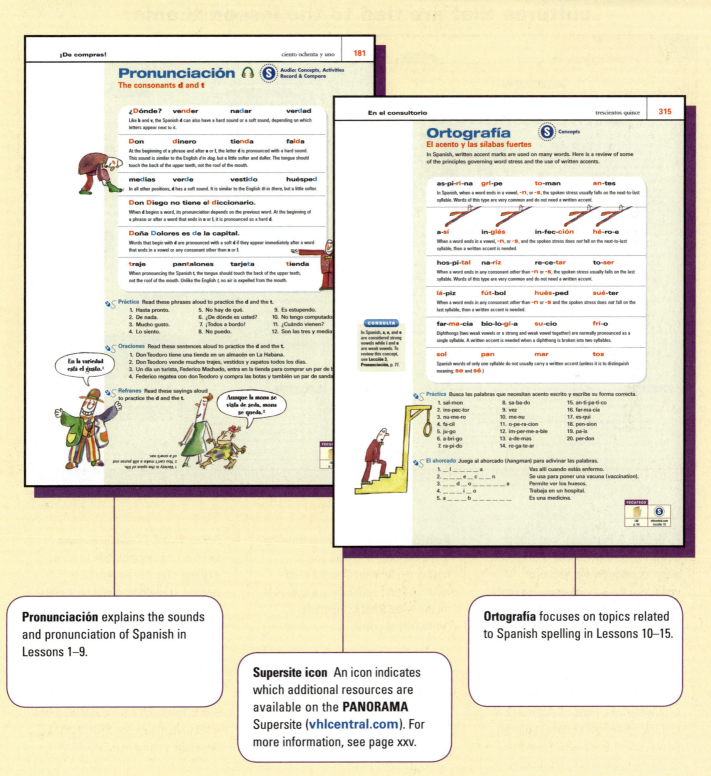

Pronunciación explains the sounds and pronunciation of Spanish in Lessons 1–9.

Supersite icon An icon indicates which additional resources are available on the **PANORAMA** Supersite (**vhlcentral.com**). For more information, see page xxv.

Ortografía focuses on topics related to Spanish spelling in Lessons 10–15.

PANORAMA at-a-glance

Cultura
shows different aspects of Hispanic cultures that are tied to the lesson theme.

En detalle & Perfil(es) Two articles on the lesson theme focus on a specific place, custom, person, group, or tradition in the Spanish-speaking world. In Spanish starting in Lesson 7, these features also provide reading practice.

Activities check your understanding of the material and lead you to further exploration. A mouse icon indicates that activities are available on the **PANORAMA** Supersite (**vhlcentral.com**).

Así se dice & El mundo hispano Lexical and comparative features expand cultural coverage to people, traditions, customs, trends, and vocabulary throughout the Spanish-speaking world.

Coverage While the **Panorama** section takes a regional approach to cultural coverage, **Cultura** is theme-driven, covering several Spanish-speaking regions in every lesson.

Flash cultura An icon lets you know that the enormously successful **Flash cultura** video offers specially shot content tied to the lesson theme.

Conexión Internet This activity leads you to research a topic related to the lesson theme on the **PANORAMA** Supersite (**vhlcentral.com**).

Estructura
presents Spanish grammar in a graphic-intensive format.

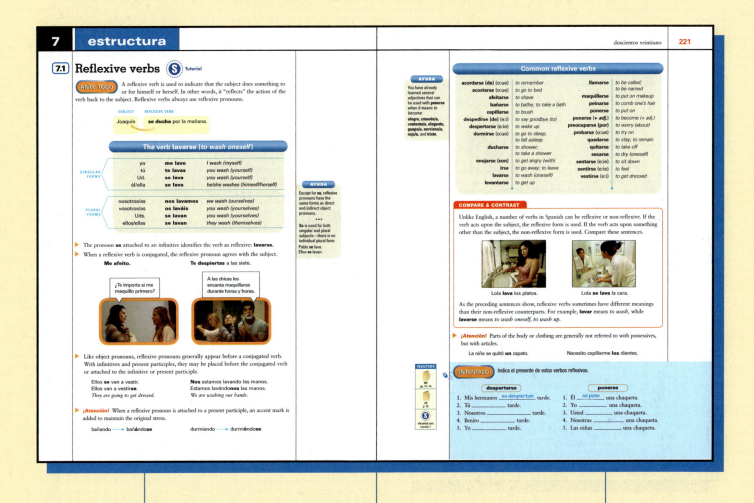

Ante todo This introduction eases you into the grammar with definitions of grammatical terms, reminders about what you already know of English grammar, and Spanish grammar you have learned in earlier lessons.

Compare & Contrast This feature focuses on aspects of grammar that native speakers of English may find difficult, clarifying similarities and differences between Spanish and English.

Diagrams To clarify concepts, clear and easy-to-grasp grammar explanations are reinforced by diagrams that colorfully present sample words, phrases, and sentences.

Charts To help you learn, colorful, easy-to-use charts call out key grammatical structures and forms, as well as important related vocabulary.

Student sidebars provide you with on-the-spot linguistic, cultural, or language-learning information directly related to the materials in front of you.

¡Inténtalo! offers an easy first step into each grammar point. A mouse icon indicates these activities are available with auto-grading on the **PANORAMA** Supersite (**vhlcentral.com**).

PANORAMA at-a-glance

Estructura
provides directed and communicative practice.

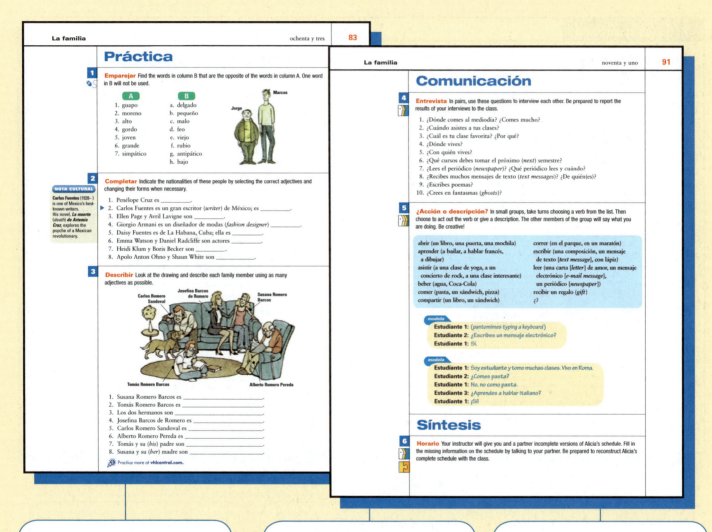

Práctica A wide range of guided, yet meaningful exercises weave current and previously learned vocabulary together with the current grammar point.

Comunicación Opportunities for creative expression use the lesson's grammar and vocabulary. These activities take place with a partner, in small groups, or with the whole class.

Síntesis activities integrate the current grammar point with previously learned points, providing built-in, consistent review and recycling as you progress through the text.

Information Gap activities engage you and a partner in problem-solving and other situations based on handouts your instructor gives you. However, you and your partner each have only half of the information you need, so you must work together to accomplish the task at hand.

Sidebars The **Notas culturales** expand coverage of the cultures of Spanish-speaking peoples and countries, while **Ayuda** sidebars provide on-the-spot language support.

NEW! Additional activities New to the Fourth Edition, the Activity Pack provides additional communicative and discrete practice for every grammar point. Your instructor will distribute these handouts for review and extra practice.

Estructura

Recapitulación reviews the grammar of each lesson and is available with auto-grading on the Supersite.

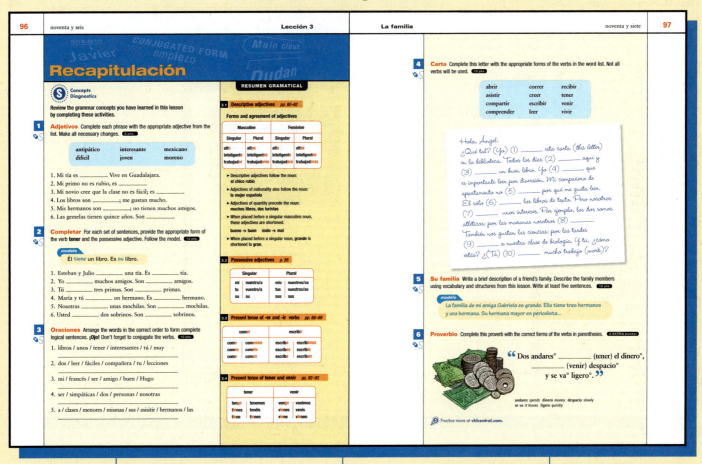

Resumen gramatical This review panel provides you with an easy-to-study summary of the basic concepts of the lesson's grammar, with page references to the full explanations.

Activities A series of activities, moving from directed to open-ended, systematically test your mastery of the lesson's grammar. The section ends with a riddle or puzzle using the grammar from the lesson.

Points Each activity is assigned a point value to help you track your progress. All **Recapitulación** sections add up to fifty points, plus two additional points for successfully completing the bonus activity.

Supersite icon An icon lets you know that **Recapitulación** can be completed online with diagnostics to help you identify where you are strong or where you might need review.

NEW! Extra practice An icon indicates when there is extra practice available online. In this case, after you finish **Recapitulación**, you can complete a set of follow-up activities to compare your results!

Adelante
Lectura focuses on reading skills and is tied to the lesson theme.

Antes de leer Valuable reading strategies and pre-reading activities strengthen your reading abilities in Spanish.

Readings Selections related to the lesson theme recycle vocabulary and grammar you have learned. The selections in Lessons 1–12 are cultural texts, while those in Lessons 13–15 are literary pieces.

Después de leer Activities include post-reading exercises that review and check your comprehension of the reading as well as expansion activities.

NEW! Selections Three readings are new to this edition. Lessons 1 and 11 now offer authentic comics by Quino and Tute, while lesson 14 now has a short story by Marco Denevi.

Adelante
In Lessons 3, 6, 9, 12, and 15, *Escritura* and *Escuchar* support writing and listening skills.

Estrategia Strategies help you prepare for the writing and listening tasks to come.

Escuchar A recorded conversation or narration develops your listening skills in Spanish. **Preparación** prepares you for listening to the recorded passage.

Escritura The **Tema** describes the writing topic and includes suggestions for approaching it.

Ahora escucha walks you through the passage, and **Comprensión** checks your listening comprehension.

PANORAMA at-a-glance

Adelante

In Lessons 3, 6, 9, 12, and 15, *En pantalla* presents authentic TV clips and short films.

En pantalla: Anuncio TV clips, all **NEW!** to this edition, give you additional exposure to authentic language. The clips include commercials, newscasts, and TV shows.

Presentation Cultural notes, video stills with captions, film posters, and vocabulary support all prepare you to view the clips and short films. Activities check your comprehension and expand on the ideas presented.

NEW! En pantalla: Cortometraje This page features authentic short films from the U.S., Mexico, Colombia, and Spain, including pre- and post-viewing support.

Supersite icon Icons lead you to the Supersite (**vhlcentral.com**), where you can view the videos and get further practice.

Panorama
presents the nations of the Spanish-speaking world.

Below the main image spread are six labeled description boxes:

El país en cifras presents interesting key facts about the featured country.

Maps point out major cities, rivers, and geographical features and situate the country in the context of its immediate surroundings and the world.

Readings A series of brief paragraphs explores facets of the country's culture such as history, places, fine arts, literature, and aspects of everyday life.

¡Increíble pero cierto! highlights an intriguing fact about the country or its people.

Conexión Internet offers Internet activities on the **PANORAMA** Supersite (**vhlcentral.com**) for additional avenues of discovery.

***Panorama cultural* Video** This video's authentic footage takes you to the featured Spanish-speaking country, letting you experience the sights and sounds of an aspect of its culture. To learn more about the video, turn to page xxviii.

Vocabulario
summarizes all the active vocabulary of the lesson.

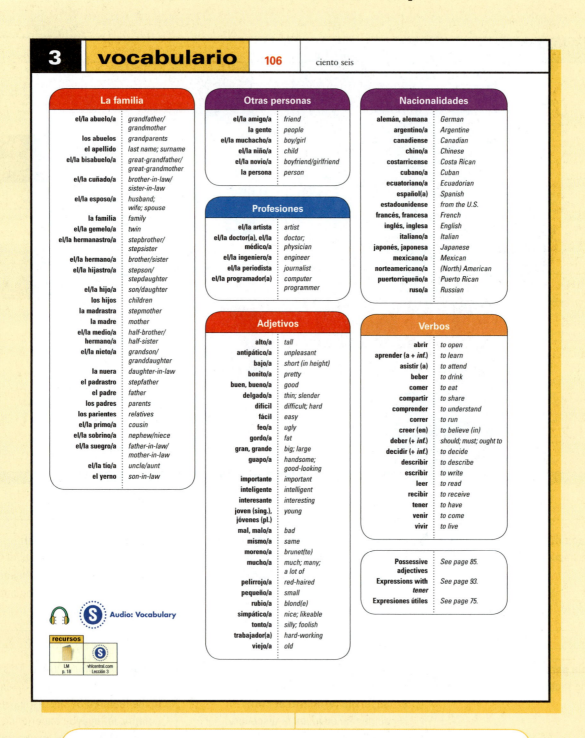

3 vocabulario 106 ciento seis

La familia

el/la abuelo/a	grandfather/grandmother
los abuelos	grandparents
el apellido	last name; surname
el/la bisabuelo/a	great-grandfather/great-grandmother
el/la cuñado/a	brother-in-law/sister-in-law
el/la esposo/a	husband; wife; spouse
la familia	family
el/la gemelo/a	twin
el/la hermanastro/a	stepbrother/stepsister
el/la hermano/a	brother/sister
el/la hijastro/a	stepson/stepdaughter
el/la hijo/a	son/daughter
los hijos	children
la madrastra	stepmother
la madre	mother
el/la medio/a hermano/a	half-brother/half-sister
el/la nieto/a	grandson/granddaughter
la nuera	daughter-in-law
el padrastro	stepfather
el padre	father
los padres	parents
los parientes	relatives
el/la primo/a	cousin
el/la sobrino/a	nephew/niece
el/la suegro/a	father-in-law/mother-in-law
el/la tío/a	uncle/aunt
el yerno	son-in-law

Otras personas

el/la amigo/a	friend
la gente	people
el/la muchacho/a	boy/girl
el/la niño/a	child
el/la novio/a	boyfriend/girlfriend
la persona	person

Profesiones

el/la artista	artist
el/la doctor(a), el/la médico/a	doctor; physician
el/la ingeniero/a	engineer
el/la periodista	journalist
el/la programador(a)	computer programmer

Nacionalidades

alemán, alemana	German
argentino/a	Argentine
canadiense	Canadian
chino/a	Chinese
costarricense	Costa Rican
cubano/a	Cuban
ecuatoriano/a	Ecuadorian
español(a)	Spanish
estadounidense	from the U.S.
francés, francesa	French
inglés, inglesa	English
italiano/a	Italian
japonés, japonesa	Japanese
mexicano/a	Mexican
norteamericano/a	(North) American
puertorriqueño/a	Puerto Rican
ruso/a	Russian

Adjetivos

alto/a	tall
antipático/a	unpleasant
bajo/a	short (in height)
bonito/a	pretty
buen, bueno/a	good
delgado/a	thin; slender
difícil	difficult; hard
fácil	easy
feo/a	ugly
gordo/a	fat
gran, grande	big; large
guapo/a	handsome; good-looking
importante	important
inteligente	intelligent
interesante	interesting
joven (sing.), jóvenes (pl.)	young
mal, malo/a	bad
mismo/a	same
moreno/a	brunet(te)
mucho/a	much; many; a lot of
pelirrojo/a	red-haired
pequeño/a	small
rubio/a	blond(e)
simpático/a	nice; likeable
tonto/a	silly; foolish
trabajador(a)	hard-working
viejo/a	old

Verbos

abrir	to open
aprender (a + *inf.*)	to learn
asistir (a)	to attend
beber	to drink
comer	to eat
compartir	to share
comprender	to understand
correr	to run
creer (en)	to believe (in)
deber (+ *inf.*)	should; must; ought to
decidir (+ *inf.*)	to decide
describir	to describe
escribir	to write
leer	to read
recibir	to receive
tener	to have
venir	to come
vivir	to live

Possessive adjectives	See page 85.
Expressions with *tener*	See page 93.
Expresiones útiles	See page 75.

Audio: Vocabulary

recursos

LM p. 18 | vhlcentral.com Lección 3

Recorded vocabulary The headset icon, the Supersite icon, and **Recursos** boxes highlight that the active lesson vocabulary is recorded for convenient study on the **PANORAMA** Supersite (**vhlcentral.com**).

The **PANORAMA** Supersite provides a wealth of resources for both students and instructors. Icons indicate exactly which resources are available on the Supersite for each strand of every lesson.

For Students
Student resources, available through a Supersite code, are provided free-of-charge with the purchase of a new student text. Here is an example of what you will find at **vhlcentral.com:**

- Activities from the student text, with auto-grading
- Additional practice for each and every textbook section
- Record and submit oral assessment activities
- Four video programs—**Fotonovela, Flash cultura, En pantalla** (**Anuncio** and **Cortometraje**), and **Panorama cultural**—in streaming video
- MP3 files for the complete **PANORAMA** Textbook and Lab Programs
- **NEW!** Oxford Spanish Mini Dictionary **OXFORD** UNIVERSITY PRESS
- Improved Flashcards with audio
- Instructor-enabled voiceboards for oral communication and threaded discussions

For Instructors
See p. xxx for a complete list of Supersite resources available to instructors.

Supersiteplus

In addition to the resources already listed, Supersite Plus offers:

- **WebSAM** The online, interactive Student Activities Manual includes audio record and submit activities, auto-grading for select activities, and a single gradebook for Supersite and WebSAM activities.
- Instructor-enabled online collaboration via instant messaging, audio and video conferencing, and whiteboard and application sharing

With **vText**, students have everything they need at the click of a mouse: textbook, practice activities, audio, video, and all Supersite resources. Plus, the instructor gradebook links assignments and grades to the **vText**.

FOTONOVELA VIDEO PROGRAM

The cast NEW!

Here are the main characters you will meet in the **Fotonovela** Video:

From Mexico,
Jimena Díaz Velázquez

From Argentina,
Juan Carlos Rossi

From Mexico,
Felipe Díaz Velázquez

From the U.S.,
Marissa Wagner

From Mexico,
María Eugenia (Maru)
Castaño Ricaurte

From Spain,
Miguel Ángel
Lagasca Martínez

Brand-new and fully integrated with your text, the **PANORAMA 4/e Fotonovela** Video is a dynamic and contemporary window into the Spanish language. The new video centers around the Díaz family, whose household includes two college-aged children and a visiting student from the U.S. Over the course of an academic year, Jimena, Felipe, Marissa, and their friends explore **el D.F.** and other parts of Mexico as they make plans for their futures. Their adventures take them through some of the greatest natural and cultural treasures of the Spanish-speaking world, as well as the highs and lows of everyday life.

The **Fotonovela** section in each textbook lesson is actually an abbreviated version of the dramatic episode featured in the video. Therefore, each **Fotonovela** section can be done before you see the corresponding video episode, after it, or as a section that stands alone.

In each dramatic segment, the characters interact using the vocabulary and grammar you are studying. As the storyline unfolds, the episodes combine new vocabulary and grammar with previously taught language, exposing you to a variety of authentic accents along the way. At the end of each episode, the **Resumen** section highlights the grammar and vocabulary you are studying.

We hope you find the new **Fotonovela** video to be an engaging and useful tool for learning Spanish!

EN PANTALLA VIDEO PROGRAM

The **PANORAMA** Supersite features an authentic TV clip and short film for Lessons 3, 6, 9, 12, and 15. TV clip formats include commercials and news stories. All clips and three of the short films are **NEW!** to the Fourth Edition, were carefully chosen to be comprehensible for students learning Spanish, and are accompanied by activities and vocabulary lists to facilitate understanding. More importantly, though, these clips and short films are a fun and motivating way to improve your Spanish!

Here are the countries represented in **En pantalla:**

Lesson 3 Chile and U.S.	Lesson 9 Chile and Mexico	Lesson 15 Argentina and Spain
Lesson 6 Mexico and Colombia	Lesson 12 Argentina and Spain	

FLASH CULTURA VIDEO PROGRAM

In the dynamic **Flash cultura** Video, young people from all over the Spanish-speaking world share aspects of life in their countries with you. The similarities and differences among Spanish-speaking countries that come up through their adventures will challenge you to think about your own cultural practices and values. The segments provide valuable cultural insights as well as linguistic input; the episodes will introduce you to a variety of accents and vocabulary as they gradually move into Spanish.

PANORAMA CULTURAL VIDEO PROGRAM

The **Panorama cultural** Video is integrated with the **Panorama** section in each lesson. Each segment is 2–3 minutes long and consists of documentary footage from each of the countries featured. The images were specially chosen for interest level and visual appeal, while the all-Spanish narrations were carefully written to reflect the vocabulary and grammar covered in the textbook.

ICONS AND *RECURSOS* BOXES

Icons

Familiarize yourself with these icons that appear throughout **PANORAMA, Fourth Edition**.

Icons legend	
Listening activity/section	Hoja de actividades
Pair activity	Textbook activity available online
Group activity	Content on the Supersite available for this section
Information Gap activity	

- The Information Gap activities and those involving **Hojas de actividades** (*activity sheets*) require handouts that your instructor will give you.

- You will see the listening icon in **Contextos**, **Pronunciación**, **Escuchar,** and **Vocabulario** sections.

- A note next to the Supersite icon will let you know exactly what type of content is available online. See p. xxv for a list of available resources.

- Additional practice on the Supersite, not included in the textbook, is indicated with this icon:

 Practice more at **vhlcentral.com.**

Recursos

Recursos boxes let you know exactly what print and technology ancillaries you can use to reinforce and expand on every section of the lessons in your textbook. They even include page numbers when applicable. See the next page for a description of the ancillaries.

Recursos boxes legend	
WB pp. 37–38 Workbook	VM pp. 219–220 Video Manual
LM p. 19 Lab Manual	PANORAMA Supersite

STUDENT ANCILLARIES

▶ **Supersite**
Student access to the Supersite (vhlcentral.com) is free with the purchase of a new student text. The Student Supersite provides:
- Select textbook and extra-practice activities
- All **PANORAMA 4/e** video programs
- Textbook Audio Program MP3s (audio recordings for the listening based textbook activities and recordings of the active vocabulary for each lesson of the student text)
- Lab Audio Program MP3s
- Study resources (online dictionary, tutorials, flashcards)
- Instructor-enabled voiceboards for oral communication and threaded discussions

See page xxv for a complete list of resources.

▶ **Supersite Plus**
The Student Supersite Plus provides:
- The **PANORAMA 4/e** Supersite
- **WebSAM**, the entire Workbook, Video Manual, and Lab Manual online, as well as a robust learning management system that completely integrates with the **PANORAMA 4/e** Supersite
- Instructor-enabled online collaboration via instant messaging, audio and video conferencing, and whiteboard and application sharing

▶ **NEW! vText**
The online virtual interactive student edition provides students with:
- Note-taking and highlighting capabilities
- Easy browsing via table of contents or page number
- Links to textbook mouse-icon activities
- Assignments and grades on the **vText** page
- Direct access to all Supersite resources

▶ **Workbook/Video Manual**
The Workbook/Video Manual contains the workbook activities for each textbook lesson, activities for the **Fotonovela** video, and pre-, while-, and post-viewing activities for the **Flash cultura** and **Panorama cultural** videos.

▶ **Lab Manual**
The Lab Manual contains lab activities for each textbook lesson for use with the Lab Audio Program.

▶ *Fotonovela* **Video DVD**
The **Fotonovela** DVD provides the complete **Fotonovela** video program with subtitles in English and Spanish.

INSTRUCTOR ANCILLARIES

▶ **Instructor's Annotated Edition (IAE)**
The expanded trim size and enhanced design make the annotations easy to reference in the classroom.

▶ **NEW! Activity Pack**
The **PANORAMA** Activity Pack offers discrete and communicative practice for individuals, pairs, and groups. Formats include multiple choice questions, information gap activities, board games, and more.

▶ **Supersite**
The password-protected Instructor Supersite allows instructors to assign and track student progress through its course management system. Instructors have full access to the Student Supersite and seamless integration with the **PANORAMA 4/e** WebSAM and vText. The Supersite now features an intuitive, user-friendly interface and tools to enhance course management, gradebook, and reporting, including:
- All-in-one gradebook
- Simple and powerful course and assignment set-up
- Reporting with customized and standard options
- Online assessment including Testing MP3 files, plus editable RTFs, and ready-to-print PDF versions
- Program audio and video with scripts and English video translations
- Voiceboards for oral communication and threaded discussions
- Lesson Plans and Instructor Resources

▶ **Supersite Plus**
Supersite Plus offers:
- The complete **PANORAMA 4/e** Supersite
- The **WebSAM** online Workbook/Lab Manual/Video Manual, with auto-graded and instructor-graded activities, and oral record-submit activities
- Online collaboration via instant messaging, audio and video conferencing, and whiteboard and application sharing

▶ **Instructor's DVD Set**
Three video DVDs (**Fotonovela, Flash cultura,** and **Panorama cultural + Cortometrajes**) are available with subtitles in English and Spanish.

▶ **Testing Program**
The Testing Program is provided in PDF and RTF formats.
- **NEW!** Volume 1 of the Testing Program contains two quizzes for each **Contextos** presentation and each **Estructura** grammar point.
- **NEW!** Volume 2 of the Testing Program contains two additional versions (**Prueba E** and **Prueba F**) of the tests for each textbook lesson.
- Volume 2 also contains quarter exams, semester exams, listening scripts, answer keys, and optional test items for culture, video, and reading sections.

PANORAMA, Fourth Edition, is the direct result of extensive reviews and continuous input from students and instructors using the Third Edition. On behalf of its authors and editors, Vista Higher Learning expresses its sincere appreciation to the many Spanish instructors and professors across the U.S. and Canada who contributed their ideas, suggestions, and recommendations via online reviews: thank you.

We especially thank those instructors who contributed their editing and writing expertise, including Martín Gaspar of the University of Wisconsin, Madison; Mercedes Hussey Pailos of Brevard Community College; and Ronna Feit of Nassau Community College/SUNY.

Reviewers

Tammy Allen
Miami University, Middletown, OH

Rosalind Arthur-Andoh
Clark Atlanta University, GA

Gilbert Bolling
Concord University, WV

Martin Camps
University of the Pacific, CA

Matt Carpenter
Yuba College, Clearlake, CA

Tulio Cedillo
Lynchburg College, VA

Lisa Celona
Tunxis Community College, CT

Richard Clark
Northwestern College, IA

Nathalie Davaut
University of South Carolina, Lancaster, SC

Chris Davison
Westminster College of Salt Lake City, UT

Lorena Delgadillo
Rowan-Cabarrus Community College, NC

Tatevik Gevorgyan
Catholic University of America, Washington, DC

Don Goetz
Northwestern Connecticut Community Technical College, CT

Julia Guerrero
Highland Community College, IL

Cecilia Herrera
University of Wisconsin, Oshkosh, WI

Josephine Hill
Jackson Community College, MI

Esther Holtermann
American University, Washington, DC

Jacqueline Horn
Loma Linda University, CA

Harriet Hutchinson
Bunker Hill Community College, Charlestown, MA

Herman Johnson
Xavier University of Louisiana, LA

Robert Lesman
Shippensburg University of Pennsylvania, PA

Lora Looney
University of Portland, OR

Frank Martínez
Nashville State Community College, TN

María Martínez
University of Manitoba,
Winnipeg, MB, Canada

Victoria Mayorga
Pierce College, Puyallup, WA

Lindsay Naramore
John Brown University, AR

Michael Nouri
University of Southern Indiana, IN

Erica Oshier
Fort Valley State University, GA

Kristin Osowski
Diablo Valley College, CA

Ruth Owens Supko
Arkansas State University, Jonesboro, AR

Jessica Perla-Collibee
Menlo College, CA

Sherrie Ray
University of Arkansas at Little Rock, AR

Caterina Reitano
University of Manitoba, Winnipeg, MB, Canada

Gabriel Rico
Victor Valley College, CA

John Riley
Greenville Technical College, Greenville, SC

Walter Rojas
Universidad del Ambiente, Costa Rica

David Salomon
Russell Sage College for Women, NY

Patricia Scarampi
Lake Forest College, IL

Nila Serrano-Proulx
Victor Valley College, CA

Jody Soberon
Southwestern Oregon Community
College, Brookings, OR

Susan Spillman
Xavier University of Louisiana, LA

Nataly Tcherepashenets
Empire State College, Center for
Distance Learning, NY

Regina Vera-Quinn
University of Waterloo, ON, Canada

Antonia Wagner
Greenville Technical College, Barton, SC

Joy Woolf
Westminster College of Salt Lake City, UT

Hola, ¿qué tal?

1

You will learn how to:
- Greet people in Spanish
- Say goodbye
- Identify yourself and others
- Talk about the time of day

Lesson Goals

In **Lección 1**, students will be introduced to the following:
- terms for greetings and goodbyes
- identifying where one is from
- courtesy expressions
- greetings in the Spanish-speaking world
- the **plaza principal**
- nouns and articles (definite and indefinite)
- numbers 0–30
- present tense of **ser**
- telling time
- recognizing cognates
- reading a comic strip
- a video about **plazas** and greetings
- demographic and cultural information about Hispanics in the United States and Canada

A primera vista Have students look at the photo and ask them what they think the young women are doing. Explain that it is common in Hispanic cultures for friends to greet each other with one or two kisses on the cheek. As a class, discuss how friends typically greet each other in North America.

Teaching Tip You will see a series of icons pointing out communicative expansions, activities, and teaching tips in the instructor annotations. Follow this key:

→●●	Interpretive communication
←●●	Presentational communication
●↔●	Interpersonal communication

A PRIMERA VISTA
- Guess what the people on the photo are saying:
 a. Adiós. b. Hola. c. salsa
- Most likely they would also say:
 a. Gracias. b. fiesta c. Buenos días.
- The women are:
 a. amigas b. chicos c. señores

INSTRUCTIONAL RESOURCES

Supersite (vhlcentral.com)
Video: *Fotonovela*, Flash cultura*, Panorama cultural**
**Also on DVD*
Audio: Textbook and Lab MP3 Files (*also on CD*)
Activity Pack: Information Gap Activities, games, additional activity handouts

Resources: Textbook Answer Key, WB/VM/LM Answer Key, Scripts, Translations, **Vocabulario adicional**, lesson plans, **Estructura** *PowerPoints*, Overheads
Testing Program: Quizzes, Tests, Exams, MP3s (*also on Test Generator CD*)

Learning Management System (Assignment Task Manager, Gradebook)
WebSAM (online Workbook/Video Manual/ Lab Manual)
Workbook/Video Manual
Lab Manual

Hola, ¿qué tal?

Más vocabulario

Buenos días.	*Good morning.*
Buenas noches.	*Good evening; Good night.*
Hasta la vista.	*See you later.*
Hasta pronto.	*See you soon.*
¿Cómo se llama usted?	*What's your name? (form.)*
Le presento a…	*I would like to introduce you to (name). (form.)*
Te presento a…	*I would like to introduce you to (name). (fam.)*
el nombre	*name*
¿Cómo estás?	*How are you? (fam.)*
No muy bien.	*Not very well.*
¿Qué pasa?	*What's happening?; What's going on?*
por favor	*please*
De nada.	*You're welcome.*
No hay de qué.	*You're welcome.*
Lo siento.	*I'm sorry.*
Gracias.	*Thank you; Thanks.*
Muchas gracias.	*Thank you very much; Thanks a lot.*

Variación léxica

Items are presented for recognition purposes only.

Buenos días.	⟷	Buenas.
De nada.	⟷	A la orden.
Lo siento.	⟷	Perdón.
¿Qué tal?	⟷	¿Qué hubo? (*Col.*)
Chau.	⟷	Ciao; Chao.

recursos
WB pp. 1–2 | LM p. 1 | S vhlcentral.com Lección 1

1
ELENA Patricia, éste es el señor Perales.
PATRICIA Encantada.
SEÑOR PERALES Igualmente. ¿De dónde es usted, señorita?
PATRICIA Soy de México. ¿Y usted?
SEÑOR PERALES De Puerto Rico.

2
TOMÁS ¿Qué tal, Alberto?
ALBERTO Regular. ¿Y tú?
TOMÁS Bien. ¿Qué hay de nuevo?
ALBERTO Nada.

3
SEÑOR VARGAS Buenas tardes, señora Wong. ¿Cómo está usted?
SEÑORA WONG Muy bien, gracias. ¿Y usted, señor Vargas?
SEÑOR VARGAS Bien, gracias.
SEÑORA WONG Hasta mañana, señor Vargas. Saludos a la señora Vargas.
SEÑOR VARGAS Adiós.

Práctica

1 Escuchar
Listen to each question or statement, then choose the correct response.

1.	a. Muy bien, gracias.	b. Me llamo Graciela. b
2.	a. Lo siento.	b. Mucho gusto. b
3.	a. Soy de Puerto Rico.	b. No muy bien. a
4.	a. No hay de qué.	b. Regular. a
5.	a. Mucho gusto.	b. Hasta pronto. b
6.	a. Nada.	b. Igualmente. a
7.	a. Me llamo Guillermo Montero.	b. Muy bien, gracias. b
8.	a. Buenas tardes. ¿Cómo estás?	b. El gusto es mío. a
9.	a. Saludos a la Sra. Ramírez.	b. Encantada. b
10.	a. Adiós.	b. Regular. b

2 Identificar
You will hear a series of expressions. Identify the expression (**a**, **b**, **c**, or **d**) that does not belong in each series.

1. ___c___ 3. ___b___
2. ___a___ 4. ___c___

3 Escoger
For each expression, write another word or phrase that expresses a similar idea.

modelo

¿Cómo estás? *¿Qué tal?*

1. De nada. *No hay de qué.*
2. Encantado. *Mucho gusto.*
3. Adiós. *Chau o Hasta luego/ mañana/pronto.*
4. Te presento a Antonio. *Éste es Antonio.*
5. Hasta la vista. *Hasta luego.*
6. Mucho gusto. *El gusto es mío.*

4 Ordenar
Work with a partner to put this scrambled conversation in order. Then act it out.

—Muy bien, gracias. Soy Rosabel.
—Soy de México. ¿Y tú?
—Mucho gusto, Rosabel.
—Hola. Me llamo Carlos. ¿Cómo estás?
—Soy de Argentina.
—Igualmente. ¿De dónde eres, Carlos?

CARLOS *Hola. Me llamo Carlos. ¿Cómo estás?*
ROSABEL *Muy bien, gracias. Soy Rosabel.*
CARLOS *Mucho gusto, Rosabel.*
ROSABEL *Igualmente. ¿De dónde eres, Carlos?*
CARLOS *Soy de México. ¿Y tú?*
ROSABEL *Soy de Argentina.*

BERTA Hasta luego, Tere.
TERESA Chau, Berta. Nos vemos mañana.

CARMEN Buenas tardes. Me llamo Carmen.
¿Cómo te llamas tú?
ANTONIO Buenas tardes. Me llamo Antonio.
Mucho gusto.
CARMEN El gusto es mío. ¿De dónde eres?
ANTONIO Soy de los Estados Unidos, de California.

5 Teaching Tip Have pairs share their responses with the class.

5 Expansion
👥↔👥 Have pairs or small groups create conversations that include the expressions used in **Actividad 5**. Ask volunteers to present their conversations to the class.

6 Teaching Tips
• Discuss the **modelo** before assigning the activity to pairs.
• 👥↔👥 After students have completed the activity, have pairs role-play the corrected mini-conversations. Ask them to substitute their own names and personal information where possible.
• Have volunteers write each mini-conversation on the board. Work as a class to identify and explain any errors.

¡Lengua viva! Have students locate examples of the titles in **Actividad 6**. Then ask them to create short sentences in which they use the titles with people they know.

5 Completar Work with a partner to complete these dialogues. *Some answers may vary. Suggested answers:*

> **modelo**
>
> **Estudiante 1:** ¿Cómo estás?
> **Estudiante 2:** _Muy bien, gracias._

1. **Estudiante 1:** _Buenos días._
 Estudiante 2: Buenos días. ¿Qué tal?
2. **Estudiante 1:** _¿Cómo te llamas?_
 Estudiante 2: Me llamo Carmen Sánchez.
3. **Estudiante 1:** _¿De dónde eres?_
 Estudiante 2: De Canadá.
4. **Estudiante 1:** Te presento a Marisol.
 Estudiante 2: _Encantado/a._

5. **Estudiante 1:** Gracias.
 Estudiante 2: _De nada._
6. **Estudiante 1:** _¿Qué tal?_
 Estudiante 2: Regular.
7. **Estudiante 1:** _¿Qué pasa?_
 Estudiante 2: Nada.
8. **Estudiante 1:** ¡Hasta la vista!
 Estudiante 2: _Answers will vary._

6 Cambiar Work with a partner and correct the second part of each conversation to make it logical. *Answers will vary.*

> **modelo**
>
> **Estudiante 1:** ¿Qué tal?
> **Estudiante 2:** *No hay de qué.* Bien. ¿Y tú?

1. **Estudiante 1:** Hasta mañana, señora Ramírez. Saludos al señor Ramírez.
 Estudiante 2: *Muy bien, gracias.*
2. **Estudiante 1:** ¿Qué hay de nuevo, Alberto?
 Estudiante 2: *Sí, me llamo Alberto. ¿Cómo te llamas tú?*
3. **Estudiante 1:** Gracias, Tomás.
 Estudiante 2: *Regular. ¿Y tú?*
4. **Estudiante 1:** Miguel, ésta es la señorita Perales.
 Estudiante 2: *No hay de qué, señorita.*
5. **Estudiante 1:** ¿De dónde eres, Antonio?
 Estudiante 2: *Muy bien, gracias. ¿Y tú?*
6. **Estudiante 1:** ¿Cómo se llama usted?
 Estudiante 2: *El gusto es mío.*
7. **Estudiante 1:** ¿Qué pasa?
 Estudiante 2: *Hasta luego, Alicia.*
8. **Estudiante 1:** Buenas tardes, señor. ¿Cómo está usted?
 Estudiante 2: *Soy de Puerto Rico.*

🔊 Practice more at **vhlcentral.com.**

¡LENGUA VIVA!

The titles **señor, señora,** and **señorita** are abbreviated **Sr., Sra.,** and **Srta.** Note that these abbreviations are capitalized, while the titles themselves are not.

•••

There is no Spanish equivalent for the English title *Ms.;* women are addressed as **señora** or **señorita.**

TEACHING OPTIONS

Extra Practice Add an auditory exercise to this vocabulary practice. Read some phrases aloud and ask if students would use them with a person of the same age or someone older. Ex: **1. Te presento a Luis.** (same age) **2. ¿Cómo estás?** (same age) **3. Buenos días, doctor Soto.** (older) **4. ¿De dónde es usted, señora?** (older) **5. Chau, Teresa.** (same age) **6. No hay de qué, señor Perales.** (older)

Game Prepare a series of response statements using language in **Contextos.** Divide the class into two teams and invite students to guess the question or statement that would have elicited each of your responses. Read one statement at a time. The first team to correctly guess the question or statement earns a point. Ex: **Me llamo Lupe Torres Garza. (¿Cómo se llama usted? / ¿Cómo te llamas?)** The team with the most points at the end wins.

Comunicación

7 **Diálogos** With a partner, complete and act out these conversations. *Answers will vary.*

> **Conversación 1**
>
> —Hola. Me llamo Teresa. ¿Cómo te llamas tú?
> —_____
>
> —Soy de Puerto Rico. ¿Y tú?
> —_____

> **Conversación 2**
>
> —_____
>
> —Muy bien, gracias. ¿Y usted, señora López?
> —_____
>
> —Hasta luego, señora. Saludos al señor López.
> —_____

> **Conversación 3**
>
> —_____
>
> —Regular. ¿Y tú?
> —_____
>
> —Nada.

8 **Conversaciones** This is the first day of class. Write four short conversations based on what the people in this scene would say. *Answers will vary.*

9 **Situaciones** In groups of three, write and act out these situations. *Answers will vary.*

1. On your way out of class on the first day of school, you strike up a conversation with the two students who were sitting next to you. You find out each student's name and where he or she is from before you say goodbye and go to your next class.
2. At the next class you meet up with a friend and find out how he or she is doing. As you are talking, your friend Elena enters. Introduce her to your friend.
3. As you're leaving the bookstore, you meet your parents' friends Mrs. Sánchez and Mr. Rodríguez. You greet them and ask how each person is. As you say goodbye, you send greetings to Mrs. Rodríguez.
4. Make up and act out a real-life situation that you and your classmates can role-play with the language you've learned.

7 Expansion
- Have students work in small groups to write a few mini-conversations modeled on this activity. Then ask them to copy the dialogues, omitting a few words or phrases. Have groups exchange papers and fill in the blanks.
- Have students rewrite **Conversaciones 1** and **3** in the formal register and **Conversación 2** in the informal register.

8 Teaching Tip To simplify, have students brainstorm who the people in the illustration are and what they are talking about. Ask students which groups would be speaking to each other in the **usted** form, and which would be using the **tú** form.

8 Expansion In pairs, have students take turns selecting a person from the drawing and providing 2-3 statements that he or she might be saying. The partner will try to guess who it is.

9 Teaching Tip To challenge students, have each group pick a situation to write and perform. Tell groups not to memorize every word of the conversation, but rather to recreate it.

The Affective Dimension Have students rehearse the situations a few times, so that they will feel more comfortable with the material and less anxious when presenting it before the class.

Section Goals

In **Fotonovela**, students will:
- receive comprehensible input from free-flowing discourse
- learn functional phrases that preview lesson grammatical structures

Instructional Resources

Supersite/DVD: *Fotonovela*
Supersite: Resources (Scripts, Translations, Answer Keys)
WebSAM
Video Manual, pp. 195–196

Video Synopsis **Marissa,**
an American college student, arrives in Mexico City for a year abroad. She meets her Mexican hosts, **Carolina** and **Roberto Díaz,** and their doorman, **Don Diego.** As **Marissa** unpacks, the **Díaz** children, **Felipe** and **Jimena,** take away her English-Spanish dictionary as a joke. **Marissa** accepts the challenge and leaves the dictionary with **Carolina.**

Teaching Tips

- In small groups, have students cover the captions and guess the plot based on the video stills. Write their predictions on the board. After students have watched the video, compare their predictions to what actually happened in the episode.
- Point out that **don** is a title of respect and neither equivalent nor related to the English name *Don.* Ask if students think **Diego** is the doorman's first or last name. (It is his first name.) Students will learn more about the titles **don** and **doña** on page 8.
- Tell students that all items in **Expresiones útiles** on page 7 are active vocabulary. Model the pronunciation of each item and have the class repeat.
- 👤↔👤 You can also practice the **Expresiones útiles** by using them in short conversations with individual students.

Bienvenida, Marissa

Marissa llega a México para pasar un año con la familia Díaz.

PERSONAJES

 MARISSA

 SRA. DÍAZ

S Video: *Fotonovela*
Record and Compare

1

MARISSA ¿Usted es de Cuba?

SRA. DÍAZ Sí, de La Habana. Y Roberto es de Mérida. Tú eres de Wisconsin, ¿verdad?

MARISSA Sí, de Appleton, Wisconsin.

2

MARISSA ¿Quiénes son los dos chicos de las fotos? ¿Jimena y Felipe?

SRA. DÍAZ Sí. Ellos son estudiantes.

DON DIEGO ¿Cómo está usted hoy, señora Carolina?

SRA. DÍAZ Muy bien, gracias. ¿Y usted?

DON DIEGO Bien, gracias.

3

DON DIEGO Buenas tardes, señora. Señorita, bienvenida a la Ciudad de México.

MARISSA ¡Muchas gracias!

5

6

4

MARISSA ¿Cómo se llama usted?

DON DIEGO Yo soy Diego. Mucho gusto.

MARISSA El gusto es mío, don Diego.

SRA. DÍAZ Ahí hay dos maletas. Son de Marissa.

DON DIEGO Con permiso.

TEACHING OPTIONS

Video Tips General suggestions for using video clips in the classroom can be found on page IAE-10 of this Instructor's Annotated Edition.

Bienvenida, Marissa →👤 Have students make a three-column chart with these headings: *Greetings, Self-Identification,* and *Courtesy Expressions.* Have students suggest two or three possible phrases for each category. Then play the **Bienvenida,** **Marissa** episode once and ask students to fill in the first column with the basic greetings that they hear. Repeat this process for the second column, where they should list the expressions the characters use to identify themselves. Play the video a third time for students to jot down courtesy expressions, such as ways to say "pleased to meet you" and "pardon me."

DON DIEGO

SR. DÍAZ

FELIPE

JIMENA

7

SR. DÍAZ ¿Qué hora es?

FELIPE Son las cuatro y veinticinco.

8

SRA. DÍAZ Marissa, te presento a Roberto, mi esposo.

SR. DÍAZ Bienvenida, Marissa.

MARISSA Gracias, señor Díaz.

9

JIMENA ¿Qué hay en esta cosa?

MARISSA Bueno, a ver, hay tres cuadernos, un mapa... ¡Y un diccionario!

JIMENA ¿Cómo se dice mediodía en inglés?

FELIPE *"Noon"*.

10

FELIPE Estás en México, ¿verdad?

MARISSA ¿Sí?

FELIPE Nosotros somos tu diccionario.

recursos

VM pp. 195–196

Ⓢ vhlcentral.com Lección 1

Expresiones útiles

Identifying yourself and others

¿Cómo se llama usted?
What's your name?
Yo soy Diego, el portero. Mucho gusto.
I'm Diego, the doorman. Nice to meet you.
¿Cómo te llamas?
What's your name?
Me llamo Marissa.
My name is Marissa.
¿Quién es...? / ¿Quiénes son...?
Who is...? / Who are...?
Es mi esposo.
He's my husband.
Tú eres..., ¿verdad?/¿cierto?/¿no?
You are..., right?

Identifying objects

¿Qué hay en esta cosa?
What's in this thing?
Bueno, a ver, aquí hay tres cuadernos...
Well, let's see, here are three notebooks...
Oye/Oiga, ¿cómo se dice *suitcase* en español?
Hey, how do you say suitcase *in Spanish?*
Se dice *maleta*.
You say maleta.

Saying what time it is

¿Qué hora es?
What time is it?
Es la una. / Son las dos.
It's one o'clock. / It's two o'clock.
Son las cuatro y veinticinco.
It's four twenty-five.

Polite expressions

Con permiso.
*Pardon me; Excuse me.
(to request permission)*
Perdón.
Pardon me; Excuse me. (to get someone's attention or excuse yourself)
¡Bienvenido/a! *Welcome!*

Expresiones útiles Identify forms of the verb **ser** and point out some subject pronouns. Identify time-telling expressions. Point out the verb form **hay** and explain that it means *there is/are*. Tell students that they will learn more about these concepts in **Estructura**.

Teaching Tip
👥 Have volunteers read individual parts of the **Fotonovela** captions aloud. Then have students work in groups of six to role-play the episode, ad-libbing when possible. Have one or two groups present the episode to the class.

Successful Language Learning Tell students that their conversational skills will grow more quickly as they learn each lesson's **Expresiones útiles**. This feature is designed to teach phrases that will be useful in conversation, and it will also help students understand key phrases in each **Fotonovela**.

Nota cultural Mexico City's metropolitan area is the largest in the hemisphere, with about 21 million people. This number is still only a fraction of Mexico's total population of 111 million. It is the most highly-populated Spanish-speaking country in the world.

TEACHING OPTIONS

Extra Practice →👤← Photocopy pages 6–7 or the **Fotonovela** Videoscript (Supersite) and white out some key words. Play the episode once, and then distribute the photocopied scripts. Play the video a second time and ask students to fill in the missing words. Go over the answers as a class.
Extra Practice Write questions and phrases from **Expresiones útiles** on the board. Ex: **Es la una. Con permiso. ¿Cómo te llamas?**

With their books closed, have students describe a context in which each question or phrase could be used.
Pairs In pairs, have students predict whom **Marissa** will get along with better: **Felipe** or **Jimena**. Have them support their opinions with specific scenes from the episode.

¿Qué pasó?

1 **¿Cierto o falso?** Indicate if each statement is **cierto** or **falso**. Then correct the false statements.

	Cierto	Falso	
1. La Sra. Díaz es de Caracas.	○	◉	La Sra. Díaz es de La Habana.
2. El Sr. Díaz es de Mérida.	◉	○	
3. Marissa es de Los Ángeles, California.	○	◉	Marissa es de Appleton, Wisconsin.
4. Jimena y Felipe son profesores.	○	◉	Jimena y Felipe son estudiantes.
5. Las dos maletas son de Jimena.	○	◉	Las dos maletas son de Marissa.
6. El Sr. Díaz pregunta "¿qué hora es?".	◉	○	
7. Hay un diccionario en la mochila (*backpack*) de Marissa.	◉	○	

2 **Identificar** Indicate which person would make each statement. One name will be used twice.

1. Son las cuatro y veinticinco, papá. Felipe
2. Roberto es mi esposo. Sra. Díaz
3. Yo soy de Wisconsin, ¿de dónde es usted? Marissa
4. ¿Qué hay de nuevo, doña Carolina? don Diego
5. Yo soy de Cuba. Sra. Díaz
6. ¿Qué hay en la mochila, Marissa? Jimena

MARISSA **FELIPE** **SRA. DÍAZ**

DON DIEGO **JIMENA**

3 **Completar** Complete the conversation between Don Diego and Marissa.

DON DIEGO Hola, (1)___señorita___.
MARISSA Hola, señor. ¿Cómo se (2)___llama___ usted?
DON DIEGO Yo me llamo Diego, ¿y (3)___usted___?
MARISSA Yo me llamo Marissa. (4)___Encantada___.
DON DIEGO (5)___Igualmente___, señorita Marissa.
MARISSA Nos (6)___vemos___, don Diego.
DON DIEGO Hasta (7)___luego/pronto/___, señorita Marissa.
 la vista

4 **Conversar** Imagine that you are chatting with a traveler you just met at the airport. With a partner, prepare a conversation using these cues. Some answers will vary.

Estudiante 1	Estudiante 2
Say "good afternoon" to your partner and ask for his or her name. →	Say hello and what your name is. Then ask what your partner's name is.
Say what your name is and that you are glad to meet your partner. →	Say that the pleasure is yours.
Ask how your partner is. →	Say that you're doing well, thank you.
Ask where your partner is from. →	Say where you're from.
Say it's one o'clock and say goodbye. →	Say goodbye.

 Practice more at **vhlcentral.com.**

Left margin (Instructor's Annotations)

1 Expansion Give students these true/false statements as items 8–10: **8. En la mochila de Marissa hay una foto de Jimena y Felipe. (Cierto.) 9. No hay cuadernos en la mochila de Marissa. (Falso.) 10. Hay cuatro personas en la familia Díaz. (Cierto.)**

2 Expansion Ask volunteers to call out additional statements that were made in the **Fotonovela**. The class should guess which character made each statement.

¡Lengua viva! Ask students how they might address **Sr. Díaz (don Roberto).**

Nota cultural Señor(a) and **señorita** may also be used with a person's first name as a sign of respect. Using these titles with a first name also shows a greater level of intimacy or warmth; **señor Díaz** sounds more formal than **señor Roberto.**

3 Teaching Tip Go over the activity by asking volunteers to take the roles of **don Diego** and **Marissa.**

4 Teaching Tip To simplify, ask students to read through the cues and jot down possible phrases for each one.

4 Possible Conversation
E1: Buenas tardes. ¿Cómo te llamas?
E2: Hola. Me llamo Felipe. Y tú, ¿cómo te llamas?
E1: Me llamo Luisa. Mucho gusto.
E2: El gusto es mío.
E1: ¿Cómo estás?
E2: Bien, gracias.
E1: ¿De dónde eres?
E2: Soy de Venezuela.
E2: Uf! Es la una. ¡Adiós!
E2: Chau.

The Affective Dimension
Point out that many people feel nervous when speaking in front of a group. Encourage students to think of anxious feelings as extra energy that will help them accomplish their goals.

Pronunciación Audio: Concepts, Activities Record & Compare

The Spanish alphabet

The Spanish and English alphabets are almost identical, with a few exceptions. For example, the Spanish letter **ñ (eñe)** doesn't occur in the English alphabet. Furthermore, the letters **k (ka)** and **w (doble ve)** are used only in words of foreign origin. Examine the chart below to find other differences.

Letra	Nombre(s)	Ejemplos	Letra	Nombre(s)	Ejemplos
a	a	adiós	m	eme	mapa
b	be	bien, problema	n	ene	nacionalidad
c	ce	cosa, cero	ñ	eñe	mañana
ch	che	chico	o	o	once
d	de	diario, nada	p	pe	profesor
e	e	estudiante	q	cu	qué
f	efe	foto	r	ere	regular, señora
g	ge	gracias, Gerardo, regular	s	ese	señor
h	hache	hola	t	te	tú
i	i	igualmente	u	u	usted
j	jota	Javier	v	ve	vista, nuevo
k	ka, ca	kilómetro	w	doble ve	walkman
l	ele	lápiz	x	equis	existir, México
ll	elle	llave	y	i griega, ye	yo
			z	zeta, ceta	zona

El alfabeto Repeat the Spanish alphabet and example words after your instructor.

Práctica Spell these words aloud in Spanish.

1. nada
2. maleta
3. quince
4. muy
5. hombre
6. por favor
7. San Fernando
8. Estados Unidos
9. Puerto Rico
10. España
11. Javier
12. Ecuador
13. Maite
14. gracias
15. Nueva York

Refranes Read these sayings aloud.

Ver es creer.[1]

En boca cerrada no entran moscas.[2]

[1] Seeing is believing. [2] Silence is golden.

recursos

LM p. 2 | vhlcentral.com Lección 1

Teaching Tip Here is the formal explanation on the Spanish alphabet from the **Real Academia Española:**
El abecedario y los dígrafos *ch, ll* y *rr* El abecedario español está hoy formado por las veintinueve letras siguientes: a, b, c, **ch**, d, e, f, g, h, i, j, k, l, **ll**, m, n, ñ, o, p, q, r, s, t, u, v, w, x, y, z. Si bien las grafías **ch** y **ll** son en propiedad dígrafos—signos ortográficos compuestos de dos letras—, vienen considerándose convencionalmente letras del abecedario español por el hecho de representar, cada una de ellas, un solo sonido. La **rr** también es un dígrafo, pero, a diferencia de la **ch** y la **ll**, no se ha considerado nunca una de las letras del abecedario porque el sonido que representa es el mismo que el que le corresponde a la **r** en posición inicial de palabra o precedida de las consonantes **n, l** o **s.**
La variante española del alfabeto latino antes expuesta fue la utilizada por la Academia desde 1803 […] en la confección de todas sus listas alfabéticas. Pero en el X Congreso de la Asociación de Academias de la Lengua Española, celebrado en 1994, se acordó adoptar el orden alfabético latino universal, en el que la **ch** y la **ll** no se consideran letras independientes.
En consecuencia, las palabras que comienzan por estas dos letras, o que las contienen, pasan a alfabetizarse en los lugares que les corresponden dentro de la **c** y de la **l**, respectivamente. Esta reforma afecta únicamente al proceso de ordenación alfabética de las palabras, no a la composición del abecedario, del que los dígrafos **ch** y **ll** siguen formando parte.

Section Goals

In **Cultura**, students will:
- read about greetings in Spanish-speaking countries
- learn informal greetings and leave-takings
- read about the **plaza principal**
- read about famous friends and couples

Instructional Resources
Supersite/DVD: *Flash cultura*
Supersite: Resources (Scripts, Translations, Answer Keys)
WebSAM
Video Manual, pp. 267–268

En detalle

Antes de leer Ask students to share how they would normally greet a friend or family member.

Lectura
- Linguists have determined that, in the U.S., friends generally remain at least eighteen inches apart while chatting. Hispanic friends would probably deem eighteen inches to be excessive.
- Show students the locations mentioned here by referring them to the maps on the inside covers of their textbooks. Explain that there may be regional variations within each country.
- Explain that an "air kiss" is limited to a grazing of cheeks.

Después de leer Call on two volunteers to stand in front of the class. Point out the natural distance between them. Then demonstrate reduced personal space in Hispanic cultures by having the volunteers face each other with their toes touching and start a conversation. Tell the rest of the class to do the same. Ask students to share their feelings on this change in personal space.

1 Expansion Ask students to write three more true/false statements for a classmate to complete.

EN DETALLE

Additional Reading
Video: *Flash cultura*

Saludos y besos en los países hispanos

In Spanish-speaking countries, kissing on the cheek is a customary way to greet friends and family members. Even when people are introduced for the first time, it is common for them to kiss, particularly in non-business settings. Whereas North Americans maintain considerable personal space when greeting, Spaniards and Latin Americans tend to decrease their personal space and give one or two kisses (**besos**) on the cheek, sometimes accompanied by a handshake or a hug. In formal business settings, where associates do not know one another on a personal level, a simple handshake is appropriate.

Greeting someone with a **beso** varies according to gender and region. Men generally greet each other with a hug or warm handshake, with the exception of Argentina, where male friends and relatives lightly kiss on the cheek. Greetings between men and women, and between women, generally include kissing, but can differ depending on the country and context. In Spain, it is customary to give **dos besos**, starting with the right cheek first. In Latin American countries, including Mexico, Costa Rica, Colombia, and Chile, a greeting consists of a single "air kiss" on the right cheek. Peruvians also "air kiss," but strangers will simply shake hands. In Colombia, female acquaintances tend to simply pat each other on the right forearm or shoulder.

Tendencias

País	Beso	País	Beso
Argentina	💋	España	💋💋
Bolivia	🚫	México	💋
Chile	💋	Paraguay	💋💋
Colombia	💋	Puerto Rico	💋
El Salvador	💋	Venezuela	💋💋💋

ACTIVIDADES

1 **¿Cierto o falso?** Indicate whether these statements are true (**cierto**) or false (**falso**). Correct the false statements.

1. Hispanic people use less personal space when greeting than in the U.S. **Cierto**
2. Men never greet with a kiss in Spanish-speaking countries. **Falso.** Argentine men can greet with a light kiss.
3. Shaking hands is not appropriate for a business setting in Latin America. **Falso.** In most business settings, people greet one another by shaking hands.

4. Spaniards greet with one kiss on the right cheek. **Falso.** They greet with one kiss on each cheek.
5. In Mexico, people greet with an "air kiss." **Cierto**
6. Gender can play a role in the type of greeting given. **Cierto**
7. If two women acquaintances meet in Colombia, they should exchange two kisses on the cheek. **Falso.** They pat one another on the right forearm or shoulder.
8. In Peru, a man and a woman meeting for the first time would probably greet each other with an "air kiss." **Falso.** They would probably shake hands.

TEACHING OPTIONS

Game Divide the class into two teams. Give situations in which people greet one another and have one member from each team identify the appropriate way to greet. Ex: Two male friends in Argentina. (light kiss on the cheek) Give one point for each correct answer. The team with the most points at the end wins.

Un beso Kisses are not only a form of greeting in Hispanic cultures. It is also common to end phone conversations and close letters or e-mails with the words **un beso** or **besos**. Additionally, friends may use **un abrazo** to end a written message. In a more formal e-mail, one can write **un saludo (cordial)** or **saludos**.

ASÍ SE DICE

Saludos y despedidas

¿Cómo te/le va?	How are things going (for you)?
¡Cuánto tiempo!	It's been a long time!
Hasta ahora.	See you soon.
¿Qué hay?	What's new?
¿Qué onda? (Méx., Arg., Chi.); ¿Qué más? (Ven., Col.)	What's going on?

EL MUNDO HISPANO

Parejas y amigos famosos

Here are some famous couples and friends from the Spanish-speaking world.

- **Jennifer López** y **Marc Anthony** (Estados Unidos/ Puerto Rico) Both singers, the couple married in 2004, and often perform together. They both starred in the **2007** film *El Cantante.*

- **Gael García Bernal** (México) y **Diego Luna** (México) These lifelong friends became famous when they starred in the 2001 Mexican film *Y tu mamá también.* They continue to work together on projects, such as the 2008 film, *Rudo y Cursi.*

- **Salma Hayek** (México) y **Penélope Cruz** (España) These two close friends developed their acting skills in their countries of origin before meeting in Hollywood.

PERFIL

La plaza principal

La Plaza Mayor de Salamanca

In the Spanish-speaking world, public space is treasured. Small city and town life revolves around the **plaza principal.** Often surrounded by cathedrals or municipal buildings like the **ayuntamiento** (*city hall*), the pedestrian **plaza** is designated as a central meeting place for family and friends. During warmer months, when outdoor cafés usually line the **plaza**, it is a popular spot to have a leisurely cup of coffee, chat, and people watch. Many town festivals, or **ferias**, also take place in this space. One of the most famous town squares is the **Plaza Mayor** in the university town of Salamanca, Spain. Students gather underneath its famous clock tower to meet up with friends or simply take a coffee break.

La Plaza de Armas, Lima, Perú

Conexión Internet

What are the **plazas principales** in large cities such as Mexico City and Caracas?

Go to **vhlcentral.com** to find more cultural information related to this **Cultura** section.

ACTIVIDADES

2 **Comprensión** Answer these questions. *Some answers may vary. Suggested answers:*

1. What are two types of buildings found on the **plaza principal**? *municipal buildings and cathedrals*
2. What two types of events or activities are common at a **plaza principal**? *meeting with friends and festivals*
3. How would Diego Luna greet his friends? *¿Qué onda?*
4. Would Salma Hayek and Jennifer López greet each other with one kiss or two? *one*

3 **Saludos** Role-play these greetings with a partner. Include a verbal greeting as well as a kiss or handshake, as appropriate. *Role-plays will vary according to student gender.*

1. friends in Mexico
2. business associates at a conference in Chile
3. friends meeting in Madrid's Plaza Mayor
4. Peruvians meeting for the first time
5. relatives in Argentina

recursos

| VM pp. 267–268 | vhlcentral.com Lección 1 |

Practice more at **vhlcentral.com.**

1.1 Nouns and articles Tutorial

Spanish nouns

ANTE TODO A noun is a word used to identify people, animals, places, things, or ideas. Unlike English, all Spanish nouns, even those that refer to non-living things, have gender; that is, they are considered either masculine or feminine. As in English, nouns in Spanish also have number, meaning that they are either singular or plural.

Nouns that refer to living things

Masculine nouns		Feminine nouns	
el hombre	*the man*	**la mujer**	*the woman*
ending in –o		*ending in –a*	
el chico	*the boy*	**la chica**	*the girl*
el pasajero	*the (male) passenger*	**la pasajera**	*the (female) passenger*
ending in –or		*ending in –ora*	
el conductor	*the (male) driver*	**la conductora**	*the (female) driver*
el profesor	*the (male) teacher*	**la profesora**	*the (female) teacher*
ending in –ista		*ending in –ista*	
el turista	*the (male) tourist*	**la turista**	*the (female) tourist*

▶ Generally, nouns that refer to males, like **el hombre**, are masculine, while nouns that refer to females, like **la mujer**, are feminine.

▶ Many nouns that refer to male beings end in **–o** or **–or**. Their corresponding feminine forms end in **–a** and **–ora**, respectively.

el conductor

la profesora

▶ The masculine and feminine forms of nouns that end in **–ista**, like **turista**, are the same, so gender is indicated by the article **el** (masculine) or **la** (feminine). Some other nouns have identical masculine and feminine forms.

el joven	**la** joven
the youth; the young man	*the youth; the young woman*
el estudiante	**la** estudiante
the (male) student	*the (female) student*

Nouns that refer to non-living things

Masculine nouns		Feminine nouns	
ending in –o		**ending in –a**	
el cuaderno	the notebook	la computadora	the computer
el diario	the diary	la cosa	the thing
el diccionario	the dictionary	la escuela	the school
el número	the number	la maleta	the suitcase
el video	the video	la palabra	the word
ending in –ma		**ending in –ción**	
el problema	the problem	la lección	the lesson
el programa	the program	la conversación	the conversation
ending in –s		**ending in –dad**	
el autobús	the bus	la nacionalidad	the nationality
el país	the country	la comunidad	the community

¡LENGUA VIVA!

The Spanish word for *video* can be pronounced with the stress on the **i** or the **e**. For that reason, you might see the word written with or without an accent: **video** or **vídeo**.

▶ As shown above, certain noun endings are strongly associated with a specific gender, so you can use them to determine if a noun is masculine or feminine.

▶ Because the gender of nouns that refer to non-living things cannot be determined by foolproof rules, you should memorize the gender of each noun you learn. It is helpful to learn each noun with its corresponding article, **el** for masculine and **la** for feminine.

▶ Another reason to memorize the gender of every noun is that there are common exceptions to the rules of gender. For example, **el mapa** (*map*) and **el día** (*day*) end in **–a**, but are masculine. **La mano** (*hand*) ends in **–o**, but is feminine.

Plural of nouns

▶ To form the plural, add **–s** to nouns that end in a vowel. For nouns that end in a consonant, add **–es**. For nouns that end in **z,** change the **z** to **c,** then add **–es**.

el chico → los chicos la nacionalidad → las nacionalidades

el diario → los diarios el país → los países

el problema → los problemas el lápiz (*pencil*) → los lápices

▶ In general, when a singular noun has an accent mark on the last syllable, the accent is dropped from the plural form.

la lección → las lecciones el autobús → los autobuses

▶ Use the masculine plural form to refer to a group that includes both males and females.

1 pasajero + 2 pasajeras = 3 pasajeros 2 chicos + 2 chicas = 4 chicos

CONSULTA

You will learn more about accent marks in **Lección 4, Pronunciación,** p. 115.

Spanish articles

ANTE TODO As you know, English often uses definite articles (*the*) and indefinite articles (*a, an*) before nouns. Spanish also has definite and indefinite articles. Unlike English, Spanish articles vary in form because they agree in gender and number with the nouns they modify.

Definite articles

▶ Spanish has four forms that are equivalent to the English definite article *the*. Use definite articles to refer to specific nouns.

Masculine		Feminine	
SINGULAR	PLURAL	SINGULAR	PLURAL
el diccionario	**los** diccionarios	**la** computadora	**las** computadoras
the dictionary	*the dictionaries*	*the computer*	*the computers*

Indefinite articles

▶ Spanish has four forms that are equivalent to the English indefinite article, which according to context may mean *a*, *an*, or *some*. Use indefinite articles to refer to unspecified persons or things.

Masculine		Feminine	
SINGULAR	PLURAL	SINGULAR	PLURAL
un pasajero	**unos** pasajeros	**una** fotografía	**unas** fotografías
a (one) passenger	*some passengers*	*a (one) photograph*	*some photographs*

¡LENGUA VIVA!
Feminine singular nouns that begin with **a-** or **ha-** require the masculine articles **el** and **un**. This is done in order to avoid repetition of the **a** sound. The plural forms still use the feminine articles.
el agua *water*
las aguas *waters*
un hacha *ax*
unas hachas *axes*

¡LENGUA VIVA!
Since **la fotografía** is feminine, so is its shortened form, **la foto**, even though it ends in **–o**.

¡INTÉNTALO! Provide a definite article for each noun in the first column and an indefinite article for each noun in the second column.

¿el, la, los o las?
1. _la_ chica
2. _el_ chico
3. _la_ maleta
4. _los_ cuadernos
5. _el_ lápiz
6. _las_ mujeres

¿un, una, unos o unas?
1. _un_ autobús
2. _unas_ escuelas
3. _una_ computadora
4. _unos_ hombres
5. _una_ señora
6. _unos_ lápices

recursos

WB
p. 3

LM
p. 3

vhlcentral.com
Lección 1

Práctica

1 **¿Singular o plural?** If the word is singular, make it plural. If it is plural, make it singular.

1. el número los números
2. un diario unos diarios
3. la estudiante las estudiantes
4. el conductor los conductores
5. el país los países
6. las cosas la cosa
7. unos turistas un turista
8. las nacionalidades la nacionalidad

9. unas computadoras una computadora
10. los problemas el problema
11. una fotografía unas fotografías
12. los profesores el profesor
13. unas señoritas una señorita
14. el hombre los hombres
15. la maleta las maletas
16. la señora las señoras

2 **Identificar** For each drawing, provide the noun with its corresponding definite and indefinite articles.

> **modelo**
> las maletas, unas maletas

1. la computadora, una computadora

2. los cuadernos, unos cuadernos

3. las mujeres, unas mujeres

4. el chico, un chico

5. la escuela, una escuela

6. las fotos, unas fotos

7. los autobuses, unos autobuses

8. el diario, un diario

Comunicación

3 **Charadas** In groups, play a game of charades. Individually, think of two nouns for each charade, for example, a boy using a computer (**un chico**; **una computadora**). The first person to guess correctly acts out the next charade. Answers will vary.

Practice more at **vhlcentral.com.**

1 **Expansion** Reverse the activity by reading the on-page answers and having students convert the singular to plural and vice versa. Make sure they close their books. Give the nouns in random order.

2 **Expansion** As an additional visual exercise, bring in photos or magazine pictures that illustrate items whose names students know. Ask students to indicate the definite article and the noun. Include a mix of singular and plural nouns. Repeat the exercise with indefinite articles.

3 **Teaching Tip** Model the game of charades by writing some new cognates on the board (Ex: **la guitarra, el teléfono, la televisión**). Act out sitting on a couch and flipping channels on a remote and invite students to guess. Emphasize that the student acting out the charade must not speak and that he or she may show the number of syllables by using fingers.

3 **Expansion** Split the class into two teams, with volunteers from each team acting out the charades. Give a point to each team for correctly guessing the charade. The team with the most points wins.

TEACHING OPTIONS

Video Show the **Fotonovela** episode again to offer more input on singular and plural nouns and articles. With their books closed, have students write down every noun and article that they hear. After viewing the video, ask volunteers to list the nouns and articles they heard. Explain that the **las** used when telling time refers to **las horas** (Ex: **Son las cinco = Son las cinco horas**).

Extra Practice To challenge students, slowly read aloud a short passage from a novel, story, poem, or newspaper article written in Spanish, preferably one with a great number of nouns and articles. As a listening exercise, have students write down every noun and article they hear, even unfamiliar ones (the articles may cue when nouns appear).

Section Goals

In **Estructura 1.2**, students will be introduced to:
• numbers 0–30
• the verb form **hay**

Instructional Resources

Supersite: Audio (Lab MP3 Files); Resources (*PowerPoints*, Activity Pack, Scripts, Answer Keys); Testing Program (Quizzes)
WebSAM
Workbook, p. 4
Lab Manual, p. 4

Teaching Tips

• Introduce numbers by asking students if they can count to ten in Spanish. Model the pronunciation of each number. Write individual numbers on the board and call on students at random to say the number.
• Say numbers aloud at random and have students hold up the appropriate number of fingers. Then reverse the drill; hold up varying numbers of fingers at random and ask students to shout out the corresponding number in Spanish.
• Emphasize the variable forms of **uno** and **veintiuno**, giving examples of each. Ex: **veintiún profesores, veintiuna profesoras.**
• Ask questions like these: **¿Cuántos estudiantes hay en la clase? (Hay _____ estudiantes en la clase.)**

1.2 # Numbers 0–30 **Tutorial**

Los números 0 a 30					
0	cero				
1	uno	**11**	once	**21**	veintiuno
2	dos	**12**	doce	**22**	veintidós
3	tres	**13**	trece	**23**	veintitrés
4	cuatro	**14**	catorce	**24**	veinticuatro
5	cinco	**15**	quince	**25**	veinticinco
6	seis	**16**	dieciséis	**26**	veintiséis
7	siete	**17**	diecisiete	**27**	veintisiete
8	ocho	**18**	dieciocho	**28**	veintiocho
9	nueve	**19**	diecinueve	**29**	veintinueve
10	diez	**20**	veinte	**30**	treinta

AYUDA

Though it is less common, the numbers 16 through 29 (except 20) can also be written as three words: **diez y seis, diez y siete…**

▶ The number **uno** (*one*) and numbers ending in **–uno**, such as **veintiuno**, have more than one form. Before masculine nouns, **uno** shortens to **un**. Before feminine nouns, **uno** changes to **una**.

 un hombre ⟶ veinti**ún** hombres **una** mujer ⟶ veinti**una** mujeres

▶ **¡Atención!** The forms **uno** and **veintiuno** are used when counting (**uno, dos, tres... veinte, veintiuno, veintidós...**). They are also used when the number *follows* a noun, even if the noun is feminine: **la lección uno**.

▶ To ask *how many people* or *things* there are, use **cuántos** before masculine nouns and **cuántas** before feminine nouns.

▶ The Spanish equivalent of both *there is* and *there are* is **hay**. Use **¿Hay...?** to ask *Is there…?* or *Are there…?* Use **no hay** to express *there is not* or *there are not*.

—**¿Cuántos** estudiantes **hay?**
How many students are there?

—**Hay** seis estudiantes en la foto.
There are six students in the photo.

—**¿Hay** chicos en la fotografía?
Are there guys in the picture?

—**Hay** tres chicas y **no hay** chicos.
There are three girls, and there are no guys.

recursos

WB p. 4

LM p. 4

S
vhlcentral.com
Lección 1

¡INTÉNTALO! Provide the Spanish words for these numbers.

1. **7** siete
2. **16** dieciséis
3. **29** veintinueve
4. **1** uno
5. **0** cero
6. **15** quince
7. **21** veintiuno
8. **9** nueve
9. **23** veintitrés
10. **11** once
11. **30** treinta
12. **4** cuatro
13. **12** doce
14. **28** veintiocho
15. **14** catorce
16. **10** diez

TEACHING OPTIONS

TPR Assign ten students a number from 0–30 and line them up in front of the class. Call out one of the numbers at random, and have the student assigned that number step forward. When two students have stepped forward, ask them to repeat their numbers. Then ask individuals to add (Say: **Suma**) or subtract (Say: **Resta**) the two numbers, giving the result in Spanish.

Game Ask students to write B-I-N-G-O across the top of a blank piece of paper. Have them draw five squares vertically under each letter and randomly fill in the squares with numbers from 0–30, without repeating any numbers. Draw numbers from a hat and call them out in Spanish. The first student to mark five in a row (horizontally, vertically, or diagonally) yells **¡Bingo!** and wins. Have the winner confirm the numbers for you in Spanish.

Práctica

1 **Contar** Following the pattern, write out the missing numbers in Spanish.

1. 1, 3, 5, ..., 29 7, 9, 11, 13, 15, 17, 19, 21, 23, 25, 27
2. 2, 4, 6, ..., 30 8, 10, 12, 14, 16, 18, 20, 22, 24, 26, 28
3. 3, 6, 9, ..., 30 12, 15, 18, 21, 24, 27
4. 30, 28, 26, ..., 0 24, 22, 20, 18, 16, 14, 12, 10, 8, 6, 4, 2
5. 30, 25, 20, ..., 0 15, 10, 5
6. 28, 24, 20, ..., 0 16, 12, 8, 4

2 **Resolver** Solve these math problems with a partner.

> **modelo**
> 5 + 3 =
> **Estudiante 1:** *cinco más tres son...*
> **Estudiante 2:** *ocho*

AYUDA
+ → **más**
− → **menos**
= → **son**

1. **2 + 15 =** Dos más quince son diecisiete.
2. **20 – 1 =** Veinte menos uno son diecinueve.
3. **5 + 7 =** Cinco más siete son doce.
4. **18 + 12 =** Dieciocho más doce son treinta.
5. **3 + 22 =** Tres más veintidós son veinticinco.
6. **6 – 3 =** Seis menos tres son tres.
7. **11 + 12 =** Once más doce son veintitrés.
8. **7 – 2 =** Siete menos dos son cinco.
9. **8 + 5 =** Ocho más cinco son trece.
10. **23 – 14 =** Veintitrés menos catorce son nueve.

3 **¿Cuántos hay?** How many persons or things are there in these drawings?

> **modelo**
> Hay tres maletas.

1. _____ Hay veinte lápices.
2. _____ Hay un hombre.

Chicos

3. _____ Hay veinticinco chicos.
4. _____ Hay una conductora.
5. _____ Hay cuatro fotos.

Chicas

6. _____ Hay treinta cuadernos.
7. _____ Hay seis turistas.
8. _____ Hay diecisiete chicas.

1 Teaching Tips
• Before beginning the activity, make sure students know each pattern: odds (**los números impares**), evens (**los números pares**), count by threes (**contar de tres en tres**).
• To simplify, write complete patterns out on the board.

1 Expansion Explain that a prime number (**un número primo**) is any number that can only be divided by itself and 1. To challenge students, ask the class to list the prime numbers up to 30. (They are: 1, 2, 3, 5, 7, 11, 13, 17, 19, 23, 29.)

2 Expansion Do simple multiplication problems. Introduce the phrases **multiplicado por** and **dividido por**. Ex: **Cinco multiplicado por cinco son...** (veinticinco). **Veinte dividido por cuatro son...** (cinco).

3 Teaching Tip Have students read the directions and the model. Cue student responses by asking questions related to the drawings. Ex: **¿Cuántos lápices hay?** (**Hay veinte lápices.**)

3 Expansion Add an additional visual aspect to this activity. Hold up or point to classroom objects and ask how many there are. Since students will not know the names of many items, a simple number or **hay** + the number will suffice to signal comprehension. Ex: —**¿Cuántos bolígrafos hay aquí?** —**(Hay) Dos.**

TEACHING OPTIONS

TPR Give ten students each a card that contains a different number from 0–30. The cards should be visible to the other students. Then call out simple math problems (addition or subtraction) involving the assigned numbers. When the first two numbers are called, each student steps forward. The student whose assigned number completes the math problem then has five seconds to join them.

Extra Practice Ask questions about your university and the town or city in which it is located. Ex: **¿Cuántos profesores hay en el departamento de español? ¿Cuántas universidades hay en _____? ¿Cuántas pizzerías hay en _____?** Encourage students to guess the number. If a number exceeds 30, write that number on the board and model its pronunciation.

Comunicación

 4 **En la clase** With a classmate, take turns asking and answering these questions about your classroom. *Answers will vary.*

1. ¿Cuántos estudiantes hay?
2. ¿Cuántos profesores hay?
3. ¿Hay una computadora?
4. ¿Hay una maleta?
5. ¿Cuántos mapas hay?

6. ¿Cuántos lápices hay?
7. ¿Hay cuadernos?
8. ¿Cuántos diccionarios hay?
9. ¿Hay hombres?
10. ¿Cuántas mujeres hay?

5 **Preguntas** With a classmate, take turns asking and answering questions about the drawing. Talk about: *Answers will vary.*

1. how many children there are
2. how many women there are
3. if there are some photographs
4. if there is a boy
5. how many notebooks there are

6. if there is a bus
7. if there are tourists
8. how many pencils there are
9. if there is a man
10. how many computers there are

 Practice more at **vhlcentral.com.**

1.3 Present tense of ser Tutorial

Subject pronouns

ANTE TODO In order to use verbs, you will need to learn about subject pronouns. A subject pronoun replaces the name or title of a person or thing and acts as the subject of a verb. In both Spanish and English, subject pronouns are divided into three groups: first person, second person, and third person.

Subject pronouns

		SINGULAR			PLURAL	
FIRST PERSON	yo	*I*		nosotros	*we* (masculine)	
				nosotras	*we* (feminine)	
SECOND PERSON	tú	*you* (familiar)		vosotros	*you* (masc., fam.)	
	usted (Ud.)	*you* (formal)		vosotras	*you* (fem., fam.)	
				ustedes (Uds.)	*you* (form.)	
THIRD PERSON	él	*he*		ellos	*they* (masc.)	
	ella	*she*		ellas	*they* (fem.)	

¡LENGUA VIVA!

In Latin America, **ustedes** is used as the plural for both **tú** and **usted**. In Spain, however, **vosotros** and **vosotras** are used as the plural of **tú**, and **ustedes** is used only as the plural of **usted**.

• • •

Usted and **ustedes** are abbreviated as **Ud.** and **Uds.**, or occasionally as **Vd.** and **Vds.**

▶ Spanish has two subject pronouns that mean *you* (singular). Use **tú** when addressing a friend, a family member, or a child you know well. Use **usted** to address a person with whom you have a formal or more distant relationship, such as a superior at work, a professor, or an older person.

Tú eres de Canadá, ¿verdad, David?	¿**Usted** es la profesora de español?
You are from Canada, right, David?	*Are you the Spanish professor?*

▶ The masculine plural forms **nosotros**, **vosotros**, and **ellos** refer to a group of males or to a group of males and females. The feminine plural forms **nosotras**, **vosotras**, and **ellas** can refer only to groups made up exclusively of females.

nosotros, vosotros, ellos

nosotros, vosotros, ellos

nosotras, vosotras, ellas

▶ There is no Spanish equivalent of the English subject pronoun *it*. Generally *it* is not expressed in Spanish.

Es un problema.	Es una computadora.
It's a problem.	*It's a computer.*

Section Goals

In **Estructura 1.3**, students will be introduced to:
• subject pronouns
• the present tense of the verb **ser**
• the uses of **ser** (to identify, to indicate possession, to describe origin, and to talk about professions or occupations)

Instructional Resources

Supersite: Audio (Lab MP3 Files); Resources (*PowerPoints*, Activity Pack, Scripts, Answer Keys); Testing Program (Quizzes)
WebSAM
Workbook, pp. 5–6
Lab Manual, p. 5

Teaching Tips

• Point to yourself and say: **Yo soy profesor(a)**. Then point to a student and ask: ¿**Tú eres profesor(a) o estudiante?** (estudiante) Say: **Sí, tú eres estudiante**. Indicate the whole class and tell them: **Ustedes son estudiantes**. Once the pattern has been established, include other subject pronouns and forms of **ser** while indicating other students. Ex: **Él es…, Ella es…, Ellos son…**
• Review familiar and formal forms of address students learned in **Contextos**.
• You may want to point out that while **usted** and **ustedes** are second person forms of address equivalent to the English *you*, they take third person verb forms.

Note: While the **vosotros/as** forms are listed in verb paradigms in **PANORAMA**, they will not be actively practiced.

TEACHING OPTIONS

Extra Practice Indicate people in the classroom and have students give subject pronouns based on their point of view. Ex: Point to yourself (**usted**), a female student (**ella**), everyone in the class (**nosotros**).
Extra Practice Ask students to indicate whether certain people would be addressed as **tú** or **usted**. Ex: A roommate, a friend's grandfather, a doctor, a neighbor's child.

Heritage Speakers Ask heritage speakers how they address elder members of their family, such as parents, grandparents, aunts, and uncles—whether they use **tú** or **usted**. Also ask them if they use **vosotros/as** (they typically will not unless they or their family are from Spain) or **voseo**. Explain that **voseo** is the use of the second-person subject pronoun **vos** instead of **tú**. It is used extensively in much of Latin America, including Argentina, Uruguay, and Costa Rica.

Teaching Tips
• Work through the explanation and the forms of **ser** in the chart. Emphasize that **es** is used for **usted**, **él**, and **ella**, and that **son** is used for **ustedes**, **ellos**, and **ellas**. Context, subject pronouns, or names will determine who is being addressed or talked about.
• Explain that **ser** is used to identify people and things. At this point there is no need to explain that **estar** also means *to be*; it will be introduced in **Lección 2**.
• Explain the meaning of **¿quién?** and ask questions about students. Ex: ____, **¿quién es ella? Sí, es ____. ¿Quién soy yo? Sí, soy el/la profesor(a)** ____. Introduce **¿qué?** and ask questions about items in the class. Ex: (*Pointing to a map*) **¿Qué es? Sí, es un mapa**.
• Point out the construction of **ser + de** to indicate possession. Stress that the construction [*apostrophe + s*] does not exist in Spanish. Pick up objects belonging to students and ask questions. Ex: **¿De quién es el cuaderno? (Es de ____.) ¿De quién son los libros? (Son de ____.)** Then hold up items from two different students and ask: **¿De quiénes son las plumas? Son de ____ y ____.**
• Introduce the contraction **de + el = del**. Emphasize that **de** does not make contractions with other definite articles, and provide examples. Ex: **Soy del estado de ____. El diccionario no es de la profesora de ____.** Also use examples of possession to illustrate the contraction. Ex: **¿Es el mapa del profesor?**

The present tense of **ser**

ANTE TODO In **Contextos** and **Fotonovela**, you have already used several present-tense forms of **ser** (*to be*) to identify yourself and others, and to talk about where you and others are from. **Ser** is an irregular verb; its forms do not follow the regular patterns that most verbs follow. You need to memorize the forms, which appear in this chart.

The verb ser (*to be*)		
SINGULAR FORMS		
yo	**soy**	*I am*
tú	**eres**	*you are* (fam.)
Ud./él/ella	**es**	*you are* (form.); *he/she is*
PLURAL FORMS		
nosotros/as	**somos**	*we are*
vosotros/as	**sois**	*you are* (fam.)
Uds./ellos/ellas	**son**	*you are* (form.); *they are*

Uses of *ser*

▶ Use **ser** to identify people and things.

—¿Quién **es** él?
Who is he?

—**Es** Felipe Díaz Velázquez.
He's Felipe Díaz Velázquez.

—¿Qué **es**?
What is it?

—**Es** un mapa de España.
It's a map of Spain.

Es Marissa.

Es una maleta.

▶ **Ser** also expresses possession, with the preposition **de**. There is no Spanish equivalent of the English construction [*noun*] + 's (*Maru's*). In its place, Spanish uses [*noun*] + **de** + [*owner*].

—¿**De** quién **es**?
Whose is it?

—**Es** el diario **de** Maru.
It's Maru's diary.

—¿**De** quién **son**?
Whose are they?

—**Son** los lápices **de** la chica.
They are the girl's pencils.

▶ When **de** is followed by the article **el**, the two combine to form the contraction **del**. **De** does *not* contract with **la**, **las**, or **los**.

—**Es** la computadora **del** conductor.
It's the driver's computer.

—**Son** las maletas **del** chico.
They are the boy's suitcases.

TEACHING OPTIONS

Extra Practice As a rapid-response drill, call out subject pronouns and have students answer with the correct form of **ser**. Ex: **tú (eres), ustedes (son)**. Reverse the drill by starting with forms of **ser**. Students must give the subject pronouns. Accept multiple answers for **es** and **son**.

TPR Have students form a circle. Toss a ball to individual students. When a student catches it, call on another to state whose ball it is. Ex: **Es de ____**. Take two balls and toss them to different students to elicit **Son de ____ y ____.**

¡LENGUA VIVA!

Some geographic locations can be referred to either with or without a definite article:
Soy de Estados Unidos./Soy de los Estados Unidos.

• • •

Sometimes a definite article is a part of a proper name, as in **El Salvador, El Paso,** and **Los Ángeles.** In these cases, **de** and **el** do not contract:
Soy de El Salvador.

▶ **Ser** also uses the preposition **de** to express origin.

¿De dónde eres?
Yo soy de Wisconsin.
¿De dónde es usted?
Yo soy de Cuba.

—**¿De** dónde **es** Juan Carlos?
Where is Juan Carlos from?

—Es **de** Argentina.
He's from Argentina.

—**¿De** dónde **es** Maru?
Where is Maru from?

—**Es de** Costa Rica.
She's from Costa Rica.

▶ Use **ser** to express profession or occupation.

Don Francisco **es conductor**.
Don Francisco is a driver.

Yo **soy estudiante**.
I am a student.

▶ Unlike English, Spanish does not use the indefinite article (**un, una**) after **ser** when referring to professions, unless accompanied by an adjective or other description.

Marta **es** profesora.
Marta is a teacher.

Marta **es una** profesora excelente.
Marta is an excellent teacher.

CONSULTA

You will learn more about adjectives in **Estructura 3.1,** pp. 80–82.

NOTA CULTURAL

Created in 1999, LAN Perú is an affiliate of the Chilean-based LAN Airlines, one of the largest carriers in South America. LAN Perú operates out of Lima, offering domestic flights and international service to select major cities in the Americas and Spain.

Somos Perú
LanPerú

recursos
WB pp. 5–6
LM p. 5
vhlcentral.com
Lección 1

¡INTÉNTALO! Provide the correct subject pronouns and the present forms of **ser**.

1. Gabriel — *él* — *es*
2. Juan y yo — *nosotros* — *somos*
3. Óscar y Flora — *ellos* — *son*
4. Adriana — *ella* — *es*
5. las turistas — *ellas* — *son*
6. el chico — *él* — *es*
7. los conductores — *ellos* — *son*
8. los señores Ruiz — *ellos* — *son*

TEACHING TIPS

• Explain **ser** + **de** to express origin. Start practicing this construction by indicating where you are from. Ex: **Soy de ____.** You may also want to further practice and contrast the contraction **del**. Ex: **Soy del estado de ____/de la región (de) ____.** Introduce **¿de dónde?** and ask students where they are from. Ex: **____, ¿de dónde eres?** After a student answers, ask another student: **¿De dónde es ____? (Es de ____.)**

• Explain the use of **ser** to describe professions or occupations. Say: **Yo soy profesor(a) de español. ¿Qué eres tú?** Response: **Soy estudiante.** Say: **Sí, eres estudiante.**

• Emphasize that the indefinite articles **un** and **una** are not used with **ser** and professions or occupations. Ex: **Él es arquitecto. Somos estudiantes.** However, stress that **un** and **una** are required if there is a descriptor present. Ex: **Él es un arquitecto importante. Somos unos estudiantes inteligentes.**

• At this point you may want to present *Vocabulario adicional: Más vocabulario para los países* from the Supersite.

TEACHING OPTIONS

Extra Practice Write cognates on the board and ask students to identify the professions of famous people. Ex: **actor/actriz, presidente, artista, pianista.** Ask: **¿Qué es Brad Pitt? (Es actor.) ¿Quién es presidente? (____ es presidente.)**
Pairs Have pairs interview each other. Write sample questions on the board. Have students report about their partners. Students should begin by saying **Él/Ella es…**

TPR Say what state you are from. Then ask individuals: **¿De dónde eres?** As students answer, have them stand in groups according to state, town, neighborhood, or street. Then point to individuals, pairs, and groups at random, and ask where people are from. Alternate direct questions (**¿De dónde son ustedes?**) with questions for the whole class to answer (**¿De dónde es ella?**). Encourage students to link arms when answering with **nosotros/as.**

Práctica

1

Pronombres What subject pronouns would you use to (a) talk *to* these people directly and (b) talk *about* them to others?

> **modelo**
> un joven tú, él

1. una chica tú, ella
2. el presidente de México Ud., él
3. tres chicas y un chico Uds., ellos
4. un estudiante tú, él
5. la señora Ochoa Ud., ella
6. dos profesoras Uds., ellas

2

Identidad y origen With a partner, take turns asking and answering these questions about the people indicated: **¿Quién es?/¿Quiénes son?** and **¿De dónde es?/¿De dónde son?**

> **modelo**
> Selena Gomez (Estados Unidos)
> **Estudiante 1:** *¿Quién es?* **Estudiante 1:** *¿De dónde es?*
> **Estudiante 2:** *Es Selena Gomez.* **Estudiante 2:** *Es de los Estados Unidos.*

1. Enrique Iglesias (España)
 E1: ¿Quién es? E2: Es Enrique Iglesias. E1: ¿De dónde es? E2: Es de España.
2. Robinson Canó (República Dominicana)
 E2: ¿Quién es? E1: Es Robinson Canó. E2: ¿De dónde es? E1: Es de (la) República Dominicana.
3. Rebecca Lobo y Martin Sheen (Estados Unidos) E1: ¿Quiénes son? E2: Son Rebecca
 Lobo y Martin Sheen. E1: ¿De dónde son? E2: Son de (los) Estados Unidos.
4. Carlos Santana y Salma Hayek (México) E2: ¿Quiénes son? E1: Son Carlos Santana y
 Salma Hayek. E2: ¿De dónde son? E1: Son de México.
5. Shakira (Colombia)
 E1: ¿Quién es? E2: Es Shakira. E1: ¿De dónde es? E2: Es de Colombia.
6. Antonio Banderas y Penélope Cruz (España) E2: ¿Quiénes son? E1: Son Antonio Banderas
 y Penélope Cruz. E2: ¿De dónde son? E1: Son de España.
7. Taylor Swift y Demi Lovato (Estados Unidos) E1: ¿Quiénes son? E2: Son Taylor Swift
 y Demi Lovato. E1: ¿De dónde son? E2: Son de (los) Estados Unidos.
8. Daisy Fuentes (Cuba) E2: ¿Quién es? E1: Es Daisy Fuentes. E2: ¿De dónde es? E1: Es de Cuba.

3

¿Qué es? Ask your partner what each object is and to whom it belongs.

> **modelo**
> **Estudiante 1:** *¿Qué es?* **Estudiante 1:** *¿De quién es?*
> **Estudiante 2:** *Es un diccionario.* **Estudiante 2:** *Es del profesor Núñez.*

1. 2. 3. 4.

1. E1: ¿Qué es?
 E2: Es una maleta.
 E1: ¿De quién es?
 E2: Es de la Sra. Valdés.

2. E1: ¿Qué es?
 E2: Es un cuaderno.
 E1: ¿De quién es?
 E2: Es de Gregorio.

3. E1: ¿Qué es?
 E2: Es una computadora.
 E1: ¿De quién es?
 E2: Es de Rafael.

4. E1: ¿Qué es?
 E2: Es un diario.
 E1: ¿De quién es?
 E2: Es de Marisa.

Comunicación

4 **Preguntas** Using the items in the word bank, ask your partner questions about the ad. Be imaginative in your responses. *Answers will vary.*

¿Cuántas?	¿De dónde?	¿Qué?
¿Cuántos?	¿De quién?	¿Quién?

SOMOS ECOTURISTA, S.A.
Los autobuses oficiales de la Ruta Maya

- 25 autobuses en total
- 30 conductores del área
- pasajeros internacionales
- mapas de la región

¡Todos a bordo!

5 **¿Quién es?** In small groups, take turns pretending to be a famous person from a Spanish-speaking country (such as Spain, Mexico, Puerto Rico, Cuba, or the United States). Use the list of professions to think of people from a variety of backgrounds. Your partners will ask you questions and try to guess who you are. *Answers will vary.*

actor *actor*	cantante *singer*	escritor(a) *writer*
actriz *actress*	deportista *athlete*	músico/a *musician*

modelo

Estudiante 3: ¿Eres de Puerto Rico?
Estudiante 1: No. Soy de Colombia.
Estudiante 2: ¿Eres hombre?
Estudiante 1: Sí. Soy hombre.
Estudiante 3: ¿Eres escritor?
Estudiante 1: No. Soy actor.
Estudiante 2: ¿Eres John Leguizamo?
Estudiante 1: ¡Sí! ¡Sí!

 Practice more at **vhlcentral.com**.

4 **Teaching Tip** If students ask, explain that the abbreviation **S.A.** in the ad stands for **Sociedad Anónima** and is equivalent to the English abbreviation *Inc.* (*Incorporated*).

4 **Expansion** Ask pairs to write four true/false statements about the ad. Call on volunteers to read their sentences. The class will indicate whether the statements are true (**cierto**) or false (**falso**) and correct the false statements.

5 **Teaching Tips**
- To simplify, have students brainstorm a list of names in the categories suggested.
- Have three students read the **modelo** aloud.

5 **Expansion** Have each group select a famous person that was mentioned during the activity and write a description of him or her. Before they begin writing, brainstorm some useful cognate adjectives that students can use and tell them to be sure not to use the person's name in their description. Then have groups take turns reading their descriptions aloud for the class to guess the person's identity. If this guessing proves too difficult, allow the class to ask for a hint (**una pista**), such as a song or movie title.

TEACHING OPTIONS

Small Groups Bring in personal photos or magazine pictures that show people. In small groups, have students invent stories about the people: who they are, where they are from, and what they do. Circulate around the room and assist with unfamiliar vocabulary as necessary, but encourage students to use terms they already know.

Game Hand out individual strips of paper with names of famous people on them. There should be several duplicates of each name. Then give descriptions of one of the famous people (**Es de _____. Es** [*profession*]**.**), including cognate adjectives if you wish (**inteligente**, **pesimista**). The first person to stand and indicate that the name they have is the one you are describing (**¡Yo lo tengo!**) wins that round.

1.4 Telling time Tutorial

 ANTE TODO In both English and Spanish, the verb *to be* (**ser**) and numbers are used to tell time.

▶ To ask what time it is, use **¿Qué hora es?** When telling time, use **es + la** with **una** and **son + las** with all other hours.

Es la una. **Son las** dos. **Son las** seis.

▶ As in English, you express time in Spanish from the hour to the half-hour by adding minutes.

Son las cuatro **y cinco.** Son las once **y veinte.**

▶ You may use either **y cuarto** or **y quince** to express fifteen minutes or quarter past the hour. For thirty minutes or half past the hour, you may use either **y media** or **y treinta.**

Es la una **y cuarto.** Son las nueve **y quince.** Son las doce **y media.** Son las siete **y treinta.**

▶ You express time from the half-hour to the hour in Spanish by subtracting minutes or a portion of an hour from the next hour.

Es la una **menos cuarto.** Son las tres **menos quince.** Son las ocho **menos veinte.** Son las tres **menos diez.**

TEACHING OPTIONS

Extra Practice Draw a large clock face on the board with numbers but without hands. Say a time and ask a volunteer to come up to the board and draw the hands to indicate that time. The rest of the class verifies that their classmate has written the correct time. Continue until several volunteers have participated.

Pairs 👤↔👤 Tell the class **tengo** means *I have*. Have pairs take turns telling each other what time their classes are this semester/ quarter. (Ex: **Tengo una clase a las…**) For each time given, the other student draws a clock face with the corresponding time. The first student verifies the time. To challenge students, give a list of course names (**las matemáticas, la biología**, etc.)

▶ To ask at what time a particular event takes place, use the phrase **¿A qué hora (...)?** To state at what time something takes place, use the construction **a la(s)** + *time*.

¿A qué hora es la clase de biología?
(At) what time is biology class?

La clase es **a las dos**.
The class is at two o'clock.

¿A qué hora es la fiesta?
(At) what time is the party?

A las ocho.
At eight.

▶ Here are some useful words and phrases associated with telling time.

¡LENGUA VIVA!

Other useful expressions for telling time:
Son las doce (del día).
It is twelve o'clock (p.m.).
Son las doce (de la noche).
It is twelve o'clock (a.m.).

Son las ocho **en punto**.
It's 8 o'clock on the dot/sharp.

Es **el mediodía**.
It's noon.

Es **la medianoche**.
It's midnight.

Son las nueve **de la mañana**.
It's 9 a.m./in the morning.

Son las cuatro y cuarto **de la tarde**.
It's 4:15 p.m./in the afternoon.

Son las diez y media **de la noche**.
It's 10:30 p.m./at night.

¿Qué hora es?

Son las cuatro menos diez.

¿Qué hora es?

Son las cuatro y veinticinco.

recursos

WB
pp. 7–8

LM
p. 6

S
vhlcentral.com
Lección 1

¡INTÉNTALO! Practice telling time by completing these sentences.

1. (1:00 a.m.) Es la _____una_____ de la mañana.
2. (2:50 a.m.) Son las tres _____menos_____ diez de la mañana.
3. (4:15 p.m.) Son las cuatro y _____cuarto/quince_____ de la tarde.
4. (8:30 p.m.) Son las ocho y _____media/treinta_____ de la noche.
5. (9:15 a.m.) Son las nueve y quince de la _____mañana_____.
6. (12:00 p.m.) Es el _____mediodía_____.
7. (6:00 a.m.) Son las seis de la _____mañana_____.
8. (4:05 p.m.) Son las cuatro y cinco de la _____tarde_____.
9. (12:00 a.m.) Es la _____medianoche_____.
10. (3:45 a.m.) Son las cuatro menos _____cuarto/quince_____ de la mañana.
11. (2:15 a.m.) Son las _____dos_____ y cuarto de la mañana.
12. (1:25 p.m.) Es la una y _____veinticinco_____ de la tarde.
13. (6:50 a.m.) Son las _____siete_____ menos diez de la mañana.
14. (10:40 p.m.) Son las once menos veinte de la _____noche_____.

Teaching Tips

• Review **¿Qué hora es?** and introduce **¿A qué hora?** and make sure students know the difference between them. Ask a few questions to contrast the constructions. Ex: **¿Qué hora es? ¿A qué hora es la clase de español?** Emphasize the difference between the questions by looking at your watch as you ask **¿Qué hora es?** and shrugging your shoulders with a quizzical look when asking **¿A qué hora es?**

• Go over **en punto, mediodía,** and **medianoche.** Explain that **medio/a** means *half*.

• Go over **de la mañana/tarde/ noche.** Ask students what time it is now.

• You may wish to explain that Spanish speakers tend to view times of day differently than English speakers do. In many countries, only after someone has eaten lunch does one say **Buenas tardes.** Similarly, with the evening, Spanish speakers tend to view 6:00 and even 7:00 as **de la tarde,** not **de la noche.**

¡Lengua viva! Introduce the Spanish equivalents for noon (**las doce del día**) and midnight (**las doce de la noche**).

TEACHING OPTIONS

Extra Practice Give half of the class slips of paper with clock faces depicting certain times. Give the corresponding times written out in Spanish to the other half of the class. Have students circulate around the room to match their times. To increase difficulty, include duplicates of each time with **de la mañana** or **de la tarde/noche** on the written-out times and a sun or a moon on the clock faces.

Heritage Speakers Ask heritage speakers if they generally tell time as presented in the text. If they use different constructions, ask them to share these with the class. Some ways Hispanics use time constructions include (1) stating the hour and the minute (**Son las diez cuarenta**) rather than using **menos,** and (2) asking the question **¿Qué horas son?** Stress, however, that the constructions presented in the text are the ones students should focus on.

Práctica

1 **Ordenar** Put these times in order, from the earliest to the latest.

a. Son las dos de la tarde. 4
b. Son las once de la mañana. 2
c. Son las siete y media de la noche. 6
d. Son las seis menos cuarto de la tarde. 5
e. Son las dos menos diez de la tarde. 3
f. Son las ocho y veintidós de la mañana. 1

2 **¿Qué hora es?** Give the times shown on each clock or watch.

modelo
Son las cuatro y cuarto/quince de la tarde.

1. Son las doce y media/treinta de la tarde. p.m.
2. Es la una de la mañana.
3. Son las cinco y cuarto/quince de la tarde. p.m.
4. Son las ocho y diez de la noche. p.m.
5. Son las cinco y media/treinta de la mañana. a.m.

6. Son las once menos cuarto/quince de la mañana. a.m.
7. Son las dos y doce de la tarde.
8. Son las siete y cinco de la mañana. a.m.
9. Son las cuatro menos cinco de la tarde. p.m.
10. Son las doce menos veinticinco de la noche.

3 **¿A qué hora?** Ask your partner at what time these events take place. Your partner will answer according to the cues provided.

modelo
la clase de matemáticas (2:30 p.m.)
Estudiante 1: ¿A qué hora es la clase de matemáticas?
Estudiante 2: Es a las dos y media de la tarde.

1. el programa *Las cuatro amigas* (11:30 a.m.)
2. el drama *La casa de Bernarda Alba* (7:00 p.m.)
3. el programa *Las computadoras* (8:30 a.m.)
4. la clase de español (10:30 a.m.)
5. la clase de biología (9:40 a.m.)
6. la clase de historia (10:50 a.m.)
7. el partido (*game*) de béisbol (5:15 p.m.)
8. el partido de tenis (12:45 p.m.)
9. el partido de baloncesto (*basketball*) (7:45 p.m.)

1. E1: ¿A qué hora es el programa *Las cuatro amigas*?
 E2: Es a las once y media/treinta de la mañana.
2. E1: ¿A qué hora es el drama *La casa de Bernarda Alba*?
 E2: Es a las siete de la noche.
3. E1: ¿A qué hora es el programa *Las computadoras*?
 E2: Es a las ocho y media/treinta de la mañana.
4. E1: ¿A qué hora es la clase de español?
 E2: Es a las diez y media/treinta de la mañana.
5. E1: ¿A qué hora es la clase de biología?
 E2: Es a las diez menos veinte de la mañana.
6. E1: ¿A qué hora es la clase de historia?
 E2: Es a las once menos diez de la mañana.
7. E1: ¿A qué hora es el partido de béisbol?
 E2: Es a las cinco y cuarto/quince de la tarde.
8. E1: ¿A qué hora es el partido de tenis?
 E2: Es a la una menos cuarto/quince de la tarde.
9. E1: ¿A qué hora es el partido de baloncesto?
 E2: Es a las ocho menos cuarto/quince de la noche.

 Practice more at **vhlcentral.com.**

Comunicación

4 **En la televisión** With a partner, take turns asking questions about these television listings.
Answers will vary.

modelo

Estudiante 1: ¿A qué hora es el documental *Las computadoras*?
Estudiante 2: Es a las nueve en punto de la noche.

TV Hoy – Programación

11:00 am Telenovela: *La casa de la familia Díaz*	**5:00 pm** Telenovela: *Tres mujeres*
12:00 pm Película: *El cóndor* (drama)	**6:00 pm** Noticias
2:00 pm Telenovela: *Dos mujeres y dos hombres*	**7:00 pm** Especial musical: *Música folklórica de México*
3:00 pm Programa juvenil: *Fiesta*	**7:30 pm** La naturaleza: *Jardín secreto*
3:30 pm Telenovela: *¡Sí, sí, sí!*	**8:00 pm** Noticiero: *Veinticuatro horas*
4:00 pm Telenovela: *El diario de la Sra. González*	**9:00 pm** Documental: *Las computadoras*

5 **Preguntas** With a partner, answer these questions based on your own knowledge. Some answers will vary.

1. Son las tres de la tarde en Nueva York. ¿Qué hora es en Los Ángeles?
Es el mediodía./ Son las doce.
2. Son las ocho y media en Chicago. ¿Qué hora es en Miami?
Son las nueve y media/treinta.
3. Son las dos menos cinco en San Francisco. ¿Qué hora es en San Antonio?
Son las cuatro menos cinco.
4. ¿A qué hora es el programa *Saturday Night Live?*; ¿A qué hora es el programa *American Idol?* Es a las once y media/treinta de la noche.; Es a las ocho de la noche.

6 **Más preguntas** Using the questions in the previous activity as a model, make up four questions of your own. Then get together with a classmate and take turns asking and answering each other's questions.
Answers will vary.

Síntesis

7 **Situación** With a partner, play the roles of a journalism student interviewing a visiting literature professor (**profesor(a) de literatura**) from Venezuela. Be prepared to act out the conversation for your classmates. Answers will vary.

Estudiante	**Profesor(a) de literatura**
Ask the professor his/her name.	→ Ask the student his/her name.
Ask the professor what time his/her literature class is.	→ Ask the student where he/she is from.
Ask how many students are in his/her class.	→ Ask to whom the notebook belongs.
Say thank you and goodbye.	→ Say thank you and you are pleased to meet him/her.

Recapitulación

Section Goal

In **Recapitulación**, students will review the grammar concepts from this lesson.

Instructional Resource
Supersite

1 Teaching Tips
- Before beginning the activity, remind students that nouns ending in -**ma** tend to be masculine, despite ending in an -**a**.
- To add an auditory aspect to this activity, read aloud a masculine or feminine noun, then call on individuals to supply the other form. Do the same for plural and singular nouns. Keep a brisk pace.

1 Expansion Have students identify the corresponding definite and indefinite articles in both singular and plural forms for all of the nouns.

2 Teaching Tips
- Have students explain why they chose their answers. Ex: 1. **Cuántas** is feminine and modifies **chicas**.
- Ask students to explain the difference between **¿Tienes un diccionario?** and **¿Tienes el diccionario?** (general versus specific).

2 Expansion
- ←👥→ Ask students to rewrite the dialogue with information from one of their own classes.
- 👥↔ Have volunteers ask classmates questions using possessives with **ser**. Ex:
 —**¿De quién es esta mochila?**
 —**Es de ella.**

 Concepts Diagnostics

Review the grammar concepts you have learned in this lesson by completing these activities.

1 Completar Complete the charts according to the models. `14 pts.`

Masculino	Femenino
el chico	la chica
el profesor	la profesora
el amigo	la amiga
el señor	la señora
el pasajero	la pasajera
el estudiante	la estudiante
el turista	la turista
el joven	la joven

Singular	Plural
una cosa	unas cosas
un libro	unos libros
una clase	unas clases
una lección	unas lecciones
un conductor	unos conductores
un país	unos países
un lápiz	unos lápices
un problema	unos problemas

2 En la clase Complete each conversation with the correct word. `11 pts.`

 César **Beatriz**

CÉSAR ¿(1) _____Cuántas_____ (Cuántos/Cuántas) chicas hay en la (2) _____clase_____ (maleta/clase)?

BEATRIZ Hay (3) _____catorce_____ (catorce/cuatro) [14] chicas.

CÉSAR Y, ¿(4) _____cuántos_____ (cuántos/cuántas) chicos hay?

BEATRIZ Hay (5) _____trece_____ (tres/trece) [13] chicos.

CÉSAR Entonces (*Then*), en total hay (6) _____veintisiete_____ (veintiséis/veintisiete) (7) _____estudiantes_____ (estudiantes/chicas) en la clase.

 Ariana **Daniel**

ARIANA ¿Tienes (*Do you have*) (8) _____un_____ (un/una) diccionario?

DANIEL No, pero (*but*) aquí (9) _____hay_____ (es/hay) uno.

ARIANA ¿De quién (10) _____es_____ (son/es)?

DANIEL (11) _____Es_____ (Son/Es) de Carlos.

1.1 Nouns and articles *pp. 12–14*

Gender of nouns

Nouns that refer to living things

	Masculine		Feminine
-o	el chico	-a	la chica
-or	el profesor	-ora	la profesora
-ista	el turista	-ista	la turista

Nouns that refer to non-living things

	Masculine		Feminine
-o	el libro	-a	la cosa
-ma	el programa	-ción	la lección
-s	el autobús	-dad	la nacionalidad

Plural of nouns
- ending in vowel + -*s* la chica → las chicas
- ending in consonant + -*es* el señor → los señores
 (-z → -ces un lápiz → unos lápices)
- Definite articles: el, la, los, las
- Indefinite articles: un, una, unos, unas

1.2 Numbers 0–30 *p. 16*

0	cero	8	ocho	16	dieciséis
1	uno	9	nueve	17	diecisiete
2	dos	10	diez	18	dieciocho
3	tres	11	once	19	diecinueve
4	cuatro	12	doce	20	veinte
5	cinco	13	trece	21	veintiuno
6	seis	14	catorce	22	veintidós
7	siete	15	quince	30	treinta

1.3 Present tense of *ser* *pp. 19–21*

yo	soy	nosotros/as	somos
tú	eres	vosotros/as	sois
Ud./él/ella	es	Uds./ellos/ellas	son

TEACHING OPTIONS

Extra Practice To add a visual aspect to this grammar review, bring in pictures from newspapers, magazines, or the Internet of nouns that students have learned. Ask them to identify the people or objects using **ser**. As a variation, ask students questions about the photos, using **hay**. Ex: **¿Cuántos/as _____ hay en la foto?**

TPR Give certain times of day and night and ask students to identify who would be awake: **vigilante** (*night watchman*), **estudiante**, or **los dos**. Have students raise their left hand for the **vigilante**, right hand for the **estudiante**, and both hands for **los dos**. Ex: **Son las cinco menos veinte de la mañana.** (left hand) **Es la medianoche.** (both hands)

3 **Presentaciones** Complete this conversation with the correct form of the verb **ser**. `6 pts.`

JUAN ¡Hola! Me llamo Juan. (1) ___Soy___ estudiante en la clase de español.

DANIELA ¡Hola! Mucho gusto. Yo (2) ___soy___ Daniela y ella (3) ___es___ Mónica. ¿De dónde (4) ___eres___ (tú), Juan?

JUAN De California. Y ustedes, ¿de dónde (5) ___son___ ?

MÓNICA Nosotras (6) ___somos___ de Florida.

1.4 **Telling time** *pp. 24–25*

Es la **una**.	It's 1:00.
Son las **dos**.	It's 2:00.
Son las **tres y diez**.	It's 3:10.
Es la una **y cuarto/ quince**.	It's 1:15.
Son las siete **y media/ treinta**.	It's 7:30.
Es la una **menos cuarto/quince**.	It's 12:45.
Son las once **menos veinte**.	It's 10:40.
Es **el mediodía**.	It's noon.
Es **la medianoche**.	It's midnight.

4 **¿Qué hora es?** Write out in words the following times, indicating whether it's morning, noon, afternoon, or night. `10 pts.`

1. It's 12:00 p.m.
Es el mediodía./Son las doce del día.

2. It's 7:05 a.m.
Son las siete y cinco de la mañana.

3. It's 9:35 p.m.
Son las diez menos veinticinco de la noche.

4. It's 5:15 p.m.
Son las cinco y cuarto/quince de la tarde.

5. It's 1:30 p.m.
Es la una y media/treinta de la tarde.

5 **¡Hola!** Write five sentences introducing yourself and talking about your classes. You may want to include: your name, where you are from, who your Spanish teacher is, the time of your Spanish class, how many students are in the class, etc. `9 pts.` Answers will vary.

6 **Canción** Use the two appropriate words from the list to complete this children's song. `2 EXTRA points!`

cinco	cuántas	cuatro	media	quiénes

" ¿ ___Cuántas___ patas°
tiene un gato°?
Una, dos, tres y
___cuatro___ . "

patas *legs* tiene un gato *does a cat have*

Practice more at **vhlcentral.com**.

3 Teaching Tip Before beginning the activity, orally review the conjugation of **ser**.

3 Expansion Ask questions about the characters in the dialogue. Ex: **¿Quién es Juan? (Juan es un estudiante en la clase de español.) ¿De dónde es? (Es de California.)**

4 Teaching Tip Go over the answers with the class and point out that items 1 and 5 may be written two ways.

4 Expansion To challenge students, give them these times as items 6–10: **6. It's 3:13 p.m., 7. It's 4:29 a.m., 8. It's 1:04 a.m., 9. It's 10:09 a.m., 10. It's 12:16 a.m.**

4 Expansion Have students write down five additional times in Spanish. Then have them get together with a partner and take turns reading the times aloud. The partner will draw a clock showing the appropriate time, plus a sun or moon to indicate a.m. or p.m. Students should check each other's drawings to verify accuracy.

5 Expansion For further practice with **ser** and **hay**, ask students to share the time and size of their other classes. Be certain to list necessary vocabulary on the board, such as **matemáticas, ciencias, literatura,** and **historia**.

6 Teaching Tip Point out the word **Una** in line 3 of the song. To challenge students, have them work in pairs to come up with an explanation for why **Una** is used. (It refers to **pata** [una pata, dos patas…]).

Lectura

NATIONAL communication cultures STANDARDS

Antes de leer

Estrategia
Recognizing cognates

As you learned earlier in this lesson, cognates are words that share similar meanings and spellings in two or more languages. When reading in Spanish, it's helpful to look for cognates and use them to guess the meaning of what you're reading. But watch out for false cognates. For example, **librería** means *bookstore*, not *library*, and **embarazada** means *pregnant*, not *embarrassed*. Look at this list of Spanish words, paying special attention to prefixes and suffixes. Can you guess the meaning of each word?

importante	oportunidad
farmacia	cultura
inteligente	activo
dentista	sociología
decisión	espectacular
televisión	restaurante
médico	policía

Examinar el texto

Glance quickly at the reading selection and guess what type of document it is. Explain your answer.

Cognados

Read the document and make a list of the cognates you find. Guess their English equivalents, then compare your answers with those of a classmate.

Practice more at **vhlcentral.com**.

Joaquín Salvador Lavado nació (*was born*) en Argentina en 1932 (mil novecientos treinta y dos). Su nombre profesional es **Quino**. Es muy popular en Latinoamérica, Europa y Canadá por sus tiras cómicas (*comic strips*). Mafalda es su serie más famosa. La protagonista, Mafalda, es una chica muy inteligente de seis años (*years*). La tira cómica ilustra las aventuras de ella y su grupo de amigos. Las anécdotas de Mafalda y los chicos también presentan temas (*themes*) importantes como la paz (*peace*) y los derechos humanos (*human rights*).

Después de leer

Preguntas

Answer these questions. Some answers may vary. Suggested answers:

1. What is Joaquín Salvador Lavado's pen name?
 Quino
2. What is Mafalda like?
 She is a precocious six-year-old.
3. Where is Mafalda in panel 1? What is she doing?
 She is in bed, counting sheep in order to fall asleep.
4. What happens to the sheep in panel 3? Why?
 It is left balancing on the hurdle because Mafalda falls asleep.
5. Why does Mafalda wake up?
 The sheep says ¡Béeee!
6. What number corresponds to the sheep in panel 5?
 veintiséis
7. In panel 6, what is Mafalda doing? How do you know?
 She is sleeping; the Zs indicate this.

© Joaquín Salvador Lavado (QUINO) Toda Mafalda – Ediciones de La Flor, 1993

Preguntas Have students work in pairs to answer the questions. Then check the answers as a class.

Los animales
• Have a volunteer read aloud the animal names in group A.
• Model the animal sounds in group B and have students repeat them so that they become comfortable making these sounds.
• Review the answers as a class. Then, ask students if any of the animal/sound combinations were surprising to them and why.
• Write the names of a few more animals (Ex: **pollito, búho, pavo**) accompanied by simple drawings on the board and have students try to guess what the sound would be in Spanish (**pío pío, uu uu, gluglú**).

Los animales

This comic strip uses a device called onomatopoeia: a word that represents the sound that it stands for. Did you know that many common instances of onomatopoeia are different from language to language? The noise a sheep makes in English is *baaaah*, but in Mafalda's language it is **béeeee**. Do you think you can match these animals with their Spanish sounds? First, practice saying aloud each animal sound in group B. Then, match each animal with its sound in Spanish. If you need help remembering the sounds the alphabet makes in Spanish, see p. 9.

A

1. _f_ **gato** 2. _d_ **perro** 3. _b_ **vacas** 4. _a_ **gallo**

 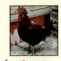

5. _c_ **rana** 6. _e_ **pato** 7. _g_ **cerdo**

B

a. kikirikí b. muuu c. croac d. guau

e. cuac cuac f. miau g. oinc

TEACHING OPTIONS

Small Groups In small groups, have students create an alternate ending for the *Mafalda* comic above. Ask them to create new content for panels 3 through 6. When they are finished, have groups share their comic strips and have the class vote for the funniest or most creative.

Heritage Speakers Ask heritage speakers if they are familiar with any other classic Spanish-language comic strips, such as *Condorito*. Have them describe the general characteristics of the main character. As a class, compare this character to *Mafalda*.

Section Goal

In **Panorama**, students will read demographic and cultural information about Hispanics in the United States and Canada.

Instructional Resources

Supersite/DVD: *Panorama cultural*
Supersite: Resources (Scripts, Translations, *PowerPoints*, Answer Keys)
WebSAM
Workbook, pp. 9–10
Video Manual, pp. 225–226

Teaching Tips

• Use **Lección 1 Panorama** overheads to assist with this presentation.

• Have students look at the map of the United States and Canada. Have volunteers read aloud the labeled cities and geographic features. Model Spanish pronunciation of names as necessary. Have students jot down as many names of places and geographic features with Hispanic origins as they can. Ask volunteers to share their lists with the class.

El país en cifras Have volunteers read the bulleted headings in **El país en cifras**. Point out cognates and clarify unfamiliar words. Explain that numerals in Spanish have a comma where English would use a decimal point (**3,5%**) and have a period where English would use a comma (**13.161.000**). Explain that **EE.UU.** is the abbreviation of **Estados Unidos**, and the doubling of the initial letters indicates plural. Model the pronunciation of **Florida** (accent on the second syllable) and point out that it is often used with an article (**la Florida**) by Spanish speakers.

¡Increíble pero cierto!

Assure students that they are not expected to produce numbers greater than 30 at this point.

Estados Unidos

El país en cifras°

▶ **Población°** de los EE.UU.: 310 millones
▶ **Población de origen hispano:** 49 millones
▶ **País de origen de hispanos en los EE.UU.:**

- 3,5% Cuba
- 9,4% otros
- 9,1% Puerto Rico
- 13,5% Centroamérica y Suramérica
- 64,5% México

SOURCE: U.S. Census Bureau

▶ **Estados con la mayor° población hispana:**

- **California** 13.161.000
- **Texas** 8.566.000
- **Florida** 3.725.173
- **Nueva York** 3.194.000
- **Illinois** 1.910.000

SOURCE: U.S. Census Bureau

Canadá

El país en cifras

▶ **Población de Canadá:** 34 millones
▶ **Población de origen hispano:** 700.000
▶ **País de origen de hispanos en Canadá:**

- 48% España
- 9,1% México
- 8,8% El Salvador
- 34,1% otros

SOURCE: Statistics Canada

▶ **Ciudades° con la mayor población hispana:**

Montreal, Toronto, Vancouver

en cifras *by the numbers* Población *Population* mayor *largest*
Ciudades *Cities* creció *grew* más *more* cada *every* niños *children*
Se estima *It is estimated* va a ser *it is going to be*

¡Increíble pero cierto!

La población hispana en los EE.UU. creció° un 3,2% entre los años 2007 (dos mil siete) y 2008 (dos mil ocho) (1,5 millones de personas más°). Hoy, uno de cada° cinco niños° en los EE.UU. es de origen hispano. Se estima° que en el año 2021 va a ser° uno de cada tres.

SOURCE: U.S. Census Bureau and The Associated Press

Mission District, en San Francisco

AK HI

CANADÁ

Vancouver Calgary

Ottawa Montre

Toronto

San Francisco Chicago Nueva York

Las Vegas **EE.UU.**

Los Ángeles Washington, D.C.

San Diego

San Antonio Océano Atlántico

Miami

MÉXICO Golfo de México

Mar Caribe

El Álamo, en San Antonio, Texas

recursos

| WB pp. 9–10 | VM pp. 225–226 | vhlcentral.com Lección 1 |

TEACHING OPTIONS

Heritage Speakers Ask heritage speakers to describe the celebrations that are held in their families' countries of origin. Ask them to tell the date when the celebration takes place, the event it commemorates, and some of the particulars of the celebration. Possible celebrations: **Cinco de Mayo, Día de la Raza, Día de los Muertos, Fiesta de San Juan, Carnaval**.

Game Divide the class into teams of five. Give teams five minutes to brainstorm place names (cities, states, lakes, rivers, mountain ranges) in the United States that have Spanish origins. One team member should jot down the names in a numbered list. After five minutes, go over the names with the class, confirming the accuracy of each name. The team with the greatest number wins.

Comida • La comida mexicana

La comida° mexicana es muy popular en los Estados Unidos. Los tacos, las enchiladas, las quesadillas y los frijoles frecuentemente forman parte de las comidas de muchos norteamericanos. También° son populares las variaciones de la comida mexicana en los Estados Unidos: el tex-mex y el cali-mex.

Lugares • La Pequeña Habana

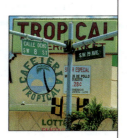

La Pequeña Habana° es un barrio° de Miami, Florida, donde viven° muchos cubanoamericanos. Es un lugar° donde se encuentran° las costumbres° de la cultura cubana, los aromas y sabores° de su comida y la música salsa. La Pequeña Habana es una parte de Cuba en los Estados Unidos.

Costumbres • Desfile puertorriqueño

Cada junio, desde° 1951 (mil novecientos cincuenta y uno), los puertorriqueños celebran su cultura con un desfile° en Nueva York. Es un gran espectáculo con carrozas° y música salsa, merengue y hip-hop. Muchos espectadores llevan° la bandera° de Puerto Rico en su ropa° o pintada en la cara°.

Comunidad • Hispanos en Canadá

En Canadá viven° muchos hispanos. Toronto y Montreal son las ciudades° con mayor° población hispana. Muchos de ellos tienen estudios universitarios° y hablan° una de las lenguas° oficiales: inglés o francés°. Los hispanos participan activamente en la vida cotidiana° y profesional de Canadá.

 ¿Qué aprendiste? Completa las frases con la información adecuada (*appropriate*).

1. Hay __49 millones__ de personas de origen hispano en los Estados Unidos.

2. Los cuatro estados con las poblaciones hispanas más grandes son (en orden) __California__, Texas, Florida y __Nueva York__.

3. Toronto, Montreal y __Vancouver__ son las ciudades con más población hispana de Canadá.

4. Las quesadillas y las enchiladas son platos (*dishes*) __mexicanos__.

5. La Pequeña __Habana__ es un barrio de Miami.

6. En Miami hay muchas personas de origen __cubano__.

7. Cada junio se celebra en Nueva York un gran desfile para personas de origen __puertorriqueño__.

8. Muchos hispanos en Canadá hablan __inglés__ o francés.

 Conexión Internet Investiga estos temas en **vhlcentral.com**.

1. Haz (*Make*) una lista de seis hispanos célebres de los EE.UU. o Canadá. Explica (*Explain*) por qué (*why*) son célebres.

2. Escoge (*Choose*) seis lugares en los Estados Unidos con nombres hispanos e investiga sobre el origen y el significado (*meaning*) de cada nombre.

Practice more at vhlcentral.com.

comida *food* También *Also* La Pequeña Habana *Little Havana* barrio *neighborhood* viven *live* lugar *place* se encuentran *are found* costumbres *customs* sabores *flavors* Cada junio desde *Each June since* desfile *parade* con carrozas *with floats* llevan *wear* bandera *flag* ropa *clothing* cara *face* viven *live* ciudades *cities* mayor *most* tienen estudios universitarios *have a degree* hablan *speak* lenguas *languages* inglés o francés *English or French* vida cotidiana *daily life*

TEACHING OPTIONS

Variación léxica Hispanic groups in the United States refer to themselves with various names. The most common of these terms, **hispano** and **latino**, refer to all people who come from Hispanic backgrounds, regardless of the country of origin of their ancestors. **Puertorriqueño**, **cubanoamericano**, and **mexicoamericano** refer to Hispanics whose ancestors came from Puerto Rico, Cuba, and Mexico, respectively.

Many Mexican Americans also refer to themselves as **chicanos**. This word has stronger socio-political connotations than **mexicoamericano**. Use of the word **chicano** implies identification with Mexican Americans' struggle for civil rights and equal opportunity in the United States. It also suggests an appreciation of the indigenous aspects of Mexican and Mexican-American culture.

Sidebar

Teaching Tip Ask volunteers to read sentences from **¡Increíble pero cierto!**, **Comida**, **Lugares**, **Costumbres**, and **Comunidad**. As necessary, model pronunciation, pause to point out cognates, and clarify unfamiliar words.

La comida mexicana Ask students if they have tried these dishes. Have students look at illustrated cookbooks or recipes to identify the ingredients and variations of the dishes mentioned in the paragraph.

La Pequeña Habana Many large cities in the United States have neighborhoods where people of Hispanic origin predominate. Encourage students to talk about the neighborhoods they know.

Desfile puertorriqueño The Puerto Rican Day Parade takes place on the weekend nearest the feast day of St. John the Baptist (**San Juan Bautista**), the patron saint of San Juan, capital of Puerto Rico.

Hispanos en Canadá The Canadian Hispanic Business Association holds a national awards program every year that honors the ten most influential Hispanic Canadians. Nominees represent countries from all over the Spanish-speaking world. Past winners have included researchers, corporate executives, judges, lawyers, entrepreneurs, musicians, artists, and politicians.

Conexión Internet Students will find supporting Internet activities and links at **vhlcentral.com**.

Teaching Tip You may want to wrap up this section by playing the *Panorama cultural* video footage for this lesson.

Instructional Resources
Supersite: Audio (Textbook & Lab MP3s); Testing Program (Tests, MP3s)
WebSAM
Lab Manual, p. 6

Teaching Tip Tell students that this is active vocabulary for which they are responsible and that it will appear on tests and exams.

Saludos

Hola.	Hello; Hi.
Buenos días.	Good morning.
Buenas tardes.	Good afternoon.
Buenas noches.	Good evening; Good night.

Despedidas

Adiós.	Goodbye.
Nos vemos.	See you.
Hasta luego.	See you later.
Hasta la vista.	See you later.
Hasta pronto.	See you soon.
Hasta mañana.	See you tomorrow.
Saludos a...	Greetings to…
Chau.	Bye.

¿Cómo está?

¿Cómo está usted?	How are you? (form.)
¿Cómo estás?	How are you? (fam.)
¿Qué hay de nuevo?	What's new?
¿Qué pasa?	What's happening?; What's going on?
¿Qué tal?	How are you?; How is it going?
(Muy) bien, gracias.	(Very) well, thanks.
Nada.	Nothing.
No muy bien.	Not very well.
Regular.	So-so; OK.

Expresiones de cortesía

Con permiso.	Pardon me; Excuse me.
De nada.	You're welcome.
Lo siento.	I'm sorry.
(Muchas) gracias.	Thank you (very much); Thanks (a lot).
No hay de qué.	You're welcome.
Perdón.	Pardon me; Excuse me.
por favor	please

Títulos

señor (Sr.); don	Mr.; sir
señora (Sra.); doña	Mrs.; ma'am
señorita (Srta.)	Miss

Presentaciones

¿Cómo se llama usted?	What's your name? (form.)
¿Cómo te llamas?	What's your name? (fam.)
Me llamo...	My name is…
¿Y usted?	And you? (form.)
¿Y tú?	And you? (fam.)
Mucho gusto.	Pleased to meet you.
El gusto es mío.	The pleasure is mine.
Encantado/a.	Delighted; Pleased to meet you.
Igualmente.	Likewise.
Éste/Ésta es...	This is…
Le presento a...	I would like to introduce you to (name). (form.)
Te presento a...	I would like to introduce you to (name). (fam.)
el nombre	name

¿De dónde es?

¿De dónde es usted?	Where are you from? (form.)
¿De dónde eres?	Where are you from? (fam.)
Soy de...	I'm from…

Palabras adicionales

¿cuánto(s)/a(s)?	how much/many?
¿de quién...?	whose…? (sing.)
¿de quiénes...?	whose…? (plural)
(no) hay	there is (not); there are (not)

Países

Argentina	Argentina
Costa Rica	Costa Rica
Cuba	Cuba
Ecuador	Ecuador
España	Spain
Estados Unidos (EE.UU.)	United States
México	Mexico
Puerto Rico	Puerto Rico

Sustantivo

el autobús	bus
la capital	capital city
el chico	boy
la chica	girl
la computadora	computer
la comunidad	community
el/la conductor(a)	driver
la conversación	conversation
la cosa	thing
el cuaderno	notebook
el día	day
el diario	diary
el diccionario	dictionary
la escuela	school
el/la estudiante	student
la foto(grafía)	photograph
el hombre	man
el/la joven	youth; young person
el lápiz	pencil
la lección	lesson
la maleta	suitcase
la mano	hand
el mapa	map
la mujer	woman
la nacionalidad	nationality
el número	number
el país	country
la palabra	word
el/la pasajero/a	passenger
el problema	problem
el/la profesor(a)	teacher
el programa	program
el/la turista	tourist
el video	video

Verbo

ser	to be

Numbers 0–30	See page 16.
Telling time	See pages 24–25.
Expresiones útiles	See page 7.

 Audio: Vocabulary

recursos

| LM p. 6 | vhlcentral.com Lección 1 |

En la universidad

2

Communicative Goals

You will learn how to:

- Talk about your classes and school life
- Discuss everyday activities
- Ask questions in Spanish
- Describe the location of people and things

Lesson Goals

In **Lección 2**, students will be introduced to the following:

- classroom- and university-related words
- names of academic courses and fields of study
- class schedules
- days of the week
- universities and majors in the Spanish-speaking world
- the **Universidad de Salamanca**
- present tense of regular –ar verbs
- forming negative sentences
- the verb **gustar**
- forming questions
- the present tense of **estar**
- prepositions of location
- numbers 31 and higher
- using text formats to predict content
- a video about the **Universidad Nacional Autónoma de México (UNAM)**
- cultural, geographic, and economic information about Spain

A primera vista Have students look at the photo. Say: **Es una foto de dos jóvenes en la universidad.** Then ask: **¿Qué son los jóvenes? (Son estudiantes.) ¿Qué hay en la mano del chico? (Hay un libro/cuaderno/diario.)**

Teaching Tip Look for these icons for additional communicative practice:

→👥←	Interpretive communication
←👥→	Presentational communication
👤↔👤	Interpersonal communication

contextos

pages 36–39
- The classroom and academic life
- Days of the week
- Fields of study and academic subjects
- Class schedules

fotonovela

pages 40–43
Felipe takes Marissa around Mexico City. Along the way, they meet some friends and discuss the upcoming semester.

cultura

pages 44–45
- Universities and majors in the Spanish-speaking world
- The University of Salamanca

estructura

pages 46–63
- Present tense of -ar verbs
- Forming questions in Spanish
- Present tense of estar
- Numbers 31 and higher
- **Recapitulación**

adelante

pages 64–67
Lectura: A brochure for a summer course in Madrid
Panorama: España

A PRIMERA VISTA

- ¿Hay dos chicos en la foto?
- ¿Hay tres cuadernos o siete?
- ¿Son turistas o estudiantes?
- ¿Qué hora es, la una de la mañana o de la tarde?

INSTRUCTIONAL RESOURCES

Supersite (vhlcentral.com)
Video: **Fotonovela*, Flash cultura*, Panorama cultural***
**Also on DVD*
Audio: Textbook and Lab MP3 Files (*also on CD*)
Activity Pack: Information Gap Activities, games, additional activity handouts

Resources: Textbook Answer Key, WB/VM/LM Answer Key, Scripts, Translations, **Vocabulario adicional**, lesson plans, **Estructura** *PowerPoints*, Overheads
Testing Program: Quizzes, Tests, Exams, MP3s (*also on Test Generator CD*)

Learning Management System (Assignment Task Manager, Gradebook)
WebSAM (online Workbook/Video Manual/Lab Manual)
Workbook/Video Manual
Lab Manual

En la universidad

Más vocabulario

la biblioteca	*library*
la cafetería	*cafeteria*
la casa	*house; home*
el estadio	*stadium*
el laboratorio	*laboratory*
la librería	*bookstore*
la residencia estudiantil	*dormitory*
la universidad	*university; college*
el/la compañero/a de clase	*classmate*
el/la compañero/a de cuarto	*roommate*
la clase	*class*
el curso	*course*
la especialización	*major*
el examen	*test; exam*
el horario	*schedule*
la prueba	*test; quiz*
el semestre	*semester*
la tarea	*homework*
el trimestre	*trimester; quarter*
la administración de empresas	*business administration*
el arte	*art*
la biología	*biology*
las ciencias	*sciences*
la computación	*computer science*
la contabilidad	*accounting*
la economía	*economics*
el español	*Spanish*
la física	*physics*
la geografía	*geography*
la música	*music*

Variación léxica

pluma ⟷ bolígrafo
pizarra ⟷ tablero (*Col.*)

el reloj
la ventana
la puerta
la profesora
el estudiante
la mesa
la calculadora
el libro
la pluma

Práctica

el mapa

la pizarra

LAS MATERIAS	COURSES
la historia	history
las humanidades	humanities
el inglés	English
las lenguas extranjeras	foreign languages
la literatura	literature
las matemáticas	mathematics
el periodismo	journalism
la psicología	psychology
la química	chemistry
la sociología	sociology

el papel

el borrador

la tiza

la papelera

el escritorio

la mochila

la estudiante

la silla

1 Escuchar Listen to Professor Morales talk about her Spanish classroom, then check the items she mentions.

puerta	☑	tiza	☑	plumas	☑
ventanas	☑	escritorios	☑	mochilas	◯
pizarra	☑	sillas	◯	papel	☑
borrador	◯	libros	☑	reloj	☑

2 Identificar You will hear a series of words. Write each one in the appropriate category.

Personas	Lugares	Materias
el estudiante	el estadio	la química
la profesora	la biblioteca	las lenguas extranjeras
el compañero de clase	la residencia estudiantil	el inglés

3 Emparejar Match each question with its most logical response. **¡Ojo!** (*Careful!*) One response will not be used.

1. ¿Qué clase es? d
2. ¿Quiénes son? g
3. ¿Quién es? e
4. ¿De dónde es? c
5. ¿A qué hora es la clase de inglés? f
6. ¿Cuántos estudiantes hay? a

a. Hay veinticinco.
b. Es un reloj.
c. Es de Perú.
d. Es la clase de química.
e. Es el señor Bastos.
f. Es a las nueve en punto.
g. Son los profesores.

4 Identificar Identify the word that does not belong in each group.

1. examen • casa • tarea • prueba casa
2. economía • matemáticas • biblioteca • contabilidad biblioteca
3. pizarra • tiza • borrador • librería librería
4. lápiz • cafetería • papel • cuaderno cafetería
5. veinte • diez • pluma • treinta pluma
6. conductor • laboratorio • autobús • pasajero laboratorio

5 ¿Qué clase es? Name the class associated with the subject matter.

> **modelo**
> los elementos, los átomos Es la clase de química.

1. Abraham Lincoln, Winston Churchill Es la clase de historia.
2. Picasso, Leonardo da Vinci Es la clase de arte.
3. Freud, Jung Es la clase de psicología.
4. África, el océano Pacífico Es la clase de geografía.
5. la cultura de España, verbos Es la clase de español.
6. Hemingway, Shakespeare Es la clase de literatura.
7. geometría, calculadora Es la clase de matemáticas.

1 Expansion Have students circle the items that they see in their own classroom.

1 Script ¿Qué hay en mi clase de español? ¡Muchas cosas! Hay una puerta y cinco ventanas. Hay una pizarra con tiza. Hay muchos escritorios para los estudiantes. En los escritorios de los estudiantes hay libros y plumas. En la mesa de la profesora hay papel. Hay un mapa y un reloj en la clase también.
Textbook MP3s

2 Teaching Tip To simplify, have students prepare for listening by predicting a few words for each category.

2 Script el estudiante, la química, el estadio, las lenguas extranjeras, la profesora, la biblioteca, el inglés, el compañero de clase, la residencia estudiantil
Textbook MP3s

3 Expansion Have student pairs ask each other the questions and answer truthfully, based on your class. Ex: **1. ¿Qué clase es? (Es la clase de español.)** For items 2–4, the questioner should indicate specific people in the classroom.

4 Expansion Have students write four additional items for a partner to complete.

5 Expansion Have the class associate famous people with these fields: **periodismo, computación, humanidades**. Then have them guess the fields associated with these people: Albert Einstein (**física**), Charles Darwin (**biología**).

Teaching Tips

• Write these questions and answers on the board, explaining their meaning as you do so:

—**¿Qué día es hoy?**

—**Hoy es ____.**

—**¿Qué día es mañana?** (Students learned **mañana** in **Lección 1.**)

—**Mañana es ____.**

—**¿Cuándo es la prueba?**

—**Es el ____.**

Then ask students the questions on the board.

• Explain that Monday is considered the first day of the week in the Spanish-speaking world and usually appears as such on calendars.

6 **Expansion** To challenge students, ask them questions such as: **Mañana es viernes… ¿qué día fue ayer? (miércoles); Ayer fue domingo… ¿qué día es mañana? (martes)**

7 **Teaching Tip** To simplify, before doing this activity, have students review the list of **sustantivos** on page 34 and numbers 0–30 on page 16.

Los días de la semana

> ¿Qué día es hoy (today)?
>
> ¿Cuándo (When) es el examen?
>
> Hoy es martes.
>
> Es el viernes.

septiembre

lunes	martes	miércoles	jueves	viernes	sábado	domingo
		1	2	3	4	5
						6
7	8	9	10			

¡LENGUA VIVA!

The days of the week are never capitalized in Spanish.

• • •

Monday is considered the first day of the week in Spanish-speaking countries.

CONSULTA

Note that September in Spanish is **septiembre**. For all of the months of the year, go to **Contextos, Lección 5,** p. 142.

6 **¿Qué día es hoy?** Complete each statement with the correct day of the week.

1. Hoy es martes. Mañana es _miércoles_. Ayer fue (*Yesterday was*) _lunes_.
2. Ayer fue sábado. Mañana es _lunes_. Hoy es _domingo_.
3. Mañana es viernes. Hoy es _jueves_. Ayer fue _miércoles_.
4. Ayer fue domingo. Hoy es _lunes_. Mañana es _martes_.
5. Hoy es jueves. Ayer fue _miércoles_. Mañana es _viernes_.
6. Mañana es lunes. Hoy es _domingo_. Ayer fue _sábado_.

7 **Analogías** Use these words to complete the analogies. Some words will not be used.

arte	día	martes	pizarra
biblioteca	domingo	matemáticas	profesor
catorce	estudiante	mujer	reloj

1. maleta ←→ pasajero ⊜ mochila ←→ _estudiante_
2. chico ←→ chica ⊜ hombre ←→ _mujer_
3. pluma ←→ papel ⊜ tiza ←→ _pizarra_
4. inglés ←→ lengua ⊜ miércoles ←→ _día_
5. papel ←→ cuaderno ⊜ libro ←→ _biblioteca_
6. quince ←→ dieciséis ⊜ lunes ←→ _martes_
7. Cervantes ←→ literatura ⊜ Dalí ←→ _arte_
8. autobús ←→ conductor ⊜ clase ←→ _profesor_
9. los EE.UU. ←→ mapa ⊜ hora ←→ _reloj_
10. veinte ←→ veintitrés ⊜ jueves ←→ _domingo_

Practice more at **vhlcentral.com.**

TEACHING OPTIONS

Extra Practice Have students prepare a day-planner for the upcoming week. Tell them to list each day of the week and the things they expect to do each day, including classes, homework, tests, appointments, and social events. Provide unfamiliar vocabulary as needed. Tell them to include the time each activity takes place. Have them exchange their day-planners with a partner and check each other's work for accuracy.

Game Have groups of five or six play a "word-chain" game in which the first group member says a word in Spanish (e.g., **estudiante**). The next student has to say a word that begins with the last letter of the first person's word (e.g., **español**). If a student cannot think of a word, he or she is eliminated and it is the next student's turn. The last student left in the game is the winner.

Comunicación

8 **Horario** Choose three courses from the chart to create your own class schedule, then discuss it with a classmate. Answers will vary.

materia	horas	días	profesor(a)
historia	9–10	lunes, miércoles	Prof. Ordóñez
biología	12–1	lunes, jueves	Profa. Dávila
periodismo	2–3	martes, jueves	Profa. Quiñones
matemáticas	2–3	miércoles, jueves	Prof. Jiménez
arte	12–1:30	lunes, miércoles	Prof. Molina

modelo

Estudiante 1: Tomo (I take) biología los lunes y jueves, de 12 a 1, con (with) la profesora Dávila.

Estudiante 2: ¿Sí? Yo no tomo biología. Yo tomo arte los lunes y miércoles, de 12 a 1:30, con el profesor Molina.

¡ATENCIÓN!

Use **el** + [day of the week] when an activity occurs on a specific day and **los** + [day of the week] when an activity occurs regularly.

El lunes tengo un examen.
On Monday I have an exam.

Los lunes y miércoles tomo biología.
On Mondays and Wednesdays I take biology.

• • •

Except for **sábados** and **domingos,** the singular and plural forms for days of the week are the same.

9 **Memoria** How well do you know your Spanish classroom? Take a good look around and then close your eyes. Your partner will ask you questions about the classroom, using these words and other vocabulary. Each person should answer six questions and switch roles every three questions. Answers will vary.

escritorio	mapa	pizarra	reloj
estudiante	mesa	profesor(a)	ventana
libro	mochila	puerta	silla

modelo

Estudiante 1: ¿Cuántas ventanas hay?

Estudiante 2: Hay cuatro ventanas.

10 **Nuevos amigos** During the first week of class, you meet a new student in the cafeteria. With a partner, prepare a conversation using these cues. Then act it out for the class. Answers will vary.

Estudiante 1

Greet your new acquaintance. → Introduce yourself.

Find out about him or her. → Tell him or her about yourself.

Ask about your partner's class schedule. → Compare your schedule to your partner's.

Say nice to meet you and goodbye. → Say nice to meet you and goodbye.

Estudiante 2

TEACHING OPTIONS

Groups Have students do **Actividad 10** in groups, imagining that they meet several new students in the cafeteria. Have the groups present this activity as a skit for the class. Give the groups time to prepare and rehearse, and tell them that they will be presenting it without a script or any other kind of notes.

Game Point out the **modelo** in **Actividad 8**. Have students write a few simple sentences that describe their own course schedules. Ex: **Tomo dos clases. Los lunes, miércoles y viernes, de 10 a 11, tomo español con la profesora Morales. Los martes y jueves, de 2:30 a 4, tomo arte con el profesor Casas.** Then collect the descriptions, shuffle them, and read them aloud. The class should guess who wrote each description.

8 **Teaching Tip** Point out the professors' names in the chart and the use of the abbreviations **Prof.** and **Profa.**

8 **Expansion** Tell students to write their name at the top of their schedules and have pairs exchange papers with another pair. Then have them repeat the activity with the new schedules, asking and answering questions in the third person. Ex: —¿Qué clases toma _____? —Los lunes y jueves _____ toma biología con la profesora Dávila.

9 **Expansion** Repeat the activity with campus-related vocabulary.

Successful Language Learning Remind the class that errors are a natural part of language learning. Point out that it is impossible to speak "perfectly" in any language. Emphasize that their spoken and written Spanish will improve if they make the effort to practice.

10 **Teaching Tip** To simplify, quickly review the basic greetings, courtesy expressions, and introductions taught in **Lección 1, Contextos,** pages 2–3.

10 **Expansion** Ask volunteers to introduce their new acquaintances to the class and present any new information they learned about their partners.

¿Qué estudias?

Felipe, Marissa, Juan Carlos y Miguel visitan Chapultepec y hablan de las clases.

PERSONAJES MARISSA FELIPE

Video: *Fotonovela*
Record and Compare

FELIPE Dos boletos, por favor.

EMPLEADO Dos boletos son 64 pesos.
FELIPE Aquí están 100 pesos.
EMPLEADO 100 menos 64 son 36 pesos de cambio.

MIGUEL Marissa, hablas muy bien el español... ¿Y dónde está tu diccionario?
MARISSA En casa de los Díaz. Felipe necesita practicar inglés.
MIGUEL ¡Ay, Maru! Chicos, nos vemos más tarde.

FELIPE Ésta es la Ciudad de México.

FELIPE Oye, Marissa, ¿cuántas clases tomas?
MARISSA Tomo cuatro clases: español, historia, literatura y también geografía. Me gusta mucho la cultura mexicana.

FELIPE Juan Carlos, ¿quién enseña la clase de química este semestre?
JUAN CARLOS El profesor Morales. Ah, ¿por qué tomo química y computación?
FELIPE Porque te gusta la tarea.

JUAN CARLOS **MIGUEL** **EMPLEADO** **MARU**

7

FELIPE Los lunes y los miércoles, economía a las 2:30. Tú tomas computación los martes en la tarde, y química, a ver... Los lunes, los miércoles y los viernes ¿a las 10? ¡Uf!

8

FELIPE Y Miguel, ¿cuándo regresa?

JUAN CARLOS Hoy estudia con Maru.

MARISSA ¿Quién es Maru?

9

MIGUEL ¿Hablas con tu mamá?

MARU Mamá habla. Yo escucho. Es la 1:30.

MIGUEL Ay, lo siento. Juan Carlos y Felipe...

MARU Ay, Felipe.

10

MARU Y ahora, ¿adónde? ¿A la biblioteca?

MIGUEL Sí, pero primero a la librería. Necesito comprar unos libros.

recursos

VM
pp. 197–198

Ⓢ
vhlcentral.com
Lección 2

Expresiones útiles

Talking about classes

¿Cuántas clases tomas?
How many classes are you taking?
Tomo cuatro clases.
I'm taking four classes.
Mi especialización es en arqueología.
My major is archeology.
Este año, espero sacar buenas notas y, por supuesto, viajar por el país.
This year, I hope / I'm hoping to get good grades. And, of course, travel through the country.

Talking about likes/dislikes

Me gusta mucho la cultura mexicana.
I like Mexican culture a lot.
Me gustan las ciencias ambientales.
I like environmental science.
Me gusta dibujar.
I like to draw.
¿Te gusta este lugar?
Do you like this place?

Paying for tickets

Dos boletos, por favor.
Two tickets, please.
Dos boletos son sesenta y cuatro pesos.
Two tickets are sixty-four pesos.
Aquí están cien pesos.
Here's a hundred pesos.
Son treinta y seis pesos de cambio.
That's thirty-six pesos change.

Talking about location and direction

¿Dónde está tu diccionario?
Where is your dictionary?
Está en casa de los Díaz.
It's at the Díaz's house.
Y ahora, ¿adónde? ¿A la biblioteca?
And now, where to? To the library?
Sí, pero primero a la librería.
Está al lado.
Yes, but first to the bookstore.
It's next door.

Expresiones útiles Identify forms of **tomar** and **estar**. Point out the questions and interrogative words. Tell students that they will learn more about these concepts in **Estructura**. Point out that **gusta** is used when what is liked is singular, and **gustan** when what is liked is plural. A detailed discussion of the **gustar** construction (see **Estructura 2.1**, page 48) is unnecessary here. Emphasize the **me/te gusta(n)** forms, as these are the only ones that will appear on tests until **Lección 7**.

Teaching Tip Have the class read through the entire **Fotonovela**, with volunteers playing the parts of **Felipe**, **Marissa, Juan Carlos, Miguel, Maru,** and the **empleado**.

TEACHING OPTIONS

Pairs Have students scan the captions and **Expresiones útiles**. They should then underline the **gustar** constructions and jot down the phrases that best describe themselves. Repeat the exercise with the verb **tomar**. Then, in pairs, have students guess which phrases their partners used to describe themselves.
Ex: —**Te gusta la tarea, ¿no?**

Extra Practice Ask pairs to write five true/false statements based on the **¿Qué estudias?** captions. Then have them exchange papers with another pair, who will complete the activity and correct the false statements. Ask volunteers to read a few statements for the class, and have students answer and point out the caption that contains the information.

¿Qué pasó?

1 Escoger Choose the answer that best completes each sentence.

1. Marissa toma (*is taking*) _____ c _____ en la universidad.
 a. español, psicología, economía y música b. historia, inglés, sociología y periodismo
 c. español, historia, literatura y geografía

2. El profesor Morales enseña (*teaches*) _____ a _____.
 a. química b. matemáticas c. historia

3. Juan Carlos toma química _____ b _____.
 a. los miércoles, jueves y viernes b. los lunes, miércoles y viernes
 c. los lunes, martes y jueves

4. Miguel necesita ir a (*needs to go to*) _____ c _____.
 a. la biblioteca b. la residencia estudiantil c. la librería

2 Identificar Indicate which person would make each statement. The names may be used more than once.

1. ¿Maru es compañera de ustedes? _____ Marissa _____
2. Mi mamá habla mucho. _____ Maru _____
3. El profesor Morales enseña la clase de química este semestre. _____ Juan Carlos _____
4. Mi diccionario está en casa de Felipe y Jimena. _____ Marissa _____
5. Necesito estudiar con Maru. _____ Miguel _____
6. Yo tomo clase de computación los martes por la tarde. _____ Juan Carlos _____

MARU

JUAN CARLOS **MARISSA**

MIGUEL

3 Completar These sentences are similar to things said in the **Fotonovela**. Complete each sentence with the correct word(s).

| Castillo de Chapultepec | estudiar | miércoles |
| clase | inglés | tarea |

1. Marissa, éste es el _____ Castillo de Chapultepec _____.
2. Felipe tiene (*has*) el diccionario porque (*because*) necesita practicar _____ inglés _____.
3. A Juan Carlos le gusta mucho la _____ tarea _____.
4. Hay clase de economía los lunes y _____ miércoles _____.
5. Miguel está con Maru para _____ estudiar _____.

4 Preguntas personales Interview a classmate about his/her university life. Answers will vary.

1. ¿Qué clases tomas en la universidad?
2. ¿Qué clases tomas los martes?
3. ¿Qué clases tomas los viernes?
4. ¿En qué clase hay más chicos?
5. ¿En qué clase hay más chicas?
6. ¿Te gusta la clase de español?

Practice more at **vhlcentral.com.**

Pronunciación 🎧 Ⓢ Audio: Concepts, Activities Record & Compare
Spanish vowels

a **e** **i** **o** **u**

Spanish vowels are never silent; they are always pronounced in a short, crisp way without the glide sounds used in English.

Álex	**clase**	**nada**	**encantada**

The letter **a** is pronounced like the *a* in *father*, but shorter.

el	**ene**	**mesa**	**elefante**

The letter **e** is pronounced like the *e* in *they*, but shorter.

Inés	**chica**	**tiza**	**señorita**

The letter **i** sounds like the *ee* in *beet*, but shorter.

hola	**con**	**libro**	**don Francisco**

The letter **o** is pronounced like the *o* in *tone*, but shorter.

uno	**regular**	**saludos**	**gusto**

The letter **u** sounds like the *oo* in *room*, but shorter.

Práctica Practice the vowels by saying the names of these places in Spain.

1. Madrid
2. Alicante
3. Tenerife
4. Toledo
5. Barcelona
6. Granada
7. Burgos
8. La Coruña

Oraciones Read the sentences aloud, focusing on the vowels.

1. Hola. Me llamo Ramiro Morgado.
2. Estudio arte en la Universidad de Salamanca.
3. Tomo también literatura y contabilidad.
4. Ay, tengo clase en cinco minutos. ¡Nos vemos!

Refranes Practice the vowels by reading these sayings aloud.

Cada loco con su tema.[2]

Del dicho al hecho hay un gran trecho.[1]

[1] Easier said than done. [2] To each his own.

recursos

LM p. 8 vhlcentral.com Lección 2

AYUDA

Although **hay** and **ay** are pronounced identically, they do not have the same meaning. As you learned in **Lección 1**, **hay** is a verb form that means *there is/are*. **Hay veinte libros**. (*There are twenty books*.) **¡Ay!** is an exclamation expressing pain, shock, or affliction: *Oh!; Oh, dear!*

Section Goal

In **Pronunciación**, students will be introduced to Spanish vowels and how they are pronounced.

Instructional Resources
Supersite: Audio (Textbook and Lab MP3 Files); Resources (Scripts, Answer Keys)
WebSAM
Lab Manual, p. 8

Teaching Tips

- Point out that the drawings above the vowels on this page indicate the approximate position of the mouth as the vowels are pronounced.
- Model the pronunciation of each vowel and have students pay attention to the shape of your mouth. Have them repeat the vowel after you. Then go through the example words.
- To practice pure vowel sounds, teach students this chant: A-E-I-O-U, ¡el burro sabe más que tú!
- Pronounce a few of the example words and have the students write them on the board with their books closed.

Práctica/Oraciones/Refranes

These exercises are recorded on the *Textbook MP3s*. You may want to play the audio so that students practice listening to Spanish spoken by speakers other than yourself.

TEACHING OPTIONS

Extra Practice Provide additional names of places in Spain. Have students spell each name aloud in Spanish, then ask them to pronounce each one. Avoid names that contain diphthongs. Ex: **Sevilla, Salamanca, Santander, Albacete, Gerona, Lugo, Badajoz, Tarragona, Logroño, Valladolid, Orense, Pamplona, Ibiza.**

Small Groups Have the class turn to the **Fotonovela**, pages 40–41, and work in groups of four to read all or part of the **Fotonovela** aloud, focusing on the correct pronunciation of the vowels. Circulate among the groups and, as needed, model the correct pronunciation and intonation of words and phrases.

Section Goals

In **Cultura**, students will:
- learn how students choose their majors and enter the university
- learn academic-related terms
- read about the **Universidad de Salamanca**
- read about university enrollment

Instructional Resources
Supersite/DVD: *Flash cultura*
Supersite: Resources (Scripts, Translations, Answer Keys)
WebSAM
Video Manual, pp. 269–270

En detalle

Antes de leer Ask students about their experiences entering the university. What were important factors in their decision of where to study? Have they chosen their majors yet? If so, how did they decide?

Lectura
- Many students tend to live at home. If they do live on campus, they usually live in a **residencia estudiantil** or a **colegio mayor**. The **colegio mayor** tends to offer more student life, similar to that of a sorority or fraternity.
- Because enrollments are high, campuses are scattered, with buildings in different areas of the city or town. Unlike an American university, where one might find a quadrangle where students gather, student life in Hispanic universities might take place in individual **facultades**.

Después de leer Ask students which university system they prefer.

1 Expansion Give students these sentences as items 11–12: 11. An undergraduate degree is often called a **licenciatura**. (**Cierto.**) 12. The majority of Hispanics that study in the U.S. are Colombian. (**Falso.** The majority are Mexican.)

EN DETALLE

Additional Reading
Video: *Flash cultura*

La elección de una carrera universitaria

Since higher education in the Spanish-speaking world is heavily state-subsidized, tuition is almost free. As a result, public universities see large enrollments. Spanish and Latin American students generally choose their **carrera universitaria** (major) when they're eighteen—which is either the year they enter the university or the year before. In order to enroll, all students must complete a high school degree, known as the **bachillerato**. In countries like Bolivia, Mexico, and Peru, the last year of high school (**colegio***) tends to be specialized in an area of study, such as the arts or natural sciences.

Students then choose their major according to their area of specialization. Similarly, university-bound students in Argentina follow the **polimodal** track during the last three years of high school. **Polimodal** refers to exposure to various disciplines, such as business, social sciences, or design. Based on this coursework, Argentine students choose their **carrera**. Finally, in Spain, students choose their major according to the score they receive on the **prueba de aptitud** (skills test or entrance exam).

University graduates receive a **licenciatura**, or bachelor's degree. In Argentina and Chile, a **licenciatura** takes four to six years to complete,

Universidad Central de Venezuela en Caracas

and may be considered equivalent to a master's degree. In Peru and Venezuela, a bachelor's degree is a five-year process. Spanish and Colombian **licenciaturas** take four to five years, although some fields, such as medicine, require six or more.

> ### Estudiantes hispanos en los EE.UU.
>
> In the 2004–05 academic year, over 13,000 Mexican students (2.3% of all international students) studied at U.S. universities. Colombians were the second-largest Spanish-speaking group, with over 7,000 students.

*¡Ojo! El **colegio** is a false cognate. In most countries, it means *high school*, but in some regions it refers to an elementary school. All undergraduate study takes place at la **universidad**.

ACTIVIDADES

1

¿Cierto o falso? Indicate whether these statements are **cierto** or **falso**. Correct the false statements.

1. Students in Spanish-speaking countries must pay large amounts of money toward their college tuition. **Falso.** At public universities tuition is almost free.
2. **Carrera** refers to any undergraduate or graduate program that students enroll in to obtain a professional degree. **Cierto.**
3. After studying at a **colegio**, students receive their **bachillerato**. **Cierto.**
4. Undergraduates study at a **colegio** or an **universidad**. **Falso.** An undergraduate student takes classes at a **universidad**.

5. In Latin America and Spain, students usually choose their majors in their second year at the university. **Falso.** They choose their majors either upon entering the university or the year before.
6. The **polimodal** system helps students choose their university major. **Cierto.**
7. In Mexico, the **bachillerato** involves specialized study. **Cierto.**
8. In Spain, majors depend on entrance exam scores. **Cierto.**
9. Venezuelans complete a **licenciatura** in five years. **Cierto.**
10. According to statistics, Colombians constitute the third-largest Latin American group studying at U.S. universities. **Falso.** Colombians are the second-largest group.

TEACHING OPTIONS

Small Groups In groups of three, have students describe the photos on this page. Ask them to write as much as they can in Spanish about the university and students pictured. Then have volunteers read their descriptions to the class.

Cultural Activity Ask student pairs to create a list of comparisons between U.S. universities and universities in Spanish-speaking countries. Encourage them to consider enrollment, student life, majors, tuition, and other significant aspects. Then survey the class and summarize the results on the board.

ASÍ SE DICE

Clases y exámenes

aprobar	to pass
la asignatura (Esp.)	la clase, la materia
la clase anual	year-long course
el examen parcial	midterm exam
la facultad	department, school
la investigación	research
el profesorado	faculty
reprobar; suspender (Esp.)	to fail
sacar buenas/ malas notas	to get good/ bad grades
tomar apuntes	to take notes

EL MUNDO HISPANO

Las universidades hispanas

It is not uncommon for universities in Spain and Latin America to have extremely large student body populations.

- **Universidad de Buenos Aires** (Argentina) 325.000 estudiantes
- **Universidad Autónoma de Santo Domingo** (República Dominicana) 180.000 estudiantes
- **Universidad Complutense de Madrid** (España) 86.200 estudiantes
- **Universidad Central de Venezuela** (Venezuela) 62.600 estudiantes

PERFIL

La Universidad de Salamanca

The University of Salamanca, established in 1218, is the oldest university in Spain. It is located in Salamanca, one of the most spectacular Renaissance cities in Europe. Salamanca is nicknamed **La Ciudad Dorada** (*The Golden City*) for the golden glow of its famous sandstone buildings, and it was declared a UNESCO World Heritage Site in 1968.

Salamanca is a true college town, as its prosperity and city life depend and revolve around the university population. Over 38,000 students from all over Spain, as well as abroad, come to study here each year. The school offers over 250 academic programs, as well as renowned Spanish courses for foreign students. To walk through the university's historic grounds is to follow the footsteps of immortal writers like Miguel de Cervantes and Miguel de Unamuno.

Conexión Internet

To which **facultad** does your major belong in Spain or Latin America?

Go to **vhlcentral.com** to find more cultural information related to this **Cultura** section.

ACTIVIDADES

2 **Comprensión** Complete these sentences.

1. The University of Salamanca was established in the year ___1218___.
2. A ___clase anual___ is a year-long course.
3. Salamanca is called ___La Ciudad Dorada___.
4. Over 300,000 students attend the ___Universidad de Buenos Aires___.
5. An ___examen parcial___ occurs about halfway through a course.

3 **La universidad en cifras** With a partner, research a Spanish or Latin American university online and find five statistics about that institution (for instance, the total enrollment, majors offered, year it was founded, etc.). Using the information you found, create a dialogue between a prospective student and a university representative. Present your dialogue to the class. Answers will vary.

recursos

VM pp. 269–270

vhlcentral.com Lección 2

 Practice more at **vhlcentral.com**.

2.1 Present tense of -ar verbs Tutorial

ANTE TODO In order to talk about activities, you need to use verbs. Verbs express actions or states of being. In English and Spanish, the infinitive is the base form of the verb. In English, the infinitive is preceded by the word *to: to study, to be.* The infinitive in Spanish is a one-word form and can be recognized by its endings: **-ar**, **-er**, or **-ir**.

-ar verb		*-er* verb		*-ir* verb	
estudiar	*to study*	**comer**	*to eat*	**escribir**	*to write*

▶ In this lesson, you will learn the forms of regular **-ar** verbs.

The verb estudiar (*to study*)

SINGULAR FORMS	yo	estudi**o**	*I study*
	tú	estudi**as**	*you* (fam.) *study*
	Ud./él/ella	estudi**a**	*you* (form.) *study; he/she studies*
PLURAL FORMS	nosotros/as	estudi**amos**	*we study*
	vosotros/as	estudi**áis**	*you* (fam.) *study*
	Uds./ellos/ellas	estudi**an**	*you* (form.) *study; they study*

> Juan Carlos estudia ciencias ambientales.

> Y tú, ¿qué estudias, Miguel?

▶ To create the forms of most regular verbs in Spanish, drop the infinitive endings (**-ar, -er, -ir**). You then add to the stem the endings that correspond to the different subject pronouns. This diagram will help you visualize verb conjugation.

Conjugation of *-ar* verbs

INFINITIVE	VERB STEM	CONJUGATED FORM
estudi**ar**	estudi-	yo estudi**o**
bail**ar**	bail-	tú bail**as**
trabaj**ar**	trabaj-	nosotros trabaj**amos**

Common -ar verbs

bailar	to dance	**estudiar**	to study
buscar	to look for	**explicar**	to explain
caminar	to walk	**hablar**	to talk; to speak
cantar	to sing	**llegar**	to arrive
cenar	to have dinner	**llevar**	to carry
comprar	to buy	**mirar**	to look (at); to watch
contestar	to answer	**necesitar (+ *inf.*)**	to need
conversar	to converse, to chat	**practicar**	to practice
desayunar	to have breakfast	**preguntar**	to ask (a question)
descansar	to rest	**preparar**	to prepare
desear (+ *inf.*)	to desire; to wish	**regresar**	to return
dibujar	to draw	**terminar**	to end; to finish
enseñar	to teach	**tomar**	to take; to drink
escuchar	to listen (to)	**trabajar**	to work
esperar (+ *inf.*)	to wait (for); to hope	**viajar**	to travel

▶ **¡Atención!** Unless referring to a person, the Spanish verbs **buscar**, **escuchar**, **esperar**, and **mirar** do not need to be followed by prepositions as they do in English.

Busco la tarea.
I'm looking for the homework.

Escucho la música.
I'm listening to the music.

Espero el autobús.
I'm waiting for the bus.

Miro la pizarra.
I'm looking at the blackboard.

COMPARE & CONTRAST

English uses three sets of forms to talk about the present: (1) the simple present (*Paco works*), (2) the present progressive (*Paco is working*), and (3) the emphatic present (*Paco does work*). In Spanish, the simple present can be used in all three cases.

Paco **trabaja** en la cafetería.
1. Paco *works* in the cafeteria.
2. Paco *is working* in the cafeteria.
3. Paco *does work* in the cafeteria.

In Spanish and English, the present tense is also sometimes used to express future action.

Marina **viaja** a Madrid mañana.
1. Marina *travels* to Madrid tomorrow.
2. Marina *will travel* to Madrid tomorrow.
3. Marina *is traveling* to Madrid tomorrow.

▶ When two verbs are used together with no change of subject, the second verb is generally in the infinitive. To make a sentence negative in Spanish, the word **no** is placed before the conjugated verb. In this case, **no** means *not*.

Deseo hablar con el señor Díaz.
I want to speak with Mr. Díaz.

Alicia **no** desea bailar ahora.
Alicia doesn't want to dance now.

▶ Spanish speakers often omit subject pronouns because the verb endings indicate who the subject is. In Spanish, subject pronouns are used for emphasis, clarification, or contrast.

—¿Qué enseñan?
What do they teach?

—**Ella** enseña arte y **él** enseña física.
She teaches art, and he teaches physics.

—¿Quién desea trabajar hoy?
Who wants to work today?

—**Yo** no deseo trabajar hoy.
I don't want to work today.

The verb gustar

▶ To express your likes and dislikes, use the expression (**no**) **me gusta** + **el/la** + [*singular noun*] or (**no**) **me gustan** + **los/las** + [*plural noun*]. Note: You may use the phrase **a mí** for emphasis, but never the subject pronoun **yo.**

Me gusta la música clásica.
I like classical music.

Me gustan las clases de español y biología.
I like Spanish and biology classes.

A mí me gustan las artes.
I like the arts.

A mí no me gusta el programa.
I don't like the program.

▶ To talk about what you like and don't like to do, use (**no**) **me gusta** + [*infinitive(s)*]. Note that the singular **gusta** is always used, even with more than one infinitive.

No me gusta viajar en autobús.
I don't like to travel by bus.

Me gusta cantar y **bailar.**
I like to sing and dance.

▶ To ask a classmate about likes and dislikes, use the pronoun **te** instead of **me.** Note: You may use **a ti** for emphasis, but never the subject pronoun **tú.**

—¿**Te gusta la geografía?**
Do you like geography?

—**Sí, me gusta. Y a ti, ¿te gusta el inglés?**
Yes, I like it. And you, do you like English?

▶ You can use this same structure to talk about other people by using the pronouns **nos, le,** and **les.** Unless your instructor tells you otherwise, only the **me** and **te** forms will appear on test materials until **Lección 7.**

Nos gusta dibujar. (nosotros)
We like to draw.

Nos gustan las clases de español e inglés. (nosotros)
We like Spanish class and English class.

No le gusta trabajar. (usted, él, ella)
You don't like to work.
He/She doesn't like to work.

Les gusta el arte. (ustedes, ellos, ellas)
You like art.
They like art.

¡INTÉNTALO! Provide the present tense forms of these verbs. The first items have been done for you.

hablar

1. Yo ___hablo___ español.
2. Ellos ___hablan___ español.
3. Inés ___habla___ español.
4. Nosotras ___hablamos___ español.
5. Tú ___hablas___ español.

gustar

1. ___Me gusta___ el café. (a mí)
2. ¿___Te gustan___ las clases? (a ti)
3. No ___te gusta___ el café. (a ti)
4. No ___me gustan___ las clases. (a mí)
5. No ___me gusta___ el café. (a mí)

Práctica

1 **Completar** Complete the conversation with the appropriate forms of the verbs in parentheses.

JUAN ¡Hola, Linda! ¿Qué tal las clases?

LINDA Bien. (1)___Tomo___ (Tomar) tres clases… química, biología y computación. Y tú, ¿cuántas clases (2)___tomas___ (tomar)?

JUAN (3)___Tomo___ (Tomar) tres también… biología, arte y literatura. El doctor Cárdenas (4)___enseña___ (enseñar) la clase de biología.

LINDA ¿Ah, sí? Lily, Alberto y yo (5)___tomamos___ (tomar) biología a las diez con la profesora Garza.

JUAN ¿(6)___Estudian___ (Estudiar) mucho ustedes?

LINDA Sí, porque hay muchos exámenes. Alberto y yo (7)___necesitamos___ (necesitar) estudiar dos horas todos los días (*every day*).

2 **Oraciones** Form sentences using the words provided. Remember to conjugate the verbs and add any other necessary words.

1. ustedes / practicar / vocabulario Ustedes practican el vocabulario.
2. ¿preparar (tú) / tarea? ¿Preparas la tarea?
3. clase de español / terminar / once La clase de español termina a las once.
4. ¿qué / buscar / ustedes? ¿Qué buscan ustedes?
5. (nosotros) buscar / pluma Buscamos una pluma.
6. (yo) comprar / calculadora Compro una calculadora.

3 **Gustos** Read what these people do. Then use the information in parentheses to tell what they like.

modelo
Yo enseño en la universidad. (las clases) Me gustan las clases.

1. Tú deseas mirar cuadros (*paintings*) de Picasso. (el arte) Te gusta el arte.
2. Soy estudiante de economía. (estudiar) Me gusta estudiar.
3. Tú estudias italiano y español. (las lenguas extranjeras) Te gustan las lenguas extranjeras.
4. No descansas los sábados. (cantar y bailar) Te gusta cantar y bailar.
5. Busco una computadora. (la computación) Me gusta la computación.

4 **Actividades** Get together with a classmate and take turns asking each other if you do these activities. Which activities does your partner like? Which do you both like? Answers will vary.

modelo
tomar el autobús
Estudiante 1: ¿Tomas el autobús?
Estudiante 2: Sí, tomo el autobús, pero (*but*) no me gusta./ No, no tomo el autobús.

bailar merengue	escuchar música rock	practicar el español
cantar bien	estudiar física	trabajar en la universidad
dibujar en clase	mirar la televisión	viajar a Europa

AYUDA

The Spanish **no** translates to both *no* and *not* in English. In negative answers to questions, you will need to use **no** twice:
¿Estudias geografía?
No, no estudio geografía.

1 **Teaching Tip** To simplify, guide the class to first identify the subject and verb ending for each item.

1 **Expansion** Go over the answers quickly as a class. Then ask volunteers to role-play the dialogue.

2 **Teaching Tip** Point out that students will need to conjugate the verbs and add missing articles and other words to complete these dehydrated sentences. Tell them that subject pronouns in parentheses are not necessary in the completed sentences. Model completion of the first sentence for the class.

2 **Expansion** Give these dehydrated sentences to the class as items 7–10: **7. (yo) desear / practicar / verbos / hoy** (Deseo practicar los verbos hoy.) **8. mi compañero de cuarto / regresar / lunes** (Mi compañero de cuarto regresa el lunes.) **9. ella / cantar / y / bailar / muy bien** (Ella canta y baila muy bien.) **10. jóvenes / necesitar / descansar / ahora** (Los jóvenes necesitan descansar ahora.)

3 **Teaching Tip** To simplify, start by reading the model aloud. Then ask students why **me** is used in the answer (the first-person singular is used in the example sentence) and why **gustan** is needed (**las clases** is plural). Have students identify the indirect object pronoun and choose **gusta** or **gustan** for each item, then complete the activity.

3 **Expansion** If you wish to practice the third-person forms, repeat the activity, providing different subjects for each item. Ex: **1. Deseamos mirar cuadros de Picasso. (Nos gusta el arte.)**

4 **Teaching Tip** Before beginning the activity, give a two- to three-minute oral rapid-response drill. Provide infinitives and subjects, and call on students to give the conjugated form.

TEACHING OPTIONS

Pairs Have individual students write five dehydrated sentences and exchange them with a partner, who will complete them. After pairs have completed their sentences, ask volunteers to share some of their dehydrated sentences. Write them on the board and have the class "hydrate" them.

Game Divide the class into two teams. Prepare brief descriptions of easily recognizable people, using **–ar** verbs. Write each name on a card, and give each team a set of names. Then read the descriptions aloud. The first team to hold up the correct name earns a point. Ex: **Ella canta, baila y viaja a muchos países. (Jennifer López)**

Comunicación

5

Describir With a partner, describe what you see in the pictures using the given verbs. Also ask your partner whether or not he/she likes one of the activities. *Answers will vary.*

> **modelo**
> enseñar
> La profesora enseña química. ¿Te gusta la química?

1. caminar, hablar, llevar
2. buscar, descansar, estudiar

3. dibujar, cantar, escuchar
4. llevar, tomar, viajar

6

Charadas In groups of three, play a game of charades using the verbs in the word bank. For example, if someone is studying, you say "**Estudias.**" The first person to guess correctly acts out the next charade. *Answers will vary.*

bailar	cantar	descansar	enseñar	mirar
caminar	conversar	dibujar	escuchar	preguntar

Síntesis

7

Conversación Get together with a classmate and pretend that you are friends who have not seen each other on campus for a few days. Have a conversation in which you catch up on things. Mention how you're feeling, what classes you're taking, what days and times you have classes, and which classes you like and don't like. *Answers will vary.*

Practice more at **vhlcentral.com.**

Teaching notes (margin)

5 Teaching Tip To challenge students, make copies of this activity with the text removed so that students can only see the illustrations. Pass out the copies and have students close their books. Write all the verbs of the activity in one list on the board. Tell students to complete the activity using three of the verbs from the board for each drawing.

5 Expansion Ask students to write additional descriptions of the drawings. Ex: **La profesora habla en clase. Hay números y letras en la pizarra. Ella explica la tarea.** Have volunteers share their descriptions with the class.

6 Teaching Tip You may want to split the class into two teams with volunteers from each team acting out the charades. Give points for correct guesses. The team with the most points at the end wins.

7 Teaching Tip Point out that, in addition to practicing –ar verbs, this activity recycles and reviews material from **Lección 1**: greetings, leave-takings, and telling time. Allow students several minutes to plan their conversation before they begin speaking.

TEACHING OPTIONS

Extra Practice Have students write a description of themselves made up of activities they like or do not like to do, using sentences containing **(no) me gusta…** Collect the descriptions and read them aloud. Have the class guess who wrote each description.
Game To add a visual aspect to this grammar practice, play **Concentración.** Choose eight infinitives taught in this section, and write each one on a separate card. On another eight cards, draw or paste a picture that illustrates the action of each infinitive. Randomly place the cards facedown in four rows of four. Play with even-numbered groups of students. In pairs, students select two cards. If the two cards match, the pair keeps them. If the cards do not match, students return them to their original position. The pair that finishes with the most cards wins.

2.2 Forming questions in Spanish 〔S〕 Tutorial

ANTE TODO There are three basic ways to ask questions in Spanish. Can you guess what they are by looking at the photos and photo captions on this page?

Te gusta mucho la tarea, ¿no?

¿Hablas con tu mamá?

¿Quién es Maru?

▶ One way to form a question is to raise the pitch of your voice at the end of a declarative sentence. When writing any question in Spanish, be sure to use an upside down question mark (**¿**) at the beginning and a regular question mark (**?**) at the end of the sentence.

Statement	**Question**
Ustedes trabajan los sábados.	¿Ustedes trabajan los sábados?
You work on Saturdays.	*Do you work on Saturdays?*
Carlota busca un mapa.	¿Carlota busca un mapa?
Carlota is looking for a map.	*Is Carlota looking for a map?*

▶ You can also form a question by inverting the order of the subject and the verb of a declarative statement. The subject may even be placed at the end of the sentence.

Statement	**Question**
SUBJECT VERB	VERB SUBJECT
Ustedes trabajan los sábados.	¿**Trabajan ustedes** los sábados?
You work on Saturdays.	*Do you work on Saturdays?*
SUBJECT VERB	VERB SUBJECT
Carlota regresa a las seis.	¿**Regresa** a las seis **Carlota**?
Carlota returns at six.	*Does Carlota return at six?*

▶ Questions can also be formed by adding the tags **¿no?** or **¿verdad?** at the end of a statement.

Statement	**Question**
Ustedes trabajan los sábados.	Ustedes trabajan los sábados, **¿no?**
You work on Saturdays.	*You work on Saturdays, don't you?*
Carlota regresa a las seis.	Carlota regresa a las seis, **¿verdad?**
Carlota returns at six.	*Carlota returns at six, right?*

Teaching Tips
- Model pronunciation by asking questions. Ex: **¿Cómo estás? ¿Cuál es tu clase favorita?**
- Point out written accent marks on interrogative words.
- Explain that **¿qué?** and **¿cuál?** are not used interchangeably. The word **¿qué?** precedes nouns while **¿cuál?** is used with verbs. Compare and contrast the following: **¿Qué clase te gusta? ¿Cuál es tu clase favorita?** Write similar questions on the board but leave out the interrogative word. Ask students whether **¿qué?** or **¿cuál?** should be used for each.
- Point out **¿cuáles?** and **¿quiénes?** and give examples for each.
- Clarify singular/plural and masculine/feminine variants for **¿cuánto/a?** and **¿cuántos/as?** Ex: **¿Cuánta tarea hay? ¿Cuántos libros hay?**
- Model the pronunciation of example sentences, asking similar questions of students. Ex: ___, **¿dónde trabajas?** Ask other students to verify their classmates' answers. Ex: ____ **trabaja en ____.**
- Explain that the answer to the question **¿por qué?** is **porque**.

Question words

Interrogative words

¿Adónde?	Where (to)?		**¿De dónde?**	From where?
¿Cómo?	How?		**¿Dónde?**	Where?
¿Cuál?, ¿Cuáles?	Which?; Which one(s)?		**¿Por qué?**	Why?
¿Cuándo?	When?		**¿Qué?**	What?; Which?
¿Cuánto/a?	How much?		**¿Quién?**	Who?
¿Cuántos/as?	How many?		**¿Quiénes?**	Who (plural)?

▶ To ask a question that requires more than a *yes* or *no* answer, use an interrogative word.

¿Cuál de ellos estudia en la biblioteca?
Which of them studies in the library?

¿Adónde caminamos?
Where are we walking?

¿Cuántos estudiantes hablan español?
How many students speak Spanish?

¿Por qué necesitas hablar con ella?
Why do you need to talk to her?

¿Dónde trabaja Ricardo?
Where does Ricardo work?

¿Quién enseña la clase de arte?
Who teaches the art class?

¿Qué clases tomas?
What classes are you taking?

¿Cuánta tarea hay?
How much homework is there?

CONSULTA

You will learn more about the difference between **qué** and **cuál** in **Estructura 9.3**, p. 292.

▶ When pronouncing this type of question, the pitch of your voice falls at the end of the sentence.

¿Cómo llegas a clase?
How do you get to class?

¿Por qué necesitas estudiar?
Why do you need to study?

▶ Notice the difference between **¿por qué?**, which is written as two words and has an accent, and **porque**, which is written as one word without an accent.

¿Por qué estudias español?
Why do you study Spanish?

¡Porque es divertido!
Because it's fun!

▶ In Spanish **no** can mean both *no* and *not*. Therefore, when answering a yes/no question in the negative, you need to use **no** twice.

¿Caminan a la universidad?
Do you walk to the university?

No, no caminamos a la universidad.
No, we do not walk to the university.

 ¡INTÉNTALO! Make questions out of these statements. Use the intonation method in column 1 and the tag **¿no?** method in column 2.

Statement	Intonation	Tag questions
1. Hablas inglés.	¿Hablas inglés?	Hablas inglés, ¿no?
2. Trabajamos mañana.	¿Trabajamos mañana?	Trabajamos mañana, ¿no?
3. Ustedes desean bailar.	¿Ustedes desean bailar?	Ustedes desean bailar, ¿no?
4. Raúl estudia mucho.	¿Raúl estudia mucho?	Raúl estudia mucho, ¿no?
5. Enseño a las nueve.	¿Enseño a las nueve?	Enseño a las nueve, ¿no?
6. Luz mira la televisión.	¿Luz mira la televisión?	Luz mira la televisión, ¿no?

recursos

WB
pp. 15–16

LM
p. 10

S
vhlcentral.com
Lección 2

TEACHING OPTIONS

Video Show the **Fotonovela** again to give students more input on forming questions. Stop the video where appropriate to discuss how certain questions, including tag questions, are formed. Have students focus on characters' rising and falling intonation in questions and statements.

Heritage Speakers Ask heritage speakers to give original statements and questions at random. Have the rest of the class determine whether each sentence is a statement or a question.
Pairs Give pairs of students five minutes to write original questions using as many interrogative words as they can. Can any pair come up with questions using all interrogative words?

Práctica

1 Preguntas Change these sentences into questions by inverting the word order.

> **modelo**
>
> Ernesto habla con su compañero de clase.
>
> ¿Habla Ernesto con su compañero de clase? /
> ¿Habla con su compañero de clase Ernesto?

1. La profesora Cruz prepara la prueba.
 ¿Prepara la profesora Cruz la prueba? / ¿Prepara la prueba la profesora Cruz?
2. Sandra y yo necesitamos estudiar.
 ¿Necesitamos Sandra y yo estudiar? / ¿Necesitamos estudiar Sandra y yo?
3. Los chicos practican el vocabulario.
 ¿Practican los chicos el vocabulario? / ¿Practican el vocabulario los chicos?
4. Jaime termina la tarea.
 ¿Termina Jaime la tarea? / ¿Termina la tarea Jaime?
5. Tú trabajas en la biblioteca. ¿Trabajas tú en la biblioteca? / ¿Trabajas en la biblioteca tú?

2 Completar Irene and Manolo are chatting in the library. Complete their conversation with the appropriate questions. Answers will vary.

IRENE Hola, Manolo. (1) ¿Cómo estás?/¿Qué tal?

MANOLO Bien, gracias. (2) ¿Y tú?

IRENE Muy bien. (3) ¿Qué hora es?

MANOLO Son las nueve.

IRENE (4) ¿Qué estudias?

MANOLO Estudio historia.

IRENE (5) ¿Por qué?

MANOLO Porque hay un examen mañana.

IRENE (6) ¿Te gusta la clase?

MANOLO Sí, me gusta mucho la clase.

IRENE (7) ¿Quién enseña la clase?

MANOLO El profesor Padilla enseña la clase.

IRENE (8) ¿Tomas psicología este semestre?

MANOLO No, no tomo psicología este (*this*) semestre.

IRENE (9) ¿A qué hora regresas a la residencia?

MANOLO Regreso a la residencia a las once.

IRENE (10) ¿Deseas tomar una soda?

MANOLO No, no deseo tomar una soda. ¡Deseo estudiar!

3 Dos profesores In pairs, create a dialogue, similar to the one in **Actividad 2**, between Professor Padilla and his colleague Professor Martínez. Use question words. Answers will vary.

> **modelo**
>
> **Prof. Padilla:** ¿Qué enseñas este semestre?
> **Prof. Martínez:** Enseño dos cursos de sociología.

Practice more at **vhlcentral.com.**

1 Teaching Tip Ask students to give both ways of forming questions for each item. Then have student pairs take turns making the statements and converting them into questions.

1 Expansion Make the even statements negative. Then have students add tag questions to the statements.

2 Expansion
◼↔◼ Have pairs of students create a similar conversation, replacing Manolo's answers with information that is true for them. Then ask volunteers to role-play their conversations for the class.

3 Teaching Tip To prepare students for the activity, have them brainstorm possible topics of conversation.

Comunicación

4 Teaching Tips

- If this is the first time students are completing an activity from the Activity Pack, explain that they need a handout.
- Distribute the *Hojas de actividades* (Activity Pack/ Supersite) and explain that students must actively approach their classmates with their *Hoja* in hand. When they find someone who answers affirmatively, that student signs his or her name.
- For survey-type activities, encourage students to ask one question per person and move on. This will promote circulation throughout the room and prevent students from remaining in clusters.

4 **Encuesta** Your instructor will give you a worksheet. Change the categories in the first column into questions, then use them to survey your classmates. Find at least one person for each category. Be prepared to report the results of your survey to the class. Answers will vary.

5 **Un juego** In groups of four or five, play a game (**un juego**) of Jeopardy®. Each person has to write two clues. Then take turns reading the clues and guessing the questions. The person who guesses correctly reads the next clue. Answers will vary.

Es algo que...	**Es un lugar donde...**	**Es una persona que...**
It's something that...	*It's a place where...*	*It's a person that...*

modelo

Estudiante 1: Es un lugar donde estudiamos.
Estudiante 2: ¿Qué es la biblioteca?

Estudiante 1: Es algo que escuchamos.
Estudiante 2: ¿Qué es la música?

Estudiante 1: Es un director de España.
Estudiante 2: ¿Quién es Pedro Almodóvar?

NOTA CULTURAL

Pedro Almodóvar is an award-winning film director from Spain. His films are full of both humor and melodrama, and their controversial subject matter has often sparked great debate. His film **Hable con ella** won the Oscar for Best Original Screenplay in 2002. His 2006 hit **Volver** was nominated for numerous awards, and won the Best Screenplay and Best Actress award for the entire female cast at the Cannes Film Festival.

4 Expansion

👤↔👤 Ask students to say the name of someone who signed their *Hoja*. Then ask that student for more information. Ex: **¿Quién estudia computación? Ah, ¿sí? ____ estudia computación. ¿Dónde estudias computación, ____? ¿Quién es el/la profesor(a)?**

5 Expansion Play this game with the entire class. Select a few students to play the contestants and to "buzz in" their answers.

6 **El nuevo estudiante** In pairs, imagine you are a transfer student and today is your first day of Spanish class. Ask your partner questions to find out all you can about the class, your classmates, and the university. Then switch roles.

modelo

Estudiante 1: Hola, me llamo Samuel. ¿Cómo te llamas?
Estudiante 2: Me llamo Laura.
Estudiante 1: ¿Quiénes son ellos?
Estudiante 2: Son Melanie y Lucas.
Estudiante 1: Y él, ¿de dónde es?
Estudiante 2: Es de California.
Estudiante 1: En la universidad hay cursos de ciencias, ¿verdad?
Estudiante 2: Sí, hay clases de biología, química y física.
Estudiante 1: ¿Cuántos exámenes hay en esta clase?
Estudiante 2: Hay dos.

6 Teaching Tip Write **la clase, los compañeros de clase,** and **la universidad** on the board. Guide students in brainstorming questions and write each one in the appropriate column.

7 Teaching Tip Brainstorm ideas for interview questions and write them on the board, or have students prepare their questions as homework for an in-class interview session.

Síntesis

7 **Entrevista** Imagine that you are a reporter for the school newspaper. Write five questions about student life at your school and use them to interview two classmates. Be prepared to report your findings to the class. Answers will vary.

2.3 Present tense of estar Tutorial

CONSULTA

To review the forms of **ser**, see **Estructura 1.3**, pp. 19–21.

ANTE TODO In **Lección 1**, you learned how to conjugate and use the verb **ser** *(to be)*. You will now learn a second verb which means *to be*, the verb **estar**. Although **estar** ends in **-ar**, it does not follow the pattern of regular **-ar** verbs. The **yo** form (**estoy**) is irregular. Also, all forms have an accented **á** except the **yo** and **nosotros/as** forms.

The verb estar (to be)

SINGULAR FORMS		
yo	est**oy**	*I am*
tú	est**ás**	*you* (fam.) *are*
Ud./él/ella	est**á**	*you* (form.) *are; he/she is*
PLURAL FORMS		
nosotros/as	est**amos**	*we are*
vosotros/as	est**áis**	*you* (fam.) *are*
Uds./ellos/ellas	est**án**	*you* (form.) *are; they are*

¡Estamos en Perú!

María está en la biblioteca.

COMPARE & CONTRAST

Compare the uses of the verb **estar** to those of the verb **ser**.

Uses of *estar*

Location
 Estoy en casa.
 I am at home.

 Marissa **está** al lado de Felipe.
 Marissa is next to Felipe.

Health
 Juan Carlos **está** enfermo hoy.
 Juan Carlos is sick today.

Well-being
 —¿Cómo **estás**, Jimena?
 How are you, Jimena?

 —**Estoy** muy bien, gracias.
 I'm very well, thank you.

Uses of *ser*

Identity
 Hola, **soy** Maru.
 Hello, I'm Maru.

Occupation
 Soy estudiante.
 I'm a student.

Origin
 —¿**Eres** de México?
 Are you from Mexico?

 —Sí, **soy** de México.
 Yes, I'm from Mexico.

Telling time
 Son las cuatro.
 It's four o'clock.

AYUDA

Use **la casa** to express *the house*, but **en casa** to express *at home*.

CONSULTA

To learn more about the difference between **ser** and **estar**, see **Estructura 5.3**, pp. 158–159.

Section Goals

In **Estructura 2.3**, students will be introduced to:
- the present tense of **estar**
- contrasts between **ser** and **estar**
- prepositions of location used with **estar**

Instructional Resources
Supersite: Audio (Lab MP3 Files); Resources (*PowerPoints*, Activity Pack, Scripts, Answer Keys); Testing Program (Quizzes)
WebSAM
Workbook, pp. 17–18
Lab Manual, p. 11

Teaching Tips

- Point out that only the **yo** and **nosotros/as** forms do not have a written accent.
- Emphasize that the principal distinction between **estar** and **ser** is that **estar** is generally used to express temporary conditions (**Álex está enfermo hoy**) and **ser** is generally used to express inherent qualities (**Álex es inteligente**).
- On the board, make a chart similar to the one in **Compare & Contrast**, but create sample sentences using the names of your students and information about them.
- Students will learn to compare **ser** and **estar** formally in **Estructura 5.3**.

TEACHING OPTIONS

TPR Have students write **ser** and **estar** on separate sheets of paper. Give statements in English and have students indicate if they would use **ser** or **estar** in each by holding up the appropriate paper. Ex: *I'm at home.* (**estar**) *I'm a student.* (**ser**) *I'm tired.* (**estar**) *I'm glad.* (**estar**) *I'm generous.* (**ser**)
Extra Practice Ask students to tell where certain people are or probably are at this moment. Ex: ¿Dónde estás? (**Estoy en la**

clase.) ¿Dónde está el presidente? (**Está en Washington, D.C.**)
Heritage Speakers Ask heritage speakers to name instances where either **ser** or **estar** may be used. They may point out more advanced uses, such as with certain adjectives: **Es aburrido** vs. **Está aburrido.** This may help to compare and contrast inherent qualities and temporary conditions.

▶ **Estar** is often used with certain prepositions to describe the location of a person or an object.

Prepositions often used with estar

al lado de	next to; beside	**delante de**	in front of
a la derecha de	to the right of	**detrás de**	behind
a la izquierda de	to the left of	**en**	in; on
allá	over there	**encima de**	on top of
allí	there	**entre**	between; among
cerca de	near	**lejos de**	far from
con	with	**sin**	without
debajo de	below	**sobre**	on; over

La tiza **está al lado de** la pluma.
The chalk is next to the pen.

Los libros **están encima del** escritorio.
The books are on top of the desk.

El laboratorio **está cerca de** la clase.
The lab is near the classroom.

Maribel **está delante de** José.
Maribel is in front of José.

La maleta **está allí**.
The suitcase is there.

El estadio no **está lejos de** la librería.
The stadium isn't far from the bookstore.

El mapa **está entre** la pizarra y la puerta.
The map is between the blackboard and the door.

Los estudiantes **están en** la clase.
The students are in class.

La calculadora **está sobre** la mesa.
The calculator is on the table.

Los turistas **están allá**.
The tourists are over there.

Hoy estudia con Maru.

La biblioteca está al lado de la librería.

 ¡INTÉNTALO! Provide the present tense forms of **estar**.

1. Ustedes _están_ en la clase.
2. José _está_ en la biblioteca.
3. Yo _estoy_ bien, gracias.
4. Nosotras _estamos_ en la cafetería.
5. Tú _estás_ en el laboratorio.
6. Elena _está_ en la librería.
7. Ellas _están_ en la clase.
8. Ana y yo _estamos_ en la clase.
9. ¿Cómo _está_ usted?
10. Javier y Maribel _están_ en el estadio.
11. Nosotros _estamos_ en la cafetería.
12. Yo _estoy_ en el laboratorio.
13. Carmen y María _están_ enfermas.
14. Tú _estás_ en la clase.

Práctica

1 **Completar** Daniela has just returned home from the library. Complete this conversation with the appropriate forms of **ser** or **estar**.

MAMÁ Hola, Daniela. ¿Cómo (1)___estás___?

▶ **DANIELA** Hola, mamá. (2)___Estoy___ bien. ¿Dónde (3)___está___ papá?
¡Ya (*Already*) (4)___son___ las ocho de la noche!

MAMÁ No (5)___está___ aquí. (6)___Está___ en la oficina.

DANIELA Y Andrés y Margarita, ¿dónde (7)___están___ ellos?

MAMÁ (8)___Están___ en el restaurante La Palma con Martín.

DANIELA ¿Quién (9)___es___ Martín?

MAMÁ (10)___Es___ un compañero de clase. (11)___Es___ de México.

DANIELA Ah. Y el restaurante La Palma, ¿dónde (12)___está___?

MAMÁ (13)___Está___ cerca de la Plaza Mayor, en San Modesto.

DANIELA Gracias, mamá. Voy (*I'm going*) al restaurante. ¡Hasta pronto!

2 **Escoger** Choose the preposition that best completes each sentence.

1. La pluma está (encima de / detrás de) la mesa. encima de
2. La ventana está (a la izquierda de / debajo de) la puerta. a la izquierda de
3. La pizarra está (debajo de / delante de) los estudiantes. delante de
4. Las sillas están (encima de / detrás de) los escritorios. detrás de
5. Los estudiantes llevan los libros (en / sobre) la mochila. en
6. La biblioteca está (sobre / al lado de) la residencia estudiantil. al lado de
7. España está (cerca de / lejos de) Puerto Rico. lejos de
8. México está (cerca de / lejos de) los Estados Unidos. cerca de
9. Felipe trabaja (con / en) Ricardo en la cafetería. con

3 **La librería** Imagine that you are in the school bookstore and can't find various items. Ask the clerk (your partner) the location of five items in the drawing. Then switch roles. Answers will vary.

modelo

Estudiante 1: ¿Dónde están los diccionarios?
Estudiante 2: Los diccionarios están debajo de los libros de literatura.

Practice more at **vhlcentral.com**.

1 **Teaching Tips**
• To simplify, guide students in choosing **ser** or **estar** for each item.
• Ask students to explain why they chose **ser** or **estar** in each case.

1 **Expansion** Ask two volunteers to role-play the conversation for the class.

2 **Expansion**
• To challenge students, rework items 1 through 6, asking questions about items in the classroom or places at the university. Ex: **¿Qué objeto está encima de la mesa? ¿Dónde está la ventana?**
• To add a visual aspect to this exercise, ask students to create simple illustrations that show the relationship of location in items 1–8.

3 **Expansion**
👤↔👤 Assign one student the role of **vendedor(a)** and another the role of **cliente/a**. Then name several of the items in the drawing and ask the participants to create mini-conversations as in the activity.

TEACHING OPTIONS

Extra Practice Add a visual aspect to this grammar practice. Use a large world map (one with Spanish labels is best), and/or the maps on the inside covers of this textbook. Ask students where countries and cities are in relation to each other on the map(s). Ex: **¿Bolivia está a la derecha de Brasil? ¿Uruguay está más cerca de Chile o de Ecuador? ¿Qué país está entre Colombia y Costa Rica?**

Small Groups 👤↔👤 Have each group member think of a country or campus location and describe it with progressively more specific statements. After each statement, the other group members guess what country/location it is; the student presenting clarifies by reacting to their guesses. Ex: —**Es un país. Está en Europa.** —**¿Es Italia?** —**No, pero está a la izquierda de Italia y Suiza. Está cerca de España.** —**¿Es Francia?** —**¡Sí, es Francia!**

Comunicación

4 **¿Dónde estás...?** Get together with a partner and take turns asking each other where you normally are at these times. Answers will vary.

> **modelo**
>
> lunes / 10:00 a.m.
>
> **Estudiante 1:** ¿Dónde estás los lunes a las diez de la mañana?
>
> **Estudiante 2:** Estoy en la clase de español.

1. sábados / 6:00 a.m.
2. miércoles / 9:15 a.m.
3. lunes / 11:10 a.m.
4. jueves / 12:30 a.m.
5. viernes / 2:25 p.m.
6. martes / 3:50 p.m.
7. jueves / 5:45 p.m.
8. miércoles / 8:20 p.m.

5 **La ciudad universitaria** You are an exchange student at a Spanish university. Tell a classmate which buildings you are looking for and ask for their location relative to where you are. Answers will vary.

> **modelo**
>
> **Estudiante 1:** ¿Está lejos la Facultad de Medicina?
>
> **Estudiante 2:** No, está cerca. Está a la izquierda de la Facultad de Administración de Empresas.

Facultad de Medicina

Facultad de Administración de Empresas

Facultad de Filosofía y Letras

Biblioteca

Tú estás aquí.

Facultad de Bellas Artes

Colegio Mayor Cervantes

Síntesis

6 **Entrevista** In groups of three, ask each other these questions. Answers will vary.

1. ¿Cómo estás?
2. ¿Dónde tomas la clase de inglés/periodismo/física/computación?
3. ¿Dónde está tu (*your*) compañero/a de cuarto ahora?
4. ¿Cuántos estudiantes hay en tu clase de historia/literatura/química/matemáticas?
5. ¿Quién(es) no está(n) en la clase hoy?
6. ¿A qué hora terminan tus clases los lunes?
7. ¿Estudias mucho?
8. ¿Cuántas horas estudias para (*for*) una prueba?

Sidebar (left column):

4 **Teaching Tips**
• Ask two volunteers to read the model aloud.
• Have students scan the days and times and ask you for any additional vocabulary.

4 **Expansion** After students have completed the activity, ask the same questions of selected individuals. Then expand on their answers by asking additional questions. Ex: —¿Dónde estás los sábados a las seis de la mañana? —Estoy en la residencia estudiantil. —¿Dónde está la residencia?

5 **Expansion**
• Have students choose a new location in the drawing and repeat the activity.
• Make copies of your campus map and distribute them to the class. Ask questions about where particular buildings are. Give yourself a starting point so that you can ask questions with as many prepositions as possible. Ex: **Estoy en la biblioteca. ¿Está lejos la librería?**
• Have students form groups of three and take turns describing the location of different places on your campus. Ex: —**Está lejos de la cafetería y la biblioteca. Está al lado de la librería y enfrente de la residencia estudiantil Hernández.** —¿Es el estadio?

6 **Expansion** Call on students to share the information they obtained with the class.

Video Show the **Fotonovela** again to give students more input. Stop the video where appropriate to discuss how **estar** and prepositions were used and to ask comprehension questions.

Pairs Write a list of well-known monuments, places, and people on the board. Ex: **el Space Needle, Bill Gates, las Cataratas del Niágara, Madonna** Have student pairs take turns asking each other the location of each item. Ex: —**¿Dónde está el Space**

Needle? —**Está en Seattle, Washginton.**

Game Divide the class into two teams. Select a student from team A to think of an item in the classroom. Team B can ask five questions about where this item is. The first student can respond only with **sí, no, caliente** (*hot*), or **frío** (*cold*). If a team guesses the item within five tries, award them a point. If not, give the other team a point. The team with the most points wins.

 Numbers 31 and higher **Tutorial**

ANTE TODO You have already learned numbers 0–30. Now you will learn the rest of the numbers.

Numbers 31–100

▶ Numbers 31–99 follow the same basic pattern as 21–29.

Numbers 31–100					
31	treinta y uno	**40**	cuarenta	**50**	cincuenta
32	treinta y dos	**41**	cuarenta y uno	**51**	cincuenta y uno
33	treinta y tres	**42**	cuarenta y dos	**52**	cincuenta y dos
34	treinta y cuatro	**43**	cuarenta y tres	**60**	sesenta
35	treinta y cinco	**44**	cuarenta y cuatro	**63**	sesenta y tres
36	treinta y seis	**45**	cuarenta y cinco	**64**	sesenta y cuatro
37	treinta y siete	**46**	cuarenta y seis	**70**	setenta
38	treinta y ocho	**47**	cuarenta y siete	**80**	ochenta
39	treinta y nueve	**48**	cuarenta y ocho	**90**	noventa
		49	cuarenta y nueve	**100**	cien, ciento

▶ **Y** is used in most numbers from **31** through **99**. Unlike numbers 21–29, these numbers must be written as three separate words.

Hay **noventa y dos** exámenes.
There are ninety-two exams.

Hay **cuarenta y dos** estudiantes.
There are forty-two students.

Hay cuarenta y siete estudiantes en la clase de geografía.

Cien menos sesenta y cuatro son treinta y seis pesos de cambio.

▶ With numbers that end in **uno** (31, 41, etc.), **uno** becomes **un** before a masculine noun and **una** before a feminine noun.

Hay **treinta y un** chicos.
There are thirty-one guys.

Hay **treinta y una** chicas.
There are thirty-one girls.

▶ **Cien** is used before nouns and in counting. The words **un, una,** and **uno** are never used before **cien** in Spanish. Use **cientos** to say *hundreds.*

Hay **cien** libros y **cien** sillas.
There are one hundred books and one hundred chairs.

¿Cuántos libros hay? **Cientos.**
How many books are there? Hundreds.

Numbers 101 and higher

▶ As shown in the chart, Spanish uses a period to indicate thousands and millions, rather than a comma, as is used in English.

Numbers 101 and higher

101	ciento uno	1.000	mil
200	doscientos/as	1.100	mil cien
300	trescientos/as	2.000	dos mil
400	cuatrocientos/as	5.000	cinco mil
500	quinientos/as	100.000	cien mil
600	seiscientos/as	200.000	doscientos/as mil
700	setecientos/as	550.000	quinientos/as cincuenta mil
800	ochocientos/as	1.000.000	un millón (de)
900	novecientos/as	8.000.000	ocho millones (de)

▶ Notice that you should use **ciento**, not **cien**, to count numbers over 100.

110 = **ciento diez** 118 = **ciento dieciocho** 150 = **ciento cincuenta**

▶ The numbers 200 through 999 agree in gender with the nouns they modify.

324 plum**as**
trescient**as** veinticuatro plum**as**

3.505 libr**os**
tres mil quinient**os** cinco libr**os**

▶ The word **mil**, which can mean *a thousand* and *one thousand*, is not usually used in the plural form to refer to an exact number, but it can be used to express the idea of *a lot, many,* or *thousands.* **Cientos** can also be used to express *hundreds* in this manner.

¡Hay **miles** de personas en el estadio!
There are thousands of people in the stadium!

Hay **cientos** de libros en la biblioteca.
There are hundreds of books in the library!

▶ To express a complex number (including years), string together all of its components.

55.422 cincuenta y cinco mil cuatrocientos veintidós

¡INTÉNTALO! Write out the Spanish equivalent of each number.

1. **102** ciento dos
2. **5.000.000** cinco millones
3. **201** doscientos uno
4. **76** setenta y seis
5. **92** noventa y dos
6. **550.300** quinientos cincuenta mil trescientos
7. **235** doscientos treinta y cinco
8. **79** setenta y nueve
9. **113** ciento trece
10. **88** ochenta y ocho
11. **17.123** diecisiete mil ciento veintitrés
12. **497** cuatrocientos noventa y siete

TEACHING OPTIONS

TPR Write number patterns on cards (one number per card) and distribute them among the class. Begin a number chain by calling out the first two numbers in the pattern. Ex: **veinticinco, cincuenta.** The students holding these cards have five seconds to get up and stand in front of the class. The rest of the class continues by calling out the numbers in the pattern for the students to join the chain. Continue until the chain is broken or complete; then begin a new pattern.

Pairs Ask students to create a list of nine items containing three numerals in the hundreds, three in the thousands, and three in the millions; each numeral should be followed by a masculine or feminine noun. Have students exchange lists with a classmate, who will read the items aloud. Partners should listen for the correct number and gender agreement. Ex: **204 personas (doscientas cuatro personas)**

Práctica y Comunicación

1 **Baloncesto** Provide these basketball scores in Spanish.

1. Ohio State 76, Michigan 65
2. Florida 92, Florida State 104
3. Stanford 83, UCLA 89
4. Purdue 81, Indiana 78
5. Princeton 67, Harvard 55
6. Duke 115, Virginia 121

1. setenta y seis, sesenta y cinco 3. ochenta y tres, ochenta y nueve 5. sesenta y siete, cincuenta y cinco
2. noventa y dos, ciento cuatro 4. ochenta y uno, setenta y ocho 6. ciento quince, ciento veintiuno

2 **Completar** Following the pattern, write out the missing numbers in Spanish.

1. 50, 150, 250 ... 1.050 trescientos cincuenta, cuatrocientos cincuenta, quinientos cincuenta, seiscientos cincuenta, setecientos cincuenta, ochocientos cincuenta, novecientos cincuenta
2. 5.000, 20.000, 35.000 ... 95.000
cincuenta mil, sesenta y cinco mil, ochenta mil
3. 100.000, 200.000, 300.000 ... 1.000.000
cuatrocientos mil, quinientos mil, seiscientos mil, setecientos mil, ochocientos mil, novecientos mil
4. 100.000.000, 90.000.000, 80.000.000 ... 0 setenta millones, sesenta millones, cincuenta millones, cuarenta millones, treinta millones, veinte millones, diez millones

3 **Resolver** In pairs, take turns reading the math problems aloud for your partner to solve.

AYUDA

+	→	**más**
−	→	**menos**
=	→	**son**

> **modelo**
> 200 + 300 =
> **Estudiante 1:** Doscientos más trescientos son...
> **Estudiante 2:** ...quinientos.

1. 1.000 + 753 = Mil más setecientos cincuenta y tres son mil setecientos cincuenta y tres.
2. 1.000.000 − 30.000 = Un millón menos treinta mil son novecientos setenta mil.
3. 10.000 + 555 = Diez mil más quinientos cincuenta y cinco son diez mil quinientos cincuenta y cinco.
4. 15 + 150 = Quince más ciento cincuenta son ciento sesenta y cinco.
5. 100.000 + 205.000 = Cien mil más doscientos cinco mil son trescientos cinco mil.
6. 29.000 − 10.000 = Veintinueve mil menos diez mil son diecinueve mil.

4 **Entrevista** Find out the telephone numbers and e-mail addresses of four classmates.
Answers will vary.

AYUDA

arroba *at* (@)
punto *dot* (.)

> **modelo**
> **Estudiante 1:** ¿Cuál es tu *(your)* número de teléfono?
> **Estudiante 2:** Es el 635-19-51.
> **Estudiante 1:** ¿Y tu dirección de correo electrónico?
> **Estudiante 2:** Es a-Smith-arroba-pe-ele-punto-e-de-u. *(asmith@pl.edu)*

Síntesis

5 **¿A qué distancia...?** Your instructor will give you and a partner incomplete charts that indicate the distances between Madrid and various locations. Fill in the missing information on your chart by asking your partner questions. Answers will vary.

> **modelo**
> **Estudiante 1:** ¿A qué distancia está Arganda del Rey?
> **Estudiante 2:** Está a veintisiete kilómetros de Madrid.

 Practice more at **vhlcentral.com.**

Recapitulación

Concepts Diagnostics

Review the grammar concepts you have learned in this lesson by completing these activities.

1 **Completar** Complete the chart with the correct verb forms. **12 pts.**

yo	tú	nosotros	ellas
compro	compras	compramos	compran
deseo	**deseas**	deseamos	desean
miro	miras	**miramos**	miran
pregunto	preguntas	preguntamos	**preguntan**

2 **Números** Write these numbers in Spanish. **8 pts.**

modelo
645: *seiscientos cuarenta y cinco*

1. **49:** cuarenta y nueve
2. **97:** noventa y siete
3. **113:** ciento trece
4. **632:** seiscientos treinta y dos
5. **1.781:** mil setecientos ochenta y uno
6. **3.558:** tres mil quinientos cincuenta y ocho
7. **1.006.015:** un millón seis mil quince
8. **67.224.370:** sesenta y siete millones doscientos veinticuatro mil trescientos setenta

3 **Preguntas** Write questions for these answers. **12 pts.**

1. —¿ De dónde es _____ Patricia?
 —Patricia es de Colombia.
2. —¿ Quién es _____ él?
 —Él es mi amigo (*friend*).
3. —¿ Cuántos idiomas hablas _____ (tú)?
 —Hablo dos idiomas (*languages*).
4. —¿ Qué desean (tomar) _____ (ustedes)?
 —Deseamos tomar café.
5. —¿ Por qué tomas biología _____?
 —Tomo biología porque me gustan las ciencias.
6. —¿ Cuándo descansa Camilo _____?
 —Camilo descansa por las mañanas.

RESUMEN GRAMATICAL

2.1 **Present tense of -ar verbs** *pp. 46–48*

estudiar	
estudio	estudiamos
estudias	estudiáis
estudia	estudian

The verb gustar

(no) me gusta + el/la + [*singular noun*]

(no) me gustan + los/las + [*plural noun*]

(no) me gusta + [*infinitive(s)*]

Note: You may use a mí for emphasis, but never yo.

To ask a classmate about likes and dislikes, use te instead of me, but never tú.

¿Te gusta la historia?

2.2 **Forming questions in Spanish** *pp. 51–52*

▶ ¿Ustedes trabajan los sábados?

▶ ¿Trabajan ustedes los sábados?

▶ Ustedes trabajan los sábados, ¿verdad?/¿no?

Interrogative words		
¿Adónde?	¿Cuánto/a?	¿Por qué?
¿Cómo?	¿Cuántos/as?	¿Qué?
¿Cuál(es)?	¿De dónde?	¿Quién(es)?
¿Cuándo?	¿Dónde?	

2.3 **Present tense of estar** *pp. 55–56*

▶ estar: estoy, estás, está, estamos, estáis, están

2.4 **Numbers 31 and higher** *pp. 59–60*

31	treinta y uno	101	ciento uno
32	treinta y dos	200	doscientos/as
	(*and so on*)	500	quinientos/as
40	cuarenta	700	setecientos/as
50	cincuenta	900	novecientos/as
60	sesenta	1.000	mil
70	setenta	2.000	dos mil
80	ochenta	5.100	cinco mil cien
90	noventa	100.000	cien mil
100	cien, ciento	1.000.000	un millón (de)

Section Goal

In **Recapitulación**, students will review the grammar concepts from this lesson.

Instructional Resource
Supersite

1 Teaching Tips
- To simplify, ask students to identify the infinitive of the verb in each row.
- Complete this activity orally as a class. Write each form on the board as students call them out.

1 Expansion Ask students to provide the third-person singular (**Ud./él/ella**) conjugations.

2 Expansion
- Ask students to write five more numbers above 31. Have them read the numbers to a partner, who will jot them down. Remind students to check each other's answers.
- To challenge students, have them complete the activity and then say what they can buy with that amount of money. Model the first item for the class. Ex: **Con 49 dólares, compro una mochila.**

3 Teaching Tips
- Remind students that all question words should carry accent marks.
- Remind students that verbs in Spanish do not require subject pronouns; they are used for emphasis or clarification.

TEACHING OPTIONS

Pairs Have students write ten questions using the interrogative words from **Estructura 2.2** to ask their partner about his/her family, house, friends, etc. Remind students that ¿**Cuánto/a?** and ¿**Cuántos/as?** should agree with their corresponding nouns. Then have students exchange papers with a classmate and answer the questions. Finally, have pairs work together to review the answers. Have them write sentences using

nosotros/as about any items they have in common.
Extra Practice On the board, write a list of landmarks (libraries, parks, churches, restaurants, hotels, and so forth) in the community. Have students choose a landmark and write a short paragraph describing its location. Ex: **El Hotel Plaza está al lado de la biblioteca. Está cerca de la catedral y delante de Sebastian's Café. Está lejos de mi casa.**

4 **Al teléfono** Complete this telephone conversation with the correct forms of the verb **estar**.

`8 pts.`

MARÍA TERESA Hola, señora López. (1) ¿____Está____ Elisa en casa?

SRA. LÓPEZ Hola, ¿quién es?

MARÍA TERESA Soy María Teresa. Elisa y yo (2) ____estamos____ en la misma (*same*) clase de literatura.

SRA. LÓPEZ ¡Ah, María Teresa! ¿Cómo (3) ____estás____?

MARÍA TERESA (4) ____Estoy____ muy bien, gracias. Y usted, ¿cómo (5) ____está____?

SRA. LÓPEZ Bien, gracias. Pues, no, Elisa no (6) ____está____ en casa. Ella y su hermano (*her brother*) (7) ____están____ en la Biblioteca Cervantes.

MARÍA TERESA ¿Cervantes?

SRA. LÓPEZ Es la biblioteca que (8) ____está____ al lado del café Bambú.

MARÍA TERESA ¡Ah, sí! Gracias, señora López.

SRA. LÓPEZ Hasta luego, María Teresa.

5 **¿Qué te gusta?** Write a paragraph of at least five sentences stating what you like and don't like about your university. If possible, explain your likes and dislikes. `10 pts.` Answers will vary.

Me gusta la clase de música porque no hay muchos exámenes. No me gusta cenar en la cafetería...

6 **Canción** Use the appropriate forms of the verb **gustar** to complete the beginning of a popular song by Manu Chao. `2 EXTRA points!`

❝ Me ____gustan____ los aviones°,
me gustas tú,
me ____gusta____ viajar,
me gustas tú,
me gusta la mañana,
me gustas tú. **❞**

aviones *airplanes*

 Practice more at **vhlcentral.com**.

TEACHING OPTIONS

Pairs Write **más, menos, multiplicado por**, and **dividido por** on the board. Model a few simple problems using numbers 31 and higher. Ex: **Cien mil trescientos menos diez mil son noventa mil trescientos. Mil dividido por veinte son cincuenta.** Then ask students to write two math problems of each type for a classmate to solve. Have partners verify each other's work.

Small Groups Tell students to think of a famous person and write five statements about their likes and dislikes from that person's point of view. Tell them to progressively give more clues to the person's identity and to end with **¿Quién soy?** Then, in small groups, have students read their statements aloud for their partners to guess. Have them respond to the guesses with more information as necessary.

4 Expansion
Ask student pairs to write a brief phone conversation based on the one in **Actividad 4**. Have volunteers role-play their dialogues for the class.

5 Teaching Tips
- Before writing their paragraphs, have students brainstorm a list of words or phrases related to universities.
- Remind students of when to use **gusta** versus **gustan**. Write a few example sentences on the board.
- Have students exchange papers with a partner to peer-edit each other's paragraphs.

6 Teaching Tip Point out the form **gustas** in lines 2, 4, and 6, and ask students to guess the translation of the phrase **me gustas tú** (*I like you*; literally, *you are pleasing to me*). Tell students that **me gustas** and **le gustas** are not used as much as their English counterparts. Most often they are used in romantic situations.

6 Canción **Manu Chao** (born 1961) is a French singer of Spanish origin. In the 80's he and his brother started the band **Mano Negra**. Since the band's breakup in 1995, he has led a successful solo career. His music, which draws on diverse influences such as punk, ska, reggae, salsa, and Algerian raï, is popular throughout Europe and Latin America. **Chao** often mixes several languages in one song.

Section Goals

In **Lectura**, students will:
- learn to use text formats to predict content
- read documents in Spanish

Instructional Resource
Supersite

Estrategia Introduce the strategy. Point out that many documents have easily identifiable formats that can help readers predict content. Have students look at the document in the **Estrategia** box and ask them to name the recognizable elements: (days of the week, time, classes). Ask what kind of document it is (a student's weekly schedule).

Cognados Have pairs of students scan **¡Español en Madrid!** and identify cognates and guess their meanings.

Examinar el texto Ask students what type of information is contained in **¡Español en Madrid!** (It is a brochure for an intensive Spanish-language summer program.) Discuss elements of the recognizable format that helped them predict the content, such as the headings, the lists of courses, and the course schedule with dates.

Lectura

Antes de leer

Estrategia

Predicting Content through Formats

Recognizing the format of a document can help you to predict its content. For instance, invitations, greeting cards, and classified ads follow an easily identifiable format, which usually gives you a general idea of the information they contain. Look at the text and identify it based on its format.

	lunes	martes	miércoles	jueves	viernes
8:30	biología		biología		biología
9:00		historia		historia	
9:30	inglés		inglés		inglés
10:00					
10:30					
11:00					
12:00					
12:30					
1:00					
2:00	arte		arte		arte

If you guessed that this is a page from a student's schedule, you are correct. You can now infer that the document contains information about a student's weekly schedule, including days, times, and activities.

Cognados

With a classmate, make a list of the cognates in the text and guess their English meanings. What do cognates reveal about the content of the document?

Examinar el texto

Look at the format of the document entitled **¡Español en Madrid!** What type of text is it? What information do you expect to find in this type of document?

Practice more at **vhlcentral.com**.

¡ESPAÑOL EN MADRID!

UAM

Programa de Cursos Intensivos de Español
Universidad Autónoma de Madrid

Después de leer

Correspondencias

Provide the letter of each item in Column B that matches the words in Column A. Two items will not be used.

A	B
1. profesores f	a. (34) 91 523 4500
2. vivienda h	b. (34) 91 524 0210
3. Madrid d	c. 23 junio–30 julio
4. número de teléfono a	d. capital cultural de Europa
5. Español 2B c	e. 16 junio–22 julio
6. número de fax g	f. especializados en enseñar español como lengua extranjera
	g. (34) 91 523 4623
	h. familias españolas

Universidad Autónoma de Madrid

Madrid, la capital cultural de Europa, y la UAM te ofrecen cursos intensivos de verano° para aprender° español como nunca antes°.

Cursos	Empieza°	Termina
Español 1A	16 junio	22 julio
Español 1B	23 junio	30 julio
Español 1C	30 junio	10 agosto
Español 2A	16 junio	22 julio
Español 2B	23 junio	30 julio
Español 3A	16 junio	22 julio
Español 3B	23 junio	30 julio

¿Dónde?
En el campus de la UAM, edificio° de la Facultad de Filosofía y Letras.

¿Quiénes son los profesores?
Son todos hablantes nativos del español y catedráticos° de la UAM especializados en enseñar el español como lengua extranjera.

¿Qué niveles se ofrecen?
Se ofrecen tres niveles° básicos:
1. Español Elemental, A, B y C
2. Español Intermedio, A y B
3. Español Avanzado, A y B

Viviendas
Para estudiantes extranjeros se ofrece vivienda° con familias españolas.

¿Cuándo?
Este verano desde° el 16 de junio hasta el 10 de agosto. Los cursos tienen una duración de 6 semanas.

Información
Para mayor información, sirvan comunicarse con la siguiente° oficina:

Universidad Autónoma de Madrid
Programa de Español como Lengua Extranjera
Ctra. Colmenar Viejo, Km. 15, 28049 Madrid, España
Tel. (34) 91 523 4500, **Fax** (34) 91 523 4623
www.uam.es

verano *summer* aprender *to learn* nunca antes *never before* edificio *building* catedráticos *professors* niveles *levels* vivienda *housing* desde *from* Empieza *Begins* siguiente *following*

¿Cierto o falso?

Indicate whether each statement is **cierto** or **falso**.
Then correct the false statements.

	Cierto	Falso
1. La Universidad Autónoma de Madrid ofrece (*offers*) cursos intensivos de italiano.	○	●
Ofrece cursos intensivos de español.		
2. La lengua nativa de los profesores del programa es el inglés.	○	●
La lengua nativa de los profesores es el español.		
3. Los cursos de español son en la Facultad de Ciencias.	○	●
Son en el edificio de la Facultad de Filosofía y Letras.		
4. Los estudiantes pueden vivir (*can live*) con familias españolas.	●	○

	Cierto	Falso
5. La universidad que ofrece los cursos intensivos está en Salamanca.	○	●
Está en Madrid.		
6. Español 3B termina en agosto.	○	●
Termina en julio.		
7. Si deseas información sobre (*about*) los cursos intensivos de español, es posible llamar al (34) 91 523 4500.	●	○
8. Español 1A empieza en julio.	○	●
Empieza en junio.		

España

Plaza Mayor en Madrid

La Sagrada Familia en Barcelona

El país en cifras

▶ **Área:** 504.750 km² (kilómetros cuadrados) o 194.884 millas cuadradas°, incluyendo las islas Baleares y las islas Canarias
▶ **Población:** 47.203.000
▶ **Capital:** Madrid—6.213.000
▶ **Ciudades° principales:** Barcelona—5.315.000, Valencia—832.000, Sevilla, Zaragoza
SOURCE: Population Division, UN Secretariat
▶ **Moneda°:** euro
▶ **Idiomas°:** español o castellano, catalán, gallego, valenciano, euskera

Gallego · Euskera · Catalán · Español · Valenciano
Regiones lingüísticas

Bandera de España

Españoles célebres
▶ **Miguel de Cervantes,** escritor° (1547–1616)
▶ **Pedro Almodóvar,** director de cine° (1949–)
▶ **Rosa Montero,** escritora y periodista° (1951–)
▶ **Fernando Alonso,** corredor de autos° (1981–)
▶ **Paz Vega,** actriz° (1976–)

millas cuadradas *square miles* Ciudades *Cities* Moneda *Currency* Idiomas *Languages* escritor *writer* cine *film* periodista *reporter* corredor de autos *race car driver* actriz *actress* pueblo *town* Cada año *Every year* Durante todo un día *All day long* se tiran *throw at each other* varias toneladas *many tons*

FRANCIA · ANDORRA · Pirineos · PORTUGAL · ESPAÑA · Madrid · Valencia · Sierra Nevada · Sevilla · Estrecho de Gibraltar · Ceuta · Melilla · MARRUECOS · La Coruña · Mar Cantábrico · San Sebastián · Zaragoza · Río Ebro · Barcelona · Salamanca · Menorca · Mallorca · Ibiza · Islas Baleares · Mar Mediterráneo

El baile flamenco

Islas Canarias · La Palma · Tenerife · Gran Canaria · Lanzarote · Gomera · Hierro · Fuerteventura

recursos
WB pp. 21–22 | VM pp. 227–228 | vhlcentral.com Lección 2

¡Increíble pero cierto!
En Buñol, un pueblo° de Valencia, la producción de tomates es un recurso económico muy importante. Cada año° se celebra el festival de *La Tomatina*. Durante todo un día°, miles de personas se tiran° tomates. Llegan turistas de todo el país, y se usan varias toneladas° de tomates.

Gastronomía • **José Andrés**

José Andrés es un chef español famoso internacionalmente°. Le gusta combinar platos° tradicionales de España con las técnicas de cocina más innovadoras°. Andrés vive° en Washington, DC, es dueño° de varios restaurantes en los EE.UU. y presenta° un programa en PBS (foto, izquierda). También° ha estado° en *Late Show with David Letterman* y *Top Chef*.

Cultura • **La diversidad**

La riqueza° cultural y lingüística de España refleja la combinación de las diversas culturas que han habitado° en su territorio durante siglos°. El español es la lengua oficial del país, pero también son oficiales el catalán, el gallego, el euskera y el valenciano.

Póster en catalán

Artes • **Velázquez y el Prado**

El Prado, en Madrid, es uno de los museos más famosos del mundo°. En el Prado hay pinturas° importantes de Botticelli, de El Greco y de los españoles Goya y Velázquez. *Las meninas* es la obra° más conocida° de Diego Velázquez, pintor° oficial de la corte real° durante el siglo° XVII.

Las meninas, Diego Velázquez, 1656

Comida • **La paella**

La paella es uno de los platos más típicos de España. Siempre se prepara° con arroz° y azafrán°, pero hay diferentes recetas°. La paella valenciana, por ejemplo, es de pollo° y conejo°, y la paella marinera es de mariscos°.

La costa de Ibiza

¿Qué aprendiste? Completa las oraciones con la información adecuada.

1. El chef español _José Andrés_ es muy famoso.
2. El arroz y el azafrán son ingredientes básicos de la _paella_.
3. El Prado está en _Madrid_.
4. José Andrés vive en _Washington, DC/EE.UU._
5. El chef José Andrés tiene un _programa_ de televisión en PBS.
6. El gallego es una de las lenguas oficiales de _España_.

Conexión Internet Investiga estos temas en **vhlcentral.com**.

Practice more at **vhlcentral.com**.

1. Busca información sobre la Universidad de Salamanca u otra universidad española. ¿Qué cursos ofrece (*does it offer*)? ¿Ofrece tu universidad cursos similares?
2. Busca información sobre un español o una española célebre (por ejemplo, un[a] político/a, un actor, una actriz, un[a] artista). ¿De qué parte de España es y por qué es célebre?

internacionalmente *internationally* platos *dishes* más innovadoras *most innovative* vive *lives* dueño *owner* presenta *hosts* También *Also* ha estado *has been* riqueza *richness* han habitado *have lived* durante siglos *for centuries* mundo *world* pinturas *paintings* obra *work* más conocida *best-known* pintor *painter* corte real *royal court* siglo *century* Siempre se prepara *It is always prepared* arroz *rice* azafrán *saffron* recetas *recipes* pollo *chicken* conejo *rabbit* mariscos *seafood*

TEACHING OPTIONS

Variación léxica Regional cultures and languages have remained strong in Spain, despite efforts made in the past to suppress them in the name of national unity. The language that has come to be called *Spanish*, **español,** is the language of the region of north central Spain called **Castilla**. Because Spain was unified under the Kingdom of Castile at the end of the Middle Ages, the language of Castile, **castellano**, became the principal language of government, business, and literature. Even today one is likely to hear Spanish speakers refer to Spanish as **castellano** or **español**. Efforts to suppress the regional languages, though often harsh, were ineffective, and after the death of the dictator **Francisco Franco** and the return of power to regional governing bodies, the regional languages of Spain were given co-official status.

José Andrés This Spanish chef (born in 1969 in Asturias) is often credited with bringing the concept of **tapas** to the U.S. In addition to his TV appearances, he has written several cookbooks and won many awards.

La diversidad Have students consult the map on the inside back cover. As you name each language (Ex: **catalán**), have students search for the corresponding region name (**Cataluña**).

Velázquez y el Prado Point out **la infanta Margarita**, the royal princess, with her attendants. The name **Las meninas** comes from the Portuguese word for "girls," used to refer to royal attendants. Reflected in the mirror are **Margarita's** parents, **los reyes Felipe IV y Mariana de Asturias**. Have students find **Velázquez** himself, standing paintbrush in hand, before an enormous canvas. You may wish to ask students to research the identity of the man in the doorway.

La paella Pairs can role-play a restaurant scene: the customer asks the waiter/waitress about the ingredients in the paella, then chooses **paella valenciana** or **paella marinera**.

Conexión Internet Students will find supporting Internet activities and links at **vhlcentral.com**.

Teaching Tip You may want to wrap up this section by playing the *Panorama cultural* video footage for this lesson.

Instructional Resources
Supersite: Audio (Textbook & Lab MP3s); Testing Program (Tests, MP3s)
WebSAM
Lab Manual, p. 12

La clase y la universidad

el/la compañero/a de clase	classmate
el/la compañero/a de cuarto	roommate
el/la estudiante	student
el/la profesor(a)	teacher
el borrador	eraser
la calculadora	calculator
el escritorio	desk
el libro	book
el mapa	map
la mesa	table
la mochila	backpack
el papel	paper
la papelera	wastebasket
la pizarra	blackboard
la pluma	pen
la puerta	door
el reloj	clock; watch
la silla	seat
la tiza	chalk
la ventana	window
la biblioteca	library
la cafetería	cafeteria
la casa	house; home
el estadio	stadium
el laboratorio	laboratory
la librería	bookstore
la residencia estudiantil	dormitory
la universidad	university; college
la clase	class
el curso, la materia	course
la especialización	major
el examen	test; exam
el horario	schedule
la prueba	test; quiz
el semestre	semester
la tarea	homework
el trimestre	trimester; quarter

Las materias

la administración de empresas	business administration
la arqueología	archeology
el arte	art
la biología	biology
las ciencias	sciences
la computación	computer science
la contabilidad	accounting
la economía	economics
el español	Spanish
la física	physics
la geografía	geography
la historia	history
las humanidades	humanities
el inglés	English
las lenguas extranjeras	foreign languages
la literatura	literature
las matemáticas	mathematics
la música	music
el periodismo	journalism
la psicología	psychology
la química	chemistry
la sociología	sociology

Preposiciones

al lado de	next to; beside
a la derecha de	to the right of
a la izquierda de	to the left of
allá	over there
allí	there
cerca de	near
con	with
debajo de	below; under
delante de	in front of
detrás de	behind
en	in; on
encima de	on top of
entre	between; among
lejos de	far from
sin	without
sobre	on; over

Palabras adicionales

¿Adónde?	Where (to)?
ahora	now
¿Cuál?, ¿Cuáles?	Which?; Which one(s)?
¿Por qué?	Why?
porque	because

Verbos

bailar	to dance
buscar	to look for
caminar	to walk
cantar	to sing
cenar	to have dinner
comprar	to buy
contestar	to answer
conversar	to converse, to chat
desayunar	to have breakfast
descansar	to rest
desear	to wish; to desire
dibujar	to draw
enseñar	to teach
escuchar la radio/ música	to listen (to) the radio/music
esperar (+ inf.)	to wait (for); to hope
estar	to be
estudiar	to study
explicar	to explain
gustar	to like
hablar	to talk; to speak
llegar	to arrive
llevar	to carry
mirar	to look (at); to watch
necesitar (+ inf.)	to need
practicar	to practice
preguntar	to ask (a question)
preparar	to prepare
regresar	to return
terminar	to end; to finish
tomar	to take; to drink
trabajar	to work
viajar	to travel

Los días de la semana

¿Cuándo?	When?
¿Qué día es hoy?	What day is it?
Hoy es…	Today is…
la semana	week
lunes	Monday
martes	Tuesday
miércoles	Wednesday
jueves	Thursday
viernes	Friday
sábado	Saturday
domingo	Sunday

Numbers 31 and higher	See pages 59–60.
Expresiones útiles	See page 41.

 Audio: Vocabulary

recursos

LM p. 12 | vhlcentral.com Lección 2

La familia

3

Communicative Goals

You will learn how to:
- **Talk about your family and friends**
- **Describe people and things**
- **Express possession**

Lesson Goals

In **Lección 3**, students will be introduced to the following:
- terms for family relationships
- names of various professions
- surnames and families in the Spanish-speaking world
- Spain's Royal Family
- descriptive adjectives
- possessive adjectives
- the present tense of common regular **-er** and **-ir** verbs
- the present tense of **tener** and **venir**
- context clues to unlock meaning of unfamiliar words
- using idea maps when writing
- how to write a friendly letter
- strategies for asking clarification in oral communication
- a television commercial for **Jumbo**, a Chilean superstore chain
- the short film **Tears & Tortillas**
- a video about two Ecuadorian families
- geographical and cultural information about Ecuador

A primera vista Here are some additional questions you can ask to personalize the photo: **¿Cuántas personas hay en tu familia? ¿De qué conversas con ellos? ¿Estudias lejos o cerca de la casa de tu familia? ¿Viajas mucho con ellos?**

Teaching Tip Look for these icons for additional communicative practice:

→👤	Interpretive communication
←👤	Presentational communication
👤↔👤	Interpersonal communication

A PRIMERA VISTA
- ¿Cuántos chicos hay en la foto?
- ¿Hay una mujer a la izquierda? ¿Y a la derecha?
- ¿Hay una cosa en la mano de la mujer?
- ¿Conversan ellos? ¿Trabajan? ¿Viajan?
- ¿Están lejos de su casa?

INSTRUCTIONAL RESOURCES

Supersite (vhlcentral.com)
Video: ***Fotonovela*, *Flash cultura*, *Anuncio*, *Cortometraje*, *Panorama cultural****
**Also on DVD*
Audio: Textbook and Lab MP3 Files (*also on CD*)
Activity Pack: Information Gap Activities, games, additional activity handouts

Resources: Textbook Answer Key, WB/VM/LM Answer Key, Scripts, Translations, **Vocabulario adicional**, lesson plans, **Estructura** *PowerPoints*, Overheads
Testing Program: Quizzes, Tests, Exams, MP3s (*also on Test Generator CD*)

Learning Management System (Assignment Task Manager, Gradebook)
WebSAM (online Workbook/Video Manual/Lab Manual)
Workbook/Video Manual
Lab Manual

La familia

La familia de **José Miguel Pérez Santoro**

mi abuelo (*my grandfather*)

Más vocabulario	
los abuelos	*grandparents*
el/la bisabuelo/a	*great-grandfather/ great-grandmother*
el/la gemelo/a	*twin*
el/la hermanastro/a	*stepbrother/stepsister*
el/la hijastro/a	*stepson/stepdaughter*
la madrastra	*stepmother*
el medio hermano/ la media hermana	*half-brother/ half-sister*
el padrastro	*stepfather*
los padres	*parents*
los parientes	*relatives*
el/la cuñado/a	*brother-in-law/ sister-in-law*
la nuera	*daughter-in-law*
el/la suegro/a	*father-in-law/ mother-in-law*
el yerno	*son-in-law*
el/la amigo/a	*friend*
el apellido	*last name; surname*
la gente	*people*
el/la muchacho/a	*boy/girl*
el/la niño/a	*child*
el/la novio/a	*boyfriend/girlfriend*
la persona	*person*
el/la artista	*artist*
el/la ingeniero/a	*engineer*
el/la doctor(a), el/la médico/a	*doctor; physician*
el/la periodista	*journalist*
el/la programador(a)	*computer programmer*

Ernesto Santoro González

mi tío (*uncle*)
hijo (*son*) de Juan y Socorro

Marina Gutiérrez de Santoro

mi tía (*aunt*)
esposa (*wife*) de Ernesto

Silvia Socorro Santoro Gutiérrez

mi prima (*cousin*)
hija (*daughter*) de Ernesto y Marina

Héctor Manuel Santoro Gutiérrez

mi primo (*cousin*)
nieto (*grandson*) de Juan y Socorro

Carmen Santoro Gutiérrez

mi prima
hija de Ernesto y Marina

Variación léxica

madre ⟷ mamá, mami (*colloquial*)
padre ⟷ papá, papi (*colloquial*)
muchacho/a ⟷ chico/a

recursos
WB pp. 23–24 | LM p. 13 | Ⓢ vhlcentral.com Lección 3

Práctica

1 Escuchar 🎧 Listen to each statement made by José Miguel Pérez Santoro, then indicate whether it is **cierto** or **falso**, based on his family tree.

	Cierto	Falso		Cierto	Falso
1.	⊘	○	6.	⊘	○
2.	⊘	○	7.	⊘	○
3.	○	⊘	8.	○	⊘
4.	⊘	○	9.	○	⊘
5.	○	⊘	10.	⊘	○

2 Personas 🎧 Indicate each word that you hear mentioned in the narration.

1. _____ cuñado
2. __✔__ tía
3. __✔__ periodista
4. __✔__ niño
5. __✔__ esposo
6. __✔__ abuelos
7. _____ ingeniera
8. __✔__ primo

3 Emparejar Provide the letter of the phrase that matches each description. Two items will not be used.

1. Mi hermano programa las computadoras. c
2. Son los padres de mi esposo. e
3. Son los hijos de mis (my) tíos. h
4. Mi tía trabaja en un hospital. a
5. Es el hijo de mi madrastra y el hijastro de mi padre. b
6. Es el esposo de mi hija. l
7. Es el hijo de mi hermana. k
8. Mi primo dibuja y pinta mucho. i
9. Mi hermanastra enseña en la universidad. j
10. Mi padre trabaja con planos (blueprints). d

a. Es médica.
b. Es mi hermanastro.
c. Es programador.
d. Es ingeniero.
e. Son mis suegros.
f. Es mi novio.
g. Es mi padrastro.
h. Son mis primos.
i. Es artista.
j. Es profesora.
k. Es mi sobrino.
l. Es mi yerno.

4 Definiciones Define these family terms in Spanish. Some answers may vary.

modelo
hijastro *Es el hijo de mi esposo/a, pero no es mi hijo.*

1. abuela
2. bisabuelo
3. tío
4. primas
5. suegra
6. cuñado
7. nietos
8. medio hermano

1. la madre de mi madre/padre
2. el abuelo de mi madre/padre
3. el hermano de mi madre/padre
4. las hijas de mis tíos/as
5. la madre de mi esposo/a
6. el esposo de mi hermana
7. los hijos de mis hijos
8. el hijo de mi padre pero no de mi madre

Family tree

Socorro González de Santoro
mi abuela (*my grandmother*)

Mirta Santoro de Pérez
mi madre (*mother*)
hija de Juan y Socorro

Rubén Ernesto Pérez Gómez
mi padre (*father*)
esposo de mi madre

José Miguel Pérez Santoro
hijo de Rubén y de Mirta

Beatriz Alicia Pérez de Morales
mi hermana (*sister*)

Felipe Morales Zapata
esposo (*husband*) de Beatriz Alicia

Víctor Miguel Morales Pérez
mi sobrino (*nephew*)
hermano (*brother*) de Anita

Anita Morales Pérez
mi sobrina (*niece*)
nieta (*granddaughter*) de mis padres

los hijos (*children*) de Beatriz Alicia y de Felipe

TEACHING OPTIONS

TPR Make a "living" family tree. Assign students different roles as family members and have students write down the term assigned to them on a sheet of paper. Arrange students as in a family tree and ask questions about relationships. Ex: **¿Quién es la madre de _____? ¿Cómo se llama el tío de _____?**

Game →🔁← Have students state the relationship between people on **José Miguel's** family tree; have their classmates guess which person they are describing. Ex: **Es la hermana de Ernesto y su padre es Juan. (Mirta) Héctor Manuel es su hermano y Beatriz Alicia es su prima. (Carmen o Silvia)** Take turns until each member of the class or group has stated a relationship.

1 Expansion To challenge students, write the false statements on the board and have students correct them by referring to the family tree.

1 Script 1. Beatriz Alicia es mi hermana. 2. Rubén es el abuelo de Víctor Miguel. 3. Silvia es mi sobrina. 4. Mirta y Rubén son los tíos de Héctor Manuel. 5. Anita es mi prima. 6. Ernesto es el hermano de mi madre. 7. Soy el tío de Anita. 8. Víctor Miguel es mi nieto. 9. Carmen, Beatriz Alicia y Marina son los nietos de Juan y Socorro. 10. El hijo de Juan y Socorro es el tío de Beatriz Alicia.
Textbook MP3s

2 Teaching Tips
• To simplify, read through the list as a class before playing the audio. Remind students to focus only on these words as they listen.
• Tell students that the words, if they appear in the narration, will not follow the sequence in the list.

2 Script Julia y Daniel son mis abuelos. Ellos viven en Montreal con mi tía Leti, que es periodista, y con mi primo César. César es un niño muy bueno y dibuja muy bien. Hoy voy a hablar por teléfono con todos ellos y con el esposo de Leti. Él es de Canadá.
Textbook MP3s

3 Expansion After students finish, ask volunteers to provide complete sentences combining elements from the numbered and lettered lists. Ex: **Los padres de mi esposo son mis suegros. Mis primos son los hijos de mis tíos.**

4 Expansion Have student pairs write five additional definitions following the pattern of those in the activity.

5 Escoger Complete the description of each photo using words you have learned in **Contextos**.
Some answers will vary. Possible answers:

1. La ___familia___ de Sara es grande.

2. Héctor y Lupita son ___novios___.

3. Maira Díaz es ___periodista___.

4. Rubén habla con su ___hijo/padre___.

5. Los dos ___hermanos___ están en el parque.

6. Irene es ___ingeniera___.

7. Elena Vargas Soto es ___artista___.

8. Don Manuel es el ___abuelo___ de Martín.

Practice more at **vhlcentral.com**.

Comunicación

6 **Una familia** With a classmate, identify the members in the family tree by asking questions about how each family member is related to Graciela Vargas García.

modelo
Estudiante 1: ¿Quién es Beatriz Pardo de Vargas?
Estudiante 2: Es la abuela de Graciela.

CONSULTA
To see the cities where these family members live, look at the map in **Panorama** on p. 104.

David Vargas Olmedo
de Quito
abuelo

Beatriz Pardo de Vargas
de Ibarra
abuela

Carlos Antonio López Ríos
de Cuenca
tío

Lupe Vargas de López
de Quito
tía

Juan Vargas Pardo
de Quito
padre

María Susana García de Vargas
de Guayaquil
madre

Ernesto López Vargas
de Loja
primo

Ramón Vargas García
de Machala
hermano

Graciela Vargas García
de Machala

Now take turns asking each other these questions. Then invent three original questions.

1. ¿Cómo se llama el primo de Graciela?　Se llama Ernesto López Vargas.
2. ¿Cómo se llama la hija de David y de Beatriz?　Se llama Lupe Vargas de López.
3. ¿De dónde es María Susana?　Es de Guayaquil.
4. ¿De dónde son Ramón y Graciela?　Son de Machala.
5. ¿Cómo se llama el yerno de David y de Beatriz?　Se llama Carlos Antonio López Ríos.
6. ¿De dónde es Carlos Antonio?　Es de Cuenca.
7. ¿De dónde es Ernesto?　Es de Loja.
8. ¿Cuáles son los apellidos del sobrino de Lupe?　Son Vargas García.

7 **Preguntas personales** With a classmate, take turns asking each other these questions.
Answers will vary.
1. ¿Cuántas personas hay en tu familia?
2. ¿Cómo se llaman tus padres? ¿De dónde son? ¿Dónde trabajan?
3. ¿Cuántos hermanos tienes? ¿Cómo se llaman? ¿Dónde estudian o trabajan?
4. ¿Cuántos primos tienes? ¿Cuáles son los apellidos de ellos? ¿Cuántos son niños y cuántos son adultos? ¿Hay más chicos o más chicas en tu familia?
5. ¿Eres tío/a? ¿Cómo se llaman tus sobrinos/as? ¿Dónde estudian o trabajan?
6. ¿Quién es tu pariente favorito?
7. ¿Tienes novio/a? ¿Tienes esposo/a? ¿Cómo se llama?

AYUDA
tu　*your* (sing.)
tus　*your* (plural)
mi　*my* (sing.)
mis　*my* (plural)
tienes　*you have*
tengo　*I have*

TEACHING OPTIONS

Extra Practice →👤← For homework, ask students to draw their own family tree or that of a fictional family. Have them label each position on the tree with the appropriate family term and the name of their family member. In class, ask students questions about their families. Ex: **¿Cómo se llama tu prima? ¿Cómo es ella? ¿Ella es estudiante? ¿Cómo se llama tu madre? ¿Quién es tu cuñado?**

Pairs 👤↔👤 Tell students to imagine that they have the opportunity to interview a famous person from a Spanish-speaking country. In pairs, using the questions in **Actividad 7** as a guide, have one student play the role of the famous person and the other student conduct the interview. Have volunteers perform their dialogues for the class to guess the famous person's identity.

6 Teaching Tip Remind students that it is common for Spanish speakers to go by two names (like **Carlos Antonio** in this chart). Students will learn about surnames on page 78; however, you may want to preview that information by pointing out how **Graciela** and her brother got their last names.

6 Expansion
- 👤↔👤 Ask students to write five statements about people in the chart (Ex: **Es la prima de Ernesto; Es una mujer de Quito.**). Then, in pairs, have them take turns reading their statements aloud. The other student should identify the person (**Es Graciela; Es Lupe**).
- Model the pronunciation of the Ecuadorian cities mentioned. Ask students to locate each on the map of Ecuador, page 104. Ask students to talk about each city based on the map. Ex: **Guayaquil y Machala son ciudades de la costa del Pacífico. Quito, Loja y Cuenca son ciudades de la cordillera de los Andes. Quito es la capital de Ecuador.**

7 Teaching Tips
- Tell students to take notes on their partner's responses. When they are finished, ask students questions about their partner's answers.
- As an alternative, first read through the questions as a class. Tell students to select a partner that they have not worked with before. Individually, have them jot down guesses to their partner's responses for a few of the questions. Students can write down any other predictions they may have about their partner's family. Then have pairs get together and complete the activity. Survey the class to find out the accuracy of the predictions.

Un domingo en familia

Marissa pasa el día en Xochimilco con la familia Díaz.

PERSONAJES

 FELIPE

 TÍA NAYELI

S Video: *Fotonovela*
Record and Compare

1

JIMENA Hola, tía Nayeli.
TÍA NAYELI ¡Hola, Jimena! ¿Cómo estás?
JIMENA Bien, gracias. Y, ¿dónde están mis primas?
TÍA NAYELI No sé. ¿Dónde están mis hijas? ¡Ah!

2

MARISSA ¡Qué bonitas son tus hijas! Y ¡qué simpáticas!

MARISSA La verdad, mi familia es pequeña.
SRA. DÍAZ ¿Pequeña? Yo soy hija única. Bueno, y ¿qué más? ¿Tienes novio?
MARISSA No. Tengo mala suerte con los novios.

3

FELIPE Soy guapo y delgado.
JIMENA Ay, ¡por favor! Eres gordo, antipático y muy feo.

5

6

4

TÍO RAMÓN ¿Tienes una familia grande, Marissa?
MARISSA Tengo dos hermanos mayores, Zack y Jennifer, y un hermano menor, Adam.

MARISSA Tía Nayeli, ¿cuántos años tienen tus hijas?
TÍA NAYELI Marta tiene ocho años y Valentina doce.

 JIMENA **MARTA** **VALENTINA** **SRA. DÍAZ** **TÍO RAMÓN** **SR. DÍAZ** MARISSA

7

SRA. DÍAZ Chicas, ¿compartimos una trajinera?

MARISSA ¡Claro que sí! ¡Qué bonitas son!

SRA. DÍAZ ¿Vienes, Jimena?

JIMENA No, gracias. Tengo que leer.

8

MARISSA Me gusta mucho este sitio. Tengo ganas de visitar otros lugares en México.

SRA. DÍAZ ¡Debes viajar a Mérida!

TÍA NAYELI ¡Sí, con tus amigos! Debes visitar a Ana María, la hermana de Roberto y de Ramón.

9

(*La Sra. Díaz habla por teléfono con la tía Ana María.*)

SRA. DÍAZ ¡Qué bien! Excelente. Sí, la próxima semana. Muchísimas gracias.

10

MARISSA ¡Gracias, Sra. Díaz!

SRA. DÍAZ Tía Ana María.

MARISSA Tía Ana María.

SRA. DÍAZ ¡Un beso, chau!

MARISSA Bye!

recursos

VM pp. 199–200

(S) vhlcentral.com Lección 3

Expresiones útiles

Talking about your family

¿Tienes una familia grande?
Do you have a big family?
Tengo dos hermanos mayores y un hermano menor.
I have two older siblings and a younger brother.
La verdad, mi familia es pequeña.
The truth is, my family is small.
¿Pequeña? Yo soy hija única.
Small? I'm an only child.

Describing people

¡Qué bonitas son tus hijas!
Y ¡qué simpáticas!
Your daughters are so pretty!
And so nice!
Soy guapo y delgado.
I'm handsome and slim.
¡Por favor! Eres gordo, antipático y muy feo.
Please! You're fat, unpleasant, and very ugly.

Talking about plans

¿Compartimos una trajinera?
Shall we share a trajinera?
¡Claro que sí! ¡Qué bonitas son!
Of course! They're so pretty!
¿Vienes, Jimena?
Are you coming, Jimena?
No, gracias. Tengo que leer.
No, thanks. I have to read.

Saying how old people are

¿Cuántos años tienen tus hijas?
How old are your daughters?
Marta tiene ocho años y Valentina doce.
Marta is eight and Valentina twelve.

Additional vocabulary

ensayo *essay*
pobrecito/a *poor thing*
próxima *next*
sitio *place*
todavía *still*
trajinera *type of barge*

Expresiones útiles Draw attention to the descriptive and possessive adjectives and the present tense forms of **tener** in the **Fotonovela** captions, **Expresiones útiles**, and as they occur in your conversation with the students. Point out that this material will be formally presented in **Estructura**. If students make errors of noun-adjective agreement or with verb conjugations, provide correct forms as needed, but do not expect them to be able to produce the forms accurately at this time.

Teaching Tip
👤↔👤 Ask students to read aloud the **Fotonovela** captions in groups of six, with one person assigned to each character. Then ask one or two groups to role-play the conversation for the class. Encourage students to ad-lib as they go.

Nota cultural The **Xochimilcas** arrived in the Valley of Mexico around 900 A.D. and settled on the hill of **Cuahilama**, southeast of present-day Mexico City. From the 14th century the **Xochimilcas** were in conflict with the Aztecs, and were finally conquered by them in the mid-15th century.

TEACHING OPTIONS

TPR →👤← As you play the **Fotonovela** episode, have students raise their right hand when they hear family-related vocabulary and their left hand when they hear a word or phrase related to professions. **Extra Practice** As a preview to **Estructura 3.1**, have students scan pages 74–75 and guide them in identifying the descriptive adjectives. Then ask students to rephrase the sentences to reflect their own families. Ex: **Mi papá es hijo único.**

Pairs 👤↔👤 Have students create a two-column chart with the heads **Marissa** and **Roberto**. Play the **Fotonovela** episode and have students jot down the names and family-related words they hear in the appropriate column. Then have them use the chart to create simple family trees for **Marissa** and **Roberto**. Finally, in pairs, have students examine the trees for accuracy and make statements describing the familial relationships.

¿Qué pasó?

1 Expansion Give these true/false statements to the class as items 7–10: **7. Jimena dice que Felipe es feo. (Cierto.) 8. Marissa tiene un novio. (Falso. Tiene mala suerte con los novios.) 9. Valentina tiene una hermana menor. (Cierto.) 10. Jimena no comparte la trajinera porque tiene que asistir a clase. (Falso. Tiene que leer.)**

2 Expansion Sra. Díaz is the only person not associated with a statement. Ask students to look at the **Fotonovela** captions and **Expresiones útiles** on pages 74–75 and invent a statement for her. Remind them not to use her exact words. Ex: **Hablo por teléfono con mi cuñada.**

Nota cultural In the 19th century, the **chinampas** fulfilled agricultural purposes. At that time, **trajineras** were used to transport crops from the islands of **Xochimilco** to markets in Mexico City.

3 Expansion Have pairs who wrote about the same family exchange papers and compare their descriptions. Ask them to share the differences with the class.

4 Teaching Tip Model the activity by providing answers based on your own family.

4 Expansion Ask volunteers to share their partners' answers with the rest of the class.

1 ¿Cierto o falso? Indicate whether each sentence is **cierto** or **falso**. Correct the false statements.

	Cierto	Falso	
1. Marissa dice que (*says that*) tiene una familia grande.	○	☑	Marissa dice que tiene una familia pequeña.
2. La Sra. Díaz tiene dos hermanos.	○	☑	La señora Díaz es hija única.
3. Marissa no tiene novio.	☑	○	
4. Valentina tiene veinte años.	○	☑	Valentina tiene doce años.
5. Marissa comparte una trajinera con la Sra. Díaz y la tía Nayeli.	☑	○	
6. A Marissa le gusta mucho Xochimilco.	☑	○	

2 Identificar Indicate which person would make each statement. The names may be used more than once. **¡Ojo!** One name will not be used.

1. Felipe es antipático y feo. *Jimena*
2. Mis hermanos se llaman Jennifer, Adam y Zack. *Marissa*
3. ¡Soy un joven muy guapo! *Felipe*
4. Mis hijas tienen ocho y doce años. *tía Nayeli*
5. ¡Qué bonitas son las trajineras! *Marissa*
6. Ana María es la hermana de Ramón y Roberto. *tía Nayeli*
7. No puedo (*I can't*) compartir una trajinera porque tengo que leer. *Jimena*
8. Tus hijas son bonitas y simpáticas, tía Nayeli. *Marissa*

SRA. DÍAZ **JIMENA**

MARISSA **FELIPE**

TÍA NAYELI

NOTA CULTURAL

Xochimilco is famous for its system of canals and **chinampas**, or artificial islands, which have been used for agricultural purposes since Pre-Hispanic times. In 1987, UNESCO declared **Xochimilco** a World Heritage Site.

NOTA CULTURAL

Trajineras are large passenger barges that you can rent in **Xochimilco**. Each boat is named and decorated and has a table and chairs so passengers can picnic while they ride.

3 Escribir In pairs, choose Marissa, Sra. Díaz, or tía Nayeli and write a brief description of her family. Be creative! *Answers will vary.*

MARISSA

SRA. DÍAZ

TÍA NAYELI

Marissa es de los EE.UU. ¿Cómo es su familia?

La Sra. Díaz es de Cuba. ¿Cómo es su familia?

La tía Nayeli es de México. ¿Cómo es su familia?

4 Conversar With a partner, use these questions to talk about your families. *Answers will vary.*

1. ¿Cuántos años tienes?
2. ¿Tienes una familia grande?
3. ¿Tienes hermanos o hermanas?
4. ¿Cuántos años tiene tu abuelo (tu hermana, tu primo, etc.)?
5. ¿De dónde son tus padres?

AYUDA

Here are some expressions to help you talk about age.

Yo tengo… años.
I am… years old.

Mi abuelo tiene… años.
My grandfather is… years old.

 Practice more at **vhlcentral.com.**

TEACHING OPTIONS

Extra Practice Ask volunteers to ad-lib the **Fotonovela** episode for the class. Assure them that it is not necessary to memorize the script or stick strictly to its content. They should try to get the general meaning across with the vocabulary and expressions they know, and they also should feel free to be creative. Give students time to prepare.

Small Groups Have groups of three interview each other about their families. Assign one person as the interviewer, one the interviewee, and the third person as the note taker. At three-minute intervals, have students switch roles. When everyone has been interviewed, have students report back to the class.

Pronunciación

Diphthongs and linking

Audio: Concepts, Activities Record & Compare

herm**a**no	**ni**ñ**a**	**cu**ñ**a**do

In Spanish, **a**, **e**, and **o** are considered strong vowels. The weak vowels are **i** and **u**.

r**ui**do	par**ie**ntes	per**io**dista

A diphthong is a combination of two weak vowels or of a strong vowel and a weak vowel. Diphthongs are pronounced as a single syllable.

m**i h**ijo	una clas**e e**xcelente

Two identical vowel sounds that appear together are pronounced like one long vowel.

l**a a**buela

co**n N**atalia	su**s s**obrinos	la**s s**illas

Two identical consonants together sound like a single consonant.

e**s i**ngeniera	mi**s a**buelos	su**s h**ijos

A consonant at the end of a word is linked with the vowel at the beginning of the next word.

m**i h**ermano	s**u e**sposa	nuestr**o a**migo

A vowel at the end of a word is linked with the vowel at the beginning of the next word.

Práctica Say these words aloud, focusing on the diphthongs.

1. historia
2. nieto
3. parientes
4. novia
5. residencia
6. prueba
7. puerta
8. ciencias
9. lenguas
10. estudiar
11. izquierda
12. ecuatoriano

Oraciones Read these sentences aloud to practice diphthongs and linking words.

1. Hola. Me llamo Anita Amaral. Soy del Ecuador.
2. Somos seis en mi familia.
3. Tengo dos hermanos y una hermana.
4. Mi papá es del Ecuador y mi mamá es de España.

Refranes Read these sayings aloud to practice diphthongs and linking sounds.

Cuando una puerta se cierra, otra se abre.[1]

Hablando del rey de Roma, por la puerta se asoma.[2]

1 When one door closes, another opens. 2 Speak of the devil and he will appear.

recursos

LM p. 14	vhlcentral.com Lección 3

recursos — LM p. 14 — vhlcentral.com Lección 3

Section Goals

In **Pronunciación**, students will be introduced to:
- the strong and weak vowels
- common diphthongs
- linking in pronunciation

Instructional Resources

Supersite: Audio (Textbook and Lab MP3 Files); Resources (Scripts, Answer Keys)
WebSAM
Lab Manual, p. 14

Teaching Tips

- Write **hermano, niña**, and **cuñado** on the board. Ask students to identify the strong and weak vowels.
- Pronounce **ruido, parientes,** and **periodista**, and have students identify the diphthong in each word. Point out that the strong vowels (**a, e, o**) do not combine with each other to form diphthongs. When two strong vowels come together, they are in different syllables.
- Pronounce **mi hermano** and **su esposa** and ask volunteers to write them on the board. Point out that the linked vowels form a diphthong and are pronounced as one syllable.
- Follow the same procedure with **es ingeniera** and **mis abuelos**. You may want to introduce linking involving the other final consonants (**l, n, r, z**). Ex: **Son hermanos. El hermano mayor está aquí. ¿Cuál es tu hermana?**
- Ask students to provide words they learned in **Lecciones 1** and **2** and **Contextos** and **Fotonovela** of this lesson that exemplify each point.

Práctica/Oraciones/Refranes

These exercises are recorded on the *Textbook MP3s.* Play the audio so that students practice listening to Spanish spoken by speakers other than yourself.

TEACHING OPTIONS

Heritage Speakers Ask heritage speakers if they know of other **refranes**. Write each **refrán** on the board and have the student who volunteered it explain what it means. Ex: **A quien Dios no le dio hijos, el diablo le da sobrinos. Más sabe el diablo por viejo que por diablo.**
Video →👤← Add an additional auditory aspect to this **Pronunciación** presentation. Play the **Fotonovela** segment and

have students identify diphthongs and linking words.
Extra Practice Here are additional sentences for extra practice with diphthongs and linking: **Los estudiantes extranjeros hablan inglés. Mi abuela Ana tiene ochenta años. Juan y Enrique son hermanos. ¿Tu esposa aprende una lengua extranjera? Tengo un examen en la clase de español hoy.** Read them aloud and have students identify diphthongs and linking words.

Flash CULTURA

Section Goals

In **Cultura**, students will:
- read about surnames and families in the Spanish-speaking world
- learn terms related to family and friends
- read about Spain's Royal Family
- read about average household size

Instructional Resources
Supersite/DVD: *Flash cultura*
Supersite: Resources (Scripts, Translations, Answer Keys)
WebSAM
Video Manual, pp. 271–272

En detalle

Antes de leer Have students brainstorm a list of famous Spanish speakers with two last names (Ex: **Gael García Bernal**).

Lectura
- **Gabriel García Márquez** is a Nobel prize-winning writer from Colombia. He and his wife also have another son (not pictured), **Gonzalo García Barcha**, an artist and graphic designer for film. **Rodrigo García Barcha** is a TV and film director (*Six Feet Under, Big Love*).
- Point out that **de** may also appear as an indicator of ancestral origin (Ex: **Ramón del Valle**). In the case of **Juan Carlos de Borbón** (page 79), **de** refers to the House of Bourbon, a European royal dynasty.
- Explain that it is common to drop the second last name in informal settings.
- Point out that it is possible to have the same maternal and paternal surnames. Ex: **María Sánchez Sánchez**

Después de leer Have students tell the class what their name would be following this naming convention.

1 Teaching Tip For each item, have students cite an example from the article or one from real life.

EN DETALLE

S Additional Reading
Video: *Flash cultura*

NATIONAL
connections
cultures
STANDARDS

¿Cómo te llamas?

In the Spanish-speaking world, it is common to have two last names: one paternal and one maternal. In some cases, the conjunctions **de** or **y** are used to connect the two. For example, in the name **Juan Martínez de Velasco,** *Martínez* is the paternal surname (**el apellido paterno**), and *Velasco* is the maternal surname (**el apellido materno**); **de** simply links the two. This convention of using two last names (**doble apellido**) is a European tradition that Spaniards brought to the Americas. It continues to be practiced in many countries, including Chile, Colombia, Mexico, Peru, and Venezuela. There are exceptions, however. In Argentina, the prevailing custom is for children to inherit only the father's last name.

Gabriel García Márquez

Mercedes Barcha Pardo

Rodrigo García Barcha

When a woman marries in a country where two last names are used, legally she retains her two maiden surnames. However, socially she may take her husband's paternal surname in place of her inherited maternal surname. For example, **Mercedes Barcha Pardo,** wife of Colombian writer **Gabriel García Márquez,** might use the names **Mercedes Barcha García** or **Mercedes Barcha de García** in social situations (although officially her name remains **Mercedes Barcha Pardo**). Adopting a husband's last name for social purposes, though widespread, is only legally recognized in Ecuador and Peru.

Most parents do not break tradition upon naming their children; regardless of the surnames the mother uses, they use the father's first surname followed by the mother's first surname, as in the name **Rodrigo García Barcha.** However, one should note that both surnames come from the grandfathers, and therefore all **apellidos** are effectively paternal.

Hijos en la casa

In Spanish-speaking countries, family and society place very little pressure on young adults to live on their own (**independizarse**), and children often live with their parents well into their thirties. For example, about 60% of Spaniards under 34 years of age live at home with their parents. This delay in moving out is both cultural and economic—lack of job security or low wages coupled with a high cost of living may make it impractical for young adults to live independently before they marry.

ACTIVIDADES

1 **¿Cierto o falso?** Indicate whether these statements are **cierto** or **falso**. Correct the false statements.

1. Most Spanish-speaking people have three last names. **Falso.** Most people have two last names.
2. Hispanic last names generally consist of the paternal last name followed by the maternal last name. **Cierto.**
3. It is common to see **de** or **y** used in a Hispanic last name. **Cierto.**
4. Someone from Argentina would most likely have two last names. **Falso.** They would use only the father's last name.
5. Generally, married women legally retain two maiden surnames. **Cierto.**
6. In social situations, a married woman often uses her husband's last name in place of her inherited paternal surname. **Falso.** She often uses it in place of her inherited maternal surname.
7. Adopting a husband's surname is only legally recognized in Peru and Ecuador. **Cierto.**
8. Hispanic last names are effectively a combination of the maternal surnames from the previous generation. **Falso.** They are a combination of the paternal surnames from the previous generation.

TEACHING OPTIONS

Los apellidos Explain that surnames began to be widely used in Europe in the Middle Ages, and that many refer to the person's profession, title, or place of origin. Using common American last names, brainstorm examples of each type. Ex: Baker, Miller (professions); Carlson (son of Carl). Explain that Hispanic surnames have similar roots. Ex: **Sastre, Zapatero, Herrero** (professions); **Fernández, Rodríguez** (-**ez** denotes "son of");

Hidalgo, Conde (titles); **Aragón, Castillo,** (places).
Large Group Write examples of Hispanic first and last names on the board. Then have students circulate around the room and introduce themselves to their classmates using a Hispanic last name. The other student must guess their mother's and father's last names. Ex: **Soy Roberto Domínguez Trujillo. (Tu padre es el señor Domínguez y tu madre es la señora Trujillo.)**

ASÍ SE DICE

Familia y amigos

el/la bisnieto/a	great-grandson/daughter
el/la chamaco/a (Méx.); el/la chamo/a (Ven.); el/la chaval(a) (Esp.); el/la pibe/a (Arg.)	el/la muchacho/a
mi colega (Esp.); mi cuate (Méx.); mi parcero/a (Col.); mi pana (Ven., P. Rico, Rep. Dom.)	my pal; my buddy
la madrina	godmother
el padrino	godfather
el/la tatarabuelo/a	great-great-grandfather/ great-great-grandmother

EL MUNDO HISPANO

Las familias

Although worldwide population trends show a decrease in average family size, households in many Spanish-speaking countries are still larger than their U.S. counterparts.

- **México** 4,0 personas
- **Colombia** 3,9 personas
- **Argentina** 3,6 personas
- **Uruguay** 3,0 personas
- **España** 2,9 personas
- **Estados Unidos** 2,6 personas

PERFIL

La familia real española

Undoubtedly, Spain's most famous family is **la familia real** (*Royal*). In 1962, then prince **Juan Carlos de Borbón**, married Princess **Sofía** of Greece. Then, in the late 1970s, **el Rey** (*King*) **Juan Carlos** and **la Reina** (*Queen*) **Sofía** returned to Spain and helped transition the country to democracy after a forty-year dictatorship. The royal couple, who enjoys immense public support, has three children: las **infantas** (*Princesses*) **Elena** and **Cristina**, and a son, **el príncipe** (*Prince*) **Felipe**, whose official title is **el Príncipe de Asturias**. In 2004, Felipe married **Letizia Ortiz Rocasolano** (now **la Princesa de Asturias**), a journalist and TV presenter. The future king and queen have two daughters, **las infantas Leonor** (born in 2005) and **Sofía** (born in 2007).

Conexión Internet

What role do **padrinos** and **madrinas** have in today's Hispanic family?

Go to **vhlcentral.com** to find more cultural information related to this **Cultura** section.

ACTIVIDADES

2 Comprensión Complete these sentences.
1. Spain's royals were responsible for guiding in ___democracy___.
2. In Spanish, your godmother is called ___la madrina___.
3. Princess Leonor is the ___granddaughter___ of Queen Sofía.
4. Uruguay's average household has ___3.0___ people.
5. If a Venezuelan calls you **mi pana**, you are that person's ___friend___.

3 Una familia famosa Create a genealogical tree of a famous family, using photos or drawings labeled with names and ages. Present the family tree to a classmate and explain who the people are and their relationships to each other.
Answers will vary.

recursos

VM pp. 271–272

vhlcentral.com Lección 3

Practice more at **vhlcentral.com**.

TEACHING OPTIONS

Cultural Comparison Have student pairs research a famous English-speaking family (such as the Kennedys) and write a brief comparison with the Spanish Royal Family. Ask students to include information about their prominence in the media, involvement in politics, and general popularity. This activity may have to be done using English.

La familia hispana Explain to students that the concept **la familia** in Spanish-speaking countries is somewhat more inclusive than it is in English. When people say **la familia**, the majority of them are referring to their extended family. Extended families, if they do not live in the same dwelling, tend to live in closer geographical proximity in Latin America than they do in the U.S. and Canada.

Section Goals

In **Estructura 3.1**, students will learn:

- forms, agreement, and position of adjectives ending in –o/–a, –e, or a consonant
- high-frequency descriptive adjectives and some adjectives of nationality

Instructional Resources

Supersite: Audio (Lab MP3 Files); Resources (*PowerPoints*, Activity Pack, Scripts, Answer Keys); Testing Program (Quizzes)
WebSAM
Workbook, pp. 25–26
Lab Manual, p. 15

Teaching Tips

- Write these adjectives on the board: **ecuatoriana, alto, bonito, viejo, trabajador.** Ask what each means and whether it is masculine or feminine. Model one of the adjectives in a sentence and ask volunteers to use the others in sentences.
- Work through the discussion of adjective forms point by point, writing examples on the board. Test comprehension as you proceed by asking volunteers to supply the correct form of adjectives for nouns you suggest. Remind students that grammatical gender does not necessarily reflect actual gender.
- Drill gender by pointing to individuals and asking the class to supply the correct form. Ex: (Pointing to male student) **¿Guapo o guapa?** (Pointing to female) **¿Simpático o simpática?** Then use adjectives ending in –e. Point to a male and say **inteligente,** then point to a female and have students provide the correct form. Continue with plurals. Keep a brisk pace.

3.1 **Descriptive adjectives** **Tutorial**

ANTE TODO Adjectives are words that describe people, places, and things. In Spanish, descriptive adjectives are used with the verb **ser** to point out characteristics such as nationality, size, color, shape, personality, and appearance.

Forms and agreement of adjectives

COMPARE & CONTRAST

In English, the forms of descriptive adjectives do not change to reflect the gender (masculine/feminine) and number (singular/plural) of the noun or pronoun they describe.

Juan is nice.	*Elena is nice.*	*They are nice.*

In Spanish, the forms of descriptive adjectives agree in gender and/or number with the nouns or pronouns they describe.

Juan es simpátic**o**.	Elena es simpátic**a**.	Ellos son simpátic**os**.

▶ Adjectives that end in **-o** have four different forms. The feminine singular is formed by changing the **-o** to **-a**. The plural is formed by adding **-s** to the singular forms.

Masculine		Feminine	
SINGULAR	PLURAL	SINGULAR	PLURAL
el muchach**o** alt**o**	los muchach**os** alt**os**	la muchach**a** alt**a**	las muchach**as** alt**as**

¡Qué bonitas son tus hijas, tía Nayeli!

Felipe es gordo, antipático y muy feo.

▶ Adjectives that end in **-e** or a consonant have the same masculine and feminine forms.

Masculine		Feminine	
SINGULAR	PLURAL	SINGULAR	PLURAL
el chico inteligent**e**	los chicos inteligent**es**	la chica inteligent**e**	las chicas inteligent**es**
el examen difíci**l**	los exámenes difíci**les**	la clase difíci**l**	las clases difíci**les**

▶ Adjectives that end in **-or** are variable in both gender and number.

Masculine		Feminine	
SINGULAR	PLURAL	SINGULAR	PLURAL
el hombre trabajad**or**	los hombres trabajad**ores**	la mujer trabajad**ora**	las mujeres trabajad**oras**

TEACHING OPTIONS

Extra Practice Have pairs of students write sentences using adjectives such as **inteligente, alto, joven**. When they have finished, ask volunteers to dictate their sentences to you to write on the board. After you have written a sentence and corrected any errors, ask volunteers to suggest a sentence that uses the antonym of the adjective.

Variación léxica Clarify that the adjective **americano/a** applies to all inhabitants of North and South America, not just citizens of the United States. Residents of the United States usually are referred to with the adjective **norteamericano/a**. In more formal contexts, such as official documents, the adjective **estadounidense** is used.

▶ Use the masculine plural form to refer to groups that include males and females.

Manuel es alt**o**. Lola es alt**a**. Manuel y Lola son alt**os**.

Common adjectives

alto/a	tall	**gordo/a**	fat	**moreno/a**	brunet(te)
antipático/a	unpleasant	**grande**	big; large	**mucho/a**	much; many;
bajo/a	short (in	**guapo/a**	handsome;		a lot of
	height)		good-looking	**pelirrojo/a**	red-haired
bonito/a	pretty	**importante**	important	**pequeño/a**	small
bueno/a	good	**inteligente**	intelligent	**rubio/a**	blond(e)
delgado/a	thin; slender	**interesante**	interesting	**simpático/a**	nice; likeable
difícil	hard; difficult	**joven**	young	**tonto/a**	silly; foolish
fácil	easy	**malo/a**	bad	**trabajador(a)**	hard-working
feo/a	ugly	**mismo/a**	same	**viejo/a**	old

Adjectives of nationality

▶ Unlike in English, Spanish adjectives of nationality are **not** capitalized. Proper names of countries, however, are capitalized.

Some adjectives of nationality

alemán, alemana	German	**francés, francesa**	French
argentino/a	Argentine	**inglés, inglesa**	English
canadiense	Canadian	**italiano/a**	Italian
chino/a	Chinese	**japonés, japonesa**	Japanese
costarricense	Costa Rican	**mexicano/a**	Mexican
cubano/a	Cuban	**norteamericano/a**	(North) American
ecuatoriano/a	Ecuadorian	**puertorriqueño**	Puerto Rican
español(a)	Spanish	**ruso/a**	Russian
estadounidense	from the U.S.		

▶ Adjectives of nationality are formed like other descriptive adjectives. Those that end in **-o** change to **-a** when forming the feminine.

chin**o** ⟶ chin**a** mexican**o** ⟶ mexican**a**

The plural is formed by adding an **-s** to the masculine or feminine form.

argentin**o** ⟶ argentin**os** cuban**a** ⟶ cuban**as**

▶ Adjectives of nationality that end in **-e** have only two forms, singular and plural.

canadiens**e** ⟶ canadiens**es** estadounidens**e** ⟶ estadounidens**es**

▶ To form the feminine of adjectives of nationality that end in a consonant, add **–a**.

alem**án** ⟶ alem**ana** españo**l** ⟶ españo**la**
japon**és** ⟶ japon**esa** inglé**s** ⟶ ingle**sa**

Position of adjectives

▶ Descriptive adjectives and adjectives of nationality generally follow the nouns they modify.

El niño **rubio** es de España.
The blond boy is from Spain.

La mujer **española** habla inglés.
The Spanish woman speaks English.

▶ Unlike descriptive adjectives, adjectives of quantity precede the modified noun.

Hay **muchos** libros en la biblioteca.
There are many books in the library.

Hablo con **dos** turistas puertorriqueños.
I am talking with two Puerto Rican tourists.

▶ **Bueno/a** and **malo/a** can appear before or after a noun. When placed before a masculine singular noun, the forms are shortened: **bueno → buen; malo → mal.**

Joaquín es un **buen** amigo.
Joaquín es un amigo **bueno.** → *Joaquín is a good friend.*

Hoy es un **mal** día.
Hoy es un día **malo.** → *Today is a bad day.*

▶ When **grande** appears before a singular noun, it is shortened to **gran,** and the meaning of the word changes: **gran** = *great* and **grande** = *big, large.*

Don Francisco es un **gran** hombre.
Don Francisco is a great man.

La familia de Inés es **grande**.
Inés' family is large.

¡LENGUA VIVA!

Like **bueno** and **grande, santo** (*saint*) is also shortened before masculine nouns (unless they begin with **To-** or **Do-**): **San Francisco, San José,** (but: **Santo Tomás, Santo Domingo**). **Santa** is used with names of female saints: **Santa Bárbara, Santa Clara.**

¡INTÉNTALO! Provide the appropriate forms of the adjectives.

simpático
1. Mi hermano es _simpático_.
2. La profesora Martínez es _simpática_.
3. Rosa y Teresa son _simpáticas_.
4. Nosotros somos _simpáticos_.

alemán
1. Hans es _alemán_.
2. Mis primas son _alemanas_.
3. Marcus y yo somos _alemanes_.
4. Mi tía es _alemana_.

difícil
1. La química es _difícil_.
2. El curso es _difícil_.
3. Las pruebas son _difíciles_.
4. Los libros son _difíciles_.

guapo
1. Su esposo es _guapo_.
2. Mis sobrinas son _guapas_.
3. Los padres de ella son _guapos_.
4. Marta es _guapa_.

recursos

WB pp. 25–26

LM p. 15

vhlcentral.com Lección 3

Práctica

1 **Emparejar** Find the words in column B that are the opposite of the words in column A. One word in B will not be used.

Marcos

Jorge

A		B
1. guapo	d	a. delgado
2. moreno	f	b. pequeño
3. alto	h	c. malo
4. gordo	a	d. feo
5. joven	e	e. viejo
6. grande	b	f. rubio
7. simpático	g	g. antipático
		h. bajo

2 **Completar** Indicate the nationalities of these people by selecting the correct adjectives and changing their forms when necessary.

1. Penélope Cruz es _____española_____.
2. Carlos Fuentes es un gran escritor (*writer*) de México; es _____mexicano_____.
3. Ellen Page y Avril Lavigne son _____canadienses_____.
4. Giorgio Armani es un diseñador de modas (*fashion designer*) _____italiano_____.
5. Daisy Fuentes es de La Habana, Cuba; ella es _____cubana_____.
6. Emma Watson y Daniel Radcliffe son actores _____ingleses_____.
7. Heidi Klum y Boris Becker son _____alemanes_____.
8. Apolo Anton Ohno y Shaun White son _____estadounidenses_____.

3 **Describir** Look at the drawing and describe each family member using as many adjectives as possible. Some answers will vary. Possible answers:

Carlos Romero Sandoval

Josefina Barcos de Romero

Susana Romero Barcos

Tomás Romero Barcos

Alberto Romero Pereda

1. Susana Romero Barcos es _____delgada, rubia_____.
2. Tomás Romero Barcos es _____pelirrojo, inteligente_____.
3. Los dos hermanos son _____jóvenes_____.
4. Josefina Barcos de Romero es _____alta, bonita, rubia_____.
5. Carlos Romero Sandoval es _____bajo, gordo_____.
6. Alberto Romero Pereda es _____viejo, bajo_____.
7. Tomás y su (*his*) padre son _____pelirrojos_____.
8. Susana y su (*her*) madre son _____altas, delgadas_____.

S Practice more at **vhlcentral.com.**

Comunicación

4

¿Cómo es? With a partner, take turns describing each item on the list. Tell your partner whether you agree (**Estoy de acuerdo**) or disagree (**No estoy de acuerdo**) with their descriptions.
Answers will vary.

> **modelo**
> San Francisco
> **Estudiante 1:** San Francisco es una ciudad (city) muy bonita.
> **Estudiante 2:** No estoy de acuerdo. Es muy fea.

1. Nueva York
2. Steve Carell
3. las canciones (songs) de Celine Dion
4. el presidente de los Estados Unidos
5. Steven Spielberg
6. la primera dama (first lady) de los Estados Unidos
7. el/la profesor(a) de español
8. las personas de Los Ángeles
9. las residencias de mi universidad
10. mi clase de español

5

Anuncio personal Write a personal ad that describes yourself and your ideal boyfriend, girlfriend, or mate. Then compare your ad with a classmate's. How are you similar and how are you different? Are you looking for the same things in a romantic partner?
Answers will vary.

SOY ALTA, morena y bonita. Soy cubana, de Holguín. Estudio arte en la universidad. Busco un chico similar. Mi novio ideal es alto, moreno, inteligente y muy simpático.

Síntesis

6

Diferencias Your instructor will give you and a partner each a drawing of a family. Describe your version of the drawing to your partner in order to find at least five differences between your picture and your partner's. Answers will vary.

> **modelo**
> **Estudiante 1:** Susana, la madre, es rubia.
> **Estudiante 2:** No, la madre es morena.

Left margin column:

4 Expansion
 Have student pairs brainstorm a list of additional famous people, places, and things. Ask them to include some plural items. Then ask students to exchange papers with another pair and discuss the people, places, and things on the lists they receive.

5 Teaching Tip Have students divide a sheet of paper into two columns, labeling one **Yo** and the other **Mi novio/a ideal** or **Mi esposo/a ideal.** Have them brainstorm Spanish adjectives for each column. Ask them to rank each adjective in the second column in terms of its importance to them.

5 Expansion
 Ask small groups to write a personal ad describing a fictional person and his or her ideal mate. Have groups exchange and respond to each other's ads.

6 Teaching Tips
- Divide the class into pairs and distribute the handouts from the Activity Pack that correspond to this Information Gap Activity (Activity Pack/Supersite). Give students ten minutes to complete this activity.
- To simplify, have students brainstorm a list of adjectives for each person in their drawing, then have them proceed with the activity.

6 Expansion
- Ask questions based on the artwork. Ex: **¿Es alto el abuelo? ¿Es delgado el hijo menor?**
- Have volunteers take turns stating the differences. Then have them invent stories based on these families.

TEACHING OPTIONS

Heritage Speakers Ask heritage speakers to describe members of their extended families. Ask the rest of the class comprehension questions.
Extra Practice Research zodiac signs on the Internet and prepare a simple personality description for each sign, using cognates and adjectives from this lesson. Divide the class into pairs and distribute the descriptions. Have students guess their partners' sign. Ex: —**Eres Aries, ¿verdad?** —**No, no soy Aries. No soy impulsiva y no soy adventurera.**
Extra Practice Encourage students to collect pictures of people from the Internet, magazines, or newspapers. Have them prepare a description of one of the pictures. Invite students to display their pictures and give their descriptions orally. The class should guess which picture is being described.

3.2 Possessive adjectives Tutorial

ANTE TODO Possessive adjectives, like descriptive adjectives, are words that are used to qualify people, places, or things. Possessive adjectives express the quality of ownership or possession.

Forms of possessive adjectives

SINGULAR FORMS	PLURAL FORMS	
mi	mis	*my*
tu	tus	*your* (fam.)
su	sus	*his, her, its, your* (form.)
nuestro/a	nuestros/as	*our*
vuestro/a	vuestros/as	*your* (fam.)
su	sus	*their, your* (form.)

COMPARE & CONTRAST

In English, possessive adjectives are invariable; that is, they do not agree in gender and number with the nouns they modify. Spanish possessive adjectives, however, do agree in number with the nouns they modify.

my cousin	*my cousins*	*my aunt*	*my aunts*
mi primo	**mis** primos	**mi** tía	**mis** tías

The forms **nuestro** and **vuestro** agree in both gender and number with the nouns they modify.

nuestr**o** prim**o**	nuestr**os** prim**os**	nuestr**a** tí**a**	nuestr**as** tí**as**

▶ Possessive adjectives are always placed before the nouns they modify.

—¿Está **tu novio** aquí?
Is your boyfriend here?

—No, **mi novio** está en la biblioteca.
No, my boyfriend is in the library.

▶ Because **su** and **sus** have multiple meanings (*your, his, her, their, its*), you can avoid confusion by using this construction instead: [*article*] + [*noun*] + **de** + [*subject pronoun*].

sus parientes ◀

los parientes **de él/ella**	*his/her relatives*
los parientes **de Ud./Uds.**	*your relatives*
los parientes **de ellos/ellas**	*their relatives*

¡INTÉNTALO! Provide the appropriate form of each possessive adjective.

1. Es _____mi_____ (*my*) libro.
2. _____Mi_____ (*My*) familia es ecuatoriana.
3. _____Tu_____ (*Your,* fam.) esposo es italiano.
4. _____Nuestro_____ (*Our*) profesor es español.
5. Es _____su_____ (*her*) reloj.
6. Es _____tu_____ (*your,* fam.) mochila.
7. Es _____su_____ (*your,* form.) maleta.
8. _____Su_____ (*Their*) sobrina es alemana.

1. _____Sus_____ (*Her*) primos son franceses.
2. _____Nuestros_____ (*Our*) primos son canadienses.
3. Son _____sus_____ (*their*) lápices.
4. _____Sus_____ (*Their*) nietos son japoneses.
5. Son _____nuestras_____ (*our*) plumas.
6. Son _____mis_____ (*my*) papeles.
7. _____Mis_____ (*My*) amigas son inglesas.
8. Son _____sus_____ (*his*) cuadernos.

Práctica

1 **La familia de Manolo** Complete each sentence with the correct possessive adjective from the options in parentheses. Use the subject of each sentence as a guide.

1. Me llamo Manolo, y _____mi_____ (nuestro, mi, sus) hermano es Federico.
2. _____Nuestra_____ (Nuestra, Sus, Mis) madre Silvia es profesora y enseña química.
3. Ella admira a _____sus_____ (tu, nuestro, sus) estudiantes porque trabajan mucho.
4. Yo estudio en la misma universidad, pero no tomo clases con _____mi_____ (mi, nuestras, tus) madre.
5. Federico trabaja en una oficina con _____nuestro_____ (mis, tu, nuestro) padre.
6. _____Su_____ (Mi, Su, Tu) oficina está en el centro de la Ciudad de México.
7. Javier y Óscar son _____mis_____ (mis, mi, sus) tíos de Oaxaca.
8. ¿Y tú? ¿Cómo es _____tu_____ (mi, su, tu) familia?

2 **Clarificar** Clarify each sentence with a prepositional phrase. Follow the model.

> **modelo**
> Su hermana es muy bonita. (ella)
> *La hermana de ella es muy bonita.*

1. Su casa es muy grande. (ellos) _____La casa de ellos es muy grande._____
2. ¿Cómo se llama su hermano? (ellas) _____¿Cómo se llama el hermano de ellas?_____
3. Sus padres trabajan en el centro. (ella) _____Los padres de ella trabajan en el centro._____
4. Sus abuelos son muy simpáticos. (él) _____Los abuelos de él son muy simpáticos._____
5. Maribel es su prima. (ella) _____Maribel es la prima de ella._____
6. Su primo lee los libros. (ellos) _____El primo de ellos lee los libros._____

3 **¿Dónde está?** With a partner, imagine that you can't remember where you put some of the belongings you see in the pictures. Your partner will help you by reminding you where your things are. Take turns playing each role. *Answers will vary.*

> **modelo**
> Estudiante 1: *¿Dónde está mi mochila?*
> Estudiante 2: *Tu mochila está encima del escritorio.*

1. 2. 3.

4. 5. 6.

Practice more at **vhlcentral.com**.

Comunicación

4 **Describir** With a partner, describe the people and places listed below. Make note of any similarities and be prepared to share them with the class. Answers will vary.

> **modelo**
>
> la biblioteca de su universidad
> *La biblioteca de nuestra universidad es muy grande. Hay muchos libros en la biblioteca. Mis amigos y yo estudiamos en la biblioteca.*

1. tu profesor favorito
2. tu profesora favorita
3. su clase de español
4. la librería de su universidad
5. tus padres
6. tus abuelos
7. tu mejor (*best*) amigo
8. tu mejor amiga
9. su universidad
10. tu país de origen

5 **Una familia famosa** Assume the identity of a member of a famous family, real or fictional (the Hiltons, Cyruses, Simpsons, Clintons, Beckhams, Jolie-Pitts, etc.) and write a description of "your" family. Be sure not to use any names! Then, in small groups, take turns reading the descriptions aloud. The other group members may ask follow-up questions to help them identify the famous person. Answers will vary.

> **modelo**
>
> **Estudiante 1:** Hay cuatro personas en mi familia. Mi padre es delgado y muy trabajador. Su trabajo (*job*) es importante; él viaja mucho. Mi madre es guapa e inteligente. Tengo una hermana mayor. Ella y yo estudiamos en una escuela privada. Nuestra casa está en la capital.
> **Estudiante 2:** ¿Son ustedes de la capital?
> **Estudiante 1:** No, somos de Chicago.
> **Estudiante 3:** ¿Eres Sasha Obama?
> **Estudiante 1:** Sí.

Síntesis

6 **Describe a tu familia** Get together with two classmates and describe your family to them in several sentences (**Mi padre es alto y moreno. Mi madre es delgada y muy bonita. Mis hermanos son...**). They will work together to try to repeat your description (**Su padre es alto y moreno. Su madre...**). If they forget any details, they can ask you questions (**¿Es alto tu hermano?**). Alternate roles until all of you have described your families. Answers will vary.

3.3 # Present tense of -er and -ir verbs **Tutorial**

ANTE TODO In **Lección 2,** you learned how to form the present tense of regular **-ar** verbs. You also learned about the importance of verb forms, which change to show who is performing the action. The chart below shows the forms from two other important groups, **-er** verbs and **-ir** verbs.

Present tense of -er and -ir verbs		
	comer *(to eat)*	**escrib**ir *(to write)*
SINGULAR FORMS		
yo	com**o**	escrib**o**
tú	com**es**	escrib**es**
Ud./él/ella	com**e**	escrib**e**
PLURAL FORMS		
nosotros/as	com**emos**	escrib**imos**
vosotros/as	com**éis**	escrib**ís**
Uds./ellos/ellas	com**en**	escrib**en**

▶ **-Er** and **-ir** verbs have very similar endings. Study the preceding chart to detect the patterns that make it easier for you to use them to communicate in Spanish.

Felipe y su tío comen.

Jimena lee.

▶ Like **-ar** verbs, the **yo** forms of **-er** and **-ir** verbs end in **-o.**

 Yo com**o**. Yo escrib**o**.

▶ Except for the **yo** form, all of the verb endings for **-er** verbs begin with **-e.**

-es	-emos	-en
-e	-éis	

▶ **-Er** and **-ir** verbs have the exact same endings, except in the **nosotros/as** and **vosotros/as** forms.

 nosotros ◀ com**emos** vosotros ◀ com**éis**
 escrib**imos** escrib**ís**

Common -er and -ir verbs

-er verbs		-ir verbs	
aprender (a + *inf.*)	*to learn*	**abrir**	*to open*
beber	*to drink*	**asistir (a)**	*to attend*
comer	*to eat*	**compartir**	*to share*
comprender	*to understand*	**decidir (+ *inf.*)**	*to decide*
correr	*to run*	**describir**	*to describe*
creer (en)	*to believe (in)*	**escribir**	*to write*
deber (+ *inf.*)	*should; must; ought to*	**recibir**	*to receive*
leer	*to read*	**vivir**	*to live*

Ellos **corren** en el parque.

Él **escribe** una carta.

¡INTÉNTALO! Provide the appropriate present tense forms of these verbs.

correr

1. Graciela _corre_.
2. Tú _corres_.
3. Yo _corro_.
4. Sara y Ana _corren_.
5. Usted _corre_.
6. Ustedes _corren_.
7. La gente _corre_.
8. Marcos y yo _corremos_.

abrir

1. Ellos _abren_ la puerta.
2. Carolina _abre_ la maleta.
3. Yo _abro_ las ventanas.
4. Nosotras _abrimos_ los libros.
5. Usted _abre_ el cuaderno.
6. Tú _abres_ la ventana.
7. Ustedes _abren_ las maletas.
8. Los muchachos _abren_ los cuadernos.

aprender

1. Él _aprende_ español.
2. Maribel y yo _aprendemos_ inglés.
3. Tú _aprendes_ japonés.
4. Tú y tu hermanastra _aprenden_ francés.
5. Mi hijo _aprende_ chino.
6. Yo _aprendo_ alemán.
7. Usted _aprende_ inglés.
8. Nosotros _aprendemos_ italiano.

recursos

WB
pp. 29–30

LM
p. 17

S
vhlcentral.com
Lección 3

Práctica

1

Completar Complete Susana's sentences about her family with the correct forms of the verbs in parentheses. One of the verbs will remain in the infinitive.

1. Mi familia y yo ___vivimos___ (vivir) en Mérida, Yucatán.
2. Tengo muchos libros. Me gusta ___leer___ (leer).
3. Mi hermano Alfredo es muy inteligente. Alfredo ___asiste___ (asistir) a clases los lunes, miércoles y viernes.
4. Los martes y jueves Alfredo y yo ___corremos___ (correr) en el Parque del Centenario.
5. Mis padres ___comen___ (comer) mucha lasaña los domingos y se quedan dormidos (*they fall asleep*).
6. Yo ___creo___ (creer) que (*that*) mis padres deben comer menos (*less*).

2

Oraciones Juan is talking about what he and his friends do after school. Form complete sentences by adding any other necessary elements.

> **modelo**
> yo / correr / amigos / lunes y miércoles
> *Yo corro con mis amigos los lunes y miércoles.*

1. Manuela / asistir / clase / yoga Manuela asiste a la clase de yoga.
2. Eugenio / abrir / correo electrónico (*e-mail*) Eugenio abre su correo electrónico.
3. Isabel y yo / leer / biblioteca Isabel y yo leemos en la biblioteca.
4. Sofía y Roberto / aprender / hablar / inglés Sofía y Roberto aprenden a hablar inglés.
5. tú / comer / cafetería / universidad Tú comes en la cafetería de la universidad.
6. mi novia y yo / compartir / libro de historia Mi novia y yo compartimos el libro de historia.

3

Consejos Mario and his family are spending a year abroad to learn Japanese. In pairs, use the words below to say what he and/or his family members are doing or should do to adjust to life in Japan. Then, create one more sentence using a verb not on the list. Answers will vary.

> **modelo**
> recibir libros / deber practicar japonés
> **Estudiante 1:** *Mario y su esposa reciben muchos libros en japonés.*
> **Estudiante 2:** *Los hijos deben practicar japonés.*

aprender japonés	decidir explorar el país
asistir a clases	escribir listas de palabras en japonés
beber sake	leer novelas japonesas
deber comer cosas nuevas	vivir con una familia japonesa
¿?	¿?

 Practice more at **vhlcentral.com.**

Comunicación

4 **Entrevista** In pairs, use these questions to interview each other. Be prepared to report the results of your interviews to the class. *Answers will vary.*

1. ¿Dónde comes al mediodía? ¿Comes mucho?
2. ¿Cuándo asistes a tus clases?
3. ¿Cuál es tu clase favorita? ¿Por qué?
4. ¿Dónde vives?
5. ¿Con quién vives?
6. ¿Qué cursos debes tomar el próximo (*next*) semestre?
7. ¿Lees el periódico (*newspaper*)? ¿Qué periódico lees y cuándo?
8. ¿Recibes muchos mensajes de texto (*text messages*)? ¿De quién(es)?
9. ¿Escribes poemas?
10. ¿Crees en fantasmas (*ghosts*)?

5 **¿Acción o descripción?** In small groups, take turns choosing a verb from the list. Then choose to act out the verb or give a description. The other members of the group will say what you are doing. Be creative! *Answers will vary.*

abrir (un libro, una puerta, una mochila)	correr (en el parque, en un maratón)
aprender (a bailar, a hablar francés, a dibujar)	escribir (una composición, un mensaje de texto [*text message*], con lápiz)
asistir (a una clase de yoga, a un concierto de rock, a una clase interesante)	leer (una carta [*letter*] de amor, un mensaje electrónico [*e-mail message*], un periódico [*newspaper*])
beber (agua, Coca-Cola)	recibir un regalo (*gift*)
comer (pasta, un sándwich, pizza)	¿?
compartir (un libro, un sándwich)	

modelo

Estudiante 1: (*pantomimes typing a keyboard*)
Estudiante 2: ¿Escribes un mensaje electrónico?
Estudiante 1: Sí.

modelo

Estudiante 1: Soy estudiante y tomo muchas clases. Vivo en Roma.
Estudiante 2: ¿Comes pasta?
Estudiante 1: No, no como pasta.
Estudiante 3: ¿Aprendes a hablar italiano?
Estudiante 1: ¡Sí!

Síntesis

6 **Horario** Your instructor will give you and a partner incomplete versions of Alicia's schedule. Fill in the missing information on the schedule by talking to your partner. Be prepared to reconstruct Alicia's complete schedule with the class. *Answers will vary.*

4 Teaching Tips
• Tell students that one of them should complete their interview before switching roles.
• This activity is also suited to a group of three students, one of whom acts as note taker. They should switch roles at the end of each interview until each student has played all three roles.

5 Teaching Tip Make sure that students understand that they have the option of acting out an activity or describing it in a creative way. Write a verb phrase on the board and model both methods. Ex: Write on the board **beber té** (*tea*). First, act out sitting primly in a chair, serving tea from a teapot, stirring in sugar, and holding the cup daintily while taking small sips. Then give a description: **Estoy en Londres. Son las cuatro de la tarde. Deseo tomar algo** (*something*).

5 Expansion Write **asociación** on the board. Have students repeat the activity, but this time they must make associations with the verbs instead of acting them out or describing them. Ex: **Santa Claus/Papá Noel (recibir un regalo); clases de tango (aprender a bailar)**

6 Teaching Tip Divide the class into pairs and distribute the handouts from the Activity Pack that correspond to this Information Gap Activity (Activity Pack/Supersite). Give students ten minutes to complete this activity.

6 Expansion
• Ask questions based on **Alicia's** schedule. Ex: **¿Qué hace Alicia a las nueve? (Ella desayuna.)**
• → Have volunteers take turns reading aloud **Alicia's** schedule. Then have them write their own schedules using as many **–er/–ir** verbs as they can.

3.4 Present tense of tener and venir — Ⓢ Tutorial

ANTE TODO The verbs **tener** (*to have*) and **venir** (*to come*) are among the most frequently used in Spanish. Because most of their forms are irregular, you will have to learn each one individually.

The verbs tener and venir		
	tener	**ven**ir
SINGULAR FORMS		
yo	ten**go**	ven**go**
tú	tien**es**	vien**es**
Ud./él/ella	tien**e**	vien**e**
PLURAL FORMS		
nosotros/as	ten**emos**	ven**imos**
vosotros/as	ten**éis**	ven**ís**
Uds./ellos/ellas	tien**en**	vien**en**

▶ The endings are the same as those of regular **-er** and **-ir** verbs, except for the **yo** forms, which are irregular: **tengo, vengo.**

▶ In the **tú, Ud.,** and **Uds.** forms, the **e** of the stem changes to **ie,** as shown below.

INFINITIVE	VERB STEM	VERB FORM
tener →	ten- →	tú t**ie**nes
		Ud./él/ella t**ie**ne
		Uds./ellos/ellas t**ie**nen
venir →	ven- →	tú v**ie**nes
		Ud./él/ella v**ie**ne
		Uds./ellos/ellas v**ie**nen

¿Tienes una familia grande, Marissa?

No, tengo una familia pequeña.

▶ Only the **nosotros** and **vosotros** forms are regular. Compare them to the forms of **comer** and **escribir** that you learned on page 88.

	tener	comer	venir	escribir
nosotros/as	ten**emos**	com**emos**	ven**imos**	escrib**imos**
vosotros/as	ten**éis**	com**éis**	ven**ís**	escrib**ís**

▶ In certain idiomatic or set expressions in Spanish, you use the construction **tener** + [*noun*] to express *to be* + [*adjective*]. This chart contains a list of the most common expressions with **tener**.

Expressions with tener

tener... años	*to be... years old*	**tener (mucha) prisa**	*to be in a (big) hurry*
tener (mucho) calor	*to be (very) hot*	**tener razón**	*to be right*
tener (mucho) cuidado	*to be (very) careful*	**no tener razón**	*to be wrong*
tener (mucho) frío	*to be (very) cold*	**tener (mucha) sed**	*to be (very) thirsty*
tener (mucha) hambre	*to be (very) hungry*	**tener (mucho) sueño**	*to be (very) sleepy*
tener (mucho) miedo (de)	*to be (very) afraid/ scared (of)*	**tener (mucha) suerte**	*to be (very) lucky*

—¿**Tienen** hambre ustedes?
Are you hungry?

—Sí, y **tenemos** sed también.
Yes, and we're thirsty, too.

▶ To express an obligation, use **tener que** (*to have to*) + [*infinitive*].

—¿Qué **tienes que** estudiar hoy?
What do you have to study today?

—**Tengo que** estudiar biología.
I have to study biology.

▶ To ask people if they feel like doing something, use **tener ganas de** (*to feel like*) + [*infinitive*].

—¿**Tienes ganas de** comer?
Do you feel like eating?

—No, **tengo ganas de** dormir.
No, I feel like sleeping.

MIciudad.com
Usted tiene que visitarnos.

¡INTÉNTALO! Provide the appropriate forms of **tener** and **venir**.

tener
1. Ellos __tienen__ dos hermanos.
2. Yo __tengo__ una hermana.
3. El artista __tiene__ tres primos.
4. Nosotros __tenemos__ diez tíos.
5. Eva y Diana __tienen__ un sobrino.
6. Usted __tiene__ cinco nietos.
7. Tú __tienes__ dos hermanastras.
8. Ustedes __tienen__ cuatro hijos.
9. Ella __tiene__ una hija.

venir
1. Mis padres __vienen__ de México.
2. Tú __vienes__ de España.
3. Nosotras __venimos__ de Cuba.
4. Pepe __viene__ de Italia.
5. Yo __vengo__ de Francia.
6. Ustedes __vienen__ de Canadá.
7. Alfonso y yo __venimos__ de Portugal.
8. Ellos __vienen__ de Alemania.
9. Usted __viene__ de Venezuela.

Teaching Tips
- Remind the class that Spanish uses **tener** + [*noun*] in many cases where English uses *to be* + [*adjective*].
- Model the use of the expressions by talking about yourself and asking students questions about themselves. Ex: **Tengo ____ años. Y tú, ¿cuántos años tienes? Esta mañana tengo frío. ¿Tienen frío ustedes? Y tú, ____, ¿tienes frío también o tienes calor? Yo no tengo sueño esta mañana. Me gusta enseñar por la mañana.**
- Present **tener que** + [*infinitive*] and **tener ganas de** + [*infinitive*] together. Go around the class asking questions that use the expressions, having students answer in complete sentences. Ex: **____, ¿tienes que estudiar más para la clase de español? ¿Tienes ganas de ir a la biblioteca ahora?**
- Give locations and have students name the **tener** expressions that they associate with those places. Accept all possible responses. Ex: **el desierto del Sahara (tener calor, tener sed); un debate político en Washington D.C. (tener razón, no tener razón)**

TEACHING OPTIONS

TPR Assign gestures to each expression with **tener**. Ex: **tener calor:** *wipe brow;* **tener cuidado:** *look around suspiciously;* **tener frío:** *wrap arms around oneself and shiver;* **tener miedo:** *hold hand over mouth in fear.* Have students stand. Say an expression at random (Ex: **Tienes sueño**) and point at a student, who should perform the appropriate gesture. Vary by pointing to more than one student (Ex: **Ustedes tienen hambre**).

Variación léxica Point out that **tener que** + [*infinitive*] not only expresses obligation, but also need. **Tengo que estudiar más** can mean either *I have to (am obligated to) study more* or *I need to study more.* Another way of expressing need is with the regular –ar verb **necesitar** + [*infinitive*]. Ex: **Necesito estudiar más.** This can also be said with **deber** + [*infinitive*]. Ex: **Debo estudiar más.**

Práctica

1 **Emparejar** Find the expression in column B that best matches an item in column A. Then, come up with a new item that corresponds with the leftover expression in column B.

A		B
1. el Polo Norte	c	a. tener calor
2. una sauna	a	b. tener sed
3. la comida salada (*salty food*)	b	c. tener frío
4. una persona muy inteligente	d	d. tener razón
5. un abuelo	g	e. tener ganas de
6. una dieta	f	f. tener hambre
		g. tener 75 años

2 **Completar** Complete the sentences with the correct forms of **tener** or **venir**.

1. Hoy nosotros ___tenemos___ una reunión familiar (*family reunion*).
2. Yo ___vengo___ en autobús de la Universidad de Quito.
3. Todos mis parientes ___vienen___, excepto mi tío Manolo y su esposa.
4. Ellos no ___tienen___ ganas de venir porque viven en Portoviejo.
5. Mi prima Susana y su novio no ___vienen___ hasta las ocho porque ella ___tiene___ que trabajar.
6. En las fiestas, mi hermana siempre (*always*) ___viene___ muy tarde (*late*).
7. Nosotros ___tenemos___ mucha suerte porque las reuniones son divertidas (*fun*).
8. Mi madre cree que mis sobrinos son muy simpáticos. Creo que ella ___tiene___ razón.

3 **Describir** Describe what these people are doing or feeling using an expression with **tener**.

1. ___Tiene (mucha) prisa.___ 2. ___Tiene (mucho) calor.___ 3. ___Tiene veintiún años.___

4. ___Tienen (mucha) hambre.___ 5. ___Tienen (mucho) frío.___ 6. ___Tiene (mucha) sed.___

 Practice more at **vhlcentral.com.**

1 Teaching Tip Go over the activity with the class, reading a statement in column A and having volunteers give the corresponding phrase in column B. Note that option **e** (**tener ganas de**) does not match any items in column A. Help students think of a word or phrase that would match it. Ex: **comer una pizza, asistir a un concierto**

1 Expansion Have pairs of students write sentences by combining elements from the two columns. Ex: **Sonia está en el Polo Norte y tiene mucho frío. José es una persona muy inteligente pero no tiene razón.**

2 Expansion Have students write the questions that would elicit the sentences in this activity. Ex: **¿Qué tienen ellos hoy? ¿Cómo viene el narrador a la reunión? ¿Quién no viene?**

3 Teaching Tip Before doing this activity as a class, have students identify which picture is referred to in each of these questions. Have them answer: **La(s) persona(s) del dibujo número ____.** Ask: **¿Quién bebe Coca-Cola? (6), ¿Quién asiste a una fiesta? (3), ¿Quiénes comen pizza? (4), ¿Quiénes esperan el autobús? (5), ¿Quién corre a la oficina? (1), ¿Quién hace ejercicio en una bicicleta? (2)**

3 Expansion Describe different situations and have students respond using **tener** expressions. Ex: **Pedro come mucho. ¿Por qué? (Porque tiene hambre.)**

TEACHING OPTIONS

Extra Practice Have students complete sentences with **tener** and **venir**. Ex: **1.** Paula y Luis no tienen hambre, pero yo sí ____ mucha hambre. (tengo) **2.** Mis padres vienen del Ecuador, pero mis hermanos y yo ____ de los Estados Unidos. (venimos) **3.** ¿Tienes frío, Marta? Pues, Carlos y yo ____ calor. (tenemos) **4.** Enrique viene de la residencia. ¿De dónde ____ tú, Angélica? (vienes) **5.** ¿Ustedes tienen que trabajar hoy? Ellos no ____ que trabajar. (tienen)

Small Groups In groups of three, ask students to write nine sentences, each of which uses a different expression with **tener**, including **tener que** + [*infinitive*] and **tener ganas de** + [*infinitive*]. Ask volunteers to write some of their group's best sentences on the board. Work with the class to read the sentences and check for accuracy.

Comunicación

4 **¿Sí o no?** Indicate whether these statements apply to you by checking either **Sí** or **No**. Answers will vary.

	Sí	No
1. Mi padre tiene 50 años.	○	○
2. Mis amigos vienen a mi casa todos los días (*every day*).	○	○
3. Vengo a la universidad los martes.	○	○
4. Tengo hambre.	○	○
5. Tengo dos computadoras.	○	○
6. Tengo sed.	○	○
7. Tengo que estudiar los domingos.	○	○
8. Tengo una familia grande.	○	○

Now interview a classmate by transforming each statement into a question. Be prepared to report the results of your interview to the class. Answers will vary.

> **modelo**
>
> **Estudiante 1:** ¿Tiene tu padre 50 años?
> **Estudiante 2:** No, no tiene 50 años. Tiene 65.

5 **Preguntas** Get together with a classmate and ask each other these questions. Answers will vary.

1. ¿Tienes que estudiar hoy?
2. ¿Cuántos años tienes? ¿Y tus hermanos/as?
3. ¿Cuándo vienes a la clase de español?
4. ¿Cuándo vienen tus amigos a tu casa, apartamento o residencia estudiantil?
5. ¿De qué tienes miedo? ¿Por qué?
6. ¿Qué tienes ganas de hacer esta noche (*tonight*)?

6 **Conversación** Use an expression with **tener** to hint at what's on your mind. Your partner will ask questions to find out why you feel that way. If your partner cannot guess what's on your mind after three attempts, tell him/her. Then switch roles. Answers will vary.

> **modelo**
>
> **Estudiante 1:** Tengo miedo.
> **Estudiante 2:** ¿Tienes que hablar en público?
> **Estudiante 1:** No.
> **Estudiante 2:** ¿Tienes un examen hoy?
> **Estudiante 1:** Sí, y no tengo tiempo para estudiar.

Síntesis

7 **Minidrama** Act out this situation with a partner: you are introducing your boyfriend/girlfriend to your extended family. To avoid any surprises before you go, talk about who is coming and what each family member is like. Switch roles. Answers will vary.

4 Teaching Tip Give students two minutes to read the statements and mark their answers. Then form pairs and model question formation. Encourage students to answer with complete sentences.

5 Teaching Tips
- You may want to provide additional vocabulary for item 5.
- Ask volunteers to summarize the responses. Record these responses on the board as a survey about the class's characteristics.

6 Teaching Tip Model the activity by giving an expression with **tener**. Ex: **Tengo mucha prisa.** Encourage students to guess the reason, using **tener** and **venir**. If they guess incorrectly, give them more specific clues. Ex: **Tengo mucho que hacer hoy. Es un día especial. (Viene un amigo a la casa.)**

7 Teaching Tip Before doing **Síntesis**, have students quickly review this material: family vocabulary on pages 70–71; descriptive adjectives on pages 80–82; possessive adjectives on page 85; and the forms of **tener** and **venir** on pages 92–93.

TEACHING OPTIONS

Small Groups 👤↔👤 Have small groups prepare skits in which one person takes a few friends to a family reunion. The introducer should make polite introductions and tell the people he or she is introducing a few facts about each other. All the people involved should attempt to make small talk.

Pairs 👤↔👤 Give pairs of students five minutes to write a conversation in which they use as many **tener** expressions as they can in a logical manner. Have the top three pairs perform their conversations for the class.

Section Goal

In **Recapitulación**, students will review the grammar concepts from this lesson.

Instructional Resource
Supersite

1 Teaching Tips
• To add an auditory aspect to the activity, have students read their answers aloud, emphasizing the adjective ending sounds –a(s) and –o(s).
• Remind students that some adjectives have the same masculine and feminine forms.

1 Expansion Ask students to rewrite the sentences to convey an opposite or different meaning. Ex: **1. Mi tía es francesa. Vive en París. 2. Mi primo no es moreno, es rubio.**

2 Teaching Tip Remind students that possessive adjectives agree in number (and in gender for **nuestro/a** and **vuestro/a**) with the nouns they modify, not with the subject. Therefore, in item 1, even though **Esteban y Julio** is a plural subject, **su** is singular to agree with **tía**.

2 Expansion
←👥→ Have students rewrite the sentences using different subjects. Encourage them to add additional sentences to each item using any of the -er/-ir verbs they have learned in this chapter. Ex: **Yo tengo una tía. Es mi tía. Ella vive en Nueva York.**

3 Teaching Tip To simplify, have students circle the subject and underline the verb before forming the sentences.

3 Expansion Have pairs create two additional dehydrated sentences for another pair to write out.

Recapitulación

S Concepts Diagnostics

Review the grammar concepts you have learned in this lesson by completing these activities.

1 Adjetivos Complete each phrase with the appropriate adjective from the list. Make all necessary changes. **6 pts.**

antipático	interesante	mexicano
difícil	joven	moreno

1. Mi tía es ___mexicana___. Vive en Guadalajara.
2. Mi primo no es rubio, es ___moreno___.
3. Mi novio cree que la clase no es fácil; es ___difícil___.
4. Los libros son ___interesantes___; me gustan mucho.
5. Mis hermanos son ___antipáticos___; no tienen muchos amigos.
6. Las gemelas tienen quince años. Son ___jóvenes___.

2 Completar For each set of sentences, provide the appropriate form of the verb **tener** and the possessive adjective. Follow the model. **12 pts.**

modelo
Él tiene un libro. Es su libro.

1. Esteban y Julio ___tienen___ una tía. Es ___su___ tía.
2. Yo ___tengo___ muchos amigos. Son ___mis___ amigos.
3. Tú ___tienes___ tres primas. Son ___tus___ primas.
4. María y tú ___tienen___ un hermano. Es ___su___ hermano.
5. Nosotras ___tenemos___ unas mochilas. Son ___nuestras___ mochilas.
6. Usted ___tiene___ dos sobrinos. Son ___sus___ sobrinos.

3 Oraciones Arrange the words in the correct order to form complete logical sentences. **¡Ojo!** Don't forget to conjugate the verbs. **10 pts.**

1. libros / unos / tener / interesantes / tú / muy
 ___Tú tienes unos libros muy interesantes.___
2. dos / leer / fáciles / compañera / tu / lecciones
 ___Tu compañera lee dos lecciones fáciles.___
3. mi / francés / ser / amigo / buen / Hugo
 ___Hugo es mi buen amigo francés./Mi buen amigo francés es Hugo.___
4. ser / simpáticas / dos / personas / nosotras
 ___Nosotras somos dos personas simpáticas.___
5. a / clases / menores / mismas / sus / asisitir / hermanos / las
 ___Sus hermanos menores asisten a las mismas clases.___

RESUMEN GRAMATICAL

3.1 Descriptive adjectives *pp. 80–82*

Forms and agreement of adjectives

Masculine		Feminine	
Singular	**Plural**	**Singular**	**Plural**
alto	altos	alta	altas
inteligente	inteligentes	inteligente	inteligentes
trabajador	trabajadores	trabajadora	trabajadoras

▶ Descriptive adjectives follow the noun:
el chico rubio

▶ Adjectives of nationality also follow the noun:
la mujer española

▶ Adjectives of quantity precede the noun:
muchos libros, dos turistas

▶ When placed before a singular masculine noun, these adjectives are shortened.
bueno → buen malo → mal

▶ When placed before a singular noun, **grande** is shortened to **gran**.

3.2 Possessive adjectives *p. 85*

Singular		Plural	
mi	nuestro/a	mis	nuestros/as
tu	vuestro/a	tus	vuestros/as
su	su	sus	sus

3.3 Present tense of -er and -ir verbs *pp. 88–89*

comer		escribir	
como	comemos	escribo	escribimos
comes	coméis	escribes	escribís
come	comen	escribe	escriben

3.4 Present tense of tener and venir *pp. 92–93*

tener		venir	
tengo	tenemos	vengo	venimos
tienes	tenéis	vienes	venís
tiene	tienen	viene	vienen

TEACHING OPTIONS

TPR Make sets of cards containing –er and –ir infinitives that are easy to act out. Divide the class into groups of five. Have students take turns drawing a card and acting out the verb for the group. Once someone has correctly guessed the verb, the group members must take turns providing the conjugated forms.

Extra Practice ←👥→ To add a visual aspect to this grammar review, bring in magazine or newspaper photos of people and places. Have students describe the people and places using descriptive adjectives.

4 **Carta** Complete this letter with the appropriate forms of the verbs in the word list. Not all verbs will be used. `10 pts.`

abrir	correr	recibir
asistir	creer	tener
compartir	escribir	venir
comprender	leer	vivir

Hola, Ángel:

¿Qué tal? (Yo) (1) ___Escribo___ esta carta (this letter) en la biblioteca. Todos los días (2) ___vengo___ aquí y (3) ___leo___ un buen libro. Yo (4) ___creo___ que es importante leer por diversión. Mi compañero de apartamento no (5) ___comprende___ por qué me gusta leer. Él sólo (6) ___abre/lee___ los libros de texto. Pero nosotros (7) ___compartimos___ unos intereses. Por ejemplo, los dos somos atléticos; por las mañanas nosotros (8) ___corremos___. También nos gustan las ciencias; por las tardes (9) ___asistimos___ a nuestra clase de biología. Y tú, ¿cómo estás? ¿(Tú) (10) ___Tienes___ mucho trabajo (work)?

5 **Su familia** Write a brief description of a friend's family. Describe the family members using vocabulary and structures from this lesson. Write at least five sentences. `12 pts.`

Answers will vary.

> **modelo**
>
> La familia de mi amiga Gabriela es grande. Ella tiene tres hermanos y una hermana. Su hermana mayor es periodista...

6 **Proverbio** Complete this proverb with the correct forms of the verbs in parentheses. `2 EXTRA points!`

66 Dos andares° ___tiene___ (tener) el dinero°,
___viene___ (venir) despacio°
y se va° ligero°. 99

andares *speeds* dinero *money* despacio *slowly*
se va *it leaves* ligero *quickly*

Practice more at **vhlcentral.com.**

Section Goals

In **Lectura**, students will:
- learn to use context clues in reading
- read context-rich selections about Hispanic families

Instructional Resource
Supersite

Estrategia Tell students that they can often infer the meaning of an unfamiliar Spanish word by looking at the word's context and by using common sense. Five types of context clues are:
- synonyms
- antonyms
- clarifications
- definitions
- additional details

Have students read the sentence **Ayer fui a ver a mi tía abuela, la hermana de mi abuela** from the letter. Point out that the meaning of **tía abuela** can be inferred from its similarity to the known word **abuela** and from the clarification that follows (**la hermana de mi abuela**).

Examinar el texto Have students read Paragraph 1 silently, without looking up the glossed words. Point out the phrase **salgo a pasear** and ask a volunteer to explain how the context might give clues to the meaning. Afterward, point out that **salgo** is the first-person singular form of **salir** (*to go out*). Tell students they will learn all the forms of **salir** in **Lección 4**.

Examinar el formato Guide students to see that the photos and captions reveal that the paragraphs are about several different families.

Lectura

Antes de leer

Estrategia
Guessing meaning from context

As you read in Spanish, you'll often come across words you haven't learned. You can guess what they mean by looking at the surrounding words and sentences. Look at the following text and guess what **tía abuela** means, based on the context.

> ¡Hola, Claudia!
> ¿Qué hay de nuevo?
> ¿Sabes qué? Ayer fui a ver a mi tía abuela, la hermana de mi abuela. Tiene 85 años, pero es muy independiente. Vive en un apartamento en Quito con su prima Lorena, quien también tiene 85 años.

If you guessed *great-aunt*, you are correct, and you can conclude from this word and the format clues that this is a letter about someone's visit with his or her great-aunt.

Examinar el texto

Quickly read through the paragraphs and find two or three words you don't know. Using the context as your guide, guess what these words mean. Then glance at the paragraphs where these words appear and try to predict what the paragraphs are about.

Examinar el formato

Look at the format of the reading. What clues do the captions, photos, and layout give you about its content?

🔹 Practice more at **vhlcentral.com**.

Gente ··· Las familias

1. Me llamo Armando y tengo setenta años, pero no me considero viejo. Tengo seis nietas y un nieto. Vivo con mi hija y tengo la oportunidad de pasar mucho tiempo con ella y con mi nieto. Por las tardes salgo a pasear° por el parque con él y por la noche le leo cuentos°.

Armando. Tiene seis nietas y un nieto.

2. Mi prima Victoria y yo nos llevamos muy bien. Estudiamos juntas° en la universidad y compartimos un apartamento. Ella es muy inteligente y me ayuda° con los estudios. Además°, es muy simpática y generosa. Si necesito cualquier° cosa, ¡ella me la compra!

Diana. Vive con su prima.

3. Me llamo Ramona y soy paraguaya, aunque° ahora vivo en los Estados Unidos. Tengo tres hijos, uno de nueve años, uno de doce y el mayor de quince. Es difícil a veces, pero mi esposo y yo tratamos° de ayudarlos y comprenderlos siempre°.

Ramona. Sus hijos son muy importantes para ella.

4. Tengo mucha suerte. Aunque mis padres están divorciados, tengo una familia muy unida. Tengo dos hermanos y dos hermanas. Me gusta hablar y salir a fiestas con ellos. Ahora tengo novio en la universidad y él no conoce a mis hermanos. ¡Espero que se lleven bien!

Ana María. Su familia es muy unida.

5. Antes quería° tener hermanos, pero ya no° es tan importante. Ser hijo único tiene muchas ventajas°: no tengo que compartir mis cosas con hermanos, no hay discusiones° y, como soy nieto único también, ¡mis abuelos piensan° que soy perfecto!

Fernando. Es hijo único.

6. Como soy joven todavía°, no tengo ni esposa ni hijos. Pero tengo un sobrino, el hijo de mi hermano, que es muy especial para mí. Se llama Benjamín y tiene diez años. Es un muchacho muy simpático. Siempre tiene hambre y por lo tanto vamos° frecuentemente a comer hamburguesas. Nos gusta también ir al cine° a ver películas de acción. Hablamos de todo. ¡Creo que ser tío es mejor que ser padre!

Santiago. Cree que ser tío es divertido.

salgo a pasear *I go take a walk* cuentos *stories* juntas *together* me ayuda *she helps me* Además *Besides* cualquier *any* aunque *although* tratamos *we try* siempre *always* quería *I wanted* ya no *no longer* ventajas *advantages* discusiones *arguments* piensan *think* todavía *still* vamos *we go* ir al cine *to go to the movies*

Después de leer

Emparejar

Glance at the paragraphs and see how the words and phrases in column A are used in context. Then find their definitions in column B.

A		B
1. me la compra	d	a. the oldest
2. nos llevamos bien	h	b. movies
3. no conoce	g	c. the youngest
4. películas	b	d. buys it for me
5. mejor que	j	e. borrows it from me
6. el mayor	a	f. we see each other
		g. doesn't know
		h. we get along
		i. portraits
		j. better than

Seleccionar

Choose the sentence that best summarizes each paragraph.

1. Párrafo 1 a
 a. Me gusta mucho ser abuelo.
 b. No hablo mucho con mi nieto.
 c. No tengo nietos.
2. Párrafo 2 c
 a. Mi prima es antipática.
 b. Mi prima no es muy trabajadora.
 c. Mi prima y yo somos muy buenas amigas.
3. Párrafo 3 a
 a. Tener hijos es un gran sacrificio, pero es muy bonito también.
 b. No comprendo a mis hijos.
 c. Mi esposo y yo no tenemos hijos.
4. Párrafo 4 c
 a. No hablo mucho con mis hermanos.
 b. Comparto mis cosas con mis hermanos.
 c. Mis hermanos y yo somos como (*like*) amigos.
5. Párrafo 5 a
 a. Me gusta ser hijo único.
 b. Tengo hermanos y hermanas.
 c. Vivo con mis abuelos.
6. Párrafo 6 b
 a. Mi sobrino tiene diez años.
 b. Me gusta mucho ser tío.
 c. Mi esposa y yo no tenemos hijos.

Emparejar If students have trouble inferring the meaning of any item, help them identify the corresponding context clues. **1. me lo presta (si no tengo dinero) 2. nos llevamos bien (compartimos un apartamento) 3. no conoce (ahora tengo novio en la universidad) 4. películas (cine) 5. mejor que (ser tío, ser padre) 6. el mayor (uno de nueve años, uno de doce; de quince)**

Seleccionar
→🔊← You might wish to ask students these listening comprehension questions: **1. ¿Cuántos años tiene Armando? (setenta) 2. ¿Con quién vive Armando? (con su hija) 3. ¿Con quién comparte un apartamento Diana? (con su prima, Victoria) 4. ¿Cómo es Victoria? (inteligente, simpática y generosa) 5. ¿De dónde es Ramona? (Es de Paraguay.) 6. ¿En qué país vive Ramona ahora? (en los Estados Unidos) 7. ¿Cómo es la familia de Ana María? (muy unida) 8. ¿Ana María tiene novio? (Sí, tiene novio.) 9. ¿Qué tiene muchas ventajas para Fernando? (ser hijo único) 10. ¿Qué piensan los abuelos de Fernando? (que él es perfecto) 11. ¿Cómo se llama el sobrino de Santiago? (Benjamín) 12. ¿Por qué comen hamburguesas con frecuencia? (porque Benjamín siempre tiene hambre)**

Teaching Tip Encourage students to record unfamiliar words and phrases that they learn in **Lectura** in their portfolios (**carpetas**).

Escritura

Estrategia

Using idea maps

How do you organize ideas for a first draft? Often, organizing ideas is the most challenging part of the process. Idea maps are useful for organizing pertinent information. Here is an example of an idea map you can use:

MAPA DE IDEAS

- 45 años
- 43 años
- moreno trabajador inteligente alto
- **Simón** *padre*
- **Rosa** *madre*
- trabajadora simpática bonita
- **Mi familia**
- **José** *hermano*
- moreno alto escucha música rock
- 15 años

Tema

Escribir un mensaje electrónico

A friend you met in a chat room for Spanish speakers wants to know about your family. Using some of the verbs and adjectives you have learned in this lesson, write a brief e-mail describing your family or an imaginary family, including:

▶ Names and relationships
▶ Physical characteristics
▶ Hobbies and interests

Here are some useful expressions for writing an e-mail or letter in Spanish:

Salutations	
Estimado/a Julio/Julia:	*Dear Julio/Julia,*
Querido/a Miguel/Ana María:	*Dear Miguel/Ana María,*

Closings	
Un abrazo,	*A hug,*
Abrazos,	*Hugs,*
Cariños,	*Much love,*
¡Hasta pronto!	*See you soon!*
¡Hasta la próxima semana!	*See you next week!*

NATIONAL communication STANDARDS

Escuchar Audio: Activities

Preparación

Based on the photograph, where do you think Cristina and Laura are? What do you think Laura is saying to Cristina?

Ahora escucha

Now you are going to hear Laura and Cristina's conversation. Use **R** to indicate which adjectives describe Cristina's boyfriend, Rafael. Use **E** for adjectives that describe Laura's boyfriend, Esteban. Some adjectives will not be used.

___ rubio	E interesante
___ feo	___ antipático
R alto	R inteligente
E trabajador	R moreno
E un poco gordo	___ viejo

Comprensión

Identificar

Which person would make each statement: Cristina or Laura?

	Cristina	Laura
1. Mi novio habla sólo de fútbol y de béisbol.	◉	○
2. Tengo un novio muy interesante y simpático.	○	◉
3. Mi novio es alto y moreno.	◉	○
4. Mi novio trabaja mucho.	○	◉
5. Mi amiga no tiene buena suerte con los muchachos.	○	◉
6. El novio de mi amiga es un poco gordo, pero guapo.	◉	○

¿Cierto o falso?

Indicate whether each sentence is **cierto** or **falso**, then correct the false statements.

	Cierto	Falso
1. Esteban es un chico interesante y simpático.	◉	○
2. Laura tiene mala suerte con los chicos. Cristina tiene mala suerte con los chicos.	○	◉
3. Rafael es muy interesante. Esteban es muy interesante.	○	◉
4. Laura y su novio hablan de muchas cosas.	◉	○

En pantalla

Anuncio

Christmas is not celebrated in winter everywhere. During the cold-weather months in North America, it's summer in the Southern Hemisphere. In Chile, for example, summer starts in December and lasts until March. Summer vacation coincides with these months, since almost all academic calendars run from early March to late December.

Vocabulario útil

quería	*I wanted*	**aprovecha**	*take advantage of*
pedirte	*to ask you*	**nuestras**	*our*
te preocupa	*it worries you*	**ofertas**	*deals, sales*
ahorrar	*to save (money)*	**calidad**	*quality*
Navidad	*Christmas*	**no cuesta**	*doesn't cost*

¿Qué hay?

For each item, write **sí** if it appears in the TV clip or **no** if it does not.

no	1. papelera		_no_	5. diccionario
sí	2. lápiz		_sí_	6. cuaderno
sí	3. mesa		_no_	7. tiza
no	4. computadora		_sí_	8. ventana

¿Qué quieres?

Write a list of things that you want for your next birthday. Then read it to the class so they know what to get you. Use as much Spanish as you can.

Answers will vary.

Lista de cumpleaños°

Quiero°...

cumpleaños *birthday* Quiero *I want* Viejito Pascuero *Santa Claus (Chile)*

Viejito Pascuero°...

¿Cómo se escribe *mountain bike*?

M... O...

Ⓢ **Video: TV Clip**

Ⓢ Practice more at **vhlcentral.com.**

Cortometraje

In the Spanish-speaking world, grandparents play an important role in the nuclear family. Even in the U.S., where retirement communities and nursing homes abound, in Latino families, members of the older generation often live with their adult children and grandchildren. This living situation is seen to bring benefits—financial, emotional, and logistical—that improve the quality of life for everyone involved. It also facilitates passing on family history and culture. In this short film, for example, the grandmother lives with her grandson, Beto.

Preparación

1. Have you or has anyone you know ever experienced something supernatural? What happened?

2. Does any of the new vocabulary in either of the lists in the next column apply to this situation? Why? Answers will vary.

Después de ver

Choose the correct answer for each question.

1. ¿Qué hace (*is she doing*) la abuela?
 a. Prepara tortillas.
 b. Come tortillas.

2. ¿Quién escucha una canción?
 a. la abuela
 b. el nieto

3. ¿Quién se aparece en la tortilla?
 a. el nieto
 b. el abuelo

4. ¿Qué tiene el nieto?
 a. sed
 b. hambre

5. ¿Cómo reacciona la abuela?
 a. Está furiosa.
 b. Tiene miedo.

 ## Conversar

Choose one of the characters and write a description of him or her. Use as many adjectives as you can and mention the person's likes and dislikes. Be creative! Then, in pairs, read your description to a partner.
Answers will vary.

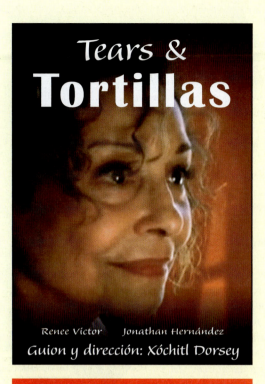

Tears & **Tortillas**

Renee Victor Jonathan Hernández
Guion y dirección: Xóchitl Dorsey

Expresiones útiles

abuelita	*Grandma*
la canción	*song*
¿Me llamaste?	*Did you call me?*

Para hablar del corto

cocinar	*to cook*
el espíritu	*spirit*
los frijoles	*beans*
la lágrima	*tear*
el milagro	*miracle*
romántico/a	*romantic*
se aparece en	*appears in*
supersticioso/a	*superstitious*

 Video: Short Film

Practice more at vhlcentral.com.

Antes de ver
- Have students guess what the film is about, based on the poster.
- Ask students to describe the woman's expression in the poster.
- Read through the **Expresiones útiles** and **Para hablar del corto** vocabulary with students to model pronunciation and practice using the terms.
- Reassure students that they do not need to understand every word they hear in the short film. Tell them to rely on visual cues and listen for cognates and words from **Expresiones útiles**.
- Explain to students that the nickname **Beto** is used for names that end in **-berto** (**Alberto**, **Humberto**, etc.).

Preparación You may want to discuss how the dead and afterlife are considered in Mexican culture.

Después de ver Using cognates and simple vocabulary, ask follow-up questions. Ex: **¿Dónde está ella? ¿Escucha música en la radio o en la computadora? ¿Cómo es la canción? ¿Romántica? ¿Bailable? ¿El nieto abre el refrigerador o el clóset?**

Conversar Before forming pairs, have students edit their descriptions, paying attention to noun-adjective and subject-verb agreement.

TEACHING OPTIONS

El cine latinoamericano In recent decades, there has been a boom of Latino filmmaking in the U.S. **Xóchitl Dorsey**, whose film is presented here, is just one of many talented independent filmmakers whose works are largely shown at film festivals. Latino film festivals, which feature films that are by or about Latinos, are held throughout the year all over the U.S. and Canada.

Pairs In pairs, have students write an alternative ending or epilogue to the film. Encourage them to be creative. Then have them act it out for the class.

Section Goal

In **Panorama**, students will receive comprehensible input by reading about the geography and culture of Ecuador.

Instructional Resources

Supersite/DVD: *Panorama cultural*
Supersite: Resources (Scripts, Translations, *PowerPoints*, Answer Keys)
WebSAM
Workbook, pp. 33–34
Video Manual, pp. 229–230

Teaching Tip

• Have students examine the map of Ecuador and look at the call-out photos and read the captions. Encourage students to mention anything they may know about Ecuador.
• Use the **Lección 3 Panorama** overheads to assist with this presentation.

El país en cifras

• Ask students to glance at the headings. Establish the kind of information contained in each and clarify unfamiliar words. Point out that most words in the headings have an English cognate.
• Point out that in September 2000, the U.S. dollar became the official currency of Ecuador.

¡Increíble pero cierto!

Mt. St. Helens in Washington and **Cotopaxi** in Ecuador are just two of a chain of volcanoes that stretches along the entire Pacific coast of North and South America, from Mt. McKinley in Alaska to **Monte Sarmiento** in the **Tierra del Fuego** of southern Chile.

Ecuador

El país en cifras

▶ **Área:** 283.560 km² (109.483 millas²), *incluyendo las islas Galápagos, aproximadamente el área de Colorado*
▶ **Población:** 14.596.000
▶ **Capital:** Quito — 2.035.000
▶ **Ciudades° principales:**
Guayaquil — 2.941.000, Cuenca, Machala, Portoviejo

SOURCE: Population Division, UN Secretariat

▶ **Moneda:** dólar estadounidense
▶ **Idiomas:** español (oficial), quichua

La lengua oficial de Ecuador es el español, pero también se hablan° otras° lenguas en el país. Aproximadamente unos 4.000.000 de ecuatorianos hablan lenguas indígenas; la mayoría° de ellos habla quichua. El quichua es el dialecto ecuatoriano del quechua, la lengua de los incas.

Bandera de Ecuador

Ecuatorianos célebres

▶ **Francisco Eugenio De Santa Cruz y Espejo,** médico, periodista y patriota (1747–1795)
▶ **Juan León Mera,** novelista (1832–1894)
▶ **Eduardo Kingman,** pintor° (1913–1998)
▶ **Rosalía Arteaga,** abogada°, política y ex vicepresidenta (1956–)

Ciudades *cities* se hablan *are spoken* otras *other* mayoría *majority* pintor *painter* abogada *lawyer* sur *south* mundo *world* pies *feet* dos veces más alto que *twice as tall as*

¡Increíble pero cierto!

El volcán Cotopaxi, situado a unos 60 kilómetros al sur° de Quito, es considerado el volcán activo más alto del mundo°. Tiene una altura de 5.897 metros (19.340 pies°). Es dos veces más alto que° el monte Santa Elena (2.550 metros o 9.215 pies) en el estado de Washington.

Muchos indígenas de Ecuador hablan quichua.

COLOMBIA
Las islas Galápagos
Indígenas del Amazonas
Río Esmeraldas
Ibarra
Quito
Portoviejo
Volcán Cotopaxi
Río Napo
Volcán Tungurahua
Río Daule
Río Pastaza
Guayaquil
Cordillera de los Andes
Volcán Chimborazo
Cuenca
Océano Pacífico
Machala
Loja
PERÚ
La ciudad de Quito y la Cordillera de los Andes

Catedral de Guayaquil

recursos
WB pp. 33–34 | VM pp. 229–230 | vhlcentral.com Lección 3

TEACHING OPTIONS

Heritage Speakers If a heritage speaker is of Ecuadorian origin or has visited Ecuador, ask him or her to share some of his or her favorite experiences there. Encourage the rest of the class to ask follow-up questions, and if a particular topic piques their interest, to find out more online.

Language Notes Remind students that **km²** is the abbreviation for **kilómetros cuadrados** and that **millas²** is the abbreviation for **millas cuadradas**. Ask a volunteer to explain why **kilómetros** takes **cuadrados** and **millas** takes **cuadradas**.

Lugares • Las islas Galápagos

Muchas personas vienen de lejos a visitar las islas Galápagos porque son un verdadero tesoro° ecológico. Aquí Charles Darwin estudió° las especies que inspiraron° sus ideas sobre la evolución. Como las Galápagos están lejos del continente, sus plantas y animales son únicos. Las islas son famosas por sus tortugas° gigantes.

Artes • Oswaldo Guayasamín

Oswaldo Guayasamín fue° uno de los artistas latinoamericanos más famosos del mundo. Fue escultor° y muralista. Su expresivo estilo viene del cubismo y sus temas preferidos son la injusticia y la pobreza° sufridas° por los indígenas de su país.

Madre y niño en azul, 1986, Oswaldo Guayasamín

Deportes • El *trekking*

El sistema montañoso de los Andes cruza° y divide Ecuador en varias regiones. La Sierra, que tiene volcanes, grandes valles y una variedad increíble de plantas y animales, es perfecta para el *trekking*. Muchos turistas visitan Ecuador cada° año para hacer° *trekking* y escalar montañas°.

Lugares • Latitud 0

Hay un monumento en Ecuador, a unos 22 kilómetros (14 millas) de Quito, donde los visitantes están en el hemisferio norte y el hemisferio sur a la vez°. Este monumento se llama la Mitad del Mundo° y es un destino turístico muy popular.

Explosión del volcán Tungurahua en 1999

¿Qué aprendiste? Completa las oraciones con la información correcta.

1. La ciudad más grande (*biggest*) de Ecuador es ____Guayaquil____.
2. La capital de Ecuador es ____Quito____.
3. Unos 4.000.000 de ecuatorianos hablan lenguas indígenas.
4. Darwin estudió el proceso de la evolución en las islas Galápagos.
5. Dos temas del arte de Guayasamín son la pobreza y la injusticia.
6. Un monumento muy popular es la Mitad del Mundo.
7. La Sierra es un lugar perfecto para el trekking.
8. El volcán Cotopaxi es el volcán activo más alto del mundo.

Conexión Internet Investiga estos temas en **vhlcentral.com**.

 Practice more at **vhlcentral.com.**

1. Busca información sobre una ciudad de Ecuador. ¿Te gustaría (*Would you like*) visitar la ciudad? ¿Por qué?
2. Haz una lista de tres animales o plantas que viven sólo en las islas Galápagos. ¿Dónde hay animales o plantas similares?

verdadero tesoro *true treasure* **estudió** *studied* **inspiraron** *inspired* **tortugas** *tortoises* **fue** *was* **escultor** *sculptor* **pobreza** *poverty* **sufridas** *suffered* **cruza** *crosses* **cada** *every* **hacer** *to do* **escalar montañas** *to climb mountains* **a la vez** *at the same time* **Mitad del Mundo** *Equatorial Line Monument (lit. Midpoint of the World)*

Las islas Galápagos
→ Bring in books, magazines, or Internet articles about the Galapagos Islands for students to read. For more information about **las islas Galápagos**, you may want to play the *Panorama cultural* video footage for this lesson.

Oswaldo Guayasamín
The name **Guayasamín** means *white bird* in Quichua. The artist took this name out of solidarity with his Incan ancestors. If possible, bring reproductions of some of **Guayasamín's** work to class. Show a variety of his paintings and encourage students to talk about what the artist's social and political stance might be.

El *trekking* Although the word **senderismo** is widely used, *trekking* is one of many English words that have been incorporated into Spanish. Generally, these are words for phenomena whose popularity originated in the English-speaking world. Some words enter Spanish without much change: **camping, marketing**. Others are modified to match Spanish spelling patterns, as **líder** (*leader*) or **mítin** (*meeting*).

Latitud 0 Bring in a globe and have students find Ecuador and point out its location on the equator.

Conexión Internet Students will find supporting Internet activities and links at **vhlcentral.com**.

TEACHING OPTIONS

Variación léxica A word that the Quichua language has contributed to English is *jerky* (salted, dried meat), which comes from the Quichua word **charqui**. The Quichua-speaking peoples of the Andean highlands had perfected techniques for "freeze-drying" both vegetable tubers and meat before the first Spaniards arrived in the region. (Freeze-dried potatoes, called **chuño**, are a staple in the diet of the inhabitants of the Andes.)

In Ecuador and throughout the rest of South America, **charqui** is the word used to name meat preserved by drying. **Charqui** is an important component in the national cuisines of South America, and in Argentina, Uruguay, and Brazil, its production is a major industry. In other parts of the Spanish-speaking world, you may hear the terms **tasajo** or **carne seca** used instead of **charqui**.

Instructional Resources
Supersite: Audio (Textbook & Lab MP3s); Testing Program (Tests, MP3s)
WebSAM
Lab Manual, p. 18

La familia

el/la abuelo/a	grandfather/grandmother
los abuelos	grandparents
el apellido	last name; surname
el/la bisabuelo/a	great-grandfather/great-grandmother
el/la cuñado/a	brother-in-law/sister-in-law
el/la esposo/a	husband; wife; spouse
la familia	family
el/la gemelo/a	twin
el/la hermanastro/a	stepbrother/stepsister
el/la hermano/a	brother/sister
el/la hijastro/a	stepson/stepdaughter
el/la hijo/a	son/daughter
los hijos	children
la madrastra	stepmother
la madre	mother
el/la medio/a hermano/a	half-brother/half-sister
el/la nieto/a	grandson/granddaughter
la nuera	daughter-in-law
el padrastro	stepfather
el padre	father
los padres	parents
los parientes	relatives
el/la primo/a	cousin
el/la sobrino/a	nephew/niece
el/la suegro/a	father-in-law/mother-in-law
el/la tío/a	uncle/aunt
el yerno	son-in-law

Otras personas

el/la amigo/a	friend
la gente	people
el/la muchacho/a	boy/girl
el/la niño/a	child
el/la novio/a	boyfriend/girlfriend
la persona	person

Profesiones

el/la artista	artist
el/la doctor(a), el/la médico/a	doctor; physician
el/la ingeniero/a	engineer
el/la periodista	journalist
el/la programador(a)	computer programmer

Adjetivos

alto/a	tall
antipático/a	unpleasant
bajo/a	short (in height)
bonito/a	pretty
buen, bueno/a	good
delgado/a	thin; slender
difícil	difficult; hard
fácil	easy
feo/a	ugly
gordo/a	fat
gran, grande	big; large
guapo/a	handsome; good-looking
importante	important
inteligente	intelligent
interesante	interesting
joven (sing.), jóvenes (pl.)	young
mal, malo/a	bad
mismo/a	same
moreno/a	brunet(te)
mucho/a	much; many; a lot of
pelirrojo/a	red-haired
pequeño/a	small
rubio/a	blond(e)
simpático/a	nice; likeable
tonto/a	silly; foolish
trabajador(a)	hard-working
viejo/a	old

Nacionalidades

alemán, alemana	German
argentino/a	Argentine
canadiense	Canadian
chino/a	Chinese
costarricense	Costa Rican
cubano/a	Cuban
ecuatoriano/a	Ecuadorian
español(a)	Spanish
estadounidense	from the U.S.
francés, francesa	French
inglés, inglesa	English
italiano/a	Italian
japonés, japonesa	Japanese
mexicano/a	Mexican
norteamericano/a	(North) American
puertorriqueño/a	Puerto Rican
ruso/a	Russian

Verbos

abrir	to open
aprender (a + *inf.*)	to learn
asistir (a)	to attend
beber	to drink
comer	to eat
compartir	to share
comprender	to understand
correr	to run
creer (en)	to believe (in)
deber (+ *inf.*)	should; must; ought to
decidir (+ *inf.*)	to decide
describir	to describe
escribir	to write
leer	to read
recibir	to receive
tener	to have
venir	to come
vivir	to live

Possessive adjectives	See page 85.
Expressions with *tener*	See page 93.
Expresiones útiles	See page 75.

 Audio: Vocabulary

recursos

LM p. 18 vhlcentral.com Lección 3

Los pasatiempos

4

Communicative Goals

You will learn how to:

- **Talk about pastimes, weekend activities, and sports**
- **Make plans and invitations**

Lesson Goals

In **Lección 4**, students will be introduced to the following:
- names of sports and other pastimes
- names of places in a city
- soccer rivalries
- Mexican golfer **Lorena Ochoa** and Argentine soccer player **Lionel Messi**
- present tense of **ir**
- the contraction **al**
- **ir a** + [*infinitive*]
- present tense of common stem-changing verbs
- verbs with irregular **yo** forms
- predicting content from visual elements
- a video about soccer in Spain
- cultural, historical, economic, and geographic information about Mexico

A primera vista Ask these additional questions to personalize the photo: **¿Te gusta practicar los deportes? ¿Crees que son importantes los pasatiempos? ¿Estudias mucho los sábados y domingos? ¿Bailas? ¿Lees? ¿Escuchas música?**

Teaching Tip Look for these icons for additional communicative practice:

→👥←	Interpretive communication
←👥←	Presentational communication
👥↔	Interpersonal communication

A PRIMERA VISTA
- ¿Es esta persona un atleta o un artista?
- ¿En qué tiene interés, en el ciclismo o en el tenis?
- ¿Es viejo? ¿Es delgado?
- ¿Tiene frío o calor?

INSTRUCTIONAL RESOURCES

Supersite (vhlcentral.com)
Video: ***Fotonovela*, Flash cultura*, Panorama cultural****
**Also on DVD*
Audio: Textbook and Lab MP3 Files (*also on CD*)
Activity Pack: Information Gap Activities, games, additional activity handouts

Resources: Textbook Answer Key, WB/VM/LM Answer Key, Scripts, Translations, **Vocabulario adicional**, lesson plans, **Estructura** *PowerPoints*, Overheads
Testing Program: Quizzes, Tests, Exams, MP3s (*also on Test Generator CD*)

Learning Management System (Assignment Task Manager, Gradebook)
WebSAM (online Workbook/Video Manual/ Lab Manual)
Workbook/Video Manual
Lab Manual

Los pasatiempos

Más vocabulario

el béisbol	baseball
el ciclismo	cycling
el esquí (acuático)	(water) skiing
el fútbol americano	football
el golf	golf
el hockey	hockey
la natación	swimming
el tenis	tennis
el vóleibol	volleyball
el equipo	team
el parque	park
el partido	game; match
la plaza	city or town square
andar en patineta	to skateboard
bucear	to scuba dive
escalar montañas (f., pl.)	to climb mountains
esquiar	to ski
ganar	to win
ir de excursión	to go on a hike
practicar deportes (m., pl.)	to play sports
escribir una carta/ un mensaje electrónico	to write a letter/ an e-mail
leer correo electrónico	to read e-mail
leer una revista	to read a magazine
deportivo/a	sports-related

Variación léxica

piscina	⟷	pileta (*Arg.*); alberca (*Méx.*)
baloncesto	⟷	básquetbol (*Amér. L.*)
béisbol	⟷	pelota (*P. Rico, Rep. Dom.*)

recursos

WB pp. 37–38 · LM p. 19 · 🄢 vhlcentral.com Lección 4

Image labels: Lee el periódico. (leer) · Pasea en bicicleta. (pasear) · la pelota · el fútbol · la jugadora · Visitan el monumento. (visitar) · Pasean. (pasear) · Toma el sol. (tomar) · Nada. (nadar) · la piscina · PARQUE MUNICIPAL

Práctica

**Patina en línea.
(patinar)**

el jugador

el baloncesto

1 **Escuchar** Indicate the letter of the activity in Column B that best corresponds to each statement you hear. Two items in Column B will not be used.

A	B
1. __b__	a. leer correo electrónico
2. __d__	b. tomar el sol
3. __f__	c. pasear en bicicleta
4. __c__	d. ir a un partido de fútbol americano
5. __g__	e. escribir una carta
6. __h__	f. practicar muchos deportes
	g. nadar
	h. ir de excursión

2 **Ordenar** Order these activities according to what you hear in the narration.

__5__	a. pasear en bicicleta	__3__	d. tomar el sol
__1__	b. nadar	__6__	e. practicar deportes
__4__	c. leer una revista	__2__	f. patinar en línea

3 **¿Cierto o falso?** Indicate whether each statement is **cierto** or **falso** based on the illustration.

	Cierto	Falso
1. Un hombre nada en la piscina.	◉	○
2. Un hombre lee una revista.	○	◉
3. Un chico pasea en bicicleta.	◉	○
4. Dos muchachos esquían.	○	◉
5. Una mujer y dos niños visitan un monumento.	◉	○
6. Un hombre bucea.	○	◉
7. Hay un equipo de hockey.	○	◉
8. Una mujer toma el sol.	◉	○

4 **Clasificar** Fill in the chart below with as many terms from **Contextos** as you can. Answers will vary.

Actividades	Deportes	Personas

1 Teaching Tip Have students check their answers with a partner before going over **Actividad 1** with the class.

1 Script 1. No me gusta nadar pero paso mucho tiempo al lado de la piscina. 2. Alicia y yo vamos al estadio a las cuatro. Creemos que nuestro equipo va a ganar. 3. Me gusta patinar en línea, esquiar y practicar el tenis. 4. El ciclismo es mi deporte favorito. 5. Me gusta mucho la natación. Paso mucho tiempo en la piscina. 6. Mi hermana es una gran excursionista.
Textbook MP3s

2 Teaching Tips
- To simplify, prepare the class for listening by having students read the list aloud.
- Ask students if the verbs in the list are conjugated or if they are infinitives. Tell them that the verbs they hear in the audio recording may be in the infinitive or conjugated form.

2 Script Hoy es sábado y mis amigos y yo estamos en el parque. Todos tenemos pasatiempos diferentes. Clara y Daniel nadan en la piscina. Luis patina en línea. Sergio y Paco toman el sol. Dalia lee una revista. Rosa y yo paseamos en bicicleta. Y tú, ¿practicas deportes?
Textbook MP3s

3 Expansion Ask students to write three additional true/false sentences based on the illustration. Have volunteers read sentences aloud for the rest of the class to answer.

4 Expansion Ask students to write three sentences using the words they listed in each category. You can cue students to elicit more responses. Ex: **¿Qué es la natación? (La natación es un deporte.)**

Teaching Tip Ask brief yes/no questions to review vocabulary in **En el centro** and **Más vocabulario**. Ex: **¿Hay muchas diversiones en el centro? No tienen ratos libres los fines de semana, ¿verdad? ¿Pasan ustedes los ratos libres en el museo?**

5 Expansion

• Have students read each item aloud and ask individuals to respond. After each answer is given, ask a different student to verify whether the answer is correct, using a complete sentence. Do the first verification yourself to model possible student responses. Ex: —**Tomamos una limonada.** —**Es un café/restaurante.** —**Sí. En un café/restaurante tomamos una limonada.**

• To challenge students, ask them to convert items into yes/no questions. Ex: **¿Tomamos una limonada en el café? (Sí.) ¿Vemos una película en el restaurante? (No.)** Have pairs take turns answering questions.

6 Teaching Tip Quickly review the verbs in the list. Make sure that students understand the meaning of **¿Qué haces…?** Tell them that they will use this phrase throughout the activity.

6 Expansion

• Ask additional questions and have volunteers answer. Ex: **¿Qué haces en la residencia estudiantil?** Suggested places: **un apartamento, la casa de un amigo/una amiga, el centro, un gimnasio**

• ↔ Write a new list of places on the board. Then, in pairs, have students perform the activity again, this time including information specific to a Spanish-speaking country. Their partner will guess where they are. Ex: —**¿Qué haces cuando estás en un restaurante?** —**Como paella.** —**¿Estás en España?** —**Sí.**

En el centro

5 Identificar Identify the place where these activities would take place.

modelo

Esquiamos. _Es una montaña._

1. Tomamos una limonada. _Es un café./Es un restaurante._
2. Vemos una película. _Es un cine._
3. Nadamos y tomamos el sol. _Es una piscina./Es un parque._
4. Hay muchos monumentos. _Es un parque./Es una ciudad./Es una plaza._
5. Comemos tacos y fajitas. _Es un restaurante._
6. Miramos pinturas (_paintings_) de Diego Rivera y Frida Kahlo. _Es un museo._
7. Hay mucho tráfico. _Es una ciudad./Es el centro._
8. Practicamos deportes. _Es un gimnasio./Es un parque._

Más vocabulario	
la diversión	_fun activity; entertainment; recreation_
el fin de semana	_weekend_
el pasatiempo	_pastime; hobby_
los ratos libres	_spare (free) time_
el videojuego	_video game_
la iglesia	_church_
el lugar	_place_
ver películas (_f., pl._)	_to watch movies_
favorito/a	_favorite_

6 Preguntar Ask a classmate what he or she does in the places mentioned below. Your classmate will respond using verbs from the word bank. _Answers will vary._

modelo

una plaza

Estudiante 1: ¿Qué haces (_do you do_) cuando estás en una plaza?
Estudiante 2: Camino por la plaza y miro a las personas.

beber	escalar	mirar	practicar
caminar	escribir	nadar	tomar
correr	leer	patinar	visitar

1. una biblioteca
2. un estadio
3. una plaza
4. una piscina
5. las montañas
6. un parque
7. un café
8. un museo

S: Practice more at vhlcentral.com.

TEACHING OPTIONS

Extra Practice ↔ Give students five minutes to write a short description of three to five sentences about a typical weekend: what they do and where, and with whom they spend time. Circulate through the class and help with unfamiliar vocabulary. Have volunteers share their paragraphs with the class. Then have the class discuss what a "typical weekend" consists of; compose a description on the board.

Game Have students tell a chain story. For example, one student begins with: **Es el sábado por la mañana y voy [al café].** The next student continues with: **Estoy en el café y tomo una Coca-Cola.** You may need to provide some phrases on the board: **voy a/al/a la…, luego, después.** The story may change location; set a time limit for each response. The game ends after ten minutes or when all students have participated.

Comunicación

7 Crucigrama Your instructor will give you and your partner an incomplete crossword puzzle. Yours has the words your partner needs and vice versa. In order to complete the puzzle, take turns giving each other clues, using definitions, examples, and phrases.

> **modelo**
>
> **2 horizontal:** Es un deporte que practicamos en la piscina.
> **6 vertical:** Es un mensaje que escribimos con lápiz o con pluma.

8 Entrevista In pairs, take turns asking and answering these questions. *Answers will vary.*

1. ¿Hay un café cerca de la universidad? ¿Dónde está?
2. ¿Cuál es tu restaurante favorito?
3. ¿Te gusta viajar y visitar monumentos? ¿Por qué?
4. ¿Te gusta ir al cine los fines de semana?
5. ¿Cuáles son tus películas favoritas?
6. ¿Te gusta practicar deportes?
7. ¿Cuáles son tus deportes favoritos? ¿Por qué?
8. ¿Cuáles son tus pasatiempos favoritos?

CONSULTA

To review expressions with **gustar**, see **Estructura 2.1**, p. 48.

9 Conversación Using the words and expressions provided, work with a partner to prepare a short conversation about pastimes. *Answers will vary.*

¿a qué hora?	¿con quién(es)?	¿dónde?
¿cómo?	¿cuándo?	¿qué?

> **modelo**
>
> **Estudiante 1:** ¿Cuándo patinas en línea?
> **Estudiante 2:** Patino en línea los domingos. Y tú, ¿patinas en línea?
> **Estudiante 1:** No, no me gusta patinar en línea. Me gusta practicar el béisbol.

10 Pasatiempos In pairs, tell each other what pastimes three of your friends and family members enjoy. Be prepared to share with the class any pastimes you noticed they have in common. *Answers will vary.*

> **modelo**
>
> **Estudiante 1:** Mi hermana pasea mucho en bicicleta, pero mis padres practican la natación. Mi hermano no nada, pero visita muchos museos.
> **Estudiante 2:** Mi primo lee muchas revistas, pero no practica muchos deportes. Mis tíos esquían y practican el golf...

TEACHING OPTIONS

Large Group Have students write down six activities they enjoy and then circulate the room to collect signatures from others who enjoy the same activities (**¿Te gusta…? Firma aquí, por favor.**). Ask volunteers to report back to the class.

Game Ask students to take out a piece of paper and write anonymously a set of activities that best corresponds to them. Collect and shuffle the slips of paper. Divide the class into two teams. Pull out and read aloud each slip of paper, and have the teams take turns guessing the student's identity.

7 Teaching Tip Model the different ways that students can give clues. Write **el gimnasio** on the board. Then write: **Es un lugar donde la gente corre. (definición) / En nuestra universidad se llama The Plex. (ejemplo) / un lugar para practicar deportes (frase)** Explain that while the definition and phrase could apply to other places, the person receiving the clue should use the empty letter spaces to figure out the answer.

7 Expansion In pairs, have students create another type of word puzzle, such as a word search. Tell them to use vocabulary related to sports and pastimes.

8 Teaching Tip Before beginning the activity, review the verb **gustar**.

8 Expansion Have the same pairs ask each other additional questions. Then ask volunteers to share their mini-conversations with the class.

9 Teaching Tip After students have asked and answered questions, ask volunteers to report their partners' activities back to the class. The partners should verify the information and provide at least one additional detail.

10 Expansion
- Ask volunteers to share any pastimes they and their partners, friends, and families have in common.
- In pairs, have students write sentences about the pastimes of a famous person without using their name. Encourage them to also recycle the descriptive adjectives and adjectives of nationality they learned in Lesson 3. Then have them work with another pair, asking questions as necessary, to guess the identity of the person being described.

Fútbol, cenotes y mole

Maru, Miguel, Jimena y Marissa visitan un cenote, mientras Felipe y Juan Carlos van a un partido de fútbol.

PERSONAJES MIGUEL PABLO

Video: *Fotonovela*
Record and Compare

1

MIGUEL Buenos días a todos.

TÍA ANA MARÍA Hola Miguel. Maru, ¿qué van a hacer hoy?

MARU Miguel y yo vamos a llevar a Marissa a un cenote.

2

MARISSA ¿No vamos a nadar? ¿Qué es un cenote?

MIGUEL Sí, sí vamos a nadar. Un cenote... difícil de explicar. Es una piscina natural en un hueco profundo.

MARU ¡Ya vas a ver! Seguro que te va a gustar.

(*unos minutos después*)

EDUARDO Hay un partido de fútbol en el parque. ¿Quieren ir conmigo?

PABLO Y conmigo. Si no consigo más jugadores, nuestro equipo va a perder.

3

ANA MARÍA Marissa, ¿qué te gusta hacer? ¿Escalar montañas? ¿Ir de excursión?

MARISSA Sí, me gusta ir de excursión y practicar el esquí acuático. Y usted, ¿qué prefiere hacer en sus ratos libres?

5

6

4

PABLO Mi mamá tiene muchos pasatiempos y actividades.

EDUARDO Sí. Ella nada y juega al tenis y al golf.

PABLO Va al cine y a los museos.

ANA MARÍA Sí, salgo mucho los fines de semana.

FELIPE ¿Recuerdas el restaurante del mole?

EDUARDO ¿Qué restaurante?

JIMENA El mole de mi tía Ana María es mi favorito.

MARU Chicos, ya es hora. ¡Vamos!

 ANA MARÍA
 MARU
 MARISSA
 EDUARDO
 FELIPE
 JUAN CARLOS
 JIMENA
DON GUILLERMO

7

(más tarde, en el parque)

PABLO No puede ser. ¡Cinco a uno!

FELIPE ¡Vamos a jugar! Si perdemos, compramos el almuerzo. Y si ganamos...

EDUARDO ¡Empezamos!

8

(mientras tanto, en el cenote)

MARISSA ¿Hay muchos cenotes en México?

MIGUEL Sólo en la península de Yucatán.

MARISSA ¡Vamos a nadar!

9

(Los chicos visitan a don Guillermo, un vendedor de paletas heladas.)

JUAN CARLOS Don Guillermo, ¿dónde podemos conseguir un buen mole?

FELIPE Eduardo y Pablo van a pagar el almuerzo. Y yo voy a pedir un montón de comida.

10

FELIPE Sí, éste es el restaurante. Recuerdo la comida.

EDUARDO Oye, Pablo... No tengo...

PABLO No te preocupes, hermanito.

FELIPE ¿Qué buscas? *(muestra la cartera de Pablo)* ¿Esto?

recursos

VM
pp. 201–202

vhlcentral.com
Lección 4

Expresiones útiles

Making invitations

Hay un partido de fútbol en el parque. ¿Quieren ir conmigo?
There's a soccer game in the park. Do you want to come with me?

¡Yo puedo jugar!
I can play!

Mmm... no quiero.
Hmm... I don't want to.

Lo siento, pero no puedo.
I'm sorry, but I can't.

¡Vamos a nadar!
Let's go swimming!

Sí, vamos.
Yes, let's go.

Making plans

¿Qué van a hacer hoy?
What are you going to do today?

Vamos a llevar a Marissa a un cenote.
We are taking Marissa to a cenote.

Vamos a comprar unas paletas heladas.
We're going to buy some popsicles.

Vamos a jugar. Si perdemos, compramos el almuerzo.
Let's play. If we lose, we'll buy lunch.

Talking about pastimes

¿Qué te gusta hacer? ¿Escalar montañas? ¿Ir de excursión?
What do you like to do? Mountain climbing? Hiking?

Sí, me gusta ir de excursión y practicar esquí acuático.
Yes, I like hiking and water skiing.

Y usted, ¿qué prefiere hacer en sus ratos libres?
And you, what do you like to do in your free time?

Salgo mucho los fines de semana.
I go out a lot on the weekends.

Voy al cine y a los museos.
I go to the movies and to museums.

Additional vocabulary

la cartera *wallet* **el hueco** *hole*
un montón de *a lot of*

¿Qué paso?

1 Escoger Choose the answer that best completes each sentence.

1. Marissa, Maru y Miguel desean _____ a __.
 a. nadar b. correr por el parque c. leer el periódico

2. A Marissa le gusta _____ c __.
 a. el tenis b. el vóleibol c. ir de excursión y practicar esquí acuático

3. A la tía Ana María le gusta _____ b __.
 a. jugar al hockey b. nadar y jugar al tenis y al golf c. hacer ciclismo

4. Pablo y Eduardo pierden el partido de _____ a __.
 a. fútbol b. béisbol c. baloncesto

5. Juan Carlos y Felipe desean _____ c __.
 a. patinar b. esquiar c. comer mole

2 Identificar Identify the person who would make each statement.

1. A mí me gusta nadar, pero no sé qué es un cenote. __Marissa__
2. Mamá va al cine y al museo en sus ratos libres. Pablo/Eduardo
3. Yo voy a pedir mucha comida. __Felipe__
4. ¿Quieren ir a jugar al fútbol con nosotros en el parque? Eduardo/Pablo
5. Me gusta salir los fines de semana. tía Ana María

MARISSA
FELIPE
EDUARDO
PABLO
TÍA ANA MARÍA

3 Preguntas Answer the questions using the information from the **Fotonovela**.

1. ¿Qué van a hacer Miguel y Maru?
 Miguel y Maru van a llevar a Marissa a un cenote.
2. ¿Adónde van Felipe y Juan Carlos mientras sus amigos van al cenote?
 Felipe y Juan Carlos van a jugar al fútbol con Pablo y Eduardo.
3. ¿Quién gana el partido de fútbol?
 Felipe y Juan Carlos ganan el partido de fútbol.
4. ¿Quiénes van al cenote con Maru y Miguel?
 Marissa y Jimena van al cenote con Maru y Miguel.

4 Conversación With a partner, prepare a conversation in which you talk about pastimes and invite each other to do some activity together. Use these expressions and also look at **Expresiones útiles** on the previous page. Answers will vary.

¿A qué hora?	**¿Dónde?** *Where?*	**Nos vemos a las siete.**
(At) What time?	**No puedo porque...**	*See you at seven.*
contigo *with you*	*I can't because...*	

▶ ¿Eres aficionado/a a...? ▶ ¿Por qué no...? ▶ ¿Qué vas a hacer esta noche?
▶ ¿Te gusta...? ▶ ¿Quieres... conmigo?

 Practice more at **vhlcentral.com**.

NOTA CULTURAL

Mole is a typical sauce in Mexican cuisine. It is made from pumpkin seeds, chile, and chocolate, and it is usually served with chicken, beef, or pork. To learn more about **mole**, go to page 252.

NOTA CULTURAL

Cenotes are deep, freshwater sinkholes found in caves throughout the Yucatán peninsula. They were formed in prehistoric times by the erosion and collapse of cave walls. The Mayan civilization considered the **cenotes** sacred, and performed rituals there. Today, they are popular destinations for swimming and diving.

NATIONAL
communication
STANDARDS

Pronunciación

**Audio: Concepts, Activities
Record & Compare**
Word stress and accent marks

pe-**lí**-cu-la	e-di-**fi**-cio	**ver**	**yo**

Every Spanish syllable contains at least one vowel. When two vowels are joined in the same syllable they form a **diphthong***. A **monosyllable** is a word formed by a single syllable.

bi-blio-**te**-ca	vi-si-**tar**	**par**-que	**fút**-bol

The syllable of a Spanish word that is pronounced most emphatically is the "stressed" syllable.

pe-**lo**-ta	pis-**ci**-na	**ra**-tos	**ha**-blan

Words that end in **n**, **s**, or a **vowel** are usually stressed on the next to last syllable.

na-ta-**ción**	pa-**pá**	in-**glés**	Jo-**sé**

If words that end in **n**, **s**, or a **vowel** are stressed on the last syllable, they must carry an accent mark on the stressed syllable.

bai-**lar**	es-pa-**ñol**	u-ni-ver-si-**dad**	tra-ba-ja-**dor**

Words that do *not* end in **n**, **s**, or a **vowel** are usually stressed on the last syllable.

béis-bol	**lá**-piz	**ár**-bol	**Gó**-mez

If words that do *not* end in **n**, **s**, or a **vowel** are stressed on the next to last syllable, they must carry an accent mark on the stressed syllable.

The two vowels that form a diphthong are either both weak or one is weak and the other is strong.

> En la unión
> está la fuerza.[2]

Práctica Pronounce each word, stressing the correct syllable. Then give the word stress rule for each word.

1. profesor
2. Puebla
3. ¿Cuántos?
4. Mazatlán
5. examen
6. ¿Cómo?
7. niños
8. Guadalajara
9. programador
10. México
11. están
12. geografía

Oraciones Read the conversation aloud to practice word stress.

MARINA Hola, Carlos. ¿Qué tal?
CARLOS Bien. Oye, ¿a qué hora es el partido de fútbol?
MARINA Creo que es a las siete.
CARLOS ¿Quieres ir?
MARINA Lo siento, pero no puedo. Tengo que estudiar biología.

> Quien ríe
> de último, ríe mejor.[1]

Refranes Read these sayings aloud to practice word stress.

1 He who laughs last, laughs best.
2 United we stand.

recursos

LM
p. 20

vhlcentral.com
Lección 4

Section Goals

In **Pronunciación**, students will be introduced to:
- the concept of word stress
- diphthongs and monosyllables
- accent marks

Instructional Resources
Supersite: Audio (Textbook and Lab MP3 Files); Resources (Scripts, Answer Keys)
WebSAM
Lab Manual, p. 20

Teaching Tips
- Write **película**, **edificio**, **ver**, and **yo** on the board. Model their pronunciation. Ask the class to identify the diphthongs and the monosyllables.
- Remind students of the strong and weak vowels that they learned about in **Lección 3**. Strong: **a, e, o**; Weak: **i, u**
- Write **biblioteca**, **visitar**, and **parque** on the board. Model their pronunciation, then ask which syllables are stressed.
- As you go through each point in the explanation, write the example words on the board, pronounce them, and have students repeat. Then, ask students to provide words they learned in **Lecciones 1–3** and **Contextos** and **Fotonovela** of this lesson that exemplify each point.

Práctica/Oraciones/Refranes
These exercises are recorded on the *Textbook MP3s*. You may want to play the audio so that students practice listening to Spanish spoken by speakers other than yourself.

TEACHING OPTIONS

Extra Practice Write on the board a list of Mexican place names. Have the class pronounce each name, paying particular attention to word stress. Ex: **Campeche, Durango, Culiacán, Tepic, Chichén Itzá, Zacatecas, Colima, Nayarit, San Luis Potosí, Sonora, Puebla, Morelos, Veracruz, Toluca, Guanajuato, Pachuca, El Tajín, Chetumal.** Model pronunciation as necessary.

Small Groups On the board, write a list of words that students already know. Then have the class work in small groups to come up with the word stress rule that applies to each word. Ex: **lápiz, equipo, pluma, Felipe, chicas, comer, mujer, tenis, hombre, libros, papel, parque, béisbol, excursión, deportes, fútbol, pasear, esquí.**

Section Goals

In **Cultura**, students will:
- read about soccer rivalries
- learn sports-related terms
- read about **Lionel Messi** and **Lorena Ochoa**
- read about renowned athletes

Instructional Resources
Supersite/DVD: *Flash cultura*
Supersite: Resources (Scripts, Translations, Answer Keys)
WebSAM
Video Manual, pp. 273–274

En detalle

Antes de leer Ask students to predict the content of this reading based on the title and photos. Have them share what they know about these teams or about other sports rivalries.

Lectura
- Use the map on page 66 to point out the locations of Barcelona and Madrid. Briefly explain that Spain's regional cultures (Basque, Catalan, Galician, etc.) were at odds with the authoritarian, centralized approach of **Franco's** regime, which banned the public use of regional languages. Point out that the nickname **Barça** is Catalan, which is why it has a cedilla to indicate a soft **c**.
- Describe the stadiums: **Camp Nou** (Catalan for *new field*) holds about 100,000 spectators and is the largest soccer stadium in Europe. Madrid's **Estadio Santiago Bernabéu,** named after an ex-player and club president, can seat about 80,000.
- Remind students that **el fútbol** is *soccer* and **el fútbol americano** is *football*.

Después de leer Ask students what facts in this reading are new or surprising to them.

1 Expansion To challenge students, ask them to write two additional items. Then have them exchange papers with a classmate and complete the activity.

EN DETALLE

Additional Reading
Video: *Flash cultura*

Real Madrid y Barça: rivalidad total

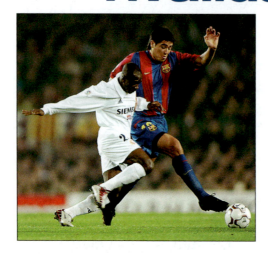

Soccer in Spain is a force to be reckoned with, and no two teams draw more attention than **Real Madrid** and the **Fútbol Club Barcelona**. Whether the venue is Madrid's **Santiago Bernabéu** or Barcelona's **Camp Nou**, the two cities shut down for the showdown, paralyzed by **fútbol** fever. A ticket to the actual game is always the hottest ticket in town.

The rivalry between **Real Madrid** and **Barça** is about more than soccer. As the two biggest, most powerful cities in Spain, Barcelona and Madrid are constantly compared to one another and have a natural rivalry. There is also a political component to the dynamic. Barcelona, with its distinct language and culture, has long struggled for increased autonomy from Madrid's centralized government. Under Francisco Franco's rule (1939–1975), when repression of the Catalan identity was at its height, a game between **Real Madrid** and **FC Barcelona** was wrapped up with all the symbolism of the regime versus the resistance, even though both teams suffered casualties in Spain's civil war and the subsequent Franco dictatorship.

Although the dictatorship is far behind, the momentum of all those decades of competition still transforms both cities into a frenzied, tense panic leading up to the game. Once the final score is announced, one of those cities is transformed again, this time into the best party in the country.

Rivalidades del fútbol

Argentina: Boca Juniors vs River Plate
México: Águilas del América vs Chivas del Guadalajara
Chile: Colo Colo vs Universidad de Chile
Guatemala: Comunicaciones vs Municipal
Uruguay: Peñarol vs Nacional
Colombia: Millonarios vs Independiente Santa Fe

ACTIVIDADES

1 ¿Cierto o falso? Indicate whether each statement is **cierto** or **falso**. Correct the false statements.

1. People from Spain don't like soccer. **Falso.** People from Spain like soccer very much.
2. Madrid and Barcelona are the most important cities in Spain. **Cierto.**
3. Santiago Bernabéu is a stadium in Barcelona. **Falso.** It is a stadium in Madrid.
4. The rivalry between Real Madrid and FC Barcelona is not only in soccer. **Cierto.**
5. Barcelona has resisted Madrid's centralized government. **Cierto.**
6. Only the FC Barcelona team was affected by the civil war. **Falso.** Both teams were affected by the civil war.
7. During Franco's regime, the Catalan culture thrived. **Falso.** Catalan culture was repressed during Franco's regime.
8. There are many famous rivalries between soccer teams in the Spanish-speaking world. **Cierto.**
9. River Plate is a popular team from Argentina. **Cierto.**
10. Comunicaciones and Peñarol are famous rivals in Guatemala. **Falso.** Comunicaciones and Municipal are important rivals in Guatemala.

TEACHING OPTIONS

Project Have small groups choose famous soccer rivalries, then split up to research and create a web page for each of the rival teams. The pages should feature each team's colors, players, home stadium, official song, and other significant or interesting information. Have the groups present their rivals' web pages to the class.

¡Goooooooool! Explain that sportscasters in the Spanish-speaking world are famous for their theatrical commentaries. One example is **Andrés Cantor**, who provides commentary for soccer matches on Spanish-language stations in the U.S. Each time a goal is scored, fans know they can hear a drawn-out bellow of **¡Goooooooool!** Cantor's call, which can last for nearly thirty seconds, was made into a ringtone for cell phones in the U.S.

ASÍ SE DICE

Los deportes

el/la árbitro/a	referee
el/la atleta	athlete
la bola; el balón	la pelota
el campeón/ la campeona	champion
la carrera	race
competir	to compete
empatar	to draw; to tie
la medalla	medal
el/la mejor	the best
mundial	worldwide
el torneo	tournament

EL MUNDO HISPANO

Atletas importantes

World-renowned Hispanic athletes:

- **Rafael Nadal** (España) is one of the best tennis players in the world. His medals include six Grand Slam singles titles and the 2008 Olympic gold medal in singles.

- **Dayron Robles** (Cuba), an Olympic champion hurdler, holds the world record in the 110-meter hurdles.

- **Carolina Ruiz Castillo** (España), an alpine skier, competed in the 2006 and 2010 Olympics.

- **Paola Milagros Espinosa Sánchez** (México) has made two Olympic appearances (2004, 2008) in diving. She and her partner, Tatiana Ortiz, took home the bronze medal in 2008.

PERFIL

Lionel Messi y Lorena Ochoa

Lionel Andrés Messi is considered one of the best soccer players of his generation. Born in 1987 in Argentina, Messi suffered a hormone deficiency that conflicted with his athletic dreams. He moved to Spain as a teenager and, at just 17, played his first game for the team **Fútbol Club Barcelona**. He is now the highest-paid player in the Spanish league.

Mexican golfer **Lorena Ochoa**, born in 1981, took up the sport at the age of five and won her first national event two years later. Winner of the LPGA Tour Player of the Year award every year from 2006-2009, Ochoa was ranked number one worldwide among female golfers when she retired in 2010.

Conexión Internet

¿Qué deportes son populares en los países hispanos?

Go to **vhlcentral.com** to find more cultural information related to this **Cultura** section.

ACTIVIDADES

2 **Comprensión** Write the name of the athlete described in each sentence.

1. Es un jugador de fútbol de Argentina. _Lionel Messi_
2. Es una chica que practica el golf. _Lorena Ochoa_
3. Es una chica española a la que le gusta esquiar. _Carolina Ruiz Castillo_
4. Es una chica mexicana que practica un deporte en la piscina. _Paola Milagros Espinosa Sánchez_

3 **¿Quién es?** Write a short paragraph describing an athlete that you like, but do not mention their name. What do they look like? What sport do they play? Where do they live? Read your description to the class to see if they can guess who they are.

Answers will vary.

recursos

VM pp. 273–274

vhlcentral.com Lección 4

Practice more at **vhlcentral.com**.

Section Goals

In **Estructura 4.1**, students will learn:
• the present tense of **ir**
• the contraction **al**
• **ir a** + [*infinitive*] to express future events
• **vamos a** to express *let's...*

Instructional Resources

Supersite: Audio (Lab MP3 Files); Resources (*PowerPoints*, Activity Pack, Scripts, Answer Keys); Testing Program (Quizzes)
WebSAM
Workbook, pp. 39–40
Lab Manual, p. 21

Teaching Tips

• Write your next day's schedule on the board. Ex: **8:00— la biblioteca; 12:00—comer.** Explain where you are going or what you are going to do, using the verb **ir.** Ask volunteers about their schedules, using forms of **ir.**
• Add a visual aspect to this grammar presentation. Write names of Spanish-speaking countries on construction paper, and pin up the papers at different points around the classroom in order to make a "map." Point to your destination "country," and as you pantomime flying there, ask students: **¿Adónde voy? (Vas a Chile.)** Once there, act out an activity, asking: **¿Qué voy a hacer? (Vas a esquiar.)**
• Practice **vamos a** to express the idea of *let's* by asking volunteers to suggest things to do. Ex: **Tengo hambre. (Vamos a la cafetería.)**

Ayuda Point out the difference in usage between **dónde** and **adónde.** Ask: **¿Adónde va el presidente de los Estados Unidos para descansar? (Va a Camp David.) ¿Dónde está Camp David? (Está en Maryland.)**

4.1 # Present tense of **ir** **Tutorial**

ANTE TODO The verb **ir** (*to go*) is irregular in the present tense. Note that, except for the **yo** form (**voy**) and the lack of a written accent on the **vosotros** form (**vais**), the endings are the same as those for regular present tense **-ar** verbs.

The verb ir (to go)

Singular forms		Plural forms	
yo	**voy**	nosotros/as	**vamos**
tú	**vas**	vosotros/as	**vais**
Ud./él/ella	**va**	Uds./ellos/ellas	**van**

▸ **Ir** is often used with the preposition **a** (*to*). If **a** is followed by the definite article **el**, they combine to form the contraction **al**. If **a** is followed by the other definite articles (**la, las, los**), there is no contraction.

a + el = al

Voy **al** parque con Juan.
I'm going to the park with Juan.

Mis amigos van **a las** montañas.
My friends are going to the mountains.

▸ The construction **ir a** + [*infinitive*] is used to talk about actions that are going to happen in the future. It is equivalent to the English *to be going* + [*infinitive*].

Va a leer el periódico.
He is going to read the newspaper.

Van a pasear por el pueblo.
They are going to walk around town.

¡Voy a ir con ellos!

Ella va al cine y a los museos.

▸ **Vamos a** + [*infinitive*] can also express the idea of *let's* (*do something*).

Vamos a pasear.
Let's take a stroll.

¡**Vamos a** ver!
Let's see!

CONSULTA

To review the contraction **de** + **el**, see **Estructura 1.3**, pp. 20–21.

AYUDA

When asking a question that contains a form of the verb **ir**, remember to use **adónde**:
¿Adónde vas?
(To) Where are you going?

recursos

WB
pp. 39–40

LM
p. 21

vhlcentral.com
Lección 4

 ¡INTÉNTALO! Provide the present tense forms of **ir.**

1. Ellos ___van___.
2. Yo ___voy___.
3. Tu novio ___va___.
4. Adela ___va___.
5. Mi prima y yo ___vamos___.
6. Tú ___vas___.
7. Ustedes ___van___.
8. Nosotros ___vamos___.
9. Usted ___va___.
10. Nosotras ___vamos___.
11. Miguel ___va___.
12. Ellas ___van___.

TEACHING OPTIONS

TPR Invent gestures to act out the activities mentioned in **Lección 4**. Ex: **leer el periódico** (act out reading and holding a newspaper), **patinar** (skate), **nadar** (move arms as if swimming). Signal individuals to gesture appropriately as you cue activities with **Vamos a.** Keep a brisk pace.
Pairs ←👥→ Have students form pairs and tell them they are going somewhere with a friend. On paper strips, write varying dollar amounts, ranging from three dollars to five thousand. Have each pair draw out a dollar amount at random and tell the class where they will go and what they will do with the money they've drawn. Encourage creativity. Ex: **Tenemos seis dólares. Vamos a McDonald's para comer. Ella va a cenar, pero yo voy a beber agua porque no tenemos más dinero./Tenemos cinco mil dólares. Vamos a cenar en París…**

Práctica Practice more at vhlcentral.com.

1 **¿Adónde van?** Everyone in your neighborhood is dashing off to various places. Say where they are going.

1. la señora Castillo / el centro La señora Castillo va al centro.
2. las hermanas Gómez / la piscina Las hermanas Gómez van a la piscina.
3. tu tío y tu papá / el partido de fútbol Tu tío y tu papá van al partido de fútbol.
4. yo / el Museo de Arte Moderno (Yo) Voy al Museo de Arte Moderno.
5. nosotros / el restaurante Miramar (Nosotros) Vamos al restaurante Miramar.

2 **¿Qué van a hacer?** These sentences describe what several students in a college hiking club are doing today. Use **ir a** + [*infinitive*] to say that they are also going to do the same activities tomorrow.

modelo

Martín y Rodolfo nadan en la piscina.
Van a nadar en la piscina mañana también.

1. Sara lee una revista. Va a leer una revista mañana también.
2. Yo practico deportes. Voy a practicar deportes mañana también.
3. Ustedes van de excursión. Van a ir de excursión mañana también.
4. El presidente del club patina. Va a patinar mañana también.
5. Tú tomas el sol. Vas a tomar el sol mañana también.
6. Paseamos con nuestros amigos. Vamos a pasear con nuestros amigos mañana también.

3 **Preguntas** With a partner, take turns asking and answering questions about where the people are going and what they are going to do there. Some answers will vary.

modelo

Estudiante 1: ¿Adónde va Estela?
Estudiante 2: Va a la Librería Sol.
Estudiante 1: Va a comprar un libro.

Estela

1. Álex y Miguel
¿Adónde van Álex y Miguel? Van al parque. Van a...

2. mi amigo ¿Adónde va mi amigo? Va al gimnasio. Va a...

3. tú ¿Adónde vas? Voy al partido de tenis. Voy a...

4. los estudiantes
¿Adónde van los estudiantes? Van al estadio. Van a...

5. profesora Torres
¿Adónde va la profesora Torres? Va a la Biblioteca Nacional. Va a...

6. ustedes ¿Adónde van ustedes? Vamos a la piscina. Vamos a...

1 **Teaching Tip** To add a visual aspect to this exercise, bring in photos of people dressed for a particular activity. As you hold up each photo, have the class say where they are going, using the verb **ir**. Ex: Show a photo of a basketball player. (**Va al gimnasio. / Va a un partido.**)

1 **Expansion** After completing the activity, extend each answer with **pero** and a different name or pronoun, and have students complete the sentence. Ex: **La señora Castillo va al centro, pero el señor Castillo... (va al trabajo).**

2 **Expansion**
• Show the same photos you used for **Actividad 1** and ask students to describe what the people are going to do. Ex: **Va a jugar al baloncesto.**
• Ask students about tomorrow's activities. Ex: **¿Qué van a hacer tus amigos mañana? ¿Qué va a hacer tu compañero/a mañana?**

3 **Expansion** Ask pairs to write a riddle using **ir a** + [*infinitive*]. Ex: **Ángela, Laura, Tomás y Manuel van a hacer cosas diferentes. Tomás va a nadar y Laura va a comer, pero no en casa. Uno de los chicos y una de las chicas van a ver una película. ¿Adónde van todos?** Then have pairs exchange papers to solve the riddles.

TEACHING OPTIONS

Heritage Speakers Ask heritage speakers to write six sentences with the verb **ir** indicating places they go on weekends either by themselves or with friends and family. Ex: **Mi familia y yo vamos a visitar a mi abuela los domingos...** Share the descriptions with the class and ask comprehension questions.
Game Have students work in teams to write a brief description of a well-known fictional character's activities for tomorrow, using the verb **ir**. Ex: **Mañana va a dormir de día. Va a caminar de noche. Va a buscar una muchacha bonita. La muchacha va a tener mucho miedo.** Have each team read their description aloud without naming the character. Teams can ask for and share more details about the person as needed. The first team to correctly identify the person (**Es Drácula.**) receives a point. The team with the most points at the end wins.

Comunicación

4

Situaciones Work with a partner and say where you and your friends go in these situations. *Answers will vary.*

1. Cuando deseo descansar…
2. Cuando mi novio/a tiene que estudiar…
3. Si mis compañeros de clase necesitan practicar el español…
4. Si deseo hablar con mis amigos…
5. Cuando tengo dinero (*money*)…
6. Cuando mis amigos y yo tenemos hambre…
7. En mis ratos libres…
8. Cuando mis amigos desean esquiar…
9. Si estoy de vacaciones…
10. Si tengo ganas de leer…

5

Encuesta Your instructor will give you a worksheet. Walk around the class and ask your classmates if they are going to do these activities today. Find one person to answer **Sí** and one to answer **No** for each item and note their names on the worksheet in the appropriate column. Be prepared to report your findings to the class.
Answers will vary.

modelo
Tú: ¿Vas a leer el periódico hoy?
Ana: Sí, voy a leer el periódico hoy.
Luis: No, no voy a leer el periódico hoy.

Actividades	Sí	No
1. comer en un restaurante chino		
2. leer el periódico	Ana	Luis
3. escribir un mensaje electrónico		
4. correr 20 kilómetros		
5. ver una película de terror		
6. pasear en bicicleta		

6

Entrevista Talk to two classmates in order to find out where they are going and what they are going to do on their next vacation. *Answers will vary.*

modelo
Estudiante 1: ¿Adónde vas de vacaciones (*on vacation*)?
Estudiante 2: Voy a Guadalajara con mis amigos.
Estudiante 3: ¿Y qué van a hacer (*to do*) ustedes en Guadalajara?
Estudiante 2: Vamos a visitar unos monumentos y museos. ¿Y tú?

Síntesis

7

Planes Make a schedule of your activities for the weekend. Then, share with a partner. *Answers will vary.*

▶ For each day, list at least three things you have to do.
▶ For each day, list at least two things you will do for fun.
▶ Tell a classmate what your weekend schedule is like. He or she will write down what you say.
▶ Switch roles to see if you have any plans in common.
▶ Take turns asking each other to participate in some of the activities you listed.

TEACHING OPTIONS

Pairs Write these times on the board: **8:00 a.m., 12:00 p.m., 12:45 p.m., 4:00 p.m., 6:00 p.m., 10:00 p.m.** Have student pairs take turns reading a time and suggesting an appropriate activity or place. Ex: **E1: Son las ocho de la mañana. E2: Vamos a correr./Vamos al gimnasio.**
Game Divide the class into teams. Name a category (Ex: **lugares públicos**) and set a time limit of two minutes. The first team member will write down one answer on a piece of paper and pass it to the next person. The paper will continue to be passed from student to student until the two minutes are up. The team with the most words wins.
Video Show the **Fotonovela** episode again to give students more input containing the verb **ir**. Stop the video where appropriate to discuss how **ir** is used to express different ideas.

4.2 Stem-changing verbs: Tutorial

e→ie, o→ue

ANTE TODO Stem-changing verbs deviate from the normal pattern of regular verbs. When stem-changing verbs are conjugated, they have a vowel change in the last syllable of the stem.

CONSULTA

To review the present tense of regular -ar verbs, see **Estructura 2.1**, p. 46.

• • •

To review the present tense of regular -er and -ir verbs, see **Estructura 3.3**, p. 88.

INFINITIVE	VERB STEM	STEM CHANGE	CONJUGATED FORM
empezar volver	empez- volv-	emp**ie**z- v**ue**lv-	emp**ie**zo v**ue**lvo

▶ In many verbs, such as **empezar** (*to begin*), the stem vowel changes from **e** to **ie**. Note that the **nosotros/as** and **vosotros/as** forms don't have a stem change.

The verb empezar (e:ie) (*to begin*)

	Singular forms		Plural forms
yo	emp**ie**zo	nosotros/as	empezamos
tú	emp**ie**zas	vosotros/as	empezáis
Ud./él/ella	emp**ie**za	Uds./ellos/ellas	emp**ie**zan

Los chicos empiezan a hablar de su visita al cenote.

Ellos vuelven a comer en el restaurante.

▶ In many other verbs, such as **volver** (*to return*), the stem vowel changes from **o** to **ue**. The **nosotros/as** and **vosotros/as** forms have no stem change.

The verb volver (o:ue) (*to return*)

	Singular forms		Plural forms
yo	v**ue**lvo	nosotros/as	volvemos
tú	v**ue**lves	vosotros/as	volvéis
Ud./él/ella	v**ue**lve	Uds./ellos/ellas	v**ue**lven

▶ To help you identify stem-changing verbs, they will appear as follows throughout the text:

> empezar (e:ie), volver (o:ue)

Common stem-changing verbs

e:ie		o:ue	
cerrar	to close	almorzar	to have lunch
comenzar (a + *inf.*)	to begin	contar	to count; to tell
empezar (a + *inf.*)	to begin	dormir	to sleep
entender	to understand	encontrar	to find
pensar	to think	mostrar	to show
perder	to lose; to miss	poder (+ *inf.*)	to be able to; can
preferir (+ *inf.*)	to prefer	recordar	to remember
querer (+ *inf.*)	to want; to love	volver	to return

▶ **Jugar** (*to play a sport or a game*) is the only Spanish verb that has a **u:ue** stem change. **Jugar** is followed by **a** + [*definite article*] when the name of a sport or game is mentioned.

Ella juega al tenis y al golf.

Los chicos juegan al fútbol.

▶ **Comenzar** and **empezar** require the preposition **a** when they are followed by an infinitive.

Comienzan a jugar a las siete.
They begin playing at seven.

Ana **empieza a** escribir una postal.
Ana is starting to write a postcard.

▶ **Pensar** + [*infinitive*] means *to plan* or *to intend to do something.* **Pensar en** means *to think about someone* or *something.*

¿**Piensan** ir al gimnasio?
Are you planning to go to the gym?

¿**En** qué **piensas**?
What are you thinking about?

¡INTÉNTALO! Provide the present tense forms of these verbs.

cerrar (e:ie)

1. Ustedes __cierran__.
2. Tú __cierras__.
3. Nosotras __cerramos__.
4. Mi hermano __cierra__.
5. Yo __cierro__.
6. Usted __cierra__.
7. Los chicos __cierran__.
8. Ella __cierra__.

dormir (o:ue)

1. Mi abuela no __duerme__.
2. Yo no __duermo__.
3. Tú no __duermes__.
4. Mis hijos no __duermen__.
5. Usted no __duerme__.
6. Nosotros no __dormimos__.
7. Él no __duerme__.
8. Ustedes no __duermen__.

Práctica

1 **Completar** Complete this conversation with the appropriate forms of the verbs. Then act it out with a partner.

PABLO Óscar, voy al centro ahora.

ÓSCAR ¿A qué hora (1)___piensas___ (pensar) volver? El partido de fútbol (2)___empieza___ (empezar) a las dos.

PABLO (3)___Vuelvo___ (Volver) a la una. (4)___Quiero___ (Querer) ver el partido.

ÓSCAR (5)¿___Recuerdas___ (Recordar) que (*that*) nuestro equipo es muy bueno? (6)¡___Puede___ (Poder) ganar!

PABLO No, (7)___pienso___ (pensar) que va a (8)___perder___ (perder). Los jugadores de Guadalajara son salvajes (*wild*) cuando (9)___juegan___ (jugar).

2 **Preferencias** With a partner, take turns asking and answering questions about what these people want to do, using the cues provided.

> **modelo**
> Guillermo: estudiar / pasear en bicicleta
> **Estudiante 1:** ¿Quiere estudiar Guillermo?
> **Estudiante 2:** No, prefiere pasear en bicicleta.

1. tú: trabajar / dormir
¿Quieres trabajar? No, prefiero dormir.
2. ustedes: mirar la televisión / jugar al dominó
¿Quieren ustedes mirar la televisión? No, preferimos jugar al dominó.
3. tus amigos: ir de excursión / descansar
¿Quieren ir de excursión tus amigos? No, mis amigos prefieren descansar.
4. tú: comer en la cafetería / ir a un restaurante
¿Quieres comer en la cafetería? No, prefiero ir a un restaurante.
5. Elisa: ver una película / leer una revista
¿Quiere ver una película Elisa? No, prefiere leer una revista.
6. María y su hermana: tomar el sol / practicar el esquí acuático
¿Quieren tomar el sol María y su hermana? No, prefieren practicar el esquí acuático.

3 **Describir** Use a verb from the list to describe what these people are doing.

almorzar	cerrar	contar	dormir	encontrar	mostrar

1. las niñas Las niñas duermen.

2. yo (Yo) Cierro la ventana.

3. nosotros (Nosotros) Almorzamos.

4. tú (Tú) Encuentras una maleta.

5. Pedro Pedro muestra una foto.

6. Teresa Teresa cuenta.

 Practice more at **vhlcentral.com.**

1 Teaching Tip

Divide the class into pairs and give them three minutes to role-play the conversation. Then have partners switch roles. Encourage students to ad-lib as they go.

1 Expansion
- To challenge students, supply them with short-answer prompts based on the conversation. They should provide questions that would elicit the answers. Ex: **A las dos. (¿A qué hora empieza el partido de fútbol?) Porque quiere ver el partido. (¿Por qué vuelve Pablo a la una?)**
- Ask questions using **pensar** + [*infinitive*], **pensar en**, and **perder** (in both senses). Ex: **¿Qué piensas hacer mañana? ¿En qué piensas ahora? ¿Cuándo pierdes las cosas?**

2 Teaching Tip To challenge students, have **Estudiante 2** be creative and use other stem-changing verbs in their responses. For example, in the model, **Estudiante 2** could also respond: **No, no puede porque va a pasear en bicicleta** or **No, porque piensa pasear en bicicleta.**

2 Expansion
Have students ask each other questions of their own using the same pattern. Ex:
—**¿Quieres jugar al baloncesto?**
—**No, prefiero jugar al tenis.**
—**¿Por qué? —¡Porque no puedo encontrar la pelota de baloncesto!**

3 Expansion Bring in photos or magazine pictures to extend this activity. Choose images that are easy to describe with common stem-changing verbs.

TEACHING OPTIONS

TPR Brainstorm gestures for stem-changing verbs. Have students act out the activity you mention. Tell them that only male students should respond to **él/ellos** and only females to **ella/ellas**. Everyone should respond to **nosotros**.
Game Arrange students in rows of five (or six if you use **vosotros**). Give the first person in each row a piece of paper and tell the class they should be silent while they are completing this activity. Call out the infinitive of a stem-changing verb. The first person writes down the **yo** form and gives the paper to the student behind, who writes the **tú** form and passes the paper on. The last person in the row holds up the paper and says, **¡Terminamos!** The first team to finish the conjugation correctly gets a point. Have students rotate positions in their row before calling out another infinitive.

Left margin annotations:

4 Teaching Tip Model the activity by asking questions about famous people. Ex: **¿Con qué frecuencia juega al fútbol americano Tom Brady?** Write the answers on the board.

4 Expansion After tallying results on the board, have students work in pairs to graph them. Have them refer to **Lectura,** pages 134–135, for models.

5 Teaching Tips
• Model the activity by stating two programs from the listing that you want to watch and asking the class to react.
• Remind students that the 24-hour clock is often used for schedules. Model a few of the program times. Then ask: **Quiero ver *Héroes* y mi amigo prefiere ver *Elsa y Fred*. ¿Hay un conflicto? (No.) ¿Por qué? (Porque *Héroes* es a las 15:00 y *Elsa y Fred* es a las 22:00.)** Give students the option of answering with the 12-hour clock.

5 Expansion
 First, guide students in identifying the shows and movies that have versions in English: **Yo soy Betty, la fea; Héroes; Hermanos y hermanas; El padrastro; 60 Minutos.** Then, have students personalize the activity by choosing their favorite programs from the list. Divide the class into pairs and have them compare and contrast their reasons for their choices.

6 Teaching Tip Divide the class into pairs and distribute the handouts from the Activity Pack (Activity Pack/Supersite) that correspond to this Information Gap Activity.

6 Expansion
 Have volunteers take turns completing the information in the puzzle. Then have students invent their own stories, using stem-changing verbs, about what happens to the same group of tourists.

4.3 Stem-changing verbs: e→i **Tutorial**

ANTE TODO You've already seen that many verbs in Spanish change their stem vowel when conjugated. There is a third kind of stem-vowel change in some verbs, such as **pedir** (*to ask for; to request*). In these verbs, the stressed vowel in the stem changes from **e** to **i**, as shown in the diagram.

INFINITIVE	VERB STEM	STEM CHANGE	CONJUGATED FORM
pedir	p**e**d-	p**i**d-	p**i**do

▶ As with other stem-changing verbs you have learned, there is no stem change in the **nosotros/as** or **vosotros/as** forms in the present tense.

The verb pedir (e:i) (*to ask for; to request*)

Singular forms		Plural forms	
yo	p**i**do	nosotros/as	pedimos
tú	p**i**des	vosotros/as	pedís
Ud./él/ella	p**i**de	Uds./ellos/ellas	p**i**den

▶ To help you identify verbs with the **e:i** stem change, they will appear as follows throughout the text:

pedir (e:i)

▶ These are the most common **e:i** stem-changing verbs:

conseguir	**decir**	**repetir**	**seguir**
to get; to obtain	*to say; to tell*	*to repeat*	*to follow; to continue; to keep (doing something)*

Pido favores cuando es necesario.
I ask for favors when it's necessary.

Javier **dice** la verdad.
Javier is telling the truth.

Sigue con su tarea.
He continues with his homework.

Consiguen ver buenas películas.
They get to see good movies.

▶ **¡Atención!** The verb **decir** is irregular in its **yo** form: **yo digo**.

▶ The **yo** forms of **seguir** and **conseguir** have a spelling change in addition to the stem change **e:i**.

Sigo su plan.
I'm following their plan.

Consigo novelas en la librería.
I get novels at the bookstore.

¡INTÉNTALO! Provide the correct forms of the verbs.

repetir (e:i)	decir (e:i)	seguir (e:i)
1. Arturo y Eva _repiten_.	1. Yo _digo_.	1. Yo _sigo_.
2. Yo _repito_.	2. Él _dice_.	2. Nosotros _seguimos_.
3. Nosotros _repetimos_.	3. Tú _dices_.	3. Tú _sigues_.
4. Julia _repite_.	4. Usted _dice_.	4. Los chicos _siguen_.
5. Sofía y yo _repetimos_.	5. Ellas _dicen_.	5. Usted _sigue_.

recursos

WB
pp. 43–44

LM
p. 23

S
vhlcentral.com
Lección 4

Práctica

1 Completar Complete these sentences with the correct form of the verb provided.

1. Cuando mi familia pasea por la ciudad, mi madre siempre (*always*) va a un café y __pide__ (pedir) una soda.
2. Pero mi padre __dice__ (decir) que perdemos mucho tiempo. Tiene prisa por llegar al Bosque de Chapultepec.
3. Mi padre tiene suerte, porque él siempre __consigue__ (conseguir) lo que (*that which*) desea.
4. Cuando llegamos al parque, mis hermanos y yo __seguimos__ (seguir) conversando (*talking*) con nuestros padres.
5. Mis padres siempre __repiten__ (repetir) la misma cosa: "Nosotros tomamos el sol aquí sin ustedes".
6. Yo siempre __pido__ (pedir) permiso para volver a casa un poco más tarde porque me gusta mucho el parque.

2 Combinar Combine words from the two columns to create sentences about yourself and people you know. *Answers will vary.*

A	B
yo	(no) pedir muchos favores
mi compañero/a de cuarto	nunca (*never*) pedir perdón
mi mejor (*best*) amigo/a	nunca seguir las instrucciones
mi familia	siempre seguir las instrucciones
mis amigos/as	conseguir libros en Internet
mis amigos/as y yo	repetir el vocabulario
mis padres	poder hablar dos lenguas
mi hermano/a	dormir hasta el mediodía
mi profesor(a) de español	siempre perder sus libros

3 Opiniones In pairs, take turns guessing how your partner completed the sentences from **Actividad 2.** If you guess incorrectly, your partner must supply the correct answer. *Answers will vary.*

> **modelo**
> **Estudiante 1:** Creo que tus padres consiguen libros en Internet.
> **Estudiante 2:** ¡No! Mi hermana consigue libros en Internet.

4 ¿Quién? Your instructor will give you a worksheet. Talk to your classmates until you find one person who does each of the activities. Use **e:ie, o:ue,** and **e:i** stem-changing verbs.

> **modelo**
> **Tú:** ¿Pides consejos con frecuencia?
> **Maira:** No, no pido consejos con frecuencia.
> **Tú:** ¿Pides consejos con frecuencia?
> **Lucas:** Sí, pido consejos con frecuencia.

 Practice more at **vhlcentral.com.**

Comunicación

5

Las películas Use these questions to interview a classmate. *Answers will vary.*

1. ¿Prefieres las películas románticas, las películas de acción o las películas de terror? ¿Por qué?
2. ¿Dónde consigues información sobre (*about*) cine y televisión?
3. ¿Dónde consigues las entradas (*tickets*) para ver una película?
4. Para decidir qué películas vas a ver, ¿sigues las recomendaciones de los críticos de cine? ¿Qué dicen los críticos en general?
5. ¿Qué cines en tu comunidad muestran las mejores (*best*) películas?
6. ¿Vas a ver una película esta semana? ¿A qué hora empieza la película?

Síntesis

6

El cine In pairs, first scan the ad and jot down all the stem-changing verbs. Then answer the questions. Be prepared to share your answers with the class. *Answers will vary.*

1. ¿Qué palabras indican que *Avatar* es una película dramática?
2. ¿Cómo son los dos personajes (*characters*) del póster? ¿Qué relación tienen?
3. ¿Te gustan las películas como ésta (*this one*)? ¿Por qué?
4. Describe tu película favorita con los verbos de la **Lección 4**.

★ ★ ★ ★ ★

Ganadora de tres premios Óscar

Cuando todas las puertas se cierran, siempre hay una oportunidad para volver a empezar.

Del productor y director de
Titanic y Terminator

Un mundo lejano puede desaparecer, su salvación está en las manos de un hombre que también puede perderlo todo... Incluso el amor.
¿Cuentan con él?

5 Teaching Tips
- Have students report to the class what their partner said. After the presentation, encourage them to ask each other questions.
- Take a class poll to find out students' film genre and local movie theater preferences.

5 Expansion To challenge students, write some key movie-related words on the board, such as **actor, actriz, argumento,** and **efectos especiales.** Explain how to use **mejor** and **peor** as adjectives. Have student pairs say which movies this year they think should win Oscars. Model by telling them: **Pienso que____ es la mejor película del año. Debe ganar porque...** Then ask students to nominate the year's worst. Have them share their opinions with the class.

6 Teaching Tips
- Write the stem-changing verbs from the ad on the board. Have students conjugate the verbs using different subjects.
- Go over student responses to item 4.

6 Expansion
👥 In pairs, have students use the verbs from the ad to write a dramatic dialogue. Have volunteers role-play their dialogues for the class.

TEACHING OPTIONS

Small Groups 👥 Select a few scenes from different Spanish-language films or plays that contain stem-changing verbs. White out the verbs and have students work in small groups to complete each dialogue. Ask them to try to identify the genre and, if possible, the title of each work. Then have volunteers act out each scene for the class, ad-libbing as appropriate.

Heritage Speakers 👥 Ask heritage speakers to start a discussion with the rest of the class about popular Spanish-language films. Brainstorm with the class a list of questions about the films, using stem-changing verbs from **Estructura 4.2** and **4.3**. Have students ask the heritage speakers the questions. Ex: **¿Dónde podemos conseguir la película aquí? ¿Dices que es tu película favorita? ¿Prefieres las películas en inglés?**

Section Goal

In **Estructura 4.4**, students will learn verbs with irregular **yo** forms.

Instructional Resources

Supersite: Audio (Lab MP3 Files); Resources (*PowerPoints*, Activity Pack, Scripts, Answer Keys); Testing Program (Quizzes)
WebSAM
Workbook, pp. 45–46
Lab Manual, p. 24

Teaching Tips

• Quickly review the present tense of **decir, tener,** and **venir,** pointing out the **–go** ending of the **yo** forms.

• Ask specific students questions to elicit the **yo** forms of the verbs. Ex: **María, ¿haces la tarea en casa o en la biblioteca? (Hago la tarea en la biblioteca.) ¿Traes un diccionario a clase? (Sí, traigo un diccionario a clase.)** As students respond, write the verbs on the board until you have listed all the irregular **yo** forms.

• Go over the uses of **salir.** Model an additional example of each use.

• You may want to tell students that in many Latin American countries (e.g., Mexico, Venezuela, Colombia, and Peru), the verb **prender** is used to express *to turn on an electrical device or appliance.*

4.4 Verbs with irregular yo forms ⑤ Tutorial

ANTE TODO In Spanish, several verbs have irregular **yo** forms in the present tense. You have already seen three verbs with the **-go** ending in the **yo** form: **decir → digo, tener → tengo,** and **venir → vengo.**

▶ Here are some common expressions with **decir.**

decir la verdad *to tell the truth*	**decir mentiras** *to tell lies*
decir que *to say that*	**decir la respuesta** *to say the answer*

▶ The verb **hacer** is often used to ask questions about what someone does. Note that when answering, **hacer** is frequently replaced with another, more specific action verb.

Verbs with irregular yo forms

	hacer *(to do; to make)*	poner *(to put; to place)*	salir *(to leave)*	suponer *(to suppose)*	traer *(to bring)*
SINGULAR FORMS	**hago**	**pongo**	**salgo**	**supongo**	**traigo**
	haces	pones	sales	supones	traes
	hace	pone	sale	supone	trae
PLURAL FORMS	hacemos	ponemos	salimos	suponemos	traemos
	hacéis	ponéis	salís	suponéis	traéis
	hacen	ponen	salen	suponen	traen

Salgo mucho los fines de semana.

Yo no salgo, yo hago la tarea y veo películas en la televisión.

▶ **Poner** can also mean *to turn on* a household appliance.

Carlos **pone** la radio. *Carlos turns on the radio.*	María **pone** la televisión. *María turns on the television.*

▶ **Salir de** is used to indicate that someone is leaving a particular place.

Hoy **salgo del** hospital. *Today I leave the hospital.*	**Sale de** la clase a las cuatro. *He leaves class at four.*

TEACHING OPTIONS

TPR Have students act out actions as you make statements with irregular **yo** forms. Ex: **Hago la tarea.** (Students imitate writing their homework.) **Pongo la radio.** (They imitate turning on a radio.)
Game Divide the class into teams of three. Each team has a piece of paper. Call out an infinitive and a person. Ex: **traer / primera persona plural.** Each team has to compose a sentence, with each member writing one part. The first team member thinks of an appropriate subject or proper name and writes it down (Ex: **nosotras**). The second writes the correct form of the verb (Ex: **traemos**). The third completes the sentence in a logical way (Ex: **el libro**). The first team to write a logical and correct sentence wins. Team members should rotate positions each time a new verb is given.

▶ **Salir para** is used to indicate someone's destination.

Mañana **salgo para** México.	Hoy **salen para** España.
Tomorrow I leave for Mexico.	*Today they leave for Spain.*

▶ **Salir con** means *to leave with someone* or *something*, or *to date someone*.

Alberto **sale con** su mochila.	Margarita **sale con** Guillermo.
Alberto is leaving with his backpack.	*Margarita is going out with Guillermo.*

The verbs ver and oír

▶ The verb **ver** (*to see*) has an irregular **yo** form. The other forms of **ver** are regular.

The verb ver (*to see*)

Singular forms		Plural forms	
yo	**veo**	nosotros/as	vemos
tú	ves	vosotros/as	veis
Ud./él/ella	ve	Uds./ellos/ellas	ven

▶ The verb **oír** (*to hear*) has an irregular **yo** form and the spelling change **i:y** in the **tú, usted, él, ella, ustedes, ellos,** and **ellas** forms. The **nosotros/as** and **vosotros/as** forms have an accent mark.

The verb oír (*to hear*)

Singular forms		Plural forms	
yo	**oigo**	nosotros/as	oímos
tú	oyes	vosotros/as	oís
Ud./él/ella	oye	Uds./ellos/ellas	oyen

▶ While most commonly translated as *to hear*, **oír** is also used in contexts where the verb *to listen* would be used in English.

Oigo a unas personas en la otra sala.	¿**Oyes** la radio por la mañana?
I hear some people in the other room.	*Do you listen to the radio in the morning?*

¡INTÉNTALO! Provide the appropriate forms of these verbs.

1. salir	Isabel __sale__.	Nosotros __salimos__.	Yo __salgo__.		
2. ver	Yo __veo__.	Uds. __ven__.	Tú __ves__.		
3. poner	Rita y yo __ponemos__.	Yo __pongo__.	Los niños __ponen__.		
4. hacer	Yo __hago__.	Tú __haces__.	Ud. __hace__.		
5. oír	Él __oye__.	Nosotros __oímos__.	Yo __oigo__.		
6. traer	Ellas __traen__.	Yo __traigo__.	Tú __traes__.		
7. suponer	Yo __supongo__.	Mi amigo __supone__.	Nosotras __suponemos__.		

Práctica

1 **Completar** Complete this conversation with the appropriate forms of the verbs. Then act it out with a partner.

ERNESTO David, ¿qué (1)___haces___ (hacer) hoy?

DAVID Ahora estudio biología, pero esta noche (2)___salgo___ (salir) con Luisa. Vamos al cine. Los críticos (3)___dicen___ (decir) que la nueva (*new*) película de Almodóvar es buena.

ERNESTO ¿Y Diana? ¿Qué (4)___hace___ (hacer) ella?

DAVID (5)___Sale___ (Salir) a comer con sus padres.

ERNESTO ¿Qué (6)___hacen___ (hacer) Andrés y Javier?

DAVID Tienen que (7)___hacer___ (hacer) las maletas. (8)___Salen___ (Salir) para Monterrey mañana.

ERNESTO Pues, ¿qué (9)___hago___ (hacer) yo?

DAVID Yo (10)___supongo___ (suponer) que puedes estudiar o (11)___ver___ (ver) la televisión.

ERNESTO No quiero estudiar. Mejor (12)___pongo___ (poner) la televisión. Mi programa favorito empieza en unos minutos.

2 **Oraciones** Form sentences using the cues provided and verbs from **Estructura 4.4**.

> **modelo**
>
> tú / _____ / cosas / en / su lugar / antes de (*before*) / salir
>
> *Tú pones las cosas en su lugar antes de salir.*

1. mis amigos / _____ / conmigo / centro Mis amigos salen conmigo al centro.
2. tú / _____ / mentiras / pero / yo _____ / verdad Tú dices mentiras, pero yo digo la verdad.
3. Alberto / _____ / música del café Pasatiempos Alberto oye la música del café Pasatiempos.
4. yo / no / _____ / muchas películas Yo no veo muchas películas.
5. domingo / nosotros / _____ / mucha / tarea El domingo nosotros hacemos mucha tarea.
6. si / yo / _____ / que / yo / querer / ir / cine / mis amigos / ir / también Si yo digo que quiero ir al cine, mis amigos van también.

3 **Describir** Use the verbs from **Estructura 4.4** to describe what these people are doing.

1. Fernán Fernán pone la mochila en el escritorio/trae una mochila.

2. los aficionados Los aficionados salen del estadio/para sus casas.

3. yo Yo traigo/salgo con una cámara.

4. nosotros Nosotros vemos el monumento.

5. la señora Vargas La señora Vargas no oye bien.

6. el estudiante El estudiante hace su tarea.

 Practice more at **vhlcentral.com**.

TEACHING OPTIONS

Game Ask students to write three sentences about themselves: two should be true and one should be false. Then, in groups of four, have students share their sentences with the group, who must decide whether that person **dice la verdad** or **dice una mentira**. Survey the class to uncover the most convincing liars.

Extra Practice Have students use five of the target verbs from **Estructura 4.4** to write sentences about their habits that others may find somewhat unusual. Ex: **Traigo doce bolígrafos en la mochila. Hago la tarea en un café en el centro. No pongo la televisión hasta las diez de la noche.**

1 Teaching Tip Quickly review the new verbs with irregular **yo** forms. Then, ask pairs to complete and role-play the conversation, encouraging them to ad-lib as they go.

1 Expansion In pairs, have students write a conversation between **David** and **Luisa** as they are waiting for the movie to start. Have volunteers act out their conversations for the class.

2 Teaching Tip To simplify, lead the class to identify key words in each sentence. Then have students choose the infinitive that best fits with the key words and name any missing words for each item. After students complete the activity individually, have volunteers write the sentences on the board.

2 Expansion
- Change the subjects of the dehydrated sentences in the activity and have students write or say aloud the new sentences.
- Ask students to form questions that would elicit the statements in **Actividad 2**. Ex: **¿Qué hago antes de salir?**
- Have students write three sentences, each using a verb from **Estructura 4.4**. Then ask them to copy their sentences onto a sheet of paper in dehydrated form, following the model of **Actividad 2**. Students should exchange papers with a partner, who writes the complete sentences. Finally, have partners check each other's work.

3 Expansion Use magazine pictures which elicit the target verbs to extend the activity. Encourage students to add further descriptions if they can.

Comunicación

4 Tu rutina In pairs, take turns asking each other these questions. *Answers will vary.*

1. ¿Qué traes a clase?
2. ¿Quiénes traen un diccionario a clase? ¿Por qué traen un diccionario?
3. ¿A qué hora sales de tu residencia estudiantil o de tu casa por la mañana? ¿A qué hora sale tu compañero/a de cuarto?
4. ¿Dónde pones tus libros cuando regresas de clase? ¿Siempre (*Always*) pones tus cosas en su lugar?
5. ¿Qué prefieres hacer, oír la radio o ver la televisión?
6. ¿Oyes música cuando estudias?
7. ¿Ves películas en casa o prefieres ir al cine?
8. ¿Haces mucha tarea los fines de semana?
9. ¿Sales con tus amigos los fines de semana? ¿A qué hora? ¿Qué hacen?
10. ¿Te gusta ver deportes en la televisión o prefieres ver otros programas? ¿Cuáles?

5 Charadas In groups, play a game of charades. Each person should think of two phrases containing the verbs **hacer, oír, poner, salir, traer,** or **ver**. The first person to guess correctly acts out the next charade. *Answers will vary.*

6 Entrevista You are doing a market research report on lifestyles. Interview a classmate to find out when he or she goes out with these people and what they do for entertainment. *Answers will vary.*

▶ los/las amigos/as
▶ el/la novio/a
▶ el/la esposo/a
▶ la familia

Síntesis

7 Situación Imagine that you are speaking with your roommate. With a partner, prepare a conversation using these cues. *Answers will vary.*

Estudiante 1	Estudiante 2
Ask your partner what he or she is doing.	→ Tell your partner that you are watching TV.
Say what you suppose he or she is watching.	→ Say that you like the show _____. Ask if he or she wants to watch.
Say no, because you are going out with friends, and tell where you are going.	→ Say you think it's a good idea, and ask what your partner and his or her friends are doing there.
Say what you are going to do, and ask your partner whether he or she wants to come along.	→ Say no and tell your partner what you prefer to do.

TEACHING OPTIONS

Pairs Have pairs of students role-play an awful first date. Students should write their script first, then present it to the class. Encourage students to use descriptive adjectives as well as the new verbs learned in **Estructura 4.4**.

Heritage Speakers Ask heritage speakers to talk about a social custom in their cultural community. Remind them to use familiar vocabulary and simple sentences.

4 Teaching Tip Model the activity by having volunteers answer the first two items.

4 Expansion
Ask volunteers to call out some of their answers. The class should speculate about the reason behind each answer and offer more information. Have the volunteer confirm or deny the speculation.
Ex: —**Traigo mi tarea a clase.**
—**Eres un(a) buen(a) estudiante.**
—**Sí, soy un(a) buen(a) estudiante porque hago mi tarea.**

5 Teaching Tips
• Model the activity by doing a charade for the class to guess. Ex: **Pongo un lápiz en la mesa.** Then divide the class into small groups.
• Ask each group to choose the best **charada**. Then have students present them to the class, who will guess the activities.

6 Teaching Tip Model the activity by giving a report on your lifestyle. Ex: **Salgo al cine con mis amigas. Me gusta comer en restaurantes con mi esposo. En familia vemos deportes en la televisión.** Remind students that a market researcher and the interviewee would address each other with the **usted** form of verbs.

7 Possible Conversation
E1: **¿Qué haces?**
E2: **Veo la tele.**
E1: **Supongo que ves** *Los Simpson.*
E2: **Sí. Me gusta el programa. ¿Quieres ver la tele conmigo?**
E1: **No puedo. Salgo con mis amigos a la plaza.**
E2: **Buena idea. ¿Qué hacen en la plaza?**
E1: **Vamos a escuchar música y a pasear. ¿Quieres venir?**
E2: **No. Prefiero descansar.**

Recapitulación

Section Goal

In **Recapitulación**, students will review the grammar concepts from this lesson.

Instructional Resource
Supersite

1 Teaching Tips
• To simplify, before students begin the activity, have them identify the stem change (if any) in each row.
• Complete this activity orally as a class.

1 Expansion Ask students to provide the remaining forms of the verbs.

2 Teaching Tip To challenge students, ask them to provide alternative verbs for the blanks. Ex: **1. vemos/miramos** Then ask: Why can't **ir** be used for item 4? (needs **a**)

2 Expansion
• Ask questions about **Cecilia's** typical day. Have students answer with complete sentences. **¿Qué hace Cecilia a las siete y media? ¿Por qué le gusta llegar temprano?**
• Write on the board the verb phrases about **Cecilia's** day. (Ex: **ver la televisión por la mañana, almorzar a las 12:30, jugar al vóleibol por la tarde**) Brainstorm a few more entries. (Ex: **hacer la tarea por la noche**) Ask students to make a two-column chart, labeled **yo** and **compañero/a**. They should initial each activity they perform. Then have them interview a partner and report back to the class.

S Concepts Diagnostics

Review the grammar concepts you have learned in this lesson by completing these activities.

1 Completar Complete the chart with the correct verb forms. **15 pts.**

Infinitive	yo	nosotros/as	ellos/as
volver	**vuelvo**	volvemos	vuelven
comenzar	comienzo	**comenzamos**	comienzan
hacer	hago	**hacemos**	**hacen**
ir	voy	vamos	van
jugar	**juego**	jugamos	juegan
repetir	repito	repetimos	**repiten**

2 Un día típico Complete the paragraph with the appropriate forms of the verbs in the word list. Not all verbs will be used. Some may be used more than once. **10 pts.**

almorzar	ir	salir
cerrar	jugar	seguir
empezar	mostrar	ver
hacer	querer	volver

¡Hola! Me llamo Cecilia y vivo en Puerto Vallarta, México. ¿Cómo es un día típico en mi vida (*life*)? Por la mañana bebo café con mis padres y juntos (*together*) (1)___vemos___ las noticias (*news*) en la televisión. A las siete y media, (yo) (2)___salgo___ de mi casa y tomo el autobús. Me gusta llegar temprano (*early*) a la universidad porque siempre (*always*) (3)___veo___ a mis amigos en la cafetería. Tomamos café y planeamos lo que (4)___queremos___ hacer cada (*each*) día. A las ocho y cuarto, mi amiga Sandra y yo (5)___vamos___ al laboratorio de lenguas. La clase de francés (6)___empieza___ a las ocho y media. ¡Es mi clase favorita! A las doce y media (yo) (7)___almuerzo___ en la cafetería con mis amigos. Después (*Afterwards*), yo (8)___sigo___ con mis clases. Por las tardes, mis amigos (9)___vuelven___ a sus casas, pero yo (10)___juego___ al vóleibol con mi amigo Tomás.

RESUMEN GRAMATICAL

4.1 Present tense of ir *p. 118*

yo	voy	nos.	vamos
tú	vas	vos.	vais
él	va	ellas	van

▶ **ir a** + [*infinitive*] = *to be going* + [*infinitive*]
▶ **a** + **el** = **al**
▶ **vamos a** + [*infinitive*] = *let's* (*do something*)

4.2 Stem-changing verbs e:ie, o:ue, u:ue *pp. 121–122*

	empezar	volver	jugar
yo	emp**ie**zo	v**ue**lvo	j**ue**go
tú	emp**ie**zas	v**ue**lves	j**ue**gas
él	emp**ie**za	v**ue**lve	j**ue**ga
nos.	empezamos	volvemos	jugamos
vos.	empezáis	volvéis	jugáis
ellas	emp**ie**zan	v**ue**lven	j**ue**gan

▶ Other e:ie verbs: **cerrar, comenzar, entender, pensar, perder, preferir, querer**
▶ Other o:ue verbs: **almorzar, contar, dormir, encontrar, mostrar, poder, recordar**

4.3 Stem-changing verbs e:i *p. 125*

	pedir		
yo	p**i**do	nos.	pedimos
tú	p**i**des	vos.	pedís
él	p**i**de	ellas	p**i**den

▶ Other e:i verbs: **conseguir, decir, repetir, seguir**

4.4 Verbs with irregular yo forms *pp. 128–129*

hacer	poner	salir	suponer	traer
hago	pongo	salgo	supongo	traigo

▶ **ver**: veo, ves, ve, vemos, veis, ven
▶ **oír**: oigo, oyes, oye, oímos, oís, oyen

TEACHING OPTIONS

Pairs Pair weaker students with more advanced students. Give each pair a numbered list of the target verbs from **Resumen gramatical** and a small plastic bag containing subject pronouns written on strips of paper. Model the first verb for students by drawing out a subject pronoun at random and conjugating the verb on the board. Ask: **¿Correcto o incorrecto?** Have students take turns and correct each other's work. Keep a brisk pace.

Extra Practice ← ↑ → Introduce the word **nunca** and have students write a short description about things they never do. Have them use as many target verbs from this lesson as possible. Ex: **Nunca veo películas románticas. Nunca pongo la televisión cuando estudio…** Collect the descriptions, shuffle them, and read them aloud. Have the class guess the person that is being described.

3 Oraciones Arrange the cues provided in the correct order to form complete sentences. Make all necessary changes. `14 pts.`

1. tarea / los / hacer / sábados / nosotros / la
 Los sábados nosotros hacemos la tarea./Nosotros hacemos la tarea los sábados.

2. en / pizza / Andrés / una / restaurante / el / pedir
 Andrés pide una pizza en el restaurante.

3. a / ? / museo / ir / ¿ / el / (tú)
 ¿(Tú) Vas al museo?

4. de / oír / amigos / bien / los / no / Elena
 Los amigos de Elena no oyen bien.

5. libros / traer / yo / clase / mis / a
 Yo traigo mis libros a clase.

6. película / ver / en / Jorge y Carlos / pensar / cine / una / el
 Jorge y Carlos piensan ver una película en el cine.

7. unos / escribir / Mariana / electrónicos / querer / mensajes
 Mariana quiere escribir unos mensajes electrónicos.

4 Escribir Write a short paragraph about what you do on a typical day. Use at least six of the verbs you have learned in this lesson. You can use the paragraph on the opposite page (**Actividad 2**) as a model. `11 pts.` Answers will vary.

> *Un día típico*
>
> Hola, me llamo Julia y vivo
> en Vancouver, Canadá. Por la
> mañana, yo...

5 Rima Complete the rhyme with the appropriate forms of the correct verbs from the list. `2 EXTRA points!`

| contar | poder |
| oír | suponer |

" Si no ___puedes___ dormir
y el sueño deseas,
lo vas a conseguir
si ___cuentas___ ovejas°. **"**

ovejas *sheep*

Practice more at **vhlcentral.com.**

3 Teaching Tip To simplify, provide the first word for each sentence.

3 Expansion Give students these sentences as items 8–11: **8. la / ? / ustedes / cerrar / ventana / ¿ / poder (¿Pueden ustedes cerrar la ventana?) 9. cine / del / tú / las / salir / once / a (Tú sales del cine a las once.) 10. el / conmigo / a / en / ellos / tenis / el / jugar / parque (Ellos juegan al tenis conmigo en el parque.) 11. que / partido / mañana / un / decir / hay / Javier (Javier dice que hay un partido mañana.)**

4 Teaching Tips
- To simplify, ask students to make a three-column chart with the headings **Por la mañana, Por la tarde,** and **Por la noche.** Have them brainstorm at least three verbs or verb phrases for each column and circle any stem-changing or irregular **yo** verbs.
- →👤← Have students exchange paragraphs with a classmate for peer editing. Ask them to underline grammatical and spelling errors.

5 Teaching Tip Point out the inverted word order in line 2 of the rhyme and ask students what the phrase would be in everyday Spanish (**y deseas el sueño**).

5 Expansion Come up with similar rhymes and have students complete them. Ex: **Si no ____ descansar y diversión deseas, lo vas a encontrar si ____ con ellas. (quieres, juegas)**

TEACHING OPTIONS

Game 👤↔👤 Make a *Bingo* card of places at school or around town, such as dorm names, libraries, cafeterias, movie theaters, and cafés. Give each student a card and model possible questions (Ex: for a cafeteria, **¿Almuerzas en ____?/¿Dónde almuerzas?**). Encourage them to circulate around the room, asking only one question per person; if they get an affirmative answer, they should write that person's name in the square. The

first student to complete a horizontal, vertical, or diagonal row and yell **¡Bingo!** is the winner.

Heritage Speakers ←👤→ Ask heritage speakers if counting sheep is common advice for sleeplessness in their families. Have them describe other insomnia remedies they have heard of or practiced.

Section Goals

In **Lectura**, students will:
- learn the strategy of predicting content by surveying the graphic elements in reading matter
- read a magazine article containing graphs and charts

Instructional Resource
Supersite

Estrategia Tell students that they can infer a great deal of information about the content of an article by surveying the graphic elements included in it. When students survey an article for its graphic elements, they should look for such things as:
- headlines or headings
- bylines
- photos
- photo captions
- graphs and tables

Examinar el texto Give students two minutes to take a look at the visual clues in the article and write down all the ideas the clues suggest.

Contestar After going over students' responses, ask them how accurate their predictions were from **Examinar el texto**.

Evaluación y predicción Write two headings on the board: **Entre los jóvenes del mundo hispano** and **Entre los jóvenes de nuestra universidad**. Ask for a show of hands to respond to your questions about the ranking of each sporting event. Tally the reponses as you proceed. Ask: **¿Quiénes creen que entre los jóvenes hispanos la Copa Mundial de Fútbol es el evento más popular? ¿Quiénes creen que los Juegos Olímpicos son el evento más popular?** Then ask: **Entre los jóvenes de nuestra universidad, ¿quiénes de ustedes creen que la Copa Mundial de Fútbol es el evento más popular?** Briefly discuss the differences indicated by student responses.

Lectura

Antes de leer

Estrategia
Predicting content from visuals

When you are reading in Spanish, be sure to look for visual clues that will orient you as to the content and purpose of what you are reading. Photos and illustrations, for example, will often give you a good idea of the main points that the reading covers. You may also encounter very helpful visuals that are used to summarize large amounts of data in a way that is easy to comprehend; these include bar graphs, pie charts, flow charts, lists of percentages, and other sorts of diagrams.

Examinar el texto

Take a quick look at the visual elements of the magazine article in order to generate a list of ideas about its content. Then compare your list with a classmate's. Are they the same or are they different? Discuss your lists and make any changes needed to produce a final list of ideas.

Contestar

Read the list of ideas you wrote in **Examinar el texto**, and look again at the visual elements of the magazine article. Then answer these questions:

1. Who is the woman in the photo, and what is her role? *María Úrsula Echevarría is the author of this article.*
2. What is the article about? *The article is about sports in the Hispanic world.*
3. What is the subject of the pie chart? *The most popular sports among college students.*
4. What is the subject of the bar graph? *Hispanic countries in world soccer championships.*

 Practice more at **vhlcentral.com**.

por María Úrsula Echevarría

El fútbol es el deporte más popular en el mundo° hispano, según° una encuesta° reciente realizada entre jóvenes universitarios. Mucha gente practica este deporte y tiene un equipo de fútbol favorito. Cada cuatro años se realiza la Copa Mundial°. Argentina y Uruguay han ganado° este campeonato° más de una vez°. Los aficionados siguen los partidos de fútbol en casa por tele y en muchos otros lugares como bares, restaurantes, estadios y clubes deportivos. Los jóvenes juegan al fútbol con sus amigos en parques y gimnasios.

Países hispanos en campeonatos mundiales de fútbol (1930–2010)

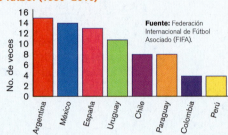

Pero, por supuesto°, en los países de habla hispana también hay otros deportes populares. ¿Qué deporte sigue al fútbol en estos países? Bueno, ¡depende del país y de otros factores!

Después de leer
Evaluación y predicción

Which of the following sporting events would be most popular among the college students surveyed? Rate them from one (most popular) to five (least popular). Which would be the most popular at your college or university? *Answers will vary.*

_____ 1. la Copa Mundial de Fútbol
_____ 2. los Juegos Olímpicos
_____ 3. el Campeonato de Wimbledon
_____ 4. la Serie Mundial de Béisbol
_____ 5. el Tour de Francia

No sólo el fútbol

En Colombia, el béisbol también es muy popular después del fútbol, aunque° esto varía según la región del país. En la costa del norte de Colombia, el béisbol es una pasión. Y el ciclismo también es un deporte que los colombianos siguen con mucho interés.

Donde el béisbol es más popular

En los países del Caribe, el béisbol es el deporte predominante. Éste es el caso en Puerto Rico, Cuba y la República Dominicana. Los niños empiezan a jugar cuando son muy pequeños. En Puerto Rico y la República Dominicana, la gente también quiere participar en otros deportes, como el baloncesto, o ver los partidos en la tele. Y para los espectadores aficionados del Caribe, el boxeo es número dos.

Deportes más populares

Fútbol (69%)
Béisbol (10%)
Baloncesto (8%)
Ciclismo (4%)
Tenis (4%)
Boxeo (3%)
Vóleibol (2%)

Donde el fútbol es más popular

En México, el béisbol es el segundo° deporte más popular después° del fútbol. Pero en Argentina, después del fútbol, el rugby tiene mucha importancia. En Perú a la gente le gusta mucho ver partidos de vóleibol. ¿Y en España? Muchas personas prefieren el baloncesto, el tenis y el ciclismo.

mundo *world* según *according to* encuesta *survey* se realiza la Copa Mundial *the World Cup is held* han ganado *have won* campeonato *championship* más de una vez *more than once* por supuesto *of course* segundo *second* después *after* aunque *although*

¿Cierto o falso?

Indicate whether each sentence is **cierto** or **falso**, then correct the false statements.

	Cierto	Falso
1. El vóleibol es el segundo deporte más popular en México. Es el béisbol.	○	◉
2. En España a la gente le gustan varios deportes como el baloncesto y el ciclismo.	◉	○
3. En la costa del norte de Colombia, el tenis es una pasión. El béisbol es una pasión.	○	◉
4. En el Caribe, el deporte más popular es el béisbol.	◉	○

Preguntas

Answer these questions in Spanish. Answers will vary.

1. ¿Dónde ven el fútbol los aficionados? Y tú, ¿cómo ves tus deportes favoritos?
2. ¿Te gusta el fútbol? ¿Por qué?
3. ¿Miras la Copa Mundial en la televisión?
4. ¿Qué deportes miras en la televisión?
5. En tu opinión, ¿cuáles son los tres deportes más populares en tu universidad? ¿En tu comunidad? ¿En tu país?
6. ¿Practicas deportes en tus ratos libres?

México

connections cultures
NATIONAL STANDARDS

El país en cifras

▶ **Área:** 1.972.550 km^2 (761.603 millas2), *casi° tres veces° el área de Texas*

La situación geográfica de México, al sur° de los Estados Unidos, ha influido en° la economía y la sociedad de los dos países. Una de las consecuencias es la emigración de la población mexicana al país vecino°. Hoy día, más de 30 millones de personas de ascendencia mexicana viven en los Estados Unidos.

▶ **Población:** 115.528.000
▶ **Capital:** México, D.F. (y su área metropolitana)—20.078.000
▶ **Ciudades principales:** Guadalajara —4.648.000, Monterrey—4.118.000, Puebla—2.460.000, Ciudad Juárez—1.470.000

SOURCE: Population Division, UN Secretariat

▶ **Moneda:** peso mexicano
▶ **Idiomas:** español (oficial), náhuatl, otras lenguas indígenas

Bandera de México

Mexicanos célebres
▶ **Benito Juárez,** héroe nacional (1806–1872)
▶ **Octavio Paz,** poeta (1914–1998)
▶ **Elena Poniatowska,** periodista y escritora (1933–)
▶ **Julio César Chávez,** boxeador (1962–)

casi *almost* veces *times* sur *south* ha influido en *has influenced* vecino *neighboring* se llenan de luz *get filled with light* flores *flowers* Muertos *Dead* se ríen *laugh* muerte *death* lo cual se refleja *which is reflected* calaveras de azúcar *sugar skulls* pan *bread* huesos *bones*

Cabo San Lucas

ESTADOS UNIDOS

Autorretrato con mono (*Self-portrait with monkey*), 1938, Frida Kahlo

Ciudad Juárez

Golfo de California
Baja California
Río Grande
Río Bravo del Norte
Sierra Madre Oriental
Sierra Madre Occidental

ESTADOS UNIDOS
MÉXICO
OCÉANO ATLÁNTICO
OCÉANO PACÍFICO
AMÉRICA DEL SUR

Monterrey

Océano Pacífico

Puerto Vallarta
Ciudad de México
Guadalajara
Puebla
Acapulco

Artesanías en Taxco, Guerrero

recursos

| WB pp. 47–48 | VM pp. 231–232 | vhlcentral.com Lección 4 |

Pirámide de Kukulcán en Chichén Itzá

¡Increíble pero cierto!

Cada dos de noviembre los cementerios de México se llenan de luz°, música y flores°. El Día de Muertos° no es un evento triste; es una fiesta en honor a las personas muertas. En ese día, los mexicanos se ríen° de la muerte°, lo cual se refleja° en detalles como las calaveras de azúcar° y el pan° de muerto —pan en forma de huesos°.

Ciudades • **México, D.F.**

La Ciudad de México, fundada° en 1525, también se llama el D.F. o Distrito Federal. Muchos turistas e inmigrantes vienen a la ciudad porque es el centro cultural y económico del país. El crecimiento° de la población es de los más altos° del mundo. El D.F. tiene una población mayor que las de Nueva York, Madrid o París.

Artes • **Diego Rivera y Frida Kahlo**

Frida Kahlo y Diego Rivera eran° artistas mexicanos muy famosos. Se casaron° en 1929. Los dos se interesaron° en las condiciones sociales de la gente indígena de su país. Puedes ver algunas° de sus obras° en el Museo de Arte Moderno de la Ciudad de México.

Historia • **Los aztecas**

Los aztecas dominaron° en México del siglo° XIV al siglo XVI. Sus canales, puentes° y pirámides con templos religiosos eran muy importantes.
El fin del imperio azteca comenzó° con la llegada° de los españoles en 1519, pero la presencia azteca sigue hoy. La Ciudad de México está situada en la capital azteca de Tenochtitlán, y muchos turistas van a visitar sus ruinas.

Economía • **La plata**

México es el mayor productor de plata° del mundo°. Estados como Zacatecas y Durango tienen ciudades fundadas cerca de los más grandes yacimientos° de plata del país. Estas ciudades fueron° en la época colonial unas de las más ricas e importantes. Hoy en día, aún° conservan mucho de su encanto° y esplendor.

Golfo de México

Península de Yucatán
Mérida
Cancún

Bahía de Campeche

Veracruz

Istmo de Tehuantepec

BELICE

GUATEMALA

 ¿Qué aprendiste? Responde a cada pregunta con una oración completa.

1. ¿Qué lenguas hablan los mexicanos?
 Los mexicanos hablan español y lenguas indígenas.

2. ¿Cómo es la población del D.F. en comparación con la de otras ciudades?
 La población del D.F. es mayor.

3. ¿En qué se interesaron Frida Kahlo y Diego Rivera? Se interesaron en las condiciones sociales de la gente indígena de su país.

4. Nombra algunas de las estructuras de la arquitectura azteca. Hay canales, puentes y pirámides con templos religiosos.

5. ¿Dónde está situada la capital de México?
 Está situada en la capital azteca de Tenochtitlán.

6. ¿Qué estados de México tienen los mayores yacimientos de plata? Zacatecas y Durango tienen los mayores yacimientos de plata.

 Conexión Internet Investiga estos temas en **vhlcentral.com.**

 Practice more at **vhlcentral.com.**

1. Busca información sobre dos lugares de México. ¿Te gustaría (*Would you like*) vivir allí? ¿Por qué?

2. Busca información sobre dos artistas mexicanos. ¿Cómo se llaman sus obras más famosas?

..

fundada *founded* **crecimiento** *growth* **más altos** *highest* **eran** *were* **Se casaron** *They got married* **se interesaron** *were interested in* **algunas** *some* **obras** *works* **dominaron** *dominated* **siglo** *century* **puentes** *bridges* **comenzó** *started* **llegada** *arrival* **plata** *silver* **mundo** *world* **yacimientos** *deposits* **fueron** *were* **aún** *still* **encanto** *charm*

Pasatiempos

andar en patineta	*to skateboard*
bucear	*to scuba dive*
escalar montañas (*f., pl.*)	*to climb mountains*
escribir una carta	*to write a letter*
escribir un mensaje electrónico	*to write an e-mail*
esquiar	*to ski*
ganar	*to win*
ir de excursión	*to go on a hike*
leer correo electrónico	*to read e-mail*
leer un periódico	*to read a newspaper*
leer una revista	*to read a magazine*
nadar	*to swim*
pasear	*to take a walk; to stroll*
pasear en bicicleta	*to ride a bicycle*
patinar (en línea)	*to (inline) skate*
practicar deportes (*m., pl.*)	*to play sports*
tomar el sol	*to sunbathe*
ver películas (*f., pl.*)	*to watch movies*
visitar monumentos (*m., pl.*)	*to visit monuments*
la diversión	*fun activity; entertainment; recreation*
el fin de semana	*weekend*
el pasatiempo	*pastime; hobby*
los ratos libres	*spare (free) time*
el videojuego	*video game*

Deportes

el baloncesto	*basketball*
el béisbol	*baseball*
el ciclismo	*cycling*
el equipo	*team*
el esquí (acuático)	*(water) skiing*
el fútbol	*soccer*
el fútbol americano	*football*
el golf	*golf*
el hockey	*hockey*
el/la jugador(a)	*player*
la natación	*swimming*
el partido	*game; match*
la pelota	*ball*
el tenis	*tennis*
el vóleibol	*volleyball*

Adjetivos

deportivo/a	*sports-related*
favorito/a	*favorite*

Lugares

el café	*café*
el centro	*downtown*
el cine	*movie theater*
el gimnasio	*gymnasium*
la iglesia	*church*
el lugar	*place*
el museo	*museum*
el parque	*park*
la piscina	*swimming pool*
la plaza	*city or town square*
el restaurante	*restaurant*

Verbos

almorzar (o:ue)	*to have lunch*
cerrar (e:ie)	*to close*
comenzar (e:ie)	*to begin*
conseguir (e:i)	*to get; to obtain*
contar (o:ue)	*to count; to tell*
decir (e:i)	*to say; to tell*
dormir (o:ue)	*to sleep*
empezar (e:ie)	*to begin*
encontrar (o:ue)	*to find*
entender (e:ie)	*to understand*
hacer	*to do; to make*
ir	*to go*
jugar (u:ue)	*to play (a sport or a game)*
mostrar (o:ue)	*to show*
oír	*to hear*
pedir (e:i)	*to ask for; to request*
pensar (e:ie)	*to think*
pensar (+ *inf.*)	*to intend*
pensar en	*to think about*
perder (e:ie)	*to lose; to miss*
poder (o:ue)	*to be able to; can*
poner	*to put; to place*
preferir (e:ie)	*to prefer*
querer (e:ie)	*to want; to love*
recordar (o:ue)	*to remember*
repetir (e:i)	*to repeat*
salir	*to leave*
seguir (e:i)	*to follow; to continue*
suponer	*to suppose*
traer	*to bring*
ver	*to see*
volver (o:ue)	*to return*

***Decir* expressions**	*See page 128.*
Expresiones útiles	*See page 113.*

recursos

LM p. 24 vhlcentral.com Lección 4

Audio: Vocabulary

Las vacaciones

5

Communicative Goals

You will learn how to:
- **Discuss and plan a vacation**
- **Describe a hotel**
- **Talk about how you feel**
- **Talk about the seasons and the weather**

A PRIMERA VISTA
- ¿Están ellos en una montaña o en un museo?
- ¿Son viejos o jóvenes?
- ¿Pasean o ven una película? ¿Andan en patineta o van de excursión?
- ¿Es posible esquiar en este lugar?

Lesson Goals

In **Lección 5**, students will be introduced to the following:
- terms for traveling and vacations
- seasons and months
- weather expressions
- ordinal numbers (1st–10th)
- **Las cataratas del Iguazú**
- **Punta del Este**, Uruguay
- **estar** with conditions and emotions
- adjectives for conditions and emotions
- present progressive of regular and irregular verbs
- comparison of the uses of **ser** and **estar**
- direct object nouns and pronouns
- personal **a**
- scanning to find specific information
- a video about **Machu Picchu**
- cultural, geographic, and historical information about Puerto Rico

A primera vista Here are some additional questions you can ask to personalize the photo: **¿Dónde te gusta pasar tus ratos libres? ¿Qué haces en tus ratos libres? ¿Te gusta explorar otras culturas? ¿Te gusta viajar a otros países? ¿Adónde quieres ir en las próximas vacaciones?**

Teaching Tip Look for these icons for additional communicative practice:

→👥	Interpretive communication
←👥	Presentational communication
👥↔	Interpersonal communication

INSTRUCTIONAL RESOURCES

Supersite (vhlcentral.com)
Video: ***Fotonovela*, Flash cultura*, Panorama cultural****
**Also on DVD*
Audio: Textbook and Lab MP3 Files (*also on CD*)
Activity Pack: Information Gap Activities, games, additional activity handouts

Resources: Textbook Answer Key, WB/VM/LM Answer Key, Scripts, Translations, **Vocabulario adicional**, lesson plans, **Estructura** *PowerPoints*, Overheads
Testing Program: Quizzes, Tests, Exams, MP3s (*also on Test Generator CD*)

Learning Management System (Assignment Task Manager, Gradebook)
WebSAM (online Workbook/Video Manual/Lab Manual)
Workbook/Video Manual
Lab Manual

Las vacaciones

Más vocabulario

la cama	bed
la habitación individual, doble	single, double room
el piso	floor (of a building)
la planta baja	ground floor
el campo	countryside
el paisaje	landscape
el equipaje	luggage
la estación de autobuses, del metro, de tren	bus, subway, train station
la llegada	arrival
el pasaje (de ida y vuelta)	(round-trip) ticket
la salida	departure; exit
la tabla de (wind)surf	surfboard/sailboard
acampar	to camp
estar de vacaciones	to be on vacation
hacer las maletas	to pack (one's suitcases)
hacer un viaje	to take a trip
hacer (wind)surf	to (wind)surf
ir de compras	to go shopping
ir de vacaciones	to go on vacation
ir en autobús (m.), auto(móvil) (m.), motocicleta (f.), taxi (m.)	to go by bus, car, motorcycle, taxi

Variación léxica

automóvil ⟷ coche (*Esp.*), carro (*Amér. L.*)
autobús ⟷ camión (*Méx.*), guagua (*Caribe*)
motocicleta ⟷ moto (*coloquial*)

recursos

WB pp. 49–50	LM p. 25	ⓢ vhlcentral.com Lección 5

la agente de viajes

el pasaporte

Confirma una reservación. (confirmar)

En la agencia de viajes

la habitación

el ascensor

el empleado

la llave

el botones

la huésped

el huésped

En el hotel

Práctica

Saca/Toma fotos.
(sacar, tomar)

BIENVENIDOS

el avión

viajero

la inspectora
de aduanas

En el aeropuerto

Pesca.
(pescar)

Monta a caballo.
(montar)

Va en barco.
(ir)

el mar

Juegan a las
cartas. (jugar)

la playa

En la playa

1 **Escuchar** 🎧 Indicate who would probably make each statement you hear. Each answer is used twice.

a. el agente de viajes
b. la inspectora de aduanas
c. un empleado del hotel

1. __a__ 4. __b__
2. __a__ 5. __c__
3. __c__ 6. __b__

2 **¿Cierto o falso?** 🎧 Mario and his wife, Natalia, are planning their next vacation with a travel agent. Indicate whether each statement is **cierto** or **falso** according to what you hear in the conversation.

	Cierto	Falso
1. Mario y Natalia están en Puerto Rico.	○	⊙
2. Ellos quieren hacer un viaje a Puerto Rico.	⊙	○
3. Natalia prefiere ir a la montaña.	○	⊙
4. Mario quiere pescar en Puerto Rico.	⊙	○
5. La agente de viajes va a confirmar la reservación.	⊙	○

3 **Escoger** Choose the best answer for each sentence.

1. Un huésped es una persona que __b__.
 a. toma fotos b. está en un hotel c. pesca en el mar
2. Abrimos la puerta con __a__.
 a. una llave b. un caballo c. una llegada
3. Enrique tiene __a__ porque va a viajar a otro (*another*) país.
 a. un pasaporte b. una foto c. una llegada
4. Antes de (*Before*) ir de vacaciones, hay que __c__.
 a. pescar b. ir en tren c. hacer las maletas
5. Nosotros vamos en __a__ al aeropuerto.
 a. autobús b. pasaje c. viajero
6. Me gusta mucho ir al campo. El __a__ es increíble.
 a. paisaje b. pasaje c. equipaje

4 **Analogías** Complete the analogies using the words below. Two words will not be used.

auto	huésped	mar	sacar
botones	llegada	pasaporte	tren

1. acampar ⟶ campo ⊜ pescar ⟶ __mar__
2. agencia de viajes ⟶ agente ⊜ hotel ⟶ __botones__
3. llave ⟶ habitación ⊜ pasaje ⟶ __tren__
4. estudiante ⟶ libro ⊜ turista ⟶ __pasaporte__
5. aeropuerto ⟶ viajero ⊜ hotel ⟶ __huésped__
6. maleta ⟶ hacer ⊜ foto ⟶ __sacar__

1 **Expansion** ←👥→ In pairs, have students select one of the statements they hear and then write a conversation based on it.

1 **Script** 1. ¡Deben ir a Puerto Rico! Allí hay unas playas muy hermosas y pueden acampar. 2. Deben llamarme el lunes para confirmar la reservación. *Script continues on page 142.*

2 **Expansion** To challenge students, give them these true/false statements as items 6–9: **6. Mario prefiere una habitación doble. (Cierto.) 7. Natalia no quiere ir a la playa. (Falso.) 8. El hotel está en la playa. (Cierto.) 9. Mario va a montar a caballo. (Falso.)**

2 **Script** MARIO: Queremos ir de vacaciones a Puerto Rico. AGENTE: ¿Desean hacer un viaje al campo? NATALIA: Yo quiero ir a la playa. M: Pues, yo prefiero una habitación doble en un hotel con un buen paisaje. A: Puedo reservar para ustedes una habitación en el hotel San Juan que está en la playa. M: Es una buena idea, así yo voy a pescar y tú vas a montar a caballo. N: Muy bien, ¿puede confirmar la reservación? A: Claro que sí. *Textbook MP3s*

3 **Expansion** Ask a volunteer to help you model making statements similar to item 1. Say: **Un turista es una persona que… (va de vacaciones).** Then ask volunteers to do the same with **una agente de viajes, un botones, una inspectora de aduanas, un empleado de hotel.**

4 **Teaching Tip** Present these items using the following formula: *Acampar* tiene la misma relación con *campo* que *pescar* tiene con… (*mar*).

TEACHING OPTIONS

Small Groups ←👥→ Have students work in groups of three to write a riddle about one of the people or objects in the **Contextos** illustrations. The group must come up with at least three descriptions of their subject. Then one of the group members reads the description to the class and asks **¿Qué soy?** Ex: **Soy un pequeño libro. Tengo una foto de una persona. Soy necesario si un viajero quiere viajar a otro país. ¿Qué soy? (Soy un pasaporte.)**

Large Groups Split the class into two evenly-numbered groups. Hand out cards at random to the members of each group. One type of card should contain a verb or verb phrase (Ex: **confirmar una reservación**). The other will contain a related noun (Ex: **el agente de viajes**). The people within the groups must find their partners.

Teaching Tips
- Use the **Lección 5 Contextos** overheads to assist with this presentation.
- Point out that the names of months are not capitalized.
- Have students look over the seasons and months of the year. Call out the names of holidays or campus events and ask students to say when they occur.
- Use magazine pictures to cover as many weather conditions as possible from this page. Begin describing one of the pictures. Then, ask volunteers questions to elicit other weather expressions. Point out the use of **mucho/a** before nouns and **muy** before adjectives.
- Drill months by calling out a month and having students name the two that follow. Ex: **abril (mayo, junio)**.
- Point out the use of **primero** for the first day of the month.
- Ask volunteers to associate seasons (or months) and general weather patterns. Ex: **En invierno, hace frío/ nieva. En marzo, hace viento.**
- Review the shortened forms **buen** and **mal** before **tiempo**.
- Point out that **Llueve** and **Nieva** can also mean *It rains* and *It snows*. **Está lloviendo** and **Está nevando** emphasize *at this moment*. Students will learn more about this concept in **Estructura 5.2**.

Las estaciones y los meses del año

el invierno: diciembre, enero, febrero

la primavera: marzo, abril, mayo

el verano: junio, julio, agosto

el otoño: septiembre, octubre, noviembre

—¿**Cuál es la fecha de hoy?**
—**Es el primero de octubre.**
—**Es el dos de marzo.**
—**Es el diez de noviembre.**

What is today's date?
It's the first of October.
It's March 2nd.
It's November 10th.

El tiempo

—¿**Qué tiempo hace?**
—**Hace buen/mal tiempo.**

How's the weather?
The weather is good/bad.

Hace (mucho) calor.
It's (very) hot.

Hace (mucho) frío.
It's (very) cold.

Llueve. (llover o:ue)
It's raining.

Está lloviendo.
It's raining.

Nieva. (nevar e:ie)
It's snowing.

Está nevando.
It's snowing.

Más vocabulario

Está (muy) nublado.	*It's (very) cloudy.*
Hace fresco.	*It's cool.*
Hace (mucho) sol.	*It's (very) sunny.*
Hace (mucho) viento.	*It's (very) windy.*

TEACHING OPTIONS

Pairs ←👤→ Have pairs of students write descriptions for each of the drawings on this page. Ask one student to write sentences for the first four drawings and the other to write sentences for the next four. When finished, ask them to check their partner's work.
TPR Introduce the question ¿**Cuándo es tu cumpleaños?** and the phrase **Mi cumpleaños es…** Allow students five minutes to ask questions and line up according to their birthdays.

Extra Practice Create a series of cloze sentences about the weather in a certain place. Ex: **En Puerto Rico _____ mucho calor. (hace) No _____ muy nublado cuando _____ sol. (está; hace) No _____ frío pero a veces _____ fresco. (hace; hace) Cuando _____ mal tiempo, _____ y _____ viento pero nunca _____. (hace; llueve; hace; nieva)**

5 **El Hotel Regis** Label the floors of the hotel.

Números ordinales

primer (before a masculine singular noun), **primero/a**	first
segundo/a	second
tercer (before a masculine singular noun), **tercero/a**	third
cuarto/a	fourth
quinto/a	fifth
sexto/a	sixth
séptimo/a	seventh
octavo/a	eighth
noveno/a	ninth
décimo/a	tenth

a. __séptimo__ piso
b. __sexto__ piso
c. __quinto__ piso
d. __cuarto__ piso
e. __tercer__ piso
f. __segundo__ piso
g. __primer__ piso
h. __planta__ baja

6 **Contestar** Look at the illustrations of the months and seasons on the previous page. In pairs, take turns asking each other these questions.

> **modelo**
> **Estudiante 1:** ¿Cuál es el primer mes de la primavera?
> **Estudiante 2:** marzo

1. ¿Cuál es el primer mes del invierno? diciembre
2. ¿Cuál es el segundo mes de la primavera? abril
3. ¿Cuál es el tercer mes del otoño? noviembre
4. ¿Cuál es el primer mes del año? enero
5. ¿Cuál es el quinto mes del año? mayo
6. ¿Cuál es el octavo mes del año? agosto
7. ¿Cuál es el décimo mes del año? octubre
8. ¿Cuál es el segundo mes del verano? julio
9. ¿Cuál es el tercer mes del invierno? febrero
10. ¿Cuál es el sexto mes del año? junio

7 **Las estaciones** Name the season that applies to the description. Some answers may vary.

1. Las clases terminan. la primavera
2. Vamos a la playa. el verano
3. Acampamos. el verano
4. Nieva mucho. el invierno
5. Las clases empiezan. el otoño
6. Hace mucho calor. el verano
7. Llueve mucho. la primavera
8. Esquiamos. el invierno
9. el entrenamiento (*training*) de béisbol la primavera
10. el Día de Acción de Gracias (*Thanksgiving*) el otoño

8 **¿Cuál es la fecha?** Give the dates for these holidays.

> **modelo**
> el día de San Valentín 14 de febrero

1. el día de San Patricio 17 de marzo
2. el día de Halloween 31 de octubre
3. el primer día de verano 20–23 de junio
4. el Año Nuevo primero de enero
5. mi cumpleaños (*birthday*) Answers will vary.
6. mi día de fiesta favorito Answers will vary.

TEACHING OPTIONS

TPR Ask ten volunteers to line up facing the class. Make sure students know the starting point and what number in line they are. At random, call out ordinal numbers. The student to which each ordinal number corresponds has three seconds to step forward. If the student does not, he or she sits down and the order changes for the rest of the students further down the line. Who will be the last student(s) standing?

Game Ask four or five volunteers to come to the front of the room and hold races. (Make it difficult to reach the finish line; for example, have students hop on one foot or recite the ordinal numbers backwards.) Teach the words **llegó** and **fue** and, after each race, ask the class to summarize the results. Ex: ____ **llegó en quinto lugar.** ____ **fue la tercera persona (en llegar).**

5 **Teaching Tips**
• Point out that for numbers greater than ten, Spanish speakers tend to use cardinal numbers instead: **Está en el piso veintiuno.**
• Add a visual aspect to this vocabulary presentation. Write out each ordinal number on a separate sheet of paper and distribute them at random among ten students. Ask them to go to the front of the class, hold up their signs, and stand in the correct order.

5 **Expansion** Ask students questions about their lives, using ordinal numbers. Ex: **¿En qué piso vives? ¿En qué piso está mi oficina?**

6 **Teaching Tip** Before beginning this activity, have students close their books. Review seasons and months of the year by asking questions. Ex: **¿Qué estación tiene los meses de junio, julio y agosto?**

6 **Expansion** Ask a student which month his or her birthday is in. Ask another student to give the season the first student's birthday falls in.

7 **Expansion** Ask volunteers to describe events, situations, or holidays that are important to them or their families. Have the class guess the event and name the season that applies.

8 **Teaching Tip** Bring in a Spanish-language calendar. Ask students to name the important events and their scheduled dates.

8 **Expansion**
• Give these holidays to students as items 7–10: **7. Independencia de los EE.UU. (4 de julio) 8. Navidad (25 de diciembre) 9. Día de Acción de Gracias (cuarto jueves de noviembre) 10. Día de los Inocentes (primero de abril)**
• Ask heritage speakers to provide other important holidays, such as saints' days.

9 **Seleccionar** Paco is talking about his family and friends. Choose the word or phrase that best completes each sentence.

1. A mis padres les gusta ir a Yucatán porque (hace sol, nieva). hace sol
2. Mi primo de Kansas dice que durante (*during*) un tornado, hace mucho (sol, viento). viento
3. Mis amigos van a esquiar si (nieva, está nublado). nieva
4. Tomo el sol cuando (hace calor, llueve). hace calor
5. Nosotros vamos a ver una película si hace (buen, mal) tiempo. mal
6. Mi hermana prefiere correr cuando (hace mucho calor, hace fresco). hace fresco
7. Mis tíos van de excursión si hace (buen, mal) tiempo. buen
8. Mi padre no quiere jugar al golf si (hace fresco, llueve). llueve
9. Cuando hace mucho (sol, frío) no salgo de casa y tomo chocolate caliente (*hot*). frío
10. Hoy mi sobrino va al parque porque (está lloviendo, hace buen tiempo). hace buen tiempo

10 **El clima** With a partner, take turns asking and answering questions about the weather and temperatures in these cities. Use the model as a guide. Answers will vary.

> **modelo**
>
> **Estudiante 1:** ¿Qué tiempo hace hoy en Nueva York?
> **Estudiante 2:** Hace frío y hace viento.
> **Estudiante 1:** ¿Cuál es la temperatura máxima?
> **Estudiante 2:** Treinta y un grados (*degrees*).
> **Estudiante 1:** ¿Y la temperatura mínima?
> **Estudiante 2:** Diez grados.

soleado lluvia nieve nublado viento

Nueva York	Miami	Chicago	París	Madrid	Tokio
Máx. 31°	Máx. 84°	Máx. 23°	Máx. 38°	Máx. 42°	Máx. 49°
Mín. 10°	Mín. 62°	Mín. 5°	Mín. 26°	Mín. 27°	Mín. 34°

Montreal	México D.F.	Cozumel	Caracas	Quito	Buenos Aires
Máx. 18°	Máx. 76°	Máx. 91°	Máx. 80°	Máx. 60°	Máx. 85°
Mín. 2°	Mín. 41°	Mín. 73°	Mín. 72°	Mín. 51°	Mín. 59°

11 **Completar** Complete these sentences with your own ideas. Answers will vary.

1. Cuando hace sol, yo…
2. Cuando llueve, mis amigos y yo…
3. Cuando hace calor, mi familia…
4. Cuando hace viento, la gente…
5. Cuando hace frío, yo…
6. Cuando hace mal tiempo, mis amigos…
7. Cuando nieva, muchas personas…
8. Cuando está nublado, mis amigos y yo…
9. Cuando hace fresco, mis padres…
10. Cuando hace buen tiempo, mis amigos…

Practice more at **vhlcentral.com.**

NOTA CULTURAL

In most Spanish-speaking countries, temperatures are given in degrees Celsius. Use these formulas to convert between **grados centígrados** and **grados Fahrenheit**.
degrees C. × 9 ÷ 5 + 32 = degrees F.
degrees F. - 32 × 5 ÷ 9 = degrees C.

CONSULTA

Calor and **frío** can apply to both weather and people. Use **hacer** to describe weather conditions or climate.
(**Hace frío en Santiago.** *It's cold in Santiago.*)
Use **tener** to refer to people.
(**El viajero tiene frío.** *The traveler is cold.*)
See **Estructura 3.4** p. 93.

Comunicación

12 **Preguntas personales** In pairs, ask each other these questions. Answers will vary.

1. ¿Cuál es la fecha de hoy? ¿Qué estación es?
2. ¿Te gusta esta estación? ¿Por qué?
3. ¿Qué estación prefieres? ¿Por qué?
4. ¿Prefieres el mar o las montañas? ¿La playa o el campo? ¿Por qué?
5. Cuando haces un viaje, ¿qué te gusta hacer y ver?
6. ¿Piensas ir de vacaciones este verano? ¿Adónde quieres ir? ¿Por qué?
7. ¿Qué deseas ver y qué lugares quieres visitar?
8. ¿Cómo te gusta viajar? ¿En avión? ¿En motocicleta...?

13 **Encuesta** Your instructor will give you a worksheet. How does the weather affect what you do? Walk around the class and ask your classmates what they prefer or like to do in the weather conditions given. Note their responses on your worksheet. Make sure to personalize your survey by adding a few original questions to the list. Be prepared to report your findings to the class.
Answers will vary.

14 **La reservación** In pairs, imagine that one of you is a receptionist at a hotel and the other is a tourist calling to make a reservation. Read only the information that pertains to you. Then role-play the situation.

Turista

Vas a viajar a Yucatán con un amigo. Llegan a Cancún el 23 de febrero y necesitan una habitación con baño privado para cuatro noches. Ustedes quieren descansar y prefieren una habitación con vista (*view*) al mar. Averigua (*Find out*) toda la información que necesitas (el costo, cuántas camas, etc.) y decide si quieres hacer la reservación o no.

Empleado/a

Trabajas en la recepción del Hotel Oceanía en Cancún. Para el mes de febrero, sólo quedan (*remain*) dos habitaciones: una individual ($168/noche) en el primer piso y una doble ($134/noche) en el quinto piso que tiene descuento porque no hay ascensor. Todas las habitaciones tienen baño privado y vista (*view*) a la piscina.

15 **Minidrama** With two or three classmates, prepare a skit about people who are on vacation or are planning a vacation. The skit should take place in one of these locations. Answers will vary.

- una agencia de viajes
- una casa
- un aeropuerto, una estación de tren/autobuses
- un hotel
- el campo o la playa

Síntesis

16 **Un viaje** You are planning a trip to Mexico and have many questions about your itinerary on which your partner, a travel agent, will advise you. Your instructor will give you and your partner each a sheet with different instructions for acting out the roles. Answers will vary.

TEACHING OPTIONS

Pairs Tell students they are part of a scientific expedition to Antarctica (**la Antártida**). Have them write a letter back home about the weather conditions and their activities there. Begin the letter for them by writing **Queridos amigos** on the board.
Game Have each student create a *Bingo* card with 25 squares (five rows of five). Tell them to write **GRATIS** (*FREE*) in the center square and the name of a different city in each of the other squares. Have them exchange cards. Call out different weather expressions. Ex: **Hace viento.** Students who think this description fits a city or cities on their card should mark the square with the weather condition. In order to win, a student must have marked five squares in a row and be able to give the weather condition for each one. Ex: **Hace mucho viento en Chicago.**

12 Expansion Have pairs imagine that one of them is a journalist and the other is a celebrity. Then have them conduct the interview using questions 3–8.

13 Teaching Tip Model the activity by asking volunteers what they enjoy doing in hot weather. Ex: **Cuando hace calor, ¿qué haces? (Nado.)** Then distribute the *Hojas de actividades* (Activity Pack/Supersite).

14 Teaching Tips
- Have students sit back-to-back to better simulate a telephone conversation.
- Survey the class to see which room was the most popular. Have volunteers explain why.

15 Teaching Tip To simplify, ask the class to brainstorm a list of people and topics that may be encountered in each situation. Write the lists on the board.

15 Expansion Have students rate the skits as most original, funniest, most realistic, etc.

16 Teaching Tip Divide the class into pairs and distribute the handouts from the Activity Pack (Activity Pack/Supersite) that correspond to this Information Gap Activity. Give students ten minutes to complete the activity.

16 Expansion Have pairs put together an ideal itinerary for someone else traveling to Mexico, like a classmate, a relative, someone famous, or **el/la profesor(a).**

Section Goals

In **Fotonovela**, students will:
- receive comprehensible input from free-flowing discourse
- learn functional phrases that preview lesson grammatical structures

Instructional Resources
Supersite/DVD: *Fotonovela*
Supersite: Resources (Scripts, Translations, Answer Keys)
WebSAM
Video Manual, pp. 203–204

Video Recap: Lección 4
Before doing this **Fotonovela** section, review the previous episode with these questions:
1. ¿Qué prefiere hacer tía Ana María en sus ratos libres? (Ella nada, juega al tenis y al golf y va al cine y a los museos.)
2. ¿Adónde van Miguel, Maru, Marissa y Jimena? (Van a un cenote.)
3. ¿Qué van a hacer Felipe y Juan Carlos? (Van a jugar al fútbol con Eduardo y Pablo.)
4. ¿Qué quieren comer los chicos después de jugar al fútbol? (Quieren comer mole.)

Video Synopsis
The friends watch the weather report on TV and discuss weather and seasons in their hometowns. **Felipe** rouses **Miguel** so they don't miss the bus to the beach. The group checks in to their hotel. At the beach, **Maru** and **Miguel** windsurf. **Miguel** gets back at **Felipe**.

Teaching Tips
- Have the class glance over the **Fotonovela** captions and list words and phrases related to tourism.
- Ask individuals how they are today, using **cansado/a** and **aburrido/a.**
- ← Ask the class to describe the perfect hotel. Ex: ¿Cómo es el hotel ideal? ¿Cómo es la habitación de hotel perfecta?

¡Vamos a la playa!

Los seis amigos hacen un viaje a la playa.

PERSONAJES

 FELIPE **JUAN CARLOS**

S Video: *Fotonovela*
Record and Compare

TÍA ANA MARÍA ¿Están listos para su viaje a la playa?
TODOS Sí.
TÍA ANA MARÍA Excelente... ¡A la estación de autobuses!
MARU ¿Dónde está Miguel?
FELIPE Yo lo traigo.

(se escucha un grito de Miguel)
FELIPE Ya está listo. Y tal vez enojado. Ahorita vamos.

FELIPE No está nada mal el hotel, ¿verdad? Limpio, cómodo... ¡Oye, Miguel! ¿Todavía estás enojado conmigo? (*a Juan Carlos*) Miguel está de mal humor. No me habla.
JUAN CARLOS ¿Todavía?

EMPLEADO Bienvenidas. ¿En qué puedo servirles?
MARU Hola. Tenemos una reservación para seis personas para esta noche.
EMPLEADO ¿A nombre de quién?
JIMENA ¿Díaz? ¿López? No estoy segura.

EMPLEADO No encuentro su nombre. Ah, no, ahora sí lo veo, aquí está. Díaz. Dos habitaciones en el primer piso para seis huéspedes.

EMPLEADO Aquí están las llaves de sus habitaciones.
MARU Gracias. Una cosa más. Mi novio y yo queremos hacer windsurf, pero no tenemos tablas.
EMPLEADO El botones las puede conseguir para ustedes.

TEACHING OPTIONS

Video Tips General suggestions for using video clips in the classroom can be found on page IAE-10 of this Instructor's Annotated Edition.

¡Vamos a la playa! → Before viewing the **¡Vamos a la playa!** episode of the **Fotonovela**, ask students to brainstorm a list of things that might happen in an episode in which the characters check into a hotel and go to the beach. Then play the **¡Vamos a la playa!** episode once without sound and have the class create a plot summary based on visual clues. Finally, show the video segment with sound and have the class correct any mistaken guesses and fill in any gaps. Ask comprehension questions as a follow-up.

MARISSA

JIMENA

MARU

MIGUEL

MAITE FUENTES

ANA MARÍA

EMPLEADO

7

JUAN CARLOS ¿Qué hace este libro aquí? ¿Estás estudiando en la playa?

JIMENA Sí, es que tengo un examen la próxima semana.

8

JUAN CARLOS Ay, Jimena. ¡No! ¿Vamos a nadar?

JIMENA Bueno, como estudiar es tan aburrido y el tiempo está tan bonito...

MARISSA Yo estoy un poco cansada. ¿Y tú? ¿Por qué no estás nadando?

FELIPE Es por causa de Miguel.

9

10

MARISSA Hmm, estoy confundida.

FELIPE Esta mañana. ¡Sigue enojado conmigo!

MARISSA No puede seguir enojado tanto tiempo.

recursos

VM
pp. 203–204

vhlcentral.com
Lección 5

Expresiones útiles

Talking with hotel personnel

¿En qué puedo servirles?
How can I help you?
Tenemos una reservación.
We have a reservation.
¿A nombre de quién?
In whose name?
¿Quizás López? ¿Tal vez Díaz?
Maybe López? Maybe Díaz?
Ahora lo veo, aquí está. Díaz.
Now I see it. Here it is. Díaz.
Dos habitaciones en el primer piso para seis huéspedes.
Two rooms on the first floor for six guests.
Aquí están las llaves.
Here are the keys.

Describing a hotel

No está nada mal el hotel.
The hotel isn't bad at all.
Todo está tan limpio y cómodo.
Everything is so clean and comfortable.
Es excelente/estupendo/fabuloso/ fenomenal/increíble/magnífico/ maravilloso/perfecto.
It's excellent/stupendous/fabulous/ phenomenal/incredible/magnificent/ marvelous/perfect.

Talking about how you feel

Yo estoy un poco cansado/a.
I am a little tired.
Estoy confundido/a. *I'm confused.*
Todavía estoy/Sigo enojado/a contigo.
I'm still angry with you.

Additional vocabulary

afuera *outside*
agradable *pleasant*
el balde *bucket*
la crema de afeitar
shaving cream
entonces *so, then*
es igual *it's the same*
el frente (frío) *(cold) front*
el grito *scream*
la temporada *period of time*

Expresiones útiles Remind students that **está**, **están**, and **estoy** are present-tense forms of the verb **estar**, which is often used with adjectives that describe conditions and emotions. Remind students that **Es** is a present-tense form of the verb **ser**, which is often used to describe characteristics of people and things and to make generalizations. Draw students' attention to video stills 7 and 9. Point out that **Estás estudiando** and **estás nadando** are examples of the present progressive, which is used to emphasize an action in progress. Finally, point out the captions for video stills 1, 4, and 6 and explain that **lo** and **las** are examples of direct object pronouns. Explain that these are words that replace direct object nouns in order to avoid repetition. Tell students that they will learn more about these concepts in **Estructura**.

Teaching Tip
👤↔👤 Have students work in groups of six to read the **Fotonovela** captions aloud (have one student read the role of both **tía Ana María** and the **empleado**). Then have one group come to the front of the class and role-play the scenes. Encourage them to use props and gestures.

Nota cultural The **Yucatán** peninsula is warm year-round, but there are rainy and dry seasons. Generally, the dry season lasts from November to April and the wet season runs from May through October. Hurricanes occur in the late summer and fall. The **Yucatán's** average temperature is 25°C to 27°C (77°F to 81°F), rarely dropping below 16°C (61°F) or rising above 49°C (120°F).

TEACHING OPTIONS

Pairs Ask pairs to write five true/false statements based on the **¡Vamos a la playa!** captions. Then have them exchange papers with another pair, who will complete the activity and correct the false statements. Ask volunteers to read a few statements for the class, who will answer and point out the caption that contains the information.

Large Groups 👤↔👤 Ask students to work in groups to rewrite the **¡Vamos a la playa!** episode using a different ending or location. Suggest new locations such as a ski resort, a big city or a campground. Allow groups time to prepare and ask them to ad-lib their new versions for the class. You may want to assign this activity as homework and have students present it in the next class period for review.

¿Qué pasó?

1 **Completar** Complete these sentences with the correct term from the word bank.

aburrido	botones	la llave
el aeropuerto	la estación de autobuses	montar a caballo
amable	habitaciones	reservación

1. Los amigos van a ___la estación de autobuses___ para ir a la playa.
2. La ___reservación___ del hotel está a nombre de los Díaz.
3. Los amigos tienen dos ___habitaciones___ para seis personas.
4. El ___botones___ puede conseguir tablas de windsurf para Maru.
5. Jimena dice que estudiar en vacaciones es muy ___aburrido___.

2 **Identificar** Identify the person who would make each statement.

EMPLEADO **MARU** **TÍA ANA MARÍA** **FELIPE** **JUAN CARLOS**

1. No lo encuentro, ¿a nombre de quién está su reservación? empleado
2. ¿Por qué estás estudiando en la playa? ¡Mejor vamos a nadar! Juan Carlos
3. Nuestra reservación es para seis personas en dos habitaciones. Maru
4. El hotel es limpio y cómodo, pero estoy triste porque Miguel no me habla. Felipe
5. Suban al autobús y ¡buen viaje a la playa! Ana María

3 **Ordenar** Place these events in the correct order.

___3___ a. El empleado busca la reservación.
___5___ b. Marissa dice que está confundida.
___1___ c. Los amigos están listos para ir a la playa.
___4___ d. El empleado da (*gives*) las llaves de las habitaciones a las chicas.
___2___ e. Miguel grita (*screams*).

4 **Conversar** With a partner, use these cues to create a conversation between a hotel employee and a guest in Mexico. Answers will vary.

Huésped	**Empleado/a**
Say hi to the employee and ask for your reservation. →	Tell the guest that you can't find his/her reservation.
Tell the employee that the reservation is in your name. →	Tell him/her that you found the reservation and that it's for a double room.
Tell the employee that the hotel is very clean and orderly. →	Say that you agree with the guest, welcome him/her and give him/her the keys.
Ask the employee to call the bellhop to help you with your luggage. →	Call the bellhop to help the guest with his/her luggage.

 Practice more at **vhlcentral.com**.

Pronunciación

Audio: Concepts, Activities Record & Compare

Spanish b and v

bueno	**vóleibol**	**biblioteca**	**vivir**

There is no difference in pronunciation between the Spanish letters **b** and **v**. However, each letter can be pronounced two different ways, depending on which letters appear next to them.

bonito	**viajar**	**también**	**investigar**

B and **v** are pronounced like the English hard *b* when they appear either as the first letter of a word, at the beginning of a phrase, or after **m** or **n**.

deber	**novio**	**abril**	**cerveza**

In all other positions, **b** and **v** have a softer pronunciation, which has no equivalent in English. Unlike the hard **b**, which is produced by tightly closing the lips and stopping the flow of air, the soft **b** is produced by keeping the lips slightly open.

bola	**vela**	**Caribe**	**declive**

In both pronunciations, there is no difference in sound between **b** and **v**. The English *v* sound, produced by friction between the upper teeth and lower lip, does not exist in Spanish. Instead, the soft **b** comes from friction between the two lips.

Verónica y su esposo cantan boleros.

When **b** or **v** begins a word, its pronunciation depends on the previous word. At the beginning of a phrase or after a word that ends in **m** or **n**, it is pronounced as a hard **b**.

Benito es de Boquerón pero vive en Victoria.

Words that begin with **b** or **v** are pronounced with a soft **b** if they appear immediately after a word that ends in a vowel or any consonant other than **m** or **n**.

Práctica Read these words aloud to practice the **b** and the **v**.

1. hablamos	4. van	7. doble	10. nublado
2. trabajar	5. contabilidad	8. novia	11. llave
3. botones	6. bien	9. béisbol	12. invierno

No hay mal que por bien no venga.[1]

Hombre prevenido vale por dos.[2]

Oraciones Read these sentences aloud to practice the **b** and the **v**.

1. Vamos a Guaynabo en autobús.
2. Voy de vacaciones a la Isla Culebra.
3. Tengo una habitación individual en el octavo piso.
4. Víctor y Eva van en avión al Caribe.
5. La planta baja es bonita también.
6. ¿Qué vamos a ver en Bayamón?
7. Beatriz, la novia de Víctor, es de Arecibo, Puerto Rico.

Refranes Read these sayings aloud to practice the **b** and the **v**.

2 An ounce of prevention equals a pound of cure.
1 Every cloud has a silver lining.

recursos	
LM p. 26	vhlcentral.com Lección 5

Section Goal

In **Pronunciación**, students will be introduced to the pronunciation of **b** and **v**.

Instructional Resources

Supersite: Audio (Textbook and Lab MP3 Files); Resources (Scripts, Answer Keys)
WebSAM
Lab Manual, p. 26

Teaching Tips

- Emphasize that **b (alta/grande)** and **v (baja/chica)** are pronounced identically in Spanish, but depending on the letter's position in a word, each can be pronounced two ways. Pronounce **vóleibol** and **vivir** and have students listen for the difference between the initial and medial sounds represented by **b** and **v**.
- Explain the cases in which **b** and **v** are pronounced like English *b* in *boy* and model the pronunciation of **bonito**, **viajar**, **también**, and **investigar**.
- Point out that before **b** or **v**, **n** is usually pronounced **m**.
- Explain that in all other positions, **b** and **v** are fricatives. Pronounce **deber**, **novio**, **abril**, and **cerveza** and stress that the friction is between the two lips.
- Remind the class that Spanish has no sound like the English **v**. Pronounce **vida**, **vacaciones**, **avión**, and **automóvil**.
- Explain that the same rules apply in connected speech. Practice with phrases like **de vacaciones** and **de ida y vuelta**.

Práctica/Oraciones/Refranes

These exercises are recorded on the *Textbook MP3s*. You may want to play the audio so that students practice listening to Spanish spoken by speakers other than yourself.

Section Goals

In **Cultura**, students will:
- read about **Las cataratas del Iguazú**
- learn travel-related terms
- read about **Punta del Este**, Uruguay
- read about popular vacation destinations in the Spanish-speaking world

Instructional Resources

Supersite/DVD: *Flash cultura*
Supersite: Resources (Scripts, Translations, Answer Keys)
WebSAM
Video Manual, pp. 275–276

En detalle

Antes de leer Ask students what kind of travel interests them. Ex: **¿Te gusta acampar o dormir en un hotel? ¿Adónde prefieres ir: a la ciudad, a las montañas…? Cuando estás de vacaciones, ¿te gusta descansar o vivir una aventura? ¿Visitar museos o observar paisajes?** Then ask students to predict what a tourist would see and do near a waterfall.

Lectura

- Explain that the **Guaraní** are an indigenous group who traditionally inhabit areas of Paraguay, northern Argentina, southern Brazil, and parts of Uruguay and Bolivia. The **Guaraní** language is one of the two official languages of Paraguay.
- The **Iguazú** Falls have been featured in many movies, most notably in *The Mission* (1986), starring Robert DeNiro and Jeremy Irons.

Después de leer Ask students through which country they would prefer to visit **Iguazú** and why.

1 Expansion Give students these true/false statements as items 11–12: 11. The **Tren Ecológico de la Selva** takes tourists to San Martín Island. (**Falso.** It takes them to the walkways.) 12. **Piedra Volada** is the tallest waterfall in Mexico. (**Cierto.**)

EN DETALLE

Additional Reading
Video: *Flash cultura*

Las cataratas del Iguazú

Imagine the impressive and majestic Niagara Falls, the most powerful waterfall in North America. Now, if you can, imagine a waterfall four times as wide and almost twice as tall that caused Eleanor Roosevelt to exclaim "Poor Niagara!" upon seeing it for the first time. Welcome to **las cataratas del Iguazú!**

Garganta del Diablo
Isla San Martín

Iguazú is located in Iguazú National Park, an area of subtropical jungle where Argentina meets Brazil. Its name comes from the indigenous Guaraní word for "great water." A UNESCO World Heritage Site, **las cataratas del Iguazú** span three kilometers and comprise 275 cascades split into two main sections by the San Martín Island. Most of the falls are about 82 meters (270 feet) high. The horseshoe-shaped cataract **Garganta del Diablo** (Devil's Throat) has the greatest water flow and is considered to be the most impressive; it also marks the border between Argentina and Brazil.

Each country offers different views and tourist options. Most visitors opt to use the numerous catwalks that are available on both sides; however, from the Argentinean side, tourists can get very close to the falls, whereas Brazil provides more panoramic views. If you don't mind getting wet, a jet boat tour is a good choice; those looking for wildlife—such as toucans, ocelots, butterflies, and jaguars—should head for San Martín Island. Brazil boasts less conventional ways to view the falls, such as helicopter rides and rappelling, while Argentina focuses on sustainability with its **Tren Ecológico de la Selva** (*Ecological Jungle Train*), an environmentally friendly way to reach the walkways.

No matter which way you choose to enjoy the falls, you are certain to be captivated.

Más cascadas° en Latinoamérica

Nombre	País	Altura°	Datos
Salto Ángel	Venezuela	979 metros	la más alta° del mundo°
Catarata del Gocta	Perú	771 metros	descubierta° en 2006
Piedra Volada	México	453 metros	la más alta de México

cascadas *waterfalls* **Altura** *Height* más alta *tallest* mundo *world* descubierta *discovered*

ACTIVIDADES

1 ¿Cierto o falso? Indicate whether these statements are **cierto** or **falso**. Correct the false statements.

1. Iguazú Falls is located on the border of Argentina and Brazil. **Cierto.**
2. Niagara Falls is four times as wide as Iguazú Falls. **Falso.** Iguazú is four times as wide as Niagara Falls.
3. Iguazú Falls has a few cascades, each about 82 meters. **Falso.** Iguazú is composed of 275 cascades about 82 meters tall.
4. Tourists visiting Iguazú can see exotic wildlife. **Cierto.**
5. *Iguazú* is the Guaraní word for "blue water." **Falso.** *Iguazú* is the Guaraní word for "great water."
6. You can access the walkways by taking the **Garganta del Diablo**. **Falso.** One way of accessing the walkways is taking the **Tren Ecológico de la Selva**.
7. It is possible for tourists to visit Iguazú Falls by air. **Cierto.**
8. **Salto Ángel** is the tallest waterfall in the world. **Cierto.**
9. There are no waterfalls in Mexico. **Falso.** The **Piedra Volada** is in Mexico.
10. For the best views of Iguazú Falls, tourists should visit the Brazilian side. **Cierto.**

TEACHING OPTIONS

La leyenda Share this legend of the **Iguazú** Falls with students: Many ages ago, in the **Iguazú** River there lived a god-serpent, **Mboí**, to whom the **Guaraní** tribes sacrificed a young woman during their annual gathering. At one such gathering, a young man named **Tarobá** instantly fell in love with **Naipí**, who was to be sacrificed. After pleading in vain to have her spared, one night **Tarobá** took **Naipí** and tried to flee with her in his canoe.

The furious **Mboí** awoke and split the river in two, forming the waterfall and trapping the pair. He transformed **Naipí** into a rock at the base of the falls and **Tarobá** into a tree perched at the edge of the abyss. Lest the lovers try to reunite, the watchful **Mboí** keeps an eternal vigil from deep under the waters of the **Garganta del Diablo**. Now ask them to think of other creation legends they know (Ex: Paul Bunyan and the Great Lakes).

ASÍ SE DICE

Viajes y turismo

el asiento del medio, del pasillo, de la ventanilla	center, aisle, window seat
el itinerario	itinerary
media pensión	breakfast and one meal included
el ómnibus (Arg., Perú)	el autobús
pensión completa	all meals included
el puente	long weekend (lit., bridge)

EL MUNDO HISPANO

Destinos populares

- **Las playas del Parque Nacional Manuel Antonio** (Costa Rica) ofrecen° la oportunidad de nadar y luego caminar por el bosque tropical°.

- **Teotihuacán** (México) Desde la época° de los aztecas, aquí se celebra el equinoccio de primavera en la Pirámide del Sol.

- **Puerto Chicama** (Perú), con sus olas° de cuatro kilómetros de largo°, es un destino para surfistas expertos.

- **Tikal** (Guatemala) Aquí puedes ver las maravillas de la selva° y ruinas de la civilización maya.

- **Las playas de Rincón** (Puerto Rico) son ideales para descansar y observar ballenas°.

ofrecen *offer* bosque tropical *rainforest* Desde la época *Since the time* olas *waves* de largo *in length* selva *jungle* ballenas *whales*

PERFIL

Punta del Este

One of South America's largest and most fashionable beach resort towns is Uruguay's **Punta del Este**, a narrow strip of land containing twenty miles of pristine beaches. Its peninsular shape gives it two very different seascapes. **La Playa Mansa**, facing the bay and therefore the more protected side, has calm waters. Here, people practice water sports like swimming, water skiing, windsurfing, and diving. **La Playa Brava**, facing the east, receives the Atlantic Ocean's powerful, wave-producing winds, making it popular for surfing, body boarding, and kite surfing. Besides the beaches, posh shopping, and world-famous nightlife, **Punta** offers its 600,000 yearly visitors yacht and fishing clubs, golf courses, and excursions to observe sea lions at the **Isla de Lobos** nature reserve.

Conexión Internet

¿Cuáles son los sitios más populares para el turismo en Puerto Rico?

Go to vhlcentral.com to find more cultural information related to this **Cultura** section.

ACTIVIDADES

2 Comprensión Complete the sentences.
1. En las playas de Rincón puedes ver ___ballenas___.
2. Cerca de 600.000 turistas visitan _Punta del Este_ cada año.
3. En el avión pides un _asiento de la ventanilla_ si te gusta ver el paisaje.
4. En Punta del Este, la gente prefiere nadar en la Playa _Mansa_.
5. El _ómnibus_ es un medio de transporte en Perú.

3 De vacaciones Spring break is coming up, and you want to go on a short vacation with some friends. Working in a small group, decide which of the locations featured on these pages best suits the group's likes and interests. Come to an agreement about how you will get there, where you prefer to stay and for how long, and what each of you will do during free time. Present your trip to the class.
Answers will vary.

Practice more at **vhlcentral.com**.

recursos
VM pp. 275–276
vhlcentral.com Lección 5

Section Goals

In **Estructura 5.1**, students will learn:
• to use **estar** to describe conditions and emotions
• adjectives that describe conditions and emotions

Instructional Resources

Supersite: Audio (Lab MP3 Files); Resources (*PowerPoints*, Activity Pack, Scripts, Answer Keys); Testing Program (Quizzes)
WebSAM
Workbook, pp. 51–52
Lab Manual, p. 27

Teaching Tips

• →👥← Ask students to find examples of **estar** used with adjectives in the **Fotonovela**. Have volunteers explain why **estar** instead of **ser** is used in each example.

• Remind students that adjectives agree in number and gender with the nouns they modify.

• Add a visual aspect to this grammar presentation. Bring in personal or magazine photos of people with varying facial expressions. Hold up each one and state the person's emotion. Ex: **Mi esposa y yo estamos contentos.**

• Point to objects and people and have volunteers supply the correct form of **estar** + [*adjective*]. Ex: Point to windows. (**Están abiertas.**)

• Use TPR to practice the adjectives. Have the class stand and signal a student. Say: ____, **estás enojado/a.** (Student will make an angry face.) Vary by indicating more than one student.

• Point out the use of **de** with **enamorado/a** and **por** with **preocupado/a**. Write cloze sentences on the board and have students complete them. Ex: **Michelle Obama está ____ Barack Obama.** (**enamorada de**)

5.1 Estar with conditions and emotions

ANTE TODO As you learned in **Lecciones 1** and **2**, the verb **estar** is used to talk about how you feel and to say where people, places, and things are located. **Estar** is also used with adjectives to talk about certain emotional and physical conditions.

▶ Use **estar** with adjectives to describe the physical condition of places and things.

La habitación **está** sucia.
The room is dirty.

La puerta **está** cerrada.
The door is closed.

▶ Use **estar** with adjectives to describe how people feel, both mentally and physically.

Yo estoy cansada.

¿Están listos para su viaje?

▶ **¡Atención!** Two important expressions with **estar** that you can use to talk about conditions and emotions are **estar de buen humor** (*to be in a good mood*) and **estar de mal humor** (*to be in a bad mood*).

Adjectives that describe emotions and conditions

abierto/a	open	**contento/a**	happy; content	**listo/a**	ready
aburrido/a	bored	**desordenado/a**	disorderly	**nervioso/a**	nervous
alegre	happy; joyful	**enamorado/a (de)**	in love (with)	**ocupado/a**	busy
avergonzado/a	embarrassed			**ordenado/a**	orderly
cansado/a	tired	**enojado/a**	mad; angry	**preocupado/a (por)**	worried (about)
cerrado/a	closed	**equivocado/a**	wrong		
cómodo/a	comfortable	**feliz**	happy	**seguro/a**	sure
confundido/a	confused	**limpio/a**	clean	**sucio/a**	dirty
				triste	sad

¡INTÉNTALO! Provide the present tense forms of **estar**, and choose which adjective best completes the sentence.

1. La biblioteca ___está___ (cerrada / nerviosa) los domingos por la noche. *cerrada*
2. Nosotros ___estamos___ muy (ocupados / equivocados) todos los lunes. *ocupados*
3. Ellas ___están___ (alegres / confundidas) porque tienen vacaciones. *alegres*
4. Javier ___está___ (enamorado / ordenado) de Maribel. *enamorado*
5. Diana ___está___ (enojada / limpia) con su novio. *enojada*
6. Yo ___estoy___ (nerviosa / abierta) por el viaje. *nerviosa*
7. La habitación siempre ___está___ (ordenada / segura) cuando vienen sus padres. *ordenada*
8. Ustedes no comprenden; ___están___ (equivocados / tristes). *equivocados*

CONSULTA
To review the present tense of **estar**, see **Estructura 2.3**, p. 55.
• • •
To review the present tense of **ser**, see **Estructura 1.3**, p. 20.

recursos

WB pp. 51–52

LM p. 27

S vhlcentral.com Lección 5

TEACHING OPTIONS

TPR Call out a sentence using an adjective and have students mime the emotion or show the condition. Ex: **Sus libros están abiertos.** (Students show their open books.) **Ustedes están alegres.** (Students act happy.) Next, call on volunteers to act out an emotion or condition and have the class tell what is going on. Ex: A student pretends to cry. (**Carlos está triste.**)

Video →👥← Replay the **Fotonovela** episode and ask comprehension questions using **estar** and adjectives expressing emotions or conditions. Ex: **¿Cómo está el hotel?** (**Está limpio y cómodo.**) **¿Está de mal humor Miguel?** (**Sí, está de mal humor.**) **¿Quién está cansado?** (**Marissa está cansada.**)

Práctica y Comunicación

1 **¿Cómo están?** Complete Martín's statements about how he and other people are feeling. In the first blank, fill in the correct form of **estar**. In the second blank, fill in the adjective that best fits the context. *Some answers may vary.*

1. Yo ___estoy___ un poco ___nervioso___ porque tengo un examen mañana.
2. Mi hermana Patricia ___está___ muy ___contenta___ porque mañana va a hacer una excursión al campo.
3. Mis hermanos Juan y José salen de la casa a las cinco de la mañana. Por la noche, siempre ___están___ muy ___cansados___ .
4. Mi amigo Ramiro ___está___ ___enamorado___ ; su novia se llama Adela.
5. Mi papá y sus colegas ___están___ muy ___ocupados___ hoy. ¡Hay mucho trabajo!
6. Patricia y yo ___estamos___ un poco ___preocupados___ por ellos porque trabajan mucho.
7. Mi amiga Mónica ___está___ un poco ___triste/enojada___ porque su novio no puede salir esta noche.
8. Esta clase no es muy interesante. ¿Tú ___estás___ ___aburrido/a___ también?

2 **Describir** Describe these people and places. *Answers will vary. Sample answers:*

1. Anabela
Está contenta/alegre/feliz.

2. Juan y Luisa
Están enojados.

3. la habitación de Teresa
Está ordenada/limpia.

4. la habitación de César
Está desordenada/sucia.

3 **Situaciones** With a partner, use **estar** to talk about how you feel in these situations.
Answers will vary.

1. Cuando hace sol…
2. Cuando tomas un examen…
3. Cuando viajas en avión…
4. Cuando estás en la clase de español…
5. Cuando ves una película con tu actor/actriz favorito/a…

4 **En la tele** In small groups, imagine that you are a family that stars on a reality TV show. You are vacationing together, but the trip isn't going well for everyone. Write the script of a scene from the show and then act it out. Use at least six adjectives from the previous page and be creative!

> **modelo**
> **Papá:** ¿Por qué estás enojada, María Rosa? El hotel es muy bonito y las habitaciones están limpias.
> **Mamá:** ¡Pero mira, Roberto! Las maletas de Elisa están abiertas y, como siempre, sus cosas están muy desordenadas.

 Practice more at **vhlcentral.com**.

5.2 The present progressive

ANTE TODO Both Spanish and English use the present progressive, which consists of the present tense of the verb *to be* and the present participle of another verb (the *-ing* form in English).

Las chicas están hablando con el empleado del hotel.

¿Estás estudiando en la playa?

▶ Form the present progressive with the present tense of **estar** and a present participle.

FORM OF **ESTAR** + PRESENT PARTICIPLE		FORM OF **ESTAR** + PRESENT PARTICIPLE	
Estoy	**pescando.**	**Estamos**	**comiendo.**
I am	*fishing.*	*We are*	*eating.*

▶ The present participle of regular **-ar**, **-er**, and **-ir** verbs is formed as follows:

INFINITIVE	STEM	ENDING	PRESENT PARTICIPLE
hablar	habl-	**-ando**	habl**ando**
comer	com-	**-iendo**	com**iendo**
escribir	escrib-	**-iendo**	escrib**iendo**

▶ **¡Atención!** When the stem of an **-er** or **-ir** verb ends in a vowel, the present participle ends in **-yendo**.

INFINITIVE	STEM	ENDING	PRESENT PARTICIPLE
leer	le-	**-yendo**	le**yendo**
oír	o-	**-yendo**	o**yendo**
traer	tra-	**-yendo**	tra**yendo**

▶ **Ir**, **poder**, and **venir** have irregular present participles (**yendo**, **pudiendo**, **viniendo**). Several other verbs have irregular present participles that you will need to learn.

▶ **-Ir** stem-changing verbs have a stem change in the present participle.

-ir stem-changing verbs

e:ie in the present tense	e → i in the present participle
preferir	prefiriendo

e:i in the present tense	e → i in the present participle
conseguir	consiguiendo

o:ue in the present tense	o → u in the present participle
dormir	durmiendo

COMPARE & CONTRAST

The use of the present progressive is much more restricted in Spanish than in English. In Spanish, the present progressive is mainly used to emphasize that an action is in progress at the time of speaking.

> Maru **está escuchando** música latina **ahora mismo**.
> *Maru is listening to Latin music right now.*

> Felipe y su amigo **todavía están jugando** al fútbol.
> *Felipe and his friend are still playing soccer.*

In English, the present progressive is often used to talk about situations and actions that occur over an extended period of time or in the future. In Spanish, the simple present tense is often used instead.

> Xavier **estudia** computación este semestre.
> *Xavier is studying computer science this semester.*

> Marissa **sale** mañana para los Estados Unidos.
> *Marissa is leaving tomorrow for the United States.*

¿Está pensando en su futuro?
Nosotros, sí.

🏛 **BANCO** CONGRESO 🏛

Preparándolo para el mañana

¡INTÉNTALO! Create complete sentences by putting the verbs in the present progressive.

1. mis amigos / descansar en la playa *Mis amigos están descansando en la playa.*
2. nosotros / practicar deportes *Estamos practicando deportes.*
3. Carmen / comer en casa *Carmen está comiendo en casa.*
4. nuestro equipo / ganar el partido *Nuestro equipo está ganando el partido.*
5. yo / leer el periódico *Estoy leyendo el periódico.*
6. él / pensar comprar una bicicleta *Está pensando comprar una bicicleta.*
7. ustedes / jugar a las cartas *Ustedes están jugando a las cartas.*
8. José y Francisco / dormir *José y Francisco están durmiendo.*
9. Marisa / leer correo electrónico *Marisa está leyendo correo electrónico.*
10. yo / preparar sándwiches *Estoy preparando sándwiches.*
11. Carlos / tomar fotos *Carlos está tomando fotos.*
12. ¿dormir / tú? *¿Estás durmiendo?*

recursos

WB
p. 53

LM
p. 28

Ⓢ
vhlcentral.com
Lección 5

Teaching Tips
- Discuss each point in the **Compare & Contrast** box.
- Write these statements on the board and ask students if they would use the present or the present progressive in Spanish for each item. 1. I'm going on vacation tomorrow. 2. She's packing her suitcase right now. 3. They are fishing in Puerto Rico this week. 4. Roberto is still working. Then ask students to translate the items. (**1. Voy de vacaciones mañana. 2. Está haciendo la maleta ahora mismo. 3. Pescan en Puerto Rico esta semana. 4. Roberto todavía está trabajando.**)
- In this lesson, students learn **todavía** to mean *still* in the present progressive tense. You may want to point out that **todavía** also means *yet*. They will be able to use that meaning in later lessons as they learn the past tenses.
- Have students rewrite the sentences in the **¡Inténtalo!** activity using the simple present. Ask volunteers to explain how the sentences change depending on whether the verb is in the present progressive or the simple present.

TEACHING OPTIONS

Pairs Have students write eight sentences in Spanish modeled after the examples in the **Compare & Contrast** box. There should be two sentences modeled after each example. Ask students to replace the verbs with blanks. Then, have students exchange papers with a partner and complete the sentences.

Extra Practice ←👤→ For homework, ask students to find five photos from a magazine or create five simple drawings of people performing different activities. For each image, have them write one sentence telling where the people are, one explaining what they are doing, and one describing how they feel. Ex: **Juan está en la biblioteca. Está estudiando. Está cansado.**

Práctica

1 **Completar** Alfredo's Spanish class is preparing to travel to Puerto Rico. Use the present progressive of the verb in parentheses to complete Alfredo's description of what everyone is doing.

1. Yo _estoy investigando_ (investigar) la situación política de la isla (*island*).
2. La esposa del profesor _está haciendo_ (hacer) las maletas.
3. Marta y José Luis _están buscando_ (buscar) información sobre San Juan en Internet.
4. Enrique y yo _estamos leyendo_ (leer) un correo electrónico de nuestro amigo puertorriqueño.
5. Javier _está aprendiendo_ (aprender) mucho sobre la cultura puertorriqueña.
6. Y tú _estás practicando_ (practicar) el español, ¿verdad?

2 **¿Qué están haciendo?** María and her friends are vacationing at a resort in San Juan, Puerto Rico. Complete her description of what everyone is doing right now.

◄ **CONSULTA**
For more information about Puerto Rico, see **Panorama**, pp. 170–171.

1. Yo
estoy escribiendo una carta.

2. Javier
está buceando en el mar.

3. Alejandro y Rebeca
están jugando a las cartas.

4. Celia y yo
estamos tomando el sol.

5. Samuel
está escuchando música.

6. Lorenzo
está durmiendo.

3 **Personajes famosos** Say what these celebrities are doing right now, using the cues provided. ◄
Answers will vary.

> **modelo**
> Celine Dion
> *Celine Dion está cantando una canción ahora mismo.*

A		B	
Stephenie Meyer	Nelly Furtado	bailar	hacer
Rachael Ray	Steve Nash	cantar	jugar
James Cameron	Las Rockettes de	correr	preparar
Venus y Serena	Nueva York	escribir	¿?
Williams	¿?	hablar	¿?
Jason Bay	¿?		

💫 Practice more at **vhlcentral.com**.

AYUDA
Stephenie Meyer: **novelas**
Rachael Ray: **televisión, negocios** (*business*)
James Cameron: **cine**
Venus y Serena Williams: **tenis**
Jason Bay: **béisbol**
Nelly Furtado: **canciones**
Steve Nash: **baloncesto**
Las Rockettes de Nueva York: **baile**

Comunicación

4

Preguntar With a partner, take turns asking each other what you are doing at these times. *Answers will vary.*

> **modelo**
> 8:00 a.m.
> **Estudiante 1:** ¡Hola, Andrés! Son las ocho de la mañana. ¿Qué estás haciendo?
> **Estudiante 2:** Estoy desayunando.

1. 5:00 a.m.	3. 11:00 a.m.	5. 2:00 p.m.	7. 9:00 p.m.
2. 9:30 a.m.	4. 12:00 p.m.	6. 5:00 p.m.	8. 11:30 p.m.

5

Describir Work with a partner and use the present progressive to describe what is going on in this Spanish beach scene. *Answers will vary.*

6

Conversar Imagine that you and a classmate are each babysitting a group of children. With a partner, prepare a telephone conversation using these cues. Be creative and add further comments. *Answers will vary.*

Estudiante 1	**Estudiante 2**
Say hello and ask what the kids are doing.	Say hello and tell your partner that two of your kids are doing their homework. Then ask what the kids at his/her house are doing.
Tell your partner that two of your kids are running and dancing in the house.	Tell your partner that one of the kids is reading.
Tell your partner that you are tired and that two of your kids are watching TV and eating pizza.	Tell your partner that one of the kids is sleeping.
Tell your partner you have to go; the kids are playing soccer in the house.	Say goodbye and good luck (**¡Buena suerte!**).

Síntesis

7

¿Qué están haciendo? A group of classmates is traveling to San Juan, Puerto Rico for a week-long Spanish immersion program. In order for the participants to be on time for their flight, you and your partner must locate them. Your instructor will give you each a handout to help you complete this task. *Answers will vary.*

TEACHING OPTIONS

Video ↤👤→ Show the **Fotonovela** episode again, pausing after each exchange. Ask students to describe what each person in the shot is doing at that moment.
TPR Write sentences with the present progressive on strips of paper. Call on volunteers to draw papers out of a hat to act out. The class should guess what the sentences are. Ex: **Yo estoy durmiendo en la cama.**

Pairs ↤👤→ Add an auditory aspect to this grammar practice. Ask students to write a short paragraph using the present progressive. Students should try to make their sentences as complex as possible. Have students dictate their sentences to a partner. After pairs have finished dictating their sentences, have them exchange papers to check for accuracy. Circulate around the room and look over students' work.

4 Teaching Tips
• To simplify, first have students outline their daily activities and at what time they do them.
• Remind students to use **a la(s)** when expressing time.

4 Expansion
👤↔👤 Reverse the activity by having students state what they are doing. Their partner should guess the time of day. Alternatively, students could say that they are doing season-specific activities (Ex: **Estoy tomando el sol.**) and their partner will guess the month.

5 Teaching Tip Use the **Lección 5 Estructura** overheads to assist with the presentation of this activity.

5 Expansion
↤👤→ In pairs, have students write a conversation between two or more of the people in the drawing. Conversations should consist of at least three exchanges.

6 Teaching Tip To simplify, before beginning their conversation, have students prepare for their roles by brainstorming two lists: one with verbs that describe what the children are doing at home and the other with adjectives that describe how the babysitter feels.

6 Expansion Ask pairs to tell each other what the parents of the two sets of children are doing. Ex: **Los padres de los niños buenos están visitando el museo. Los padres de los niños malos están en una fiesta.**

7 Teaching Tip Divide the class into pairs and distribute the handouts from the Activity Pack (Activity Pack/Supersite) that correspond to this Information Gap Activity.

7 Expansion Have pairs discuss what each program participant is doing in flight. Ex: **Pedro está leyendo una novela.**

5.3 Ser and estar (S) Tutorial

ANTE TODO You have already learned that **ser** and **estar** both mean *to be* but are used for different purposes. These charts summarize the key differences in usage between **ser** and **estar**.

Uses of ser

1. Nationality and place of origin	Juan Carlos **es** argentino. **Es** de Buenos Aires.
2. Profession or occupation	Adela **es** agente de viajes. Francisco **es** médico.
3. Characteristics of people and things ...	José y Clara **son** simpáticos. El clima de Puerto Rico **es** agradable.
4. Generalizations....................	¡**Es** fabuloso viajar! **Es** difícil estudiar a la una de la mañana.
5. Possession	**Es** la pluma de Jimena. **Son** las llaves del señor Díaz.
6. What something is made of	La bicicleta **es** de metal. Los pasajes **son** de papel.
7. Time and date	Hoy **es** martes. **Son** las dos. Hoy **es** el primero de julio.
8. Where or when an event takes place ..	El partido **es** en el estadio Santa Fe. La conferencia **es** a las siete.

¡ATENCIÓN!

Ser de expresses not only origin (**Es de Buenos Aires.**) and possession (**Es la pluma de Maru.**), but also what material something is made of (**La bicicleta es de metal.**).

Ellos son mis amigos.

Miguel está enojado conmigo.

Uses of estar

1. Location or spatial relationships	El aeropuerto **está** lejos de la ciudad. Tu habitación **está** en el tercer piso.
2. Health	¿Cómo **estás**? **Estoy** bien, gracias.
3. Physical states and conditions.......	El profesor **está** ocupado. Las ventanas **están** abiertas.
4. Emotional states	Marissa **está** feliz hoy. **Estoy** muy enojado con Maru.
5. Certain weather expressions	**Está** lloviendo. **Está** nublado.
6. Ongoing actions (progressive tenses) ..	**Estamos** estudiando para un examen. Ana **está** leyendo una novela.

Ser and estar with adjectives

▶ With many descriptive adjectives, **ser** and **estar** can both be used, but the meaning will change.

Juan **es** delgado.	Ana **es** nerviosa.
Juan is thin.	*Ana is a nervous person.*
Juan **está** más delgado hoy.	Ana **está** nerviosa por el examen.
Juan looks thinner today.	*Ana is nervous because of the exam.*

▶ In the examples above, the statements with **ser** are general observations about the inherent qualities of Juan and Ana. The statements with **estar** describe conditions that are variable.

▶ Here are some adjectives that change in meaning when used with **ser** and **estar**.

With ser	With estar
El chico **es listo**.	El chico **está listo**.
The boy is smart.	*The boy is ready.*
La profesora **es mala**.	La profesora **está mala**.
The professor is bad.	*The professor is sick.*
Jaime **es aburrido**.	Jaime **está aburrido**.
Jaime is boring.	*Jaime is bored.*
Las peras **son verdes**.	Las peras **están verdes**.
Pears are green.	*The pears are not ripe.*
El gato **es muy vivo**.	El gato **está vivo**.
The cat is very lively.	*The cat is alive.*
Iván **es un hombre seguro**.	Iván no **está seguro**.
Iván is a confident man.	*Iván is not sure.*

¡INTÉNTALO! Form complete sentences by using the correct form of **ser** or **estar** and making any other necessary changes.

1. Alejandra / cansado
 Alejandra *está cansada.*
2. ellos / pelirrojo
 Ellos son pelirrojos.
3. Carmen / alto
 Carmen es alta.
4. yo / la clase de español
 Estoy en la clase de español.
5. película / a las once
 La película es a las once.
6. hoy / viernes
 Hoy es viernes.

7. nosotras / enojado
 Nosotras estamos enojadas.
8. Antonio / médico
 Antonio es médico.
9. Romeo y Julieta / enamorado
 Romeo y Julieta están enamorados.
10. libros / de Ana
 Los libros son de Ana.
11. Marisa y Juan / estudiando
 Marisa y Juan están estudiando.
12. partido de baloncesto / gimnasio
 El partido de baloncesto es en el gimnasio.

recursos

WB
pp. 54–55

LM
p. 29

(S)
vhlcentral.com
Lección 5

Práctica

1 Teaching Tip Have students identify the use(s) of **ser** or **estar** for each item.

1 Expansion To challenge students, ask them to use each adjective in a sentence. If the adjective can take both verbs, have them provide two sentences.

2 Teaching Tip To simplify, ask students to point out context clues that will help them determine whether to use **ser** or **estar**. Ex: The word **hoy** in line 2 suggests that **guapo** is a variable physical state.

2 Expansion Have pairs write a continuation of the conversation and then present it to the class.

3 Teaching Tip Use the **Lección 5 Estructura** overheads to assist with the presentation of this activity.

3 Expansion Add another visual aspect to this grammar practice. Bring in photos or magazine pictures that show many different people performing a variety of activities. Have students use **ser** and **estar** to write short descriptions of the scenes.

1 **¿Ser o estar?** Indicate whether each adjective takes **ser** or **estar**. **¡Ojo!** Three of them can take both verbs.

	ser	estar			ser	estar
1. delgada	●	●	5. seguro	●	●	
2. canadiense	●	○	6. enojada	○	●	
3. enamorado	○	●	7. importante	●	○	
4. lista	●	●	8. avergonzada	○	●	

2 **Completar** Complete this conversation with the appropriate forms of **ser** and **estar**.

EDUARDO ¡Hola, Ceci! ¿Cómo (1)____estás____?

CECILIA Hola, Eduardo. Bien, gracias. ¡Qué guapo (2)____estás____ hoy!

EDUARDO Gracias. (3)____Eres____ muy amable. Oye, ¿qué (4)____estás____ haciendo? (5)¿____Estás____ ocupada?

CECILIA No, sólo le (6)____estoy____ escribiendo una carta a mi prima Pilar.

EDUARDO ¿De dónde (7)____es____ ella?

CECILIA Pilar (8)____es____ de Ecuador. Su papá (9)____es____ médico en Quito. Pero ahora Pilar y su familia (10)____están____ de vacaciones en Ponce, Puerto Rico.

EDUARDO Y… ¿cómo (11)____es____ Pilar?

CECILIA (12)____Es____ muy lista. Y también (13)____es____ alta, rubia y muy bonita.

3 **En el parque** With a partner, take turns describing the people in the drawing. Your descriptions should answer the questions provided. *Answers will vary.*

1. ¿Quiénes son?
2. ¿Dónde están?
3. ¿Cómo son?
4. ¿Cómo están?
5. ¿Qué están haciendo?
6. ¿Qué estación es?
7. ¿Qué tiempo hace?
8. ¿Quiénes están de vacaciones?

Practice more at **vhlcentral.com.**

TEACHING OPTIONS

Extra Practice Have students write a paragraph about a close friend, including the person's physical appearance, general disposition, place of birth, birthday, profession, and where the friend is now. Ask volunteers to share their descriptions with the class.

Pairs Ask pairs to role-play this scenario: Student A is at the beach with some friends while Student B is at home. Student A calls Student B, trying to convince him or her to come to the beach. Students should try to employ as many uses of **ser** and **estar** in their scenario as possible. After acting out the scene once, have students switch roles.

Comunicación

4 **Describir** With a classmate, take turns describing these people. Mention where they are from, what they are like, how they are feeling, and what they are doing right now. Answers will vary.

> **modelo**
>
> tu compañero/a de cuarto
>
> *Mi compañera de cuarto es de San Juan, Puerto Rico. Es muy inteligente. Está cansada pero está estudiando porque tiene un examen.*

1. tu mejor (*best*) amigo/a
2. tu actor/actriz favorito/a
3. tu profesor(a) favorito/a
4. tu novio/a o esposo/a
5. tus abuelos
6. tus padres

5 **Adivinar** Get together with a partner and take turns describing a celebrity using these items as a guide. Don't mention the celebrity's name. Can your partner guess who you are describing?
 Answers will vary.

- descripción física
- cómo está ahora
- origen
- dónde está ahora
- qué está haciendo ahora
- profesión u ocupación

6 **En el aeropuerto** In groups of three, take turns assuming the identity of a character from this drawing. Your partners will ask you questions using **ser** and **estar** until they figure out who you are.
 Answers will vary.

> **modelo**
>
> **Estudiante 3:** *¿Dónde estás?*
> **Estudiante 1:** *Estoy cerca de la puerta.*
> **Estudiante 2:** *¿Qué estás haciendo?*
> **Estudiante 1:** *Estoy escuchando a otra persona.*
> **Estudiante 3:** *¿Eres uno de los pasajeros?*
> **Estudiante 1:** *No, soy empleado del aeropuerto.*
> **Estudiante 2:** *¿Eres Camilo?*

Síntesis

7 **Conversación** In pairs, imagine that you and your partner are two of the characters in the drawing in **Actividad 6**. After boarding, you are seated next to each other and strike up a conversation. Act out what you would say to your fellow passenger. Answers will vary.

4 Expansion Have pairs select two descriptions to present to the class.

5 Teaching Tip Model the activity for the class. You may want to tell students to use **una persona** to create ambiguity in their descriptions. Ex: **Es una persona alta…**

6 Teaching Tip Use the **Lección 5 Estructura** overheads to assist with the presentation of this activity.

6 Expansion
←👥→ Have students pick one of the individuals pictured and write a one-paragraph description, employing as many different uses of **ser** and **estar** as possible.

7 Teaching Tips
- ←👥→ To simplify, first have students write a character description for the person they will be playing. Then, as a class, brainstorm topics of conversation.
- Make sure that students use **ser** and **estar**, the present progressive, and stem-changing verbs in their conversations, as well as vacation-, pastime-, and family-related vocabulary.

The Affective Dimension
Encourage students to consider pair and group activities as a cooperative venture in which group members support and motivate each other.

Small Groups ←👥→ Have students work in small groups to write a television commercial for a vacation resort in the Spanish-speaking world. Ask them to employ as many uses of **ser** and **estar** as they can. If possible, after they have written the commercial, have them tape it to show to the class.

TPR Call on a volunteer and whisper the name of a celebrity in his or her ear. The volunteer acts out verbs and characteristics and uses props to elicit descriptions from the class. Ex: The volunteer points to the U.S. on a map. (**Es de los Estados Unidos.**) He or she then indicates a short, thin man. (**Es un hombre atlético y delgado.**) He or she acts out riding a bicycle. (**Está paseando en bicicleta. ¿Es Lance Armstrong?**)

Section Goals

In **Estructura 5.4**, students will study:

- direct object nouns
- the personal **a**
- direct object pronouns

Instructional Resources

Supersite: Audio (Lab MP3 Files); Resources (*PowerPoints*, Activity Pack, Scripts, Answer Keys); Testing Program (Quizzes)
WebSAM
Workbook, p. 56
Lab Manual, p. 30

Teaching Tips

- Write these sentences on the board: —¿Quién tiene el pasaporte? —Juan lo tiene. Underline **pasaporte** and explain that it is a direct object noun. Then underline **lo** and explain that it is the masculine singular direct object pronoun. Translate both sentences. Continue with: —¿Quién saca fotos? —Simón las saca. —¿Quién tiene la llave? —Pilar la tiene.
- Read this exchange aloud: —¿Haces las maletas? —No, no hago las maletas. —¿Por qué no haces las maletas? —No hago las maletas porque las maletas no están aquí. Ask students if the exchange sounds natural to them. Then write it on the board and ask students to use direct object pronouns to avoid repetition. If students try to say **no las están** in the last sentence, point out that direct object pronouns cannot replace the subject of a verb. The only option is to eliminate the subject: **no están.**
- Ask individuals questions to elicit the personal a: ¿Visitas a tu abuela los fines de semana? ¿Llamas a tu padre los sábados?
- Ask questions to elicit third-person direct object pronouns. Ex: ¿Quién ve el lápiz de Marcos? ¿Quién quiere estos diccionarios?

5.4 Direct object nouns and pronouns Tutorial

SUBJECT	VERB	DIRECT OBJECT NOUN
Juan Carlos y Jimena *Juan Carlos and Jimena*	están tomando *are taking*	fotos. *photos.*

▶ A direct object noun receives the action of the verb directly and generally follows the verb. In the example above, the direct object noun answers the question *What are Juan Carlos and Jimena taking?*

▶ When a direct object noun in Spanish is a person or a pet, it is preceded by the word **a.** This is called the personal **a**; there is no English equivalent for this construction.

La señora Díaz visita **a** la doctora Salas.
Mrs Díaz is visiting Dr. Salas.

La señora Díaz visita el café Delicias.
Mrs. Díaz is visiting the Delicias café.

▶ In the first sentence above, the personal **a** is required because the direct object is a person. In the second sentence, the personal **a** is not required because the direct object is a place, not a person.

Miguel no me habla.

No tenemos tablas de windsurf.

El botones las puede conseguir para ustedes.

▶ Direct object pronouns are words that replace direct object nouns. Like English, Spanish uses a direct object pronoun to avoid repeating a noun already mentioned.

	DIRECT OBJECT			DIRECT OBJECT PRONOUN
Maribel hace	las maletas.		Maribel	las hace.
Felipe compra	el sombrero.		Felipe	lo compra.
Vicky tiene	la llave.		Vicky	la tiene.

Direct object pronouns

SINGULAR		PLURAL	
me	*me*	**nos**	*us*
te	*you* (fam.)	**os**	*you* (fam.)
lo	*you* (m., form.)	**los**	*you* (m., form.)
	him; it (m.)		*them* (m.)
la	*you* (f., form.)	**las**	*you* (f., form.)
	her; it (f.)		*them* (f.)

TEACHING OPTIONS

TPR Call out a series of sentences with direct object nouns, some of which require the personal **a** and some of which do not. Ex: **Visito muchos museos. Visito a mis tíos.** Have students raise their hands if the personal **a** is used.

Extra Practice Write six sentences on the board that have direct object nouns. Use two verbs in the simple present tense, two in the present progressive, and two using **ir a** + [*infinitive*]. Draw a line through the direct objects as students call them out. Have students state which pronouns to write to replace them. Then, draw an arrow from each pronoun to where it goes in the sentence, as indicated by students.

▶ In affirmative sentences, direct object pronouns generally appear before the conjugated verb. In negative sentences, the pronoun is placed between the word **no** and the verb.

Adela practica **el tenis**.	Gabriela no tiene **las llaves**.
Adela **lo** practica.	Gabriela **no las** tiene.
Carmen compra **los pasajes**.	Diego no hace **las maletas**.
Carmen **los** compra.	Diego **no las** hace.

▶ When the verb is an infinitive construction, such as **ir a** + [*infinitive*], the direct object pronoun can be placed before the conjugated form or attached to the infinitive.

Ellos van a escribir **unas postales**.
- Ellos **las** van a escribir.
- Ellos van a escribir**las**.

Lidia quiere ver **una película**.
- Lidia **la** quiere ver.
- Lidia quiere ver**la**.

▶ When the verb is in the present progressive, the direct object pronoun can be placed before the conjugated form or attached to the present participle. **¡Atención!** When a direct object pronoun is attached to the present participle, an accent mark is added to maintain the proper stress.

Gerardo está leyendo **la lección**.
- Gerardo **la** está leyendo.
- Gerardo está leyéndo**la**.

Toni está mirando **el partido**.
- Toni **lo** está mirando.
- Toni está mirándo**lo**.

CONSULTA

To learn more about accents, see **Lección 4, Pronunciación**, p. 115, **Lección 10, Ortografía**, p. 315, and **Lección 11, Ortografía**, p. 349.

¡INTÉNTALO! Choose the correct direct object pronoun for each sentence.

1. Tienes el libro de español. *c*
 a. La tienes. b. Los tienes. c. Lo tienes.
2. Voy a ver el partido de baloncesto. *a*
 a. Voy a verlo. b. Voy a verte. c. Voy a vernos.
3. El artista quiere dibujar a Luisa y a su mamá. *c*
 a. Quiere dibujarme. b. Quiere dibujarla. c. Quiere dibujarlas.
4. Marcos busca la llave. *b*
 a. Me busca. b. La busca. c. Las busca.
5. Rita me lleva al aeropuerto y también lleva a Tomás. *a*
 a. Nos lleva. b. Las lleva. c. Te lleva.
6. Puedo oír a Gerardo y a Miguel. *b*
 a. Puedo oírte. b. Puedo oírlos. c. Puedo oírlo.
7. Quieren estudiar la gramática. *c*
 a. Quieren estudiarnos. b. Quieren estudiarlo. c. Quieren estudiarla.
8. ¿Practicas los verbos irregulares? *a*
 a. ¿Los practicas? b. ¿Las practicas? c. ¿Lo practicas?
9. Ignacio ve la película. *a*
 a. La ve. b. Lo ve. c. Las ve.
10. Sandra va a invitar a Mario a la excursión. También me va a invitar a mí. *c*
 a. Los va a invitar. b. Lo va a invitar. c. Nos va a invitar.

recursos
WB p. 56
LM p. 30
vhlcentral.com Lección 5

Práctica

1 Simplificar Professor Vega's class is planning a trip to Costa Rica. Describe their preparations by changing the direct object nouns into direct object pronouns.

> **modelo**
> La profesora Vega tiene su pasaporte.
> La profesora Vega lo tiene.

1. Gustavo y Héctor confirman las reservaciones. Gustavo y Héctor las confirman.
2. Nosotros leemos los folletos (brochures). Nosotros los leemos.
3. Ana María estudia el mapa. Ana María lo estudia.
4. Yo aprendo los nombres de los monumentos de San José. Yo los aprendo.
5. Alicia escucha a la profesora. Alicia la escucha.
6. Miguel escribe las direcciones para ir al hotel. Miguel las escribe.
7. Esteban busca el pasaje. Esteban lo busca.
8. Nosotros planeamos una excursión. Nosotros la planeamos.

2 Vacaciones Ramón is going to San Juan, Puerto Rico with his friends, Javier and Marcos. Express his thoughts more succinctly using direct object pronouns.

> **modelo**
> Quiero hacer una excursión.
> Quiero hacerla./La quiero hacer.

1. Voy a hacer mi maleta. Voy a hacerla./La voy a hacer.
2. Necesitamos llevar los pasaportes. Necesitamos llevarlos./Los necesitamos llevar.
3. Marcos está pidiendo el folleto turístico. Marcos está pidiéndolo./Marcos lo está pidiendo.
4. Javier debe llamar a sus padres. Javier debe llamarlos./Javier los debe llamar.
5. Ellos desean visitar el Viejo San Juan. Ellos desean visitarlo./Ellos lo desean visitar.
6. Puedo llamar a Javier por la mañana. Puedo llamarlo./Lo puedo llamar.
7. Prefiero llevar mi cámara. Prefiero llevarla./La prefiero llevar.
8. No queremos perder nuestras reservaciones de hotel. No queremos perderlas./No las queremos perder.

3 ¿Quién? The Garza family is preparing to go on a vacation to Puerto Rico. Based on the clues, answer the questions. Use direct object pronouns in your answers.

> **modelo**
> ¿Quién hace las reservaciones para el hotel? (el Sr. Garza)
> El Sr. Garza las hace.

1. ¿Quién compra los pasajes para el vuelo (flight)? (la Sra. Garza) La Sra. Garza los compra.
2. ¿Quién tiene que hacer las maletas de los niños? (María) María tiene que hacerlas./María las tiene que hacer.
3. ¿Quiénes buscan los pasaportes? (Antonio y María) Antonio y María los buscan.
4. ¿Quién va a confirmar las reservaciones de hotel? (la Sra. Garza) La Sra. Garza va a confirmarlas./La Sra. Garza las va a confirmar.
5. ¿Quién busca la cámara? (María) María la busca.
6. ¿Quién compra un mapa de Puerto Rico? (Antonio) Antonio lo compra.

Practice more at **vhlcentral.com**.

Comunicación

4 **Entrevista** Take turns asking and answering these questions with a classmate. Be sure to use direct object pronouns in your responses. *Answers will vary.*

1. ¿Ves mucho la televisión?
2. ¿Cuándo vas a ver tu programa favorito?
3. ¿Quién prepara la comida (*food*) en tu casa?
4. ¿Te visita mucho tu familia?
5. ¿Visitas mucho a tus abuelos?
6. ¿Nos entienden nuestros padres a nosotros?
7. ¿Cuándo ves a tus amigos/as?
8. ¿Cuándo te llaman tus amigos/as?

5 **Los pasajeros** Get together with a partner and take turns asking each other questions about the drawing. Use the word bank and direct object pronouns. *Answers will vary.*

AYUDA

For travel-related vocabulary, see **Contextos**, pp. 140–141.

> **modelo**
> **Estudiante 1:** ¿Quién está leyendo el libro?
> **Estudiante 2:** Susana lo está leyendo./Susana está leyéndolo.

buscar	confirmar	escribir	leer	tener	vender
comprar	encontrar	escuchar	llevar	traer	¿?

Sra. Sánchez Orlando Sr. López
Marta Sr. Sánchez Susana Miguelito

Síntesis

6 **Adivinanzas** In pairs, take turns describing a person, place, or thing for your partner to guess. Each of you should give at least five descriptions. *Answers will vary.*

> **modelo**
> **Estudiante 1:** Lo uso para (*I use it to*) escribir en mi cuaderno.
> No es muy grande y tiene borrador. ¿Qué es?
> **Estudiante 2:** ¿Es un lápiz?
> **Estudiante 1:** ¡Sí!

4 Teaching Tip Ask students to record their partner's answers. After the interviews, have students review answers in groups and report the most common responses to the class.

4 Expansion 👤↔👤 Have students write five additional questions, then continue their interviews. Encourage students to comment on their partner's answers.

5 Teaching Tip Before assigning the activity, ask individual students to identify different objects in the picture that might be used as direct objects in questions and answers.

5 Expansion
• Reverse the activity by having students say what the people are doing. Their partner will guess who it is. Ex: **Está escribiendo en su cuaderno. (Es Miguelito.)**
• ←👤→ Have students use **ser** and **estar** to write descriptions of the people in the drawing.

6 Teaching Tip To simplify this activity, have students first write out their descriptions.

6 Expansion ←👤→ Have pairs write out five additional riddles. Have volunteers read them aloud for the class to answer.

Recapitulación

Concepts Diagnostics

Review the grammar concepts you have learned in this lesson by completing these activities.

1 **Completar** Complete the chart with the correct present participle of these verbs. **8 pts.**

Infinitive	Present participle	Infinitive	Present participle
hacer	haciendo	estar	estando
acampar	acampando	ser	siendo
tener	teniendo	vivir	viviendo
venir	viniendo	estudiar	estudiando

2 **Vacaciones en París** Complete this paragraph about Julia's trip to Paris with the correct form of **ser** or **estar**. **12 pts.**

Hoy (1) __es__ (es/está) el 3 de julio y voy a París por tres semanas. (Yo) (2) __Estoy__ (Soy/Estoy) muy feliz porque voy a ver a mi mejor amiga. Ella (3) __es__ (es/está) de Puerto Rico, pero ahora (4) __está__ (es/está) viviendo en París. También (yo) (5) __estoy__ (soy/estoy) un poco nerviosa porque (6) __es__ (es/está) mi primer viaje a Francia. El vuelo (*flight*) (7) __es__ (es/está) hoy por la tarde, pero ahora (8) __está__ (es/está) lloviendo. Por eso (9) __estamos__ (somos/estamos) preocupadas, porque probablemente el avión va a salir tarde. Mi equipaje ya (10) __está__ (es/está) listo. (11) __Es__ (Es/Está) tarde y me tengo que ir. ¡Va a (12) __ser__ (ser/estar) un viaje fenomenal!

3 **¿Qué hacen?** Respond to these questions by indicating what people do with the items mentioned. Use direct object pronouns. **5 pts.**

modelo
¿Qué hacen ellos con la película? (ver)
La ven.

1. ¿Qué haces tú con el libro de viajes? (leer) __Lo leo.__
2. ¿Qué hacen los turistas en la ciudad? (explorar) __La exploran.__
3. ¿Qué hace el botones con el equipaje? (llevar) __Lo lleva (a la habitación).__
4. ¿Qué hace la agente con las reservaciones? (confirmar) __Las confirma.__
5. ¿Qué hacen ustedes con los pasaportes? (mostrar) __Los mostramos.__

RESUMEN GRAMATICAL

5.1 **Estar with conditions and emotions** *p. 152*

► Yo est**oy** aburrido/a, feliz, nervioso/a.
► El cuarto **está** desordenado, limpio, ordenado.
► Estos libros est**án** abiertos, cerrados, sucios.

5.2 **The present progressive** *pp. 154–155*

► The present progressive is formed with the present tense of **estar** plus the present participle.

Forming the present participle

infinitive	stem	ending	present participle
hablar	habl-	-ando	habl**ando**
comer	com-	-iendo	com**iendo**
escribir	escrib-	-iendo	escrib**iendo**

-ir stem-changing verbs

	infinitive	present participle
e:ie	preferir	pref**i**riendo
e:i	conseguir	cons**i**guiendo
o:ue	dormir	d**u**rmiendo

► Irregular present participles: yendo (ir), pudiendo (poder), viniendo (venir)

5.3 **Ser and estar** *pp. 158–159*

► Uses of **ser**: nationality, origin, profession or occupation, characteristics, generalizations, possession, what something is made of, time and date, time and place of events
► Uses of **estar**: location, health, physical states and conditions, emotional states, weather expressions, ongoing actions
► Many adjectives can be used with both **ser** and **estar**, but the meaning of the adjectives will change.

Juan **es** delgado. Juan **está** más delgado hoy.
Juan is thin. *Juan looks thinner today.*

TEACHING OPTIONS

Extra Practice Add an auditory aspect to this grammar review. Go around the room and read a sentence with a direct object. Each student must repeat the sentence using a direct object pronoun. Ex: **María y Jennifer están comprando sus libros para la clase. (María y Jennifer los están comprando./María y Jennifer están comprándolos.)**
TPR Divide the board into two columns, with the heads **ser**

and **estar**. Ask a volunteer to stand in front of each verb. The rest of the class should take turns calling out a use of **ser** or **estar**. The volunteer standing in front of the correct verb should step forward and give an example sentence. Ex: nationality or origin (**Soy norteamericano/a.**) After each volunteer has given two sentences, call on different students to take their places. Continue this way until everyone has had a turn.

4 **Opuestos** Complete these sentences with the appropriate form of the verb **estar** and an antonym for the underlined adjective. **5 pts.**

> **modelo**
>
> Mis respuestas están <u>bien</u>, pero las de Susana *están mal*.

1. Las tiendas están <u>abiertas</u>, pero la agencia de viajes _está_ _cerrada_.

2. No me gustan las habitaciones <u>desordenadas</u>. Incluso (*Even*) mi habitación de hotel _está_ _ordenada_.

3. Nosotras estamos <u>tristes</u> cuando trabajamos. Hoy comienzan las vacaciones y _estamos_ _contentas/alegres/felices_

4. En esta ciudad los autobuses están <u>sucios</u>, pero los taxis _están_ _limpios_.

5. —El avión sale a las 5:30, ¿verdad? —No, estás <u>confundida</u>. Yo _estoy_ _seguro/a_ de que el avión sale a las 5:00.

5.4 **Direct object nouns and pronouns** *pp. 162–163*

Direct object pronouns

Singular		Plural	
me	lo	nos	los
te	la	os	las

In affirmative sentences:
Adela practica **el tenis**. → Adela **lo** practica.

In negative sentences: Adela **no lo** practica.

With an infinitive:
Adela **lo** va a practicar./Adela va a practicar**lo**.

With the present progressive:
Adela **lo** está practicando./Adela está practicándo**lo**.

5 **En la playa** Describe what these people are doing. Complete the sentences using the present progressive tense. **8 pts.**

1. El Sr. Camacho _está pescando_.

2. Felicia _está paseando en barco_.

3. Leo _está montando a caballo_.

4. Nosotros _estamos jugando a las cartas_.

6 **Antes del viaje** Write a paragraph of at least six sentences describing the time right before you go on a trip. Say how you feel and what you are doing. You can use **Actividad 2** as a model. **12 pts.** Answers will vary.

> **modelo**
>
> Hoy es viernes, 27 de octubre. Estoy en mi habitación...

7 **Refrán** Complete this Spanish saying by filling in the missing present participles. Refer to the translation and the drawing. **2 EXTRA points!**

¡LA CIUDAD ESTÁ MUY SUCIA!

66 Se consigue más

haciendo que

diciendo . **99**

(You can accomplish more by doing than by saying.)

 Practice more at **vhlcentral.com.**

TEACHING OPTIONS

TPR →👤👤 Prepare five anonymous descriptions of easily recognizable people, using **ser** and **estar**. Write each name on a separate card and give each student a set of cards. Read the descriptions aloud and have students hold up the corresponding name. Ex: **Es cantante y autora de libros infantiles. Es rubia y delgada. No es muy joven, pero no es vieja. Es de Michigan, pero ahora está en Inglaterra. Está divorciada de Guy Ritchie. (Madonna)**

Extra Practice Give students these items to make sentences with the present progressive. **1.** con / madre / hablar / yo / mi / estar (Yo estoy hablando con mi madre.) **2.** nuestro / equipaje / buscar / nosotros / estar (Nosotros estamos buscando nuestro equipaje.) **3.** ¿ / llover / playa / la / estar / en / ? (¿Está lloviendo en la playa?) **4.** el / Nueva York / pasaje / ella / para / comprar / estar (Ella está comprando el pasaje para Nueva York.)

4 **Expansion**
👤↔👤 Have students create three sentences about their own lives, using antonyms. Ex: **Mi hermano es desordenado, pero yo soy muy ordenado.** Tell them to make one of the sentences false. Then, in pairs, have students read their sentences aloud. Their partner should try to guess which statement is false.

5 **Expansion** To challenge students, have them imagine that the people in the illustration are now in a hotel. Ask students to say what they are doing. Ex: **Leo está mirando un programa sobre caballos.**

6 **Teaching Tips**
• →👤← Have students exchange papers with a partner for peer editing.
• To make this activity more challenging, require students to include at least two examples each of **ser**, **estar**, and direct object pronouns.

7 **Teaching Tip** Explain the use of the impersonal **se** and explain that **Se consigue** means *You can accomplish* (as in the translation) or *One can accomplish*. Students will learn the impersonal **se** in **Estructura 10.3**.

7 **Expansion**
←👤→ To challenge students, have them work in pairs to create a short dialogue that ends with this saying. Encourage them to be creative.

Section Goals

In **Lectura**, students will:
- learn the strategy of scanning to find specific information in reading matter
- read a brochure about ecotourism in Puerto Rico

Instructional Resource
Supersite

Estrategia Explain to students that a good way to get an idea of what an article or other text is about is to scan it before reading. Scanning means running one's eyes over a text in search of specific information that can be used to infer the content of the text. Explain that scanning a text before reading it is a good way to improve Spanish reading comprehension.

The Affective Dimension
Point out to students that becoming familiar with cognates will help them feel less overwhelmed when they encounter new Spanish texts.

Examinar el texto Do the activity orally as a class. Some cognates that give a clue to the content of the text are: **turismo ecológico, teléfono, TV por cable, Internet, hotel, aire acondicionado, perfecto, Parque Nacional Foresta, Museo de Arte Nativo, Reserva, Biosfera, Santuario.** These clues should tell a reader scanning the text that it is about a hotel promoting ecotourism.

Preguntas Ask the questions orally of the class. Possible responses: 1. travel brochure 2. Puerto Rico 3. photos of beautiful tropical beaches, bays, and forests; The document is trying to attract the reader. 4. **Hotel Vistahermosa** in Lajas, Puerto Rico; attract guests

Atracciones cercanas

Playa Grande ¿Busca la playa perfecta? Playa Grande es la playa que está buscando. Usted puede pescar, sacar fotos, nadar y pasear en bicicleta. Playa Grande es un paraíso para el turista que quiere practicar deportes acuáticos. El lugar es bonito e interesante y usted va a tener muchas oportunidades para descansar y disfrutar en familia.

Valle Niebla Ir de excursión, tomar café, montar a caballo, caminar, hacer picnics. Más de cien lugares para acampar.

Bahía Fosforescente Sacar fotos, salidas de noche, excursión en barco. Una maravillosa experiencia llena de luz°.

Arrecifes de Coral Sacar fotos, bucear, explorar. Es un lugar único en el Caribe.

Playa Vieja Tomar el sol, pasear en bicicleta, jugar a las cartas, escuchar música. Ideal para la familia.

Parque Nacional Foresta Sacar fotos, visitar el Museo de Arte Nativo. Reserva Mundial de la Biosfera.

Santuario de las Aves Sacar fotos, observar aves°, seguir rutas de excursión.

llena de luz *full of light* aves *birds*

Después de leer

Listas

Which amenities of Hotel Vistahermosa would most interest these potential guests? Explain your choices. Answers will vary.

1. dos padres con un hijo de seis años y una hija de ocho años

2. un hombre y una mujer en su luna de miel (*honeymoon*)

3. una persona en un viaje de negocios (*business trip*)

Conversaciones

With a partner, take turns asking each other these questions. Answers will vary.

1. ¿Quieres visitar el Hotel Vistahermosa? ¿Por qué?
2. Tienes tiempo de visitar sólo tres de las atracciones turísticas que están cerca del hotel. ¿Cuáles vas a visitar? ¿Por qué?
3. ¿Qué prefieres hacer en Valle Niebla? ¿En Playa Vieja? ¿En el Parque Nacional Foresta?

Situaciones

You have just arrived at Hotel Vistahermosa. Your classmate is the concierge. Use the phrases below to express your interests and ask for suggestions about where to go. Answers will vary.

1. montar a caballo
2. bucear
3. pasear en bicicleta
4. pescar
5. observar aves

Contestar

Answer these questions. Answers will vary.

1. ¿Quieres visitar Puerto Rico? Explica tu respuesta.

2. ¿Adónde quieres ir de vacaciones el verano que viene? Explica tu respuesta.

Listas
- Ask these comprehension questions. **1. ¿El Hotel Vistahermosa está situado cerca de qué mar? (el mar Caribe) 2. ¿Qué playa es un paraíso para el turista? (la Playa Grande) 3. ¿Dónde puedes montar a caballo? (en el Valle Niebla)**
- 👥 Encourage discussion of each of the items by asking questions such as: **En tu opinión, ¿qué tipo de atracciones buscan los padres con hijos de seis y ocho años? ¿Qué esperan de un hotel? Y una pareja en su luna de miel, ¿qué tipo de atracciones espera encontrar en un hotel? En tu opinión, ¿qué busca una persona en un viaje de negocios?**

Conversaciones Ask individuals about what their partners said. Ex: **¿Por qué (no) quiere _____ visitar el Hotel Vistahermosa? ¿Qué atracciones quiere ver?** Ask other students: **Y tú, ¿quieres visitar el Parque Nacional Foresta o prefieres visitar otro lugar?**

Situaciones
- Give students a couple of minutes to review **Más vocabulario** on page 140 and **Expresiones útiles** on page 147.
- To challenge students, add to the list activities such as **sacar fotos, correr, nadar,** and **ir de excursión.**

Contestar Have volunteers explain how the reading selection might influence their choice of a vacation destination for next summer.

Pairs Have pairs of students work together to read the brochure aloud and write three questions about it. After they have finished, ask pairs to exchange papers with another pair, who will work together to answer them. Alternatively, you might pick pairs to read their questions to the class. Ask volunteers to answer them.

Small Groups →👥← To practice scanning written material to infer its content, bring in short, simple Spanish-language magazine or newspaper articles you have read. Have small groups scan the articles to determine what they are about. Have them write down all the clues that help them. When each group has come to a decision, ask it to present its findings to the class. Confirm the accuracy of the inferences.

Puerto Rico

NATIONAL
connections
cultures
STANDARDS

El país en cifras

▸ **Área**: 8.959 km² (3.459 millas²)
menor° que el área de Connecticut

▸ **Población**: 4.074.000
Puerto Rico es una de las islas más densamente pobladas° del mundo. Más de la mitad de la población vive en San Juan, la capital.

▸ **Capital**: San Juan—2.763.000

SOURCE: Population Division, UN Secretariat

▸ **Ciudades principales**: Arecibo, Bayamón, Fajardo, Mayagüez, Ponce

▸ **Moneda**: dólar estadounidense

▸ **Idiomas**: español (oficial); inglés (oficial)
Aproximadamente la cuarta parte de la población puertorriqueña habla inglés, pero en las zonas turísticas este porcentaje es mucho más alto. El uso del inglés es obligatorio para documentos federales.

Bandera de Puerto Rico

Puertorriqueños célebres

▸ **Raúl Juliá,** actor (1940–1994)
▸ **Roberto Clemente,** beisbolista (1934–1972)
▸ **Julia de Burgos,** escritora (1914–1953)
▸ **Benicio del Toro,** actor y productor (1967–)
▸ **Rosie Pérez,** actriz y bailarina (1964–)

menor *less* pobladas *populated* río subterráneo *underground river* más largo *longest* cuevas *caves* bóveda *vault* fortaleza *fort* caber *fit*

Faro en Arecibo

Playa en San Juan

Océano Atlántico

San Juan ⭐

Arecibo

Bayamón

Río Grande de Añasco

Mayagüez

Cordillera Central

Sierra de Cayey

Ponce

Mar Caribe

Iglesia en Ponce

Pescadores en Mayagüez

recursos

WB pp. 57–58

VM pp. 233–234

vhlcentral.com Lección 5

OCÉANO ATLÁNTICO

PUERTO RICO

OCÉANO PACÍFICO

¡Increíble pero cierto!

El río Camuy es el tercer río subterráneo° más largo° del mundo y tiene el sistema de cuevas° más grande del hemisferio occidental. La Cueva de los Tres Pueblos es una gigantesca bóveda°, tan grande que toda la fortaleza° del Morro puede caber° en su interior.

Section Goal

In **Panorama**, students will read about the geography, history, and culture of Puerto Rico.

Instructional Resources
Supersite/DVD: *Panorama cultural*
Supersite: Resources (Scripts, Translations, *PowerPoints*, Answer Keys)
WebSAM
Workbook, pp. 57–58
Video Manual, pp. 233–234

Teaching Tips
• Use the **Lección 5 Panorama** overheads to assist with this presentation.
• Have students look at the map of Puerto Rico. Discuss Puerto Rico's location in relation to the U.S. mainland and the other Caribbean islands. Encourage students to describe what they see in the photos on this page.

El país en cifras After reading **Puertorriqueños célebres**, ask volunteers who are familiar with these individuals to tell a little more about each one. **Rita Moreno** is the only Hispanic female performer to have won an Oscar, a Tony, an Emmy, and a Grammy. You might also mention novelist **Rosario Ferré**, whose *House on the Lagoon* (*La casa de la laguna*) gives a fictional portrait of a large part of Puerto Rican history.

¡Increíble pero cierto! The **río Camuy** caves are actually a series of karstic sinkholes, formed by water sinking into and eroding limestone. Another significant cave in this system is **Cueva Clara**, located in the **Parque de las Cavernas del Río Camuy**. The entrance of the 170-foot-high cave resembles the façade of a cathedral.

TEACHING OPTIONS

Heritage Speakers ←👥→ Encourage heritage speakers of Puerto Rican descent who have visited or lived on the island to share their impressions of it with the class. Ask them to describe people they knew or met, places they saw, and experiences they had. Have the class ask follow-up questions.
El béisbol Baseball is a popular sport in Puerto Rico, home of the Winter League. **Roberto Clemente,** a player with the Pittsburgh

Pirates who died tragically in a plane crash, was the first Latino to be inducted into the Baseball Hall of Fame. He is venerated all over the island with buildings and monuments. There are numerous Major League Baseball players that were born in Puerto Rico, such as **Carlos Beltrán, Iván Rodríguez, Jorge Posada, Carlos Delgado,** and **Fernando Cabrera**.

Lugares • **El Morro**

El Morro es una fortaleza que se construyó para proteger° la bahía° de San Juan desde principios del siglo° XVI hasta principios del siglo XX. Hoy día muchos turistas visitan este lugar, convertido en un museo. Es el sitio más fotografiado de Puerto Rico. La arquitectura de la fortaleza es impresionante. Tiene misteriosos túneles, oscuras mazmorras° y vistas fabulosas de la bahía.

Artes • **Salsa**

La salsa, un estilo musical de origen puertorriqueño y cubano, nació° en el barrio latino de la ciudad de Nueva York. Dos de los músicos de salsa más famosos son Tito Puente y Willie Colón, los dos de Nueva York. Las estrellas° de la salsa en Puerto Rico son Felipe Rodríguez y Héctor Lavoe. Hoy en día, Puerto Rico es el centro internacional de este estilo musical. El Gran Combo de Puerto Rico es una de las orquestas de salsa más famosas del mundo°.

Isla de Culebra

Fajardo

Isla de Vieques

Ciencias • **El Observatorio de Arecibo**

El Observatorio de Arecibo tiene uno de los radiotelescopios más grandes del mundo. Gracias a este telescopio, los científicos° pueden estudiar las propiedades de la Tierra°, la Luna° y otros cuerpos celestes. También pueden analizar fenómenos celestiales como los quasares y pulsares, y detectar emisiones de radio de otras galaxias, en busca de inteligencia extraterrestre.

Historia • **Relación con los Estados Unidos**

Puerto Rico pasó a ser° parte de los Estados Unidos después de° la guerra° de 1898 y se hizo° un estado libre asociado en 1952. Los puertorriqueños, ciudadanos° estadounidenses desde° 1917, tienen representación política en el Congreso, pero no votan en las elecciones presidenciales y no pagan impuestos° federales. Hay un debate entre los puertorriqueños: ¿debe la isla seguir como estado libre asociado, hacerse un estado como los otros° o volverse° independiente?

 ¿Qué aprendiste? Responde a las preguntas con una oración completa.

1. ¿Cuál es la moneda de Puerto Rico? *La moneda de Puerto Rico es el dólar estadounidense.*
2. ¿Qué idiomas se hablan (*are spoken*) en Puerto Rico? *Se hablan español e inglés en Puerto Rico.*
3. ¿Cuál es el sitio más fotografiado de Puerto Rico? *El Morro es el sitio más fotografiado de Puerto Rico.*
4. ¿Qué es el Gran Combo? *Es una orquesta de Puerto Rico.*
5. ¿Qué hacen los científicos en el Observatorio de Arecibo? *Los científicos estudian las propiedades de la Tierra y la Luna y detectan emisiones de otras galaxias.*

 Conexión Internet Investiga estos temas en **vhlcentral.com**.

Practice more at **vhlcentral.com.**

1. Describe a dos puertorriqueños famosos. ¿Cómo son? ¿Qué hacen? ¿Dónde viven? ¿Por qué son célebres?
2. Busca información sobre lugares en los que se puede hacer ecoturismo en Puerto Rico. Luego presenta un informe a la clase.

proteger *protect* bahía *bay* siglo *century* mazmorras *dungeons* nació *was born* estrellas *stars* mundo *world* científicos *scientists* Tierra *Earth* Luna *Moon* pasó a ser *became* después de *after* guerra *war* se hizo *became* ciudadanos *citizens* desde *since* pagan impuestos *pay taxes* otros *others* volverse *to become*

El Morro
- Remind students that at the time **El Morro** was built, piracy was a major concern for Spain and its Caribbean colonies. If possible, show other photos of **El Morro**, San Juan Bay, and **Viejo San Juan**.
- For additional information about **El Morro** and **Viejo San Juan**, you may want to play the *Panorama cultural* video footage for this lesson.

Salsa With students, listen to **salsa** or **merengue** from the Dominican Republic, and **rumba** or **mambo** from Cuba. Encourage them to identify common elements in the music (strong percussion patterns rooted in African traditions, alternating structure of soloist and ensemble, incorporation of Western instruments and musical vocabulary). Then, have them point out contrasts.

El Observatorio de Arecibo The Arecibo Ionospheric Observatory has the world's most sensitive radio telescope. It can detect objects up to 13 billion light years away. The telescope dish is 1,000 feet in diameter and covers 20 acres. The dish is made of about 40,000 aluminum mesh panels.

Relación con los Estados Unidos Point out that only Puerto Ricans living on the island vote in plebiscites (or referenda) on the question of the island's political relationship with the United States.

Conexión Internet Students will find supporting Internet activities and links at **vhlcentral.com**.

TEACHING OPTIONS

Variación léxica When the first Spanish colonists arrived on the island they were to name Puerto Rico, they found it inhabited by the Taínos, who called the island **Boriquen**. Puerto Ricans still use **Borinquén** to refer to the island, and they frequently call themselves **boricuas**. The Puerto Rican national anthem is *La borinqueña*. Some other Taíno words that have entered Spanish (and English) are **huracán**, **hamaca**, **canoa**, and **iguana**. **Juracán** was the name of the Taíno god of the winds whose anger stirred up the great storms that periodically devastated the island. The hammock, of course, was the device the Taínos slept in, and canoes were the boats made of great hollowed-out logs with which they paddled between islands. The Taíno language also survives in many Puerto Rican place names: **Arecibo, Bayamón, Guayama, Sierra de Cayey, Yauco**, and **Coamo**.

Los viajes y las vacaciones

acampar	to camp
confirmar una reservación	to confirm a reservation
estar de vacaciones (*f. pl.*)	to be on vacation
hacer las maletas	to pack (one's suitcases)
hacer un viaje	to take a trip
hacer (wind)surf	to (wind)surf
ir de compras (*f. pl.*)	to go shopping
ir de vacaciones	to go on vacation
ir en autobús (*m.*), auto(móvil) (*m.*), avión (*m.*), barco (*m.*), moto(cicleta) (*f.*), taxi (*m.*)	to go by bus, car, plane, boat, motorcycle, taxi
jugar a las cartas	to play cards
montar a caballo (*m.*)	to ride a horse
pescar	to fish
sacar/tomar fotos (*f. pl.*)	to take photos
el/la agente de viajes	travel agent
el/la inspector(a) de aduanas	customs inspector
el/la viajero/a	traveler
el aeropuerto	airport
la agencia de viajes	travel agency
el campo	countryside
el equipaje	luggage
la estación de autobuses, del metro, de tren	bus, subway, train station
la llegada	arrival
el mar	sea
el paisaje	landscape
el pasaje (de ida y vuelta)	(round-trip) ticket
el pasaporte	passport
la playa	beach
la salida	departure; exit
la tabla de (wind)surf	surfboard/sailboard

El hotel

el ascensor	elevator
el/la botones	bellhop
la cama	bed
el/la empleado/a	employee
la habitación individual, doble	single, double room
el hotel	hotel
el/la huésped	guest
la llave	key
el piso	floor (of a building)
la planta baja	ground floor

Adjetivos

abierto/a	open
aburrido/a	bored; boring
alegre	happy; joyful
amable	nice; friendly
avergonzado/a	embarrassed
cansado/a	tired
cerrado/a	closed
cómodo/a	comfortable
confundido/a	confused
contento/a	happy; content
desordenado/a	disorderly
enamorado/a (de)	in love (with)
enojado/a	mad; angry
equivocado/a	wrong
feliz	happy
limpio/a	clean
listo/a	ready; smart
nervioso/a	nervous
ocupado/a	busy
ordenado/a	orderly
preocupado/a (por)	worried (about)
seguro/a	sure; safe; confident
sucio/a	dirty
triste	sad

Los números ordinales

primer, primero/a	first
segundo/a	second
tercer, tercero/a	third
cuarto/a	fourth
quinto/a	fifth
sexto/a	sixth
séptimo/a	seventh
octavo/a	eighth
noveno/a	ninth
décimo/a	tenth

Palabras adicionales

ahora mismo	right now
el año	year
¿Cuál es la fecha (de hoy)?	What is the date (today)?
de buen/mal humor	in a good/bad mood
la estación	season
el mes	month
todavía	yet; still

Seasons, months, and dates	See page 142.
Weather expressions	See page 142.
Direct object pronouns	See page 162.
Expresiones útiles	See page 147.

recursos
LM p. 30 | vhlcentral.com Lección 5

Audio: Vocabulary

¡De compras!

6

Communicative Goals

You will learn how to:
- Talk about and describe clothing
- Express preferences in a store
- Negotiate and pay for items you buy

A PRIMERA VISTA
- ¿Está comprando algo la chica?
- ¿Crees que busca una maleta o una blusa?
- ¿Está contenta o enojada?
- ¿Cómo es la chica?

Lesson Goals

In **Lección 6**, students will be introduced to the following:
- terms for clothing and shopping
- colors
- open-air markets
- Venezuelan clothing designer **Carolina Herrera**
- the verbs **saber** and **conocer**
- indirect object pronouns
- preterite tense of regular verbs
- demonstrative adjectives and pronouns
- skimming a document
- how to report an interview
- writing a report
- listening for linguistic cues
- a television commercial for the Mexican supermarket **Comercial Mexicana**
- the short film *Parking Lot*
- a video about open-air markets
- cultural, geographic, economic, and historical information about Cuba

A primera vista Here are some additional questions you can ask to personalize the photo: **¿Te gusta ir de compras? ¿Por qué? ¿Estás de buen humor cuando vas de compras? ¿Piensas ir de compras este fin de semana? ¿Adónde? ¿Qué compras cuando estás de vacaciones?**

Teaching Tip Look for these icons for additional communicative practice:

→👥←	Interpretive communication
←👥→	Presentational communication
👥↔👥	Interpersonal communication

INSTRUCTIONAL RESOURCES

Supersite (vhlcentral.com)
Video: *Fotonovela*, Flash cultura*, Anuncio, Cortometraje*, Panorama cultural**
**Also on DVD*
Audio: Textbook and Lab MP3 Files (*also on CD*)
Activity Pack: Information Gap Activities, games, additional activity handouts

Resources: Textbook Answer Key, WB/VM/LM Answer Key, Scripts, Translations, **Vocabulario adicional**, lesson plans, **Estructura** *PowerPoints*, Overheads
Testing Program: Quizzes, Tests, Exams, MP3s (*also on Test Generator CD*)

Learning Management System (Assignment Task Manager, Gradebook)
WebSAM (online Workbook/Video Manual/ Lab Manual)
Workbook/Video Manual
Lab Manual

¡De compras!

Más vocabulario

el abrigo	coat
los calcetines (el calcetín)	sock(s)
el cinturón	belt
las gafas (de sol)	(sun)glasses
los guantes	gloves
el impermeable	raincoat
la ropa	clothing; clothes
la ropa interior	underwear
las sandalias	sandals
el traje	suit
el vestido	dress
los zapatos de tenis	sneakers
el regalo	gift
el almacén	department store
el centro comercial	shopping mall
el mercado (al aire libre)	(open-air) market
el precio (fijo)	(fixed; set) price
la rebaja	sale
la tienda	shop; store
costar (o:ue)	to cost
gastar	to spend (money)
pagar	to pay
regatear	to bargain
vender	to sell
hacer juego (con)	to match (with)
llevar	to wear; to take
usar	to wear; to use

Variación léxica

calcetines ⟷ medias (*Amér. L.*)
cinturón ⟷ correa (*Col., Venez.*)
gafas/lentes ⟷ espejuelos (*Cuba, P.R.*), anteojos (*Arg., Chile*)
zapatos de tenis ⟷ zapatillas de deporte (*Esp.*), zapatillas (*Arg., Perú*)

recursos
WB pp. 59–60 | LM p. 31 | Ⓢ vhlcentral.com Lección 6

los pantalones cortos
el traje de baño
los pantalones
la camiseta
el dependiente/el vendedor
la camisa
la clienta
el dinero en efectivo
la blusa
la bolsa
el suéter
la falda
las medias

el sombrero

Caballeros

un par de zapatos

los zapatos

la chaqueta

la caja

la cartera

la dependienta/la vendedora

la corbata

la tarjeta de crédito

los (blue)jeans

la bota

Práctica

1 Escuchar Listen to Juanita and Vicente talk about what they're packing for their vacations. Indicate who is packing each item. If both are packing an item, write both names. If neither is packing an item, write an **X**.

1. abrigo _Vicente_
2. zapatos de tenis _Juanita, Vicente_
3. impermeable _X_
4. chaqueta _Vicente_
5. sandalias _Juanita_
6. bluejeans _Juanita, Vicente_
7. gafas de sol _Vicente_
8. camisetas _Juanita, Vicente_
9. traje de baño _Juanita_
10. botas _Vicente_
11. pantalones cortos _Juanita_
12. suéter _Vicente_

2 ¿Lógico o ilógico? Listen to Guillermo and Ana talk about vacation destinations. Indicate whether each statement is **lógico** or **ilógico**.

1. _ilógico_
2. _lógico_
3. _ilógico_
4. _lógico_

3 Completar Anita is talking about going shopping. Complete each sentence with the correct word(s), adding definite or indefinite articles when necessary.

caja	medias	tarjeta de crédito
centro comercial	par	traje de baño
dependientas	ropa	vendedores

1. Hoy voy a ir de compras al _centro comercial_.
2. Voy a ir a la tienda de ropa para mujeres. Siempre hay muchas rebajas y las _dependientas_ son muy simpáticas.
3. Necesito comprar _un par_ de zapatos.
4. Y tengo que comprar _un traje de baño_ porque el sábado voy a la playa con mis amigos.
5. También voy a comprar unas _medias_ para mi mamá.
6. Voy a pagar todo (*everything*) en _la caja_.
7. Pero hoy no tengo dinero. Voy a tener que usar mi _tarjeta de crédito_.
8. Mañana voy al mercado al aire libre. Me gusta regatear con los _vendedores_.

4 Escoger Choose the item in each group that does not belong.

1. almacén • centro comercial • mercado • (sombrero)
2. camisa • camiseta • blusa • (botas)
3. jeans • (bolsa) • falda • pantalones
4. abrigo • suéter • (corbata) • chaqueta
5. mercado • tienda • almacén • (cartera)
6. (pagar) • llevar • hacer juego (con) • usar
7. botas • sandalias • zapatos • (traje)
8. vender • regatear • (ropa interior) • gastar

1 Expansion Have students form pairs and discuss what the weather will be like at each destination. Then have them name three more articles that each person should pack.

1 Script JUANITA: Hola. Me llamo Juanita. Mi familia y yo salimos de vacaciones mañana y estoy haciendo mis maletas. Para nuestra excursión al campo ya tengo bluejeans, camisetas y zapatos de tenis. También vamos a la playa… ¡no puedo esperar! *Script continues on page 176.*

2 Teaching Tip You may want to do this activity as a TPR exercise. Have students raise their right hands if they hear a logical statement and their left hands if they hear an illogical statement.

2 Script 1. Este verano quiero ir de vacaciones a un lugar caliente, con playas y mucho, mucho sol; por eso, necesito comprar un abrigo y botas. 2. A mí me gustaría visitar Costa Rica en la estación de lluvias. Hace mucho calor, pero llueve muchísimo. Voy a necesitar mi impermeable todo el tiempo. 3. Mi lugar favorito para ir de vacaciones es Argentina en invierno. Me gusta esquiar en las montañas. No puedo ir sin mis sandalias ni mi traje de baño. 4. En mi opinión, el lugar ideal para ir de vacaciones es mi club. Allí juego mi deporte favorito, el tenis y también asisto a fiestas elegantes. Por eso siempre llevo mis zapatos de tenis y a veces traje y corbata. *Textbook MP3s*

3 Expansion Ask students to write three additional fill-in-the-blank sentences for a partner to complete.

4 Expansion Go over the answers quickly in class. After each answer, have volunteers indicate why a particular item does not belong. Ex: **1. Un sombrero no es un lugar donde compras cosas.**

1 Script (continued)

Para ir a la playa necesito un traje de baño, pantalones cortos y sandalias. ¿Qué más necesito? Creo que es todo. VICENTE: Buenos días. Soy Vicente. Estoy haciendo mis maletas porque mi familia y yo vamos a las montañas a esquiar. Los primeros dos días vamos a hacer una excursión por las montañas. Necesito zapatos de tenis, camisetas, una chaqueta y bluejeans. El tercer día vamos a esquiar. Necesito un abrigo, un suéter y botas… y gafas de sol.
Textbook MP3s

Teaching Tips

- Read the color words aloud, slowly, one at a time. Point to each drawing and ask: **¿De qué color es esta camiseta?** Ask about combinations. Ex: **Si combino rojo y azul, ¿qué color resulta? (morado)**
- Point to objects in the classroom and clothes you and students are wearing to elicit color words.
- Give dates and have students name the colors that they associate with each one. Ex: **el 14 de febrero (rojo, rosado); el 31 de octubre (negro, anaranjado)** You may want to repeat the process with brand names. Ex: FedEx **(anaranjado, morado, blanco)**
- Point out that color words are adjectives and agree in number and gender with the nouns they modify.

5 Expansion Add a visual aspect to this activity. Show magazine pictures of various products (cars, computers, etc.) and ask questions. Ex: **¿Es cara o barata esta computadora? (Es barata.)**

6 Expansion Point to individuals and ask other students what color of clothing each is wearing. Ex: ____, **¿de qué color es la falda de ____? (Es ____.)**

Los colores

amarillo/a anaranjado/a azul

blanco/a gris marrón, café morado/a negro/a

rojo/a rosado/a verde

¡LENGUA VIVA!

The names of colors vary throughout the Spanish-speaking world. For example, in some countries, **anaranjado/a** may be referred to as **naranja, morado/a** as **púrpura,** and **rojo/a** as **colorado/a.**

Other terms that will prove helpful include **claro** (*light*) and **oscuro** (*dark*): **azul claro, azul oscuro.**

Adjetivos

barato/a	*cheap*
bueno/a	*good*
cada	*each*
caro/a	*expensive*
corto/a	*short (in length)*
elegante	*elegant*
hermoso/a	*beautiful*
largo/a	*long*
loco/a	*crazy*
nuevo/a	*new*
otro/a	*other; another*
pobre	*poor*
rico/a	*rich*

5 **Contrastes** Complete each phrase with the opposite of the underlined word.

1. una corbata <u>barata</u> • unas camisas… caras
2. unas vendedoras <u>malas</u> • unos dependientes… buenos
3. un vestido <u>corto</u> • una falda… larga
4. un hombre muy <u>pobre</u> • una mujer muy… rica
5. una cartera <u>nueva</u> • un cinturón… viejo
6. unos trajes <u>hermosos</u> • unos jeans… feos
7. un impermeable <u>caro</u> • unos suéteres… baratos
8. unos calcetines <u>blancos</u> • unas medias… negras

CONSULTA

Like other adjectives you have seen, colors must agree in gender and number with the nouns they modify.
Ex: **las camisas verdes, el vestido amarillo.**
For a review of descriptive adjectives, see **Estructura 3.1,** pp. 80–81.

6 **Preguntas** Answer these questions with a classmate.

1. ¿De qué color es la rosa de Texas? Es amarilla.
2. ¿De qué color es la bandera (*flag*) de Canadá? Es roja y blanca.
3. ¿De qué color es la casa donde vive el presidente de los EE.UU.? Es blanca.
4. ¿De qué color es el océano Atlántico? Es azul.
5. ¿De qué color es la nieve? Es blanca.
6. ¿De qué color es el café? Es marrón./Es café.
7. ¿De qué color es el dólar de los EE.UU.? Es verde y blanco.
8. ¿De qué color es la cebra (*zebra*)? Es negra y blanca.

 Practice more at **vhlcentral.com.**

TEACHING OPTIONS

Pairs Ask student pairs to write a physical description of a well-known TV or cartoon character. Then have them read their descriptions for the rest of the class to guess. Ex: **Soy bajo y un poco gordo. Llevo pantalones cortos azules y una camiseta roja. Tengo el pelo amarillo. También soy amarillo. ¿Quién soy?** (Bart Simpson)

Game Add a visual aspect to this vocabulary practice by playing

Concentración. On eight cards, write descriptions of clothing, including colors. Ex: **unos pantalones negros** On another eight cards, draw pictures that match the descriptions. Shuffle the cards and place them face-down in four rows of four. In pairs, students select two cards. If the cards match, the pair keeps them. If the cards do not match, students replace them in their original position. The pair with the most cards at the end wins.

Comunicación

7 **Las maletas** With a classmate, answer these questions about the drawings.

1. ¿Qué ropa hay al lado de la maleta de Carmela?
 Hay una camiseta, unos pantalones cortos y un traje de baño.
2. ¿Qué hay en la maleta?
 Hay un sombrero y un par de sandalias.
3. ¿De qué color son las sandalias?
 Las sandalias son rojas.
4. ¿Adónde va Carmela?
 Va a la playa.

CONSULTA

To review weather, see **Lección 5, Contextos**, p. 142.

▶ 5. ¿Qué tiempo va a hacer?
 Va a hacer sol./ Va a hacer calor.
6. ¿Qué hay al lado de la maleta de Pepe?
 Hay un par de calcetines, un par de guantes, un suéter y una chaqueta.
7. ¿Qué hay en la maleta?
 Hay dos pantalones.
8. ¿De qué color es el suéter?
 El suéter es rosado.

NOTA CULTURAL

Bariloche is a popular resort for skiing in South America. Located in Argentina's Patagonia region, the town is also known for its chocolate factories and its beautiful lakes, mountains, and forests.

▶ 9. ¿Qué va a hacer Pepe en Bariloche?
 Va a esquiar.
10. ¿Qué tiempo va a hacer?
 Va a hacer frío./ Va a nevar.

8 **El viaje** Get together with two classmates and imagine that the three of you are going on vacation. Pick a destination and then draw three suitcases. Write in each one what clothing each person is taking. Present your drawings to the rest of the class, answering these questions. *Answers will vary.*

- ¿Adónde van?
- ¿Qué tiempo va a hacer allí?
- ¿Qué van a hacer allí?
- ¿Qué hay en sus maletas?
- ¿De qué color es la ropa que llevan?

9 **Preferencias** Take turns asking and answering these questions with a classmate. *Answers will vary.*

1. ¿Adónde vas a comprar ropa? ¿Por qué?
2. ¿Qué tipo de ropa prefieres? ¿Por qué?
3. ¿Cuáles son tus colores favoritos?
4. En tu opinión, ¿es importante comprar ropa nueva frecuentemente? ¿Por qué?
5. ¿Gastas mucho dinero en ropa cada mes? ¿Buscas rebajas?
6. ¿Regateas cuando compras ropa? ¿Usas tarjetas de crédito?

TEACHING OPTIONS

Pairs Have students form pairs and tell them they are going on a shopping spree. On paper strips, write varying dollar amounts, from ten dollars to three thousand, and distribute them. Have pairs discuss what they will buy. Encourage creativity. Ex: **Tenemos quince dólares y vamos a Old Navy. Ella va a comprar medias amarillas. Yo voy a comprar un sombrero en rebaja.**
Extra Practice Add an auditory aspect to this vocabulary practice. Ask students to write an anonymous description of the article of clothing or outfit that best defines them. Collect the papers, shuffle them, and read the descriptions aloud for the class to guess.
Pairs Have pairs take turns describing classmates' clothing and guessing the person. Ex: **Esta persona lleva jeans y una blusa marrón. Lleva sandalias blancas. (Es ____.)**

7 **Teaching Tip** For questions 1 and 6, tell students to include the color for each piece of clothing.

7 **Expansion**
- In pairs, have students discuss what essential items might be missing from the suitcases. Students may agree or disagree with their partner's suggestions. Ex: **—Pepe debe llevar unas botas y unas gafas de sol. —Sí, Pepe necesita unas botas para esquiar.**
- Ask volunteers what kind of clothing they would take with them to these destinations: **Seattle en la primavera, la Florida en el verano, Toronto en el invierno, San Francisco en el otoño.**

8 **Teaching Tip** One class period before doing this activity, assign groups and have them discuss where they are going.

8 **Expansion** Have students guess where the groups are going, based on the content of the suitcases. Facilitate guessing by asking items 2–5 from the list.

9 **Expansion**
- Ask students to report the findings of their interviews to the class. Ex: ____ va a H&M para comprar ropa porque allí la ropa no es cara. Prefiere ropa informal…
- Have students work with different partners. Tell students to assume the identity of a famous person and explain their clothing preferences, using questions similar to those in **Actividad 9**.

En el mercado

Los chicos van de compras al mercado. ¿Quién hizo la mejor compra?

 communication cultures NATIONAL STANDARDS

PERSONAJES **FELIPE** **JUAN CARLOS**

S Video: *Fotonovela* **Record and Compare**

1

MARISSA Oigan, vamos al mercado.

JUAN CARLOS ¡Sí! Los chicos en un equipo y las chicas en otro.

FELIPE Tenemos dos horas para ir de compras.

MARU Y don Guillermo decide quién gana.

2

JIMENA Esta falda azul es muy elegante.

MARISSA ¡Sí! Además, este color está de moda.

MARU Éste rojo es de algodón.

(*Las chicas encuentran unas bolsas.*)

VENDEDOR Ésta de rayas cuesta 190 pesos, ésta 120 pesos y ésta 220 pesos.

3

MARISSA ¿Me das aquella blusa rosada? Me parece que hace juego con esta falda, ¿no? ¿No tienen otras tallas?

JIMENA Sí, aquí. ¿Qué talla usas?

MARISSA Uso talla 4.

JIMENA La encontré. ¡Qué ropa más bonita!

5

6

(*En otra parte del mercado*)

FELIPE Juan Carlos compró una camisa de muy buena calidad.

MIGUEL (*a la vendedora*) ¿Puedo ver ésos, por favor?

VENDEDORA Sí, señor. Le doy un muy buen precio.

4

VENDEDOR Son 530 por las tres bolsas. Pero como ustedes son tan bonitas, son 500 pesos.

MARU Señor, no somos turistas ricas. Somos estudiantes pobres.

VENDEDOR Bueno, son 480 pesos.

MARISSA	JIMENA	MARU	MIGUEL	DON GUILLERMO	VENDEDORA	VENDEDOR

7

JUAN CARLOS Miren, mi nueva camisa. Elegante, ¿verdad?

FELIPE A ver, Juan Carlos... te queda bien.

8

MARU ¿Qué compraste?

MIGUEL Sólo esto.

MARU ¡Qué bonitos aretes! Gracias, mi amor.

9

JUAN CARLOS Y ustedes, ¿qué compraron?

JIMENA Bolsas.

MARU Acabamos de comprar tres bolsas por sólo 480 pesos. ¡Una ganga!

10

FELIPE Don Guillermo, usted tiene que decidir quién gana. ¿Los chicos o las chicas?

DON GUILLERMO El ganador es... Miguel. ¡Porque no compró nada para él, sino para su novia!

recursos

VM pp. 205–206

vhlcentral.com Lección 6

Expresiones útiles

Talking about clothing

¡Qué ropa más bonita!
What nice clothing!
Esta falda azul es muy elegante.
This blue skirt is very elegant.
Está de moda.
It's in style.
Éste rojo es de algodón/lana.
This red one is cotton/wool.
Ésta de rayas/lunares/cuadros es de seda.
This striped / polka-dotted / plaid one is silk.
Es de muy buena calidad.
It's very good quality.
¿Qué talla usas/llevas?
What size do you wear?
Uso/Llevo talla 4.
I wear a size 4.
¿Qué número calza?
What size shoe do you wear?
Yo calzo siete.
I wear a size seven.

Negotiating a price

¿Cuánto cuesta?
How much does it cost?
Demasiado caro/a.
Too expensive.
Es una ganga.
It's a bargain.

Saying what you bought

¿Qué compraste?/¿Qué compró usted?
What did you buy?
Sólo compré esto.
I only bought this.
¡Qué bonitos aretes!
What beautiful earrings!
Y ustedes, ¿qué compraron?
And you guys, what did you buy?

Additional vocabulary

híjole *wow*

Expresiones útiles

- Point out the verb forms **compraste, compró, compré,** and **compraron.** Tell the class that these are forms of the verb **comprar** in the preterite tense, which is used to talk about events in the past. Tell them that **Esta** is an example of a demonstrative adjective, which is used to single out particular nouns; explain that the accented forms, **Éste** and **Ésta,** are pronouns. Tell students that **esto** is one of three neuter demonstrative pronouns. Have students scan the **Fotonovela** captions for other demonstratives. Also point out the captions for stills 3 and 4 and explain that **Me** and **Le** are examples of indirect object pronouns, which show *to whom* or *for whom* an action is done. Tell students that they will learn more about these concepts in **Estructura.**

- Help students with adjective placement and agreement when talking about clothing. Ask them to translate these phrases: 1. a white tie with gray and brown stripes (**una corbata blanca con rayas grises y marrones**) 2. black wool pants (**unos pantalones negros de lana**) 3. a yellow cotton shirt with purple polka dots (**una camisa amarilla de algodón con lunares morados**) 4. a red silk dress (**un vestido rojo de seda**) Discuss different possibilities for adjective placement and how it affects agreement. Ex: **Un vestido rojo de seda** versus **Un vestido de seda roja.**

Nota cultural When bargaining in open-air markets, one can typically expect to arrive at an agreed price of about 10 to 20% lower than the original. Bargaining is usually a friendly, pleasant experience and an expected and welcome ritual.

TEACHING OPTIONS

TPR Ask students to write **clientes** and **vendedores** on separate sheets on paper. Read aloud phrases from **Expresiones útiles** and have them hold up the paper(s) that correspond(s) to the people that would say that expression. Ex: **¿Qué número calza usted? (vendedores)**

Small Groups Have the class work in small groups to write statements about the **Fotonovela.** Then ask groups to exchange papers and write out a question that would have elicited each statement. Ex: **Miguel compra unos aretes para su novia. (¿Qué compra Miguel para su novia?)**

¿Qué pasó?

1 ¿Cierto o falso? Indicate whether each sentence is **cierto** or **falso**. Correct the false statements.

	Cierto	Falso
1. Jimena dice que la falda azul no es elegante.	○	⊘ Jimena dice que la falda azul es muy elegante.
2. Juan Carlos compra una camisa.	⊘	○
3. Marissa dice que el azul es un color que está de moda.	⊘	○
4. Miguel compra unas sandalias para Maru.	○	⊘ Miguel compra unos aretes para Maru.

2 Identificar Provide the first initial of the person who would make each statement.

M 1. ¿Te gusta cómo se me ven mis nuevos aretes?
F 2. Juan Carlos compró una camisa de muy buena calidad.
M 3. No podemos pagar 500, señor, eso es muy caro.
J 4. Aquí tienen ropa de muchas tallas.
J 5. Esta falda me gusta mucho, el color azul es muy elegante.
F 6. Hay que darnos prisa, sólo tenemos dos horas para ir de compras.

MARU

FELIPE

JIMENA

3 Completar Answer the questions using the information in the **Fotonovela**.

1. ¿Qué talla es Marissa? Marissa usa talla 4.
2. ¿Cuánto les pide el vendedor por las tres bolsas? Las bolsas cuestan 500 pesos.
3. ¿Cuál es el precio que pagan las tres amigas por las bolsas? El precio que pagan es 480 pesos.
4. ¿Qué dice Juan Carlos sobre su nueva camisa? Juan Carlos dice que su nueva camisa es elegante.
5. ¿Quién ganó al hacer las compras? ¿Por qué? Ganó Miguel porque le compró unos aretes a su novia.

4 Conversar With a partner, role-play a conversation between a customer and a salesperson in an open-air market. Use these expressions and also look at **Expresiones útiles** on the previous page. Answers will vary.

¿Qué desea?	Estoy buscando...	Prefiero el/la rojo/a.
What would you like?	*I'm looking for...*	*I prefer the red one.*

Cliente/a	**Vendedor(a)**
Say good afternoon.	→ Greet the customer and ask what he/she would like.
Explain that you are looking for a particular item of clothing.	→ Show him/her some items and ask what he/she prefers.
Discuss colors and sizes.	→ Discuss colors and sizes.
Ask for the price and begin bargaining.	→ Tell him/her a price. Negotiate a price.
Settle on a price and purchase the item.	→ Accept a price and say thank you.

Ⓢ Practice more at **vhlcentral.com**.

Pronunciación

S Audio: Concepts, Activities
Record & Compare

The consonants d and t

¿Dónde? ven**d**er na**d**ar ver**d**a**d**

Like **b** and **v**, the Spanish **d** can also have a hard sound or a soft sound, depending on which letters appear next to it.

Don **d**inero tien**d**a fal**d**a

At the beginning of a phrase and after **n** or **l**, the letter **d** is pronounced with a hard sound. This sound is similar to the English *d* in *dog*, but a little softer and duller. The tongue should touch the back of the upper teeth, not the roof of the mouth.

me**d**ias ver**d**e vesti**d**o hués**p**e**d**

In all other positions, **d** has a soft sound. It is similar to the English *th* in *there*, but a little softer.

Don **D**iego no tiene el **d**iccionario.

When **d** begins a word, its pronunciation depends on the previous word. At the beginning of a phrase or after a word that ends in **n** or **l**, it is pronounced as a hard **d**.

Doña **D**olores es **d**e la capital.

Words that begin with **d** are pronounced with a soft **d** if they appear immediately after a word that ends in a vowel or any consonant other than **n** or **l**.

traje pan**t**alones tarje**t**a **t**ienda

When pronouncing the Spanish **t**, the tongue should touch the back of the upper teeth, not the roof of the mouth. Unlike the English *t*, no air is expelled from the mouth.

 Práctica Read these phrases aloud to practice the **d** and the **t**.

1. Hasta pronto.
2. De nada.
3. Mucho gusto.
4. Lo siento.
5. No hay de qué.
6. ¿De dónde es usted?
7. ¡Todos a bordo!
8. No puedo.
9. Es estupendo.
10. No tengo computadora.
11. ¿Cuándo vienen?
12. Son las tres y media.

Oraciones Read these sentences aloud to practice the **d** and the **t**.

1. Don Teodoro tiene una tienda en un almacén en La Habana.
2. Don Teodoro vende muchos trajes, vestidos y zapatos todos los días.
3. Un día un turista, Federico Machado, entra en la tienda para comprar un par de botas.
4. Federico regatea con don Teodoro y compra las botas y también un par de sandalias.

Refranes Read these sayings aloud to practice the **d** and the **t**.

En la variedad está el gusto.[1]

Aunque la mona se vista de seda, mona se queda.[2]

[1] *Variety is the spice of life.*
[2] *You can't make a silk purse out of a sow's ear.*

recursos

LM
p. 32

S
vhlcentral.com
Lección 6

TEACHING OPTIONS

Extra Practice Write some additional proverbs on the board and have the class practice saying each one. Ex: **De tal padre, tal hijo.** (*Like father, like son.*) **El que tiene tejado de cristal no tira piedras al vecino.** (*People who live in glass houses shouldn't throw stones.*) **Cuatro ojos ven más que dos.** (*Two heads are better than one.*) **Donde come uno, comen dos, y donde comen dos, comen todos.** (*There's always room for one more at the table.*)

Extra Practice Write on the board the names of these famous Cuban literary figures: **José Martí, Julián del Casal, Gertrudis Gómez de Avellaneda,** and **Dulce María Loynaz.** Say the names aloud and have the class repeat. Then ask volunteers to explain the pronunciation of each **d** and **t** in these names.

Section Goal

In **Pronunciación**, students will be introduced to the pronunciation of the letters **d** and **t**.

Instructional Resources
Supersite: Audio (Textbook and Lab MP3 Files); Resources (Scripts, Answer Keys)
WebSAM
Lab Manual, p. 32

Teaching Tips
- Explain that **d** has a hard sound at the beginning of a phrase or after **n** or **l**. Write **don, dinero, tienda,** and **falda** on the board and have the class pronounce them.
- Explain that **d** has a soft sound in all other positions. Pronounce **medias, verde, vestido,** and **huésped** and have the class repeat.
- Point out that within phrases, **d** at the beginning of a word has a hard or soft sound depending on the last sound of the preceding word. Read the examples aloud and have the class repeat.
- Explain that **t** is pronounced with the tongue at the back of the upper teeth and that, unlike English, no air is expelled from the mouth. Pronounce **traje, pantalones, tarjeta,** and **tienda** and have the class repeat. Then pronounce pairs of similar-sounding Spanish and English words, having students focus on the difference between the **t** sounds: ti/*tea*; tal/*tall*; todo/*toad*; tema/*tame*; tela/*tell*.

Práctica/Oraciones/ Refranes These exercises are recorded on the *Textbook MP3s.* You may want to play the audio so that students practice listening to Spanish spoken by speakers other than yourself.

EN DETALLE

Additional Reading
Video: *Flash cultura*

Los mercados al aire libre

Mercados al aire libre are an integral part of commerce and culture in the Spanish-speaking world. Whether they take place daily or weekly, these markets are an important forum where tourists, locals, and vendors interact. People come to the marketplace to shop, socialize, taste local foods, and watch street performers. Wandering from one **puesto** (*stand*) to the next, one can browse fresh fruits and vegetables, clothing, CDs and DVDs, and **artesanías** (*crafts*). Some markets offer a mix of products, while others specialize in food, fashion, or used merchandise, such as antiques and books.

When shoppers see an item they like, they can bargain with the vendor. Friendly bargaining is an expected ritual and may result in a significantly lower price. When selling food, vendors may give the customer a little extra of what they purchase; this free addition is known as **la ñapa.**

Many open-air markets are also tourist attractions. The market in Otavalo, Ecuador, is world-famous and has taken place every Saturday since pre-Incan times. This market is well-known for the colorful textiles woven by the **otavaleños,** the indigenous people of the area. One can also find leather goods and wood carvings from nearby

Mercado de Otavalo

towns. Another popular market is **El Rastro,** held every Sunday in Madrid, Spain. Sellers set up **puestos** along the streets to display their wares, which range from local artwork and antiques to inexpensive clothing and electronics.

Otros mercados famosos

Mercado	Lugar	Productos
Feria Artesanal de Recoleta	Buenos Aires, Argentina	artesanías
Mercado Central	Santiago, Chile	mariscos°, pescado°, frutas, verduras°
Tianguis Cultural del Chopo	Ciudad de México, México	ropa, música, revistas, libros, arte, artesanías
El mercado de Chichicastenango	Chichicastenango, Guatemala	frutas y verduras, flores°, cerámica, textiles

mariscos *seafood* pescado *fish* verduras *vegetables* flores *flowers*

ACTIVIDADES

1 **¿Cierto o falso?** Indicate whether these statements are **cierto** or **falso.** Correct the false statements.

1. Generally, open-air markets specialize in one type of goods. **Falso.** They sell a variety of goods.
2. Bargaining is commonplace at outdoor markets. **Cierto.**
3. Only new goods can be found at open-air markets. **Falso.** They sell both new and used goods.
4. A Spaniard in search of antiques could search at **El Rastro.** **Cierto.**
5. If you are in Guatemala and want to buy ceramics, you can go to Chichicastenango. **Cierto.**
6. A **ñapa** is a tax on open-air market goods. **Falso.** A **ñapa** is a free addition sometimes given to customers.
7. The **otavaleños** weave colorful textiles to sell on Saturdays. **Cierto.**
8. Santiago's **Mercado Central** is known for books and music. **Falso.** It's known for seafood, fish, fruits, and vegetables.

ASÍ SE DICE

La ropa

la chamarra (Méx.)	la chaqueta
de manga corta/larga	*short/long-sleeved*
los mahones (P. Rico); el pantalón de mezclilla (Méx.); los tejanos (Esp.); los vaqueros (Arg., Cuba, Esp., Uru.)	los bluejeans
la marca	*brand*
la playera (Méx.); la remera (Arg.)	la camiseta

EL MUNDO HISPANO

Diseñadores de moda

- **Adolfo Domínguez** (España) Su ropa tiene un estilo minimalista y práctico. Usa telas° naturales y cómodas en sus diseños.

- **Silvia Tcherassi** (Colombia) Los colores vivos y las líneas asimétricas de sus vestidos y trajes muestran influencias tropicales.

- **Óscar de la Renta** (República Dominicana) Diseña ropa opulenta para la mujer clásica.

- **Narciso Rodríguez** (EE.UU.) En sus diseños delicados y finos predominan los colores blanco y negro. Hizo° el vestido de boda° de Carolyn Bessette Kennedy.

telas *fabrics* Hizo *He made* de boda *wedding*

PERFIL

Carolina Herrera

In 1980, at the urging of some friends, **Carolina Herrera** created a fashion collection as a "test." The Venezuelan designer received such a favorable response that within one year she moved her family from Caracas to New York City and created her own label, Carolina Herrera, Ltd.

"I love elegance and intricacy, but whether it is in a piece of clothing or a fragrance, the intricacy must appear as simplicity," Herrera once stated. She quickly found that many sophisticated women agreed; from the start, her sleek and glamorous

designs have been in constant demand. Over the years, Herrera has grown her brand into a veritable fashion empire that encompasses her fashion and bridal collections, cosmetics, perfume, and accessories that are sold around the globe.

Conexión Internet

¿Qué marcas de ropa son populares en el mundo hispano?

Go to **vhlcentral.com** to find more cultural information related to this **Cultura** section.

ACTIVIDADES

2 **Comprensión** Complete these sentences.

1. Adolfo Domínguez usa telas _naturales_ y _cómodas_ en su ropa.
2. Si hace fresco en el D.F., puedes llevar una _chamarra_.
3. La diseñadora _Carolina Herrera_ hace ropa, perfumes y más.
4. La ropa de _Silvia Tcherassi_ muestra influencias tropicales.
5. Los _mahones_ son una ropa casual en Puerto Rico.

3 **Mi ropa favorita** Write a brief description of your favorite article of clothing. Mention what store it is from, the brand, colors, fabric, style, and any other information. Then get together with a small group, collect the descriptions, and take turns reading them aloud at random. Can the rest of the group guess whose favorite piece of clothing is being described? *Answers will vary.*

recursos

VM pp. 277–278	vhlcentral.com Lección 6

Practice more at **vhlcentral.com.**

Section Goals

In **Estructura 6.1**, students will learn:

• the uses of **saber** and **conocer**
• more uses of the personal **a**
• other verbs conjugated like **conocer**

Instructional Resources

Supersite: Audio (Lab MP3 Files); Resources (*PowerPoints*, Activity Pack, Scripts, Answer Keys); Testing Program (Quizzes)
WebSAM
Workbook, p. 61
Lab Manual, p. 33

Teaching Tips

• Use the **Lección 6 Estructura** overheads to assist with this presentation.
• Point out the irregular **yo** forms of **saber** and **conocer**.
• Divide the board into two columns with the headings **saber** and **conocer**. In the first column, write the uses of **saber** and model them by asking individuals what they know how to do and what factual information they know. Ex: _____, ¿sabes bailar salsa? ¿Sabes mi número de teléfono? In the second column, write the uses of **conocer** and model them by asking individuals about people and places they know. Ex: _____, ¿conoces Cuba? ¿Conoces a Anier García?
• Further distinguish the uses of **saber** and **conocer** by making statements such as: **Sé quién es el presidente de este país, pero no lo conozco.**
• Point out the first **¡Atención!** bullet. Ask volunteers to write the full conjugation of these verbs on the board.
• Point out the similar **yo** form for **conocer, parecer, ofrecer, conducir,** and **traducir.**
• Ask questions using the new verbs. Ex: ¿Quiénes conducen? ¿Qué carro conduces?

6.1 Saber and conocer Tutorial

ANTE TODO Spanish has two verbs that mean *to know*: **saber** and **conocer**. They cannot be used interchangeably. Note the irregular **yo** forms.

The verbs saber and conocer

		saber (to know)	conocer (to know)
SINGULAR FORMS	yo	sé	conozco
	tú	sabes	conoces
	Ud./él/ella	sabe	conoce
PLURAL FORMS	nosotros/as	sabemos	conocemos
	vosotros/as	sabéis	conocéis
	Uds./ellos/ellas	saben	conocen

▶ **Saber** means *to know a fact or piece(s) of information* or *to know how to do something.*

No **sé** tu número de teléfono.
I don't know your telephone number.

Mi hermana **sabe** hablar francés.
My sister knows how to speak French.

▶ **Conocer** means *to know* or *be familiar/acquainted* with a person, place, or thing.

¿**Conoces** la ciudad de Nueva York?
Do you know New York City?

No **conozco** a tu amigo Esteban.
I don't know your friend Esteban.

▶ When the direct object of **conocer** is a person or pet, the personal **a** is used.

¿Conoces La Habana?
Do you know Havana?

but

¿Conoces **a** Celia Cruz?
Do you know Celia Cruz?

▶ **¡Atención!** **Parecer** (*to seem*) and **ofrecer** (*to offer*) are conjugated like **conocer**.

▶ **¡Atención!** **Conducir** (*to drive*) and **traducir** (*to translate*) also have an irregular **yo** form, but since they are **-ir** verbs, they are conjugated differently from **conocer**.

conducir		con**duzco**, conduces, conduce, condu**cimos**, condu**cís**, conducen
traducir		tra**duzco**, traduces, traduce, tradu**cimos**, tradu**cís**, traducen

 ¡INTÉNTALO! Provide the appropriate forms of these verbs.

saber

1. José no ___sabe___ la hora.
2. Sara y yo ___sabemos___ jugar al tenis.
3. ¿Por qué no ___sabes___ tú estos verbos?
4. Mis padres ___saben___ hablar japonés.
5. Yo ___sé___ a qué hora es la clase.
6. Usted no ___sabe___ dónde vivo.
7. Mi hermano no ___sabe___ nadar.
8. Nosotros ___sabemos___ muchas cosas.

conocer

1. Usted y yo ___conocemos___ bien Miami.
2. ¿Tú ___conoces___ a mi amigo Manuel?
3. Sergio y Taydé ___conocen___ mi pueblo.
4. Emiliano ___conoce___ a mis padres.
5. Yo ___conozco___ muy bien el centro.
6. ¿Ustedes ___conocen___ la tienda Gigante?
7. Nosotras ___conocemos___ una playa hermosa.
8. ¿Usted ___conoce___ a mi profesora?

recursos

WB p. 61

LM p. 33

vhlcentral.com Lección 6

TEACHING OPTIONS

TPR Divide the class into two teams, **saber** and **conocer**, and have them line up. Indicate the first member of each team and call out a sentence in English that uses *to know*. (Ex: We know the answer.) The team member whose verb corresponds to the English sentence has to step forward and provide the Spanish translation.

Extra Practice Ask students to jot down three things they know how to do well (**saber** + [*infinitive*] + **bien**). Collect the papers, shuffle them, and read the sentences aloud. Have the rest of the class guess who wrote the sentences.

Práctica y Comunicación

1 **Completar** Indicate the correct verb for each sentence.

1. Mis hermanos (conocen/saben) conducir, pero yo no (sé/conozco).
2. —¿(Conocen/Saben) ustedes dónde está el estadio? —No, no lo (conocemos/sabemos).
3. —¿(Conoces/Sabes) a Lady Gaga? —Bueno, (sé/conozco) quién es, pero no la (conozco/sé).
4. Mi profesora (sabe/conoce) Cuba y también (conoce/sabe) bailar salsa.

2 **Combinar** Combine elements from each column to create sentences. Answers will vary.

A	B	C
Shakira	(no) conocer	Conan O'Brien
los Yankees	(no) saber	cantar y bailar
el primer ministro		La Habana Vieja
de Canadá		muchas personas importantes
mis amigos y yo		hablar dos lenguas extranjeras
tú		jugar al béisbol

3 **Preguntas** In pairs, ask each other these questions. Answer with complete sentences.
Answers will vary.

1. ¿Conoces a un(a) cantante famoso/a? ¿Te gusta cómo canta?
2. En tu familia, ¿quién sabe cantar bien? ¿Tu opinión es objetiva?
3. Y tú, ¿conduces bien o mal? ¿Y tus amigos?
4. Si un(a) amigo/a no conduce muy bien, ¿le ofreces crítica constructiva?
5. ¿Cómo parece estar el/la profesor(a) hoy? ¿Y tus compañeros de clase?

4 **Entrevista** Jot down three things you know how to do, three people you know, and three places you are familiar with. Then, in a small group, find out what you have in common. Answers will vary.

> **modelo**
> **Estudiante 1:** ¿Conocen ustedes a David Lomas?
> **Estudiante 2:** Sí, conozco a David. Vivimos en la misma residencia estudiantil.
> **Estudiante 3:** No, no lo conozco. ¿Cómo es?

5 **Anuncio** In groups, read the ad and answer these questions. Answers will vary.

1. Busquen ejemplos de los verbos **saber** y **conocer**.
2. ¿Qué saben del Centro Comercial Oviedo?
3. ¿Qué pueden hacer en el Centro Comercial Oviedo?
4. ¿Conocen otros centros comerciales similares? ¿Cómo se llaman? ¿Dónde están?
5. ¿Conocen un centro comercial en otro país? ¿Cómo es?...

El sabe dónde **comer** lo que más le gusta.

El sabe cómo **jugar** cuatro horas seguidas.

El sabe dónde está su **regalo** de cumpleaños.

El sabe dónde **divertirse**...

... y usted sabe dónde puede encontrar un poco de todo. ¿Conoce algún otro lugar como éste?

CENTRO COMERCIAL **MÁLAGA** SABE LO QUE TE GUSTA.

Practice more at **vhlcentral.com.**

1 **Teaching Tip** To challenge students, write this activity on the board as cloze sentences.

1 **Expansion** Give students these sentences as items 5–8: **5. No (sé/conozco) a qué hora es el examen. (sé) 6. (Conoces/ Sabes) las cataratas de Iguazú, ¿verdad? (Conoces) 7. ¿Quieren (saber/conocer) dónde va a ser la fiesta? (saber) 8. Esta noche voy a salir con mi novia, pero mis padres no lo (conocen/saben). Todavía no la (conocen/saben)... ¡no (conocen/saben) quién es ella! (saben, conocen, saben)**

2 **Teaching Tip** To simplify, before beginning the activity, read through column C and have students determine whether each item takes the verb **saber** or **conocer.**

2 **Expansion**
• Add more elements to column A (Ex: **yo, mis padres, mi profesor(a) de español**) and continue the activity.
• Ask students questions about what certain celebrities know how to do or whom they know. Ex: **Brad Pitt, ¿conoce a Angelina Jolie? (Sí, la conoce.) David Ortiz, ¿sabe jugar al béisbol? (Sí, sabe jugarlo.)**

3 **Expansion** In pairs, have students create three additional questions using the verbs **conducir, ofrecer,** and **traducir.** Then have pairs join other pairs to ask and answer their questions.

4 **Teaching Tip** To simplify, have students divide a sheet of paper into three columns with the headings **Sé, Conozco a,** and **Conozco.** Then have them complete their lists.

5 **Expansion** Ask each group to create an advertisement using two examples each of **saber** and **conocer.**

6.2 Indirect object pronouns (S) Tutorial

ANTE TODO In **Lección 5**, you learned that a direct object receives the action of the verb directly. In contrast, an indirect object receives the action of the verb indirectly.

	SUBJECT	I.O. PRONOUN	VERB	DIRECT OBJECT	INDIRECT OBJECT
	Roberto	**le**	presta	cien pesos	**a Luisa.**
	Roberto		*lends*	*100 pesos*	*to Luisa.*

An indirect object is a noun or pronoun that answers the question *to whom* or *for whom* an action is done. In the preceding example, the indirect object answers this question:
¿A quién le presta Roberto cien pesos? *To whom does Roberto lend 100 pesos?*

Indirect object pronouns

Singular forms		Plural forms	
me	(to, for) *me*	**nos**	(to, for) *us*
te	(to, for) *you* (fam.)	**os**	(to, for) *you* (fam.)
le	(to, for) *you* (form.)	**les**	(to, for) *you* (form.)
	(to, for) *him; her*		(to, for) *them*

▶ **¡Atención!** The forms of indirect object pronouns for the first and second persons (**me, te, nos, os**) are the same as the direct object pronouns. Indirect object pronouns agree in number with the corresponding nouns, but not in gender.

Bueno, le doy un descuento.

Acabo de mostrarles que sí sabemos regatear.

Using indirect object pronouns

▶ Spanish speakers commonly use both an indirect object pronoun and the noun to which it refers in the same sentence. This is done to emphasize and clarify to whom the pronoun refers.

I.O. PRONOUN	INDIRECT OBJECT	I.O. PRONOUN	INDIRECT OBJECT
Ella **le** vende la ropa **a Elena.**		**Les** prestamos el dinero **a Inés y a Álex.**	

▶ Indirect object pronouns are also used without the indirect object noun when the person for whom the action is being done is known.

Ana **le** presta la falda **a Elena.**
Ana lends her skirt to Elena.

También **le** presta unos jeans.
She also lends her a pair of jeans.

▶ Indirect object pronouns are usually placed before the conjugated form of the verb. In negative sentences the pronoun is placed between **no** and the conjugated verb.

Martín **me** compra un regalo. Eva **no me** escribe cartas.
Martín is buying me a gift. *Eva doesn't write me letters.*

CONSULTA

For more information on accents, see **Lección 4, Pronunciación**, p. 115, **Lección 10, Ortografía**, p. 315, and **Lección 11, Ortografía**, p. 349.

▶ When a conjugated verb is followed by an infinitive or the present progressive, the indirect object pronoun may be placed before the conjugated verb or attached to the infinitive or present participle. **¡Atención!** When an indirect object pronoun is attached to a present participle, an accent mark is added to maintain the proper stress.

Él no quiere **pagarte**./ Él está **escribiéndole** una postal a ella./
Él no **te** quiere pagar. Él **le** está escribiendo una postal a ella.
He does not want to pay you. *He is writing a postcard to her.*

▶ Because the indirect object pronouns **le** and **les** have multiple meanings, Spanish speakers often clarify to whom the pronouns refer with the preposition **a** + [*pronoun*] or **a** + [*noun*].

UNCLARIFIED STATEMENTS **CLARIFIED STATEMENTS**
Yo **le** compro un abrigo. Yo **le** compro un abrigo **a usted/él/ella**.

Ella **le** describe un libro. Ella **le** describe un libro **a Juan**.

UNCLARIFIED STATEMENTS **CLARIFIED STATEMENTS**
Él **les** vende unos sombreros. Él **les** vende unos sombreros **a ustedes/ellos/ellas**.

Ellos **les** hablan muy claro. Ellos **les** hablan muy claro **a los clientes**.

▶ The irregular verbs **dar** (*to give*) and **decir** (*to say; to tell*) are often used with indirect object pronouns.

The verbs dar and decir

	Singular forms				Plural forms	
	dar	**decir**			**dar**	**decir**
yo	**doy**	**digo**	nosotros/as		**damos**	**decimos**
tú	**das**	**dices**	vosotros/as		**dais**	**decís**
Ud./él/ella	**da**	**dice**	Uds./ellos/ellas		**dan**	**dicen**

Me dan una fiesta cada año. **Te digo** la verdad.
They give (throw) me a party every year. *I'm telling you the truth.*

Voy a **darle** consejos. No **les digo** mentiras a mis padres.
I'm going to give her advice. *I don't tell lies to my parents.*

recursos

WB
pp. 62–63

LM
p. 34

S

vhlcentral.com
Lección 6

¡INTÉNTALO! Use the cues in parentheses to provide the correct indirect object pronoun for each sentence.

1. Juan ____le____ quiere dar un regalo. (*to Elena*)
2. María ____nos____ prepara un café. (*for us*)
3. Beatriz y Felipe ____me____ escriben desde (*from*) Cuba. (*to me*)
4. Marta y yo ____les____ compramos unos guantes. (*for them*)
5. Los vendedores ____te____ venden ropa. (*to you, fam. sing.*)
6. La dependienta ____nos____ muestra los guantes. (*to us*)

Teaching Tips
• Point out that the position of indirect object pronouns in a sentence is the same as that of direct object pronouns.
• Ask individuals questions using indirect object pronouns. Ex: **¿A quién le ofreces ayuda? ¿Les das consejos a tus amigos? ¿Qué te dicen tus padres que no debes hacer? ¿Les dices mentiras a tus padres? ¿Cuándo vas a escribirles a tus abuelos?** Have students respond with complete sentences and ask follow-up questions if necessary.
• After going over the **¡Inténtalo!** orally with the class, ask students which items might require clarification (items 1 and 4). Ask them what they would add to each sentence in order to clarify **le** or **les**.
• As a comprehension check, have students write answers to these questions: **1. Es el cumpleaños de tu mejor amigo. ¿Qué vas a comprarle? 2. ¿A quiénes les hablas todos los días? 3. ¿Quién te presta dinero cuando lo necesitas? 4. ¿Quién les está enseñando español a ustedes?**
• In pairs, have students write the dialogue of an argument between two roommates, using **dar** and **decir**. Have volunteers role-play their conversations for the class. Encourage them to be creative and act out the argument with props, if possible.

Práctica

NOTA CULTURAL

Cuban writer and patriot **José Martí** (1853–1895) was born in **La Habana Vieja**, the old colonial center of Havana. Founded by Spanish explorers in the early 1500s, Havana, along with San Juan, Puerto Rico, served as a major stopping point for Spaniards traveling to Mexico and South America.

1 Completar Fill in the blanks with the correct pronouns to complete Mónica's description of her family's holiday shopping.

1. Juan y yo ____le____ damos una blusa a nuestra hermana Gisela.
2. Mi tía ____nos____ da a nosotros una mesa para la casa.
3. Gisela ____le____ da dos corbatas a su novio.
4. A mi mamá yo ____le____ doy un par de guantes negros.
5. A mi profesora ____le____ doy dos libros de José Martí.
6. Juan ____les____ da un regalo a mis padres.
7. Mis padres ____me____ dan un traje nuevo a mí.
8. Y a ti, yo ____te____ doy un regalo también. ¿Quieres verlo?

2 En La Habana Describe what happens on Pascual's trip to Cuba based on the cues provided.

1. ellos / cantar / canción / (mí)
Ellos me cantan una canción (a mí).

2. él / comprar / libros / (sus hijos) / Plaza de Armas
Él les compra libros (a sus hijos) en la Plaza de Armas.

3. yo / preparar el almuerzo (lunch) / (ti)
Yo te preparo el almuerzo (a ti).

4. él / explicar cómo llegar / (conductor)
Él le explica cómo llegar (al conductor).

5. mi novia / sacar / foto / (nosotros)
Mi novia nos saca una foto (a nosotros).

6. el guía (guide) / mostrar / catedral de San Cristóbal / (ustedes)
El guía les muestra la catedral de San Cristóbal (a ustedes).

NOTA CULTURAL

La Habana Vieja, Cuba, is the site of another well-known outdoor market. Located in the **Plaza de la Catedral**, it is a place where Cuban painters, artists, and sculptors sell their work, and other vendors offer handmade crafts and clothing.

3 Combinar Use an item from each column and an indirect object pronoun to create logical sentences. Answers will vary.

> **modelo**
>
> Mis padres les dan regalos a mis primos.

A	B	C	D
yo	comprar	mensajes electrónicos	mí
el dependiente	dar	corbata	ustedes
el profesor Arce	decir	dinero en efectivo	clienta
la vendedora	escribir	tarea	novia
mis padres	explicar	problemas	primos
tú	pagar	regalos	ti
nosotros/as	prestar	ropa	nosotros
¿?	vender	¿?	¿?

: Practice more at **vhlcentral.com.**

1 Teaching Tip Before beginning the activity, have students identify the indirect object in each sentence.

1 Expansion Have students write four sentences about themselves, leaving out the indirect object pronoun. Ex: **Yo ____ doy un regalo a mis padres. Mi tío ____ compra una moto a mí…** Then have them exchange papers with a classmate and complete the sentences.

2 Teaching Tips
- To simplify, read through the cues for each item and have students identify the indirect object pronoun that is needed. Then have them write the complete sentences.
- Point out that students will need to add articles to some sentences.

2 Expansion Divide the class into small groups. Have each student pick a photo (photos 1, 2, 4, and 5 are most appropriate) to present to the group as a verbal portrait, including an introductory sentence that sets the scene, followed by a body and conclusion. The verbal portrait should answer the questions *who, what, where, when*, and *why* with regard to what is seen in the photo. After each group member has presented his or her photo, the group chooses one to present to the class.

3 Expansion Have students convert three of their statements into questions, using **¿Quién?, ¿A quién?,** and **¿Qué?** Have pairs take turns asking and answering their questions. Ex: **¿Quién les vende la ropa? (el dependiente) ¿A quiénes les das regalos? (a mis primos) ¿Qué te explican tus padres? (los problemas)**

TEACHING OPTIONS

Heritage Speakers Ask heritage speakers to share any typical words or phrases that one would hear in a radio ad. Then have students work in pairs to create a radio commercial for their favorite clothing store. Have them tell customers what they can buy, for whom, and at what price.

Pairs Ask students to write five questions that elicit indirect object pronouns. In pairs, have students ask their partner questions and write down their partner's answers. Then ask pairs to review the questions and answers for accuracy.

Pairs Brainstorm on the board a list of things that parents tell high school-age or college-age children they should or should not do. Then have pairs ask each other if their parents tell them these things and summarize their findings for the class. Ex: **Nuestros padres nos dicen que no debemos tomar mucho café.**

Comunicación

4 **Entrevista** In pairs, take turns asking and answering for whom you do these activities. Use the model as a guide. *Answers will vary.*

cantar canciones de amor (*love songs*)	escribir mensajes electrónicos
comprar ropa	mostrar fotos de un viaje
dar una fiesta	pedir dinero
decir mentiras	preparar comida (*food*) mexicana

modelo

escribir mensajes electrónicos
Estudiante 1: ¿A quién le escribes mensajes electrónicos?
Estudiante 2: Le escribo mensajes electrónicos a mi hermano.

5 **¡Somos ricos!** You and your classmates chipped in on a lottery ticket and you won! Now you want to spend money on your loved ones. In groups of three, discuss what each person is buying for family and friends. *Answers will vary.*

modelo

Estudiante 1: Quiero comprarle un vestido de Carolina Herrera a mi madre.
Estudiante 2: Y yo voy a darles un automóvil nuevo a mis padres.
Estudiante 3: Voy a comprarles una casa a mis padres, pero a mis amigos no les voy a dar nada.

6 **Entrevista** Use these questions to interview a classmate. *Answers will vary.*

1. ¿Qué tiendas, almacenes o centros comerciales prefieres?
2. ¿A quién le compras regalos cuando hay rebajas?
3. ¿A quién le prestas dinero cuando lo necesita?
4. Quiero ir de compras. ¿Cuánto dinero me puedes prestar?
5. ¿Te dan tus padres su tarjeta de crédito cuando vas de compras?

Síntesis

7 **Minidrama** In groups of three, take turns playing the roles of two shoppers and a clerk in a clothing store. The shoppers should talk about the articles of clothing they are looking for and for whom they are buying the clothes. The clerk should recommend several items based on the shoppers' descriptions. Use these expressions and also look at **Expresiones útiles** on page 179. *Answers will vary.*

Me queda grande/pequeño.	¿Está en rebaja?
It's big/small on me.	*Is it on sale?*
¿Tiene otro color?	También estoy buscando...
Do you have another color?	*I'm also looking for...*

4 **Teaching Tips**
• Have two volunteers read the model aloud. Then go through the phrases in the word bank and model question formation.
• To challenge students, have them ask follow-up questions for each item. Ex: **¿A quién le compras ropa? ¿Qué ropa le compras? ¿Dónde la compras?**

4 **Expansion**
In small groups, give students five minutes to brainstorm as many questions as they can using different forms of the verbs in the word bank. Invite two groups to come to the front of the class. Each pair takes a turn asking the other its questions. Encourage students to ask follow-up questions.

5 **Teaching Tip** Give each group a different lottery pay-out. Remind students they have to split it equally among the group members.

5 **Expansion** Have students research one of the different lotteries in Spain, such as **el Gordo** or **ONCE**. Have them write a brief description of how the lottery works, what it costs, and how much recent winners received.

6 **Teaching Tip** Take a class survey of the answers and write the results on the board.

6 **Expansion** Have students work in pairs and write a conversation between a parent and a child, using item 4 as a starting point. Ask students to role-play their dialogues for the class.

7 **Teaching Tip** To simplify, have students begin by brainstorming phrases for their role. Remind them that, except for the dialogue *between* the two shoppers, they should use **usted** in their conversations.

TEACHING OPTIONS

Small Groups Have students write a conversation. One friend tries to convince the other to go shopping with him or her this weekend. The other friend explains that he or she cannot and lists all the things he or she is going to do. Students should include as many different indirect object pronouns as possible.
Pairs Ask students to imagine that they are going on an extended trip. Have them make a list of five things they are

going to do (e.g., things they are going to buy for themselves or others) before leaving. Ex: **Voy a comprarme unos zapatos.**
Extra Practice Add a visual aspect to this grammar practice. Bring in personal or magazine photos that elicit statements with indirect object pronouns. Have students write descriptions of what is happening in each image. Ex: **La mujer está diciéndole a su hijo que tiene que comer el brócoli....**

6.3 Preterite tense of regular verbs Tutorial

ANTE TODO In order to talk about events in the past, Spanish uses two simple tenses: the preterite and the imperfect. In this lesson, you will learn how to form the preterite tense, which is used to express actions or states completed in the past.

Preterite of regular -ar, -er, and -ir verbs

		-ar verbs **comprar**	-er verbs **vender**	-ir verbs **escribir**
SINGULAR FORMS	yo	compr**é** *I bought*	vend**í** *I sold*	escrib**í** *I wrote*
	tú	compr**aste**	vend**iste**	escrib**iste**
	Ud./él/ella	compr**ó**	vend**ió**	escrib**ió**
PLURAL FORMS	nosotros/as	compr**amos**	vend**imos**	escrib**imos**
	vosotros/as	compr**asteis**	vend**isteis**	escrib**isteis**
	Uds./ellos/ellas	compr**aron**	vend**ieron**	escrib**ieron**

▶ **¡Atención!** The **yo** and **Ud./él/ella** forms of all three conjugations have written accents on the last syllable to show that it is stressed.

▶ As the chart shows, the endings for regular **-er** and **-ir** verbs are identical in the preterite.

¿Qué compraste?

Compré estos aretes.

▶ Note that the **nosotros/as** forms of regular **-ar** and **-ir** verbs in the preterite are identical to the present tense forms. Context will help you determine which tense is being used.

En invierno **compramos** ropa.
In the winter, we buy clothing.

Anoche **compramos** unos zapatos.
Last night we bought some shoes.

▶ **-Ar** and **-er** verbs that have a stem change in the present tense are regular in the preterite. They do *not* have a stem change.

	PRESENT	PRETERITE
cerrar (e:ie)	La tienda **cierra** a las seis.	La tienda **cerró** a las seis.
volver (o:ue)	Carlitos **vuelve** tarde.	Carlitos **volvió** tarde.
jugar (u:ue)	Él **juega** al fútbol.	Él **jugó** al fútbol.

▶ **¡Atención!** **-Ir** verbs that have a stem change in the present tense also have a stem change in the preterite.

Section Goals

In **Estructura 6.3**, students will learn:
• the preterite of regular verbs
• spelling changes in the preterite for different verbs
• words commonly used with the preterite tense

Instructional Resources
Supersite: Audio (Lab MP3 Files); Resources (*PowerPoints*, Activity Pack, Scripts, Answer Keys); Testing Program (Quizzes)
WebSAM
Workbook, pp. 64–65
Lab Manual, p. 35

Teaching Tips

• →👥← Introduce the preterite by describing some things you did yesterday, using the first-person preterite of known regular verbs. Use adverbs that signal the preterite (page 191). Ex: **Ayer compré una chaqueta nueva. Bueno, entré en el almacén y compré una. Y de repente, vi un sombrero. Decidí comprarlo también.** Each time you introduce a preterite form, write it on the board.

• After you have used several regular first-person preterites, expand by asking students questions. Ex: **Ayer compré un sombrero. Y tú, _____, ¿qué compraste ayer? (Compré un libro.)** Ask other students about their classmates' answers. Ex: **¿Qué compró _____ ayer? (Compró un libro.)**

Extra Practice For practice with discrimination between preterite forms, call out preterite forms of regular verbs and point to individuals to provide the corresponding subject pronoun. Ex: **comimos (nosotros/as), creyeron (ustedes/ellos/ellas), llegué (yo), leíste (tú).**
Pairs 👤↔👤 Tell students to have a conversation about what they did last weekend. Make sure they include things they did by

themselves and with others. Then, in groups of four, have them share their partner's weekend activities.
Small Groups Give each group of five a list of verbs, including some with spelling changes. Student A chooses a verb from the list and gives the **yo** form. Student B gives the **tú** form, and so on. Students work their way down the list, alternating who begins the conjugation chain.

▶ Verbs that end in **-car**, **-gar**, and **-zar** have a spelling change in the first person singular (**yo** form) in the preterite.

bus**car**	bus**c-**	**qu-**	yo bus**qué**
llegar	**lle**g-	**gu-**	yo lle**gué**
empe**zar**	empe**z-**	**c-**	yo empe**cé**

▶ Except for the **yo** form, all other forms of **-car**, **-gar**, and **-zar** verbs are regular in the preterite.

▶ Three other verbs—**creer**, **leer**, and **oír**—have spelling changes in the preterite. The **i** of the verb endings of **creer**, **leer**, and **oír** carries an accent in the **yo**, **tú**, **nosotros/as**, and **vosotros/as** forms, and changes to **y** in the **Ud./él/ella** and **Uds./ellos/ellas** forms.

creer	cre-	cre**í**, cre**íste**, cre**yó**, cre**ímos**, cre**ísteis**, cre**yeron**
leer	le-	le**í**, le**íste**, le**yó**, le**ímos**, le**ísteis**, le**yeron**
oír	o-	o**í**, o**íste**, o**yó**, o**ímos**, o**ísteis**, o**yeron**

▶ **Ver** is regular in the preterite, but none of its forms has an accent.

ver ⟶ vi, viste, vio, vimos, visteis, vieron

Words commonly used with the preterite

anoche	last night	**pasado/a** (*adj.*)	last; past
anteayer	the day before	**el año pasado**	last year
	yesterday	**la semana pasada**	last week
ayer	yesterday	**una vez**	once; one time
de repente	suddenly	**dos veces**	twice; two times
desde... hasta...	from... until...	**ya**	already

Ayer llegué a Santiago de Cuba. **Anoche** oí un ruido extraño.
Yesterday I arrived in Santiago de Cuba. *Last night I heard a strange noise.*

▶ **Acabar de** + [*infinitive*] is used to say that something has just occurred. Note that **acabar** is in the present tense in this construction.

Acabo de comprar una falda. **Acabas de ir** de compras.
I just bought a skirt. *You just went shopping.*

recursos

WB
pp. 64–65

LM
p. 35

S
vhlcentral.com
Lección 6

 ¡INTÉNTALO! Provide the appropriate preterite forms of the verbs.

	comer	salir	comenzar	leer
1. ellas	comieron	salieron	comenzaron	leyeron
2. tú	comiste	saliste	comenzaste	leíste
3. usted	comió	salió	comenzó	leyó
4. nosotros	comimos	salimos	comenzamos	leímos
5. yo	comí	salí	comencé	leí

Teaching Tips
- Point out that verbs ending in **-car** and **-gar** are regular and have logical spelling changes in the **yo** form in order to preserve the hard **c** and **g** sounds.
- Students will learn the preterite of **dar** in **Estructura 9.1**. If you wish to present it for recognition only at this point, you can tell them that the endings are identical to **ver** in the preterite.
- Provide sentence starters using the present indicative and have students complete them in a logical manner. Ex: **Todos los días los estudiantes llegan temprano, pero anteayer… (llegaron tarde.)**
- Practice verbs with spelling changes in the preterite by asking students about things they read, heard, and saw yesterday. Ex: **¿Leíste las noticias ayer? ¿Quiénes vieron el pronóstico del tiempo? Yo oí que va a llover hoy. ¿Qué oyeron ustedes?**
- Add a visual aspect to this grammar presentation. Use magazine pictures to demonstrate **acabar de**. Ex: **¿Quién acaba de ganar? (Serena Williams acaba de ganar.) ¿Qué acaban de ver ellos? (Acaban de ver una película.)**

TEACHING OPTIONS

Game Divide the class into teams of six and have them sit in rows. Call out the infinitive of a verb. The first person writes the preterite **yo** form on a sheet of paper and passes it to the second person, who writes the **tú** form, and so on. The sixth checks spelling. If all forms are correct, the team gets a point. Continue play, having team members rotate positions for each round. The team with the most points after six rounds wins.

Extra Practice Have students write down five things they did yesterday. Ask students questions about what they did to elicit as many different conjugations as possible. Ex: _____, ¿leíste las noticias ayer? ¿Quién más leyó las noticias ayer?... _____ y _____, ustedes dos leyeron las noticias ayer, ¿verdad? ¿Quiénes leyeron las noticias ayer?

Práctica

1 **Completar** Andrea is talking about what happened last weekend. Complete each sentence by choosing the correct verb and putting it in the preterite.

1. El viernes a las cuatro de la tarde, la profesora Mora ___asistió___ (asistir, costar, usar) a una reunión (*meeting*) de profesores.
2. A la una, yo ___llegué___ (llegar, bucear, llevar) a la tienda con mis amigos.
3. Mis amigos y yo ___compramos___ (comprar, regatear, gastar) dos o tres cosas.
4. Yo ___compré___ (costar, comprar, escribir) unos pantalones negros y mi amigo Mateo ___compró___ (gastar, pasear, comprar) una camisa azul.
5. Después, nosotros ___comimos___ (llevar, vivir, comer) cerca de un mercado.
6. A las tres, Pepe ___habló___ (hablar, pasear, nadar) con su novia por teléfono.
7. El sábado por la tarde, mi mamá ___escribió___ (escribir, beber, vivir) una carta.
8. El domingo mi tía ___decidió___ (decidir, salir, escribir) comprarme un traje.
9. A las cuatro de la tarde, mi tía ___encontró___ (beber, salir, encontrar) el traje y después nosotras ___vimos___ (acabar, ver, salir) una película.

2 **Preguntas** Imagine that you have a pesky friend who keeps asking you questions. Respond that you already did or have just done what he/she asks. Make sure you and your partner take turns playing the role of the pesky friend and responding to his/her questions.

modelo

leer la lección
Estudiante 1: ¿Leíste la lección?
Estudiante 2: Sí, ya la leí./Sí, acabo de leerla.

1. escribir el mensaje electrónico
2. lavar (*to wash*) la ropa
3. oír las noticias (*news*)
4. comprar pantalones cortos
5. practicar los verbos
6. pagar la cuenta (*bill*)
7. empezar la composición
8. ver la película *Diarios de motocicleta*

1. E1: ¿Escribiste el mensaje electrónico?
 E2: Sí, ya lo escribí./Acabo de escribirlo.
2. E1: ¿Lavaste la ropa?
 E2: Sí, ya la lavé./Acabo de lavarla.
3. E1: ¿Oíste las noticias?
 E2: Sí, ya las oí./Acabo de oírlas.
4. E1: ¿Compraste pantalones cortos?
 E2: Sí, ya los compré./Acabo de comprarlos.
5. E1: ¿Practicaste los verbos?
 E2: Sí, ya los practiqué./Acabo de practicarlos.
6. E1: ¿Pagaste la cuenta?
 E2: Sí, ya la pagué./Acabo de pagarla.
7. E1: ¿Empezaste la composición?
 E2: Sí, ya la empecé./Acabo de empezarla.
8. E1: ¿Viste la película Diarios de motocicleta?
 E2: Sí, ya la vi./Acabo de verla.

NOTA CULTURAL

Based on Ernesto "Che" Guevara's diaries, *Diarios de motocicleta* (2004) traces the road trip of Che (played by Gael García Bernal) with his friend Alberto Granado (played by Rodrigo de la Serna) through Argentina, Chile, Peru, Colombia, and Venezuela.

3 **¿Cuándo?** Use the time expressions from the word bank to talk about when you and others did the activities listed. Answers will vary.

anoche	anteayer	el mes pasado	una vez
ayer	la semana pasada	el año pasado	dos veces

1. mi compañero/a de cuarto: llegar tarde a clase
2. mi mejor (*best*) amigo/a: salir con un(a) chico/a guapo/a
3. mis padres: ver una película
4. yo: llevar un traje/vestido
5. el presidente/primer ministro de mi país: asistir a una conferencia internacional
6. mis amigos y yo: comer en un restaurante
7. ¿?: comprar algo (*something*) bueno, bonito y barato

 Practice more at **vhlcentral.com.**

Comunicación

4 **Ayer** Jot down at what time you did these activities yesterday. Then get together with a classmate and find out at what time he or she did these activities. Be prepared to share your findings with the class.

Answers will vary.

1. desayunar
2. empezar la primera clase
3. almorzar
4. ver a un(a) amigo/a
5. salir de clase
6. volver a la residencia/casa

5 **Las vacaciones** Imagine that you took these photos on a vacation with friends. Get together with a partner and use the pictures to tell him or her about your trip. Answers will vary.

6 **El fin de semana** Your instructor will give you and your partner different incomplete charts about what four employees at **Almacén Gigante** did last weekend. After you fill out the chart based on each other's information, you will fill out the final column about your partner. Answers will vary.

Síntesis

7 **Conversación** Get together with a partner and have a conversation about what you did last week using verbs from the word bank. Don't forget to include school activities, shopping, and pastimes. Answers will vary.

acampar	comer	gastar	tomar
asistir	comprar	hablar	trabajar
bailar	correr	jugar	vender
beber	escribir	leer	ver
buscar	estudiar	oír	viajar

TEACHING OPTIONS

Large Group Have students stand up. Tell them to create a story chain about a student who had a very bad day. Begin the story by saying: **Ayer, Rigoberto pasó un día desastroso.** In order to sit down, students must contribute to the story. Call on a student to tell how **Rigoberto** began his day. The second person tells what happened next, and so on, until only one student remains. That person must conclude the story.

Extra Practice For homework, have students make a "to do" list at the beginning of their day. Then, ask students to return to their lists at the end of the day and write sentences stating which activities they completed. Ex: **limpiar mi habitación; No, no limpié mi habitación.**

4 Teaching Tips
- After forming pairs, model question formation and possible responses for the first two items.
- 👤↔👤 Encourage students to ask follow-up questions. Ex: **1. ¿Dónde desayunaste, en casa o en la cafetería? ¿Qué comiste?**

5 Teaching Tips
- You may wish to provide extra vocabulary. Ex: **los helados/las paletas, el picnic**
- 👤↔👤 Have students first state where they traveled and when. Then have them identify the people in the photos, stating their names and their relationship to them and describing their personalities. Finally, students should tell what everyone did on the trip. Encourage students to ask each other follow-up questions to learn more about their partner's trip.

5 Expansion
←👤→ After completing the activity orally, have students write a paragraph about their vacation, basing their account on the photos.

6 Teaching Tip Divide the class into pairs and distribute the handouts from the Activity Pack (Activity Pack/Supersite) that correspond to this Information Gap Activity. Give students ten minutes to complete the activity.

6 Expansion Have students tell the class about any activities that both their partner and one of the **Almacén Gigante** employees did. Ex: **La señora Zapata leyó un libro y _____ también. Los dos leyeron un libro.**

7 Teaching Tips
- ←👤→ Have volunteers rehearse their conversation, then present it to the class.
- Have volunteers report to the class what their partners did last week.

6.4 Demonstrative adjectives and pronouns

comparisons — NATIONAL STANDARDS

Demonstrative adjectives **S** Tutorial

ANTE TODO In Spanish, as in English, demonstrative adjectives are words that "demonstrate" or "point out" nouns. Demonstrative adjectives precede the nouns they modify and, like other Spanish adjectives you have studied, agree with them in gender and number. Observe these examples and then study the chart below.

esta camisa **ese** vendedor **aquellos** zapatos
this shirt *that salesman* *those shoes (over there)*

Demonstrative adjectives				
Singular		**Plural**		
MASCULINE	FEMININE	MASCULINE	FEMININE	
este	**esta**	**estos**	**estas**	*this; these*
ese	**esa**	**esos**	**esas**	*that; those*
aquel	**aquella**	**aquellos**	**aquellas**	*that; those (over there)*

▶ There are three sets of demonstrative adjectives. To determine which one to use, you must establish the relationship between the speaker and the noun(s) being pointed out.

▶ The demonstrative adjectives **este, esta, estos,** and **estas** are used to point out nouns that are close to the speaker and the listener.

Me gustan estos zapatos.

▶ The demonstrative adjectives **ese, esa, esos,** and **esas** are used to point out nouns that are not close in space and time to the speaker. They may, however, be close to the listener.

Prefiero esos zapatos.

▶ The demonstrative adjectives **aquel**, **aquella**, **aquellos**, and **aquellas** are used to point out nouns that are far away from the speaker and the listener.

Aquel auto es de mi hermana.

Demonstrative pronouns

▶ Demonstrative pronouns are identical to their corresponding demonstrative adjectives, with the exception that they traditionally carry an accent mark on the stressed vowel. The **Real Academia** now requires this accent only for clarification but it is still commonly used.

Demonstrative pronouns			
Singular		**Plural**	
MASCULINE	FEMININE	MASCULINE	FEMININE
éste	ésta	éstos	éstas
ése	ésa	ésos	ésas
aquél	aquélla	aquéllos	aquéllas

—¿Quieres comprar **este suéter**?
Do you want to buy this sweater?

—No, no quiero **éste**. Quiero **ése**.
No, I don't want this one. I want that one.

—¿Vas a leer **estas revistas**?
Are you going to read these magazines?

—Sí, voy a leer **éstas**. También voy a leer **aquéllas**.
Yes, I'm going to read these. I'll also read those (over there).

▶ **¡Atención!** Like demonstrative adjectives, demonstrative pronouns agree in gender and number with the corresponding noun.

Este libro es de Pablito. **Éstos** son de Juana.

▶ There are three neuter demonstrative pronouns: **esto**, **eso**, and **aquello**. These forms refer to unidentified or unspecified nouns, situations, ideas, and concepts. They do not change in gender or number and never carry an accent mark.

—¿Qué es **esto**? —**Eso** es interesante. —**Aquello** es bonito.
What's this? *That's interesting.* *That's pretty.*

recursos

WB pp. 66–68

LM p. 36

Ⓢ
vhlcentral.com
Lección 6

¡INTÉNTALO! Provide the correct form of the demonstrative adjective for these nouns.

1. la falda / este _____ esta falda _____
2. los estudiantes / este _____ estos estudiantes _____
3. los países / aquel _____ aquellos países _____
4. la ventana / ese _____ esa ventana _____
5. los periodistas / ese _____ esos periodistas _____
6. el chico / aquel _____ aquel chico _____
7. las sandalias / este _____ estas sandalias _____
8. las chicas / aquel _____ aquellas chicas _____

Práctica

1

Cambiar Make the singular sentences plural and the plural sentences singular.

> **modelo**
> Estas camisas son blancas.
> *Esta camisa es blanca.*

1. Aquellos sombreros son muy elegantes. *Aquel sombrero es muy elegante.*
2. Ese abrigo es muy caro. *Esos abrigos son muy caros.*
3. Estos cinturones son hermosos. *Este cinturón es hermoso.*
4. Esos precios son muy buenos. *Ese precio es muy bueno.*
5. Estas faldas son muy cortas. *Esta falda es muy corta.*
6. ¿Quieres ir a aquel almacén? *¿Quieres ir a aquellos almacenes?*
7. Esas blusas son baratas. *Esa blusa es barata.*
8. Esta corbata hace juego con mi traje. *Estas corbatas hacen juego con mis trajes.*

2

Completar Here are some things people might say while shopping. Complete the sentences with the correct demonstrative pronouns.

1. No me gustan esos zapatos. Voy a comprar ____éstos____. (*these*)
2. ¿Vas a comprar ese traje o ____éste____? (*this one*)
3. Esta guayabera es bonita, pero prefiero ____ésa____. (*that one*)
4. Estas corbatas rojas son muy bonitas, pero ____ésas____ son fabulosas. (*those*)
5. Estos cinturones cuestan demasiado. Prefiero ____aquéllos____. (*those over there*)
6. ¿Te gustan esas botas o ____éstas____? (*these*)
7. Esa bolsa roja es bonita, pero prefiero ____aquélla____. (*that one over there*)
8. No voy a comprar estas botas; voy a comprar ____aquéllas____. (*those over there*)
9. ¿Prefieres estos pantalones o ____ésos____? (*those*)
10. Me gusta este vestido, pero voy a comprar ____ése____. (*that one*)
11. Me gusta ese almacén, pero ____aquél____ es mejor (*better*). (*that one over there*)
12. Esa blusa es bonita, pero cuesta demasiado. Voy a comprar ____ésta____. (*this one*)

3

Describir With your partner, look for two items in the classroom that are one of these colors: **amarillo, azul, blanco, marrón, negro, verde, rojo.** Take turns pointing them out to each other, first using demonstrative adjectives, and then demonstrative pronouns. *Answers will vary.*

> **modelo**
> azul
> **Estudiante 1:** *Esta silla es azul. Aquella mochila es azul.*
> **Estudiante 2:** *Ésta es azul. Aquélla es azul.*

Now use demonstrative adjectives and pronouns to discuss the colors of your classmates' clothing. One of you can ask a question about an article of clothing, using the wrong color. Your partner will correct you and point out that color somewhere else in the room.

> **modelo**
> **Estudiante 1:** *¿Esa camisa es negra?*
> **Estudiante 2:** *No, ésa es azul. Aquélla es negra.*

 Practice more at **vhlcentral.com.**

TEACHING OPTIONS

Pairs 👤↔👤 Have pairs role-play a dialogue between friends shopping for clothes. Student A tries to convince the friend that the clothes he or she wants to buy are not attractive. Student A suggests other items of clothing, but the friend does not agree. Students should use as many demonstrative adjectives and pronouns as possible.
Game Divide the class into two teams. Post pictures of different versions of the same object (Ex: sedan, sports car, all-terrain vehicle) on the board. Assign each a dollar figure, but do not share the prices with the class. Team A guesses the price of each object, using demonstrative adjectives and pronouns. Team B either agrees or guesses a higher or lower price. The team that guesses the closest price, wins. Ex: **Este carro cuesta $20.000, ése cuesta $35.000 y aquél cuesta $18.000.**

Comunicación

4

Conversación With a classmate, use demonstrative adjectives and pronouns to ask each other questions about the people around you. Use expressions from the word bank and/or your own ideas.

Answers will vary.

¿A qué hora…?	¿Cuántos años tiene(n)…?
¿Cómo es/son…?	¿De dónde es/son…?
¿Cómo se llama…?	¿De quién es/son...?
¿Cuándo…?	¿Qué clases toma(n)…?

modelo

Estudiante 1: *¿Cómo se llama esa chica?*

Estudiante 2: *Se llama Rebeca.*

Estudiante 1: *¿A qué hora llegó aquel chico a la clase?*

Estudiante 2: *A las nueve.*

5

En una tienda Imagine that you and a classmate are in Madrid shopping at Zara. Study the floor plan, then have a conversation about your surroundings. Use demonstrative adjectives and pronouns.

Answers will vary.

modelo

Estudiante 1: *Me gusta este suéter azul.*

Estudiante 2: *Yo prefiero aquella chaqueta.*

Síntesis

6

Diferencias Your instructor will give you and a partner each a drawing of a store. They are almost identical, but not quite. Use demonstrative adjectives and pronouns to find seven differences.

Answers will vary.

modelo

Estudiante 1: *Aquellas gafas de sol son feas, ¿verdad?*

Estudiante 2: *No. Aquellas gafas de sol son hermosas.*

TEACHING OPTIONS

Pairs Ask students to write a conversation between two people sitting at a busy sidewalk café in the city. They are watching the people who walk by, asking each other questions about what the passersby are doing, and making comments on their clothing. Students should use as many demonstrative adjectives and pronouns as possible in their conversations. Invite several pairs to present their conversations to the class.

Small Groups Ask students to bring in pictures of their families, a sports team, a group of friends, etc. Have them take turns asking about and identifying the people in the pictures. Ex: —¿Quién es aquella mujer? —¿Cuál? —Aquélla con la camiseta roja. —Es mi…

4 Teaching Tip To challenge students, have both partners ask a question for each item in the word bank and at least one other question using an interrogative expression that is not included. Encourage students to ask follow-up questions.

5 Expansion Divide the class into small groups and have students role-play a situation between a salesperson and two customers. The customers should ask about the different items of clothing pictured and the salesperson will answer. They talk about how the items fit and their cost. The customers then express their preferences and decide which items to buy.

6 Teaching Tip Divide the class into pairs and distribute the handouts from the Activity Pack (Activity Pack/Supersite) that correspond with this Information Gap Activity. Give students ten minutes to complete the activity.

6 Expansion Have pairs work together with another pair to compare the seven responses that confirmed the seven differences. Ex: **No. Aquellas gafas de sol no son feas. Aquéllas son hermosas.** Ask a few groups to share some of the sentences with the class.

Recapitulación

S Concepts Diagnostics

Review the grammar concepts you have learned in this lesson by completing these activities.

1 **Completar** Complete the chart with the correct preterite or infinitive form of the verbs. **15 pts.**

Infinitive	yo	ella	ellos
tomar	tomé	tomó	**tomaron**
abrir	abrí	**abrió**	abrieron
comprender	comprendí	comprendió	comprendieron
leer	**leí**	leyó	leyeron
pagar	pagué	pagó	pagaron

2 **En la tienda** Look at the drawing and complete the conversation with demonstrative adjectives and pronouns. **7 pts.**

CLIENTE Buenos días, señorita. Deseo comprar (1) _____esta_____ corbata.

VENDEDORA Muy bien, señor. ¿No le interesa mirar (2) _____aquellos_____ trajes que están allá? Hay unos que hacen juego con la corbata.

CLIENTE (3) _____Aquéllos_____ de allá son de lana, ¿no? Prefiero ver (4) _____ese_____ traje marrón que está detrás de usted.

VENDEDORA Estupendo. Como puede ver, es de seda. Cuesta seiscientos cincuenta dólares.

CLIENTE Ah... eh... no, creo que sólo voy a comprar la corbata, gracias.

VENDEDORA Bueno... si busca algo más económico, hay rebaja en (5) _____aquellos_____ sombreros. Cuestan sólo treinta dólares.

CLIENTE ¡Magnífico! Me gusta (6) _____aquél_____, el blanco que está hasta arriba (*at the top*). Y quiero pagar todo con (7) _____esta_____ tarjeta.

VENDEDORA Sí, señor. Ahora mismo le traigo el sombrero.

RESUMEN GRAMATICAL

6.1 **Saber and conocer** *p. 184*

saber	conocer
sé	conozco
sabes	conoces
sabe	conoce
sabemos	conocemos
sabéis	conocéis
saben	conocen

► saber = to know facts/how to do something
► conocer = to know a person, place, or thing

6.2 **Indirect object pronouns** *pp. 186–187*

Indirect object pronouns

Singular	Plural
me	nos
te	os
le	les

► dar = doy, das, da, damos, dais, dan
► decir (e:i) = digo, dices, dice, decimos, decís, dicen

6.3 **Preterite tense of regular verbs** *pp. 190–191*

comprar	vender	escribir
compré	vendí	escribí
compraste	vendiste	escribiste
compró	vendió	escribió
compramos	vendimos	escribimos
comprasteis	vendisteis	escribisteis
compraron	vendieron	escribieron

Verbs with spelling changes in the preterite

► -car: buscar → yo busqué
► -gar: llegar → yo llegué
► -zar: empezar → yo empecé
► creer: creí, creíste, creyó, creímos, creísteis, creyeron
► leer: leí, leíste, leyó, leímos, leísteis, leyeron
► oír: oí, oíste, oyó, oímos, oísteis, oyeron
► ver: vi, viste, vio, vimos, visteis, vieron

3 **¿Saber o conocer?** Complete each dialogue with the correct form of **saber** or **conocer**. `10 pts.`

1. —¿Qué <u>sabes</u> hacer tú?
 —(Yo) <u>Sé</u> jugar al fútbol.
2. —¿<u>Conoces</u> tú esta tienda de ropa?
 —No, (yo) no la <u>conozco</u>. ¿Es buena?
3. —¿Tus padres no <u>conocen</u> a tu novio?
 —No, ¡ellos no <u>saben</u> que tengo novio!
4. —Mi compañero de cuarto todavía no me <u>conoce</u> bien.
 —Y tú, ¿lo quieres <u>conocer</u> a él?
5. —¿<u>Saben</u> ustedes dónde está el mercado?
 —No, nosotros no <u>conocemos</u> bien esta ciudad.

4 **Oraciones** Form complete sentences using the information provided. Use indirect object pronouns and the present tense of the verbs. `10 pts.`

1. Javier / prestar / el abrigo / a Maripili
 Javier le presta el abrigo a Maripili.
2. nosotros / vender / ropa / a los clientes
 Nosotros les vendemos ropa a los clientes.
3. el vendedor / traer / las camisetas / a mis amigos y a mí
 El vendedor nos trae las camisetas (a mis amigos y a mí).
4. yo / querer dar / consejos / a ti
 Yo quiero darte consejos (a ti)./Yo te quiero dar consejos (a ti).
5. ¿tú / ir a comprar / un regalo / a mí?
 ¿Tú vas a comprarme un regalo (a mí)?/¿Tú me vas a comprar un regalo (a mí)?

5 **Mi última compra** Write a short paragraph describing the last time you went shopping. Use at least four verbs in the preterite tense. `8 pts.` *Answers will vary.*

> **modelo**
> *El viernes pasado, busqué unos zapatos en el centro comercial...*

6 **Poema** Write the missing words to complete the excerpt from the poem *Romance sonámbulo* by Federico García Lorca. `2 EXTRA points!`

❝Verde que <u>te</u> quiero verde.
Verde viento. Verdes ramas°.
El barco sobre la mar
y el caballo en la montaña, [...]
Verde que te quiero <u>verde</u> (*green*). ❞

ramas *branches*

 Practice more at **vhlcentral.com.**

Demonstrative adjectives and pronouns *pp. 194–195*

Demonstrative adjectives

Singular		Plural	
Masc.	**Fem.**	**Masc.**	**Fem.**
este	esta	estos	estas
ese	esa	esos	esas
aquel	aquella	aquellos	aquellas

Demonstrative pronouns

Singular		Plural	
Masc.	**Fem.**	**Masc.**	**Fem.**
éste	ésta	éstos	éstas
ése	ésa	ésos	ésas
aquél	aquélla	aquéllos	aquéllas

3 **Teaching Tip** Ask students to explain why they chose **saber** or **conocer** in each case.

3 **Expansion** Have students choose one dialogue from this activity and write a continuation. Encourage them to use at least one more example each of **saber** and **conocer**.

4 **Teaching Tips**
- Ask a volunteer to model the first sentence for the class.
- Before forming sentences, have students identify the indirect object in each item.
- Remind students of the possible positions for indirect object pronouns when using an infinitive.

4 **Expansion**
- Ask students to create three dehydrated sentences similar to those in **Actividad 4**. Have them exchange papers with a classmate and form complete sentences.
- For items 1–4, have students write questions that would elicit these statements. Ex: **1. ¿A quién le presta el abrigo Javier?/¿Qué le presta Javier a Maripili?** For item 5, have them write a response.

5 **Teaching Tip** To add a visual aspect to this activity, have students create a time line of what they did when they went shopping.

6 **Teaching Tips**
- Tell students to read through the whole excerpt before filling in the blanks.
- Have a volunteer read the excerpt aloud.

TEACHING OPTIONS

Extra Practice Add an auditory aspect to this grammar review. Read each of these sentences twice, pausing after the second time for students to write: **1. Ayer empecé a leer sobre los diseñadores hispanos. 2. Ellas buscaron unas bolsas en el mercado al aire libre. 3. El dependiente vendió cinco camisetas. 4. Nosotras oímos una explosión. 5. El joven le leyó el libro a su hermanito. 6. Raúl vio una película anoche.**

Game Divide the class into two teams. Indicate a member of each team and call out a color. The first student to find an object or article of clothing in the room, point to it, and use the correct form of a demonstrative adjective earns a point for their team. Ex: **¡Aquella camiseta es morada!** The team with the most points at the end wins.

Lectura

NATIONAL communication cultures STANDARDS

Antes de leer

Estrategia

Skimming

Skimming involves quickly reading through a document to absorb its general meaning. This allows you to understand the main ideas without having to read word for word. When you skim a text, you might want to look at its title and subtitles. You might also want to read the first sentence of each paragraph.

Examinar el texto

Look at the format of the reading selection. How is it organized? What does the organization of the document tell you about its content?

Buscar cognados

Scan the reading selection to locate at least five cognates. Based on the cognates, what do you think the reading selection is about? *Answers will vary.*
Suggested answers for 1-5: elegancia, blusas, accesorios, pantalones, precio.

1. _____ 4. _____
2. _____ 5. _____
3. _____

The reading selection is about ___a sale in a store___.

Impresiones generales

Now skim the reading selection to understand its general meaning. Jot down your impressions. What new information did you learn about the document by skimming it? Based on all the information you now have, answer these questions in Spanish.

1. Who created this document? *un almacén/una tienda*
2. What is its purpose? *vender ropa*
3. Who is its intended audience? *gente que quiere comprar ropa*

Practice more at **vhlcentral.com.**

Corona

¡Corona tiene las ofertas más locas del verano!

La tienda más elegante de la ciudad con precios increíbles

Carteras
ELEGANCIA
Colores anaranjado, blanco, rosado y amarillo
Ahora: 15.000 pesos
50% de rebaja

Sandalias de playa
GINO
Números del 35 al 38
A sólo 12.000 pesos
50% de descuento

Faldas largas
ROPA BONITA
Algodón. De distintos colores
Talla mediana
Precio especial:
8.000 pesos

Blusas de seda
BAMBÚ
De cuadros y de lunares
Ahora: 21.000 pesos
40% de rebaja

Vestido de algodón
PANAMÁ
Colores blanco, azul y verde
Ahora: 18.000 pesos
30% de rebaja

Accesorios
BELLEZA
Cinturones, gafas de sol, sombreros, medias
Diversos estilos
Todos con un 40% de rebaja

Lunes a sábado de 9 a 21 horas.
Domingo de 10 a 14 horas.

¡Grandes rebajas!

Real° Liquidación°

¡La rebaja está de moda en Corona!

y con la tarjeta de crédito más conveniente del mercado.

Chaquetas
CASINO
Microfibra. Colores negro,
café y gris
Tallas: P, M, G, XG
Ahora: 22.500 pesos

Zapatos
COLOR
Italianos y franceses
Números del 40 al 45
A sólo 20.000 pesos

Pantalones
OCÉANO
Colores negro, gris y café
Ahora: 11.500 pesos
30% de rebaja

Ropa interior
ATLÁNTICO
Tallas: P, M, G
Colores blanco,
negro y gris
40% de rebaja

Traje inglés
GALES
Modelos originales
Ahora: 105.000 pesos
30% de rebaja

Accesorios
GUAPO
Gafas de sol, corbatas,
cinturones, calcetines
Diversos estilos
Todos con un 40%
de rebaja

Real *Royal* Liquidación *Clearance sale* caballeros *gentlemen*

Por la compra de 40.000 pesos, puede llevar un regalo gratis.

- Un hermoso cinturón de señora
- Un par de calcetines
- Una corbata de seda
- Una bolsa para la playa
- Una mochila
- Unas medias

Después de leer

Completar

Complete this paragraph about the reading selection with the correct forms of the words from the word bank.

almacén	hacer juego	tarjeta de crédito
caro	increíble	tienda
dinero	pantalones	verano
falda	rebaja	zapato

En este anuncio de periódico, el _____almacén_____ Corona anuncia la liquidación de _____verano_____ con grandes _____rebajas_____. Con muy poco _____dinero_____ usted puede conseguir ropa fina y elegante. Si no tiene dinero en efectivo, puede utilizar su _____tarjeta de crédito_____ y pagar luego. Para el caballero con gustos refinados, hay _____zapatos_____ importados de París y Roma. La señora elegante puede encontrar blusas de seda que _____hacen juego_____ con todo tipo de _____pantalones/faldas_____ o _____faldas/pantalones_____. Los precios de esta liquidación son realmente _____increíbles_____.

¿Cierto o falso?

Indicate whether each statement is **cierto** or **falso**. Correct the false statements.

1. Hay sandalias de playa. Cierto.
2. Las corbatas tienen una rebaja del 30%. Falso. Tienen una rebaja del 40%.
3. El almacén Corona tiene un departamento de zapatos. Cierto.
4. Normalmente las sandalias cuestan 22.000 pesos. Falso. Normalmente cuestan 24.000 pesos.
5. Cuando gastas 30.000 pesos en la tienda, llevas un regalo gratis. Falso. Cuando gastas 40.000 pesos en la tienda, llevas un regalo gratis.
6. Tienen carteras amarillas. Cierto.

Preguntas

In pairs, take turns asking and answering these questions. Answers will vary.

1. Imagina que vas a ir a la tienda Corona. ¿Qué departamentos vas a visitar? ¿El departamento de ropa para señoras, el departamento de ropa para caballeros…?
2. ¿Qué vas a buscar en Corona?
3. ¿Hay tiendas similares a la tienda Corona en tu pueblo o ciudad? ¿Cómo se llaman? ¿Tienen muchas gangas?

Escritura

Estrategia

How to report an interview

There are several ways to prepare a written report about an interview. For example, you can transcribe the interview verbatim, you can simply summarize it, or you can summarize it but quote the speakers occasionally. In any event, the report should begin with an interesting title and a brief introduction, which may include the five Ws (*what, where, when, who, why*) and the H (*how*) of the interview. The report should end with an interesting conclusion. Note that when you transcribe dialogue in Spanish, you should pay careful attention to format and punctuation.

Writing dialogue in Spanish

• If you need to transcribe an interview verbatim, you can use speakers' names to indicate a change of speaker.

CARMELA	¿Qué compraste? ¿Encontraste muchas gangas?
ROBERTO	Sí, muchas. Compré un suéter, una camisa y dos corbatas. Y tú, ¿qué compraste?
CARMELA	Una blusa y una falda muy bonitas. ¿Cuánto costó tu camisa?
ROBERTO	Sólo diez dólares. ¿Cuánto costó tu blusa?
CARMELA	Veinte dólares.

• You can also use a dash (*raya*) to mark the beginning of each speaker's words.

—¿Qué compraste?
—Un suéter y una camisa muy bonitos. Y tú, ¿encontraste muchas gangas?
—Sí... compré dos blusas, tres camisetas y un par de zapatos.
—¡A ver!

Tema

Escribe un informe

Write a report for the school newspaper about an interview you conducted with a student about his or her shopping habits and clothing preferences. First, brainstorm a list of interview questions. Then conduct the interview using the questions below as a guide, but feel free to ask other questions as they occur to you.

Examples of questions:

▶ ¿Cuándo vas de compras?

▶ ¿Adónde vas de compras?

▶ ¿Con quién vas de compras?

▶ ¿Qué tiendas, almacenes o centros comerciales prefieres?

▶ ¿Compras ropa de catálogos o por Internet?

▶ ¿Prefieres comprar ropa cara o barata? ¿Por qué? ¿Te gusta buscar gangas?

▶ ¿Qué ropa llevas cuando vas a clase?

▶ ¿Qué ropa llevas cuando sales a bailar?

▶ ¿Qué ropa llevas cuando practicas un deporte?

▶ ¿Cuáles son tus colores favoritos? ¿Compras mucha ropa de esos colores?

▶ ¿Les das ropa a tu familia o a tus amigos/as?

Escuchar **Audio: Activities**

Estrategia
Listening for linguistic cues

You can enhance your listening comprehension by listening for specific linguistic cues. For example, if you listen for the endings of conjugated verbs, or for familiar constructions, such as **acabar de** + [*infinitive*] or **ir a** + [*infinitive*], you can find out whether an event already took place, is taking place now, or will take place in the future. Verb endings also give clues about who is participating in the action.

To practice listening for linguistic cues, you will now listen to four sentences. As you listen, note whether each sentence refers to a past, present, or future action. Also jot down the subject of each sentence.

Preparación

Based on the photograph, what do you think Marisol has recently done? What do you think Marisol and Alicia are talking about? What else can you guess about their conversation from the visual clues in the photograph?

Ahora escucha

Now you are going to hear Marisol and Alicia's conversation. Make a list of the clothing items that each person mentions. Then put a check mark after the item if the person actually purchased it.

Marisol	Alicia
1. pantalones ✓	1. falda
2. blusa ✓	2. blusa
3. _____	3. zapatos
4. _____	4. cinturón

Practice more at **vhlcentral.com.**

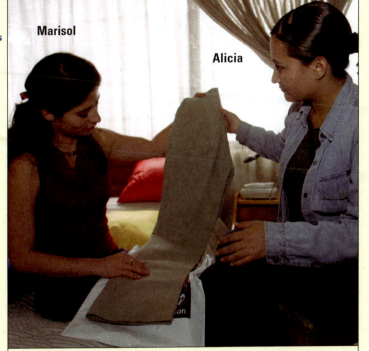

Marisol

Alicia

Comprensión

¿Cierto o falso?

Indicate whether each statement is **cierto** or **falso**. Then correct the false statements.

1. Marisol y Alicia acaban de ir de compras juntas (*together*). Falso. Marisol acaba de ir de compras.
2. Marisol va a comprar unos pantalones y una blusa mañana. Falso. Marisol ya los compró.
3. Marisol compró una blusa de cuadros. Cierto.
4. Alicia compró unos zapatos nuevos hoy. Falso. Alicia va a comprar unos zapatos nuevos.
5. Alicia y Marisol van a ir al café. Cierto.
6. Marisol gastó todo el dinero de la semana en ropa nueva. Cierto.

Preguntas

Discuss the following questions with a classmate. Be sure to explain your answers. Answers will vary.

1. ¿Crees que Alicia y Marisol son buenas amigas? ¿Por qué?
2. ¿Cuál de las dos estudiantes es más ahorradora (*frugal*)? ¿Por qué?
3. ¿Crees que a Alicia le gusta la ropa que Marisol compró?
4. ¿Crees que la moda es importante para Alicia? ¿Para Marisol? ¿Por qué?
5. ¿Es importante para ti estar a la moda? ¿Por qué?

Section Goals
In **Escuchar**, students will:
• listen for specific linguistic cues in oral sentences
• answer questions based on a recorded conversation

Instructional Resources
Supersite: Audio (Textbook MP3s); Resources (Scripts)

Estrategia
Script 1. Acabamos de pasear por la ciudad y encontramos unos monumentos fenomenales. 2. Estoy haciendo las maletas. 3. Carmen y Alejandro decidieron ir a un restaurante. 4. Mi familia y yo vamos a ir a la playa.

Teaching Tip Ask students to look at the photo of **Marisol** and **Alicia** and predict what they are talking about.

Ahora escucha
Script MARISOL: Oye, Alicia, ¿qué estás haciendo?
ALICIA: Estudiando no más. ¿Qué hay de nuevo?
M: Acabo de comprarme esos pantalones que andaba buscando.
A: ¿Los encontraste en el centro comercial? ¿Y cuánto te costaron?
M: Míralos. ¿Te gustan? En el almacén Melo tienen tremenda rebaja. Como estaban baratos me compré una blusa también. Es de cuadros, pero creo que hace juego con los pantalones por el color rojo. ¿Qué piensas?
A: Es de los mismos colores que la falda y la blusa que llevaste cuando fuimos al cine anoche. La verdad es que te quedan muy bien esos colores. ¿No encontraste unos zapatos y un cinturón para completar el juego?
M: No lo digas ni de chiste. Mi tarjeta de crédito está que

no aguanta más. Y trabajé poco la semana pasada. ¡Acabo de gastar todo el dinero para la semana!
A: ¡Ay, chica! Fui al centro comercial el mes pasado y encontré unos zapatos muy, pero muy de moda. Muy caros... pero buenos. No me los compré porque no los tenían en mi número. Voy a comprarlos cuando lleguen más... el vendedor me va a llamar.

M: Ajá... ¿Y va a invitarte a salir con él?
A: ¡Ay! ¡No seas así! Ven, vamos al café. Te ves muy bien y no hay que gastar eso aquí.
M: De acuerdo. Vamos.

(Script continues at far left in the bottom panels.)

En pantalla

NATIONAL communication cultures STANDARDS

Anuncio

Grocery stores in Mexico make one-stop shopping easy! Similar to the concept of a *Super-Walmart* in the U.S., most **supermercados°** in Mexico sell appliances, clothing, medicine, gardening supplies, electronics, and toys in addition to groceries. Large chains, like **Comercial Mexicana**, and smaller grocery stores alike typically sell a variety of products, allowing customers to satisfy all of their routine weekly shopping needs in one trip. Watch the **En pantalla** videoclip to see how one customer takes advantage of one-stop shopping at his local supermarket.

Vocabulario útil	
con lo que ahorré	with what I saved
corazón	sweetheart
de peluche	stuffed (toy)
dragón	ragon
¿Me lo compras?	Would you buy it for me?

Comprensión

Indicate whether each statement is **cierto** or **falso**.

	Cierto	Falso
1. El niño quiere un elefante de peluche.	○	☑
2. La señora usa un vestido rojo.	○	☑
3. El niño sigue a la señora hasta la caja.	☑	○
4. La señora no es la mamá del niño.	☑	○

📖 Conversar

With a partner, use these cues to create a conversation in Spanish between two friends at a clothing store.

Answers will vary.

Estudiante 1: Would you buy me a(n)...?
Estudiante 2: No, because it costs...
Estudiante 1: Please! I always (**siempre**) buy you...
Estudiante 2: OK, I will buy you this... How much does it cost?
Estudiante 1: It's on sale! It only costs....

supermercados *supermarkets*

Comercial mexicana

¿Me lo compras?

No, corazón.

¿Me lo compras, me lo compras, me lo compras?

Ⓢ **Video: TV Clip**

Ⓢ Practice more at **vhlcentral.com.**

Cortometraje

The short film *Parking Lot* takes place in a parking lot in Bogotá, Colombia. A woman thinks she recognizes an old boyfriend named Santiago, but the man denies knowing her. Pay attention to the action, body language, and music. Which character is more believable? An incoming call on the man's cell phone introduces an additional piece to the puzzle.

Preparación

Answer the following questions. Answers will vary.

1. Piensa en alguien (*someone*) que no has visto (*you haven't seen*) en mucho tiempo. ¿Quién es? ¿Te gusta la idea de ver a esta persona? ¿Por qué?

2. ¿Sería (*Would it be*) fácil reconocer (*recognize*) a esta persona? Explica por qué.

3. ¿Crees que esta persona te reconocería a ti? ¿Por qué?

Después de ver

Place these events in chronological order.

<u> 3 </u> a. La mujer y el hombre se toman una foto con el teléfono celular.

<u> 4 </u> b. El hombre entra en el coche.

<u> 5 </u> c. El hombre habla por teléfono.

<u> 1 </u> d. La mujer le dice al hombre que está muy cambiado.

<u> 2 </u> e. La mujer le toma la mano al hombre.

Conversar

En parejas, supongan que el hombre del estacionamiento es Santiago, el ex novio de la mujer. Escriban una lista de las razones por las que él no admite quién es. Comparen su lista con la de otra pareja y hablen de sus ideas.
Answers will vary.

UN FILM DE ALVARO D. RUIZ

PARKING *lot*

Expresiones útiles

¿En qué andas?	*What are you up to?*
lo que pasa es que	*what's happening is (that); the thing is (that)*
me está confundiendo (con)	*you're mistaking me for*
me hubiera encantado	*I would have loved*
qué pena	*what a shame*
te pareces muchísimo (a)	*you look a lot like*

Para hablar del corto

la barba	*beard*
el coche	*car*
la cola de caballo	*ponytail*
se encuentra con	*runs into*
el estacionamiento	*parking lot*
estar muy cambiado/a	*to look very different*
el (teléfono) celular	*cell phone*

 Video: Short Film

 Practice more at **vhlcentral.com**.

Cuba

NATIONAL connections cultures STANDARDS

El país en cifras

▶ **Área:** 110.860 km² (42.803 millas²), *aproximadamente el área de Pensilvania*
▶ **Población:** 11.213.000
▶ **Capital:** La Habana—2.100.000

La Habana Vieja fue declarada° Patrimonio° Cultural de la Humanidad por la UNESCO en 1982. Este distrito es uno de los lugares más fascinantes de Cuba. En La Plaza de Armas, se puede visitar el majestuoso Palacio de Capitanes Generales, que ahora es un museo. En la calle° Obispo, frecuentada por el autor Ernest Hemingway, hay hermosos cafés, clubes nocturnos y tiendas elegantes.

▶ **Ciudades principales:** Santiago de Cuba; Camagüey; Holguín; Guantánamo
SOURCE: Population Division, UN Secretariat
▶ **Moneda:** peso cubano
▶ **Idiomas:** español (oficial)

Bandera de Cuba

Cubanos célebres

▶ **Carlos Finlay,** doctor y científico (1833–1915)
▶ **José Martí,** político y poeta (1853–1895)
▶ **Fidel Castro,** ex primer ministro, ex comandante en jefe° de las fuerzas armadas (1926–)
▶ **Zoé Valdés,** escritora (1959–)
▶ **Ibrahim Ferrer,** músico (1927–2005)

fue declarada *was declared* Patrimonio *Heritage* calle *street* comandante en jefe *commander in chief* liviano *light* colibrí abeja *bee hummingbird* ave *bird* mundo *world* miden *measure* pesan *weigh*

recursos

| WB pp. 69–70 | VM pp. 235–236 | vhlcentral.com Lección 6 |

¡Increíble pero cierto!

Pequeño y liviano°, el colibrí abeja° de Cuba es una de las más de 320 especies de colibrí y es también el ave° más pequeña del mundo°. Menores que muchos insectos, estas aves minúsculas miden° 5 centímetros y pesan° sólo 1,95 gramos.

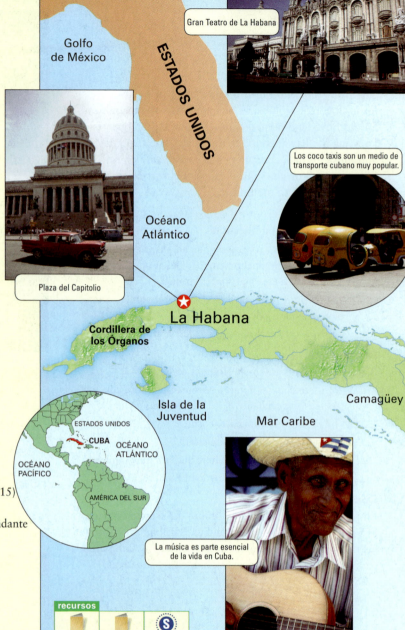
Gran Teatro de La Habana
Golfo de México
ESTADOS UNIDOS
Océano Atlántico
Plaza del Capitolio
Los coco taxis son un medio de transporte cubano muy popular.
La Habana
Cordillera de los Órganos
Isla de la Juventud
Mar Caribe
Camagüey
ESTADOS UNIDOS
CUBA
OCÉANO ATLÁNTICO
OCÉANO PACÍFICO
AMÉRICA DEL SUR
La música es parte esencial de la vida en Cuba.

Baile • **Ballet Nacional de Cuba**

La bailarina Alicia Alonso fundó el Ballet Nacional de Cuba en 1948, después de° convertirse en una estrella° internacional en el Ballet de Nueva York y en Broadway. El Ballet Nacional de Cuba es famoso en todo el mundo por su creatividad y perfección técnica.

Economía • **La caña de azúcar y el tabaco**

La caña de azúcar° es el producto agrícola° que más se cultiva en la isla y su exportación es muy importante para la economía del país. El tabaco, que se usa para fabricar los famosos puros° cubanos, es otro cultivo° de mucha importancia.

Gente • **Población**

La población cubana tiene raíces° muy heterogéneas. La inmigración a la isla fue determinante° desde la colonia hasta mediados° del siglo° XX. Los cubanos de hoy son descendientes de africanos, europeos, chinos y antillanos, entre otros.

Música • **Buena Vista Social Club**

En 1997 nace° el fenómeno musical conocido como *Buena Vista Social Club*. Este proyecto reúne° a un grupo de importantes músicos de Cuba, la mayoría ya mayores, con una larga trayectoria interpretando canciones clásicas del son° cubano. Ese mismo año ganaron un *Grammy*. Hoy en día estos músicos son conocidos en todo el mundo, y personas de todas las edades bailan al ritmo° de su música.

Holguín

Santiago de Cuba
Guantánamo

Sierra Maestra

 ¿Qué aprendiste? Responde a las preguntas con una oración completa.

1. ¿Qué autor está asociado con la Habana Vieja? Ernest Hemingway está asociado con la Habana Vieja.
2. ¿Por qué es famoso el Ballet Nacional de Cuba? Es famoso por su creatividad y perfección técnica.
3. ¿Cuáles son los dos cultivos más importantes para la economía cubana? Los cultivos más importantes son la caña de azúcar y el tabaco.
4. ¿Qué fabrican los cubanos con la planta del tabaco? Los cubanos fabrican puros.
5. ¿De dónde son muchos de los inmigrantes que llegaron a Cuba? Son de África, de Europa, de China y de las Antillas, entre otros lugares.
6. ¿En qué año ganó un *Grammy* el disco *Buena Vista Social Club*? Ganó un *Grammy* en 1997.

 Conexión Internet Investiga estos temas en **vhlcentral.com**.

Practice more at **vhlcentral.com**.

1. Busca información sobre un(a) cubano/a célebre. ¿Por qué es célebre? ¿Qué hace? ¿Todavía vive en Cuba?
2. Busca información sobre una de las ciudades principales de Cuba. ¿Qué atracciones hay en esta ciudad?

..

después de *after* estrella *star* caña de azúcar *sugar cane* agrícola *farming* puros *cigars* cultivo *crop* raíces *roots* determinante *deciding* mediados *halfway through* siglo *century* nace *is born* reúne *gets together* son *Cuban musical genre* ritmo *rhythm*

TEACHING OPTIONS

Language Notes Some Cuban songs mention beings with names that do not sound Spanish, such as **Obatalá, Elegguá,** and **Babaluayé**. These are divinities (**orichas**) of the Afro-Cuban religion, which has its origins in Yoruba-speaking West Africa. Forcibly converted to Catholicism upon their arrival in Cuba, Africans developed a syncretized religion in which they worshiped the gods they had brought from Africa in the form of Catholic saints. **Babaluayé,** for instance, is worshiped as **San Lázaro**. **Obatalá** is **Nuestra Señora de las Mercedes**. Cuban popular music is deeply rooted in the songs and dances with which Afro-Cubans expressed their devotion to the **orichas.**

Instructional Resources
Supersite: Audio (Textbook & Lab MP3s); Testing Program (Tests, MP3s)
WebSAM
Lab Manual, p. 36

La ropa

el abrigo	coat
los (blue)jeans	jeans
la blusa	blouse
la bolsa	purse; bag
la bota	boot
los calcetines (el calcetín)	sock(s)
la camisa	shirt
la camiseta	t-shirt
la cartera	wallet
la chaqueta	jacket
el cinturón	belt
la corbata	tie
la falda	skirt
las gafas (de sol)	(sun)glasses
los guantes	gloves
el impermeable	raincoat
las medias	pantyhose; stockings
los pantalones	pants
los pantalones cortos	shorts
la ropa	clothing; clothes
la ropa interior	underwear
las sandalias	sandals
el sombrero	hat
el suéter	sweater
el traje	suit
el traje de baño	bathing suit
el vestido	dress
los zapatos de tenis	sneakers

Verbos

conducir	to drive
conocer	to know; to be acquainted with
ofrecer	to offer
parecer	to seem
saber	to know; to know how
traducir	to translate

Ir de compras

el almacén	department store
la caja	cash register
el centro comercial	shopping mall
el/la cliente/a	customer
el/la dependiente/a	clerk
el dinero	money
(en) efectivo	cash
el mercado (al aire libre)	(open-air) market
un par (de zapatos)	a pair (of shoes)
el precio (fijo)	(fixed; set) price
la rebaja	sale
el regalo	gift
la tarjeta de crédito	credit card
la tienda	shop; store
el/la vendedor(a)	salesperson
costar (o:ue)	to cost
gastar	to spend (money)
hacer juego (con)	to match (with)
llevar	to wear; to take
pagar	to pay
regatear	to bargain
usar	to wear; to use
vender	to sell

Adjetivos

barato/a	cheap
bueno/a	good
cada	each
caro/a	expensive
corto/a	short (in length)
elegante	elegant
hermoso/a	beautiful
largo/a	long
loco/a	crazy
nuevo/a	new
otro/a	other; another
pobre	poor
rico/a	rich

Los colores

el color	color
amarillo/a	yellow
anaranjado/a	orange
azul	blue
blanco/a	white
gris	gray
marrón, café	brown
morado/a	purple
negro/a	black
rojo/a	red
rosado/a	pink
verde	green

Palabras adicionales

acabar de (+ inf.)	to have just done something
anoche	last night
anteayer	the day before yesterday
ayer	yesterday
de repente	suddenly
desde	from
dos veces	twice; two times
hasta	until
pasado/a (adj.)	last; past
el año pasado	last year
la semana pasada	last week
prestar	to lend; to loan
una vez	once; one time
ya	already

Indirect object pronouns	See page 186.
Demonstrative adjectives and pronouns	See page 194.
Expresiones útiles	See page 179.

 Audio: Vocabulary

La rutina diaria

Communicative Goals

You will learn how to:
- **Describe your daily routine**
- **Talk about personal hygiene**
- **Reassure someone**

Lesson Goals

In **Lección 7**, students will be introduced to the following:
- terms for daily routines
- reflexive verbs
- adverbs of time
- the custom of **la siesta**
- drinking **mate** as part of a daily routine
- indefinite and negative words
- preterite of **ser** and **ir**
- verbs like **gustar**
- predicting content from the title
- a video about **tapas**
- cultural, geographic, and historical information about Peru

A primera vista Here are some additional questions you can ask to personalize the photo: **¿Con quién vives? ¿Qué le dices antes de salir de casa? ¿Qué tipo de ropa llevas para ir a tus clases? ¿Les prestas esta ropa a tus amigos/as? ¿Qué ropa usaste en el verano? ¿Y en el invierno?**

Teaching Tip Look for these icons for additional communicative practice:

Icon	
→👤←	Interpretive communication
←👤→	Presentational communication
👤↔👤	Interpersonal communication

contextos

pages 210–213
- Daily routine
- Personal hygiene
- Time expressions

fotonovela

pages 214–217
Marissa, Felipe, and Jimena all compete for space in front of the mirror as they get ready to go out on Friday night.

cultura

pages 218–219
- La siesta
- Ir de tapas

estructura

pages 220–235
- Reflexive verbs
- Indefinite and negative words
- Preterite of **ser** and **ir**
- Verbs like **gustar**
- Recapitulación

adelante

pages 236–239
Lectura: An e-mail from Guillermo
Panorama: Perú

A PRIMERA VISTA
- ¿Está él en casa o en una tienda?
- ¿Está contento o enojado?
- ¿Cómo es él?
- ¿Qué colores hay en la foto?

INSTRUCTIONAL RESOURCES

Supersite (vhlcentral.com)
Video: **Fotonovela*, Flash cultura*, Panorama cultural***
*Also on DVD
Audio: Textbook and Lab MP3 Files (*also on CD*)
Activity Pack: Information Gap Activities, games, additional activity handouts

Resources: Textbook Answer Key, WB/VM/LM Answer Key, Scripts, Translations, **Vocabulario adicional**, lesson plans, **Estructura** *PowerPoints*, Overheads
Testing Program: Quizzes, Tests, Exams, MP3s (*also on Test Generator CD*)

Learning Management System (Assignment Task Manager, Gradebook)
WebSAM (online Workbook/Video Manual/Lab Manual)
Workbook/Video Manual
Lab Manual

La rutina diaria

Más vocabulario

el baño, el cuarto de baño	bathroom
el inodoro	toilet
el jabón	soap
el despertador	alarm clock
el maquillaje	makeup
la rutina diaria	daily routine
bañarse	to bathe; to take a bath
cepillarse el pelo	to brush one's hair
dormirse (o:ue)	to go to sleep; to fall asleep
lavarse la cara	to wash one's face
levantarse	to get up
maquillarse	to put on makeup
antes (de)	before
después	afterwards; then
después (de)	after
durante	during
entonces	then
luego	then
más tarde	later
por la mañana	in the morning
por la noche	at night
por la tarde	in the afternoon; in the evening
por último	finally

Variación léxica

afeitarse	↔	rasurarse (Méx., Amér. C.)
ducha	↔	regadera (Col., Méx., Venez.)
ducharse	↔	bañarse (Amér. L.)
pantuflas	↔	chancletas (Méx., Col.); zapatillas (Esp.)

recursos

WB pp. 73–74 | LM p. 37 | (S) vhlcentral.com Lección 7

Se viste. (vestirse)

Se despierta. (despertarse)

En la habitación por la mañana

el espejo

Se afeita. (afeitarse)

Se pone crema de afeitar. (ponerse)

el lavabo

la crema de afeitar

la ducha

Se ducha. (ducharse)

el champú

En el baño por la mañana

Se peina. (peinarse)

Se acuesta. (acostarse)

En la habitación por la noche

Se lava las manos. (lavarse las manos)

Se cepilla los dientes. (cepillarse los dientes)

la toalla

las pantuflas

la pasta de dientes

En el baño por la noche

Práctica

1 **Escuchar** 🎧 Escucha las oraciones e indica si cada oración es **cierta** o **falsa**, según el dibujo.

1. _falsa_
2. _cierta_
3. _falsa_
4. _cierta_
5. _falsa_
6. _falsa_
7. _falsa_
8. _cierta_
9. _falsa_
10. _cierta_

2 **Ordenar** 🎧 Escucha la rutina diaria de Marta. Después ordena los verbos según lo que escuchaste.

5 a. almorzar
2 b. ducharse
4 c. peinarse
7 d. ver la televisión
3 e. desayunar
8 f. dormirse
1 g. despertarse
6 h. estudiar en la biblioteca

3 **Seleccionar** Selecciona la palabra que no está relacionada con cada grupo.

1. lavabo • toalla • despertador • jabón _despertador_
2. manos • antes de • después de • por último _manos_
3. acostarse • jabón • despertarse • dormirse _jabón_
4. espejo • lavabo • despertador • entonces _entonces_
5. dormirse • toalla • vestirse • levantarse _toalla_
6. pelo • cara • manos • inodoro _inodoro_
7. espejo • champú • jabón • pasta de dientes _espejo_
8. maquillarse • vestirse • peinarse • dientes _dientes_
9. baño • dormirse • despertador • acostarse _baño_
10. ducharse • luego • bañarse • lavarse _luego_

4 **Identificar** Con un(a) compañero/a, identifica las cosas que cada persona necesita. Sigue el modelo. Some answers will vary.

modelo
Jorge / lavarse la cara
Estudiante 1: ¿Qué necesita Jorge para lavarse la cara?
Estudiante 2: Necesita jabón y una toalla.

1. Mariana / maquillarse _maquillaje y un espejo_
2. Gerardo / despertarse _un despertador_
3. Celia / bañarse _jabón y una toalla_
4. Gabriel / ducharse _una ducha, una toalla y jabón_
5. Roberto / afeitarse _un espejo y crema de afeitar_
6. Sonia / lavarse el pelo _champú y una toalla_
7. Vanesa / lavarse las manos _un lavabo, jabón y una toalla_
8. Manuel / vestirse _su ropa/una camiseta/unos pantalones/etc._
9. Simón / acostarse _una cama_
10. Daniela / cepillarse los dientes _pasta de dientes y cepillo de dientes_

TEACHING OPTIONS

Pairs 👥 Have students write out three daily routine activities without showing them to their partner. The partner will ask questions that contain adverbs of time in order to guess the action. Ex: —**¿Es antes o después de ducharse?** —**Antes de ducharse.** —**¿Es levantarse?** —**Sí.**

Small Groups Write verbs and verb phrases used to describe daily routines on separate note cards. Divide the class into small groups and give each group a set of cards. Students should work together to determine the most logical sequence in which the actions may occur.

1 **Teaching Tip** Go over **Actividad 1** with the class. Then, have volunteers correct the false statements.

1 **Script** 1. Hay dos despertadores en la habitación de las chicas. 2. Un chico se pone crema de afeitar en la cara. 3. Una de las chicas se ducha. 4. Uno de los chicos se afeita. 5. Hay una toalla en la habitación de las chicas. 6. Una de las chicas se maquilla. 7. Las chicas están en el baño. 8. Uno de los chicos se cepilla los dientes en el baño. 9. Uno de los chicos se viste. 10. Una de las chicas se despierta.
Textbook MP3s

2 **Teaching Tip** To simplify, point out that the verbs in the list are in the infinitive form and tell students that they will hear them in conjugated (third-person singular) form. Before listening, have volunteers provide the third-person singular form of each verb.

2 **Script** Normalmente, Marta por la mañana se despierta a las siete, pero no puede levantarse hasta las siete y media. Se ducha y después se viste. Luego desayuna y se cepilla los dientes. Después, se peina y se maquilla. Entonces sale para sus clases. Después de las clases almuerza con sus amigos y por la tarde estudia en la biblioteca. Regresa a casa, cena y ve un poco la televisión. Por la noche, generalmente se acuesta a las diez y por último, se duerme.
Textbook MP3s

3 **Expansion** Go over the answers and explain why a particular item does not belong. Ex: **El lavabo, la toalla y el jabón son para lavarse. El despertador es para despertarse.**

4 **Expansion** Have students make statements about the people's actions, then ask a question. Ex: **Jorge se lava la cara. ¿Qué necesita?**

5 **La rutina de Andrés** Ordena esta rutina de una manera lógica.

a. Se afeita después de cepillarse los dientes. __4__
b. Se acuesta a las once y media de la noche. __9__
c. Por último, se duerme. __10__
d. Después de afeitarse, sale para las clases. __5__
e. Asiste a todas sus clases y vuelve a su casa. __6__
f. Andrés se despierta a las seis y media de la mañana. __1__
g. Después de volver a casa, come un poco. Luego estudia en su habitación. __7__
h. Se viste y entonces se cepilla los dientes. __3__
i. Se cepilla los dientes antes de acostarse. __8__
j. Se ducha antes de vestirse. __2__

6 **La rutina diaria** Con un(a) compañero/a, mira los dibujos y describe lo que hacen Ángel y Lupe.

Some answers may vary. Suggested answers:

1.
Ángel se afeita y mira la televisión.

2.
Lupe se maquilla y escucha la radio.

3.
Ángel se ducha y canta.

4.
Lupe se baña y lee.

5.
Ángel se lava la cara con jabón.

6.
Lupe se lava el pelo con champú en la ducha.

7.
Ángel se cepilla el pelo.

8.
Lupe se cepilla los dientes.

 Practice more at **vhlcentral.com.**

Comunicación

7 **La farmacia** Lee el anuncio y responde a las preguntas con un(a) compañero/a.

Answers will vary.

LA FARMACIA NUEVO SOL tiene todo
lo que necesitas para la vida diaria.

Esta semana tenemos grandes rebajas.

Con poco dinero puedes comprar lo que necesitas para el cuarto de baño ideal.

Para los hombres ofrecemos…
Excelentes cremas de afeitar de Guapo y Máximo

Para las mujeres ofrecemos…
Nuevo maquillaje de Marisol y jabones de baño Ilusiones y Belleza

Y para todos tenemos los mejores jabones, pastas de dientes y cepillos de dientes.

¡Visita LA FARMACIA NUEVO SOL!
Tenemos los mejores precios. Visita nuestra tienda muy cerca de tu casa.

1. ¿Qué tipo de tienda es? Es una farmacia.
2. ¿Qué productos ofrecen para las mujeres? maquillaje, jabones de baño
3. ¿Qué productos ofrecen para los hombres? cremas de afeitar
4. Haz (*Make*) una lista de los verbos que asocias con los productos del anuncio.
5. ¿Dónde compras tus productos de higiene? Answers will vary.
6. ¿Tienes una tienda favorita? ¿Cuál es? Answers will vary.

Suggested answers: afeitarse, maquillarse, cepillarse los dientes, ducharse/bañarse

8 **Rutinas diarias** Trabajen en parejas para describir la rutina diaria de dos o tres de estas personas. Pueden usar palabras de la lista. *Answers will vary.*

antes (de)	entonces	primero
después (de)	luego	tarde
durante el día	por último	temprano

- un(a) profesor(a) de la universidad
- un(a) turista
- un hombre o una mujer de negocios (*businessman/woman*)
- un vigilante nocturno (*night watchman*)
- un(a) jubilado/a (*retired person*)
- el presidente/primer ministro de tu país
- un niño de cuatro años
- Daniel Espinosa

¡Necesito arreglarme!

Es viernes por la tarde y Marissa, Jimena y Felipe se preparan para salir.

PERSONAJES MARISSA JIMENA

Video: *Fotonovela*
Record and Compare

MARISSA ¿Hola? ¿Está ocupado?
JIMENA Sí. Me estoy lavando la cara.
MARISSA Necesito usar el baño.

MARISSA Tengo que terminar de arreglarme. Voy al cine esta noche.
JIMENA Yo también tengo que salir. ¿Te importa si me maquillo primero? Me voy a encontrar con mi amiga Elena en una hora.

JIMENA No te preocupes, Marissa. Llegaste primero. Entonces, te arreglas el pelo y después me maquillo.
FELIPE ¿Y yo? Tengo crema de afeitar en la cara. No me voy a ir. Estoy aquí y aquí me quedo.

JIMENA ¡Felipe! ¿Qué estás haciendo?
FELIPE Me estoy afeitando. ¿Hay algún problema?
JIMENA ¡Siempre haces lo mismo!
FELIPE Pues, yo no vi a nadie aquí.

JIMENA ¿Por qué no te afeitaste por la mañana?
FELIPE Porque cada vez que quiero usar el baño, una de ustedes está aquí. O bañándose o maquillándose.

MARISSA Tú ganas. ¿Adónde vas a ir esta noche, Felipe?
FELIPE Juan Carlos y yo vamos a ir a un café en el centro. Siempre hay música en vivo. (*Se despide.*) Me siento guapísimo. Todavía me falta cambiarme la camisa.

FELIPE

7

MARISSA ¿Adónde vas esta noche?

JIMENA A la biblioteca.

MARISSA ¡Es viernes! ¡Nadie debe estudiar los viernes! Voy a ver una película de Pedro Almodóvar con unas amigas.

8

MARISSA ¿Por qué no vienen tú y Elena al cine con nosotras? Después, podemos ir a ese café y molestar a Felipe.

9

JIMENA No sé.

MARISSA ¿Cuándo fue la última vez que viste a Juan Carlos?

JIMENA Cuando fuimos a Mérida.

10

MARISSA A ti te gusta ese chico.

JIMENA No tengo idea de qué estás hablando. Si no te importa, nos vemos en el cine.

recursos

VM
pp. 207–208

vhlcentral.com
Lección 7

Expresiones útiles

Talking about getting ready

Necesito arreglarme.
I need to get ready.
Me estoy lavando la cara.
I'm washing my face.
¿Te importa si me maquillo primero?
Is it OK with you if I put on my makeup first?
Tú te arreglas el pelo y después yo me maquillo.
You fix your hair and then I'll put on my makeup.
Todavía me falta cambiarme la camisa.
I still have to change my shirt.

Reassuring someone

Tranquilo/a.
Relax.
No te preocupes.
Don't worry.

Talking about past actions

¿Cuándo fue la última vez que viste a Juan Carlos?
When was the last time you saw Juan Carlos?
Cuando fuimos a Mérida.
When we went to Mérida.

Talking about likes and dislikes

Me fascinan las películas de Almodóvar.
I love Almodóvar's movies.
Me encanta la música en vivo.
I love live music.
Me molesta compartir el baño.
It bothers me to share the bathroom.

Additional vocabulary

encontrarse con *to meet up with*
molestar *to bother*
nadie *no one*

Expresiones útiles Draw attention to the verb forms **fue** and **fuimos** in the caption of video still 9. Tell students that these are preterite forms of the verbs **ser** and **ir,** respectively. Then explain that the context clarifies which verb is used. Point out the phrases **Me estoy lavando, me maquillo, te arreglas,** and **No te preocupes.** Tell the class that these are forms of the reflexive verbs **lavarse, maquillarse, arreglarse,** and **preocuparse.** Then, point out the phrases **Me fascinan, Me encanta,** and **Me molesta.** Explain that these are examples of verbs that have constructions similar to that of **gustar.** Finally, draw attention to the caption for video still 3 and point out the words **algún, Siempre,** and **nadie.** Explain that **algún** and **Siempre** are indefinite words and **nadie** is a negative word. Tell students that they will learn more about these concepts in **Estructura.**

Teaching Tip
👤↔👤 Have students get together in groups of three to role-play the episode. Encourage students to ad-lib when possible. Then, ask one or two groups to present the episode to the class.

Nota cultural In the Spanish-speaking world, young people tend to dress more formally than their U.S. counterparts, not only for parties, but also to go see a movie or attend class. This concept is known as **lucir bien** (*to look good*). In some countries, for people of all ages, dressing in an overly casual manner may result in poorer service at certain establishments.

TEACHING OPTIONS

TPR Ask students to write **Marissa, Jimena,** and **Felipe** on separate pieces of paper. Read aloud statements from the perspective of the characters and have students hold up the corresponding name. Ex: **Me quiero arreglar el pelo. (Marissa) Mi hermano se está afeitando. (Jimena) Me pongo roja porque tengo vergüenza. (Jimena) Me siento muy guapo. (Felipe)**
Small Groups 👤↔👤 Ask students to select one of the characters

and write a short description about what they think his or her daily routine is like. Then have students who picked the same character get together to find similarities and differences in their descriptions.
Pairs Ask pairs of students to work together to create six true/false sentences about the **Fotonovela.** Have pairs exchange papers and complete the activity.

¿Qué pasó?

¿Cierto o falso?
1 ¿**Cierto o falso?** Indica si lo que dicen estas oraciones es **cierto** o **falso**. Corrige las oraciones falsas.

1. Marissa va a ver una película de Pedro Almodóvar con unas amigas.
 Cierto.
2. Jimena se va a encontrar con Elena en dos horas.
 Falso. Jimena se va a encontrar con Elena en una hora.
3. Felipe se siente muy feo después de afeitarse.
 Falso. Felipe se siente guapísimo después de afeitarse.
4. Jimena quiere maquillarse.
 Cierto.
5. Marissa quiere ir al café para molestar a Juan Carlos.
 Falso. Marissa quiere ir al café para molestar a Felipe.

Identificar
2 **Identificar** Identifica quién puede decir estas oraciones. Puedes usar cada nombre más de una vez.

1. No puedo usar el baño porque siempre están aquí, o bañándose o maquillándose. _____Felipe_____
2. Quiero arreglarme el pelo porque voy al cine esta noche. _____Marissa_____
3. Hoy voy a ir a la biblioteca. _____Jimena_____
4. ¡Necesito arreglarme! _____Marissa/Jimena/Felipe_____
5. Te gusta Juan Carlos. _____Marissa_____
6. ¿Por qué quieres afeitarte cuando estamos en el baño? _____Jimena/Marissa_____

MARISSA

FELIPE

JIMENA

Ordenar
3 **Ordenar** Ordena correctamente los planes que tiene Marissa.

__5__ a. Voy al café.
__2__ b. Me arreglo el pelo.
__6__ c. Molesto a Felipe.
__3__ d. Me encuentro con unas amigas.
__1__ e. Entro al baño.
__4__ f. Voy al cine.

En el baño
4 **En el baño** Trabajen en parejas para representar los papeles de dos compañeros/as de cuarto que deben usar el baño al mismo tiempo para hacer su rutina diaria. Usen las instrucciones como guía.
Answers will vary.

Estudiante 1	Estudiante 2
Di (*Say*) que quieres arreglarte porque vas a ir al cine.	→ Di (*Say*) que necesitas arreglarte porque te vas a encontrar con tus amigos/as.
Pregunta si puedes secarte el pelo.	→ Responde que no porque necesitas lavarte la cara.
Di que puede lavarse la cara, pero que después necesitas secarte el pelo.	→ Di que puede secarse el pelo, pero que después necesitas peinarte.

NATIONAL
communication
STANDARDS

Practice more at **vhlcentral.com.**

1 Expansion Give students these true/false statements as items 6–7: **6. Felipe va a encontrarse con Juan Carlos en una discoteca. (Falso. Ellos van a encontrarse en un café.) 7. La última vez que Jimena vio a Juan Carlos fue ayer. (Falso. Fue en Mérida.)**

Nota cultural Internationally renowned, Spanish filmmaker **Pedro Almodóvar's** films are generally characterized by complex narratives and themes of family, identity, and desire. He has won numerous awards, and the1988 film *Mujeres al borde de un ataque de nervios*, his first movie to have major international success, was adapted as a musical.

2 Expansion Give students these sentences as items 7–8: **7. Quiero ponerme otra camisa. (Felipe) 8. Debes venir al cine. (Marissa)**

3 Expansion Ask pairs to imagine another character's plans and list them using the **yo** form of the verbs, as in the activity. Then have pairs share their lists with the class.

4 Possible Conversation
E1: Quiero arreglarme porque voy a ir al cine.
E2: Pues, necesito arreglarme porque voy a encontrarme con mis amigos.
E1: ¿Puedo secarme el pelo?
E2: No, porque necesito lavarme la cara.
E1: Está bien. Puedes lavarte la cara, pero después necesito secarme el pelo.
E2: De acuerdo. Puedes secarte el pelo, pero después necesito peinarme.

TEACHING OPTIONS

Extra Practice →👤← Add an auditory aspect to this vocabulary practice. Ask students to close their books. Then read aloud the sentences from **Actividad 3**, in the correct order. Read each sentence twice slowly to give students an opportunity to write them down. Then read them again at normal speed, without pausing, to allow students to check for accuracy or fill in any gaps. Ask comprehension questions as a follow-up.

Small Groups 👤↔👤 Have students get together in small groups to discuss and compare their daily routines. Have them use as many of the words and expressions from this lesson as they can. Then ask for a few volunteers to describe the daily routine of one of their group members.

Pronunciación

Audio: Concepts, Activities Record & Compare

The consonant r

ropa	**r**utina	**r**ico	**R**amón

In Spanish, **r** has a strong trilled sound at the beginning of a word. No English words have a trill, but English speakers often produce a trill when they imitate the sound of a motor.

gusta**r**	du**r**ante	p**r**imero	c**r**ema

In any other position, **r** has a weak sound similar to the English *tt* in *better* or the English *dd* in *ladder*. In contrast to English, the tongue touches the roof of the mouth behind the teeth.

piza**rr**a	co**rr**o	ma**rr**ón	abu**rr**ido

The letter combination **rr**, which only appears between vowels, always has a strong trilled sound.

ca**r**o	ca**rr**o	pe**r**o	pe**rr**o

Between vowels, the difference between the strong trilled **rr** and the weak **r** is very important, as a mispronunciation could lead to confusion between two different words.

Práctica Lee las palabras en voz alta, prestando (*paying*) atención a la pronunciación de la **r** y la **rr**.

1. Perú	4. madre	7. rubio	10. tarde
2. Rosa	5. comprar	8. reloj	11. cerrar
3. borrador	6. favor	9. Arequipa	12. despertador

Oraciones Lee las oraciones en voz alta, prestando atención a la pronunciación de la **r** y la **rr**.

1. Ramón Robles Ruiz es programador. Su esposa Rosaura es artista.
2. A Rosaura Robles le encanta regatear en el mercado.
3. Ramón nunca regatea… le aburre regatear.
4. Rosaura siempre compra cosas baratas.
5. Ramón no es rico, pero prefiere comprar cosas muy caras.
6. ¡El martes Ramón compró un carro nuevo!

Refranes Lee en voz alta los refranes, prestando atención a la **r** y a la **rr**.

Perro que ladra no muerde.[1]

No se ganó Zamora en una hora.[2]

2 Rome wasn't built in a day.
1 A dog's bark is worse than its bite.

recursos

LM p. 38	vhlcentral.com Lección 7

EN DETALLE

La siesta

¿Sientes cansancio° después de comer?

¿Te cuesta° volver al trabajo° o a clase después del almuerzo? Estas sensaciones son normales. A muchas personas les gusta relajarse° después de almorzar. Este momento de descanso es **la siesta**. La siesta es popular en los países hispanos y viene de una antigua costumbre° del área del Mediterráneo. La palabra *siesta* viene del latín, es una forma corta de decir "sexta hora". La sexta hora del día es después del mediodía, el momento de más calor. Debido al° calor y al cansancio, los habitantes de España, Italia, Grecia y Portugal tienen la costumbre de dormir la siesta desde hace° más de° dos mil años. Los españoles y los portugueses llevaron la costumbre a los países americanos.

Aunque hoy día esta costumbre está desapareciendo en las grandes ciudades, la siesta todavía es importante en la cultura hispana. En pueblos pequeños, por ejemplo, muchas oficinas° y tiendas tienen la costumbre de cerrar por dos o tres horas después del mediodía. Los empleados van a su casa, almuerzan con sus familias, duermen la siesta o hacen actividades, como ir al gimnasio, y luego regresan al trabajo entre las 2:30 y las 4:30 de la tarde.

Los estudios científicos explican que una siesta corta después de almorzar ayuda° a trabajar más y mejor° durante la tarde. Pero ¡cuidado! Esta siesta debe durar° sólo entre veinte y cuarenta minutos. Si dormimos más, entramos en la fase de sueño profundo y es difícil despertarse.

Hoy, algunas empresas° de los EE.UU., Canadá, Japón, Inglaterra y Alemania tienen salas° especiales donde los empleados pueden dormir la siesta.

¿Dónde duermen la siesta?

■ Costumbre antigua
■ Costumbre nueva

En los lugares donde la siesta es una costumbre antigua, las personas la duermen en su casa. En los países donde la siesta es una costumbre nueva, la gente duerme en sus lugares de trabajo o en centros de siesta.

Sientes cansancio *Do you feel tired* **Te cuesta** *Is it hard for you* **trabajo** *work* **relajarse** *to relax* **antigua costumbre** *old custom* **Debido al** *Because (of)* **desde hace** *for* **más de** *more than* **aunque** *although* **está desapareciendo** *is disappearing* **oficinas** *offices* **ayuda** *helps* **mejor** *better* **durar** *last* **algunas empresas** *some businesses* **salas** *rooms*

ACTIVIDADES

1 **¿Cierto o falso?** Indica si lo que dicen las oraciones es **cierto** o **falso**. Corrige la información falsa.

1. La costumbre de la siesta empezó en Asia. **Falso.** La costumbre de la siesta empezó en el área del Mediterráneo.
2. La palabra *siesta* está relacionada con la sexta hora del día. **Cierto.**
3. Los españoles y los portugueses llevaron la costumbre de la siesta a Latinoamérica. **Cierto.**
4. La siesta ayuda a trabajar más y mejor durante la tarde. **Cierto.**
5. Los horarios de trabajo de las grandes ciudades hispanas son los mismos que los pueblos pequeños. **Falso.** En las grandes ciudades hispanas la costumbre de la siesta está desapareciendo.
6. Una siesta larga siempre es mejor que una siesta corta. **Falso.** La siesta debe durar entre veinte y cuarenta minutos.
7. En los Estados Unidos, los empleados de algunas empresas pueden dormir la siesta en el trabajo. **Cierto.**
8. Es fácil despertar de un sueño profundo. **Falso.** Es difícil despertar de un sueño profundo.

ASÍ SE DICE

El cuidado personal

el aseo; el excusado; el servicio; el váter (Esp.)	el baño
el cortaúñas	nail clippers
el desodorante	deodorant
el enjuague bucal	mouthwash
el hilo dental/ la seda dental	dental floss
la máquina de afeitar/ de rasurar (Méx.)	electric razor

EL MUNDO HISPANO

Costumbres especiales

- **México y El Salvador** Los vendedores pasan por las calles anunciando a gritos° su mercancía°: tanques de gas y flores° en México; pan y tortillas en El Salvador.

- **Costa Rica** Para encontrar las direcciones°, los costarricenses usan referencias a anécdotas, lugares o características geográficas. Por ejemplo: *200 metros norte de la iglesia Católica, frente al° supermercado Mi Mega.*

- **Argentina** En Tigre, una ciudad junto al Río° de la Plata, la gente usa barcos particulares°, barcos colectivos° y barcos-taxi para ir de una isla a otra. Todas las mañanas, un barco colectivo recoge° a los niños y los lleva a la escuela.

gritos *shouts* mercancía *merchandise* flores *flowers* direcciones *addresses* frente al *opposite* río *river* particulares *private* barcos colectivos *collective boats* recoge *picks up*

PERFIL

El mate

El mate es una parte muy importante de la rutina diaria en muchos países. Es una bebida° muy similar al té que se consume en Argentina, Uruguay y Paraguay. Tradicionalmente se bebe caliente° con una *bombilla*° y en un recipiente° que también se llama *mate*. Por ser amarga, algunos le agregan° azúcar para suavizar su sabor°. El mate se puede tomar a cualquier°

hora y en cualquier lugar, aunque en Argentina las personas prefieren sentarse en círculo e ir pasando el mate de mano en mano mientras° conversan. Los uruguayos, por otra parte, acostumbran llevar el agua° caliente para el mate en un termo°

bajo el brazo° y lo beben mientras caminan. Si ves a una persona con un termo bajo el brazo y un mate en la mano, ¡es casi seguro que es de Uruguay!

bebida *drink* caliente *hot* bombilla *straw (in Argentina)* recipiente *container* amarga *bitter* le agregan *add* suavizar su sabor *soften its flavor* cualquier *any* mientras *while* agua *water* termo *thermos* bajo el brazo *under their arm*

Conexión Internet

¿Qué costumbres son populares en los países hispanos?

Go to **vhlcentral.com** to find more cultural information related to this **Cultura** section.

ACTIVIDADES

2 **Comprensión** Completa las oraciones.

1. Uso _el hilo dental/la seda dental_ para limpiar (*to clean*) entre los dientes.
2. En _El Salvador_ las personas compran pan y tortillas a los vendedores que pasan por la calle.
3. El _mate_ es una bebida similar al té.
4. Los uruguayos beben mate mientras _caminan_.

3 **¿Qué costumbres tienes?** Escribe cuatro oraciones sobre una costumbre que compartes con tus amigos o con tu familia (por ejemplo: ir al cine, ir a eventos deportivos, leer, comer juntos, etc.). Explica qué haces, cuándo lo haces y con quién. Answers will vary.

recursos

VM pp. 279–280

vhlcentral.com Lección 7

 Practice more at **vhlcentral.com.**

Section Goals

In **Estructura 7.1**, students will learn:
• the conjugation of reflexive verbs
• common reflexive verbs

Instructional Resources
Supersite: Audio (Lab MP3 Files); Resources (*PowerPoints*, Activity Pack, Scripts, Answer Keys); Testing Program (Quizzes)
WebSAM
Workbook, pp. 75–76
Lab Manual, p. 39

Teaching Tips

• Model the first-person reflexive by talking about yourself. Ex: **Me levanto muy temprano. Me levanto a las cinco de la mañana.** Then model the second person by asking questions with a verb you have already used in the first person. Ex: **Y tú, _____, ¿a qué hora te levantas? (Me levanto a las ocho.)**

• Introduce the third person by making statements and asking questions about what a student has told you. Ex: _____ **se levanta muy tarde, ¿no? (Sí, se levanta muy tarde.)**

• Add a visual aspect to this grammar presentation. Use magazine pictures to clarify meanings between third-person singular and third-person plural forms. Ex: **Se lava las manos** and **Se lavan las manos.**

• On the board summarize the three possible positions for reflexive pronouns. You may want to demonstrate this visually by using an **X** to represent the reflexive pronoun: **X verbo conjugado, infinitivoX, gerundioX.** Remind students that they have already learned these positions for direct and indirect object pronouns.

7.1 # Reflexive verbs **Tutorial**

ANTE TODO A reflexive verb is used to indicate that the subject does something to or for himself or herself. In other words, it "reflects" the action of the verb back to the subject. Reflexive verbs always use reflexive pronouns.

SUBJECT REFLEXIVE VERB
Joaquín **se ducha** por la mañana.

The verb lavarse (*to wash oneself*)

	SINGULAR FORMS		
	yo	**me lavo**	*I wash (myself)*
	tú	**te lavas**	*you wash (yourself)*
	Ud.	**se lava**	*you wash (yourself)*
	él/ella	**se lava**	*he/she washes (himself/herself)*

	PLURAL FORMS		
	nosotros/as	**nos lavamos**	*we wash (ourselves)*
	vosotros/as	**os laváis**	*you wash (yourselves)*
	Uds.	**se lavan**	*you wash (yourselves)*
	ellos/ellas	**se lavan**	*they wash (themselves)*

▶ The pronoun **se** attached to an infinitive identifies the verb as reflexive: **lavarse.**

▶ When a reflexive verb is conjugated, the reflexive pronoun agrees with the subject.

Me afeito. **Te despiertas** a las siete.

¿Te importa si me maquillo primero?

A las chicas les encanta maquillarse durante horas y horas.

▶ Like object pronouns, reflexive pronouns generally appear before a conjugated verb. With infinitives and present participles, they may be placed before the conjugated verb or attached to the infinitive or present participle.

Ellos **se** van a vestir. **Nos** estamos lavando las manos.
Ellos van a vestir**se**. Estamos lavándo**nos** las manos.
They are going to get dressed. *We are washing our hands.*

▶ **¡Atención!** When a reflexive pronoun is attached to a present participle, an accent mark is added to maintain the original stress.

bañando ⟶ bañándose durmiendo ⟶ durmiéndose

TEACHING OPTIONS

Extra Practice To provide oral practice with reflexive verbs, create sentences that follow the pattern of the sentences in the examples. Say the sentence, have students repeat it, then say a different subject, varying the gender and number. Have students then say the sentence with the new subject, changing pronouns and verb forms as necessary.

Extra Practice ←👥→ Have students describe daily routines in their families. Encourage heritage speakers to use their own linguistic variation of words presented in this lesson. Ex: **regarse** (e:ie), **pintarse**. Have students work together to compare and contrast activities as well as lexical variations.

AYUDA

You have already learned several adjectives that can be used with **ponerse** when it means *to become*: **alegre, cómodo/a, contento/a, elegante, guapo/a, nervioso/a, rojo/a**, and **triste**.

Common reflexive verbs

acordarse (de) (o:ue)	to remember	**llamarse**	to be called; to be named
acostarse (o:ue)	to go to bed		
afeitarse	to shave	**maquillarse**	to put on makeup
bañarse	to bathe; to take a bath	**peinarse**	to comb one's hair
cepillarse	to brush	**ponerse**	to put on
despedirse (de) (e:i)	to say goodbye (to)	**ponerse (+ adj.)**	to become (+ adj.)
despertarse (e:ie)	to wake up	**preocuparse (por)**	to worry (about)
dormirse (o:ue)	to go to sleep; to fall asleep	**probarse** (o:ue)	to try on
ducharse	to shower; to take a shower	**quedarse**	to stay; to remain
		quitarse	to take off
		secarse	to dry (oneself)
enojarse (con)	to get angry (with)	**sentarse** (e:ie)	to sit down
irse	to go away; to leave	**sentirse** (e:ie)	to feel
lavarse	to wash (oneself)	**vestirse** (e:i)	to get dressed
levantarse	to get up		

COMPARE & CONTRAST

Unlike English, a number of verbs in Spanish can be reflexive or non-reflexive. If the verb acts upon the subject, the reflexive form is used. If the verb acts upon something other than the subject, the non-reflexive form is used. Compare these sentences.

Lola **lava** los platos.

Lola **se lava** la cara.

As the preceding sentences show, reflexive verbs sometimes have different meanings than their non-reflexive counterparts. For example, **lavar** means *to wash*, while **lavarse** means *to wash oneself, to wash up*.

▶ **¡Atención!** Parts of the body or clothing are generally not referred to with possessives, but with articles.

La niña se quitó **un** zapato. Necesito cepillarme **los** dientes.

recursos

WB
pp. 75–76

LM
p. 39

S

vhlcentral.com
Lección 7

¡INTÉNTALO! Indica el presente de estos verbos reflexivos.

despertarse

1. Mis hermanos _se despiertan_ tarde.
2. Tú _te despiertas_ tarde.
3. Nosotros _nos despertamos_ tarde.
4. Benito _se despierta_ tarde.
5. Yo _me despierto_ tarde.

ponerse

1. Él _se pone_ una chaqueta.
2. Yo _me pongo_ una chaqueta.
3. Usted _se pone_ una chaqueta.
4. Nosotras _nos ponemos_ una chaqueta.
5. Las niñas _se ponen_ una chaqueta.

TEACHING OPTIONS

TPR Model gestures for a few of the reflexive verbs. Ex: **acordarse** (tap side of head), **acostarse** (lay head on folded hands). Have students stand. Begin by practicing as a class using only the **nosotros** form, saying expressions at random. (Ex: **Nos lavamos la cara.**) Then vary the verb forms and point to the student who should perform the appropriate gesture. Keep a brisk pace. Vary by pointing to more than one student. (Ex: **Ustedes se peinan.**)

Pairs ← 👤 → Have students write a short account of their daily routine. Then have pairs compare and contrast their routines using a Venn diagram (see **Lección 9, Escritura**). Have the pair label the circles with their names and write **Los/Las dos** where they overlap. Then have them list their activities in the appropriate section. Remind them to use the **nosotros/as** form for verbs under **Los/Las dos**.

Teaching Tips

• Go through the list of common reflexive verbs asking students closed-answer questions.
Ex: **¿Te acuerdas de tu primer día en la universidad? (Sí, me acuerdo.) ¿Los niños se acuestan tarde o temprano? (Los niños se acuestan temprano.)**

• Emphasize that, with reflexive verbs, the person *doing* the action also *receives* the action. Contrast the difference between reflexive and non-reflexive verbs by giving examples from your life.
Ex: **Los lunes, me despierto muy temprano, a las cinco. A las seis, despierto a mi hijo. Primero, me ducho y después baño a mi hijo…** (You may want to use a doll or other visual aspect for this presentation.)

• To practice reflexive verbs in the preterite and periphrastic future (**ir a** + [*infinitive*]), talk about what you did yesterday and plan to do tomorrow.
Ex: **Ayer me levanté a las seis. Pero el sábado me voy a levantar a las nueve.** Then ask volunteers to talk about what they did and plan to do.

• Survey the class about the products they use daily, using reflexive verbs. Ex: ____, **¿te cepillas los dientes con *Crest* o *Colgate*? ¿Te lavas el pelo con *Pantene*? ¿Te lavas con *Dove* o *Lever 2000*?** Practice other forms by having students summarize the results. Ex: **Nick, Kim y Antoine se lavan con *Irish Spring*. Lucas y yo nos cepillamos los dientes con *Tom's*.**

• Ask volunteers to translate sentences such as: *He dresses the children at seven. He gets dressed at seven.*

¡Atención! Point out that the possessive article is not used with parts of the body and clothing. Especially with reflexive verbs, the pronoun eliminates any ambiguity.

Práctica

1 Nuestra rutina

La familia de Blanca sigue la misma rutina todos los días. Según Blanca, ¿qué hacen ellos?

> **modelo**
>
> mamá / despertarse a las 5:00
> *Mamá se despierta a las cinco.*

1. Roberto y yo / levantarse a las 7:00 Roberto y yo nos levantamos a las siete.
2. papá / ducharse primero y / luego afeitarse Papá se ducha primero y luego se afeita.
3. yo / lavarse la cara y / vestirse antes de tomar café Yo me lavo la cara y me visto antes de tomar café.
4. mamá / peinarse y / luego maquillarse Mamá se peina y luego se maquilla.
5. todos (nosotros) / sentarse a la mesa para comer Todos nos sentamos a la mesa para comer.
6. Roberto / cepillarse los dientes después de comer Roberto se cepilla los dientes después de comer.
7. yo / ponerse el abrigo antes de salir Yo me pongo el abrigo antes de salir.
8. nosotros / despedirse de mamá Nosotros nos despedimos de mamá.

2 La fiesta elegante

Selecciona el verbo apropiado y completa las oraciones con la forma correcta.

1. Tú ____lavas____ (lavar / lavarse) el auto antes de ir a la fiesta.
2. Nosotros no ____nos acordamos____ (acordar / acordarse) de comprar los regalos.
3. Para llegar a tiempo, Raúl y Marta ____acuestan____ (acostar / acostarse) a los niños antes de salir.
4. Yo ____me siento____ (sentir / sentirse) cómoda en mi vestido nuevo.
5. Mis amigos siempre ____se visten____ (vestir / vestirse) con ropa muy elegante.
6. Los cocineros ____prueban____ (probar / probarse) la comida antes de servirla.
7. Usted ____se preocupa____ (preocupar / preocuparse) mucho por llegar antes que (*before*) los demás invitados, ¿no?
8. En general, ____me afeito____ (afeitar / afeitarse) yo mismo, pero hoy es un día especial y el barbero (*barber*) me ____afeita____ (afeitar / afeitarse). ¡Será una fiesta inolvidable!

3 Describir

Mira los dibujos y describe lo que estas personas hacen. Some answers may vary.

1. el joven El joven se quita/se pone los zapatos.

2. Carmen Carmen se duerme./se acuesta. /se despierta.

3. Juan Juan se pone/se quita la camiseta.

4. ellos Ellos se despiden/se saludan.

5. Estrella Estrella se maquilla.

6. Toni Toni se enoja con el perro.

Comunicación

4 **Preguntas personales** En parejas, túrnense para hacerse estas preguntas. Answers will vary.

1. ¿A qué hora te levantas durante la semana?
2. ¿A qué hora te levantas los fines de semana?
3. ¿Prefieres levantarte tarde o temprano? ¿Por qué?
4. ¿Te enojas frecuentemente con tus amigos?
5. ¿Te preocupas fácilmente? ¿Qué te preocupa?
6. ¿Qué te pone contento/a?
7. ¿Qué haces cuando te sientes triste?
8. ¿Y cuando te sientes alegre?
9. ¿Te acuestas tarde o temprano durante la semana?
10. ¿A qué hora te acuestas los fines de semana?

5 **Charadas** En grupos, jueguen a las charadas. Cada persona debe pensar en dos oraciones con verbos reflexivos. La primera persona que adivina la charada dramatiza la siguiente. Answers will vary.

6 **Debate** En grupos, discutan este tema: ¿Quiénes necesitan más tiempo para arreglarse (*to get ready*) antes de salir, los hombres o las mujeres? Hagan una lista de las razones (*reasons*) que tienen para defender sus ideas e informen a la clase. Answers will vary.

7 **La coartada** Hoy se cometió un crimen entre las 7 y las 11 de la mañana. En parejas, imaginen que uno de ustedes es un sospechoso y el otro un policía investigador. El policía le pregunta al sospechoso qué hace habitualmente a esas horas y el sospechoso responde. Luego, el policía presenta las respuestas del sospechoso ante el jurado (la clase) y entre todos deciden si es culpable o no. Answers will vary.

Síntesis

8 **La familia ocupada** Tú y tu compañero/a asisten a un programa de verano en Lima, Perú. Viven con la familia Ramos. Tu profesor(a) te va a dar la rutina incompleta que la familia sigue en las mañanas. Trabaja con tu compañero/a para completarla. Answers will vary.

> **modelo**
> **Estudiante 1:** ¿Qué hace el señor Ramos a las seis y cuarto?
> **Estudiante 2:** El señor Ramos se levanta.

 Practice more at **vhlcentral.com**.

TEACHING OPTIONS

Game 👥↔👥 Working in teams, students should tell each other about the strangest, funniest, or most exciting thing they have done. The team then chooses one account and writes it down. Collect the papers, shuffle them, and read the descriptions aloud. The class has two minutes to ask team members questions to find out who did the activity.
Extra Practice →👥← Add an auditory aspect to this grammar

practice. Prepare descriptions of five celebrities or fictional characters, using reflexives. Write their names in random order on the board. Then read the descriptions aloud and have students match each one to a name. Ex: **Es seria; se preocupa por temas importantes, como la justicia. Siempre se viste de rojo. Quiere a su hermano, pero con frecuencia se enoja con él. Tiene una hermana menor que se llama Maggie. (Lisa Simpson)**

4 Expansion
👥↔👥 Ask volunteers to call out some of their answers. The class should add information by speculating on the reason behind each answer. Ex: **Hablas por teléfono con tus amigos cuando te sientes triste porque ellos te comprenden muy bien.** Have the volunteer confirm or refute the speculation.

5 Teaching Tip Ask each group to present their best **charada** to the class.

6 Teaching Tip Before assigning groups, go over some of the things men and women do to get ready to go out. Ex: **Las mujeres se maquillan. Los hombres se afeitan.** Then ask students to indicate their opinion on the question and divide the class into groups accordingly.

7 Teaching Tip You may want to give students more details of the crime.

8 Teaching Tip Divide the class into pairs and distribute the handouts from the Activity Pack (Activity Pack/Supersite) that correspond to this Information Gap Activity. Give students ten minutes to complete this activity.

8 Expansion Ask small groups to imagine that they all live in the same house and have them put together a message board to reflect their different schedules.

Section Goals

In **Estructura 7.2**, students will learn:

• high-frequency indefinite and negative words

• the placement and use of indefinite and negative words

Instructional Resources

Supersite: Audio (Lab MP3 Files); Resources (*PowerPoints*, Activity Pack, Scripts, Answer Keys); Testing Program (Quizzes)
WebSAM
Workbook, pp. 77–78
Lab Manual, p. 40

Teaching Tips

• Write **alguien** and **nadie** on the board and ask questions about what students are wearing. Ex: **Hoy alguien lleva una camiseta verde. ¿Quién es? ¿Alguien lleva pantalones anaranjados?**

• Present negative words by complaining dramatically in a whining tone. Ex: **Nadie me llama por teléfono. Nunca recibo un mensaje electrónico de ningún estudiante. Ni mi esposo ni mis hijos se acuerdan de mi cumpleaños.** Then smile radiantly and state the opposite. Ex: **Alguien me llama por teléfono.**

• Add a visual aspect to this grammar presentation. Use magazine pictures to compare and contrast indefinite and negative words. Ex: **La señora tiene algo en las manos. ¿El señor tiene algo también? No, el señor no tiene nada.**

• Have students say they do the opposite of what you do. Ex: **Yo siempre canto en la ducha. (Nosotros no cantamos nunca en la ducha.)**

• Point out that **uno/a(s)** can be used as an indefinite pronoun. Ex: **¿Tienes un lápiz? Sí, tengo uno.**

7.2 # Indefinite and negative words **Tutorial**

ANTE TODO Indefinite words refer to people and things that are not specific, for example, *someone* or *something*. Negative words deny the existence of people and things or contradict statements, for instance, *no one* or *nothing*. Spanish indefinite words have corresponding negative words, which are opposite in meaning.

Indefinite and negative words

Indefinite words		Negative words	
algo	*something; anything*	**nada**	*nothing; not anything*
alguien	*someone; somebody; anyone*	**nadie**	*no one; nobody; not anyone*
alguno/a(s), algún	*some; any*	**ninguno/a, ningún**	*no; none; not any*
o... o	*either... or*	**ni... ni**	*neither... nor*
siempre	*always*	**nunca, jamás**	*never, not ever*
también	*also; too*	**tampoco**	*neither; not either*

▶ There are two ways to form negative sentences in Spanish. You can place the negative word before the verb, or you can place **no** before the verb and the negative word after.

Nadie se levanta temprano.
No one gets up early.

No se levanta nadie temprano.
No one gets up early.

Ellos **nunca gritan**.
They never shout.

Ellos **no gritan nunca**.
They never shout.

¿Hay algún problema?

Siempre haces esto.

▶ Because they refer to people, **alguien** and **nadie** are often used with the personal **a**. The personal **a** is also used before **alguno/a, algunos/as,** and **ninguno/a** when these words refer to people and they are the direct object of the verb.

—Perdón, señor, ¿busca usted **a alguien**?
—No, gracias, señorita, no busco **a nadie**.

—Tomás, ¿buscas **a alguno** de tus hermanos?
—No, mamá, no busco **a ninguno**.

▶ **¡Atención!** Before a masculine, singular noun, **alguno** and **ninguno** are shortened to **algún** and **ningún**.

—¿Tienen ustedes **algún** amigo peruano?
—No, no tenemos **ningún** amigo peruano.

AYUDA

Alguno/a, algunos/as are not always used in the same way English uses *some* or *any*. Often, **algún** is used where *a* would be used in English.

¿Tienes algún libro que hable de los incas?
Do you have a book that talks about the Incas?

Note that **ninguno/a** is rarely used in the plural.

—**¿Visitaste algunos museos?**
—**No, no visité ninguno.**

TEACHING OPTIONS

Extra Practice Write cloze sentences on the board and have the students complete them with an indefinite or negative word. Ex: **Los vegetarianos no comen hamburguesas _____ . (nunca) Las madres _____ se preocupan por sus hijos. (siempre) En las fiestas ella no es sociable, _____ baila _____ habla con _____. (ni, ni, nadie)**

Pairs Have students take turns giving one-word indefinite and negative word prompts and having the other respond in complete sentences. Ex: **E1: siempre E2: Siempre le mando un mensaje electrónico a mi madre por la mañana. E1: tampoco E2: Yo no me levanto temprano tampoco.**

COMPARE & CONTRAST

In English, it is incorrect to use more than one negative word in a sentence. In Spanish, however, sentences frequently contain two or more negative words. Compare these Spanish and English sentences.

Nunca le escribo a **nadie**.
I never write to anyone.

No me preocupo por **nada nunca**.
I do not ever worry about anything.

As the preceding sentences show, once an English sentence contains one negative word (for example, *not* or *never*), no other negative word may be used. Instead, indefinite (or affirmative) words are used. In Spanish, however, once a sentence is negative, no other affirmative (that is, indefinite) word may be used. Instead, all indefinite ideas must be expressed in the negative.

▶ **Pero** is used to mean *but*. The meaning of **sino** is *but rather* or *on the contrary*. It is used when the first part of the sentence is negative and the second part contradicts it.

Los estudiantes no se acuestan
temprano **sino** tarde.
*The students don't go to bed
early, but rather late.*

Esas gafas son caras,
pero bonitas.
*Those glasses are expensive,
but pretty.*

María no habla francés
sino español.
*María doesn't speak French,
but rather Spanish.*

José es inteligente, **pero**
no saca buenas notas.
*José is intelligent but
doesn't get good grades.*

¡INTÉNTALO! Cambia las oraciones para que sean negativas.

1. Siempre se viste bien.
 _____Nunca_____ se viste bien.
 _____No_____ se viste bien _____nunca_____.
2. Alguien se ducha.
 _____Nadie_____ se ducha.
 _____No_____ se ducha _____nadie_____.
3. Ellas van también.
 Ellas _____tampoco_____ van.
 Ellas _____no_____ van _____tampoco_____.
4. Alguien se pone nervioso.
 _____Nadie_____ se pone nervioso.
 _____No_____ se pone nervioso _____nadie_____.
5. Tú siempre te lavas las manos.
 Tú _____nunca / jamás_____ te lavas las manos.
 Tú _____no_____ te lavas las manos _____nunca / jamás_____.
6. Voy a traer algo.
 _____No_____ voy a traer _____nada_____.
7. Juan se afeita también.
 Juan _____tampoco_____ se afeita.
 Juan _____no_____ se afeita _____tampoco_____.
8. Mis amigos viven en una residencia o en casa.
 Mis amigos _____no_____ viven _____ni_____ en una residencia _____ni_____ en casa.
9. La profesora hace algo en su escritorio.
 La profesora _____no_____ hace _____nada_____ en su escritorio.
10. Tú y yo vamos al mercado.
 _____Ni_____ tú _____ni_____ yo vamos al mercado.
11. Tienen un espejo en su casa.
 _____No_____ tienen _____ningún_____ espejo en su casa.
12. Algunos niños se ponen sus abrigos.
 _____Ningún_____ niño se pone su abrigo.

recursos

WB
pp. 77–78

LM
p. 40

vhlcentral.com
Lección 7

Teaching Tips

- Emphasize that there is no limit to the number of negative words that can be strung together in a sentence in Spanish. Ex: **No hablo con nadie nunca de ningún problema, ni con mi familia ni con mis amigos.**
- Ask volunteers questions about their activities since the last class, reiterating the answers. Ex: **¿Quién compró algo nuevo? Sólo dos personas. Nadie más compró algo nuevo. Yo no compré nada nuevo tampoco.**
- Elicit negative responses by asking questions whose answers will clearly be negative. Ex: **¿Alguien lleva zapatos de lunares? (No, nadie lleva zapatos de lunares.) ¿Piensas comprar un barco mañana? (No, no pienso comprar ninguno/ningún barco.) ¿Tienes nietos? (No, no tengo ninguno/ningún nieto.)**
- Give examples of **pero** and **sino** using the seating of the students. Ex: ____ se sienta al lado de ____ , pero no al lado de ____ . No se sienta a la izquierda de ____ , sino a la derecha. ____ no se sienta al lado de la ventana, pero está cerca de la puerta.

TEACHING OPTIONS

Video Show the **Fotonovela** again to give students more input containing indefinite and negative words. Stop the video where appropriate to discuss how these words are used.
Pairs Have pairs create sentences about your community using affirmative and negative words. Ex: **En nuestra ciudad no hay ningún mercado al aire libre. Hay algunos restaurantes de tapas. El equipo de béisbol juega bien, pero no gana muchos partidos.**

Small Groups Give small groups five minutes to write a description of **un señor muy, pero muy antipático**. Tell them to use as many indefinite and negative words as possible to describe what makes this person so unpleasant. Encourage exaggeration and creativity.

Práctica

1 **¿Pero o sino?** Forma oraciones sobre estas personas usando **pero** o **sino**.

> **modelo**
> muchos estudiantes viven en residencias estudiantiles / muchos de ellos quieren vivir fuera del *(off)* campus
> *Muchos estudiantes viven en residencias estudiantiles, pero muchos de ellos quieren vivir fuera del campus.*

1. Marcos nunca se despierta temprano / siempre llega puntual a clase
 Marcos nunca se despierta temprano, pero siempre llega puntual a clase.
2. Lisa y Katarina no se acuestan temprano / muy tarde
 Lisa y Katarina no se acuestan temprano sino muy tarde.
3. Alfonso es inteligente / algunas veces es antipático
 Alfonso es inteligente, pero algunas veces es antipático.
4. los directores de la residencia no son ecuatorianos / peruanos
 Los directores de la residencia no son ecuatorianos sino peruanos.
5. no nos acordamos de comprar champú / compramos jabón
 No nos acordamos de comprar champú, pero compramos jabón.
6. Emilia no es estudiante / profesora
 Emilia no es estudiante sino profesora.
7. no quiero levantarme / tengo que ir a clase
 No quiero levantarme, pero tengo que ir a clase.
8. Miguel no se afeita por la mañana / por la noche
 Miguel no se afeita por la mañana sino por la noche.

2 **Completar** Completa esta conversación. Usa expresiones negativas en tus respuestas. Luego, dramatiza la conversación con un(a) compañero/a. *Answers will vary.*

AURELIO Ana María, ¿encontraste algún regalo para Eliana?
ANA MARÍA (1) *No, no encontré ningún regalo/nada para Eliana.*

AURELIO ¿Viste a alguna amiga en el centro comercial?
ANA MARÍA (2) *No, no vi a ninguna amiga/ninguna/nadie en el centro comercial.*

AURELIO ¿Me llamó alguien?
ANA MARÍA (3) *No, nadie te llamó./No, no te llamó nadie.*

AURELIO ¿Quieres ir al teatro o al cine esta noche?
ANA MARÍA (4) *No, no quiero ir ni al teatro ni al cine.*

AURELIO ¿No quieres salir a comer?
ANA MARÍA (5) *No, no quiero salir a comer (tampoco).*

AURELIO ¿Hay algo interesante en la televisión esta noche?
ANA MARÍA (6) *No, no hay nada interesante en la televisión.*

AURELIO ¿Tienes algún problema?
ANA MARÍA (7) *No, no tengo ningún problema/ninguno.*

 Practice more at **vhlcentral.com.**

Comunicación

3 **Opiniones** Completa estas oraciones de una manera lógica. Luego, compara tus respuestas con las de un(a) compañero/a. *Answers will vary.*

1. Mi habitación es _____, pero _____.
2. Por la noche me gusta _____, pero _____.
3. Un(a) profesor(a) ideal no es _____, sino _____.
4. Mis amigos son _____, pero _____.

4 **En el campus** En parejas, háganse preguntas sobre qué hay en su universidad: residencias bonitas, departamento de ingeniería, cines, librerías baratas, estudiantes guapos/as, equipo de fútbol, playa, clases fáciles, museo, profesores/as estrictos/as. Sigan el modelo. *Answers will vary.*

> **modelo**
> **Estudiante 1:** ¿Hay algunas residencias bonitas?
> **Estudiante 2:** Sí, hay una/algunas. Está(n) detrás del estadio.
>
> **Estudiante 1:** ¿Hay algún museo?
> **Estudiante 2:** No, no hay ninguno.

5 **Quejas** En parejas, hagan una lista de cinco quejas (*complaints*) comunes que tienen los estudiantes. Usen expresiones negativas. *Answers will vary.*

> **modelo**
> Nadie me entiende.

Ahora hagan una lista de cinco quejas que los padres tienen de sus hijos.

> **modelo**
> Nunca limpian sus habitaciones.

6 **Anuncios** En parejas, lean el anuncio y contesten las preguntas.
Some answers will vary.

1. ¿Es el anuncio positivo o negativo? ¿Por qué? *Answers will vary.*
2. ¿Qué palabras indefinidas hay? *algún, siempre, algo*
3. Escriban el texto del anuncio cambiando todo por expresiones negativas. *¿No buscas ningún producto especial? ¡Nunca hay nada para nadie en las tiendas García!*

Ahora preparen su propio (*own*) anuncio usando expresiones afirmativas y negativas.

¿Buscas algún producto especial?

¡Siempre hay algo para todos en las tiendas García!

Síntesis

7 **Encuesta** Tu profesor(a) te va a dar una hoja de actividades para hacer una encuesta. Circula por la clase y pídeles a tus compañeros que comparen las actividades que hacen durante la semana con las que hacen durante los fines de semana. Escribe las respuestas. *Answers will vary.*

3 Teaching Tip Before assigning the activity, give some personal examples using different subjects. Ex: **Mi hijo es inteligente, pero no le gusta estudiar. Mi amiga no es norteamericana, sino española.**

3 Expansion Give students these sentences as items 5–6: **5. Mis padres no son ____ sino ____. 6. Mi compañero/a de cuarto es ____ pero ____.**

4 Teaching Tip To simplify, before beginning the activity, practice question formation for each topic as a class.

4 Expansion Have pairs of students create three additional sentences about your school.

5 Expansion Divide the class into all-male and all-female groups. Then have each group make two different lists: **Quejas que tienen los hombres de las mujeres** and **Quejas que tienen las mujeres de los hombres.** After five minutes, compare and contrast the answers and perceptions.

6 Expansion Have pairs work with another pair to create an ad that combines the best aspects of each of their individual ads. Then have them present their final product to the class.

7 Teaching Tip Distribute the *Hojas de actividades* from the Activity Pack/Supersite that correspond to this activity.

7 Expansion Have students write a short paragraph summarizing the information obtained through the **encuesta.** Ex: **Nadie va a la biblioteca durante el fin de semana, pero muchos vamos durante la semana. No estudiamos los sábados sino los domingos....**

Section Goal

In **Estructura 7.3**, students will learn the preterite of **ser** and **ir**.

Instructional Resources
Supersite: Audio (Lab MP3 Files); Resources (*PowerPoints*, Activity Pack, Scripts, Answer Keys); Testing Program (Quizzes)
WebSAM
Workbook, p. 79
Lab Manual, p. 41

Teaching Tips
• Ask volunteers to answer questions such as: **¿Fuiste al cine el sábado pasado? ¿Cómo fue la película? ¿Fueron tus amigos y tú a alguna fiesta durante el fin de semana? ¿Fue agradable la fiesta? ¿Quiénes fueron?**
• Contrast the preterite of **ser** and **ir** by saying pairs of sentences. Ex: **1. Anteayer fue sábado. Fui al supermercado el sábado. 2. Ayer fue domingo. No fui al supermercado ayer. 3. ¿Fueron ustedes al partido de fútbol el sábado? ¿Fue divertido el partido?**
• Point out that although the preterite forms of **ser** and **ir** are identical, there is rarely any confusion because context clarifies which verb is used.

7.3 Preterite of ser and ir Tutorial

ANTE TODO In **Lección 6**, you learned how to form the preterite tense of regular **-ar**, **-er**, and **-ir** verbs. The following chart contains the preterite forms of **ser** (*to be*) and **ir** (*to go*). Since these forms are irregular, you will need to memorize them.

Preterite of ser and ir		
	ser *(to be)*	**ir** *(to go)*
SINGULAR FORMS		
yo	**fui**	**fui**
tú	**fuiste**	**fuiste**
Ud./él/ella	**fue**	**fue**
PLURAL FORMS		
nosotros/as	**fuimos**	**fuimos**
vosotros/as	**fuisteis**	**fuisteis**
Uds./ellos/ellas	**fueron**	**fueron**

AYUDA Note that, whereas regular **-er** and **-ir** verbs have accent marks in the **yo** and **Ud./él/ella** forms of the preterite, **ser** and **ir** do not.

▶ Since the preterite forms of **ser** and **ir** are identical, context clarifies which of the two verbs is being used.

Él **fue** a comprar champú y jabón.
He went to buy shampoo and soap.

¿Cómo **fue** la película anoche?
How was the movie last night?

¡INTÉNTALO! Completa las oraciones usando el pretérito de **ser** e **ir**.

ir
1. Los viajeros _fueron_ a Perú.
2. Patricia _fue_ a Cuzco.
3. Tú _fuiste_ a Iquitos.
4. Gregorio y yo _fuimos_ a Lima.
5. Yo _fui_ a Trujillo.
6. Ustedes _fueron_ a Arequipa.
7. Mi padre _fue_ a Lima.
8. Nosotras _fuimos_ a Cuzco.
9. Él _fue_ a Machu Picchu.
10. Usted _fue_ a Nazca.

ser
1. Usted _fue_ muy amable.
2. Yo _fui_ muy cordial.
3. Ellos _fueron_ simpáticos.
4. Nosotros _fuimos_ muy tontos.
5. Ella _fue_ antipática.
6. Tú _fuiste_ muy generoso.
7. Ustedes _fueron_ cordiales.
8. La gente _fue_ amable.
9. Tomás y yo _fuimos_ muy felices.
10. Los profesores _fueron_ buenos.

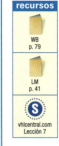
recursos
WB p. 79
LM p. 41
vhlcentral.com Lección 7

TEACHING OPTIONS

Video Replay the **Fotonovela** segment and have students listen for preterite forms of **ser** and **ir**. Stop the video with each example to illustrate how context makes the meaning of the verb clear.
Pairs Have pairs of students work together to solve this logical reasoning problem. **Mis compañeros de casa, Julia y Fernando, y yo fuimos de vacaciones durante el mes de julio a Puerto Rico, a Chile y a México. Julia fue a un viaje de esquí, pero Fernando y yo fuimos a lugares donde hace sol. El viaje de Fernando fue desagradable porque pasó un huracán y fue imposible nadar en el Pacífico durante esos días. Por suerte, mi viaje fue muy agradable. ¿Adónde fui? (a Puerto Rico) ¿Adónde fueron Julia y Fernando? (Julia fue a Chile y Fernando fue a México.)**

Práctica y Comunicación

1 **Completar** Completa estas conversaciones con la forma correcta del pretérito de **ser** o **ir**. Indica el infinitivo de cada forma verbal.

NOTA CULTURAL

La ciudad peruana de **El Callao**, fundada en 1537, fue por muchos años el puerto (*port*) más activo de la costa del Pacífico en Suramérica. En el siglo XVIII, se construyó (*was built*) una fortaleza allí para proteger (*protect*) la ciudad de los ataques de piratas y bucaneros.

Conversación 1

			ser	ir
RAÚL	¿Adónde (1) _fueron_ ustedes de vacaciones?		○	◉
PILAR	(2) _Fuimos_ a Perú.		○	◉
RAÚL	¿Cómo (3) _fue_ el viaje?		◉	○
▶ PILAR	¡(4) _Fue_ estupendo! Machu Picchu y El Callao son increíbles.		◉	○
RAÚL	¿(5) _Fue_ caro el viaje?		◉	○
PILAR	No, el precio (6) _fue_ muy bajo. Sólo costó tres mil dólares.		◉	○

Conversación 2

			ser	ir
ISABEL	Tina y Vicente (7) _fueron_ novios, ¿no?		◉	○
LUCÍA	Sí, pero ahora no. Anoche Tina (8) _fue_ a comer con Gregorio		○	◉
	y la semana pasada ellos (9) _fueron_ al partido de fútbol.		○	◉
ISABEL	¿Ah sí? Javier y yo (10) _fuimos_ al partido y no los vimos.		○	◉

2 **Descripciones** Forma oraciones con estos elementos. Usa el pretérito. *Answers will vary.*

A	B	C	D
yo	(no) ir	a un restaurante	ayer
tú	(no) ser	en autobús	anoche
mi compañero/a		estudiante	anteayer
nosotros		muy simpático/a	la semana pasada
mis amigos		a la playa	el año pasado
ustedes		dependiente/a en una tienda	

3 **Preguntas** En parejas, túrnense para hacerse estas preguntas. *Answers will vary.*

1. ¿Cuándo fuiste al cine por última vez? ¿Con quién fuiste?
2. ¿Fuiste en auto, en autobús o en metro? ¿Cómo fue el viaje?
3. ¿Cómo fue la película?
4. ¿Fue una película de terror, de acción o un drama?
5. ¿Fue una de las mejores películas que viste? ¿Por qué?
6. ¿Fueron buenos los actores o no? ¿Cuál fue el mejor?
7. ¿Adónde fuiste/fueron después?
8. ¿Fue una buena idea ir al cine?
9. ¿Fuiste feliz ese día?

4 **El viaje** En parejas, escriban un diálogo de un(a) viajero/a hablando con el/la agente de viajes sobre un viaje que hizo recientemente. Usen el pretérito de **ser** e **ir**. *Answers will vary.*

> **modelo**
>
> **Agente:** *¿Cómo fue el viaje?*
> **Viajero:** *El viaje fue maravilloso/horrible…*

 Practice more at **vhlcentral.com**.

1 **Teaching Tip** Before assigning the activity, write cloze sentences on the board and ask volunteers to fill in the blanks. Ex: **¿Cómo ____ los guías turísticos durante tu viaje? (fueron) ¿Quién ____ con Marcela al baile? (fue)**

1 **Expansion**
👥↔👥 Ask small groups to write four questions based on the conversations. Have groups exchange papers to discuss and answer the questions they receive. Then have them confirm their answers with the group who wrote the questions.

2 **Expansion** Ask a volunteer to say one of his or her sentences aloud. Point to another student, and call out an interrogative word in order to cue a question. Ex: **E1: No fui a un restaurante anoche.** Say: **¿Adónde? E2: ¿Adónde fuiste? E1: Fui al cine.**

3 **Expansion**
👥↔👥 Have students form new pairs and describe the movie that their first partner saw, based on the information they learned from items 3–6. The other student should guess what movie it was, asking for more information as needed.

4 **Expansion**
←👤→ Ask pairs to write a similar conversation within a different context (Ex: **un día horrible**).

TEACHING OPTIONS

Small Groups 👥↔👥 Have small groups of students role-play a TV interview with astronauts who have just returned from a long stay on Mars. Have students review previous lesson vocabulary lists as necessary in preparation. Give groups sufficient time to plan and practice their skits. When all groups have completed the activity, ask a few of them to perform their role-play for the class.

TPR Read aloud a series of sentences using **ser** and **ir** in the preterite. Have students raise their right hand if the verb is **ser**, and their left hand for **ir**. Ex: **Yo fui camarero a los dieciocho años.** (right hand)

7.4 Verbs like gustar (S) Tutorial

ANTE TODO In **Lección 2**, you learned how to express preferences with **gustar**. You will now learn more about the verb **gustar** and other similar verbs. Observe these examples.

Me gusta ese champú.

> **ENGLISH EQUIVALENT**
> *I like that shampoo.*
> **LITERAL MEANING**
> *That shampoo is pleasing to me.*

¿Te gustaron las clases?

> **ENGLISH EQUIVALENT**
> *Did you like the classes?*
> **LITERAL MEANING**
> *Were the classes pleasing to you?*

▶ As the examples show, constructions with **gustar** do not have a direct equivalent in English. The literal meaning of this construction is *to be pleasing to (someone)*, and it requires the use of an indirect object pronoun.

INDIRECT OBJECT PRONOUN	VERB	SUBJECT		SUBJECT	VERB	DIRECT OBJECT
Me	**gusta**	ese champú.		I	like	that shampoo.

▶ In the diagram above, observe how in the Spanish sentence the object being liked **(ese champú)** is really the subject of the sentence. The person who likes the object, in turn, is an indirect object because it answers the question: *To whom is the shampoo pleasing?*

¿Te gusta Juan Carlos?

Me gustan los cafés que tienen música en vivo.

▶ Other verbs in Spanish are used in the same way as **gustar**. Here is a list of the most common ones.

Verbs like gustar

aburrir	to bore	**importar**	to be important to; to matter
encantar	to like very much; to love (inanimate objects)	**interesar**	to be interesting to; to interest
faltar	to lack; to need	**molestar**	to bother; to annoy
fascinar	to fascinate; to like very much	**quedar**	to be left over; to fit (clothing)

▶ The most commonly used verb forms of **gustar** and similar verbs are the third person (singular and plural). When the object or person being liked is singular, the singular form (**gusta**) is used. When two or more objects or persons are being liked, the plural form (**gustan**) is used. Observe the following diagram:

| me, te, le, nos, os, les | SINGULAR | encanta / interesó | → | la película / el concierto |
| | PLURAL | importan / fascinaron | → | las vacaciones / los museos de Lima |

▶ To express what someone likes or does not like to do, use an appropriate verb followed by an infinitive. The singular form is used even if there is more than one infinitive.

Nos molesta comer a las nueve. *It bothers us to eat at nine o'clock.*

Les encanta bailar y **cantar** en las fiestas. *They love to dance and sing at parties.*

▶ As you learned in **Lección 2**, the construction a + [*pronoun*] (**a mí, a ti, a usted, a él,** etc.) is used to clarify or to emphasize who is pleased, bored, etc. The construction **a** + [*noun*] can also be used before the indirect object pronoun to clarify or to emphasize who is pleased.

A los turistas les gustó mucho Machu Picchu. *The tourists liked Machu Picchu a lot.*

A ti te gusta cenar en casa, pero **a mí** me aburre. *You like eating dinner at home, but I get bored.*

▶ **¡Atención!** **Mí** (*me*) has an accent mark to distinguish it from the possessive adjective **mi** (*my*).

¡INTÉNTALO! Indica el pronombre de objeto indirecto y la forma del tiempo presente adecuados en cada oración.

fascinar

1. A él _le fascina_ viajar.
2. A mí _me fascina_ bailar.
3. A nosotras _nos fascina_ cantar.
4. A ustedes _les fascina_ leer.
5. A ti _te fascina_ correr y patinar.
6. A ellos _les fascinan_ los aviones.
7. A mis padres _les fascina_ caminar.
8. A usted _le fascina_ jugar al tenis.
9. A mi esposo y a mí _nos fascina_ dormir.
10. A Alberto _le fascina_ dibujar y pintar.
11. A todos _nos/les fascina_ opinar.
12. A Pili _le fascinan_ los sombreros.

aburrir

1. A ellos _les aburren_ los deportes.
2. A ti _te aburren_ las películas.
3. A usted _le aburren_ los viajes.
4. A mí _me aburren_ las revistas.
5. A Jorge y a Luis _les aburren_ los perros.
6. A nosotros _nos aburren_ las vacaciones.
7. A ustedes _les aburre_ el béisbol.
8. A Marcela _le aburren_ los libros.
9. A mis amigos _les aburren_ los museos.
10. A ella _le aburre_ el ciclismo.
11. A Omar _le aburre_ ir de compras.
12. A ti y a mí _nos aburre_ el baile.

Teaching Tips

• Write a model sentence on the board such as those found in the examples. Ex: **A Carlos le encanta la pasta dental *Crest*.** Then change the noun and ask volunteers to say the new sentence. Ex: **A nosotros (A nosotros nos encanta la pasta dental *Crest*.)**

• Ask students about their preferences, using verbs that follow the pattern of **gustar**. Ex: **A mí me encantan las lenguas, pero me aburren las matemáticas. ¿Qué les interesa a ustedes? ¿Qué les aburre?**

• Point out the third bullet on this page. Give students some sample phrases to complete. Ex: **A ____ me encantan las películas. A ____ les aburre ir de compras. A ____ le gusta viajar.** Explain that some phrases have many possible answers.

TEACHING OPTIONS

Large Group Have the class sit in a circle. Student A begins by saying **Me encanta** and an activity he or she enjoys. Ex: **Me encanta correr.** Student B reports what student A said and adds his or her own favorite activity. **A Frank le encanta correr. A mí me fascina bailar.** Student C reports the preferences of the first two students and adds his or her own, and so forth. This activity may be used with any verb that follows the pattern of **gustar**.

Extra Practice → 🔊 To add an auditory aspect to this grammar presentation, read a series of sentences aloud, pausing for students to write. Ex: **1. A todos en mi familia nos encanta viajar. 2. Nos gusta viajar en avión, pero nos molestan los aviones pequeños. 3. A mi hijo le interesan las culturas latinoamericanas, a mi esposo le encantan los países de Asia y a mí me fascina Europa.** Ask comprehension questions as a follow-up.

Práctica

1 Teaching Tip To simplify, have students identify the subject in each sentence before filling in the blanks.

1 Expansion
←👤→ Have students use the verbs in the activity to write a paragraph describing their own musical tastes.

2 Expansion Repeat the activity using the preterite. Invite students to provide additional details. Ex: **1. A Ramón le molestó el despertador ayer. 2. A nosotros nos encantó esquiar en Vail.**

3 Teaching Tip To challenge students, have them add new items to columns A and C and then complete the activity.

3 Expansion Ask students to create two additional sentences using verbs from column B. Have students read their sentences aloud. After everyone has had a turn, ask the class how many similar or identical sentences they heard and what they were.

1 **Completar** Completa las oraciones con todos los elementos necesarios.

1. ___A___ Adela _le encanta_ (encantar) la música de Tito "El Bambino".
2. A ___mí___ me _interesa_ (interesar) la música de otros países.
3. A mis amigos _les encantan_ (encantar) las canciones (*songs*) de Calle 13.
4. A Juan y ___a___ Rafael no les _molesta_ (molestar) la música alta (*loud*).
5. ___A___ nosotros _nos fascinan_ (fascinar) los grupos de pop latino.
6. ___Al___ señor Ruiz _le interesa_ (interesar) más la música clásica.
7. A ___mí___ me _aburre_ (aburrir) la música clásica.
8. ¿A ___ti___ te _falta_ (faltar) dinero para el concierto de Carlos Santana?
9. No. Ya compré el boleto y _me quedan_ (quedar) cinco dólares.
10. ¿Cuánto dinero te _queda_ (quedar) a ___ti___?

NOTA CULTURAL

Hoy día, la música latina es popular en los EE.UU. gracias a artistas como **Shakira**, de nacionalidad colombiana, y **Tito "El Bambino"**, puertorriqueño. Otros artistas, como **Carlos Santana** y **Gloria Estefan**, difundieron (*spread*) la música latina en los años 60, 70, 80 y 90.

2 **Describir** Mira los dibujos y describe lo que está pasando. Usa los verbos de la lista. *Answers will vary. Suggested answers:*

aburrir	faltar	molestar
encantar	interesar	quedar

1. a Ramón — A Ramón le molesta despertarse temprano.

2. a nosotros — A nosotros nos encanta esquiar.

3. a ti — A ti no te queda bien este vestido. A ti te queda mal/grande este vestido.

4. a Sara — A Sara le interesan los libros de arte moderno.

3 **Gustos** Forma oraciones con los elementos de las columnas. *Answers will vary.*

> **modelo**
> A ti te interesan las ruinas de Machu Picchu.

A	B	C
yo	aburrir	despertarse temprano
tú	encantar	mirarse en el espejo
mi mejor amigo/a	faltar	la música rock
mis amigos y yo	fascinar	las pantuflas rosadas
Bart y Homero Simpson	interesar	la pasta de dientes con menta (*mint*)
Shakira	molestar	las ruinas de Machu Picchu
Antonio Banderas		los zapatos caros

 Practice more at **vhlcentral.com**.

TEACHING OPTIONS

Large Groups Have students stand and form a circle. Begin by tossing a ball to a student, who should state a complaint using a verb like **gustar** (Ex: **Me falta dinero para comprar los libros**) and then toss the ball to another student. The next student should offer advice (Ex: **Debes pedirle dinero a tus padres**) and throw the ball to another person, who will air another complaint. Repeat the activity with positive statements (**Me fascinan las películas**

cómicas) and advice (**Debes ver las películas de Will Ferrell**).
Extra Practice Write sentences like these on the board. Have students copy them and draw faces (☺/☹) to indicate the feelings expressed. Ex: **1. Me encantan las enchiladas verdes. 2. Me aburren las matemáticas. 3. Me fascina la ópera italiana. 4. No me falta dinero para comprar un auto. 5. Me queda pequeño el sombrero.**

Comunicación

4 **Preguntas** En parejas, túrnense para hacer y contestar estas preguntas. Answers will vary.

1. ¿Te gusta levantarte temprano o tarde? ¿Por qué? ¿Y a tu compañero/a de cuarto?
2. ¿Te gusta acostarte temprano o tarde? ¿Y a tu compañero/a de cuarto?
3. ¿Te gusta dormir la siesta?
4. ¿Te encanta acampar o prefieres quedarte en un hotel cuando estás de vacaciones?
5. ¿Qué te gusta hacer en el verano?
6. ¿Qué te fascina de esta universidad? ¿Qué te molesta?
7. ¿Te interesan más las ciencias o las humanidades? ¿Por qué?
8. ¿Qué cosas te aburren?

5 **Completar** Trabajen en parejas. Túrnense para completar estas frases de una manera lógica.

Answers will vary.

1. A mi novio/a le fascina(n)…
2. A mi mejor (*best*) amigo/a no le interesa(n)…
3. A mis padres les importa(n)…
4. A nosotros nos molesta(n)…
5. A mis hermanos les aburre(n)…
6. A mi compañero/a de cuarto le aburre(n)…
7. A los turistas les interesa(n)…
8. A los jugadores profesionales les encanta(n)…
9. A nuestro/a profesor(a) le molesta(n)…
10. A mí me importa(n)…

6 **La residencia** Tú y tu compañero/a de clase son los directores de una residencia estudiantil en Perú. Su profesor(a) les va a dar a cada uno de ustedes las descripciones de cinco estudiantes. Con la información tienen que escoger quiénes van a ser compañeros de cuarto. Después, completen la lista.

Answers will vary.

Síntesis

7 **Situación** Trabajen en parejas para representar los papeles de un(a) cliente/a y un(a) dependiente/a en una tienda de ropa. Usen las instrucciones como guía. Answers will vary.

Dependiente/a	Cliente/a
Saluda al/a la cliente/a y pregúntale en qué le puedes servir.	Saluda al/a la dependiente/a y dile (*tell him/her*) qué quieres comprar y qué colores prefieres.
Pregúntale si le interesan los estilos modernos y empieza a mostrarle la ropa.	Explícale que los estilos modernos te interesan. Escoge las cosas que te interesan.
Habla de los gustos del/de la cliente/a.	Habla de la ropa (me queda(n) bien/mal, me encanta(n)…).
Da opiniones favorables al/a la cliente/a (las botas te quedan fantásticas…).	Decide cuáles son las cosas que te gustan y qué vas a comprar.

4 Teaching Tip Take a class survey of the answers and write the results on the board. Ask volunteers to use verbs like **gustar** to summarize them.

5 Teaching Tip For items that start with **A mi(s)…**, have pairs compare their answers and then report to the class: first, the answers they had in common; then, the answers that differed. Ex: **A mis padres les importan los estudios, pero a los padres de _____ les importa más el dinero.**

6 Teaching Tip Divide the class into pairs and distribute the handouts from the Activity Pack (Activity Pack/Supersite) that correspond to this Information Gap Activity. Give students ten minutes to complete this activity.

6 Expansion
• Have pairs circulate around the classroom and compare their matches.
• Have pairs choose one of the students and write his or her want ad looking for a suitable roommate.

7 Teaching Tip To simplify, have students prepare for their roles by brainstorming a list of words and phrases. Remind students to use the formal register in this conversation.

7 Expansion
Ask pairs to role-play their conversation for the class or have them record it.

Recapitulación

Section Goal

In **Recapitulación**, students will review the grammar concepts from this lesson.

Instructional Resource
Supersite

1 Expansion To challenge students, ask them to provide the infinitive and the third-person singular form of each verb.

2 Teaching Tip To challenge students, eliminate the first sentence in each item. Have them complete the sentences based on context alone and explain which verb is used.

2 Expansion Ask students to create four additional sentences using the preterite of **ser** and **ir**. Then have pairs exchange papers for peer editing.

3 Teaching Tips
• To simplify, have students begin by identifying the subject in each sentence.
• Remind students of the different positions for reflexive pronouns and the need for an infinitive after a phrase like **antes de** or a conjugated verb, such as **puedo**.

S Concepts Diagnostics

Completa estas actividades para repasar los conceptos de gramática que aprendiste en esta lección.

1 Completar Completa la tabla con la forma correcta de los verbos. **6 pts.**

yo	tú	nosotros	ellas
me levanto	te levantas	nos levantamos	se levantan
me afeito	**te afeitas**	nos afeitamos	se afeitan
me visto	te vistes	**nos vestimos**	se visten
me seco	te secas	nos secamos	**se secan**

2 Hoy y ayer Cambia los verbos del presente al pretérito. **5 pts.**

1. Vamos de compras hoy. ___Fuimos___ de compras hoy.
2. Por último, voy a poner el despertador. Por último, ___fui___ a poner el despertador.
3. Lalo es el primero en levantarse. Lalo ___fue___ el primero en levantarse.
4. ¿Vas a tu habitación? ¿___Fuiste___ a tu habitación?
5. Ustedes son profesores. Ustedes ___fueron___ profesores.

3 Reflexivos Completa cada conversación con la forma correcta de los verbos reflexivos. **11 pts.**

TOMÁS Yo siempre (1) ___me baño___ (bañarse) antes de (2) ___acostarme___ (acostarse). Esto me relaja porque no (3) ___me duermo___ (dormirse) fácilmente. Y así puedo (4) ___levantarme___ (levantarse) más tarde. Y tú, ¿cuándo (5) ___te duchas___ (ducharse)?

LETI Pues por la mañana, para poder (6) ___despertarme___ (despertarse).

DAVID ¿Cómo (7) ___se siente___ (sentirse) Pepa hoy?

MARÍA Todavía está enojada.

DAVID ¿De verdad? Ella nunca (8) ___se enoja___ (enojarse) con nadie.

BETO ¿(Nosotros) (9) ___Nos vamos___ (Irse) de esta tienda? Estoy cansado.

SARA Pero antes vamos a (10) ___probarnos___ (probarse) estos sombreros. Si quieres, después (nosotros) (11) ___nos sentamos___ (sentarse) un rato.

RESUMEN GRAMATICAL

7.1 Reflexive verbs *pp. 220–221*

lavarse	
me lavo	nos lavamos
te lavas	os laváis
se lava	se lavan

7.2 Indefinite and negative words *pp. 224–225*

Indefinite words	Negative words
algo	nada
alguien	nadie
alguno/a(s), algún	ninguno/a, ningún
o... o	ni... ni
siempre	nunca, jamás
también	tampoco

7.3 Preterite of ser and ir *p. 228*

▶ The preterite of **ser** and **ir** are identical. Context will determine the meaning.

ser and ir	
fui	fuimos
fuiste	fuisteis
fue	fueron

7.4 Verbs like gustar *pp. 230–231*

aburrir	importar
encantar	interesar
faltar	molestar
fascinar	quedar

	SINGULAR	
me, te, le, nos, os, les	encanta / interesó	la película / el concierto
	PLURAL	
	importan / fascinaron	las vacaciones / los museos

▶ Use the construction a + [*noun/pronoun*] to clarify the person in question.

A mí me encanta ver películas, ¿y a ti?

TEACHING OPTIONS

TPR Divide the class into two teams, **ser** and **ir**, and have them line up. Indicate the first member of each team and call out a sentence in Spanish. Ex: **Fuimos al parque.** The team member whose verb corresponds to the sentence has five seconds to step forward and provide the English translation.
Game Play **Concentración**. On eight note cards, write simple sentences using a variety of reflexive and non-reflexive verbs.

(Ex: **Nos cepillamos los dientes. Lavamos el auto los sábados.**) On another eight cards, draw or paste a picture of an item that matches each description (Ex: a tube of toothpaste, a car). Place the cards face-down in four rows of four. Have pairs take turns selecting two cards; if they match, the pair keeps them, and if not, they return the cards to their original positions. The pair with the most cards at the end wins.

4 **Conversaciones** Completa cada conversación de manera lógica con palabras de la lista. No tienes que usar todas las palabras. **8 pts.**

algo	nada	ningún	siempre
alguien	nadie	nunca	también
algún	ni... ni	o... o	tampoco

1. —¿Tienes __algún__ plan para esta noche?

 —No, prefiero quedarme en casa. Hoy no quiero ver a __nadie__.

 —Yo __también__ me quedo. Estoy muy cansado.

2. —¿Puedo entrar? ¿Hay __alguien__ en el cuarto de baño?

 —Sí. ¡Un momento! Ahora mismo salgo.

3. —¿Puedes prestarme __algo__ para peinarme? No encuentro __ni__ mi cepillo __ni__ mi peine.

 —Lo siento, yo __tampoco__ encuentro los míos (*mine*).

4. —¿Me prestas tu maquillaje?

 —Lo siento, no tengo. __Nunca__ me maquillo.

5 **Oraciones** Forma oraciones completas con los elementos dados (*given*). Usa el presente de los verbos. **8 pts.**

1. David y Juan / molestar / levantarse temprano _A David y a Juan les molesta levantarse temprano._
2. Lucía / encantar / las películas de terror _A Lucía le encantan las películas de terror._
3. todos (nosotros) / importar / la educación _A todos nos importa la educación._
4. tú / aburrir / ver / la televisión _A ti te aburre ver la televisión._

6 **Rutinas** Escribe seis oraciones que describan las rutinas de dos personas que conoces. **12 pts.** _Answers will vary._

> **modelo**
> Mi tía se despierta temprano, pero mi primo...

7 **Adivinanza** Completa la adivinanza con las palabras que faltan y adivina la respuesta. **¡2 puntos EXTRA!**

❝Cuanto más° __te seca__ (*it dries you*),
más se moja°. ❞
¿Qué es? __La toalla__

Cuanto más *The more* se moja *it gets wet*

 Practice more at **vhlcentral.com.**

4 Expansion
Have students write additional mini-conversations using the remaining indefinite and negative words from the word bank.

5 Teaching Tip Remind students to use the personal **a** in their answers.

5 Expansion Give students these sentences as items 5–8: **5.** yo / faltar / dinero (**A mí me falta dinero.**) **6.** Pedro y yo / fascinar / cantar y bailar (**A Pedro y a mí nos fascina cantar y bailar.**) **7.** usted / quedar / muy bien / esas gafas de sol (**A usted le quedan muy bien esas gafas de sol.**) **8.** ¿ / ustedes / interesar / conocer / otros países / ? (**¿A ustedes les interesa conocer otros países?**)

6 Expansion
Have volunteers share their sentences with the class. Encourage classmates to ask them follow-up questions. Ex: **¿Por qué se despierta temprano tu tía?**

7 Expansion
To challenge students, have them work in small groups to create a riddle using grammar and/or vocabulary from this lesson. Have groups share their riddles with the class.

TEACHING OPTIONS

Game Play a game of **Diez Preguntas**. Ask a volunteer to think of a person in the class. Other students get one chance each to ask a question using indefinite and negative words. Ex: **¿Es alguien que siempre llega temprano a clase?**

Extra Practice Have students imagine they are a famous singer or actor. Then have them write eight sentences from the point of view of that person using verbs like **gustar** and indefinite and negative words. Ex: **Jennifer López: Me encanta la música pop pero me aburre la música clásica. Tampoco me interesa la música** *country*.... Ask volunteers to share some of their sentences and see if the rest of the class agrees with their statements.

S **Audio:** Reading
Additional Reading

Section Goals

In **Lectura**, students will:
- learn the strategy of predicting content from the title
- read an e-mail in Spanish

Instructional Resource
Supersite

Estrategia Tell students that they can often predict the content of a newspaper article from its headline. Display or make up several cognate-rich headlines from Spanish newspapers. Ex: **Decenas de miles recuerdan la explosión atómica en Hiroshima; Lanzamiento de musicahoy.net, sitio para profesionales y aficionados a la música; Científicos anuncian que Plutón ya no es planeta.** Ask students to predict the content of each article.

Examinar el texto Survey the class to find out the most common predictions. Were most of them about a positive or negative experience?

Compartir
👤↔👤 Have pairs discuss how they are able to tell what the content will be by looking at the format of the text.

Cognados Discuss how scanning the text for cognates can help predict the content.

Lectura

Antes de leer

Estrategia
Predicting content from the title

Prediction is an invaluable strategy in reading for comprehension. For example, we can usually predict the content of a newspaper article from its headline. We often decide whether to read the article based on its headline. Predicting content from the title will help you increase your reading comprehension in Spanish.

Examinar el texto

Lee el título de la lectura y haz tres predicciones sobre el contenido. Escribe tus predicciones en una hoja de papel. Answers will vary.

Compartir

Comparte tus ideas con un(a) compañero/a de clase.

Cognados

Haz una lista de seis cognados que encuentres en la lectura. Answers will vary.

1. _____
2. _____
3. _____
4. _____
5. _____
6. _____

¿Qué te dicen los cognados sobre el tema de la lectura?

 Practice more at **vhlcentral.com.**

Anterior Siguiente Responder Responder a todos

De:	Guillermo Zamora
Para:	Lupe; Marcos; Sandra; Jorge
Asunto:	¡Qué día!

Hola, chicos:

La semana pasada me di cuenta° de que necesito organizar mejor° mi rutina… pero especialmente debo prepararme mejor para los exámenes. Me falta disciplina, me molesta no tener control de mi tiempo y nunca deseo repetir los eventos de la semana pasada. 🙁

El miércoles pasé todo el día 😴 y toda la noche estudiando para el examen de biología del jueves por la mañana. Me aburre la biología y no empecé a estudiar hasta el día antes del examen. El jueves a las 8, después de no dormir en toda la noche, fui exhausto al examen. Fue difícil, pero afortunadamente° me acordé de todo el material. Esa noche me acosté temprano y dormí mucho. 😴

Me desperté a las 7, y fue extraño° ver a mi compañero de cuarto, Andrés, preparándose para ir a dormir. Como° siempre se enferma°, tiene problemas para dormir y no hablamos mucho, no le comenté nada. Fui al baño a cepillarme los dientes

TEACHING OPTIONS

Extra Practice Ask students to skim the selection and find sentences with verbs like **gustar**. Have them use the **le** and **les** pronouns to rewrite the sentences and talk about **Guillermo** and **Andrés**. Encourage students to say more about the characters by creating additional sentences of the **gustar** type.
Extra Practice Ask heritage speakers if they use e-mail regularly to keep in touch with friends and family in their families' countries

of origin. Ask them if they have ever used Spanish-language versions of popular web-based e-mail applications. Then have the class log onto some Spanish-language versions of e-mail providers, such as Yahoo. Have them list cognates and loan words from English. Then ask students to compare pages from different countries (such as **ar.yahoo.com** and **pe.yahoo.com**) and note any differences in wording.

Reenviar · Marcar · Imprimir · Redactar · Bandeja entrada

para ir a clase. ¿Y Andrés? Él se acostó. "Debe estar enfermo°, ¡otra vez!", pensé.

Mi clase es a las 8, y fue necesario hacer las cosas rápido. Todo empezó a ir mal… eso pasa siempre cuando uno tiene prisa. Cuando busqué mis cosas para el baño, no las encontré. Entonces me duché sin jabón, me cepillé los dientes sin cepillo de dientes y me peiné con las manos. Tampoco encontré ropa limpia y usé la sucia. Rápido, tomé mis libros. ¿Y Andrés? Roncando°… ¡a las 7:50!

Cuando salí corriendo para la clase, la prisa no me permitió ver el campus desierto. Cuando llegué a la clase, no vi a nadie. No vi al profesor ni a los estudiantes. Por último miré mi reloj, y vi la hora. Las 8 en punto… ¡de la noche!

¡Dormí 24 horas!

Guillermo

me di cuenta *I realized* **mejor** *better* **afortunadamente** *fortunately*
extraño *strange* **Como** *Since* **se enferma** *he gets sick* **enfermo** *sick*
Roncando *Snoring*

Después de leer

Seleccionar
Selecciona la respuesta correcta.

1. ¿Quién es el/la narrador(a)? c
 a. Andrés
 b. una profesora
 c. Guillermo
2. ¿Qué le molesta al narrador? b
 a. Le molestan los exámenes de biología.
 b. Le molesta no tener control de su tiempo.
 c. Le molesta mucho organizar su rutina.
3. ¿Por qué está exhausto? c
 a. Porque fue a una fiesta la noche anterior.
 b. Porque no le gusta la biología.
 c. Porque pasó la noche anterior estudiando.
4. ¿Por qué no hay nadie en clase? a
 a. Porque es de noche.
 b. Porque todos están de vacaciones.
 c. Porque el profesor canceló la clase.
5. ¿Cómo es la relación de Guillermo y Andrés? b
 a. Son buenos amigos.
 b. No hablan mucho.
 c. Tienen una buena relación.

Ordenar
Ordena los sucesos de la narración. Utiliza los números del 1 al 9.

a. Toma el examen de biología. __2__
b. No encuentra sus cosas para el baño. __5__
c. Andrés se duerme. __7__
d. Pasa todo el día y toda la noche estudiando para un examen. __1__
e. Se ducha sin jabón. __6__
f. Se acuesta temprano. __3__
g. Vuelve a su cuarto después de las 8 de la noche. __9__
h. Se despierta a las 7 y su compañero de cuarto se prepara para dormir. __4__
i. Va a clase y no hay nadie. __8__

Contestar
Contesta estas preguntas. Answers will vary.

1. ¿Cómo es tu rutina diaria? ¿Muy organizada?
2. ¿Cuándo empiezas a estudiar para los exámenes?
3. ¿Tienes compañero/a de cuarto? ¿Es tu amigo/a?
4. Para comunicarte con tus amigos/as, ¿prefieres el teléfono o el correo electrónico? ¿Por qué?

Perú

El país en cifras

▸ **Área:** 1.285.220 km² (496.224 millas²), *un poco menos que el área de Alaska*
▸ **Población:** 31.197.000
▸ **Capital:** Lima —9.659.000
▸ **Ciudades principales:** Arequipa —848.000, Trujillo, Chiclayo, Callao, Iquitos

SOURCE: Population Division, UN Secretariat

Iquitos es un puerto muy importante en el río Amazonas. Desde Iquitos se envían° muchos productos a otros lugares, incluyendo goma°, nueces°, madera°, arroz°, café y tabaco. Iquitos es también un destino popular para los ecoturistas que visitan la selva°.

▸ **Moneda:** nuevo sol
▸ **Idiomas:** español (oficial); quechua, aimara y otras lenguas indígenas (oficiales en los territorios donde se usan)

Bandera de Perú

Peruanos célebres
▸ **Clorinda Matto de Turner,** escritora (1854–1909)
▸ **César Vallejo,** poeta (1892–1938)
▸ **Javier Pérez de Cuéllar,** diplomático (1920–)
▸ **Mario Vargas Llosa,** escritor (1936–)

Mario Vargas Llosa, Premio Nobel de Literatura 2010

se envían *are shipped* goma *rubber* nueces *nuts* madera *timber* arroz *rice* selva *jungle* Hace más de *More than... ago* grabó *engraved* tamaño *size*

Bailando marinera norteña en Trujillo
Calle en la ciudad de Iquitos
Pasaje Santa Rosa de Lima
Mercado indígena en Cuzco

recursos
WB pp. 83–84 | VM pp. 237–238 | vhlcentral.com Lección 7

¡Increíble pero cierto!
Hace más de° dos mil años la civilización nazca de Perú grabó° más de dos mil kilómetros de líneas en el desierto. Los dibujos sólo son descifrables desde el aire. Uno de ellos es un cóndor del tamaño° de un estadio. Las Líneas de Nazca son uno de los grandes misterios de la humanidad.

Lugares • Lima

Lima es una ciudad moderna y antigua° a la vez°. La Iglesia de San Francisco es notable por su arquitectura barroca colonial. También son fascinantes las exhibiciones sobre los incas en el Museo Oro del Perú y en el Museo Nacional de Antropología y Arqueología. Barranco, el barrio° bohemio de la ciudad, es famoso por su ambiente cultural y sus bares y restaurantes.

Historia • Machu Picchu

A 80 kilómetros al noroeste de Cuzco está Machu Picchu, una ciudad antigua del Imperio inca. Está a una altitud de 2.350 metros (7.710 pies), entre dos cimas° de los Andes. Cuando los españoles llegaron a Perú y recorrieron la región, nunca encontraron Machu Picchu. En 1911, el arqueólogo estadounidense Hiram Bingham la descubrió. Todavía no se sabe ni cómo se construyó° una ciudad a esa altura, ni por qué los incas la abandonaron. Sin embargo°, esta ciudad situada en desniveles° naturales es el ejemplo más conocido de la arquitectura inca.

Artes • La música andina

Machu Picchu aún no existía° cuando se originó la música cautivadora° de las culturas indígenas de los Andes. Los ritmos actuales de la música andina tienen influencias españolas y africanas. Varios tipos de flauta°, entre ellos la quena y la zampoña, caracterizan esta música. En las décadas de los sesenta y los setenta se popularizó un movimiento para preservar la música andina, y hasta° Simon y Garfunkel incorporaron a su repertorio la canción *El cóndor pasa.*

Economía • Llamas y alpacas

Perú se conoce por sus llamas, alpacas, guanacos y vicuñas, todos ellos animales mamíferos° parientes del camello. Estos animales todavía tienen una enorme importancia en la economía del país. Dan lana para exportar a otros países y para hacer ropa, mantas°, bolsas y otros artículos artesanales. La llama se usa también para la carga y el transporte.

 ¿Qué aprendiste? Responde a las preguntas con una oración completa.

1. ¿Qué productos envía Iquitos a otros lugares? Iquitos envía goma, nueces, madera, arroz, café y tabaco a otros lugares.
2. ¿Cuáles son las lenguas oficiales de Perú? Las lenguas oficiales de Perú son el español, el quechua, el aimara y otras lenguas indígenas.
3. ¿Por qué es notable la Iglesia de San Francisco en Lima? Es notable por su arquitectura barroca colonial.
4. ¿Qué información sobre Machu Picchu no se sabe todavía? No se sabe ni cómo se construyó ni por qué la abandonaron.
5. ¿Qué son la quena y la zampoña? Son tipos de flauta.
6. ¿Qué hacen los peruanos con la lana de sus llamas y alpacas? La exportan a otros países y hacen ropa, mantas, bolsas y otros artículos artesanales.

 Conexión Internet Investiga estos temas en **vhlcentral.com**.

1. Investiga la cultura incaica. ¿Cuáles son algunos de los aspectos interesantes de su cultura?
2. Busca información sobre dos artistas, escritores o músicos peruanos y presenta un breve informe a tu clase.

Practice more at **vhlcentral.com**.

antigua *old* **a la vez** *at the same time* **barrio** *neighborhood* **cimas** *summits* **se construyó** *was built* **Sin embargo** *However* **desniveles** *uneven pieces of land* **aún no existía** *didn't exist yet* **cautivadora** *captivating* **flauta** *flute* **hasta** *even* **mamíferos** *mammalian* **mantas** *blankets*

BRASIL

BOLIVIA

Instructional Resources
Supersite: Audio (Textbook & Lab MP3s); Testing Program (Tests, MP3s)
WebSAM
Lab Manual, p. 42

Los verbos reflexivos

acordarse (de) (o:ue)	to remember
acostarse (o:ue)	to go to bed
afeitarse	to shave
bañarse	to bathe; to take a bath
cepillarse el pelo	to brush one's hair
cepillarse los dientes	to brush one's teeth
despedirse (de) (e:i)	to say goodbye (to)
despertarse (e:ie)	to wake up
dormirse (o:ue)	to go to sleep; to fall asleep
ducharse	to shower; to take a shower
enojarse (con)	to get angry (with)
irse	to go away; to leave
lavarse la cara	to wash one's face
lavarse las manos	to wash one's hands
levantarse	to get up
llamarse	to be called; to be named
maquillarse	to put on makeup
peinarse	to comb one's hair
ponerse	to put on
ponerse (+ *adj.*)	to become (+ *adj.*)
preocuparse (por)	to worry (about)
probarse (o:ue)	to try on
quedarse	to stay; to remain
quitarse	to take off
secarse	to dry oneself
sentarse (e:ie)	to sit down
sentirse (e:ie)	to feel
vestirse (e:i)	to get dressed

Palabras de secuencia

antes (de)	before
después	afterwards; then
después (de)	after
durante	during
entonces	then
luego	then
más tarde	later (on)
por último	finally

Palabras afirmativas y negativas

algo	something; anything
alguien	someone; somebody; anyone
alguno/a(s), algún	some; any
jamás	never; not ever
nada	nothing; not anything
nadie	no one; nobody; not anyone
ni... ni	neither... nor
ninguno/a, ningún	no; none; not any
nunca	never; not ever
o... o	either... or
siempre	always
también	also; too
tampoco	neither; not either

En el baño

el baño, el cuarto de baño	bathroom
el champú	shampoo
la crema de afeitar	shaving cream
la ducha	shower
el espejo	mirror
el inodoro	toilet
el jabón	soap
el lavabo	sink
el maquillaje	makeup
la pasta de dientes	toothpaste
la toalla	towel

Verbos similares a gustar

aburrir	to bore
encantar	to like very much; to love (inanimate objects)
faltar	to lack; to need
fascinar	to fascinate; to like very much
importar	to be important to; to matter
interesar	to be interesting to; to interest
molestar	to bother; to annoy
quedar	to be left over; to fit (clothing)

Palabras adicionales

el despertador	alarm clock
las pantuflas	slippers
la rutina diaria	daily routine
por la mañana	in the morning
por la noche	at night
por la tarde	in the afternoon; in the evening

Expresiones útiles	See page 215.

recursos

LM p. 42 — vhlcentral.com Lección 7

Audio: Vocabulary

La comida

Communicative Goals

You will learn how to:
- **Order food in a restaurant**
- **Talk about and describe food**

Lesson Goals

In **Lección 8**, students will be introduced to the following:
- food terms
- meal-related words
- fruits and vegetables native to the Americas
- Spanish chef **Ferran Adrià**
- preterite of stem-changing verbs
- double object pronouns
- converting **le** and **les** to **se** with double object pronouns
- comparisons
- superlatives
- reading for the main idea
- a video about Latin food in the U.S.
- cultural, geographic, and historical information about Guatemala

A primera vista Here are some additional questions you can ask to personalize the photo: **¿Dónde te encanta comer? ¿Por qué? ¿Fuiste a algún lugar especial para comer la semana pasada? ¿Compras comida? ¿Dónde? ¿Prefieres cocinar o comer en un restaurante?**

Teaching Tip Look for these icons for additional communicative practice:

	Interpretive communication
	Presentational communication
	Interpersonal communication

A PRIMERA VISTA
- ¿Dónde está ella?
- ¿Qué hace?
- ¿Es parte de su rutina diaria?
- ¿Qué colores hay en la foto?

INSTRUCTIONAL RESOURCES

Supersite (vhlcentral.com)
Video: *Fotonovela*, Flash cultura*, Panorama cultural**
**Also on DVD*
Audio: Textbook and Lab MP3 Files (*also on CD*)
Activity Pack: Information Gap Activities, games, additional activity handouts

Resources: Textbook Answer Key, WB/VM/LM Answer Key, Scripts, Translations, **Vocabulario adicional**, lesson plans, **Estructura** *PowerPoints*, Overheads
Testing Program: Quizzes, Tests, Exams, MP3s (*also on Test Generator CD*)

Learning Management System (Assignment Task Manager, Gradebook)
WebSAM (online Workbook/Video Manual/Lab Manual)
Workbook/Video Manual
Lab Manual

La comida

Más vocabulario

el/la camarero/a	waiter/waitress
la comida	food; meal
la cuenta	bill
el/la dueño/a	owner; landlord
los entremeses	hors d'oeuvres; appetizers
el menú	menu
el plato (principal)	(main) dish
la propina	tip
la sección de (no) fumar	(non) smoking section
el agua (mineral)	(mineral) water
la bebida	drink
la cerveza	beer
la leche	milk
el refresco	soft drink; soda
el ajo	garlic
las arvejas	peas
los cereales	cereal; grains
los frijoles	beans
el melocotón	peach
el pollo (asado)	(roast) chicken
el queso	cheese
el sándwich	sandwich
el yogur	yogurt
el aceite	oil
la margarina	margarine
la mayonesa	mayonnaise
el vinagre	vinegar
delicioso/a	delicious
sabroso/a	tasty; delicious
saber	to taste; to know
saber a	to taste like

Variación léxica

camarones ⟷ gambas (*Esp.*)

camarero ⟷ mesero (*Amér. L.*), mesonero (*Ven.*), mozo (*Arg., Chile, Urug., Perú*)

refresco ⟷ gaseosa (*Amér. C., Amér. S.*)

Las frutas
la pera
la banana
las uvas
la naranja
el limón
el maíz
Las verduras
la cebolla
la lechuga
el champiñón
la zanahoria
el tomate

recursos

WB pp. 85–86	LM p. 43	🅢 vhlcentral.com Lección 8

Práctica

LAS CARNES

el pollo
el pavo
el jamón
la carne de res

Pescados y mariscos

el atún
la chuleta (de cerdo)
el salmón
los camarones (el camarón)
la langosta

1 Escuchar Indica si las oraciones que vas a escuchar son **ciertas** o **falsas**, según el dibujo. Después, corrige las falsas.

1. Cierta _____
2. Falsa. El hombre compra una naranja.
3. Cierta _____
4. Falsa. El pollo es una carne y la zanahoria es una verdura.
5. Cierta _____
6. Falsa. El hombre y la mujer no compran vinagre.
7. Falsa. La naranja es una fruta.
8. Falsa. La chuleta de cerdo es una carne.
9. Falsa. El limón es una fruta y el jamón es una carne.
10. Cierta _____

2 Seleccionar Paulino y Pilar van a cenar a un restaurante. Escucha la conversación y selecciona la respuesta que mejor completa cada oración.

1. Paulino le pide el ___menú___ (menú / plato) al camarero.
2. El plato del día es (atún / salmón) ___atún___.
3. Pilar ordena ___agua mineral___ (leche / agua mineral) para beber.
4. Paulino quiere un refresco de ___naranja___ (naranja / limón).
5. Paulino hoy prefiere ___la chuleta___ (el salmón / la chuleta).
6. Dicen que la carne en ese restaurante es muy ___sabrosa___ (sabrosa / mala).
7. Pilar come salmón con ___zanahorias___ (zanahorias / champiñones).

3 Identificar Identifica la palabra que no está relacionada con cada grupo.

1. champiñón • cebolla • propina • zanahoria ___propina___
2. camarones • ajo • atún • salmón ___ajo___
3. aceite • leche • refresco • agua mineral ___aceite___
4. jamón • chuleta de cerdo • vinagre • carne de res ___vinagre___
5. cerveza • lechuga • arvejas • frijoles ___cerveza___
6. carne • pescado • mariscos • camarero ___camarero___
7. pollo • naranja • limón • melocotón ___pollo___
8. maíz • queso • tomate • champiñón ___queso___

4 Completar Completa las oraciones con las palabras más lógicas.

1. ¡Me gusta mucho este plato! Sabe ___b___.
 a. mal b. delicioso c. antipático
2. Camarero, ¿puedo ver el ___c___, por favor?
 a. aceite b. maíz c. menú
3. Carlos y yo bebemos siempre agua ___b___.
 a. cómoda b. mineral c. principal
4. El plato del día es ___a___.
 a. pollo asado b. mayonesa c. ajo
5. Margarita es vegetariana. Ella come ___a___.
 a. frijoles b. chuletas c. jamón
6. Mi hermana le da ___c___ a su niña.
 a. ajo b. vinagre c. yogur

TEACHING OPTIONS

Game Add a visual aspect to this vocabulary practice by playing **Concentración**. On eight cards, write names of food items. On another eight cards, draw or paste a picture that matches each food item. Place the cards face-down in four rows of four. In pairs, students select two cards. If the two cards match, the pair keeps them. If the two cards do not match, students replace them in their original positions. The pair with the most cards at the end wins.

Game Play a modified version of **20 Preguntas**. Ask a volunteer to think of a food item from the drawing or vocabulary list. Other students get one chance each to ask a yes/no question until someone guesses the item correctly. Limit attempts to ten questions per item. You may want to write some phrases on the board to cue students' questions. Ex: **¿Es una fruta? ¿Es roja?**

1 Expansion Have students write three additional true/false statements for a partner to answer.

1 Script 1. La langosta está cerca de los camarones. 2. El hombre compra una pera. 3. La lechuga es una verdura. 4. El pollo y la zanahoria son carnes. 5. La cebolla está cerca del maíz. 6. El hombre y la mujer compran vinagre. 7. La naranja es una verdura. 8. La chuleta de cerdo es pescado. 9. El limón y el jamón son frutas. 10. El pavo está cerca del pollo. *Textbook MP3s*

2 Teaching Tip To challenge students, write the cloze sentences on the board without the choices in parentheses. Have students copy them and complete them as they listen.

2 Script PAULINO: Camarero, ¿puedo ver el menú, por favor? CAMARERO: Sí, señor. Hoy el plato del día es atún con champiñones. ¿Qué les traigo de beber? PILAR: Yo voy a beber agua mineral. PA: Para mí, un refresco de naranja, por favor. C: ¿Quieren unos entremeses? El queso es muy sabroso. PA: Sí, queremos el queso. PI: Mira, Paulino, tienen el salmón en salsa de tomate que te gusta. PA: Sí, pero hoy prefiero la chuleta de cerdo. Dicen que la carne en este restaurante sabe deliciosa. PI: Muy bien, entonces yo voy a comer el salmón en salsa de tomate y zanahorias. *Textbook MP3s*

3 Expansion Have students indicate why a particular item does not belong. Ex: **El champiñón, la cebolla y la zanahoria son verduras. La propina no es una verdura.**

4 Expansion Give additional statements. Ex: **Un vegetariano no come ____. (carne)**

Teaching Tips

- 👥↔👥 Involve the class in a conversation about meals. Say: **Por lo general, desayuno sólo café con leche y pan tostado, pero cuando tengo mucha hambre desayuno dos huevos y una salchicha también. ____, ¿qué desayunas tú?** Ask follow-up questions to continue the discussion.

- Use the **Lección 8 Contextos** overheads to assist with this vocabulary presentation.

- Have students look at the illustrations on this page and say: **Mira el desayuno aquí. ¿Qué desayuna esta persona?** Then continue to **el almuerzo** and **la cena.** Have students identify the food items and talk about their eating habits, including what, when, and where they eat. Say: **Yo siempre desayuno en casa, pero casi nunca almuerzo en casa. ¿A qué hora almuerzan ustedes por lo general?**

- Ask students to tell you their favorite foods to eat for each of the three meals. Ex: ____, **¿qué te gusta desayunar?** Introduce additional items such as **los espaguetis, la pasta, la pizza.**

Nota cultural Point out that in Spanish-speaking countries, **el almuerzo,** also called **la comida,** usually is the main meal of the day, consists of several courses, and is enjoyed at a leisurely pace. **La cena** is typically much lighter than **el almuerzo.**

Note: At this point you may want to present *Vocabulario adicional: Más vocabulario relacionado con la comida* from the Supersite.

el desayuno

el jugo (de fruta)

el café

el pan (tostado)

el azúcar

la mantequilla

la salchicha

el huevo

el almuerzo

el té helado

la manzana

la hamburguesa

el pan

las papas/patatas fritas

la cena

la sal

la pimienta

la sopa

el vino tinto

el arroz

la ensalada

los espárragos

el bistec

NOTA CULTURAL

En Guatemala, un desayuno típico incluye huevos, frijoles, fruta, tortillas, jugo y café.

Otros desayunos populares son:

madalenas (*muffins*) España

pan dulce (*assorted breads/pastries*) México

champurradas (*sugar cookies*) Guatemala

gallo pinto (*fried rice and beans*) Costa Rica

perico (*scrambled eggs with peppers and onions*) Venezuela

Más vocabulario

escoger	*to choose*
merendar (e:ie)	*to snack*
probar (o:ue)	*to taste; to try*
recomendar (e:ie)	*to recommend*
servir (e:i)	*to serve*
el té	*tea*
el vino blanco	*white wine*

TEACHING OPTIONS

Small Groups ←👥→ In small groups, have students create a menu for a special occasion. Ask them to describe what they are going to serve for **el entremés, el plato principal,** and **bebidas.** Write **el postre** on the board and explain that it means *dessert.* Explain that in Spanish-speaking countries fresh fruit and cheese are common as dessert, but you may also want to introduce the words **el pastel** (*pie, cake*) and **el helado** (*ice*

cream). Have groups present their menus to the class.

Extra Practice →👥← Add an auditory aspect to this vocabulary presentation. Prepare descriptions of five to seven different meals, with a mix of breakfasts, lunches, and dinners. As you read each description aloud, have students write down what you say as a dictation and then guess the meal it describes.

5 **Completar** Trabaja con un(a) compañero/a de clase para relacionar cada producto con el grupo alimenticio (*food group*) correcto.

> modelo
>
> _La carne_ es del grupo uno.

el aceite	las bananas	los cereales	la leche
el arroz	el café	los espárragos	el pescado
el azúcar	la carne	los frijoles	el vino

1. _La leche_ y el queso son del grupo cuatro.
2. _Los frijoles_ son del grupo ocho.
3. _El pescado_ y el pollo son del grupo tres.
4. _El aceite_ es del grupo cinco.
5. _El azúcar_ es del grupo dos.
6. Las manzanas y _las bananas_ son del grupo siete.
7. _El café_ es del grupo seis.
8. _Los cereales_ son del grupo diez.
9. _Los espárragos_ y los tomates son del grupo nueve.
10. El pan y _el arroz_ son del grupo diez.

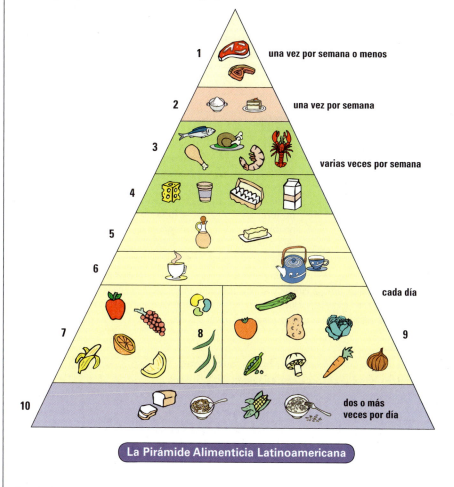

1 — una vez por semana o menos
2 — una vez por semana
3 — varias veces por semana
4
5
6
7 8 9 — cada día
10 — dos o más veces por día

La Pirámide Alimenticia Latinoamericana

5 **Teaching Tip** Ask students to compare foods at the base of the pyramid with those at the top. (The foods at the bottom of the pyramid are essential dietary requirements. Closer to the top, the food items become less essential to daily requirements but help to balance out a diet.)

5 **Expansion**
- Ask additional questions about the **pirámide alimenticia.** Ask: **¿Qué se debe comer varias veces por semana? ¿Qué se debe comer todos los días? ¿Cuáles son los productos que aparecen en el grupo cuatro? ¿Y en el grupo siete?** Get students to have a discussion about what they eat. **¿Comen ustedes carne sólo una vez a la semana o menos? ¿Qué comidas comen ustedes dos veces o más al día? ¿Toman café todos los días?**
- Ask students if they know which food groups and food products comprise the food pyramid used in this country. If you can get a copy of one, bring it to class and have pairs compare similarities and differences between the dietary requirements.

TEACHING OPTIONS

Heritage Speakers Ask heritage speakers to talk about food items or dishes unique to their families' countries of origin that are not typically found in this country. Have them describe what the item looks and tastes like. If the item is a dish, they should briefly describe how to prepare it if they know how to do so. Have the class ask follow-up questions to find out more information, such as when and where these items are eaten.

Extra Practice Have students draw food pyramids based not on what they should eat, but on what they actually do eat. Encourage them to include drawings or magazine cutouts to enhance the visual presentation. Then have students present their pyramids to the class.

6 **¿Cierto o falso?** Consulta la Pirámide Alimenticia Latinoamericana de la página 245 e indica si lo que dice cada oración es **cierto** o **falso**. Si la oración es falsa, escribe las comidas que sí están en el grupo indicado.

modelo

El queso está en el grupo diez.
Falso. En ese grupo están el maíz, el pan, los cereales y el arroz.

1. La manzana, la banana, el limón y las arvejas están en el grupo siete.
 Falso. En ese grupo están la manzana, las uvas, la banana, la naranja y el limón.
2. En el grupo cuatro están los huevos, la leche y el aceite.
 Falso. En ese grupo están los huevos, la leche, el queso y el yogur.
3. El azúcar está en el grupo dos.
 Cierto.
4. En el grupo diez están el pan, el arroz y el maíz.
 Cierto.
5. El pollo está en el grupo uno.
 Falso. En ese grupo están la carne de res/el bistec/el jamón y la chuleta de cerdo.
6. En el grupo nueve están la lechuga, el tomate, las arvejas, la naranja, la papa, los espárragos y la cebolla. Falso. En ese grupo están la lechuga, el tomate, las arvejas, la zanahoria, la papa, los espárragos, la cebolla y el champiñón.
7. El café y el té están en el mismo grupo.
 Cierto.
8. En el grupo cinco está el arroz.
 Falso. En ese grupo están el aceite y la mantequilla.
9. El pescado, el yogur y el bistec están en el grupo tres.
 Falso. En ese grupo están el pescado, el pollo, el pavo, los camarones y la langosta.

7 **Combinar** Combina palabras de cada columna, en cualquier (*any*) orden, para formar diez oraciones lógicas sobre las comidas. Añade otras palabras si es necesario. Answers will vary.

modelo

La camarera nos sirve la ensalada.

A	B	C
el/la camarero/a	almorzar	la sección de no fumar
el/la dueño/a	escoger	el desayuno
mi familia	gustar	la ensalada
mi novio/a	merendar	las uvas
mis amigos y yo	pedir	el restaurante
mis padres	preferir	el jugo de naranja
mi hermano/a	probar	el refresco
el/la médico/a	recomendar	el plato
yo	servir	el arroz

NOTA CULTURAL

El arroz es un alimento básico en el Caribe, Centroamérica y México, entre otros países. Aparece frecuentemente como acompañamiento del plato principal y muchas veces se sirve con frijoles. Un plato muy popular en varios países es **el arroz con pollo** (*chicken and rice casserole*).

8 **Un menú** En parejas, usen la Pirámide Alimenticia Latinoamericana de la página 245 para crear un menú para una cena especial. Incluyan alimentos de los diez grupos para los entremeses, los platos principales y las bebidas. Luego presenten el menú a la clase. Answers will vary.

modelo

La cena especial que vamos a preparar es deliciosa. Primero, hay dos entremeses: ensalada César y sopa de langosta. El plato principal es salmón con salsa de ajo y espárragos. También vamos a servir arroz…

 Practice more at **vhlcentral.com**.

Comunicación

9 **Conversación** En parejas, túrnense para hacerse estas preguntas. *Answers will vary.*

1. ¿Meriendas mucho durante el día? ¿Qué comes? ¿A qué hora?
2. ¿Qué te gusta cenar?
3. ¿A qué hora, dónde y con quién almuerzas?
4. ¿Cuáles son las comidas más (*most*) típicas de tu almuerzo?
5. ¿Desayunas? ¿Qué comes y bebes por la mañana?
6. ¿Qué comida te gusta más? ¿Qué comida no conoces y quieres probar?
7. ¿Comes cada día alimentos de los diferentes grupos de la pirámide alimenticia? ¿Cuáles son las comidas y bebidas más frecuentes en tu dieta?
8. ¿Qué comida recomiendas a tus amigos? ¿Por qué?
9. ¿Eres vegetariano/a? ¿Crees que ser vegetariano/a es una buena idea? ¿Por qué?
10. ¿Te gusta cocinar (*to cook*)? ¿Qué comidas preparas para tus amigos? ¿Para tu familia?

10 **Describir** Con dos compañeros/as de clase, describe las dos fotos, contestando estas preguntas. *Answers will vary.*

▶ ¿Quiénes están en las fotos?

▶ ¿Dónde están?

▶ ¿Qué hora es?

▶ ¿Qué comen y qué beben?

11 **Crucigrama** Tu profesor(a) les va a dar a ti y a tu compañero/a un crucigrama (*crossword puzzle*) incompleto. Tú tienes las palabras que necesita tu compañero/a y él/ella tiene las palabras que tú necesitas. Tienen que darse pistas (*clues*) para completarlo. No pueden decir la palabra; deben utilizar definiciones, ejemplos y frases. *Answers will vary.*

> **modelo**
> **6 vertical:** Es un condimento que normalmente viene con la sal.
> **12 horizontal:** Es una fruta amarilla.

9 **Teaching Tip** Ask the same questions of individual students. Ask other students to restate what their partners answered.

9 **Expansion**
Have pairs join other pairs and share their answers to items 6 and 7. Then have them decide which student is the most adventurous eater of the group and report back to the class. You may wish to teach the phrase **el/la más aventurero/a del grupo,** thus previewing superlatives, which are presented in **Estructura 8.4.**

10 **Expansion**
Add an additional visual aspect to this vocabulary practice. Using magazine pictures that show dining situations, have students describe what is going on: who the people are, what they are eating and drinking, and so forth.

11 **Teaching Tip** Divide the class into pairs and distribute the handouts from the Activity Pack (Activity Pack/Supersite) that correspond to this Information Gap Activity. Give students ten minutes to complete this activity.

11 **Expansion** Have groups create another type of word puzzle, such as a word-find, to share with the class. It should contain additional food- and meal-related vocabulary.

TEACHING OPTIONS

Small Groups In small groups, ask students to prepare brief skits related to food. The skits may involve being in a market, in a restaurant, in a café, inviting people over for dinner, and so forth. Allow groups time to rehearse before performing their skits for the class, who will vote for the most creative one.

Game Play a game of continuous narration. One student begins with: **Voy a preparar** (*name of dish*) **y voy al mercado. Necesito comprar...** and names one food item. The next student then repeats the entire narration, adding another food item. Continue on with various students. When the possibilities for that particular dish are used up, have another student begin with another dish.

Section Goals

In **Fotonovela**, students will:
- receive comprehensible input from free-flowing discourse
- learn functional phrases that preview lesson grammatical structures

Instructional Resources

Supersite/DVD: *Fotonovela*
Supersite: Resources (Scripts, Translations, Answer Keys)
WebSAM
Video Manual, pp. 209–210

Video Recap: Lección 7

Before doing this **Fotonovela** section, review the previous episode with these questions:
1. ¿Adónde va a ir Marissa? (Va al cine.) 2. ¿Qué necesita hacer antes de salir? (Necesita arreglarse el pelo.) 3. ¿Qué está haciendo Felipe en el baño? (Está afeitándose.) 4. ¿Qué planes tiene Jimena? ¿Adónde decide ir al final? (Tiene que estudiar en la biblioteca. Decide ir al cine con Marissa.)

Video Synopsis

Miguel and **Maru** are at one of Mexico City's best restaurants enjoying a romantic dinner to celebrate their second anniversary. **Felipe** and **Juan Carlos** show up and, while **Juan Carlos** distracts the waiter, **Felipe** serves the couple their food, making a mess of the table. To set things right with the manager, they must pay for dinner and wash the dishes.

Teaching Tips

- Have the class predict the content of this episode based on its title and the video stills.
- Quickly review the predictions and ask the class a few questions to help them summarize this episode.

Una cena... romántica

Maru y Miguel quieren tener una cena romántica, pero les espera una sorpresa.

PERSONAJES

MARU MIGUEL

S Video: *Fotonovela*
Record and Compare

1

MARU No sé qué pedir. ¿Qué me recomiendas?

MIGUEL No estoy seguro. Las chuletas de cerdo se ven muy buenas.

MARU ¿Vas a pedirlas?

MIGUEL No sé.

2

MIGUEL ¡Qué bonitos! ¿Quién te los dio?

MARU Me los compró un chico muy guapo e inteligente.

MIGUEL ¿Es tan guapo como yo?

MARU Sí, como tú, guapísimo.

MIGUEL Por nosotros.

MARU Dos años.

3

(El camarero llega a la mesa.)

CAMARERO ¿Les gustaría saber nuestras especialidades del día?

MARU Sí, por favor.

CAMARERO Para el entremés, tenemos ceviche de camarón. De plato principal ofrecemos bistec con verduras a la plancha.

5

6

4

MARU Voy a probar el jamón.

CAMARERO Perfecto. ¿Y para usted, caballero?

MIGUEL Pollo asado con champiñones y papas, por favor.

CAMARERO Excelente.

(en otra parte del restaurante)

JUAN CARLOS Disculpe. ¿Qué me puede contar del pollo? ¿Dónde lo consiguió el chef?

CAMARERO ¡Oiga! ¿Qué está haciendo?

TEACHING OPTIONS

Video Tips General suggestions for using video clips in the classroom can be found on page IAE-10 of this Instructor's Annotated Edition.

Una cena... romántica ➜ Play the first half of the **Una cena... romántica** segment and have the class give you a description of what they see. Write their observations on the board, pointing out any inaccuracies. Repeat this process to allow the class to pick up more details of the plot. Then ask students to use the information they have accumulated to guess what happens in the rest of the segment. Write their predictions on the board. Then play the entire segment and, through discussion, help the class summarize the plot.

CAMARERO **JUAN CARLOS** **FELIPE** **GERENTE**

7

FELIPE Los espárragos están sabrosísimos esta noche. Usted pidió el pollo, señor. Estos champiñones saben a mantequilla.

8

GERENTE ¿Qué pasa aquí, Esteban?

CAMARERO Lo siento señor. Me quitaron la comida.

GERENTE (*a Felipe*) Señor, ¿quién es usted? ¿Qué cree que está haciendo?

9

JUAN CARLOS Felipe y yo les servimos la comida a nuestros amigos. Pero desafortunadamente, salió todo mal.

FELIPE Soy el peor camarero del mundo. ¡Lo siento! Nosotros vamos a pagar la comida.

JUAN CARLOS ¿Nosotros?

10

FELIPE Todo esto fue idea tuya, Juan Carlos.

JUAN CARLOS ¿Mi idea? ¡Felipe! (*al gerente*) Señor, él es más responsable que yo.

GERENTE Tú y tú, vamos.

recursos

VM pp. 209–210
vhlcentral.com Lección 8

Expresiones útiles

Ordering food

¿Qué me recomiendas?
What do you recommend?
Las chuletas de cerdo se ven muy buenas.
The pork chops look good.
¿Les gustaría saber nuestras especialidades del día?
Would you like to hear our specials?
Para el entremés, tenemos ceviche de camarón.
For an appetizer, we have shrimp ceviche.
De plato principal ofrecemos bistec con verduras a la plancha.
For a main course, we have beef with grilled vegetables.
Voy a probar el jamón.
I am going to try the ham.

Describing people and things

¡Qué bonitos! ¿Quién te los dio?
How pretty! Who gave them to you?
Me los compró un chico muy guapo e inteligente.
A really handsome, intelligent guy bought them for me.
¿Es tan guapo como yo?
Is he as handsome as I am?
Sí, como tú, guapísimo.
Yes, like you, gorgeous.
Soy el peor camarero del mundo.
I am the worst waiter in the world.
Él es más responsable que yo.
He is more responsible than I am.

Additional vocabulary

el/la gerente *manager*
caballero *gentleman, sir*

¿Qué pasó?

1 **Escoger** Escoge la respuesta que completa mejor cada oración.

1. Miguel lleva a Maru a un restaurante para __c__.
 a. almorzar b. desayunar c. cenar
2. El camarero les ofrece __b__ como plato principal.
 a. ceviche de camarón b. bistec con verduras a la plancha
 c. pescado, arroz y ensalada
3. Miguel va a pedir __a__.
 a. pollo asado con champiñones y papas
 b. langosta al horno c. pescado con verduras a la mantequilla
4. Felipe les lleva la comida a sus amigos y prueba __c__.
 a. el jamón y los vinos b. el atún y la lechuga
 c. los espárragos y los champiñones

2 **Identificar** Indica quién puede decir estas oraciones.

1. Qué desastre. Soy un camarero muy malo. *Felipe*
2. Les recomiendo el bistec con verduras a la plancha. *camarero*
3. Tal vez escoja las chuletas de cerdo, creo que son muy sabrosas. *Miguel*
4. ¿Qué pasa aquí? *gerente*
5. Dígame las especialidades del día, por favor. *Maru/Miguel*
6. No fue mi idea. Felipe es más responsable que yo. *Juan Carlos*

FELIPE **MARU** **JUAN CARLOS**

CAMARERO **MIGUEL** **GERENTE**

3 **Preguntas** Contesta estas preguntas sobre la **Fotonovela**. *Some answers may vary. Sample answers:*

1. ¿Por qué fueron Maru y Miguel a un restaurante?
 Maru y Miguel fueron a un restaurante para tener una cena romántica.
2. ¿Qué entremés es una de las especialidades del día?
 El ceviche de camarón es el entremés del día.
3. ¿Qué pidió Maru?
 Maru pidió vino, sopa de frijoles y jamón con espárragos.
4. ¿Quiénes van a pagar la cuenta?
 Juan Carlos y Felipe van a pagar la cuenta.

4 **En el restaurante** *Answers will vary.*

1. Prepara con un(a) compañero/a una conversación en la que le preguntas si conoce algún buen restaurante en tu comunidad. Tu compañero/a responde que él/ella sí conoce un restaurante que sirve una comida deliciosa. Lo/La invitas a cenar y tu compañero/a acepta. Determinan la hora para verse en el restaurante y se despiden.

2. Trabaja con un(a) compañero/a para representar los papeles de un(a) cliente/a y un(a) camarero/a en un restaurante. El/La camarero/a te pregunta qué te puede servir y tú preguntas cuál es la especialidad de la casa. El/La camarero/a te dice cuál es la especialidad y te recomienda algunos platos del menú. Tú pides entremeses, un plato principal y escoges una bebida. El/La camarero/a te sirve la comida y tú le das las gracias.

 Practice more at **vhlcentral.com.**

Pronunciación

Audio: Concepts, Activities Record & Compare

ll, ñ, c, and z

pollo	llave	ella	cebolla

Most Spanish speakers pronounce the letter **ll** like the *y* in *yes*.

mañana	señor	baño	niña

The letter **ñ** is pronounced much like the *ny* in *canyon*.

café	colombiano	cuando	rico

Before **a**, **o**, or **u**, the Spanish **c** is pronounced like the *c* in *car*.

cereales	delicioso	conducir	conocer

Before **e** or **i**, the Spanish **c** is pronounced like the *s* in *sit*. (In parts of Spain, **c** before **e** or **i** is pronounced like the *th* in *think*.)

zeta	zanahoria	almuerzo	cerveza

The Spanish **z** is pronounced like the *s* in *sit*. (In parts of Spain, **z** is pronounced like the *th* in *think*.)

Práctica Lee las palabras en voz alta.

1. mantequilla
2. cuñada
3. aceite
4. manzana
5. español
6. cepillo
7. zapato
8. azúcar
9. quince
10. compañera
11. almorzar
12. calle

Oraciones Lee las oraciones en voz alta.

1. Mi compañero de cuarto se llama Toño Núñez. Su familia es de la ciudad de Guatemala y de Quetzaltenango.
2. Dice que la comida de su mamá es deliciosa, especialmente su pollo al champiñón y sus tortillas de maíz.
3. Creo que Toño tiene razón porque hoy cené en su casa y quiero volver mañana para cenar allí otra vez.

Refranes Lee los refranes en voz alta.

Panza llena, corazón contento.[2]

Las apariencias engañan.[1]

1 Looks can be deceiving. 2 A full belly makes a happy heart.

recursos

LM p. 44 — vhlcentral.com Lección 8

Flash CULTURA

Section Goals

In **Cultura**, students will:
- read about fruits and vegetables native to the Americas
- learn food-related terms
- read about Spanish chef **Ferran Adrià**
- read about typical dishes from Peru, Spain, and Colombia

Instructional Resources
Supersite/DVD: *Flash cultura*
Supersite: Resources (Scripts, Translations, Answer Keys)
WebSAM
Video Manual, pp. 281–282

En detalle
Antes de leer Ask students if they can name any fruits and vegetables that are native to North America.

Lectura
- The Aztec and Maya's beverage made of cacao, chile, and other spices was far thicker and more bitter than the hot chocolate most North Americans consume today.
- Point out that many words, such as **tomate, chocolate, aguacate, tamale,** and **mole** are of Nahuatl origin, the language of the Aztecs. **Papa** comes from the Quechua word for *potato.* Explain that **salsa** is a general term for *sauce.*
- Explain that **tamales** are corn dough (usually filled with meat or cheese), which is wrapped in plant leaves or corn husks and steamed. **Arepas** are a type of thin corn cake, and **mole** is a Mexican sauce made of chile peppers, spices, and unsweetened chocolate.

Después de leer Ask students if they were surprised to learn that these foods were unknown to Europe and the rest of the world until about 500 years ago. Ask them to name dishes they would miss without these fruits and vegetables.

1 Expansion Ask students to write three additional true/false statements for a classmate to answer.

EN DETALLE

Additional Reading
Video: *Flash cultura*

NATIONAL connections cultures STANDARDS

Frutas y verduras de América

Imagínate una pizza sin salsa° de tomate o una hamburguesa sin papas fritas. Ahora piensa que quieres ver una película, pero las palomitas de maíz° y el chocolate no existen. ¡Qué mundo° tan insípido°! Muchas de las comidas más populares del mundo tienen ingredientes esenciales que son originarios del continente llamado Nuevo Mundo. Estas frutas y verduras no fueron introducidas en Europa sino hasta° el siglo° XVI.

El tomate, por ejemplo, era° usado como planta ornamental cuando llegó por primera vez a Europa porque pensaron que era venenoso°. El maíz, por su parte, era ya la base de la comida de muchos países latinoamericanos muchos siglos antes de la llegada de los españoles.

La papa fue un alimento° básico para los incas. Incluso consiguieron deshidratarla para almacenarla° por largos períodos de tiempo. El cacao (planta con la que se hace el chocolate) fue muy importante para los aztecas y los mayas. Ellos usaban sus semillas° como moneda° y como ingrediente de diversas salsas. También las molían° para preparar una bebida, mezclándolas° con agua ¡y con chile! El aguacate°, la guayaba°, la papaya, la piña y el maracuyá (o fruta de la pasión) son otros ejemplos de frutas originarias de América que son hoy día conocidas en todo el mundo.

Mole

> **¿En qué alimentos encontramos estas frutas y verduras?**
>
> **Tomate:** pizza, ketchup, salsa de tomate, sopa de tomate
>
> **Maíz:** palomitas de maíz, tamales, tortillas, arepas (Colombia y Venezuela), pan
>
> **Papa:** papas fritas, frituras de papa°, puré de papas°, sopa de papas, tortilla de patatas (España)
>
> **Cacao:** mole (México), chocolatinas°, cereales, helados°, tartas°
>
> **Aguacate:** guacamole (México), coctel de camarones, sopa de aguacate, nachos, enchiladas hondureñas

salsa *sauce* palomitas de maíz *popcorn* mundo *world* insípido *flavorless* hasta *until* siglo *century* era *was* venenoso *poisonous* alimento *food* almacenarla *to store it* semillas *seeds* moneda *currency* las molían *they used to grind them* mezclándolas *mixing them* aguacate *avocado* guayaba *guava* frituras de papa *chips* puré de papas *mashed potatoes* chocolatinas *chocolate bars* helados *ice cream* tartas *cakes*

ACTIVIDADES

1 **¿Cierto o falso?** Indica si lo que dicen las oraciones es cierto o falso. Corrige la información falsa.

1. El tomate se introdujo a Europa como planta ornamental. **Cierto.**
2. Los incas sólo consiguieron almacenar las papas por poco tiempo. **Falso.** Los incas pudieron almacenar las papas por largo tiempo.
3. Los aztecas y los mayas usaron las papas como moneda. **Falso.** Los aztecas y los mayas usaron las semillas de cacao como moneda.
4. El maíz era una comida poco popular en Latinoamérica. **Falso.** El maíz era muy popular en Latinoamérica.
5. El aguacate era el alimento básico de los incas. **Falso.** La papa era el alimento básico de los incas.
6. En México se hace una salsa con chocolate. **Cierto.**
7. El aguacate, la guayaba, la papaya, la piña y el maracuyá son originarios de América. **Cierto.**
8. Las arepas se hacen con cacao. **Falso.** Las arepas se hacen con maíz.
9. El aguacate es un ingrediente del cóctel de camarones. **Cierto.**
10. En España hacen una tortilla con papas. **Cierto.**

TEACHING OPTIONS

Game Have students make a *Bingo* card of fruits and vegetables mentioned in **Contextos** and on page 252, with one "free" square in the middle. Draw cards with different dishes and call them out. Have students cover the square on their card of the fruit or vegetable that is used in that dish. Ex: **tortilla de patatas** (Student covers **la papa**). The winner is the first student to fill a row (horizontally, vertically, or diagonally) and yell *¡Bingo!*

Extra Practice ←🔁→ Tell students to imagine they are Europeans who traveled to the Americas 500 years ago and are tasting a fruit or vegetable for the first time. Have them write a letter to a friend or family member describing the look and taste of the fruit or vegetable. Encourage them to use verbs like **gustar** in the letter. You may want to brainstorm a list of possible adjectives on the board for students to use in their descriptions.

Práctica

1 Escoger Escoge la palabra correcta para comparar a dos hermanas muy diferentes. Haz los cambios necesarios.

1. Lucila es más alta y más bonita ___que___ Tita. (de, más, menos, que)
2. Tita es más delgada porque come ___más___ verduras que su hermana. (de, más, menos, que)
3. Lucila es más ___simpática___ que Tita porque es alegre. (listo, simpático, bajo)
4. A Tita le gusta comer en casa. Va a ___menos___ restaurantes que su hermana. (más, menos, que) Es tímida, pero activa. Hace ___más___ ejercicio (*exercise*) que su hermana. (más, tanto, menos) Todos los días toma más ___de___ cinco vasos (*glasses*) de agua mineral. (que, tan, de)
5. Lucila come muchas papas fritas y se preocupa ___menos___ que Tita por comer frutas. (de, más, menos) ¡Son ___tan___ diferentes! Pero se llevan (*they get along*) muy bien. (como, tan, tanto)

2 Emparejar Compara a Mario y a Luis, los novios de Lucila y Tita, completando las oraciones de la columna A con las palabras o frases de la columna B.

A

1. Mario es ___tan interesante___ como Luis.
2. Mario viaja tanto ___como___ Luis.
3. Luis toma ___tantas___ clases de cocina (*cooking*) como Mario.
4. Luis habla ___francés___ tan bien como Mario.
5. Mario tiene tantos ___amigos extranjeros___ como Luis.
6. ¡Qué casualidad (*coincidence*)! Mario y Luis también son hermanos, pero no hay tanta ___diferencia___ entre ellos como entre Lucila y Tita.

B

tantas
diferencia
tan interesante
amigos extranjeros
como
francés

3 Oraciones Combina elementos de las columnas A, B y C para hacer comparaciones. Escribe oraciones completas. Answers will vary.

> **modelo**
> Arnold Schwarzenegger tiene tantos autos como Jennifer Aniston.
> Jennifer Aniston es menos musculosa que Arnold Schwarzenegger.

A	B	C
la comida japonesa	costar	la gente de Montreal
el fútbol	saber	la música *country*
Arnold Schwarzenegger	ser	el brócoli
el pollo	tener	el presidente de los EE.UU.
la gente de Vancouver	¿?	la comida italiana
la primera dama (*lady*) de los EE.UU.		el hockey
las universidades privadas		Jennifer Aniston
las espinacas		las universidades públicas
la música rap		la carne de res

Practice more at **vhlcentral.com**.

Irregular comparisons

▶ Some adjectives have irregular comparative forms.

Irregular comparative forms

Adjective		Comparative form	
bueno/a	good	mejor	better
malo/a	bad	peor	worse
grande	big	mayor	bigger
pequeño/a	small	menor	smaller
joven	young	menor	younger
viejo/a	old	mayor	older

CONSULTA

To review how descriptive adjectives like **bueno**, **malo**, and **grande** shorten before nouns, see **Estructura 3.1**, p. 82.

▶ When **grande** and **pequeño/a** refer to age, the irregular comparative forms, **mayor** and **menor**, are used. However, when these adjectives refer to size, the regular forms, **más grande** and **más pequeño/a**, are used.

Yo soy **menor** que tú.
I'm younger than you.

Pedí un plato **más pequeño**.
I ordered a smaller dish.

Nuestro hijo es **mayor** que el hijo de los Andrade.
Our son is older than the Andrades' son.

La ensalada de Isabel es **más grande** que ésa.
Isabel's salad is bigger than that one.

▶ The adverbs **bien** and **mal** have the same irregular comparative forms as the adjectives **bueno/a** and **malo/a**.

Julio nada **mejor** que los otros chicos.
Julio swims better than the other boys.

Ellas cantan **peor** que las otras chicas.
They sing worse than the other girls.

¡INTÉNTALO! Escribe el equivalente de las palabras en inglés.

1. Ernesto mira más televisión ___que___ (*than*) Alberto.
2. Tú eres ___menos___ (*less*) simpático que Federico.
3. La camarera sirve ___tanta___ (*as much*) carne como pescado.
4. Recibo ___más___ (*more*) propinas que tú.
5. No estudio ___tanto como___ (*as much as*) tú.
6. ¿Sabes jugar al tenis tan bien ___como___ (*as*) tu hermana?
7. ¿Puedes beber ___tantos___ (*as many*) refrescos como yo?
8. Mis amigos parecen ___tan___ (*as*) simpáticos como ustedes.

recursos

WB
pp. 91–92

LM
p. 47

vhlcentral.com
Lección 8

Teaching Tips

• Practice the differences between **grande—mayor** and **pequeño/a—menor** when referring to age by having two students stand. Ask **E1: ____, ¿cuántos años tienes? (E1: Tengo dieciocho años.)** Then ask **E2: Y tú, ____, ¿cuántos años tienes? (E2: Tengo diecinueve años.)** Now ask the class: **¿Quién es mayor? ¿Y quién es más grande?**

• Ask questions and give examples to practice irregular comparative forms. Ex: (pointing to two students) **Lisa tiene diecinueve años y Shawn tiene veintiún años. ¿Lisa es mayor que Shawn? (No, Lisa es menor que Shawn.)** Then ask questions about celebrities. Ex: **¿Quién canta mejor, Lady Gaga o Rihanna?** Have students state their opinions in complete sentences. Ex: **Lady Gaga canta mejor que Rihanna.**

TEACHING OPTIONS

Large Groups Divide the class into groups of six. Give cards with adjectives listed on page 263 to one group. Give cards with the corresponding irregular comparative form to another group. Students must find their partners. To avoid confusion, make duplicate cards of **mayor** and **menor**.

Pairs Write on the board the heading **Nuestra universidad vs.** [*another nearby university*]. Underneath, write a list of categories.

Ex: **la ciudad universitaria, los estudiantes, las residencias estudiantiles, el equipo de fútbol americano** Have pairs take turns making comparisons about the universities. Encourage them to be creative and to use a variety of comparative forms. Ex: **Los estudiantes de nuestra universidad estudian tanto como los estudiantes de** [*other university*].

Comparisons of equality

▶ This construction is used to make comparisons of equality.

| tan + [adjective / adverb] + como | | tanto/a(s) + [singular noun / plural noun] + como |

¿Es tan guapo como yo?

¿Aquí vienen tantos mexicanos como extranjeros?

▶ **¡Atención!** Note that unlike **tan**, **tanto** acts as an adjective and therefore agrees in number and gender with the noun it modifies.

Estas uvas son **tan ricas como** aquéllas. Yo probé **tantos platos como** él.
These grapes are as tasty as those ones (are). *I tried as many dishes as he did.*

▶ **Tan** and **tanto** can also be used for emphasis, rather than to compare, with these meanings: **tan** *so*, **tanto** *so much*, **tantos/as** *so many*.

¡Tu almuerzo es **tan** grande! ¡Comes **tantas** manzanas!
Your lunch is so big! *You eat so many apples!*

¡Comes **tanto**! ¡Preparan **tantos** platos!
You eat so much! *They prepare so many dishes!*

▶ Comparisons of equality with verbs are formed by placing **tanto como** after the verb. Note that in this construction **tanto** does not change in number or gender.

[verb] + **tanto como**

Tú viajas **tanto como** mi tía. Ellos hablan **tanto como** mis hermanas.
You travel as much as my aunt (does). *They talk as much as my sisters.*

Sabemos **tanto como** ustedes. No estudio **tanto como** Felipe.
We know as much as you (do). *I don't study as much as Felipe (does).*

8.3 # Comparisons Tutorial

 ANTE TODO Both Spanish and English use comparisons to indicate which of two people or things has a lesser, equal, or greater degree of a quality.

Comparisons

menos interesante	más grande	tan sabroso como
less interesting	*bigger*	*as delicious as*

Comparisons of inequality

▶ Comparisons of inequality are formed by placing **más** (*more*) or **menos** (*less*) before adjectives, adverbs, and nouns and **que** (*than*) after them.

$$\text{más/menos} + \boxed{\begin{array}{c}\textit{adjective}\\\textit{adverb}\\\textit{noun}\end{array}} + \text{que}$$

▶ **¡Atención!** Note that while English has a comparative form for short adjectives (*taller*), such forms do not exist in Spanish (**más** alto).

adjectives

Los bistecs son **más caros que** el pollo.	Estas uvas son **menos ricas que** esa pera.
Steaks are more expensive than chicken.	*These grapes are less tasty than that pear.*

adverbs

Me acuesto **más tarde que** tú.	Luis se despierta **menos temprano que** yo.
I go to bed later than you (do).	*Luis wakes up less early than I (do).*

nouns

Juan prepara **más platos que** José.	Susana come **menos carne que** Enrique.
Juan prepares more dishes than José (does).	*Susana eats less meat than Enrique (does).*

La ensalada es menos cara que la sopa.

¿El pollo es más rico que el jamón?

▶ When the comparison involves a numerical expression, **de** is used before the number instead of **que**.

Hay más **de** cincuenta naranjas.	Llego en menos **de** diez minutos.
There are more than fifty oranges.	*I'll be there in less than ten minutes.*

▶ With verbs, this construction is used to make comparisons of inequality.

$$\boxed{\textit{verb}} + \text{más/menos que}$$

Mis hermanos **comen más que** yo.	Arturo **duerme menos que** su padre.
My brothers eat more than I (do).	*Arturo sleeps less than his father (does).*

Comunicación

3 **Contestar** Trabajen en parejas. Túrnense para hacer preguntas, usando las palabras interrogativas **¿Quién?** o **¿Cuándo?**, y para responderlas. Sigan el modelo. Answers will vary.

> **modelo**
>
> nos enseña español
>
> **Estudiante 1:** ¿Quién nos enseña español?
>
> **Estudiante 2:** La profesora Camacho nos lo enseña.

1. te puede explicar (*explain*) la tarea cuando no la entiendes
2. les vende el almuerzo a los estudiantes
3. vas a comprarme boletos (*tickets*) para un concierto
4. te escribe mensajes de texto
5. nos prepara los entremeses
6. me vas a prestar tu computadora
7. te compró esa bebida
8. nos va a recomendar el menú de la cafetería
9. le enseñó español al/a la profesor(a)
10. me vas a mostrar tu casa o apartamento

4 **Preguntas** En parejas, túrnense para hacerse estas preguntas. Answers will vary.

> **modelo**
>
> **Estudiante 1:** ¿Les prestas tu casa a tus amigos? ¿Por qué?
>
> **Estudiante 2:** No, no se la presto a mis amigos porque no son muy responsables.

1. ¿Me prestas tu auto? ¿Ya le prestaste tu auto a otro/a amigo/a?
2. ¿Quién te presta dinero cuando lo necesitas?
3. ¿Les prestas dinero a tus amigos? ¿Por qué?
4. ¿Nos compras el almuerzo a mí y a los otros compañeros de clase?
5. ¿Les mandas correo electrónico a tus amigos? ¿Y a tu familia?
6. ¿Les das regalos a tus amigos? ¿Cuándo?
7. ¿Quién te va a preparar la cena esta noche?
8. ¿Quién te va a preparar el desayuno mañana?

Síntesis

5 **Regalos de Navidad** Tu profesor(a) te va a dar a ti y a un(a) compañero/a una parte de la lista de los regalos de Navidad (*Christmas gifts*) que Berta pidió y los regalos que sus parientes le compraron. Conversen para completar sus listas. Answers will vary.

> **modelo**
>
> **Estudiante 1:** ¿Qué le pidió Berta a su mamá?
>
> **Estudiante 2:** Le pidió una computadora. ¿Se la compró?
>
> **Estudiante 1:** Sí, se la compró.

NOTA CULTURAL

Las fiestas navideñas (*Christmas season*) en los países hispanos duran hasta enero. En muchos lugares celebran **la Navidad** (*Christmas*), pero no se dan los regalos hasta el seis de enero, **el Día de los Reyes Magos** (*Three Kings' Day/The Feast of the Epiphany*).

3 **Teaching Tips**
- To simplify, begin by reading through the items and guiding students in choosing **quién** or **cuándo** for each one.
- Continue the **modelo** exchange by asking: **¿Cuándo nos lo enseña? (Nos lo enseña los lunes, miércoles, jueves y viernes.)**
- To challenge students, have them ask follow-up questions using other interrogative words.

3 **Expansion**
👤↔👤 Ask questions of individual students. Then ask them why they answered as they did. Students answer using double object pronouns. Ex: **¿Quién te enseña español? (Usted me lo enseña.) ¿Por qué? (Usted me lo enseña porque es profesor(a) de español.)**

4 **Teaching Tip** Ask the questions of individual students. Then verify class comprehension by asking other students to repeat the information given.

5 **Teaching Tip** Divide the class into pairs and distribute the handouts from the Activity Pack (Activity Pack/Supersite) that correspond to this Information Gap Activity. Give students ten minutes to complete this activity.

5 **Expansion** Ask students to find a new partner and have them make a list of the gifts they each received for their last birthday or other occasion. Then have students point to each item on their list and, using double object pronouns, tell their partner who bought it for them. Ex: **zapatos nuevos (Me los compró mi prima.)**

TEACHING OPTIONS

Heritage Speakers ←👤→ Ask heritage speakers if they or their families celebrate **el Día de los Reyes Magos** (The Feast of the Epiphany, January 6). Ask them to expand on the information given in the **Nota cultural** box and to tell whether **el Día de los Reyes** is more important for them than **la Navidad**.

Large Groups Divide the class into two groups. Give each member of the first group a strip of paper with a question on it. Ex: **¿Te compró ese suéter tu novia?** Give each member of the second group a piece of paper with an answer to one of the questions. Ex: **Sí, ella me lo compró.** Students must find their partners. Take care not to create sentences that can have more than one match.

Práctica

1 **Responder** Imagínate que trabajas de camarero/a en un restaurante. Responde a los pedidos (*requests*) de estos clientes usando pronombres.

> **modelo**
>
> Sra. Gómez: Una ensalada, por favor.
> Sí, señora. Enseguida *(Right away)* se la traigo.

AYUDA

Here are some other useful expressions:

ahora mismo
right now

inmediatamente
immediately

¡A la orden!
At your service!

¡Ya voy!
I'm on my way!

1. Sres. López: La mantequilla, por favor. Sí, señores. Enseguida se la traigo.
2. Srta. Rivas: Los camarones, por favor. Sí, señorita. Enseguida se los traigo.
3. Sra. Lugones: El pollo asado, por favor. Sí, señora. Enseguida se lo traigo.
4. Tus compañeros/as de cuarto: Café, por favor. Sí, chicos/as. Enseguida se lo traigo.
5. Tu profesor(a) de español: Papas fritas, por favor. Sí, profesor(a). Enseguida se las traigo.
6. Dra. González: La chuleta de cerdo, por favor. Sí, doctora. Enseguida se la traigo.
7. Tu padre: Los champiñones, por favor. Sí, papá. Enseguida te los traigo.
8. Dr. Torres: La cuenta, por favor. Sí, doctor. Enseguida se la traigo.

2 **¿Quién?** La señora Cevallos está planeando una cena. Se pregunta cómo va a resolver ciertas situaciones. En parejas, túrnense para decir lo que ella está pensando. Cambien los sustantivos subrayados por pronombres de objeto directo y hagan los otros cambios necesarios.

> **modelo**
>
> ¡No tengo carne! ¿Quién va a traerme <u>la carne</u> del supermercado? (mi esposo)
> Mi esposo va a traérmela./Mi esposo me la va a traer.

NOTA CULTURAL

Los vinos de Chile son conocidos internacionalmente. **Concha y Toro** es el productor y exportador más grande de vinos de Chile. Las zonas más productivas de vino están al norte de Santiago, en el Valle Central.

1. ¡Las invitaciones! ¿Quién les manda <u>las invitaciones</u> a los invitados (*guests*)?
 (mi hija) Mi hija se las manda.
2. No tengo tiempo de ir a la bodega. ¿Quién me puede comprar <u>el vino</u>?
 (mi hijo) Mi hijo puede comprármelo./Mi hijo me lo puede comprar.
3. ¡Ay! No tengo suficientes platos (*plates*). ¿Quién puede prestarme <u>los platos</u> que necesito? (mi mamá) Mi mamá puede prestármelos./Mi mamá me los puede prestar.
4. Nos falta mantequilla. ¿Quién nos trae <u>la mantequilla</u>?
 (mi cuñada) Mi cuñada nos la trae.
5. ¡Los entremeses! ¿Quién está preparándonos <u>los entremeses</u>?
 (Silvia y Renata) Silvia y Renata están preparándonoslos./Silvia y Renata nos los están preparando.
6. No hay suficientes sillas. ¿Quién nos trae <u>las sillas</u> que faltan?
 (Héctor y Lorena) Héctor y Lorena nos las traen.
7. No tengo tiempo de pedirle el aceite a Mónica. ¿Quién puede pedirle <u>el aceite</u>?
 (mi hijo) Mi hijo puede pedírselo./Mi hijo se lo puede pedir.
8. ¿Quién va a servirles <u>la cena</u> a los invitados?
 (mis hijos) Mis hijos van a servírsela./Mis hijos se la van a servir.
9. Quiero poner buena música de fondo (*background*). ¿Quién me va a recomendar <u>la música</u>? (mi esposo) Mi esposo va a recomendármela./Mi esposo me la va a recomendar.
10. ¡Los postres! ¿Quién va a preparar <u>los postres</u> para los invitados?
 (Sra. Villalba) La señora Villalba va a preparárselos./La señora Villalba se los va a preparar.

 Practice more at **vhlcentral.com.**

1 **Teaching Tip** Do the activity with the whole class, selecting a student to play the role of customer and another to play the role of server for each item.

Ayuda Model the helpful phrases in sentences. Point out that **Ahora mismo, Inmediatamente,** and **Ya** can replace **Enseguida** in the **modelo** for **Actividad 1.**

2 **Expansion**
- For each item, change the subject in parentheses so that students practice different forms of the verbs.
- Add a visual aspect to this activity. Hold up magazine pictures and ask students to state who is doing what to or for whom. Ex: **La señora les muestra la casa a los jóvenes. Se la muestra a los jóvenes.**

TEACHING OPTIONS

Heritage Speakers Ask heritage speakers to talk about a favorite gift they received. Write **regalar** on the board and explain that it means *to give (a gift)*. Have students talk about what they received, who gave it to them (**regalar**), and why. Ask the rest of the class comprehension questions.
Game Play **Concentración**. Write sentences that use double object pronouns on each of eight cards. Ex: **Óscar se las**

muestra. On another eight cards, draw or paste a picture that matches each sentence. Ex: A photo of a boy showing photos to his grandparents. Place the cards face-down in four rows of four. In pairs, students select two cards. If the two cards match, the pair keeps them. If they do not match, students replace them in their original position. The pair with the most cards at the end wins.

▶ Because **se** has multiple meanings, Spanish speakers often clarify to whom the pronoun refers by adding **a usted, a él, a ella, a ustedes, a ellos,** or **a ellas.**

¿El sombrero? Carlos **se** lo vendió **a ella.**
The hat? Carlos sold it to her.

¿Las verduras? Ellos **se** las compran **a usted.**
The vegetables? They are buying them for you.

▶ Double object pronouns are placed before a conjugated verb. With infinitives and present participles, they may be placed before the conjugated verb or attached to the end of the infinitive or present participle.

DOUBLE OBJECT PRONOUNS
Te lo voy a mostrar.

DOUBLE OBJECT PRONOUNS
Voy a mostrár**telo.**

DOUBLE OBJECT PRONOUNS
Nos las están comprando.

DOUBLE OBJECT PRONOUNS
Están comprándo**noslas.**

Mi abuelo **me lo** está leyendo.
Mi abuelo está leyéndo**melo.**

El camarero **se los** va a servir.
El camarero va a servír**selos.**

▶ As you can see above, when double object pronouns are attached to an infinitive or a present participle, an accent mark is added to maintain the original stress.

¡INTÉNTALO! Escribe el pronombre de objeto directo o indirecto que falta en cada oración.

Objeto directo

1. ¿La ensalada? El camarero nos _____la_____ sirvió.
2. ¿El salmón? La dueña me _____lo_____ recomienda.
3. ¿La comida? Voy a prepárarte_____la_____.
4. ¿Las bebidas? Estamos pidiéndose_____las_____.
5. ¿Los refrescos? Te _____los_____ puedo traer ahora.
6. ¿Los platos de arroz? Van a servírnos_____los_____ después.

Objeto indirecto

1. ¿Puedes traerme tu plato? No, no _____te_____ lo puedo traer.
2. ¿Quieres mostrarle la carta? Sí, voy a mostrár_____se_____la ahora.
3. ¿Les serviste la carne? No, no _____se_____ la serví.
4. ¿Vas a leerle el menú? No, no _____se_____ lo voy a leer.
5. ¿Me recomiendas la langosta? Sí, _____te_____ la recomiendo.
6. ¿Cuándo vas a prepararnos la cena? _____Se_____ la voy a preparar en una hora.

recursos

WB pp. 89–90

LM p. 46

vhlcentral.com
Lección 8

8.2 Double object pronouns Tutorial

ANTE TODO In **Lecciones 5** and **6**, you learned that direct and indirect object pronouns replace nouns and that they often refer to nouns that have already been referenced. You will now learn how to use direct and indirect object pronouns together. Observe the following diagram.

Indirect Object Pronouns			Direct Object Pronouns	
me	nos	**+**	lo	los
te	os		la	las
le (se)	les (se)			

▶ When direct and indirect object pronouns are used together, the indirect object pronoun always precedes the direct object pronoun.

I.O.		D.O.		DOUBLE OBJECT PRONOUNS
La camarera **me** muestra **el menú**.	→			La camarera **me lo** muestra.
The waitress shows me the menu.				*The waitress shows it to me.*

I.O.		D.O.		DOUBLE OBJECT PRONOUNS
Nos sirven **los platos**.	→			**Nos los** sirven.
They serve us the dishes.				*They serve them to us.*

I.O.		D.O.		DOUBLE OBJECT PRONOUNS
Maribel **te** pidió **una hamburguesa**.	→			Maribel **te la** pidió.
Maribel ordered a hamburger for you.				*Maribel ordered it for you.*

¿Quién te los dio?

Me los compró un chico muy guapo.

▶ In Spanish, two pronouns that begin with the letter **l** cannot be used together. Therefore, the indirect object pronouns **le** and **les** always change to **se** when they are used with **lo, los, la,** and **las**.

I.O.		D.O.		DOUBLE OBJECT PRONOUNS
Le escribí **la carta**.	→			**Se la** escribí.
I wrote him the letter.				*I wrote it to him.*

I.O.		D.O.		DOUBLE OBJECT PRONOUNS
Les sirvió **los sándwiches**.	→			**Se los** sirvió.
He served them the sandwiches.				*He served them to them.*

Comunicación

3 **El almuerzo** Trabajen en parejas. Túrnense para completar las oraciones de César de una manera lógica. *Answers will vary.*

> **modelo**
>
> Mi compañero de cuarto se despertó temprano, pero yo...
> *Mi compañero de cuarto se despertó temprano, pero yo me desperté tarde.*

1. Yo llegué al restaurante a tiempo, pero mis amigos...
2. Beatriz pidió la ensalada de frutas, pero yo...
3. Yolanda les recomendó el bistec, pero Eva y Paco...
4. Nosotros preferimos las papas fritas, pero Yolanda...
5. El camarero sirvió la carne, pero yo...
6. Beatriz y yo pedimos café, pero Yolanda y Paco...
7. Eva se sintió enferma, pero Paco y yo...
8. Nosotros repetimos postre (*dessert*), pero Eva...
9. Ellos salieron tarde, pero yo...
10. Yo me dormí temprano, pero mi compañero de cuarto...

¡LENGUA VIVA!

In Spanish, the verb **repetir** is used to express *to have a second helping* (of something).

Cuando mi mamá prepara sopa de champiñones, yo siempre repito.

When my mom makes mushroom soup, I always have a second helping.

4 **Entrevista** Trabajen en parejas y túrnense para entrevistar a su compañero/a. *Answers will vary.*

1. ¿Te acostaste tarde o temprano anoche? ¿A qué hora te dormiste? ¿Dormiste bien?
2. ¿A qué hora te despertaste esta mañana? Y, ¿a qué hora te levantaste?
3. ¿A qué hora vas a acostarte esta noche?
4. ¿Qué almorzaste ayer? ¿Quién te sirvió el almuerzo?
5. ¿Qué cenaste ayer?
6. ¿Cenaste en un restaurante recientemente? ¿Con quién(es)?
7. ¿Qué pediste en el restaurante? ¿Qué pidieron los demás?
8. ¿Se durmió alguien en alguna de tus clases la semana pasada? ¿En qué clase?

Síntesis

5 **Describir** En grupos, estudien la foto y las preguntas. Luego, describan la primera (¿y la última?) cita de César y Libertad. *Answers will vary.*

▶ ¿Adónde salieron a cenar?

▶ ¿Qué pidieron?

▶ ¿Les gustó la comida?

▶ ¿Quién prefirió una cena vegetariana? ¿Por qué?

▶ ¿Cómo se vistieron?

▶ ¿De qué hablaron? ¿Les gustó la conversación?

▶ ¿Van a volver a verse? ¿Por qué?

CONSULTA

To review words commonly associated with the preterite, such as **anoche**, see **Estructura 6.3**, p. 191.

3 **Expansion** Have students share their sentences with the class. Ask other students comprehension questions based on what was said.

4 **Expansion**
- To practice the formal register, have students ask you the same questions.
- After interviewing a classmate, have students form new pairs and report on their interviewee's answers.

5 **Expansion**
- ←🔺→ Have groups present their description to the class in the form of a narration.
- 🔺↔🔺 Have students imagine that, in the middle of the date, either **César** or **Libertad** goes to the restroom to make a cellphone call to a friend. In pairs, have students write the dialogue of the phone call. Have a few volunteers role-play their conversations for the class.

Consulta In addition to pointing out words and expressions that may signal the preterite, remind students about transition words that help to move the flow of a narration (Ex: **primero, después, luego, también**).

TEACHING OPTIONS

Pairs 🔺↔🔺 In pairs, have students take turns telling each other about a memorable experience in a restaurant, whether it was a date, dinner with family or friends, and so forth. Encourage students to take notes as their partners narrate. Then have students reveal to the class what their partners told them.

Extra Practice ←🔺→ Add a visual aspect to this grammar practice. As you hold up magazine pictures that show restaurant scenes, have students describe them in the past tense, using the preterite. You may want to write on the board some stem-changing –**ir** verbs that might apply to the situations pictured in the photographs.

Práctica

1 **Completar** Completa estas oraciones para describir lo que pasó anoche en el restaurante El Famoso.

1. Paula y Humberto Suárez llegaron al restaurante El Famoso a las ocho y ___siguieron___ (seguir) al camarero a una mesa en la sección de no fumar.
2. El señor Suárez ___pidió___ (pedir) una chuleta de cerdo.
3. La señora Suárez ___prefirió___ (preferir) probar los camarones.
4. De tomar, los dos ___pidieron___ (pedir) vino tinto.
5. El camarero ___repitió___ (repetir) el pedido (*the order*) para confirmarlo.
6. La comida tardó mucho (*took a long time*) en llegar y los señores Suárez ___se durmieron___ (dormirse) esperando la comida.
7. A las nueve y media el camarero les ___sirvió___ (servir) la comida.
8. Después de comer la chuleta, el señor Suárez ___se sintió___ (sentirse) muy mal.
9. Pobre señor Suárez... ¿por qué no ___pidió___ (pedir) los camarones?

2 **El camarero loco** En el restaurante La Hermosa trabaja un camarero muy distraído que siempre comete muchos errores. Indica lo que los clientes pidieron y lo que el camarero les sirvió.

> **modelo**
> Armando / papas fritas
> Armando pidió papas fritas, pero el camarero le sirvió maíz.

1. nosotros / jugo de naranja Nosotros pedimos jugo de naranja, pero el camarero nos sirvió papas.

2. Beatriz / queso Beatriz pidió queso, pero el camarero le sirvió uvas.

3. tú / arroz Tú pediste arroz, pero el camarero te sirvió arvejas/sopa.

4. Elena y Alejandro / atún Elena y Alejandro pidieron atún, pero el camarero les sirvió camarones/mariscos.

5. usted / agua mineral Usted pidió agua mineral, pero el camarero le sirvió vino tinto.

6. yo / hamburguesa Yo pedí una hamburguesa, pero el camarero me sirvió zanahorias.

 Practice more at **vhlcentral.com.**

Section Goal

In **Estructura 8.1**, students will be introduced to the preterite of stem-changing verbs.

Instructional Resources

Supersite: Audio (Lab MP3 Files); Resources (*PowerPoints*, Activity Pack, Scripts, Answer Keys); Testing Program (Quizzes)
WebSAM
Workbook, pp. 87–88
Lab Manual, p. 45

Teaching Tips

• Review present-tense forms of –ir stem-changing verbs like **pedir** and **dormir**. Also review formation of the preterite of regular –ir verbs, using **escribir** and **recibir**.

• Give model sentences that use these verbs in the preterite, emphasizing stem-changing forms. Ex: **Me dormí temprano anoche, pero mi compañero de cuarto se durmió muy tarde.**

• Ask students questions using stem-changing –ir verbs in the preterite. Ex: **¿Cuántas horas dormiste anoche?** Then have other students summarize the answers. Ex: ____ **durmió seis horas, pero ____ durmió ocho. ____ y ____ durmieron cinco horas.**

• Point out that **morir** means *to die* and provide sample sentences using third-person preterite forms of the verb. Ex: **No tengo bisabuelos. Ya murieron.**

• Other –ir verbs that change their stem vowel in the preterite are **conseguir, despedirse, divertirse, pedir, preferir, repetir, seguir, sentir, sugerir,** and **vestirse**.

8.1 Preterite of stem-changing verbs Tutorial

ANTE TODO As you learned in **Lección 6**, –ar and –er stem-changing verbs have no stem change in the preterite. –Ir stem-changing verbs, however, do have a stem change. Study the following chart and observe where the stem changes occur.

CONSULTA
There are a few high-frequency irregular verbs in the preterite. You will learn more about them in **Estructura 9.1**, p. 286.

Preterite of –ir stem-changing verbs		
	servir (to serve)	**dormir** (to sleep)
SINGULAR FORMS		
yo	serví	dormí
tú	serviste	dormiste
Ud./él/ella	sirvió	durmió
PLURAL FORMS		
nosotros/as	servimos	dormimos
vosotros/as	servisteis	dormisteis
Uds./ellos/ellas	sirvieron	durmieron

▶ Stem-changing –ir verbs, in the preterite only, have a stem change in the third-person singular and plural forms. The stem change consists of either **e** to **i** or **o** to **u**.

(e → i) pedir: p**i**dió, p**i**dieron (o → u) morir (*to die*): m**u**rió, m**u**rieron

¿Quién pidió el jamón?

Yo lo pedí.

¡INTÉNTALO! Cambia cada infinitivo al pretérito.

1. Yo _serví, dormí, pedí..._. (servir, dormir, pedir, preferir, repetir, seguir)
 preferí, repetí, seguí

2. Usted _____. (morir, conseguir, pedir, sentirse, despedirse, vestirse)
 murió, consiguió, pidió, se sintió, se despidió, se vistió

3. Tú _____. (conseguir, servir, morir, pedir, dormir, repetir)
 conseguiste, serviste, moriste, pediste, dormiste, repetiste

4. Ellas _____. (repetir, dormir, seguir, preferir, morir, servir)
 repitieron, durmieron, siguieron, prefirieron, murieron, sirvieron

5. Nosotros _____. (seguir, preferir, servir, vestirse, despedirse, dormirse)
 seguimos, preferimos, servimos, nos vestimos, nos despedimos, nos dormimos

6. Ustedes _____. (sentirse, vestirse, conseguir, pedir, despedirse, dormirse)
 se sintieron, se vistieron, consiguieron, pidieron, se despidieron, se durmieron

7. Él _____. (dormir, morir, preferir, repetir, seguir, pedir)
 durmió, murió, prefirió, repitió, siguió, pidió

recursos

WB
pp. 87–88

LM
p. 45

vhlcentral.com
Lección 8

TEACHING OPTIONS

Large Groups Have the class stand and form a circle. Call out a name or subject pronoun and an infinitive that has a stem change in the preterite (Ex: **Miguel/seguir**). Toss a ball to a student, who will say the correct form (Ex: **siguió**) and toss the ball back to you. Then name another pronoun and infinitive and throw the ball to another student. To challenge students, include some infinitives without a stem change in the preterite.

Pairs Ask students to work in pairs to come up with ten original sentences in which they use the **Ud./él/ella** and **Uds./ellos/ellas** preterite forms of stem-changing –ir verbs. Point out that students should try to use vocabulary items from **Contextos** in their sentences. Ask pairs to share their sentences with the class.

ASÍ SE DICE

La comida

el banano (Col.), el cambur (Ven.), el guineo (Nic.), el plátano (Amér. L., Esp.)	la banana
el choclo (Amér. S., el elote (Méx.), el jojoto (Ven.), la mazorca (Esp.)	*corncob*
las caraotas (Ven.), los porotos (Amér. S.), las habichuelas (P. R.)	los frijoles
el durazno (Méx.)	el melocotón
el jitomate (Méx.)	el tomate

EL MUNDO HISPANO

Algunos platos típicos

- **Ceviche peruano:** Es un plato de pescado crudo° que se marina° en jugo de limón, con sal, pimienta, cebolla y ají°. Se sirve con lechuga, maíz, camote° y papa amarilla.

- **Gazpacho andaluz:** Es una sopa fría típica del sur de España. Se hace con verduras crudas y molidas°: tomate, ají, pepino° y ajo. También lleva pan, sal, aceite y vinagre.

- **Sancocho colombiano:** Es una sopa de pollo, pescado o carne con plátano, maíz, zanahoria, yuca, papas, cebolla, cilantro y ajo. Se sirve con arroz blanco.

crudo *raw* se marina *gets marinated* ají *pepper* camote *sweet potato* molidas *mashed* pepino *cucumber*

PERFIL

Ferran Adrià: arte en la cocina°

¿Qué haces si un amigo te invita a comer croquetas líquidas o paella de *Kellogg's*? ¿Piensas que es una broma°? ¡Cuidado! Puedes estar perdiendo la oportunidad de probar los platos de uno de los chefs más innovadores del mundo°: **Ferran Adrià**.

Este artista de la cocina basa su éxito° en la creatividad y en la química. Adrià modifica combinaciones de ingredientes y juega con contrastes de gustos y sensaciones: frío-caliente, crudo-cocido°, dulce°-salado°... A partir de nuevas técnicas, altera° la textura° de los alimentos sin alterar su sabor°. Sus platos sorprendentes° y divertidos atraen a muchos nuevos chefs a su academia de cocina experimental. Quizás un día compraremos° en el supermercado té esférico°, carne líquida y espuma° de tomate.

Aire de zanahorias

cocina *kitchen* broma *joke* mundo *world* éxito *success* cocido *cooked* dulce *sweet* salado *savory* sabor *taste* sorprendentes *surprising* compraremos *we will buy* esférico *spheric* espuma *foam*

Conexión Internet

¿Qué platos comen los hispanos en los Estados Unidos?

Go to **vhlcentral.com** to find more cultural information related to this **Cultura** section.

ACTIVIDADES

2 Comprensión Empareja cada palabra con su definición.

1. fruta amarilla d
2. sopa típica de Colombia c
3. ingrediente del ceviche e
4. chef español b

a. gazpacho
b. Ferran Adrià
c. sancocho
d. guineo
e. pescado

3 ¿Qué plato especial hay en tu región? Escribe cuatro oraciones sobre un plato típico de tu región. Explica los ingredientes que contiene y cómo se sirve. Answers will vary.

recursos

VM pp. 281–282

vhlcentral.com Lección 8

 Practice more at **vhlcentral.com.**

TEACHING OPTIONS

Large Group Get students out of their seats. Give volunteers each a name of a fruit or vegetable (tell them to keep it secret) and have them stand at different points in the classroom. Then have the rest of the class circulate around the room and ask questions to guess what the volunteer represents. Ex: **¿Es fruta o verdura? ¿De qué color? ¿En qué platos se come?**

Game Play a *Jeopardy*-style game. Divide the class into three teams and have one representative from each team stand up. Read a definition and the first team representative to raise his or her hand must answer in the form of a question. Ex: **Es una sopa típica de Colombia. (¿Qué es el sancocho?)** Each correct answer earns one point. The team with the most points at the end wins.

Así se dice
- Model the pronunciation of each term and have students repeat it.
- To challenge students, add these words to the list: **el chícharo, el guisante** (*pea*); **el hongo, la seta** (*mushroom*); **el melón de agua (Cuba), la patilla (Col.)** (*watermelon*).
- Point out that **plátano** is also used for *plantain*.

Perfil
Time Magazine named **Ferran Adrià** one of the most innovative people of the twenty-first century for his unique food creations and cooking style, known as molecular gastronomy. His meals typically consist of 25 to 30 small courses, allowing guests to try a variety of flavors and textures in one sitting. According to his philosophy, a successful marriage of two flavors is often achieved tapping into the "psychological palate" or memory of different food experiences. In 2006, 2007, and 2008, *Restaurant* magazine named **El Bulli** the number one restaurant in the world.

El mundo hispano
- Point out that in **ceviche**, the fish or seafood gets "cooked" by the acidity of the lemon or lime juice.
- Ask students: **¿Alguna vez probaron el ceviche, el gazpacho o el sancocho? De los ingredientes que tienen, ¿cuáles son originarios de las Américas? ¿Conocen platos similares?**

2 Expansion
Have pairs choose one of the dishes or ingredients from the activity and ask them to create a recipe using the item. Ask volunteers to present their recipes to the class.

3 Expansion
Ask students to create a **menu del día** in which they describe the dishes and suggest complementary dishes (appetizers, drinks, or dessert).

Comunicación

4 **Intercambiar** En parejas, hagan comparaciones sobre diferentes cosas. Pueden usar las sugerencias de la lista u otras ideas. *Answers will vary.*

AYUDA

You can use these adjectives in your comparisons:

bonito/a
caro/a
elegante
interesante
inteligente

modelo

Estudiante 1: Los pollos de *Pollitos del Corral* son muy ricos.
Estudiante 2: Pues yo creo que los pollos de *Rostipollos* son tan buenos como los pollos de *Pollitos del Corral*.
Estudiante 1: Ummm... no tienen tanta mantequilla como los pollos de *Pollitos del Corral*. Tienes razón. Son muy sabrosos.

restaurantes en tu ciudad/pueblo
cafés en tu comunidad
tiendas en tu ciudad/pueblo

periódicos en tu ciudad/pueblo
revistas favoritas
libros favoritos

comidas favoritas
los profesores
los cursos que toman

5 **Conversar** En grupos, túrnense para hacer comparaciones entre ustedes mismos (*yourselves*) y una persona de cada categoría de la lista. *Answers will vary.*

▶ una persona de tu familia
▶ un(a) amigo/a especial
▶ una persona famosa

Síntesis

6 **La familia López** En grupos, túrnense para hablar de Sara, Sabrina, Cristina, Ricardo y David y hacer comparaciones entre ellos. *Answers will vary.*

modelo

Estudiante 1: Sara es tan alta como Sabrina.
Estudiante 2: Sí, pero David es más alto que ellas.
Estudiante 3: En mi opinión, él es guapo también.

Sidebar

4 Expansion Ask pairs of volunteers to present one of their conversations to the class. Then survey the class to see with which of the students the class agrees more.

5 Teaching Tip Model the activity by making a few comparisons between yourself and a celebrity.

5 Expansion Ask a volunteer to share his or her comparisons. Then make comparisons between yourself and the student or yourself and the person the student mentioned. Continue to do this with different students, asking them to make similar comparisons as well.

6 Expansion Add an interpretive aspect to this activity. Have students create a drawing of a family similar to the one on this page. Tell them not to let anyone see their drawings. Then divide the class into pairs and have them describe their drawings to one another. Each student must draw the family described by his or her partner.

TEACHING OPTIONS

Extra Practice Add an auditory aspect to this grammar practice. Prepare short descriptions of five easily recognizable people in which you compare them to other well-known people. Write their names on the board in random order. Then read the descriptions aloud and have students match them to the appropriate name. Ex: **Esta persona trabaja en películas de Hollywood. Es tan buen actor como Tom Cruise, pero tiene** más hijos que él. Su pareja es más bonita que Jennifer **Aniston. (Brad Pitt)**

TPR Give the same types of objects to different students but in different numbers. For example, hand out three books to one student, one book to another, and four to another. Then call on individuals to make comparisons between the students based on the number of objects they have.

8.4 Superlatives Tutorial

ANTE TODO Both English and Spanish use superlatives to express the highest or lowest degree of a quality.

el/la mejor	**el/la peor**	**el/la más alto/a**
the best	*the worst*	*the tallest*

▶ This construction is used to form superlatives. Note that the noun is always preceded by a definite article and that **de** is equivalent to the English *in* or *of*.

$$\boxed{\text{el/la/los/las} + \fbox{noun} + \textbf{más/menos} + \fbox{adjective} + \textbf{de}}$$

▶ The noun can be omitted if the person, place, or thing referred to is clear.

¿El restaurante Las Delicias?
 Es **el más elegante** de la ciudad.
The restaurant Las Delicias?
 It's the most elegant (one) in the city.

Recomiendo el pollo asado.
 Es **el más sabroso** del menú.
I recommend the roast chicken.
 It's the most delicious on the menu.

▶ Here are some irregular superlative forms.

Irregular superlatives

Adjective		Superlative form	
bueno/a	*good*	**el/la mejor**	*(the) best*
malo/a	*bad*	**el/la peor**	*(the) worst*
grande	*big*	**el/la mayor**	*(the) biggest*
pequeño/a	*small*	**el/la menor**	*(the) smallest*
joven	*young*	**el/la menor**	*(the) youngest*
viejo/a	*old*	**el/la mayor**	*(the) eldest*

▶ The absolute superlative is equivalent to *extremely*, *super*, or *very*. To form the absolute superlative of most adjectives and adverbs, drop the final vowel, if there is one, and add **-ísimo/a(s)**.

malo → mal- → **malísimo** mucho → much- → **muchísimo**

¡El bistec está **malísimo**! Comes **muchísimo**.

▶ Note these spelling changes.

ri**c**o → ri**qu**ísimo lar**g**o → lar**gu**ísimo feli**z** → feli**c**ísimo

fá**c**il → fa**c**ilísimo joven → joven**c**ísimo trabajador → trabajador**c**ísimo

¡ATENCIÓN!

While **más** alone means *more*, after **el, la, los** or **las**, it means *most*. Likewise, **menos** can mean *less* or *least*.

Es **el café más rico del** país.

It's the most delicious coffee in the country.

Es **el menú menos caro de** todos éstos.

It is the least expensive menu of all of these.

CONSULTA

The rule you learned in **Estructura 8.3** (p. 263) regarding the use of **mayor/menor** with age, but not with size, is also true with superlative forms.

¡INTÉNTALO! Escribe el equivalente de las palabras en inglés.

1. Marisa es <u>la más inteligente</u> (*the most intelligent*) de todas.
2. Ricardo y Tomás son <u>los menos aburridos</u> (*the least boring*) de la fiesta.
3. Miguel y Antonio son <u>los peores</u> (*the worst*) estudiantes de la clase.
4. Mi profesor de biología es <u>el mayor</u> (*the oldest*) de la universidad.

recursos

WB
pp. 93–94

LM
p. 48

vhlcentral.com
Lección 8

Práctica y Comunicación

1 **El más...** Responde a las preguntas afirmativamente. Usa las palabras entre paréntesis.

> **modelo**
> El cuarto está sucísimo, ¿no? (residencia)
> *Sí, es el más sucio de la residencia.*

1. El almacén Velasco es buenísimo, ¿no? (centro comercial) Sí, es el mejor del centro comercial.
2. La silla de tu madre es comodísima, ¿no? (casa) Sí, es la más cómoda de la casa.
3. Ángela y Julia están nerviosísimas por el examen, ¿no? (clase) Sí, son las más nerviosas de la clase.
4. Jorge es jovencísimo, ¿no? (mis amigos) Sí, es el menor de mis amigos.

2 **Completar** Tu profesor(a) te va a dar una hoja de actividades con descripciones de José Valenzuela Carranza y Ana Orozco Hoffman. Completa las oraciones con las palabras de la lista. Some answers may vary. Suggested answers:

altísima	del	mayor	peor
atlética	guapísimo	mejor	periodista
bajo	la	menor	trabajadorcísimo
de	más	Orozco	Valenzuela

1. José tiene 22 años; es el __menor__ y el más __bajo__ de su familia. Es __guapísimo__ y __trabajadorcísimo__. Es el mejor __periodista__ de la ciudad y el __peor__ jugador de baloncesto.
2. Ana es la más __atlética__ y __la__ mejor jugadora de baloncesto del estado. Es la __mayor__ de sus hermanos (tiene 28 años) y es __altísima__. Estudió la profesión __más__ difícil __de__ todas: medicina.
3. Jorge es el __mejor__ jugador de videojuegos de su familia.
4. Mauricio es el menor de la familia __Orozco__.
5. El abuelo es el __mayor__ de todos los miembros de la familia Valenzuela.
6. Fifí es la perra más antipática __del__ mundo.

3 **Superlativos** Trabajen en parejas para hacer comparaciones. Usen los superlativos. Answers will vary.

> **modelo**
> Angelina Jolie, Bill Gates, Jimmy Carter
> **Estudiante 1:** *Bill Gates es el más rico de los tres.*
> **Estudiante 2:** *Sí, ¡es riquísimo! Y Jimmy Carter es el mayor de los tres.*

1. Guatemala, Argentina, España
2. Jaguar, Prius, Smart
3. la comida mexicana, la comida francesa, la comida árabe
4. Paris Hilton, Meryl Streep, Katie Holmes
5. Ciudad de México, Buenos Aires, Nueva York
6. *Don Quijote de la Mancha, Cien años de soledad, Como agua para chocolate*
7. el fútbol americano, el golf, el béisbol
8. las películas románticas, las películas de acción, las películas cómicas

 Practice more at **vhlcentral.com**.

1 Expansion
- Give these sentences to students as items 5–7: **5. Esas películas son malísimas, ¿no? (Hollywood) (Sí, son las peores de Hollywood.) 6. El centro comercial Galerías es grandísimo, ¿no? (ciudad) (Sí, es el mayor de la ciudad.) 7. Tus bisabuelos son viejísimos, ¿no? (familia) (Sí, son los mayores de mi familia.)**
- To challenge students, after they have completed the activity, have them repeat it by answering in the negative. Ex: **1. No, es el peor del centro comercial.**

2 Teaching Tip Distribute the *Hojas de actividades* (Activity Pack/Supersite) that correspond to this activity.

2 Expansion
In pairs, have students select a family member or a close friend and describe him or her using comparatives and superlatives. Ask volunteers to share their descriptions with the class.

3 Teaching Tips
- To simplify, read through the items with students and, in English, brainstorm points of comparison between the three people or things. For item 6, briefly describe these novels for students who are not familiar with them.
- Encourage students to create as many superlatives as they can for each item. Have volunteers share their most creative statements with the class.

TEACHING OPTIONS

Extra Practice Add an auditory aspect to this grammar practice. Prepare ten superlative sentences and read them aloud slowly, pausing after each sentence to allow students to write the direct opposite. Ex: **Ernesto es el menor de la familia. (Ernesto es el mayor de la familia.)**

Pairs Bring in clothing catalogs and have students work in pairs to create superlative statements about the prices of different items. Ask volunteers to share some of their statements with the class. You may want to have students review clothing-related vocabulary from **Lección 6**.

Recapitulación

 Concepts Diagnostics

Completa estas actividades para repasar los conceptos de gramática que aprendiste en esta lección.

1 Completar Completa la tabla con la forma correcta del pretérito. **9 pts.**

Infinitive	yo	usted	ellos
dormir	dormí	durmió	durmieron
servir	serví	sirvió	sirvieron
vestirse	me vestí	se vistió	se vistieron

2 La cena Completa la conversación con el pretérito de los verbos. **7 pts.**

PAULA ¡Hola, Daniel! ¿Qué tal el fin de semana?

DANIEL Muy bien. Marta y yo (1) conseguimos (conseguir) hacer muchas cosas, pero lo mejor fue la cena del sábado.

PAULA Ah, ¿sí? ¿Adónde fueron?

DANIEL Al restaurante Vistahermosa. Es elegante, así que (nosotros) (2) nos vestimos (vestirse) bien.

PAULA Y, ¿qué platos (3) pidieron (pedir, ustedes)?

DANIEL Yo (4) pedí (pedir) camarones y Marta (5) prefirió (preferir) el pollo. Y al final, el camarero nos (6) sirvió (servir) flan.

PAULA ¡Qué rico!

DANIEL Sí. Pero después de la cena Marta no (7) se sintió (sentirse) bien.

3 Camareros Genaro y Úrsula son camareros en un restaurante. Completa la conversación que tienen con su jefe usando pronombres. **8 pts.**

JEFE Úrsula, ¿le ofreciste agua fría al cliente de la mesa 22?

ÚRSULA Sí, (1) se la ofrecí de inmediato.

JEFE Genaro, ¿los clientes de la mesa 5 te pidieron ensaladas?

GENARO Sí, (2) me las pidieron.

ÚRSULA Genaro, ¿recuerdas si ya me mostraste los vinos nuevos?

GENARO Sí, ya (3) te los mostré.

JEFE Genaro, ¿van a pagarte la cuenta los clientes de la mesa 5?

GENARO Sí, (4) me la van a pagar/van a pagármela ahora mismo.

RESUMEN GRAMATICAL

8.1 Preterite of stem-changing verbs *p. 254*

servir	dormir
serví	dormí
serviste	dormiste
sirvió	durmió
servimos	dormimos
servisteis	dormisteis
sirvieron	durmieron

8.2 Double object pronouns *pp. 257–258*

Indirect Object Pronouns: me, te, le (se), nos, os, les (se)

Direct Object Pronouns: lo, la, los, las

Le escribí la carta. → Se la escribí.

Nos van a servir los platos. → Nos los van a servir./ Van a servírnoslos.

8.3 Comparisons *pp. 261–263*

Comparisons of inequality

más/menos +	adj., adv., n.	+ que

verb + más/menos + que

Comparisons of equality

tan +	adj., adv.	+ como
tanto/a(s) +	noun	+ como

verb + tanto como

Irregular comparative forms

bueno/a	mejor
malo/a	peor
grande	mayor
pequeño/a	menor
joven	menor
viejo/a	mayor

4 **El menú** Observa el menú y sus características.
Completa las oraciones basándote en los elementos dados.
Usa comparativos y superlativos. **14 pts.**

8.4	Superlatives		*p. 266*

el/la/ los/las +	*noun*	+ más/ menos +	*adjective*	+ de

▶ Irregular superlatives follow the same pattern as irregular comparatives.

Ensaladas	*Precio*	*Calorías*
Ensalada de tomates	$9.00	170
Ensalada de mariscos	$12.99	325
Ensalada de zanahorias	$9.00	200
Platos principales		
Pollo con champiñones	$13.00	495
Cerdo con papas	$10.50	725
Atún con espárragos	$18.95	495

1. ensalada de mariscos / otras ensaladas / costar
 La ensalada de mariscos _____cuesta más que_____ las otras ensaladas.
2. pollo con champiñones / cerdo con papas / calorías
 El pollo con champiñones tiene _____menos calorías que_____ el cerdo con papas.
3. atún con espárragos / pollo con champiñones / calorías
 El atún con espárragos tiene _____tantas calorías como_____ el pollo con champiñones.
4. ensalada de tomates / ensalada de zanahorias / caro
 La ensalada de tomates es _____tan cara como_____ la ensalada de zanahorias.
5. cerdo con papas / platos principales / caro
 El cerdo con papas es _____el menos caro de_____ los platos principales.
6. ensalada de zanahorias / ensalada de tomates / costar
 La ensalada de zanahorias _____cuesta tanto como_____ la ensalada de tomates.
7. ensalada de mariscos / ensaladas / caro
 La ensalada de mariscos es _____la más cara de_____ las ensaladas.

5 **Dos restaurantes** ¿Cuál es el mejor restaurante que conoces? ¿Y el peor? Escribe un párrafo de
por lo menos (*at least*) seis oraciones donde expliques por qué piensas así. Puedes hablar de la calidad
de la comida, el ambiente, los precios, el servicio, etc. **12 pts.** Answers will vary.

6 **Adivinanza** Completa la adivinanza y adivina la respuesta. **¡2 puntos EXTRA!**

❝En el campo yo nací°,
mis hermanos son
los _____ajos_____ (*garlic, pl.*),
y aquél que llora° por mí
me está partiendo°
en pedazos°. **❞**
¿Quién soy? _____La cebolla_____

nací *was born* llora *cries* partiendo *cutting* pedazos *pieces*

Practice more at **vhlcentral.com**.

Teaching Tips / Expansion (right column)

4 **Teaching Tips**
- Remind students that the comparative **tanto/a** must agree in gender and number with the noun it modifies.
- To challenge students, have pairs ask each other questions about the menu using comparatives and superlatives. Ex: **¿Qué ensalada cuesta tanto como la ensalada de tomates? (La ensalada de zanahorias cuesta tanto como la ensalada de tomates.)**

5 **Teaching Tip** To help students organize their ideas, have them divide their paper into two columns: **mejor** and **peor**. Under each category, have students list the different reasons why their chosen restaurants are the best or worst.

6 **Expansion**
←👤→ Have students work in small groups to create an original riddle related to food. Have groups read their riddles for the class to guess.

TEACHING OPTIONS

TPR Have students write a celebrity's name, a place, and a thing on separate slips of paper. Collect the papers in three envelopes, separated by category. Then divide the class into two teams, **comparativos** and **superlativos**, and have them line up. Draw out two or three slips of paper (alternate randomly) and read the terms aloud. The corresponding team member has five seconds to step forward and create a logical comparison or superlative statement.

Pairs ←👤→ Have pairs imagine they went to a restaurant where the server mixed up all the orders. Call on pairs to share their experiences, using **pedir** and **servir** as well as double object pronouns. Ex: **Fui a un restaurante italiano. Pedí la pasta primavera. ¡El camarero me sirvió la sopa de mariscos! ¡Y me la sirvió fría! Mi compañero pidió langosta, pero el camarero no se la sirvió. ¡Le sirvió una chuleta de cerdo!**

Section Goals

In **Lectura**, students will:
- learn to identify the main idea in a text
- read a content-rich menu and restaurant review

Instructional Resource
Supersite

Estrategia Tell students that recognizing the main idea of a text will help them unlock the meaning of unfamiliar words and phrases they come across while reading. Tell them to first check the title, where the main idea is often expressed. Then have them read the topic sentence of each paragraph before they read the full text to get a sense of the main idea.

Examinar el texto First, have students scan the menu. Ask how the title and subheadings help predict the content. Ask volunteers to state the meaning of each category of food served. Then have students scan the newspaper article. Ask them how the title and the format (the box with ratings) of the text give clues to the content.

Identificar la idea principal Ask students to read the column heading and the title of the article and predict the subject of the article and the author's purpose. Then have students read the topic sentence of the first paragraph and state the main idea. Finally, have them read the entire paragraph.

Lectura

communication cultures / *NATIONAL STANDARDS*

Antes de leer

Estrategia
Reading for the main idea

As you know, you can learn a great deal about a reading selection by looking at the format and looking for cognates, titles, and subtitles. You can skim to get the gist of the reading selection and scan it for specific information. Reading for the main idea is another useful strategy; it involves locating the topic sentences of each paragraph to determine the author's purpose for writing a particular piece. Topic sentences can provide clues about the content of each paragraph, as well as the general organization of the reading. Your choice of which reading strategies to use will depend on the style and format of each reading selection.

Examinar el texto

En esta sección tenemos dos textos diferentes. ¿Qué estrategias puedes usar para leer la crítica culinaria°? ¿Cuáles son las apropiadas para familiarizarte con el menú? Utiliza las estrategias más eficaces° para cada texto. ¿Qué tienen en común? ¿Qué tipo de comida sirven en el restaurante?

Identificar la idea principal

Lee la primera frase de cada párrafo de la crítica culinaria del restaurante **La feria del maíz**. Apunta° el tema principal de cada párrafo. Luego lee todo el primer párrafo. ¿Crees que el restaurante le gustó al autor de la crítica culinaria? ¿Por qué? Ahora lee la crítica entera. En tu opinión, ¿cuál es la idea principal de la crítica? ¿Por qué la escribió el autor? Compara tus opiniones con las de un(a) compañero/a.

crítica culinaria *restaurant review* eficaces *efficient*
Apunta *Jot down*

 Practice more at **vhlcentral.com**.

MENÚ

Entremeses
Tortilla servida con
- Ajiaceite (chile, aceite) • Ajicomino (chile, comino)

Pan tostado servido con
- Queso frito a la pimienta • Salsa de ajo y mayonesa

Sopas
- Tomate • Cebolla • Verduras • Pollo y huevo
- Carne de res • Mariscos

Entradas
Tomaticán
(tomate, papas, maíz, chile, arvejas y zanahorias)

Tamales
(maíz, azúcar, ajo, cebolla)

Frijoles enchilados
(frijoles negros, carne de cerdo o de res, arroz, chile)

Chilaquil
(tortilla de maíz, queso, hierbas y chile)

Tacos
(tortillas, pollo, verduras y salsa)

Cóctel de mariscos
(camarones, langosta, vinagre, sal, pimienta, aceite)

Postres°
- Plátanos caribeños • Cóctel de frutas al ron°
- Uvate (uvas, azúcar de caña y ron) • Flan napolitano
- Helado° de piña y naranja • Pastel° de yogur

Después de leer

Preguntas

En parejas, contesten estas preguntas sobre la crítica culinaria de **La feria del maíz**.

1. ¿Quién es el dueño y chef de **La feria del maíz**?
 Ernesto Sandoval
2. ¿Qué tipo de comida se sirve en el restaurante?
 tradicional
3. ¿Cuál es el problema con el servicio?
 Se necesitan más camareros.
4. ¿Cómo es el ambiente del restaurante?
 agradable
5. ¿Qué comidas probó el autor? las tortillas, el ajiaceite, la sopa de mariscos, los tamales, los tacos de pollo y los plátanos caribeños
6. ¿Quieren ir ustedes al restaurante **La feria del maíz**? ¿Por qué? Answers will vary.

23F

Gastronomía
Por Eduardo Fernández

La feria del maíz

La feria del maíz
13 calle 4-41 Zona 1
La Antigua, Guatemala
2329912

lunes a sábado
10:30am-11:30pm
domingo 10:00am-10:00pm

Comida ︙︙︙︙︙

Servicio ︙︙︙

Ambiente ︙︙︙︙

Precio ︙︙

Sobresaliente°. En el nuevo restaurante **La feria del maíz** va a encontrar la perfecta combinación entre la comida tradicional y el encanto° de la vieja ciudad de Antigua. Ernesto Sandoval, antiguo jefe de cocina° del famoso restaurante **El fogón**, está teniendo mucho éxito° en su nueva aventura culinaria.

El gerente°, el experimentado José Sierra, controla a la perfección la calidad del servicio. El camarero que me atendió esa noche fue muy amable en todo momento. Sólo hay que comentar que,

debido al éxito inmediato de **La feria del maíz**, se necesitan más camareros para atender a los clientes de una forma más eficaz. En esta ocasión, el mesero se tomó unos veinte minutos en traerme la bebida.

Afortunadamente, no me importó mucho la espera entre plato y plato, pues el ambiente es tan agradable que me sentí como en casa. El restaurante mantiene el estilo colonial de Antigua. Por dentro°, es elegante y rústico a la vez. Cuando el tiempo lo permite, se puede comer también en el patio, donde hay muchas flores.

El servicio de camareros y el ambiente agradable del local pasan a un segundo plano cuando llega la comida, de una calidad extraordinaria. Las tortillas de casa se sirven con un ajiaceite delicioso. La sopa

de mariscos es excelente y los tamales, pues, tengo que confesar que son mejores que los de mi abuelita. También recomiendo los tacos de pollo, servidos con un mole buenísimo. De postre, don Ernesto me preparó su especialidad, unos plátanos caribeños sabrosísimos.

Los precios pueden parecer altos° para una comida tradicional, pero la calidad de los productos con que se cocinan los platos y el exquisito ambiente de **La feria del maíz** garantizan° una experiencia inolvidable°.

Bebidas
- Cerveza negra • Chilate (bebida de maíz, chile y cacao)
- Jugos de fruta • Agua mineral • Té helado
- Vino tinto/blanco • Ron

Postres *Desserts* **ron** *rum* **Helado** *Ice cream* **Pastel** *Cake* **Sobresaliente** *Outstanding* **encanto** *charm* **jefe de cocina** *head chef* **éxito** *success* **gerente** *manager* **Por dentro** *Inside* **altos** *high* **garantizan** *guarantee* **inolvidable** *unforgettable*

Preguntas
- Have students quickly review the article before answering the questions. Suggest that pairs take turns answering them. The student who does not answer a question should find the line of text that contains the answer.
- Give students these questions as items 7–9: **7. ¿Cómo fue el camarero que atendió al crítico? (Fue muy amable, pero estaba muy ocupado con otros clientes del restaurante.) 8. ¿Cuál fue la opinión del crítico con respecto a la comida? (La encontró toda de muy alta calidad.) 9. ¿Cómo son los precios de La feria del maíz? (Son altos, pero la calidad de la comida los justifica.)**

Un(a) guía turístico/a

Tú eres un(a) guía turístico/a en Guatemala. Estás en el restaurante **La feria del maíz** con un grupo de turistas norteamericanos. Ellos no hablan español y quieren pedir de comer, pero necesitan tu ayuda. Lee nuevamente el menú e indica qué error comete cada turista.

1. La señora Johnson es diabética y no puede comer azúcar. Pide sopa de verduras y tamales. No pide nada de postre.
 No debe pedir los tamales porque tienen azúcar.
2. Los señores Petit son vegetarianos y piden sopa de tomate, frijoles enchilados y plátanos caribeños.
 No deben pedir los frijoles enchilados porque tienen carne.

3. El señor Smith, que es alérgico al chocolate, pide tortilla servida con ajiaceite, chilaquil y chilate para beber.
 No debe pedir chilate porque tiene cacao.
4. La adorable hija del señor Smith tiene sólo cuatro años y le gustan mucho las verduras y las frutas naturales. Su papá le pide tomaticán y un cóctel de frutas.
 No debe pedir el cóctel de frutas porque tiene ron.
5. La señorita Jackson está a dieta y pide uvate, flan napolitano y helado.
 No debe pedir postres porque está a dieta.

Un(a) guía turístico/a Have students select an alternative food for the customer to order that would better suit his/her dietary needs.

The Affective Dimension
A source of discomfort in travel can be unfamiliar foods. Tell students that by learning about the foods of a country they are going to visit they can make that part of their visit even more enjoyable.

TEACHING OPTIONS

Large Groups Ask students to review the items in **Un(a) guía turístico/a**, write a conversation, and role-play the scene involving a tour guide eating lunch in a Guatemalan restaurant with several tourists. Have them work in groups of eight to assign the following roles: **camarero, guía turístico/a, la señora Johnson, los señores Petit, el señor Smith, la hija del señor Smith,** and **la señorita Jackson**. Have groups perform their skits for the class.

Variación léxica Tell students that the adjective of place or nationality for Guatemala is **guatemalteco/a**. Guatemalans often use a more colloquial term, **chapín**, as a synonym for **guatemalteco/a**.

Teaching Tips

- Use the **Lección 8 Panorama** overheads to assist with this presentation.
- As students examine the map in their books, point out that Guatemala has three main climatic regions: the tropical Pacific and Caribbean coasts, the highlands (southwest), and jungle lowlands (north). Ask volunteers to read aloud the names of the cities, mountains, and rivers of Guatemala. Point out that indigenous languages are the source of many place names.

El país en cifras As you read about the languages of Guatemala, you might point out that while some Guatemalans are monolingual in either Spanish or a Mayan language, many are bilingual, speaking an indigenous language and Spanish.

¡Increíble pero cierto! Guatemala is internationally renowned for the wealth and diversity of its textile arts. Each village has a traditional, "signature" weaving style that allows others to quickly identify where each beautiful piece comes from.

Guatemala

NATIONAL STANDARDS — connections cultures

El país en cifras

▸ **Área:** 108.890 km² (42.042 millas²), *un poco más pequeño que Tennessee*

▸ **Población:** 16.227.000

▸ **Capital:** Ciudad de Guatemala—1.281.000

▸ **Ciudades principales:** Quetzaltenango, Escuintla, Mazatenango, Puerto Barrios
SOURCE: Population Division, UN Secretariat

▸ **Moneda:** quetzal

▸ **Idiomas:** español (oficial), lenguas mayas, xinca, garífuna
El español es la lengua de un 60 por ciento° de la población; el otro 40 por ciento tiene como lengua materna el xinca, el garífuna o, en su mayoría°, una de las lenguas mayas (cakchiquel, quiché y kekchícomo, entre otras). Una palabra que las lenguas mayas tienen en común es ixim, que significa 'maíz', un cultivo° de mucha importancia en estas culturas.

Bandera de Guatemala

Guatemaltecos célebres

▸ **Carlos Mérida,** pintor (1891–1984)
▸ **Miguel Ángel Asturias,** escritor (1899–1974)
▸ **Margarita Carrera,** poeta y ensayista (1929–)
▸ **Rigoberta Menchú Tum,** activista (1959–), premio Nobel de la Paz° en 1992

por ciento *percent* en su mayoría *most of them* cultivo *crop*
Paz *Peace* telas *fabrics* tinte *dye* aplastados *crushed*
hace... destiñan *keeps the colors from running*

Map labels:
ESTADOS UNIDOS · OCÉANO ATLÁNTICO · GUATEMALA · OCÉANO PACÍFICO · AMÉRICA DEL SUR

Palacio Nacional de la Cultura en la Ciudad de Guatemala

MÉXICO · Sierra de Lacandón · Río Usumacinta · Lago Petén Itzá · Río de la Pasión

Mujeres indígenas limpiando cebollas

Sierra Madre · Lago de Atitlán · Quetzaltenango · Sierra de las Minas · Lago de Izabal · Río Motag[...]

⭐Guatemala · Antigua Guatemala · Mazatenango · Escuintla

Iglesia de la Merced en Antigua Guatemala

EL SALVADOR · Océano Pacífico

recursos
WB pp. 95–96 | VM pp. 239–240 | 🅢 vhlcentral.com Lección 8

¡Increíble pero cierto!

¿Qué "ingrediente" secreto se encuentra en las telas° tradicionales de Guatemala? ¡El mosquito! El excepcional tinte° de estas telas es producto de una combinación de flores y de mosquitos aplastados°. El insecto hace que los colores no se destiñan°. Quizás es por esto que los artesanos representan la figura del mosquito en muchas de sus telas.

Ciudades • **Antigua Guatemala**

Antigua Guatemala fue fundada en 1543. Fue una capital de gran importancia hasta 1773, cuando un terremoto° la destruyó. Sin embargo, conserva el carácter original de su arquitectura y hoy es uno de los centros turísticos del país. Su celebración de la Semana Santa° es, para muchas personas, la más importante del hemisferio.

Naturaleza • **El quetzal**

El quetzal simbolizó la libertad para los antiguos° mayas porque creían° que este pájaro° no podía° vivir en cautiverio°. Hoy el quetzal es el símbolo nacional. El pájaro da su nombre a la moneda nacional y aparece también en los billetes° del país. Desafortunadamente, está en peligro° de extinción. Para su protección, el gobierno mantiene una reserva ecológica especial.

Historia • **Los mayas**

Desde 1500 a.C. hasta 900 d.C., los mayas habitaron gran parte de lo que ahora es Guatemala. Su civilización fue muy avanzada. Los mayas fueron arquitectos y constructores de pirámides, templos y observatorios. También descubrieron° y usaron el cero antes que los europeos, e inventaron un calendario complejo° y preciso.

Artesanía • **La ropa tradicional**

La ropa tradicional de los guatemaltecos se llama *huipil* y muestra el amor° de la cultura maya por la naturaleza. Ellos se inspiran en las flores°, plantas y animales para crear sus diseños° de colores vivos° y formas geométricas. El diseño y los colores de cada *huipil* indican el pueblo de origen y a veces también el sexo y la edad° de la persona que lo lleva.

¿Qué aprendiste? Responde a cada pregunta con una oración completa.

1. ¿Qué significa la palabra *ixim*?
 La palabra *ixim* significa "maíz".
2. ¿Quién es Rigoberta Menchú?
 Rigoberta Menchú es una activista de Guatemala.
3. ¿Qué pájaro representa a Guatemala?
 El quetzal representa a Guatemala.
4. ¿Qué simbolizó el quetzal para los mayas?
 El quetzal simbolizó la libertad para los mayas.
5. ¿Cuál es la moneda nacional de Guatemala?
 La moneda nacional de Guatemala es el quetzal.
6. ¿De qué fueron arquitectos los mayas?
 Los mayas fueron arquitectos de pirámides, templos y observatorios.

7. ¿Qué celebración de la Antigua Guatemala es la más importante del hemisferio para muchas personas? La celebración de la Semana Santa de la Antigua Guatemala es la más importante del hemisferio.
8. ¿Qué descubrieron los mayas antes que los europeos? Los mayas descubrieron el cero antes que los europeos.
9. ¿Qué muestra la ropa tradicional de los guatemaltecos? La ropa muestra el amor a la naturaleza.
10. ¿Qué indica un *huipil* con su diseño y sus colores? Con su diseño y colores, un *huipil* indica el pueblo de origen, el sexo y la edad de la persona.

Conexión Internet Investiga estos temas en **vhlcentral.com**.

1. Busca información sobre Rigoberta Menchú. ¿De dónde es? ¿Qué libros publicó? ¿Por qué es famosa?
2. Estudia un sitio arqueológico de Guatemala para aprender más sobre los mayas y prepara un breve informe para tu clase.

Practice more at **vhlcentral.com**.

terremoto *earthquake* Semana Santa *Holy Week* antiguos *ancient* creían *they believed* pájaro *bird* no podía *couldn't*
cautiverio *captivity* los billetes *bills* peligro *danger* descubrieron *they discovered* complejo *complex* amor *love* flores *flowers*
diseños *designs* vivos *bright* edad *age*

Antigua Guatemala
→🔁← Have students use tour books and the Internet to read more about **Semana Santa** celebrations in this Guatemalan city, usually referred to simply as Antigua. Also, you may want to play the *Panorama cultural* video footage for this lesson that focuses on Antigua and Chichicastenango.

El quetzal Recent conservation efforts in Guatemala, Costa Rica, and other Central American nations have focused on preserving the cloud forests (**bosques nubosos**) that are home to the **quetzal**.

Los mayas Today ethnobotanists work with Mayan traditional healers to learn about medicinal uses of plants of the region.

La ropa tradicional Many indigenous Guatemalans still wear traditional clothing richly decorated with embroidery. The **huipil** is a long, sleeveless tunic worn by women. A distinctively woven **faja**, or waist sash, identifies the town or village each woman comes from.

Conexión Internet Students will find supporting Internet activities and links at **vhlcentral.com**.

TEACHING OPTIONS

Worth Noting Spanish is a second language for more than 40% of Guatemalans. Students may be interested to learn that Guatemala has many bilingual education programs, where native languages are used in addition to Spanish for instructional purposes. There are also many government-sponsored Spanish as a Second Language (SSL) programs, offered through schools and radio or television. Speakers of Guatemala's indigenous languages often encounter problems similar to those found by other learners of Spanish: difficulty with agreement of number and gender.

Las comidas

el/la camarero/a	waiter/waitress
la comida	food; meal
la cuenta	bill
el/la dueño/a	owner; landlord
el menú	menu
la propina	tip
la sección de (no) fumar	(non) smoking section
el almuerzo	lunch
la cena	dinner
el desayuno	breakfast
los entremeses	hors d'oeuvres; appetizers
el plato (principal)	(main) dish
delicioso/a	delicious
rico/a	tasty; delicious
sabroso/a	tasty; delicious

Las frutas

la banana	banana
las frutas	fruits
el limón	lemon
la manzana	apple
el melocotón	peach
la naranja	orange
la pera	pear
la uva	grape

Las verduras

las arvejas	peas
la cebolla	onion
el champiñón	mushroom
la ensalada	salad
los espárragos	asparagus
los frijoles	beans
la lechuga	lettuce
el maíz	corn
las papas/patatas (fritas)	(fried) potatoes; French fries
el tomate	tomato
las verduras	vegetables
la zanahoria	carrot

La carne y el pescado

el atún	tuna
el bistec	steak
los camarones	shrimp
la carne	meat
la carne de res	beef
la chuleta (de cerdo)	(pork) chop
la hamburguesa	hamburger
el jamón	ham
la langosta	lobster
los mariscos	shellfish
el pavo	turkey
el pescado	fish
el pollo (asado)	(roast) chicken
la salchicha	sausage
el salmón	salmon

Otras comidas

el aceite	oil
el ajo	garlic
el arroz	rice
el azúcar	sugar
los cereales	cereal; grains
el huevo	egg
la mantequilla	butter
la margarina	margarine
la mayonesa	mayonnaise
el pan (tostado)	(toasted) bread
la pimienta	black pepper
el queso	cheese
la sal	salt
el sándwich	sandwich
la sopa	soup
el vinagre	vinegar
el yogur	yogurt

Las bebidas

el agua (mineral)	(mineral) water
la bebida	drink
el café	coffee
la cerveza	beer
el jugo (de fruta)	(fruit) juice
la leche	milk
el refresco	soft drink; soda
el té (helado)	(iced) tea
el vino (blanco/ tinto)	(white/red) wine

Verbos

escoger	to choose
merendar (e:ie)	to snack
morir (o:ue)	to die
pedir (e:i)	to order (food)
probar (o:ue)	to taste; to try
recomendar (e:ie)	to recommend
saber	to taste; to know
saber a	to taste like
servir (e:i)	to serve

Las comparaciones

como	like; as
más de (+ number)	more than
más… que	more… than
menos de (+ number)	fewer than
menos… que	less… than
tan… como	as… as
tantos/as… como	as many… as
tanto… como	as much… as
el/la mayor	the eldest
el/la mejor	the best
el/la menor	the youngest
el/la peor	the worst
mejor	better
peor	worse

Expresiones útiles	See page 249.

recursos

LM p. 48 | vhlcentral.com Lección 8

 Audio: Vocabulary

Las fiestas

9

Lesson Goals

In **Lección 9**, students will be introduced to the following:
- terms for parties and celebrations
- words for stages of life and personal relationships
- **Semana Santa** celebrations
- Chile's International Music Festival in **Viña del Mar**
- irregular preterites
- verbs that change meaning in the preterite
- uses of **¿qué?** and **¿cuál?**
- pronouns after prepositions
- recognizing word families
- using a Venn diagram to organize information
- writing a comparative analysis
- using context to infer the meaning of unfamiliar words
- a television commercial about **Las Fiestas Patrias** and other celebrations in Chile
- the short film **Iker pelos tiesos**
- a video about **las fiestas de la calle San Sebastián** in San Juan, Puerto Rico
- cultural, geographic, and economic information about Chile

A primera vista Here are some additional questions you can ask to personalize the photo: **¿Fuiste a una fiesta importante el año pasado? ¿Cuál fue la ocasión? ¿Sirvieron comida en la fiesta? ¿Qué sirvieron? En tu opinión, ¿son divertidos los matrimonios? ¿Por qué?**

Teaching Tip Look for these icons for additional communicative practice:

→👤←	Interpretive communication
←👤→	Presentational communication
👤↔👤	Interpersonal communication

A PRIMERA VISTA
- ¿Se conocen ellos?
- ¿Cómo se sienten, alegres o tristes?
- ¿Está el hombre más contento que la mujer?
- ¿De qué color es su ropa?

INSTRUCTIONAL RESOURCES

Supersite (vhlcentral.com)
Video: **Fotonovela*, Flash cultura*, Anuncio, Cortometraje*, Panorama cultural***
**Also on DVD*
Audio: Textbook and Lab MP3 Files (*also on CD*)
Activity Pack: Information Gap Activities, games, additional activity handouts

Resources: Textbook Answer Key, WB/VM/LM Answer Key, Scripts, Translations, **Vocabulario adicional**, lesson plans, **Estructura** *PowerPoints*, Overheads
Testing Program: Quizzes, Tests, Exams, MP3s (*also on Test Generator CD*)

Learning Management System (Assignment Task Manager, Gradebook)
WebSAM (online Workbook/Video Manual/Lab Manual)
Workbook/Video Manual
Lab Manual

Las fiestas

Más vocabulario

la alegría	happiness
la amistad	friendship
el amor	love
el beso	kiss
la sorpresa	surprise
el aniversario (de bodas)	(wedding) anniversary
la boda	wedding
el cumpleaños	birthday
el día de fiesta	holiday
el divorcio	divorce
el matrimonio	marriage
la Navidad	Christmas
la quinceañera	young woman celebrating her fifteenth birthday
el/la recién casado/a	newlywed
cambiar (de)	to change
celebrar	to celebrate
divertirse (e:ie)	to have fun
graduarse (de/en)	to graduate (from/in)
invitar	to invite
jubilarse	to retire (from work)
nacer	to be born
odiar	to hate
pasarlo bien/mal	to have a good/bad time
reírse (e:i)	to laugh
relajarse	to relax
sonreír (e:i)	to smile
sorprender	to surprise
juntos/as	together
¡Felicidades!/ ¡Felicitaciones!	Congratulations!

Variación léxica

pastel ⟷ torta *(Arg., Col., Venez.)*
comprometerse ⟷ prometerse *(Esp.)*

recursos

WB pp. 97–98	LM p. 49	S vhlcentral.com Lección 9

la pareja

el pastel (de chocolate)

la botella de vino

el flan de caramelo

las galletas

los postres

el champán

los dulces

FELIZ CUMPLEAÑOS

brindar

el invitado

regalar

Relaciones personales

casarse (con)	to get married (to)
comprometerse (con)	to get engaged (to)
divorciarse (de)	to get divorced (from)
enamorarse (de)	to fall in love (with)
llevarse bien/mal (con)	to get along well/ badly (with)
romper (con)	to break up (with)
salir (con)	to go out (with); to date
separarse (de)	to separate (from)
tener una cita	to have a date; to have an appointment

el helado

Práctica

1 **Escuchar** 🎧 Escucha la conversación e indica si las oraciones son **ciertas** o **falsas**.

1. A Silvia no le gusta mucho el chocolate. Falsa.
2. Silvia sabe que sus amigos le van a hacer una fiesta. Falsa.
3. Los amigos de Silvia le compraron un pastel de chocolate. Cierta.
4. Los amigos brindan por Silvia con refrescos. Falsa.
5. Silvia y sus amigos van a comer helado. Cierta.
6. Los amigos de Silvia le van a servir flan y galletas. Falsa.

2 **Ordenar** 🎧 Escucha la narración y ordena las oraciones de acuerdo con los eventos de la vida de Beatriz.

5 a. Beatriz se compromete con Roberto.
4 b. Beatriz se gradúa.
3 c. Beatriz sale con Emilio.
2 d. Sus padres le hacen una gran fiesta.
6 e. La pareja se casa.
1 f. Beatriz nace en Montevideo.

3 **Emparejar** Indica la letra de la frase que mejor completa cada oración.

a. cambió de	d. nos divertimos	g. se llevan bien
b. lo pasaron mal	e. se casaron	h. sonrió
c. nació	f. se jubiló	i. tenemos una cita

1. María y sus compañeras de cuarto _g_. Son buenas amigas.
2. Pablo y yo _d_ en la fiesta. Bailamos y comimos mucho.
3. Manuel y Felipe _b_ en el cine. La película fue muy mala.
4. ¡Tengo una nueva sobrina! Ella _c_ ayer por la mañana.
5. Mi madre _a_ profesión. Ahora es artista.
6. Mi padre _f_ el año pasado. Ahora no trabaja.
7. Jorge y yo _i_ esta noche. Vamos a ir a un restaurante muy elegante.
8. Jaime y Laura _e_ el septiembre pasado. La boda fue maravillosa.

4 **Definiciones** En parejas, definan las palabras y escriban una oración para cada ejemplo. Answers will vary. Suggested answers below.

modelo
romper (con) una pareja termina la relación
Marta rompió con su novio.

1. regalar — dar un regalo
2. helado — una comida fría y dulce
3. pareja — dos personas enamoradas
4. invitado — una persona que va a una fiesta
5. casarse — ellos deciden estar juntos para siempre
6. pasarlo bien — divertirse
7. sorpresa — la persona no sabe lo que va a pasar
8. amistad — la relación entre dos personas que se llevan bien

1 Script (continued) E3: ¿El helado es de la cafetería o lo compraste cerca de la residencia estudiantil? E2: Lo compré en la tienda que está al lado de nuestra residencia. Es mejor que el helado de la cafetería. E1: Psstt… aquí viene Silvia… E1, E2, E3: ¡Sorpresa! ¡Sorpresa, Silvia! ¡Felicidades! E4: ¡Qué sorpresa! E1: Y ahora, ¡brindamos por nuestra amiga! E3: ¿Con qué brindamos? ¿Con el champán? E1: ¡Cómo no! ¡Por nuestra amiga Silvia, la más joven de todos nosotros!
Textbook MP3s

Teaching Tips
• 👥↔👤 Engage students in a conversation about the stages in **Sergio's** life. Say: **Miren al bebé en el primer dibujo. ¡Qué contento está! ¿Qué hace en el segundo dibujo? Está paseando en un triciclo, ¿no? ¿Quiénes se acuerdan de su niñez?** Continue until you have covered all the vocabulary in **Más vocabulario**.
• Make true/false statements and have students correct the false ones. Ex: **Un soltero es un hombre que no está casado. (Cierto.) La vejez ocurre antes de la niñez. (Falso. La vejez ocurre después de la madurez.)**

5 Expansion Have students create original sentences that describe events from **Más vocabulario** on page 276. Their partner has to name the event described. Ex: **Lourdes y Mario llevan diez años de casados. (el aniversario de bodas)**

¡Lengua viva! In the United States, **fiestas de quince años** have become big business. For many immigrants, giving an elaborate party represents a way to affirm both cultural identity and socioeconomic status.

6 Expansion In pairs, have students take turns making statements about celebrities, using the answers. Ex: **La muerte de Heath Ledger fue en el 2008.**

Las etapas de la vida de Sergio

el nacimiento

la niñez

la adolescencia

la juventud

la madurez

la vejez

Más vocabulario

la edad	age
el estado civil	marital status
las etapas de la vida	the stages of life
la muerte	death
casado/a	married
divorciado/a	divorced
separado/a	separated
soltero/a	single
viudo/a	widower/widow

5 Las etapas de la vida Identifica las etapas de la vida que se describen en estas oraciones.

1. Mi abuela se jubiló y se mudó (*moved*) a Viña del Mar. la vejez
2. Mi padre trabaja para una compañía grande en Santiago. la madurez
3. ¿Viste a mi nuevo sobrino en el hospital? Es precioso y ¡tan pequeño! el nacimiento
4. Mi abuelo murió este año. la vejez/la muerte
5. Mi hermana celebró su fiesta de quince años. la adolescencia
6. Mi hermana pequeña juega con muñecas (*dolls*). la niñez

6 Cambiar En parejas, imaginen que son dos hermanos/as de diferentes edades. Cada vez que el/la hermano/a menor dice algo, se equivoca. El/La hermano/a mayor lo/la corrige (*corrects him/her*), cambiando las expresiones subrayadas (*underlined*). Túrnense para ser mayor y menor, decir algo equivocado y corregir.

> **modelo**
> **Estudiante 1:** La niñez es cuando trabajamos mucho.
> **Estudiante 2:** No, te equivocas (*you're wrong*). La madurez es cuando trabajamos mucho.

1. El nacimiento es el fin de la vida. La muerte
2. La juventud es la etapa cuando nos jubilamos. La vejez
3. A los sesenta y cinco años, muchas personas comienzan a trabajar. se jubilan
4. Julián y nuestra prima se divorcian mañana. se casan
5. Mamá odia a su hermana. quiere/se lleva bien con
6. El abuelo murió, por eso la abuela es separada. viuda
7. Cuando te gradúas de la universidad, estás en la etapa de la adolescencia. la juventud
8. Mi tío nunca se casó; es viudo. soltero

🔊 Practice more at **vhlcentral.com.**

NOTA CULTURAL

Viña del Mar es una ciudad en la costa de Chile, situada al oeste de Santiago. Tiene playas hermosas, excelentes hoteles, casinos y buenos restaurantes. El poeta Pablo Neruda pasó muchos años allí.

¡LENGUA VIVA!

The term **quinceañera** refers to a girl who is celebrating her 15th birthday. The party is called **la fiesta de quince años**.

AYUDA

Other ways to contradict someone:

No es verdad.
It's not true.

Creo que no.
I don't think so.

¡Claro que no!
Of course not!

¡Qué va!
No way!

TEACHING OPTIONS

Small Groups 👥↔👤 In small groups, have students perform a skit whose content describes and/or displays a particular stage of life (youth, old age, etc.) or marital status (married, single, divorced). The rest of the class has to try to figure out what the group is displaying.

Game Play a modified version of **20 Preguntas**. Ask a volunteer to think of a famous person. Other students get one chance each to ask a yes/no question until someone guesses the name correctly. Limit attempts to ten questions per famous person. Point out that students can narrow down their selection by using vocabulary about the stages of life and marital status.

Comunicación

7 **Una fiesta** Trabaja con dos compañeros/as para planear una fiesta. Recuerda incluir la siguiente información. *Answers will vary.*

1. ¿Qué tipo de fiesta es? ¿Dónde va a ser? ¿Cuándo va a ser?
2. ¿A quiénes van a invitar?
3. ¿Qué van a comer? ¿Quiénes van a llevar o a preparar la comida?
4. ¿Qué van a beber? ¿Quiénes van a traer las bebidas?
5. ¿Cómo planean entretener a los invitados? ¿Van a bailar o a jugar algún juego?
6. Después de la fiesta, ¿quiénes van a limpiar (*to clean*)?

8 **Encuesta** Tu profesor(a) va a darte una hoja de actividades. Haz las preguntas de la hoja a dos o tres compañeros/as de clase para saber qué actitudes tienen en sus relaciones personales. Luego comparte los resultados de la encuesta con la clase y comenta tus conclusiones. *Answers will vary.*

Preguntas	Nombres	Actitudes
1. ¿Te importa la amistad? ¿Por qué?		
2. ¿Es mejor tener un(a) buen(a) amigo/a o muchos/as amigos/as?		
3. ¿Cuáles son las características que buscas en tus amigos/as?		
4. ¿Tienes novio/a? ¿A qué edad es posible enamorarse?		
5. ¿Deben las parejas hacer todo juntos? ¿Deben tener las mismas opiniones? ¿Por qué?		

¡LENGUA VIVA!

While a **buen(a) amigo/a** is a *good friend*, the term **amigo/a íntimo/a** refers to a *close friend*, or a *very good friend*, without any romantic overtones.

9 **Minidrama** En parejas, consulten la ilustración de la página 278 y luego, usando las palabras de la lista, preparen un minidrama para representar las etapas de la vida de Sergio. Pueden inventar más información sobre su vida. *Answers will vary.*

amor	celebrar	enamorarse	romper
boda	comprometerse	graduarse	salir
cambiar	cumpleaños	jubilarse	separarse
casarse	divorciarse	nacer	tener una cita

7 Teaching Tip To simplify, create a seven-column chart on the board with the headings **Lugar, Fecha y hora, Invitados, Comida, Bebidas, Actividades,** and **Limpieza.** Have groups brainstorm a few items for each category.

7 Expansion
- ←👤→ Ask volunteer groups to describe the party they have just planned.
- ←👤→ Have students make invitations for their party. Ask the class to judge which invitation is the cleverest, funniest, most elegant, etc.

8 Teaching Tip Distribute the *Hojas de actividades* (Activity Pack/Supersite). Give students ten minutes to ask other group members the questions.

8 Expansion Take a survey of the attitudes found in the entire class. Ex: **¿Quiénes creen que es más importante tener un buen amigo que muchos amigos? ¿Quiénes creen que es más importante tener muchos amigos que un buen amigo?**

9 Teaching Tip To simplify, read through the word list as a class and have students name the stage(s) of life that correspond to each word.

9 Expansion After all skits have been presented, have the class vote on the most original, funniest, truest to life, etc.

TEACHING OPTIONS

Extra Practice ←👤→ Add a visual aspect to this vocabulary practice. Using magazine pictures, display images that pertain to parties or celebrations, stages of life, or interpersonal relations. Have students describe the pictures and make guesses about who the people are, how they are feeling, and so forth.

Extra Practice →👤← Add an auditory aspect to this vocabulary practice. As a listening comprehension activity, prepare short

descriptions of five easily recognizable people. Use as much active lesson vocabulary as possible. Write their names on the board in random order. Then read the descriptions aloud and have students match each one to the appropriate name. Ex: **Me casé tres veces. Me divorcié dos veces y ahora estoy casada con otro cantante latino. Yo canto, pero también soy actriz y tengo mi propia marca de perfumes. (Jennifer López)**

El Día de Muertos

La familia Díaz conmemora el Día de Muertos.

PERSONAJES MARISSA JIMENA FELIPE JUAN CARLOS

S Video: *Fotonovela*
Record and Compare

1

MAITE FUENTES El Día de Muertos se celebra en México el primero y el segundo de noviembre. Como pueden ver, hay calaveras de azúcar, flores, música y comida por todas partes. Ésta es una fiesta única que todos deben ver por lo menos una vez en la vida.

2

MARISSA *Holy moley!* ¡Está delicioso!
TÍA ANA MARÍA Mi mamá me enseñó a prepararlo. El mole siempre fue el plato favorito de mi papá. Mi hijo Eduardo nació el día de su cumpleaños. Por eso le pusimos su nombre.

MARISSA ¿Cómo se conocieron?
TÍA ANA MARÍA En la fiesta de un amigo. Fue amor a primera vista.
MARISSA (*Señala la foto.*) La voy a llevar al altar.

3

TÍO RAMÓN ¿Dónde están mis hermanos?
JIMENA Mi papá y Felipe están en el otro cuarto. Esos dos antipáticos no quieren decirnos qué están haciendo. Y la tía Ana María...
TÍO RAMÓN ... está en la cocina.

5

4

TÍA ANA MARÍA Marissa, ¿le puedes llevar esa foto que está ahí a Carolina? La necesita para el altar.
MARISSA Sí. ¿Son sus padres?
TÍA ANA MARÍA Sí, el día de su boda.

6

TÍA ANA MARÍA Ramón, ¿cómo estás?
TÍO RAMÓN Bien, gracias. ¿Y Mateo? ¿No vino contigo?
TÍA ANA MARÍA No. Ya sabes que me casé con un doctor y, pues, trabaja muchísimo.

 SRA. DÍAZ **SR. DÍAZ** **TÍA ANA MARÍA** **TÍO RAMÓN** **TÍA NAYELI** **DON DIEGO** **MARTA** VALENTINA MAITE FUENTES

SR. DÍAZ Familia Díaz, deben prepararse...

FELIPE ... ¡para la sorpresa de sus vidas!

JUAN CARLOS Gracias por invitarme.

SR. DÍAZ Juan Carlos, como eres nuestro amigo, ya eres parte de la familia.

(En el cementerio)

JIMENA Yo hice las galletas y el pastel. ¿Dónde los puse?

MARTA Postres... ¿Cuál prefiero? ¿Galletas? ¿Pastel? ¡Dulces!

VALENTINA Me gustan las galletas.

SR. DÍAZ Brindamos por ustedes, mamá y papá.

TÍO RAMÓN Todas las otras noches estamos separados. Pero esta noche estamos juntos.

TÍA ANA MARÍA Con gratitud y amor.

recursos

VM pp. 211–212 | vhlcentral.com Lección 9

Expresiones útiles

Discussing family history

El mole siempre fue el plato favorito de mi papá.
Mole was always my dad's favorite dish.
Mi hijo Eduardo nació el día de su cumpleaños.
My son Eduardo was born on his birthday.
Por eso le pusimos su nombre.
That's why we named him after him (after my father).
¿Cómo se conocieron sus padres?
How did your parents meet?
En la fiesta de un amigo. Fue amor a primera vista.
At a friend's party. It was love at first sight.

Talking about a party/celebration

Ésta es una fiesta única que todos deben ver por lo menos una vez.
This is a unique celebration that everyone should see at least once.
Gracias por invitarme.
Thanks for inviting me.
Brindamos por ustedes.
A toast to you.

Additional vocabulary

alma *soul*
altar *altar*
ángel *angel*
calavera de azúcar *skull made out of sugar*
cementerio *cemetery*
cocina *kitchen*
disfraz *costume*

Expresiones útiles Draw attention to **pusimos** and explain that it is an irregular preterite form of the verb **poner**. Then point out the forms **vino** (video still 6) and **hice** and **puse** (video still 9) and tell students that these are irregular preterite forms of the verbs **venir, hacer,** and **poner**. Finally, draw attention to the phrase **Cómo se conocieron** and explain that **conocer** in the preterite means *to meet*. Tell students that they will learn more about these concepts in **Estructura**.

Teaching Tip Go through the **Fotonovela**, asking volunteers to read the various parts.

Nota cultural **El Día de Muertos** is an example of a holiday that blends indigenous and Catholic customs and beliefs. In pre-Columbian times, this celebration of deceased ancestors was a month-long festival that fell in the ninth month of the Aztec calendar, in August. The Spaniards moved it to coincide with the Catholic holidays of All Saints' Day and All Souls' Day.

¿Qué pasó?

1 Completar Completa las oraciones con la información correcta, según la **Fotonovela**.

1. El Día de Muertos es una ___fiesta___ única que todos deben ver.
2. La tía Ana María preparó ___mole___ para celebrar.
3. Marissa lleva la ___foto___ al altar.
4. Jimena hizo las ___galletas___ y el ___pastel___.
5. Marta no sabe qué ___postre___ prefiere.

2 Identificar Identifica quién puede decir estas oraciones. Vas a usar un nombre dos veces.

SR. DÍAZ **MAITE FUENTES**

JUAN CARLOS **VALENTINA**

TÍA ANA MARÍA

1. Mis padres se conocieron en la fiesta de un amigo. *tía Ana María*
2. El Día de Muertos se celebra con flores, calaveras de azúcar, música y comida. *Maite Fuentes*
3. Gracias por invitarme a celebrar este Día de Muertos. *Juan Carlos*
4. Los de la foto son mis padres el día de su boda. *tía Ana María*
5. A mí me gustan mucho las galletas. *Valentina*
6. ¡Qué bueno que estás aquí, Juan Carlos! Eres uno más de la familia. *Sr. Díaz*

3 Seleccionar Selecciona algunas de las opciones de la lista para completar las oraciones.

amor	días de fiesta	pasarlo bien	salieron
el champán	divorciarse	postres	se enamoraron
cumpleaños	flan	la quinceañera	una sorpresa

1. El Sr. Díaz y Felipe prepararon ___una sorpresa___ para la familia.
2. Los ___días de fiesta___, como el Día de Muertos, se celebran con la familia.
3. Eduardo, el hijo de Ana María, nació el día del ___cumpleaños___ de su abuelo.
4. La tía Ana María siente gratitud y ___amor___ hacia (*toward*) sus padres.
5. Los días de fiesta también son para ___pasarlo bien___ con los amigos.
6. El Día de Muertos se hacen muchos ___postres___.
7. Los padres de la tía Ana María ___se enamoraron___ a primera vista.

4 Una cena Trabajen en grupos para representar una conversación en una cena de Año Nuevo. *Answers will vary.*

- Una persona brinda por el año que está por comenzar y por estar con su familia y amigos.
- Cada persona del grupo habla de cuál es su comida favorita en año nuevo.
- Después de la cena, una persona del grupo dice que es hora de (*it's time to*) comer las uvas.
- Cada persona del grupo dice qué desea para el año que empieza.
- Después, cada persona del grupo debe desear Feliz Año Nuevo a las demás.

Practice more at **vhlcentral.com**.

NOTA CULTURAL

Comer doce uvas a las doce de la noche del 31 de diciembre de cada año es una costumbre que nació en España y que también se observa en varios países de Latinoamérica. Se debe comer una uva por cada una de las 12 campanadas (*strokes*) del reloj y se cree que (*it's believed that*) quien lo hace va a tener un año próspero.

Pronunciación

Audio: Concepts, Activities Record & Compare

The letters h, j, and g

helado	hombre	hola	hermosa

The Spanish **h** is always silent.

José	jubilarse	dejar	pareja

The letter **j** is pronounced much like the English *h* in *his*.

agencia	general	Gil	Gisela

The letter **g** can be pronounced three different ways. Before **e** or **i**, the letter **g** is pronounced much like the English *h*.

Gustavo, gracias por llamar el domingo.

At the beginning of a phrase or after the letter **n**, the Spanish **g** is pronounced like the English *g* in *girl*.

Me gradué en agosto.

In any other position, the Spanish **g** has a somewhat softer sound.

Guerra	conseguir	guantes	agua

In the combinations **gue** and **gui**, the **g** has a hard sound and the **u** is silent. In the combination **gua**, the **g** has a hard sound and the **u** is pronounced like the English *w*.

Práctica Lee las palabras en voz alta, prestando atención a la **h**, la **j** y la **g**.

1. hamburguesa	5. geografía	9. seguir	13. Jorge
2. jugar	6. magnífico	10. gracias	14. tengo
3. oreja	7. espejo	11. hijo	15. ahora
4. guapa	8. hago	12. galleta	16. guantes

Oraciones Lee las oraciones en voz alta, prestando atención a la **h**, la **j** y la **g**.
1. Hola. Me llamo Gustavo Hinojosa Lugones y vivo en Santiago de Chile.
2. Tengo una familia grande; somos tres hermanos y tres hermanas.
3. Voy a graduarme en mayo.
4. Para celebrar mi graduación, mis padres van a regalarme un viaje a Egipto.
5. ¡Qué generosos son!

Refranes Lee los refranes en voz alta, prestando atención a la **h**, la **j** y la **g**.

A la larga, lo más dulce amarga.[1]

El hábito no hace al monje.[2]

1 Too much of a good thing. 2 The clothes don't make the man.

recursos

LM p. 50 vhlcentral.com Lección 9

Section Goal

In **Pronunciación**, students will be introduced to the pronunciation of **h**, **j**, and **g**.

Instructional Resources
Supersite: Audio (Textbook and Lab MP3 Files); Resources (Scripts, Answer Keys)
WebSAM
Lab Manual, p. 50

Teaching Tips
• Ask the class how the Spanish **h** is pronounced. Ask volunteers to pronounce the example words. Contrast the pronunciations of the English *hotel* and the Spanish **hotel**.
• Explain that **j** is pronounced much like the English *h*.
• Draw attention to the fact that the letter **g** is pronounced like the English *h* before **e** or **i**. Write the example words on the board and ask volunteers to pronounce them.
• Point out that the letter **g** is pronounced like the English *g* in *good* at the beginning of a phrase or after the letter **n**.
• Explain that in any other position, particularly between vowels, **g** has a softer sound.
• Tell the class that in the combinations **gue** and **gui**, **g** has a hard sound and **u** is not pronounced. Explain that in the combinations **gua** and **guo**, the **u** sounds like the English *w*.

Práctica/Oraciones/Refranes
These exercises are recorded on the *Textbook MP3s*. You may want to play the audio so that students practice listening to Spanish spoken by speakers other than yourself.

TEACHING OPTIONS

Extra Practice Write the names of these Chilean cities on the board and ask for a volunteer to pronounce each one: **Santiago, Antofagasta, Rancagua, Coihaique.** Repeat the process with the names of these Chilean writers: **Alberto Blest Gana, Vicente Huidobro, Gabriela Mistral, Juan Modesto Castro.**

Pairs Have students work in pairs to read aloud the sentences in **Actividad 6, Cambiar,** page 278. Remind them to pay attention to the pronunciation of the letters **h**, **j**, and **g**. Encourage students to help their partners if they have trouble pronouncing a particular word.

EN DETALLE

Additional Reading
Video: *Flash cultura*

Semana Santa: vacaciones y tradición

¿Te imaginas pasar veinticuatro horas tocando un tambor° entre miles de personas? Así es como mucha gente celebra el Viernes Santo° en el pequeño pueblo de **Calanda**, España.

De todas las celebraciones hispanas, la Semana Santa° es una de las más espectaculares y únicas.

Procesión en Sevilla, España

Semana Santa es la semana antes de Pascua°, una celebración religiosa que conmemora la Pasión de Jesucristo. Generalmente, la gente tiene unos días de vacaciones en esta semana. Algunas personas aprovechan° estos días para viajar, pero otras prefieren participar en las tradicionales celebraciones religiosas en las calles. En **Antigua**, Guatemala, hacen alfombras° de flores° y altares; también organizan Vía Crucis° y danzas. En las famosas procesiones y desfiles° religiosos de **Sevilla**, España, los fieles°

sacan a las calles imágenes religiosas. Las imágenes van encima de plataformas ricamente decoradas con abundantes flores y velas°. En la procesión, los penitentes llevan túnicas y unos sombreros cónicos que les cubren° la cara°. En sus manos llevan faroles° o velas encendidas.

Si visitas algún país hispano durante la Semana Santa, debes asistir a un desfile. Las playas y las discotecas pueden esperar hasta la semana siguiente.

Alfombra de flores en Antigua, Guatemala

Otras celebraciones famosas

Ayacucho, Perú: Además de alfombras de flores y procesiones, aquí hay una antigua tradición llamada "quema de la chamiza"°.

Iztapalapa, Ciudad de México: Es famoso el Vía Crucis del cerro° de la Estrella. Es una representación del recorrido° de Jesucristo con la cruz°.

Popayán, Colombia: En las procesiones "chiquitas" los niños llevan imágenes que son copias pequeñas de las que llevan los mayores.

tocando un tambor *playing a drum* Viernes Santo *Good Friday* Semana Santa *Holy Week* Pascua *Easter Sunday* aprovechan *take advantage of* alfombras *carpets* flores *flowers* Vía Crucis *Stations of the Cross* desfiles *parades* fieles *faithful* velas *candles* cubren *cover* cara *face* faroles *lamps* quema de la chamiza *burning of brushwood* cerro *hill* recorrido *route* cruz *cross*

ACTIVIDADES

1 **¿Cierto o falso?** Indica si lo que dicen las oraciones sobre Semana Santa en países hispanos es **cierto** o **falso**. Corrige las falsas.

1. La Semana Santa se celebra después de Pascua.
 Falso. La Semana Santa es la semana antes de Pascua.
2. Las personas tienen días libres durante la Semana Santa.
 Cierto.
3. Todas las personas asisten a las celebraciones religiosas.
 Falso. Algunas personas aprovechan estos días para viajar.
4. En los países hispanos, las celebraciones se hacen en las calles.
 Cierto.

5. En Antigua y en Ayacucho es típico hacer alfombras de flores.
 Cierto.
6. En Sevilla, sacan imágenes religiosas a las calles.
 Cierto.
7. En Sevilla, las túnicas cubren la cara.
 Falso. Los sombreros cónicos cubren la cara.
8. En la procesión en Sevilla algunas personas llevan flores en sus manos.
 Falso. En sus manos llevan faroles o velas encendidas.
9. El Vía Crucis de Iztapalapa es en el interior de una iglesia.
 Falso. Es en el cerro de la Estrella.
10. Las procesiones "chiquitas" son famosas en Sevilla, España.
 Falso. Son famosas en Popayán, Colombia.

ASÍ SE DICE

Fiestas y celebraciones

la despedida de soltero/a	*bachelor(ette) party*
el día feriado/festivo	el día de fiesta
disfrutar	*to enjoy*
festejar	celebrar
los fuegos artificiales	*fireworks*
pasarlo en grande	divertirse mucho
la vela	*candle*

EL MUNDO HISPANO

Celebraciones latinoamericanas

- **Oruro, Bolivia** Durante el carnaval de Oruro se realiza la famosa Diablada, una antigua danza° que muestra la lucha° entre el Bien y el Mal: ángeles contra° demonios.

- **Panchimalco, El Salvador** La primera semana de mayo, Panchimalco se cubre de flores y de color. También hacen el Desfile de las palmas° y bailan danzas antiguas.

- **Quito, Ecuador** El mes de agosto es el Mes de las Artes. Danza, teatro, música, cine, artesanías° y otros eventos culturales inundan la ciudad.

- **San Pedro Sula, Honduras** En junio se celebra la Feria Juniana. Hay comida típica, bailes, desfiles, conciertos, rodeos, exposiciones ganaderas° y eventos deportivos y culturales.

danza *dance* lucha *fight* contra *versus* palmas *palm leaves* artesanías *handcrafts* exposiciones ganaderas *cattle shows*

PERFIL

Festival de Viña del Mar

En 1959 unos estudiantes de **Viña del Mar**, Chile, celebraron una fiesta en una casa de campo conocida como la Quinta Vergara donde hubo° un espectáculo° musical. En 1960 repitieron el evento. Asistió tanta gente que muchos vieron el espectáculo parados° o sentados en el suelo°. Algunos se subieron a los árboles°.

Años después, se convirtió en el **Festival Internacional de la Canción**. Este evento se celebra en febrero, en el mismo lugar donde empezó. ¡Pero ahora nadie necesita subirse a un árbol para verlo! Hay un anfiteatro con capacidad para quince mil personas.

En el festival hay concursos° musicales y conciertos de artistas famosos como Calle 13 y Nelly Furtado.

Nelly Furtado

hubo *there was* espectáculo *show* parados *standing* suelo *floor* se subieron a los árboles *climbed trees* concursos *competitions*

Conexión Internet

¿Qué celebraciones hispanas hay en los Estados Unidos y Canadá?

Go to **vhlcentral.com** to find more cultural information related to this **Cultura** section.

ACTIVIDADES

2 **Comprensión** Responde a las preguntas.

1. ¿Cuántas personas por día pueden asistir al Festival de Viña del Mar? quince mil
2. ¿Qué es la Diablada? Es una antigua danza que muestra la lucha entre el bien y el mal.
3. ¿Qué celebran en Quito en agosto? Celebran el Mes de las Artes.
4. Nombra dos atracciones en la Feria Juniana de San Pedro Sula. Answers will vary.
5. ¿Qué es la Quinta Vergara? una casa de campo donde empezó el Festival de Viña del Mar

3 **¿Cuál es tu celebración favorita?** Escribe un pequeño párrafo sobre la celebración que más te gusta de tu comunidad. Explica cómo se llama, cuándo ocurre y cómo es. Answers will vary.

recursos

VM pp. 283–284
vhlcentral.com Lección 9

Practice more at **vhlcentral.com.**

Section Goal

In **Estructura 9.1**, students will be introduced to the irregular preterites of several common verbs.

Instructional Resources

Supersite: Audio (Lab MP3 Files); Resources (*PowerPoints*, Activity Pack, Scripts, Answer Keys); Testing Program (Quizzes)
WebSAM
Workbook, pp. 99–100
Lab Manual, p. 51

Teaching Tips

- Quickly review the present tense of a stem-changing verb such as **pedir**. Write the paradigm on the board and ask volunteers to point out the stem-changing forms.
- Work through the preterite paradigms of **tener, venir,** and **decir**, modeling the pronunciation.
- 🧍↔🧍 Add a visual aspect to this grammar presentation. Use magazine pictures to ask about social events in the past. Ex: **¿Con quién vino este chico a la fiesta? (Vino con esa chica rubia.) ¿Qué se puso esta señora para ir a la boda? (Se puso un sombrero.) ¿Qué trajo esta chica a clase? (Trajo una mochila.) ¿Y qué hizo? (Se durmió.)**
- Write the preterite paradigm for **estar** on the board. Then erase the initial **es-** for each form and point out that the preterite of **estar** and **tener** are identical except for the initial **es-**.

9.1 Irregular preterites 🅢 Tutorial

ANTE TODO You already know that the verbs **ir** and **ser** are irregular in the preterite. You will now learn other verbs whose preterite forms are also irregular.

Preterite of tener, venir, and decir

		tener (u-stem)	venir (i-stem)	decir (j-stem)
SINGULAR FORMS	yo	tuve	vine	dije
	tú	tuviste	viniste	dijiste
	Ud./él/ella	tuvo	vino	dijo
PLURAL FORMS	nosotros/as	tuvimos	vinimos	dijimos
	vosotros/as	tuvisteis	vinisteis	dijisteis
	Uds./ellos/ellas	tuvieron	vinieron	dijeron

▶ **¡Atención!** The endings of these verbs are the regular preterite endings of **-er/-ir** verbs, except for the **yo** and **usted/él/ella** forms. Note that these two endings are unaccented.

▶ These verbs observe similar stem changes to **tener, venir,** and **decir.**

INFINITIVE	U-STEM	PRETERITE FORMS
poder	pud-	pude, pudiste, pudo, pudimos, pudisteis, pudieron
poner	pus-	puse, pusiste, puso, pusimos, pusisteis, pusieron
saber	sup-	supe, supiste, supo, supimos, supisteis, supieron
estar	estuv-	estuve, estuviste, estuvo, estuvimos, estuvisteis, estuvieron

INFINITIVE	I-STEM	PRETERITE FORMS
querer	quis-	quise, quisiste, quiso, quisimos, quisisteis, quisieron
hacer	hic-	hice, hiciste, hizo, hicimos, hicisteis, hicieron

INFINITIVE	J-STEM	PRETERITE FORMS
traer	traj-	traje, trajiste, trajo, trajimos, trajisteis, trajeron
conducir	conduj-	conduje, condujiste, condujo, condujimos, condujisteis, condujeron
traducir	traduj-	traduje, tradujiste, tradujo, tradujimos, tradujisteis, tradujeron

▶ **¡Atención!** Most verbs that end in **-cir** are **j**-stem verbs in the preterite. For example, **producir → produje, produjiste,** etc.

> **Produjimos** un documental sobre los accidentes en la casa.
> *We produced a documentary about accidents in the home.*

▶ Notice that the preterites with **j**-stems omit the letter **i** in the **ustedes/ellos/ellas** form.

> Mis amigos **trajeron** comida a la fiesta.
> *My friends brought food to the party.*

> Ellos **dijeron** la verdad.
> *They told the truth.*

Extra Practice Do a pattern practice drill. Name an infinitive and ask individuals to provide conjugations for the different subject pronouns and/or names you provide. Reverse the activity by saying a conjugated form and asking students to give an appropriate subject pronoun.

Game Divide the class into two teams. Indicate one team member at a time, alternating between teams. Give a verb in its infinitive form and a subject pronoun (Ex: **querer/tú**). The team member should give the correct preterite form (Ex: **quisiste**). Give one point per correct answer. Deduct one point for each wrong answer. The team with the most points at the end wins.

The preterite of **dar**

	SINGULAR FORMS		PLURAL FORMS
yo	d**i**	nosotros/as	d**imos**
tú	d**iste**	vosotros/as	d**isteis**
Ud./él/ella	d**io**	Uds./ellos/ellas	d**ieron**

▶ The endings for **dar** are the same as the regular preterite endings for **-er** and **-ir** verbs, except that there are no accent marks.

La camarera me **dio** el menú.
The waitress gave me the menu.

Le **di** a Juan algunos consejos.
I gave Juan some advice.

Los invitados le **dieron** un regalo.
The guests gave him/her a gift.

Nosotros **dimos** una gran fiesta.
We gave a great party.

▶ The preterite of **hay** (*inf.* **haber**) is **hubo** (*there was; there were*).

CONSULTA

Note that there are other ways to say *there was* or *there were* in Spanish. See **Estructura 10.1**, p. 342.

Marissa le dio la foto a la Sra. Díaz.

Hubo una celebración en casa de los Díaz.

¡INTÉNTALO! Escribe la forma correcta del pretérito de cada verbo que está entre paréntesis.

1. (querer) tú _quisiste_
2. (decir) usted _dijo_
3. (hacer) nosotras _hicimos_
4. (traer) yo _traje_
5. (conducir) ellas _condujeron_
6. (estar) ella _estuvo_
7. (tener) tú _tuviste_
8. (dar) ella y yo _dimos_
9. (traducir) yo _traduje_
10. (haber) ayer _hubo_
11. (saber) usted _supo_
12. (poner) ellos _pusieron_

13. (venir) yo _vine_
14. (poder) tú _pudiste_
15. (querer) ustedes _quisieron_
16. (estar) nosotros _estuvimos_
17. (decir) tú _dijiste_
18. (saber) ellos _supieron_
19. (hacer) él _hizo_
20. (poner) yo _puse_
21. (traer) nosotras _trajimos_
22. (tener) yo _tuve_
23. (dar) tú _diste_
24. (poder) ustedes _pudieron_

recursos

WB pp. 99–100

LM p. 51

vhlcentral.com Lección 9

Teaching Tips

• ➡️🔄 Use the preterite forms of all these verbs by talking about what you did in the recent past and then asking students questions that involve them in a conversation about what they did in the recent past. You may want to avoid the preterite of **poder, saber,** and **querer** for the moment. Ex: **El sábado pasado tuve que ir a la fiesta de cumpleaños de mi sobrina. Cumplió siete años. Le di un bonito regalo. ____, ¿tuviste que ir a una fiesta el sábado? ¿No? Pues, ¿qué hiciste el sábado?**

• Point out that **dar** has the same preterite endings as **ver**.

• Drill the preterite of **dar** by asking students about what they gave their family members for their last birthdays or other special occasion. Ex: **¿Qué le diste a tu hermano para su cumpleaños?** Then ask what other family members gave them. Ex: **¿Qué te dio tu padre? ¿Y tu madre?**

• 🔄🔄 In a dramatically offended tone, say: **Di una fiesta el sábado. Los invité a todos ustedes y ¡no vino nadie!** Complain about all the work you did to prepare for the party. Ex: **Limpié toda la casa, preparé tortilla española, fui al supermercado y compré refrescos, puse la mesa con platos bonitos, puse música salsa…** Then write **¿Por qué no viniste a mi fiesta?** and **Lo siento, profesor(a), no pude venir a su fiesta porque tuve que…** on the board and give students one minute to write a creative or humorous excuse. Have volunteers read their excuses aloud. Ex: **Lo siento, profesor, no pude venir a su fiesta porque tuve que lavarme el pelo…**

TEACHING OPTIONS

Video ➡️🔄 Show the **Fotonovela** again to give students more input containing irregular preterite forms. Stop the video where appropriate to discuss how certain verbs were used and to ask comprehension questions.

Extra Practice 🔄🔄 Have students write down six things they brought to class today. Then have them circulate around the room, asking other students if they also brought those items (**¿Trajiste tus llaves a clase hoy?**). When they find a student that answers **sí,** they ask that student to sign his or her name next to that item (**Firma aquí, por favor.**). Can students get signatures for all the items they brought to class?

Práctica

1 Completar Completa estas oraciones con el pretérito de los verbos entre paréntesis.

1. El sábado ___hubo___ (haber) una fiesta sorpresa para Elsa en mi casa.
2. Sofía ___hizo___ (hacer) un pastel para la fiesta y Miguel ___trajo___ (traer) un flan.
3. Los amigos y parientes de Elsa ___vinieron___ (venir) y ___trajeron___ (traer) regalos.
4. El hermano de Elsa no ___vino___ (venir) porque ___tuvo___ (tener) que trabajar.
5. Su tía María Dolores tampoco ___pudo___ (poder) venir.
6. Cuando Elsa abrió la puerta, todos gritaron: "¡Feliz cumpleaños!" y su esposo le ___dio___ (dar) un beso.
7. Elsa no ___supo___ (saber) cómo reaccionar (*react*). ___Estuvo___ (Estar) un poco nerviosa al principio, pero pronto sus amigos ___pusieron___ (poner) música y ella ___pudo___ (poder) relajarse bailando con su esposo.
8. Al final de la noche, todos ___dijeron___ (decir) que se divirtieron mucho.

2 Describir En parejas, usen verbos de la lista para describir lo que estas personas hicieron. Deben dar por lo menos dos oraciones por cada dibujo. *Some answers may vary. Suggested answers:*

dar	hacer	tener	traer
estar	poner	traducir	venir

1. el señor López
El señor López le dio/trajo dinero a su hijo.

2. Norma
Norma puso el pavo en la mesa. /Norma trajo el pavo a la mesa.

3. anoche nosotros
Anoche nosotros tuvimos/hicimos/dimos una fiesta de Navidad./Anoche nosotros estuvimos en una fiesta de Navidad.

4. Roberto y Elena
Roberto y Elena le trajeron/dieron un regalo a su amigo.

Practice more at **vhlcentral.com.**

Comunicación

3 **Preguntas** En parejas, túrnense para hacerse y responder a estas preguntas. Answers will vary.

1. ¿Fuiste a una fiesta de cumpleaños el año pasado? ¿De quién?
2. ¿Quiénes fueron a la fiesta?
3. ¿Quién condujo el auto?
4. ¿Cómo estuvo el ambiente de la fiesta?
5. ¿Quién llevó regalos, bebidas o comida? ¿Llevaste algo especial?
6. ¿Hubo comida? ¿Quién la hizo? ¿Hubo champán?
7. ¿Qué regalo hiciste tú? ¿Qué otros regalos trajeron los invitados?
8. ¿Cuántos invitados hubo en la fiesta?
9. ¿Qué tipo de música hubo?
10. ¿Qué te dijeron algunos invitados de la fiesta?

4 **Encuesta** Tu profesor(a) va a darte una hoja de actividades. Para cada una de las actividades de la lista, encuentra a alguien que hizo esa actividad en el tiempo indicado. Answers will vary.

> **modelo**
> traer dulces a clase
> **Estudiante 1:** ¿Trajiste dulces a clase?
> **Estudiante 2:** Sí, traje galletas y helado a la fiesta del fin del semestre.

Actividades **Nombres**

1. ponerse un disfraz (costume) de Halloween
2. traer dulces a clase
3. conducir su auto a clase
4. estar en la biblioteca ayer
5. dar un regalo a alguien ayer
6. poder levantarse temprano esta mañana
7. hacer un viaje a un país hispano en el verano
8. tener una cita anoche
9. ir a una fiesta el fin de semana pasado
10. tener que trabajar el sábado pasado

Síntesis

5 **Conversación** En parejas, preparen una conversación en la que uno/a de ustedes va a visitar a su hermano/a para explicarle por qué no fue a su fiesta de graduación y para saber cómo estuvo la fiesta. Incluyan esta información en la conversación: Answers will vary.

- cuál fue el menú
- quiénes vinieron a la fiesta y quiénes no pudieron venir
- quiénes prepararon la comida o trajeron algo
- si él/ella tuvo que preparar algo
- lo que la gente hizo antes y después de comer
- cómo lo pasaron, bien o mal

TEACHING OPTIONS

Extra Practice ←🔁→ Ask students to write a brief composition on the **Fotonovela** from this lesson. Students should write about where the characters went, what they did, what they said to each other, and so forth. (Note: Students should stick to completed actions in the past [*preterite*]. The use of the imperfect for narrating a story will not be presented until **Lección 10**.)

Large Groups Divide the class into two groups. To each member of the first group, give a strip of paper with a question. Ex: **¿Quién me trajo el pastel de cumpleaños?** To each member of the second group, give a strip of paper with the answer to that question. Ex: **Marta te lo trajo.** Students must find their partners.

3 Teaching Tip
←🔁→ Instead of having students take turns, ask them to go through all the questions with their partner, taking notes about the information the partner gives them. Later, have them write a third-person description of their partner's experiences.

3 Expansion To practice the formal register, call on different students to ask you the questions in the activity. Ex: **¿Fue usted a una fiesta de cumpleaños el año pasado? (Sí, fui a la fiesta de cumpleaños de Lisa.)**

4 Teaching Tip Distribute the *Hojas de actividades* (Activity Pack/Supersite). Point out that to get information, students must form questions using the **tú** forms of the infinitives. Ex: **¿Trajiste dulces a clase?**

4 Expansion Write items 1–10 on the board and ask for a show of hands for each item. Ex: **¿Quién trajo dulces a clase?** Write tally marks next to each item to find out which activity was the most popular.

Nota cultural Halloween is celebrated in some Spanish-speaking countries, but it is not part of Hispanic culture. However, **El Día de todos los Santos** (November 1st) and **el Día de los Muertos** (November 2nd), which was featured in the **Fotonovela**, are two fall holidays that are deeply rooted in the culture.

5 Expansion
←🔁→ Have pairs work in groups of four to write a paragraph combining the most interesting or unusual aspects of each pair's conversation. Ask a group representative to read the paragraph to the class, who will vote for the most creative or funniest paragraph.

9.2 Verbs that change meaning in the preterite

 Tutorial

ANTE TODO The verbs **conocer, saber, poder,** and **querer** change meanings when used in the preterite. Because of this, each of them corresponds to more than one verb in English, depending on its tense.

Verbs that change meaning in the preterite

Present	Preterite
conocer	
to know; to be acquainted with	*to meet*
Conozco a esa pareja. / *I know that couple.*	**Conocí** a esa pareja ayer. / *I met that couple yesterday.*
saber	
to know information; to know how to do something	*to find out; to learn*
Sabemos la verdad. / *We know the truth.*	**Supimos** la verdad anoche. / *We found out (learned) the truth last night.*
poder	
to be able; can	*to manage; to succeed (could and did)*
Podemos hacerlo. / *We can do it.*	**Pudimos** hacerlo ayer. / *We managed to do it yesterday.*
querer	
to want; to love	*to try*
Quiero ir, pero tengo que trabajar. / *I want to go but I have to work.*	**Quise** evitarlo, pero fue imposible. / *I tried to avoid it, but it was impossible.*

¡ATENCIÓN!

In the preterite, the verbs **poder** and **querer** have different meanings, depending on whether they are used in affirmative or negative sentences.

pude *I succeeded*
no pude *I failed (to)*
quise *I tried (to)*
no quise *I refused (to)*

¡INTÉNTALO! Elige la respuesta más lógica.

1. Yo no hice lo que me pidieron mis padres. ¡Tengo mis principios! a
 a. No quise hacerlo. b. No supe hacerlo.

2. Hablamos por primera vez con Nuria y Ana en la boda. a
 a. Las conocimos en la boda. b. Les dijimos en la boda.

3. Por fin hablé con mi hermano después de llamarlo siete veces. b
 a. No quise hablar con él. b. Pude hablar con él.

4. Josefina se acostó para relajarse. Se durmió inmediatamente. a
 a. Pudo relajarse. b. No pudo relajarse.

5. Después de mucho buscar, encontraste la definición en el diccionario. b
 a. No supiste la respuesta. b. Supiste la respuesta.

6. Las chicas fueron a la fiesta. Cantaron y bailaron mucho. a
 a. Ellas pudieron divertirse. b. Ellas no supieron divertirse.

recursos

WB p. 101
LM p. 52
vhlcentral.com Lección 9

Práctica y Comunicación

1 **Carlos y Eva** Forma oraciones con los siguientes elementos. Usa el pretérito y haz todos los cambios necesarios. Al final, inventa la razón del divorcio de Carlos y Eva.

1. anoche / mi esposa y yo / saber / que / Carlos y Eva / divorciarse
Anoche mi esposa y yo supimos que Carlos y Eva se divorciaron.

2. los / conocer / viaje / isla de Pascua
Los conocimos en un viaje a la isla de Pascua.

3. no / poder / hablar / mucho / con / ellos / ese día
No pudimos hablar mucho con ellos ese día.

4. pero / ellos / ser / simpático / y / nosotros / hacer planes / vernos / con más / frecuencia
Pero ellos fueron simpáticos y nosotros hicimos planes para vernos con más frecuencia.

5. yo / poder / encontrar / su / número / teléfono / páginas / amarillo
Yo pude encontrar su número de teléfono en las páginas amarillas.

6. (yo) querer / llamar / los / ese día / pero / no / tener / tiempo
Quise llamarlos ese día, pero no tuve tiempo.

7. cuando / los / llamar / nosotros / poder / hablar / Eva
Cuando los llamé, nosotros pudimos hablar con Eva.

8. nosotros / saber / razón / divorcio / después / hablar / ella
Nosotros supimos la razón del divorcio después de hablar con ella.

9. _____
Answers will vary.

2 **Completar** Completa estas frases de una manera lógica. *Answers will vary.*

1. Ayer mi compañero/a de cuarto supo…
2. Esta mañana no pude…
3. Conocí a mi mejor amigo/a en…
4. Mis padres no quisieron…
5. Mi mejor amigo/a no pudo…
6. Mi novio/a y yo nos conocimos en…
7. La semana pasada supe…
8. Ayer mis amigos quisieron…

3 **Telenovela** En parejas, escriban el diálogo para una escena de una telenovela (*soap opera*). La escena trata de una situación amorosa entre tres personas: Mirta, Daniel y Raúl. Usen el pretérito de **conocer, poder, querer** y **saber** en su diálogo. *Answers will vary.*

PASIÓN — SUSPENSO AVENTURA — VENGANZA

LA MUJER DOBLE

Síntesis

4 **Conversación** En una hoja de papel, escribe dos listas: las cosas que hiciste durante el fin de semana y las cosas que quisiste hacer, pero no pudiste. Luego, compara tu lista con la de un(a) compañero/a, y expliquen ambos por qué no pudieron hacer esas cosas. *Answers will vary.*

 Practice more at **vhlcentral.com**.

9.3 ¿Qué? and ¿cuál? Tutorial

ANTE TODO You've already learned how to use interrogative words and phrases. As you know, **¿qué?** and **¿cuál?** or **¿cuáles?** mean *what?* or *which?* However, they are not interchangeable.

▶ **¿Qué?** is used to ask for a definition or an explanation.

¿Qué es el flan?
What is flan?

¿Qué estudias?
What do you study?

▶ **¿Cuál(es)?** is used when there is more than one possibility to choose from.

¿Cuál de los dos prefieres, el vino o el champán?
Which of these (two) do you prefer, wine or champagne?

¿Cuáles son tus medias, las negras o las blancas?
Which ones are your socks, the black ones or the white ones?

▶ **¿Cuál?** cannot be used before a noun; in this case, **¿qué?** is used.

¿Qué sorpresa te dieron tus amigos?
What surprise did your friends give you?

¿Qué colores te gustan?
What colors do you like?

▶ **¿Qué?** used before a noun has the same meaning as **¿cuál?**

¿Qué regalo te gusta?
What (Which) gift do you like?

¿Qué dulces quieren ustedes?
What (Which) sweets do you want?

Review of interrogative words and phrases

¿a qué hora?	at what time?	**¿cuántos/as?**	how many?
¿adónde?	(to) where?	**¿de dónde?**	from where?
¿cómo?	how?	**¿dónde?**	where?
¿cuál(es)?	what?; which?	**¿por qué?**	why?
¿cuándo?	when?	**¿qué?**	what?; which?
¿cuánto/a?	how much?	**¿quién(es)?**	who?

¡INTÉNTALO! Completa las preguntas con **¿qué?** o **¿cuál(es)?**, según el contexto.

1. ¿ _Cuál_ de los dos te gusta más?
2. ¿ _Cuál_ es tu teléfono?
3. ¿ _Qué_ tipo de pastel pediste?
4. ¿ _Qué_ es una galleta?
5. ¿ _Qué_ haces ahora?
6. ¿ _Cuáles_ son tus platos favoritos?
7. ¿ _Qué_ bebidas te gustan más?
8. ¿ _Qué_ es esto?
9. ¿ _Cuál_ es el mejor?
10. ¿ _Cuál_ es tu opinión?
11. ¿ _Qué_ fiestas celebras tú?
12. ¿ _Qué_ botella de vino prefieres?
13. ¿ _Cuál_ es tu helado favorito?
14. ¿ _Qué_ pones en la mesa?
15. ¿ _Qué_ restaurante prefieres?
16. ¿ _Qué_ estudiantes estudian más?
17. ¿ _Qué_ quieres comer esta noche?
18. ¿ _Cuál_ es la sorpresa mañana?
19. ¿ _Qué_ postre prefieres?
20. ¿ _Qué_ opinas?

recursos

WB p. 102

LM p. 53

vhlcentral.com
Lección 9

Práctica y Comunicación

1 **Completar** Tu clase de español va a crear un sitio web. Completa estas preguntas con alguna(s) palabra(s) interrogativa(s). Luego, con un(a) compañero/a, hagan y contesten las preguntas para obtener la información para el sitio web.

1. ¿_____Cuál_____ es la fecha de tu cumpleaños?
2. ¿_Dónde/Cuándo/A qué hora_ naciste?
3. ¿_____Cuál_____ es tu estado civil?
4. ¿_Cómo/Cuándo/Dónde_ te relajas?
5. ¿_____Quién/Cómo_____ es tu mejor amigo/a?
6. ¿_____Qué_____ cosas te hacen reír?
7. ¿_____Qué_____ postres te gustan? ¿_____Cuál_____ te gusta más?
8. ¿_____Qué_____ problemas tuviste en la primera cita con alguien?

2 **Una invitación** En parejas, lean esta invitación. Luego, túrnense para hacer y contestar preguntas con **qué** y **cuál** basadas en la información de la invitación. Answers will vary.

> **modelo**
> **Estudiante 1:** ¿Cuál es el nombre del padre de la novia?
> **Estudiante 2:** Su nombre es Fernando Sandoval Valera.

> *Fernando Sandoval Valera* *Lorenzo Vásquez Amaral*
> *Isabel Arzipe de Sandoval* *Elena Soto de Vásquez*
>
> *tienen el agrado de invitarlos*
> *a la boda de sus hijos*
>
> *María Luisa y José Antonio*
>
> *La ceremonia religiosa tendrá lugar*
> *el sábado 10 de junio a las dos de la tarde*
> *en el Templo de Santo Domingo*
> *(Calle Santo Domingo, 961).*
>
> *Después de la ceremonia, sírvanse pasar a la recepción en el salón*
> *de baile del Hotel Metrópoli (Sotero del Río, 465).*

3 **Quinceañera** Trabaja con un(a) compañero/a. Uno/a de ustedes es el/la director(a) del salón de fiestas "Renacimiento". La otra persona es el padre/la madre de Sandra, quien quiere hacer la fiesta de quince años de su hija gastando menos de $25 por invitado. Su profesor(a) va a darles la información necesaria para confirmar la reservación. Answers will vary.

> **modelo**
> **Estudiante 1:** ¿Cuánto cuestan los entremeses?
> **Estudiante 2:** Depende. Puede escoger champiñones por 50 centavos o
> camarones por dos dólares.
> **Estudiante 1:** ¡Uf! A mi hija le gustan los camarones, pero son muy caros.
> **Estudiante 2:** Bueno, también puede escoger quesos por un dólar por invitado.

 Practice more at **vhlcentral.com.**

Section Goals

In **Estructura 9.4**, students will be introduced to:
- pronouns as objects of prepositions
- the pronoun-preposition combinations **conmigo** and **contigo**

Instructional Resources
Supersite: Audio (Lab MP3 Files); Resources (*PowerPoints*, Activity Pack, Scripts, Answer Keys); Testing Program (Quizzes)
WebSAM
Workbook, pp. 103–104
Lab Manual, p. 54

Teaching Tips
- Review the chart "Prepositions often used with **estar**" in **Estructura 2.3**. Use prepositional pronouns as you describe yourself and others in relation to people and things. Say: **¿Quién está delante de mí? Sí, ____ está delante de mí. ¿Y quién está detrás de ella? Sí, ____ está detrás de ella.**
- Ask students which pronouns they recognize and which are new. Ask the class to deduce the rules for pronouns after prepositions.
- Point out that students have been using these pronouns with the preposition **a** since **Lección 2**, when they learned the verb **gustar**.
- Practice **conmigo** and **contigo** by making invitations and having students decline. Ex: **____, ¿quieres ir conmigo al museo? (No, no quiero ir contigo.)** In a sad tone, say: **Nadie quiere ir conmigo a ningún lado.**

9.4 Pronouns after prepositions Tutorial

ANTE TODO In Spanish, as in English, the object of a preposition is the noun or pronoun that follows a preposition. Observe the following diagram.

	Prepositional pronouns	
	Singular	**Plural**
preposition +	**mí** me	**nosotros/as** us
	ti you (fam.)	**vosotros/as** you (fam.)
	Ud. you (form.)	**Uds.** you (form.)
	él him	**ellos** them (m.)
	ella her	**ellas** them (f.)

▸ Note that, except for **mí** and **ti,** these pronouns are the same as the subject pronouns. **¡Atención!** **Mí** (*me*) has an accent mark to distinguish it from the possessive adjective **mi** (*my*).

▸ The preposition **con** combines with **mí** and **ti** to form **conmigo** and **contigo,** respectively.

—¿Quieres venir **conmigo** a Concepción? —Sí, gracias, me gustaría ir **contigo.**
Do you want to come with me to Concepción? *Yes, thanks, I would like to go with you.*

▸ The preposition **entre** is followed by **tú** and **yo** instead of **ti** and **mí.**

Papá va a sentarse **entre tú y yo.**
Dad is going to sit between you and me.

CONSULTA
For more prepositions, refer to **Estructura 2.3,** p. 56.

¡INTÉNTALO! Completa estas oraciones con las preposiciones y los pronombres apropiados.

1. *(with him)* No quiero ir __con él__.
2. *(for her)* Las galletas son __para ella__.
3. *(for me)* Los mariscos son __para mí__.
4. *(with you, pl. form.)* Preferimos estar __con ustedes__.
5. *(with you, sing. fam.)* Me gusta salir __contigo__.
6. *(with me)* ¿Por qué no quieres tener una cita __conmigo__?
7. *(for her)* La cuenta es __para ella__.
8. *(for them, m.)* La habitación es muy pequeña __para ellos__.
9. *(with them, f.)* Anoche celebré la Navidad __con ellas__.
10. *(for you, sing. fam.)* Este beso es __para ti__.
11. *(with you, sing. fam.)* Nunca me aburro __contigo__.
12. *(with you, pl. form.)* ¡Qué bien que vamos __con ustedes__!
13. *(for you, sing. fam.)* __Para ti__ la vida es muy fácil.
14. *(for them, f.)* __Para ellas__ no hay sorpresas.

recursos

WB pp. 103–104
LM p. 54
vhlcentral.com Lección 9

Práctica y Comunicación

1 **Completar** David sale con sus amigos a comer. Para saber quién come qué, lee el mensaje electrónico que David le envió (*sent*) a Cecilia dos días después y completa el diálogo en el restaurante con los pronombres apropiados.

> **modelo**
>
> **Camarero:** Los camarones en salsa verde, ¿para quién son?
> **David:** Son para _____ella_____.

Para: Cecilia	Asunto: El menú

Hola, Cecilia:

¿Recuerdas la comida del viernes? Quiero repetir el menú en mi casa el miércoles. Ahora voy a escribir lo que comimos, luego me dices si falta algún plato. Yo pedí el filete de pescado y Maribel camarones en salsa verde. Tatiana pidió un plato grandísimo de machas a la parmesana. Diana y Silvia pidieron langostas, ¿te acuerdas? Y tú, ¿qué pediste? Ah, sí, un bistec grande con papas. Héctor también pidió un bistec, pero más pequeño. Miguel pidió pollo y vino tinto para todos. Y la profesora comió ensalada verde porque está a dieta. ¿Falta algo? Espero tu mensaje. Hasta pronto. David.

CAMARERO El filete de pescado, ¿para quién es?

DAVID Es para (1)_____mí_____.

CAMARERO Aquí está. ¿Y las machas a la parmesana y las langostas?

DAVID Las machas son para (2)_____ella_____.

SILVIA Y DIANA Las langostas son para (3)_____nosotras_____.

CAMARERO Tengo un bistec grande…

DAVID Cecilia, es para (4)_____ti_____, ¿no es cierto? Y el bistec más pequeño es para (5)_____él_____.

CAMARERO ¿Y la botella de vino?

MIGUEL Es para todos (6)_____nosotros_____, y el pollo es para (7)_____mí_____.

CAMARERO (*a la profesora*) Entonces la ensalada verde es para (8)_____usted_____.

2 **Compartir** Tu profesor(a) va a darte una hoja de actividades en la que hay un dibujo. En parejas, hagan preguntas para saber dónde está cada una de las personas en el dibujo. Ustedes tienen dos versiones diferentes de la ilustración. Al final deben saber dónde está cada persona. Answers will vary.

> **modelo**
>
> **Estudiante 1:** ¿Quién está al lado de Óscar?
> **Estudiante 2:** Alfredo está al lado de él.

Alfredo	Dolores	Graciela	Raúl
Sra. Blanco	Enrique	Leonor	Rubén
Carlos	Sra. Gómez	Óscar	Yolanda

Practice more at **vhlcentral.com.**

Section Goal

In **Recapitulación**, students will review the grammar concepts from this lesson.

Instructional Resource
Supersite

1 **Teaching Tip** Ask students to identify which verb changes meaning in the preterite.

1 **Expansion**
• To challenge students, ask them to provide the **tú** and **ustedes** forms of the verbs.
• Have students provide the conjugations of **conocer, dar,** and **venir.**

2 **Teaching Tip** To simplify, have students circle the subject of each verb before filling in the blanks.

2 **Expansion**
←👤→ Have students work in pairs to write a response e-mail from **Omar.** Tell them to use the preterite tense to ask for more details about the party. Ex: **¿Qué más tuviste que hacer para preparar la fiesta? ¿Qué regalos te dieron tus amigos?**

Recapitulación

S Concepts Diagnostics

Completa estas actividades para repasar los conceptos de gramática que aprendiste en esta lección.

1 **Completar** Completa la tabla con el pretérito de los verbos. **9 pts.**

Infinitive	yo	ella	nosotros
conducir	conduje	condujo	condujimos
hacer	hice	hizo	hicimos
saber	supe	supo	supimos

2 **Mi fiesta** Completa este mensaje electrónico con el pretérito de los verbos de la lista. Vas a usar cada verbo sólo una vez. **10 pts.**

dar	haber	tener
decir	hacer	traer
estar	poder	venir
	poner	

Hola, Omar:

Como tú no (1) ___pudiste___ venir a mi fiesta de cumpleaños, quiero contarte cómo fue. El día de mi cumpleaños, muy temprano por la mañana, mis hermanos me (2) ___dieron___ una gran sorpresa: ellos (3) ___pusieron___ un regalo delante de la puerta de mi habitación: ¡una bicicleta roja preciosa! Mi madre nos preparó un desayuno riquísimo. Después de desayunar, mis hermanos y yo (4) ___tuvimos___ que limpiar toda la casa, así que (*therefore*) no (5) ___hubo___ más celebración hasta la tarde. A las seis y media (nosotros) (6) ___hicimos___ una barbacoa en el patio de la casa. Todos los invitados (7) ___trajeron___ bebidas y regalos. (8) ___Vinieron___ todos mis amigos, excepto tú, ¡qué pena! :-(La fiesta (9) ___estuvo___ muy animada hasta las diez de la noche, cuando mis padres (10) ___dijeron___ que los vecinos (*neighbors*) iban a (*were going to*) protestar y entonces todos se fueron a sus casas.

RESUMEN GRAMATICAL

9.1 **Irregular preterites** *pp. 286–287*

u-stem	estar poder poner saber tener	estuv- pud- pus- sup- tuv-	
i-stem	hacer querer venir	hic- quis- vin-	-e, -iste, -o, -imos, -isteis, -(i)eron
j-stem	conducir decir traducir traer	conduj- dij- traduj- traj-	

► Preterite of **dar:** di, diste, dio, dimos, disteis, dieron

► Preterite of **hay** (*inf.* **haber**): **hubo**

9.2 **Verbs that change meaning in the preterite** *p. 290*

Present	Preterite
conocer	
to know; to be acquainted with	to meet
saber	
to know info.; to know how to do something	to find out; to learn
poder	
to be able; can	to manage; to succeed
querer	
to want; to love	to try

9.3 **¿Qué? and ¿cuál?** *p. 292*

► Use **¿qué?** to ask for a definition or an explanation.

► Use **¿cuál(es)?** when there is more than one possibility to choose from.

► **¿Cuál?** cannot be used before a noun; use **¿qué?** instead.

► **¿Qué?** used before a noun has the same meaning as **¿cuál?**

TEACHING OPTIONS

TPR Have students stand and form a circle. Call out an infinitive from **Resumen gramatical** and a subject pronoun (Ex: **poder/ nosotros**) and toss a ball to a student, who will give the correct preterite form (Ex: **pudimos**). He or she then tosses the ball to another student, who must use the verb correctly in a sentence before throwing the ball back to you. Ex: **No pudimos comprar los regalos**.

Small Groups ←👤→ Tell small groups to imagine that one of them has received an anonymous birthday gift from a secret admirer. Have them create a dialogue in which friends ask questions about the gift and the potential admirer. Students must use at least two irregular preterites, two examples of **¿qué?** or **¿cuál?**, and three pronouns after prepositions.

3 **¿Presente o pretérito?** Escoge la forma correcta de los verbos en paréntesis. `6 pts.`

1. Después de muchos intentos (*tries*), (podemos/pudimos) hacer una piñata.
2. —¿Conoces a Pepe?
 —Sí, lo (conozco/conocí) en tu fiesta.
3. Como no es de aquí, Cristina no (sabe/supo) mucho de las celebraciones locales.
4. Yo no (quiero/quise) ir a un restaurante grande, pero tú decides.
5. Ellos (quieren/quisieron) darme una sorpresa, pero Nina me lo dijo todo.
6. Mañana se terminan las vacaciones; por fin (podemos/pudimos) volver a la escuela.

9.4 **Pronouns after prepositions** *p. 294*

Prepositional pronouns

	Singular	Plural
Preposition +	mí	nosotros/as
	ti	vosotros/as
	Ud.	Uds.
	él	ellos
	ella	ellas

► Exceptions: **conmigo, contigo, entre tú y yo**

4 **Preguntas** Escribe una pregunta para cada respuesta con los elementos dados. Empieza con **qué**, **cuál** o **cuáles** de acuerdo con el contexto y haz los cambios necesarios. `8 pts.`

1. —¿? / pastel / querer —Quiero el pastel de chocolate. 1. ¿Qué pastel quieres?
2. —¿? / ser / sangría —La sangría es una bebida típica española. 2. ¿Qué es la sangría?
3. —¿? / ser / restaurante favorito —Mis restaurantes favoritos son Dalí y Jaleo. 3. ¿Cuáles son tus restaurantes favoritos?
4. —¿? / ser / dirección electrónica —Mi dirección electrónica es paco@email.com. 4. ¿Cuál es tu dirección electrónica?

5 **¿Dónde me siento?** Completa la conversación con los pronombres apropiados. `7 pts.`

JUAN A ver, te voy a decir dónde te vas a sentar. Manuel, ¿ves esa silla? Es para ___ti___. Y esa otra silla es para tu novia, que todavía no está aquí.

MANUEL Muy bien, yo la reservo para ___ella___.

HUGO ¿Y esta silla es para ___mí___ (*me*)?

JUAN No, Hugo. No es para ___ti___. Es para Carmina, que viene con Julio.

HUGO No, Carmina y Julio no pueden venir. Hablé con ___ellos___ y me avisaron.

JUAN Pues ellos se lo pierden (*it's their loss*). ¡Más comida para ___nosotros___ (*us*)!

CAMARERO Aquí tienen el menú. Les doy un minuto y enseguida estoy con ___ustedes___.

6 **Cumpleaños feliz** Escribe cinco oraciones que describan cómo celebraste tu último cumpleaños. Usa el pretérito y los pronombres que aprendiste en esta lección. `10 pts.` Answers will vary.

7 **Poema** Completa este fragmento del poema *Elegía nocturna* de Carlos Pellicer con el pretérito de los verbos entre paréntesis. `¡2 puntos EXTRA!`

> " Ay de mi corazón° que nadie ___quiso___ (querer)
> tomar de entre mis manos desoladas.
> Tú ___viniste___ (venir) a mirar sus llamaradas°
> y le miraste arder° claro° y sereno. "

corazón *heart* llamaradas *flames* arder *to burn* claro *clear*

 Practice more at **vhlcentral.com**.

3 **Teaching Tip** To challenge students, ask them to explain why they chose the preterite or present tense in each case.

4 **Expansion** Give students these answers as items 5–8:
5. —¿? / libro / comprar —Voy a comprar el libro de viajes. (¿Qué libro vas a comprar?)
6. —¿? / ser / última película / ver —Vi la película *Los abrazos rotos*. (¿Cuál fue la última película que viste?)
7. —¿? / ser / número de la suerte —Mi número de la suerte es el ocho. (¿Cuál es tu número de la suerte?)
8. —¿? / ser / nacimiento —El nacimiento es la primera etapa de la vida. (¿Qué es el nacimiento?)

5 **Expansion** Have four volunteers role-play the dialogue for the class. Encourage them to ad-lib as they present.

6 **Teaching Tip** To simplify, have students begin by making an idea map. In the center circle, have them write **Mi último cumpleaños**. Help them brainstorm labels for the surrounding circles, such as **lugar, invitados, comida, regalos,** etc. You also may want to provide a list of infinitives that students may use in their descriptions.

7 **Teaching Tip** You may want to point out the example of **leísmo** in line 4 (**le miraste**). Explain that some Spanish speakers tend to use **le** or **les** as direct object pronouns. In this case, **le** replaces the direct object pronoun **lo**, which refers to **mi corazón**.

Nota cultural Mexican poet **Carlos Pellicer** mixes in his works the splendor of nature with the most intimate emotions. Some of his most important works are *Práctica de vuelo, Hora de junio,* and *Camino*. Also a museologist, he helped create the **Museo Casa de Frida Kahlo** and the **Anahuacalli**, which exhibits pre-Hispanic art donated by **Diego Rivera**.

TEACHING OPTIONS

Game Divide the class into two teams and have them line up. Indicate the first member of each team and call out a sentence. Ex: **Me gusta el color gris.** The first student to reach the board and write a corresponding question using the proper interrogative form earns a point for his or her team. Ex: **¿Qué color te gusta?** or **¿Cuál es tu color preferido?** The team with the most points at the end wins.
Pairs Add a visual aspect to this grammar review. Have pairs choose a photo of a person from a magazine and invent an imaginary list of the ten most important things that happened to that person in his or her lifetime. Tell them to use at least four preterites from this lesson. Ex: **Conoció al presidente de los Estados Unidos. Ganó la lotería y le dio todo el dinero a su mejor amigo.** Have pairs present their photos and lists to the class, who will ask follow-up questions. Ex: **¿Por qué le dio todo el dinero a un amigo?**

Section Goals

In **Lectura**, students will:
• learn to use word families to infer meaning in context
• read content-rich texts

Instructional Resource
Supersite

Estrategia Write **conocer** on the board and remind students of the meaning *to know, be familiar with*. Next to it, write **conocimiento** and **conocido**. Tell students that recognizing the family relationship between a known word and unfamiliar words can help them infer the meaning of the words they do not yet know. Guide students to see that **conocimiento** is a noun meaning *knowledge, familiarity* and **conocido** is an adjective form of the verb meaning *known* or *well-known*.

Examinar el texto Have students scan the text for clues to its contents. Ask volunteers to tell what kind of text it is and how they know. Headlines (**titulares**), photos, and layout (**diseño de la página**) reveal that it is the society section (**notas sociales**) of a newspaper.

Raíces Have students fill in the rest of the chart after they have read **Vida social**.

Lectura

communication cultures NATIONAL STANDARDS

Antes de leer

Estrategia
Recognizing word families

Recognizing root words can help you guess the meaning of words in context, ensuring better comprehension of a reading selection. Using this strategy will enrich your Spanish vocabulary as you will see below.

Examinar el texto

Familiarízate con el texto usando las estrategias de lectura más efectivas para ti. ¿Qué tipo de documento es? ¿De qué tratan° las cuatro secciones del documento? Explica tus respuestas.

Raíces°

Completa el siguiente cuadro° para ampliar tu vocabulario. Usa palabras de la lectura de esta lección y vocabulario de las lecciones anteriores. ¿Qué significan las palabras que escribiste en el cuadro? Some answers may vary. Suggested answers:

Verbos	Sustantivos	Otras formas
1. agradecer *to thank, to be grateful for*	agradecimiento/ gracias *gratitude/thanks*	agradecido *grateful, thankful*
2. estudiar	estudiante *student*	estudiado *studied*
3. celebrar *to celebrate*	celebración *celebration*	celebrado
4. bailar *to dance*	baile	bailable *danceable*
5. bautizar	bautismo *baptism*	bautizado *baptized*

¿De qué tratan...? *What are... about?* **Raíces** *Roots* **cuadro** *chart*

 Practice more at **vhlcentral.com**.

Vida social

Matrimonio
Espinoza Álvarez-
Reyes Salazar

El día sábado 17 de junio a las 19 horas, se celebró el matrimonio de Silvia Reyes y Carlos Espinoza en la catedral de Santiago. La ceremonia fue oficiada por el pastor Federico Salas y participaron los padres de los novios, el señor Jorge Espinoza y señora y el señor José Alfredo Reyes y señora. Después de la ceremonia, los padres de los recién casados ofrecieron una fiesta bailable en el restaurante La Misión.

Bautismo

José María recibió el bautismo el 26 de junio.

Sus padres, don Roberto Lagos Moreno y doña María Angélica Sánchez, compartieron la alegría de la fiesta con todos sus parientes y amigos. La ceremonia religiosa tuvo lugar° en la catedral de Aguas Blancas. Después de la ceremonia, padres, parientes y amigos celebraron una fiesta en la residencia de la familia Lagos.

TEACHING OPTIONS

Heritage Speakers Ask heritage speakers to share with the class other terms they use to refer to various types of celebrations. Possible responses: wedding: **boda, casamiento**; graduation: **graduación, promoción**; baptism: **bautizo**; birthday: **cumpleaños, día del santo**.

Extra Practice Here are some related words of which at least one form will be familiar to students. Guide them to recognize the relationship between words and meanings. **idea, ideal, idealismo, idealizar, idear, ideario, idealista • conservar, conservación, conserva, conservador • bueno, bondad, bondadoso, bonito • habla, hablador, hablar, hablante, hablado**

Fiesta de quince años

32B

El doctor don Amador Larenas Fernández y la señora Felisa Vera de Larenas celebraron los quince años de su hija Ana Ester junto a sus parientes y amigos. La quinceañera reside en la ciudad de Valparaíso y es estudiante del Colegio Francés. La fiesta de presentación en sociedad de la señorita Ana Ester fue el día viernes 2 de mayo a las 19 horas en el Club Español. Entre los invitados especiales asistieron el alcalde° de la ciudad, don Pedro Castedo, y su esposa. La música estuvo a cargo de la Orquesta Americana. ¡Feliz cumpleaños, le deseamos a la señorita Ana Ester en su fiesta bailable!

Expresión de gracias
Carmen Godoy Tapia

Agradecemos° sinceramente a todas las personas que nos acompañaron en el último adiós a nuestra apreciada esposa, madre, abuela y tía, la señora Carmen Godoy Tapia. El funeral tuvo lugar el día 28 de junio en la ciudad de Viña del Mar. La vida de Carmen Godoy fue un ejemplo de trabajo, amistad, alegría y amor para todos nosotros. Su esposo, hijos y familia agradecen de todo corazón° su asistencia° al funeral a todos los parientes y amigos.

tuvo lugar *took place* alcalde *mayor* Agradecemos *We thank*
de todo corazón *sincerely* asistencia *attendance*

Después de leer

Corregir 🔵🟢
Escribe estos comentarios otra vez para corregir la información errónea.

1. El alcalde y su esposa asistieron a la boda de Silvia y Carlos. El alcalde y su esposa asistieron a la fiesta de quince años de Ana Ester.
2. Todos los anuncios (*announcements*) describen eventos felices. Tres de los anuncios tratan de eventos felices. Uno trata de una muerte.
3. Felisa Vera de Larenas cumple quince años. Ana Ester Larenas cumple quince años.
4. Roberto Lagos y María Angélica Sánchez son hermanos. Roberto Lagos y María Angélica Sánchez están casados/son esposos.
5. Carmen Godoy Tapia les dio las gracias a las personas que asistieron al funeral. La familia de Carmen Godoy Tapia les dio las gracias a las personas que asistieron al funeral.

Identificar 🔵🟢
Escribe el nombre de la(s) persona(s) descrita(s) (*described*).

1. Dejó viudo a su esposo el 28 de junio. Carmen Godoy Tapia
2. Sus padres y todos los invitados brindaron por él, pero él no entendió por qué. José María
3. El Club Español les presentó una cuenta considerable. don Amador Larenas Fernández y doña Felisa Vera de Larenas
4. Unió a los novios en santo matrimonio. el pastor Federico Salas
5. Su fiesta de cumpleaños se celebró en Valparaíso. Ana Ester

Un anuncio
Trabajen en grupos pequeños para inventar un anuncio breve sobre una celebración importante. Puede ser una graduación, un matrimonio o una gran fiesta en la que ustedes participan. Incluyan la siguiente información. Answers will vary.
1. nombres de los participantes
2. la fecha, la hora y el lugar
3. qué se celebra
4. otros detalles de interés

Section Goals

In **Escritura**, students will:
- create a Venn diagram to organize information
- learn words and phrases that signal similarity and difference
- write a comparative analysis

Instructional Resource
Supersite

Estrategia Explain that a graphic organizer, such as a Venn diagram, is a useful way to record information and visually organize details to be compared and contrasted in a comparative analysis. On the board, draw a Venn diagram with the headings **La boda de mi hermano, El bautismo de mi sobrina**, and the subheadings **Diferencias** and **Similitudes**. Tell students they are going to complete a Venn diagram to compare two celebrations. Discuss with the class how these events are alike and how they are different, using some of the terms to signal similarities and differences.

Tema Explain to students that to write a comparative analysis, they will need to use words or phrases that signal similarities (**similitudes**) and differences (**diferencias**). Model the pronunciation of the words and expressions under **Escribir una composición**. Then have volunteers use them in sentences to express the similarities and differences listed in the Venn diagram.

Escritura

Estrategia

Planning and writing a comparative analysis

Writing any kind of comparative analysis requires careful planning. Venn diagrams are useful for organizing your ideas visually before comparing and contrasting people, places, objects, events, or issues. To create a Venn diagram, draw two circles that overlap one another and label the top of each circle. List the differences between the two elements in the outer rings of the two circles, then list their similarities where the two circles overlap. Review the following example.

Diferencias y similitudes

Boda de Silvia Reyes y Carlos Espinoza

Diferencias:
1. Primero hay una celebración religiosa.
2. Se celebra en un restaurante.

Similitudes:
1. Las dos fiestas se celebran por la noche.
2. Las dos fiestas son bailables.

Fiesta de quince años de Ana Ester Larenas Vera

Diferencias:
1. Se celebra en un club.
2. Vienen invitados especiales.

La lista de palabras y expresiones a la derecha puede ayudarte a escribir este tipo de ensayo (*essay*).

Tema

Escribir una composición

Compara una celebración familiar (como una boda, una fiesta de cumpleaños o una graduación) a la que tú asististe recientemente con otro tipo de celebración. Utiliza palabras y expresiones de esta lista.

Para expresar similitudes

además; también	*in addition; also*
al igual que	*the same as*
como	*as; like*
de la misma manera	*in the same manner (way)*
del mismo modo	*in the same manner (way)*
tan + [*adjetivo*] + como	*as + [adjective] + as*
tanto/a(s) + [*sustantivo*] + como	*as many/much + [noun] + as*

Para expresar diferencias

a diferencia de	*unlike*
a pesar de	*in spite of*
aunque	*although*
en cambio	*on the other hand*
más/menos… que	*more/less … than*
no obstante	*nevertheless; however*
por el contrario	*on the contrary*
por otro lado	*on the other hand*
sin embargo	*nevertheless; however*

EVALUATION: Composición

Criteria	Scale
Content	1 2 3 4
Organization	1 2 3 4
Use of comparisons/contrasts	1 2 3 4
Use of vocabulary	1 2 3 4
Accuracy	1 2 3 4

Scoring	
Excellent	18–20 points
Good	14–17 points
Satisfactory	10–13 points
Unsatisfactory	< 10 points

Escuchar

 Audio: Activities

Estrategia

Guessing the meaning of words through context

When you hear an unfamiliar word, you can often guess its meaning by listening to the words and phrases around it.

 To practice this strategy, you will now listen to a paragraph. Jot down the unfamiliar words that you hear. Then listen to the paragraph again and jot down the word or words that give the most useful clues to the meaning of each unfamiliar word.

Invitation

*Margarita Robles de García
y Roberto García Olmos*

*Piden su presencia en la celebración
del décimo aniversario de bodas
el día 13 de marzo
con una misa en la Iglesia Virgen del Coromoto
a las 6:30*

*seguida por cena y baile
en el restaurante El Campanero,
Calle Principal, Las Mercedes
a las 8:30*

Preparación

Lee la invitación. ¿De qué crees que van a hablar Rosa y Josefina?

Ahora escucha

Ahora escucha la conversación entre Josefina y Rosa. Cuando oigas una de las palabras de la columna A, usa el contexto para identificar el sinónimo o la definición en la columna B.

A	B
d 1. festejar	a. conmemoración religiosa de una muerte
c 2. dicha	b. tolera
h 3. bien parecido	c. suerte
g 4. finge (fingir)	d. celebrar
b 5. soporta (soportar)	e. me divertí
e 6. yo lo disfruté (disfrutar)	f. horror
	g. crea una ficción
	h. guapo

 Practice more at **vhlcentral.com.**

Comprensión

¿Cierto o falso?

Lee cada oración e indica si lo que dice es **cierto** o **falso**. Corrige las oraciones falsas.

1. No invitaron a mucha gente a la fiesta de Margarita y Roberto porque ellos no conocen a muchas personas.
 Falso. Fueron muchos invitados.

2. Algunos fueron a la fiesta con pareja y otros fueron sin compañero/a. Cierto.

3. Margarita y Roberto decidieron celebrar el décimo aniversario porque no hicieron una fiesta el día de su boda. Falso. Celebraron el décimo aniversario porque les gustan las fiestas.

4. Rafael les parece interesante a Rosa y a Josefina. Cierto.

5. Josefina se divirtió mucho en la fiesta porque bailó toda la noche con Rafael. Falso. Josefina se divirtió mucho, pero bailó con otros, no con Rafael.

Preguntas

Responde a estas preguntas con oraciones completas.
Answers will vary.

1. ¿Son solteras Rosa y Josefina? ¿Cómo lo sabes?

2. ¿Tienen las chicas una amistad de mucho tiempo con la pareja que celebra su aniversario? ¿Cómo lo sabes?

familia, ¿llegaste a conocer al cuñado de Magalí? Es soltero, ¿no? Quise bailar con él, pero no me sacó a bailar.
R: Hablas de Rafael. Es muy bien parecido; ¡ese pelo...! Estuve hablando con él después del brindis. Me dijo que no le gusta ni el champán ni el vino; él finge tomar cuando

brindan porque no lo soporta. No te sacó a bailar porque él y Susana estaban juntos en la fiesta.
J: De todos modos, aun sin Rafael, bailé toda la noche. Lo pasé muy, pero muy bien.

Section Goals

In **En pantalla**, students will:
- read about **las Fiestas Patrias** in Chile
- watch a television commercial about **las Fiestas Patrias** and other celebrations in Chile
- read about the short film *Iker pelos tiesos*
- watch the short film *Iker pelos tiesos*

Instructional Resources
Supersite/DVD: *En pantalla*
Supersite: Resources (Scripts, Translations)

Introduction To check comprehension, have students indicate whether these statements are **cierto** or **falso** and have them correct the false statements. **1. Durante las Fiestas Patrias todos los niños tienen que ir a la escuela.** (Falso. Durante las Fiestas Patrias se cierran casi todas las escuelas.) **2. Las empanadas y los asados son bailes típicos de Chile.** (Falso. Son platos tradicionales de Chile.) **3. Los chilenos vuelan volantines durante las Fiestas Patrias.** (Cierto.)

Antes de ver
- Have students look at the video stills, read the captions, and predict what is being celebrated in each visual.
- Read through the **Vocabulario útil** with students and model the pronunciation.

Seleccionar
- For items 1–3, have students name a holiday that they associate with the three related words.
- Have students write a sentence using each of the words that doesn't belong.

Fiesta
Have students imagine that one of their friends is timid and reluctant to come to the party. Ask them to write a dialogue in which they try to convince their friend to come.

En pantalla

Anuncio

Desfiles°, música, asados°, fuegos artificiales° y baile son los elementos de una buena fiesta. ¿Celebrar durante toda una semana? ¡Eso sí que es una fiesta espectacular! El 18 de septiembre Chile conmemora su independencia de España y los chilenos demuestran su orgullo° nacional durante una semana llena de celebraciones. Durante las Fiestas Patrias° casi todas las oficinas° y escuelas se cierran para que la gente se reúna° a festejar. Desfiles y rodeos representan la tradición de los vaqueros° del país, y la gente baila cueca, el baile nacional. Las familias y los amigos se reúnen para preparar y disfrutar platos tradicionales como las empanadas y asados. Otra de las tradiciones de estas fiestas es hacer volar cometas°, llamadas volantines. Mira el video para descubrir cómo se celebran otras fiestas en Chile.

Vocabulario útil	
conejo	*bunny*
disfraces	*costumes*
mariscal	*traditional Chilean soup with raw seafood*
sustos	*frights*
vieja (Chi.)	*mother*

Seleccionar

Selecciona la palabra que no está relacionada con cada grupo.

1. disfraces • noviembre • arbolito • sustos *arbolito*
2. volantines • arbolito • regalos • diciembre *volantines*
3. conejo • enero • huevitos • chocolates *enero*
4. septiembre • volantines • disfraces • asado *disfraces*

Fiesta

Trabajen en grupos de tres. Imaginen que van a organizar una fiesta para celebrar el 4 de julio. Escriban una invitación electrónica para invitar a sus parientes y amigos a la fiesta. Describan los planes que tienen para la fiesta y díganles a sus amigos qué tiene que traer cada uno. *Answers will vary.*

Desfiles/Paradas *Parades* asados *barbecues* fuegos artificiales *fireworks* orgullo *pride* Fiestas Patrias *Independence Day celebrations* oficinas *offices* se reúna *would get together* vaqueros *cowboys* cometas/volantines *kites*

FIESTAS PATRIAS
CHILEVISION

Noviembre: disfraces, dulces…

Mayo: besito, tarjeta, tecito con la mamá…

Septiembre… Septiembre: familia, parada militar…

Video: TV Clip

Practice more at **vhlcentral.com.**

TEACHING OPTIONS

Small Groups Have small groups create a commercial similar to the one for **Chilevisión**, but that includes other important holidays. Allow groups to choose any Spanish-speaking country they want, including the U.S. and Canada. Have groups bring in visuals to represent each celebration and hold up the visuals as they read the script aloud for the class. Each group member should read a portion of the script.

Heritage Speakers If heritage speakers have attended parties for young people in a Spanish-speaking country (such as a **miniteca** in Colombia), have them describe certain aspects of the party. Is it common to bring food or drink to a friend's party? Are parties more or less formal than in the U.S.? Do people dance or just listen to music? Have the rest of the class compare and contrast these customs with their own.

Cortometraje

Para Iker, cada persona se parece a un animal. Por ejemplo, su papá es un oso°. A Iker le habría gustado° ser un oso también, pero él es otro animal. Y eso es algo que nadie sabe en la escuela. ¿Qué puede pasar si° sus compañeros descubren el secreto de Iker?

 Preparación

En parejas, túrnense para hacerse estas preguntas. *Answers will vary.*

1. ¿Tienes rasgos particulares? ¿Cuáles son de tu apariencia física? ¿Cuáles son de tu personalidad?
2. ¿Cuáles de tus rasgos son buenos? ¿Cuáles son malos? ¿Cómo determinas que son buenos o malos?
3. ¿Qué rasgos te hacen una persona única?
4. ¿Es común alguno de esos rasgos en tu familia? ¿Cuál?
5. ¿Qué animal crees que serías (*you would be*) según (*according to*) tus rasgos? Explica tu respuesta.

Después de ver

Escoge la opción que completa mejor cada oración.

1. En la familia de Iker, _b_ el mismo rasgo.
 a. no hay dos personas con
 b. él y su abuelo comparten
 c. el abuelo y Tito tienen
2. Para Iker, su _b_ es un perico.
 a. hermana b. mamá c. maestra (*teacher*)
3. Iker se sintió _a_ cuando su compañero le dijo que le gustaba su peinado.
 a. aliviado (*relieved*) b. cohibido c. enojado
4. Al final, Iker estaba _c_ de mostrar su pelo tal y como es.
 a. avergonzado b. nervioso c. orgulloso

 Conversar

En parejas, respondan a estas preguntas con oraciones completas. *Answers will vary.*

1. ¿Se han sentido ustedes cohibidos/as alguna vez? ¿Qué pasó?
2. ¿Cuáles son las ventajas (*advantages*) de presentarse ante el mundo tal y como son?
3. ¿Creen que la percepción que tienen de ustedes mismos/as influye en (*influences*) la manera en que ven a los demás? Expliquen su respuesta.

oso *bear* le habría gustado *he would have liked* si *if*

Iker pelos tiesos

Escrito y Dirigido por:
Sandra García Velten

Expresiones útiles	
devolver	to return, to give back
disimular	to hide, to disguise
me hubiera gustado	I would have liked
meter	to put (something) in, to introduce
el peinado	hairstyle
salir (igual) a	to take after
si supieran	if they knew
tieso/a	stiff

Para hablar del corto	
burlarse (de)	to make fun (of)
esconder(se)	to hide (oneself)
la fuerza	strength
orgulloso/a	proud
pelear(se)	to fight (with one another)
el rasgo	feature, characteristic
sentirse cohibido/a	to feel self-conscious

 Video: Short Film

 Practice more at **vhlcentral.com**.

Antes de ver
- Have students look at the poster and ask them if the boy's hair reminds them of any animal.
- Read through the **Expresiones útiles** and **Para hablar del corto** vocabulary with students to model pronunciation and practice using the terms.
- Reassure students that they do not need to understand every word they hear in the short film. Tell them to rely on visual cues and to listen for cognates and words from **Expresiones útiles**.
- Ask students to predict how the film will end.

Preparación Have pairs ask each other questions 1–4. Then have them assess their partner's answers up to that point and predict what their partner will answer for item 5.

Después de ver As a variant, have students close their books. Then provide these items as cloze sentences. Rather than the multiple-choice options, give students a word bank.

Conversar
Once pairs have completed the activity, have students debate the notion that we all, to some extent, conform to society with regard to our physical appearance.

TEACHING OPTIONS

Small Groups Teach students the Mexican slang expressions that they will hear in the film, such as **órale**. In small groups, have them write mini-conversations that incorporate the expressions. Have volunteers read their dialogues to the class.

Large Groups Divide the class into two groups and tell them to imagine that they are administrators at Iker's school. Some parents have complained about the school uniform policy. Have one group argue for the abolishment of school uniforms and one group argue that the dress code should remain in effect. As part of their arguments, students should consider the increase in bullying incidents at the school over the past year.

Chile

connections cultures NATIONAL STANDARDS

El país en cifras

▶ **Área:** 756.950 km² (292.259 millas²), *dos veces el área de Montana*

▶ **Población:** 17.926.000
Aproximadamente el 80 por ciento de la población del país es urbana.

▶ **Capital:** Santiago de Chile—6.237.000

▶ **Ciudades principales:** Valparaíso— 911.000, Concepción, Viña del Mar, Temuco

SOURCE: Population Division, UN Secretariat

▶ **Moneda:** peso chileno

▶ **Idiomas:** español (oficial), mapuche

Bandera de Chile

Chilenos célebres

▶ **Bernardo O'Higgins,** militar° y héroe nacional (1778–1842)

▶ **Gabriela Mistral,** Premio Nobel de Literatura, 1945; poeta y diplomática (1889–1957)

▶ **Pablo Neruda,** Premio Nobel de Literatura, 1971; poeta (1904–1973)

▶ **Isabel Allende,** novelista (1942–)

Pablo Neruda

militar *soldier* terremoto *earthquake* heridas *wounded* hogar *home* desierto *desert* el más seco *the driest* mundo *world* han tenido *have had* ha sido usado *has been used* Marte *Mars*

¡Increíble pero cierto!

El desierto° de Atacama, en el norte de Chile, es el más seco° del mundo°. Con más de cien mil km² de superficie, algunas zonas de este desierto nunca han tenido° lluvia. Atacama ha sido usado° como escenario para representar a Marte° en películas y series de televisión.

PERÚ

La costa de Viña del Mar

Pampa del Tamarugal

BOLIVIA

Cordillera de los Andes

Edificio antiguo en Santiago

El puerto de Valparaíso

Océano Pacífico

Viña del Mar
Valparaíso

Santiago de Chile

ARGENTINA

Concepción

Temuco

Una celebración en Temuco

Torres del Paine

Lago Buenos Aires

Océano Atlántico

Punta Arenas

recursos

Estrecho de Magallanes

Isla Grande de Tierra del Fuego

WB pp. 105–106 | VM pp. 241–242 | S vhlcentral.com Lección 9

Section Goal

In **Panorama**, students will read about the geography, culture, and economy of Chile.

Instructional Resources

Supersite/DVD: *Panorama cultural*

Supersite: Resources (Scripts, Translations, *PowerPoints*, Answer Keys)

WebSAM

Workbook, pp. 105–106

Video Manual, pp. 241–242

Teaching Tips

• Use the **Lección 9 Panorama** overheads to assist with this presentation.

• Ask students to look at the map of Chile and have them talk about the physical features of the country. Point out that Chile is about 2,700 miles from north to south, but no more than 276 miles from east to west. Point out that Chile has a variety of climates.

El país en cifras After reading **Chilenos célebres,** give students more information about **Bernardo O'Higgins.** They can probably guess correctly that his father was an Irish immigrant, but should also know that he is considered one of the founders of modern Latin America, along with **Simón Bolívar** and **José de San Martín.** These "founding fathers" are called **los próceres.**

¡Increíble pero cierto! The Atacama Desert covers the northern third of the country. It is considered one of the best places in the world for astronomical observations, due to its high altitude, absence of cloud cover, dry air, and lack of light pollution and radio interference.

TEACHING OPTIONS

Heritage Speakers →🗣← Invite heritage speakers to select a poem by **Pablo Neruda** to read aloud for the class. Many of the *Odas elementales,* such as *Oda a la alcachofa, Oda al tomate,* and *Oda a la cebolla,* are written in simple language. Prepare copies of the poem beforehand and go over unfamiliar vocabulary.

Worth Noting Though Chile is the second smallest Spanish-speaking country in South America, it has about 2,700 miles of coastline. Some of the highest peaks in the Andes lie on the border with Argentina, and the volcanoes that lie along the Atacama Desert are the tallest in the world. Chile's agricultural region is a valley the size of central California's. The southern archipelago is cool, foggy, and rainy, like the Alaska panhandle. It is estimated that Chile has about 6,000 islands.

Lugares • **La isla de Pascua**

La isla de Pascua° recibió ese nombre porque los exploradores holandeses° llegaron a la isla por primera vez el día de Pascua de 1722. Ahora es parte del territorio de Chile. La isla de Pascua es famosa por los *moái*, estatuas enormes que representan personas con rasgos° muy exagerados. Estas estatuas las construyeron los *rapa nui*, los antiguos habitantes de la zona. Todavía no se sabe mucho sobre los *rapa nui*, ni tampoco se sabe por qué decidieron abandonar la isla.

Deportes • **Los deportes de invierno**

Hay muchos lugares para practicar deportes de invierno en Chile porque las montañas nevadas de los Andes ocupan gran parte del país. El Parque Nacional Villarrica, por ejemplo, situado al pie de un volcán y junto a° un lago, es un sitio popular para el esquí y el *snowboard*. Para los que prefieren deportes más extremos, el centro de esquí Valle Nevado organiza excursiones para practicar heliesquí.

Ciencias • **Astronomía**

Los observatorios chilenos, situados en los Andes, son lugares excelentes para las observaciones astronómicas. Científicos° de todo el mundo van a Chile para estudiar las estrellas° y otros cuerpos celestes. Hoy día Chile está construyendo nuevos observatorios y telescopios para mejorar las imágenes del universo.

Economía • **El vino**

La producción de vino comenzó en Chile en el siglo° XVI. Ahora la industria del vino constituye una parte importante de la actividad agrícola del país y la exportación de sus productos está aumentando° cada vez más. Los vinos chilenos son muy apreciados internacionalmente por su gran variedad, sus ricos y complejos sabores° y su precio moderado. Los más conocidos son los vinos de Aconcagua y del valle del Maipo.

 ¿Qué aprendiste? Responde a cada pregunta con una oración completa.

1. ¿Qué porcentaje (*percentage*) de la población chilena es urbana?
 El 80 por ciento de la población chilena es urbana.
2. ¿Qué son los *moái*? ¿Dónde están? Los *moái* son estatuas enormes. Están en la isla de Pascua.
3. ¿Qué deporte extremo ofrece el centro de esquí Valle Nevado?
 Ofrece la práctica de heliesquí.
4. ¿Por qué van a Chile científicos de todo el mundo? Porque los observatorios chilenos son excelentes para las observaciones astronómicas.
5. ¿Cuándo comenzó la producción de vino en Chile?
 Comenzó en el siglo XVI.
6. ¿Por qué son apreciados internacionalmente los vinos chilenos? Son apreciados por su variedad, sus ricos y complejos sabores y su precio moderado.

 Conexión Internet Investiga estos temas en **vhlcentral.com**.

1. Busca información sobre Pablo Neruda e Isabel Allende. ¿Dónde y cuándo nacieron? ¿Cuáles son algunas de sus obras (*works*)? ¿Cuáles son algunos de los temas de sus obras?
2. Busca información sobre sitios donde los chilenos y los turistas practican deportes de invierno en Chile. Selecciona un sitio y descríbeselo a tu clase.

 Practice more at **vhlcentral.com**.

La isla de Pascua *Easter Island* holandeses *Dutch* rasgos *features* junto a *beside* Científicos *Scientists* estrellas *stars*
siglo *century* aumentando *increasing* complejos sabores *complex flavors*

La isla de Pascua With its vibrant Polynesian culture, Easter Island is unlike anywhere else in Chile. Located 2,000 miles from the nearest island and 4,000 from the Chilean coast, it is one of the most isolated places on earth. Until the 1960s, it was visited once a year by a Chilean warship bringing supplies. Now there are regular air connections to Santiago. For more information about **la isla de Pascua,** you may want to play the *Panorama cultural* video footage for this lesson.

Los deportes de invierno Remind students that some of the highest mountains in South America lie along the border Chile shares with Argentina. In the south is the **Parque Nacional Torres del Paine**, a national park featuring ice caverns, deep glacial trenches, and other spectacular features.

Astronomía In 1962, the Cerro Tololo Inter-American Observatory was founded as a joint project between Chilean and American astronomers. Since that time, so many other major telescopes have been installed for research purposes that Chile is home to the highest concentration of telescopes in the world.

El vino ←→ Invite students to research the wine-growing regions of Chile and to compare them to those of California, Spain, or other wine-producing areas. Encourage students to share their findings with the class.

Conexión Internet Students will find supporting Internet activities and links at **vhlcentral.com**.

TEACHING OPTIONS

Worth Noting The native Mapuche people of southern Chile are a small minority of the Chilean population today, but have maintained a strong cultural identity since the time of their first contact with Europeans. In fact, they resisted conquest so well that it was only in the late nineteenth century that the government of Chile could assert sovereignty over the region south of the Bío-Bío River. However, the majority of Chileans are of European descent. Chilean Spanish is much less infused with indigenous lexical items than the Spanish of countries such as Guatemala and Mexico, where the larger indigenous population has made a greater impact on the language.

Las celebraciones

el aniversario (de bodas)	(wedding) anniversary
la boda	wedding
el cumpleaños	birthday
el día de fiesta	holiday
la fiesta	party
el/la invitado/a	guest
la Navidad	Christmas
la quinceañera	young woman celebrating her fifteenth birthday
la sorpresa	surprise
brindar	to toast (drink)
celebrar	to celebrate
divertirse (e:ie)	to have fun
invitar	to invite
pasarlo bien/mal	to have a good/bad time
regalar	to give (a gift)
reírse (e:i)	to laugh
relajarse	to relax
sonreír (e:i)	to smile
sorprender	to surprise

Los postres y otras comidas

la botella (de vino)	bottle (of wine)
el champán	champagne
los dulces	sweets; candy
el flan (de caramelo)	baked (caramel) custard
la galleta	cookie
el helado	ice cream
el pastel (de chocolate)	(chocolate) cake; pie
el postre	dessert

Las relaciones personales

la amistad	friendship
el amor	love
el divorcio	divorce
el estado civil	marital status
el matrimonio	marriage
la pareja	(married) couple; partner
el/la recién casado/a	newlywed
casarse (con)	to get married (to)
comprometerse (con)	to get engaged (to)
divorciarse (de)	to get divorced (from)
enamorarse (de)	to fall in love (with)
llevarse bien/mal (con)	to get along well/ badly (with)
odiar	to hate
romper (con)	to break up (with)
salir (con)	to go out (with); to date
separarse (de)	to separate (from)
tener una cita	to have a date; to have an appointment
casado/a	married
divorciado/a	divorced
juntos/as	together
separado/a	separated
soltero/a	single
viudo/a	widower/widow

Las etapas de la vida

la adolescencia	adolescence
la edad	age
el estado civil	marital status
las etapas de la vida	the stages of life
la juventud	youth
la madurez	maturity; middle age
la muerte	death
el nacimiento	birth
la niñez	childhood
la vejez	old age
cambiar (de)	to change
graduarse (de/en)	to graduate (from/in)
jubilarse	to retire (from work)
nacer	to be born

Palabras adicionales

la alegría	happiness
el beso	kiss
conmigo	with me
contigo	with you
¡Felicidades!/ ¡Felicitaciones!	Congratulations!
¡Feliz cumpleaños!	Happy birthday!

Expresiones útiles	See page 281.

 Audio: Vocabulary

En el consultorio

10

Communicative Goals

You will learn how to:

- Describe how you feel physically
- Talk about health and medical conditions

Lesson Goals

In **Lección 10**, students will be introduced to the following:

- names of parts of the body
- health-related terms
- medical-related vocabulary
- health services in Spanish-speaking countries
- healers and shamans
- the imperfect tense
- uses of the preterite and imperfect tenses
- impersonal **se** constructions
- using **se** for unplanned events
- forming adverbs using [*adjective*] + **–mente**
- common adverbs and adverbial expressions
- activating background knowledge
- a video about hospitals in Argentina
- cultural, geographic, and economic information about Costa Rica and Nicaragua

A primera vista Ask these additional questions: **¿Cuándo fue la última vez que viste a tu médico/a? ¿Estuviste en su consultorio la semana pasada? ¿Cuáles son las mejores comidas para sentirte bien?**

Teaching Tip Look for these icons for additional communicative practice:

→👤←	Interpretive communication
←👤→	Presentational communication
👤↔👤	Interpersonal communication

A PRIMERA VISTA

- ¿Están en una farmacia o en un hospital?
- ¿El hombre es médico o dentista?
- ¿Qué hace él, una operación o un examen médico?
- ¿Crees que la paciente está nerviosa?

INSTRUCTIONAL RESOURCES

Supersite (vhlcentral.com)
Video: ***Fotonovela*, Flash cultura*, Panorama cultural****
**Also on DVD*
Audio: Textbook and Lab MP3 Files (*also on CD*)
Activity Pack: Information Gap Activities, games, additional activity handouts

Resources: Textbook Answer Key, WB/VM/LM Answer Key, Scripts, Translations, **Vocabulario adicional**, lesson plans, **Estructura** *PowerPoints*, Overheads
Testing Program: Quizzes, Tests, Exams, MP3s (*also on Test Generator CD*)

Learning Management System (Assignment Task Manager, Gradebook)
WebSAM (online Workbook/Video Manual/Lab Manual)
Workbook/Video Manual
Lab Manual

Section Goals

In **Contextos**, students will learn and practice:
- names of parts of the body
- vocabulary for talking about illnesses and accidents
- vocabulary associated with medical visits

Instructional Resources

Supersite: Audio (Textbook and Lab MP3 Files); Resources (Overheads, **Vocabulario adicional**, Activity Pack, Scripts, Answer Keys); Testing Program (Quizzes)
WebSAM
Workbook, pp. 109–110
Lab Manual, p. 55

Teaching Tips

- →🧍← Pretend to have had an accident-filled day. Ex: **Ayer pasé un día horrible. Fui a pasear en bicicleta y me caí. Me lastimé las rodillas y los brazos. Luego, cuando llegué a casa, me di con la puerta y me lastimé el ojo. Esta mañana cerré la puerta del auto y me lastimé el dedo.** Then ask comprehension questions about what hurts. Ex: **¿Me duele la garganta? (No.)** Finally, ask students about likely treatment options.
- Use the **Lección 10 Contextos** overheads to assist with this presentation.
- ←🧍→ Have students refer to the scene and the vocabulary boxes as you give yes/no statements about the new vocabulary. Ex: **¿Sí o no? La enfermera le toma la temperatura a la paciente. (Sí.) La doctora le pone una inyección al hombre. (No.)** Then ask volunteers to describe what is going on in the scene, using as much of the new vocabulary as possible.

En el consultorio

Más vocabulario

la clínica	clinic
el consultorio	doctor's office
el/la dentista	dentist
el examen médico	physical exam
la farmacia	pharmacy
el hospital	hospital
la operación	operation
la sala de emergencia(s)	emergency room
el cuerpo	body
el oído	(sense of) hearing; inner ear
el accidente	accident
la salud	health
el síntoma	symptom
caerse	to fall (down)
darse con	to bump into; to run into
doler (o:ue)	to hurt
enfermarse	to get sick
estar enfermo/a	to be sick
poner una inyección	to give an injection
recetar	to prescribe
romperse (la pierna)	to break (one's leg)
sacar(se) un diente	to have a tooth removed
sufrir una enfermedad	to suffer an illness
torcerse (o:ue) (el tobillo)	to sprain (one's ankle)
toser	to cough

Variación léxica

gripe ⟷ gripa (Col., Gua., Méx.)
resfriado ⟷ catarro (Cuba, Esp., Gua.)
sala de emergencia(s) ⟷ sala de urgencias (Arg., Col., Esp., Méx.)
romperse ⟷ quebrarse (Arg., Gua.)

recursos

WB pp. 109–110	LM p. 55	🅢 vhlcentral.com Lección 10

el corazón

el paciente

SALIDA

el ojo

la nariz

la doctora

la cabeza

la oreja

el cuello

la boca

la garganta

el estómago

el dedo

la rodilla

el dedo del pie

Síntomas y condiciones médicas

el dolor (de cabeza)	(head)ache; pain
la gripe	flu
el resfriado	cold
la tos	cough
congestionado/a	congested; stuffed up
embarazada	pregnant
grave	grave; serious
mareado/a	dizzy; nauseated
médico/a	medical
saludable	healthy
sano/a	healthy
tener dolor (m.)	to have pain
tener fiebre	to have a fever

TPR Play a game of **Simón dice.** Write **toquen** on the board and explain that it means *touch.* Start by saying: **Simón dice… que toquen la nariz.** Students are to touch their noses and keep their hands there until instructed to do otherwise. Work through various parts of the body. Be sure to give instructions occasionally without saying **Simón dice…**

Variación léxica Point out differences in health-related vocabulary, as well as some false cognates. **Embarazada** means *pregnant,* not *embarrassed.* You may also want to present **constipado/a** and explain that it does not mean *constipated,* but rather *congested* or *stuffed up.* Point out that, whereas in English people have ten fingers and ten toes, in Spanish people have twenty **dedos: diez dedos de las manos y diez de los pies.**

la radiografía

el hueso

la enfermera

la paciente

Estornuda.

Toma la temperatura.

el brazo

la pierna

el tobillo

La medicina

el antibiótico	antibiotic
la aspirina	aspirin
la pastilla	pill; tablet
la receta	prescription

Práctica

1 Escuchar 🎧 Escucha las preguntas y selecciona la respuesta más adecuada.

a. Tengo dolor de cabeza y fiebre.
b. No fui a la clase porque estaba (*I was*) enfermo.
c. Me caí la semana pasada jugando al tenis.
d. Debes ir a la farmacia.
e. Porque tengo gripe.
f. Sí, tengo mucha tos por las noches.
g. Lo llevaron directamente a la sala de emergencia.
h. No sé. Todavía tienen que tomarme la temperatura.

1. ___c___ 3. ___g___ 5. ___f___ 7. ___a___
2. ___e___ 4. ___d___ 6. ___h___ 8. ___b___

2 Seleccionar 🎧 Escucha la conversación entre Daniel y su doctor y selecciona la respuesta que mejor complete cada oración.

1. Daniel cree que tiene ___a___.
 a. gripe b. un resfriado c. la temperatura alta
2. A Daniel le duele la cabeza, estornuda, tose y ___c___.
 a. se cae b. tiene fiebre c. está congestionado
3. El doctor le ___b___.
 a. pone una inyección b. toma la temperatura
 c. mira el oído
4. A Daniel no le gustan ___a___.
 a. las inyecciones b. los antibióticos c. las visitas al doctor
5. El doctor dice que Daniel tiene ___b___.
 a. gripe b. un resfriado c. fiebre
6. Después de la consulta Daniel va a ___c___.
 a. la sala de emergencia b. la clínica c. la farmacia

3 Completar Completa las oraciones con una palabra de la misma familia de la palabra subrayada. Usa la forma correcta de cada palabra.

1. Cuando <u>oyes</u> algo, usas el ___oído___.
2. Cuando te <u>enfermas</u>, te sientes ___enfermo/a___ y necesitas ir al consultorio para ver a la ___enfermera___.
3. ¿Alguien ___estornudó___? Creo que oí un <u>estornudo</u> (*sneeze*).
4. No puedo <u>arrodillarme</u> (*kneel down*) porque me lastimé la ___rodilla___ en un accidente de coche.
5. ¿Vas al ___consultorio___ para <u>consultar</u> al médico?
6. Si te rompes un <u>diente</u>, vas al ___dentista___.

4 Contestar Mira el dibujo y contesta las preguntas. Answers will vary.

1. ¿Qué hace la doctora? 4. ¿Qué hace el paciente?
2. ¿Qué hay en la pared (*wall*)? 5. ¿A quién le duele la garganta?
3. ¿Qué hace la enfermera? 6. ¿Qué tiene la paciente?

TEACHING OPTIONS

Game Play **Concentración**. On eight cards, write names for parts of the body or items found in a doctor's office. On another eight cards, draw or paste a picture that matches each word. Place the cards facedown in four rows of four. In pairs, students select two cards. If the cards match, the pair keeps them. If the cards do not match, they replace them in their original position. The pair with the most cards at the end wins.

Heritage Speakers ←🛉→ Ask heritage speakers to describe a visit they made to a doctor's office. Verify comprehension by having students relate what was said. On the board, write any nonactive vocabulary that students may use, such as **auscultar los pulmones, sacar la lengua, tomar la presión arterial, la sangre,** and so forth.

1 Teaching Tip Before playing the audio, have students read through the list of responses. Explain that not all the questions are directed at the same person.

1 Script 1. ¿Cuándo te caíste? 2. ¿Por qué vas al médico? 3. ¿Adónde llevaron a Juan después del accidente? 4. ¿Adónde debo ir para conseguir estas pastillas? 5. ¿Tienes mucha tos? 6. ¿Tienes fiebre? 7. ¿Cuáles son sus síntomas, señor? 8. Ayer no te vi en la clase de biología. ¿Por qué? *Textbook MP3s*

2 Teaching Tip To challenge students, write the activity items on the board as cloze sentences. Have students complete them as they listen to the audio.

2 Script DANIEL: Hola, doctor. Me siento enfermo. Creo que tengo gripe. DOCTOR: ¿Cuándo te enfermaste? DA: La semana pasada. DO: ¿Cuáles son tus síntomas? DA: Me duele la cabeza, estornudo y tengo mucha tos por las noches. Ah, y también estoy congestionado. DO: Voy a tomarte la temperatura. DA: ¿Me va a poner una inyección, doctor? No me gustan las inyecciones. DO: No tienes fiebre y, tranquilo, no necesitas inyecciones. Esto es un simple resfriado. Voy a recetarte unas pastillas y pronto tu salud va a mejorar. DA: Gracias, doctor. Voy a pasar por la farmacia al salir de la consulta. *Textbook MP3s*

3 Teaching Tip Have students identify the part of speech of each underlined word and each fill-in-the-blank answer.

3 Expansion Have students write two additional cloze sentences for a partner to complete.

4 Teaching Tip Have pairs play a memory game. Have them study the drawing for 30 seconds, then ask each other the questions.

5 **Asociaciones** Trabajen en parejas para identificar las partes del cuerpo que ustedes asocian con estas actividades. Sigan el modelo. Answers will vary.

> **modelo**
> nadar
> **Estudiante 1:** Usamos los brazos para nadar.
> **Estudiante 2:** Usamos las piernas también.

1. hablar por teléfono
2. tocar el piano
3. correr en el parque
4. escuchar música
5. ver una película
6. toser
7. llevar zapatos
8. comprar perfume
9. estudiar biología
10. comer pollo asado

6 **Cuestionario** Contesta el cuestionario seleccionando las respuestas que reflejen mejor tus experiencias. Suma (*Add*) los puntos de cada respuesta y anota el resultado. Después, con el resto de la clase, compara y analiza los resultados del cuestionario y comenta lo que dicen de la salud y de los hábitos de todo el grupo. Answers will vary.

¿Tienes buena salud?

27–30 puntos	Salud y hábitos excelentes
23–26 puntos	Salud y hábitos buenos
22 puntos o menos	Salud y hábitos problemáticos

1. ¿Con qué frecuencia te enfermas? (resfriados, gripe, etc.)
Cuatro veces por año o más. (1 punto)
Dos o tres veces por año. (2 puntos)
Casi nunca. (3 puntos)

2. ¿Con qué frecuencia tienes dolores de estómago o problemas digestivos?
Con mucha frecuencia. (1 punto)
A veces. (2 puntos)
Casi nunca. (3 puntos)

3. ¿Con qué frecuencia sufres de dolores de cabeza?
Frecuentemente. (1 punto)
A veces. (2 puntos)
Casi nunca. (3 puntos)

4. ¿Comes verduras y frutas?
No, casi nunca como verduras ni frutas. (1 punto)
Sí, a veces. (2 puntos)
Sí, todos los días. (3 puntos)

5. ¿Eres alérgico/a a algo?
Sí, a muchas cosas. (1 punto)
Sí, a algunas cosas. (2 puntos)
No. (3 puntos)

6. ¿Haces ejercicios aeróbicos?
No, casi nunca hago ejercicios aeróbicos. (1 punto)
Sí, a veces. (2 puntos)
Sí, con frecuencia. (3 puntos)

7. ¿Con qué frecuencia te haces un examen médico?
Nunca o casi nunca. (1 punto)
Cada dos años. (2 puntos)
Cada año y/o antes de empezar a practicar un deporte. (3 puntos)

8. ¿Con qué frecuencia vas al dentista?
Nunca voy al dentista. (1 punto)
Sólo cuando me duele un diente. (2 puntos)
Por lo menos una vez por año. (3 puntos)

9. ¿Qué comes normalmente por la mañana?
No como nada por la mañana. (1 punto)
Tomo una bebida dietética. (2 puntos)
Como cereal y fruta. (3 puntos)

10. ¿Con qué frecuencia te sientes mareado/a?
Frecuentemente. (1 punto)
A veces. (2 puntos)
Casi nunca. (3 puntos)

 Practice more at **vhlcentral.com.**

Comunicación

7 **¿Qué les pasó?** Trabajen en un grupo de dos o tres personas. Hablen de lo que les pasó y de cómo se sienten las personas que aparecen en los dibujos. Answers will vary.

1. Adela 2. Francisco 3. Pilar

4. Pedro 5. Cristina 6. Félix

8 **Un accidente** Cuéntale a la clase de un accidente o una enfermedad que tuviste. Incluye información que conteste estas preguntas. Answers will vary.

✔ ¿Qué ocurrió?
✔ ¿Dónde ocurrió?
✔ ¿Cuándo ocurrió?
✔ ¿Cómo ocurrió?
✔ ¿Quién te ayudó y cómo?
✔ ¿Tuviste algún problema después del accidente o después de la enfermedad?
✔ ¿Cuánto tiempo tuviste el problema?

9 **Crucigrama** Tu profesor(a) les va a dar a ti y a un(a) compañero/a un crucigrama *(crossword)* incompleto. Tú tienes las palabras que necesita tu compañero/a y él/ella tiene las palabras que tú necesitas. Tienen que darse pistas para completarlo. No pueden decir la palabra necesaria; deben utilizar definiciones, ejemplos y frases. Answers will vary.

modelo
10 horizontal: La usamos para hablar.
14 vertical: Es el médico que examina los dientes.

Successful Language Learning Tell students to imagine situations in which they commonly see a doctor and to think about what they would say in Spanish in each of these situations.

7 Expansion
- Ask students to list the various possibilities of what happened to these people and how they feel. Have them name possible treatments for each.
- Bring in magazine pictures related to illness, medicine, and medical appointments. Have students describe what is going on in the images.

8 Teaching Tip Model this activity by talking about an illness or accident you had.

8 Expansion To practice more verb forms, have students discuss with a partner illnesses or accidents that someone they know had.

9 Teaching Tip Divide the class into pairs and distribute the handouts from the Activity Pack (Activity Pack/Supersite) that correspond to this Information Gap Activity. Give students ten minutes to complete this activity.

9 Expansion Have pairs use words from the crossword to role-play a visit to a doctor's office.

TEACHING OPTIONS

Pairs For homework, ask students to draw an alien or other fantastic being. In the next class period, have students describe the alien to a classmate, who will draw it according to the description. Ex: **Tiene una cabeza grande y tres piernas delgadas con pelo en las rodillas. Encima de la cabeza tiene ocho ojos pequeños y uno grande…** Then have students compare the drawings for accuracy.

Extra Practice Write **Mido ____ pies y ____ pulgadas** on the board and explain what it means. Then have students write physical descriptions of themselves using as much vocabulary from this lesson as they can. Collect the papers, shuffle them, and read the descriptions aloud. The rest of the class has to guess who is being described.

¡Qué dolor!

Jimena no se siente bien y tiene que ir al doctor.

PERSONAJES ELENA JIMENA

Video: *Fotonovela*
Record and Compare

1

ELENA ¿Cómo te sientes?

JIMENA Me duele un poco la garganta. Pero no tengo fiebre.

ELENA Creo que tienes un resfriado. Te voy a llevar a casa.

2

ELENA ¿Don Diego ya fue a la farmacia? ¿Cuánto tiempo hace que lo llamaste?

JIMENA Hace media hora. Ay, qué cosas, de niña apenas me enfermaba. No perdí ni un solo día de clases.

ELENA Yo tampoco.

ELENA Nunca tenía resfriados, pero me rompí el brazo dos veces. Mi hermana y yo estábamos paseando en bicicleta y casi me di con un señor que caminaba por la calle. Me caí y me rompí el brazo.

3

JIMENA ¿Qué es esto?

ELENA Es té de jengibre. Cuando me dolía el estómago, mi mamá siempre me hacía tomarlo. Se dice que es bueno para el dolor de estómago.

JIMENA Pero no me duele el estómago.

4

JIMENA Hola, don Diego. Gracias por venir.

DON DIEGO Fui a la farmacia. Aquí están las pastillas para el resfriado. Se debe tomar una cada seis horas con las comidas. Y no se deben tomar más de seis pastillas al día.

5

6

(*La Sra. Díaz llama a Jimena.*)

JIMENA Hola, mamá. Don Diego me trajo los medicamentos... ¿Al doctor? ¿Estás segura? Allá nos vemos. (*A Elena*) Mi mamá ya hizo una cita para mí con el Dr. Meléndez.

DON DIEGO **SRA. DÍAZ** **DR. MELÉNDEZ**

SRA. DÍAZ ¿Te pusiste un suéter anoche?

JIMENA No, mamá. Se me olvidó.

SRA. DÍAZ Doctor, esta jovencita salió anoche, se le olvidó ponerse un suéter y parece que le dio un resfriado.

DR. MELÉNDEZ Jimena, ¿cuáles son tus síntomas?

JIMENA Toso con frecuencia y me duele la garganta.

DR. MELÉNDEZ ¿Cuánto tiempo hace que tienes estos síntomas?

JIMENA Hace dos días que me duele la garganta.

DR. MELÉNDEZ Muy bien. Aquí no tienes infección. No tienes fiebre. Te voy a mandar algo para la garganta. Puedes ir por los medicamentos inmediatamente a la farmacia.

SRA. DÍAZ Doctor, ¿cómo está? ¿Es grave?

DR. MELÉNDEZ No, no es nada grave. Jimena, la próxima vez, escucha a tu mamá. ¡Tienes que usar suéter!

recursos

VM pp. 213–214 | vhlcentral.com Lección 10

Expresiones útiles

Discussing medical conditions

¿Cómo te sientes?
How do you feel?
Me duele un poco la garganta.
My throat hurts a little.
No me duele el estómago.
My stomach doesn't hurt.
De niño/a apenas me enfermaba.
As a child, I rarely got sick.
¡Soy alérgico/a a chile!
I'm allergic to chili powder!

Discussing remedies

Se dice que el té de jengibre es bueno para el dolor de estómago.
They say ginger tea is good for stomach aches.
Aquí están las pastillas para el resfriado.
Here are the pills for your cold.
Se debe tomar una cada seis horas.
You should take one every six hours.

Expressions with hacer

Hace + [*period of time*] **que** + [*present /preterite*]
¿Cuánto tiempo hace que tienes estos síntomas?
How long have you had these symptoms?
Hace dos días que me duele la garganta.
My throat has been hurting for two days.
¿Cuánto tiempo hace que lo llamaste?
How long has it been since you called him?
Hace media hora.
It's been a half hour (since I called).

Additional vocabulary

canela *cinnamon*
miel *honey*
terco *stubborn*

Expresiones útiles Point out the phrase **apenas me enfermaba**. Explain that **apenas** is an adverb, and that **me enfermaba** is an imperfect tense form, used here to talk about habitual events in the past. Then draw attention to **Se dice que** and **Se debe tomar** and explain that these are examples of impersonal constructions with **se**. Finally, point out **Se me olvidó** and **se le olvidó** under video still 7 and tell students that **se** is also used to describe unplanned or accidental events. Tell students that they will learn more about these concepts in **Estructura**.

Teaching Tip

👥↔👤 Ask students to read the **Fotonovela** captions in groups of five. Ask one or two groups to role-play the dialogue for the class.

Nota cultural In Celsius, normal body temperature is 37 degrees. If a temperature reading is above 37 but below 38, it is considered **febrícula**, or low-grade fever. Any temperature from 38 to 40 degrees Celsius is considered a fever (**fiebre**).

TEACHING OPTIONS

Pairs 👤↔👤 On the board, write the paradigms for **hace** + [*time period*] + **que** + [*present*] and **hace** + [*time period*] + **que** + [*preterite*]. Ask a few comprehension questions to contrast their uses. Ex: **¿Cuánto tiempo hace que te graduaste de la escuela secundaria? ¿Cuánto tiempo hace que eres estudiante universitario?** Then write two lists on the board, one with activities (Ex: **ir al dentista, leer un buen libro, ver una película extranjera,** **hacerse un examen médico, comer comida orgánica**) and one with time expressions (Ex: **un año, un mes, una semana, dos días, una hora**). Then have pairs interview each other to find out how long it has been since they have done these activities. Ex: **—¿Cuánto tiempo hace que fuiste al dentista? —Hace dos años que fui al dentista./Fui al dentista hace dos años.** Have students report to the class about their partners' activities.

¿Qué pasó?

1 **¿Cierto o falso?** Decide si lo que dicen estas oraciones sobre Jimena es **cierto** o **falso**. Corrige las oraciones falsas.

	Cierto	Falso
1. Dice que de niña apenas se enfermaba.	✓	○
2. Tiene dolor de garganta y fiebre.	○	✓ — Tiene dolor de garganta, pero no tiene fiebre.
3. Olvidó ponerse un suéter anoche.	✓	○
4. Hace tres días que le duele la garganta.	○	✓ — Hace dos días que le duele la garganta.
5. El doctor le dice que tiene una infección.	○	✓ — El doctor le dice que no tiene una infección.

2 **Identificar** Identifica quién puede decir estas oraciones.

1. Como dice tu mamá, tienes que usar suéter. Dr. Meléndez
2. Por pasear en bicicleta me rompí el brazo dos veces. Elena
3. ¿Cuánto tiempo hace que toses y te duele la garganta? Dr. Meléndez
4. Tengo cita con el Dr. Meléndez. Jimena
5. Dicen que el té de jengibre es muy bueno para los dolores de estómago. Elena
6. Nunca perdí un día de clases porque apenas me enfermaba. Jimena

DR. MELÉNDEZ

ELENA

JIMENA

3 **Ordenar** Pon estos sucesos en el orden correcto.

a. Jimena va a ver al doctor. **4**
b. El doctor le dice a la Sra. Díaz que no es nada serio. **6**
c. Elena le habla a Jimena de cuando se rompió el brazo. **2**
d. El doctor le receta medicamentos. **5**
e. Jimena le dice a Elena que le duele la garganta. **1**
f. Don Diego le trae a Jimena las pastillas para el resfriado. **3**

4 **En el consultorio** Trabajen en parejas para representar los papeles de un(a) médico/a y su paciente. Usen las instrucciones como guía.

El/La médico/a	**El/La paciente**
Pregúntale al / a la paciente qué le pasó.	→ Dile que te caíste en casa. Describe tu dolor.
Pregúntale cuánto tiempo hace que se cayó.	→ Describe la situación. Piensas que te rompiste el dedo.
Mira el dedo. Debes recomendar un tratamiento (*treatment*) al / a la paciente.	→ Debes hacer preguntas al / a la médico/a sobre el tratamiento (*treatment*).

 Practice more at **vhlcentral.com.**

Ortografía

 Concepts

El acento y las sílabas fuertes

In Spanish, written accent marks are used on many words. Here is a review of some of the principles governing word stress and the use of written accents.

as-pi-ri-na **gri-pe** **to-man** **an-tes**

In Spanish, when a word ends in a vowel, **-n**, or **-s**, the spoken stress usually falls on the next-to-last syllable. Words of this type are very common and do not need a written accent.

a-sí **in-glés** **in-fec-ción** **hé-ro-e**

When a word ends in a vowel, **-n**, or **-s**, and the spoken stress does *not* fall on the next-to-last syllable, then a written accent is needed.

hos-pi-tal **na-riz** **re-ce-tar** **to-ser**

When a word ends in any consonant *other* than **-n** or **-s**, the spoken stress usually falls on the last syllable. Words of this type are very common and do not need a written accent.

lá-piz **fút-bol** **hués-ped** **sué-ter**

When a word ends in any consonant *other* than **-n** or **-s** and the spoken stress does *not* fall on the last syllable, then a written accent is needed.

far-ma-cia **bio-lo-gí-a** **su-cio** **frí-o**

Diphthongs (two weak vowels or a strong and weak vowel together) are normally pronounced as a single syllable. A written accent is needed when a diphthong is broken into two syllables.

sol **pan** **mar** **tos**

Spanish words of only one syllable do not usually carry a written accent (unless it is to distinguish meaning: **se** and **sé**.)

CONSULTA

In Spanish, **a**, **e**, and **o** are considered strong vowels while **i** and **u** are weak vowels. To review this concept, see **Lección 3**, **Pronunciación**, p. 77.

Práctica Busca las palabras que necesitan acento escrito y escribe su forma correcta.

1. sal-mon salmón
2. ins-pec-tor
3. nu-me-ro número
4. fa-cil fácil
5. ju-go
6. a-bri-go
7. ra-pi-do rápido
8. sa-ba-do sábado
9. vez
10. me-nu menú
11. o-pe-ra-cion operación
12. im-per-me-a-ble
13. a-de-mas además
14. re-ga-te-ar
15. an-ti-pa-ti-co antipático
16. far-ma-cia
17. es-qui esquí
18. pen-sion pensión
19. pa-is país
20. per-don perdón

El ahorcado Juega al ahorcado (*hangman*) para adivinar las palabras.

1. _ l _ _ _ _ _ a Vas allí cuando estás enfermo. clínica
2. _ _ _ _ e _ c _ _ n Se usa para poner una vacuna (*vaccination*). inyección
3. _ _ _ d _ o _ _ _ _ _ _ a Permite ver los huesos. radiografía
4. _ _ _ _ i _ o Trabaja en un hospital. médico
5. a _ _ _ _ b _ _ _ _ _ _ _ Es una medicina. antibiótico

recursos

| LM p. 56 | vhlcentral.com Lección 10 |

Section Goals

In **Ortografía**, students will review:
- word stress
- the use of written accent marks

Instructional Resources
Supersite: Audio (Lab MP3 Files); Resources (Scripts, Answer Keys)
WebSAM
Lab Manual, p. 56

Teaching Tips

- You may want to explain that all words in which the spoken stress falls on the antepenultimate or preantepenultimate syllable will carry a written accent, regardless of the word's final letter.
- As you go through each point in the explanation, write the example words on the board, pronounce them, and have students repeat. Then, ask students to provide words they learned in previous lessons that exemplify each point.
- Make a list of unfamiliar words on the board, leaving out any written accent marks. Pronounce them, and ask students if a written accent mark is needed, and if so, where it should be placed. Include words that carry a written accent mark as well as some that do not.
- Point out that **Ortografía** replaces **Pronunciación** in the Student Edition for **Lecciones 10–15**, but not in the Lab Manual. The **Recursos** box references the **Pronunciación** sections found in all lessons of the Lab Manual.

TEACHING OPTIONS

Extra Practice Add an auditory aspect to this **Ortografía** section. Have students close their books. Then read aloud the questions in **Actividad 6, Cuestionario,** page 310. Say each sentence twice slowly and once at normal speed to give students enough time to write. Then have them open their books and check their work.

Pairs Ask students to work in pairs and explain why each word in the **Práctica** activity does or does not have a written accent mark. The same process can be followed with the words in the **El ahorcado** activity.

Section Goals

In **Cultura**, students will:
- read about health services in Spanish-speaking countries
- learn health-related terms
- read about **curanderos** and **chamanes**
- read about home remedies and medicinal plants

Instructional Resources

Supersite/DVD: *Flash cultura*
Supersite: Resources (Scripts, Translations, Answer Keys)
WebSAM
Video Manual, pp. 285–286

En detalle

Antes de leer Ask students about their experiences with health care while traveling. Ex: **¿Alguna vez te enfermaste durante un viaje? ¿Dónde? ¿Fuiste al hospital o al médico? ¿Quién lo pagó?**

Lectura
- Point out that many over-the-counter health care products in the U.S. are available by request at pharmacies in Spanish-speaking countries (e.g., facial cleansers, sunscreen, contact lens solution).
- Tell students that most pharmacies are closed on Sundays.
- While traditional pharmacies are privately owned and consist of a small counter and retail space, large chain pharmacies are entering the market, especially in Latin America.

Después de leer
- Ask students which three factors described in the article would be most important in devising an ideal health care system.

1 Expansion Give students these true/false statements as items 9–10: **9. El sistema de salud en Cuba no es muy desarrollado. (Falso. Es muy desarrollado.) 10. Las farmacias generalmente tienen un horario comercial. (Cierto.)**

EN DETALLE

(S) Additional Reading
Video: *Flash cultura*

Servicios de salud

¿Sabías que en los países hispanos no necesitas pagar por los servicios de salud?
Ésta es una de las diferencias que hay entre países como los Estados Unidos y los países hispanos.

En la mayor parte de estos países, el gobierno ofrece servicios médicos muy baratos o gratuitos° a sus ciudadanos°. Los turistas y extranjeros también pueden tener acceso a los servicios médicos a bajo° costo. La Seguridad Social y organizaciones similares son las responsables de gestionar° estos servicios.

Naturalmente, esto no funciona igual° en todos los países. En Ecuador, México y Perú, la situación varía según las regiones. Los habitantes de las ciudades y pueblos grandes tienen acceso a más servicios médicos, mientras que quienes viven en pueblos remotos sólo cuentan con° pequeñas clínicas.

Por su parte, Costa Rica, Colombia, Cuba y España tienen sistemas de salud muy desarrollados°.

Cruz verde de farmacia en Madrid, España

Las farmacias

Farmacia de guardia: Las farmacias generalmente tienen un horario comercial. Sin embargo°, en cada barrio° hay una farmacia de guardia que abre las veinticuatro horas del día.

Productos farmacéuticos: Todavía hay muchas farmacias tradicionales que están más especializadas en medicinas y productos farmacéuticos. No venden una gran variedad de productos.

Recetas: Muchos medicamentos se venden sin receta médica. Los farmacéuticos aconsejan° a las personas sobre problemas de salud y les dan las medicinas.

Cruz° verde: En muchos países, las farmacias tienen como símbolo una cruz verde. Cuando la cruz verde está encendida°, la farmacia está abierta.

En España, por ejemplo, todas las personas tienen acceso a ellos y en muchos casos son completamente gratuitos. Según un informe de la Organización Mundial de la Salud, el sistema de salud español ocupa el séptimo° lugar del mundo. Esto se debe no sólo al buen funcionamiento° del sistema, sino también al nivel de salud general de la población. Impresionante, ¿no?

Consulta médica en la República Dominicana

gratuitos *free (of charge)* ciudadanos *citizens* bajo *low* gestionar *to manage* igual *in the same way* cuentan con *have* desarrollados *developed* séptimo *seventh* funcionamiento *operation* Sin embargo *However* barrio *neighborhood* aconsejan *advise* Cruz *Cross* encendida *lit (up)*

ACTIVIDADES

1 **¿Cierto o falso?** Indica si lo que dicen las oraciones es **cierto** o **falso**. Corrige la información falsa.

1. En los países hispanos los gobiernos ofrecen servicios de salud accesibles a sus ciudadanos. **Cierto.**
2. En los países hispanos los extranjeros tienen que pagar mucho dinero por los servicios médicos. **Falso.** Los extranjeros tienen acceso a los servicios médicos a bajo costo.
3. El sistema de salud español es uno de los mejores del mundo. **Cierto.**
4. Las farmacias de guardia abren sólo los sábados y domingos. **Falso.** Las farmacias de guardia abren las 24 horas del día.
5. En los países hispanos las farmacias venden una gran variedad de productos. **Falso.** En los países hispanos las farmacias están más especializadas en medicinas y productos farmacéuticos.
6. Los farmacéuticos de los países hispanos aconsejan a los enfermos y venden algunas medicinas sin necesidad de receta. **Cierto.**
7. En México y otros países, los pueblos remotos cuentan con grandes centros médicos. **Falso.** Cuentan con pequeñas clínicas.
8. Muchas farmacias usan una cruz verde como símbolo. **Cierto.**

TEACHING OPTIONS

Cultural Comparison ←👤→ Ask students to write a short paragraph in which they compare the health care systems in the U.S. or Canada with those of different Spanish-speaking countries. You may want to have students review comparisons (**Estructura 8.3**) before writing.

Pairs 👤↔👤 Ask pairs to write a dialogue in which a foreign tourist in Costa Rica goes to the emergency room due to an injury. Have them use vocabulary from **Contextos** and **Expresiones útiles**. Have students role-play their dialogues for the class.

ASÍ SE DICE

La salud

el chequeo (Esp., Méx.)	el examen médico
la droguería (Col.)	la farmacia
la herida	*injury; wound*
la píldora	la pastilla
los primeros auxilios	*first aid*
la sangre	*blood*

EL MUNDO HISPANO

Remedios caseros° y plantas medicinales

- **Achiote°** En Suramérica se usa para curar inflamaciones de garganta. Las hojas° de achiote se cuecen° en agua, se cuelan° y se hacen gárgaras° con esa agua.

- **Ají** En Perú se usan cataplasmas° de las semillas° de ají para aliviar los dolores reumáticos y la tortícolis°.

- **Azúcar** En Nicaragua y otros países centroamericanos se usa el azúcar para detener° la sangre en pequeñas heridas.

- **Sábila (aloe vera)** En Latinoamérica, el jugo de las hojas de sábila se usa para reducir cicatrices°. Se recomienda aplicarlo sobre la cicatriz dos veces al día, durante varios meses.

Remedios caseros *Home remedies* Achiote *Annatto* hojas *leaves* se cuecen *are cooked* se cuelan *they are drained* gárgaras *gargles* cataplasmas *pastes* semillas *seeds* tortícolis *stiff neck* detener *to stop* cicatrices *scars*

PERFILES

Curanderos° y chamanes

¿Quieres ser doctor(a), juez(a)°, político/a o psicólogo/a? En algunas sociedades de las Américas **los curanderos** y **los chamanes** no tienen que escoger entre estas profesiones porque ellos son mediadores de conflictos y dan consejos a la comunidad. Su opinión es muy respetada.

Códice Florentino, México, siglo XVI

Desde las culturas antiguas° de las Américas muchas personas piensan que la salud del cuerpo y de la mente sólo puede existir si hay un equilibrio entre el ser humano y la naturaleza. Los curanderos y los chamanes son quienes cuidan este equilibrio.

Los curanderos se especializan más en enfermedades físicas, mientras que los chamanes están más

Cuzco, Perú

relacionados con los males° de la mente y el alma°. Ambos° usan plantas, masajes y rituales y sus conocimientos se basan en la tradición, la experiencia, la observación y la intuición.

Curanderos *Healers* juez(a) *judge* antiguas *ancient* males *illnesses* alma *soul* Ambos *Both*

Conexión Internet

¿Cuáles son algunos hospitales importantes del mundo hispano?

Go to **vhlcentral.com** to find more cultural information related to this **Cultura** section.

ACTIVIDADES

2 **Comprensión** Responde a las preguntas.

1. ¿Cómo se les llama a las farmacias en Colombia? *droguerías*
2. ¿Qué parte del achiote se usa para curar la garganta? *las hojas*
3. ¿Cómo se aplica la sábila para reducir cicatrices? *Se aplica sobre la cicatriz dos veces al día.*
4. En algunas partes de las Américas, ¿quiénes mantienen el equilibrio entre el ser humano y la naturaleza? *los chamanes y curanderos*
5. ¿Qué usan los curanderos y chamanes para curar? *Usan plantas, masajes y rituales.*

3 **¿Qué haces cuando tienes gripe?** Escribe cuatro oraciones sobre las cosas que haces cuando tienes gripe. Explica si vas al médico, si tomas medicamentos o si sigues alguna dieta especial. Después, comparte tu texto con un(a) compañero/a. *Answers will vary.*

recursos

VM pp. 285–286

vhlcentral.com Lección 10

 Practice more at **vhlcentral.com.**

TEACHING OPTIONS

TPR Divide the class into two teams, **remedios naturales** and **medicina moderna**, and have them stand at opposite sides of the room. Read a medical scenario aloud. The team whose name defines the situation most accurately has five seconds to step forward. Ex: **1. Juan sufre de dolores de cabeza. Hoy tiene una migraña. Decide comprar vitamina B2. (remedios naturales) 2. María tiene mucha ansiedad. Además siente estrés por su**

trabajo. Toma pastillas calmantes. (medicina moderna)
Small Groups Have small groups create a television commercial for a new natural product. Encourage them to include a customer testimonial stating how long they have had these symptoms (**hace** + [*time period*] + **que** + [*present*]), when they started using the product (**hace** + [*time period*] + **que** + [*preterite*]), and how they feel now.

Así se dice

- You may want to point out that in Spain a **droguería** is not a pharmacy, but rather a shop selling cleaning and decorating materials, as well as cosmetics.
- To challenge students, add these health-related words to the list: **la espalda** (*back*); **la fractura** (*fracture*); **el hombro** (*shoulder*); **el jarabe** (*cough syrup*); **la lengua** (*tongue*); **la muñeca** (*wrist*); **sangrar** (*to bleed*); **tener escalofríos** (*to have chills*); **el vendaje** (*bandage*).
- Practice new vocabulary by asking questions. Ex: **¿Vas todos los años a hacerte un chequeo?**

Perfiles Curanderos

sometimes experience discrimination in the medical field. However, recently, some medical doctors have grown to understand the beliefs of **los curanderos** and are working with them to help support their ceremonies and natural care while providing additional modern medical attention.

El mundo hispano

- Ask students: **¿Conocen otros remedios caseros o naturales?**
- Ask heritage speakers to describe home remedies used in their families.

2 **Expansion** Give students these questions as items 6–8: **6. ¿Para qué se usa el azúcar en Centroamérica? (para detener la sangre) 7. ¿Quiénes curan los males de la mente y el alma? (los chamanes) 8. ¿En qué se basan los conocimientos de los curanderos y chamanes? (en la tradición, la experiencia, la observación y la intuición)**

3 **Teaching Tip** As a variant, have students create a list of recommendations for a friend who has the flu. Ex: **Debes tomar sopa de pollo con verduras.**

Section Goal

In **Estructura 10.1**, students will learn the imperfect tense.

Instructional Resources
Supersite: Audio (Lab MP3 Files); Resources (*PowerPoints*, Activity Pack, Scripts, Answer Keys); Testing Program (Quizzes)
WebSAM
Workbook, pp. 111–112
Lab Manual, p. 57

Teaching Tips
• Explain to students that they can already express the past with the preterite tense, and now they are learning the imperfect tense, which also expresses the past but in a different way.
• As you work through the discussion of the imperfect, test comprehension by asking volunteers to supply the correct form of verbs for the subjects you name. Ex: **romper/nosotros (rompíamos)**
• Point out that **había** is impersonal and can be followed by a singular or plural noun. Ex: **Había una enfermera. Había muchos pacientes.**

¡Atención! To demonstrate that the accents on –**er** and –**ir** verbs break diphthongs, write **farmacia** and **vendia** on the board. Ask volunteers to pronounce each word, and have the class identify which needs a written accent to break the diphthong (**vendía**).

10.1 The imperfect tense (S) Tutorial

ANTE TODO In **Lecciones 6–9,** you learned the preterite tense. You will now learn the imperfect, which describes past activities in a different way.

The imperfect of regular verbs

		cantar	beber	escribir
SINGULAR FORMS	yo	cant**aba**	beb**ía**	escrib**ía**
	tú	cant**abas**	beb**ías**	escrib**ías**
	Ud./él/ella	cant**aba**	beb**ía**	escrib**ía**
PLURAL FORMS	nosotros/as	cant**ábamos**	beb**íamos**	escrib**íamos**
	vosotros/as	cant**abais**	beb**íais**	escrib**íais**
	Uds./ellos/ellas	cant**aban**	beb**ían**	escrib**ían**

De niña apenas me enfermaba.

Cuando me dolía el estómago, mi mamá me daba té de jengibre.

▶ There are no stem changes in the imperfect.

entender (e:ie)
servir (e:i)
doler (o:ue)

Entendíamos japonés.
We used to understand Japanese.
El camarero les **servía** el café.
The waiter was serving them coffee.
A Javier le **dolía** el tobillo.
Javier's ankle was hurting.

▶ The imperfect form of **hay** is **había** *(there was; there were; there used to be).*

▶ **¡Atención!** **Ir, ser,** and **ver** are the only verbs that are irregular in the imperfect.

The imperfect of irregular verbs

		ir	ser	ver
SINGULAR FORMS	yo	ib**a**	er**a**	ve**ía**
	tú	ib**as**	er**as**	ve**ías**
	Ud./él/ella	ib**a**	er**a**	ve**ía**
PLURAL FORMS	nosotros/as	íb**amos**	ér**amos**	ve**íamos**
	vosotros/as	ib**ais**	er**ais**	ve**íais**
	Uds./ellos/ellas	ib**an**	er**an**	ve**ían**

TEACHING OPTIONS

Extra Practice To provide oral practice with the imperfect tense, change the subjects in **¡Inténtalo!** on page 319. Have students give the appropriate forms for each infinitive listed. **Large Groups** Write a list of activities on the board. Ex: **1. tenerle miedo a la oscuridad 2. ir a la escuela en autobús 3. llevar el almuerzo a la escuela 4. comer brócoli 5. ser atrevido/a en clase 6. creer en Santa Claus** Have students copy the list on a sheet of paper and check off the items that they used to do when they were in the second grade. Then have them circulate around the room and find other students that used to do the same activities. Ex: **¿Le tenías miedo a la oscuridad?** When they find a student who used to do the same activity, have them write that student's name next to the item. Then have students report back to the class. Ex: **Mark y yo creíamos en Santa Claus.**

CONSULTA

You will learn more about the contrast between the preterite and the imperfect in **Estructura 10.2,** pp. 322–323.

Uses of the imperfect

▶ As a general rule, the imperfect is used to describe actions which are seen by the speaker as incomplete or "continuing," while the preterite is used to describe actions which have been completed. The imperfect expresses what was happening at a certain time or how things used to be. The preterite, in contrast, expresses a completed action.

—¿Qué te **pasó**?
What happened to you?

—¿Dónde **vivías** de niño?
Where did you live as a child?

—Me **torcí** el tobillo.
I sprained my ankle.

—**Vivía** en San José.
I lived in San José.

▶ These expressions are often used with the imperfect because they express habitual or repeated actions: **de niño/a** (*as a child*), **todos los días** (*every day*), **mientras** (*while*).

Uses of the imperfect

1. Habitual or repeated actions	**Íbamos** al parque los domingos. *We used to go to the park on Sundays.*
2. Events or actions that were in progress	Yo **leía** mientras él **estudiaba**. *I was reading while he was studying.*
3. Physical characteristics.	**Era** alto y guapo. *He was tall and handsome.*
4. Mental or emotional states	**Quería** mucho a su familia. *He loved his family very much.*
5. Telling time.	**Eran** las tres y media. *It was 3:30.*
6. Age .	Los niños **tenían** seis años. *The children were six years old.*

¡INTÉNTALO! Indica la forma correcta de cada verbo en el imperfecto.

1. Mis hermanos _____veían_____ (ver) televisión todas las tardes.
2. Yo _____viajaba_____ (viajar) en el tren de las 3:30.
3. ¿Dónde _____vivía_____ (vivir) Samuel de niño?
4. Tú _____hablabas_____ (hablar) con Javier.
5. Leonardo y yo _____corríamos_____ (correr) por el parque.
6. Ustedes _____iban_____ (ir) a la clínica.
7. Nadia _____bailaba_____ (bailar) merengue.
8. ¿Cuándo _____asistías_____ (asistir) tú a clase de español?
9. Yo _____era_____ (ser) muy feliz.
10. Nosotras _____comprendíamos_____ (comprender) las preguntas.

recursos

WB
pp. 111–112

LM
p. 57

S
vhlcentral.com
Lección 10

Práctica

1 Completar Primero, completa las oraciones con el imperfecto de los verbos. Luego, pon las oraciones en orden lógico y compáralas con las de un(a) compañero/a.

a. El doctor dijo que no ___era___ (ser) nada grave. __7__
b. El doctor ___quería___ (querer) ver la nariz del niño. __6__
c. Su mamá ___estaba___ (estar) dibujando cuando Miguelito entró llorando. __3__
d. Miguelito ___tenía___ (tener) la nariz hinchada (*swollen*). Fueron al hospital. __4__
e. Miguelito no ___iba___ (ir) a jugar más. Ahora quería ir a casa a descansar. __8__
f. Miguelito y sus amigos ___jugaban___ (jugar) al béisbol en el patio. __2__
g. ___Eran___ (Ser) las dos de la tarde. __1__
h. Miguelito le dijo a la enfermera que ___le dolía___ (dolerle) la nariz. __5__

2 Transformar Forma oraciones completas para describir lo que hacían Julieta y César. Usa las formas correctas del imperfecto y añade todas las palabras necesarias.

1. Julieta y César / ser / paramédicos
 Julieta y César eran paramédicos.
2. trabajar / juntos y / llevarse / muy bien
 Trabajaban juntos y se llevaban muy bien.
3. cuando / haber / accidente, / siempre / analizar / situación / con cuidado
 Cuando había un accidente, siempre analizaban la situación con cuidado.
4. preocuparse / mucho / por / pacientes
 Se preocupaban mucho por los pacientes.
5. si / paciente / tener / mucho / dolor, / ponerle / inyección
 Si el paciente tenía mucho dolor, le ponían una inyección.

3 En la escuela de medicina Usa los verbos de la lista para completar las oraciones con las formas correctas del imperfecto. Algunos verbos se usan más de una vez. Some answers may vary.
Suggested answers:

caerse	enfermarse	ir	querer	tener
comprender	estornudar	pensar	sentirse	tomar
doler	hacer	poder	ser	toser

1. Cuando Javier y Victoria ___eran___ estudiantes de medicina, siempre ___tenían___ que ir al médico.
2. Cada vez que él ___tomaba___ un examen, a Javier le ___dolía___ mucho la cabeza.
3. Cuando Victoria ___hacía___ ejercicios aeróbicos, siempre ___se sentía___ mareada.
4. Todas las primaveras, Javier ___estornudaba/tosía___ mucho porque es alérgico al polen.
5. Victoria también ___se caía___ de su bicicleta camino a la escuela.
6. Después de comer en la cafetería, a Victoria siempre le ___dolía___ el estómago.
7. Javier ___quería/pensaba___ ser médico para ayudar a los demás.
8. Pero no ___comprendía___ por qué él ___se enfermaba___ con tanta frecuencia.
9. Cuando Victoria ___tenía___ fiebre, no ___podía___ ni leer el termómetro.
10. A Javier ___le dolían___ los dientes, pero nunca ___quería___ ir al dentista.
11. Victoria ___tosía/estornudaba___ mucho cuando ___se sentía___ congestionada.
12. Javier y Victoria ___pensaban___ que nunca ___iban___ a graduarse.

 Practice more at **vhlcentral.com.**

Comunicación

4 **Entrevista** Trabajen en parejas. Un(a) estudiante usa estas preguntas para entrevistar a su compañero/a. Luego compartan los resultados de la entrevista con la clase. Answers will vary.

1. Cuando eras estudiante de primaria, ¿te gustaban tus profesores/as?
2. ¿Veías mucha televisión cuando eras niño/a?
3. Cuando tenías diez años, ¿cuál era tu programa de televisión favorito?
4. Cuando eras niño/a, ¿qué hacía tu familia durante las vacaciones?
5. ¿Cuántos años tenías en 2005?
6. Cuando estabas en el quinto año escolar, ¿qué hacías con tus amigos/as?
7. Cuando tenías once años, ¿cuál era tu grupo musical favorito?
8. Antes de tomar esta clase, ¿sabías hablar español?

5 **Describir** En parejas, túrnense para describir cómo eran sus vidas cuando eran niños. Pueden usar las sugerencias de la lista u otras ideas. Luego informen a la clase sobre la vida de su compañero/a. Answers will vary.

> **modelo**
> De niña, mi familia y yo siempre íbamos a Tortuguero. Tomábamos un barco desde Limón, y por las noches mirábamos las tortugas (*turtles*) en la playa. Algunas veces teníamos suerte, porque las tortugas venían a poner (*lay*) huevos. Otras veces, volvíamos al hotel sin ver ninguna tortuga.

- las vacaciones
- ocasiones especiales
- qué hacías durante el verano
- celebraciones con tus amigos/as
- celebraciones con tu familia
- cómo era tu escuela
- cómo eran tus amigos/as
- los viajes que hacías
- a qué jugabas
- qué hacías cuando te sentías enfermo/a

NOTA CULTURAL

El Parque Nacional Tortuguero está en la costa del Caribe, al norte de la ciudad de Limón, en Costa Rica. Varias especies de tortuga (*turtle*) van a las playas del parque para poner (*lay*) sus huevos. Esto ocurre de noche, y hay guías que llevan pequeños grupos de turistas a observar este fenómeno biológico.

Síntesis

6 **En el consultorio** Tu profesor(a) te va a dar una lista incompleta con los pacientes que fueron al consultorio del doctor Donoso ayer. En parejas, conversen para completar sus listas y saber a qué hora llegaron las personas al consultorio y cuáles eran sus problemas. Answers will vary.

4 Teaching Tip
←👤→ To simplify, have students record the results of their interviews in a Venn diagram, which they can use to present the information to the class.

5 Teaching Tips
• After students have completed the activity in pairs, divide the class into small groups. Then, after each student reports to the class, have groups decide on a follow-up question to ask.
• ←👤→ You may want to assign this activity as a short written composition.

6 Teaching Tip Divide the class into pairs and distribute the handouts from the Activity Pack (Activity Pack/Supersite) that correspond to this Information Gap Activity. Give students ten minutes to complete this activity.

6 Expansion
←👤→ Have pairs write Dr. Donoso's advice for three of the patients. Then have them read the advice to the class and compare it with what other pairs wrote for the same patients.

TEACHING OPTIONS

Large Groups 👤↔👤 Label the four corners of the room **La Revolución Americana, Tiempos prehistóricos, El Imperio Romano,** and **El Japón de los samurai.** Have students go to the corner that best represents the historical period they would visit if they could. Each group should then discuss their reasons for choosing that period using the imperfect tense. A spokesperson will report the group's responses to the rest of the class.

Game 👤↔👤 Divide the class into teams of three. Each team should choose a historical or fictional villain. When it is their turn, they will give the class one hint. The other teams are allowed three questions, which must be answered truthfully. At the end of the question/answer session, teams must guess the person's identity. Award one point for each correct guess and two to any team able to stump the class.

Section Goal

In **Estructura 10.2**, students will compare and contrast the uses and meanings of the preterite and imperfect tenses.

Instructional Resources

Supersite: Audio (Lab MP3 Files); Resources (*PowerPoints*, Activity Pack, Scripts, Answer Keys); Testing Program (Quizzes)
WebSAM
Workbook, pp. 113–116
Lab Manual, p. 58

Teaching Tips

- Draw a simple time line on the board. Mark the year you were born and the present year. Invite students to guess how old you were at key points in your life. Ex: **¿Qué creen ustedes? ¿Cuántos años tenía yo cuando aprendí a conducir?** Mark the appropriate spot on the time line and write the corresponding phrase (**Aprendí a conducir.**).
- Give personalized examples as you contrast the preterite and the imperfect. Ex: **La semana pasada tuve que ir al dentista. Me dolía mucho el diente.**
- 👥↔👤 Involve the class in a conversation about what they did in the past. Ask: **_____, ¿paseabas en bicicleta cuando eras niño/a? ¿Te caíste alguna vez? _____, ¿cuando eras niño/a iba tu familia de vacaciones todos los años? ¿Adónde iban?**
- ←👤→ Add a visual aspect to this grammar presentation. Create or bring in a series of simple drawings. As you hold up each one, have students narrate the events in English and say whether they would use the preterite or imperfect in each case. Ex: 1. The man was sleeping (imperfect). It was midnight (imperfect). The door was open (imperfect). 2. It was 12:05. (imperfect). The man heard a noise (preterite)… Then have volunteers narrate the scenes in Spanish.

The preterite and the imperfect **Tutorial**

ANTE TODO Now that you have learned the forms of the preterite and the imperfect, you will learn more about how they are used. The preterite and the imperfect are not interchangeable. In Spanish, the choice between these two tenses depends on the context and on the point of view of the speaker.

Me rompí el brazo cuando estaba paseando en bicicleta.

Tenía dolor de cabeza, pero me tomé una aspirina y se me fue.

COMPARE & CONTRAST

Use the preterite to...

1. Express actions that are viewed by the speaker as completed
 Sandra **se rompió** la pierna.
 Sandra broke her leg.

 Fueron a Buenos Aires ayer.
 They went to Buenos Aires yesterday.

2. Express the beginning or end of a past action
 La película **empezó** a las nueve.
 The movie began at nine o'clock.

 Ayer **terminé** el proyecto para la clase de química.
 Yesterday I finished the project for chemistry class.

3. Narrate a series of past actions or events
 La doctora me **miró** los oídos, me **hizo** unas preguntas y **escribió** la receta.
 The doctor looked in my ears, asked me some questions, and wrote the prescription.

 Me di con la mesa, **me caí** y **me lastimé** el pie.
 I bumped into the table, I fell, and I injured my foot.

Use the imperfect to...

1. Describe an ongoing past action with no reference to its beginning or end
 Sandra **esperaba** al doctor.
 Sandra was waiting for the doctor.

 El médico **se preocupaba** por sus pacientes.
 The doctor worried about his patients.

2. Express habitual past actions and events
 Cuando **era** joven, **jugaba** al tenis.
 When I was young, I used to play tennis.

 De niño, Eduardo **se enfermaba** con mucha frecuencia.
 As a child, Eduardo used to get sick very frequently.

3. Describe physical and emotional states or characteristics
 La chica **quería** descansar. **Se sentía** mal y **tenía** dolor de cabeza.
 The girl wanted to rest. She felt ill and had a headache.

 Ellos **eran** altos y **tenían** ojos verdes.
 They were tall and had green eyes.

 Estábamos felices de ver a la familia.
 We were happy to see our family.

AYUDA

These words and expressions, as well as similar ones, commonly occur with the preterite: **ayer, anteayer, una vez, dos veces, tres veces, el año pasado, de repente.** They usually imply that an action has happened at a specific point in time. For a review, see **Estructura 6.3**, p. 191.

AYUDA

These words and expressions, as well as similar ones, commonly occur with the imperfect: **de niño/a, todos los días, mientras, siempre, con frecuencia, todas las semanas.** They usually express habitual or repeated actions in the past.

TEACHING OPTIONS

Extra Practice Write in English a simple, humorous retelling of a well-known fairy tale. Read it to the class, pausing after each verb in the past to ask the class whether the imperfect or preterite would be used in Spanish. Ex: *Once upon a time there was a girl named Little Red Riding Hood. She wanted to take lunch to her ailing grandmother. She put a loaf of bread, a wedge of cheese, and a bottle of Beaujolais in a basket and set off through the*

woods. Meanwhile, farther down the path, a big, ugly, snaggle-toothed wolf was leaning against a tree, filing his nails…
Pairs On separate slips of paper, have students write six personalized statements, one for each of the uses of the preterite and imperfect in **Compare & Contrast**. Have them shuffle the slips and exchange them with a partner, who will identify which preterite or imperfect use each of the sentences illustrates.

▶ The preterite and the imperfect often appear in the same sentence. In such cases, the imperfect describes what *was happening*, while the preterite describes the action that "interrupted" the ongoing activity.

Miraba la tele cuando **sonó** el teléfono.
I was watching TV when the phone rang.

Felicia **leía** el periódico cuando **llegó** Ramiro.
Felicia was reading the newspaper when Ramiro arrived.

▶ You will also see the preterite and the imperfect together in narratives such as fiction, news, and the retelling of events. The imperfect provides background information, such as time, weather, and location, while the preterite indicates the specific events that occurred.

Eran las dos de la mañana y el detective ya no **podía** mantenerse despierto. **Se bajó** lentamente del coche, **estiró** las piernas y **levantó** los brazos hacia el cielo oscuro.
It was two in the morning, and the detective could no longer stay awake. He slowly stepped out of the car, stretched his legs, and raised his arms toward the dark sky.

La luna **estaba** llena y no **había** en el cielo ni una sola nube. De repente, el detective **escuchó** un grito espeluznante proveniente del parque.
The moon was full and there wasn't a single cloud in the sky. Suddenly, the detective heard a piercing scream coming from the park.

Un médico colombiano desarrolló una vacuna contra la malaria

En 1986, el doctor colombiano Manuel Elkin Patarroyo creó la primera vacuna sintética para combatir la malaria. Esta enfermedad parecía haberse erradicado hacía décadas en muchas partes del mundo. Sin embargo, justo cuando Patarroyo terminó de elaborar la inmunización, los casos de malaria empezaban a aumentar de nuevo. En mayo de 1993, el doctor colombiano cedió la patente de la vacuna a la Organización Mundial de la Salud en nombre de Colombia. Los grandes laboratorios farmacéuticos presionaron a la OMS porque querían la vacuna. Las presiones no tuvieron éxito y, en 1995, el doctor Patarroyo y la OMS pactaron continuar con el acuerdo incial: la vacuna seguía siendo propiedad de la OMS.

 ¡INTÉNTALO! Elige el pretérito o el imperfecto para completar la historia. Explica por qué se usa ese tiempo verbal en cada ocasión. *Answers for the second part will vary.*

1. ___Eran___ (Fueron/Eran) las doce.
2. ___Había___ (Hubo/Había) mucha gente en la calle.
3. A las doce y media, Tomás y yo ___entramos___ (entramos/entrábamos) en el restaurante Tárcoles.
4. Todos los días yo ___almorzaba___ (almorcé/almorzaba) con Tomás al mediodía.
5. El camarero ___llegó___ (llegó/llegaba) inmediatamente con el menú.
6. Nosotros ___empezamos___ (empezamos/empezábamos) a leerlo.
7. Yo ___pedí___ (pedí/pedía) el pescado.
8. De repente, el camarero ___volvió___ (volvió/volvía) a nuestra mesa.
9. Y nos ___dio___ (dio/daba) una mala noticia.
10. Desafortunadamente, no ___tenían___ (tuvieron/tenían) más pescado.
11. Por eso Tomás y yo ___decidimos___ (decidimos/decidíamos) comer en otro lugar.
12. ___Llovía___ (Llovió/Llovía) mucho cuando ___salimos___ (salimos/salíamos) del restaurante.
13. Así que ___regresamos___ (regresamos/regresábamos) al restaurante Tárcoles.
14. Esta vez, ___pedí___ (pedí/pedía) arroz con pollo.

recursos

WB pp. 113–116

LM p. 58

S vhlcentral.com Lección 10

TEACHING OPTIONS

Pairs ←🔽→ Ask students to narrate the most interesting, embarrassing, exciting, or annoying thing that has happened to them recently. Tell them to describe what happened and how they felt, using the preterite and the imperfect.
Video ➔🔽← Show the **Fotonovela** again to give students more input about the use of the imperfect. Stop the video at appropriate moments to contrast the use of preterite and imperfect tenses.

Heritage Speakers ←🔽→ Have heritage speakers work with other students in pairs to write a simple summary of this lesson's **Fotonovela**. First, as a class, briefly summarize the episode in English and write which verbs would be in the imperfect or preterite. Then have pairs write their paragraphs. They should set the scene, and describe where the characters were, what they were doing, and what happened.

Práctica

1 **En el periódico** Completa esta noticia con las formas correctas del pretérito o el imperfecto.

Un accidente trágico

Ayer temprano por la mañana (1) **hubo** (haber) un trágico accidente en el centro de San José cuando el conductor de un autobús no (2) **vio** (ver) venir un carro. La mujer que (3) **manejaba** (manejar) el carro (4) **murió** (morir) al instante y los paramédicos (5) **tuvieron** (tener) que llevar al pasajero al hospital porque (6) **sufrió** (sufrir) varias fracturas. El conductor del autobús (7) **dijo** (decir) que no (8) **vio** (ver) el carro hasta el último momento porque (9) **estaba** (estar) muy nublado y (10) **llovía** (llover). Él (11) **intentó** (intentar) (*to attempt*) dar un viraje brusco (*to swerve*), pero (12) **perdió** (perder) el control del autobús y no (13) **pudo** (poder) evitar (*to avoid*) el accidente. Según nos informaron, no (14) **se lastimó** (lastimarse) ningún pasajero del autobús.

◀ **AYUDA**

Reading Spanish-language newspapers is a good way to practice verb tenses. You will find that both the imperfect and the preterite occur with great regularity. Many newsstands carry international papers, and many Spanish-language newspapers (such as Spain's *El País*, Mexico's *Reforma*, and Argentina's *Clarín*) are on the Web.

2 **Seleccionar** Utiliza el tiempo verbal adecuado, según el contexto. *Answers will vary. Suggested answers:*

1. La semana pasada, Manolo y Aurora **querían** (querer) dar una fiesta. **Decidieron** (Decidir) invitar a seis amigos y servirles mucha comida.
2. Manolo y Aurora **estaban** (estar) preparando la comida cuando Elena **llamó** (llamar). Como siempre, **tenía** (tener) que estudiar para un examen.
3. A las seis, **volvió** (volver) a sonar el teléfono. Su amigo Francisco tampoco **podía** (poder) ir a la fiesta, porque **tenía** (tener) fiebre. Manolo y Aurora **se sentían** (sentirse) muy tristes, pero **tenían** (tener) que preparar la comida.
4. Después de otros quince minutos, **sonó** (sonar) el teléfono. Sus amigos, los señores Vega, **estaban** (estar) en camino (*en route*) al hospital: a su hijo le **dolía** (doler) mucho el estómago. Sólo dos de los amigos **podían** (poder) ir a la cena.
5. Por supuesto, **iban** (ir) a tener demasiada comida. Finalmente, cinco minutos antes de las ocho, **llamaron** (llamar) Ramón y Javier. Ellos **pensaban** (pensar) que la fiesta **era** (ser) la próxima semana.
6. Tristes, Manolo y Aurora **se sentaron** (sentarse) a comer solos. Mientras **comían** (comer), pronto **llegaron** (llegar) a la conclusión de que **era** (ser) mejor estar solos: ¡La comida **estaba** (estar) malísima!

3 **Completar** Completa las frases de una manera lógica. Usa el pretérito o el imperfecto. En parejas, comparen sus respuestas. *Answers will vary.*

1. De niño/a, yo...
2. Yo conducía el auto mientras...
3. Anoche mi novio/a...
4. Ayer el/la profesor(a)...
5. La semana pasada un(a) amigo/a...
6. Con frecuencia mis padres...
7. Esta mañana en la cafetería...
8. Hablábamos con el doctor cuando...

 Practice more at **vhlcentral.com**.

Comunicación

4 **Entrevista** Usa estas preguntas para entrevistar a un(a) compañero/a acerca de su primer(a) novio/a. Si quieres, puedes añadir otras preguntas. Answers will vary.

1. ¿Quién fue tu primer(a) novio/a?
2. ¿Cuántos años tenías cuando lo/la conociste?
3. ¿Cómo era él/ella?
4. ¿Qué le gustaba hacer? ¿Tenían ustedes los mismos pasatiempos?
5. ¿Por cuánto tiempo salieron ustedes?
6. ¿Adónde iban cuando salían?
7. ¿Pensaban casarse?
8. ¿Cuándo y por qué rompieron?

5 **La sala de emergencias** En parejas, miren la lista e inventen qué les pasó a estas personas que están en la sala de emergencias. Answers will vary.

> **modelo**
>
> Eran las tres de la tarde. Como todos los días, Pablo jugaba al fútbol con sus amigos. Estaba muy contento. De repente, se cayó y se rompió el brazo. Entonces fue a la sala de emergencias.

Paciente	Edad	Hora	Estado
1. Pablo Romero	9 años	15:20	hueso roto (el brazo)
2. Estela Rodríguez	45 años	15:25	tobillo torcido
3. Lupe Quintana	29 años	15:37	embarazada, dolores
4. Manuel López	52 años	15:45	infección de garganta
5. Marta Díaz	3 años	16:00	congestión, fiebre
6. Roberto Salazar	32 años	16:06	dolor de oído
7. Marco Brito	18 años	16:18	daño en el cuello, posible fractura
8. Ana María Ortiz	66 años	16:29	reacción alérgica a un medicamento

6 **Situación** Anoche alguien robó (*stole*) el examen de la **Lección 10** de la oficina de tu profesor(a) y tú tienes que averiguar quién lo hizo. Pregúntales a tres compañeros dónde estaban, con quién estaban y qué hicieron entre las ocho y las doce de la noche. Answers will vary.

Síntesis

7 **La primera vez** En grupos, cuéntense cómo fue la primera vez que les pusieron una inyección, se rompieron un hueso, pasaron la noche en un hospital, estuvieron mareados/as, etc. Incluyan estos datos en su conversación: una descripción del tiempo que hacía, sus edades, qué pasó y cómo se sentían.

Answers will vary.

TEACHING OPTIONS

Small Groups Have small groups write a skit and perform it for the class. Three students walk into the campus clinic. Each explains to the nurse what happened and why he or she should be seen first. Students should use the preterite and imperfect. **Game** Create a short narrative in the past based on a well-known story. Allow space between sentences so they may be easily cut into strips. Then make a copy of the narrative and edit it, changing all preterites to imperfects and vice versa. Make two copies of each version and cut the sentences apart. Place a complete set of both the versions into two separate bags, mix the strips up, and challenge two teams to reconstruct the correct version. The team that does so first wins.

4 Teaching Tips
• In order to be sensitive to those who haven't had a romantic relationship, you may wish to change the context to a first friendship. Items 5–8 should be adjusted accordingly (Ex: **¿Por cuánto tiempo fueron amigos/as?**).
• To simplify, have students prepare a few notes to help them with their responses.

4 Expansion
→🔸← Have students write a summary of their partners' responses, omitting all names. Collect the summaries, then read them to the class. Have students guess who had the relationship described in the summary.

5 Teaching Tip Remind students that the 24-hour clock is often used for schedules. Go through a few of the times and ask volunteers to provide the equivalent in the 12-hour clock.

5 Expansion
→🔸← Have pairs share their answers with the class, without mentioning the patient's name. The class must guess who it is.

6 Expansion
←🔸→ Have groups decide who is the most likely thief. Ask them to prepare a police report explaining why they believe their suspect is the culprit.

7 Teaching Tip To simplify, before assigning groups, have students list information they can include in their descriptions, such as their age, the time, the date, what the weather was like, and so forth. Then have them list the events of the day in the order they happened.

7 Expansion
←🔸→ Have students decide who in their group is the most accident-prone on the basis of his or her responses. Ask the group to prepare a doctor's account of his or her treatments.

Constructions with se Tutorial

ANTE TODO In **Lección 7,** you learned how to use **se** as the third person reflexive pronoun (**Él se despierta. Ellos se visten. Ella se baña.**). **Se** can also be used to form constructions in which the person performing the action is not expressed or is de-emphasized.

Impersonal constructions with se

▶ In Spanish, verbs that are not reflexive can be used with **se** to form impersonal constructions. These are statements in which the person performing the action is not defined.

Se habla español en Costa Rica.
Spanish is spoken in Costa Rica.

Se puede leer en la sala de espera.
You can read in the waiting room.

Se hacen operaciones aquí.
They perform operations here.

Se necesitan medicinas enseguida.
They need medicine right away.

▶ **¡Atención!** Note that the third person singular verb form is used with singular nouns and the third person plural form is used with plural nouns.

Se vende ropa. **Se venden** camisas.

▶ You often see the impersonal **se** in signs, advertisements, and directions.

SE PROHÍBE NADAR

Se necesitan programadores
Grupo Tecno
Tel. 778-34-34

ENTRADA

Se entra por la izquierda

Se for unplanned events

¿Te pusiste un suéter anoche?

No, mamá. Se me olvidó.

▶ **Se** also describes accidental or unplanned events. In this construction, the person who performs the action is de-emphasized, implying that the accident or unplanned event is not his or her direct responsibility. Note this construction.

se + [**INDIRECT OBJECT PRONOUN**] + [**VERB**] + [**SUBJECT**]

Se me cayó la pluma.

In this type of construction, what would normally be the direct object of the sentence becomes the subject, and it agrees with the verb, not with the indirect object pronoun.

I.O. PRONOUN	VERB		SUBJECT
Se	me, te, le, nos, os, les	quedó / cayó / dañó (SINGULAR)	la receta. / la taza. / el radio.
		rompieron / olvidaron / perdieron (PLURAL)	las botellas. / las pastillas. / las llaves.

These verbs are the ones most frequently used with **se** to describe unplanned events.

Verbs commonly used with se

caer	to fall; to drop	**perder (e:ie)**	to lose
dañar	to damage; to break down	**quedar**	to be left behind
olvidar	to forget	**romper**	to break

Se me perdió el teléfono de la farmacia.
I lost the pharmacy's phone number.

Se nos olvidaron los pasajes.
We forgot the tickets.

▶ **¡Atención!** While Spanish has a verb for *to fall* (**caer**), there is no direct translation for *to drop*. **Dejar caer** (*To let fall*) or a **se** construction is often used to mean *to drop*.

El médico **dejó caer** la aspirina.
The doctor dropped the aspirin.

A mí **se me cayeron** los cuadernos.
I dropped the notebooks.

▶ To clarify or emphasize who the person involved in the action is, this construction commonly begins with the preposition **a** + [*noun*] or **a** + [*prepositional pronoun*].

Al paciente se le perdió la receta.
The patient lost his prescription.

A ustedes se les quedaron los libros en casa.
You left the books at home.

CONSULTA

For an explanation of prepositional pronouns, refer to **Estructura 9.4**, p. 294.

¡INTÉNTALO! Completa las oraciones con **se** impersonal y los verbos en presente.

A

1. _Se enseñan_____ (enseñar) cinco lenguas en esta universidad.
2. _Se come_____ (comer) muy bien en Las Delicias.
3. _Se venden_____ (vender) muchas camisetas allí.
4. _Se sirven_____ (servir) platos exquisitos cada noche.

Completa las oraciones con **se** y los verbos en pretérito.

B

1. _Se me rompieron_____ (*I broke*) las gafas.
2. _Se te cayeron_____ (*You* (fam., sing.) *dropped*) las pastillas.
3. _Se les perdió_____ (*They lost*) la receta.
4. _Se le quedó_____ (*You* (form., sing.) *left*) aquí la radiografía.

recursos

WB pp. 117–118

LM p. 59

S vhlcentral.com Lección 10

Teaching Tips

• Test comprehension by asking volunteers to change sentences from plural to singular and vice versa. Ex: **Se me perdieron las llaves. (Se me perdió la llave.)**

• Have students finish sentences using a construction with **se** to express an unplanned event. Ex: **1. Al doctor ____. (se le cayó el termómetro) 2. A la profesora ____. (se le quedaron los papeles en casa)**

• 👥 Involve students in a conversation about unplanned events that happened to them recently. Say: **Se me olvidaron las gafas de sol esta mañana. Y a ti, ____, ¿se te olvidó algo esta mañana? ¿Qué se te olvidó?** Continue with other verbs. Ex: **¿A quién se le perdió algo importante esta semana? ¿Qué se te perdió?**

Successful Language Learning Tell students that this construction has no exact equivalent in English. Tell them to examine the examples in the textbook and make up some of their own in order to get a feel for how this construction works.

TEACHING OPTIONS

Video 👥 Show the **Fotonovela** again to give students more input containing constructions with **se**. Have students write down as many of the examples as they can. After viewing, have students edit their lists and cross out any reflexive verbs that they mistakenly understood to be constructions with **se**.
Heritage Speakers 👥 Ask heritage speakers to write a fictional or true account of a day in which everything went wrong. Ask them to include as many constructions with **se** as possible. Have them read their accounts aloud to the class, who will summarize the events.
Extra Practice Have students use **se** constructions to make excuses in different situations. Ex: You did not bring in a composition to class. (**Se me dañó la computadora.**)

Práctica

1 **¿Cierto o falso?** Lee estas oraciones sobre la vida en 1901. Indica si lo que dice cada oración es **cierto** o **falso**. Luego corrige las oraciones falsas.

1. Se veía mucha televisión. *Falso. No se veía televisión. Se leía mucho.*
2. Se escribían muchos libros. *Cierto.*
3. Se viajaba mucho en tren. *Cierto.*
4. Se montaba a caballo. *Cierto.*
5. Se mandaba correo electrónico. *Falso. No se mandaba correo electrónico. Se mandaban cartas y postales.*
6. Se preparaban comidas en casa. *Cierto.*
7. Se llevaban minifaldas. *Falso. No se llevaban minifaldas. Se llevaban faldas largas.*
8. Se pasaba mucho tiempo con la familia. *Cierto.*

2 **Traducir** Traduce estos letreros (*signs*) y anuncios al español.

1. Nurses needed *Se necesitan enfermeros/as*
2. Eating and drinking prohibited *Se prohíbe comer y beber*
3. Programmers sought *Se buscan programadores*
4. English is spoken *Se habla inglés*
5. Computers sold *Se venden computadoras*
6. No talking *Se prohíbe hablar*
7. Teacher needed *Se necesita profesor(a)*
8. Books sold *Se venden libros*
9. Do not enter *Se prohíbe entrar*
10. Spanish is spoken *Se habla español*

3 **¿Qué pasó?** Mira los dibujos e indica lo que pasó en cada uno. *Some answers will vary. Suggested answers:*

1. camarero / pastel
Al camarero se le cayó el pastel.

2. Sr. Álvarez / espejo
Al señor Álvarez se le rompió el espejo.

3. Arturo / tarea
A Arturo se le olvidó la tarea.

4. Sra. Domínguez / llaves
A la Sra. Domínguez se le perdieron las llaves.

5. Carla y Lupe / botellas de vino
A Carla y a Lupe se les rompieron las botellas de vino.

6. Juana / platos
A Juana se le rompieron los platos.

🅢 Practice more at **vhlcentral.com.**

TEACHING OPTIONS

Comunicación

4 **¿Distraído/a yo?** Trabajen en parejas y usen estas preguntas para averiguar cuál de los/las dos es más distraído/a (*absentminded*). Answers will vary.

¿Alguna vez…

1. se te olvidó invitar a alguien a una fiesta o comida? ¿A quién?
2. se te quedó algo importante en la casa? ¿Qué?
3. se te perdió algo importante durante un viaje? ¿Qué?
4. se te rompió algo muy caro? ¿Qué?

¿Sabes…

5. si se permite el ingreso (*admission*) de perros al parque cercano a la universidad?
6. si en el supermercado se aceptan cheques?
7. dónde se arreglan zapatos y botas?
8. qué se sirve en la cafetería de la universidad los lunes?

5 **Opiniones** En parejas, terminen cada oración con ideas originales. Después, comparen los resultados con la clase para ver qué pareja tuvo las mejores ideas. Answers will vary.

1. No se tiene que dejar propina cuando…
2. Antes de viajar, se debe…
3. Si se come bien, …
4. Para tener una vida sana, se debe…
5. Se sirve la mejor comida en…
6. Se hablan muchas lenguas en…

Síntesis

6 **Anuncios** En grupos, preparen dos anuncios de televisión para presentar a la clase. Usen el imperfecto y por lo menos dos construcciones con **se** en cada uno. Answers will vary.

> **modelo**
> Se me cayeron unos libros en el pie y me dolía mucho. Pero ahora no, gracias a SuperAspirina 500. ¡Dos pastillas y se me fue el dolor! Se puede comprar SuperAspirina 500 en todas las farmacias Recetamax.

4 Teaching Tip Encourage students to give detailed responses. Model this by choosing from the first set of questions and providing as many details as possible. Ex: **Una vez cuando era adolescente se me rompió un plato muy caro de mi abuela. Pero ella no se enojó. Me dijo: No te preocupes por el plato. ¿Te lastimaste?**

4 Expansion
↔️👥→ Have each pair decide on the most unusual answer to the questions. Ask the student who gave it to describe the event to the class.

5 Expansion Ask pairs to write similar beginnings to three different statements using **se** constructions. Have pairs exchange papers and finish each other's sentences.

6 Expansion
↔️👥→ After all the groups have presented their ads, have each group write a letter of complaint. Their letter should be directed to one of the other groups, claiming false advertising.

TEACHING OPTIONS

Extra Practice Write these sentence fragments on the board and ask students to supply at least two logical endings using a construction with **se**. **1. Cuando ella subía al avión, ____. (se le cayó la maleta; se le torció el pie) 2. Una vez, cuando yo comía en un restaurante elegante, ____. (se me rompió un vaso; se me perdió la tarjeta de crédito) 3. Ayer cuando yo venía a clase,** ____. (se me dañó la bicicleta; me caí y se me rompió el brazo) **4. Cuando era niño/a, siempre ____. (se me olvidaban las cosas; se me perdían las cosas) 5. El otro día cuando yo lavaba los platos, ____. (se me rompieron tres vasos; se me acabó el detergente)**

10.4 Adverbs Tutorial

 ANTE TODO Adverbs are words that describe how, when, and where actions take place. They can modify verbs, adjectives, and even other adverbs. In previous lessons, you have already learned many Spanish adverbs, such as the ones below.

aquí	hoy	nunca
ayer	mal	siempre
bien	muy	temprano

▶ The most common adverbs end in -**mente**, equivalent to the English ending *-ly*.

verdaderamente *truly, really* **generalmente** *generally* **simplemente** *simply*

▶ To form these adverbs, add -**mente** to the feminine form of the adjective. If the adjective does not have a special feminine form, just add -**mente** to the standard form. **¡Atención!** Adjectives do not lose their accents when adding -**mente**.

ADJECTIVE	FEMININE FORM	SUFFIX	ADVERB
seguro	segura	-mente	seguramente
fabuloso	fabulosa	-mente	fabulosamente
enorme		-mente	enormemente
fácil		-mente	fácilmente

▶ Adverbs that end in -**mente** generally follow the verb, while adverbs that modify an adjective or another adverb precede the word they modify.

Maira dibuja **maravillosamente**.
Maira draws wonderfully.

Sergio está **casi siempre** ocupado.
Sergio is almost always busy.

Common adverbs and adverbial expressions

a menudo	*often*	**así**	*like this; so*	**menos**	*less*
a tiempo	*on time*	**bastante**	*enough; rather*	**muchas veces**	*a lot; many times*
a veces	*sometimes*	**casi**	*almost*		
además (de)	*furthermore; besides*	**con frecuencia**	*frequently*	**poco**	*little*
				por lo menos	*at least*
apenas	*hardly; scarcely*	**de vez en cuando**	*from time to time*	**pronto**	*soon*
		despacio	*slowly*	**rápido**	*quickly*

 ¡INTÉNTALO! Transforma los adjetivos en adverbios.

1. alegre **alegremente**
2. constante **constantemente**
3. gradual **gradualmente**
4. perfecto **perfectamente**
5. real **realmente**
6. frecuente **frecuentemente**
7. tranquilo **tranquilamente**
8. regular **regularmente**
9. maravilloso **maravillosamente**
10. normal **normalmente**
11. básico **básicamente**
12. afortunado **afortunadamente**

recursos

WB pp. 119–120

LM p. 60

vhlcentral.com Lección 10

Práctica

1 **Escoger** Completa la historia con los adverbios adecuados.

1. La cita era a las dos, pero llegamos ___tarde___. (mientras, nunca, tarde)
2. El problema fue que ___ayer___ se nos dañó el despertador. (aquí, ayer, despacio)
3. La recepcionista no se enojó porque sabe que normalmente llego ___a tiempo___. (a veces, a tiempo, poco)
4. ___Por lo menos___ el doctor estaba listo. (Por lo menos, Muchas veces, Casi)
5. ___Apenas___ tuvimos que esperar cinco minutos. (Así, Además, Apenas)
6. El doctor dijo que nuestra hija Irene necesitaba cambiar su rutina diaria ___inmediatamente___. (temprano, menos, inmediatamente)
▶ 7. El doctor nos explicó ___bien___ las recomendaciones del Cirujano General (*Surgeon General*) sobre la salud de los jóvenes. (de vez en cuando, bien, apenas)
8. ___Afortunadamente___ nos dijo que Irene estaba bien, pero tenía que hacer más ejercicio y comer mejor. (Bastante, Afortunadamente, A menudo)

Comunicación

2 **Aspirina** Lee el anuncio y responde a las preguntas con un(a) compañero/a. *Answers will vary.*

No hay tiempo para el dolor de cabeza.

Si tienes prisa, o simplemente quieres que tu dolor de cabeza se vaya muy pronto, piensa en Capalivia. Se asimila mejor y actúa rápidamente. Ya no se puede perder tiempo por un dolor de cabeza.

ASPIRINA

1. ¿Cuáles son los adverbios que aparecen en el anuncio?
2. Según el anuncio, ¿cuáles son las ventajas (*advantages*) de este tipo de aspirina?
3. ¿Tienen ustedes dolores de cabeza? ¿Qué toman para curarlos?
4. ¿Qué medicamentos ven con frecuencia en los anuncios de televisión? Escriban descripciones de varios de estos anuncios. Usen adverbios en sus descripciones.

 Practice more at **vhlcentral.com**.

Recapitulación

Section Goal

In **Recapitulación**, students will review the grammar concepts from this lesson.

Instructional Resource
Supersite

1 Teaching Tip Ask students to identify the infinitive for each row.

1 Expansion Ask students to provide the forms for **ir**, **ver**, and **doler**.

2 Expansion
• To challenge students, have them create sentences to express the opposite meaning for each item. Ex: **1. Pablito se cae muy poco.**
• ←👤→ Ask students to write a paragraph in which they use at least five of the listed adverbs. Then have them exchange papers with a partner for peer editing.

S Concepts Diagnostics

Completa estas actividades para repasar los conceptos de gramática que aprendiste en esta lección.

1 Completar Completa el cuadro con la forma correcta del imperfecto. **12 pts.**

yo/Ud./él/ella	tú	nosotros	Uds./ellos/ellas
era	eras	éramos	eran
cantaba	**cantabas**	cantábamos	cantaban
venía	venías	**veníamos**	venían
quería	querías	queríamos	**querían**

2 Adverbios Escoge el adverbio correcto de la lista para completar estas oraciones. Lee con cuidado las oraciones; los adverbios sólo se usan una vez. No vas a usar uno de los adverbios. **8 pts.**

a menudo	apenas	fácilmente
a tiempo	casi	maravillosamente
además	despacio	por lo menos

1. Pablito se cae ___a menudo___; un promedio (*average*) de cuatro veces por semana.

2. No me duele nada y no sufro de ninguna enfermedad; me siento ___maravillosamente___ bien.

3. —Doctor, ¿cómo supo que tuve una operación de garganta?
 —Muy ___fácilmente___, lo leí en su historial médico.

4. ¿Le duele mucho la espalda (*back*)? Entonces tiene que levantarse ___despacio___.

5. Ya te sientes mucho mejor, ¿verdad? Mañana puedes volver al trabajo; tu temperatura es ___casi___ normal.

6. Es importante hacer ejercicio con regularidad, ___por lo menos___ tres veces a la semana.

7. El examen médico no comenzó ni tarde ni temprano. Comenzó ___a tiempo___, a las tres de la tarde.

8. Parece que ya te estás curando del resfriado. ___Apenas___ estás congestionada.

RESUMEN GRAMATICAL

10.1 The imperfect tense *pp. 318–319*

The imperfect of regular verbs

cantar	beber	escribir
cantaba	bebía	escribía
cantabas	bebías	escribías
cantaba	bebía	escribía
cantábamos	bebíamos	escribíamos
cantabais	bebíais	escribíais
cantaban	bebían	escribían

► There are no stem changes in the imperfect:
entender (e:ie) → entendía; servir (e:i) → servía;
doler (o:ue) → dolía

► The imperfect of hay is había.

► Only three verbs are irregular in the imperfect.
ir: iba, ibas, iba, íbamos, ibais, iban
ser: era, eras, era, éramos, erais, eran
ver: veía, veías, veía, veíamos, veíais, veían

10.2 The preterite and the imperfect *pp. 322–323*

Preterite	Imperfect
1. Completed actions	1. Ongoing past action
Fueron a Buenos Aires ayer.	De niño, usted **jugaba** al fútbol.
2. Beginning or end of past action	2. Habitual past actions
La película **empezó** a las nueve.	Todos los domingos yo **visitaba** a mi abuela.
3. Series of past actions or events	3. Description of states or characteristics
Me **caí** y me **lastimé** el pie.	Ella **era** alta. **Quería** descansar.

10.3 Constructions with se *pp. 326–327*

Impersonal constructions with se

	prohíbe fumar.
Se	habla español.
	hablan varios idiomas.

TEACHING OPTIONS

TPR Divide the class into three groups: **-ar** verbs, **-er** verbs, and **-ir** verbs. Read a series of sentences that contain the imperfect tense. Have groups stand up when their verb form is used. Ex: **Mi escuela primaria tenía un patio grande.** (**-er** verb group stands)

Extra Practice ←👤→ Ask students to use the preterite and imperfect to write a paragraph about an imaginary scenario in which a celebrity got injured and went to the emergency room. Have students describe the person's age, where he or she was, the weather, the time, what he or she was doing when the accident occurred, and what happened at the hospital. Ask volunteers to read their paragraphs aloud.

3 **Un accidente** Escoge el imperfecto o el pretérito según el contexto para completar esta conversación. **10 pts.**

NURIA Hola, Felipe. ¿Estás bien? ¿Qué es eso? ¿(1) (**Te lastimaste**/Te lastimabas) el pie?

FELIPE Ayer (2) (**tuve**/tenía) un pequeño accidente.

NURIA Cuéntame. ¿Cómo (3) (**pasó**/pasaba)?

FELIPE Bueno, (4) (**fueron**/eran) las cinco de la tarde y (5) (llovió/**llovía**) mucho cuando (6) (**salí**/salía) de la casa en mi bicicleta. No (7) (**vi**/veía) a una chica que (8) (caminó/**caminaba**) en mi dirección, y los dos (9) (**nos caímos**/nos caíamos) al suelo (*ground*).

NURIA Y la chica, ¿está bien ella?

FELIPE Sí. Cuando llegamos al hospital, ella sólo (10) (tuvo/**tenía**) dolor de cabeza.

Se for unplanned events		
Se	me, te, le, nos, os, les	cayó la taza.
		dañó el radio.
		rompieron las botellas.
		olvidaron las llaves.

10.4 **Adverbs** *p. 330*

Formation of adverbs		
fácil	→	fácilmente
seguro	→	seguramente
verdadero	→	verdaderamente

4 **Oraciones** Escribe oraciones con **se** a partir de los elementos dados (*given*). Usa el tiempo especificado entre paréntesis y añade pronombres cuando sea necesario. **10 pts.**

> **modelo**
>
> Carlos / quedar / la tarea en casa (pretérito)
> *A Carlos se le quedó la tarea en casa.*

1. en la farmacia / vender / medicamentos (presente) En la farmacia se venden medicamentos.

2. ¿(tú) / olvidar / las llaves / otra vez? (pretérito) ¿Se te olvidaron las llaves otra vez?

3. (yo) / dañar / la computadora (pretérito) Se me dañó la computadora.

4. en esta clase / prohibir / hablar inglés (presente) En esta clase se prohíbe hablar inglés.

5. ellos / romper / las gafas / en el accidente (pretérito) A ellos se les rompieron las gafas en el accidente.

5 **En la consulta** Escribe al menos cinco oraciones sobre tu última visita al médico. Incluye cinco verbos en pretérito y cinco en imperfecto. Habla de qué te pasó, cómo te sentías, cómo era el/la doctor(a), qué te dijo, etc. Usa tu imaginación. **10 pts.** Answers will vary.

6 **Refrán** Completa el refrán con las palabras que faltan. **¡2 puntos EXTRA!**

❝Lo que ___bien___ (*well*) se aprende, nunca ___se___ pierde. **❞**

 Practice more at **vhlcentral.com**.

3 **Teaching Tip** To challenge students, have them explain why they used the preterite and imperfect in each case and how the meaning might change if the other tense were used.

4 **Teaching Tip** For items 2, 3, and 5, have volunteers rewrite the sentences on the board using other subjects. Ex: **2. (nosotros) ¿Se nos olvidaron las llaves otra vez?**

4 **Expansion** Give students these additional items: **6. (yo) / caer / el vaso de cristal (pretérito) (Se me cayó el vaso de cristal.) 7. (ustedes) / quedar / las maletas en el aeropuerto (pretérito) (A ustedes se les quedaron las maletas en el aeropuerto.) 8. en esta tienda / hablar / español e italiano (presente) (En esta tienda se hablan español e italiano.)**

5 **Teaching Tip**
👤↔👤 After writing their paragraphs, have students work in pairs and ask each other follow-up questions about their visits.

6 **Teaching Tips**
- Have volunteers give additional examples of situations in which one might use this expression.
- Ask students to give the English equivalent of this phrase. (*What is well learned is never lost.*) Ask them how this expression might relate to their own lives and studies.

TEACHING OPTIONS

Extra Practice Write questions on the board that elicit the impersonal **se**. Have pairs write two responses for each question. Ex: **¿Qué se hace para mantener la salud? ¿Dónde se come bien en esta ciudad? ¿Cuándo se dan fiestas en esta universidad? ¿Dónde se consiguen los jeans más baratos?**

Game Divide the class into two teams and have them line up. Point to the first member of each team and call out an adjective that can be changed into an adverb (Ex: **lento**). The first student to reach the board and correctly write the adverb (**lentamente**) earns a point for his or her team. If the student can also write an "opposite" adverb (Ex: **rápidamente**), he or she earns a bonus point. The team with the most points at the end wins.

Section Goals

In **Lectura**, students will:
- learn to activate background knowledge to understand a reading selection
- read a content-rich text on health care while traveling

Instructional Resource
Supersite

Estrategia Tell students that they will find it easier to understand the content of a reading selection on a particular topic by reviewing what they know about the subject before reading. Then ask students to brainstorm ways to stay healthy while traveling. Possible responses: do not drink tap water, do not eat raw fruit or vegetables, pack personal medical supplies that may not be available at the destination.

Examinar el texto Students should mention that the text is an interview (**entrevista**) by a journalist (**periodista**) of an author (**autora**) whose book is about staying healthy while traveling.

Conocimiento previo
←👤→ Have small groups write a paragraph summarizing ways to safeguard health while traveling. Their recommendations should be based on their collective experiences. If no one in the group can relate personally to a given situation, encourage students to draw on the experiences of people they know. Have groups share their paragraphs with the class.

The Affective Dimension
Remind students that they will probably feel less anxious about reading in Spanish if they follow the suggestions in the **Estrategia** sections, which are designed to reinforce and increase reading comprehension skills.

Lectura

Antes de leer

Estrategia
Activating background knowledge

Using what you already know about a particular subject will often help you better understand a reading selection. For example, if you read an article about a recent medical discovery, you might think about what you already know about health in order to understand unfamiliar words or concepts.

Examinar el texto

Utiliza las estrategias de lectura que tú consideras más efectivas para hacer algunas observaciones preliminares acerca del texto. Después trabajen en parejas para comparar sus observaciones acerca del texto. Luego contesten estas preguntas:

- Analicen el formato del texto: ¿Qué tipo de texto es? ¿Dónde creen que se publicó este artículo?
- ¿Quiénes son Carla Baron y Tomás Monterrey?
- Miren la foto del libro. ¿Qué sugiere el título del libro sobre su contenido?

Conocimiento previo

Ahora piensen en su conocimiento previo° sobre el cuidado de la salud en los viajes. Consideren estas preguntas:

- ¿Viajaron alguna vez a otro estado o a otro país?
- ¿Tuvieron problemas durante sus viajes con el agua, la comida o el clima del lugar?
- ¿Olvidaron poner en su maleta algún medicamento que después necesitaron?
- Imaginen que su compañero/a se va de viaje. Díganle por lo menos cinco cosas que debe hacer para prevenir cualquier problema de salud.

conocimiento previo *background knowledge*

 Practice more at **vhlcentral.com.**

Libro de la semana

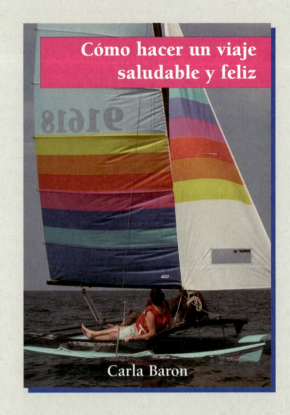

Cómo hacer un viaje saludable y feliz

Carla Baron

Después de leer

Correspondencias
Busca las correspondencias entre los problemas y las recomendaciones.

Problemas
1. el agua ___b___
2. el sol ___d___
3. la comida ___a___
4. la identificación ___e___
5. el clima ___c___

Recomendaciones
a. Hay que adaptarse a los ingredientes desconocidos (*unknown*).
b. Toma sólo productos purificados (*purified*).
c. Es importante llevar ropa adecuada cuando viajas.
d. Lleva loción o crema con alta protección solar.
e. Lleva tu pasaporte.

TEACHING OPTIONS

Heritage Speakers 👤↔👤 Ask heritage speakers to state consequences for a tourist who does not follow the recommendations in **Correspondencias**. Ex: **a. La persona prueba una comida picante y le da dolor de estómago.** After each consequence is stated, have volunteers suggest an appropriate course of action or treatment. Ex: **Debe ir a una farmacia y comprar unas pastillas, como** *Tums*. Encourage

heritage speakers to respond to the students' suggestions.
Small Groups ←👤→ Ask small groups to select a country they would like to visit. Have them research and write a report about what food and beverage precautions should be taken (**precauciones que se deben tomar**) by visitors to that country. They should mention precautions such as not eating undercooked meat, unwashed fruits, and not drinking tap water.

Entrevista a Carla Baron
por Tomás Monterrey

Tomás: ¿Por qué escribió su libro *Cómo hacer un viaje saludable y feliz*?

Carla: Me encanta viajar, conocer otras culturas y escribir. Mi primer viaje lo hice cuando era estudiante universitaria. Todavía recuerdo el día en que llegamos a San Juan, Puerto Rico. Era el panorama ideal para unas vacaciones maravillosas, pero al llegar a la habitación del hotel, bebí mucha agua de la llave° y luego pedí un jugo de frutas con mucho hielo°. El clima en San Juan es tropical y yo tenía mucha sed y calor. Los síntomas llegaron en menos de media hora: pasé dos días con dolor de estómago y corriendo al cuarto de baño cada diez minutos. Desde entonces, siempre que viajo sólo bebo agua mineral y llevo un pequeño bolso con medicinas necesarias, como pastillas para el dolor y también bloqueador solar, una crema repelente de mosquitos y un desinfectante.

Tomás: ¿Son reales° las situaciones que se narran en su libro?

Carla: Sí, son reales y son mis propias° historias°. A menudo los autores crean caricaturas divertidas de un turista en dificultades. ¡En mi libro la turista en dificultades soy yo!

Tomás: ¿Qué recomendaciones puede encontrar el lector en su libro?

Carla: Bueno, mi libro es anecdótico y humorístico, pero el tema de la salud se trata° de manera seria. En general, se dan recomendaciones sobre ropa adecuada para cada sitio, consejos para protegerse del sol, y comidas y bebidas adecuadas para el turista que viaja al Caribe o Suramérica.

Tomás: ¿Tiene algún consejo para las personas que se enferman cuando viajan?

Carla: Muchas veces los turistas toman el avión sin saber nada acerca del país que van a visitar. Ponen toda su ropa en la maleta, toman el pasaporte, la cámara fotográfica y ¡a volar°! Es necesario tomar precauciones porque nuestro cuerpo necesita adaptarse al clima, al sol, a la humedad, al agua y a la comida. Se trata de° viajar, admirar las maravillas del mundo y regresar a casa con hermosos recuerdos. En resumen, el secreto es "prevenir en vez de° curar".

llave *faucet* hielo *ice* reales *true* propias *own* historias *stories*
se trata *is treated* ¡a volar! *Off they go!* Se trata de *It's a question of*
en vez de *instead of*

Seleccionar
Selecciona la respuesta correcta.

1. El tema principal de este libro es ___d___.
 a. Puerto Rico b. la salud y el agua c. otras culturas
 d. el cuidado de la salud en los viajes
2. Las situaciones narradas en el libro son ___a___.
 a. autobiográficas b. inventadas c. ficticias
 d. imaginarias
3. ¿Qué recomendaciones no vas a encontrar en este libro? ___d___
 a. cómo vestirse adecuadamente
 b. cómo prevenir las quemaduras solares
 c. consejos sobre la comida y la bebida
 d. cómo dar propina en los países del Caribe o de Suramérica
4. En opinión de la señorita Baron, ___b___.
 a. es bueno tomar agua de la llave y beber jugo de frutas con mucho hielo
 b. es mejor tomar solamente agua embotellada (*bottled*)
 c. los minerales son buenos para el dolor abdominal
 d. es importante visitar el cuarto de baño cada diez minutos
5. ¿Cuál de estos productos no lleva la autora cuando viaja a otros países? ___c___
 a. desinfectante
 b. crema repelente
 c. detergente
 d. pastillas medicinales

Section Goal

In **Panorama**, students will read about the geography, culture, and economy of Costa Rica.

Instructional Resources

Supersite/DVD: *Panorama cultural*

Supersite: Resources (Scripts, Translations, *PowerPoints*, Answer Keys)

WebSAM

Workbook, pp. 121–122

Video Manual, pp. 243–244

Teaching Tips

• Use the **Lección 10 Panorama** overheads to assist with this presentation.

• Have students look at the map of Costa Rica. Encourage them to mention the physical features that they notice. Discuss the map and the images in the call-out photos.

El país en cifras After each section, ask students questions about the content. Ex: **¿Entre qué masas de agua está Costa Rica? Las ciudades principales, ¿en qué lado de la cordillera Central están?** When reading about Costa Rica's population, point out that the country has over a 90% literacy rate, the best in Latin America. Point out that **Óscar Arias** received the Nobel Peace Prize for his work in resolving civil wars in the other Central American countries during the 1970s.

¡Increíble pero cierto! Costa Rica has one of the most long-standing democratic traditions in the Americas. Although it has no army, it does have a national police force and a rural guard.

Costa Rica

NATIONAL connections cultures STANDARDS

El país en cifras

▶ **Área:** 51.100 km² (19.730 millas²), *aproximadamente el área de Virginia Occidental°*

▶ **Población:** 4.957.000

Costa Rica es el país de Centroamérica con la población más homogénea. El 94% de sus habitantes es blanco y mestizo°. Más del 50% de la población es de ascendencia° española y un alto porcentaje tiene sus orígenes en otros países europeos.

▶ **Capital:** San José —1.655.000

▶ **Ciudades principales:** Alajuela, Cartago, Puntarenas, Heredia

SOURCE: Population Division, UN Secretariat

▶ **Moneda:** colón costarricense

▶ **Idioma:** español (oficial)

Bandera de Costa Rica

Costarricenses célebres

▶ **Carmen Lyra,** escritora (1888–1949)

▶ **Chavela Vargas,** cantante (1919–)

▶ **Óscar Arias Sánchez,** ex presidente de Costa Rica (1941–)

▶ **Claudia Poll,** nadadora° olímpica (1941–)

Óscar Arias recibió el Premio Nobel de la Paz en 1987.

Virginia Occidental *West Virginia* mestizo *of indigenous and white parentage* ascendencia *descent* nadadora *swimmer* ejército *army* gastos *expenditures* invertir *to invest* cuartel *barracks*

¡Increíble pero cierto!

Costa Rica es el único país latinoamericano que no tiene ejército°. Sin gastos° militares, el gobierno puede invertir° más dinero en la educación y las artes. En la foto aparece el Museo Nacional de Costa Rica, antiguo cuartel° del ejército.

Mercado Central en San José
NICARAGUA
Vista del volcán Arenal
Río San Juan
Río Tempisque
Cordillera de Guanacaste
Cordillera Central
Volcán Arenal
Cordillera de Tilarán
Alajuela
Puntarenas
Heredia
Río Grande de Tárcoles
Volcán Irazú
San José
Cartago
Cordillera
Edificio Metálico en San José
Océano Pacífico

ESTADOS UNIDOS
OCÉANO ATLÁNTICO
COSTA RICA
OCÉANO PACÍFICO
AMÉRICA DEL SUR

Basílica de Nuestra Señora de los Ángeles en Cartago

recursos

| WB pp. 121–122 | VM pp. 243–244 | vhlcentral.com Lección 10 |

MUSEO NACIONAL

Lugares • **Los parques nacionales**

El sistema de parques nacionales de Costa Rica ocupa aproximadamente el 12% de su territorio y fue establecido° para la protección de su biodiversidad. En los parques, los ecoturistas pueden admirar montañas, cataratas° y una gran variedad de plantas exóticas. Algunos ofrecen también la oportunidad de ver quetzales°, monos°, jaguares, armadillos y mariposas° en su hábitat natural.

Mar Caribe

Economía • **Las plantaciones de café**

Costa Rica fue el primer país centroamericano en desarrollar° la industria del café. En el siglo° XIX, los costarricenses empezaron a exportar esta semilla a Inglaterra°, lo que significó una contribución importante a la economía de la nación. Actualmente, más de 50.000 costarricenses trabajan en el cultivo del café. Este producto representa cerca del 15% de sus exportaciones anuales.

Limón

Sociedad • **Una nación progresista**

Costa Rica es un país progresista. Tiene un nivel de alfabetización° del 96%, uno de los más altos de Latinoamérica. En 1870, esta nación centroamericana abolió la pena de muerte° y en 1948 eliminó el ejército e hizo obligatoria y gratuita° la educación para todos sus ciudadanos.

manca

PANAMÁ

 ¿Qué aprendiste? Responde a las preguntas con oraciones completas.

1. ¿Cómo se llama la capital de Costa Rica?
 La capital de Costa Rica se llama San José.
2. ¿Quién es Claudia Poll?
 Claudia Poll es una nadadora olímpica.
3. ¿Qué porcentaje del territorio de Costa Rica ocupan los parques nacionales?
 Los parques nacionales ocupan aproximadamente el 12% del territorio de Costa Rica.
4. ¿Para qué se establecieron los parques nacionales? Los parques nacionales se establecieron para proteger los ecosistemas de la región y su biodiversidad.
5. ¿Qué pueden ver los turistas en los parques nacionales? En los parques nacionales, los turistas pueden ver cataratas, montañas y muchas plantas exóticas.
6. ¿Cuántos costarricenses trabajan en las plantaciones de café hoy día?
 Más de 50.000 costarricenses trabajan en las plantaciones de café hoy día.
7. ¿Cuándo eliminó Costa Rica la pena de muerte?
 Costa Rica eliminó la pena de muerte en 1870.

Parque Morazán
en San José

 Conexión Internet Investiga estos temas en **vhlcentral.com**.

Practice more at
vhlcentral.com.

1. Busca información sobre Óscar Arias Sánchez. ¿Quién es? ¿Por qué se le considera (*is he considered*) un costarricense célebre?
2. Busca información sobre los artistas de Costa Rica. ¿Qué artista, escritor o cantante te interesa más? ¿Por qué?

..

establecido *established* **cataratas** *waterfalls* **quetzales** *type of tropical bird* **monos** *monkeys* **mariposas** *butterflies*
en desarrollar *to develop* **siglo** *century* **Inglaterra** *England* **nivel de alfabetización** *literacy rate* **pena de muerte** *death penalty* **gratuita** *free*

Nicaragua

NATIONAL connections cultures STANDARDS

El país en cifras

▶ **Área:** 129.494 km² (49.998 millas²), *aproximadamente el área de Nueva York. Nicaragua es el país más grande de Centroamérica. Su terreno es muy variado e incluye bosques° tropicales, montañas, sabanas° y marismas°, además de unos 40 volcanes.*

▶ **Población:** 6.265.000

▶ **Capital:** Managua—1.015.000
Managua está en una región de una notable inestabilidad geológica, con muchos volcanes y terremotos°. En décadas recientes, los nicaragüenses han decidido° que no vale la pena° construir rascacielos° porque no resisten los terremotos.

▶ **Ciudades principales:** León, Masaya, Granada
SOURCE: Population Division, UN Secretariat

▶ **Moneda:** córdoba

▶ **Idiomas:** español (oficial); lenguas indígenas y criollas (oficiales); inglés

Bandera de Nicaragua

Nicaragüenses célebres

▶ **Rubén Darío,** poeta (1867–1916)
▶ **Violeta Barrios de Chamorro,** política y ex-presidenta (1929–)
▶ **Daniel Ortega,** político y presidente (1945–)
▶ **Gioconda Belli,** poeta (1948–)

bosques *forests* sabanas *grasslands* marismas *marshes* terremotos *earthquakes* han decidido *have decided* no vale la pena *it's not worthwhile* rascacielos *skyscrapers* agua dulce *fresh water* Surgió *Emerged* maravillas *wonders*

Iglesia en León

Teatro Nacional Rubén Darío en Managua

Calle en Granada

Violeta Barrios de Chamorro

recursos

| WB p. 123–124 | VM pp. 245–246 | vhlcentral.com Lección 10 |

Río Coco

HONDURAS

Cordillera Isabelia
Saslaya
Chachagón
Piu
Río Tuma
Río Grande
Cordillera Dariense

León
Sierra Madre
Lago de Managua
Managua
Masaya
Lago de Nicaragua
Granada
Isla Zapatera
Concepción
Maderas
Isla Ometepe
Archipiélago de Solentiname
Río San Juan

Océano Pacífico

COSTA RICA

ESTADOS UNIDOS
OCÉANO ATLÁNTICO
NICARAGUA
OCÉANO PACÍFICO
AMÉRICA DEL SUR

¡Increíble pero cierto!

Ometepe, que en náhuatl significa "dos montañas", es la isla más grande del mundo en un lago de agua dulce°. Surgió° en el Lago de Nicaragua por la actividad de los volcanes Maderas y Concepción. Por su valor natural y arqueológico, fue nominada para las siete nuevas maravillas° del mundo en 2009.

Historia • Las huellas° de Acahualinca

La región de Managua se caracteriza por tener un gran número de sitios prehistóricos. Las huellas de Acahualinca son uno de los restos° más famosos y antiguos°. Se formaron hace más de 6.000 años, a orillas° del lago de Managua. Las huellas, tanto de humanos como de animales, se dirigen° hacia una misma dirección, lo que ha hecho° pensar a los expertos que éstos corrían hacia° el lago para escapar de una erupción volcánica.

Artes • Ernesto Cardenal (1925–)

Ernesto Cardenal, poeta, escultor y sacerdote° católico, es uno de los escritores más famosos de Nicaragua, país conocido° por sus grandes poetas. Ha escrito° más de 35 libros y es considerado uno de los principales autores de Latinoamérica. Desde joven creyó en el poder de la poesía para mejorar la sociedad y trabajó por establecer la igualdad° y la justicia en su país. En los años 60, Cardenal estableció la comunidad artística del archipiélago de Solentiname en el lago de Nicaragua. Fue ministro de cultura del país desde 1979 hasta 1988 y participó en la fundación de Casa de los Tres Mundos, una organización creada para el intercambio cultural internacional.

Naturaleza • El lago de Nicaragua

El lago de Nicaragua, con un área de más de 8.000 km² (3.100 millas²), es el lago más grande de Centroamérica. Tiene más de 400 islas e islotes° de origen volcánico, entre ellas la isla Zapatera. Allí se han encontrado° numerosos objetos de cerámica y estatuas prehispánicos. Se cree que la isla era un centro ceremonial indígena.

¿Qué aprendiste? Responde a cada pregunta con una oración completa.

1. ¿Por qué no hay muchos rascacielos en Managua?
 No hay muchos rascacielos en Managua porque no resisten los terremotos.
2. Nombra dos poetas de Nicaragua.
 Rubén Darío y Gioconda Belli/Ernesto Cardenal son dos poetas de Nicaragua.
3. ¿Qué significa Ometepe en náhuatl?
 Ometepe significa "dos montañas" en náhuatl.
4. ¿Cuál es una de las teorías sobre la formación de las huellas de Acahualinca?
 Una teoría dice que las personas y los animales corrían para escapar de la erupción del volcán.
5. ¿Por qué es famoso el archipiélago de Solentiname?
 El archipiélago de Solentiname es famoso porque es el sitio de la comunidad artística establecida por Cardenal.
6. ¿Qué cree Ernesto Cardenal acerca de la poesía?
 Cardenal cree que la poesía puede mejorar la sociedad.
7. ¿Cómo se formaron las islas del lago de Nicaragua?
 Las islas se formaron por erupciones volcánicas.
8. ¿Qué hay de interés arqueológico en la isla Zapatera?
 En la isla Zapatera hay muchos objetos de cerámica y estatuas prehispánicos./Se cree que la isla era un centro ceremonial indígena.

Conexión Internet Investiga estos temas en **vhlcentral.com**.

1. ¿Dónde se habla inglés en Nicaragua y por qué?
2. ¿Qué información hay ahora sobre la economía y/o los derechos humanos en Nicaragua?

 Practice more at **vhlcentral.com**.

...
huellas *footprints* restos *remains* antiguos *ancient* orillas *shores* se dirigen *are headed* ha hecho *has made* hacia *toward*
sacerdote *priest* conocido *known* Ha escrito *He has written* igualdad *equality* islotes *islets* se han encontrado *have been found*

Las huellas de Acahualinca The **huellas de Acahualinca** consist of the prints of bison, otter, deer, lizards, and birds—as well as humans. The prints were preserved in soft mud, then covered with volcanic ash, which became petrified.

Ernesto Cardenal After completing undergraduate courses in Nicaragua, **Ernesto Cardenal** studied in Mexico and in the United States, where he worked with the religious poet Thomas Merton at the Trappist seminary in Kentucky. He later studied theology in Colombia and was ordained in Nicaragua in 1965. Shortly after that, **Cardenal** founded the faith-based community of artists on the Solentiname Islands.

El lago de Nicaragua Environmental groups in Nicaragua have been concerned about the recent introduction of a variety of **tilapia** into Lake Nicaragua. Although **tilapia** are native to the lake, this variety is a more prolific species. Environmentalists are concerned that the Nicaraguan-Norwegian joint venture responsible for this initiative has not done an adequate environmental impact study, and that the delicate and unique ecology of the lake may be negatively impacted.

Conexión Internet Students will find supporting Internet activities and links at **vhlcentral.com**.

Teaching Tip You may want to wrap up this section by playing the *Panorama cultural* video footage for this lesson.

El cuerpo

la boca	mouth
el brazo	arm
la cabeza	head
el corazón	heart
el cuello	neck
el cuerpo	body
el dedo	finger
el dedo del pie	toe
el estómago	stomach
la garganta	throat
el hueso	bone
la nariz	nose
el oído	(sense of) hearing; inner ear
el ojo	eye
la oreja	(outer) ear
el pie	foot
la pierna	leg
la rodilla	knee
el tobillo	ankle

La salud

el accidente	accident
el antibiótico	antibiotic
la aspirina	aspirin
la clínica	clinic
el consultorio	doctor's office
el/la dentista	dentist
el/la doctor(a)	doctor
el dolor (de cabeza)	(head)ache; pain
el/la enfermero/a	nurse
el examen médico	physical exam
la farmacia	pharmacy
la gripe	flu
el hospital	hospital
la infección	infection
el medicamento	medication
la medicina	medicine
la operación	operation
el/la paciente	patient
la pastilla	pill; tablet
la radiografía	X-ray
la receta	prescription
el resfriado	cold (illness)
la sala de emergencia(s)	emergency room
la salud	health
el síntoma	symptom
la tos	cough

Verbos

caerse	to fall (down)
dañar	to damage; to break down
darse con	to bump into; to run into
doler (o:ue)	to hurt
enfermarse	to get sick
estar enfermo/a	to be sick
estornudar	to sneeze
lastimarse (el pie)	to injure (one's foot)
olvidar	to forget
poner una inyección	to give an injection
prohibir	to prohibit
recetar	to prescribe
romper	to break
romperse (la pierna)	to break (one's leg)
sacar(se) un diente	to have a tooth removed
ser alérgico/a (a)	to be allergic (to)
sufrir una enfermedad	to suffer an illness
tener dolor (m.)	to have a pain
tener fiebre	to have a fever
tomar la temperatura	to take someone's temperature
torcerse (o:ue) (el tobillo)	to sprain (one's ankle)
toser	to cough

Adjetivos

congestionado/a	congested; stuffed-up
embarazada	pregnant
grave	grave; serious
mareado/a	dizzy; nauseated
médico/a	medical
saludable	healthy
sano/a	healthy

Adverbios

a menudo	often
a tiempo	on time
a veces	sometimes
además (de)	furthermore; besides
apenas	hardly; scarcely
así	like this; so
bastante	enough; rather
casi	almost
con frecuencia	frequently
de niño/a	as a child
de vez en cuando	from time to time
despacio	slowly
menos	less
mientras	while
muchas veces	a lot; many times
poco	little
por lo menos	at least
pronto	soon
rápido	quickly
todos los días	every day

Expresiones útiles	See page 313.

 Audio: Vocabulary

recursos

LM p. 60	vhlcentral.com Lección 10

La tecnología

11

Communicative Goals

You will learn how to:

- Talk about using technology and electronics
- Use common expressions on the telephone
- Talk about car trouble

Lesson Goals

In **Lección 11**, students will be introduced to the following:

- terms related to technology, electronics, and the Internet
- terms related to cars and their accessories
- cell phone use in Spanish-speaking countries
- text messaging
- familiar (**tú**) commands
- uses of **por** and **para**
- reciprocal reflexive verbs
- stressed possessive adjectives and pronouns
- recognizing borrowed words
- a video about technology in Peru
- cultural, geographic, and historical information about Argentina and Uruguay

A primera vista Here are some additional questions you can ask: ¿**Te gustan las computadoras?** ¿**Para qué usas Internet?** ¿**Cómo te comunicas con tus amigos?** ¿**Por chat, por teléfono o se escriben mensajes electrónicos?** ¿**Cómo se escribían tus abuelos cuando no existía el correo electrónico?**

Teaching Tip Look for these icons for additional communicative practice:

→👥←	Interpretive communication
←👥→	Presentational communication
👤↔👤	Interpersonal communication

A PRIMERA VISTA

- ¿Qué hace la chica?
- ¿Crees que usa su computadora con frecuencia?
- ¿Es una chica saludable?
- ¿Qué partes del cuerpo se ven en la foto?

INSTRUCTIONAL RESOURCES

Supersite (vhlcentral.com)
Video: **Fotonovela*, Flash cultura*, Panorama cultural***
*Also on DVD
Audio: Textbook and Lab MP3 Files (*also on CD*)
Activity Pack: Information Gap Activities, games, additional activity handouts

Resources: Textbook Answer Key, WB/VM/LM Answer Key, Scripts, Translations, **Vocabulario adicional**, lesson plans, **Estructura** *PowerPoints*, Overheads
Testing Program: Quizzes, Tests, Exams, MP3s (*also on Test Generator CD*)

Learning Management System (Assignment Task Manager, Gradebook)
WebSAM (online Workbook/Video Manual/ Lab Manual)
Workbook/Video Manual
Lab Manual

Section Goals

In **Contextos**, students will learn and practice:

• vocabulary related to technology, electronics, and the Internet

• terms related to cars and their accessories

Instructional Resources

Supersite: Audio (Textbook and Lab MP3 Files); Resources (Overheads, **Vocabulario adicional**, Activity Pack, Scripts, Answer Keys); Testing Program (Quizzes)
WebSAM
Workbook, pp. 125–126
Lab Manual, p. 61

Teaching Tips

• 👥↔👤 To engage students in a conversation, ask them about electronic items they have. Ex: **¿Quiénes tienen cámara digital? ¿Quiénes tienen un *fax*? ¿Quiénes tienen teléfono celular? ¿Cuántas veces al día lo usas? ¿Para qué lo usas?**

• Use the **Lección 11 Contextos** overheads to assist with this presentation.

• As students look at the illustration, ask questions to elicit computer vocabulary and ask them about their computer use. Ex: **¿Es portátil la computadora? ¿Qué se usa para mover el cursor? ¿Quiénes navegan en la red? ¿Cuál es tu sitio web favorito?**

• Give students true/false statements about electronic devices and have them react. Ex: **El control remoto se usa con el televisor. (Cierto.)**

• Explain to students that Spanish speakers sometimes adopt and use English words in place of their Spanish counterparts. This is especially true with words having to do with technology. For example, in Argentina, Chile, and Puerto Rico, **el mouse** is heard more frequently than **el ratón**. **El email** is also often used instead of **el correo electrónico** by many Spanish speakers.

La tecnología

Más vocabulario

la cámara digital/de video	digital/video camera
el canal	(TV) channel
el correo de voz	voice mail
el estéreo	stereo
el *fax*	fax (machine)
la pantalla táctil	touch screen
el reproductor de CD	CD player
la televisión por cable	cable television
el video	video
el archivo	file
arroba	@ symbol
el blog	blog
la conexión inalámbrica	wireless connection
la dirección electrónica	e-mail address
Internet	Internet
el mensaje de texto	text message
la página principal	home page
el programa de computación	software
la red	network; Web
el sitio web	website
apagar	to turn off
borrar	to erase
descargar	to download
escanear	to scan
funcionar	to work
grabar	to record
guardar	to save
imprimir	to print
llamar	to call
navegar (en Internet)	to surf (the Internet)
poner, prender	to turn on
sonar (o:ue)	to ring
descompuesto/a	not working; out of order
lento/a	slow
lleno/a	full

Variación léxica

computadora ⟷ ordenador (*Esp.*), computador (*Col.*)

descargar ⟷ bajar (*Arg., Col., Esp., Ven.*)

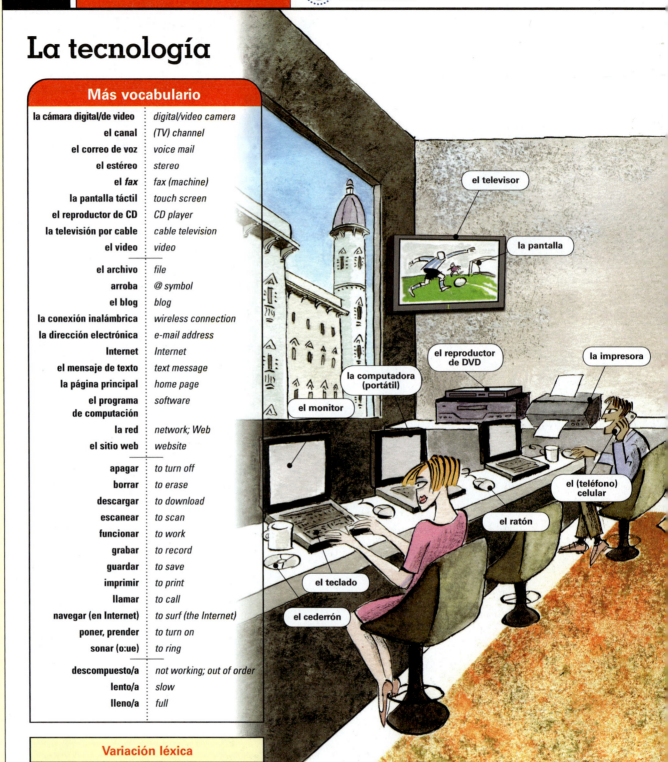

el televisor

la pantalla

el reproductor de DVD

la impresora

la computadora (portátil)

el monitor

el (teléfono) celular

el ratón

el teclado

el cederrón

recursos

WB pp. 125–126	LM p. 61	vhlcentral.com Lección 11

TEACHING OPTIONS

Large Group 👥↔👥 Ask students to write down a list of six electronic devices they have or use frequently. If possible, have them specify the brand name. Then have students circulate around the room and ask others if they have the same items. If someone answers affirmatively, the student should get the person's signature (**Firma aquí, por favor**). Students should try to get a different signature for each item.

Game Add a visual aspect to this vocabulary practice. Play **Concentración**. On eight cards, write names of electronic items. On another eight cards, draw or paste a picture that matches each name. Place the cards facedown in four rows of four. In pairs, students select two cards. If the cards match, the pair keeps them. If the cards do not match, students replace them in their original position. The pair with the most cards at the end wins.

Práctica

1 **Escuchar** Escucha la conversación entre dos amigas. Después completa las oraciones.

1. María y Ana están en _____b_____.
 a. una tienda b. un cibercafé c. un restaurante
2. A María le encantan _____b_____.
 a. los celulares b. las cámaras digitales c. los cibercafés
3. Ana prefiere guardar las fotos en _____c_____.
 a. la pantalla b. un archivo c. un cederrón
4. María quiere tomar un café y _____c_____.
 a. poner la computadora b. sacar fotos digitales
 c. navegar en Internet
5. Ana paga por el café y _____a_____.
 a. el uso de Internet b. la impresora c. el cederrón

2 **¿Cierto o falso?** Escucha las oraciones e indica si lo que dice cada una es **cierto** o **falso**, según el dibujo.

1. ___cierto___ 5. ___cierto___
2. ___falso___ 6. ___falso___
3. ___falso___ 7. ___cierto___
4. ___cierto___ 8. ___falso___

3 **Oraciones** Escribe oraciones usando estos elementos. Usa el pretérito y añade las palabras necesarias.

1. yo / descargar / fotos / Internet
 Yo descargué las fotos digitales por Internet.
2. tú / apagar / televisor / diez / noche
 Tú apagaste el televisor a las diez de la noche.
3. Daniel y su esposa / comprar / computadora portátil / ayer
 Daniel y su esposa compraron una computadora portátil ayer.
4. Sara y yo / ir / cibercafé / para / navegar en Internet
 Sara y yo fuimos al cibercafé para navegar en Internet.
5. Jaime / decidir / comprar / reproductor de MP3
 Jaime decidió comprar un reproductor de MP3.
6. teléfono celular / sonar / pero / yo / no contestar
 El teléfono celular sonó, pero yo no contesté.

4 **Preguntas** Mira el dibujo y contesta las preguntas. Answers will vary.

1. ¿Qué tipo de café es?
2. ¿Cuántas impresoras hay? ¿Cuántos ratones?
3. ¿Por qué vinieron estas personas al café?
4. ¿Qué hace el camarero?
5. ¿Qué hace la mujer en la computadora? ¿Y el hombre?
6. ¿Qué máquinas están cerca del televisor?
7. ¿Dónde hay un cibercafé en tu comunidad?
8. ¿Por qué puedes tú necesitar un cibercafé?

Cibercafé CORRIENTES

el control remoto

el reproductor de MP3

el disco compacto

1 Script (continued)

A: Claro que sí. También imprimo fotos, pero no voy a imprimirlas ahora. Prefiero guardarlas en un cederrón. M: Buena idea. Ahí está mi café. Voy a navegar en Internet mientras tomo mi cafecito. A: Bueno. Tengo que irme. Voy a pagar por el café y el uso de Internet. ¿No es muy caro, verdad? M: Para nada, es muy barato. Hasta luego. A: Chau. Nos vemos.
Textbook MP3s

Teaching Tips

• Using cognate vocabulary, ask students about cars. Ex: **¿Quiénes tienen carro? ¿Qué tipo de carro es? ¿Cuántas veces al mes tienes que llenar el tanque? ¿Cuánto cuesta la gasolina ahora?**

• Use the **Lección 11 Contextos** overheads to assist with this vocabulary presentation.

• Have students refer to the illustration on this page as you give true/false statements. Ex: **Un mecánico limpia el parabrisas. (Falso.)**

5 Teaching Tip Before
beginning the activity, ask several brief yes/no questions to test comprehension. Ex: **¿Sí o no? ¿Se usa el baúl para llenar el tanque? (No.)**

5 Expansion Have students
create three similar sentence starters for a partner to complete. Write some on the board and have the class complete them.

6 Expansion

👥↔👥 Ask groups to discuss car troubles they have had. Possible subjects are: a visit to the mechanic, a car accident, getting a speeding ticket, etc. Write helpful vocabulary on the board. Ex: **ponerle una multa, exceder la velocidad máxima,** etc. Have each group pick the strangest or funniest story to share with the class.

En la gasolinera

Más vocabulario

la autopista, la carretera	highway
la calle	street
la circulación, el tráfico	traffic
el garaje, el taller (mecánico)	(mechanic's) garage; repair shop
la licencia de conducir	driver's license
el/la mecánico/a	mechanic
la policía	police (force)
la velocidad máxima	speed limit
arrancar	to start
arreglar	to fix; to arrange
bajar(se) de	to get off of/out of (a vehicle)
conducir, manejar	to drive
estacionar	to park
parar	to stop
subir(se) a	to get on/into (a vehicle)

5 Completar Completa estas oraciones con las palabras correctas.

1. Para poder conducir legalmente, necesitas… *una licencia de conducir.*
2. Puedes poner las maletas en… *el baúl.*
3. Si tu carro no funciona, debes llevarlo a… *un mecánico/taller.*
4. Para llenar el tanque de tu coche, necesitas ir a… *la gasolinera.*
5. Antes de un viaje largo, es importante revisar… *el aceite.*
6. Otra palabra para autopista es… *carretera.*
7. Mientras hablas por teléfono celular, no es buena idea… *manejar/conducir.*
8. Otra palabra para coche es… *carro.*

6 Conversación Completa la conversación con las palabras de la lista.

el aceite	la gasolina	llenar	el parabrisas	el taller
el baúl	las llantas	manejar	revisar	el volante

EMPLEADO Bienvenido al (1)___*taller*___ mecánico *Óscar*. ¿En qué le puedo servir?

JUAN Buenos días. Quiero (2)___*llenar*___ el tanque y revisar (3)___*el aceite*___, por favor.

EMPLEADO Con mucho gusto. Si quiere, también le limpio (4)___*el parabrisas*___.

JUAN Sí, gracias. Está un poquito sucio. La próxima semana tengo que (5)___*manejar*___ hasta Buenos Aires. ¿Puede cambiar (6)___*las llantas*___? Están gastadas (*worn*).

EMPLEADO Claro que sí, pero voy a tardar (*it will take me*) un par de horas.

JUAN Mejor regreso mañana. Ahora no tengo tiempo. ¿Cuánto le debo por (7)___*la gasolina*___?

EMPLEADO Sesenta pesos. Y veinticinco por (8)___*revisar*___ y cambiar el aceite.

🔎 Practice more at **vhlcentral.com.**

¡LENGUA VIVA!

Aunque **carro** es el término que se usa en la mayoría de países hispanos, no es el único. En España, por ejemplo, se dice **coche**, y en Argentina, Chile y Uruguay se dice **auto**.

CONSULTA

For more information about **Buenos Aires**, see **Panorama**, p. 370.

TEACHING OPTIONS

TPR Draw a car on the board. Be sure to include identifiable parts (windshield, steering wheel, etc.). Make sticky notes that contain the Spanish names for these items. Have students place the notes on the corresponding parts of the car.
Variación léxica Ask students if they can explain why a trunk is called **maletera** in Peru (it is where one puts the **maletas**) or a **cajuela** in Mexico (it is related to the words **caja** and **cajón**).

TPR Divide the class into small groups. Have students take turns miming actions involving technology or parts of a car. The other group members should guess the object being used. Ex: A student mimes clicking a mouse. (**el ratón**)
Heritage Speakers ↔👤 Ask heritage speakers to describe car trends in their families' countries of origin. What brands are available? What size models are most popular?

Comunicación

7 **Preguntas** Trabajen en grupos y túrnense para contestar estas preguntas. Después compartan sus respuestas con la clase. Answers will vary.

1. a. ¿Tienes un teléfono celular? ¿Para qué lo usas?
 b. ¿Qué utilizas más: el teléfono o el correo electrónico? ¿Por qué?
 c. En tu opinión, ¿cuáles son las ventajas (*advantages*) y desventajas de los diferentes modos de comunicación?
2. a. ¿Con qué frecuencia usas la computadora?
 b. ¿Para qué usas Internet?
 c. ¿Tienes tu propio blog? ¿Cómo es?
3. a. ¿Miras la televisión con frecuencia? ¿Qué programas ves?
 b. ¿Dónde miras tus programas favoritos, en la tele o en la computadora?
 c. ¿Ves películas en la computadora? ¿Cuál es tu película favorita de todos los tiempos (*of all time*)?
 d. ¿A través de (*By*) qué medio escuchas música? ¿Radio, estéreo, reproductor de MP3 o computadora?
4. a. ¿Tienes licencia de conducir?
 b. ¿Cuánto tiempo hace que la conseguiste?
 c. ¿Tienes carro? Descríbelo.
 d. ¿Llevas tu carro al taller? ¿Para qué?

NOTA CULTURAL

Algunos sitios web utilizan códigos para identificar su país de origen. Éstos son los códigos para algunos países hispanohablantes:

Argentina .ar
Colombia .co
España .es
México .mx
Venezuela .ve

CONSULTA

To review expressions like **hace… que**, see **Lección 10, Expresiones útiles**, p. 313.

8 **Postal** En parejas, lean la tarjeta postal. Después contesten las preguntas. Answers will vary.

19 julio de 1979

Hola, Paco:

¡Saludos! Estamos de viaje por unas semanas. La Costa del Sol es muy bonita. No hemos encontrado (we haven't found) a tus amigos porque nunca están en casa cuando llamamos. El teléfono suena y suena y nadie contesta. Vamos a seguir llamando.

Sacamos muchas fotos muy divertidas. Cuando regresemos y las revelemos (get them developed), te las voy a enseñar. Las playas son preciosas. Hasta ahora el único problema fue que la oficina en la cual reservamos un carro perdió nuestros papeles y tuvimos que esperar mucho tiempo.

También tuvimos un pequeño problema con el hotel. La agencia de viajes nos reservó una habitación en un hotel que está muy lejos de todo. No podemos cambiarla, pero no me importa mucho. A pesar de eso, estamos contentos.

Tu hermana, Gabriela

EUROPA 12 PTA

ESPAÑA

Francisco Jiménez
San Lorenzo 3250
Rosario, Argentina 2000

1. ¿Cuáles son los problemas que ocurren en el viaje de Gabriela?
2. Con la tecnología de hoy, ¿existen los mismos problemas cuando se viaja? ¿Por qué?
3. Hagan una comparación entre la tecnología de los años 70 y 80 y la de hoy.
4. Imaginen que la hija de Gabriela escribe un correo electrónico sobre el mismo tema con fecha de hoy. Escriban ese correo, incorporando la tecnología actual (teléfonos celulares, Internet, cámaras digitales, etc.). Inventen nuevos problemas.

7 Teaching Tip For item 2, if few or no students have their own blogs, ask them if they follow any and what they are about. Encourage them to seek out some blogs related to learning Spanish as a foreign language.

7 Expansion Write names of different communication devices on the board (Ex: **teléfono celular**, *fax*, **computadora**). Then survey the class to find out how many people own or use these items. Analyze the trends of the class.

8 Teaching Tip Possible answers: **1.** Gabriela no encuentra a los amigos de Paco porque nunca están en casa, tuvo que esperar mucho por el carro y su hotel estaba muy lejos de todo. **2.** No existen los mismos problemas porque existen el correo de voz y los teléfonos celulares, se puede reservar un carro en Internet y se puede buscar información sobre un hotel en la red antes del viaje.

8 Expansion ←🏃→ Ask groups to write a postcard similar to the one in the activity, except that in theirs the problems encountered during the trip are a direct result of the existence of technology, not its absence.

Note: At this point you may want to present *Vocabulario adicional: Más vocabulario para el carro y la tecnología* from the Supersite.

TEACHING OPTIONS

Extra Practice ←🏃→ For homework, have students do an Internet research project on technology and technology terminology in the Spanish-speaking world. Suggest possible topics and websites where students may look for information. Have students write out their reports and present them to the class.

Large Groups 🏃↔🏃 Stage a debate about the role of technology in today's world. Divide the class into two groups and assign each side a position. Propose this debate topic: **La tecnología: ¿beneficio o no?** Allow groups time to plan their arguments before staging the debate.

En el taller

El coche de Miguel está descompuesto y Maru tiene problemas con su computadora.

 Video: *Fotonovela*
Record and Compare

PERSONAJES

 MIGUEL JORGE

1

MIGUEL ¿Cómo lo ves?

JORGE Creo que puedo arreglarlo. ¿Me pasas la llave?

2

JORGE ¿Y dónde está Maru?

MIGUEL Acaba de enviarme un mensaje de texto: "Última noticia sobre la computadora portátil: todavía está descompuesta. Moni intenta arreglarla. Voy para allá".

JORGE ¿Está descompuesta tu computadora?

MIGUEL No, la mía no, la suya. Una amiga la está ayudando.

JORGE Un mal día para la tecnología, ¿no?

3

MIGUEL Ella está preparando un proyecto para ver si puede hacer sus prácticas profesionales en el Museo de Antropología.

JORGE ¿Y todo está en la computadora?

MIGUEL Y claro.

4

MARU Buenos días, Jorge.

JORGE ¡Qué gusto verte, Maru! ¿Cómo está la computadora?

MARU Mi amiga Mónica recuperó muchos archivos, pero muchos otros se borraron.

5

6

MARU Estamos en una triste situación. Yo necesito una computadora nueva, y Miguel necesita otro coche.

JORGE Y un televisor nuevo para mí, por favor.

MARU

7

MARU ¿Qué vamos a hacer, Miguel?

MIGUEL Tranquila, cariño. Por eso tenemos amigos como Jorge y Mónica. Nos ayudamos los unos a los otros.

8

JORGE ¿No te sientes afortunada, Maru? No te preocupes. Sube.

MIGUEL ¡Por fin!

MARU Gracias, Jorge. Eres el mejor mecánico de la ciudad.

9

MIGUEL ¿Cuánto te debo por el trabajo?

JORGE Hombre, no es nada. Guárdalo para el coche nuevo. Eso sí, recomiéndame con tus amigos.

MIGUEL Gracias, Jorge.

10

JORGE No manejes en carretera. Revisa el aceite cada 1.500 kilómetros y asegúrate de llenarle el tanque... No manejes con el cofre abierto. Nos vemos.

Expresiones útiles

Giving instructions to a friend

¿Me pasas la llave?
Can you pass me the wrench?
No lo manejes en carretera.
Don't drive it on the highway.
Revisa el aceite cada 1.500 kilómetros.
Check the oil every 1,500 kilometers.
Asegúrate de llenar el tanque.
Make sure to fill up the tank.
No manejes con el cofre abierto.
Don't drive with the hood open.
Recomiéndame con tus amigos.
Recommend me to your friends.

Taking a phone call

Aló./Bueno./Diga.
Hello.
¿Quién habla?/ ¿De parte de quién?
Who is speaking/calling?
Con él/ella habla.
Speaking.
¿Puedo dejar un recado?
May I leave a message?

Reassuring someone

Tranquilo/a, cariño.
Relax, sweetie.
Nos ayudamos los unos a los otros.
We help each other out.
No te preocupes.
Don't worry.

Additional vocabulary

entregar *to hand in*
el intento *attempt*
la noticia *news*
el proyecto *project*
recuperar *to recover*

recursos

VM
pp. 215–216

vhlcentral.com
Lección 11

¿Qué pasó?

1 Seleccionar Selecciona las respuestas que completan correctamente estas oraciones.

1. Jorge intenta arreglar __b__.
 a. la computadora de Maru b. el coche de Miguel c. el teléfono celular de Felipe
2. Maru dice que se borraron muchos __a__ de su computadora.
 a. archivos b. sitios web c. mensajes de texto
3. Jorge dice que necesita un __c__.
 a. navegador GPS b. reproductor de DVD c. televisor
4. Maru dice que Jorge es el mejor __a__.
 a. mecánico de la ciudad b. amigo del mundo c. compañero de la clase
5. Jorge le dice a Miguel que no maneje su coche en __c__.
 a. el tráfico b. el centro de la ciudad c. la carretera

2 Identificar Identifica quién puede decir estas oraciones.

 MARU
 MIGUEL
 JORGE

1. Cómprate un coche nuevo y recomiéndame con tus amigos. Jorge
2. El mensaje de texto de Maru dice que su computadora todavía está descompuesta. Miguel
3. Mi amiga Mónica me ayudó a recuperar muchos archivos, pero necesito una computadora nueva. Maru
4. No conduzcas con el cofre abierto y recuerda que el tanque debe estar lleno. Jorge
5. Muchos de los archivos de mi computadora se borraron. Maru

3 Problema mecánico Trabajen en parejas para representar los papeles de un(a) mecánico/a y un(a) cliente/a que está llamando al taller porque su carro está descompuesto. Usen las instrucciones como guía. Answers will vary.

Mecánico/a	Cliente/a
Contesta el teléfono con un saludo y el nombre del taller.	Saluda y explica que tu carro está descompuesto.
Pregunta qué tipo de problema tiene exactamente.	Explica que tu carro no arranca cuando hace frío.
Di que debe traer el carro al taller.	Pregunta cuándo puedes llevarlo.
Ofrece una hora para revisar el carro.	Acepta la hora que ofrece el/la mecánico/a.
Da las gracias y despídete.	Despídete y cuelga (*hang up*) el teléfono.

Ahora cambien los papeles y representen otra conversación. Ustedes son un(a) técnico/a y un(a) cliente/a. Usen estas ideas:

el celular no guarda mensajes
la computadora no descarga fotos
la impresora imprime muy lentamente
el reproductor de DVD está descompuesto

 Practice more at **vhlcentral.com**.

Ortografía

S Concepts

La acentuación de palabras similares

Although accent marks usually indicate which syllable in a word is stressed, they are also used to distinguish between words that have the same or similar spellings.

Él maneja **el** coche. **Sí**, voy **si** quieres.

Although one-syllable words do not usually carry written accents, some *do* have accent marks to distinguish them from words that have the same spelling but different meanings.

Sé cocinar. **Se** baña. ¿Tomas **té**? **Te** duermes.

Sé (*I know*) and **té** (*tea*) have accent marks to distinguish them from the pronouns **se** and **te**.

para **mí** **mi** cámara **Tú** lees. **tu** estéreo

Mí (*Me*) and **tú** (*you*) have accent marks to distinguish them from the possessive adjectives **mi** and **tu**.

¿**Por qué** vas? Voy **porque** quiero.

Several words of more than one syllable also have accent marks to distinguish them from words that have the same or similar spellings.

Éste es rápido. **Este** tren es rápido.

Demonstrative pronouns have accent marks to distinguish them from demonstrative adjectives.

¿**Cuándo** fuiste? Fui **cuando** me llamó.
¿**Dónde** trabajas? Voy al taller **donde** trabajo.

Adverbs have accent marks when they are used to convey a question.

Práctica Marca los acentos en las palabras que los necesitan.

ANA Alo, soy Ana. ¿Que tal? *Aló/¿Qué?*
JUAN Hola, pero… ¿por que me llamas tan tarde? *¿por qué?*
ANA Porque mañana tienes que llevarme a la universidad. Mi auto esta dañado. *está*
JUAN ¿Como se daño? *¿Cómo?/dañó*
ANA Se daño el sabado. Un vecino (*neighbor*) choco con (*crashed into*) el. *dañó/sábado/chocó/él*

Crucigrama Utiliza las siguientes pistas (*clues*) para completar el crucigrama. ¡Ojo con los acentos!

Horizontales
1. Él _____ levanta.
4. No voy _____ no puedo.
7. Tú _____ acuestas.
9. ¿_____ es el examen?
10. Quiero este video y _____.

Verticales
2. ¿Cómo _____ usted?
3. Eres _____ mi hermano.
5. ¿_____ tal?
6. Me gusta _____ suéter.
8. Navego _____ la red.

	¹S	²E			³C				
		S	⁴P	O	R	⁵Q	U	⁶E	
		⁷T	⁸E		M		U		S
	⁹C	U	Á	N	D	O	¹⁰É	S	E

recursos

LM p. 62

S vhlcentral.com Lección 11

EN DETALLE

Additional Reading
Video: *Flash cultura*

El teléfono cellular

¿Cómo te comunicas con tus amigos y familia? En algunos países hispanos, el servicio de teléfono común° es bastante caro, por lo que el teléfono celular, más accesible y barato, es el favorito de mucha gente.

El servicio más popular entre los jóvenes es el sistema de tarjetas prepagadas°, porque no requiere de un contrato ni de cuotas° extras. En muchos países, puedes encontrar estas tarjetas en cualquier° tienda o recargar el saldo° de tu celular por Internet.

Los celulares de los años 80, grandes e incómodos, eran un símbolo de estatus y estaban limitados al uso de la voz°. Las funciones que entonces° sólo existían en la ciencia ficción, ahora son una realidad. Los celulares de hoy tienen muchas funciones: cámara de fotos o de video,

agenda electrónica°, navegador GPS, juegos, conexión a Internet, reproductor de MP3… Con los teléfonos actuales se puede interactuar en las redes sociales° de Internet y, gracias a la tecnología táctil, acceder a sus aplicaciones de forma diferente y rápida.

Con la evolución de los celulares, muchas personas han dejado de usar ciertos aparatos°: ¿para qué una cámara, un reproductor de música y un celular separados si puedes tener todo en uno°?

El uso de los celulares

- En el mundo se intercambian cerca de 500 mil millones de mensajes de texto al año.
- En los EE.UU., el 53% de los hispanos con celular lo usan para conectarse a Internet y el 84% de los hispanos menores de 30 años tiene un celular.
- América Latina tiene 179 millones de usuarios de teléfonos celulares. De ellos, el 73% utiliza programas de mensajería instantánea, el 82% navega por Internet y el 55% transfiere datos como videos y fotos.

común *ordinary* prepagadas *prepaid* cuotas *fees* cualquier *any* recargar el saldo *to buy more minutes* voz *voice* en ese entonces *back then* agenda electrónica *PDA* redes sociales *social Networks* aparatos *appliances* todo en uno *all in one*

ACTIVIDADES

1 **¿Cierto o falso?** Indica si lo que dicen estas oraciones es **cierto** o **falso**. Corrige la información falsa.

1. El teléfono común es un servicio caro en algunos países. Cierto.
2. Muchas personas usan más el teléfono celular que el teléfono común. Cierto.
3. Es difícil encontrar tarjetas prepagadas en los países hispanos. Falso. Puedes encontrar tarjetas prepagadas en cualquier tienda o recargar tu saldo por Internet.
4. En los años 80 los celulares eran un símbolo de estatus. Cierto.
5. Los primeros teléfonos celulares eran muy cómodos y pequeños. Falso. Los primeros teléfonos celulares eran grandes e incómodos.
6. Hoy en día muy pocas personas usan el celular para sacar fotos y oír música. Falso. Hoy en día muchas personas usan el celular para sacar fotos y oír música.
7. En los EE.UU., el 12% de los hispanos usa el celular para conectarse a Internet. Falso. En los EE.UU., el 53% de los hispanos usa el celular para conectarse a Internet.

ASÍ SE DICE

La tecnología

los audífonos (Méx., Col.), los auriculares (Arg.), los cascos (Esp.)	headset; earphones
el móvil (Esp.)	el celular
el manos libres (Amér. S.)	hands-free system
la memoria	memory
mensajear (Méx.)	enviar y recibir mensajes de texto

EL MUNDO HISPANO

Las bicimotos

- **Argentina** El *ciclomotor* se usa mayormente° para repartir a domicilio° comidas y medicinas.

- **Perú** La *motito* se usa mucho para el reparto a domicilio de pan fresco todos los días.

- **México** La *Vespa* se usa para evitar° el tráfico en grandes ciudades.

- **España** La población usa el *Vespino* para ir y volver al trabajo cada día.

- **Puerto Rico** Una *scooter* es el medio de transporte favorito en las zonas rurales.

- **República Dominicana** Las *moto-taxis* son el medio de transporte más económico, ¡pero no olvides el casco°!

mayormente *mainly* repartir a domicilio *home delivery of* evitar *to avoid* casco *helmet*

PERFIL

Los mensajes de texto

¿Qué tienen en común un **mensaje de texto** y un telegrama?: la necesidad de decir lo máximo en el menor espacio posible —y rápidamente—. Así como los abuelos se las arreglaron° para hacer más baratos sus telegramas, que se cobraban° por número de palabras, ahora los jóvenes buscan ahorrar° espacio, tiempo y dinero, en sus mensajes de texto. Esta economía del lenguaje dio origen al **lenguaje chat**, una forma de escritura muy creativa y compacta. Olvídate de la gramática, la puntuación y la ortografía: es tan flexible que evoluciona° todos los días con el uso que cada quien° le da, aunque° hay muchas palabras y expresiones ya establecidas°. Fácilmente encontrarás° abreviaturas (**xq?**, "¿Por qué?"; **tkm**, "Te quiero mucho."), sustitución de sonidos por números (**a2**, "Adiós."; **5mntrios**, "Sin comentarios."), símbolos (**ad+**, "además") y omisión de vocales y acentos (**tb**, "también"; **k tl?**, "¿Qué tal?"). Ahora que lo sabes, si un amigo te envía: **cont xfa, m dbs $!°**, puedes responderle: **ntp, ns vms + trd°**.

se las arreglaron *they managed to* se cobraban *were charged* ahorrar *to save* evoluciona *evolves* cada quien *each person* aunque *although* establecidas *fixed* encontrarás *you will find* cont xfa, m dbs $! Contesta, por favor, ¡me debes dinero! ntp, ns vms +trd No te preocupes, nos vemos más tarde.

Conexión Internet

¿Qué sitios web son populares entre los jóvenes hispanos?	Go to **vhlcentral.com** to find more cultural information related to this **Cultura** section.

ACTIVIDADES

2 **Comprensión** Responde a las preguntas.

1. ¿Cuáles son tres formas de decir *headset*? los audífonos, los auriculares, los cascos
2. ¿Para qué se usan las bicimotos en Argentina? para repartir a domicilio comidas y medicinas
3. ¿Qué dio origen al "lenguaje chat"? la necesidad de ahorrar espacio, tiempo y dinero
4. ¿Es importante escribir los acentos en los mensajes de texto? No. La gramática, la ortografía y la puntuación no importan en un mensaje de texto.

3 **¿Cómo te comunicas?** Escribe un párrafo breve en donde expliques qué utilizas para comunicarte con tus amigos/as (correo electrónico, redes sociales, teléfono, etc.) y de qué hablan cuando se llaman por teléfono. Answers will vary.

recursos

VM pp. 287–288	vhlcentral.com Lección 11

 Practice more at **vhlcentral.com.**

Así se dice

- Model the pronunciation of each term.
- To challenge students, add these words to the list: **el navegador** (*browser*); **la señal** (*signal*); **tener la batería baja** (*to have a low battery*).
- Ask students questions using these terms. Ex: **Si hablas por teléfono mientras manejas, ¿usas un manos libres? Nunca mensajeas mientras conduces, ¿verdad?**

Perfil

- Have students look up additional Spanish text messaging abbreviations in an online Spanish SMS dictionary. Ask them to decipher the meaning of the phrase **hexo x ti y xa ti** (**hecho por ti y para ti**) with regard to an online dictionary in which anyone can make entries. Then, have students make a list of the abbreviations they would use most when texting.

El mundo hispano

- Ask: **¿Alguna vez paseaste en bicimoto? ¿Qué te parece este modo de transporte?**
- Have students write three fill-in-the-blank sentences about this section for a partner to complete.

2 **Expansion** Ask additional comprehension questions. Ex: **¿Para qué necesita memoria un móvil?** (para guardar fotos, videos y mensajes de texto)

3 **Teaching Tip**
→👥← Allow students ten minutes to write a rough draft of their paragraph without looking up any words or grammar. Then have students work with a classmate to peer-edit their text and consult any necessary resources.

3 **Expansion**
←👥→ To challenge students, have them also explain how they expect their methods of communication will be different in ten years, using **ir a +** [*infinitive*].

TEACHING OPTIONS

Pairs ←👥→ For homework, ask student pairs to write a short dialogue between two people using text messages. If necessary, have them research additional text message abbreviations on the Internet. Encourage humor and creativity. In the next class period, have pairs exchange dialogues with another pair, who will decipher the conversation.

TPR Call out true/false statements about the information presented on pages 350–351. If the statement is true, have students raise their right hand, and if it is false, have students raise their left hand. To challenge students, have volunteers correct the false statements.
Heritage Speakers ←👥→ If heritage speakers have family in Spanish-speaking countries, ask them to discuss cell phone use there.

Section Goals

In **Estructura 11.1**, students will learn:
- affirmative **tú** commands
- negative **tú** commands

Instructional Resources

Supersite: Audio (Lab MP3 Files); Resources (*PowerPoints*, Activity Pack, Scripts, Answer Keys); Testing Program (Quizzes)
WebSAM
Workbook, pp. 127–128
Lab Manual, p. 63

Teaching Tips

- Model the use of informal commands with simple examples using TPR and gestures. Ex: Point to a student and say: _____ , **levántate. Gracias, ahora siéntate.** Give other commands using **camina, vuelve, toca,** and **corre.**
- Help students recognize that the affirmative **tú** command forms of regular verbs are the same as the third-person singular forms.
- Emphasize that **tú** commands are spoken to people one addresses as **tú.**

11.1 Familiar commands (S) Tutorial

ANTE TODO In Spanish, the command forms are used to give orders or advice. You use **tú** commands (**mandatos familiares**) when you want to give an order or advice to someone you normally address with the familiar **tú**.

Affirmative tú commands

Infinitive	Present tense él/ella form	Affirmative tú command
hablar	habla	**habla** (tú)
guardar	guarda	**guarda** (tú)
prender	prende	**prende** (tú)
volver	vuelve	**vuelve** (tú)
pedir	pide	**pide** (tú)
imprimir	imprime	**imprime** (tú)

▶ Affirmative **tú** commands usually have the same form as the **él/ella** form of the present indicative.

Guarda el documento antes de cerrarlo.
Save the document before closing it.

Imprime tu tarea para la clase de inglés.
Print your homework for English class.

▶ There are eight irregular affirmative **tú** commands.

Irregular affirmative tú commands

decir	**di**	salir	**sal**
hacer	**haz**	ser	**sé**
ir	**ve**	tener	**ten**
poner	**pon**	venir	**ven**

¡Sal ahora mismo!
Leave at once!

Haz los ejercicios.
Do the exercises.

▶ Since **ir** and **ver** have the same **tú** command (**ve**), context will determine the meaning.

Ve al cibercafé con Yolanda.
Go to the cybercafé with Yolanda.

Ve ese programa… es muy interesante.
See that program… it's very interesting.

Súbete al coche y préndelo.

No lo manejes en la carretera.

▶ The negative **tú** commands are formed by dropping the final -**o** of the **yo** form of the present tense. For -**ar** verbs, add -**es**. For -**er** and -**ir** verbs, add -**as**.

Negative tú commands

Infinitive	Present tense yo form	Negative tú command
hablar	hablo	**no hables** (tú)
guardar	guardo	**no guardes** (tú)
prender	prendo	**no prendas** (tú)
volver	vuelvo	**no vuelvas** (tú)
pedir	pido	**no pidas** (tú)

Héctor, **no pares** el carro aquí.
Héctor, don't stop the car here.

No prendas la computadora todavía.
Don't turn on the computer yet.

▶ Verbs with irregular **yo** forms maintain the same irregularity in their negative **tú** commands. These verbs include **conducir, conocer, decir, hacer, ofrecer, oír, poner, salir, tener, traducir, traer, venir,** and **ver**.

No pongas el cederrón en la computadora.
Don't put the CD-ROM in the computer.

No conduzcas tan rápido.
Don't drive so fast.

▶ Note also that stem-changing verbs keep their stem changes in negative **tú** commands.

No p**ie**rdas tu celular.
Don't lose your cell phone.

No v**ue**lvas a esa gasolinera.
Don't go back to that gas station.

No rep**i**tas las instrucciones.
Don't repeat the instructions.

▶ Verbs ending in -**car**, -**gar**, and -**zar** have a spelling change in the negative **tú** commands.

sa**car**	c → **qu**	no sa**qu**es
apa**gar**	g → **gu**	no apa**gu**es
almor**zar**	z → **c**	no almuer**c**es

▶ The following verbs have irregular negative **tú** commands.

Irregular negative tú commands

dar	**no des**
estar	**no estés**
ir	**no vayas**
saber	**no sepas**
ser	**no seas**

¡INTÉNTALO! Indica los mandatos familiares afirmativos y negativos de estos verbos.

1. correr — _Corre_ más rápido. / No _corras_ más rápido.
2. llenar — _Llena_ el tanque. / No _llenes_ el tanque.
3. salir — _Sal_ ahora. / No _salgas_ ahora.
4. descargar — _Descarga_ ese documento. / No _descargues_ ese documento.
5. levantarse — _Levántate_ temprano. / No _te levantes_ temprano.
6. hacerlo — _Hazlo_ ya. / No _lo hagas_ ahora.

Práctica

1 **Expansion** Continue this activity orally with the class, using regular verbs. Call out a negative command and designate individuals to make corresponding affirmative commands. Ex: **No sirvas la comida ahora. (Sirve la comida ahora./Sírvela ahora.)**

1 **Completar** Tu mejor amigo no entiende nada de tecnología y te pide ayuda. Completa los comentarios de tu amigo con el mandato de cada verbo.

1. No ___vengas___ en una hora. ___Ven___ ahora mismo. (venir)
2. ___Haz___ tu tarea después. No la ___hagas___ ahora. (hacer)
3. No ___vayas___ a la tienda a comprar papel para la impresora. ___Ve___ a la cafetería a comprarme algo de comer. (ir)
4. No ___me digas___ que no puedes abrir un archivo. ___Dime___ que el programa de computación funciona sin problemas. (decirme)
5. ___Sé___ generoso con tu tiempo y no ___seas___ antipático si no entiendo fácilmente. (ser)
6. ___Ten___ mucha paciencia y no ___tengas___ prisa. (tener)
7. ___Apaga___ tu teléfono celular, pero no ___apagues___ la computadora. (apagar)

2 **Expansion**
Ask volunteers to role-play the exchanges between **Pedro** and **Marina**. Encourage them to ad-lib and add more to the exchanges as they go along.

2 **Cambiar** Pedro y Marina no pueden ponerse de acuerdo (*agree*) cuando viajan en su carro. Cuando Pedro dice que algo es necesario, Marina expresa una opinión diferente. Usa la información entre paréntesis para formar las órdenes que Marina le da a Pedro.

> **modelo**
> **Pedro:** Necesito revisar el aceite del carro. (seguir hasta el próximo pueblo)
> **Marina:** *No revises el aceite del carro. Sigue hasta el próximo pueblo.*

1. Necesito conducir más rápido. (parar el carro) No conduzcas más rápido. Para el carro.
2. Necesito poner el radio. (hablarme) No pongas el radio. Háblame.
3. Necesito almorzar ahora. (comer más tarde) No almuerces ahora. Come más tarde.
4. Necesito sacar los discos compactos. (manejar con cuidado) No saques… Maneja…
5. Necesito estacionar el carro en esta calle. (pensar en otra opción) No estaciones… Piensa…
6. Necesito volver a esa gasolinera. (arreglar el carro en un taller) No vuelvas… Arregla…
7. Necesito leer el mapa. (pedirle ayuda a aquella señora) No leas… Pídele…
8. Necesito dormir en el carro. (acostarse en una cama) No duermas… Acuéstate…

3 **Teaching Tip** To simplify, review the vocabulary in the word bank by asking students to make associations with each word. Ex: **imprimir (documento), descargar (programa)**

3 **Problemas** Tú y tu compañero/a trabajan en el centro de computadoras de la universidad. Muchos estudiantes están llamando con problemas. Denles órdenes para ayudarlos a resolverlos.

Answers will vary. Suggested answers:

> **modelo**
> **Problema:** *No veo nada en la pantalla.*
> **Tu respuesta:** *Prende la pantalla de tu computadora.*

apagar…	descargar…	grabar…	imprimir…	prender…
borrar…	funcionar…	guardar…	navegar…	volver…

1. No me gusta este programa de computación. Descarga otro.
2. Tengo miedo de perder mi documento. Guárdalo.
3. Prefiero leer este sitio web en papel. Imprímelo.
4. Mi correo electrónico funciona muy lentamente. Borra los mensajes más viejos.
5. Busco información sobre los gauchos de Argentina. Navega en Internet.
6. Tengo demasiados archivos en mi computadora. Borra algunos archivos.
7. Mi computadora se congeló (*froze*). Apaga la computadora y luego préndela.
8. Quiero ver las fotos del cumpleaños de mi hermana. Descárgalas.

Practice more at **vhlcentral.com.**

NOTA CULTURAL

Los gauchos (*nomadic cowboys*), conocidos por su habilidad (*skill*) para montar a caballo y utilizar el lazo, viven en la Región Pampeana, una llanura muy extensa ubicada en el centro de Argentina y dedicada a la agricultura (*agriculture*).

TEACHING OPTIONS

TPR Have pairs of students brainstorm a list of actions that can be mimed. Then have them give each other **tú** commands based on the actions. Call on several pairs to demonstrate their actions for the class. When a repertoire of mimable actions is established, do TPR with the class using these commands/actions.
Pairs Tell students to imagine that they belong to their grandparents' generation and are not very familiar with new technology. Have them write three questions about electronic devices to ask a partner, who will answer using affirmative and negative commands. If the response uses a negative command, it should be followed by an affirmative command. Ex: **¿Debo apagar la computadora cada vez que salgo de la casa? (No, no la apagues. Pero guarda todos tus documentos.)** Students should ask follow-up questions when necessary.

Comunicación

4 **Órdenes** Circula por la clase e intercambia mandatos negativos y afirmativos con tus compañeros/as. Debes seguir las órdenes que ellos te dan o reaccionar apropiadamente. Answers will vary.

> **modelo**
>
> **Estudiante 1:** Dame todo tu dinero.
> **Estudiante 2:** No, no quiero dártelo. Muéstrame tu cuaderno.
> **Estudiante 1:** Aquí está.
> **Estudiante 3:** Ve a la pizarra y escribe tu nombre.
> **Estudiante 4:** No quiero. Hazlo tú.

5 **Anuncios** Miren este anuncio. Luego, en grupos pequeños, preparen tres anuncios adicionales para tres escuelas que compiten (*compete*) con ésta. Answers will vary.

INFORMÁTICA ARGENTINA

Toma nuestros cursos y aprende a usar la computadora

abre y lee tus archivos

imprime tus documentos

entra al campo de la tecnología

¡Ponte en contacto con nosotros llamando al **11-4-129-1508** HOY!

Síntesis

6 **¡Tanto que hacer!** Tu profesor(a) te va a dar una lista de diligencias (*errands*). Algunas las hiciste tú y algunas las hizo tu compañero/a. Las diligencias que ya hicieron tienen esta marca ✔. Pero quedan cuatro diligencias por hacer. Dale órdenes a tu compañero/a y él/ella responde para confirmar si hay que hacerla o si ya la hizo. Answers will vary.

> **modelo**
>
> **Estudiante 1:** Llena el tanque.
> **Estudiante 2:** Ya llené el tanque. / ¡Ay, no! Tenemos que llenar el tanque.

4 Teaching Tip To simplify, ask students to brainstorm a list of what they might ask their classmates to do.

4 Expansion Have volunteers report to the class what they were asked to do, what they did, and what they did not do.

5 Teaching Tip Ask comprehension questions about the ad. **¿Qué se anuncia? (cursos de informática) ¿Cómo puedes informarte? (llamar por teléfono) ¿Dónde se encuentra este tipo de anuncio? (en periódicos y revistas)**

5 Expansion Post the finished ads in different places around the classroom. Have groups circulate and write one question for each poster. Then have group members ask their questions. Group answers should include a **tú** command.

6 Teaching Tips
- Divide the class into pairs and distribute the handouts from the Activity Pack (Activity Pack/Supersite) that correspond to this Information Gap Activity. Give students ten minutes to complete this activity.
- Ask volunteers to give examples of **tú** commands that college students usually give to their roommates. Ex: **Saca la basura. Apaga la tele. No te acuestes en el sofá.**

Section Goal

In **Estructura 11.2**, students will learn when to use **por** and **para**.

Instructional Resources

Supersite: Audio (Lab MP3 Files); Resources (*PowerPoints*, Activity Pack, Scripts, Answer Keys); Testing Program (Quizzes)
WebSAM
Workbook, pp. 129–130
Lab Manual, p. 64

Teaching Tips

• Bring in magazine advertisements or write popular sayings on the board and have students identify the uses of **por** and **para**. Ex: **Habla hasta por los codos; Para un mundo más justo; Calabaza, calabaza, cada uno para su casa; Por la boca muere el pez.**

• Ask students to translate phrases requiring **por**. Ex: *talk by phone, send information by e-mail, walk across campus, walk along Bécquer Street, arrive in the afternoon/in the morning, be worried about the accident/about your friend, drive 30 miles per hour, study for four hours.*

11.2 Por and para Tutorial

ANTE TODO Unlike English, Spanish has two words that mean *for*: **por** and **para**. These two prepositions are not interchangeable. Study the following charts to see how they are used.

▶ **Por** and **para** are most commonly used to describe aspects of movement, time, and action, but in different circumstances.

Por	Para
Movement	
Through or by a place	**Towards a destination**
La excursión nos llevó **por** el centro.	Mis amigos van **para** el estadio.
The tour took us through downtown.	*My friends are going to the stadium.*
Time	
Duration of an event	**Action deadline**
Ana navegó la red **por** dos horas.	Tengo que escribir un ensayo **para** mañana.
Ana surfed the net for two hours.	*I have to write an essay by tomorrow.*
Action	
Reason or motive for an action or circumstance	**Indication of for whom something is intended or done**
Llegué a casa tarde **por** el tráfico.	Estoy preparando una sorpresa **para** Eduardo.
I got home late because of the traffic.	*I'm preparing a surprise for Eduardo.*

▶ Here is a complete list of all of the uses of **por** and **para**.

Por is used to indicate...

1. **Movement: Motion or a general location** . . (around, through, along, by)
Pasamos **por** el parque y **por** el río.
We passed by the park and along the river.

2. **Time: Duration of an action** (for, during, in)
Estuve en la Patagonia **por** un mes.
I was in Patagonia for a month.

3. **Action: Reason or motive for an action** . . (because of, on account of, on behalf of)
Lo hizo **por** su familia.
She did it on behalf of her family.

4. **Object of a search** (for, in search of)
Vengo **por** ti a las ocho.
I'm coming for you at eight.
Manuel fue **por** su cámara digital.
Manuel went in search of his digital camera.

5. **Means by which something is done** . . . (by, by way of, by means of)
Ellos viajan **por** la autopista.
They travel by (by way of) the highway.

6. **Exchange or substitution** (for, in exchange for)
Le di dinero **por** el reproductor de MP3.
I gave him money for the MP3 player.

7. **Unit of measure** (per, by)
José manejaba a 120 kilómetros **por** hora.
José was driving 120 kilometers per hour.

¡ATENCIÓN!

Por is also used in several idiomatic expressions, including:

por aquí *around here*
por ejemplo *for example*
por eso *that's why; therefore*
por fin *finally*

AYUDA

Remember that when giving an exact time, **de** is used instead of **por** before **la mañana, la tarde,** or **la noche**.
La clase empieza a las nueve **de** la mañana.

• • •

In addition to **por**, **durante** is also commonly used to mean *for* when referring to time.
Esperé al mecánico **durante** cincuenta minutos.

TEACHING OPTIONS

TPR Call out a sentence, omitting either **por** or **para**. If students think **por** should be used in the sentence, they raise one hand. If they think **para** should be used, they raise two hands. Avoid cases where either **por** or **para** could be used. Ex: **Tengo que leer el capítulo 11 _____ mañana.** (two hands) **Elena trabaja _____ la noche.** (one hand) **Estuve en Buenos Aires _____ el mes de marzo.** (one hand)

Extra Practice ←■→ Ask students to write a paragraph about a time when communication technology failed them. Remind them to use new vocabulary and at least two uses each of **por** and **para**. Have students exchange their papers for peer editing.

Para is used to indicate...

1. Movement: Destination *(toward, in the direction of)*	Salimos **para** Córdoba el sábado. *We are leaving for Córdoba on Saturday.*
2. Time: Deadline or a specific time in the future . *(by, for)*	Él va a arreglar el carro **para** el viernes. *He will fix the car by Friday.*
3. Action: Purpose or goal + *[infinitive]* *(in order to)*	Juan estudia **para** (ser) mecánico. *Juan is studying to be a mechanic.*
4. Purpose + *[noun]* *(for, used for)*	Es una llanta **para** el carro. *It's a tire for the car.*
5. The recipient of something *(for)*	Compré una impresora **para** mi hijo. *I bought a printer for my son.*
6. Comparison with others or an opinion . . *(for, considering)*	**Para** un joven, es demasiado serio. *For a young person, he is too serious.* **Para** mí, esta lección no es difícil. *For me, this lesson isn't difficult.*
7. In the employment of *(for)*	Sara trabaja **para** Telecom Argentina. *Sara works for Telecom Argentina.*

▶ In many cases it is grammatically correct to use either **por** or **para** in a sentence. The meaning of the sentence is different, however, depending on which preposition is used.

Caminé **por** el parque.
I walked through the park.

Caminé **para** el parque.
I walked to (toward) the park.

Trabajó **por** su padre.
He worked for (in place of) his father.

Trabajó **para** su padre.
He worked for his father('s company).

¡INTÉNTALO! Completa estas oraciones con las preposiciones **por** o **para**.

1. Fuimos al cibercafé ___por___ la tarde.
2. Necesitas un navegador GPS ___para___ encontrar la casa de Luis.
3. Entraron ___por___ la puerta.
4. Quiero un pasaje ___para___ Buenos Aires.
5. ___Para___ arrancar el carro, necesito la llave.
6. Arreglé el televisor ___para___ mi amigo.
7. Estuvieron nerviosos ___por___ el examen.
8. ¿No hay una gasolinera ___por___ aquí?
9. El reproductor de MP3 es ___para___ usted.
10. Juan está enfermo. Tengo que trabajar ___por___ él.
11. Estuvimos en Canadá ___por___ dos meses.
12. ___Para___ mí, el español es fácil.
13. Tengo que estudiar la lección ___para___ el lunes.
14. Voy a ir ___por___ la carretera.
15. Compré dulces ___para___ mi novia.
16. Compramos el auto ___por___ un buen precio.

recursos

WB
pp. 129–130

LM
p. 64

vhlcentral.com
Lección 11

Práctica

1 **Completar** Completa este párrafo con las preposiciones **por** o **para**.

El mes pasado mi esposo y yo hicimos un viaje a Buenos Aires y sólo pagamos dos mil dólares (1)__por__ los pasajes. Estuvimos en Buenos Aires (2)__por__ una semana y paseamos por toda la ciudad. Durante el día caminamos (3)__por__ la plaza San Martín, el microcentro y el barrio de La Boca, donde viven muchos artistas. (4)__Por__ la noche fuimos a una tanguería, que es una especie de teatro, (5)__para__ mirar a la gente bailar tango. Dos días después decidimos hacer una excursión (6)__por__ las pampas (7)__para__ ver el paisaje y un rodeo con gauchos. Alquilamos (*We rented*) un carro y manejamos (8)__por__ todas partes y pasamos unos días muy agradables. El último día que estuvimos en Buenos Aires fuimos a Galerías Pacífico (9)__para__ comprar recuerdos (*souvenirs*) (10)__para__ nuestros hijos y nietos. Compramos tantos regalos que tuvimos que pagar impuestos (*duties*) en la aduana al regresar.

2 **Oraciones** Crea oraciones originales con los elementos de las columnas. Une los elementos usando **por** o **para**. Answers will vary.

> **modelo**
> Fuimos a Mar del Plata por razones de salud para visitar a un especialista. ◄

(no) fue al mercado	por/para	comprar frutas	por/para	¿?
(no) fuimos a las montañas	por/para	tres días	por/para	¿?
(no) fuiste a Mar del Plata	por/para	razones de salud	por/para	¿?
(no) fueron a Buenos Aires	por/para	tomar el sol	por/para	¿?

3 **Describir** Usa **por** o **para** y el tiempo presente para describir estos dibujos. Answers will vary.

TALLER JUÁREZ

LA ESTANCIA

1. _____
2. _____
3. _____

100 K/h

PARQUE

4. _____
5. _____
6. _____

Ⓢ Practice more at **vhlcentral.com.**

Comunicación

4 **Descripciones** Usa **por** o **para** y completa estas frases de manera lógica. Luego, compara tus respuestas con las de un(a) compañero/a. *Answers will vary.*

1. En casa, hablo con mis amigos…
2. Mi padre/madre trabaja…
3. Ayer fui al taller…
4. Los miércoles tengo clases…
5. A veces voy a la biblioteca…
6. Esta noche tengo que estudiar…
7. Necesito… dólares…
8. Compré un regalo…
9. Mi mejor amigo/a estudia…
10. Necesito hacer la tarea…

5 **Situación** En parejas, dramaticen esta situación. Utilicen muchos ejemplos de **por** y **para**.
Answers will vary.

Hijo/a	Padre/Madre
Pídele dinero a tu padre/madre.	→ Pregúntale a tu hijo/a para qué lo necesita.
Dile que quieres comprar un carro.	→ Pregúntale por qué necesita un carro.
Explica tres razones por las que necesitas un carro.	→ Explica por qué sus razones son buenas o malas.
Dile que por no tener un carro tu vida es muy difícil.	→ Decide si vas a darle el dinero y explica por qué.

Síntesis

6 **Una subasta** (*auction*) Cada estudiante debe traer a la clase un objeto o una foto del objeto para vender. En grupos, túrnense para ser el/la vendedor(a) y los postores (*bidders*). Para empezar, el/la vendedor(a) describe el objeto y explica para qué se usa y por qué alguien debe comprarlo.
Answers will vary.

modelo

Vendedora: Aquí tengo un reproductor de CD. Pueden usarlo para disfrutar su música favorita o para escuchar canciones en español. Sólo hace un año que lo compré y todavía funciona perfectamente. ¿Quién ofrece $ 1.500 para empezar?

Postor(a) 1: Pero los reproductores de CD son anticuados. Te doy $ 20.

Vendedora: Ah, pero éste es muy especial porque viene con el CD que grabé cuando quería ser cantante de ópera.

Postor(a) 2: Ah, ¡entonces te doy $ 100!

TEACHING OPTIONS

Small Groups ←🔺→ Have students create a television advertisement for a car or piece of technological equipment. Students should describe the item; explain why the customer should buy it; tell how much it costs; explain that the item is on sale only until a certain date; and detail any possible trade-ins. Students should use **por** and **para** as much as possible in their ad.

Extra Practice For students still having trouble distinguishing between **por** and **para**, have them create a mnemonic device, like a story or chant, for remembering the different uses. Ex: **Vine por la tarde y busqué por el parque, por el río y por el centro. Busqué por horas. Viajé por carro, por tren y por avión.** Do the same for **para**.

4 Teaching Tip Model the activity by completing item 1 in two different ways.

4 Expansion Have students create new sentences, employing additional uses of **por** and **para**.

5 Teaching Tip
←🔺→ Ask students questions about the car in the picture. Ex: **¿Te gusta este carro? ¿Cuánto se paga por un carro así? ¿A cuántas millas por hora corre este carro?** Have students write their answers using complete sentences.

5 Expansion
• 🔺↔🔺 Ask volunteers to role-play their conversation for the class.
• ←🔺→ Show a picture of an old used car and ask students to create a new conversation. The parents are offering to buy their son/daughter this car instead of the one shown in the activity.

6 Teaching Tips
• 🔺↔🔺 Before the bidding begins, display the items to be auctioned off and name them. Invite students to walk around with their group members and discuss what the items are, their purposes, and how much they will pay for them.
• ←🔺→ Have groups prepare the opening statements for the items their members brought. Students then take turns opening up the bidding for the entire class. Non-group members may bid on each item. Group members should place bids to keep the bidding alive.

Section Goal

In **Estructura 11.3**, students will learn the use of reciprocal reflexives.

Instructional Resources
Supersite: Audio (Lab MP3 Files); Resources (*PowerPoints*, Activity Pack, Scripts, Answer Keys); Testing Program (Quizzes)
WebSAM
Workbook, pp. 131–132
Lab Manual, p. 65

Teaching Tips
- Ask a volunteer to explain what reflexive verbs are. Ask other students to provide examples. Review reflexive verbs and pronouns by asking students questions about their personal routine. Ex: **Yo me desperté a las seis de la mañana. Y tú, _____, ¿a qué hora te despertaste?**
- After going over the example sentences, ask students questions that contain or require reciprocal constructions. Ex: **¿Los estudiantes y los profesores siempre se saludan? ¿Se ven ustedes con frecuencia durante la semana? En las elecciones, ¿los candidatos siempre se respetan?**
- ← 🛉 → Add a visual aspect to this grammar presentation. Hold up images of pairs of celebrities and have students write descriptions about them, using reciprocal reflexives. Remind students they can use the present, preterite, or imperfect tense. Ex: Photos of Jennifer Aniston and Brad Pitt (**Antes se querían mucho, pero ahora no se hablan....**)

11.3 Reciprocal reflexives Tutorial

ANTE TODO In **Lección 7**, you learned that reflexive verbs indicate that the subject of a sentence does the action to itself. Reciprocal reflexives, on the other hand, express a shared or reciprocal action between two or more people or things. In this context, the pronoun means *(to) each other* or *(to) one another.*

Luis y Marta **se** miran en el espejo.
Luis and Marta look at themselves in the mirror.

Luis y Marta **se** miran.
Luis and Marta look at each other.

▶ Only the plural forms of the reflexive pronouns (**nos, os, se**) are used to express reciprocal actions because the action must involve more than one person or thing.

Cuando **nos vimos** en la calle, **nos abrazamos**.
When we saw each other on the street, we hugged (one another).

Ustedes **se** van a **encontrar** en el cibercafé, ¿no?
You are meeting (each other) at the cybercafé, right?

Nos ayudamos cuando usamos la computadora.
We help each other when we use the computer.

Las amigas **se saludaron** y **se besaron**.
The friends greeted each other and kissed (one another).

¡ATENCIÓN!
Here is a list of common verbs that can express reciprocal actions:
abrazar(se) *to hug; to embrace (each other)*
ayudar(se) *to help (each other)*
besar(se) *to kiss (each other)*
encontrar(se) *to meet (each other); to run into (each other)*
saludar(se) *to greet (each other)*

 ¡INTÉNTALO! Indica el reflexivo recíproco adecuado de estos verbos en el presente o el pretérito.

presente

1. (escribir) Los novios _se escriben_.
 Nosotros _nos escribimos_.
 Ana y Ernesto _se escriben_.
2. (escuchar) Mis tíos _se escuchan_.
 Nosotros _nos escuchamos_.
 Ellos _se escuchan_.
3. (ver) Nosotros _nos vemos_.
 Fernando y Tomás _se ven_.
 Ustedes _se ven_.
4. (llamar) Ellas _se llaman_.
 Mis hermanos _se llaman_.
 Pepa y yo _nos llamamos_.

pretérito

1. (saludar) Nicolás y tú _se saludaron_.
 Nuestros vecinos _se saludaron_.
 Nosotros _nos saludamos_.
2. (hablar) Los amigos _se hablaron_.
 Elena y yo _nos hablamos_.
 Ustedes _se hablan_.
3. (conocer) Alberto y yo _nos conocimos_.
 Ustedes _se conocieron_.
 Ellos _se conocieron_.
4. (encontrar) Ana y Javier _se encontraron_.
 Los primos _se encontraron_.
 Mi hermana y yo _nos encontramos_.

recursos
WB pp. 131–132
LM p. 65
vhlcentral.com Lección 11

TEACHING OPTIONS

Extra Practice ← 🛉 → Have students describe what they and their significant other or best friend do together, or what their friends do together. Have them use these verbs: **llamarse por teléfono, verse, decirse, ayudarse, encontrarse, reunirse.** Ex: **Mi amigo y yo siempre nos ayudamos con las tareas. Nos reunimos en la biblioteca o en mi casa y estudiamos por horas. Cuando hay examen de español, nos hacemos preguntas sobre**

el vocabulario y la gramática.
Pairs 🛉↔🛉 Have students write a conversation in which they discuss two friends who are romantically involved, but have had a misunderstanding. Ask them to incorporate these verbs: **conocerse, encontrarse, quererse, hablarse, enojarse, besarse, mirarse,** and **entenderse.** Have pairs role-play their conversations for the class.

Práctica y Comunicación

1 **Un amor recíproco** Describe a Laura y a Elián usando los verbos recíprocos.

modelo

> Laura veía a Elián todos los días. Elián veía a Laura todos los días.
> *Laura y Elián se veían todos los días.*

1. Laura conocía bien a Elián. Elián conocía bien a Laura.
 Laura y Elián se conocían bien.
2. Laura miraba a Elián con amor. Elián la miraba con amor también.
 Laura y Elián se miraban con amor.
3. Laura entendía bien a Elián. Elián entendía bien a Laura.
 Laura y Elián se entendían bien.
4. Laura hablaba con Elián todas las noches por teléfono. Elián hablaba
 con Laura todas las noches por teléfono.
 Laura y Elián se hablaban todas las noches por teléfono.
5. Laura ayudaba a Elián con sus problemas. Elián la ayudaba también
 con sus problemas.
 Laura y Elián se ayudaban con sus problemas.

2 **Describir** Mira los dibujos y describe lo que estas personas hicieron. Answers will vary.
Suggested answers:

1. Las hermanas ___se abrazaron___.

2. Ellos ___se besaron___.

3. Gilberto y Mercedes ___no se miraron___ /
___no se hablaron___ / ___se enojaron___.

4. Tú y yo ___nos saludamos___ /
___nos encontramos en la calle___

NATIONAL communication STANDARDS

3 **Preguntas** En parejas, túrnense para hacerse estas preguntas. Answers will vary.

1. ¿Se vieron tú y tu mejor amigo/a ayer? ¿Cuándo se ven ustedes normalmente?
2. ¿Dónde se encuentran tú y tus amigos?
3. ¿Se ayudan tú y tu mejor amigo/a con sus problemas?
4. ¿Se entienden bien tus compañeros de clase?
5. ¿Dónde se conocieron tú y tu mejor amigo/a? ¿Cuánto tiempo hace que se
 conocen ustedes?
6. ¿Cuándo se dan regalos tú y tu novio/a?
7. ¿Se escriben tú y tus amigos mensajes de texto o prefieren llamarse por teléfono?
8. ¿Siempre se llevan bien tú y tu compañero/a de cuarto? Explica.

 Practice more at **vhlcentral.com**.

1 Teaching Tip To simplify, before beginning the activity, review conjugations of the imperfect tense.

1 Expansion
- ←👤→ Have students expand upon the sentences to create a story about **Laura** and **Elián** falling in love.
- Have students rewrite the sentences, imagining that they are talking about themselves and their significant other, a close friend, or a relative.

2 Teaching Tip
←👤→ Have pairs choose a drawing and create the story of what the characters did leading up to the moment pictured and what they did after that. Ask pairs to share their stories and have the class vote for the most original or funniest one.

3 Teaching Tips
- To simplify, ask students to read through the questions and prepare short answers before talking to their partners.
- 👤↔👤 Have students ask follow-up questions. Ex: **¿A qué hora se vieron ayer? ¿Dónde se vieron? ¿Por qué se vieron ayer? ¿Para qué se ven ustedes normalmente?**
- Encourage students to verify what they hear by paraphrasing or summarizing their partner's responses.

TEACHING OPTIONS

Game Divide the class into small teams and write a verb on the board. Teams have twenty seconds to come up with a famous couple or two famous people or entities that behave or feel that way toward each other. The verb may be conjugated in the present, imperfect, or preterite tense. Ex: **quererse (Romeo y Julieta se querían.)** All teams with a correct answer earn one point. The team with the most points at the end wins.

Extra Practice Call on volunteers to act out a reciprocal action. The class will guess the action, using the correct verb in a sentence.
Heritage Speakers ←👤→ Ask heritage speakers to summarize the action of their favorite love story, soap opera, or television drama. They should use as many reciprocal reflexives as possible in their summaries. Ask the class comprehension questions as a follow-up.

11.4 Stressed possessive adjectives and pronouns (S) Tutorial

ANTE TODO Spanish has two types of possessive adjectives: the unstressed (or short) forms you learned in **Lección 3** and the stressed (or long) forms. The stressed forms are used for emphasis or to express *of mine, of yours,* and so on.

Stressed possessive adjectives

Masculine singular	Feminine singular	Masculine plural	Feminine plural	
mío	mía	míos	mías	*my; (of) mine*
tuyo	tuya	tuyos	tuyas	*your; (of) yours (fam.)*
suyo	suya	suyos	suyas	*your; (of) yours (form.); his; (of) his; her; (of) hers; its*
nuestro	nuestra	nuestros	nuestras	*our; (of) ours*
vuestro	vuestra	vuestros	vuestras	*your; (of) yours (fam.)*
suyo	suya	suyos	suyas	*your; (of) yours (form.); their; (of) theirs*

▶ **¡Atención!** Used with **un/una**, these possessives are similar in meaning to the English expression *of mine/yours/*etc.

> Juancho es **un** amigo **mío**. Ella es **una** compañera **nuestra**.
> *Juancho is a friend of mine.* *She is a classmate of ours.*

▶ Stressed possessive adjectives agree in gender and number with the nouns they modify. While unstressed possessive adjectives are placed before the noun, stressed possessive adjectives are placed after the noun they modify.

> **su** impresora la impresora **suya**
> *her printer* *her printer*
>
> **nuestros** televisores los televisores **nuestros**
> *our television sets* *our television sets*

▶ A definite article, an indefinite article, or a demonstrative adjective usually precedes a noun modified by a stressed possessive adjective.

> Me encantan { **unos** discos compactos **tuyos**. *I love some of your CDs.*
> **los** discos compactos **tuyos**. *I love your CDs.*
> **estos** discos compactos **tuyos**. *I love these CDs of yours.*

▶ Since **suyo, suya, suyos,** and **suyas** have more than one meaning, you can avoid confusion by using the construction: [*article*] + [*noun*] + **de** + [*subject pronoun*].

> **el** teclado **suyo** el teclado **de él/ella/usted** *his/her keyboard*
> el teclado **de ustedes/ellos/ellas** *your keyboard*

CONSULTA

This is the same construction you learned in **Lección 3** for clarifying **su** and **sus**. To review unstressed possessive adjectives, see **Estructura 3.2**, p. 85.

Possessive pronouns

▶ Possessive pronouns are used to replace a noun + [*possessive adjective*]. In Spanish, the possessive pronouns have the same forms as the stressed possessive adjectives, but they are preceded by a definite article.

la cámara **nuestra** **la nuestra**
el navegador GPS **tuyo** **el tuyo**
los archivos **suyos** **los suyos**

▶ A possessive pronoun agrees in number and gender with the noun it replaces.

—Aquí está **mi coche**. ¿Dónde está **el tuyo**?
Here's my car. Where is yours?

—¿Tienes **las revistas** de Carlos?
Do you have Carlos' magazines?

—**El mío** está en el taller de mi hermano.
Mine is at my brother's garage.

—No, pero tengo **las nuestras**.
No, but I have ours.

¿También está descompuesta tu computadora?

No, la mía no, la suya.

¡INTÉNTALO! Indica las formas tónicas (*stressed*) de estos adjetivos posesivos y los pronombres posesivos correspondientes.

		adjetivos	pronombres
1.	su cámara digital	la cámara digital suya	la suya
2.	mi televisor	el televisor mío	el mío
3.	nuestros discos compactos	los discos compactos nuestros	los nuestros
4.	tus calculadoras	las calculadoras tuyas	las tuyas
5.	su monitor	el monitor suyo	el suyo
6.	mis videos	los videos míos	los míos
7.	nuestra impresora	la impresora nuestra	la nuestra
8.	tu estéreo	el estéreo tuyo	el tuyo
9.	nuestro cederrón	el cederrón nuestro	el nuestro
10.	mi computadora	la computadora mía	la mía

recursos

WB
pp. 133–134

LM
p. 66

S
vhlcentral.com
Lección 11

Práctica

1 Oraciones
Forma oraciones con estas palabras. Usa el presente y haz los cambios necesarios.

1. un / amiga / suyo / vivir / Mendoza *Una amiga suya vive en Mendoza.*
2. ¿me / prestar / calculadora / tuyo? *¿Me prestas la calculadora tuya?*
3. el / coche / suyo / nunca / funcionar / bien *El coche suyo nunca funciona bien.*
4. no / nos / interesar / problemas / suyo *No nos interesan los problemas suyos.*
5. yo / querer / cámara digital / mío / ahora mismo *Yo quiero la cámara digital mía ahora mismo.*
6. un / amigos / nuestro / manejar / como / loco *Unos amigos nuestros manejan como locos.*

2 ¿Es suyo?
Un policía ha capturado (*has captured*) al hombre que robó (*robbed*) en tu casa. Ahora quiere saber qué cosas son tuyas. Túrnate con un(a) compañero/a para hacer el papel del policía y usa las pistas (*clues*) para contestar las preguntas.

modelo
no/viejo
Policía: Esta impresora, ¿es suya?
Estudiante: No, no es mía. La mía era más vieja.

1. sí E1: Este estéreo, ¿es suyo?
E2: Sí, es mío.

2. no/pequeño E1: Este televisor, ¿es suyo?
E2: No, no es mío. El mío era más pequeño.

3. sí E1: Estos teléfonos celulares, ¿son suyos?
E2: Sí, son míos.

4. sí E1: Esta computadora portátil, ¿es suya?
E2: Sí, es mía.

5. no/grande E1: Esta cámara de video, ¿es suya?
E2: No, no es mía. La mía era más grande.

6. no/caro E1: Estos reproductores de MP3, ¿son suyos?
E2: No, no son míos. Los míos eran más caros.

3 Conversaciones
Completa estas conversaciones con las formas adecuadas de los pronombres posesivos.

1. —La casa de ellos estaba en la Avenida Alvear. ¿Dónde estaba la casa de ustedes?
 — __La nuestra__ estaba en la calle Bolívar.
2. —A Carmen le encanta su monitor nuevo.
 —¿Sí? A José no le gusta __el suyo__.
3. —Puse mis discos aquí. ¿Dónde pusiste __los tuyos__, Alfonso?
 —Puse __los míos__ en el escritorio.
4. —Se me olvidó traer mis llaves. ¿Trajeron ustedes __las suyas__?
 —No, dejamos __las nuestras__ en casa.
5. —Yo compré mi computadora en una tienda y Marta compró __la suya__ en Internet. Y __la tuya__, ¿dónde la compraste?
 — __La mía__ es de Cíbermax.

 Practice more at **vhlcentral.com.**

1 Expansion Have students write four additional dehydrated sentences that use stressed possessive adjectives or pronouns. Have them exchange papers with a classmate, who will "rehydrate" them.

2 Expansion Have students continue the activity, using these items: **el navegador GPS, las calculadoras, el reproductor de DVD, los ratones**

3 Teaching Tip To simplify, have students begin by scanning the conversations and writing the English translation of the word for each blank. Ex: 1. *Ours.* Then have them underline the noun that the pronoun refers to and state its gender and number. Ex: 1. **la casa**; feminine singular.

3 Expansion
👥↔👥 Have students create conversations modeled after the ones in the activity and perform them for the class. Each one should consist of at least six lines and use as many stressed possessive adjectives and pronouns as possible.

TEACHING OPTIONS

Large Groups 👥↔👥 Have students bring in a photo of their favorite car and tell them to imagine that everyone in town is picking up his or her car at the mechanic's shop at the same time. Have students role-play a scene between the mechanic and several customers. The mechanic tries to determine to whom each car belongs.

Pairs 👥↔👥 Have pairs make a wish list consisting of ten items that they need for next year, then give it to another pair. Students must then divide the items between themselves, deciding who gets what on the list, and justifying their claim. Ex: —**La bicicleta nueva es mía. La necesito para ir a la universidad.** —**Bueno, entonces el navegador GPS es mío porque acabo de comprar un automóvil nuevo.** Students should try to use at least one possessive adjective or pronoun in their claims.

Comunicación

4 **Vendedores competitivos** Trabajen en grupos de tres. Uno/a de ustedes va a una tienda a comprar un aparato tecnológico (reproductor de MP3, computadora portátil, monitor, etc.). Los/as otros/as dos son empleados/as de dos marcas rivales y compiten para convencer al/a la cliente/a de que compre su producto. Usen los adjetivos posesivos y túrnense para comprar y vender. ¿Quién es el/la mejor vendedor/a? *Answers will vary.*

> **modelo**
> **Estudiante 1:** *Buenos días, quiero comprar un reproductor de MP3.*
> **Estudiante 2:** *Tengo lo que necesita. El mío, tiene capacidad para 500 canciones.*
> **Estudiante 3:** *El tuyo es muy viejo, con el mío también puedes ver videos…*

5 **Comparar** Trabajen en parejas. Intenta (*Try to*) convencer a tu compañero/a de que algo que tú tienes es mejor que lo que él/ella tiene. Pueden hablar de sus carros, reproductores de MP3, teléfonos celulares, clases, horarios o trabajos. *Answers will vary.*

> **modelo**
> **Estudiante 1:** *Mi computadora tiene una pantalla de quince pulgadas (inches). ¿Y la tuya?*
> **Estudiante 2:** *La mía es mejor porque tiene una pantalla de diecisiete pulgadas.*
> **Estudiante 1:** *Pues la mía…*

Síntesis

6 **Inventos locos** En grupos pequeños, imaginen que construyeron un aparato tecnológico revolucionario. Dibujen su invento y descríbanlo contestando estas preguntas. Incluyan todos los detalles que crean (*that you believe*) necesarios. Luego, compártanlo con la clase. Utilicen los posesivos, **por** y **para** y el vocabulario de **Contextos**. *Answers will vary.*

> **modelo**
> *Nuestro aparato se usa para cocinar huevos y funciona de una manera muy fácil…*

- ¿Para qué se usa?
- ¿Cómo es?
- ¿Cuánto cuesta?
- ¿Qué personas van a comprar este aparato?

4 Teaching Tip Encourage students to bring in personal items to use as props, or have them print out photos of the items.

5 Teaching Tip Before beginning the activity, have students make a list of objects to compare. Then have them brainstorm as many different qualities or features of those objects as they can. Finally, have them list adjectives that they might use to compare the objects they have chosen.

5 Expansion Have pairs who had a heated discussion perform it for the class.

6 Expansion To challenge students, have them create a television or radio ad for their invention.

Extra Practice
- Write the names of four different means of communication on slips of paper and post them in different corners of the room: **el correo electrónico, el teléfono, el mensaje de texto, una carta.** Tell students to pick their preferred means of communication and go to that corner. Then have each group write five reasons for their choice as well as one reason why they did not choose any of the others, using stressed possessive adjectives and pronouns.
- Write a cloze paragraph on the board and have students complete it with the correct stressed possessive adjectives and pronouns. To simplify, add a word bank.

Section Goal

In **Recapitulación**, students will review the grammar concepts from this lesson.

Instructional Resource
Supersite

1 Teaching Tip Remind students that the **–s** ending is only present in negative familiar commands.

1 Expansion
To challenge students, have them write mini-dialogues that include these command forms.

2 Teaching Tip Ask students to identify the rule associated with each use of **por** or **para** in the sentences.

2 Expansion Ask questions using **por** and **para**. Ex: **¿Hablan mucho por *Skype*? ¿Para qué clase estudian más, la clase de español o la clase de matemáticas?**

3 Expansion Make plural nouns singular and singular nouns plural in each question and have students repeat the activity. Ex: **1. ¿Éstos son mis bolígrafos? (Sí, son los tuyos.)**

Recapitulación

S Concepts Diagnostics

Completa estas actividades para repasar los conceptos de gramática que aprendiste en esta lección.

1 Completar Completa la tabla con las formas de los mandatos familiares. **8 pts.**

Infinitivo	Mandato	
	Afirmativo	**Negativo**
comer	come	no comas
hacer	haz	no hagas
sacar	saca	no saques
venir	ven	no vengas
ir	ve	no vayas

2 Por y para Completa el diálogo con **por** o **para**. **10 pts.**

MARIO Hola, yo trabajo (1) ___para___ el periódico de la universidad. ¿Puedo hacerte unas preguntas?

INÉS Sí, claro.

MARIO ¿Navegas mucho (2) ___por___ la red?

INÉS Sí, todos los días me conecto a Internet (3) ___para___ leer mi correo y navego (4) ___por___ una hora. También me gusta hablar (5) ___por___ *Skype* con mis amigos. Es muy bueno y, (6) ___para___ mí, es divertido.

MARIO ¿Y qué piensas sobre hacer la tarea en la computadora?

INÉS En general, me parece bien, pero (7) ___por___ ejemplo, anoche hice unos ejercicios (8) ___para___ la clase de álgebra y al final me dolieron los ojos. (9) ___Por___ eso a veces prefiero hacer la tarea a mano.

MARIO Muy bien. Muchas gracias (10) ___por___ tu tiempo.

3 Posesivos Completa las oraciones y confirma de quién son las cosas. **6 pts.**

1. —¿Éste es mi bolígrafo? —Sí, es el ___tuyo___ (*fam.*).
2. —¿Ésta es la cámara de tu papá? —Sí, es la ___suya___.
3. —¿Ese teléfono es de Pilar? —Sí, es el ___suyo___.
4. —¿Éstos son los cederrones de ustedes? —No, no son ___nuestros___.
5. —¿Ésta es tu computadora portátil? —No, no es ___mía___.
6. —¿Ésas son mis fotos? —Sí, son las ___suyas___ (*form.*).

RESUMEN GRAMATICAL

11.1 Familiar commands *pp. 352–353*

tú commands		
Infinitive	**Affirmative**	**Negative**
guardar	guarda	no guardes
volver	vuelve	no vuelvas
imprimir	imprime	no imprimas

▸ Irregular **tú** command forms

dar → no des	saber → no sepas
decir → di	salir → sal
estar → no estés	ser → sé, no seas
hacer → haz	tener → ten
ir → ve, no vayas	venir → ven
poner → pon	

▸ Verbs ending in **-car, -gar, -zar** have a spelling change in the negative **tú** commands:

sacar → no saques
apagar → no apagues
almorzar → no almuerces

11.2 Por and para *pp. 356–357*

▸ Uses of **por**:

motion or general location; duration; reason or motive; object of a search; means by which something is done; exchange or substitution; unit of measure

▸ Uses of **para**:

destination; deadline; purpose or goal; recipient of something; comparison or opinion; in the employment of.

11.3 Reciprocal reflexives *p. 360*

▸ Reciprocal reflexives express a shared or reciprocal action between two or more people or things. Only the plural forms (**nos, os, se**) are used.

Cuando **nos** vimos en la calle, **nos** abrazamos.

▸ Common verbs that can express reciprocal actions:

abrazar(se), ayudar(se), besar(se), conocer(se), encontrar(se), escribir(se), escuchar(se), hablar(se), llamar(se), mirar(se), saludar(se), ver(se)

TEACHING OPTIONS

Pairs Have pairs create a short survey about technology use. Encourage them to use **por** and **para**, as well as adverbs like **a menudo, normalmente**, etc. Then have them exchange their surveys with another pair and complete them. Ask volunteers to share their survey results with the class.

Extra Practice Tell students that you are a new student in class who likes to take people's things. Go around the room and gather students' belongings (books, pens, bags, etc.). In each case, insist that the item is yours. Ex: **Esta mochila es mía.** Have students protest and take their item back. Ex: **Esta mochila no es tuya, es mía.** Have other students contribute by asking, **¿Esta mochila es suya o es mía?**

4 **Ángel y diablito** A Juan le gusta pedir consejos a su ángel y a su diablito imaginarios. Completa las respuestas con mandatos familiares desde las dos perspectivas. `8 pts.`

1. Estoy manejando. ¿Voy más rápido?
 Á No, no ____vayas____ más rápido.
 D Sí, ____ve____ más rápido.

2. Es el reproductor de música de mi hermana. ¿Lo pongo en mi mochila?
 Á No, no ___lo pongas___ en tu mochila.
 D Sí, ___ponlo___ en tu mochila.

3. Necesito estirar (*to stretch*) las piernas. ¿Doy un paseo?
 Á Sí, ____da____ un paseo.
 D No, no ____des____ un paseo.

4. Mi amigo necesita imprimir algo. ¿Apago la impresora?
 Á No, no ___apagues___ la impresora.
 D Sí, ___apaga___ la impresora.

11.4	**Stressed possessive adjectives and pronouns**

pp. 362–363

Stressed possessive adjectives	
Masculine	**Feminine**
mío(s)	mía(s)
tuyo(s)	tuya(s)
suyo(s)	suya(s)
nuestro(s)	nuestra(s)
vuestro(s)	vuestra(s)
suyo(s)	suya(s)

la impresora **suya** → la **suya**

las llaves **mías** → las **mías**

5 **Oraciones** Forma oraciones para expresar acciones recíprocas con el tiempo indicado. `6 pts.`

> **modelo**
> tú y yo / conocer / bien (presente) *Tú y yo nos conocemos bien.*

1. José y Paco / llamar / una vez por semana (imperfecto)
 José y Paco se llamaban una vez por semana.
2. mi novia y yo / ver / todos los días (presente)
 Mi novia y yo nos vemos todos los días.
3. los compañeros de clase / ayudar / con la tarea (pretérito)
 Los compañeros de clase se ayudaron con la tarea.
4. tú y tu mamá / escribir / por correo electrónico / cada semana (imperfecto)
 Tú y tu mamá se escribían por correo electrónico cada semana.
5. mis hermanas y yo / entender / perfectamente (presente)
 Mis hermanas y yo nos entendemos perfectamente.
6. los profesores / saludar / con mucho respeto (pretérito)
 Los profesores se saludaron con mucho respeto.

6 **La tecnología** Escribe al menos seis oraciones diciéndole a un(a) amigo/a qué hacer para tener "una buena relación" con la tecnología. Usa mandatos familiares afirmativos y negativos. `12 pts.`

Answers will vary.

7 **Saber compartir** Completa la expresión con los dos pronombres posesivos que faltan.

`¡2 puntos EXTRA!`

> **"** Lo que° es ___mío___ es ___tuyo/suyo___. **"**

Lo que *What*

 Practice more at **vhlcentral.com.**

4 **Teaching Tip**
👥↔👥 Have volunteers role-play each exchange for the class. Encourage them to ad-lib as they go.

4 **Expansion** Give students these situations as items 5–8:
5. Mi amigo tiene las respuestas del examen final de historia. ¿Se las pido? (No, no se las pidas.; Sí, pídeselas.) 6. Es el cumpleaños de mi compañero de cuarto. ¿Le compro algo? (Sí, cómprale algo.; No, no le compres nada.) 7. Rompí la computadora portátil de mi padre. ¿Se lo digo? (Sí, díselo.; No, no se lo digas.) 8. No tengo nada de dinero. ¿Busco trabajo? (Sí, búscalo.; No, no lo busques.)

5 **Expansion** Have students create two additional dehydrated sentences. Then have them exchange papers with a classmate and complete the exercise.

6 **Teaching Tip**
←👤→ To challenge students, have them first write a letter from the point of view of the friend who needs help with technology. Then have students write their suggestions according to the problems outlined in the letter.

7 **Teaching Tip** Explain that this expression takes the masculine possessive form because it does not refer to anything specific, as denoted by **lo que**.

TEACHING OPTIONS

Game Divide the class into two teams, **por** and **para**, and have them line up. Choose a volunteer to go first from each team and say an English sentence using an equivalent of **por** or **para**. Ex: Yesterday I got sick and my brother worked *for* me. The student whose team corresponds to the correct Spanish equivalent of *for* has five seconds to step forward and give the Spanish translation. Ex: **Ayer me enfermé y mi hermano trabajó *por* mí.** Award one point for every

correct answer. The team with the most points at the end wins.
Small Groups 👤↔👤 As a class, brainstorm a list of infinitives that can be made reciprocal (**llamar, abrazar, conocer**, etc.) and write them on the board. In small groups, have students create a dialogue using at least six of these infinitives. Then have students act out their dialogues for the class. Encourage students to use lesson vocabulary.

Section Goals

In **Lectura**, students will:
- learn to recognize borrowed words
- increase their reading comprehension in Spanish by using borrowed words to predict content
- read a content-rich text with borrowed words

Instructional Resource
Supersite

Estrategia Tell students that recognizing words borrowed from English will help them understand unfamiliar texts.

Examinar el texto If students struggle answering these questions, have them focus on the character in red shorts and what he is holding and saying.

Buscar Invite students to speculate as to why so many words related to technology are loan words from English.

Sobre el autor Juan Matías Loiseau has also made two award-winning short films, *El Ángel de Dorotea* (2005) and *Abismos* (2006).

Lectura

NATIONAL · STANDARDS · communication cultures

Antes de leer

Estrategia
Recognizing borrowed words

One way languages grow is by borrowing words from each other. English words that relate to technology often are borrowed by Spanish and other languages throughout the world. Sometimes the words are modified slightly to fit the sounds of the languages that borrow them. When reading in Spanish, you can often increase your understanding by looking for words borrowed from English or other languages you know.

Examinar el texto

Observa la tira cómica°. ¿De qué trata°? ¿Cómo lo sabes? Answers will vary.

Buscar

Esta lectura contiene una palabra tomada° del inglés. Trabaja con un(a) compañero/a para encontrarla.

el celular

Repasa° las palabras nuevas relacionadas con la tecnología que aprendiste en **Contextos** y expande la lista de palabras tomadas del inglés. Answers will vary.

_____ _____
_____ _____
_____ _____

Sobre el autor

Juan Matías Loiseau (1974). Más conocido como Tute, este artista nació en Buenos Aires, Argentina. Estudió diseño gráfico, humorismo y cine. Sus tiras cómicas se publican en Estados Unidos, Francia y toda Latinoamérica.

tira cómica *comic strip* ¿De qué trata? *What is it about?*
tomada *taken* Repasa *Review*

(S) Practice more at **vhlcentral.com.**

TEACHING OPTIONS

Pairs ←👤→ Have pairs of students work together to create an alternate ending to this comic. Then have students get together in groups and share their new endings. Have the group select one to present to the class.

Game ←👤→ Have students write a short description of a type of new technology that has changed their lives. Tell them to present the most general clues first, moving toward more specific clues. Ex: **Con esto puedo enviarles mensajes cortos a mis amigos. Y los amigos míos pueden contestarme inmediatamente. Uso el celular sin usar minutos. (mensajes de texto)** Have students read their descriptions for the class to guess.

Después de leer

Comprensión 🔊💬

Indica si las oraciones son **ciertas** o **falsas**. Corrige las falsas.

Cierto	Falso	
✓	_____	1. Hay tres personajes en la tira cómica: un usuario de teléfono, un amigo y un empleado de la empresa (*company*) telefónica.
_____	✓	2. El nuevo servicio de teléfono incluye las llamadas telefónicas únicamente. También viene con un tipo que te sigue a todos lados.
_____	✓	3. El empleado duerme en su casa. Duerme al lado de la cama del usuario.
✓	_____	4. El contrato de teléfono dura (*lasts*) un año.
_____	✓	5. El usuario y el amigo están trabajando (*working*). Están de vacaciones.

Preguntas 🔊💬

Responde a estas preguntas con oraciones completas. Usa el pretérito y el imperfecto.

1. ¿Al usuario le gustaba usar el teléfono celular todo el tiempo?
 No, al usuario le molestaba usar el celular todo el tiempo.

2. ¿Por qué el usuario decidió tirar el teléfono al mar?
 Porque el celular y el tipo lo tenían harto.

3. Según el amigo, ¿para qué tenía el usuario que tirar el teléfono celular al mar?
 El usuario tenía que tirar el teléfono al mar para recuperar su libertad.

4. ¿Qué ocurrió cuando el usuario tiró el teléfono?
 El empleado fue a buscar el teléfono.

5. ¿Qué le dijo el empleado al usuario cuando salió del mar?
 El empleado le dijo que tenía una llamada perdida.

Conversar

En grupos pequeños, hablen de estos temas.
Answers will vary.

1. ¿Se sienten identificados/as con el usuario de teléfono de la tira cómica? ¿Por qué?

2. ¿Cuáles son los aspectos positivos y los negativos de tener teléfono celular?

3. ¿Cuál es para ustedes el límite que debe tener la tecnología en nuestras vidas?

te viene *comes with* **tipo** *guy, dude* **te avisa** *alerts you* **escuchás** *listen (Arg.)* **distraídos** *careless* **piso** *floor* **bolsa de dormir** *sleeping bag* **darle de baja** *to suspend* **harto** *fed up* **revolear** *throw it away with energy (S. America)* **bien hecho** *well done* **llamada perdida** *missed call*

Comprensión Have students write three additional true/false statements for a classmate to complete.

Preguntas
- Have students work in pairs to answer these questions.
- Assign a number to each panel in the comic. Then have students identify the panel(s) where they found the information needed for their answers.

Conversar For item 2, survey the class and write their answers on the board in a two-column chart with the headings **Lo positivo** and **Lo negativo**. Then ask the class to determine which column wins out overall.

TEACHING OPTIONS

Large Groups ← → Ask students to work in groups of six. Tell them to improvise and create a humorous story as a group. Ask one person in the group to start it off by giving an introductory sentence, such as: **Ayer estuvimos en el coche y ocurrió algo muy raro.** Have the others add sentences with additional details to complete the story. Encourage students to be creative and make the story as long as they wish.

Pairs ← → In pairs, have students create a comic strip about cars or car accessories. Tell them that they may use the same main character as the comic on these pages, or they may develop new character(s). Have students present their comics to the class.

Section Goal

In **Panorama**, students will read about the geography, history, and culture of Argentina.

Instructional Resources
Supersite/DVD: *Panorama cultural*
Supersite: Resources (Scripts, Translations, *PowerPoints*, Answer Keys)
WebSAM
Workbook, pp. 135–136
Video Manual, pp. 247–248

Teaching Tips
• Use the **Lección 11 Panorama** overheads to assist with this presentation.
• Have students look at the map of Argentina and guide them to recognize Argentina's great size and the variety of topographical features, such as mountains (**los Andes**), vast plains (**las pampas**), and large rivers.
• Point out that Argentina is one of the largest beef producers in the world and that **gauchos** have played an important role in the culture of the country. Bariloche is an important winter recreation area. Remind students that June–August is winter in the southern hemisphere.

El país en cifras Patagonia is very sparsely populated, but Buenos Aires is a metropolis about the size of New York City. Invite students to mention anything they know about Argentina.

¡Increíble pero cierto!
Avenida 9 de Julio is so wide that pedestrians need a few minutes and several green lights to cross it (there are stoplights to control pedestrian traffic). To help alleviate this, some urban planners have advocated making the central part of the avenue subterranean.

Argentina

connections cultures NATIONAL STANDARDS

El país en cifras

▶ **Área:** 2.780.400 km² (1.074.000 millas²)
Argentina es el país de habla española más grande del mundo. Su territorio es dos veces el tamaño° de Alaska.
▶ **Población:** 42.548.000
▶ **Capital:** Buenos Aires (y su área metropolitana) —13.401.000
En el gran Buenos Aires vive más del treinta por ciento de la población total del país. La ciudad es conocida° como el "París de Suramérica" por su estilo parisino°.

Buenos Aires

▶ **Ciudades principales:**
Córdoba —1.552.000, Rosario —1.280.000, Mendoza —956.000
SOURCE: Population Division, UN Secretariat
▶ **Moneda:** peso argentino
▶ **Idiomas:** español (oficial), lenguas indígenas

Bandera de Argentina

Argentinos célebres
▶ **Jorge Luis Borges,** escritor (1899–1986)
▶ **María Eva Duarte de Perón ("Evita"),** primera dama° (1919–1952)
▶ **Mercedes Sosa,** cantante (1935–2009)
▶ **Leandro "Gato" Barbieri,** saxofonista (1932–)

tamaño *size* conocida *known* parisino *Parisian* primera dama *First Lady*
ancha *wide* mide *it measures* campo *field*

Gaucho de las pampas

ESTADOS UNIDOS
OCÉANO ATLÁNTICO
OCÉANO PACÍFICO
AMÉRICA DEL SUR
ARGENTINA

BOLIVIA
PARAGUAY
Las catar... del Igua...
San Miguel de Tucumán
Córdoba
URUGUA...
La Cordillera de los Andes
Aconcagua
Mendoza
Rosario
Río Paraná
CHILE
Buenos Aires
La Pampa
Mar del Plata
San Carlos de Bariloche
Monte Fitz Roy (Chaltén)
Patagonia
Océano Atlántico
Vista de San Carlos de Bariloche
Tierra del Fuego

recursos
WB pp. 135–136 VM pp. 247–248 vhlcentral.com Lección 11

¡Increíble pero cierto!
La Avenida 9 de Julio en Buenos Aires es la calle más ancha° del mundo. De lado a lado mide° cerca de 140 metros, lo que es equivalente a un campo° y medio de fútbol. Su nombre conmemora el Día de la Independencia de Argentina.

BRASIL

Historia • Inmigración europea

Se dice que Argentina es el país más "europeo" de toda Latinoamérica. Después del año 1880, inmigrantes italianos, alemanes, españoles e ingleses llegaron para establecerse en esta nación. Esta diversidad cultural ha dejado° una profunda huella° en la música, el cine y la arquitectura argentinos.

Artes • El tango

El tango es uno de los símbolos culturales más importantes de Argentina. Este género° musical es una mezcla de ritmos de origen africano, italiano y español, y se originó a finales del siglo XIX entre los porteños°. Poco después se hizo popular entre el resto de los argentinos y su fama llegó hasta París. Como baile, el tango en un principio° era provocativo y violento, pero se hizo más romántico durante los años 30. Hoy día, este estilo musical tiene adeptos° en muchas partes del mundo°.

Lugares • Las cataratas del Iguazú

Las famosas cataratas° del Iguazú se encuentran entre las fronteras de Argentina, Paraguay y Brasil, al norte de Buenos Aires. Cerca de ellas confluyen° los ríos Iguazú y Paraná. Estas extensas caídas de agua tienen hasta 80 metros (262 pies) de altura° y en época° de lluvias llegan a medir 4 kilómetros (2,5 millas) de ancho. Situadas en el Parque Nacional Iguazú, las cataratas son un destino° turístico muy visitado.

¿Qué aprendiste? Responde a cada pregunta con una oración completa.

1. ¿Qué porcentaje de la población de Argentina vive en el gran Buenos Aires?
Más del treinta por ciento de la población de Argentina vive en el gran Buenos Aires.
2. ¿Quién era Mercedes Sosa?
Mercedes Sosa era una cantante argentina.
3. Se dice que Argentina es el país más europeo de Latinoamérica. ¿Por qué? Se dice que Argentina es el país más europeo de Latinoamérica porque muchos inmigrantes europeos se establecieron allí.
4. ¿Qué tipo de baile es uno de los símbolos culturales más importantes de Argentina?
El tango es uno de los símbolos culturales más importantes de Argentina.
5. ¿Dónde y cuándo se originó el tango?
El tango se originó entre los porteños a finales del siglo XIX.
6. ¿Cómo era el baile del tango originalmente?
El tango era un baile provocativo y violento.
7. ¿En qué parque nacional están las cataratas del Iguazú?
Las cataratas del Iguazú están en el Parque Nacional Iguazú.

Artesano en
Buenos Aires

Conexión Internet Investiga estos temas en **vhlcentral.com**.

1. Busca información sobre el tango. ¿Te gustan los ritmos y sonidos del tango? ¿Por qué? ¿Se baila el tango en tu comunidad?
2. ¿Quiénes fueron Juan y Eva Perón y qué importancia tienen en la historia de Argentina?

Practice more at **vhlcentral.com**.

ha dejado *has left* huella *mark* género *genre* porteños *people of Buenos Aires* en un principio *at first* adeptos *followers* mundo *world* cataratas *waterfalls* confluyen *converge* altura *height* época *season* destino *destination*

Inmigración europea Among the waves of immigrants were thousands of European Jews. An interesting chapter in the history of the **pampas** features Jewish **gauchos**. A generous, pre-Zionist philanthropist purchased land for Jews who settled on the Argentine grasslands. At one time, the number of Yiddish-language newspapers in Argentina was second only to that in New York City.

El tango Carlos Gardel (1890–1935) is considered the great classic interpreter of **tango**. If possible, bring in a recording of his version of a **tango** such as *Cuesta abajo* or *Volver*. **Astor Piazzola** (1921–1992) was a modern exponent of **tango**. His **tango nuevo** has found interpreters such as cellist Yo-Yo Ma and the Kronos Quartet. For more information about **el tango**, you may want to play the *Panorama cultural* video footage for this lesson.

Las cataratas del Iguazú At just over ten miles away, **Puerto Iguazú** is the closest city to the falls. Other nearby attractions include the **Itaipú** dam, which is the world's biggest hydroelectric facility, and the **Parque de las Aves**, where one can observe many near-extinct and exotic species of birds.

Conexión Internet Students will find supporting Internet activities and links at **vhlcentral.com**.

Uruguay

NATIONAL STANDARDS — connections cultures

El país en cifras

▶ **Área:** 176.220 km² (68.039 millas²), *el tamaño° del estado de Washington*

▶ **Población:** 3.430.000

▶ **Capital:** Montevideo—1.644.000

Casi la mitad° de la población de Uruguay vive en Montevideo. Situada en la desembocadura° del famoso Río de la Plata, esta ciudad cosmopolita e intelectual es también un destino popular para las vacaciones, debido a sus numerosas playas de arena° blanca que se extienden hasta la ciudad de Punta del Este.

▶ **Ciudades principales:** Salto, Paysandú, Las Piedras, Rivera
SOURCE: Population Division, UN Secretariat

▶ **Moneda:** peso uruguayo

▶ **Idiomas:** español (oficial)

Bandera de Uruguay

Uruguayos célebres

▶ **Horacio Quiroga,** escritor (1878–1937)

▶ **Juana de Ibarbourou,** escritora (1892–1979)

▶ **Mario Benedetti,** escritor (1920–2009)

▶ **Cristina Peri Rossi,** escritora y profesora (1941–)

tamaño *size* mitad *half* desembocadura *mouth* arena *sand* avestruz *ostrich* ave no voladora *flightless bird* medir *measure* cotizado *valued*

Gaucho uruguayo

BRASIL

Río Arapey
Rivera
Salto
Río Uruguay
Cuchilla de Haedo
Paysandú
Río Negro
Embalse del Río Negro
Río Negro
Cuchilla Grande
Laguna Merín
Río Yí
Cuchilla Grande Inferior
Colonia
Las Piedras
Río de la Plata
Montevideo
Punta del Este

ESTADOS UNIDOS
OCÉANO PACÍFICO
OCÉANO ATLÁNTICO
AMÉRICA DEL SUR
URUGUAY

Entrada a la Ciudad Vieja, Colonia del Sacramento

recursos
WB pp. 137–138
VM pp. 249–250
vhlcentral.com Lección 11

¡Increíble pero cierto!

En Uruguay hay muchos animales curiosos, entre ellos el ñandú. De la misma familia del avestruz°, el ñandú es el ave no voladora° más grande del hemisferio occidental. Puede llegar a medir° dos metros. Normalmente, va en grupos de veinte o treinta y vive en el campo. Es muy cotizado° por su carne, sus plumas y sus huevos.

Costumbres • La carne y el mate

En Uruguay y Argentina, la carne es un elemento esencial de la dieta diaria. Algunos platillos representativos de estas naciones son el asado°, la parrillada° y el chivito°. El mate, una infusión similar al té, también es típico de la región. Esta bebida de origen indígena está muy presente en la vida social y familiar de estos países aunque, curiosamente, no se puede consumir en bares o restaurantes.

Deportes • El fútbol

El fútbol es el deporte nacional de Uruguay. El primer equipo de balompié° uruguayo se formó en 1891 y en 1930 el país suramericano fue la sede° de la primera Copa Mundial de esta disciplina. El equipo nacional ha conseguido grandes éxitos° a lo largo de los años: dos campeonatos olímpicos, en 1923 y 1928, y dos campeonatos mundiales, en 1930 y 1950. De hecho, Uruguay y Argentina han presentado su candidatura binacional para que la Copa Mundial de Fútbol de 2030 se celebre en sus países.

Costumbres • El Carnaval

El Carnaval de Montevideo es el de mayor duración en el mundo. A lo largo de 40 días, los uruguayos disfrutan de° los desfiles° y la música que inundan las calles de su capital. La celebración más conocida es el Desfile de las Llamadas, en el que participan bailarines al ritmo del candombe, una danza de tradición africana.

¿Qué aprendiste? Responde a cada pregunta con una oración completa.

1. ¿Qué tienen en común los uruguayos célebres mencionados en la página anterior (*previous*)?
 Son escritores.
2. ¿Cuál es el elemento esencial de la dieta uruguaya?
 La carne es esencial en la dieta uruguaya.
3. ¿Qué es el ñandú?
 El ñandú es un ave no voladora que vive en Uruguay.
4. ¿Qué es el mate?
 El mate es una bebida indígena que es similar al té.
5. ¿Cuándo se formó el primer equipo uruguayo de fútbol?
 En 1891 se formó el primer equipo de fútbol uruguayo.
6. ¿Cuándo se celebró la primera Copa Mundial de fútbol?
 La primera Copa Mundial se celebró en 1930.
7. ¿Cómo se llama la celebración más conocida del Carnaval de Montevideo?
 La celebración más conocida del Carnaval de Montevideo se llama el Desfile de las Llamadas.
8. ¿Cuántos días dura el Carnaval de Montevideo?
 El Carnaval de Montevideo dura unos cuarenta días.

Edificio del Parlamento en Montevideo

Conexión Internet Investiga estos temas en **vhlcentral.com**.

1. Uruguay es conocido como un país de muchos escritores. Busca información sobre uno de ellos y escribe una biografía.
2. Investiga cuáles son las comidas y bebidas favoritas de los uruguayos. Descríbelas e indica cuáles te gustaría probar y por qué.

 Practice more at **vhlcentral.com**.

asado *barbecued beef* parrillada *barbecue* chivito *goat* balompié *soccer* sede *site* éxitos *successes* disfrutan de *enjoy* desfiles *parades*

La carne y el mate Uruguay's national dishes are **parrillada** and **chivito**. **Parillada** consists of different cuts of meat and offal cooked on a grill or open fire. Sometimes it includes **pamplona**, meat rolled and stuffed with ham, cheese, and peppers. A **chivito** is a sandwich made with thinly sliced filet mignon, tomatoes, mozzarella, olives, and mayonnaise.

El fútbol Uruguayan women have begun to make their mark in soccer. Although the International Federation of Football Association (FIFA) established a women's league in 1982, it was not until 1985 that the first women's league—from Brazil—was formally established. The women's league of Uruguay was formed in 1996 and now participates in international soccer play.

El Carnaval Along with the rest of Latin America, Uruguay participated in the slave trade during the colonial period. African-influenced **candombe** music is popular with Uruguayans from all sectors of society.

Conexión Internet Students will find supporting Internet activities and links at **vhlcentral.com**.

Teaching Tip You may want to wrap up this section by playing the *Panorama cultural* video footage for this lesson.

TEACHING OPTIONS

Worth Noting Uruguay is similar to its larger, more powerful neighbor, Argentina, in many ways: Uruguayans also love the **tango** and **yerba mate,** many play the Argentine card game **truco,** and most are devoted carnivores. Historically, raising cattle, the culture of the **gaucho,** and the great cattle ranches called **estancias** have been important elements in the Uruguayan culture. Another, less pleasant, similarity was in the Dirty War (**Guerra sucia**) waged by an Uruguayan military dictatorship against domestic dissidents during the 1970s and 80s. In 1984 the military allowed the election of a civilian government. Today, presidential and parliamentary elections are held every five years. Uruguay has a multi-party system in which three political parties dominate.

La tecnología

la cámara digital/ de video	digital/video camera
el canal	(TV) channel
el cibercafé	cybercafé
el control remoto	remote control
el correo de voz	voice mail
el disco compacto	CD
el estéreo	stereo
el fax	fax (machine)
la pantalla táctil	touch screen
el radio	radio (set)
el reproductor de CD	CD player
el reproductor de MP3	MP3 player
el (teléfono) celular	(cell) phone
la televisión por cable	cable television
el televisor	televison set
el video	video
apagar	to turn off
funcionar	to work
llamar	to call
poner, prender	to turn on
sonar (o:ue)	to ring
descompuesto/a	not working; out of order
lento/a	slow
lleno/a	full

La computadora

el archivo	file
la arroba	@ symbol
el blog	blog
el cederrón	CD-ROM
la computadora (portátil)	(portable) computer; (laptop)
la conexión inalámbrica	wireless (connection)
la dirección electrónica	e-mail address
el disco compacto	CD
la impresora	printer
Internet	Internet
el mensaje de texto	text message
el monitor	(computer) monitor
la página principal	home page
la pantalla	screen
el programa de computación	software
el ratón	mouse
la red	network; Web
el reproductor de DVD	DVD player
el sitio web	website
el teclado	keyboard
borrar	to erase
descargar	to download
escanear	to scan
grabar	to record
guardar	to save
imprimir	to print
navegar (en Internet)	to surf (the Internet)

El carro

la autopista, la carretera	highway
el baúl	trunk
la calle	street
el capó, el cofre	hood
el carro, el coche	car
la circulación, el tráfico	traffic
el garaje, el taller (mecánico)	garage; (mechanic's) repair shop
la gasolina	gasoline
la gasolinera	gas station
la licencia de conducir	driver's license
la llanta	tire
el/la mecánico/a	mechanic
el navegador GPS	GPS
el parabrisas	windshield
la policía	police (force)
la velocidad máxima	speed limit
el volante	steering wheel
arrancar	to start
arreglar	to fix; to arrange
bajar(se) de	to get off of/out of (a vehicle)
conducir, manejar	to drive
estacionar	to park
llenar (el tanque)	to fill (the tank)
parar	to stop
revisar (el aceite)	to check (the oil)
subir(se) a	to get on/into (a vehicle)

Verbos

abrazar(se)	to hug; to embrace (each other)
ayudar(se)	to help (each other)
besar(se)	to kiss (each other)
encontrar(se) (o:ue)	to meet (each other); to run into (each other)
saludar(se)	to greet (each other)

Otras palabras y expresiones

por aquí	around here
por ejemplo	for example
por eso	that's why; therefore
por fin	finally

Por and **para**	See pages 356–357.
Stressed possessive adjectives and pronouns	See pages 362–363.
Expresiones útiles	See page 347.

recursos
LM p. 66 | vhlcentral.com Lección 11

Audio: Vocabulary

La vivienda

12

A PRIMERA VISTA

- ¿Están los chicos en casa?
- ¿Viven en una casa o en un apartamento?
- ¿Ya comieron o van a comer?
- ¿Están de buen humor o de mal humor?

Lesson Goals

In **Lección 12**, students will be introduced to the following:
- terms for parts of a house
- names of common household objects
- terms for household chores
- central patios
- floating islands in Lake Titicaca
- relative pronouns
- formal (**usted/ustedes**) commands
- object pronouns with formal commands
- present subjunctive
- subjunctive with verbs and expressions of will and influence
- locating the main parts of a sentence
- using linking words
- writing a lease agreement
- using visual cues while listening
- a television commercial for **Comfort**, a fabric softener
- the short film *036*
- a video about the **Museo Casa de Frida Kahlo**
- cultural and geographic information about Panama and El Salvador

A primera vista Here are some additional questions you can ask to personalize the photo: **¿Dónde vives? ¿Con quién vives? ¿Cómo es tu casa? ¿Qué haces en casa por la noche? ¿Qué haces los fines de semana? ¿Tienes computadora en casa? ¿Qué otros aparatos tecnológicos tienes?**

Teaching Tip Look for these icons for additional communicative practice:

→👥←	Interpretive communication
←👥→	Presentational communication
👤↔👤	Interpersonal communication

INSTRUCTIONAL RESOURCES

Supersite (vhlcentral.com)
Video: *Fotonovela*, Flash cultura*, Anuncio, Cortometraje*, Panorama cultural**
**Also on DVD*
Audio: Textbook and Lab MP3 Files (*also on CD*)
Activity Pack: Information Gap Activities, games, additional activity handouts

Resources: Textbook Answer Key, WB/VM/LM Answer Key, Scripts, Translations, **Vocabulario adicional**, lesson plans, **Estructura** PowerPoints, Overheads
Testing Program: Quizzes, Tests, Exams, MP3s (*also on Test Generator CD*)

Learning Management System (Assignment Task Manager, Gradebook)
WebSAM (online Workbook/Video Manual/Lab Manual)
Workbook/Video Manual
Lab Manual

Section Goals

In **Contextos**, students will learn and practice:
• names of rooms in a house
• names of common household objects
• terms for household chores

Instructional Resources

Supersite: Audio (Textbook and Lab MP3 Files); Resources (Overheads, **Vocabulario adicional**, Activity Pack, Scripts, Answer Keys); Testing Program (Quizzes)
WebSAM
Workbook, pp. 139–140
Lab Manual, p. 67

Teaching Tips

• Use the **Lección 12 Contextos** overheads to assist with this presentation.
• As students look at the illustration in their books, describe the house, naming the kinds of rooms and introducing those that are not shown. Ex: **Ésta es la casa de los Hernández. Hay una sala grande, un dormitorio, una oficina, una cocina y un altillo. También hay un cuarto de baño, un sótano, un patio y un garaje, pero no vemos estos cuartos en la ilustración.**
• Ask open-ended questions about the house and housework pictured in the illustration. Ex: **¿Dónde se pone la comida después de regresar del supermercado?** Ask personalized questions. Ex: **____, ¿vives en una residencia o en un apartamento? ¿Cuántos cuartos hay?**

Note: At this point you may want to present *Vocabulario adicional: Más vocabulario para el hogar* from the Supersite.

La vivienda

Más vocabulario

las afueras	suburbs; outskirts
el alquiler	rent (payment)
el ama (*m., f.*) de casa	housekeeper; caretaker
el barrio	neighborhood
el edificio de apartamentos	apartment building
el/la vecino/a	neighbor
la vivienda	housing
el balcón	balcony
la entrada	entrance
la escalera	stairs; stairway
el garaje	garage
el jardín	garden; yard
el patio	patio; yard
el sótano	basement; cellar
la cafetera	coffee maker
el electrodoméstico	electrical appliance
el horno (de microondas)	(microwave) oven
la lavadora	washing machine
la luz	light; electricity
la secadora	clothes dryer
la tostadora	toaster
el cartel	poster
la mesita de noche	night stand
los muebles	furniture
alquilar	to rent
mudarse	to move (from one house to another)

Variación léxica

dormitorio ⟷ aposento (*Rep. Dom.*); recámara (*Méx.*)

apartamento ⟷ departamento (*Arg., Chile, Méx.*); piso (*Esp.*)

lavar los platos ⟷ lavar/fregar los trastes (*Amér. C., Rep. Dom.*)

recursos

WB pp. 139–140	LM p. 67	S vhlcentral.com Lección 12

el altillo

el dormitorio

la cómoda

el armario

el cuadro/ la pintura

Hace la cama. (hacer)

la almohada

la manta

Los quehaceres domésticos

arreglar	to neaten; to straighten up
barrer el suelo	to sweep the floor
cocinar	to cook
ensuciar	to get (something) dirty
hacer quehaceres domésticos	to do household chores
lavar (el suelo, los platos)	to wash (the floor, the dishes)
limpiar la casa	to clean the house
planchar la ropa	to iron the clothes
quitar la mesa	to clear the table
quitar el polvo	to dust

la sala

las cortinas

la lámpara

la mesita

el sofá

Pasa la aspiradora. (pasar)

la alfombra

TEACHING OPTIONS

Extra Practice Ask students to complete these analogies.
1. aspiradora : ____ :: lavadora : ropa (alfombra)
 (*Aspiradora* es a ____ como *lavadora* es a ropa.)
2. frío : calor :: congelador : ____ (horno)
3. cama : alcoba :: ____ : oficina (escritorio)
4. platos : cocina :: carro : ____ (garaje)

Heritage Speakers Ask heritage speakers to tell the class any other terms their families use to refer to rooms in a home or household appliances. Ex: **el lavaplatos = el lavavajillas; el altillo = el ático, el desván.**

Práctica

la oficina
- el sillón
- la pared
- el estante
- Sacude los muebles. (sacudir)

la cocina
- el refrigerador
- el congelador
- la cocina, la estufa
- el horno
- el lavaplatos
- Saca la basura. (sacar)

1 **Escuchar** 🎧 Escucha la conversación y completa las oraciones.

1. Pedro va a limpiar primero ___la sala___.
2. Paula va a comenzar en ___la cocina___.
3. Pedro va a ___planchar la ropa___ en el sótano.
4. Pedro también va a limpiar ___la oficina___.
5. Ellos están limpiando la casa porque ___la madre de Pedro viene a visitarlos___.

2 **Respuestas** 🎧 Escucha las preguntas y selecciona la respuesta más adecuada. Una respuesta no se va a usar.

___3___ a. Sí, la alfombra estaba muy sucia.
___5___ b. No, porque todavía se están mudando.
___1___ c. Sí, sacudí la mesa y el estante.
_____ d. Sí, puse el pollo en el horno.
___2___ e. Hice la cama, pero no limpié los muebles.
___4___ f. Sí, después de sacarla de la secadora.

3 **Escoger** Escoge la letra de la respuesta correcta.

1. Cuando quieres tener una lámpara y un despertador cerca de tu cama, puedes ponerlos en ___c___.
 a. el barrio b. el cuadro c. la mesita de noche
2. Si no quieres vivir en el centro de la ciudad, puedes mudarte ___b___.
 a. al alquiler b. a las afueras c. a la vivienda
3. Guardamos (*We keep*) los pantalones, las camisas y los zapatos en ___b___.
 a. la secadora b. el armario c. el patio
4. Para subir de la planta baja al primer piso, usas ___c___.
 a. la entrada b. el cartel c. la escalera
5. Ponemos cuadros y pinturas en ___a___.
 a. las paredes b. los quehaceres c. los jardines

4 **Definiciones** En parejas, identifiquen cada cosa que se describe. Luego inventen sus propias descripciones de algunas palabras y expresiones de **Contextos**.

> **modelo**
> **Estudiante 1:** Es donde pones los libros.
> **Estudiante 2:** el estante

1. Es donde pones la cabeza cuando duermes. la/una almohada
2. Es el quehacer doméstico que haces después de comer. lavar los platos/ quitar la mesa
3. Algunos de ellos son las cómodas y los sillones. los muebles
4. Son las personas que viven en tu barrio. los vecinos
5. _____
6. _____

el comedor

5 **Completar** Completa estas frases con las palabras más adecuadas.

1. Para tomar vino necesitas… *una copa*
2. Para comer una ensalada necesitas… *un tenedor/un plato*
3. Para tomar café necesitas… *una taza*
4. Para poner la comida en la mesa necesitas… *un plato/poner la mesa*
5. Para limpiarte la boca después de comer necesitas… *una servilleta*
6. Para cortar (*to cut*) un bistec necesitas… *un cuchillo (y un tenedor)*
7. Para tomar agua necesitas… *un vaso/una copa*
8. Para tomar sopa necesitas… *una cuchara/un plato*

6 **Los quehaceres** Trabajen en grupos para indicar quién hace estos quehaceres domésticos en sus casas. Luego contesten las preguntas. *Answers will vary.*

barrer el suelo	lavar los platos	planchar la ropa
cocinar	lavar la ropa	sacar la basura
hacer las camas	pasar la aspiradora	sacudir los muebles

modelo
Estudiante 1: *¿Quién pasa la aspiradora en tu casa?*
Estudiante 2: *Mi hermano y yo pasamos la aspiradora.*

1. ¿Quién hace más quehaceres, tú o tus compañeros/as?
2. ¿Quiénes hacen la mayoría de los quehaceres, los hombres o las mujeres?
3. ¿Piensas que debes hacer más quehaceres? ¿Por qué?

Practice more at **vhlcentral.com.**

Comunicación

7 **La vida doméstica** En parejas, describan las habitaciones que ven en estas fotos. Identifiquen y describan cinco muebles o adornos (*accessories*) de cada foto y digan dos quehaceres que se pueden hacer en cada habitación. Answers will vary.

8 **Mi apartamento** Dibuja el plano (*floor plan*) de un apartamento amueblado (*furnished*) imaginario y escribe los nombres de las habitaciones y de los muebles. En parejas, siéntense espalda contra espalda (*sit back to back*). Uno/a de ustedes describe su apartamento mientras su compañero/a lo dibuja según la descripción. Cuando terminen, miren el segundo dibujo. ¿Es similar al dibujo original? Hablen de los cambios que se necesitan hacer para mejorar el dibujo. Repitan la actividad intercambiando papeles. Answers will vary.

CONSULTA

To review bathroom-related vocabulary, see **Lección 7, Contextos,** p. 210.

9 **¡Corre, corre!** Tu profesor(a) va a darte una serie incompleta de dibujos que forman una historia. Tú y tu compañero/a tienen dos series diferentes. Descríbanse los dibujos para completar la historia. Answers will vary.

> **modelo**
>
> **Estudiante 1:** Marta quita la mesa.
> **Estudiante 2:** Francisco...

TEACHING OPTIONS

Extra Practice Have students complete this cloze activity. **La vida doméstica de un estudiante universitario puede ser un desastre, ¿no? Nunca hay tiempo para hacer los _____ (quehaceres) domésticos. Sólo _____ (pasa) la aspiradora una vez al semestre y nunca _____ (sacude) los muebles. Los _____ (platos) sucios se acumulan en la _____ (cocina). Saca la ropa de la _____ (secadora) y se la pone sin _____ (planchar). Y,** ¿por qué hacer la _____ (cama)? Se va a acostar en ella de nuevo este mismo día, ¿no?

Game Have students bring in real estate ads. Ask teams of three to write a description of a property. Teams then take turns reading their descriptions aloud. Other teams guess the price. The team that guesses the amount closest to the real price without going over scores one point.

7 Teaching Tip
Model the activity using magazine pictures. Have students guess which photo you are describing. Ex: **¡Qué comedor más desordenado! ¡Es un desastre! Alguien debe quitar los platos sucios de la mesa. También es necesario sacudir los muebles y pasar la aspiradora.**

8 Teaching Tips
• Draw a floor plan of a four-room apartment on the board. Ask volunteers to describe it.
• Have students draw their floor plans before you assign pairs. Make sure they understand the activity so that their floor plans do not become too complicated.

8 Expansion
• Have students make the suggested changes to their floor plans and repeat the activity again with a different partner.
• Have pairs repeat the activity, drawing floor plans of their actual homes or apartments.
• In pairs, tell students to imagine that they are interior decorators. Give each pair the same catalogue from IKEA or Pottery Barn, but set different budgets. Tell them they must design the apartment of their dreams without going over the spending limit. Have students describe their dream houses to the class while volunteers draw them on the board.

9 Teaching Tip Divide the class into pairs and distribute the handouts from the Activity Pack (Activity Pack/Supersite) that correspond to this Information Gap Activity.

9 Expansion
Have pairs tell each other about an occasion when they have had to clean up their home for a particular reason. Encourage pairs to ask each other questions to find out additional information. Then ask volunteers to share their partners' stories with the class.

Los quehaceres

Jimena y Felipe deben limpiar el apartamento para poder ir de viaje con Marissa.

PERSONAJES

 JIMENA FELIPE

S Video: *Fotonovela* Record and Compare

1

SR. DÍAZ Quieren ir a Yucatán con Marissa, ¿verdad?

SRA. DÍAZ Entonces, les sugiero que arreglen este apartamento. Regresamos más tarde.

SR. DÍAZ Les aconsejo que preparen la cena para las 8:30.

2

MARISSA ¿Qué pasa?

JIMENA Nuestros papás quieren que Felipe y yo arreglemos toda la casa.

FELIPE Y que, además, preparemos la cena.

MARISSA ¡Pues, yo les ayudo!

(Don Diego llega a ayudar a los chicos.)

FELIPE Tenemos que limpiar la casa hoy.

JIMENA ¿Nos ayuda, don Diego?

DON DIEGO Claro. Recomiendo que se organicen en equipos para limpiar.

3

MARISSA Mis padres siempre quieren que mis hermanos y yo ayudemos con los quehaceres. No me molesta ayudar. Pero odio limpiar el baño.

JIMENA Lo que más odio yo es sacar la basura.

5

6

4

JUAN CARLOS Hola, Jimena. ¿Está Felipe? *(a Felipe)* Te olvidaste del partido de fútbol.

FELIPE Juan Carlos, ¿verdad que mi papá te considera como de la familia?

JUAN CARLOS Sí.

MARISSA Yo lleno el lavaplatos... después de vaciarlo.

DON DIEGO Juan Carlos, ¿por qué no terminas de pasar la aspiradora? Y Felipe, tú limpia el polvo. ¡Ya casi acaban!

SRA. DÍAZ

SR. DÍAZ

MARISSA

JUAN CARLOS

DON DIEGO

7

(Los chicos preparan la cena y ponen la mesa.)

JUAN CARLOS ¿Dónde están los tenedores?

JIMENA Allá.

JUAN CARLOS ¿Y las servilletas?

MARISSA Aquí están.

8

FELIPE La sala está tan limpia. Le pasamos la aspiradora al sillón y a las cortinas. ¡Y también a las almohadas!

JIMENA Yucatán, ¡ya casi llegamos!

9

(Papá y mamá regresan a casa.)

SRA. DÍAZ ¡Qué bonita está la casa!

SR. DÍAZ Buen trabajo, muchachos. ¿Qué hay para cenar?

JIMENA Quesadillas. Vengan.

10

SRA. DÍAZ Don Diego, quédese a cenar con nosotros. Venga.

SR. DÍAZ Sí, don Diego. Pase.

DON DIEGO Gracias.

Expresiones útiles

Making recommendations

Le(s) sugiero que arregle(n) este apartamento.
I suggest you tidy up this apartment.
Le(s) aconsejo que prepare(n) la cena para las ocho y media.
I recommend that you have dinner ready for eight thirty.

Organizing work

Recomiendo que se organicen en equipos para limpiar.
I recommend that you divide yourselves into teams to clean.
Yo lleno el lavaplatos... después de vaciarlo.
I'll fill the dishwasher... after I empty it.
¿Por qué no terminas de pasar la aspiradora?
Why don't you finish vacuuming?
¡Ya casi acaban!
You're almost finished!
Felipe, tú quita el polvo.
Felipe, you dust.

Making polite requests

Don Diego, quédese a cenar con nosotros.
Don Diego, stay and have dinner with us.
Venga.
Come on.
Don Diego, pase.
Don Diego, come in.

Additional vocabulary

el plumero *duster*

recursos

VM
pp. 217–218

vhlcentral.com
Lección 12

¿Qué pasó?

1 **¿Cierto o falso?** Indica si lo que dicen estas oraciones es **cierto** o **falso**. Corrige las oraciones falsas.

		Cierto	Falso
1.	Felipe y Jimena tienen que preparar el desayuno. *Felipe y Jimena tienen que preparar la cena.*	○	⊘
2.	Don Diego ayuda a los chicos organizando los quehaceres domésticos.	⊘	○
3.	Jimena le dice a Juan Carlos dónde están los tenedores.	⊘	○
4.	A Marissa no le molesta limpiar el baño. *Marissa odia limpiar el baño.*	○	⊘
5.	Juan Carlos termina de lavar los platos. *Juan Carlos termina de pasar la aspiradora.*	○	⊘

2 **Identificar** Identifica quién puede decir estas oraciones.

1. Yo les ayudo, no me molesta hacer quehaceres domésticos. *Marissa*
2. No me gusta sacar la basura, pero es necesario hacerlo. *Jimena*
3. Es importante que termines de pasar la aspiradora, Juan Carlos. *Don Diego*
4. ¡La casa está muy limpia! ¡Qué bueno que pasamos la aspiradora! *Felipe*
5. ¡Buen trabajo, chicos! ¿Qué vamos a cenar? *Sr. Díaz*

 JIMENA **DON DIEGO**
 FELIPE
 SR. DÍAZ **MARISSA**

3 **Completar** Los chicos y don Diego están haciendo los quehaceres. Adivina en qué cuarto está cada uno de ellos.

1. Jimena limpia el congelador. Jimena está en ____la cocina____.
2. Don Diego limpia el escritorio. Don Diego está en ____la oficina____.
3. Felipe pasa la aspiradora debajo de la mesa y las sillas. Felipe está en ____el comedor____.
4. Juan Carlos sacude el sillón. Juan Carlos está en ____la sala____.
5. Marissa hace la cama. Marissa está en ____el dormitorio/ la alcoba____.

4 **Mi casa** Dibuja el plano de una casa o de un apartamento. Puede ser el plano de la casa o del apartamento donde vives o de donde te gustaría (*you would like*) vivir. Después, trabajen en parejas y describan lo que se hace en cuatro de las habitaciones. Para terminar, pídanse (*ask for*) ayuda para hacer dos quehaceres domésticos. Pueden usar estas frases en su conversación. *Answers will vary.*

Quiero mostrarte…	Al fondo hay…
Ésta es (la cocina).	Quiero que me ayudes a (sacar la basura).
Allí yo (preparo la comida).	Por favor, ayúdame con…

Practice more at **vhlcentral.com.**

Ortografía (S) Concepts
Mayúsculas y minúsculas

Here are some of the rules that govern the use of capital letters (**mayúsculas**) and lowercase letters (**minúsculas**) in Spanish.

Los estudiantes llegaron al aeropuerto a las dos. **L**uego fueron al hotel.

In both Spanish and English, the first letter of every sentence is capitalized.

Rubén **B**lades **P**anamá **C**olón los **A**ndes

The first letter of all proper nouns (names of people, countries, cities, geographical features, etc.) is capitalized.

Cien años de soledad *Don Quijote de la Mancha*
El País *Muy Interesante*

The first letter of the first word in titles of books, films, and works of art is generally capitalized, as well as the first letter of any proper names. In newspaper and magazine titles, as well as other short titles, the initial letter of each word is often capitalized.

la **s**eñora Ramos **d**on Francisco
el **p**residente **S**ra. Vives

Titles associated with people are *not* capitalized unless they appear as the first word in a sentence. Note, however, that the first letter of an abbreviated title is capitalized.

Último **Á**lex **MENÚ** **PERDÓN**

Accent marks should be retained on capital letters. In practice, however, this rule is often ignored.

lunes **v**iernes **m**arzo **p**rimavera

The first letter of days, months, and seasons is <u>not</u> capitalized.

español **e**stadounidense **j**aponés **p**anameños

The first letter of nationalities and languages is <u>not</u> capitalized.

Profesor Herrera, ¿es cierto que somos venenosas°?

Sí, Pepito. ¿Por qué lloras?

Práctica Corrige las mayúsculas y minúsculas incorrectas.

1. soy lourdes romero. Soy Colombiana.
 Soy Lourdes Romero. Soy colombiana.
2. éste Es mi Hermano álex.
 Éste es mi hermano Álex.
3. somos De panamá. Somos de Panamá.
4. ¿es ud. La sra. benavides?
 ¿Es Ud. la Sra. Benavides?
5. ud. Llegó el Lunes, ¿no?
 Ud. llegó el lunes, ¿no?

Palabras desordenadas Lee el diálogo de las serpientes. Ordena las letras para saber de qué palabras se trata. Después escribe las letras indicadas para descubrir por qué llora Pepito.

m n a a P á ◯ _ _ _ _ _
s t e m r a ◯ _ _ _ _ _
i g s l é n _ _ _ ◯ _ _
y a U r u g u _ _ _ ◯ _ _ _
r o ñ e s a _ _ _ _ _ ◯

¡ _ orque _ e acabo de morder° la _ en _ u _ !

¡Porque me acabo de morder la lengua!
Respuestas: Panamá, martes, inglés, Uruguay, señora.

venenosas *venomous* **morder** *to bite*

recursos

LM p. 68 (S) vhlcentral.com Lección 12

Section Goal

In **Ortografía**, students will learn about the rules for capitalization in Spanish.

Instructional Resources
Supersite: Audio (Lab MP3 Files); Resources (Scripts, Answer Keys)
WebSAM
Lab Manual, p. 68

Teaching Tips
- Explain that in a few Spanish city and country names the definite article is considered part of the name, and is thus capitalized. Ex: **La Habana, La Coruña, La Haya, El Salvador**.
- As in English, Spanish titles of books, film, and works of art are italicized in print; however, capitalization rules differ. In Spanish, only the first word and any proper noun gets an initial capital. Spanish treatment of the names of newspapers and magazines is the same as in English; they are italicized in print and each word is capitalized. Tell students that *El País* is a Spanish newspaper and *Muy Interesante* is a popular science magazine.
- After going through the explanation, write example titles, names, sentences, etc., all in lowercase on the board. Then, ask pairs to decide which letters should be capitalized.
- Point out that **Ortografía** replaces **Pronunciación** in the Student Edition for **Lecciones 10–15**, but not in the Lab Manual. The **Recursos** box references the **Pronunciación** sections found in all lessons of the Lab Manual.

TEACHING OPTIONS

Extra Practice Have students scan the reading on the next page. Have them circle all the capital letters and explain why each is capitalized. Then point out the words **árabe, españoles,** and **islámica** and have volunteers explain why they are not capitalized.
Extra Practice Add an auditory aspect to this **Ortografía** section. Read this sentence aloud for students to write down: **El doctor Guzmán, el amigo panameño de la señorita Rivera, llegó a Quito**

el lunes, doce de mayo. To allow students time to write, read the sentence twice slowly and once at full speed. Tell the class to abbreviate all titles. Have volunteers write their version of the sentence on the board, and as a class correct any mistakes they may have made.

EN DETALLE

Additional Reading
Video: *Flash cultura*

El patio central

En las tardes cálidas° de Oaxaca, México; Córdoba, España, o Popayán, Colombia, es un placer sentarse en **el patio central** de una casa y tomar un refresco disfrutando de° una buena conversación. De influencia árabe, esta característica arquitectónica° fue traída° a las Américas por los españoles. En la época° colonial, se construyeron casas, palacios, monasterios, hospitales y escuelas con patio central. Éste es un espacio privado e íntimo en donde se puede disfrutar del sol y de la brisa° estando aislado° de la calle.

El centro del patio es un espacio abierto. Alrededor de° él, separado por columnas, hay un pasillo cubierto°. Así, en el patio hay zonas de sol y de sombra°. El patio es una parte importante de la vivienda familiar y su decoración se cuida° mucho. En el centro del patio muchas veces hay una fuente°, plantas e incluso árboles°. El agua es un elemento muy importante en la cultura islámica porque

simboliza la purificación del cuerpo y del alma°. Por esta razón y para disminuir° la temperatura, el agua en estas construcciones es muy importante. El agua y la vegetación ayudan a mantener la temperatura fresca y el patio proporciona° luz y ventilación a todas las habitaciones.

La distribución

Las casas con patio central eran usualmente las viviendas de familias adineradas°. Son casas de dos o tres pisos. Los cuartos de la planta baja son las áreas comunes: cocina, comedor, sala, etc., y tienen puertas al patio. En los pisos superiores están las habitaciones privadas de la familia.

cálidas *hot* disfrutando de *enjoying* arquitectónica *architectural* traída *brought* época *era* brisa *breeze* aislado *isolated* Alrededor de *Surrounding* cubierto *covered* sombra *shade* se cuida *is looked after* fuente *fountain* árboles *trees* alma *soul* disminuir *lower* proporciona *provides* adineradas *wealthy*

ACTIVIDADES

1 **¿Cierto o falso?** Indica si lo que dicen las oraciones es **cierto** o **falso**. Corrige las falsas.

1. Los patios centrales de Latinoamérica tienen su origen en la tradición indígena. **Falso.** Los patios centrales tienen su origen en la arquitectura árabe.
2. Los españoles llevaron a América el concepto del patio. **Cierto.**
3. En la época colonial las casas eran las únicas construcciones con patio central. **Falso.** Se construyeron casas, palacios, monasterios, hospitales y escuelas.
4. El patio es una parte importante en estas construcciones, y es por eso que se le presta atención a su decoración. **Cierto.**
5. El patio central es un lugar de descanso que da luz y ventilación a las habitaciones. **Cierto.**
6. Las fuentes en los patios tienen importancia por razones culturales y porque bajan la temperatura. **Cierto.**
7. En la cultura española el agua simboliza salud y bienestar del cuerpo y del alma. **Falso.** En la cultura islámica el agua simboliza salud y bienestar del cuerpo y del alma.
8. Las casas con patio central eran para personas adineradas. **Cierto.**
9. Los cuartos de la planta baja son privados. **Falso.** Los cuartos de la planta baja son las áreas comunes.
10. Las alcobas están en los pisos superiores. **Cierto.**

ASÍ SE DICE

La vivienda

el ático, el desván	el altillo
la cobija (Col., Méx.), la frazada (Arg., Cuba, Ven.)	la manta
el escaparate (Cuba, Ven.), el ropero (Méx.)	el armario
el fregadero	*kitchen sink*
el frigidaire (Perú); el frigorífico (Esp.), la nevera	el refrigerador
el lavavajillas (Arg., Esp., Méx.)	el lavaplatos

EL MUNDO HISPANO

Los muebles

- **Mecedora°** La mecedora es un mueble típico de Latinoamérica, especialmente de la zona del Caribe. A las personas les gusta relajarse mientras se mecen° en el patio.

- **Mesa camilla** Era un mueble popular en España hasta hace algunos años. Es una mesa con un bastidor° en la parte inferior° para poner un brasero°. En invierno, las personas se sentaban alrededor de la mesa camilla para conversar, jugar a las cartas o tomar café.

- **Hamaca** Se cree que los taínos hicieron las primeras hamacas con fibras vegetales. Su uso es muy popular en toda Latinoamérica para dormir y descansar.

Mecedora *Rocking chair* **se mecen** *they rock themselves*
bastidor *frame* **inferior** *bottom* **brasero** *container for hot coals*

PERFIL

Las islas flotantes del lago Titicaca

Bolivia y Perú comparten **el lago Titicaca**, donde viven **los uros**, uno de los pueblos indígenas más antiguos de América. Hace muchos años, los uros fueron a vivir al lago escapando de **los incas**. Hoy en día, siguen viviendo allí en cuarenta **islas flotantes** que ellos mismos hacen con unos juncos° llamados **totora**. Primero tejen° grandes plataformas. Luego, con el mismo material, construyen sus casas sobre las plataformas. La totora es resistente, pero con el tiempo el agua la pudre°. Los habitantes de las islas

necesitan renovar continuamente las plataformas y las casas. Sus muebles y sus barcos también están hechos° de juncos. Los uros viven de la pesca y del turismo; en las islas hay unas tiendas donde venden artesanías° hechas con totora.

PERÚ

Lago Titicaca

BOLIVIA

juncos *reeds* **tejen** *they weave* **la pudre** *rots it*
hechos *made* **artesanías** *handcrafts*

Conexión Internet

¿Cómo son las casas modernas en los países hispanos?

Go to **vhlcentral.com** to find more cultural information related to this **Cultura** section.

ACTIVIDADES

2 **Comprensión** Responde a las preguntas.

1. Tu amigo mexicano te dice: "La **cobija** azul está en el **ropero**". ¿Qué quiere decir? La manta azul está en en el armario.

2. ¿Quiénes hicieron las primeras hamacas? ¿Qué material usaron? los taínos; fibras vegetales

3. ¿Qué grupo indígena vive en el lago Titicaca? Los uros viven en el lago Titicaca.

4. ¿Qué pueden comprar los turistas en las islas flotantes del lago Titicaca? Pueden comprar artesanías hechas con totora.

3 **Viviendas tradicionales** Escribe cuatro oraciones sobre una vivienda tradicional que conoces. Explica en qué lugar se encuentra, de qué materiales está hecha y cómo es. Answers will vary.

recursos

VM pp. 289–290

vhlcentral.com Lección 12

Practice more at **vhlcentral.com**.

Así se dice
- Model the pronunciation of each term and have students repeat it.
- Explain that compound words like **lavavajillas** are often masculine: **el lavavajillas, los lavavajillas**.
- To challenge students, add these household-related words to the list: **arrendar (Chi., Col.), rentar (Cuba, Méx, P. Rico)** (*to rent*); **la chimenea** (*fireplace*); **el corredor** (*hallway*); **el gavetero (Cuba, Pan., P. Rico)** (*dresser, bureau*); **la licuadora, la batidora (Cuba, Esp., Rep. Dom., Ven.)** (*blender*); **las persianas** (*blinds*); **el plato hondo, el tazón** (*bowl*); **el tragaluz, la claraboya** (*skylight*).

Perfil
- Have students share any facts from the reading that are new or surprising to them.
- Ask students: **¿Les interesa visitar estas islas? ¿Cuáles son las ventajas y desventajas de vivir en un sitio así?**

El mundo hispano
- If possible, bring in photos of the three pieces of furniture.
- Ask students if they have similar furniture in their homes.

2 **Expansion** Give students these questions as items 5–8:
**5. ¿Por qué los uros se fueron a vivir al lago Titicaca? (Para escapar de los incas.)
6. ¿Cuántas islas flotantes hay entre Bolivia y Perú? (cuarenta)
7. ¿Cómo se hace la base de las casas flotantes? (Se tejen con totora.) 8. ¿Por qué se usaba una mesa camilla en invierno y no en verano? (Daba calor a los pies.)**

3 **Teaching Tip** To add a visual aspect to this activity, have students find a photo of a traditional dwelling and use the photo as a basis for their written description.

TEACHING OPTIONS

Small Groups In small groups, have students research the floating islands of Lake Titicaca and make a poster or collage. Tell them to include information about the **uro** way of life, tourism, and any other significant details about the islands. Have groups present their posters to the class.

Extra Practice Ask students to write a short description of their favorite room in their family's house or apartment. Encourage them to give details about the furniture and decorations. Have them share their paragraphs with a partner, who will ask clarifying questions about the room.

12.1 Relative pronouns Tutorial

ANTE TODO In both English and Spanish, relative pronouns are used to combine two sentences or clauses that share a common element, such as a noun or pronoun. Study this diagram.

Mis padres me regalaron **la aspiradora**.
My parents gave me the vacuum cleaner.

La aspiradora funciona muy bien.
The vacuum cleaner works really well.

La aspiradora **que** me regalaron mis padres funciona muy bien.
The vacuum cleaner that my parents gave me works really well.

Lourdes es muy inteligente.
Lourdes is very intelligent.

Lourdes estudia español.
Lourdes is studying Spanish.

Lourdes, **quien** estudia español, es muy inteligente.
Lourdes, who studies Spanish, is very intelligent.

Eso fue todo lo que dijimos.

Mi papá se lleva bien con Juan Carlos, quien es como mi hermano.

▶ Spanish has three frequently-used relative pronouns. **¡Atención!** Even though interrogative words (**qué**, **quién**, etc.) always carry an accent, relative pronouns never carry a written accent.

que	*that; which; who*
quien(es)	*who; whom; that*
lo que	*that which; what*

▶ **Que** is the most frequently used relative pronoun. It can refer to things or to people. Unlike its English counterpart, *that*, **que** is never omitted.

¿Dónde está la cafetera **que** compré?
Where is the coffee maker (that) I bought?

El hombre **que** limpia es Pedro.
The man who is cleaning is Pedro.

▶ The relative pronoun **quien** refers only to people, and is often used after a preposition or the personal **a. Quien** has only two forms: **quien** (singular) and **quienes** (plural).

¿Son las chicas **de quienes** me hablaste la semana pasada?
Are they the girls (that) you told me about last week?

Eva, **a quien** conocí anoche, es mi nueva vecina.
Eva, whom I met last night, is my new neighbor.

Section Goal

In **Estructura 12.1**, students will learn the relative pronouns **que, quien(es), lo que** and their uses.

Instructional Resources
Supersite: Audio (Lab MP3 Files); Resources (*PowerPoints*, Activity Pack, Scripts, Answer Keys); Testing Program (Quizzes)
WebSAM
Workbook, pp. 141–142
Lab Manual, p. 69

Teaching Tips
• Have students look at the **Fotonovela** on pages 380–381. Ask questions about the episode. Restate each student response as a sentence using a relative pronoun. Write the sentences on the board and underline the relative pronouns. Ex:
1. ¿Quiénes van a arreglar la casa? (Felipe y Jimena) Sí, ellos son las personas que van a limpiar la casa. 2. ¿Qué cuarto tiene lavaplatos? (la cocina) Sí, la cocina es el cuarto que tiene lavaplatos.
• Compare and contrast the use of **que** and **quien** by writing some examples on the board. Ex: **Es la chica que vino con Carlos a mi fiesta. Es la chica a quien conocí en mi fiesta.** Have students deduce the rule.

TEACHING OPTIONS

Extra Practice Write these sentences on the board, and have students supply the correct relative pronoun.
1. Hay una escalera ____ sube al primer piso. (que)
2. Elena es la muchacha a ____ le presté la aspiradora. (quien)
3. ¿Dónde pusiste la ropa ____ acabas de quitarte? (que)
4. ¿Cuáles son los estudiantes a ____ les alquilas tu casa? (quienes)

5. La cómoda ____ compramos la semana pasada está en el dormitorio de mi hermana. (que)
Heritage Speakers Using complex sentences with relative pronouns, have heritage speakers describe a location in their families' communities where people can get together. Ex: town square, park, café, etc.

¡LENGUA VIVA!

In English, it is generally recommended that *who(m)* be used to refer to people, and that *that* and *which* be used to refer to things. In Spanish, however, it is perfectly acceptable to use **que** when referring to people.

▶ **Quien(es)** is occasionally used instead of **que** in clauses set off by commas.

Lola, **quien** es cubana, es médica.
Lola, who is Cuban, is a doctor.

Su tía, **que** es alemana, ya llegó.
His aunt, who is German, already arrived.

▶ Unlike **que** and **quien(es)**, **lo que** doesn't refer to a specific noun. It refers to an idea, a situation, or a past event and means *what, that which,* or *the thing that.*

Lo que me molesta es el calor.
What bothers me is the heat.

Lo que quiero es una casa.
What I want is a house.

Este supermercado tiene todo **lo que** necesito.

A Samuel no le gustó **lo que** le dijo Violeta.

¡INTÉNTALO! Completa estas oraciones con pronombres relativos.

1. Voy a utilizar los platos ___que___ me regaló mi abuela.
2. Ana comparte un apartamento con la chica a ___quien___ conocimos en la fiesta de Jorge.
3. Esta oficina tiene todo ___lo que___ necesitamos.
4. Puedes estudiar en el dormitorio ___que___ está a la derecha de la cocina.
5. Los señores ___que___ viven en esa casa acaban de llegar de Centroamérica.
6. Los niños a ___quienes___ viste en nuestro jardín son mis sobrinos.
7. La piscina ___que___ ves desde la ventana es la piscina de mis vecinos.
8. Fue Úrsula ___quien___ ayudó a mamá a limpiar el refrigerador.
9. Ya te dije que fue mi padre ___quien___ alquiló el apartamento.
10. ___Lo que___ te dijo Pablo no es cierto.
11. Tengo que sacudir los muebles ___que___ están en el altillo una vez al mes.
12. No entiendo por qué no lavaste los vasos ___que___ te dije.
13. La mujer a ___quien___ saludaste vive en las afueras.
14. ¿Sabes ___lo que___ necesita este dormitorio? ¡Unas cortinas!
15. No quiero volver a hacer ___lo que___ hice ayer.
16. No me gusta vivir con personas a ___quienes___ no conozco.

recursos

WB
pp. 141–142

LM
p. 69

Ⓢ
vhlcentral.com
Lección 12

Teaching Tips

• Test comprehension as you proceed by asking volunteers to answer questions about students and objects in the classroom. Ex: **¿Cómo se llama la estudiante que se sienta detrás de ____? ¿Cómo se llaman los estudiantes a quienes acabo de hacer una pregunta? ¿Dónde está la tarea que ustedes hicieron para hoy?**

• Add a visual aspect to this grammar presentation. Line up four to five pictures. Ask questions that use relative pronouns or elicit them in student answers. Ex: **¿Quién está comiendo una hamburguesa? (El muchacho que está sentado en la playa está comiendo una hamburguesa.) ¿Quién sabe lo que está haciendo esta muchacha? (Está quitando la mesa.)**

• 👥↔👥 Ask students to make two short lists: **Lo que tengo en mi dormitorio** and **Lo que quiero tener en mi dormitorio.** Ask volunteers to read part of their lists to the class. Encourage a conversation by asking questions such as: **¿Es esto lo que tienes en tu dormitorio? ¿Es un ____ lo que quieres tú?**

TEACHING OPTIONS

Video →👥← Show the **Fotonovela** again to give students more input containing relative pronouns. Stop the video where appropriate to discuss how relative pronouns were used.
Game ←👥→ Ask students to bring in some interesting pictures from magazines or the Internet, but tell them not to show these photos to one another. Divide the class into teams of three. Each team should pick a picture. One student will write an accurate

description of it, and the others will write imaginary descriptions. Tell them to use relative pronouns in the descriptions. Each team will read its three descriptions aloud without showing the picture. Give the rest of the class two minutes to ask questions about the descriptions before guessing which is the accurate one. Award one point for a correct guess and two points to the team able to fool the class.

Práctica

1 Combinar Combina elementos de la columna A y la columna B para formar oraciones lógicas.

A	B
1. Ése es el hombre ___d___.	a. con quien bailaba es mi vecina
2. Rubén Blades, ___c___.	b. que te compró Cecilia
3. No traje ___e___.	c. quien es de Panamá, es un cantante muy bueno
4. ¿Te gusta la manta ___b___?	d. que arregló mi lavadora
5. ¿Cómo se llama el programa ___g___?	e. lo que necesito para la clase de matemáticas
6. La mujer ___a___.	f. que comiste en el restaurante
	g. que escuchaste en la radio anoche

2 Completar Completa la historia sobre la casa que Jaime y Tina quieren comprar, usando los pronombres relativos **que, quien, quienes** o **lo que**.

1. Jaime y Tina son los chicos a ___quienes___ conocí la semana pasada.

2. Quieren comprar una casa ___que___ está en las afueras de la ciudad.

3. Es una casa ___que___ era de una artista famosa.

4. La artista, a ___quien___ yo conocía, murió el año pasado y no tenía hijos.

5. Ahora se vende la casa con todos los muebles ___que___ ella tenía.

6. La sala tiene una alfombra ___que___ ella trajo de Kuwait.

7. La casa tiene muchos estantes, ___lo que___ a Tina le encanta.

3 Oraciones Javier y Ana acaban de casarse y han comprado (*they have bought*) una casa y muchas otras cosas. Combina sus declaraciones para formar una sola oración con los pronombres relativos **que, quien(es)** y **lo que**.

> **modelo**
>
> Vamos a usar los vasos nuevos mañana. Los pusimos en el comedor.
>
> *Mañana vamos a usar los vasos nuevos que pusimos en el comedor.*

1. Tenemos una cafetera nueva. Mi prima nos la regaló.
 Tenemos una cafetera nueva que mi prima nos regaló.
2. Tenemos una cómoda nueva. Es bueno porque no hay espacio en el armario.
 Tenemos una cómoda nueva, lo que es bueno porque no hay espacio en el armario.
3. Esos platos no nos costaron mucho. Están encima del horno.
 Esos platos que están encima del horno no nos costaron mucho.
4. Esas copas me las regaló mi amiga Amalia. Ella viene a visitarme mañana.
 Esas copas me las regaló mi amiga Amalia, quien/que viene a visitarme mañana.
5. La lavadora está casi nueva. Nos la regalaron mis suegros.
 La lavadora que nos regalaron mis suegros está casi nueva.
6. La vecina nos dio una manta de lana. Ella la compró en México.
 La vecina nos dio una manta de lana que compró en México.

Practice more at **vhlcentral.com**.

Comunicación

4 **Entrevista** En parejas, túrnense para hacerse estas preguntas. *Answers will vary.*

1. ¿Qué es lo que más te gusta de vivir en las afueras o en la ciudad?
2. ¿Cómo son las personas que viven en tu barrio?
3. ¿Cuál es el quehacer doméstico que pagarías (*you would pay*) por no hacer?
4. ¿Quién es la persona que hace los quehaceres domésticos en tu casa?
5. ¿Hay vecinos que te caen bien? ¿Quiénes?
6. ¿De qué vecino es el coche que más te gusta?
7. ¿Cuál es el barrio de tu ciudad que más te gusta y por qué?
8. ¿Quién es la persona a quien le pedirías (*you would ask*) que te ayude con los quehaceres?
9. ¿Cuál es el lugar de la casa donde te sientes más cómodo/a? ¿Por qué?
10. ¿Qué es lo que más te gusta de tu barrio?
11. ¿Qué hace el vecino que más llama la atención?
12. ¿Qué es lo que menos te gusta de tu barrio?

5 **Adivinanza** En grupos, túrnense para describir distintas partes de una vivienda usando pronombres relativos. Los demás compañeros tienen que hacer preguntas hasta que adivinen (*they guess*) la palabra. *Answers will vary.*

> **modelo**
> **Estudiante 1:** Es lo que tenemos en el dormitorio.
> **Estudiante 2:** ¿Es el mueble que usamos para dormir?
> **Estudiante 1:** No. Es lo que usamos para guardar la ropa.
> **Estudiante 3:** Lo sé. Es la cómoda.

Síntesis

6 **Definir** En parejas, definan las palabras. Usen los pronombres relativos **que, quien(es)** y **lo que.** Luego compartan sus definiciones con la clase. *Answers will vary.*

alquiler	flan	patio	tenedor
amigos	guantes	postre	termómetro
aspiradora	jabón	sillón	vaso
enfermera	manta	sótano	vecino

> **modelo**
> lavadora Es lo que se usa para lavar la ropa.
> pastel Es un postre que comes en tu cumpleaños.

12.2 Formal (usted/ustedes) commands (S) Tutorial

ANTE TODO As you learned in **Lección 11**, the command forms are used to give orders or advice. Formal commands are used with people you address as **usted** or **ustedes**. Observe these examples, then study the chart.

AYUDA

By learning formal commands, it will be easier for you to learn the subjunctive forms that are presented in **Estructura 12.3**, p. 394.

Hable con ellos, don Francisco.
Talk with them, Don Francisco.

Coma frutas y verduras.
Eat fruits and vegetables.

Laven los platos ahora mismo.
Wash the dishes right now.

Beban menos té y café.
Drink less tea and coffee.

Formal commands (Ud. and Uds.)

Infinitive	Present tense yo form	Ud. command	Uds. command
limpiar	limpio	limpie	limpien
barrer	barro	barra	barran
sacudir	sacudo	sacuda	sacudan
decir (e:i)	digo	diga	digan
pensar (e:ie)	pienso	piense	piensen
volver (o:ue)	vuelvo	vuelva	vuelvan
servir (e:i)	sirvo	sirva	sirvan

▶ The **usted** and **ustedes** commands, like the negative **tú** commands, are formed by dropping the final **-o** of the **yo** form of the present tense. For **-ar** verbs, add **-e** or **-en**. For **-er** and **-ir** verbs, add **-a** or **-an**.

Don Diego, quédese a cenar con nosotros.

No se preocupen, yo los ayudo.

▶ Verbs with irregular **yo** forms maintain the same irregularity in their formal commands. These verbs include **conducir, conocer, decir, hacer, ofrecer, oír, poner, salir, tener, traducir, traer, venir,** and **ver.**

Oiga, don Manolo...
Listen, Don Manolo...

¡Salga inmediatamente!
Leave immediately!

Ponga la mesa, por favor.
Set the table, please.

Hagan la cama antes de salir.
Make the bed before leaving.

▶ Note also that verbs maintain their stem changes in **usted** and **ustedes** commands.

e:ie	o:ue	e:i
No **pierda** la llave.	**Vuelva** temprano, joven.	**Sirva** la sopa, por favor.
Cierren la puerta.	**Duerman** bien, chicos.	**Repitan** las frases.

Section Goals

In **Estructura 12.2**, students will learn:
• formal (**usted/ustedes**) commands
• use of object pronouns with formal commands

Instructional Resources
Supersite: Audio (Lab MP3 Files); Resources (*PowerPoints*, Activity Pack, Scripts, Answer Keys); Testing Program (Quizzes)
WebSAM
Workbook, pp. 143–144
Lab Manual, p. 70

Teaching Tips
• Model the use of formal commands with simple examples using TPR and gestures. Ex: **Levántense. Siéntense.** Then point to individual students and give commands in an exaggerated formal tone. Ex: **Señor(ita) _____, levántese.** Give other commands using **salga/salgan, vuelva/vuelvan,** and **venga/vengan.**
• Write these sentences on the board, contrasting their meaning with the examples in the text: **Habla con ellos. Come frutas y verduras. Lavan los platos ahora mismo. Beben menos té y café.**
• Have volunteers give the command forms for other verbs, such as **alquilar, correr,** or **imprimir.**

TEACHING OPTIONS

Video Replay the **Fotonovela**, having students focus on formal commands. Ask them to write down each formal command that they hear. Then form groups of three and have students compare their lists.
Extra Practice Describe situations and have students call out **ustedes** commands that would be used. Ex: A mother sending her kids off to overnight camp. (**Cepíllense los dientes antes de**

dormir.) An aerobics class. (**Levanten los brazos.**)
TPR Have students stand. Using the verbs presented in the discussion of formal commands, give commands at random (Ex: **Barra el suelo.**) and point to a student who should perform the appropriate gesture. Keep a brisk pace. Vary by pointing to more than one student. Ex: **Pongan la mesa.**

AYUDA

These spelling changes are necessary to ensure that the words are pronounced correctly. See **Lección 8, Pronunciación,** p. 251, and **Lección 9, Pronunciación,** p. 283.

• • •

It may help you to study the following five series of syllables. Note that, within each series, the consonant sound doesn't change.

ca que qui co cu
za ce ci zo zu
ga gue gui go gu
ja ge gi jo ju

▶ Verbs ending in **-car, -gar,** and **-zar** have a spelling change in the command forms.

sa**car**	c → qu	sa**qu**e, sa**qu**en
ju**gar**	g → gu	jue**gu**e, jue**gu**en
almor**zar**	z → c	almuer**c**e, almuer**c**en

▶ These verbs have irregular formal commands.

Infinitive	Ud. command	Uds. command
dar	**dé**	**den**
estar	**esté**	**estén**
ir	**vaya**	**vayan**
saber	**sepa**	**sepan**
ser	**sea**	**sean**

▶ To make a formal command negative, simply place **no** before the verb.

No ponga las maletas en la cama. **No ensucien** los sillones.
Don't put the suitcases on the bed. *Don't dirty the armchairs.*

▶ In affirmative commands, reflexive, indirect and direct object pronouns are always attached to the end of the verb.

Siénten**se**, por favor. Acuésten**se** ahora.
Síga**me**, Laura. Pónganlas en el suelo, por favor.

▶ **¡Atención!** When a pronoun is attached to an affirmative command that has two or more syllables, an accent mark is added to maintain the original stress.

limpie ⟶ **límpielo** lean ⟶ **léanlo**
diga ⟶ **dígamelo** sacudan ⟶ **sacúdanlos**

▶ In negative commands, these pronouns always precede the verb.

No **se** preocupe. No **los** ensucien.
No **me lo** dé. No **nos las** traigan.

▶ **Usted** and **ustedes** can be used with the command forms to strike a more formal tone. In such instances, they follow the command form.

Muéstrele usted la foto a su amigo. **Tomen ustedes** esta mesa.
Show the photo to your friend. *Take this table.*

recursos

WB
pp. 143–144

LM
p. 70

vhlcentral.com
Lección 12

 ¡INTÉNTALO! Indica los mandatos (*commands*) afirmativos y negativos correspondientes.

1. escucharlo (Ud.) _____Escúchelo_____. _____No lo escuche_____.
2. decírmelo (Uds.) _____Díganmelo_____. _____No me lo digan_____.
3. salir (Ud.) _____Salga_____. _____No salga_____.
4. servírnoslo (Uds.) _____Sírvannoslo_____. _____No nos lo sirvan_____.
5. barrerla (Ud.) _____Bárrala_____. _____No la barra_____.
6. hacerlo (Ud.) _____Hágalo_____. _____No lo haga_____.

Teaching Tips

• Ask volunteers to write formal command forms of other verbs with spelling changes on the board. Ex: **empezar (empiece); comenzar (comience); buscar (busque); pagar (pague); llegar (llegue).**

• Test comprehension as you proceed by asking volunteers to supply the correct form of other infinitives you name.

• Point out that the written accent mark on **dé** serves to distinguish the verb form from the preposition **de**.

• Point out that the affirmative answer for item 4 of **¡Inténtalo!** is spelled with a double n: **Sírvannoslo**.

TEACHING OPTIONS

Extra Practice Write a list of situations on the board using singular and plural forms. Ex: **La cocina está sucia. Mis amigos y yo tenemos hambre. Tenemos miedo.** Then have students write responses in the form of commands. Ex: **Límpiela. Hagan la cena. No tengan miedo.**

Heritage Speakers Ask heritage speakers to make a list of ten commands they would hear in their homes that may not be heard elsewhere. Ex: **Sírvale el café al niño. Acuéstese después de almorzar.**

Práctica

1 Completar La señora González quiere mudarse de casa. Ayúdala a organizarse. Indica el mandato formal de cada verbo.

1. __Lea__ los anuncios del periódico y __guárdelos__. (Leer, guardarlos)
2. __Vaya__ personalmente y __vea__ las casas usted misma. (Ir, ver)
3. Decida qué casa quiere y __llame__ al agente. __Pídale__ un contrato de alquiler. (llamar, Pedirle)
4. __Contrate__ un camión *(truck)* para ese día y __pregúnteles__ la hora exacta de llegada. (Contratar, preguntarles)
5. El día de la mudanza *(On moving day)* __esté__ tranquila. __Vuelva__ a revisar su lista para completar todo lo que tiene que hacer. (estar, Volver)
6. Primero, __dígales__ a todos en casa que usted va a estar ocupada. No __les diga__ que usted va a hacerlo todo. (decirles, decirles)
7. __Saque__ tiempo para hacer las maletas tranquilamente. No __les haga__ las maletas a los niños más grandes. (Sacar, hacerles)
8. No __se preocupe__. __Sepa__ que todo va a salir bien. (preocuparse, Saber)

2 ¿Qué dicen? Mira los dibujos y escribe un mandato lógico para cada uno. Usa palabras que aprendiste en **Contextos**. Answers will vary. Suggested answers:

1. _Abran sus libros, por favor._

2. _Cierre la puerta. ¡Hace frío!_

3. _Traiga usted la cuenta, por favor._

4. _La cocina está sucia. Bárranla, por favor._

5. _Duerma bien, niña._

6. _Arreglen el cuarto, por favor. Está desordenado._

 Practice more at **vhlcentral.com.**

Comunicación

3 **Solucionar** Trabajen en parejas. Un(a) estudiante presenta los problemas de la columna A y el/la otro/a los de la columna B. Usen mandatos formales y túrnense para ofrecer soluciones. *Answers will vary.*

> **modelo**
>
> **Estudiante 1:** Vilma se torció un tobillo jugando al tenis. Es la tercera vez.
> **Estudiante 2:** *No juegue más al tenis. / Vaya a ver a un especialista.*

A	B
1. Se me perdió el libro de español con todas mis notas.	1. Mis hijas no se levantan temprano. Siempre llegan tarde a la escuela.
2. A Vicente se le cayó la botella de vino para la cena.	2. A mi abuela le robaron *(stole)* las maletas. Era su primer día de vacaciones.
3. ¿Cómo? ¿Se le olvidó traer el traje de baño a la playa?	3. Nuestra casa es demasiado pequeña para nuestra familia.
4. Se nos quedaron los boletos en la casa. El avión sale en una hora.	4. Me preocupo constantemente por Roberto. Trabaja demasiado.

4 **Conversaciones** En parejas, escojan dos situaciones y preparen conversaciones para presentar a la clase. Usen mandatos formales. *Answers will vary.*

> **modelo**
>
> **Lupita:** Señor Ramírez, siento mucho llegar tan tarde. Mi niño se enfermó. ¿Qué debo hacer?
> **Sr. Ramírez:** *No se preocupe. Siéntese y descanse un poco.*

SITUACIÓN 1 Profesor Rosado, no vine la semana pasada porque el equipo jugaba en Boquete. ¿Qué debo hacer para ponerme al día *(catch up)*?

SITUACIÓN 2 Los invitados de la boda llegan a las cuatro de la tarde, las mesas están sin poner y el champán sin servir. Son las tres de la tarde y los camareros apenas están llegando. ¿Qué deben hacer los camareros?

SITUACIÓN 3 Mi novio es un poco aburrido. No le gustan ni el cine, ni los deportes, ni salir a comer. Tampoco habla mucho. ¿Qué puedo hacer?

▶ **SITUACIÓN 4** Tengo que preparar una presentación para mañana sobre el Canal de Panamá. ¿Por dónde comienzo?

NOTA CULTURAL

El 31 de diciembre de 1999, los Estados Unidos cedió el control del **Canal de Panamá** al gobierno de Panamá, terminando así con casi cien años de administración estadounidense.

Síntesis

5 **Presentar** En grupos, preparen un anuncio de televisión para presentar a la clase. El anuncio debe tratar de un detergente, un electrodoméstico o una agencia inmobiliaria *(real estate agency)*. Usen mandatos, los pronombres relativos (**que, quien(es)** o **lo que**) y el **se** impersonal. *Answers will vary.*

> **modelo**
>
> *Compre el lavaplatos Destellos. Tiene todo lo que usted desea. Es el lavaplatos que mejor funciona. Venga a verlo ahora mismo… No pierda ni un minuto más. Se aceptan tarjetas de crédito.*

3 Teaching Tip Ask volunteers to offer other suggestions for the problem in the **modelo**. Ex: **Tenga usted más cuidado. Compre nuevos zapatos de tenis.**

3 Expansion Ask pairs to pick their most humorous or unusual response to present to the class.

4 Expansion Have pairs write an additional scenario on a sheet of paper. Then ask them to exchange papers with another pair and give them two minutes to prepare a new dialogue. Have them act out their dialogues for the authors.

5 Teaching Tip Divide the class into small groups. Have them choose a product or business and brainstorm positive attributes that they want to advertise.

5 Expansion
• Ask groups to present their commercials to the class.
• Have groups make a video of their ads outside of class. Encourage them to be as creative as possible.

The Affective Dimension
When presenting the television commercial, students may feel more comfortable speaking if they assume the personae of celebrity endorsers.

TEACHING OPTIONS

Heritage Speakers Have heritage speakers write a brief description of a kitchen item commonly found in their homes, but not typically in other communities. Ex: **comal, molcajete, cafetera exprés, paellera**. Ask the rest of the class to write a description of the most unusual kitchen item in their homes. Collect all the descriptions, shuffle them, and read them aloud. Have the class guess which items are more typical of Spanish-speaking households. Then, have heritage speakers use formal commands to give the basic steps of a recipe that uses one of the items.
Pairs Have pairs of students write a list of commands for the president of your school. Ex: **Por favor, no suba el costo de la matrícula. Permita más fiestas en las residencias.** Then have them write a list of plural commands for their fellow students. Ex: **No hablen en la biblioteca.**

12.3 # The present subjunctive Tutorial

NATIONAL STANDARDS comparisons

ANTE TODO With the exception of commands, all the verb forms you have been using have been in the indicative mood. The indicative is used to state facts and to express actions or states that the speaker considers to be real and definite. In contrast, the subjunctive mood expresses the speaker's attitudes toward events, as well as actions or states the speaker views as uncertain or hypothetical.

Por favor, quiten los platos de la mesa.

Les aconsejo que preparen la cena.

▶ The present subjunctive is formed very much like **usted**, **ustedes** and *negative* **tú** commands. From the **yo** form of the present indicative, drop the **-o** ending, and replace it with the subjunctive endings.

INFINITIVE	PRESENT INDICATIVE	VERB STEM	PRESENT SUBJUNCTIVE
hablar	**hablo**	**habl-**	**hable**
comer	**como**	**com-**	**coma**
escribir	**escribo**	**escrib-**	**escriba**

▶ The present subjunctive endings are:

-ar verbs		-er and -ir verbs	
-e	-emos	-a	-amos
-es	-éis	-as	-áis
-e	-en	-a	-an

Present subjunctive of regular verbs

		hablar	comer	escribir
SINGULAR FORMS	yo	habl**e**	com**a**	escrib**a**
	tú	habl**es**	com**as**	escrib**as**
	Ud./él/ella	habl**e**	com**a**	escrib**a**
PLURAL FORMS	nosotros/as	habl**emos**	com**amos**	escrib**amos**
	vosotros/as	habl**éis**	com**áis**	escrib**áis**
	Uds./ellos/ellas	habl**en**	com**an**	escrib**an**

▶ Verbs with irregular **yo** forms show the same irregularity in all forms of the present subjunctive.

Infinitive	Present indicative	Verb stem	Present subjunctive
conducir	conduzco	**conduzc-**	**conduzca**
conocer	conozco	**conozc-**	**conozca**
decir	digo	**dig-**	**diga**
hacer	hago	**hag-**	**haga**
ofrecer	ofrezco	**ofrezc-**	**ofrezca**
oír	oigo	**oig-**	**oiga**
parecer	parezco	**parezc-**	**parezca**
poner	pongo	**pong-**	**ponga**
tener	tengo	**teng-**	**tenga**
traducir	traduzco	**traduzc-**	**traduzca**
traer	traigo	**traig-**	**traiga**
venir	vengo	**veng-**	**venga**
ver	veo	**ve-**	**vea**

▶ To maintain the **-c, -g,** and **-z** sounds, verbs ending in **-car, -gar,** and **-zar** have a spelling change in all forms of the present subjunctive.

sacar: sa**qu**e, sa**qu**es, sa**qu**e, sa**qu**emos, sa**qu**éis, sa**qu**en

jugar: jue**gu**e, jue**gu**es, jue**gu**e, ju**gu**emos, ju**gu**éis, jue**gu**en

almorzar: almuer**c**e, almuer**c**es, almuer**c**e, almor**c**emos, almor**c**éis, almuer**c**en

Present subjunctive of stem-changing verbs

▶ **-Ar** and **-er** stem-changing verbs have the same stem changes in the subjunctive as they do in the present indicative.

pensar (e:ie): p**ie**nse, p**ie**nses, p**ie**nse, pensemos, penséis, p**ie**nsen

mostrar (o:ue): m**ue**stre, m**ue**stres, m**ue**stre, mostremos, mostréis, m**ue**stren

entender (e:ie): ent**ie**nda, ent**ie**ndas, ent**ie**nda, entendamos, entendáis, ent**ie**ndan

volver (o:ue): v**ue**lva, v**ue**lvas, v**ue**lva, volvamos, volváis, v**ue**lvan

▶ **-Ir** stem-changing verbs have the same stem changes in the subjunctive as they do in the present indicative, but in addition, the **nosotros/as** and **vosotros/as** forms undergo a stem change. The unstressed **e** changes to **i,** while the unstressed **o** changes to **u.**

pedir (e:i): p**i**da, p**i**das, p**i**da, p**i**damos, p**i**dáis, p**i**dan

sentir (e:ie): s**ie**nta, s**ie**ntas, s**ie**nta, s**i**ntamos, s**i**ntáis, s**ie**ntan

dormir (o:ue): d**ue**rma, d**ue**rmas, d**ue**rma, d**u**rmamos, d**u**rmáis, d**ue**rman

Irregular verbs in the present subjunctive

▶ These five verbs are irregular in the present subjunctive.

		dar	estar	ir	saber	ser
SINGULAR FORMS	yo	dé	esté	vaya	sepa	sea
	tú	des	estés	vayas	sepas	seas
	Ud./él/ella	dé	esté	vaya	sepa	sea
PLURAL FORMS	nosotros/as	demos	estemos	vayamos	sepamos	seamos
	vosotros/as	deis	estéis	vayáis	sepáis	seáis
	Uds./ellos/ellas	den	estén	vayan	sepan	sean

▶ **¡Atención!** The subjunctive form of **hay** (_there is, there are_) is also irregular: **haya**.

General uses of the subjunctive

▶ The subjunctive is mainly used to express: 1) will and influence, 2) emotion, 3) doubt, disbelief, and denial, and 4) indefiniteness and nonexistence.

▶ The subjunctive is most often used in sentences that consist of a main clause and a subordinate clause. The main clause contains a verb or expression that triggers the use of the subjunctive. The conjunction **que** connects the subordinate clause to the main clause.

Main clause	Connector	Subordinate clause

Es muy importante que **vayas** al hotel ahora mismo.

▶ These impersonal expressions are always followed by clauses in the subjunctive:

Es bueno que… _It's good that…_	**Es mejor que…** _It's better that…_	**Es malo que…** _It's bad that…_
Es importante que… _It's important that…_	**Es necesario que…** _It's necessary that…_	**Es urgente que…** _It's urgent that…_

 ¡INTÉNTALO! Indica el presente de subjuntivo de estos verbos.

1. (alquilar, beber, vivir) que yo _____ alquile, beba, viva
2. (estudiar, aprender, asistir) que tú _____ estudies, aprendas, asistas
3. (encontrar, poder, tener) que él _____ encuentre, pueda, tenga
4. (hacer, pedir, dormir) que nosotras _____ hagamos, pidamos, durmamos
5. (dar, hablar, escribir) que ellos _____ den, hablen, escriban
6. (pagar, empezar, buscar) que ustedes _____ paguen, empiecen, busquen
7. (ser, ir, saber) que yo _____ sea, vaya, sepa
8. (estar, dar, oír) que tú _____ estés, des, oigas

recursos

WB
pp. 145–146

LM
p. 71

vhlcentral.com
Lección 12

Práctica y Comunicación

1 **Completar** Completa las oraciones con el presente de subjuntivo de los verbos entre paréntesis. Luego empareja las oraciones del primer grupo con las del segundo grupo.

A

1. Es mejor que ___cenemos___ en casa. (nosotros, cenar) __b__
2. Es importante que ___visites___ las casas colgadas de Cuenca. (tú, visitar) __c__
3. Señora, es urgente que le ___saque___ el diente. Tiene una infección. (yo, sacar) __e__
4. Es malo que Ana les ___dé___ tantos dulces a los niños. (dar) __a__
5. Es necesario que ___lleguen___ a la una de la tarde. (ustedes, llegar) __f__
6. Es importante que ___nos acostemos___ temprano. (nosotros, acostarse) __d__

B

a. Es importante que ___coman___ más verduras. (ellos, comer)
b. No, es mejor que ___salgamos___ a comer. (nosotros, salir)
c. Y yo creo que es bueno que ___vaya___ a Madrid después. (yo, ir)
d. En mi opinión, no es necesario que ___durmamos___ tanto. (nosotros, dormir)
e. ¿Ah, sí? ¿Es necesario que me ___tome___ un antibiótico también? (yo, tomar)
f. Para llegar a tiempo, es necesario que ___almorcemos___ temprano. (nosotros, almorzar)

2 **Minidiálogos** En parejas, completen los minidiálogos con expresiones impersonales de una manera lógica. *Answers will vary.*

> **modelo**
>
> **Miguelito:** Mamá, no quiero arreglar mi cuarto.
> **Sra. Casas:** *Es necesario que lo arregles. Y es importante que sacudas los muebles también.*

1. **MIGUELITO** Mamá, no quiero estudiar. Quiero salir a jugar con mis amigos.
 SRA. CASAS _____

2. **MIGUELITO** Mamá, es que no me gustan las verduras. Prefiero comer pasteles.
 SRA. CASAS _____

3. **MIGUELITO** ¿Tengo que poner la mesa, mamá?
 SRA. CASAS _____

4. **MIGUELITO** No me siento bien, mamá. Me duele todo el cuerpo y tengo fiebre.
 SRA. CASAS _____

3 **Entrevista** Trabajen en parejas. Entrevístense usando estas preguntas. Expliquen sus respuestas. *Answers will vary.*

1. ¿Es importante que las personas sepan una segunda lengua? ¿Por qué?
2. ¿Es urgente que los norteamericanos aprendan otras lenguas?
3. Si un(a) norteamericano/a quiere aprender francés, ¿es mejor que lo aprenda en Francia?
4. ¿Es necesario que una persona sepa decir "te amo" en la lengua nativa de su pareja?
5. ¿Es importante que un cantante de ópera entienda italiano?

Practice more at **vhlcentral.com.**

TEACHING OPTIONS

Heritage Speakers Have heritage speakers think of any major social differences between their own cultural communities and mainstream culture. Invite them to share these comparisons with the class using impersonal expressions. Ex: **Aquí, es necesario que llames antes de ir a visitar a un amigo. En mi cultura, es normal que lleguemos sin llamar a la casa de un amigo....**

Small Groups Divide the class into groups of four. Assign each group one of these personal characteristics: **apariencia física, dinero, inteligencia, personalidad.** Have groups use the subjunctive to write a short paragraph about the importance or unimportance of this trait for certain individuals. Ex: **Para ser presidente, es importante que la persona tenga carisma....**

1 **Expansion**

After students have paired the sentences from each group, have them continue a couple of the short conversations with three more sentences using the subjunctive. Ex: **No es posible que encontremos un restaurante con mesas disponibles a las siete. Es mejor que salgamos ahora mismo para no tener ese problema. Sin embargo, es importante que no manejemos muy rápido; no quiero causar un accidente.**

2 **Teaching Tip** To simplify, before assigning the activity, have students brainstorm impersonal expressions that a mother would say to her young son.

2 **Expansion**

• Ask volunteers to share their mini-dialogues with the rest of the class. Encourage them to ad-lib as they go.

• Ask questions about **Miguelito** and his mother. Ex: **Para la señora Casas, ¿es necesario que Miguelito coma pasteles? (No. Es necesario que Miguelito coma las verduras.) ¿Qué quiere Miguelito? (Quiere salir a jugar con sus amigos.)** Have a volunteer explain why the second response does not take the subjunctive. (There isn't a change of subject and **que** is absent.)

3 **Expansion**

Ask students to report on their partner's answers using complete sentences and explanations. Ex: **¿Qué opina _____ sobre los cantantes de ópera? ¿Cree que es importante que entiendan italiano?** Ask follow-up questions as necessary.

Section Goals

In **Estructura 12.4**, students will learn:

• the subjunctive with verbs and expressions of will and influence
• common verbs of will and influence

Instructional Resources

Supersite: Audio (Lab MP3 Files); Resources (*PowerPoints*, Activity Pack, Scripts, Answer Keys); Testing Program (Quizzes)
WebSAM
Workbook, pp. 147–148
Lab Manual, p. 72

Teaching Tips

• Write the word **Recomendaciones** on the board. Ask volunteers for household tips and write them on the board in the infinitive form, followed by the student's name in parentheses. Ex: **hacer todos los quehaceres los sábados** (Paul); **lavar los platos a mano** (Sara) When you have approximately ten suggestions, begin rephrasing them using verbs of will and influence with subordinate clauses. Ex: **Paul nos aconseja que hagamos todos los quehaceres los sábados. Sara recomienda que lavemos los platos a mano.** After you have modeled several responses, ask volunteers to continue. Give them cues such as: **¿Qué sugiere _____?**
• Go through the lists of verbs of will and influence and impersonal expressions that generally take the subjunctive, giving examples of their use.
• Have a volunteer read the advertisement for **Dentabrit** and explain what the subject of each clause is.

12.4 Subjunctive with verbs of will and influence Tutorial

ANTE TODO You will now learn how to use the subjunctive with verbs and expressions of will and influence.

Quiero que tengas dientes más blancos.

▶ Verbs of will and influence are often used when someone wants to affect the actions or behavior of other people.

Enrique **quiere** que salgamos a cenar.
Enrique wants us to go out to dinner.

Paola **prefiere** que cenemos en casa.
Paola prefers that we have dinner at home.

▶ Here is a list of widely used verbs of will and influence.

Verbs of will and influence

aconsejar	*to advise*	**pedir** (e:i)	*to ask (for)*
desear	*to wish; to desire*	**preferir** (e:ie)	*to prefer*
importar	*to be important; to matter*	**prohibir**	*to prohibit*
		querer (e:ie)	*to want*
insistir (en)	*to insist (on)*	**recomendar** (e:ie)	*to recommend*
mandar	*to order*	**rogar** (o:ue)	*to beg; to plead*
necesitar	*to need*	**sugerir** (e:ie)	*to suggest*

▶ Some impersonal expressions, such as **es necesario que, es importante que, es mejor que,** and **es urgente que,** are considered expressions of will or influence.

▶ When the main clause contains an expression of will or influence, the subjunctive is required in the subordinate clause, provided that the two clauses have different subjects.

Main clause ——— Connector ——— Subordinate clause
VERB OF WILL — SUBJUNCTIVE
Mi mamá **prefiere** que yo **saque** la basura.

¡ATENCIÓN!

In English, verbs or expressions of will and influence often use a construction with an infinitive, such as *I want you to go.* This is not the case in Spanish, where the subjunctive would be used in a subordinate clause.

TEACHING OPTIONS

Small Groups Have small groups write nine sentences, each of which uses a different verb of will and influence with the subjunctive. Ask volunteers to write some of their group's best sentences on the board. Work with the class to read the sentences and check for accuracy.

Extra Practice Have students finish these sentence starters. **1.** Yo insisto en que mis amigos… **2.** No quiero que mi familia… **3.** Para mí es importante que el amor… **4.** Prefiero que mi residencia… **5.** Mi novio/a no quiere que yo… **6.** Los profesores siempre recomiendan a los estudiantes que… **7.** El doctor sugiere que nosotros… **8.** Mi madre me ruega que… **9.** El policía manda que los estudiantes… **10.** El fotógrafo prefiere que la gente…

Les sugiero que arreglen este apartamento.

Recomiendo que se organicen en equipos.

▶ Indirect object pronouns are often used with the verbs **aconsejar, importar, mandar, pedir, prohibir, recomendar, rogar,** and **sugerir.**

Te aconsejo que estudies.
I advise you to study.

Le sugiero que vaya a casa.
I suggest that he go home.

Les recomiendo que barran el suelo.
I recommend that you sweep the floor.

Le ruego que no venga.
I'm begging you not to come.

▶ Note that all the forms of **prohibir** in the present tense carry a written accent, except for the **nosotros/as** form: **prohíbo, prohíbes, prohíbe, prohibimos, prohibís, prohíben.**

Ella les **prohíbe** que miren la televisión.
She prohibits them from watching TV.

Nos **prohíben** que nademos en la piscina.
They prohibit that we swim in the swimming pool.

▶ The infinitive is used with words or expressions of will and influence if there is no change of subject in the sentence.

No quiero **sacudir** los muebles.
I don't want to dust the furniture.

Paco prefiere **descansar.**
Paco prefers to rest.

Es importante **sacar** la basura.
It's important to take out the trash.

No es necesario **quitar** la mesa.
It's not necessary to clear the table.

¡INTÉNTALO! Completa cada oración con la forma correcta del verbo entre paréntesis.

1. Te sugiero que __vayas__ (ir) con ella al supermercado.
2. Él necesita que yo le __preste__ (prestar) dinero.
3. No queremos que tú __hagas__ (hacer) nada especial para nosotros.
4. Mis papás quieren que yo __limpie__ (limpiar) mi cuarto.
5. Nos piden que la __ayudemos__ (ayudar) a preparar la comida.
6. Quieren que tú __saques__ (sacar) la basura todos los días.
7. Quiero __descansar__ (descansar) esta noche.
8. Es importante que ustedes __limpien__ (limpiar) los estantes.
9. Su tía les manda que __pongan__ (poner) la mesa.
10. Te aconsejo que no __salgas__ (salir) con él.
11. Mi tío insiste en que mi prima __haga__ (hacer) la cama.
12. Prefiero __ir__ (ir) al cine.
13. Es necesario __estudiar__ (estudiar).
14. Recomiendo que ustedes __pasen__ (pasar) la aspiradora.

recursos

WB
pp. 147–148

LM
p. 72

S
vhlcentral.com
Lección 12

Teaching Tips
• 👥↔👥 Elicit indirect object pronouns with verbs of influence by making statements that give advice and asking students for advice. Ex: **Yo siempre les aconsejo a mis estudiantes que estudien mucho. ¿Qué me recomiendan ustedes a mí?** Continue: **1. Mi coche no arranca cuando hace mucho frío. ¿Qué me recomiendas, _____? 2. Mi apartamento está siempre desordenado. ¿Qué me aconsejan? 3. Voy a tener huéspedes este fin de semana. ¿Qué nos sugieren que hagamos?** Ask follow-up questions as appropriate.
• Write these sentences on the board: **Quiero que almuerces en la cafetería. Quiero almorzar en la cafetería.** Ask a volunteer to explain why an infinitive is used in the second sentence instead of the subjunctive.

TEACHING OPTIONS

Extra Practice Create sentences that follow the pattern of the sentences in ¡Inténtalo! Say the sentence, have students repeat it, then give a different subject pronoun for the subordinate clause, varying the person and number. Have students then say the sentence with the new subject, changing pronouns and verbs as necessary.

TPR Have students stand. At random, call out implied commands using statements with verbs of will or influence and actions that can be mimed. Ex: **Quiero que laves los platos. Insisto en que hagas la cama.** When you make a statement, point to a student to mime the action. Also use plural statements and point to more than one student. When you use negative statements, students should do nothing. Keep a brisk pace.

Práctica

1 Completar Completa el diálogo con verbos de la lista.

cocina	haga	quiere	sea
comas	ponga	saber	ser
diga	prohíbe	sé	vaya

IRENE Tengo problemas con Vilma. Sé que debo hablar con ella. ¿Qué me recomiendas que le (1)___diga___?

JULIA Pues, necesito (2)___saber___ más antes de darte consejos.

IRENE Bueno, para empezar me (3)___prohíbe___ que traiga dulces a la casa.

JULIA Pero chica, tiene razón. Es mejor que tú no (4)___comas___ cosas dulces.

IRENE Sí, ya lo sé. Pero quiero que (5)___sea___ más flexible. Además, insiste en que yo (6)___haga___ todo en la casa.

JULIA Yo (7)___sé___ que Vilma (8)___cocina___ y hace los quehaceres todos los días.

IRENE Sí, pero siempre que hay fiesta me pide que (9)___ponga___ los cubiertos y las copas en la mesa y que (10)___vaya___ al sótano por las servilletas y los platos. ¡Es lo que más odio: ir al sótano!

JULIA Mujer, ¡Vilma sólo (11)___quiere___ que ayudes en la casa!

2 Aconsejar En parejas, lean lo que dice cada persona. Luego den consejos lógicos usando verbos como **aconsejar, recomendar** y **prohibir**. Sus consejos deben ser diferentes de lo que la persona quiere hacer. Answers will vary.

> **modelo**
> **Isabel:** Quiero conseguir un comedor con los muebles más caros del mundo.
> **Consejo:** *Te aconsejamos que consigas unos muebles menos caros.*

1. **DAVID** — Pienso poner el cuadro del lago de Maracaibo en la cocina.
2. **SARA** — Voy en bicicleta a comprar unas copas de cristal.
3. **SR. ALARCÓN** — Insisto en comenzar a arreglar el jardín en marzo.
4. **SRA. VILLA** — Quiero ver las tazas y los platos de la tienda El Ama de Casa Feliz.
5. **DOLORES** — Voy a poner servilletas de tela (*cloth*) para los cuarenta invitados.
6. **SR. PARDO** — Pienso poner todos mis muebles nuevos en el altillo.
7. **SRA. GONZÁLEZ** — Hay una fiesta en casa esta noche, pero no quiero limpiarla.
8. **CARLITOS** — Hoy no tengo ganas de hacer las camas ni de quitar la mesa.

3 Preguntas En parejas, túrnense para contestar las preguntas. Usen el subjuntivo. Answers will vary.

1. ¿Te dan consejos tus amigos/as? ¿Qué te aconsejan? ¿Aceptas sus consejos? ¿Por qué?
2. ¿Qué te sugieren tus profesores que hagas antes de terminar los cursos que tomas?
3. ¿Insisten tus amigos/as en que salgas mucho con ellos?
4. ¿Qué quieres que te regalen tu familia y tus amigos/as en tu cumpleaños?
5. ¿Qué le recomiendas tú a un(a) amigo/a que no quiere salir los sábados con su novio/a?
6. ¿Qué les aconsejas a los nuevos estudiantes de tu universidad?

Practice more at **vhlcentral.com**.

> **NOTA CULTURAL**
>
> En el **lago de Maracaibo,** en Venezuela, hay casas suspendidas sobre el agua que se llaman **palafitos**. Este tipo de construcciones les recordó a los conquistadores la ciudad de Venecia, Italia, de donde viene el nombre "Venezuela", que significa "pequeña Venecia".

Comunicación

4 **Inventar** En parejas, preparen una lista de seis personas famosas. Un(a) estudiante da el nombre de una persona famosa y el/la otro/a le da un consejo. *Answers will vary.*

> **modelo**
>
> **Estudiante 1:** Judge Judy.
> **Estudiante 2:** Le recomiendo que sea más simpática con la gente.
> **Estudiante 2:** Orlando Bloom.
> **Estudiante 1:** Le aconsejo que haga más películas.

5 **Hablar** En parejas, miren la ilustración. Imaginen que Gerardo es su hermano y necesita ayuda para arreglar su casa y resolver sus problemas románticos y económicos. Usen expresiones impersonales y verbos como **aconsejar, sugerir** y **recomendar**. *Answers will vary.*

> **modelo**
>
> Es mejor que arregles el apartamento más a menudo.
> Te aconsejo que no dejes para mañana lo que puedes hacer hoy.

Síntesis

6 **La doctora Salvamórez** Hernán tiene problemas con su novia y le escribe a la doctora Salvamórez, columnista del periódico *Panamá y su gente*. Ella responde a las cartas de personas con problemas románticos. En parejas, lean el mensaje de Hernán y después usen el subjuntivo para escribir los consejos de la doctora. *Answers will vary.*

> Estimada doctora Salvamórez:
>
> Mi novia nunca quiere que yo salga de casa. No le molesta que vengan mis amigos a visitarme. Pero insiste en que nosotros sólo miremos los programas de televisión que ella quiere. Necesita saber dónde estoy en cada momento, y yo necesito que ella me dé un poco de independencia. ¿Qué hago?
>
> Hernán

4 Teaching Tip Ask volunteers to read the **modelo** aloud and provide other suggestions for Judge Judy and Orlando Bloom.

4 Expansion Ask each pair to pick its favorite response and share it with the class, who will vote for the most clever, shocking, or humorous suggestion.

5 Teaching Tips
• Use the **Lección 12 Estructura** overheads to assist with the presentation of this activity.
• Ask volunteers to describe the drawing, naming everything they see and all the chores that need to be done.

5 Expansion Have students change partners and take turns playing the roles of **Gerardo** and his sibling giving him advice. Ex: **Te sugiero que pongas la pizza en la basura....**

6 Expansion
• Have pairs compare their responses in groups of four. Ask groups to choose which among all of the suggestions are the most likely to work for **Hernán** and have them share these with the class.
• Have pairs choose a famous couple in history or fiction. Ex: Elizabeth Bennet and Mr. Darcy or Napoleon and Josephine. Then have them write a letter from one of the couples to **doctora Salvamórez**. Finally, have them exchange their letters with another pair and write the corresponding responses from the doctor.

Section Goal

In **Recapitulación**, students will review the grammar concepts from this lesson.

Instructional Resource
Supersite

1 Expansion Give students additional verbs to conjugate in the subjunctive. Ex: **comer, dar, estar, saber, traer.**

2 Expansion
• Have volunteers take turns reading aloud portions of the brochure.
• To challenge students, ask them to work in pairs to write four pieces of advice for a real estate agent, using impersonal expressions. Ex: **Es importante que sea honesto....** Have a few pairs read their sentences for the class.

Extra Practice
On note cards or sticky notes, write names of well-known characters from literature, film, or television. Making sure that students do not see the name assigned to them, stick a note on the back of each student's shirt. Have students circulate around the room, giving each other hints about the identity of their characters, using the subjunctive. Tell students to be sure to use only the present tense in the main clause. Ex: **Tu madre dice que es importante que te cases con el conde París. / Tu novio te pide que te cases con él en secreto. / Deseas que toda tu familia crea que estás muerta. (Julieta Capuleto)**

Recapitulación

Concepts Diagnostics

Completa estas actividades para repasar los conceptos de gramática que aprendiste en esta lección.

1 Completar Completa el cuadro con la forma correspondiente del presente de subjuntivo. **12 pts.**

yo/él/ella	tú	nosotros/as	Uds./ellos/ellas
limpie	limpies	limpiemos	limpien
venga	**vengas**	vengamos	vengan
quiera	quieras	**queramos**	quieran
ofrezca	ofrezcas	ofrezcamos	**ofrezcan**

2 El apartamento ideal Completa este folleto (*brochure*) informativo con la forma correcta del presente de subjuntivo. **8 pts.**

> ### ¿Eres joven y buscas tu primera vivienda? Te ofrezco estos consejos:
>
> ■ Te sugiero que primero (tú) (1) __escribas__ (escribir) una lista de las cosas que quieres en un apartamento.
>
> ■ Quiero que después (2) __pienses__ (pensar) muy bien cuáles son tus prioridades. Es necesario que cada persona (3) __tenga__ (tener) sus prioridades claras, porque el hogar (*home*) perfecto no existe.
>
> ■ Antes de decidir en qué área quieren vivir, les aconsejo a ti y a tu futuro/a compañero/a de apartamento que (4) __salgan__ (salir) a ver la ciudad y que (5) __conozcan__ (conocer) los distintos barrios y las afueras.
>
> ■ Pidan que el agente les (6) __muestre__ (mostrar) todas las partes de cada casa.
>
> ■ Finalmente, como consumidores, es importante que nosotros (7) __sepamos__ (saber) bien nuestros derechos (*rights*); por eso, deben insistir en que todos los puntos del contrato (8) __estén__ (estar) muy claros antes de firmarlo (*signing it*).
>
> ### ¡Buena suerte!

RESUMEN GRAMATICAL

12.1 Relative pronouns *pp. 386–387*

Relative pronouns	
que	*that; which; who*
quien(es)	*who; whom; that*
lo que	*that which; what*

12.2 Formal commands *pp. 390–391*

Formal commands (Ud. and Uds.)		
Infinitive	**Present tense yo form**	**Ud(s). command**
limpiar	limpi**o**	limpi**e(n)**
barrer	barr**o**	barr**a(n)**
sacudir	sacud**o**	sacud**a(n)**

► Verbs with stem changes or irregular **yo** forms maintain the same irregularity in the formal commands:

hacer: yo ha**go** → Ha**g**an la cama.

Irregular formal commands	
dar	dé (Ud.); den (Uds.)
estar	esté(n)
ir	vaya(n)
saber	sepa(n)
ser	sea(n)

12.3 The present subjunctive *pp. 394–396*

Present subjunctive of regular verbs		
hablar	**comer**	**escribir**
habl**e**	com**a**	escrib**a**
habl**es**	com**as**	escrib**as**
habl**e**	com**a**	escrib**a**
habl**emos**	com**amos**	escrib**amos**
habl**éis**	com**áis**	escrib**áis**
habl**en**	com**an**	escrib**an**

3 **Relativos** Completa las oraciones con **lo que**, **que** o **quien**. [8 pts.]

1. Me encanta la alfombra __que__ está en el comedor.
2. Mi amiga Tere, con __quien__ trabajo, me regaló ese cuadro.
3. Todas las cosas __que__ tenemos vienen de la casa de mis abuelos.
4. Hija, no compres más cosas. __Lo que__ debes hacer ahora es organizarlo todo.
5. La agencia de decoración de __que__ le hablé se llama Casabella.
6. Esas flores las dejaron en la puerta mis nuevos vecinos, a __quienes__ aún (*yet*) no conozco.
7. Leonor no compró nada, porque __lo que__ le gustaba era muy caro.
8. Mi amigo Aldo, a __quien__ visité ayer, es un cocinero excelente.

Irregular verbs in the present subjunctive		
dar		dé, des, dé, demos, deis, den
estar	est- +	-é, -és, -é, -emos, -éis, -én
ir	vay- +	
saber	sep- +	-a, -as, -a, -amos, -áis, -an
ser	se- +	

12.4 **Subjuntive with verbs of will and influence**
pp. 398–399

▶ Verbs of will and influence: **aconsejar, desear, importar, insistir (en), mandar, necesitar, pedir** (e:i), **preferir** (e:ie), **prohibir, querer** (e:ie), **recomendar** (e:ie), **rogar** (o:ue), **sugerir** (e:ie)

4 **Preparando la casa** Martín y Ángela van a hacer un curso de verano en Costa Rica y una vecina va a cuidarles (*take care of*) la casa mientras ellos no están. Completa las instrucciones de la vecina con mandatos formales. Usa cada verbo una sola vez y agrega pronombres de objeto directo o indirecto si es necesario. [10 pts.]

arreglar	dejar	hacer	pedir	sacudir
barrer	ensuciar	limpiar	poner	tener

Primero, (1) __hagan__ ustedes las maletas. Las cosas que no se llevan a Costa Rica, (2) __pónganlas__ en el altillo. Ángela, (3) __arregle/limpie__ las habitaciones y Martín, (4) __limpie/arregle__ usted la cocina y el baño. Después, los dos (5) __barran__ el suelo y (6) __sacudan__ los muebles de toda la casa. Ángela, no (7) __deje__ sus joyas (*jewelry*) en el apartamento. (8) __Tengan__ cuidado ¡y no (9) __ensucien__ nada antes de irse! Por último, (10) __pídanle__ a alguien que recoja (*pick up*) su correo.

5 **Los quehaceres** A tu compañero/a de cuarto no le gusta ayudar con los quehaceres. Escribe al menos seis oraciones dándole consejos para hacer más divertidos los quehaceres. [12 pts.]

Answers will vary.

modelo
Te sugiero que pongas música mientras lavas los platos…

6 **El circo** Completa esta famosa frase que tiene su origen en el circo (*circus*). [¡2 puntos EXTRA!]

" ¡ __Pasen__ (Pasar) ustedes y __vean__ (ver)! El espectáculo va a comenzar. "

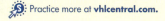 Practice more at **vhlcentral.com**.

3 **Teaching Tip** Have students circle the noun or idea to which each relative pronoun refers.

3 **Expansion**
• Ask volunteers to give the corresponding questions for each item. Ex: **1. ¿Qué alfombra te encanta?**
• Have students work in pairs to create four additional sentences using relative pronouns.

4 **Teaching Tips**
• To simplify, have students begin by scanning the paragraph and identifying which blanks call for **usted** commands and which call for **ustedes** commands.
• Tell students that some answers will contain object pronouns (items 2 and 10).

5 **Teaching Tip**
👥↔️👥 Before beginning this activity, have pairs discuss their own habits regarding chores.

5 **Expansion** Have students imagine they have two roommates and ask them to rewrite their sentences using **ustedes** commands.

6 **Expansion** To challenge students, ask them to write two **ustedes** commands for people attending a circus and one **usted** command for the master of ceremonies.

TEACHING OPTIONS

Extra Practice Call out formal commands. Ex: **Sacudan los muebles.** Have students respond by naming the infinitive and subject. Ex: **sacudir, ustedes.** Reverse the drill by calling out verb phrases and either **usted** or **ustedes.** Have students give the command form.
Large Groups Review present subjunctive and vocabulary from previous lessons. Divide the class into two teams and have

them line up. Name a person or group of people. Ex: **estudiantes de informática, Miley Cyrus, un niño en su primer día de la escuela primaria.** Then point to the first member of team A, who has three seconds to create a piece of advice. Ex: **Quiero que apaguen las computadoras.** Then the first member of team B has to give another sentence. Continue until the chain is broken, then name a new person.

Section Goals

In **Lectura**, students will:
- learn to locate the main parts of a sentence
- read a content-rich text with long sentences

Instructional Resource
Supersite

Estrategia Tell students that if they have trouble reading long sentences in Spanish, they should pause to identify the main verb of the sentence and its subject. They should then reread the entire sentence.

Examinar el texto Students should see from the layout (cover page with title, photo, and phone numbers; interior pages with an introduction and several headings followed by short paragraphs) that this is a brochure. Revealing cognates are: **información** (cover) and **residencia oficial del Presidente de Panamá** (introduction).

¿Probable o improbable? Ask volunteers to read aloud each item and give the answer. Have a volunteer rephrase the improbable statement so that it is probable.

Oraciones largas Ask pairs to create a couple of long sentences. Have them point out the main verb and subject.

Lectura

NATIONAL communication cultures STANDARDS

Antes de leer

Estrategia

Locating the main parts of a sentence

Did you know that a text written in Spanish is an average of 15% longer than the same text written in English? Since the Spanish language tends to use more words to express ideas, you will often encounter long sentences when reading in Spanish. Of course, the length of sentences varies with genre and with authors' individual styles. To help you understand long sentences, identify the main parts of the sentence before trying to read it in its entirety. First locate the main verb of the sentence, along with its subject, ignoring any words or phrases set off by commas. Then reread the sentence, adding details like direct and indirect objects, transitional words, and prepositional phrases.

Examinar el texto

Mira el formato de la lectura. ¿Qué tipo de documento es? ¿Qué cognados encuentras en la lectura? ¿Qué te dicen sobre el tema de la selección?

¿Probable o improbable?

Mira brevemente el texto e indica si estas oraciones son probables o improbables.

1. Este folleto° es de interés turístico. probable
2. Describe un edificio moderno cubano. improbable
3. Incluye algunas explicaciones de arquitectura. probable
4. Espera atraer° a visitantes al lugar. probable

Oraciones largas

Mira el texto y busca algunas oraciones largas. Con un(a) compañero/a, identifiquen las partes principales de la oración y después examinen las descripciones adicionales. ¿Qué significan las oraciones?

folleto *brochure* atraer *to attract* épocas *time periods*

Bienvenidos al Palacio de las Garzas

El palacio está abierto de martes a domingo.
Para más información,
llame al teléfono 507-226-7000.
También puede solicitar° un folleto
a la casilla° 3467,
Ciudad de Panamá, Panamá.

Después de leer

Ordenar

Pon estos eventos en el orden cronológico adecuado.

- 3 El palacio se convirtió en residencia presidencial.
- 2 Durante diferentes épocas°, maestros, médicos y banqueros ejercieron su profesión en el palacio.
- 4 El Dr. Belisario Porras ocupó el palacio por primera vez.
- 1 Los españoles construyeron el palacio.
- 5 Se renovó el palacio.
- 6 Los turistas pueden visitar el palacio de martes a domingo.

Practice more at **vhlcentral.com.**

TEACHING OPTIONS

Heritage Speakers ←👥→ Ask heritage speakers to give a brief presentation about a famous government building in their family's home country. Tell them to include recommendations about what rooms and objects are particularly noteworthy and should not be missed. If possible, they should illustrate their presentation with photographs or brochures.

Extra Practice ←👥→ Ask students to write ten statements using the subjunctive to describe their dream house (**la casa de mis sueños**). Ex: **Para mí es importante que haya una piscina de tamaño olímpico en la casa de mis sueños. Recomiendo que la cocina sea grande porque me gusta cocinar. Es necesario que tenga varios dormitorios porque siempre tengo huéspedes.** Have students share their sentences with a partner.

El Palacio de las Garzas° es la residencia oficial del Presidente de Panamá desde 1903. Fue construido en 1673 para ser la casa de un gobernador español. Con el paso de los años fue almacén, escuela, hospital, aduana, banco y por último, palacio presidencial.

En la actualidad el edificio tiene tres pisos, pero los planos originales muestran una construcción de un piso con un gran patio en el centro. La restauración del palacio comenzó en el año 1922 y los trabajos fueron realizados por el arquitecto Villanueva-Myers y el pintor Roberto Lewis. El palacio, un monumento al estilo colonial, todavía conserva su elegancia y buen gusto, y es una de las principales atracciones turísticas del barrio Casco Viejo°.

Planta baja

EL PATIO DE LAS GARZAS

Una antigua puerta de hierro° recibe a los visitantes. El patio interior todavía conserva los elementos originales de la construcción: piso de mármol°, columnas cubiertas° de nácar° y una magnífica fuente° de agua en el centro. Aquí están las nueve garzas que le dan el nombre al palacio y que representan las nueve provincias de Panamá.

Primer piso

EL SALÓN AMARILLO

Aquí el turista puede visitar una galería de cuarenta y un retratos° de gobernadores y personajes ilustres de Panamá. La principal atracción de este salón es el sillón presidencial, que se usa especialmente cuando hay cambio de presidente. Otros atractivos de esta área son el comedor Los Tamarindos, que se destaca° por la elegancia de sus muebles y sus lámparas de cristal, y el Patio Andaluz, con sus coloridos mosaicos que representan la unión de la cultura indígena y la española.

EL SALÓN DR. BELISARIO PORRAS

Este elegante y majestuoso salón es uno de los lugares más importantes del Palacio de las Garzas. Lleva su nombre en honor al Dr. Belisario Porras, quien fue tres veces presidente de Panamá (1912–1916, 1918–1920 y 1920–1924).

Segundo piso

Es el área residencial del palacio y el visitante no tiene acceso a ella. Los armarios, las cómodas y los espejos de la alcoba fueron comprados en Italia y Francia por el presidente Porras, mientras que las alfombras, cortinas y frazadas° son originarias de España.

solicitar *request* casilla *post office box* Garzas *Herons* Casco Viejo *Old Quarter*
hierro *iron* mármol *marble* cubiertas *covered* nácar *mother-of-pearl*
fuente *fountain* retratos *portraits* se destaca *stands out* frazadas *blankets*

Preguntas

Contesta las preguntas.

1. ¿Qué sala es notable por sus muebles elegantes y sus lámparas de cristal? el comedor Los Tamarindos
2. ¿En qué parte del palacio se encuentra la residencia del presidente? en el segundo piso
3. ¿Dónde empiezan los turistas su visita al palacio? en el Patio de las Garzas
4. ¿En qué lugar se representa artísticamente la rica herencia cultural de Panamá? en el Patio Andaluz
5. ¿Qué salón honra la memoria de un gran panameño? el Salón Dr. Belisario Porras
6. ¿Qué partes del palacio te gustaría (*would you like*) visitar? ¿Por qué? Explica tu respuesta. Answers will vary.

Conversación

En grupos de tres o cuatro estudiantes, hablen sobre lo siguiente: Answers will vary.

1. ¿Qué tiene en común el Palacio de las Garzas con otras residencias presidenciales u otras casas muy grandes?
2. ¿Te gustaría vivir en el Palacio de las Garzas? ¿Por qué?
3. Imagina que puedes diseñar tu palacio ideal. Describe los planos para cada piso del palacio.

Escritura

Estrategia

Using linking words

You can make your writing sound more sophisticated by using linking words to connect simple sentences or ideas and create more complex sentences. Consider these passages, which illustrate this effect:

Without linking words

En la actualidad el edificio tiene tres pisos. Los planos originales muestran una construcción de un piso con un gran patio en el centro. La restauración del palacio comenzó en el año 1922. Los trabajos fueron realizados por el arquitecto Villanueva-Myers y el pintor Roberto Lewis.

With linking words

En la actualidad el edificio tiene tres pisos, pero los planos originales muestran una construcción de un piso con un gran patio en el centro. La restauración del palacio comenzó en el año 1922 y los trabajos fueron realizados por el arquitecto Villanueva-Myers y el pintor Roberto Lewis.

Linking words	
cuando	when
mientras	while
o	or
pero	but
porque	because
pues	since
que	that; who; which
quien(es)	who
sino	but (rather)
y	and

Tema

Escribir un contrato de arrendamiento°

Eres el/la administrador(a)° de un edificio de apartamentos. Prepara un contrato de arrendamiento para los nuevos inquilinos°. El contrato debe incluir estos detalles:

▶ la dirección° del apartamento y del/de la administrador(a)
▶ las fechas del contrato
▶ el precio del alquiler y el día que se debe pagar
▶ el precio del depósito
▶ información y reglas° acerca de:
 la basura
 el correo
 los animales domésticos
 el ruido°
 los servicios de electricidad y agua
 el uso de electrodomésticos
▶ otros aspectos importantes de la vida comunitaria

contrato de arrendamiento *lease* administrador(a) *manager* inquilinos *tenants*
dirección *address* reglas *rules* ruido *noise*

EVALUATION: Contrato

Criteria	Scale
Content	1 2 3 4
Organization	1 2 3 4
Use of vocabulary	1 2 3 4
Use of linking words	1 2 3 4
Grammatical accuracy	1 2 3 4

Scoring	
Excellent	18–20 points
Good	14–17 points
Satisfactory	10–13 points
Unsatisfactory	< 10 points

Escuchar Audio: Activities

Preparación

Mira el dibujo. ¿Qué pistas te da para comprender la conversación que vas a escuchar? ¿Qué significa *bienes raíces*?

Ahora escucha

Mira los anuncios de esta página y escucha la conversación entre el señor Núñez, Adriana y Felipe. Luego indica si cada descripción se refiere a la casa ideal de Adriana y Felipe, a la casa del anuncio o al apartamento del anuncio.

Frases	La casa ideal	La casa del anuncio	El apartamento del anuncio
Es barato.	___	___	✔
Tiene cuatro alcobas.	___	✔	___
Tiene una oficina.	✔	___	___
Tiene un balcón.	___	___	✔
Tiene una cocina moderna.	___	✔	___
Tiene un jardín muy grande.	___	✔	___
Tiene un patio.	✔	___	___

18G

Bienes raíces

Se vende.
4 alcobas, 3 baños, cocina moderna, jardín con árboles frutales.
B/. 225.000

Se alquila.
2 alcobas, 1 baño. Balcón.
Urbanización Las Brisas. B/. 525

Comprensión

Preguntas

1. ¿Cuál es la relación entre el señor Núñez, Adriana y Felipe? ¿Cómo lo sabes? El Sr. Núñez es el padre de Adriana y Felipe es su esposo.

2. ¿Qué diferencia de opinión hay entre Adriana y Felipe sobre dónde quieren vivir? Felipe prefiere vivir en la ciudad, pero Adriana quiere vivir en las afueras.

3. Usa la información de los dibujos y la conversación para entender lo que dice Adriana al final. ¿Qué significa "todo a su debido tiempo"? Answers will vary.

Conversación

En parejas, túrnense para hacer y responder a las preguntas. Answers will vary.

1. ¿Qué tienen en común el apartamento y la casa del anuncio con el lugar donde tú vives?

2. ¿Qué piensas de la recomendación del señor Núñez?

3. ¿Qué tipo de sugerencias te da tu familia sobre dónde vivir?

4. ¿Dónde prefieres vivir tú, en un apartamento o en una casa? Explica por qué.

 Practice more at **vhlcentral.com**.

En pantalla

Anuncio

En los países hispanos el costo del servicio de electricidad y de los electrodomésticos es muy caro. Es por eso que no es muy común tener muchos electrodomésticos. Por ejemplo, en los lugares donde hace mucho calor, mucha gente no tiene aire acondicionado°; utiliza los ventiladores°, que usan menos electricidad. Muchas personas lavan la ropa a mano o barren el piso en vez de usar una lavadora o una aspiradora.

Vocabulario útil

mascota	*pet*
un poco asustado	*a bit scared*
suavizante	*(fabric) softener*
suavizar	*to soften*

Preparación

¿Lavas tu ropa, cocinas, barres? ¿Te piden que hagas algunos quehaceres domésticos en casa? Answers will vary.

Preguntas

Contesta estas preguntas.

1. ¿Qué le encanta al osito (*little bear*) *Softy*?
 A *Softy* le encanta la ropa suave.
2. ¿Por qué se lastimó cuando se cayó sobre las toallas?
 Porque la mujer no usó un suavizante de buena calidad.
3. Según el anuncio, ¿qué es lo que un suavizante barato no puede hacer? No puede suavizar tan bien como uno de buena calidad.
4. ¿Cómo se siente *Softy* cuando llega el médico: tranquilo o asustado? Se siente asustado.
5. ¿Qué le recomienda el médico a la mujer? Que use siempre Comfort.

Consejos

Cuando la mujer visita a *Softy* en el hospital, el médico le da consejos y órdenes sobre cómo tratar a su mascota. En parejas, preparen una lista de los consejos y órdenes que el médico le da. Usen el subjuntivo y el imperativo.
Answers will vary.

aire acondicionado *air conditioning* ventiladores *fans*

¡Hola! Soy *Softy* y me encanta la ropa suave.

¡Ay, mi brazo!

Si usted quiere a su mascota, tiene que usar siempre Comfort.

(S) **Video: TV Clip**

(S) Practice more at **vhlcentral.com**.

Cortometraje

La burocracia puede ser complicada y frustrante, con sus reglas° y su jerarquía impenetrables. En *036* vemos cómo una chica española llega a una oficina del gobierno preparada para presentar° todos los documentos necesarios para hacerse trabajadora autónoma. La chica "se bate en duelo°" con el oficinista° como si se tratara de° una película del Lejano Oeste°. Él cree que ella no tiene todos los documentos, pero la chica sabe lo que hace.

 ### Preparación

En parejas, contesten estas preguntas. *Answers will vary.*

1. ¿Qué es la burocracia?
2. ¿En qué tipo de oficinas es común?
3. ¿En qué circunstancias es necesario presentar documentos?

Después de ver

Completa cada oración con una palabra de la lista.

un café	ganas	el impreso
la determinación	una grapadora	la oficina

1. Cuando llega la chica a ___la oficina___, un chico sale frustrado.
2. El oficinista se sirve ___un café___ antes de dejarla hablar.
3. El oficinista no tiene ___ganas___ de ayudarla.
4. ___La determinación___ de la chica es más fuerte que la del oficinista.
5. Al final la chica sorprende a todos cuando saca ___una grapadora___.

 ### Conversar

Entrevista a un(a) compañero/a y pregúntale cuándo tuvo que confrontarse con la burocracia. ¿Qué sucedió? Comparen sus experiencias con la de la chica del cortometraje. *Answers will vary.*

Carolina Bang
Tomás del Estal

036

un corto de Juan Fernando Andrés Parrilla y Esteban Roel García Vázquez

Expresiones útiles

la casilla	*box (on a form)*
cumplimentar	*to fill out*
el DNI	Documento Nacional de Identidad
darse de alta	*to register*
grapado/a	*stapled*
la Hacienda	*IRS equivalent in Spain*
el impreso	*form*
el/la trabajador(a) autónomo/a	*self-employed worker*

Para hablar del corto

desafiar	*to challenge*
la grapadora	*stapler*
perseverar	*to persevere*
sellar	*to stamp*
terco/a	*stubborn*

 Video: Short Film

Practice more at vistas.vhlcentral.com.

reglas *rules* presentar *submit* se bate en duelo *fights a duel* oficinista *office worker* como si se tratara de *as if it were* Lejano Oeste *Wild West*

Section Goal

In **Panorama**, students will read about the geography and culture of Panama.

Instructional Resources

Supersite/DVD: *Panorama cultural*
Supersite: Resources (Scripts, Translations, *PowerPoints*, Answer Keys)
WebSAM
Workbook, pp. 149–150
Video Manual, pp. 251–252

Teaching Tips

• Use the **Lección 12 Panorama** overheads to assist with this presentation.

• Have students look at the map of Panama and discuss the physical features of the country. Point out the bodies of water that run along the coasts of Panama, and the canal that cuts through the isthmus (**istmo**). Then, have students look at the call-out photos and read the captions. Point out that the Kuna live on the San Blas Islands in the Caribbean Sea.

El país en cifras

Mention that the national currency, the balboa, is named for **Vasco Núñez de Balboa**, who explored the Isthmus of Panama in 1501. Tell students that **chibcha** is a major indigenous language group, with dialects spoken by people from central Colombia through eastern Nicaragua. After reading about the **Panameños célebres**, ask students to share what they know about the individuals.

¡Increíble pero cierto!

The opening of the Panama Canal not only dramatically reduced the distance ships had to travel to get from the Atlantic Ocean to the Pacific, it also provided a much safer route than the stormy, perilous route around Cape Horn and through the Straits of Magellan.

Panamá

NATIONAL connections cultures STANDARDS

El país en cifras

▶ **Área:** 78.200 km² (30.193 millas²), *aproximadamente el área de Carolina del Sur*

▶ **Población:** 3.773.000

▶ **Capital:** La Ciudad de Panamá —1.527.000

▶ **Ciudades principales:** Colón, David

SOURCE: Population Division, UN Secretariat

▶ **Moneda:** balboa; es equivalente al dólar estadounidense.
En Panamá circulan los billetes de dólar estadounidense. El país centroamericano, sin embargo, acuña° su propia moneda. "El peso" es una moneda grande equivalente a cincuenta centavos°. La moneda de cinco centavos es llamada frecuentemente "real".

▶ **Idiomas:** español (oficial), lenguas indígenas, inglés
Muchos panameños son bilingües. La lengua materna del 14% de los panameños es el inglés.

Bandera de Panamá

Panameños célebres

▶ **Mariano Rivera,** beisbolista (1969–)

▶ **Mireya Moscoso,** política (1946–)

▶ **Rubén Blades,** músico y político (1948–)

acuña *mints* centavos *cents*
peaje *toll* promedio *average*

recursos
WB pp. 149–150 | VM pp. 251–252 | (S) vhlcentral.com Lección 12

Mujer kuna lavando una mola

Un turista disfruta del bosque tropical colgado de un cable.

COSTA RICA
Lago Gatún
Canal de Panamá
Bocas del Toro
Mar Caribe
Colón
Islas San Blas
Cordillera de San Blas
Río Chepo
Serranía de Tabasará
David
Ciudad de Panamá
Océano Pacífico
Río Cobre
Isla del Rey
Isla de Coiba
Golfo de Panamá

ESTADOS UNIDOS
OCÉANO ATLÁNTICO
PANAMÁ
AMÉRICA DEL SUR

Ruinas de un fuerte panameño

¡Increíble pero cierto!

¿Conocías estos datos sobre el Canal de Panamá?

• Gracias al Canal de Panamá, el viaje en barco de Nueva York a Tokio es 3.000 millas más corto.

• Su construcción costó 639 millones de dólares.

• Hoy lo usan en promedio 39 barcos al día.

• El peaje° promedio° cuesta 54.000 dólares.

Tokio
Nueva York
PANAMÁ

Lugares • El Canal de Panamá

El Canal de Panamá conecta el océano Pacífico con el océano Atlántico. La construcción de este cauce° artificial empezó en 1903 y concluyó diez años después. Es una de las principales fuentes° de ingresos° del país, gracias al dinero que aportan los más de 14.000 buques° que transitan anualmente por esta ruta y a las actividades comerciales que se han desarrollado° en torno a° ella.

Artes • La mola

La mola es una forma de arte textil de los kunas, una tribu indígena que vive principalmente en las islas San Blas. Esta pieza artesanal se confecciona con fragmentos de tela° de colores vivos. Algunos de sus diseños son abstractos, inspirados en las formas del coral, y otros son geométricos, como en las molas más tradicionales. Antiguamente, estos tejidos se usaban sólo como ropa, pero hoy día también sirven para decorar las casas.

Naturaleza • El mar

Panamá, cuyo° nombre significa "lugar de muchos peces°", es un país muy frecuentado por los aficionados del buceo y la pesca. El territorio panameño cuenta con una gran variedad de playas en los dos lados del istmo°, con el mar Caribe a un lado y el océano Pacífico al otro. Algunas zonas costeras están destinadas al turismo. Otras están protegidas por la diversidad de su fauna marina, en la que abundan los arrecifes° de coral, como el Parque Nacional Marino Isla Bastimentos.

COLOMBIA

 ¿Qué aprendiste? Responde a cada pregunta con una oración completa.

1. ¿Cuál es la lengua materna del catorce por ciento de los panameños?
 El inglés es la lengua materna del catorce por ciento de los panameños.
2. ¿A qué unidad monetaria (*monetary unit*) es equivalente el balboa?
 El balboa es equivalente al dólar estadounidense.
3. ¿Qué océanos une el Canal de Panamá?
 El Canal de Panamá une los océanos Atlántico y Pacífico.
4. ¿Quién es Mariano Rivera?
 Mariano Rivera es un beisbolista panameño.
5. ¿Qué son las molas?
 Las molas son una forma de arte textil de los kunas.
6. ¿Cómo son los diseños de las molas?
 Algunos diseños son abstractos y otros son geométricos.
7. ¿Para qué se usan las molas?
 Las molas se usan como ropa y para decorar las casas.
8. ¿Cómo son las playas de Panamá?
 Son muy variadas; unas están destinadas al turismo, otras tienen valor ecológico.
9. ¿Qué significa "Panamá"?
 "Panamá" significa "lugar de muchos peces".

Vista de la Ciudad de Panamá

 Conexión Internet Investiga estos temas en **vhlcentral.com**.

1. Investiga la historia de las relaciones entre Panamá y los Estados Unidos y la decisión de devolver (*give back*) el Canal de Panamá. ¿Estás de acuerdo con la decisión? Explica tu opinión.
2. Investiga sobre los kunas u otro grupo indígena de Panamá. ¿En qué partes del país viven? ¿Qué lenguas hablan? ¿Cómo es su cultura?

 Practice more at **vhlcentral.com**.

cauce *channel* fuentes *sources* ingresos *income* buques *ships* han desarrollado *have developed* en torno a *around* tela *fabric* cuyo *whose* peces *fish* istmo *isthmus* arrecifes *reefs*

El Salvador

El país en cifras

▸ **Área:** 21.040 km² (8.124 millas²), el tamaño° de Massachusetts
▸ **Población:** 6.383.000

El Salvador es el país centroamericano más pequeño y el más densamente poblado°. Su población, al igual que la de Honduras, es muy homogénea: casi el 90 por ciento es mestiza.

▸ **Capital:** San Salvador—1.691.000
▸ **Ciudades principales:** Soyapango, Santa Ana, San Miguel, Mejicanos

SOURCE: Population Division, UN Secretariat

▸ **Moneda:** dólar estadounidense
▸ **Idiomas:** español (oficial), náhuatl, lenca

Bandera de El Salvador

Salvadoreños célebres

▸ **Óscar Romero,** arzobispo° y activista por los derechos humanos° (1917–1980)
▸ **Claribel Alegría,** poeta, novelista y cuentista (1924–)
▸ **Roque Dalton,** poeta, ensayista y novelista (1935–1975)
▸ **María Eugenia Brizuela,** política (1956–)

Óscar Romero

tamaño *size* poblado *populated* arzobispo *archbishop*
derechos humanos *human rights* laguna *lagoon* sirena *mermaid*

¡Increíble pero cierto!

El rico folclor salvadoreño se basa sobre todo en sus extraordinarios recursos naturales. Por ejemplo, según una leyenda, las muertes que se producen en la laguna° de Alegría tienen su explicación en la existencia de una sirena° solitaria que vive en el lago y captura a los jóvenes atractivos.

Ruinas de Tazumal

Catedral Metropolitana de San Salvador

GUATEMALA

HONDURAS

Lago de Guija
Río de la Paz
Santa Ana
Mejicanos
Volcán de San Salvador
San Salvador
Soyapango
Río Lempa
Ilobasco
Río Torola
Volcán de San Vicente
Río Goascorán
La Libertad
Volcán de San Miguel
San Miguel
Océano Pacífico
Golfo de Fonseca

Chorros de la Calera en Juayúa

ESTADOS UNIDOS
OCÉANO ATLÁNTICO
EL SALVADOR
OCÉANO PACÍFICO
AMÉRICA DEL SUR

recursos
WB pp. 151–152 | VM pp. 253–254 | vhlcentral.com Lección 12

Section Goal

In **Panorama**, students will read about the geography and culture of El Salvador.

Instructional Resources

Supersite/DVD: *Panorama cultural*
Supersite: Resources (Scripts, Translations, *PowerPoints*, Answer Keys)
WebSAM
Workbook, pp. 151–152
Video Manual, pp. 253–254

Teaching Tips

• Use the **Lección 12 Panorama** overheads to assist with this presentation.
• Have students look at the map of El Salvador.
• Draw students' attention to the number of active volcanoes in El Salvador. Tell students that because of the fertility of El Salvador's volcanic soil, the country has a strong agricultural sector. Have students look at the inset map as you point out that El Salvador is the only Central American country without coastline on the Gulf of Mexico. Look at the photos and ask volunteers to read the captions.

El país en cifras In the early 1970s, El Salvador's overpopulation, chronic economic problems, and lack of social justice resulted in social disturbances that the government put down with brutal force.

¡Increíble pero cierto! In the town of Concepción de Ataco, another legend claims that on the **Cerro la Empalizada** there is a cave containing plants that disorient anyone who steps on them.

TEACHING OPTIONS

Worth Noting Government repression in El Salvador intensified resistance, and by the mid-1970s a civil war was being fought between government forces and the **FMLN,** an armed guerrilla movement. Among the many martyrs of the war was the Archbishop of San Salvador, **Óscar Romero.** A descendent of the privileged class in El Salvador, **Romero** came to champion the cause of peace and social justice for the poor. This position made him the target of reactionary elements. On March 24, 1980, Archbishop **Romero** was assassinated while giving mass in the Cathedral of San Salvador. His life and death became an inspiration for those seeking social justice. Still, it was only in 1991 that a cease-fire brought an end to the civil war.

Deportes • El surfing

El Salvador es uno de los destinos favoritos en Latinoamérica para la práctica del surfing. Cuenta con 300 kilómetros de costa a lo largo del océano Pacífico y sus olas° altas son ideales para quienes practican este deporte. De sus playas, La Libertad es la más visitada por surfistas de todo el mundo, gracias a que está muy cerca de la capital salvadoreña. Sin embargo, los fines de semana muchos visitantes prefieren viajar a la Costa del Bálsamo, donde se concentra menos gente.

Naturaleza • El Parque Nacional Montecristo

El Parque Nacional Montecristo se encuentra en la región norte del país. Se le conoce también como El Trifinio porque se ubica° en el punto donde se unen las fronteras de Guatemala, Honduras y El Salvador. Este bosque reúne a muchas especies vegetales y animales, como orquídeas, monos araña°, pumas, quetzales y tucanes. Además, las copas° de sus enormes árboles forman una bóveda° que impide° el paso de la luz solar. Este espacio natural se encuentra a una altitud de 2.400 metros (7.900 pies) sobre el nivel del mar y recibe 200 centímetros (80 pulgadas°) de lluvia al año.

Artes • La artesanía de Ilobasco

Ilobasco es un pueblo conocido por sus artesanías. En él se elaboran objetos con arcilla° y cerámica pintada a mano, como juguetes°, adornos° y utensilios de cocina. Además, son famosas sus "sorpresas", que son pequeñas piezas° de cerámica en cuyo interior se representan escenas de la vida diaria. Los turistas realizan excursiones para ver la elaboración, paso a paso°, de estos productos.

 ¿Qué aprendiste? Responde a cada pregunta con una oración completa.

1. ¿Qué tienen en común las poblaciones de El Salvador y Honduras?
 Las poblaciones de los dos países son muy homogéneas.

2. ¿Qué es el náhuatl?
 El náhuatl es un idioma que se habla en El Salvador.

3. ¿Quién es María Eugenia Brizuela?
 Es una política salvadoreña.

4. Hay muchos lugares ideales para el surfing en El Salvador. ¿Por qué? Porque El Salvador recibe algunas de las mejores olas del océano Pacífico.

5. ¿A qué altitud se encuentra el Parque Nacional Montecristo? Se encuentra a una altitud de 2.400 metros.

6. ¿Cuáles son algunos de los animales y las plantas que viven en este parque?
 Hay orquídeas, monos araña, pumas, quetzales y tucanes.

7. ¿Por qué se le llama El Trifinio al Parque Nacional Montecristo? Porque es el punto donde se unen Guatemala, Honduras y El Salvador.

8. ¿Por qué es famoso el pueblo de Ilobasco?
 Es famoso por los objetos de arcilla y por los artículos de cerámica pintados a mano.

9. ¿Qué se puede ver en un viaje a Ilobasco?
 Se puede ver la fabricación de los artículos de cerámica paso a paso.

10. ¿Qué son las "sorpresas" de Ilobasco?
 Las "sorpresas" son pequeñas piezas de cerámica con escenas de la vida diaria en su interior.

 Conexión Internet Investiga estos temas en **vhlcentral.com**.

1. El Parque Nacional Montecristo es una reserva natural; busca información sobre otros parques o zonas protegidas en El Salvador. ¿Cómo son estos lugares? ¿Qué tipos de plantas y animales se encuentran allí?

2. Busca información sobre museos u otros lugares turísticos en San Salvador (u otra ciudad de El Salvador).

 Practice more at **vhlcentral.com**.

olas *waves* se ubica *it is located* monos araña *spider monkeys* copas *tops* bóveda *cap* impide *blocks* pulgadas *inches* arcilla *clay* juguetes *toys* adornos *ornaments* piezas *pieces* paso a paso *step by step*

El surfing Tell students that **La Libertad** is a relatively small town that sees a large influx of beachgoers, not just surfers, during the weekends and holidays. Black volcanic sand covers the beach of **La Libertad**. About five miles east lies Zunzal beach, which, during Holy Week (**Semana Santa**) each year, is the site of international surfing competitions.

El Parque Nacional Montecristo The Montecristo cloud forest (**bosque nuboso**) is a protected area at the point where El Salvador, Honduras, and Guatemala meet. The point, at the summit of Montecristo, is called **El Trifinio**. Visitors only have access to Montecristo between November 1st and June 1st. The rest of the year it is closed to visitors for the animals' reproductive season.

La artesanía de Ilobasco Ilobasco is a crafts village that specializes in ceramics. **Sorpresas** are one of the most famous items. They are miniscule, intricate scenes and figures inside egg-shaped shells about the size of a walnut.

Conexión Internet Students will find supporting Internet activities and links at **vhlcentral.com**.

Variación léxica **Pupusa** is the name given to the Salvadoran version of the **tortilla**. In fact, **pupusas** are made by putting a filling such as red beans, onions, garlic, and cheese on one uncooked **tortilla**, laying another **tortilla** over it, and pressing the two together so they adhere, and then frying both in hot oil until the **pupusa** is golden and crunchy. Served sizzling from the fryer, **pupusas** are delicious. They are so popular that

in El Salvador there are many shops, called **pupuserías**, that specialize in them. And if you visit a neighborhood in the United States where Salvadorans have settled, you will inevitably find a **pupusería**. You may want to play the *Panorama cultural* video footage for this lesson that shows how **pupusas** are made.

Las viviendas

las afueras	suburbs; outskirts
el alquiler	rent (payment)
el ama (*m., f.*) de casa	housekeeper; caretaker
el barrio	neighborhood
el edificio de apartamentos	apartment building
el/la vecino/a	neighbor
la vivienda	housing
alquilar	to rent
mudarse	to move (from one house to another)

Los cuartos y otros lugares

el altillo	attic
el balcón	balcony
la cocina	kitchen
el comedor	dining room
el dormitorio	bedroom
la entrada	entrance
la escalera	stairs; stairway
el garaje	garage
el jardín	garden; yard
la oficina	office
el pasillo	hallway
el patio	patio; yard
la sala	living room
el sótano	basement; cellar

Los muebles y otras cosas

la alfombra	carpet; rug
la almohada	pillow
el armario	closet
el cartel	poster
la cómoda	chest of drawers
las cortinas	curtains
el cuadro	picture
el estante	bookcase; bookshelves
la lámpara	lamp
la luz	light; electricity
la manta	blanket
la mesita	end table
la mesita de noche	night stand
los muebles	furniture
la pared	wall
la pintura	painting; picture
el sillón	armchair
el sofá	couch; sofa

Los electrodomésticos

la cafetera	coffee maker
la cocina, la estufa	stove
el congelador	freezer
el electrodoméstico	electric appliance
el horno (de microondas)	(microwave) oven
la lavadora	washing machine
el lavaplatos	dishwasher
el refrigerador	refrigerator
la secadora	clothes dryer
la tostadora	toaster

La mesa

la copa	wineglass; goblet
la cuchara	(table or large) spoon
el cuchillo	knife
el plato	plate
la servilleta	napkin
la taza	cup
el tenedor	fork
el vaso	glass

Los quehaceres domésticos

arreglar	to neaten; to straighten up
barrer el suelo	to sweep the floor
cocinar	to cook
ensuciar	to get (something) dirty
hacer la cama	to make the bed
hacer quehaceres domésticos	to do household chores
lavar (el suelo, los platos)	to wash (the floor, the dishes)
limpiar la casa	to clean the house
pasar la aspiradora	to vacuum
planchar la ropa	to iron the clothes
poner la mesa	to set the table
quitar la mesa	to clear the table
quitar el polvo	to dust
sacar la basura	to take out the trash
sacudir los muebles	to dust the furniture

Verbos y expresiones verbales

aconsejar	to advise
insistir (en)	to insist (on)
mandar	to order
recomendar (e:ie)	to recommend
rogar (o:ue)	to beg; to plead
sugerir (e:ie)	to suggest
Es bueno que…	It's good that…
Es importante que…	It's important that…
Es malo que…	It's bad that…
Es mejor que…	It's better that…
Es necesario que…	It's necessary that…
Es urgente que…	It's urgent that…

Relative pronouns	See page 386.
Expresiones útiles	See page 381.

recursos

LM p. 72 — vhlcentral.com Lección 12

Audio: Vocabulary

La naturaleza

13

Communicative Goals

You will learn how to:

- Talk about and discuss the environment
- Express your beliefs and opinions about issues

Lesson Goals

In **Lección 13**, students will be introduced to the following:

- terms to describe nature, the environment, conservation, and recycling
- the Andes mountain range
- Colombia's Santa Marta mountain range
- subjunctive with verbs and expressions of emotion
- subjunctive with verbs and expressions of doubt, disbelief, and denial
- expressions of certainty
- conjunctions followed by the infinitive
- forming regular past participles
- irregular past participles
- past participles used as adjectives
- identifying a text's purpose
- a video about nature in Costa Rica
- cultural, geographic, and historical information about Colombia and Honduras

A primera vista Ask these additional questions: **¿Te interesa la ecología? ¿Te gusta entrar en contacto con la naturaleza? ¿Cómo te sientes cuando estás fuera de la ciudad? ¿Te preocupa la ecología de la región donde vives?**

Teaching Tip Look for these icons for additional communicative practice:

→👥←	Interpretive communication
←👥→	Presentational communication
👥↔👥	Interpersonal communication

A PRIMERA VISTA

- ¿Son estas personas excursionistas?
- ¿Es importante que usen ropa cómoda?
- ¿Se llevan bien o mal?
- ¿Les interesa la naturaleza?

INSTRUCTIONAL RESOURCES

Supersite (vhlcentral.com)
Video: *Fotonovela*, Flash cultura*, Panorama cultural**
**Also on DVD*
Audio: Textbook and Lab MP3 Files (*also on CD*)
Activity Pack: Information Gap Activities, games, additional activity handouts

Resources: Textbook Answer Key, WB/VM/LM Answer Key, Scripts, Translations, **Vocabulario adicional**, lesson plans, **Estructura** *PowerPoints*, Overheads
Testing Program: Quizzes, Tests, Exams, MP3s (*also on Test Generator CD*)

Learning Management System (Assignment Task Manager, Gradebook)
WebSAM (online Workbook/Video Manual/ Lab Manual)
Workbook/Video Manual
Lab Manual

La naturaleza

Más vocabulario

el bosque (tropical)	(tropical; rain) forest
el desierto	desert
la naturaleza	nature
la planta	plant
la selva, la jungla	jungle
la tierra	land; soil
el cielo	sky
la estrella	star
la luna	moon
el calentamiento global	global warming
el cambio climático	climate change
la conservación	conservation
la contaminación (del aire; del agua)	(air; water) pollution
la deforestación	deforestation
la ecología	ecology
el/la ecologista	ecologist
el ecoturismo	ecotourism
la energía (nuclear; solar)	(nuclear; solar) energy
la extinción	extinction
la fábrica	factory
el medio ambiente	environment
el peligro	danger
el recurso natural	natural resource
la solución	solution
el gobierno	government
la ley	law
la (sobre)población	(over)population
ecologista	ecological
puro/a	pure
renovable	renewable

Variación léxica

hierba ⟷ pasto (*Perú*); grama (*Venez., Col.*); zacate (*Méx.*)

el ave, el pájaro
el cráter
el volcán
el pez (sing.), los peces (pl.)
la vaca
el árbol
la hierba
la flor
el perro
el gato

la nube

el sol

el valle

el sendero

el lago

la piedra

el río

Más vocabulario

el animal	*animal*
la ballena	*whale*
el mono	*monkey*
la tortuga (marina)	*(sea) turtle*

Práctica

1 **Escuchar** Mientras escuchas estas oraciones, anota los sustantivos (*nouns*) que se refieren a las plantas, los animales, la tierra y el cielo.

Plantas	Animales	Tierra	Cielo
flores	perro	volcán	sol
hierba	tortugas marinas	bosques tropicales	nubes
árboles	peces	campo	estrellas

2 **¿Cierto o falso?** Escucha las oraciones e indica si lo que dice cada una es **cierto** o **falso**, según el dibujo.

1. _cierto_
2. _falso_
3. _falso_
4. _cierto_
5. _cierto_
6. _falso_

3 **Seleccionar** Selecciona la palabra que no está relacionada.

1. estrella • gobierno • luna • sol _gobierno_
2. lago • río • mar • peligro _peligro_
3. vaca • ballena • pájaro • población _población_
4. cielo • cráter • aire • nube _cráter_
5. desierto • solución • selva • bosque _solución_
6. flor • hierba • renovable • árbol _renovable_

4 **Definir** Trabaja con un(a) compañero/a para definir o describir cada palabra. Sigue el modelo. Answers will vary.

> **modelo**
> **Estudiante 1:** ¿Qué es el cielo?
> **Estudiante 2:** El cielo está sobre la tierra y tiene nubes.

1. la población
2. un mono
3. el calentamiento global
4. la naturaleza
5. un desierto
6. la extinción
7. la ecología
8. un sendero

5 **Describir** Trabajen en parejas para describir estas fotos.
Answers will vary.

1 **Teaching Tip** To simplify, have students brainstorm a few words for each category before listening.

1 **Script** 1. Mi novio siempre me compra flores para nuestro aniversario. 2. Cuando era pequeño, jugaba con mi perro todo el tiempo. 3. En los desiertos casi no hay hierba. 4. Algunos científicos dicen que la temperatura del sol va a aumentar en los próximos años. 5. Hoy día, en Latinoamérica hay seis especies de tortugas marinas en peligro de extinción. *Script continues on page 418.*

Script continues on page 418.

2 **Teaching Tip** To challenge students, have them correct the false statements.

2 **Script** 1. Hay un gato jugando con un perro. 2. La vaca está en un sendero de la montaña. 3. No hay nubes sobre el valle. 4. La vaca está comiendo hierba. 5. Una pareja come sobre la hierba. 6. Las piedras están lejos del río.
Textbook MP3s

3 **Expansion** Have students state a category for the related words. Ex: **1. cosas que están en el cielo**

4 **Expansion** Have pairs read their definitions aloud in random order for the class to guess which term is being described.

5 **Teaching Tip** To simplify, give students these guidelines to help them prepare their descriptions: objects in the photos, colors, what the weather is like, the time of day, the location where the photo was taken.

5 **Expansion**
←🏃→ Ask students to imagine the photos were taken on a recent vacation. Have them write a brief essay about their vacation, incorporating their descriptions.

1 Script (continued)

6. Durante la tormenta, las nubes grises cubrían toda la ciudad. 7. En el mar Caribe hay muchos peces exóticos. 8. Algunas noches vamos al campo para ver las estrellas. 9. El Puracé es un volcán activo en los Andes colombianos. 10. Los árboles de los bosques tropicales contienen las curas para muchas enfermedades.

Textbook MP3s

Teaching Tips

• Use the **Lección 13 Contextos** overheads to assist with this vocabulary presentation.

• 👥↔👤 Involve students in a discussion about recycling and conservation. Ask volunteers to describe what is happening in the drawing. Ask: **¿Qué hace la señora de la izquierda? (Recicla una lata de aluminio.)** Cover the active vocabulary, then ask about students' own experiences and opinions. Ex: **¿Tiene un buen programa de reciclaje nuestra ciudad? ¿Qué hacen ustedes para reducir la contaminación del medio ambiente? ¿Qué hace la universidad? ¿Cómo estamos afectados por la contaminación en nuestra ciudad/región? ¿Cuál es el mayor problema ecológico de nuestra región? ¿Qué evitan ustedes por razones ecológicas?**

6 Expansion

• 👥↔👤 Ask questions to engage students in a conversation that requires them to recycle the activity vocabulary. Ex: **¿Qué debemos hacer para mantener las calles limpias? ¿Para qué trabajan los científicos? ¿Por qué es necesario que trabajemos para proteger el medio ambiente?**

• ↔👤→ Have students write five additional sentences, using different forms of the verbs. Ask volunteers to share their sentences with the class.

Recicla la lata de aluminio. (reciclar)

el envase de plástico

Recoge la botella de vidrio. (recoger)

El reciclaje

Más vocabulario

cazar	to hunt
conservar	to conserve
contaminar	to pollute
controlar	to control
cuidar	to take care of
dejar de (+ *inf.*)	to stop (doing something)
desarrollar	to develop
descubrir	to discover
destruir	to destroy
estar afectado/a (por)	to be affected (by)
estar contaminado/a	to be polluted
evitar	to avoid
mejorar	to improve
proteger	to protect
reducir	to reduce
resolver (o:ue)	to resolve; to solve
respirar	to breathe

6 Completar Selecciona la palabra o la expresión adecuada para completar cada oración.

contaminar	destruyen	reciclamos
controlan	están afectadas	recoger
cuidan	mejoramos	resolver
descubrir	proteger	se desarrollaron

1. Si vemos basura en las calles, la debemos __recoger__.
2. Los científicos trabajan para __descubrir__ nuevas soluciones.
3. Es necesario que todos trabajemos juntos para __resolver__ los problemas del medio ambiente.
4. Debemos __proteger__ el medio ambiente porque hoy día está en peligro.
5. Muchas leyes nuevas __controlan__ el nivel de emisiones que producen las fábricas.
6. Las primeras civilizaciones __se desarrollaron__ cerca de los ríos y los mares.
7. Todas las personas __están afectadas__ por la contaminación.
8. Los turistas deben tener cuidado de no __contaminar__ los lugares que visitan.
9. Podemos conservar los recursos si __reciclamos__ el aluminio, el vidrio y el plástico.
10. La contaminación y la deforestación __destruyen__ el medio ambiente.

 Practice more at **vhlcentral.com.**

TEACHING OPTIONS

Pairs Have pairs of students write each vocabulary word from this page on index cards. Pairs then shuffle the cards and take turns drawing from the stack. The student who draws a card then must make a comment about conservation or the environment, using the word he or she has drawn. The other student writes down the comment. After students finish the stack, call on volunteers to share their comments.

Small Groups 👥↔👥 Divide the class into groups of three or four. Have each group make a list of eight environmental problems in the region. Ask groups to trade lists. Have them write solutions to the problems on the list they receive, and then give the lists back to the original group. After reading the solutions, the original groups should give reasons why the solutions are viable or not.

Comunicación

7 **¿Es importante?** En parejas, lean este párrafo y contesten las preguntas.
Some answers will vary. Suggested answers:

Los problemas del medio ambiente

importantísimo
muy importante
importante
poco importante
no es importante

la deforestación | los animales en peligro de extinción | la contaminación del aire | la contaminación del agua | la basura en las ciudades

Para celebrar El día de la Tierra, una estación de radio colombiana hizo una pequeña encuesta entre estudiantes universitarios, donde les preguntaron sobre los problemas del medio ambiente. Se les preguntó cuáles creían que eran los cinco problemas más importantes del medio ambiente. Ellos también tenían que decidir el orden de importancia de estos problemas, del uno al cinco.

Los resultados probaron (*proved*) que la mayoría de los estudiantes están preocupados por la contaminación del aire. Muchos mencionaron que no hay aire puro en las ciudades. El problema número dos para los estudiantes es que los ríos y los lagos están afectados por la contaminación. La deforestación quedó como el problema número tres, la basura en las ciudades como el número cuatro y los animales en peligro de extinción como el cinco.

1. ¿Según la encuesta, qué problema consideran más grave? ¿Qué problema consideran menos grave? la contaminación del aire; los animales en peligro de extinción

2. ¿Cómo creen ustedes que se puede evitar o resolver el problema más importante?

3. ¿Es necesario resolver el problema menos importante? ¿Por qué?

4. ¿Consideran ustedes que existen los mismos problemas en su comunidad? Den algunos ejemplos.

8 **Situaciones** Trabajen en grupos pequeños para representar estas situaciones. Answers will vary.

1. Unos/as representantes de una agencia ambiental (*environmental*) hablan con el/la presidente/a de una fábrica que está contaminando el aire o el río de la zona.

2. Un(a) guía de ecoturismo habla con un grupo sobre cómo disfrutar (*enjoy*) de la naturaleza y conservar el medio ambiente.

3. Un(a) representante de la universidad habla con un grupo de nuevos estudiantes sobre la campaña (*campaign*) ambiental de la universidad y trata de reclutar (*tries to recruit*) miembros para un club que trabaja para la protección del medio ambiente.

9 **Escribir una carta** Trabajen en parejas para escribir una carta a una fábrica real o imaginaria que esté contaminando el medio ambiente. Expliquen las consecuencias que sus acciones van a tener para el medio ambiente. Sugiéranle algunas ideas para que solucione el problema. Utilicen por lo menos diez palabras de **Contextos**. Answers will vary.

7 **Expansion**
Divide the class into groups of five to discuss questions 2–4. Groups should reach a consensus for each question, then report back to the class.

8 **Teaching Tip**
Divide the class into small groups. Have each group choose a situation, but make sure that each situation is selected by at least one group. Have students take turns playing each role. After groups have had time to prepare their situations, ask volunteers to present them to the class.

9 **Teaching Tips**
• Remind students that a business letter in Spanish begins with a salutation, such as **Estimado(s) señor(es)**, and ends with a closing such as **Atentamente**.
• With the class, brainstorm a list of agencies or companies that are known not to be environmentally conscious. Ask the class to categorize the companies by how they harm the environment. Then divide the class into pairs and have them choose a company for the activity. Alternately, you can vary the activity to have it focus on green companies.

TEACHING OPTIONS

Heritage Speakers Ask heritage speakers to interview family members or people in their community about the environmental challenges in their families' countries of origin. Encourage them to find out how the problems affect the land and the people. Have students report their findings to the class.
Large Groups Prepare two sets of index cards, one with environmental problems and the other with possible solutions.

Ex: **la destrucción de los bosques – reducir las áreas de deforestación; la contaminación de los ríos – controlar el tipo de sustancias que hay en el agua.** Shuffle the two sets of cards and distribute them. Have students with problem cards circulate around the room, asking their classmates questions until they find a viable solution.

Aventuras en la naturaleza

Las chicas visitan un santuario de tortugas, mientras los chicos pasean por la selva.

PERSONAJES

MARISSA **JIMENA**

Video: *Fotonovela*
Record and Compare

1

MARISSA Querida tía Ana María, lo estoy pasando muy bien. Es maravilloso que México tenga tantos programas estupendos para proteger a las tortugas. Hoy estamos en Tulum, y ¡el paisaje es espectacular! Con cariño, Marissa.

2

MARISSA Estoy tan feliz de que estés aquí conmigo.

JIMENA Es mucho más divertido cuando se viaja con amigos.

(*Llegan Felipe y Juan Carlos*)

JIMENA ¿Qué pasó?

JUAN CARLOS No lo van a creer.

FELIPE Juan Carlos encontró al grupo. ¡Yo esperaba encontrarlos también! ¡Pero nunca vinieron por mí! Yo estaba asustado. Regresé al lugar de donde salimos y esperé. Me perdí todo el recorrido.

3

GUÍA A menos que protejamos a los animales de la contaminación y la deforestación, en poco tiempo muchos de ellos van a estar extintos. Por favor, síganme y eviten pisar las plantas.

5

4

FELIPE Nos retrasamos sólo cinco minutos... Qué extraño. Estaban aquí hace unos minutos.

JUAN CARLOS ¿Adónde se fueron?

FELIPE No creo que puedan ir muy lejos.

(*Se separan para buscar al grupo.*)

6

FELIPE Decidí seguir un río y...

MARISSA No es posible que un guía continúe el recorrido cuando hay dos personas perdidas.

JIMENA Vamos a ver, chicos, ¿qué pasó? Díganos la verdad.

 JUAN CARLOS **FELIPE** **GUÍA**

JUAN CARLOS Felipe se cayó. Él no quería contarles.

JIMENA ¡Lo sabía!

FELIPE Y ustedes, ¿qué hicieron hoy?

JIMENA Marissa y yo fuimos al santuario de las tortugas.

MARISSA Aprendimos sobre las normas que existen para proteger a las tortugas marinas.

JIMENA Pero no cabe duda de que necesitamos aprobar más leyes para mantenerlas protegidas.

MARISSA Fue muy divertido verlas tan cerca.

JUAN CARLOS Entonces se divirtieron. ¡Qué bien!

JIMENA Gracias, y tú, pobrecito, pasaste todo el día con mi hermano. Siempre te mete en problemas.

recursos

VM pp. 219–220

vhlcentral.com Lección 13

Expresiones útiles

Talking about the environment

Aprendimos sobre las normas que existen para proteger a las tortugas marinas.
We learned about the regulations that exist to protect sea turtles.

Afortunadamente, ahora la población está aumentando.
Fortunately, the population is now growing.

No cabe duda de que necesitamos aprobar más leyes para mantenerlas protegidas.
There is no doubt that we need to pass more laws to keep them protected.

Es maravilloso que México tenga tantos programas estupendos para proteger a las tortugas.
It's marvelous that Mexico has so many wonderful programs to protect the turtles.

A menos que protejamos a los animales de la contaminación y la deforestación, en poco tiempo muchos de ellos van a estar extintos.
Unless we protect animals from pollution and habitat loss, soon many of them will be extinct.

Additional vocabulary

aumentar
to grow; to get bigger
meterse en problemas
to get into trouble
perdido/a
lost
el recorrido
tour
sobre todo
above all

¿Qué pasó?

1

Seleccionar Selecciona la respuesta más lógica para completar cada oración.

1. México tiene muchos programas para _____ c _____ a las tortugas.
 a. destruir b. reciclar c. proteger
2. Según la guía, muchos animales van a estar en peligro de _____ b _____ si no los protegemos.
 a. reciclaje b. extinción c. deforestación
3. La guía les pide a los visitantes que eviten pisar _____ a _____.
 a. las plantas b. las piedras c. la tierra
4. Felipe no quería contarles a las chicas que se _____ c _____.
 a. divirtió b. alegró c. cayó
5. Jimena dice que debe haber más _____ b _____ para proteger a las tortugas.
 a. playas b. leyes c. gobiernos

2

Identificar Identifica quién puede decir estas oraciones. Puedes usar algunos nombres más de una vez.

1. Fue divertido ver a las tortugas y aprender las normas para mantenerlas protegidas. Marissa/Jimena
2. Tenemos que evitar la contaminación y la deforestación. guía
3. Estoy feliz de estar aquí. Tulum es maravilloso. Marissa
4. Es una lástima que me pierda el recorrido. Felipe
5. No es posible que esa historia que nos dices sea verdad. Jimena/Marissa
6. No van a creer lo que le sucedió a Felipe. Juan Carlos
7. Tenemos que cuidar las plantas y los animales. guía
8. Ojalá que mi hermano no se meta en más problemas. Jimena

FELIPE MARISSA

JIMENA

GUÍA JUAN CARLOS

3

Preguntas Responde a estas preguntas usando la información de **Fotonovela**.

1. ¿Qué lugar visitan Marissa y Jimena?
 Marissa y Jimena visitan un santuario de tortugas.
2. ¿Adónde fueron Juan Carlos y Felipe?
 Juan Carlos y Felipe fueron a la selva.
3. Según la guía, ¿por qué muchos animales están en peligro de extinción?
 Muchos animales están en peligro de extinción por la contaminación y la deforestación.
4. ¿Por qué Jimena y Marissa no creen la historia de Felipe?
 Porque no es posible que un guía continúe el recorrido cuando hay dos personas perdidas.
5. ¿Qué esperaba Felipe cuando estaba perdido?
 Felipe esperaba encontrar al grupo.

4

El medio ambiente En parejas, discutan algunos problemas ambientales y sus posibles soluciones. Usen estas preguntas y frases en su conversación.
Answers will vary.

- ¿Hay problemas de contaminación donde vives?
- Tenemos un problema muy grave de contaminación de...
- ¿Cómo podemos resolver los problemas de la contaminación?

Practice more at **vhlcentral.com**.

1 **Teaching Tip** To challenge students, write these sentences on the board without the multiple choice items and have students complete them.

2 **Expansion** Have pairs of students write questions or statements that could have elicited these comments.

Nota cultural **Tulum** is the third most-visited archeological site in Mexico, after **Teotihuacán** and **Chichén Itzá**.

3 **Expansion** Ask students to write three additional questions for a classmate to answer.

4 **Possible Conversation**
E1: ¿Hay problemas de contaminación donde vives?
E2: Sí, tenemos un problema muy grave de contaminación en los ríos. Hay muchos papeles, botellas y latas en ellos. En las montañas, los ríos no están tan afectados por la contaminación pero en las ciudades, sí. ¿En tu región hay problemas de contaminación?
E1: Sí, tenemos un problema gravísimo de contaminación del aire. Esto causa enfermedades para los habitantes.
E2: Qué terrible. ¿Cómo podemos resolver los problemas de la contaminación?
E1: Bueno, nosotros ahora tenemos un programa de reciclaje. También algunas personas tratan de no usar el auto. Usan el metro o caminan.

The Affective Dimension
Many students feel nervous when called on to give an answer or to read aloud. You can minimize anxiety by asking for volunteers and by having students work in pairs or groups.

TEACHING OPTIONS

Extra Practice →👤← Add an auditory aspect to this vocabulary practice. Use the sentences in **Actividad 1** or **Actividad 2** for a dictation activity. Have students close their books, then read each sentence twice slowly and once at regular speed. Then have students open their books and check their work for accuracy. Ask comprehension questions as a follow-up.

Small Groups ←👤→ Have students work in groups of three to write a short article about their environmental concerns for a local newsletter (**boletín informativo**). Their articles should include a description of a few environmental problems and some suggestions for solving them. Have groups share their articles with the class.

Ortografía

 Concepts

Los signos de puntuación

In Spanish, as in English, punctuation marks are important because they help you express your ideas in a clear, organized way.

> **No podía ver las llaves. Las buscó por los estantes, las mesas, las sillas, el suelo; minutos después, decidió mirar por la ventana. Allí estaban…**

The **punto y coma (;)**, the **tres puntos (…)**, and the **punto (.)** are used in very similar ways in Spanish and English.

> **Argentina, Brasil, Paraguay y Uruguay son miembros de Mercosur.**

In Spanish, the **coma (,)** is not used before **y** or **o** in a series.

| 13,5% | 29,2° | 3.000.000 | $2.999,99 |

In numbers, Spanish uses a **coma** where English uses a decimal point and a **punto** where English uses a comma.

 Cómo te llamas ¿Dónde está? ¡Ven aquí! Hola

Questions in Spanish are preceded and followed by **signos de interrogación (¿ ?)**, and exclamations are preceded and followed by **signos de exclamación (¡ !)**.

Práctica Lee el párrafo e indica los signos de puntuación necesarios. *Answers will vary.*

Ayer recibí la invitación de boda de Marta mi amiga colombiana inmediatamente empecé a pensar en un posible regalo fui al almacén donde Marta y su novio tenían una lista de regalos había de todo copas cafeteras tostadoras finalmente decidí regalarles un perro ya sé que es un regalo extraño pero espero que les guste a los dos

¿Palabras de amor? El siguiente diálogo tiene diferentes significados (*meanings*) dependiendo de los signos de puntuación que utilices y el lugar donde los pongas. Intenta encontrar los diferentes significados. *Answers will vary.*

JULIÁN	me quieres
MARISOL	no puedo vivir sin ti
JULIÁN	me quieres dejar
MARISOL	no me parece mala idea
JULIÁN	no eres feliz conmigo
MARISOL	no soy feliz

recursos

LM p. 74 vhlcentral.com Lección 13

Section Goal

In **Ortografía**, students will learn the use of punctuation marks in Spanish.

Instructional Resources
Supersite: Audio (Lab MP3 Files); Resources (Scripts, Answer Keys)
WebSAM
Lab Manual, p. 74

Teaching Tips

• Explain that there is no space before or between ellipsis marks in Spanish. There is, however, a space after the third ellipsis point when used within a sentence.

• Model reading the numerical examples. Ex: **13,5% = trece coma cinco por ciento.** Write numbers on the board for translations into Spanish. Ex: 89.3%; 5,020,307; $13.50

• Explain that the inverted question mark or exclamation point does not always come at the beginning of a sentence, but where the question or exclamation begins. Ex:
—**¿Cómo estás, Mirta?**
—**¡Bien! Y tú, ¿cómo estás?**
—**Ay, ¡me duele la cabeza!**

• Point out that **Ortografía** replaces **Pronunciación** in the Student Edition for **Lecciones 10–15**, but not in the Lab Manual. The **Recursos** box references the **Pronunciación** sections found in all lessons of the Lab Manual.

¿Palabras de amor? Two possibilities for punctuation:

J: ¿Me quieres?
M: ¡No puedo vivir sin ti!
J: ¿Me quieres dejar?
M: No. Me parece mala idea.
J: ¿No eres feliz conmigo?
M: No. Soy feliz.

J: ¿Me quieres?
M: No. Puedo vivir sin ti.
J: ¡Me quieres dejar!
M: No me parece mala idea.
J: ¿No eres feliz conmigo?
M: No soy feliz.

TEACHING OPTIONS

Pairs Have pairs write example sentences for each of the four punctuation rules in **Ortografía**. Ask volunteers to write their sentences on the board and have the class identify the rules.
Video Photocopy the **Fotonovela** Videoscript (Supersite) and white out the punctuation in order to make a master for a cloze activity. Distribute the photocopies and, as you replay the episode, have students mark the punctuation.

Extra Practice To simplify the **¿Palabras de amor?** activity, write *A woman without her man is nothing* on the board and point out how it can be punctuated in two ways to express opposite meanings. After completing the dialogues, have students work in pairs to dramatize both versions. Ask a few pairs to role-play the contrasting dialogues for the class.

EN DETALLE

Additional Reading
Video: *Flash cultura*

¡Los Andes se mueven!

Los Andes, la cadena° de montañas más extensa de América, son conocidos como "la espina dorsal° de Suramérica". Sus 7.240 kilómetros (4.500 millas) van desde el norte° de la región entre Venezuela y Colombia, hasta el extremo sur°, entre Argentina y Chile, y pasan por casi todos los países suramericanos. La cordillera° de los Andes, formada hace 27 millones de años, es la segunda más alta del mundo, después de la del Himalaya (aunque° esta última es mucho más "joven", ya que se formó hace apenas cinco millones de años).

Para poder atravesar° de un lado a otro de los Andes, existen varios pasos o puertos° de montaña. Situados a grandes alturas°, son generalmente estrechos° y peligrosos. En algunos de ellos hay, también, vías ferroviarias°.

De acuerdo con° varias instituciones científicas, la cordillera de los Andes se eleva° y se hace más angosta° cada año. La capital de Chile se acerca° a la capital de Argentina a un ritmo° de 19,4 milímetros por año. Si ese ritmo se mantiene°, Santiago y Buenos Aires podrían unirse° en unos... 63 millones de años, ¡casi el mismo tiempo que ha transcurrido° desde la extinción de los dinosaurios!

Los Andes en números

3 Cordilleras que forman los Andes: Las cordilleras Central, Occidental y Oriental

900 (A.C.°) Año aproximado en que empezó el desarrollo° de la cultura chavín, en los Andes peruanos

600 Número aproximado de volcanes que hay en los Andes

6.960 Metros (22.835 pies) de altura del Aconcagua (Argentina), el pico° más alto de los Andes

Arequipa, Perú

cadena *range* espina dorsal *spine* norte *north* sur *south* cordillera *mountain range* aunque *although* atravesar *to cross* puertos *passes* alturas *heights* estrechos *narrow* vías ferroviarias *railroad tracks* De acuerdo con *According to* se eleva *rises* angosta *narrow* se acerca *gets closer* ritmo *rate* se mantiene *keeps going* podrían unirse *could join together* ha transcurrido *has gone by* A.C. *Before Christ* desarrollo *development* pico *peak*

ACTIVIDADES

1 **Escoger** la opción que completa mejor cada oración.

1. Los Andes son la cadena montañosa más extensa del...
 a. mundo. b. continente americano. c. hemisferio norte.
2. "La espina dorsal de Suramérica" es...
 a. los Andes. b. el Himalaya. c. el Aconcagua.
3. La cordillera de los Andes se extiende...
 a. de este a oeste. b. de sur a oeste. c. de norte a sur.
4. El Himalaya y los Andes tienen...
 a. diferente altura. b. la misma altura. c. el mismo color.
5. Es posible atravesar los Andes por medio de...
 a. montañas b. puertos c. aviones
6. En algunos de los puertos de montaña de los Andes hay...
 a. puertas. b. vías ferroviarias. c. cordilleras.
7. En 63 millones de años, Buenos Aires y Santiago podrían...
 a. separarse. b. desarrollarse. c. unirse.
8. El Aconcagua es...
 a. una montaña. b. un grupo indígena. c. un volcán.

ASÍ SE DICE

La naturaleza

el arco iris	rainbow
la cascada; la catarata	waterfall
el cerro; la colina; la loma	hill
la cima; la cumbre; el tope (Col.)	summit; mountain top
la maleza; los rastrojos (Col.); la yerba mala (Cuba); los hierbajos (Méx.); los yuyos (Arg.)	weeds
la niebla	fog

EL MUNDO HISPANO

Cuerpos° de agua

- **Lago de Maracaibo** es el lago natural más grande de Suramérica y tiene una conexión directa y natural con el mar.

- **Lago Titicaca** es el lago navegable más alto del mundo. Se encuentra a más de 3.800 metros de altitud.

- **Bahía Mosquito** es una bahía bioluminiscente. En sus aguas viven unos microorganismos que emiten luz° cuando sienten que algo agita° el agua.

Cuerpos *Bodies* emiten luz *emit light* agita *shakes*

PERFIL

La Sierra Nevada de Santa Marta

La Sierra Nevada de Santa Marta es una cadena de montañas en la costa norte de Colombia. Se eleva abruptamente desde las costas del mar Caribe y en apenas 42 kilómetros llega a una altura de 5.775 metros (18.947 pies) en sus picos nevados°. Tiene las montañas más altas de Colombia y es la formación montañosa costera° más alta del mundo.

Los pueblos indígenas que habitan allí lograron° mantener los frágiles ecosistemas de estas montañas a través de° un sofisticado sistema de terrazas° y senderos empedrados° que permitieron° el control de las aguas en una región de muchas

lluvias, evitando° así la erosión de la tierra. La Sierra fue nombrada Reserva de la Biosfera por la UNESCO en 1979.

nevados *snowcapped* costera *coastal* lograron *managed* a través de *by means of* terrazas *terraces* empedrados *cobblestone* permitieron *allowed* evitando *avoiding*

Conexión Internet

¿Dónde se puede hacer ecoturismo en Latinoamérica?

Go to vhlcentral.com to find more cultural information related to this **Cultura** section.

ACTIVIDADES

2 **Comprensión** Indica si lo que dice cada oración es **cierto** o **falso**. Corrige la información falsa.

1. En Colombia, *weeds* se dice **hierbajos**. **Falso.** Se dice rastrojos.
2. El lago Titicaca es el más grande del mundo. **Falso.** Es el lago navegable más alto del mundo.
3. La Sierra Nevada de Santa Marta es la formación montañosa costera más alta del mundo. **Cierto.**
4. Los indígenas destruyeron el ecosistema de Santa Marta. **Falso.** Lograron mantener los ecosistemas de las montañas.

3 **Maravillas de la naturaleza** Escribe un párrafo breve donde describas alguna maravilla de la naturaleza que has (*you have*) visitado y que te impresionó. Puede ser cualquier (*any*) sitio natural: un río, una montaña, una selva, etc. Answers will vary.

recursos

VM pp. 291–292

vhlcentral.com Lección 13

 Practice more at **vhlcentral.com.**

Section Goals

In **Estructura 13.1**, students will learn:

• how to use the subjunctive with verbs and expressions of emotion
• common verbs and expressions of emotion

Instructional Resources
Supersite: Audio (Lab MP3 Files); Resources (*PowerPoints*, Activity Pack, Scripts, Answer Keys); Testing Program (Quizzes)
WebSAM
Workbook, pp. 157–158
Lab Manual, p. 75

Teaching Tips
• Ask students to call out some of the verbs that, when placed in the main clause, trigger the subjunctive in the subordinate clause (see **Estructura 12.4**). List the verbs on the board and ask students to use them in sentences as a review of the conjugation of regular –**ar**, –**er**, and –**ir** verbs.
• Model the use of some common verbs and expressions of emotion. Ex: **Me molesta mucho que recojan la basura sólo una vez a la semana. Me sorprende que algunas personas no se preocupen por el medio ambiente. Es ridículo que produzcamos tanta basura.** Then ask volunteers to use other verbs and expressions in sentences.

13.1 The subjunctive with verbs of emotion

ANTE TODO In the previous lesson, you learned how to use the subjunctive with expressions of will and influence. You will now learn how to use the subjunctive with verbs and expressions of emotion.

Main clause Subordinate clause

Marta **espera** yo **vaya** al lago este fin de semana.

▶ When the verb in the main clause of a sentence expresses an emotion or feeling, such as hope, fear, joy, pity, surprise, etc., the subjunctive is required in the subordinate clause.

Nos alegramos de que te **gusten** las flores.
We are happy that you like the flowers.

Siento que tú no **puedas** venir mañana.
I'm sorry that you can't come tomorrow.

Temo que Ana no **pueda** ir mañana con nosotros.
I'm afraid that Ana won't be able to go with us tomorrow.

Le **sorprende** que Juan **sea** tan joven.
It surprises him that Juan is so young.

Es una lástima que ellos no estén aquí con nosotros.

Me alegro de que te divirtieras.

Common verbs and expressions of emotion

alegrarse (de)	to be happy	**tener miedo (de)**	to be afraid (of)
esperar	to hope; to wish	**es extraño**	it's strange
gustar	to be pleasing; to like	**es una lástima**	it's a shame
molestar	to bother	**es ridículo**	it's ridiculous
sentir (e:ie)	to be sorry; to regret	**es terrible**	it's terrible
sorprender	to surprise	**es triste**	it's sad
temer	to be afraid; to fear	**ojalá (que)**	I hope (that); I wish (that)

Me molesta que la gente no **recicle** el plástico.
It bothers me that people don't recycle plastic.

Es triste que **tengamos** problemas como el cambio climático.
It's sad that we have problems like climate change.

CONSULTA

Certain verbs of emotion, like **gustar, molestar,** and **sorprender,** require indirect object pronouns. For more examples, see **Estructura 7.4,** pp. 230–231.

TEACHING OPTIONS

Large Groups Have students circulate around the room, interviewing each other about their hopes and fears for the future of the environment. Ex: **¿Qué deseas para el futuro del medio ambiente? (Deseo que encontremos una solución al problema de la contaminación.) ¿Qué es lo que más temes? (Temo que destruyamos los bosques tropicales.)** Encourage students to use the common verbs and expressions of emotion.

Extra Practice Ask students to imagine that they have just finished watching a documentary about the effects of pollution. Have them write five responses to what they saw and heard, using different verbs or expressions of emotion in each sentence. Ex: **Me sorprende que el río esté contaminado....**

▶ As with expressions of will and influence, the infinitive, not the subjunctive, is used after an expression of emotion when there is no change of subject from the main clause to the subordinate clause. Compare these sentences.

Temo **llegar** tarde.
I'm afraid I'll arrive late.

Temo que mi novio **llegue** tarde.
I'm afraid my boyfriend will arrive late.

▶ The expression **ojalá (que)** means *I hope* or *I wish*, and it is always followed by the subjunctive. Note that the use of **que** with this expression is optional.

Ojalá (que) se conserven
nuestros recursos naturales.
*I hope (that) our natural resources
will be conserved.*

Ojalá (que) recojan la
basura hoy.
*I hope (that) they collect the
garbage today.*

Ojalá que

su aseguradora escuche
sus necesidades con la
misma atención.

COLMENA
salud - medicina
Con su familia, por su futuro.

Por fin usted se puede poner en manos
de una compañía confiable.

¡INTÉNTALO! Completa las oraciones con las formas correctas de los verbos.

1. Ojalá que ellos _descubran_ (descubrir) nuevas formas de energía.
2. Espero que Ana nos _ayude_ (ayudar) a recoger la basura en la carretera.
3. Es una lástima que la gente no _recicle_ (reciclar) más.
4. Esperamos _proteger_ (proteger) a las tortugas marinas que llegan a esta playa.
5. Me alegro de que mis amigos _quieran_ (querer) conservar la naturaleza.
6. Espero que tú _vengas_ (venir) a la reunión (*meeting*) del Club de Ecología.
7. Es malo _contaminar_ (contaminar) el medio ambiente.
8. A mis padres les gusta que nosotros _participemos_ (participar) en la reunión.
9. Es terrible que nuestras ciudades _estén_ (estar) afectadas por la contaminación.
10. Ojalá que yo _pueda_ (poder) hacer algo para reducir el calentamiento global.

Práctica

1 Completar Completa el diálogo con palabras de la lista. Compara tus respuestas con las de un(a) compañero/a.

Bogotá, Colombia

alegro	molesta	salga
encuentren	ojalá	tengo miedo de
estén	puedan	vayan
lleguen	reduzcan	visitar

OLGA Me alegro de que Adriana y Raquel (1)__vayan__ a Colombia. ¿Van a estudiar?

SARA Sí. Es una lástima que (2)__lleguen__ una semana tarde. Ojalá que la universidad las ayude a buscar casa. (3)__Tengo miedo de__ que no consigan dónde vivir.

OLGA Me (4)__molesta__ que seas tan pesimista, pero sí, yo también espero que (5)__encuentren__ gente simpática y que hablen mucho español.

SARA Sí, ojalá. Van a hacer un estudio sobre la deforestación en las costas. Es triste que en tantos países los recursos naturales (6)__estén__ en peligro.

OLGA Pues, me (7)__alegro__ de que no se queden mucho en la capital por la contaminación. (8)__Ojalá__ tengan tiempo de viajar por el país.

SARA Sí, espero que (9)__puedan__ ir a Medellín. Sé que también quieren (10)__visitar__ la Catedral de Sal de Zipaquirá.

2 Transformar Transforma estos elementos en oraciones completas para formar un diálogo entre Juan y la madre de Raquel. Añade palabras si es necesario. Luego, con un(a) compañero/a, presenta el diálogo a la clase.

1. Juan, / esperar / (tú) escribirle / Raquel. / Ser / tu / novia. / Ojalá / no / sentirse / sola *Juan, espero que (tú) le escribas a Raquel. Es tu novia. Ojalá (que) no se sienta sola.*

2. molestarme / (usted) decirme / lo que / tener / hacer. / Ahora / mismo / le / estar / escribiendo *Me molesta que (Ud.) me diga lo que tengo que hacer. Ahora mismo le estoy escribiendo.*

3. alegrarme / oírte / decir / eso. / Ser / terrible / estar / lejos / cuando / nadie / recordarte *Me alegra oírte decir eso. Es terrible estar lejos cuando nadie te recuerda.*

4. señora, / ¡yo / tener / miedo de / (ella) no recordarme / mí! / Ser / triste / estar / sin / novia *Señora, ¡yo tengo miedo de que (ella) no me recuerde a mí! Es triste estar sin novia.*

5. ser / ridículo / (tú) sentirte / así. / Tú / saber / ella / querer / casarse / contigo *Es ridículo que te sientas así. Tú sabes que ella quiere casarse contigo.*

6. ridículo / o / no, / sorprenderme / (todos) preocuparse / ella / y / (nadie) / acordarse de / mí *Ridículo o no, me sorprende que todos se preocupen por ella y nadie se acuerde de mí.*

 Practice more at **vhlcentral.com.**

Comunicación

3

Comentar En parejas, túrnense para formar oraciones sobre su comunidad, sus clases, su gobierno o algún otro tema, usando expresiones como **me alegro de que, temo que** y **es extraño que.** Luego, reaccionen a los comentarios de su compañero/a. Answers will vary.

> **modelo**
>
> **Estudiante 1:** *Me alegro de que vayan a limpiar el río.*
> **Estudiante 2:** *Yo también. Me preocupa que el agua del río esté tan sucia.*

4

Contestar Lee el mensaje electrónico que Raquel le escribió a su novio, Juan. Luego, en parejas, contesten el mensaje usando expresiones como **me sorprende que, me molesta que** y **es una lástima que.** Answers will vary.

De:	Raquel
Para:	Juan
Asunto:	¡Hola!

Hola, Juan:

Mi amor, siento no escribirte más frecuentemente. La verdad es que estoy muy ocupada todo el tiempo. No sabes cuánto me estoy divirtiendo en Colombia. Me sorprende haber podido adaptarme tan bien. Es bueno tener tanto trabajo. Aprendo mucho más aquí que en el laboratorio de la universidad. Me encanta que me den responsabilidades y que compartan sus muchos conocimientos conmigo. Ay, pero pienso mucho en ti. Qué triste es que no podamos estar juntos por tanto tiempo. Ojalá que los días pasen rápido. Bueno, querido, es todo por ahora. Escríbeme pronto.

Te quiero y te extraño mucho,

Raquel

AYUDA

Echar de menos (a alguien) and **extrañar (a alguien)** are two ways of saying *to miss (someone).*

Síntesis

5

No te preocupes Estás muy preocupado/a por los problemas del medio ambiente y le comentas a tu compañero/a todas tus preocupaciones. Él/Ella va a darte la solución adecuada para tus preocupaciones. Su profesor(a) les va a dar una hoja distinta a cada uno/a con la información necesaria para completar la actividad. Answers will vary.

> **modelo**
>
> **Estudiante 1:** *Me molesta que las personas tiren basura en las calles.*
> **Estudiante 2:** *Por eso es muy importante que los políticos hagan leyes*
> *para conservar las ciudades limpias.*

13.2 The subjunctive with doubt, disbelief, and denial

 Tutorial

ANTE TODO Just as the subjunctive is required with expressions of emotion, influence, and will, it is also used with expressions of doubt, disbelief, and denial.

Main clause		Subordinate clause
Dudan	que	su hijo les **diga** la verdad.

▶ The subjunctive is always used in a subordinate clause when there is a change of subject and the expression in the main clause implies negation or uncertainty.

No creo que puedan ir muy lejos.

No es posible que el guía continúe el recorrido sin ustedes.

▶ Here is a list of some common expressions of doubt, disbelief, or denial.

Expressions of doubt, disbelief, or denial

dudar	to doubt	**no es seguro**	it's not certain
negar (e:ie)	to deny	**no es verdad**	it's not true
no creer	not to believe	**es imposible**	it's impossible
no estar seguro/a (de)	not to be sure	**es improbable**	it's improbable
no es cierto	it's not true; it's not certain	**(no) es posible**	it's (not) possible
		(no) es probable	it's (not) probable

El gobierno **niega** que el agua **esté** contaminada.
The government denies that the water is polluted.

Dudo que el gobierno **resuelva** el problema.
I doubt that the government will solve the problem.

Es probable que **haya** menos bosques y selvas en el futuro.
It's probable that there will be fewer forests and jungles in the future.

No es verdad que mi hermano **estudie** ecología.
It's not true that my brother studies ecology.

¡LENGUA VIVA!
In English, the expression *it is probable* indicates a fairly high degree of certainty. In Spanish, however, **es probable** implies uncertainty and therefore triggers the subjunctive in the subordinate clause: **Es probable que venga Elena (pero quizás no puede).**

▶ The indicative is used in a subordinate clause when there is no doubt or uncertainty in the main clause. Here is a list of some expressions of certainty.

Expressions of certainty

no dudar	not to doubt	estar seguro/a (de)	to be sure
no cabe duda de	there is no doubt	es cierto	it's true; it's certain
no hay duda de	there is no doubt	es seguro	it's certain
no negar (e:ie)	not to deny	es verdad	it's true
creer	to believe	es obvio	it's obvious

No negamos que **hay** demasiados carros en las carreteras.
We don't deny that there are too many cars on the highways.

No hay duda de que el Amazonas **es** uno de los ríos más largos.
There is no doubt that the Amazon is one of the longest rivers.

Es verdad que Colombia **es** un país bonito.
It's true that Colombia is a beautiful country.

Es obvio que las ballenas **están** en peligro de extinción.
It's obvious that whales are in danger of extinction.

▶ In affirmative sentences, the verb **creer** expresses belief or certainty, so it is followed by the indicative. In negative sentences, however, when doubt is implied, **creer** is followed by the subjunctive.

Creo que **debemos** usar exclusivamente la energía solar.
I believe we should use solar energy exclusively.

No creo que **haya** vida en el planeta Marte.
I don't believe that there is life on planet Mars.

▶ The expressions **quizás** and **tal vez** are usually followed by the subjunctive because they imply doubt about something.

Quizás haga sol mañana.
Perhaps it will be sunny tomorrow.

Tal vez veamos la luna esta noche.
Perhaps we will see the moon tonight.

¡INTÉNTALO! Completa estas oraciones con la forma correcta del verbo.

recursos
WB pp. 159–160
LM p. 76
vhlcentral.com Lección 13

1. Dudo que ellos _trabajen_ (trabajar).
2. Es cierto que él _come_ (comer) mucho.
3. Es imposible que ellos _salgan_ (salir).
4. Es probable que ustedes _ganen_ (ganar).
5. No creo que ella _vuelva_ (volver).
6. Es posible que nosotros _vayamos_ (ir).
7. Dudamos que tú _recicles_ (reciclar).
8. Creo que ellos _juegan_ (jugar) al fútbol.
9. No niego que ustedes _estudian_ (estudiar).
10. Es posible que ella no _venga_ (venir) a casa.
11. Es probable que Lucio y Carmen _duerman_ (dormir).
12. Es posible que mi prima Marta _llame_ (llamar).
13. Tal vez Juan no nos _oiga_ (oír).
14. No es cierto que Paco y Daniel nos _ayuden_ (ayudar).

Práctica

1 Expansion

 Have pairs prepare another conversation between **Raúl** and his father using expressions of doubt, disbelief, and denial, as well as expressions of certainty. Have pairs role-play their conversations for the class.

2 Expansion

• Continue the activity by making other false statements. Ex: **Voy a hacer una excursión a la Patagonia mañana. Mi abuela sólo come pasteles y cebollas.**

• Tell students to write five statements about themselves or people they know, three of which should be false and two of which should be true. Have them read their sentences to a partner, who will react using statements of certainty or disbelief, and try to determine which statements are true.

1 **Escoger** Escoge las respuestas correctas para completar el diálogo. Luego dramatiza el diálogo con un(a) compañero/a.

RAÚL Ustedes dudan que yo realmente (1)__estudie__ (estudio/estudie). No niego que a veces me (2)__divierto__ (divierto/divierta) demasiado, pero no cabe duda de que (3)__tomo__ (tomo/tome) mis estudios en serio. Estoy seguro de que cuando me vean graduarme van a pensar de manera diferente. Creo que no (4)__tienen__ (tienen/tengan) razón con sus críticas.

PAPÁ Es posible que tu mamá y yo no (5)__tengamos__ (tenemos/tengamos) razón. Es cierto que a veces (6)__dudamos__ (dudamos/dudemos) de ti. Pero no hay duda de que te (7)__pasas__ (pasas/pases) toda la noche en Internet y oyendo música. No es nada seguro que (8)__estés__ (estás/estés) estudiando.

RAÚL Es verdad que (9)__uso__ (uso/use) mucho la computadora pero, ¡piensen! ¿No es posible que (10)__sea__ (es/sea) para buscar información para mis clases? ¡No hay duda de que Internet (11)__es__ (es/sea) el mejor recurso del mundo! Es obvio que ustedes (12)__piensan__ (piensan/piensen) que no hago nada, pero no es cierto.

PAPÁ No dudo que esta conversación nos (13)__va__ (va/vaya) a ayudar. Pero tal vez esta noche (14)__puedas__ (puedes/puedas) trabajar sin música. ¿Está bien?

2 **Dudas** Carolina es una chica que siempre miente. Expresa tus dudas sobre lo que Carolina está diciendo ahora. Usa las expresiones entre paréntesis para tus respuestas.

modelo
El próximo año Marta y yo vamos de vacaciones por diez meses. (dudar)
Dudo que vayan de vacaciones por ese tiempo. ¡Ustedes no son ricas!

1. Estoy escribiendo una novela en español. (no creer)
No creo que estés escribiendo una novela en español.
2. Mi tía es la directora de PETA. (no ser verdad)
No es verdad que tu tía sea la directora de PETA.
3. Dos profesores míos juegan para los Osos *(Bears)* de Chicago. (ser imposible)
Es imposible que dos profesores tuyos jueguen para los Osos de Chicago.
4. Mi mejor amiga conoce al chef Bobby Flay. (no ser cierto)
No es cierto que tu mejor amiga conozca al chef Bobby Flay.
5. Mi padre es dueño del Centro Rockefeller. (no ser posible)
No es posible que tu padre sea dueño del Centro Rockefeller.
6. Yo ya tengo un doctorado *(doctorate)* en lenguas. (ser improbable)
Es improbable que ya tengas un doctorado en lenguas.

 Practice more at **vhlcentral.com.**

AYUDA
Here are some useful expressions to say that you don't believe someone.
¡Qué va!
¡Imposible!
¡No te creo!
¡Es mentira!

TEACHING OPTIONS

Large Groups Divide the class into large groups to stage an environmental debate. Some groups should play the role of environmental advocates while others represent industrialists and big business. Have students take turns presenting a policy platform for the group they represent. When they have finished, opposing groups express their doubts, disbeliefs, and denials.

Heritage Speakers Ask heritage speakers to write a paragraph about a current event or political issue in their cultural community. Ask them to be sure to include expressions of certainty as well as expressions of doubt, disbelief, or denial. Have them read their paragraphs to the class, who will react using the subjunctive with emotions, certainty, or disbelief.

Comunicación

3 **Entrevista** En parejas, imaginen que trabajan para un periódico y que tienen que hacerle una entrevista a la ecologista Mary Axtmann, quien colaboró en la fundación de la organización Ciudadanos Pro Bosque San Patricio, en Puerto Rico. Escriban seis preguntas para la entrevista después de leer las declaraciones de Mary Axtmann. Al final, inventen las respuestas de Axtmann. Answers will vary.

Declaraciones de Mary Axtmann:

"... que el bosque es un recurso ecológico educativo para la comunidad."

"El Bosque San Patricio es un pulmón (*lung*) que produce oxígeno para la ciudad."

"El Bosque San Patricio está en medio de la ciudad de San Juan. Por eso digo que este bosque es una esmeralda (*emerald*) en un mar de concreto."

"El bosque pertenece (*belongs*) a la comunidad."

"Nosotros salvamos este bosque mediante la propuesta (*proposal*) y no la protesta."

4 **Adivinar** Escribe cinco oraciones sobre tu vida presente y futura. Cuatro deben ser falsas y sólo una debe ser cierta. Presenta tus oraciones al grupo. El grupo adivina cuál es la oración cierta y expresa sus dudas sobre las oraciones falsas. Answers will vary.

modelo

Estudiante 1: Quiero irme un año a la selva a trabajar.
Estudiante 2: Dudo que te guste vivir en la selva.
Estudiante 3: En cinco años voy a ser presidente de los Estados Unidos.
Estudiante 2: No creo que seas presidente de los Estados Unidos en cinco años. ¡Tal vez en treinta!

Síntesis

5 **Intercambiar** En grupos, escriban un párrafo sobre los problemas del medio ambiente en su estado o en su comunidad. Compartan su párrafo con otro grupo, que va a ofrecer opiniones y soluciones. Luego presenten su párrafo, con las opiniones y soluciones del otro grupo, a la clase. Answers will vary.

TEACHING OPTIONS

Small Groups In groups of three, have students pretend they are on a live newscast of a local news station. Give each group a breaking news story and have one student play the reporter that interviews the other two about what is happening. The interviewees should use the expressions from the lesson when responding to the reporter's questions. Possible news stories: protest in favor of animal rights, a volcano about to erupt, a local ecological problem.

Game Divide the class into two teams. Team A writes sentences with expressions of certainty, while team B writes sentences with expressions of doubt, disbelief, or denial. Put all the sentences in a hat. Each team takes turns drawing sentences and stating the opposite of what the sentence says. The team with the most correct sentences at the end wins.

3 **Teaching Tip** Before starting, have the class brainstorm different topics that might be discussed with Mary Axtmann.

3 **Expansion** Ask pairs to role-play their interviews for the class.

4 **Teaching Tip** Tell groups to choose a secretary, who will write down the group members' true statements and present them to the class.

5 **Teaching Tip** Assign students to groups of four. Ask group members to appoint a mediator to lead the discussion, a secretary to write the paragraph, a proofreader to check what was written, and a stenographer to take notes on the opinions and solutions of the other group.

5 **Expansion** Have students create a poster illustrating the environmental problems in their community and proposing possible solutions.

13.3 The subjunctive with conjunctions Tutorial

ANTE TODO Conjunctions are words or phrases that connect other words and clauses in sentences. Certain conjunctions commonly introduce adverbial clauses, which describe *how, why, when,* and *where* an action takes place.

Main clause	Conjunction	Adverbial clause
Vamos a visitar a Carlos	**antes de que**	**regrese** a California.

Muchos animales van a estar en peligro de extinción, a menos que los protejamos.

Marissa habla con Jimena antes de que lleguen los chicos.

▶ With certain conjunctions, the subjunctive is used to express a hypothetical situation, uncertainty as to whether an action or event will take place, or a condition that may or may not be fulfilled.

▶ Here is a list of the conjunctions that always require the subjunctive.

Conjunctions that require the subjunctive

a menos que	*unless*	en caso (de) que	*in case (that)*
antes (de) que	*before*	para que	*so that*
con tal (de) que	*provided that*	sin que	*without*

Voy a recoger el envase **en caso de que pueda** reciclarse.
I'm going to pick up the container in case it can be recycled.

Voy al supermercado **para que tengas** algo de comer.
I'm going to the store so that you'll have something to eat.

Algunos animales van a morir **a menos que** haya leyes para protegerlos.
Some animals are going to die unless there are laws to protect them.

Ellos nos llevan a la selva **para que** veamos las plantas tropicales.
They are taking us to the jungle so we can see the tropical plants.

▶ The infinitive, not **que** + [*subjunctive*], is used after the prepositions **antes de, para,** and **sin** when there is no change of subject. **¡Atención!** While you may use a present participle with the English equivalent of these conjunctions, in Spanish you cannot.

Te llamamos **antes de salir** de la casa.
We will call you before leaving the house.

Te llamamos mañana **antes de que salgas.**
We will call you tomorrow before you leave.

Section Goals

In **Estructura 13.3**, students will learn:
• conjunctions that require the subjunctive
• when the infinitive follows a conjunction
• conjunctions followed by the subjunctive or the indicative

Instructional Resources
Supersite: Audio (Lab MP3 Files); Resources (*PowerPoints*, Activity Pack, Scripts, Answer Keys); Testing Program (Quizzes)
WebSAM
Workbook, pp. 161–162
Lab Manual, p. 77

Teaching Tips
• →🔲← To introduce conjunctions that require the subjunctive, make a few statements about yourself. Ex: **Nunca llego a clase tarde a menos que tenga un problema con mi carro. Siempre leo mi correo electrónico antes de que empiece mi primera clase. Camino a clase con tal de que no llueva.** Write each conjunction on the board as you go.
• Have volunteers read the captions to the video stills. Help them identify the conjunctions in the sentences and the subjunctive verbs in the subordinate clauses.

TEACHING OPTIONS

Extra Practice ←🔲→ Write these partial sentences on the board. Have students complete them with true or invented information about their own lives. **1. Voy a terminar los estudios con tal de que..., 2. Necesito $500 en caso de que..., 3. Puedo salir este sábado a menos que..., 4. El mundo cambia sin que..., 5. Debo... antes de que..., 6. Mis padres... para que yo...** Encourage students to expand on their answers with additional information when possible.

Video →🔲← Have students divide a sheet of paper into four columns, labeling them **Voluntad, Emoción, Duda,** and **Conjunción**. Replay the **Fotonovela** episode. Have them listen for each use of the subjunctive, marking the example they hear in the appropriate column.
Extra Practice ←🔲→ Play the episode again, then have students write a short summary that includes each use of the subjunctive.

Conjunctions with subjunctive or indicative

> Voy a formar un club de ecología tan pronto como vuelva al DF.

> Cuando veo basura, la recojo.

Conjunctions used with subjunctive or indicative

cuando	*when*	**hasta que**	*until*
después de que	*after*	**tan pronto como**	*as soon as*
en cuanto	*as soon as*		

▶ With the conjunctions above, use the subjunctive in the subordinate clause if the main clause expresses a future action or command.

> Vamos a resolver el problema **cuando desarrollemos** nuevas tecnologías.
> *We are going to solve the problem when we develop new technologies.*

> **Después de que** ustedes **tomen** sus refrescos, reciclen las botellas.
> *After you drink your soft drinks, recycle the bottles.*

▶ With these conjunctions, the indicative is used in the subordinate clause if the verb in the main clause expresses an action that habitually happens, or that happened in the past.

> Contaminan los ríos **cuando construyen** nuevos edificios.
> *They pollute the rivers when they build new buildings.*

> Contaminaron el río **cuando construyeron** ese edificio.
> *They polluted the river when they built that building.*

¡INTÉNTALO! Completa las oraciones con las formas correctas de los verbos.

1. Voy a estudiar ecología cuando ___vuelva___ (volver) a la universidad.
2. No podemos evitar el cambio climático, a menos que todos ___trabajemos___ (trabajar) juntos.
3. No podemos conducir sin ___contaminar___ (contaminar) el aire.
4. Siempre recogemos mucha basura cuando ___vamos___ (ir) al parque.
5. Elisa habló con el presidente del Club de Ecología después de que ___terminó___ (terminar) la reunión.
6. Vamos de excursión para ___observar___ (observar) los animales y las plantas.
7. La contaminación va a ser un problema muy serio hasta que nosotros ___cambiemos___ (cambiar) nuestros sistemas de producción y transporte.
8. El gobierno debe crear más parques nacionales antes de que los bosques y ríos ___estén___ (estar) completamente contaminados.
9. La gente recicla con tal de que no ___sea___ (ser) difícil.

recursos

WB pp. 161–162

LM p. 77

Ⓢ vhlcentral.com Lección 13

Práctica

1 **Completar** La señora Montero habla de una excursión que quiere hacer con su familia. Completa las oraciones con la forma correcta de cada verbo.

1. Voy a llevar a mis hijos al parque para que ___aprendan___ (aprender) sobre la naturaleza.
2. Voy a pasar todo el día allí a menos que ___haga___ (hacer) mucho frío.
3. Podemos explorar el parque en bicicleta sin ___caminar___ (caminar) demasiado.
4. Vamos a bajar al cráter con tal de que no se ___prohíba___ (prohibir).
5. Siempre llevamos al perro cuando ___vamos___ (ir) al parque.
6. No pensamos ir muy lejos en caso de que ___llueva___ (llover).
7. Vamos a almorzar a la orilla (*shore*) del río cuando nosotros ___terminemos___ (terminar) de preparar la comida.
8. Mis hijos van a dejar todo limpio antes de ___salir___ (salir) del parque.

2 **Frases** Completa estas frases de una manera lógica. *Answers will vary.*

1. No podemos controlar la contaminación del aire a menos que...
2. Voy a reciclar los productos de papel y de vidrio en cuanto...
3. Debemos comprar coches eléctricos tan pronto como...
4. Protegemos los animales en peligro de extinción para que...
5. Mis amigos y yo vamos a recoger la basura de la universidad después de que...
6. No podemos desarrollar nuevas fuentes (*sources*) de energía sin...
7. Hay que eliminar la contaminación del agua para...
8. No podemos proteger la naturaleza sin que...

3 **Organizaciones colombianas** En parejas, lean las descripciones de las organizaciones de conservación. Luego expresen en sus propias (*own*) palabras las opiniones de cada organización.
Answers will vary.

Organización:
Fundación Río Orinoco

Problema:
La destrucción de los ríos

Solución:
Programa para limpiar las orillas de los ríos y reducir la erosión y así proteger los ríos

Organización:
Oficina de Turismo Internacional

Problema:
Necesidad de mejorar la imagen del país en el mercado turístico internacional

Solución:
Plan para promover el ecoturismo en los 54 parques nacionales, usando agencias de publicidad e implementando un plan agresivo de conservación

Organización:
Asociación Nabusimake-Pico Colón

Problema:
Un lugar turístico popular en la Sierra Nevada de Santa Marta necesita mejor mantenimiento

Solución:
Programa de voluntarios para limpiar y mejorar los senderos

> **AYUDA**
>
> Here are some expressions you can use as you complete **Actividad 3**.
>
> **Se puede evitar... con tal de que...**
> **Es necesario... para que...**
> **Debemos prohibir... antes de que...**
> **No es posible... sin que...**
> **Vamos a... tan pronto como...**
> **A menos que... no vamos a...**

 Practice more at **vhlcentral.com.**

Comunicación

4 **Preguntas** En parejas, túrnense para hacerse estas preguntas. *Answers will vary.*

1. ¿Qué haces cada noche antes de acostarte?
2. ¿Qué haces después de salir de la universidad?
3. ¿Qué hace tu familia para que puedas asistir a la universidad?
4. ¿Qué piensas hacer tan pronto como te gradúes?
5. ¿Qué quieres hacer mañana, a menos que haga mal tiempo?
6. ¿Qué haces en tus clases sin que los profesores lo sepan?

5 **Comparar** En parejas, comparen una actividad rutinaria que ustedes hacen con algo que van a hacer en el futuro. Usen palabras de la lista. *Answers will vary.*

antes de	después de que	hasta que	sin (que)
antes de que	en caso de que	para (que)	tan pronto como

> **modelo**
>
> **Estudiante 1:** El sábado vamos al lago. Tan pronto como volvamos, vamos a estudiar para el examen.
> **Estudiante 2:** Todos los sábados llevo a mi primo al parque para que juegue. Pero el sábado que viene, con tal de que no llueva, lo voy a llevar a las montañas.

Síntesis

6 **Tres en raya** *(Tic-Tac-Toe)* Formen dos equipos. Con el vocabulario de esta lección, una persona comienza una frase y otra persona de su equipo la termina usando palabras de la gráfica. El primer equipo que forme tres oraciones seguidas *(in a row)* gana el tres en raya. Hay que usar la conjunción o la preposición y el verbo correctamente. Si no, ¡no cuenta! *Answers will vary.*

¡LENGUA VIVA!

Tic-Tac-Toe has various names in the Spanish-speaking world, including **tres en raya, tres en línea, ta-te-ti, gato, la vieja,** and **triqui-triqui**.

> **modelo**
>
> *Equipo 1*
> **Estudiante 1:** Dudo que podamos eliminar la deforestación…
> **Estudiante 2:** sin que nos ayude el gobierno.
> *Equipo 2*
> **Estudiante 1:** Creo que podemos conservar nuestros recursos naturales…
> **Estudiante 2:** con tal de que todos hagamos algo para ayudar.

cuando	con tal de que	para que
antes de que	para	sin que
hasta que	en caso de que	antes de

4 **Expansion** When pairs have finished asking and answering the questions, work with the whole class, asking several individuals each of the questions and asking other students to react to their responses.
Ex: _____ **hace aeróbicos antes de acostarse. ¿Quién más hace ejercicio? ¡Uf! Hacer ejercicio a esa hora me parece excesivo. ¿Quiénes ven la tele? ¿Nadie lee un libro antes de acostarse?**

5 **Teaching Tip**
👥↔👤 Have partners compare the routines of other people they know and what they are going to do in the future. Have them do the same with celebrities, making guesses about their routines.

6 **Teaching Tips**
• Have groups prepare *Tic-Tac-Toe* cards like the one shown in the activity.
• Regroup the students to do a second round of *Tic-Tac-Toe*.

TEACHING OPTIONS

Heritage Speakers Ask heritage speakers if they played *Tic-Tac-Toe* when growing up. What did they call it? Have them look at the names listed in **¡Lengua viva!** to see if any are familiar. Ask them the names of other childhood games they played and to describe them. Are the games similar to those played by other students in the class?

Pairs 👥↔👤 Ask partners to interview each other about what they must do today for their future goals to become a reality. Students should state what their goals are, the necessary conditions to achieve them, and talk about obstacles they may encounter. Students should use as many conjunctions as possible in their interviews. Have pairs present their interviews to the class.

13.4 Past participles used as adjectives

ANTE TODO In **Lección 5**, you learned about present participles (**estudiando**). Both Spanish and English have past participles. The past participles of English verbs often end in **–ed** (*to turn → turned*), but many are also irregular (*to buy → bought; to drive → driven*).

▶ In Spanish, regular **–ar** verbs form the past participle with **–ado**. Regular **–er** and **–ir** verbs form the past participle with **–ido**.

INFINITIVE	STEM	PAST PARTICIPLE
bailar	bail-	**bailado**
comer	com-	**comido**
vivir	viv-	**vivido**

▶ **¡Atención!** The past participles of **–er** and **–ir** verbs whose stems end in **–a, –e,** or **–o** carry a written accent mark on the **i** of the **–ido** ending.

caer	**caído**	reír	**reído**
creer	**creído**	sonreír	**sonreído**
leer	**leído**	traer	**traído**
oír	**oído**		

Irregular past participles

abrir	**abierto**	morir	**muerto**
decir	**dicho**	poner	**puesto**
describir	**descrito**	resolver	**resuelto**
descubrir	**descubierto**	romper	**roto**
escribir	**escrito**	ver	**visto**
hacer	**hecho**	volver	**vuelto**

▶ In Spanish, as in English, past participles can be used as adjectives. They are often used with the verb **estar** to describe a condition or state that results from an action. Like other Spanish adjectives, they must agree in gender and number with the nouns they modify.

Me gusta usar papel **reciclado.**
I like to use recycled paper.

La mesa está **puesta** y la cena está **servida.**
The table is set and dinner is served.

AYUDA

You already know several past participles used as adjectives:
aburrido, interesado, nublado, perdido, etc.
• • •
Note that all irregular past participles except **dicho** and **hecho** end in **–to.**

¡INTÉNTALO!

Indica la forma correcta del participio pasado de estos verbos.

1. hablar ___hablado___
2. beber ___bebido___
3. decidir ___decidido___
4. romper ___roto___
5. escribir ___escrito___
6. cantar ___cantado___
7. oír ___oído___
8. traer ___traído___
9. correr ___corrido___
10. leer ___leído___
11. ver ___visto___
12. hacer ___hecho___

recursos

WB pp. 163-164

LM p. 78

vhlcentral.com Lección 13

Práctica

1

Completar Completa las oraciones con la forma adecuada del participio pasado del verbo que está entre paréntesis.

1. Nuestra excursión a la selva ya está ___preparada___ (preparar).
2. Todos los detalles están ___escritos___ (escribir) en español.
3. Tenemos que comprar los pasajes, pero Sara no encuentra el mapa. ¡Ay no! Creo que estamos ___perdidos___ (perder).
4. Sabemos que la agencia de viajes está en una plaza muy ___conocida___ (conocer), la Plaza Bolívar. Está ___abierta___ (abrir) de nueve a tres.
5. El nombre de la agencia está ___escrito___ (escribir) en la entrada y en la acera (*sidewalk*).
6. Pero ya son las tres y diez... qué mala suerte. Seguramente la oficina ya está ___cerrada___ (cerrar).

2

Preparativos Tú y tu compañero/a van a hacer un viaje. Túrnense para hacerse estas preguntas sobre los preparativos (*preparations*). Usen el participio pasado en sus respuestas.

> **modelo**
>
> **Estudiante 1:** *¿Compraste los pasajes de avión?*
> **Estudiante 2:** *Sí, los pasajes ya están comprados.*

1. ¿Hiciste las maletas?
 Sí, las maletas ya están hechas.
2. ¿Confirmaste las reservaciones para el hotel?
 Sí, las reservaciones ya están confirmadas.
3. ¿Compraste tus medicinas?
 Sí, las/mis medicinas ya están compradas.
4. ¿Lavaste la ropa?
 Sí, la ropa ya está lavada.
5. ¿Apagaste todas las luces?
 Sí, las luces ya están apagadas.
6. ¿Cerraste bien la puerta?
 Sí, la puerta ya está cerrada.

Comunicación

3

Describir Tú y un(a) compañero/a son agentes de policía y tienen que investigar un crimen. Miren el dibujo y describan lo que encontraron en la habitación del señor Villalonga. Usen el participio pasado en la descripción. Luego, comparen su descripción con la de otra pareja. Answers will vary.

> **modelo**
>
> *La puerta del baño no estaba cerrada.*

Recapitulación

RESUMEN GRAMATICAL

Concepts Diagnostics

Completa estas actividades para repasar los conceptos de gramática que aprendiste en esta lección.

1 **Completar** Completa la tabla con la forma correcta de los verbos. **6 pts.**

Infinitivo	Participio (f.)	Infinitivo	Participio (m.)
completar	completada	hacer	hecho
cubrir	cubierta	pagar	pagado
decir	dicha	perder	perdido
escribir	escrita	poner	puesto

2 **Subjuntivo con conjunciones** Escoge la forma correcta del verbo para completar las oraciones. **6 pts.**

1. En cuanto (empiecen/empiezan) las vacaciones, vamos a viajar.
2. Por favor, llámeme a las siete y media en caso de que no (me despierto/me despierte).
3. Toni va a usar su bicicleta hasta que los coches híbridos (cuesten/cuestan) menos dinero.
4. Estudiantes, pueden entrar al parque natural con tal de que (van/vayan) todos juntos.
5. Debemos conservar el agua antes de que no (queda/quede) nada para beber.
6. Siempre quiero vender mi coche cuando (yo) (piense/pienso) en la contaminación.

3 **Creer o no creer** Completa esta conversación con la forma correcta del presente de indicativo o de subjuntivo, según el contexto. **6 pts.**

CAROLA Creo que (1) _____debemos_____ (nosotras, deber) escribir nuestra presentación sobre el reciclaje.

MÓNICA Hmm, no estoy segura de que el reciclaje (2) _____sea_____ (ser) un buen tema. No hay duda de que la gente ya (3) _____sabe_____ (saber) reciclar.

CAROLA Sí, pero dudo que todos lo (4) _____practiquen_____ (practicar).

MÓNICA ¿Sabes, Néstor? El sábado vamos a ir a limpiar la playa con un grupo de voluntarios. ¿Quieres ir?

NÉSTOR No creo que (5) _____pueda_____ (yo, poder) ir, tengo que estudiar.

CAROLA ¿Estás seguro? ¡Es imposible que (6) _____vayas_____ (tú, ir) a estudiar todo el fin de semana!

NÉSTOR Bueno, sí, tengo un par de horas en la tarde para ir a la playa...

RESUMEN GRAMATICAL

13.1 The subjunctive with verbs of emotion
pp. 426-427

Verbs and expressions of emotion

alegrarse (de)	tener miedo (de)
esperar	es extraño
gustar	es una lástima
molestar	es ridículo
sentir (e:ie)	es terrible
sorprender	es triste
temer	ojalá (que)

Main clause		Subordinate clause
Marta espera	que	yo vaya al lago mañana.
Ojalá		comamos en casa.

13.2 The subjunctive with doubt, disbelief, and denial
pp. 430-431

Expressions of doubt, disbelief, or denial (used with subjunctive)

dudar	no es verdad
negar (e:ie)	es imposible
no creer	es improbable
no estar seguro/a (de)	(no) es posible
no es cierto	(no) es probable
no es seguro	

Expressions of certainty (used with indicative)

no dudar	estar seguro/a (de)
no cabe duda de	es cierto
no hay duda de	es seguro
no negar (e:ie)	es verdad
creer	es obvio

► The infinitive is used after these expressions when there is no change of subject.

13.3 The subjunctive with conjunctions
pp. 434-435

Conjunctions that require the subjunctive

a menos que	en caso (de) que
antes (de) que	para que
con tal (de) que	sin que

TEACHING OPTIONS

TPR Divide the class into two teams, **indicativo** and **subjuntivo**, and have them line up. Point to the first member of each team and call out an expression of doubt, disbelief, denial, or certainty. The student whose team corresponds to the mood has four seconds to step forward and give an example sentence. Ex: **es posible** (The student from the **subjuntivo** team steps forward. Example sentence: **Es posible que el río esté contaminado.**)

Extra Practice Tell students to imagine they are the president of their school's nature club. Have them prepare a short speech in which they try to convince new students about the importance of the environment and nature. Have them use at least three expressions with the subjunctive.

Extra Practice Call out infinitives and have volunteers give the correct past participle.

4 **Oraciones** Escribe oraciones con estos elementos. Usa el subjuntivo y el participio pasado cuando sea necesario. **20 pts.**

1. ser ridículo / los coches / contaminar tanto
Es ridículo que los coches contaminen tanto.

2. el gobierno / ir a proteger / las ciudades / afectar / por los tornados El gobierno va a proteger las ciudades afectadas por los tornados.

3. no caber duda de / tú y yo / poder / hacer mucho más
No cabe duda de que tú y yo podemos hacer mucho más.

4. los ecologistas / temer / los recursos naturales / desaparecer / poco a poco Los ecologistas temen que los recursos naturales desaparezcan poco a poco.

5. (yo) no estar seguro / los niños / poder ir / porque / el parque / estar / cerrar No estoy seguro de que los niños puedan ir porque el parque está cerrado.

6. (yo) alegrarse de / en mi ciudad / reciclarse / el plástico y el vidrio Me alegro de que en mi ciudad se reciclen el plástico y el vidrio.

7. (nosotros) no creer que / la casa / estar / abrir
No creemos que la casa esté abierta.

8. estar prohibido / tocar o dar de comer a / estos animales / proteger Está prohibido tocar o dar de comer a estos animales protegidos.

9. es improbable / existir / leyes / contra la deforestación
Es improbable que existan leyes contra la deforestación.

10. ojalá que / la situación / mejorar / día a día
Ojalá que la situación mejore día a día.

5 **Escribir** Escribe un diálogo de al menos seis oraciones en el que un(a) amigo/a hace comentarios pesimistas sobre la situación del medio ambiente en tu ciudad o región y tú respondes con comentarios y reacciones optimistas. Usa verbos y expresiones de esta lección. **12 pts.** Answers will vary.

6 **Canción** Completa estos versos de una canción de Juan Luis Guerra. **¡2 puntos EXTRA!**

“ Ojalá que ___llueva___ (llover) café en el campo.
Pa'° que todos los niños ___canten___ (cantar) en el campo. ”

Pa' *short for* Para

 Practice more at **vhlcentral.com.**

► The infinitive is used after the prepositions **antes de, para,** and **sin** when there is no change of subject.

Te llamamos **antes de salir** de casa.

Te llamamos mañana **antes de que salgas**.

Conjunctions used with subjunctive or indicative	
cuando	hasta que
después de que	tan pronto como
en cuanto	

13.4 **Past participles used as adjectives** *p. 438*

Past participles		
Infinitive	Stem	Past participle
bailar	bail-	bail**ado**
comer	com-	com**ido**
vivir	viv-	viv**ido**

Irregular past participles			
abrir	**abierto**	morir	**muerto**
decir	**dicho**	poner	**puesto**
describir	**descrito**	resolver	**resuelto**
descubrir	**descubierto**	romper	**roto**
escribir	**escrito**	ver	**visto**
hacer	**hecho**	volver	**vuelto**

► Like common adjectives, past participles must agree with the noun they modify.

Hay unas postales **escritas** en español.

4 Expansion Ask students to create three additional dehydrated sentences. Then have them exchange papers with a classmate and hydrate the sentences.

5 Teaching Tip Remind students that, with the exception of **ojalá**, the word **que** must be present and there must be a change of subject in order to use the subjunctive.

6 Expansion Have students create their own song verse by replacing **llueva café** and **canten** with other verbs in the subjunctive. Ex: **nieve helado** and **bailen**

Section Goals

In **Lectura**, students will:
- learn that recognizing the purpose of a text can help them to understand it
- read two fables

Instructional Resource
Supersite

Estrategia Tell students that recognizing the writer's purpose will help them comprehend an unfamiliar text.

Examinar los textos Have students scan the texts, using the reading strategies they have learned to determine the authors' purposes. Then have them work with a partner to answer the questions. Students should recognize that the texts are fables because the characters are animals.

Predicciones
- Tell pairs that where their predictions differ they should refer back to the texts for resolution.
- Give students these additional predictions: **5. Los textos son infantiles. 6. Se trata de una historia romántica.**

Determinar el propósito
- Tell students to take notes about the characters as they read. Remind students that they should be able to retell the stories in their own words.
- ←👤→ Ask students who generally reads fables. Ex: **Por lo general, ¿las fábulas se escriben para niños, adultos o ambos?** Then have them write a few sentences explaining their answer.

Lectura

NATIONAL communication cultures STANDARDS

Antes de leer

Estrategia

Recognizing the purpose of a text

When you are faced with an unfamiliar text, it is important to determine the writer's purpose. If you are reading an editorial in a newspaper, for example, you know that the journalist's objective is to persuade you of his or her point of view. Identifying the purpose of a text will help you better comprehend its meaning.

Examinar los textos

Primero, utiliza la estrategia de lectura para familiarizarte con los textos. Después contesta estas preguntas y compara tus respuestas con las de un(a) compañero/a. Answers will vary.
- ¿De qué tratan los textos?°
- ¿Son fábulas°, poemas, artículos de periódico…?
- ¿Cómo lo sabes?

Predicciones

Lee estas predicciones sobre la lectura e indica si estás de acuerdo° con ellas. Después compara tus opiniones con las de un(a) compañero/a. Answers will vary.
1. Los textos son del género° de ficción.
2. Los personajes son animales.
3. La acción de los textos tiene lugar en un zoológico.
4. Hay alguna moraleja°.

Determinar el propósito

Con un(a) compañero/a, hablen de los posibles propósitos° de los textos.
Consideren estas preguntas: Answers will vary.
- ¿Qué te dice el género de los textos sobre los posibles propósitos de los textos?
- ¿Piensas que los textos pueden tener más de un propósito? ¿Por qué?

¿De qué tratan los textos? *What are the texts about?*
fábulas *fables* estás de acuerdo *you agree*
género *genre* moraleja *moral* propósitos *purposes*

 Practice more at **vhlcentral.com.**

Sobre los autores

Félix María Samaniego (1745–1801) nació en España y escribió las *Fábulas morales* que ilustran de manera humorística el carácter humano. Los protagonistas de muchas de sus fábulas son animales que hablan.

El perro y el cocodrilo

Bebiendo un perro en el Nilo°,
al mismo tiempo corría.
"Bebe quieto°", le decía
un taimado° cocodrilo.

Díjole° el perro prudente:
"Dañoso° es beber y andar°;
pero ¿es sano el aguardar
a que me claves el diente°? "

¡Oh qué docto° perro viejo!
Yo venero° su sentir°
en esto de no seguir
del enemigo el consejo.

TEACHING OPTIONS

Pairs ←👤→ Pair more advanced students with those who have weaker language skills. Ask pairs to write a short description of the events in one of the fables presented here. Encourage them to use transitional words and expressions, such as **primero, finalmente, por eso,** and **entonces**.

Heritage Speakers 👤↔👤 Ask heritage speakers to describe any fables in Spanish with which they are familiar. If possible, have them bring in copies of the text. Then have a class discussion comparing the protagonists and moral of the fable to those in this **Lectura** section.

Tomás de Iriarte (1750–1791) nació en las islas Canarias y tuvo gran éxito° con su libro *Fábulas literarias*. Su tendencia a representar la lógica a través de° símbolos de la naturaleza fue de gran influencia para muchos autores de su época°.

El pato° y la serpiente

A orillas° de un estanque°,
diciendo estaba un pato:
"¿A qué animal dio el cielo°
los dones que me ha dado°?

"Soy de agua, tierra y aire:
cuando de andar me canso°,
si se me antoja, vuelo°;
si se me antoja, nado".

Una serpiente astuta
que le estaba escuchando,
le llamó con un silbo°,
y le dijo "¡Seo° guapo!

"No hay que echar tantas plantas°;
pues ni anda como el gamo°,
ni vuela como el sacre°,
ni nada como el barbo°;

"y así tenga sabido
que lo importante y raro°
no es entender de todo,
sino ser diestro° en algo".

Nilo *Nile* quieto *in peace* taimado *sly* Díjole *Said to him* Dañoso *Harmful* andar *to walk* ¿es sano... diente? *Is it good for me to wait for you to sink your teeth into me?* docto *wise* venero *revere* sentir *wisdom* éxito *success* a través de *through* época *time* pato *duck* orillas *banks* estanque *pond* cielo *heaven* los dones... dado *the gifts that it has given me* me canso *I get tired* si se... vuelo *if I feel like it, I fly* silbo *hiss* Seo *Señor* No hay... plantas *There's no reason to boast* gamo *deer* sacre *falcon* barbo *barbel (a type of fish)* raro *rare* diestro *skillful*

Después de leer

Comprensión 🔵📄
Escoge la mejor opción para completar cada oración.
1. El cocodrilo _____ perro.
 a. está preocupado por el (b.) quiere comerse al
 c. tiene miedo del
2. El perro _____ cocodrilo.
 (a.) tiene miedo del b. es amigo del
 c. quiere quedarse con el
3. El pato cree que es un animal _____.
 a. muy famoso b. muy hermoso
 (c.) de muchos talentos
4. La serpiente cree que el pato es _____.
 a. muy inteligente (b.) muy tonto c. muy feo

Preguntas 🔵📄
Responde a las preguntas. Answers will vary.
1. ¿Qué representa el cocodrilo?

2. ¿Qué representa el pato?

3. ¿Cuál es la moraleja (*moral*) de "El perro y el cocodrilo"?

4. ¿Cuál es la moraleja de "El pato y la serpiente"?

Coméntalo
En parejas, túrnense para hacerse estas preguntas. ¿Estás de acuerdo con las moralejas de estas fábulas? ¿Por qué? ¿Cuál de estas fábulas te gusta más? ¿Por qué? ¿Conoces otras fábulas? ¿Cuál es su propósito? Answers will vary.

Escribir
Escribe una fábula para compartir con la clase. Puedes escoger algunos animales de la lista o escoger otros. ¿Qué características deben tener estos animales? Answers will vary.
- una abeja (*bee*)
- un gato
- un mono
- un burro
- un perro
- una tortuga
- un águila (*eagle*)
- un pavo real (*peacock*)

Comprensión
- To simplify, before beginning the activity, call on volunteers to explain the fables in their own words using Spanish.
- Encourage students to justify their answers by citing the text.

Preguntas For items 1 and 2, have the class brainstorm a list of adjectives to describe each animal.

Coméntalo For additional class discussion, have students imagine they must rewrite fables with the same morals, but using other animals as the protagonists. Ask students: **¿Qué animales escogen para sustituir a estos animales? ¿Cómo cambia la historia?**

Escribir
- Before writing, encourage students to outline their fables. Have them include the characters, the setting, the basic plot, and the moral in their outlines.
- If needed, supply additional vocabulary for students to describe the animals' characteristics. Ex: **sabio, perezoso, terco, fiel, lento, inquieto, orgulloso, egoísta, (im)paciente**

TEACHING OPTIONS

Extra Practice To challenge students, have them write a story from the viewpoint of the dog, the crocodile, the duck, or the snake, in which they explain their encounter with another animal and what they learned from the experience. You may want to review the imperfect and preterite tenses before assigning this activity.

Small Groups If time and resources permit, bring in other fables in Spanish, such as **Samaniego's *El herrero y el perro*** or ***La abeja haragana*** by **Horacio Quiroga**. Have students work in small groups to read and analyze one fable in terms of its characters and moral. Then have volunteers summarize their analyses for the class.

Colombia

NATIONAL connections cultures STANDARDS

El país en cifras

▶ **Área:** 1.138.910 km² (439.734 millas²), *tres veces el área de Montana*

▶ **Población:** 49.385.000

De todos los países de habla hispana, sólo México tiene más habitantes que Colombia. Casi toda la población colombiana vive en las áreas montañosas y la costa occidental° del país. Aproximadamente el 55% de la superficie° del país está sin poblar°.

▶ **Capital:** Bogotá —9.521.000

▶ **Ciudades principales:** Medellín —4.019.000, Cali —2.627.000, Barranquilla —2.015.000, Cartagena —1.076.000

SOURCE: Population Division, UN Secretariat

Medellín

▶ **Moneda:** peso colombiano

▶ **Idiomas:** español (oficial); lenguas indígenas, criollas y gitanas

Bandera de Colombia

Colombianos célebres

▶ **Edgar Negret,** escultor°, pintor (1920–)
▶ **Juan Pablo Montoya,** automovilista (1975–)
▶ **Fernando Botero,** pintor, escultor (1932–)
▶ **Shakira,** cantante (1977–)

occidental *western* superficie *surface* sin poblar *unpopulated*
escultor *sculptor* dioses *gods* arrojaban *threw* oro *gold*
cacique *chief* llevó *led*

Baile típico de Cartagena

Palacio de San Francisco, Bogotá

Barranquilla
Cartagena
Mar Caribe
PANAMÁ
Sierra Nevada de Santa Marta
VENEZUELA
Río Magdalena
Cordillera Occidental de los Andes
Cordillera Central de los Andes
Medellín
Río Meta
COLOMBIA
ESTADOS UNIDOS
OCÉANO ATLÁNTICO
OCÉANO PACÍFICO
AMÉRICA DEL SUR
Volcán Nevado del Huila
Cali
Bogotá
Cordillera Oriental de los Andes
Océano Pacífico
Cultivo de caña de azúcar cerca de Cali
ECUADOR
PERÚ

recursos

| WB pp. 165–166 | VM pp. 255–256 | vhlcentral.com Lección 13 |

Laguna de Guatavita

¡Increíble pero cierto!

En el siglo XVI los exploradores españoles oyeron la leyenda de El Dorado. Esta leyenda cuenta que los indios, como parte de un ritual en honor a los dioses°, arrojaban° oro° a la laguna de Guatavita y el cacique° se sumergía en sus aguas cubierto de oro. Aunque esto era cierto, muy pronto la exageración llevó° al mito de una ciudad de oro.

Section Goal

In **Panorama**, students will read about the geography, history, and culture of Colombia.

Instructional Resources

Supersite/DVD: *Panorama cultural*
Supersite: Resources (Scripts, Translations, *PowerPoints*, Answer Keys)
WebSAM
Workbook, pp. 165–166
Video Manual, pp. 255–256

Teaching Tips

• Use the **Lección 13 Panorama** overheads to assist with this presentation.

• Have students look at the map of Colombia and talk about the physical features of the country. Point out the three parallel ranges of the Andes in the west. After students look at the call-out photos and read the captions, point out that there are no major cities in the eastern half of the country. Ask students to suggest reasons for the lack of population in that area.

El país en cifras After reading the **Población** section, ask students what the impact might be of having 55% of the nation's territory unpopulated, and the sort of problems this might create for a national government. Point out that, although Spanish is the official language, over 60 indigenous languages are spoken in Colombia.

¡Increíble pero cierto! In their desperation to recover the gold from Lake Guatavita, Spaniards made several attempts to drain the lake. Around 1545, **Hernán Pérez de Quesada** set up a bucket brigade that lowered the water level by a few meters, allowing a small amount of gold to be gathered.

TEACHING OPTIONS

La música One of Colombia's contributions to Latin popular music is the dance called the **cumbia.** The **cumbia** was born out of the fusion of musical elements contributed by each of Colombia's three main ethnic groups: indigenous Andeans, Africans, and Europeans. According to ethnomusicologists, the flutes and wind instruments characteristically used in the **cumbia** derive from indigenous Andean music, the rhythms have their origin in African music, and the melodies are shaped by popular Spanish melodies. **Cumbias** are popular outside of Colombia, particularly in Mexico. Another Colombian dance, native to the Caribbean coast, is the **vallenato,** a fusion of African and European elements. If possible, bring in examples of **cumbias** and **vallenatos** for the class to listen to and compare and contrast.

Lugares • El Museo del Oro

El famoso Museo del Oro del Banco de la República fue fundado° en Bogotá en 1939 para preservar las piezas de orfebrería° de la época precolombina. Tiene más de 30.000 piezas de oro y otros materiales; en él se pueden ver joyas°, ornamentos religiosos y figuras que representaban ídolos. El cuidado con el que se hicieron los objetos de oro refleja la creencia° de las tribus indígenas de que el oro era la expresión física de la energía creadora° de los dioses.

Literatura • Gabriel García Márquez (1928–)

Gabriel García Márquez, ganador del Premio Nobel de Literatura en 1982, es uno de los escritores contemporáneos más importantes del mundo. García Márquez publicó su primer cuento° en 1947, cuando era estudiante universitario. Su libro más conocido, *Cien años de soledad*, está escrito en el estilo° literario llamado "realismo mágico", un estilo que mezcla° la realidad con lo irreal y lo mítico°.

Historia • Cartagena de Indias

Los españoles fundaron la ciudad de Cartagena de Indias en 1533 y construyeron a su lado la fortaleza° más grande de las Américas, el Castillo de San Felipe de Barajas. En la ciudad de Cartagena se conservan muchos edificios de la época colonial, como iglesias, monasterios, palacios y mansiones. Cartagena es conocida también por el Festival Internacional de Música y su prestigioso Festival Internacional de Cine.

Costumbres • El Carnaval

Durante el Carnaval de Barranquilla, la ciudad vive casi exclusivamente para esta fiesta. Este festival es una fusión de las culturas que han llegado° a las costas caribeñas de Colombia y de sus grupos autóctonos°. El evento más importante es la Batalla° de las Flores, un desfile° de carrozas° decoradas con flores. En 2003, la UNESCO declaró este carnaval como Patrimonio de la Humanidad°.

BRASIL

¿Qué aprendiste? Responde a cada pregunta con una oración completa.

1. ¿Cuáles son las principales ciudades de Colombia? Bogotá, Medellín, Cali, Barranquilla y Cartagena son las ciudades principales de Colombia.
2. ¿Qué país de habla hispana tiene más habitantes que Colombia? México tiene más habitantes que Colombia.
3. ¿Quién es Edgar Negret? Edgar Negret es un escultor y pintor colombiano.
4. ¿Cuándo oyeron los españoles la leyenda de El Dorado? En el siglo XVI los españoles oyeron la leyenda.
5. ¿Para qué fue fundado el Museo del Oro? El museo fue fundado para preservar las piezas de orfebrería de la época precolombina.
6. ¿Quién ganó el Premio Nobel de Literatura en 1982? Gabriel García Márquez lo ganó.
7. ¿Qué construyeron los españoles al lado de la ciudad de Cartagena de Indias? Construyeron el Castillo de San Felipe de Barajas.
8. ¿Cuál es el evento más importante del Carnaval de Barranquilla? El evento más importante es la Batalla de las Flores.

Conexión Internet Investiga estos temas en **vhlcentral.com**.

Practice more at **vhlcentral.com.**

1. Busca información sobre las ciudades más grandes de Colombia. ¿Qué lugares de interés hay en estas ciudades? ¿Qué puede hacer un(a) turista en estas ciudades?
2. Busca información sobre pintores y escultores colombianos como Edgar Negret, Débora Arango o Fernando Botero. ¿Cuáles son algunas de sus obras más conocidas? ¿Cuáles son sus temas?

fundado *founded* orfebrería *goldsmithing* joyas *jewels* creencia *belief* creadora *creative* cuento *story* estilo *style* mezcla *mixes* mítico *mythical* fortaleza *fortress* han llegado *have arrived* autóctonos *indigenous* Batalla *Battle* desfile *parade* carrozas *floats* Patrimonio de la Humanidad *World Heritage*

TEACHING OPTIONS

Worth Noting Colombia, like other mountainous countries near the equator, does not experience the four seasons that are known in parts of the United States and Canada. The average temperature of a given location does not vary much during the course of a year. Climate, however, changes dramatically with elevation, the higher altitudes being cooler than the low-lying ones. While the average temperature at sea level is 86°, 57° is the average temperature in Bogotá, the third highest capital in the world, behind La Paz, Bolivia, and Quito, Ecuador. When Colombians speak of **verano** or **invierno**, they are referring to the dry season (**verano**) and the rainy season (**invierno**). When these seasons occur varies from one part of the country to another. In the Andean region, the **verano**, or dry season, generally falls between December and March.

Honduras

NATIONAL connections cultures STANDARDS

El país en cifras

▶ **Área:** 112.492 km² (43.870 millas²),
 un poco más grande que Tennessee

▶ **Población:** 8.386.000
*Cerca del 90 por ciento de la población de
Honduras es mestiza. Todavía hay pequeños
grupos indígenas como los jicaque, los misquito
y los paya, que han mantenido su cultura sin
influencias exteriores y que no hablan español.*

▶ **Capital:** Tegucigalpa—1.181.000

Tegucigalpa

▶ **Ciudades principales:** San Pedro Sula,
 El Progreso, La Ceiba

SOURCE: Population Division, UN Secretariat

▶ **Moneda:** lempira

▶ **Idiomas:** español (oficial), lenguas indígenas, inglés

Bandera de Honduras

Hondureños célebres

▶ **José Antonio Velásquez,** pintor (1906–1983)
▶ **Argentina Díaz Lozano,** escritora (1912–1999)
▶ **Carlos Roberto Reina,** juez° y presidente
 del país (1926–2003)
 Roberto Sosa, escritor (1930–)

juez *judge* presos *prisoners* madera *wood* hamacas *hammocks*

Guacamayo

Artículos de paja en un
mercado de artesanías

Islas de la Bahía Mar Caribe

Golfo de Honduras

GUATEMALA La Ceiba Santa Fe

San Pedro Sula Río Ulúa Sierra Rijol Sierra de Payas Laguna de Caratasca

Sierra Espíritu Santo El Progreso Río Patuca

Sierra Grita Sierra Villasanta Río Guyambre Montañas de Colón

Lago de Yojoa

Tegucigalpa Río Coco

EL SALVADOR Río Choluteca

Océano Pacífico **NICARAGUA**

Baile tradicional

ESTADOS UNIDOS

OCÉANO ATLÁNTICO

HONDURAS

OCÉANO PACÍFICO AMÉRICA DEL SUR

recursos

WB pp. 167–168 VM pp. 257–258 S vhlcentral.com Lección 13

¡Increíble pero cierto!

¿Irías de compras a una prisión? Hace un tiempo,
cuando la Penitenciaría Central de Tegucigalpa aún
funcionaba, los presos° hacían objetos de madera°,
hamacas° y hasta instrumentos musicales y los
vendían en una tienda dentro de la prisión. Allí, los
turistas podían regatear con este especial grupo
de artesanos.

TEACHING OPTIONS

Worth Noting It was in Honduras, on his fourth voyage, that Christopher Columbus first set foot on the mainland of the continent now known as the Americas. On August 14, 1502, the navigator landed at a site near the town of Trujillo and named the country **Honduras** (*Depths*) because of the deep waters along the northern Caribbean coast.

Extra Practice ←👤→ Have students choose one of the people listed in **Hondureños célebres** and find out more about his or her work. They should report their findings to the class.

Lugares • Copán

Copán es una zona arqueológica muy importante de Honduras. Fue construida por los mayas y se calcula que en el año 400 d. C. albergaba° a una ciudad con más de 150 edificios y una gran cantidad de plazas, patios, templos y canchas° para el juego de pelota°. Las ruinas más famosas del lugar son los edificios adornados con esculturas pintadas a mano, los cetros° ceremoniales de piedra y el templo Rosalila.

Economía • Las plantaciones de bananas

Desde hace más de cien años, las bananas son la exportación principal de Honduras y han tenido un papel fundamental en su historia. En 1899, la Standard Fruit Company empezó a exportar bananas del país centroamericano hacia Nueva Orleans. Esta fruta resultó tan popular en los Estados Unidos que generó grandes beneficios° para esta compañía y para la United Fruit Company, otra empresa norteamericana. Estas trasnacionales intervinieron muchas veces en la política hondureña debido° al enorme poder° económico que alcanzaron° en la nación.

San Antonio de Oriente, 1957,
José Antonio Velásquez

Artes • José Antonio Velásquez (1906–1983)

José Antonio Velásquez fue un famoso pintor hondureño. Es catalogado como primitivista° porque sus obras° representan aspectos de la vida cotidiana. En la pintura° de Velásquez es notorio el énfasis en los detalles°, la falta casi total de los juegos de perspectiva y la pureza en el uso del color. Por todo ello, el artista ha sido comparado con importantes pintores europeos del mismo género° como Paul Gauguin o Emil Nolde.

 ¿Qué aprendiste? Responde a cada pregunta con una oración completa.

1. ¿Qué es el lempira?
El lempira es la moneda nacional de Honduras.
2. ¿Por qué es famoso Copán?
Porque es el sitio arqueológico más importante de Honduras.
3. ¿Dónde está el templo Rosalila?
El templo Rosalila está en Copán.
4. ¿Cuál es la exportación principal de Honduras?
Las bananas son la exportación principal de Honduras.
5. ¿Qué fue la Standard Fruit Company? La Standard Fruit Company fue una compañía estadounidense que exportaba bananas de Honduras e intervino muchas veces en la política hondureña.
6. ¿Cómo es el estilo de José Antonio Velásquez?
El estilo de Velásquez es primitivista.
7. ¿Qué temas trataba Velásquez en su pintura?
Velásquez pintaba aspectos de la vida cotidiana.

 Conexión Internet Investiga estos temas en **vhlcentral.com**.

1. ¿Cuáles son algunas de las exportaciones principales de Honduras, además de las bananas? ¿A qué países exporta Honduras sus productos?
2. Busca información sobre Copán u otro sitio arqueológico en Honduras. En tu opinión, ¿cuáles son los aspectos más interesantes del sitio?

 Practice more at **vhlcentral.com**.

albergaba *housed* canchas *courts* juego de pelota *pre-Columbian ceremonial ball game* cetros *scepters* beneficios *profits*
debido a *due to* poder *power* alcanzaron *reached* primitivista *primitivist* obras *works* pintura *painting* detalles *details* género *genre*

Copán Recent archeological studies have focused on the abrupt disappearance of the Mayans from Copán around the ninth century C.E. Findings indicate that the Mayan dynasty suffered a sudden collapse that left the Copán valley virtually depopulated within a century. For more information about Copán, you may want to play the *Panorama cultural* video footage for this lesson.

Las plantaciones de bananas When Hurricane Mitch struck Central America in November 1998, it not only wiped out much of the infrastructure of Honduras, but also destroyed 60% of the projected agricultural exports. Today's agricultural problems are due to rampant deforestation and consequent drought and soil erosion.

José Antonio Velásquez The primitive style established by **José Antonio Velásquez** is now being carried on by his son, **Tulio Velásquez. Tulio**, who was taught by his father, had his first exhibition in 1959. Since then, his primitive art has been exhibited throughout the Americas, in Europe, and in Asia. Have students view works by each artist and then write a brief comparison of their styles.

Conexión Internet Students will find supporting Internet activities and links at **vhlcentral.com**.

TEACHING OPTIONS

Worth Noting Honduras was among the hardest hit of the Central American nations when Hurricane Mitch struck in late October 1998. Major roadways and bridges were destroyed, entire communities were covered in mud, and an air of hopelessness and desperation pervaded the country. With one of the lowest per capita income levels and one of the highest illiteracy rates in Central America, Hondurans were already

struggling before the devastation of the hurricane. Since then, the economy has grown about 7% per year, but half of the population still remains below the poverty line.
Heritage Speakers ◄■► Ask heritage speakers to research one of the Honduran topics mentioned in **Panorama** and write a three-paragraph essay about it. They may then present their findings orally to the class.

Instructional Resources

Supersite: Audio (Textbook & Lab MP3s); Testing Program (Tests, MP3s)

WebSAM

Lab Manual, p. 78

La naturaleza

el árbol	tree
el bosque (tropical)	(tropical; rain) forest
el cielo	sky
el cráter	crater
el desierto	desert
la estrella	star
la flor	flower
la hierba	grass
el lago	lake
la luna	moon
la naturaleza	nature
la nube	cloud
la piedra	stone
la planta	plant
el río	river
la selva, la jungla	jungle
el sendero	trail; path
el sol	sun
la tierra	land; soil
el valle	valley
el volcán	volcano

Los animales

el animal	animal
el ave, el pájaro	bird
la ballena	whale
el gato	cat
el mono	monkey
el perro	dog
el pez (sing.), los peces (pl.)	fish
la tortuga (marina)	(sea) turtle
la vaca	cow

 Audio: Vocabulary

recursos

LM p. 78 | vhlcentral.com Lección 13

El medio ambiente

el calentamiento global	global warming
el cambio climático	climate change
la conservación	conservation
la contaminación (del aire; del agua)	(air; water) pollution
la deforestación	deforestation
la ecología	ecology
el/la ecologista	ecologist
el ecoturismo	ecotourism
la energía (nuclear, solar)	(nuclear, solar) energy
el envase	container
la extinción	extinction
la fábrica	factory
el gobierno	government
la lata	(tin) can
la ley	law
el medio ambiente	environment
el peligro	danger
la (sobre)población	(over)population
el reciclaje	recycling
el recurso natural	natural resource
la solución	solution
cazar	to hunt
conservar	to conserve
contaminar	to pollute
controlar	to control
cuidar	to take care of
dejar de (+ *inf.*)	to stop (doing something)
desarrollar	to develop
descubrir	to discover
destruir	to destroy
estar afectado/a (por)	to be affected (by)
estar contaminado/a	to be polluted
evitar	to avoid
mejorar	to improve
proteger	to protect
reciclar	to recycle
recoger	to pick up
reducir	to reduce
resolver (o:ue)	to resolve; to solve
respirar	to breathe
de aluminio	(made) of aluminum
de plástico	(made) of plastic
de vidrio	(made) of glass
ecologista	ecological
puro/a	pure
renovable	renewable

Las emociones

alegrarse (de)	to be happy
esperar	to hope; to wish
sentir (e:ie)	to be sorry; to regret
temer	to fear
es extraño	it's strange
es una lástima	it's a shame
es ridículo	it's ridiculous
es terrible	it's terrible
es triste	it's sad
ojalá (que)	I hope (that); I wish (that)

Las dudas y certezas

(no) creer	(not) to believe
(no) dudar	(not) to doubt
(no) negar (e:ie)	(not) to deny
es imposible	it's impossible
es improbable	it's improbable
es obvio	it's obvious
No cabe duda de	There is no doubt that…
No hay duda de	There is no doubt that…
(no) es cierto	it's (not) certain
(no) es posible	it's (not) possible
(no) es probable	it's (not) probable
(no) es seguro	it's (not) certain
(no) es verdad	it's (not) true

Conjunciones

a menos que	unless
antes (de) que	before
con tal (de) que	provided (that)
cuando	when
después de que	after
en caso (de) que	in case (that)
en cuanto	as soon as
hasta que	until
para que	so that
sin que	without
tan pronto como	as soon as

Past participles used as adjectives	See page 438.
Expresiones útiles	See page 421.

En la ciudad

Communicative Goals

You will learn how to:

- Give advice to others
- Give and receive directions
- Discuss daily errands and city life

Lesson Goals

In **Lección 14**, students will be introduced to the following:
- names of commercial establishments
- banking terminology
- citing locations
- city transportation
- Mexican architect **Luis Barragán**
- subjunctive in adjective clauses
- **nosotros/as** commands
- future tense
- identifying point of view
- a video about Mexico City's subway system
- geographic, economic, and historical information about Venezuela and the Dominican Republic

A primera vista Here are some additional questions you can ask based on the photo: **¿Cómo es la vida en la ciudad? ¿Y en el campo? ¿Dónde prefieres vivir? ¿Por qué? ¿Es posible que una ciudad esté completamente libre de contaminación? ¿Cómo? ¿Qué responsabilidades tienen las personas que viven en una ciudad para proteger el medio ambiente?**

Teaching Tip Look for these icons for additional communicative practice:

→👤←	Interpretive communication
←👤→	Presentational communication
👤↔👤	Interpersonal communication

A PRIMERA VISTA
- ¿Viven estas personas en un bosque, un pueblo o una ciudad?
- ¿Dónde están, en una calle o en un sendero?
- ¿Es posible que estén afectadas por la contaminación? ¿Por qué?
- ¿Está limpio o sucio el lugar donde están?

INSTRUCTIONAL RESOURCES

Supersite (vhlcentral.com)
Video: ***Fotonovela*, *Flash cultura*, *Panorama cultural***
Also on DVD
Audio: Textbook and Lab MP3 Files (*also on CD*)
Activity Pack: Information Gap Activities, games, additional activity handouts

Resources: Textbook Answer Key, WB/VM/LM Answer Key, Scripts, Translations, **Vocabulario adicional**, lesson plans, **Estructura** *PowerPoints*, Overheads
Testing Program: Quizzes, Tests, Exams, MP3s (*also on Test Generator CD*)

Learning Management System (Assignment Task Manager, Gradebook)
WebSAM (online Workbook/Video Manual/Lab Manual)
Workbook/Video Manual
Lab Manual

En la ciudad

Más vocabulario

la frutería	fruit store
la heladería	ice cream shop
la pastelería	pastry shop
la pescadería	fish market
la cuadra	(city) block
la dirección	address
la esquina	corner
el estacionamiento	parking lot
derecho	straight (ahead)
enfrente de	opposite; facing
hacia	toward
cruzar	to cross
doblar	to turn
hacer diligencias	to run errands
quedar	to be located
el cheque (de viajero)	(traveler's) check
la cuenta corriente	checking account
la cuenta de ahorros	savings account
ahorrar	to save (money)
cobrar	to cash (a check)
depositar	to deposit
firmar	to sign
llenar (un formulario)	to fill out (a form)
pagar a plazos	to pay in installments
pagar al contado/ en efectivo	to pay in cash
pedir prestado/a	to borrow
pedir un préstamo	to apply for a loan
ser gratis	to be free of charge

Variación léxica

cuadra	⟷	manzana (*Esp.*)
estacionamiento	⟷	aparcamiento (*Esp.*)
doblar	⟷	girar; virar; dar vuelta
hacer diligencias	⟷	hacer mandados

recursos

WB pp. 169–170 | LM p. 79 | **S** vhlcentral.com Lección 14

la peluquería, el salón de belleza
el banco
el supermercado
la panadería
la joyería
el cajero automático
Indica cómo llegar. (indicar)
Está perdida. (estar)

Práctica

el letrero

la carnicería

la zapatería

la lavandería

1 **Escuchar** 🎧 Mira el dibujo. Luego escucha las oraciones e indica si lo que dice cada una es **cierto** o **falso**.

	Cierto	Falso		Cierto	Falso
1.	○	⊘	6.	⊘	○
2.	⊘	○	7.	⊘	○
3.	○	⊘	8.	○	⊘
4.	⊘	○	9.	○	⊘
5.	○	⊘	10.	⊘	○

2 **¿Quién la hizo?** 🎧 Escucha la conversación entre Telma y Armando. Escribe el nombre de la persona que hizo cada diligencia o una X si nadie la hizo. Una diligencia la hicieron los dos.

1. abrir una cuenta corriente Armando
2. abrir una cuenta de ahorros Telma
3. ir al banco Armando, Telma
4. ir a la panadería X
5. ir a la peluquería Telma
6. ir al supermercado Armando

3 **Seleccionar** Indica dónde haces estas diligencias.

banco	joyería	pescadería
carnicería	lavandería	salón de belleza
frutería	pastelería	zapatería

1. comprar galletas pastelería
2. comprar manzanas frutería
3. lavar la ropa lavandería
4. comprar mariscos pescadería
5. comprar pollo carnicería
6. comprar sandalias zapatería

4 **Completar** Completa las oraciones con las palabras más adecuadas.

1. El banco me regaló un reloj. Fue ____gratis____.
2. Me gusta ____ahorrar____ dinero, pero no me molesta gastarlo.
3. La cajera me dijo que tenía que ____firmar____ el cheque en el dorso (*on the back*) para cobrarlo.
4. Para pagar con un cheque, necesito tener dinero en mi ____cuenta corriente____.
5. Mi madre va a un ____cajero automático____ para obtener dinero en efectivo cuando el banco está cerrado.
6. Cada viernes, Julio lleva su cheque al banco y lo ____cobra____ para tener dinero en efectivo.
7. Ana ____deposita____ su cheque en su cuenta de ahorros.
8. Cuando viajas, es buena idea llevar cheques ____de viajero____.

ESTE SUR NORTE OESTE

TEACHING OPTIONS

Game Add a visual aspect to this vocabulary presentation by playing **Concentración**. On eight cards, write names of types of commercial establishments. On another eight cards, draw or paste a picture that matches each commercial establishment. Place the cards facedown in four rows of four. In pairs, students select two cards. If the cards match, the pair keeps them. If the cards do not match, students replace them in their original

position. The pair with the most cards at the end wins.
Pairs Have each student write a shopping list with ten items. Have students include items found in different stores. Then have them exchange their shopping list with a partner. Each student tells his or her partner where to go to get each item. Ex: **unas botas (Para comprar unas botas, tienes que ir a la zapatería que queda en la calle ____.)**

1 **Teaching Tip** Have students check their answers by reading each statement in the script to the class and asking volunteers to say whether it is true or false. To challenge students, have them correct the false statements.

1 **Script** 1. El supermercado queda al este de la plaza, al lado de la joyería. 2. La zapatería está al lado de la carnicería. 3. El banco queda al sur de la plaza. 4. Cuando sales de la zapatería, la lavandería está a su lado. 5. La carnicería está al lado del banco. *Script continues on page 452.*

2 **Teaching Tip** Do this listening exercise as a TPR activity. Have students raise their right hand if **Armando** did the errand, their left hand if it was **Telma**, or both hands if both people did it.

2 **Script** TELMA: Hola, Armando, ¿qué tal? ARMANDO: Pues bien. Acabo de hacer unas diligencias. Fui a la carnicería y al supermercado. ¿Y tú? Estás muy guapa. ¿Fuiste a la peluquería? T: Sí, fui al nuevo salón de belleza que está enfrente de la panadería. También fui al banco. A: ¿A qué banco fuiste? T: Fui al banco Mercantil. Está aquí en la esquina. A: Ah, ¿sí? Yo abrí una cuenta corriente ayer, ¡y fue gratis! T: Sí, yo abrí una cuenta de ahorros esta mañana y no me cobraron nada. *Textbook MP3s*

3 **Expansion** After students finish, ask them what else can be bought or done in each establishment. Ex: **¿Qué más podemos comprar en la pastelería?**

4 **Expansion**
👥↔👥 Ask students to compare and contrast aspects of banking. Ex: ATM vs. traditional tellers; paying bills online vs. by check; savings account vs. checking account. Have them work in groups of three to make a list of **Ventajas** and **Desventajas**.

1 **Script (continued)**

6. Cuando sales de la joyería, el cajero automático está a su lado. 7. No hay ninguna heladería cerca de la plaza. 8. La joyería está al oeste de la peluquería. 9. Hay una frutería al norte de la plaza. 10. No hay ninguna pastelería cerca de la plaza.

Textbook MP3s

Teaching Tips

• Use the **Lección 14 Contextos** overheads to assist with this vocabulary presentation.

• 👥↔👥 Ask students questions about the scene to elicit active vocabulary. Ex: **¿Qué hace la señora en la ventanilla? Y las personas que esperan detrás de ella, ¿qué hacen?** Then, involve students in a conversation about sending mail and the post office. Ex: **Necesito estampillas. ¿Dónde está la oficina de correos que está más cerca de aquí? A mí me parece que la carta es una forma de escritura en vías de extinción. Desde que uso el correo electrónico y los mensajes de texto, casi nunca escribo cartas. ¿Quiénes todavía escriben cartas?**

5 **Expansion**

• 👥↔👥 After you have gone over the activity, have pairs role-play the conversation, encouraging them to ad-lib as they go.

• ↔👥 Have pairs create short conversations similar to the one presented in the activity, but set in a different place of business. Ex: **el salón de belleza, la pescadería**

6 **Teaching Tips**

• To simplify, create a word bank of useful phrases on the board. Ask volunteers to suggest expressions and grammatical constructions that will help students develop their role-plays.

• Go over the new vocabulary by asking questions. Ex: **¿Cuándo pedimos un préstamo? ¿Los cheques son para una cuenta corriente o una cuenta de ahorros?**

Manda/Envía un paquete. (mandar, enviar)

la estampilla, el sello

Hacen cola. (hacer)

SELLOS

el cartero

el correo

Echa una carta al buzón. (echar)

el sobre

En el correo

5 **Conversación** Completa la conversación entre Juanita y el cartero con las palabras más adecuadas.

CARTERO Buenas tardes, ¿es usted la señorita Ramírez? Le traigo un (1) _____paquete_____.

JUANITA Sí, soy yo. ¿Quién lo envía?

CARTERO La señora Brito. Y también tiene dos (2) _____cartas_____.

JUANITA Ay, pero ¡ninguna es de mi novio! ¿No llegó nada de Manuel Fuentes?

CARTERO Sí, pero él echó la carta al (3) _____buzón_____ sin poner un (4) _____sello_____ en el sobre.

JUANITA Entonces, ¿qué recomienda usted que haga?

CARTERO Sugiero que vaya al (5) _____correo_____. Con tal de que pague el costo del sello, se le puede dar la carta sin ningún problema.

JUANITA Uy, otra diligencia, y no tengo mucho tiempo esta tarde para (6) _____hacer_____ cola en el correo, pero voy enseguida. ¡Ojalá que sea una carta de amor!

6 **En el banco** Tú eres un(a) empleado/a de banco y tu compañero/a es un(a) estudiante universitario/a que necesita abrir una cuenta corriente. En parejas, hagan una lista de las palabras que pueden necesitar para la conversación. Después lean estas situaciones y modifiquen su lista original según la situación. Answers will vary.

• una pareja de recién casados quiere pedir un préstamo para comprar una casa

• una persona quiere información de los servicios que ofrece el banco

• un(a) estudiante va a estudiar al extranjero (*abroad*) y quiere saber qué tiene que hacer para llevar su dinero de una forma segura

• una persona acaba de ganar 50 millones de dólares en la lotería y quiere saber cómo invertirlos (*invest them*)

Ahora, escojan una de las cuatro situaciones y represéntenla para la clase.

 Practice more at **vhlcentral.com.**

Comunicación

7 Diligencias En parejas, decidan quién va a hacer cada diligencia y cuál es la manera más rápida de llegar a los diferentes lugares desde el campus. Answers will vary.

AYUDA

Note these different meanings:

quedar to be located; to be left over; to fit

quedarse to stay, to remain

> **cobrar unos cheques**
>
> **Estudiante 1:** Yo voy a cobrar unos cheques. ¿Cómo llego al banco?
> **Estudiante 2:** Conduce hacia el norte hasta cruzar la calle Oak.
> El banco queda en la esquina a la izquierda.

1. enviar un paquete
2. comprar botas nuevas
3. comprar un pastel de cumpleaños
4. lavar unas camisas
5. comprar helado
6. cortarse (to cut) el pelo

8 El Hatillo Trabajen en parejas para representar los papeles de un(a) turista que está perdido/a en El Hatillo y de un(a) residente de la ciudad que quiere ayudarlo/la. Answers will vary.

NOTA CULTURAL

El Hatillo es un municipio del área metropolitana de Caracas. Forma parte del Patrimonio Cultural de Venezuela y es muy popular por su arquitectura pintoresca, sus restaurantes y sus tiendas de artesanía.

Legend:
- Plaza Bolívar
- Plaza Sucre
- banco
- Casa de la Cultura
- farmacia
- iglesia
- terminal
- escuela
- estacionamiento
- joyería
- zapatería
- café Primavera

El Hatillo

(map with calle Miranda, calle 2 de Mayo, calle Escalona, calle La Paz, calle Sta. Rosalía, calle Bolívar, calle Sucre, calle Comercio, calle Bella Vista, calle El Matadero)

> **Plaza Sucre, café Primavera**
>
> **Estudiante 1:** Perdón, ¿por dónde queda la Plaza Sucre?
> **Estudiante 2:** Del café Primavera, camine derecho por la calle Sucre
> hasta cruzar la calle Comercio…

1. Plaza Bolívar, farmacia
2. Casa de la Cultura, Plaza Sucre
3. banco, terminal
4. estacionamiento (este), escuela
5. Plaza Sucre, estacionamiento (oeste)
6. joyería, banco
7. farmacia, joyería
8. zapatería, iglesia

9 Cómo llegar En grupos, escriban un minidrama en el que unos/as turistas están preguntando cómo llegar a diferentes sitios de la comunidad en la que ustedes viven.
Answers will vary.

Teaching Tips / Sidebar

7 Teaching Tip
Draw a map of your campus and nearby streets that includes symbols of public buildings. Ask students to use the map to answer your questions and direct you to different locations. Ex: **¿En qué calle queda el banco más cercano? Estoy en la esquina de ____ y ____. ¿Me pueden indicar cómo llegar a _____?**

8 Teaching Tips
- Go over the icons in the map's legend, finding the place each represents.
- Explain that the task is to give directions to the first place from the second place. Ask students to find **Plaza Sucre** and **café Primavera** on the map.

8 Expansion
Ask students to read about **El Hatillo** on the Internet and report back to the class with their findings.

9 Teaching Tips
- As a class, brainstorm different tourist sites in and around your area. Write them on the board.
- Using one of the places listed on the board, model the activity by asking volunteers to give driving directions from campus.

TEACHING OPTIONS

TPR Have students work in pairs. One partner is blindfolded and the other gives directions for getting from one place in the classroom to another. Ex: **¿Quieres llegar de tu escritorio a la puerta? Bueno, camina derecho cinco pasos. Da tres pasos a la izquierda. Luego dobla a la derecha y camina cuatro pasos para que no choques con el escritorio. Estás cerca de la puerta. Sigue derecho dos pasos más. Allí está la puerta.**

Game Divide the class into teams of three. Each must write directions to a particular commercial establishment close to campus. The teams read their directions, and the other teams try to guess what errand they are running. Each team that guesses correctly wins a point. The team with the most points wins.

Corriendo por la ciudad

Maru necesita entregar unos documentos en el Museo de Antropología.

PERSONAJES

 MARU MIGUEL

S Video: *Fotonovela*
Record and Compare

1

MARU Miguel, ¿estás seguro de que tu coche está estacionado en la calle de Independencia? Estoy en la esquina de Zaragoza y Francisco Sosa. OK. Estoy enfrente del salón de belleza.

2

MIGUEL Dobla a la avenida Hidalgo. Luego cruza la calle Independencia y dobla a la derecha. El coche está enfrente de la pastelería.

MARU ¡Ahí está! Gracias, cariño. Hablaremos luego.

3

MARU Vamos, arranca. Pensé que podías aguantar unos kilómetros más. Necesito un coche que funcione bien. (*en el teléfono*) Miguel, tu coche está descompuesto. Voy a pasar al banco porque necesito dinero, y luego me iré en taxi al museo.

4

MARU Hola, Moni. Lo siento, tengo que ir a entregar un paquete y todavía tengo que ir a un cajero.

MÓNICA ¡Uf! Y la cola está súper larga.

MARU ¿Me puedes prestar algo de dinero?

MÓNICA Déjame ver cuánto tengo. Estoy haciendo diligencias, y me gasté casi todo el efectivo en la carnicería y en la panadería y en la frutería.

5

6

MÓNICA ¿Estás bien? Te ves pálida. Sentémonos un minuto.

MARU ¡No tengo tiempo! Tengo que llegar al Museo de Antropología. Necesito entregar...

MÓNICA ¡Ah, sí, tu proyecto!

Section Goals

In **Fotonovela**, students will:
• receive comprehensible input from free-flowing discourse
• learn functional phrases that preview lesson grammatical structures

Instructional Resources
Supersite/DVD: *Fotonovela*
Supersite: Resources (Scripts, Translations, Answer Keys)
WebSAM
Video Manual, pp. 221–222

Video Recap: Lección 13
Before doing this **Fotonovela** section, review the previous one with these questions:
1. ¿Adónde fueron Marissa y Jimena? (Fueron al santuario de tortugas.) 2. ¿Qué aprendieron allí? (Aprendieron sobre las normas para proteger a las tortugas.) 3. ¿Qué le pasó a Felipe durante el recorrido por la selva? (Se cayó.) 4. ¿Qué mentira les dijo Felipe a las chicas? (Les dijo que se perdió todo el recorrido.)

Video Synopsis **Maru** is racing against the clock to deliver her application for an internship at the **Museo de Antropología**. However, with **Miguel's** car broken down again, long lines at the bank, and heavy traffic, **Maru** needs her friend **Mónica's** help to meet the deadline.

Teaching Tip Ask students to predict what they would see and hear in an episode in which one of the characters runs into trouble when trying to get somewhere on time in a big city. Then, ask them a few questions to help them summarize this episode.

TEACHING OPTIONS

Video Tips General suggestions for using video clips in the classroom can be found on page IAE-10 of this Instructor's Annotated Edition.

Corriendo por la ciudad →👤← Play the **Corriendo por la ciudad** episode without sound and ask the class to summarize what they see. Then, ask them to predict the content of the episode and write their predictions on the board. Then play the entire episode with sound. Finally, through questions and discussion, lead the class to an accurate summary of the plot.

MÓNICA

MÓNICA ¿Puedes mandarlo por correo? El correo está muy cerca de aquí.

MARU El plazo para mandarlo por correo se venció la semana pasada. Tengo que entregarlo personalmente.

MARU ¿Me podrías prestar tu coche?

MÓNICA Estás muy nerviosa para manejar con este tráfico. Te acompaño. ¡No!, mejor, yo te llevo. Mi coche está en el estacionamiento de la calle Constitución.

MARU En esta esquina dobla a la derecha. En el semáforo, a la izquierda y sigue derecho.

MÓNICA Hay demasiado tráfico. No sé si podemos...

MARU Hola, Miguel. No, no hubo más problemas. Lo entregué justo a tiempo. Nos vemos más tarde. (*a Mónica*) ¡Vamos a celebrar!

recursos

VM
pp. 221–222

vhlcentral.com
Lección 14

Expresiones útiles

Getting/giving directions

Estoy en la esquina de Zaragoza y Francisco Sosa.
I'm at the corner of Zaragoza and Francisco Sosa.
Dobla a la avenida Hidalgo.
Turn on Hidalgo Avenue.
Luego cruza la calle Independencia y dobla a la derecha.
Then cross Independencia Street and turn right.
El coche está enfrente de la pastelería.
The car is in front of the bakery.
En el semáforo, a la izquierda y sigue derecho.
Left at the light, then straight ahead.

Talking about errands

Voy a pasar al banco porque necesito dinero.
I'm going to the bank because I need money.
No tengo tiempo.
I don't have time.
Estoy haciendo diligencias, y me gasté casi todo el efectivo.
I'm running errands, and I spent most of my cash.

Asking for a favor

¿Me puedes prestar algo de dinero?
Could you lend me some money?
¿Me podrías prestar tu coche?
Could I borrow your car?

Talking about deadlines

Tengo que entregar mi proyecto.
I have to turn in my project.
El plazo para mandarlo por correo se venció la semana pasada.
The deadline to mail it in passed last week.

Additional vocabulary

acompañar *to accompany*
aguantar *to endure, to hold up*
ándale *come on*
pálido/a *pale*
¿Qué onda? *What's up?*

¿Qué pasó?

1 Expansion Give students these true/false statements as items 5–6: **5. Maru va al museo en taxi. (Falso. Mónica la lleva en su coche.) 6. Hay mucha gente en el cajero. (Cierto.)**

Nota cultural For timely delivery of correspondence in Mexico City, courier services are often used within the city limits, rather than the postal service. Some companies even have their own in-house messengers for such purposes.

2 Teaching Tip Write these sentences on separate slips of paper so that students can arrange them in the correct sequence.

3 Expansion Have pairs come up with an additional situation and then make a list of the errands that **Maru, Mónica,** and **Miguel** need to do in order to complete the task. Then have them read the list of errands aloud so the class can guess what the situation might be.

4 Possible Conversation
E1: **Voy al supermercado y a la heladería. ¿Quieres ir conmigo?**
E2: **Sí, en cuanto termine mi almuerzo, te acompaño.**
E1: **Tengo que pasar por el banco porque necesito dinero.**
E2: **Yo también necesito ir al banco. ¿Hay un banco por aquí con cajero automático?**
E1: **Hay un cajero automático a tres cuadras de aquí. Queda en la calle Libertad.**
E2: **También necesito ir a la lavandería y al correo para mandar unas cartas.**
E1: **No hay problema... el correo y la lavandería están cerca del banco.**
E2: **Oye, ¿qué vas a hacer esta noche?**
E1: **Voy a ir a la fiesta que celebran para un amigo. ¿Quieres ir?**
E2: **¡Sí, gracias!**

1 ¿Cierto o falso? Decide si lo que dicen estas oraciones es **cierto** o **falso**. Corrige las oraciones falsas.

	Cierto	Falso
1. Miguel dice que su coche está estacionado enfrente de la carnicería.	○	◉
2. Maru necesita pasar al banco porque necesita dinero.	◉	○
3. Mónica gastó el efectivo en la joyería y el supermercado.	○	◉
4. Maru puede mandar el paquete por correo.	○	◉

1. Miguel dice que su coche está estacionado enfrente de la pastelería.
3. Mónica gastó el efectivo en la carnicería, la panadería y la frutería.
4. Maru no puede mandar el paquete por correo.

CONSULTA
To review the use of verbs like **necesitar**, see **Estructura 12.4**, p. 398.

2 Ordenar Pon los sucesos de la **Fotonovela** en el orden correcto.

a. Maru le pide dinero prestado a Mónica. __3__
b. Maru entregó el paquete justo a tiempo (*just in time*). __6__
c. Mónica dice que hay una cola súper larga en el banco. __2__
d. Mónica lleva a Maru en su coche. __4__
e. Maru dice que se irá en taxi al museo. __1__
f. Maru le dice a Mónica que doble a la derecha en la esquina. __5__

3 Otras diligencias En parejas, hagan una lista de las diligencias que Miguel, Maru y Mónica necesitan hacer para completar estas actividades. *Answers will vary.*

1. enviar un paquete por correo
2. pedir una beca (*scholarship*)
3. visitar una nueva ciudad
4. abrir una cuenta corriente
5. celebrar el cumpleaños de Mónica
6. comprar una nueva computadora portátil

MARU

MIGUEL **MÓNICA**

4 Conversación Un(a) compañero/a y tú son vecinos/as. Uno/a de ustedes acaba de mudarse y necesita ayuda porque no conoce la ciudad. Los/Las dos tienen que hacer algunas diligencias y deciden hacerlas juntos/as. Preparen una conversación breve incluyendo planes para ir a estos lugares. *Answers will vary.*

> **modelo**
>
> **Estudiante 1:** Necesito lavar mi ropa. ¿Sabes dónde queda una lavandería?
> **Estudiante 2:** Sí. Aquí a dos cuadras hay una. También tengo que lavar mi ropa. ¿Qué te parece si vamos juntos?

▶ un banco
▶ una lavandería
▶ un supermercado
▶ una heladería
▶ una panadería

AYUDA
primero *first*
luego *then*
¿Sabes dónde queda...? *Do you know where...is?*
¿Qué te parece? *What do you think?*
¡Cómo no! *But of course!*

Practice more at **vhlcentral.com.**

Ortografía ⓢ Concepts

Las abreviaturas

In Spanish, as in English, abbreviations are often used in order to save space and time while writing. Here are some of the most commonly used abbreviations in Spanish.

usted ⟶ **Ud.** ustedes ⟶ **Uds.**

As you have already learned, the subject pronouns **usted** and **ustedes** are often abbreviated.

don ⟶ **D.** doña ⟶ **Dña.** doctor(a) ⟶ **Dr(a).**
señor ⟶ **Sr.** señora ⟶ **Sra.** señorita ⟶ **Srta.**

These titles are frequently abbreviated.

centímetro ⟶ **cm** metro ⟶ **m** kilómetro ⟶ **km**
litro ⟶ **l** gramo ⟶ **g, gr** kilogramo ⟶ **kg**

The abbreviations for these units of measurement are often used, but without periods.

por ejemplo ⟶ **p. ej.** página(s) ⟶ **pág(s).**

These abbreviations are often seen in books.

derecha ⟶ **dcha.** izquierda ⟶ **izq., izqda.**
código postal ⟶ **C.P.** número ⟶ **n.°**

These abbreviations are often used in mailing addresses.

Sra. Emilia F. Bazán
Cía. Romero, S.A.
9396
Calle Lozano, n.° 37
Caracas, Venezuela

Banco ⟶ **Bco.** Compañía ⟶ **Cía.**
cuenta corriente ⟶ **c/c.** Sociedad Anónima (*Inc.*) ⟶ **S.A.**

These abbreviations are frequently used in the business world.

Práctica Escribe otra vez esta información usando las abreviaturas adecuadas.

1. doña María Dña. María
2. señora Pérez Sra. Pérez
3. Compañía Mexicana de Inversiones Cía. Mexicana de Inversiones
4. usted Ud.
5. Banco de Santander Bco. de Santander
6. doctor Medina Dr. Medina
7. Código Postal 03697 C.P. 03697
8. cuenta corriente número 20-453 c/c., n.° 20-453

Emparejar En la tabla hay nueve abreviaturas. Empareja los cuadros necesarios para formarlas. S.A., Bco., cm, Dña., c/c., dcha., Srta., C.P., Ud.

S.	c.	C.	c	co.	U
B	c/	Sr	A.	D	dc
ta.	P.	ña.	ha.	m	d.

recursos
LM p. 80
vhlcentral.com Lección 14

Section Goal

In **Ortografía**, students will learn some common Spanish abbreviations.

Instructional Resources
Supersite: Audio (Lab MP3 Files); Resources (Scripts, Answer Keys)
WebSAM
Lab Manual, p. 80

Teaching Tips
- Point out that the abbreviations **Ud.** and **Uds.** begin with a capital letter, though the spelled-out forms do not.
- Write **D.**, **Dña.**, **Dr.**, **Dra.**, **Sr.**, **Sra.**, and **Srta.** on the board. Again, point out that the abbreviations begin with a capital letter, though the spelled-out forms do not.
- Point out that the period in **n.°** does not appear at the end of the abbreviation.
- Point out that **Ortografía** replaces **Pronunciación** in the Student Edition for **Lecciones 10–15**, but not in the Lab Manual. The **Recursos** box references the **Pronunciación** sections found in all lessons of the Lab Manual.

Successful Language Learning Tell students that the ability to recognize common abbreviations will make it easier for them to interpret written information in a Spanish-speaking country.

TEACHING OPTIONS

Pairs Working in pairs, have students write an imaginary mailing address that uses as many abbreviations as possible. Then have a few pairs write their work on the board and ask for volunteers to read the addresses aloud.

Extra Practice Write a list of abbreviations on the board; each abbreviation should have one letter missing. Have the class fill in the missing letters and tell you what each abbreviation stands for. Ex: **U__.**, **D__a.**, **g__**, **Bc__.**, **d__ha.**, **p__gs.**, **__zq.**, **S.__.**

Section Goals

In **Cultura**, students will:
- read about city transportation
- learn transportation-related terms
- read about Mexican architect **Luis Barragán**
- read about nicknames for Latin American and Spanish cities

Instructional Resources

Supersite/DVD: *Flash cultura*
Supersite: Resources (Scripts, Translations, Answer Keys)
WebSAM
Video Manual, pp. 293–294

En detalle

Antes de leer

←👤→ Ask students to predict the content of this reading based on the title, photo, and map. Have them share with the class their experiences with public transportation.

Lectura
- Explain that most bus and subway stations have detailed maps with colors and station names in order to facilitate system use. Many stations are named after a neighborhood, an important building, or a monument in the area.
- Of the 175 stations in Mexico City's subway system, at least two downtown stations are attractions in themselves. **Insurgentes** is packed with market stalls and is a popular place for shopping. Near the national palace, **Pino Suárez** houses an Aztec pyramid, which was unearthed during the **metro's** construction.

Después de leer Ask students to give examples of U.S. or Canadian cities that have transit systems, and if possible what type (**autobús, metro, tranvía,** or **tren**).

❶ **Expansion** Ask students to write three additional true/false statements for a partner to complete.

EN DETALLE

S Additional Reading
Video: *Flash cultura*

connections cultures NATIONAL STANDARDS

Paseando en metro

Hoy es el primer día de Teresa en la Ciudad de México. Debe tomar el metro para ir del centro de la ciudad a Coyoacán, en el sur. Llega a la estación Zócalo y compra un pasaje por el equivalente a veintitrés centavos° de dólar, ¡qué ganga! Con este pasaje puede ir a cualquier° parte de la ciudad o del área metropolitana.

No sólo en México, sino también en ciudades de Venezuela, Chile, Argentina y España, hay sistemas de transporte público eficientes y

muy económicos. También suele haber° varios tipos de transporte: autobús, metro, tranvía°, microbús y tren. Generalmente se pueden comprar abonos° de uno o varios días para un determinado tipo de transporte. En algunas ciudades también existen abonos de transporte combinados que permiten usar, por ejemplo, el metro y el autobús o el autobús y el tren. En estas ciudades, los metros, autobuses y trenes pasan con mucha frecuencia. Las paradas° y estaciones están bien señalizadas°.

Vaya°, Teresa ya está llegando a Coyoacán. Con lo que ahorró en el pasaje del metro, puede comprarse un helado de mango y unos esquites° en el jardín Centenario.

El metro

El primer metro de Suramérica que se abrió al público fue el de Buenos Aires, Argentina (1° de diciembre de 1913); el último, el de Valparaíso, Chile (23 de noviembre de 2005).

Ciudad	Pasajeros/Día (aprox.)
México D.F., México	4.500.000
Madrid, España	2.500.000
Santiago, Chile	2.500.000
Buenos Aires, Argentina	1.700.000
Caracas, Venezuela	1.650.000
Medellín, Colombia	500.000
Guadalajara, México	165.000

centavos *cents* **cualquier** *any* **suele haber** *there usually are* **tranvía** *streetcar* **abonos** *passes* **paradas** *stops* **señalizadas** *labeled* **Vaya** *Well* **esquites** *toasted corn kernels*

ACTIVIDADES

1 **¿Cierto o falso?** Indica si lo que dice cada oración es **cierto** o **falso**. Corrige la información falsa.

1. En la Ciudad de México, el pasaje de metro cuesta 23 dólares. **Falso.** Cuesta 23 centavos de dólar.
2. En México, un pasaje se puede usar sólo para ir al centro de la ciudad. **Falso.** Se puede ir a cualquier parte de la ciudad o del área metropolitana.
3. En Chile hay varios tipos de transporte público. **Cierto.**
4. En ningún caso los abonos de transporte sirven para más de un tipo de transporte. **Falso.** Hay abonos combinados que permiten usar distintos tipos de transporte.
5. Los trenes, autobuses y metros pasan con mucha frecuencia. **Cierto.**
6. Hay pocos letreros en las paradas y estaciones. **Falso.** Las paradas y estaciones están bien señalizadas.
7. Los servicios de metro de México y España son los que mayor cantidad de viajeros transporta cada día. **Cierto.**
8. La ciudad de Buenos Aires tiene el sistema de metro más viejo de Latinoamérica. **Cierto.**
9. El metro que lleva menos tiempo en servicio es el de la ciudad de Medellín, Colombia **Falso.** Es el de Valparaíso, Chile.

TEACHING OPTIONS

Small Groups ←👤→ Have students work in small groups, research one of the transportation systems mentioned in the reading, and create an informational poster. Tell them to include a system map, the pricing scheme, a brief history, and any other significant information. Have groups present their posters to the class.

Pairs 👤↔👤 In pairs, have students use the Internet to research a map of a Spanish-speaking city's subway system and write a dialogue between a tourist trying to get to a museum and a subway ticket agent. Encourage students to use formal commands. Have pairs role-play their dialogues for the class.

ASÍ SE DICE

En la ciudad

el parqueadero (Col., Pan.) el parqueo (Bol., Cuba, Amér. C.)	el estacionamiento
dar un aventón (Méx.); dar botella (Cuba)	to give (someone) a ride
el subterráneo, el subte (Arg.)	el metro

EL MUNDO HISPANO

Apodos de ciudades

Así como Nueva York es la Gran Manzana, muchas ciudades hispanas tienen un apodo°.

- **La tacita de plata°** A Cádiz, España, se le llama así por sus edificios blancos de estilo árabe.

- **Ciudad de la eterna primavera** Arica, Chile; Cuernavaca, México, y Medellín, Colombia, llevan este sobrenombre por su clima templado° durante todo el año.

- **La docta°** Así se conoce a la ciudad argentina de Córdoba por su gran tradición universitaria.

- **La ciudad de los reyes** Así se conoce Lima, Perú, porque fue la capital del Virreinato° del Perú y allí vivían los virreyes°.

- **La arenosa** Barranquilla, Colombia, se le llama así por sus orillas del río cubiertas° de arena.

apodo *nickname* plata *silver* templado *mild* docta *erudite* Virreinato *Viceroyalty* virreyes *viceroys* cubiertas *covered*

PERFIL

Luis Barragán: arquitectura y emoción

Para el arquitecto mexicano **Luis Barragán** (1902–1988) los sentimientos° y emociones que despiertan sus diseños eran muy importantes. Afirmaba° que la arquitectura tiene una dimensión espiritual. Para él, era belleza, inspiración, magia°, serenidad, misterio, silencio, privacidad, asombro°...

Casa Barragán, Ciudad de México, 1947-1948

Las obras de Barragán muestran un suave° equilibrio entre la naturaleza y la creación humana. Su estilo también combina la arquitectura tradicional mexicana con conceptos modernos. Una característica de sus casas son las paredes

envolventes° de diferentes colores con muy pocas ventanas.

En 1980, Barragán obtuvo° el Premio Pritzker, algo así como el Premio Nobel de Arquitectura. Está claro que este artista logró° que sus casas transmitieran sentimientos especiales.

sentimientos *feelings* Afirmaba *He stated* magia *magic* asombro *amazement* suave *smooth* envolventes *enveloping* obtuvo *received* logró *managed*

Conexión Internet

¿Qué otros arquitectos combinan las construcciones con la naturaleza?

Go to **vhlcentral.com** to find more cultural information related to this **Cultura** section.

ACTIVIDADES

2 **Comprensión** Responde a las preguntas.

1. ¿En qué país estás si te dicen "Dame botella al parqueo"? en Cuba
2. ¿Qué ciudades tienen clima templado todo el año? Arica, Chile; Cuernavaca, México, y Medellín, Colombia
3. ¿Qué es más importante en los diseños de Barragán: la naturaleza o la creación humana? Son igual de importantes.
4. ¿Qué premio obtuvo Barragán y cuándo? Barragán obtuvo el Premio Pritzker en 1980.

3 **¿Qué ciudad te gusta?** Escribe un párrafo breve sobre el sentimiento que despiertan las construcciones que hay en una ciudad o un pueblo que te guste mucho. Explica cómo es y cómo te sientes cuando estás allí. Inventa un apodo para este lugar. Answers will vary.

recursos

VM pp. 293–294

vhlcentral.com Lección 14

Practice more at vhlcentral.com.

TEACHING OPTIONS

Large Groups 👥↔👥 Divide the class into two groups. Give each member of the first group a card with a nickname from **El mundo hispano**. Give each member of the second group a card with the reason for the nickname. Have students circulate around the room, asking questions until they find their partners. Finally, have the class form a "map" of the cities. Ask pairs to read their cards aloud.

Extra Practice ←👥→ If time and resources permit, have students use the Internet or library to find and copy a picture of one of **Luis Barragán's** buildings or spaces. Ask them to write five sentences describing the photo. Also tell them to include their personal opinions. Encourage students to compare the work to another building or space with which they are familiar.

Section Goal

In **Estructura 14.1**, students will learn the use of the subjunctive in adjective clauses.

Instructional Resources

Supersite: Audio (Lab MP3 Files); Resources (*PowerPoints*, Activity Pack, Scripts, Answer Keys); Testing Program (Quizzes)
WebSAM
Workbook, pp. 171–172
Lab Manual, p. 81

Teaching Tips

• Add a visual aspect to this grammar presentation. Use magazine pictures to compare and contrast the uses of the indicative and subjunctive in adjective clauses. Ex: **Esta casa tiene una fuente en el jardín. Yo busco una casa que tenga piscina. Este señor come insectos vivos. ¿Conocen a alguien que coma insectos vivos?**

• Ask volunteers to answer questions that describe their wishes. Ex: **¿Qué buscas en una casa? ¿Qué buscas en un(a) compañero/a de cuarto?**

• Ask volunteers to read the captions to the video stills and point out the subordinate adjective clause and its antecedent, then indicate whether the indicative or subjunctive is used in the clause, and why.

• Make sure to point out the role of the indefinite article vs. the definite article in determining the use of the subjunctive in adjective clauses. Show students the two sentences in **¡Atención!** and have them explain why the subjunctive is used in one, but not the other.

14.1 The subjunctive in adjective clauses

S Tutorial

ANTE TODO In **Lección 13**, you learned that the subjunctive is used in adverbial clauses after certain conjunctions. You will now learn how the subjunctive can be used in adjective clauses to express that the existence of someone or something is uncertain or indefinite.

¿Conoces una joyería que esté cerca?

No, no conozco ninguna joyería que esté cerca de aquí.

▶ The subjunctive is used in an adjective (or subordinate) clause that refers to a person, place, thing, or idea that either does not exist or whose existence is uncertain or indefinite. In the examples below, compare the differences in meaning between the statements using the indicative and those using the subjunctive.

¡ATENCIÓN!

Adjective clauses are subordinate clauses that modify a noun or pronoun in the main clause of a sentence. That noun or pronoun is called the *antecedent*.

Indicative	Subjunctive
Necesito **el libro** que **tiene** información sobre Venezuela. *I need the book that has information about Venezuela.*	Necesito **un libro** que **tenga** información sobre Venezuela. *I need a book that has information about Venezuela.*
Quiero vivir en **esta casa** que **tiene** jardín. *I want to live in this house that has a garden.*	Quiero vivir en **una casa** que **tenga** jardín. *I want to live in a house that has a garden.*
En mi barrio, hay **una heladería** que **vende** helado de mango. *In my neighborhood, there's an ice cream shop that sells mango ice cream.*	En mi barrio no hay **ninguna heladería** que **venda** helado de mango. *In my neighborhood, there is no ice cream shop that sells mango ice cream.*

▶ When the adjective clause refers to a person, place, thing, or idea that is clearly known, certain, or definite, the indicative is used.

Quiero ir **al supermercado** que **vende** productos venezolanos.
I want to go to the supermarket that sells Venezuelan products.

Busco **al profesor** que **enseña** japonés.
I'm looking for the professor who teaches Japanese.

Conozco **a alguien** que **va** a esa peluquería.
I know someone who goes to that beauty salon.

Tengo **un amigo** que **vive** cerca de mi casa.
I have a friend who lives near my house.

¡ATENCIÓN!

Observe the important role that the indefinite article vs. the definite article plays in determining the use of the subjunctive in adjective clauses. Read the following sentences and notice why they are different:

¿Conoces un restaurante italiano que *esté* cerca de mi casa?

¿Conoces el restaurante italiano que *está* cerca de mi casa?

▶ The personal **a** is not used with direct objects that are hypothetical people. However, as you learned in **Lección 7**, **alguien** and **nadie** are always preceded by the personal **a** when they function as direct objects.

Necesitamos **un empleado** que **sepa** usar computadoras.
We need an employee who knows how to use computers.

Necesitamos **al empleado** que **sabe** usar computadoras.
We need the employee who knows how to use computers.

Buscamos **a alguien** que **pueda** cocinar.
We're looking for someone who can cook.

No conocemos **a nadie** que **pueda** cocinar.
We don't know anyone who can cook.

▶ The subjunctive is commonly used in questions with adjective clauses when the speaker is trying to find out information about which he or she is uncertain. However, if the person who responds to the question knows the information, the indicative is used.

—¿Hay un parque que **esté** cerca de nuestro hotel?
Is there a park that's near our hotel?

—Sí, hay un parque que **está** muy cerca del hotel.
Yes, there's a park that's very near the hotel.

▶ **¡Atención!** Here are some verbs which are commonly followed by adjective clauses in the subjunctive:

Verbs commonly used with subjunctive

buscar	haber
conocer	necesitar
encontrar	querer

SECCIÓN AMARILLA
Busque cualquier información que necesite.

¡INTÉNTALO! Escoge entre el subjuntivo y el indicativo para completar cada oración.

1. Necesito una persona que ___pueda___ (puede/pueda) cantar bien.
2. Buscamos a alguien que ___tenga___ (tiene/tenga) paciencia.
3. ¿Hay restaurantes aquí que ___sirvan___ (sirven/sirvan) comida japonesa?
4. Tengo una amiga que ___saca___ (saca/saque) fotografías muy bonitas.
5. Hay una carnicería que ___está___ (está/esté) cerca de aquí.
6. No vemos ningún apartamento que nos ___interese___ (interesa/interese).
7. Conozco a un estudiante que ___come___ (come/coma) hamburguesas todos los días.
8. ¿Hay alguien que ___diga___ (dice/diga) la verdad?

TEACHING OPTIONS

Pairs Ask pairs to rewrite the sentences in the ¡Inténtalo! activity with the unused verbs (**puede, tiene, sirven, saque, esté, interesa, coma, dice**) and change the main clauses accordingly.
Extra Practice Ask students to imagine that they have the opportunity to build their ideal community. Have them write a paragraph describing what they need, want, and are looking for in this place, taking into account the climate, inhabitants,

cultural and employment opportunities, architecture, leisure activities, geography, and so on. Their descriptions should include only sentences in the subjunctive. Refer them to the verbs in the list to help them develop their ideas.

Práctica

1

Completar Completa estas oraciones con la forma correcta del indicativo o del subjuntivo de los verbos entre paréntesis.

1. Buscamos un hotel que ___tenga___ (tener) piscina.
2. ¿Sabe usted dónde ___queda___ (quedar) el Correo Central?
3. ¿Hay algún buzón por aquí donde yo ___pueda___ (poder) echar una carta?
4. Ana quiere ir a la carnicería que ___está___ (estar) en la avenida Lecuna.
5. Encontramos un restaurante que ___sirve___ (servir) comida típica venezolana.
6. ¿Conoces a alguien que ___sepa___ (saber) mandar un *fax* por computadora?
7. Llamas al empleado que ___entiende___ (entender) este nuevo programa de computación.
8. No hay nada en este mundo que ___sea___ (ser) gratis.

2

Oraciones Marta está haciendo diligencias en Caracas con una amiga. Forma oraciones con estos elementos, usando el presente de indicativo o de subjuntivo. Haz los cambios que sean necesarios.

1. yo / conocer / un / panadería / que / vender / pan / cubano
 Yo conozco una panadería que vende pan cubano.
2. ¿hay / alguien / que / saber / dirección / de / un / buen / carnicería?
 ¿Hay alguien que sepa la dirección de una buena carnicería?
3. yo / querer / comprarle / mi / hija / un / zapatos / que / gustar
 Yo quiero comprarle a mi hija unos zapatos que le gusten.
4. ella / no / encontrar / nada / que / gustar / en / ese / zapatería
 Ella no encuentra nada que le guste en esa zapatería.
5. ¿tener / dependientas / algo / que / ser / más / barato?
 ¿Tienen las dependientas algo que sea más barato?
6. ¿conocer / tú / alguno / banco / que / ofrecer / cuentas / corrientes / gratis?
 ¿Conoces tú algún banco que ofrezca cuentas corrientes gratis?
7. nosotras / no / conocer / nadie / que / hacer / tanto / diligencias / como / nosotras
 Nosotras no conocemos a nadie que haga tantas diligencias como nosotras.
8. nosotras / necesitar / un / línea / de / metro / que / nos / llevar / a / casa
 Nosotras necesitamos una línea de metro que nos lleve a casa.

NOTA CULTURAL

El **metro** de Caracas empezó a funcionar en 1983, después de varios años de intensa publicidad para promoverlo (*promote it*). El arte fue un recurso importante en la promoción del metro. En las estaciones se pueden admirar obras (*works*) de famosos escultores venezolanos como Carlos Cruz-Diez y Jesús Rafael Soto.

3

Anuncios clasificados En parejas, lean estos anuncios y luego describan el tipo de persona u objeto que se busca. Answers will vary.

CLASIFICADOS

VENDEDOR(A) Se necesita persona dinámica y responsable con buena presencia. Experiencia mínima de un año. Horario de trabajo flexible. Llamar a Joyería Aurora de 10 a 13h y de 16 a 18h. Tel: 263-7553

PELUQUERÍA UNISEX Se busca persona con experiencia en peluquería y maquillaje para trabajar tiempo completo. Llamar de 9 a 13: 30h. Tel: 261-3548

COMPARTIR APARTAMENTO Se necesita compañera para compartir apartamento de 2 alcobas en el Chaco. Alquiler $500 por mes. No fumar. Llamar al 951-3642 entre 19 y 22h.

CLASES DE INGLÉS Profesor de Inglaterra con diez años de experiencia ofrece clases para grupos o instrucción privada para individuos. Llamar al 933-4110 de 16:30 a 18:30.

SE BUSCA CONDOMINIO Se busca condominio en Sabana Grande con 3 alcobas, 2 baños, sala, comedor y aire acondicionado. Tel: 977-2018.

EJECUTIVO DE CUENTAS Se requiere joven profesional con al menos dos años de experiencia en el sector financiero. Se ofrecen beneficios excelentes. Enviar currículum vitae al Banco Unión, Avda. Urdaneta 263, Caracas.

Comunicación

4

Subjuntivo Completa estas frases de una manera lógica. Luego, con un(a) compañero/a, túrnense para comparar sus respuestas. Answers will vary.

> **modelo**
> **Estudiante 1:** Tengo una novia que sabe bailar tango. ¿Y tú?
> **Estudiante 2:** Yo tengo un novio que habla alemán.

1. Deseo un trabajo (*job*) que…
2. Algún día espero tener un apartamento/una casa que…
3. Mis padres buscan un carro que…, pero yo quiero un carro que…
4. Tengo un(a) novio/a que…
5. Un(a) consejero/a (*advisor*) debe ser una persona que…
6. Me gustaría (*I would like*) conocer a alguien que…
7. En esta clase no hay nadie que…
8. No tengo ningún profesor que…

5

Encuesta Tu profesor(a) va a darte una hoja de actividades. Circula por la clase y pregúntales a tus compañeros/as si conocen a alguien que haga cada actividad de la lista. Si responden que sí, pregúntales quién es y anota sus respuestas. Luego informa a la clase de los resultados de tu encuesta.
Answers will vary.

6

¿Compatibles? Vas a mudarte a un apartamento con dos dormitorios. Como no quieres pagar la renta tú solo/a, estás buscando a un(a) compañero/a para que viva contigo. Escribe un anuncio buscando a alguien con cuatro características que consideres importantes y pégalo en la pared de la clase. Puedes usar algunas de estas opciones u otras en tu anuncio y no olvides usar el subjuntivo. Answers will vary.

- cocinar
- escuchar hip-hop
- estar informado/a
- gustarle la política/el arte/los deportes
- llevarse bien con los animales
- ser vegetariano/a / limpio/a / optimista
- tener paciencia

> **modelo**
> Busco a alguien a quien no le guste el fútbol, que sea vegetariano, juegue videojuegos y le fascine la ciencia ficción.

Luego lee los anuncios de tus compañeros/as. ¿Con quién(es) podrías compartir tu apartamento? Busca tres candidatos/as y entrevístalos/las en dos minutos. Túrnate para entrevistar y ser entrevistado. ¿Encontraste a la persona ideal para que viva contigo? Answers will vary.

Síntesis

7

Busca los cuatro Tu profesor(a) te va a dar una hoja con ocho anuncios clasificados y a tu compañero/a otra hoja con ocho anuncios distintos a los tuyos. Háganse preguntas para encontrar los cuatro anuncios de cada hoja que tienen su respuesta en la otra. Answers will vary.

Practice more at **vhlcentral.com.**

4 Teaching Tip Model the activity by giving a personal example. Write a sentence starter on the board and then complete it. Ex: **No conozco ningún restaurante cercano que…** (No conozco ningún restaurante cercano que tenga un patio grande.)

4 Expansion Assign students to groups of six and ask them to pick two responses and make a visual representation of them. Designate a student from each group to show the visual for the class to guess what the response was. Guesses should include an adjective clause.

5 Teaching Tip Distribute the *Hojas de actividades* (Activity Pack/Supersite) that correspond to this activity.

5 Expansion ←👤→ Have pairs write six original sentences with adjective clauses based on the answers of the **encuesta**. Three sentences should have subordinate clauses in the subjunctive and three in the indicative.

6 Teaching Tip 👤↔👤 During the interview phase of the activity, encourage students to ask follow-up questions to gather more information that will aid them in determining compatibility. For example, if the interviewee generally likes animals and the interviewer has a cat, they should make sure that the potential roommate doesn't have any issues with cats.

7 Teaching Tip Divide the class into pairs and distribute the handouts from the Activity Pack (Activity Pack/Supersite) that correspond to this Information Gap Activity.

7 Expansion ←👤→ Have pairs write counterparts for two of the ads that do not have them. One ad should be for someone seeking to buy something and the other should be a "for sale" ad.

Section Goal
In **Estructura 14.2**, students will learn **nosotros/as** commands.

Instructional Resources
Supersite: Audio (Lab MP3 Files); Resources (*PowerPoints*, Activity Pack, Scripts, Answer Keys); Testing Program (Quizzes)
WebSAM
Workbook, pp. 173–174
Lab Manual, p. 82

Teaching Tips
• Model the **nosotros/as** commands by making suggestions to the class. Begin by having students respond to **tú** and **ustedes** commands, and then add commands for the class as a whole. Ex: ____ , abre el libro. ____ y ____ , abran el libro. Ahora todos, abramos el libro. Abrámoslo.
• Check comprehension by asking volunteers to convert **vamos a** + [*infinitive*] suggestions into **nosotros/as** commands.

Successful Language Learning
Ask students to think about how they might use the **nosotros/as** commands when they are out with a group of Spanish speakers.

14.2 Nosotros/as commands Tutorial

ANTE TODO You have already learned familiar (**tú**) commands and formal (**usted/ustedes**) commands. You will now learn **nosotros/as** commands, which are used to give orders or suggestions that include yourself and other people.

▶ **Nosotros/as** commands correspond to the English *Let's*.

Nosotros/as commands

Infinitive	Nosotros/as form of present subjunctive	Nosotros/as command
cruzar	crucemos	**(no) crucemos**
comer	comamos	**(no) comamos**
escribir	escribamos	**(no) escribamos**
pedir	pidamos	**(no) pidamos**
salir	salgamos	**(no) salgamos**
volver	volvamos	**(no) volvamos**

▶ As the chart shows, both affirmative and negative **nosotros/as** commands are generally formed by using the first-person plural form of the present subjunctive.

Crucemos la calle.
Let's cross the street.

No crucemos la calle.
Let's not cross the street.

▶ The affirmative *Let's* + [*verb*] command may also be expressed with **vamos a** + [*infinitive*]. Remember, however, that **vamos a** + [*infinitive*] can also mean *we are going to (do something)*. Context and tone of voice determine which meaning is being expressed.

Vamos a cruzar la calle.
Let's cross the street.

Vamos a trabajar mucho.
We're going to work a lot.

▶ To express *Let's go*, the present indicative form of **ir** (**vamos**) is used, not the subjunctive. For the negative command, however, the subjunctive is used.

Vamos a la pescadería.
Let's go to the fishmarket.

No **vayamos** a la pescadería.
Let's not go to the fish market.

CONSULTA
Remember that stem-changing **–ir** verbs have an additional stem change in the **nosotros/as** and **vosotros/as** forms of the present subjunctive. To review these forms, see **Estructura 12.3**, p. 395.

Pensemos, ¿adónde fuiste hoy?

¡Eso es! ¡El carro de Miguel! Vamos.

TEACHING OPTIONS

TPR Brainstorm gestures related to this lesson's vocabulary. Have students stand. At random, call out **nosotros/as** commands. All students should perform the appropriate gesture. Keep a brisk pace. Ex: **Echemos una carta al buzón. Hagamos cola. Firmemos un cheque. Paguemos en efectivo. Pidamos un préstamo. Llenemos un formulario.**

Extra Practice To provide oral practice with **nosotros/as** commands, create sentences with **vamos a** before the name of a business. Ex: **Vamos al banco. Vamos a la peluquería.** Say the sentence, have students repeat it, then call on individual students to add an appropriate **nosotros/as** command form. Ex: **Saquemos dinero. Cortémonos el pelo.**

▶ Object pronouns are always attached to affirmative **nosotros/as** commands. A written accent is added to maintain the original stress.

Firmemos el cheque. ——————→ **Firmémoslo.**
Let's sign the check. *Let's sign it.*

Escribamos a Ana y Raúl. ————→ **Escribámosles.**
Let's write Ana and Raúl. *Let's write them.*

▶ Object pronouns are placed in front of negative **nosotros/as** commands.

No **les paguemos** el préstamo. No **se lo digamos** a ellos.
Let's not pay them the loan. *Let's not tell them.*

No **lo compremos.** No **se la presentemos.**
Let's not buy it. *Let's not introduce her to him.*

▶ When **nos** or **se** is attached to an affirmative **nosotros/as** command, the final **–s** is dropped from the verb ending.

Sentémonos allí. **Démoselo** a ella.
Let's sit there. *Let's give it to her.*

▶ The **nosotros/as** command form of **irse** (*to go away*) is **vámonos**. Its negative form is **no nos vayamos**.

¡Vámonos de vacaciones! **No nos vayamos** de aquí.
Let's go away on vacation! *Let's not go away from here.*

¡Hagamos un viaje!

¡Compremos un caballo!

¡Pidamos un préstamo!

BANCOSUR. LLÁMANOS.

recursos

WB
pp. 173–174

LM
p. 82

Ⓢ
vhlcentral.com
Lección 14

¡INTÉNTALO! Indica los mandatos afirmativos y negativos de la primera persona del plural (**nosotros/as**) de estos verbos.

1. estudiar — *estudiemos, no estudiemos*
2. cenar — *cenemos, no cenemos*
3. leer — *leamos, no leamos*
4. decidir — *decidamos, no decidamos*
5. decir — *digamos, no digamos*
6. cerrar — *cerremos, no cerremos*
7. levantarse — *levantémonos, no nos levantemos*
8. irse — *vámonos, no nos vayamos*
9. depositar — *depositemos, no depositemos*
10. quedarse — *quedémonos, no nos quedemos*
11. pedir — *pidamos, no pidamos*
12. vestirse — *vistámonos, no nos vistamos*

Práctica

1 **Completar** Completa esta conversación con mandatos de **nosotros/as.** Luego, representa la conversación con un(a) compañero/a.

MARÍA Sergio, ¿quieres hacer diligencias ahora o por la tarde?

SERGIO No (1)_las dejemos_ (dejarlas) para más tarde. (2)_Hagámoslas_ (Hacerlas) ahora. ¿Qué tenemos que hacer?

MARÍA Necesito comprar sellos.

SERGIO Yo también. (3)_Vamos_ (Ir) al correo.

MARÍA Pues, antes de ir al correo, necesito sacar dinero de mi cuenta corriente.

SERGIO Bueno, (4)_busquemos_ (buscar) un cajero automático.

MARÍA ¿Tienes hambre?

SERGIO Sí. (5)_Crucemos_ (Cruzar) la calle y (6)_entremos_ (entrar) en ese café.

MARÍA Buena idea.

SERGIO ¿Nos sentamos aquí?

MARÍA No, no (7)_nos sentemos_ (sentarse) aquí; (8)_sentémonos_ (sentarse) enfrente de la ventana.

SERGIO ¿Qué pedimos?

MARÍA (9)_Pidamos_ (Pedir) café y pan dulce.

2 **Responder** Responde a cada mandato de **nosotros/as** según las indicaciones entre paréntesis. Sustituye los sustantivos por los objetos directos e indirectos.

> **modelo**
> Vamos a vender el carro.
> *Sí, vendámoslo./No, no lo vendamos.*

1. Vamos a levantarnos a las seis. (sí)
 Sí, levantémonos a las seis.
2. Vamos a enviar los paquetes. (no)
 No, no los enviemos.
3. Vamos a depositar el cheque. (sí)
 Sí, depositémoslo.
4. Vamos al supermercado. (no)
 No, no vayamos al supermercado.
5. Vamos a mandar esta postal a nuestros amigos. (no)
 No, no se la mandemos.
6. Vamos a limpiar la habitación. (sí)
 Sí, limpiémosla.
7. Vamos a mirar la televisión. (no)
 No, no la miremos.
8. Vamos a bailar. (sí)
 Sí, bailemos.
9. Vamos a pintar la sala. (no)
 No, no la pintemos.
10. Vamos a comprar estampillas. (sí)
 Sí, comprémoslas.

 Practice more at **vhlcentral.com.**

Comunicación

3 **Preguntar** Tú y tu compañero/a están de vacaciones en Caracas y se hacen sugerencias para resolver las situaciones que se presentan. Inventen mandatos afirmativos o negativos de **nosotros/as.**
Answers will vary.

> **modelo**
>
> Se nos olvidaron las tarjetas de crédito.
> *Paguemos en efectivo./No compremos más regalos.*

A

1. El museo está a sólo una cuadra de aquí.
2. Tenemos hambre.
3. Hay mucha cola en el cine.

B

1. Tenemos muchos cheques de viajero.
2. Tenemos prisa para llegar al cine.
3. Estamos cansados y queremos dormir.

4 **Decisiones** Trabajen en grupos pequeños. Ustedes están en Caracas por dos días. Lean esta página de una guía turística sobre la ciudad y decidan qué van a hacer hoy por la mañana, por la tarde y por la noche. Hagan oraciones con mandatos afirmativos o negativos de **nosotros/as.**
Answers will vary.

> **modelo**
>
> *Visitemos el Museo de Arte Contemporáneo Sofía Imber*
> *esta tarde. Quiero ver las esculturas de Jesús Rafael Soto.*

GUÍA DE *Caracas*

MUSEOS
- **Museo de Arte Colonial** Avenida Panteón
- **Museo de Arte Contemporáneo Sofía Imber** Parque Central. Esculturas de Jesús Rafael Soto y pinturas de Miró, Chagall y Picasso.
- **Galería de Arte Nacional** Parque Central. Colección de más de 4.000 obras de arte venezolano.

SITIOS DE INTERÉS
- **Plaza Bolívar**
- **Jardín Botánico** Avenida Interna UCV. De 8:00 a 5:00.
- **Parque del Este** Avenida Francisco de Miranda. Parque más grande de la ciudad con terrario.
- **Casa Natal de Simón Bolívar** Esquina de Sociedad de la avenida Universitaria. Casa colonial donde nació El Libertador.

RESTAURANTES
- **El Barquero** Avenida Luis Roche
- **Restaurante El Coyuco** Avenida Urdaneta
- **Restaurante Sorrento** Avenida Francisco Solano
- **Café Tonino** Avenida Andrés Bello

Síntesis

5 **Situación** Tú y un(a) compañero/a viven juntos/as en un apartamento y tienen problemas económicos. Describan los problemas y sugieran algunas soluciones. Hagan oraciones con mandatos afirmativos o negativos de **nosotros/as.** *Answers will vary.*

> **modelo**
>
> *Hagamos un presupuesto (budget).*
> *Es importante que no gastemos tanto dinero.*

TEACHING OPTIONS

Heritage Speakers ← 🔴 → Ask heritage speakers to write a conversation using **nosotros/as** commands. The topic of the conversation should be typical errands they run in their communities. Have them read their conversations to the class, making sure to note any new vocabulary on the board.
Pairs ← 🔴 → Have pairs create a guide for their favorite city, based on the **Guía de Caracas** in **Actividad 4**. Have them exchange their guides with another pair. That pair should decide which places they will visit and which they will avoid. Have them express their preferences using **nosotros/as** commands.
Pairs 🔴 ↔ 🔴 Have students create a dialogue in which two friends are deciding which local restaurant to go to for dinner. Students should use **nosotros/as** commands as much as possible. Have pairs perform their role-plays for the class.

3 **Expansion** To challenge students, ask them to expand their answers with a reason for their choice. Ex: **Paguemos en efectivo porque tenemos suficiente dinero.**

4 **Expansion**
← 🔴 → Have groups bring in tourist information for another city in the Spanish-speaking world and repeat the activity. Encourage them to make copies of this information for the class. They should then present to the class their suggestions for what to do, using **nosotros/as** commands.

5 **Teaching Tip** To simplify, have students brainstorm different financial problems and solutions encountered by roommates sharing an apartment. Write their responses on the board.

5 **Expansion**
🔴 ↔ 🔴 Call on pairs to perform their **Situación** for the class. Encourage them to ad-lib as they go.

Section Goals

In **Estructura 14.3**, students will learn:
- the future tense
- irregular verbs in the future
- the future as a means of expressing conjecture or probability

Instructional Resources
Supersite: Audio (Lab MP3 Files); Resources (*PowerPoints,* Activity Pack, Scripts, Answer Keys); Testing Program (Quizzes)
WebSAM
Workbook, pp. 175–176
Lab Manual, p. 83

Teaching Tips
- Review the **ir a** + [*infinitive*] construction to express the future in Spanish. Then, work through the paradigm for the formation of the future. Go over regular and irregular verbs in the future point by point, calling students' attention to the information in **¡Atención!**
- Ask students about their future activities using **ir a** + [*infinitive*]. After they answer, repeat the information using the future. Ex: **¿A qué hora van a almorzar ustedes?** (Vamos a almorzar a la una.) **Ustedes almorzarán a la una.**
- Check for understanding by asking volunteers to give different forms of verbs not listed. Ex: **ahorrar, ofrecer, vivir**

14.3 # The future **Tutorial**

ANTE TODO You have already learned ways of expressing the near future in Spanish. You will now learn how to form and use the future tense. Compare the different ways of expressing the future in Spanish and English.

Present indicative	Present subjunctive
Voy al cine mañana.	Ojalá **vaya al cine** mañana.
I'm going to the movies tomorrow.	*I hope I go to the movies tomorrow.*

ir a + [*infinitive*]	Future
Voy a ir al cine.	**Iré** al cine.
I'm going to go to the movies.	*I will go to the movies.*

▶ In Spanish, the future is a simple tense that consists of one word, whereas in English it is made up of the auxiliary verb *will* or *shall*, and the main verb.

Future tense

		estudiar	aprender	recibir
SINGULAR FORMS	yo	estudiar**é**	aprender**é**	recibir**é**
	tú	estudiar**ás**	aprender**ás**	recibir**ás**
	Ud./él/ella	estudiar**á**	aprender**á**	recibir**á**
PLURAL FORMS	nosotros/as	estudiar**emos**	aprender**emos**	recibir**emos**
	vosotros/as	estudiar**éis**	aprender**éis**	recibir**éis**
	Uds./ellos/ellas	estudiar**án**	aprender**án**	recibir**án**

▶ **¡Atención!** Note that all of the future endings have a written accent except the **nosotros/as** form.

¿Cuándo **recibirás** la carta?	Mañana **aprenderemos** más.
When will you receive the letter?	*Tomorrow we will learn more.*

▶ The future endings are the same for regular and irregular verbs. For regular verbs, simply add the endings to the infinitive. For irregular verbs, add the endings to the irregular stem.

Irregular verbs in the future

INFINITIVE	STEM	FUTURE FORMS
decir	dir-	dir**é**
hacer	har-	har**é**
poder	podr-	podr**é**
poner	pondr-	pondr**é**
querer	querr-	querr**é**
saber	sabr-	sabr**é**
salir	saldr-	saldr**é**
tener	tendr-	tendr**é**
venir	vendr-	vendr**é**

CONSULTA
To review **ir a** + [*infinitive*], see **Estructura 4.1**, p. 118.

TEACHING OPTIONS

Extra Practice To provide oral practice, create sentences using the future. Say a sentence, have students repeat it, then change the subject. Have students then say the sentence with the new subject, changing the verb as necessary.
Heritage Speakers Ask heritage speakers to share any song excerpts they know that use the future, such as *No seré* by **Julieta Venegas**, *El día de mi suerte* by **Héctor Lavoe**, or *Viviré* by

Juan Luis Guerra. Have the class analyze the use of the future.
Game Divide the class into teams of five. Each team should have a piece of paper. Give an infinitive in Spanish. The first team member will write the **yo** form of the verb and pass the paper to the second member, who will write the **tú** form, and so forth. The first team to finish the entire paradigm correctly wins a point. The team with the most points at the end wins.

▶ The future of **hay** (*inf.* **haber**) is **habrá** (*there will be*).

La próxima semana **habrá** un nuevo director.	**Habrá** más formularios en el correo.
Next week there will be a new director.	*There will be more forms at the post office.*

▶ Although the English word *will* can refer to future time, it also refers to someone's willingness to do something. In this case, Spanish uses **querer** + [*infinitive*], not the future tense.

¿Quieres llamarme, por favor?	**¿Quieren ustedes escucharnos**, por favor?
Will you please call me?	*Will you please listen to us?*

COMPARE & CONTRAST

In Spanish, the future tense has an additional use: expressing conjecture or probability. English sentences involving expressions such as *I wonder, I bet, must be, may, might,* and *probably* are often translated into Spanish using the *future of probability.*

—¿Dónde **estarán** mis llaves?	—¿Qué hora **será**?
I wonder where my keys are.	*What time can it be? (I wonder what time it is.)*
—**Estarán** en la cocina.	—**Serán** las once o las doce.
They're probably in the kitchen.	*It must be (It's probably) eleven or twelve.*

Note that although the future tense is used, these verbs express conjecture about *present* conditions, events, or actions.

CONSULTA

To review these conjunctions of time, see **Estructura 13.3**, p. 435.

▶ The future may also be used in the main clause of sentences in which the present subjunctive follows a conjunction of time such as **cuando, después (de) que, en cuanto, hasta que,** and **tan pronto como.**

Cuando llegues a casa, **hablaremos**.	Nos verás en cuanto entres en la cafetería.
When you get home, we will talk.	*You'll see us as soon as you enter the cafeteria.*

¡INTÉNTALO! Conjuga los verbos entre paréntesis en futuro.

1. (dejar, correr, pedir) yo _____ *dejaré, correré, pediré*
2. (cobrar, beber, vivir) tú _____ *cobrarás, beberás, vivirás*
3. (hacer, poner, venir) Lola _____ *hará, pondrá, vendrá*
4. (tener, decir, querer) nosotros _____ *tendremos, diremos, querremos*
5. (ir, ser, estar) ustedes _____ *irán, serán, estarán*
6. (firmar, comer, repetir) usted _____ *firmará, comerá, repetirá*
7. (saber, salir, poder) yo _____ *sabré, saldré, podré*
8. (encontrar, jugar, servir) tú _____ *encontrarás, jugarás, servirás*

recursos

WB
pp. 175–176

LM
p. 83

vhlcentral.com
Lección 14

Teaching Tips

• Go over the future of **haber**. Remind students that **habrá** is the only form and does not agree with any element in a sentence.
• Go over the explanation of **querer** + [*infinitive*].
• Explain the use of the future for expressing conjecture, which English generally expresses with the present tense. Add a visual aspect to this grammar presentation. Use magazine pictures to get students to speculate about what people are thinking or going to do. Ex: **¿Qué estará pensando la mujer que hace cola en el banco? (Estará pensando en su cita en el salón de belleza.)**
• Go over the use of the future in the main clause of sentences in which the present subjunctive follows a conjunction of time. Check for understanding by asking individuals to supply the main clause to prompts of present subjunctive clauses. Ex: **En cuanto pueda…; Tan pronto como me lo digas…**
• Ask students to answer questions about the future of the **Fotonovela** characters. Ex: **¿Quién tendrá la profesión más interesante? ¿Por qué? ¿Quién será más feliz?**

TEACHING OPTIONS

Pairs Ask students to write ten academic resolutions for the upcoming semester, using the future. Ex: **Haré dos o tres borradores de cada composición. Practicaré el español con los estudiantes hispanos.** Have students share their resolutions with a partner, who will then report back to the class. Ex: ____ **hará dos o tres borradores de cada composición.**

Extra Practice Ask students to finish these sentences logically: **1. Tan pronto como termine mis estudios,… 2. El día que gane la lotería,… 3. Cuando lleguen las vacaciones,… 4. Hasta que tenga mi propio (*own*) apartamento,…** Encourage them to expand their answers with additional information where appropriate.

Práctica

1 **Planes** Celia está hablando de sus planes. Repite lo que dice, usando el tiempo futuro.

> **modelo**
> Hoy voy a hacer unas compras.
> *Hoy haré unas compras.*

1. Voy a pasar por el banco a cobrar un cheque. *Pasaré por el banco a cobrar un cheque.*
2. Mi hermana va a venir conmigo al supermercado. *Mi hermana vendrá conmigo al supermercado.*
3. Vamos a buscar las mejores rebajas. *Buscaremos las mejores rebajas.*
4. Voy a comprarme unas botas. *Me compraré unas botas.*
5. Después voy a volver a casa y me voy a duchar. *Después volveré a casa y me ducharé.*
6. Seguramente mis amigos me van a llamar para salir esta noche. *Seguramente mis amigos me llamarán para salir esta noche.*

2 **¿Quién será?** En parejas, imaginen que están en un café y ven entrar a un hombre o una mujer. Imaginen cómo será su vida y utilicen el futuro de probabilidad en su conversación. Usen estas preguntas como guía y después lean su conversación delante de la clase. *Answers will vary.*

> **modelo**
> **Estudiante 1:** *¿Será simpático?*
> **Estudiante 2:** *Creo que no, está muy serio. Será antipático.*

- ¿Estará soltero/a?
- ¿Cuántos años tendrá?
- ¿Vivirá por aquí cerca?
- ¿Será famoso/a?
- ¿Será de otro país?
- ¿Con quién vivirá?
- ¿Estará esperando a alguien? ¿A quién?

3 **¿Qué pasará?** Imagina que tienes que adivinar (*to predict*) el futuro de tu compañero/a. Túrnense para hablar sobre cada una de estas categorías usando el futuro. *Answers will vary.*

> **modelo**
> **Estudiante 1:** *¿Seré rico? ¿Tendré una casa grande?*
> **Estudiante 2:** *Mmm... tendrás muy poco dinero durante los próximos cinco años, pero después serás muy, muy rico con una casa enorme. Luego te mudarás a una isla desierta (deserted) donde conocerás a...*

- amor
- dinero
- salud
- trabajo
- vivienda

TEACHING OPTIONS

Small Groups Divide the class into small groups. Have students take turns telling the group three things they will do next summer or next year. Ex: **Viajaré a Europa. Trabajaré en un banco.** Have students report back to the class what their group members will do.

Extra Practice To provide more practice with the future, give students oral prompts with a future date. Ex: **En el año 2020...** Provide the prompt and then call on individual students to complete the sentence using the future. (**...nadie manejará un coche. ... usted vivirá en Costa Rica.**)

Comunicación

4 **Conversar** Tú y tu compañero/a viajarán a la República Dominicana por siete días. Indiquen lo que harán y no harán. Digan dónde, cómo, con quién o en qué fechas lo harán, usando el anuncio (*ad*) como guía. Pueden usar sus propias ideas también. Answers will vary.

> **modelo**
>
> **Estudiante 1:** ¿Qué haremos el martes?
> **Estudiante 2:** Visitaremos el Jardín Botánico.
> **Estudiante 1:** Pues, tú visitarás el Jardín Botánico y yo caminaré por el Mercado Modelo.

¡Bienvenido a la República Dominicana!

Se divertirá desde el momento en que llegue al **Aeropuerto Internacional de las Américas**.

• Visite la ciudad colonial de **Santo Domingo** con su interesante arquitectura.

• Vaya al **Jardín Botánico** y disfrute de nuestra abundante naturaleza.

• En el **Mercado Modelo** no va a poder resistir la tentación de comprar artesanías.

• No deje de escalar el **Pico Duarte** (se recomiendan 3 días).

• ¿Le gusta bucear? **Cabarete** tiene todo el equipo que usted necesita.

• ¿Desea nadar? **Punta Cana** le ofrece hermosas playas.

5 **Planear** En grupos pequeños, hagan planes para empezar un negocio (*business*). Elijan una de las opciones y usen las preguntas como guía. Finalmente, presenten su plan a la clase. Answers will vary.

> un supermercado un salón de belleza una heladería

1. ¿Cómo se llamará?
2. ¿Cuánta gente trabajará en este lugar? ¿Qué hará cada persona?
3. ¿En qué parte de la ciudad estará? ¿Cómo llegará la gente?
4. ¿Quién será el/la director(a)? ¿Por qué?
5. ¿Van a necesitar un préstamo? ¿Cómo lo pedirán?
6. Este/a supermercado / salón de belleza / heladería será el/la mejor de la ciudad porque...

Síntesis

6 **El futuro de Cristina** Tu profesor(a) va a darte una serie incompleta de dibujos sobre el futuro de Cristina. Tú y tu compañero/a tienen dos series diferentes. Háganse preguntas y respondan de acuerdo a los dibujos para completar la historia. Answers will vary.

> **modelo**
>
> **Estudiante 1:** ¿Qué hará Cristina en el año 2020?
> **Estudiante 2:** Ella se graduará en el año 2020.

4 Teaching Tips
• Give pairs time to read the ad before they complete the activity.
• ←👥→ If you have any students of Dominican heritage in your class or if any of your students have visited the Dominican Republic, ask them to share what they know about the places named in the ad.

4 👥↔👥 Expansion Have several pairs role-play their conversations to the class.

5 Expansion Have groups develop visual aids to accompany their presentation.

6 Teaching Tip Divide the class into pairs and distribute the handouts from the Activity Pack (Activity Pack/Supersite) that correspond to this Information Gap Activity. Give students ten minutes to complete the activity.

6 Expansion
• ←👥→ Have students change partners, and have the new pairs use the future to retell the story without looking at the drawings. Later, ask students if the second version of the story differed from the first one.
• ←👥→ Have pairs pick a person who is currently in the news and write predictions about his or her future. Ask pairs to share their predictions with the class.

TEACHING OPTIONS

Large Groups Have students stand in a circle. Name an infinitive and subject pronoun. Ex: **tener/ustedes.** Throw a ball to a student, who must give the correct simple future form (Ex: **tendrán**) and toss the ball back to you. Keep a brisk pace.

Large Groups ←👥→ Assign a century to each corner of the room. Ex: 23rd century. Tell students they are going to go into the future in a time machine (**máquina del tiempo**). They should pick which year they would like to visit and go to that corner. Once assembled, each group should develop a summary of life in their century. After groups have finished, call on a spokesperson in each group to report to the class.

Recapitulación

(S) **Concepts Diagnostics**

Completa estas actividades para repasar los conceptos de gramática que aprendiste en esta lección.

1 **Completar** Completa el cuadro con la forma correspondiente del futuro. **10 pts.**

Infinitive	yo	ella	nosotros
ahorrar	ahorraré	ahorrará	ahorraremos
decir	diré	dirá	diremos
poner	pondré	pondrá	pondremos
querer	querré	querrá	querremos
salir	saldré	saldrá	saldremos

2 **Los novios** Completa este diálogo entre dos novios con mandatos en la forma de **nosotros/as**. **10 pts.**

SIMÓN ¿Quieres ir al cine mañana?

CARLA Sí, ¡qué buena idea! (1) __Compremos__ (Comprar) los boletos (*tickets*) por teléfono.

SIMÓN No, mejor (2) __pidámoselos__ (pedírselos) gratis a mi prima, quien trabaja en el cine.

CARLA ¡Fantástico!

SIMÓN Y también quiero visitar la nueva galería de arte el fin de semana que viene.

CARLA ¿Por qué esperar? (3) __Visitémosla__ (Visitarla) esta tarde.

SIMÓN Bueno, pero primero tengo que limpiar mi apartamento.

CARLA No hay problema. (4) __Limpiémoslo__ (Limpiarlo) juntos.

SIMÓN Muy bien. ¿Y tú no tienes que hacer diligencias hoy? (5) __Hagámoslas__ (Hacerlas) también.

CARLA Sí, tengo que ir al correo y al banco. (6) __Vamos__ (Ir) al banco hoy, pero no (7) __vayamos__ (ir) al correo todavía. Antes tengo que escribir una carta.

SIMÓN ¿Una carta misteriosa? (8) __Escribámosla__ (Escribirla) ahora.

CARLA No, mejor no (9) __la escribamos__ (escribirla) hasta que regresemos de la galería donde venden un papel reciclado muy lindo (*cute*).

SIMÓN ¿Papel lindo? ¿Pues para quién es la carta?

CARLA No importa. (10) __Empecemos__ (Empezar) a limpiar.

RESUMEN GRAMATICAL

14.1 The subjunctive in adjective clauses *pp. 460–461*

▶ When adjective clauses refer to something that is known, certain, or definite, the indicative is used.

Necesito **el libro** que **tiene** fotos.

▶ When adjective clauses refer to something that is uncertain or indefinite, the subjunctive is used.

Necesito **un libro** que **tenga** fotos.

14.2 Nosotros/as commands *pp. 464–465*

▶ Same as **nosotros/as** form of present subjunctive.

Affirmative	Negative
Démosle un libro a Lola.	No le demos un libro a Lola.
Démoselo.	No se lo demos.

▶ While the subjunctive form of the verb **ir** is used for the negative **nosotros/as** command, the indicative is used for the affirmative command.

No **vayamos** a la plaza. | **Vamos** a la plaza.

14.3 The future *pp. 468–469*

Future tense of **estudiar***	
estudiaré	estudiaremos
estudiarás	estudiaréis
estudiará	estudiarán

*Same ending for -ar, -er, and -ir verbs.
▶ The future of hay is habrá (*there will be*).
▶ The future can also express conjecture or probability.

Irregular verbs in the future		
Infinitive	**Stem**	**Future forms**
decir	**dir-**	diré
hacer	**har-**	haré
poder	**podr-**	podré
poner	**pondr-**	pondré
querer	**querr-**	querré
saber	**sabr-**	sabré
salir	**saldr-**	saldré
tener	**tendr-**	tendré
venir	**vendr-**	vendré

3 **Frases** Escribe oraciones con los elementos que se dan. Usa el tiempo futuro. `10 pts.`

1. Lorenzo y yo / ir / al banco / mañana / y / pedir / un préstamo Lorenzo y yo iremos al banco mañana y pediremos un préstamo.
2. la empleada del banco / hacernos / muchas preguntas / y / también / darnos / un formulario La empleada del banco nos hará muchas preguntas y también nos dará un formulario.
3. Lorenzo / llenar / el formulario / y / yo / firmarlo Lorenzo llenará el formulario y yo lo firmaré.
4. nosotros / salir / del banco / contentos / porque el dinero / llegar / a nuestra cuenta / muy pronto Nosotros saldremos del banco contentos porque el dinero llegará a nuestra cuenta muy pronto.
5. los dos / tener / que trabajar mucho / para pagar el préstamo / pero nuestros padres / ayudarnos Los dos tendremos que trabajar mucho para pagar el préstamo, pero nuestros padres nos ayudarán.

4 **Verbos** Escribe los verbos en el presente de indicativo o de subjuntivo. `10 pts.`

1. —¿Sabes dónde hay un restaurante donde nosotros (1) ___podamos___ (poder) comer paella valenciana? —No, no conozco ninguno que (2) ___sirva___ (servir) paella, pero conozco uno que (3) se especializa (especializarse) en tapas españolas.
2. Busco vendedores que (4) ___sean___ (ser) educados. No estoy seguro de conocer a alguien que (5) ___tenga___ (tener) esa característica. Pero ahora que lo pienso, ¡sí! Tengo dos amigos que (6) ___trabajan___ (trabajar) en el almacén Excelencia. Los voy a llamar. Y debo decirles que necesitamos que (ellos) (7) ___sepan___ (saber) hablar inglés.
3. Se busca apartamento que (8) ___esté___ (estar) bien situado, que (9) ___cueste___ (costar) menos de $800 al mes y que (10) ___permita___ (permitir) tener perros.

5 **La ciudad ideal** Escribe un párrafo de al menos cinco oraciones describiendo cómo es la comunidad ideal donde te gustaría (*you would like*) vivir en el futuro y compárala con la comunidad donde vives ahora. Usa cláusulas adjetivas y el vocabulario de esta lección. `10 pts.` Answers will vary.

6 **Adivinanza** Completa la adivinanza y adivina la respuesta. `¡2 puntos EXTRA!`

"Me llegan las cartas
y no sé ___leer___ (*to read*)
y, aunque° me las como,
no mancho° el papel.**"**
¿Quién soy? ___el buzón___

aunque *although* **no mancho** *I don't stain*

 Practice more at **vhlcentral.com.**

3 **Teaching Tip** Before beginning the activity, ask students to identify the irregular verbs in the future tense.

3 **Expansion** To challenge students, tell them to imagine that **Rita's** week did not go as she had planned. Have them rewrite **Rita's** description, using the past perfect and past subjunctive. Ex: **Me molestó que el traje que había pedido por Internet no llegara el lunes.**

4 **Teaching Tip** Before students complete the activity, have them circle the verbs in the main clause of each sentence with a blank.

5 **Teaching Tips**
- Have students make a Venn diagram with the headings **Mi comunidad, Mi comunidad ideal,** and **Las dos**. Have them fill in each area with short phrases to include in their paragraphs.
- → Have students exchange their papers for peer editing.

6 **Expansion** To challenge students, have them work in small groups to create a riddle about an object or place found in the city.

TEACHING OPTIONS

Heritage Speakers ← → Ask heritage speakers to compare a city or town from their families' countries of origin with their current hometown. What forms of transportation are available? Is there a downtown area? Where do people tend to live and work? Encourage classmates to ask follow-up questions.

Game Divide the class into two teams. Write a main clause on the board. Ex: **Busco un apartamento…** and have one member from each team come to the board and complete the sentence with subordinate clauses in the indicative or subjunctive. Each correct answer earns one point. The team with the most points at the end wins.

Section Goals

In **Lectura**, students will:
- learn the strategy of identifying a narrator's point of view
- read an authentic narrative in Spanish

Instructional Resource
Supersite

Estrategia
→👤← Tell students that recognizing the point of view from which a narrative is told will help them comprehend it. Write examples of first-person and omniscient narratives on the board and ask students to identify the point of view in each.

Examinar el texto
→👤← Ask students to read the first two paragraphs of *Esquina peligrosa* and determine whether the narrative is written from the first- or third-person point of view. Call on a volunteer to explain what clues in the text help reveal the narrator.

Punto de vista
Have students complete this activity in pairs. First have them find the corresponding sentences in the text. Then have them fill in the blanks with the **yo** form of the verbs.

Lectura

NATIONAL STANDARDS connections cultures

Antes de leer

Estrategia
Identifying point of view

You can understand a narrative more completely if you identify the point of view of the narrator. You can do this by simply asking yourself from whose perspective the story is being told. Some stories are narrated in the first person. That is, the narrator is a character in the story, and everything you read is filtered through that person's thoughts, emotions, and opinions. Other stories have an omniscient narrator who is not one of the story's characters and who reports the thoughts and actions of all the characters.

Examinar el texto

Lee brevemente este cuento escrito por Marco Denevi. ¿Crees que se narra en primera persona o tiene un narrador omnisciente? ¿Cómo lo sabes?

Answers will vary.

Punto de vista

Éstos son fragmentos de *Esquina peligrosa* en los que se cambió el punto de vista° a primera persona. Completa cada oración de manera lógica.

1. Le ___ordené___ a mi chofer que me condujese hasta aquel barrio...
2. Al doblar la esquina ___vi___ el almacén, el mismo viejo y sombrío almacén donde ___yo___ había trabajado como dependiente...
3. El recuerdo de ___mi___ niñez me puso nostálgico. Se ___me___ humedecieron los ojos.
4. Yo ___tomé___ la canasta de mimbre, ___fui___ llenándola con paquetes [...] y ___salí___ a hacer el reparto.

punto de vista *point of view*

 Practice more at **vhlcentral.com**.

Marco Denevi (1922–1998) fue un escritor y dramaturgo argentino. Estudió derecho y más tarde se convirtió en escritor. Algunas de sus obras, como *Rosaura a las diez*, han sido° llevadas al cine. Denevi se caracteriza por su gran creatividad e ingenio, que jamás dejan de sorprender al lector°.

Esquina peligrosa

Marco Denevi

El señor Epidídimus, el magnate de las finanzas°, uno de los hombres más ricos del mundo, sintió un día el vehemente deseo de visitar el barrio donde había vivido cuando era niño y trabajaba como dependiente de almacén.

Le ordenó a su chofer que lo condujese hasta aquel barrio humilde° y remoto. Pero el barrio estaba tan cambiado que el señor Epidídimus no lo reconoció. En lugar de calles de tierra había bulevares asfaltados°, y las míseras casitas de antaño° habían sido reemplazadas por torres de departamentos°.

Al doblar una esquina vio el almacén, el mismo viejo y sombrío° almacén donde él había trabajado como dependiente cuando tenía doce años.

—Deténgase aquí—le dijo al chofer. Descendió del automóvil y entró en el almacén. Todo se conservaba igual que en la época de su infancia: las estanterías, la anticuada caja registradora°, la balanza de pesas° y, alrededor, el mudo asedio° de la mercadería.

El señor Epidídimus percibió el mismo olor de sesenta años atrás: un olor picante y agridulce a jabón

_____ ❧ _____

TEACHING OPTIONS

Pairs 👤↔👤 Have pairs of students reread *Esquina peligrosa* and write four discussion questions about the selection. When they have finished, have them exchange questions with another pair, who can work together to discuss and answer them.

Small Groups 👤↔👤 Have students generate a list of other short stories or excerpts of longer works that contain fantastical elements on the board. Then, in small groups, have students choose a text and compare and contrast its fantastical qualities with *Esquina peligrosa*.

> han sido *have been* lector *reader* finanzas *finance* humilde *humble, modest* asfaltados *paved with asphalt* antaño *yesteryear* torres de departamentos *apartment buildings* sombrío *somber* anticuada caja registradora *old-fashioned cash register* balanza de pesas *scale* mudo asedio *silent siege* aserrín *sawdust* acaroína *pesticide* penumbra del fondo *half-light from the back* reparto *delivery* lodazal *bog*

amarillo, a aserrín° húmedo, a vinagre, a aceitunas, a acaroína°. El recuerdo de su niñez lo puso nostálgico. Se le humedecieron los ojos. Le pareció que retrocedía en el tiempo.

Desde la penumbra del fondo° le llegó la voz ruda del patrón:

—¿Estas son horas de venir? Te quedaste dormido, como siempre.

El señor Epidídimus tomó la canasta de mimbre, fue llenándola con paquetes de azúcar, de yerba y de fideos, y salió a hacer el reparto°.

La noche anterior había llovido y las calles de tierra estaban convertidas en un lodazal°.

(1974)

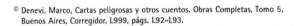

© Denevi, Marco, *Cartas peligrosas y otros cuentos. Obras Completas, Tomo 5*, Buenos Aires, Corregidor, L999, págs. L92–L93.

Después de leer

Comprensión 🌐

Indica si las oraciones son **ciertas** o **falsas**. Corrige las falsas.

Cierto	Falso	
	✓	1. El señor Epidídimus tiene una tienda con la que gana poco dinero. Es un magnate de las finanzas, uno de los hombres más ricos del mundo.
✓		2. Epidídimus vivía en un barrio humilde cuando era pequeño.
✓		3. Epidídimus le ordenó al chofer que lo llevara a un barrio de gente con poco dinero.
✓		4. Cuando Epidídimus entró al almacén se acordó de experiencias pasadas.
	✓	5. Epidídimus les dio órdenes a los empleados del almacén. Su patrón le ordenó hacer el reparto.

Interpretación

Responde a estas preguntas con oraciones completas.
Answers will vary.

1. ¿Es rico o pobre Epidídimus? ¿Cómo lo sabes?

2. ¿Por qué Epidídimus va al almacén?

3. ¿De quién es la voz "ruda" que Epidídimus escucha? ¿Qué orden crees que le dio a Epidídimus?

4. ¿Qué hace Epidídimus al final?

Coméntalo

En parejas, hablen de sus impresiones y conclusiones. Tomen como guía estas preguntas. *Answers will vary.*

- ¿Te sorprendió el final de este cuento? ¿Por qué?
- ¿Qué va a hacer Epidídimus el resto del día?
- ¿Crees que Epidídimus niño estaba soñando o Epidídimus adulto estaba recordando?
- ¿Por qué crees que el cuento se llama *Esquina peligrosa*?

Comprensión Have students write five additional true/false statements for a partner to complete. Make sure students correct the false statements.

Interpretación Have students work in pairs to complete this activity. Ask them to support their answers with fragments from the text.

Coméntalo ←👥→ Ask students to explain their opinions. For the third question, survey the class to see which is the most popular interpretation.

Venezuela

NATIONAL STANDARDS
connections
cultures

El país en cifras

▶ **Área:** 912.050 km^2 (352.144 millas2), *aproximadamente dos veces el área de California*
▶ **Población:** 31.292.000
▶ **Capital:** Caracas —3.292.000
▶ **Ciudades principales:** Maracaibo —2.357.000, Valencia —1.905.000, Barquisimeto —1.273.000, Maracay —1.138.000

SOURCE: Population Division, UN Secretariat

▶ **Moneda:** bolívar
▶ **Idiomas:** español (oficial), lenguas indígenas (oficiales)

El yanomami es uno de los idiomas indígenas que se habla en Venezuela. La cultura de los yanomami tiene su centro en el sur de Venezuela, en el bosque tropical. Son cazadores° y agricultores y viven en comunidades de hasta 400 miembros.

Bandera de Venezuela

Venezolanos célebres

▶ **Teresa Carreño,** compositora y pianista (1853–1917)
▶ **Rómulo Gallegos,** escritor y político (1884–1969)
▶ **Andrés Eloy Blanco,** poeta (1897–1955)
▶ **Baruj Benacerraf,** científico (1920–)

En 1980, Baruj Benacerraf, junto con dos de sus colegas, recibió el Premio Nobel por sus investigaciones en el campo° de la inmunología y las enfermedades autoinmunes. Nacido en Caracas, Benacerraf también vivió en París y reside ahora en los Estados Unidos.

cazadores *hunters* campo *field* caída *drop* Salto Ángel *Angel Falls* catarata *waterfall* la dio a conocer *made it known*

Isla Margarita

Maracaibo
Lago de Maracaibo
Valencia
⭐ Caracas
Cordillera Central de la Costa
Río Orinoco
Macizo de las Guayanas
GUYAN...
Río Orinoco
BRASIL

Vista de Caracas

ESTADOS UNIDOS
OCÉANO ATLÁNTICO
OCÉANO PACÍFICO
VENEZUELA

Una piragua

recursos

| WB pp. 177–178 | VM pp. 259–260 | vhlcentral.com Lección 14 |

¡Increíble pero cierto!

Con una caída° de 979 metros (3.212 pies) desde la meseta de Auyan Tepuy, Salto Ángel°, en Venezuela, es la catarata° más alta del mundo, ¡diecisiete veces más alta que las cataratas del Niágara! James C. Angel la dio a conocer° en 1935. Los indígenas de la zona la denominan "Kerepakupai Merú".

Economía • **El petróleo**

La industria petrolera° es muy importante para la economía venezolana. La mayor concentración de petróleo del país se encuentra debajo del lago Maracaibo. En 1976 se nacionalizaron las empresas° petroleras y pasaron a ser propiedad° del estado con el nombre de *Petróleos de Venezuela*. Este producto representa más del 70% de las exportaciones del país, siendo los Estados Unidos su principal comprador°.

Actualidades • **Caracas**

El *boom* petrolero de los años cincuenta transformó a Caracas en una ciudad cosmopolita. Sus rascacielos° y excelentes sistemas de transporte la hacen una de las ciudades más modernas de Latinoamérica. El metro, construido en 1983, es uno de los más modernos del mundo y sus extensas carreteras y autopistas conectan la ciudad con el interior del país. El corazón de la capital es el Parque Central, una zona de centros comerciales, tiendas, restaurantes y clubes.

Historia • **Simón Bolívar (1783–1830)**

A principios del siglo° XIX, el territorio de la actual Venezuela, al igual que gran parte de América, todavía estaba bajo el dominio de la Corona° española. El general Simón Bolívar, nacido en Caracas, es llamado "El Libertador" porque fue el líder del movimiento independentista suramericano en el área que hoy es Venezuela, Colombia, Ecuador, Perú y Bolivia.

 ¿Qué aprendiste? Responde a cada pregunta con una oración completa.

1. ¿Cuál es la moneda de Venezuela?
 La moneda de Venezuela es el bolívar.
2. ¿Quién fue Rómulo Gallegos?
 Rómulo Gallegos fue un escritor y político venezolano.
3. ¿Cuándo se dio a conocer el Salto Ángel?
 El Salto Ángel se dio a conocer en 1935.
4. ¿Cuál es el producto más exportado de Venezuela?
 El producto más exportado de Venezuela es el petróleo.
5. ¿Qué ocurrió en 1976 con las empresas petroleras?
 En 1976 las empresas petroleras se nacionalizaron.
6. ¿Cómo se llama la capital de Venezuela?
 La capital de Venezuela se llama Caracas.
7. ¿Qué hay en el Parque Central de Caracas?
 Hay centros comerciales, tiendas, restaurantes y clubes.
8. ¿Por qué es conocido Simón Bolívar como "El Libertador"?
 Simón Bolívar es conocido como "El Libertador" porque fue el líder del movimiento independentista suramericano.

Sombreros y hamacas en Ciudad Bolívar

 Conexión Internet Investiga estos temas en **vhlcentral.com**.

1. Busca información sobre Simón Bolívar. ¿Cuáles son algunos de los episodios más importantes de su vida? ¿Crees que Bolívar fue un estadista (*statesman*) de primera categoría? ¿Por qué?
2. Prepara un plan para un viaje de ecoturismo por el Orinoco. ¿Qué quieres ver y hacer durante la excursión?

 Practice more at **vhlcentral.com**.

industria petrolera *oil industry* empresas *companies* propiedad *property* comprador *buyer* rascacielos *skyscrapers*
siglo *century* Corona *Crown*

El petróleo Students may be surprised to learn that Venezuela is among the world's top ten crude oil producers, with 73 billion barrels of petroleum reserves. Venezuela may have up to as much as 1.2 trillion barrels of extra-heavy oil, including bitumen.

Caracas Both Caracas and Houston, Texas, are major urban areas fueled by oil booms. Students may find it interesting to compare how these cities have developed. Houston's urban development is limited only by the coastline, allowing it to sprawl in all other directions; Caracas is hemmed into a narrow valley by two mountain ranges, leading to its dense development and its many high-rises.

Simón Bolívar The life of **Simón Bolívar** has inspired artists of every sort: from painters and sculptors to musicians and writers. In 1989, Colombian Nobel winner **Gabriel García Márquez** published *El general en su laberinto*, his vision of **Bolívar** toward the end of his life, as he muses about his accomplishments and disappointments.

Conexión Internet Students will find supporting Internet activities and links at **vhlcentral.com**.

Teaching Tip You may want to wrap up this section by playing the *Panorama cultural* video footage for this lesson.

TEACHING OPTIONS

Worth Noting Tell students that the **Salto Ángel**, besides being the highest uninterrupted waterfall in the world, falls from a **tepuy**, a flat-topped, sandstone mountain with vertical sides. Because of the isolation that results from the great elevation and the vertical sides, the top of each **tepuy** is a unique ecosystem, featuring plants and animals of different species that grow nowhere else on earth, including the tops of neighboring **tepuyes**. The chilly,

damp climate atop a **tepuy** differs so markedly from the tropical climate at its base that **tepuy**-dwelling species cannot survive on the **sabana** below and vice versa.
Heritage Speakers Ask heritage speakers whose families are of Venezuelan origin or students who have visited there to tell the class about their experiences in the country.

La República Dominicana

NATIONAL STANDARDS connections cultures

El país en cifras

▶ **Área:** 48.730 km² (18.815 millas²), *el área combinada de New Hampshire y Vermont*

▶ **Población:** 10.867.000

La isla La Española, llamada así tras° el primer viaje de Cristóbal Colón, estuvo bajo el completo dominio de la corona° española hasta 1697, cuando la parte oeste de la isla pasó a ser propiedad° francesa. Hoy día está dividida políticamente en dos países, la República Dominicana en la zona este y Haití en el oeste.

SOURCE: Population Division, UN Secretariat

▶ **Capital:** Santo Domingo—2.381.000

▶ **Ciudades principales:** Santiago de los Caballeros, La Vega, Puerto Plata, San Pedro de Macorís

▶ **Moneda:** peso dominicano

▶ **Idiomas:** español (oficial), criollo haitiano

Bandera de la República Dominicana

Dominicanos célebres

▶ **Juan Pablo Duarte,** político y padre de la patria° (1813–1876)

▶ **Celeste Woss y Gil,** pintora (1891–1985)

▶ **Juan Luis Guerra,** compositor y cantante de merengue (1957–)

tras *after* corona *crown* propiedad *property*
padre de la patria *founding father* restos *remains* siglo *century*
tumbas *graves* navegante *sailor* reemplazó *replaced*

Hombres tocando los palos en una misa en Nochebuena

Catedral de Santa María la Menor

Océano Atlántico

Isla La Española

Puerto Plata

Santiago

Pico Duarte

HAITÍ

Río Yuna

La Vega

Bahía Escocesa

Cordillera Central

Río San Juan

Sierra de Neiba

Sierra de Baoruco

Bahía de Ocoa

San Pedro de Macorís

Santo Domingo

Mar Caribe

ESTADOS UNIDOS

LA REPÚBLICA DOMINICANA

OCÉANO PACÍFICO

OCÉANO ATLÁNTICO

AMÉRICA DEL SUR

Trabajadores del campo recogen la cosecha de ajos

recursos

WB pp. 179–180

VM pp. 261–262

S vhlcentral.com Lección 14

¡Increíble pero cierto!

Los restos° de Cristóbal Colón pasaron por varias ciudades desde su muerte en el siglo° XVI hasta el siglo XIX. Por esto, se conocen dos tumbas° de este navegante°: una en la Catedral de Sevilla, España y otra en el Museo Faro a Colón en Santo Domingo, que reemplazó° la tumba inicial en la catedral de la capital dominicana.

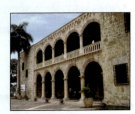

Ciudades • **Santo Domingo**

La zona colonial de Santo Domingo, ciudad fundada en 1496, posee° algunas de las construcciones más antiguas del hemisferio. Gracias a las restauraciones°, la arquitectura de la ciudad es famosa no sólo por su belleza sino también por el buen estado de sus edificios. Entre sus sitios más visitados se cuentan° la Calle de las Damas, llamada así porque allí paseaban las señoras de la corte del Virrey; el Alcázar de Colón, un palacio construido entre 1510 y 1514 por Diego Colón, hijo de Cristóbal; y la Fortaleza° Ozama, la más vieja de las Américas, construida entre 1502 y 1508.

Deportes • **El béisbol**

El béisbol es un deporte muy practicado en el Caribe. Los primeros países hispanos en tener una liga fueron Cuba y México, donde se empezó a jugar al béisbol en el siglo XIX. Hoy día este deporte es una afición° nacional en la República Dominicana. Pedro Martínez (foto, derecha) y David Ortiz son sólo dos de los muchísimos beisbolistas dominicanos que han alcanzado° enorme éxito° e inmensa popularidad entre los aficionados.

Artes • **El merengue**

El merengue, un ritmo originario de la República Dominicana, tiene sus raíces° en el campo. Tradicionalmente las canciones hablaban de los problemas sociales de los campesinos°. Sus instrumentos eran la guitarra, el acordeón, el guayano° y la tambora, un tambor° característico del lugar. Entre 1930 y 1960, el merengue se popularizó en las ciudades; adoptó un tono más urbano, en el que se incorporaron instrumentos como el saxofón y el bajo°, y empezaron a formarse grandes orquestas. Uno de los cantantes y compositores de merengue más famosos es Juan Luis Guerra.

 ¿Qué aprendiste? Responde a cada pregunta con una oración completa.

1. ¿Quién es Juan Luis Guerra?
 Juan Luis Guerra es un compositor y cantante de merengue.
2. ¿Cuándo se fundó la ciudad de Santo Domingo?
 Santo Domingo se fundó en 1496.
3. ¿Qué es el Alcázar de Colón?
 El Alcázar de Colón es un palacio construido entre 1510 y 1514 por Diego Colón, hijo de Cristóbal.
4. Nombra dos beisbolistas famosos de la República Dominicana.
 Dos beisbolistas famosos de la República Dominicana son Pedro Martínez y David Ortiz.
5. ¿De qué hablaban las canciones de merengue tradicionales?
 Las canciones de merengue tradicionales hablaban de los problemas sociales de los campesinos.
6. ¿Qué instrumentos se utilizaban para tocar (*play*) el merengue?
 Se utilizaban la guitarra, el acordeón, el guayano y la tambora.
7. ¿Cuándo se transformó el merengue en un estilo urbano?
 El merengue se transformó en un estilo urbano entre los años 1930 y 1960.
8. ¿Qué cantante ha ayudado a internacionalizar el merengue?
 Juan Luis Guerra ha ayudado a internacionalizar el merengue.

 Conexión Internet Investiga estos temas en **vhlcentral.com**.

 Practice more at **vhlcentral.com.**

1. Busca más información sobre la isla La Española. ¿Cómo son las relaciones entre la República Dominicana y Haití?
2. Busca más información sobre la zona colonial de Santo Domingo: la Catedral de Santa María, la Casa de Bastidas o el Panteón Nacional. ¿Cómo son estos edificios? ¿Te gustan? Explica tus respuestas.

posee *possesses* restauraciones *restorations* se cuentan *are included* Fortaleza *Fortress* afición *pastime* han alcanzado *have reached*
éxito *success* raíces *roots* campesinos *rural people* guayano *metal scraper* tambor *drum* bajo *bass*

Santo Domingo UNESCO has declared Santo Domingo a World Heritage site because of the abundance of historical architecture. Efforts are being made to restore buildings to their original grandeur, and to "correct" restorations made in the past that were not true to original architectural styles.

El béisbol The Dominican Republic has the second-highest number of players in Major League Baseball (only the U.S. has more). The Dominican Republic has its own baseball league (comprised of six teams), whose season lasts from October to January. Many major and minor league players play in the Dominican League during their off-season.

El merengue The **merengue** represents a fusion of the cultures that make up the Dominican Republic's heritage. The gourd scraper—or **güiro**—comes from the indigenous Arawak people, the **tambora**—a drum unique to the Dominican Republic—is part of the nation's African legacy, the stringed instruments were adapted from the Spanish guitar, and the accordion was introduced by German merchants. For more information about **merengue**, you may want to play the ***Panorama cultural*** video footage for this lesson.

Conexión Internet Students will find supporting Internet activities and links at **vhlcentral.com**.

TEACHING OPTIONS

Worth Noting →👤← Students may enjoy learning more about Latin American baseball. They can check out reports of Caribbean League baseball games on the Internet, which follow Dominican, Cuban, and Venezuelan teams among others. Encourage students to create a bilingual dictionary of baseball

terms such as **jardinero** *(outfielder)*, **jardín** *(outfield)*, **cuadrangular/jonrón** *(home run)*, **batear** *(to hit)*, **pichear** *(to pitch)*, **anotar carreras** *(to score runs)*, **ponchar** *(to strike out)*, **la goma** *(home plate)*, **el montículo** *(mound)*, and so forth. Encourage sports fans to identify Latin Americans currently playing in the Major Leagues.

En la ciudad

el banco	bank
la carnicería	butcher shop
el correo	post office
el estacionamiento	parking lot
la frutería	fruit store
la heladería	ice cream shop
la joyería	jewelry store
la lavandería	laundromat
la panadería	bakery
la pastelería	pastry shop
la peluquería, el salón de belleza	beauty salon
la pescadería	fish market
el supermercado	supermarket
la zapatería	shoe store
hacer cola	to stand in line
hacer diligencias	to run errands

En el banco

el cajero automático	ATM
el cheque (de viajero)	(traveler's) check
la cuenta corriente	checking account
la cuenta de ahorros	savings account
ahorrar	to save (money)
cobrar	to cash (a check)
depositar	to deposit
firmar	to sign
llenar (un formulario)	to fill out (a form)
pagar a plazos	to pay in installments
pagar al contado/ en efectivo	to pay in cash
pedir prestado/a	to borrow
pedir un préstamo	to apply for a loan
ser gratis	to be free of charge

Cómo llegar

la cuadra	(city) block
la dirección	address
la esquina	corner
el letrero	sign
cruzar	to cross
doblar	to turn
estar perdido/a	to be lost
indicar cómo llegar	to give directions
quedar	to be located
(al) este	(to the) east
(al) norte	(to the) north
(al) oeste	(to the) west
(al) sur	(to the) south
derecho	straight (ahead)
enfrente de	opposite; facing
hacia	toward

Expresiones útiles	See page 455.

En el correo

el cartero	mail carrier
el correo	mail/post office
la estampilla, el sello	stamp
el paquete	package
el sobre	envelope
echar (una carta) al buzón	to put (a letter) in the mailbox; to mail
enviar, mandar	to send; to mail

recursos

LM
p. 83

vhlcentral.com
Lección 14

Audio: Vocabulary

El bienestar

15

Communicative Goals

You will learn how to:
- Talk about health, well-being, and nutrition
- Talk about physical activities

A PRIMERA VISTA
- ¿Está la chica en un gimnasio o en un lugar al aire libre?
- ¿Practica ella deportes frecuentemente?
- ¿Es activa o sedentaria?
- ¿Es probable que le importe su salud?

Lesson Goals

In **Lección 15**, students will be introduced to the following:
- terms for health and exercise
- nutrition terms
- natural spas
- the health benefits of fruit
- conditional
- present perfect
- past perfect
- making inferences
- organizing information logically when writing
- writing a personal wellness plan
- listening for the gist and for cognates
- a public service announcement for **Edenor**, Argentina's largest distributor of electricity
- the short film *Cloe*
- a video about places to relax and ways to deal with stress in Madrid, Spain
- cultural, geographic, and historical information about Bolivia and Paraguay

A primera vista Here are some additional questions you can ask: **¿Crees que tienes buena salud? ¿Vas al gimnasio regularmente? ¿Usas tu carro para hacer diligencias, o caminas? ¿Qué haces cuando te sientes nervioso/a o cansado/a? ¿Es importante que desayunes todas las mañanas? ¿Cuántas horas duermes cada noche?**

Teaching Tip Look for these icons for additional communicative practice:

→👥	Interpretive communication
←👥→	Presentational communication
👥↔	Interpersonal communication

Section Goals

In **Contextos**, students will learn and practice:
- vocabulary used to talk about health and exercise
- vocabulary used to discuss nutrition and a healthy diet

Instructional Resources

Supersite: Audio (Textbook and Lab MP3 Files); Resources (Overheads, **Vocabulario adicional**, Activity Pack, Scripts, Answer Keys); Testing Program (Quizzes)
WebSAM
Workbook, pp. 181–182
Lab Manual, p. 85

Teaching Tips

- Use the **Lección 15 Contextos** overheads to assist with this presentation.
- Write **hacer ejercicio** on the board, then ask personalized questions, writing new vocabulary on the board: Ex: **¿Quiénes hacen ejercicio regularmente? ¿Hacen ejercicios aeróbicos? ¿Quiénes levantan pesas?**
- 👤↔👤 Give the people in the illustration names and make statements and ask questions about their activities. Ex: **El señor Garza es teleadicto. Él no hace ejercicio. Ve televisión y come papitas. ¿Es activo o sedentario? ¿Lleva una vida sana?** After you have gone over the active vocabulary, ask students personalized questions to engage the class in a discussion about their exercise habits. Ex: **¿Qué hacen para aliviar el estrés? ¿Creen que se puede hacer demasiada gimnasia? ¿Creen que es más importante ser flexible o ser fuerte?**
- Point out the *No smoking* sign at the top right of the drawing. Explain that the infinitive, instead of a command form, is often found on public signs to express prohibitions or instructions.

El bienestar

Más vocabulario

adelgazar	to lose weight; to slim down
aliviar el estrés	to reduce stress
aliviar la tensión	to reduce tension
apurarse, darse prisa	to hurry; to rush
aumentar de peso, engordar	to gain weight
calentarse (e:ie)	to warm up
disfrutar (de)	to enjoy; to reap the benefits (of)
entrenarse	to practice; to train
estar a dieta	to be on a diet
estar en buena forma	to be in good shape
hacer gimnasia	to work out
llevar una vida sana	to lead a healthy lifestyle
mantenerse en forma	to stay in shape
sufrir muchas presiones	to be under a lot of pressure
tratar de (+ *inf.*)	to try (to do something)
la droga	drug
el/la drogadicto/a	drug addict
activo/a	active
débil	weak
en exceso	in excess; too much
flexible	flexible
fuerte	strong
sedentario/a	sedentary; related to sitting
tranquilo/a	calm; quiet
el bienestar	well-being

Variación léxica

hacer ejercicios aeróbicos ⟷ hacer aeróbic *(Esp.)*

el/la entrenador(a) ⟷ el/la monitor(a)

recursos

WB pp. 181–182	LM p. 85	Ⓢ vhlcentral.com Lección 15

GIMNASIO SUCRE

el teleadicto

Hace ejercicios de estiramiento. (hacer)

la clase de ejercicios aeróbicos

Suda. (sudar)

Hace ejercicio. (hacer)

el entrenador

el músculo

la cinta caminadora

TEACHING OPTIONS

TPR Ask students to stand. Call out commands based on the lesson vocabulary. Ex: **¡Levanten pesas! ¡Hagan ejercicios aeróbicos! ¡Apúrense! ¡Descansen!** Working with students, invent a gesture to mime each activity. When you have invented gestures to cover all the vocabulary, carry out a TPR activity with the class. Keep a brisk pace. Vary singular and plural commands.

Heritage Speakers Have volunteers read the words in the **Variación léxica** box aloud. Ask heritage speakers if they can name any additional terms related to fitness, health, and well-being. Ex: **tener mucho estrés, estar estresado/a; trotar**

No fumar.

el masaje

Hacen ejercicios aeróbicos.
(hacer)

Levanta pesas.
(levantar)

Práctica

1 **Escuchar** 🎧 Mira el dibujo. Luego escucha las oraciones e indica si lo que se dice en cada oración es **cierto** o **falso**.

	Cierto	Falso		Cierto	Falso
1.	○	◉	6.	○	◉
2.	○	◉	7.	○	◉
3.	◉	○	8.	◉	○
4.	◉	○	9.	○	◉
5.	◉	○	10.	○	◉

2 **Seleccionar** 🎧 Escucha el anuncio del gimnasio Sucre. Marca con una **X** los servicios que se ofrecen.

X 1. dietas para adelgazar
____ 2. programa para aumentar de peso
X 3. clases de gimnasia
X 4. entrenador personal
X 5. masajes
____ 6. programa para dejar de fumar

3 **Identificar** Identifica el antónimo (*antonym*) de cada palabra.

apurarse	fuerte
disfrutar	mantenerse en forma
engordar	sedentario
estar enfermo	sufrir muchas presiones
flexible	tranquilo

1. activo *sedentario*
2. adelgazar *engordar*
3. aliviar el estrés *sufrir muchas presiones*
4. débil *fuerte*
5. ir despacio *apurarse*
6. estar sano *estar enfermo*
7. nervioso *tranquilo*
8. ser teleadicto *mantenerse en forma*

4 **Combinar** Combina elementos de cada columna para formar ocho oraciones lógicas sobre el bienestar.

1. David levanta pesas *h*
2. Estás en buena forma *d*
3. Felipe se lastimó *f*
4. José y Rafael *e*
5. Mi hermano *a*
6. Sara hace ejercicios de *b*
7. Mis primas están a dieta *c*
8. Para llevar una vida sana, *g*

a. aumentó de peso.
b. estiramiento.
c. porque quieren adelgazar.
d. porque haces ejercicio.
e. sudan mucho en el gimnasio.
f. un músculo de la pierna.
g. no se debe fumar.
h. y corre mucho.

1 **Teaching Tip** Check answers by reading each statement and asking volunteers to say whether it is true or false. To challenge students, have them provide the correct information for each false statement.

1 **Script** 1. Se puede fumar dentro del gimnasio. 2. El teleadicto está en buena forma. 3. Los músculos del entrenador son grandes. 4. La mujer que está corriendo también está sudando.
Script continues on page 484.

2 **Teaching Tip** Tell students to listen to the audio without looking at the drawing.

2 **Script** Si quieres estar en buena forma, aliviar el estrés o adelgazar, el gimnasio Sucre te ofrece una serie de programas que se adaptarán a tus gustos. Tenemos un equipo de entrenadores que te pueden ayudar a mantenerte en forma con las clases de ejercicios aeróbicos y de gimnasia. Si sufres muchas presiones y lo que necesitas es un servicio más especial, puedes trabajar con un entrenador personal en nuestros programas privados de pesas, masajes y dietas para adelgazar.
Textbook MP3s

3 **Expansion** Have students use each pair of opposite terms in sentences.
Ex: **José está muy nervioso porque no estudió para el examen. Roberto estudió por dos horas; por eso está tranquilo.**

4 **Expansion** Have students create original endings for the sentence starters in the left column.

Note: At this point you may want to present *Vocabulario adicional: Más vocabulario para el bienestar* from the Supersite.

la proteína **la grasa** **el colesterol** **los minerales** **las vitaminas**

La nutrición

5 **Completar** Completa cada oración con la palabra adecuada.

1. Después de hacer ejercicio, como pollo o bistec porque contienen ___b___.
 a. drogas b. proteínas c. grasa
2. Para ___c___, es necesario consumir comidas de todos los grupos alimenticios (*nutrition groups*).
 a. aliviar el estrés b. correr c. comer una dieta equilibrada
3. Mis primas ___a___ una buena comida.
 a. disfrutan de b. tratan de c. sudan
4. Mi entrenador no come queso ni papas fritas porque contienen ___c___.
 a. dietas b. vitaminas c. mucha grasa
5. Mi padre no come mantequilla porque él necesita reducir ___b___.
 a. la nutrición b. el colesterol c. el bienestar
6. Mi novio cuenta ___c___ porque está a dieta.
 a. las pesas b. los músculos c. las calorías

CONSULTA
To review what you have learned about nutrition and food groups, see **Contextos, Lección 8**, pp. 242–245.

6 **La nutrición** En parejas, hablen de los tipos de comida que comen y las consecuencias que tienen para su salud. Luego compartan la información con la clase. Answers will vary.

1. ¿Cuántas comidas con mucha grasa comes regularmente? ¿Piensas que debes comer menos comidas de este tipo? ¿Por qué?
2. ¿Compras comidas con muchos minerales y vitaminas? ¿Necesitas consumir más comidas que los contienen? ¿Por qué?
3. ¿Algún miembro de tu familia tiene problemas con el colesterol? ¿Qué haces para evitar problemas con el colesterol?
4. ¿Eres vegetariano/a? ¿Conoces a alguien que sea vegetariano/a? ¿Qué piensas de la idea de no comer carne u otros productos animales? ¿Es posible comer una dieta equilibrada sin comer carne? Explica.
5. ¿Tomas cafeína en exceso? ¿Qué ventajas (*advantages*) y desventajas tiene la cafeína? Da ejemplos de productos que contienen cafeína y de productos descafeinados.
6. ¿Llevas una vida sana? ¿Y tus amigos? ¿Crees que, en general, los estudiantes llevan una vida sana? ¿Por qué?

Practice more at **vhlcentral.com**.

TEACHING OPTIONS

TPR Add an auditory aspect to this vocabulary practice. Have students write **bueno** on one piece of paper and **malo** on another. Prepare a series of statements about healthy and unhealthy habits. As you read each statement, have students hold up the corresponding paper. Ex: **Antes de hacer ejercicio, siempre como comidas con mucha grasa.** (malo) **Consumo muy poco alcohol.** (bueno)

Small groups In groups of three or four, have students take turns miming actions involving fitness, health, and well-being. The other group members should guess the verb or verb phrase. Ex: A student mimes lifting weights. (**Estás levantando pesas.**)

Comunicación

7 **Un anuncio** En grupos de cuatro, imaginen que son dueños/as de un gimnasio con un equipo (*equipment*) moderno, entrenadores cualificados y un(a) nutricionista. Preparen y presenten un anuncio para la televisión que hable del gimnasio y atraiga (*attracts*) a una gran variedad de nuevos clientes. No se olviden de presentar esta información: Answers will vary.

▶ las ventajas de estar en buena forma
▶ el equipo que tienen
▶ los servicios y clases que ofrecen
▶ las características únicas
▶ la dirección y el teléfono
▶ el precio para los socios (*members*)

8 **Recomendaciones para la salud** En parejas, imaginen que están preocupados/as por los malos hábitos de un(a) amigo/a que no está bien últimamente (*lately*). Escriban y representen una conversación en la cual hablen de lo que está pasando en la vida de su amigo/a y los cambios que necesita hacer para llevar una vida sana. Answers will vary.

9 **El teleadicto** Con un(a) compañero/a, representen los papeles de un(a) nutricionista y un(a) teleadicto/a. La persona sedentaria habla de sus malos hábitos para la comida y de que no hace ejercicio. También dice que toma demasiado café y que siente mucho estrés. El/La nutricionista le sugiere una dieta equilibrada con bebidas descafeinadas y una rutina para mantenerse en buena forma. El/La teleadicto/a le da las gracias por su ayuda. Answers will vary.

10 **El gimnasio perfecto** Tú y tu compañero/a quieren encontrar el gimnasio perfecto. Su profesor(a) les va a dar a cada uno/a de ustedes el anuncio de un gimnasio. Túrnense para hacerse preguntas sobre las actividades que se ofrecen en cada uno. Al final, decidan cuál es el mejor gimnasio y compartan su decisión con la clase. Answers will vary.

11 **¿Quién es?** Trabajen en grupos. Cada uno/a de ustedes va a elegir a una persona famosa por temas de salud y bienestar. Los demás miembros del grupo deben hacer preguntas hasta descubrir a quién eligió cada quien. Recuerden usar el vocabulario de la lección. Answers will vary.

> **modelo**
>
> **Estudiante 1:** ¿Haces ejercicio todos los días?
> **Estudiante 2:** Sí, sobre todo hago ejercicios aeróbicos. ¡Me encanta la música!
> **Estudiante 3:** ¿Comes una dieta equilibrada?
> **Estudiante 2:** Sí, y hace más de 40 años que perdí más de 100 libras (*pounds*) de peso.
> **Estudiante 1:** ¡Ya sé! ¡Eres Richard Simmons!

TEACHING OPTIONS

Pairs 👥 Tell students to imagine that they are personal wellness consultants. (If you wish, have them take on the persona of one of the people mentioned in **Actividad 11**.) Have them give their partner a set of ten guidelines on how to begin a comprehensive health program. Suggestions should be made regarding diet, aerobic exercise, strength training, flexibility training, and stress management. Have students switch roles.

Extra Practice 👥 Ask students to write down five personal goals for achieving or maintaining a healthy lifestyle. Then have them write a brief paragraph explaining why they want to attain these goals and how they plan to achieve them. Call on volunteers to share their goals with the class.

7 Teaching Tips
• Have students visit health clubs in your area to gather brochures and/or fitness magazines to help them brainstorm ideas.
• Have groups write their advertisement so that each student gets to speak for an equal amount of time.

8 Teaching Tips
• Suggest that students use expressions of doubt followed by the subjunctive or expressions of certainty. Review the expressions on pages 430–431 as needed.
• 👥 Have partners discuss at least five bad habits their friend has, explain why he or she has them, and what he or she tried to do to overcome them. Then, have students discuss ways of successfully overcoming each habit.

9 Teaching Tip Before doing this activity, review the verbs and expressions of will and influence on pages 398–399.

9 Expansion
👥 Have students conduct a follow-up interview which takes place one month after the initial meeting.

10 Teaching Tip Divide the class into pairs and distribute the handouts from the Activity Pack (Activity Pack/Supersite) that correspond to this activity.

10 Expansion
• 👥 Have pairs work in groups to discuss which gym they would join and why.
• 👥 Have groups compare these gyms with your campus gym.

11 Teaching Tip Encourage students to think of people from all areas of health, including nutrition, exercise, and mental well-being. To simplify, provide a list of names on the board. Ex: Richard Simmons, Jillian Michaels, Dr. Oz, Oprah, Dr. Phil, Billy Blanks, Bethenny Frankel, Jackie Warner, Michael Pollan

Section Goals

In **Fotonovela**, students will:
• receive comprehensible input from free-flowing discourse
• learn functional phrases that preview lesson grammatical structures

Instructional Resources
Supersite/DVD: *Fotonovela*
Supersite: Resources (Scripts, Translations, Answer Keys)
WebSAM
Video Manual, pp. 223–224

Video Recap: Lección 14
Before doing this **Fotonovela** section, review the previous episode with these questions:
1. **¿Por qué Maru no está en Yucatán con los otros chicos?** (Tuvo que entregar su proyecto.)
2. **¿Por qué Maru dice que necesita un coche que funcione bien?** (Porque el coche de Miguel está descompuesto.)
3. **¿Qué quiere Maru que Mónica le preste?** (Quiere que Mónica le preste dinero para tomar un taxi.)
4. **¿Dónde dejó Maru el proyecto?** (Lo dejó en el coche de Miguel.)
5. **¿Cómo llegó Maru al Museo de Antropología?** (Mónica la llevó.)

Video Synopsis
Marissa, Felipe, Jimena, and **Juan Carlos** visit the famous Mayan ruins of **Chichén Itzá.** After exploring the archeological site, they visit a spa to escape the sun and unwind. **Juan Carlos** and **Jimena** finally connect.

Teaching Tips
• Ask students to read only the first statement in each caption. Then have them predict the content of the episode, based only on those sentences. Write down their predictions.
• 👥↔👥 Quickly review the predictions students made about the episode. Through discussion, help the class summarize the plot.

Chichén Itzá

Los chicos exploran Chichén Itzá y se relajan en un spa.

PERSONAJES **MARISSA** **FELIPE**

S Video: *Fotonovela*
Record and Compare

1

MARISSA ¡Chichén Itzá es impresionante! Qué lástima que Maru y Miguel no estén con nosotros. Sobre todo Maru.

FELIPE Ha estado bajo mucha presión.

MARISSA Podría quedarme aquí para siempre. ¿Ustedes ya habían venido antes?

FELIPE Sí. Nuestros papás nos trajeron cuando éramos niños.

2

FELIPE El otro día le gané a Juan Carlos en el parque.

JUAN CARLOS Estaba mirando hacia otro lado, cuando me di cuenta, Felipe ya había empezado a correr.

(en otro lugar de las ruinas)

JUAN CARLOS ¡Hace calor!

JIMENA ¡Sí! Hay que estar en buena forma para recorrer las ruinas.

3

5

4

JUAN CARLOS Siempre había llevado una vida sana antes de entrar a la universidad.

JIMENA Tienes razón. La universidad hace que seamos muy sedentarios.

JUAN CARLOS ¡Busquemos a Felipe y a Marissa!

6

FELIPE ¡Gané!

JIMENA Qué calor. Tengo una idea. Vamos.

TEACHING OPTIONS

Video Tips General suggestions for using video clips in the classroom can be found on page IAE-10 of this Instructor's Annotated Edition.

Chichén Itzá ➔👥← To introduce the class to this **Fotonovela** episode, first play the video without any sound so students can concentrate on the action. Have students tell you what they saw and make predictions about the content of the video. Then, play the episode with sound and have students jot down notes about the plot. Next, have the class work in small groups to compare notes and prepare summaries of the episode. Ask one or two groups to read their summaries to the class. Finally, discuss the plot with the class and check for accuracy.

JUAN CARLOS **JIMENA** **EMPLEADA**

EMPLEADA Ofrecemos varios servicios para aliviar el estrés: masajes, saunas...

FELIPE Me gustaría un masaje.

MARISSA Yo prefiero un baño mineral.

JUAN CARLOS ¿Crees que tendrías un poco de tiempo libre la semana que viene? Me gustaría invitarte a salir.

JIMENA ¿Sin Felipe?

JUAN CARLOS Sin Felipe.

EMPLEADA ¿Ya tomaron una decisión?

JIMENA Sí.

recursos

VM pp. 223–224

vhlcentral.com Lección 15

Expresiones útiles

Wishing a friend were with you

Qué lástima que no estén con nosotros.
What a shame that they aren't with us.
Sobre todo Maru.
Especially Maru.
Él/Ella ha estado bajo mucha presión.
He/She has been under a lot of pressure.
Creo que ellos ya habían venido antes.
I think they had already come (here) before.

Talking about trips

¿Ustedes ya habían venido antes?
Had you been (here) before?
Sí. He querido regresar desde que leí el *Chilam Balam*.
Yes. I have wanted to come back ever since I read the Chilam Balam.
¿Recuerdas cuando nos trajo papá?
Remember when Dad brought us?
Al llegar a la cima, comenzaste a llorar.
When we got to the top, you started to cry.

Talking about well-being

Siempre había llevado una vida sana antes de entrar a la universidad.
I had always maintained a healthy lifestyle before starting college.
Ofrecemos varios servicios para aliviar el estrés.
We offer many services to relieve stress.
Me gustaría un masaje.
I would like a massage.

Additional vocabulary

la cima *top, peak*
el escalón *step*
el muro *wall*
tomar una decisión *to make a decision*

Expresiones útiles Draw attention to the sentence **Me gustaría un masaje**. Tell students that **gustaría** is an example of the conditional, which they saw in **Lección 8** (**¿Les gustaría saber cuáles son las especialidades del día?**). The conditional is formed much like the future tense. Point out that **ha estado** and **He querido** are examples of the present perfect, which combines a present-tense form of the verb **haber** with the past participle of another verb. Finally, explain that **habían venido** and **había llevado** are examples of the past perfect, which combines an imperfect-tense form of **haber** with a past participle. Tell students that they will learn more about these concepts in **Estructura**.

Teaching Tips
- Have the class read through the entire **Fotonovela**, with volunteers playing the various parts.
- Point out **Me gustaría invitarte a salir** from the caption for video still 9. Ask students to translate it into English using the sentence **Me gustaría un masaje** from **Expresiones útiles** as a guide.
- Explain that the conditional is used to express *what you would do* or *what would happen* under certain circumstances and that they will learn more about its use in **Estructura**.

Nota cultural **Chichén Itzá** is a large pre-Columbian archaeological site built by the Mayans in Mexico. Now a UNESCO World Heritage Site, it attracts thousands of tourists from all over the world each year. While at one time visitors were given open access to **Chichén Itzá**, this is now limited due to the erosion and destruction of many structures.

¿Qué pasó?

1 **Seleccionar** Selecciona la respuesta que completa mejor cada oración.

1. Felipe y Marissa piensan que Maru ____c____.
 a. debe hacer ejercicio b. aumentó de peso c. ha estado bajo mucha presión
2. Felipe y Jimena visitaron Chichén Itzá ____b____.
 a. para aliviar el estrés b. cuando eran niños c. para llevar una vida sana
3. Jimena dice que la universidad hace a los estudiantes ____b____.
 a. comer una dieta equilibrada b. ser sedentarios c. levantar pesas
4. En el spa ofrecen servicios para ____b____.
 a. sudar b. aliviar el estrés c. ser flexibles
5. Felipe elige que le den un ____c____.
 a. baño mineral b. almuerzo c. masaje

2 **Identificar** Identifica quién puede decir estas oraciones.

1. No me di cuenta (*I didn't realize*) de que habías empezado a correr, por eso ganaste. Juan Carlos
2. Miguel y Maru no visitaron Chichén Itzá, ¡qué lástima que no estén con nosotros! Marissa
3. Se necesita estar en buena forma para visitar este tipo de lugares. Jimena
4. Los masajes, saunas y baños minerales que ofrecemos alivian la tensión. empleada
5. Si salimos, no invites a Felipe. Jimena
6. Yo corro más rápido que Juan Carlos. Felipe

MARISSA

FELIPE

JIMENA

JUAN CARLOS

EMPLEADA

3 **Inventar** En parejas, hagan descripciones de los personajes de la **Fotonovela**. Utilicen las oraciones, la lista de palabras y otras expresiones que sepan. Answers will vary.

aliviar el estrés	hacer ejercicios de estiramiento	masaje
bienestar	llevar una vida sana	teleadicto/a
grasa	mantenerse en forma	vitamina

> **modelo**
> **Estudiante 1:** Felipe es activo, flexible y fuerte.
> **Estudiante 2:** Marissa siempre hace ejercicios de estiramiento. Está en buena forma y lleva una vida muy sana...

1. A Juan Carlos le duelen los músculos después de hacer gimnasia.
2. Maru a veces sufre presiones y estrés en la universidad.
3. A Jimena le encanta salir con amigos o leer un buen libro.
4. Felipe trata de comer una dieta equilibrada.
5. Juan Carlos no es muy flexible.

 Practice more at **vhlcentral.com.**

Ortografía (S) Concepts

Las letras b y v

Since there is no difference in pronunciation between the Spanish letters **b** and **v**, spelling words that contain these letters can be tricky. Here are some tips.

nom**b**re	**b**lusa	a**b**soluto	descu**b**rir

The letter **b** is always used before consonants.

bon ita	**b**otella	**b**uscar	**b**ien estar

At the beginning of words, the letter **b** is usually used when it is followed by the letter combinations -**on**, -**or**, -**ot**, -**u**, -**ur**, -**us**, -**ien**, and -**ene**.

adelgaza**b**a	disfruta**b**an	i**b**as	í**b**amos

The letter **b** is used in the verb endings of the imperfect tense for -**ar** verbs and the verb **ir**.

voy	**v**amos	estu**v**o	tu**v**ieron

The letter **v** is used in the present tense forms of **ir** and in the preterite forms of **estar** and **tener**.

oct**avo**	hu**evo**	act**iva**	gr**ave**

The letter **v** is used in these noun and adjective endings: -**avo/a**, -**evo/a**, -**ivo/a**, -**ave**, -**eve**.

 Práctica Completa las palabras con las letras **b** o **v**.

1. Una _v_ez me lastimé el _b_razo cuando esta_b_a _b_uceando.
2. Manuela se ol_v_idó sus li_b_ros en el auto_b_ús.
3. Ernesto tomó el _b_orrador y se puso todo _b_lanco de tiza.
4. Para tener una _v_ida sana y saluda_b_le, necesitas tomar _v_itaminas.
5. En mi pue_b_lo hay un _b_ule_v_ar que tiene muchos ár_b_oles.

 El ahorcado (*Hangman*) Juega al ahorcado para adivinar las palabras.

1. _n_ u _b_ e _s_ Están en el cielo. nubes
2. _b_ u z ó _n_ Relacionado con el correo buzón
3. _b_ o _t_ e _l l_ a Está llena de líquido. botella
4. _n_ i _e v_ e Fenómeno meteorológico nieve
5. _v_ e _n t a n a s_ Los "ojos" de la casa ventanas

recursos	
LM p. 86	vhlcentral.com Lección 15

Section Goals

In **Cultura**, students will:
• read about natural spas
• learn exercise-related terms
• read about the health benefits of papaya and pineapple
• read about popular beliefs regarding health

Instructional Resources
Supersite/DVD: *Flash cultura*
Supersite: Resources (Scripts, Translations, Answer Keys)
WebSAM
Video Manual, pp. 295–296

En detalle
Antes de leer Have students look at the photos and describe what they see. Then ask: **¿Alguna vez han ido a un balneario? ¿Por qué creen que las personas van a los balnearios?**

Lectura
• While people of all ages visit spas, the elderly have discovered specific health benefits. In places like Villa Elisa, Argentina, many go to thermal baths to reduce swelling in their joints and relieve backaches.
• Point out the word **lodoterapia**. Have a volunteer explain what it means and how this word is formed.
• Point out the chart and ask students what information it shows.

Después de leer
←👥→ Ask students which spa they would like to visit. Have them write a short paragraph of 3 to 4 sentences explaining why.

1 Expansion Have students rephrase each statement as a question. Ex: **2. ¿Desde cuándo se conocen los tratamientos con agua y lodo?**

EN DETALLE

(S) **Additional Reading**
Video: *Flash cultura*

Spas naturales

¿Hay algo mejor que un buen baño° para descansar y aliviar la tensión? Y si el baño se toma en una terma°, el beneficio° es mayor. Los tratamientos con agua y lodo° para mejorar la salud y el bienestar son populares en las Américas desde hace muchos siglos°. Las termas son manantiales° naturales de agua caliente. La temperatura facilita la absorción de minerales y otros elementos que contiene el agua y que son buenos para la salud. El agua de las termas se usa en piscinas, baños y duchas o en el sitio natural en el que surge°: pozas°, estanques° o cuevas°.

Ecotermales en Arenal, Costa Rica

Volcán de lodo El Totumo, Colombia

En Baños de San Vicente, en Ecuador, son muy populares los tratamientos° con lodo volcánico.

El lodo caliente se extiende por el cuerpo; así la piel° absorbe los minerales beneficiosos para la salud; también se usa para dar masajes. La lodoterapia es útil para tratar varias enfermedades, además hace que la piel se vea radiante.

En Costa Rica, la actividad volcánica también ha dado° origen a fuentes° y pozas termales. Si te gusta cuidarte y amas la naturaleza, recuerda estos nombres: Las Hornillas y Las Pailas. Son pozas naturales de aguas termales que están cerca del volcán Rincón de la Vieja. Un baño termal en medio de un paisaje tan hermoso es una experiencia única.

baño *bath* **terma** *hot spring* **beneficio** *benefit* **lodo** *mud* **siglos** *centuries* **manantiales** *springs* **surge** *springs forth* **pozas** *small pools* **estanques** *ponds* **cuevas** *caves* **tratamientos** *treatments* **piel** *skin* **ha dado** *has given* **fuentes** *springs* **balnearios** *spas* **cascadas** *waterfalls* **algas** *seaweed* **temazcales** *steam and medicinal herb baths*

Otros balnearios°

Todos ofrecen piscinas, baños, pozas y duchas de aguas termales y además...

Lugar	Servicios
El Edén y Yanasara, Curgos (Perú)	cascadas° de aguas termales
Montbrió del Camp, Tarragona (España)	baños de algas°
Puyuhuapi (Chile)	duchas de agua de mar; baños de algas
Termas de Río Hondo, Santiago del Estero (Argentina)	baños de lodo
Tepoztlán, Morelos (México)	temazcales° aztecas
Uyuni, Potosí (Bolivia)	baños de sal

ACTIVIDADES

1 **¿Cierto o falso?** Indica si lo que dicen las oraciones es cierto o falso. Corrige la información falsa.

1. Las aguas termales son beneficiosas para algunas enfermedades, incluido el estrés. **Cierto.**
2. Los tratamientos con agua y lodo se conocen sólo desde hace pocos años. **Falso.** Son populares desde hace muchos siglos.
3. Las termas son manantiales naturales de agua caliente. **Cierto.**
4. La lodoterapia es un tratamiento con barro. **Cierto.**

5. La temperatura de las aguas termales no afecta la absorción de los minerales. **Falso.** Facilita la absorción de minerales y otros elementos.
6. Mucha gente va a Baños de San Vicente, Ecuador, por sus playas. **Falso.** Mucha gente va por los tratamientos con lodo.
7. Las Hornillas son pozas de aguas termales en Costa Rica. **Cierto.**
8. Montbrió del Camp ofrece baños de sal. **Falso.** Montbrió del Camp ofrece baños de algas.
9. Es posible ver aguas termales en forma de cascadas. **Cierto.**
10. Tepoztlán ofrece temazcales aztecas. **Cierto.**

TEACHING OPTIONS

TPR Call out true/false statements about the reading. If the statement is true, have students raise one hand. If the statement is false, have students raise both hands. To challenge students, have volunteers correct the false information.

Small Groups ←👥→ Have students work in small groups. Tell them to imagine that they are planning a trip to one of the spas mentioned in the reading. Have them do additional Internet research and find out how to travel there, the services offered, and the prices. Then have groups present their itineraries to the class.

Así se dice
- Model the pronunciation of each term and have students repeat it.
- To challenge students, add these exercise-related words to the list: **estar cachas (Esp.)** (*to be very muscular*); **la (máquina) elíptica** (*elliptical machine*); **la fatiga** (*fatigue*); **rebajar** (*to lose weight*); **la resistencia** (*endurance*); **trotar, hacer footing (Esp.)** (*to jog*).
- 👥↔👤 Ask students personalized questions to involve them in a discussion using the new vocabulary. Ex: **¿Qué haces si te da un calambre muscular? (Hago ejercicios de estiramiento.)**

ASÍ SE DICE

El ejercicio

los abdominales	sit-ups
la bicicleta estática	stationary bicycle
el calambre muscular	(muscular) cramp
el (fisi)culturismo; la musculación (Esp.)	bodybuilding
las flexiones de pecho; las lagartijas (Méx.; Col.); las planchas (Esp.)	push-ups
la cinta (trotadora) (Arg.; Chile)	la cinta caminadora

EL MUNDO HISPANO

Creencias° sobre la salud

- **Colombia** Como algunos suelos son de baldosas°, se cree que si uno anda descalzo° se enfrían° los pies y esto puede causar un resfriado o artritis.

- **Cuba** Por la mañana, muchas madres sacan a sus bebés a los patios y a las puertas de las casas. La creencia es que unos cinco minutos de sol ayudan a fijar° el calcio en los huesos y aumentan la inmunidad contra las enfermedades.

- **México** Muchas personas tienen la costumbre de tomar a diario un vaso de jugo del cactus conocido como "nopal". Se dice que es bueno para reducir el colesterol y el azúcar en la sangre y que ayuda a adelgazar.

Creencias *Beliefs* baldosas *tiles* anda descalzo *walks barefoot* se enfrían *get cold* fijar *to set*

PERFIL

Las frutas y la salud

Desde hace muchos años se conocen las propiedades de la papaya para tratar problemas digestivos. Esta fruta originaria de las Américas contiene una enzima, la papaína, que actúa de forma semejante° a como lo hacen los jugos gástricos. Una porción de papaya o un vaso de jugo de esta fruta ayuda a la digestión. La papaya también es rica en vitaminas A y C.

La piña° también es una fruta natural de las Américas que es buena para la digestión. La piña contiene bromelina, una enzima que, como la papaína, ayuda a digerir° las proteínas. Esta deliciosa fruta contiene también ácido cítrico, vitaminas y minerales. Además, tiene efectos diuréticos y antiinflamatorios que pueden aliviar las enfermedades reumáticas. La piña ofrece una ayuda fácil y sabrosa para perder peso por su contenido en fibra y su efecto diurético. Una rodaja° o un vaso de jugo de piña fresca antes de comer

puede ayudar en cualquier° dieta para adelgazar.

semejante *similar* piña *pineapple* digerir *to digest* rodaja *slice* cualquier *any*

Conexión Internet

¿Qué sistemas de ejercicio son más populares entre los hispanos?

Go to **vhlcentral.com** to find more cultural information related to this **Cultura** section.

Perfil
- Take a quick survey of the class to find out who likes papaya and pineapple. If possible, bring in papaya and pineapple juice for students to sample.
- Papaya is also called **fruta bomba** (Cuba), **lechosa** (Dominican Republic, Puerto Rico), and **lechoso** (Venezuela). Pineapple is known as **ananá** in Uruguay.

El mundo hispano Ask students if any of these popular beliefs are surprising to them.

2 Expansion Give students these questions as items 5–6:
5. ¿Qué vitaminas contiene la papaya? (las vitaminas A y C)
6. Si eres parte del ejército español, es probable que hagas planchas. ¿Qué haces? (flexiones de pecho)

3 Teaching Tip
- Review vocabulary for daily routines from **Lección 7**.
- To simplify, before coming to class, have students brainstorm a list of interview questions to ask their partners.

3 Expansion
👤↔👤 Call on volunteers to summarize their partners' responses for the class.

ACTIVIDADES

2 Comprensión Responde a las preguntas.

1. Una argentina te dice: "Voy a usar la cinta." ¿Qué va a hacer?
 Va a usar la cinta caminadora.
2. Según los colombianos, ¿qué efectos negativos tiene el no usar zapatos en casa? Puede causar un resfriado o artritis.
3. ¿Cómo se llama la enzima de la papaya que ayuda a la digestión? la papaína
4. ¿Cómo se aconseja consumir la piña en dietas de adelgazamiento? una rodaja o un vaso de jugo de piña fresca antes de comer

3 Para sentirte mejor Entrevista a un(a) compañero/a sobre las cosas que hace todos los días y las cosas que hace al menos una o dos veces a la semana para sentirse mejor. Hablen sobre actividades deportivas, la alimentación y lo que hacen en sus ratos libres. Answers will vary.

recursos

VM pp. 295–296	vhlcentral.com Lección 15

 Practice more at **vhlcentral.com.**

TEACHING OPTIONS

Heritage Speakers 👥↔👤 Ask heritage speakers to talk about popular health beliefs or foods with healing properties that they have encountered in their communities or heard from their relatives.

Pairs Divide the class into pairs. Have students take turns quizzing each other about the health beliefs and practices mentioned on these pages. Write a question on the board for stu-

dents to use as a model. Ex: **¿Para qué sirve la lodoterapia?**

Game Play a *Jeopardy*-style game. Divide the class into three teams and have one member from each team stand up. Read a definition. Ex: **Es una enzima de la papaya.** The first student to raise his or her hand must answer in the form of a question. Ex: **¿Qué es la papaína?** Each correct answer earns one point. The team with the most points wins.

15.1 The conditional (S) Tutorial

ANTE TODO The conditional tense in Spanish expresses what you *would do* or what *would happen* under certain circumstances.

The conditional tense

		visitar	comer	escribir
SINGULAR FORMS	yo	visitar**ía**	comer**ía**	escribir**ía**
	tú	visitar**ías**	comer**ías**	escribir**ías**
	Ud./él/ella	visitar**ía**	comer**ía**	escribir**ía**
PLURAL FORMS	nosotros/as	visitar**íamos**	comer**íamos**	escribir**íamos**
	vosotros/as	visitar**íais**	comer**íais**	escribir**íais**
	Uds./ellos/ellas	visitar**ían**	comer**ían**	escribir**ían**

Me gustaría un masaje.

¿Crees que tendrías un poco de tiempo libre?

▶ The conditional tense is formed much like the future tense. The endings are the same for all verbs, both regular and irregular. For regular verbs, you simply add the appropriate endings to the infinitive. **¡Atención!** All forms of the conditional have an accent mark.

▶ For irregular verbs, add the conditional endings to the irregular stems.

INFINITIVE	STEM	CONDITIONAL		INFINITIVE	STEM	CONDITIONAL
decir	dir-	dir**ía**		querer	querr-	querr**ía**
hacer	har-	har**ía**		saber	sabr-	sabr**ía**
poder	podr-	podr**ía**		salir	saldr-	saldr**ía**
poner	pondr-	pondr**ía**		tener	tendr-	tendr**ía**
haber	habr-	habr**ía**		venir	vendr-	vendr**ía**

▶ While in English the conditional is a compound verb form made up of the auxiliary verb *would* and a main verb, in Spanish it is a simple verb form that consists of one word.

Yo no **iría** a ese gimnasio.
I would not go to that gym.

¿**Vendrías** conmigo a la clase de yoga?
Would you come to yoga class with me?

¡ATENCIÓN!

The polite expressions **Me gustaría...** (*I would like...*) and **Te gustaría** (*You would like...*) are commonly used examples of the conditional.

AYUDA

The infinitive of **hay** is **haber**, so its conditional form is **habría**.

Section Goals

In **Estructura 15.1** students will learn:
- to use the conditional
- to make polite requests and hypothesize about past conditions

Instructional Resources

Supersite: Audio (Lab MP3 Files); Resources (*PowerPoints*, Activity Pack, Scripts, Answer Keys); Testing Program (Quizzes)
WebSAM
Workbook, pp. 183–184
Lab Manual, p. 87

Teaching Tips

- 👤↔👤 Ask students to imagine they are on the trip with the **Fotonovela** characters. Ask them what they would like to do there. Ex: **¿Qué te gustaría hacer o ver en México? A mí me gustaría ir de excursión. ¿Y a ti?** Tell students that **gustaría** is a polite form of **gustar** that they already know. The conditional can be used to make polite requests.
- Ask volunteers to read the captions to the video stills and indicate which verbs are in the conditional.
- Point out that, as in the future, there is only one set of endings in the conditional.
- Check for understanding by citing an infinitive and a subject pronoun while pointing to a specific student. The student should respond with the conditional form. Ex: **decir / nosotros (diríamos); venir / tú (vendrías)**
- Ask students what the future form of **hay** is. Then ask them what they would expect the conditional form to be (**habrá/habría**).

TEACHING OPTIONS

TPR In teams of five, have students line up several feet from the board. Call out an infinitive. The first team members race to the board and write the **yo** form of the verb in the conditional, then pass the chalk to the next team members, who write the **tú** form, and so on. The team that finishes first and has all the forms correct wins the round.

Extra Practice ←👤→ Ask students to write a short paragraph describing what they would do over the next six months if they could do anything their hearts desired and money and time were no object. Ex: **Yo viajaría por todo el mundo...** Call on volunteers to read their paragraphs aloud, then ask the class comprehension questions about what was said. Ex: **¿Qué harían _____ y _____?**

▶ The conditional is commonly used to make polite requests.

¿Podrías abrir la ventana, por favor?
Would you open the window, please?

¿Sería tan amable de venir a mi oficina?
Would you be so kind as to come to my office?

AYUDA

Keep in mind the two parallel combinations shown in the example sentences:
1) present tense in main clause → future tense in subordinate clause
2) past tense in main clause → conditional tense in subordinate clause

▶ In Spanish, as in English, the conditional expresses the future in relation to a past action or state of being. In other words, the future indicates what *will happen* whereas the conditional indicates what *would happen*.

Creo que mañana **hará** sol.
I think it will be sunny tomorrow.

Creía que hoy **haría** sol.
I thought it would be sunny today.

▶ The English *would* is often used with a verb to express the conditional, but it can also mean *used to*, in the sense of past habitual action. To express past habitual actions, Spanish uses the imperfect, not the conditional.

Íbamos al parque los sábados.
We would go to the park on Saturdays.

Antes, me **entrenaba** todos los días.
Before, I used to work out every day.

Sin ti, no sé qué haría.

Sólo tú sabes ordenar mi vida.

Sin ti perdería la cabeza.
Sin ti no podría estar al día.
Todo lo resuelves con la mayor elegancia.
Sólo tú sabes ordenar mi vida.

COMPARE & CONTRAST

In **Lección 14**, you learned the *future of probability*. Spanish also has the *conditional of probability*, which expresses conjecture or probability about a past condition, event, or action. Compare these Spanish and English sentences.

Serían las once de la noche cuando Elvira me llamó.
It must have been (It was probably) 11 p.m. when Elvira called me.

Sonó el teléfono. **¿Llamaría** Emilio para cancelar nuestra cita?
The phone rang. I wondered if it was Emilio calling to cancel our date.

Note that English conveys conjecture or probability with phrases such as *I wondered if*, *probably*, and *must have been*. In contrast, Spanish gets these same ideas across with conditional forms.

¡INTÉNTALO! Indica la forma apropiada del condicional de los verbos.

recursos

WB
pp. 183–184

LM
p. 87

Ⓢ
vhlcentral.com
Lección 15

1. Yo _escucharía, leería, me apuraría_ (escuchar, leer, apurarse)
2. Tú _te mantendrías, comprenderías, compartirías_ (mantenerse, comprender, compartir)
3. Marcos _pondría, vendría, querría_ (poner, venir, querer)
4. Nosotras _seríamos, sabríamos, iríamos_ (ser, saber, ir)
5. Ustedes _adelgazarían, deberían, sufrirían_ (adelgazar, deber, sufrir)
6. Ella _saldría, podría, haría_ (salir, poder, hacer)
7. Yo _tendría, trataría, fumaría_ (tener, tratar, fumar)
8. Tú _dirías, verías, engordarías_ (decir, ver, engordar)

Teaching Tips

• Discuss the use of the conditional in polite requests. Remind students of the forms **me gustaría** and **te gustaría**, which they have already seen in the **Fotonovela**. You might point out that usage tends to occur in set expressions, such as **¿Podrías… ? ¿Sería usted tan amable de… ? ¿Tendrían ustedes la bondad de… ? ¿Me harías el favor de… ?**

• Explain the concept of the conditional as *the future of the past*. Explain that the conditional is used to express some action that was yet to occur at some past time, and give examples. Ex: **1. Creo que me mantendré en forma. Creía que me mantendría en forma. 2. Sé que adelgazarás. Sabía que adelgazarías.**

• Remind students of the future of probability. Point out that the conditional of probability functions just like it, but in the context of the past. Compare the second example in the Compare & Contrast box to the following: **Suena el teléfono. ¿Llamará Emilio para cancelar nuestra cita?**

TEACHING OPTIONS

Extra Practice Tell students to imagine that their families have come into a great deal of money. Ask them to write ten sentences describing what they and their family members would do with the money. Students should try to use as many different verbs and conjugations as possible. Ex: **Mi familia y yo ayudaríamos a los artistas de nuestra ciudad…**

Pairs Have students work together to role-play interviewing a personal trainer. Interviewers should ask the trainer what he or she would do to help get them in shape. Have students switch roles.

Práctica

Teaching Tips
- To simplify, have students begin by underlining the infinitives with irregular stems.
- →👤← Ask six volunteers to write the completed sentences on the board. Have the class check for accurate spelling and grammar.

1 **¡A ponerse en forma!** Víctor y Emilia quieren apuntarse (*enroll*) a un gimnasio y están hablando con el gerente. Completa las oraciones con el condicional del verbo.

VÍCTOR Buenas tardes. Necesitamos información sobre el gimnasio.

GERENTE Por supuesto. Me (1)___encantaría___ (encantar) ayudar.

EMILIA Primero, ¿ (2)___podría___ (poder) usted decirnos cuánto cuesta al mes?

GERENTE (3)___Costaría___ (costar) setenta dólares por persona.

VÍCTOR Y además del uso de las máquinas, ¿qué otros servicios (4)___estarían___ (estar) incluidos?

GERENTE Ustedes (5)___tendrían___ (tener) un entrenador particular (*personal*) que los (6)___ayudaría___ (ayudar) a estar en buena forma y les (7)___recomendaría___ (recomendar) qué clases de ejercicios les (8)___serían___ (ser) más beneficiosos.

EMILIA Víctor, ¿qué piensas? ¿Tú (9)___irías___ (ir) al gimnasio dos veces por semana?

Expansion Ask questions about the responses to practice all forms of the conditional. Ex: **¿Qué le diría ____ a la persona de enfrente? (Le diría que no puede ver nada.) ¿Qué harían ____ y ____ en esta situación? (Asistirían a otra clase.)**

2 **¿Qué harías?** En parejas, pregúntense qué harían en las siguientes situaciones. Answers will vary.

> **modelo**
> ¡No me perdería mi clase de ejercicios aeróbicos por nada del mundo! Me movería a un lado para poder ver bien al instructor y hablaría con la persona de enfrente amablemente.

Estás en una clase de ejercicios aeróbicos y la persona de enfrente no te deja ver.

Vas al banco a depositar un cheque y te das cuenta de (*you realize*) que en tu cuenta hay por error un millón de dólares que no es tuyo.

Estás manejando por el desierto y te quedas sin gasolina.

Vuelves a tu apartamento después de tus clases y tu ex novio/a no te deja entrar.

Teaching Tip Before you divide the class into pairs, allow individuals sufficient time to write out their eight ideas. Then have students work with a partner to give advice. Tell them to take turns sharing their ideas.

3 **Presidente por un día** Imagina que eres el/la presidente/a de tu universidad por un día. Escribe ocho cosas que harías en esa situación. Usa el condicional. Luego compara tus ideas con las de un(a) compañero/a. Answers will vary.

> **modelo**
> Yo tendría un jet privado para mis viajes.

conocer	hacer	poner
dar	invertir en	sufrir
disfrutar	mejorar	tener

Expansion →👤← Have partners choose their three best ideas to present to the class. Write them on the board, then ask the class to vote on which are the most creative or interesting.

 Practice more at **vhlcentral.com.**

TEACHING OPTIONS

Pairs 👤↔👤 Have students take turns asking each other for favors, using courtesy expressions with the conditional. Partners respond by saying whether they will do the favor; if they cannot, they should make up an excuse. Ex: **¿Me podrías recoger del gimnasio a las cinco de la tarde? (Lo siento, pero no puedo. Tengo una clase de química hasta las cinco y media.)**

Large Groups Ask students to think about what they would do if they were training for the Olympics. Have them pick an event and a Spanish-speaking country to represent. Ex: **Sería de Paraguay. Nadaría los 200 metros.** Then go around asking each student to read his or her sentence aloud, but have them listen carefully to their classmates so they can first restate what their classmates said.

Comunicación

4 **Conversaciones** Tu profesor(a) te dará una hoja de actividades. En ella se presentan dos listas con diferentes problemas que supuestamente tienen los estudiantes. En parejas, túrnense para explicar los problemas de su lista; uno/a cuenta lo que le pasa y el/la otro/a dice lo que haría en esa situación usando la frase "Yo en tu lugar..." (*If I were you...*) Answers will vary.

> **AYUDA**
>
> Here are two ways of saying *If I were you:*
> **Si yo fuera tú...**
> **Yo en tu lugar...**

> *modelo*
>
> **Estudiante 1:** ¡Qué problema! Mi novio/a no me habla desde el domingo.
> **Estudiante 2:** Yo en tu lugar, no le diría nada por unos días para ver qué pasa.

5 **Roberto en el gimnasio** Roberto es una persona muy sedentaria. El médico le dice que tiene que adelgazar para mejorar su salud. Dile ocho cosas que tú harías si fueras él. Usa el condicional. Después, compara tus sugerencias con las del resto de la clase. Answers will vary.

> *modelo*
>
> Si yo fuera tú, vería menos la televisión y haría gimnasia.

Síntesis

6 **Encuesta** Tu profesor(a) te dará una hoja de actividades. Circula por la clase y pregúntales a tres compañeros/as qué actividad(es) de las que se describen les gustaría realizar. Usa el condicional de los verbos. Anota las respuestas e informa a la clase de los resultados de la encuesta. Answers will vary.

> *modelo*
>
> **Estudiante 1:** ¿Dejarías de fumar?
> **Estudiante 2:** Claro que sí. Sería difícil al principio, pero podría hacerlo.

Actividades	Nombre de tu compañero/a y su respuesta	Nombre de tu compañero/a y su respuesta	Nombre de tu compañero/a y su respuesta
1. tomar vitaminas			
2. adelgazar			
3. levantar pesas			
4. entrenarse para un maratón			
5. comer una dieta equilibrada			
6. mantenerse en forma			

4 **Teaching Tip** Distribute the *Hojas de actividades* (Activity Pack/Supersite) that correspond to this activity.

4 **Expansion** 👥↔👤 Working as a class, name a problem from one of the lists and ask several volunteers to share the suggestions they received. Encourage other students to comment on the suggestions.

5 **Teaching Tip** Go over the directions with the class. Work with the class to brainstorm a list of Roberto's problems. Write them on the board. Then give students time to write eight pieces of advice.

5 **Suggestion** Remind students that **y** changes to **e** in front of a word starting with **i**, as seen in the model.

6 **Teaching Tip** Distribute the *Hojas de actividades* (Activity Pack/Supersite) that correspond to this activity.

6 **Expansion** Encourage students to add two more activities to their list.

15.2 # The present perfect 🅢 Tutorial

ANTE TODO In **Lección 13**, you learned how to form past participles. You will now learn how to form the present perfect indicative (**el pretérito perfecto de indicativo**), a compound tense that uses the past participle. The present perfect is used to talk about what someone *has done*. In Spanish, it is formed with the present tense of the auxiliary verb **haber** and a past participle.

Maru ha estado bajo mucha presión.

He querido regresar desde que leí el *Chilam Balam*.

Present indicative of haber

Singular forms		Plural forms	
yo	**he**	nosotros/as	**hemos**
tú	**has**	vosotros/as	**habéis**
Ud./él/ella	**ha**	Uds./ellos/ellas	**han**

Tú no **has aumentado** de peso.
You haven't gained weight.

Yo ya **he leído** esos libros.
I've already read those books.

¿**Ha asistido** Juan a la clase de yoga?
Has Juan attended the yoga class?

Hemos conocido al entrenador.
We have met the trainer.

▶ The past participle does not change in form when it is part of the present perfect tense; it only changes in form when it is used as an adjective.

Clara **ha abierto** las ventanas.
Clara has opened the windows.

Yo **he cerrado** la puerta del gimnasio.
I've closed the door to the gym.

Las ventanas están **abiertas.**
The windows are open.

La puerta del gimnasio está **cerrada.**
The door to the gym is closed.

▶ In Spanish, the present perfect indicative generally is used just as in English: to talk about what someone has done or what has occurred. It usually refers to the recent past.

He trabajado cuarenta horas esta semana.
I have worked forty hours this week.

¿Cuál es el último libro que **has leído**?
What is the last book that you have read?

▶ In English, the auxiliary verb and the past participle are often separated. In Spanish, however, these two elements—**haber** and the past participle—cannot be separated by any word.

Siempre **hemos vivido** en Bolivia.
We have always lived in Bolivia.

Usted nunca **ha venido** a mi oficina.
You have never come to my office.

¿Y Juan Carlos todavía no te ha invitado a salir?

Últimamente hemos sufrido muchas presiones en la universidad.

▶ The word **no** and any object or reflexive pronouns are placed immediately before **haber**.

Yo **no he comido** la merienda.
I haven't eaten the snack.

¿Por qué **no la has comido**?
Why haven't you eaten it?

Susana ya **se ha entrenado**.
Susana has already trained.

Ellos **no lo han terminado**.
They haven't finished it.

▶ Note that *to have* can be either a main verb or an auxiliary verb in English. As a main verb, it corresponds to **tener,** while as an auxiliary, it corresponds to **haber.**

Tengo muchos amigos.
I have a lot of friends.

He sufrido muchas presiones.
I have been under a lot of pressure.

▶ To form the present perfect of **hay,** use the third-person singular of **haber (ha) + habido.**

Ha habido muchos problemas con la nueva entrenadora.
There have been a lot of problems with the new trainer.

Ha habido un accidente en la calle Central.
There has been an accident on Central Street.

recursos

WB
pp. 185–186

LM
p. 88

vhlcentral.com
Lección 15

¡INTÉNTALO! Indica el pretérito perfecto de indicativo de estos verbos.

1. (disfrutar, comer, vivir) yo <u>he disfrutado, he comido, he vivido</u>
2. (traer, adelgazar, compartir) tú <u>has traído, has adelgazado, has compartido</u>
3. (venir, estar, correr) usted <u>ha venido, ha estado, ha corrido</u>
4. (leer, resolver, poner) ella <u>ha leído, ha resuelto, ha puesto</u>
5. (decir, romper, hacer) ellos <u>han dicho, han roto, han hecho</u>
6. (mantenerse, dormirse) nosotros <u>nos hemos mantenido, nos hemos dormido</u>
7. (estar, escribir, ver) yo <u>he estado, he escrito, he visto</u>
8. (vivir, correr, morir) él <u>ha vivido, ha corrido, ha muerto</u>

Teaching Tips
• Ask students questions in the present perfect with indirect and direct objects. Have students respond using the correct pronoun and placement. Ex: ____, ¿has estudiado bien la lección? (Sí, la he estudiado bien.) ____, ¿has entendido todo lo que te he dicho? (No, no lo he entendido todo.) ¿Todos me han entregado el trabajo de hoy? (Sí, todos se lo hemos entregado.)

• Explain that, although an adverb can never appear between **haber** and its past participle, it may appear in other positions in the sentence to change emphasis. Ex: **Hemos vivido siempre en Bolivia. Siempre hemos vivido en Bolivia.**

• Tell students that the present perfect used with **alguna vez** means *ever*. Ex: ¿Alguna vez has corrido un maratón? *(Have you ever run a marathon?)* ¿Has ido alguna vez a la India? *(Have you ever gone to India?)*

• Before assigning the **¡Inténtalo!** to the class, do a quick review of irregular past participles.

• Practice adverb placement by supplying an adverb for each item in the **¡Inténtalo!** activity. Ex: **siempre (Siempre he disfrutado./He disfrutado siempre.)**

TEACHING OPTIONS

Large Groups Divide the class into groups. Have students write down five fitness activities. Then have them ask each of their group members if they have ever done those activities and record their answers. Ex: **¿Has levantado pesas? ¿Has tomado clases en un gimnasio? ¿Has corrido en un maratón? ¿Has nadado en el océano?** Encourage students to respond to their partner's answers and ask follow-up questions.

Extra Practice Draw a time line on the board. On the far right of the line, write **el presente.** Just to the left of that point, write **el pasado muy reciente.** To the left of that, write **el pasado reciente.** Then to the far left, write **el pasado.** Make a statement using the preterite, the present perfect, or **acabar de** + [*infinitive*]. Have students indicate on the time line when the action took place.

Práctica

1 Completar Estas oraciones describen cómo es la vida de unos estudiantes. Completa las oraciones con el pretérito perfecto de indicativo de los verbos de la lista.

adelgazar	comer	llevar
aumentar	hacer	sufrir

1. Luisa _____ha sufrido_____ muchas presiones este año.
2. Juan y Raúl _____han aumentado_____ de peso porque no hacen ejercicio.
3. Pero María y yo _____hemos adelgazado_____ porque trabajamos en exceso y nos olvidamos de comer.
4. Desde siempre, yo _____he llevado_____ una vida muy sana.
5. Pero tú y yo no _____hemos hecho_____ gimnasia este semestre.

2 ¿Qué has hecho? Indica si has hecho lo siguiente. *Answers will vary.*

> **modelo**
>
> escalar una montaña
> Sí, he escalado varias montañas./No, no he escalado nunca una montaña.

1. jugar al baloncesto
2. viajar a Bolivia
3. conocer a una persona famosa
4. levantar pesas
5. comer un insecto
6. recibir un masaje
7. aprender varios idiomas
8. bailar salsa
9. ver una película en español
10. escuchar música latina
11. estar despierto/a 24 horas
12. bucear

AYUDA

You may use some of these expressions in your answers:
una vez *once*
un par de veces *a couple of times*
algunas veces *a few times*
varias veces *several times*
muchas veces *many times, often*

3 La vida sana En parejas, túrnense para hacer preguntas sobre el tema de la vida sana. Sean creativos. *Answers will vary.*

> **modelo**
>
> encontrar un gimnasio
> **Estudiante 1:** ¿Has encontrado un buen gimnasio cerca de tu casa?
> **Estudiante 2:** Yo no he encontrado un gimnasio, pero sé que debo buscar uno.

1. tratar de estar en forma
2. estar a dieta los últimos dos meses
3. dejar de tomar refrescos
4. hacerse una prueba del colesterol
5. entrenarse cinco días a la semana
6. cambiar de una vida sedentaria a una vida activa
7. tomar vitaminas por las noches y por las mañanas
8. hacer ejercicio para aliviar la tensión
9. consumir mucha proteína
10. dejar de fumar

 Practice more at **vhlcentral.com.**

Comunicación

4 **Descripción** En parejas, describan lo que han hecho y no han hecho estas personas. Usen la imaginación. Answers will vary.

1. Jorge y Raúl

2. Luisa

3. Jacobo

4. Natalia y Diego

5. Ricardo

6. Carmen

5 **Describir** En parejas, identifiquen a una persona que lleva una vida muy sana. Puede ser una persona que conocen o un personaje que aparece en una película o programa de televisión. Entre los dos, escriban una descripción de lo que esta persona ha hecho para llevar una vida sana. Answers will vary.

> **modelo**
> Mario López siempre ha hecho todo lo posible para mantenerse en forma. Él...

Síntesis

6 **Situación** Trabajen en parejas para representar una conversación entre un(a) enfermero/a de la clínica de la universidad y un(a) estudiante. Answers will vary.

- El/La estudiante no se siente nada bien.
- El/La enfermero/a debe averiguar de dónde viene el problema e investigar los hábitos del/de la estudiante.
- El/La estudiante le explica lo que ha hecho en los últimos meses y cómo se ha sentido.
- Luego el/la enfermero/a le da recomendaciones de cómo llevar una vida más sana.

TEACHING OPTIONS

Game Have students write three important things they have done over the past year on a slip of paper and put it in a box. Ex: **Este año he creado un blog.** Have students draw a paper from the box, then circulate around the room, asking students if they have done the activities listed, until they find the person who wrote the slip of paper. The first person to find a match wins.

Heritage Speakers Have heritage speakers interview a Spanish-speaking immigrant to find out how that person's life has changed since moving to this country. Tell them to find out if the interviewee's physical activity and diet have changed and report this information to the class. Have the rest of the class react and state to what degree the interviewee's lifestyle is typical of this country.

4 Teaching Tip
To simplify, before beginning the activity, ask volunteers to describe the people in the drawings and how they think they feel.

4 Expansion
In small groups, have students choose one of the drawings to elaborate on, using the preterite, present perfect, and present indicative. To begin, each student should take a turn telling a part of the story using the preterite, then as the story moves into the recent past, each group member should add to the story using the present perfect. To finish, the group should decide together what the people have just done and what they are going to do next. You may wish to assign one group member as the secretary to record the stories so that they can be shared with the class. Ex: **Carmen fue de vacaciones a Chile... En Portillo ella ha esquiado en una montaña... Carmen acaba de quitarse las botas de esquí y ahora va a almorzar en un restaurante.**

5 Teaching Tip
Have pairs describe eight things their chosen person has done that exemplify a healthy lifestyle. Remind them to include introductory and concluding statements in their descriptions.

5 Expansion
Have students choose someone who is the exact opposite of the healthy person they chose earlier and write a description of what that person has done that exemplifies an unhealthy lifestyle.

6 Expansion
While pairs are performing their role-plays for the class, stop the action after the patient has described his or her symptoms and what he or she has done in the last few months. Ask the class to make a diagnosis. Then have the pair finish their presentation.

15.3 # The past perfect **Tutorial**

ANTE TODO The past perfect indicative (**el pretérito pluscuamperfecto de indicativo**) is used to talk about what someone *had done* or what *had occurred* before another past action, event, or state. Like the present perfect, the past perfect uses a form of **haber**—in this case, the imperfect—plus the past participle.

Past perfect indicative			
	cerrar	**perder**	**asistir**
SINGULAR FORMS			
yo	**había** cerrado	**había** perdido	**había** asistido
tú	**habías** cerrado	**habías** perdido	**habías** asistido
Ud./él/ella	**había** cerrado	**había** perdido	**había** asistido
PLURAL FORMS			
nosotros/as	**habíamos** cerrado	**habíamos** perdido	**habíamos** asistido
vosotros/as	**habíais** cerrado	**habíais** perdido	**habíais** asistido
Uds./ellos/ellas	**habían** cerrado	**habían** perdido	**habían** asistido

Antes de 2010, **había vivido** en La Paz.
Before 2010, I had lived in La Paz.

Cuando llegamos, Luis ya **había salido.**
When we arrived, Luis had already left.

▶ The past perfect is often used with the word **ya** (*already*) to indicate that an action, event, or state had already occurred before another. Remember that, unlike its English equivalent, **ya** cannot be placed between **haber** and the past participle.

Ella **ya había salido** cuando llamaron.
She had already left when they called.

Cuando llegué, Raúl **ya se había acostado.**
When I arrived, Raúl had already gone to bed.

▶ **¡Atención!** The past perfect is often used in conjunction with **antes de** + [*noun*] or **antes de** + [*infinitive*] to describe when the action(s) occurred.

Antes de este año, nunca **había estudiado español.**
Before this year, I had never studied Spanish.

Luis **me había llamado antes de venir.**
Luis had called me before he came.

¡INTÉNTALO! Indica el pretérito pluscuamperfecto de indicativo de cada verbo.

1. Nosotros ya ___*habíamos cenado*___ (cenar) cuando nos llamaron.
2. Antes de tomar esta clase, yo no ___*había estudiado*___ (estudiar) nunca el español.
3. Antes de ir a México, ellos nunca ___*habían ido*___ (ir) a otro país.
4. Eduardo nunca ___*se había entrenado*___ (entrenarse) tanto en invierno.
5. Tú siempre ___*habías llevado*___ (llevar) una vida sana antes del año pasado.
6. Antes de conocerte, yo ya te ___*había visto*___ (ver) muchas veces.

recursos

WB pp. 187–188

LM p. 89

vhlcentral.com Lección 15

Práctica

1 **Completar** Completa los minidiálogos con las formas correctas del pretérito pluscuamperfecto de indicativo.

1. **SARA** Antes de cumplir los 15 años, ¿ __habías estudiado__ (estudiar) tú otra lengua?
 JOSÉ Sí, __había tomado__ (tomar) clases de inglés y de italiano.

▶ 2. **DOLORES** Antes de ir a Argentina, ¿ __habían probado__ (probar) tú y tu familia el mate?
 TOMÁS Sí, ya __habíamos tomado__ (tomar) mate muchas veces.

3. **ANTONIO** Antes de este año, ¿ __había corrido__ (correr) usted en un maratón?
 SRA. VERA No, nunca lo __había hecho__ (hacer).

4. **SOFÍA** Antes de su enfermedad, ¿ __había sufrido__ (sufrir) muchas presiones tu tío?
 IRENE Sí... y él nunca __se había mantenido__ (mantenerse) en buena forma.

2 **Tu vida** Indica si ya habías hecho estas cosas antes de cumplir los dieciséis años. Answers will vary.

1. hacer un viaje en avión
2. escalar una montaña
3. escribir un poema
4. filmar un video
5. enamorarte
6. tomar clases de aeróbicos
7. montar a caballo
8. ir de pesca
9. manejar un carro
10. cantar frente a 50 o más personas

Comunicación

3 **Gimnasio Olímpico** En parejas, lean el anuncio y contesten las preguntas.

Hasta el año pasado, siempre había mirado la tele sentado en el sofá durante mis ratos libres. ¡Era sedentario y teleadicto! Jamás había practicado ningún deporte y había aumentado mucho de peso.

Este año, he empezado a llevar una dieta equilibrada y voy al gimnasio todos los días. He comenzado a ser una persona muy activa y he adelgazado. Disfruto de una vida sana. ¡Me siento muy feliz!

Manténgase en forma.

¡Acabo de descubrir una nueva vida!

¡Venga al Gimnasio Olímpico hoy mismo!

1. Identifiquen los elementos del pretérito pluscuamperfecto de indicativo en el anuncio. había mirado; había practicado; había aumentado
2. ¿Cómo era la vida del hombre cuando llevaba una vida sedentaria? ¿Cómo es ahora? Answers will vary.
3. ¿Se identifican ustedes con algunos de los hábitos, presentes o pasados, de este hombre? ¿Con cuáles? Answers will vary.
4. ¿Qué les recomienda el hombre del anuncio a los lectores? ¿Creen que les da buenos consejos? Answers will vary.

Practice more at **vhlcentral.com.**

Recapitulación

 Concepts Diagnostics

Completa estas actividades para repasar los conceptos de gramática que aprendiste en esta lección.

1 Verbos Completa el cuadro con la forma correcta de los verbos. `12 pts.`

Infinitivo	tú	nosotros	ellas
tratar	tratarías	**trataríamos**	tratarían
querer	**querrías**	querríamos	**querrían**
poder	podrías	**podríamos**	podrían
haber	**habrías**	habríamos	**habrían**
vivir	vivirías	viviríamos	vivirían

2 Completar Completa el cuadro con el pretérito perfecto de los verbos. `6 pts.`

Infinitivo	yo	él	ellas
tratar	he tratado	ha tratado	han tratado
entrenarse	me he entrenado	se ha entrenado	se han entrenado

3 Diálogo Completa la conversación con la forma adecuada del condicional de los verbos. `8 pts.`

aconsejar	encantar	ir	poder
dejar	gustar	llover	volver

OMAR ¿Sabes? La demostración de yoga al aire libre fue un éxito. Yo creía que (1) __llovería__, pero hizo sol.

NIDIA Ah, me alegro. Te dije que Jaime y yo (2) __iríamos__, pero tuvimos un imprevisto (*something came up*) y no pudimos. Y a Laura, ¿la viste allí?

OMAR Sí, ella vino. Al contrario que tú, al principio me dijo que ella y su marido no (3) __podrían__ venir, pero al final aparecieron (*showed up*). Necesitaba relajarse un poco; está muy estresada con su trabajo.

NIDIA Yo le (4) __aconsejaría__ que busque otra cosa. En su lugar, (5) __dejaría__ esa compañía y (6) __volvería__ a escribir un libro.

OMAR Estoy de acuerdo. Oye, esta noche voy a ir al gimnasio. ¿(7) __Te gustaría__ venir conmigo?

NIDIA Sí, (8) __me encantaría/__ __me gustaría__. ¿A qué hora vamos?

OMAR A las siete y media.

RESUMEN GRAMATICAL

15.1 **The conditional** *pp. 492–493*

The conditional tense* of **disfrutar**	
disfrutaría	disfrutaríamos
disfrutarías	disfrutaríais
disfrutaría	disfrutarían

*Same ending for **-ar, - er,** and **-ir** verbs.

▶ Verbs with irregular conditional: **decir, haber, hacer, poder, poner, querer, saber, salir, tener, venir**

15.2 **The present perfect** *pp. 496–497*

Present indicative of **haber**	
he	hemos
has	habéis
ha	han

Present perfect: present tense of **haber** + past participle

Present perfect indicative	
he empezado	**hemos** empezado
has empezado	**habéis** empezado
ha empezado	**han** empezado

He empezado a ir al gimnasio con regularidad.
I have begun to go to the gym regularly.

15.3 **The past perfect** *p. 500*

Past perfect: imperfect tense of **haber** + past participle

Past perfect indicative	
había vivido	**habíamos** vivido
habías vivido	**habíais** vivido
había vivido	**habían** vivido

Antes de 2011, yo ya **había vivido** en tres países diferentes.
Before 2011, I had already lived in three different countries.

4 Preguntas Completa las preguntas para estas respuestas usando el pretérito perfecto de indicativo. **8 pts.**

modelo

—¿Has llamado a tus padres? —Sí, los llamé ayer.

1. —¿Tú __has hecho__ ejercicio esta mañana en el gimnasio? —No, hice ejercicio en el parque.
2. —Y ustedes, ¿__han desayunado__ ya? —Sí, desayunamos en el hotel.
3. —Y Juan y Felipe, ¿adónde __han ido__ ? —Fueron al cine.
4. —Paco, ¿(nosotros) __hemos recibido__ la cuenta del gimnasio? —Sí, la recibimos la semana pasada.
5. —Señor Martín, ¿__ha pescado__ algo ya? —Sí, pesqué uno grande. Ya me puedo ir a casa contento.
6. —Inés, ¿__has visto__ mi pelota de fútbol? —Sí, la vi esta mañana en el coche.
7. —Yo no __he tomado__ café todavía. ¿Alguien quiere acompañarme? —No, gracias. Yo ya tomé mi café en casa.
8. —¿Ya te __ha dicho__ el doctor que puedes comer chocolate? —Sí, me lo dijo ayer.

5 Antes de graduarse Di lo que cada una de estas personas ya había hecho o no había hecho todavía antes de graduarse de la universidad. Sigue el modelo. **6 pts.**

modelo

yo / ya conocer a muchos amigos
Yo ya había conocido a muchos amigos.

1. Margarita / ya dejar de fumar
Margarita ya había dejado de fumar.
2. tú / ya aprender a mantenerse en forma
Tú ya habías aprendido a mantenerte en forma.
3. Julio / ya casarse
Julio ya se había casado.
4. Mabel y yo / ya practicar yoga
Mabel y yo ya habíamos practicado yoga.
5. los hermanos Falsero / todavía no perder un partido de voleyball
Los hermanos Falsero todavía no habían perdido un partido de voleyball.
6. yo / ya entrenarse para el maratón
Yo ya me había entrenado para el maratón.

6 Manteniéndote en forma Escribe al menos cinco oraciones para describir cómo te has mantenido en forma este semestre. Di qué cosas han cambiado este semestre en relación con el año pasado. Por ejemplo, ¿qué cosas has hecho o practicado este semestre que nunca habías probado antes? **10 pts.** Answers will vary.

7 Poema Completa este fragmento de un poema de Nezahualcóyotl con el pretérito perfecto de indicativo de los verbos. **¡2 puntos EXTRA!**

" __He llegado__ (Llegar) aquí,
soy Yoyontzin.
Sólo busco las flores
sobre la tierra, __he venido__ (venir)
a cortarlas. "

Practice more at **vhlcentral.com.**

4 Teaching Tips
- Call on volunteers to read the model aloud.
- To simplify, have students begin by identifying the subject and infinitive for each blank.

4 Expansion Have students change the response for each item to the present perfect. Ex: **1. No, he hecho ejercicio en el parque.**

5 Expansion Give students these sentence cues as items 7-8: **7. nosotros / ya sufrir muchas presiones (Nosotros ya habíamos sufrido muchas presiones.) 8. Óscar / ya ir al gimnasio (Óscar ya había ido al gimnasio.)**

6 Teaching Tip To simplify, before students begin writing, encourage them to list their ideas under two columns: **El año pasado** and **Este semestre**. Have students brainstorm a few verbs in the past perfect for the first column and in the present perfect for the second.

7 Expansion Have students write a personalized version of the poem fragment. Ex: **He llegado aquí, soy ____. Sólo busco ____. He ____ a ____.**

TEACHING OPTIONS

Extra Practice Prepare sentences that use the present perfect. Say each sentence, have students repeat it, then say a different subject, varying the number. Have students then say the sentence with the new subject, making any necessary changes.

Game Divide the class into teams of five and have them sit in rows. Give the first student in each row a piece of paper. Call out an infinitive and have the first team member write the past perfect **yo** form of the verb and pass the paper to the second team member, who writes the **tú** form, and so forth. The first team to complete the paradigm correctly earns a point. The team with the most points at the end wins.

Lectura

Antes de leer

Estrategia
Making inferences

For dramatic effect and to achieve a smoother writing style, authors often do not explicitly supply the reader with all the details of a story or poem. Clues in the text can help you infer those things the writer chooses not to state in a direct manner. You simply "read between the lines" to fill in the missing information and draw conclusions. To practice making inferences, read these statements:

A Liliana le encanta ir al gimnasio. Hace años que empezó a levantar pesas.

Based on this statement alone, what inferences can you draw about Liliana?

El autor

Ve a la página 445 de tu libro y lee la biografía de Gabriel García Márquez.

El título

Sin leer el texto del cuento (*story*), lee el título. Escribe cinco oraciones que empiecen con la frase "Un día de éstos". Answers will vary.

El cuento

Éstas son algunas palabras que vas a encontrar al leer *Un día de éstos*. Busca su significado en el diccionario. Según estas palabras, ¿de qué piensas que trata (*is about*) el cuento? Answers will vary.

alcalde	lágrimas
dentadura postiza	muela
displicente	pañuelo
enjuto	rencor
guerrera	teniente

Practice more at **vhlcentral.com**.

Un día de éstos
Gabriel García Márquez

El lunes amaneció tibio° y sin lluvia. Don Aurelio Escovar, dentista sin título y buen madrugador°, abrió su gabinete° a las seis. Sacó de la vidriera° una dentadura postiza° montada aún° en el molde de yeso° y puso sobre la mesa un puñado° de instrumentos que ordenó de mayor a menor, como en una exposición. Llevaba una camisa a rayas, sin cuello, cerrada arriba con un botón dorado°, y los pantalones sostenidos con cargadores° elásticos. Era rígido, enjuto, con una mirada que raras veces correspondía a la situación, como la mirada de los sordos°.

Cuando tuvo las cosas dispuestas sobre la mesa rodó la fresa° hacia el sillón de resortes y se sentó a pulir° la dentadura postiza. Parecía no pensar en lo que hacía, pero trabajaba con obstinación, pedaleando en la fresa incluso cuando no se servía de ella.

Después de las ocho hizo una pausa para mirar el cielo por la ventana y vio dos gallinazos° pensativos que se secaban al sol en el caballete° de la casa vecina. Siguió trabajando con la idea de que antes del almuerzo volvería a llover°. La voz destemplada° de su hijo de once años lo sacó de su abstracción.

—Papá.

—Qué.

—Dice el alcalde que si le sacas una muela.

—Dile que no estoy aquí.

Estaba puliendo un diente de oro°. Lo retiró a la distancia del brazo y lo examinó con los ojos a medio cerrar. En la salita de espera volvió a gritar su hijo.

—Dice que sí estás porque te está oyendo.

El dentista siguió examinando el diente. Sólo cuando lo puso en la mesa con los trabajos terminados, dijo:

amaneció tibio *dawn broke warm* madrugador *early riser* gabinete *office* vidriera *glass cabinet* dentadura postiza *dentures* montada aún *still set* yeso *plaster* puñado *handful* dorado *gold* sostenidos con cargadores *held by suspenders* sordos *deaf* rodó la fresa *he turned the drill* pulir *to polish* gallinazos *vultures* caballete *ridge* volvería a llover *it would rain again* voz destemplada *harsh voice* oro *gold* cajita de cartón *small cardboard box* puente *bridge* te pega un tiro *he will shoot you* Sin apresurarse *Without haste* gaveta *drawer* Hizo girar *He turned* apoyada *resting* umbral *threshold* mejilla *cheek* hinchada *swollen* barba *beard* marchitos *faded* hervían *were boiling* pomos de loza *china bottles* cancel de tela *cloth screen* se acercaba *was approaching* talones *heels* mandíbula *jaw* cautelosa *cautious* cacerola *saucepan* pinzas *pliers* escupidera *spittoon* aguamanil *washstand* cordal *wisdom tooth* gatillo *pliers* se aferró *clung* barras *arms* descargó *unloaded* vacío helado *icy hollowness* riñones *kidneys* no soltó un suspiro *he didn't let out a sigh* muñeca *wrist* amarga ternura *bitter tenderness* teniente *lieutenant* crujido *crunch* a través de *through* sudoroso *sweaty* jadeante *panting* se desabotonó *he unbuttoned* a tientas *blindly* bolsillo *pocket* trapo *cloth* cielorraso desfondado *ceiling with the paint sagging* telaraña polvorienta *dusty spiderweb* haga buches de *rinse your mouth out with* vaina *thing*

—Mejor.

Volvió a operar la fresa. De una cajita de cartón° donde guardaba las cosas por hacer, sacó un puente° de varias piezas y empezó a pulir el oro.

—Papá.

—Qué.

Aún no había cambiado de expresión.

—Dice que si no le sacas la muela te pega un tiro°.

Sin apresurarse°, con un movimiento extremadamente tranquilo, dejó de pedalear en la fresa, la retiró del sillón y abrió por completo la gaveta° inferior de la mesa. Allí estaba el revólver.

—Bueno —dijo—. Dile que venga a pegármelo.

Hizo girar° el sillón hasta quedar de frente a la puerta, la mano apoyada° en el borde de la gaveta. El alcalde apareció en el umbral°. Se había afeitado la mejilla° izquierda, pero en la otra, hinchada° y dolorida, tenía una barba° de cinco días. El dentista vio en sus ojos marchitos° muchas noches de desesperación. Cerró la gaveta con la punta de los dedos y dijo suavemente:

—Siéntese.

—Buenos días —dijo el alcalde.

—Buenos —dijo el dentista.

Mientras hervían° los instrumentos, el alcalde apoyó el cráneo en el cabezal de la silla y se sintió mejor. Respiraba un olor glacial. Era un gabinete pobre: una vieja silla de madera, la fresa de pedal y una vidriera con pomos de loza°. Frente a la silla, una ventana con un cancel de tela° hasta la altura de un hombre. Cuando sintió que el dentista se acercaba°, el alcalde afirmó los talones° y abrió la boca.

Don Aurelio Escovar le movió la cabeza hacia la luz. Después de observar la muela dañada, ajustó la mandíbula° con una presión cautelosa° de los dedos.

—Tiene que ser sin anestesia —dijo.

—¿Por qué?

—Porque tiene un absceso.

El alcalde lo miró en los ojos.

—Está bien —dijo, y trató de sonreír. El dentista no le correspondió. Llevó a la mesa de trabajo la cacerola° con los instrumentos hervidos y los sacó del agua con unas pinzas° frías, todavía sin apresurarse. Después rodó la escupidera° con la punta del zapato y fue a lavarse las manos en el aguamanil°. Hizo todo sin mirar al alcalde. Pero el alcalde no lo perdió de vista.

Era una cordal° inferior. El dentista abrió las piernas y apretó la muela con el gatillo° caliente. El alcalde se aferró a las barras° de la silla, descargó toda su fuerza en los pies y sintió un vacío helado° en los riñones°, pero no soltó un suspiro°. El dentista sólo movió la muñeca°. Sin rencor, más bien con una amarga ternura°, dijo:

—Aquí nos paga veinte muertos, teniente°.

El alcalde sintió un crujido° de huesos en la mandíbula y sus ojos se llenaron de lágrimas. Pero no suspiró hasta que no sintió salir la muela. Entonces la vio a través de° las lágrimas. Le pareció tan extraña a su dolor, que no pudo entender la tortura de sus cinco noches anteriores. Inclinado sobre la escupidera, sudoroso°, jadeante°, se desabotonó° la guerrera y buscó a tientas° el pañuelo en el bolsillo° del pantalón. El dentista le dio un trapo° limpio.

—Séquese las lágrimas —dijo.

El alcalde lo hizo. Estaba temblando. Mientras el dentista se lavaba las manos, vio el cielorraso desfondado° y una telaraña polvorienta° con huevos de araña e insectos muertos. El dentista regresó secándose. "Acuéstese —dijo— y haga buches de° agua de sal." El alcalde se puso de pie, se despidió con un displicente saludo militar, y se dirigió a la puerta estirando las piernas, sin abotonarse la guerrera.

—Me pasa la cuenta —dijo.

—¿A usted o al municipio?

El alcalde no lo miró. Cerró la puerta, y dijo, a través de la red metálica:

—Es la misma vaina°.

Después de leer

Comprensión

Completa las oraciones con la palabra o expresión correcta.

1. Don Aurelio Escovar es ____dentista____ sin título.
2. Al alcalde le duele _una muela /una cordal_.
3. Aurelio Escovar y el alcalde se llevan _____mal_____.
4. El alcalde amenaza (*threatens*) al dentista con pegarle un ____tiro____.
5. Finalmente, Aurelio Escovar ___le saca___ la muela al alcalde.
6. El alcalde llevaba varias noches sin _____dormir_____.

Interpretación

En parejas, respondan a estas preguntas. Luego comparen sus respuestas con las de otra pareja. Answers will vary.

1. ¿Cómo reacciona don Aurelio cuando escucha que el alcalde amenaza con pegarle un tiro? ¿Qué les dice esta actitud sobre las personalidades del dentista y del alcalde?
2. ¿Por qué creen que don Aurelio y el alcalde no se llevan bien?
3. ¿Creen que era realmente necesario no usar anestesia?
4. ¿Qué piensan que significa el comentario "aquí nos paga veinte muertos, teniente"? ¿Qué les dice esto del alcalde y su autoridad en el pueblo?
5. ¿Cómo se puede interpretar el saludo militar y la frase final del alcalde "es la misma vaina"?

Section Goals

In **Escritura**, students will:
- learn to organize information logically
- integrate lesson vocabulary and structures
- write a personal wellness plan in Spanish

Instructional Resource
Supersite

Estrategia Have students brainstorm details of maintaining a personal wellness plan that includes nutrition, exercise, and stress reduction. Then have a volunteer tell about his or her plan, and guide students in organizing the information in three different ways: chronologically, sequentially, and in order of importance.

Tema
👤↔👤 Review the three suggested categories of details to include. Then, have volunteers make up questions or use the ones on this page to interview you regarding your personal wellness plan.

Successful Language Learning Point out to students that this strategy will help them improve their writing in both Spanish and English.

Escritura

Estrategia
Organizing information logically

Many times a written piece may require you to include a great deal of information. You might want to organize your information in one of three different ways:

▶ chronologically (e.g., events in the history of a country)
▶ sequentially (e.g., steps in a recipe)
▶ in order of importance

Organizing your information beforehand will make both your writing and your message clearer to your readers. If you were writing a piece on weight reduction, for example, you would need to organize your ideas about two general areas: eating right and exercise. You would need to decide which of the two is more important according to your purpose in writing the piece. If your main idea is that eating right is the key to losing weight, you might want to start your piece with a discussion of good eating habits. You might want to discuss the following aspects of eating right in order of their importance:

▶ quantities of food
▶ selecting appropriate foods from the food pyramid
▶ healthy recipes
▶ percentage of fat in each meal
▶ calorie count
▶ percentage of carbohydrates in each meal
▶ frequency of meals

You would then complete the piece by following the same process to discuss the various aspects of the importance of getting exercise.

Tema

Escribir un plan personal de bienestar

Desarrolla un plan personal para mejorar tu bienestar, tanto físico como emocional. Tu plan debe describir:

1. lo que has hecho para mejorar tu bienestar y llevar una vida sana
2. lo que no has podido hacer todavía
3. las actividades que debes hacer en los próximos meses

Considera también estas preguntas:

La nutrición
▶ ¿Comes una dieta equilibrada?
▶ ¿Consumes suficientes vitaminas y minerales?
▶ ¿Consumes demasiada grasa?
▶ ¿Quieres aumentar de peso o adelgazar?
▶ ¿Qué puedes hacer para mejorar tu dieta?

El ejercicio
▶ ¿Haces ejercicio? ¿Con qué frecuencia?
▶ ¿Vas al gimnasio? ¿Qué tipo de ejercicios haces allí?
▶ ¿Practicas algún deporte?
▶ ¿Qué puedes hacer para mejorar tu bienestar físico?

El estrés
▶ ¿Sufres muchas presiones?
▶ ¿Qué actividades o problemas te causan estrés?
▶ ¿Qué haces (o debes hacer) para aliviar el estrés y sentirte más tranquilo/a?
▶ ¿Qué puedes hacer para mejorar tu bienestar emocional?

NATIONAL communication STANDARDS

EVALUATION: Plan personal de bienestar

Criteria	Scale
Content	1 2 3 4
Organization	1 2 3 4
Use of vocabulary	1 2 3 4
Accuracy and mechanics	1 2 3 4
Creativity	1 2 3 4

Scoring	
Excellent	18–20 points
Good	14–17 points
Satisfactory	10–13 points
Unsatisfactory	< 10 points

Escuchar Audio: Activities

Preparación

Mira la foto. ¿Qué pistas° te da de lo que vas a oír? Answers will vary.

Ahora escucha

Escucha lo que dice Ofelia Cortez de Bauer. Anota algunos de los cognados que escuchas y también la idea general del discurso°. Answers will vary.

Idea general: _____

Ahora contesta las siguientes preguntas.

1. ¿Cuál es el género° del discurso?
2. ¿Cuál es el tema?
3. ¿Cuál es el propósito°?

pistas *clues* discurso *speech* género *genre* propósito *purpose*
público *audience* debía haber incluido *should have included*

 Practice more at **vhlcentral.com.**

Comprensión

¿Cierto o falso?

Indica si lo que dicen estas oraciones es **cierto** o **falso**. Corrige las oraciones falsas.

	Cierto	Falso
1. La señora Bauer habla de la importancia de estar en buena forma y de hacer ejercicio.	◉	○
2. Según ella, lo más importante es que lleves el programa sugerido por los expertos.	○	◉
Lo más importante es que lleves un programa variado que te guste.		
3. La señora Bauer participa en actividades individuales y de grupo.	◉	○
4. El único objetivo del tipo de programa que ella sugiere es adelgazar.	○	◉
Los objetivos de su programa son: condicionar el sistema cardiopulmonar, aumentar la fuerza muscular y mejorar la flexibilidad.		

Preguntas

Responde a las preguntas. Answers will vary.

1. Imagina que el programa de radio sigue. Según las pistas que ella dio, ¿qué vas a oír en la segunda parte?
2. ¿A qué tipo de público° le interesa el tema del que habla la señora Bauer?
3. ¿Sigues los consejos de la señora Bauer? Explica tu respuesta.
4. ¿Qué piensas de los consejos que ella da? ¿Hay otra información que ella debía haber incluido°?

NATIONAL communication STANDARDS

con un buen calentamiento al comienzo. Tres días por semana corro en el parque, o si hace mal tiempo, uso una caminadora en el gimnasio. Luego levanto pesas y termino haciendo estiramientos de los músculos. Los fines de semana me mantengo activa pero hago una variedad de cosas de acuerdo a lo que quiere hacer la familia. A veces practico la natación; otras, vamos de excursión al campo, por ejemplo. Como les había

dicho la semana pasada, como unas 1.600 calorías al día, mayormente alimentos con poca grasa y sin sal. Disfruto mucho del bienestar que estos hábitos me producen. Ahora iremos a unos anuncios de nuestros patrocinadores. Cuando regresemos, voy a contestar sus preguntas acerca del ejercicio, la dieta o el bienestar en general. El teléfono es el 43.89.76. No se vayan. Ya regresamos con mucha más información.

En pantalla

NATIONAL communication cultures STANDARDS

Anuncio

En 1990, el periodista argentino Víctor Sueiro vio "un túnel oscuro°, una luz blanca intensa que se hizo más fuerte" y sintió "una paz° total". Durante cuarenta segundos, una muerte clínica causada por un paro cardíaco° lo llevó a tener esa famosa visión. Después de "volver de la muerte", se dedicó° a escribir sobre el fin de la vida, los ángeles y misterios similares, y sus libros tuvieron gran éxito. A continuación vas a ver a Sueiro en un anuncio que, con humor, nos hace una invitación ecológica.

Vocabulario útil

derrochando	*wasting*
energía eléctrica	*electric energy*
el más allá	*the afterlife*
una luz blanca	*a white light*

Preparación

¿Conoces a alguien a quien le ocurrió algo que parecía sobrenatural (*supernatural*)? Explica qué ocurrió, si es posible... Answers will vary.

Preguntas

Contesta las preguntas con oraciones completas.

1. ¿Qué vio Víctor Sueiro cuando fue al más allá?
 Sueiro vio una luz blanca.
2. ¿Qué le piden que haga? ¿Por qué?
 Le piden que vuelva al más allá para que apague la luz y vuelva.
3. ¿Por qué es importante que apague la luz? Es importante que apague la luz para que no se gaste/derroche la energía eléctrica.
4. ¿Qué hace Víctor Sueiro cuando despierta?
 Apaga la televisión y la luz.

Creencias

Víctor Sueiro estuvo clínicamente muerto por 40 segundos. Luego escribió un libro que decía que no debíamos tener miedo del más allá porque hay una luz hermosa al final. ¿Qué opinas de su historia? Usa el subjuntivo en tus respuestas. Answers will vary.

modelo

Dudo que haya una luz hermosa. No creo que Sueiro recuerde lo que vio...

oscuro *dark* paz *peace* paro cardíaco *cardiac arrest* se dedicó *he devoted himself*

▌Edenor

Tenemos información de que usted fue al más allá y volvió. ¿Es correcto?

¿Qué me está pidiendo?

¿Qué hacemos?

 Video: TV Clip

Practice more at **vhlcentral.com.**

Cortometraje

A veces, nos encontramos con alguien que conocemos pero no nos acordamos muy bien de cómo. El chico protagonista de *Cloe*, Dani, toma esta idea y la utiliza para acercarse a hablar con una chica en un café. Según él, se conocieron hace un par de años: su amigo Coque dio una fiesta de disfraces en su apartamento en La Latina, un barrio de Madrid.

Preparación

¿Alguna vez le has hablado a un desconocido (*stranger*) que creías conocer? ¿Alguna vez te ha hablado un desconocido que creía conocerte? ¿Qué sucedió?
Answers will vary.

Después de ver

Indica si lo que dice cada oración es **cierto** o **falso**. Corrige las oraciones falsas.

1. La chica protagonista se llama Cloe. *Falso. Se llama Marta.*

2. La chica dice que se conocieron en una fiesta de Navidad.
 Falso. La chica dice que se conocieron en una fiesta de disfraces.

3. El chico dice que en la fiesta iba disfrazado del Lobo Feroz.
 Falso. El chico dice que no iba disfrazado de nada.

4. La chica no conoce al chico. *Cierto.*

5. Al final, el chico se da cuenta de que ella también le ha mentido. *Cierto.*

Conversar

Imagina que la conversación entre el chico y la chica se desarrolla de otra manera y la historia acaba de manera diferente. En parejas, escriban un final diferente para el corto. Luego, compártanlo con la clase. *Answers will vary.*

Un corto de **Manuela Moreno**

CLOE

Protagonizado por **Manuela Burló** y **Tony Bernetti**
Una producción de MOMENTO

Expresiones útiles

la Caperucita Roja	*Little Red Riding Hood*
en la punta de la lengua	*on the tip of one's tongue*
la fiesta de disfraces	*costume party*
ir vestido de algo	*to dress up as something*
el Lobo Feroz	*Big Bad Wolf*
se pasó un poco	*he went too far*
el tipo éste	*this guy*
la trenza	*braid*

Para hablar del corto

caradura	*cheeky*
encontrarse con (alguien)	*to run into (someone)*
fingir	*to pretend*
mentir (e:ie)	*to lie*

 Video: Short Film

 Practice more at **vhlcentral.com.**

Antes de ver

- Have students look at the poster and ask them what they think the short film will be about.
- Read through the **Expresiones útiles** and **Para hablar del corto** vocabulary with students to model pronunciation and practice using the terms.
- Reassure students that they do not need to understand every word they hear in the short film. Tell them to rely on visual cues and listen for cognates and words from **Expresiones útiles**.

Preparación Give students a few moments to think of examples from their own experiences. Allow them to ask you for additional vocabulary.

Después de ver
Have students write two additional true/false statements for a partner to answer.

Conversar
👥↔👤 After students have presented their alternate endings, have the class discuss their reactions and opinions.

TEACHING OPTIONS

Worth Noting *Cloe* (2010) was written and directed by Spanish filmmaker **Manuela Moreno**. She has three other short films: *Camas* (2010), *Quiero estar el resto de mi vida contigo* (2009), and *Dolores* (2008).

Pairs 👤↔👤 Have pairs role-play a conversation in which two strangers pretend to know each other. Tell them to think about where they run into each other and how they could have met before.

Bolivia

NATIONAL connections cultures STANDARDS

El país en cifras

▶ **Área:** 1.098.580 km² (424.162 millas²), *equivalente al área total de Francia y España*

▶ **Población:** 10.854.000

Los indígenas quechua y aimará constituyen más de la mitad° de la población de Bolivia. Estos grupos indígenas han mantenido sus culturas y lenguas tradicionales. Las personas de ascendencia° indígena y europea representan la tercera parte de la población. Los demás son de ascendencia europea nacida en Latinoamérica. Una gran mayoría de los bolivianos, más o menos el 70%, vive en el altiplano°.

▶ **Capital:** La Paz, sede° del gobierno, capital administrativa—1.840.000; Sucre, sede del Tribunal Supremo, capital constitucional y judicial

▶ **Ciudades principales:** Santa Cruz de la Sierra—1.916.000, Cochabamba, Oruro, Potosí

SOURCE: Population Division, UN Secretariat

▶ **Moneda:** peso boliviano

▶ **Idiomas:** español (oficial), aimará (oficial), quechua (oficial)

Bandera de Bolivia

Bolivianos célebres

▶ **Jesús Lara,** escritor (1898–1980)
▶ **Víctor Paz Estenssoro,** político y presidente (1907–2001)
▶ **María Luisa Pacheco,** pintora (1919–1982)
▶ **Matilde Casazola,** poeta (1942–)

mitad *half* ascendencia *descent* altiplano *high plateau* sede *seat*
paraguas *umbrella* cascada *waterfall*

¡Increíble pero cierto!

La Paz es la capital más alta del mundo. Su aeropuerto está situado a una altitud de 4.061 metros (13.325 pies). Ah, y si viajas en carro hasta La Paz, ¡no te olvides del paraguas°! En la carretera, que cruza 9.000 metros de densa selva, te encontrarás con una cascada°.

Lugares • El lago Titicaca

Titicaca, situado en los Andes de Bolivia y Perú, es el lago navegable más alto del mundo, a una altitud de 3.810 metros (12.500 pies). Con un área de más de 8.300 kilómetros² (3.200 millas²), también es el segundo lago más grande de Suramérica, después del lago de Maracaibo (Venezuela). La mitología inca cuenta que los hijos del dios° Sol emergieron de las profundas aguas del lago Titicaca para fundar su imperio°.

Artes • La música andina

La música andina, compartida por Bolivia, Perú, Ecuador, Chile y Argentina, es el aspecto más conocido de su folclore. Hay muchos conjuntos° profesionales que dan a conocer° esta música popular, de origen indígena, alrededor° del mundo. Algunos de los grupos más importantes y que llevan más de treinta años actuando en escenarios internacionales son Los Kjarkas (Bolivia), Inti Illimani (Chile), Los Chaskis (Argentina) e Illapu (Chile).

Historia • Tiahuanaco

Tiahuanaco, que significa "Ciudad de los dioses", es un sitio arqueológico de ruinas preincaicas situado cerca de La Paz y del lago Titicaca. Se piensa que los antepasados° de los indígenas aimará fundaron este centro ceremonial hace unos 15.000 años. En el año 1100, la ciudad tenía unos 60.000 habitantes. En este sitio se pueden ver el Templo de Kalasasaya, el Monolito Ponce, el Templete Subterráneo, la Puerta del Sol y la Puerta de la Luna. La Puerta del Sol es un impresionante monumento que tiene tres metros de alto y cuatro de ancho° y que pesa unas 10 toneladas.

 ¿Qué aprendiste? Responde a las preguntas con una oración completa.

1. ¿Qué idiomas se hablan en Bolivia? En Bolivia se hablan español, quechua y aimará.
2. ¿Dónde vive la mayoría de los bolivianos? La mayoría de los bolivianos vive en el altiplano.
3. ¿Cuál es la capital administrativa de Bolivia? La capital administrativa de Bolivia es La Paz.
4. Según la mitología inca, ¿qué ocurrió en el lago Titicaca? Los hijos del dios Sol emergieron del lago para fundar el imperio inca.
5. ¿De qué países es la música andina? La música andina es de Bolivia, Perú, Ecuador, Chile y Argentina.
6. ¿Qué origen tiene esta música? Es música de origen indígena.
7. ¿Cómo se llama el sitio arqueológico situado cerca de La Paz y el lago Titicaca? El sitio arqueológico situado cerca de La Paz y el lago Titicaca se llama Tiahuanaco.
8. ¿Qué es la Puerta del Sol? La Puerta del Sol es un monumento que está en Tiahuanaco.

 Conexión Internet Investiga estos temas en **vhlcentral.com**.

Practice more at **vhlcentral.com**.

1. Busca información sobre un(a) boliviano/a célebre. ¿Cuáles son algunos de los episodios más importantes de su vida? ¿Qué ha hecho esta persona? ¿Por qué es célebre?
2. Busca información sobre Tiahuanaco u otro sitio arqueológico en Bolivia. ¿Qué han descubierto los arqueólogos en ese sitio?

dios *god* imperio *empire* conjuntos *groups* dan a conocer *make known* alrededor *around* antepasados *ancestors* ancho *wide*

El lago Titicaca Sitting more than two miles above sea level, Lake Titicaca is larger than the area of Delaware and Rhode Island combined. Five major river systems feed into the lake, which has forty-one islands. Lake Titicaca is also the largest lake in South America as measured by water volume.

La música andina Andean music is characterized by its plaintive, haunting melodies, often based in a minor or pentatonic scale.

Tiahuanaco The pre-Incan civilization that flourished at **Tiahuanaco** was probably a theocracy, governed by priest-kings. The primary deity was **Viracocha**, a sky and thunder god worshipped throughout much of the Andean world. The Tiahuanacan head of state was viewed as **Viracocha's** embodiment on earth.

Conexión Internet Students will find supporting Internet activities and links at **vhlcentral.com**.

Teaching Tip You may want to wrap up this section by playing the *Panorama cultural* video footage for this lesson.

TEACHING OPTIONS

Worth Noting Teams of scientists have extracted sediment samples from Titicaca's lakebed to study the history of climatological change in the region. Such research helps scientists build models to analyze contemporary trends in global climate change.

Worth Noting Students might enjoy learning this indigenous riddle about the **armadillo**, the animal whose outer shell is used to make the **charango**, a small guitar used in Andean music.
Vive en el cerro, lejos del mar.
De concha el saco sin abrochar.
Cuando se muere... ¡pues a cantar!

Section Goal

In **Panorama**, students will read about the geography and culture of Paraguay.

Instructional Resources

Supersite/DVD: *Panorama cultural*

Supersite: Resources (Scripts, Translations, *PowerPoints*, Answer Keys)

WebSAM

Workbook, pp. 191–192

Video Manual, pp. 265–266

Teaching Tips

• Use the **Lección 15 Panorama** overheads to assist with this presentation.

• Have students look at the map of Paraguay. Note that the major population centers lie east of the Paraguay River, which divides the country in two. West of the river is the **Gran Chaco**, a sparsely populated and largely infertile region.

El país en cifras As you read **Idiomas**, point out that **guaraní** is also spoken in neighboring Bolivia, Brazil, and Argentina. However, as an officially bilingual nation, Paraguay has the largest concentration of **guaraní** speakers. As students read **Paraguayos célebres**, let them know that writer **Augusto Roa Bastos** is well known throughout Latin America as both a poet and novelist. His novels *Yo, el Supremo* and *Hijo de hombre* deal with the turbulent and difficult history of Paraguay.

¡Increíble pero cierto!
→👥← Like Paraguay, several other Spanish-speaking countries impose fines on citizens for not voting. Ask students to research and name these countries. Ask the class if they think that such a measure should be implemented here to improve voter turnout at the polls.

Paraguay

El país en cifras

▸ **Área:** 406.750 km² (157.046 millas²), *el tamaño° de California*

▸ **Población:** 7.007.000

▸ **Capital:** Asunción—2.277.000

▸ **Ciudades principales:** Ciudad del Este, San Lorenzo, Lambaré, Fernando de la Mora

SOURCE: Population Division, UN Secretariat

▸ **Moneda:** guaraní

▸ **Idiomas:** español (oficial), guaraní (oficial)

Las tribus indígenas que habitaban la zona antes de la llegada de los españoles hablaban guaraní. Ahora el 90 por ciento de los paraguayos habla esta lengua, que se usa con frecuencia en canciones, poemas, periódicos y libros. Varios institutos y asociaciones, como el Teatro Guaraní, se dedican a preservar la cultura y la lengua guaraníes.

Bandera de Paraguay

Paraguayos célebres

▸ **Agustín Barrios,** guitarrista y compositor (1885–1944)

▸ **Josefina Plá,** escritora y ceramista (1909–1999)

▸ **Augusto Roa Bastos,** escritor (1917–2005)

▸ **Olga Blinder,** pintora (1921–2008)

recursos		
WB pp. 191–192	VM pp. 265–266	vhlcentral.com Lección 15

tamaño *size* multara *fined*

Paraguayo con alfombras típicas del país

Agricultor indígena de la tribu maca

Itapúa

¡Increíble pero cierto!

¿Te imaginas qué pasaría si el gobierno multara° a los ciudadanos que no van a votar? En Paraguay es una obligación. Ésta es una ley nacional, que otros países también tienen, para obligar a los ciudadanos a participar en las elecciones. En Paraguay los ciudadanos que no van a votar tienen que pagar una multa al gobierno.

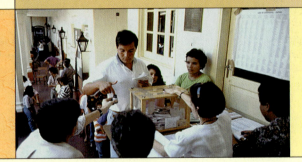

TEACHING OPTIONS

Worth Noting ←👥→ Give students exposure to the **guaraní** language by sharing the names of these typical Paraguayan dishes: **chipa** (a baked good flavored with **anís**), **kiveve** (a stew made from **andaí,** a type of squash), and **pastel mandi'o** (turnovers made with the South American staple, manioc flour, and filled with **so'o ku'í,** chopped meat). Invite students who have visited or lived in Paraguay to share other information

about traditional Paraguayan fare. Be sure to have them mention the national drink of Paraguay (as well as Uruguay, Argentina, and Rio Grande do Sul in Brazil), **yerba mate.** This is an infusion made from the leaves of a tree native to Paraguay and is sometimes called *Paraguayan tea* in English.

Artesanía • El ñandutí

La artesanía° más famosa de Paraguay se llama ñandutí y es un encaje° hecho a mano originario de Itauguá. En guaraní, la palabra ñandutí significa telaraña° y esta pieza recibe ese nombre porque imita el trazado° que crean los arácnidos. Estos encajes suelen ser° blancos, pero también los hay de colores, con formas geométricas o florales.

Ciencias • La represa Itaipú

La represa° Itaipú es una instalación hidroeléctrica que se encuentra en la frontera entre Paraguay y Brasil. Su construcción inició en 1974 y duró 8 años. La cantidad de concreto que se utilizó durante los primeros cinco años de esta obra fue similar a la que se necesita para construir un edificio de 350 pisos. Cien mil trabajadores paraguayos participaron en el proyecto. En 1984 se puso en funcionamiento la Central Hidroeléctrica de Itaipú y gracias a su cercanía con las famosas Cataratas de Iguazú, muchos turistas la visitan diariamente.

Naturaleza • Los ríos Paraguay y Paraná

Los ríos Paraguay y Paraná sirven de frontera natural entre Argentina y Paraguay, y son las principales rutas de transporte de este último país. El Paraná tiene unos 3.200 kilómetros navegables, y por esta ruta pasan barcos de más de 5.000 toneladas, los cuales viajan desde el estuario° del Río de la Plata hasta la ciudad de Asunción. El río Paraguay divide el Gran Chaco de la meseta° Paraná, donde vive la mayoría de los paraguayos.

 ¿Qué aprendiste? Responde a cada pregunta con una oración completa.

1. ¿Quién fue Augusto Roa Bastos?
 Augusto Roa Bastos fue un escritor paraguayo.
2. ¿Cómo se llama la moneda de Paraguay?
 La moneda de Paraguay se llama guaraní.
3. ¿Qué es el ñandutí?
 El ñandutí es un tipo de encaje.
4. ¿De dónde es originario el ñandutí?
 El ñandutí es originario de Itauguá.
5. ¿Qué forma imita el ñandutí?
 Imita la forma de una telaraña.
6. En total, ¿cuántos años tomó la construcción de la represa Itaipú?
 La construcción de la represa Itaipú tomó 8 años.
7. ¿A cuántos paraguayos dio trabajo la construcción de la represa?
 La construcción de la represa dio trabajo a 100.000 paraguayos.
8. ¿Qué países separan los ríos Paraguay y Paraná? Los ríos Paraguay y Paraná separan Argentina y Paraguay.
9. ¿Qué distancia se puede navegar por el Paraná?
 Se pueden navegar 3.200 kilómetros.

 Conexión Internet Investiga estos temas en **vhlcentral.com**.

1. Busca información sobre Alfredo Stroessner, el ex presidente de Paraguay. ¿Por qué se le considera un dictador?
2. Busca información sobre la historia de Paraguay. En tu opinión, ¿cuáles fueron los episodios decisivos en su historia?

 Practice more at **vhlcentral.com**.

···

artesanía *crafts*　**encaje** *lace*　**telaraña** *spiderweb*　**trazado** *outline; design*　**suelen ser** *are usually*　**represa** *dam*　**estuario** *estuary*　**meseta** *plateau*

El ñandutí In recent years, the number of traditional **ñandutí** makers has been in serious decline. Many artisans of Itauguá have turned to more profitable sources of income. In an effort to keep this traditional art alive, formal instruction in the skill of making **ñandutí** has been incorporated in the curriculum of local handicraft schools.

La represa Itaipú The Itaipú dam project is a joint venture between Brazil and Paraguay, and has been remarkably successful. In 2008, the plant supplied 90% of Paraguay's energy and 19% of that consumed by Brazil.

Los ríos Paraguay y Paraná The Paraná River was a highway for the settlement of Paraguay. Along its banks, between the sixteenth and late eighteenth centuries, the Jesuits organized their **guaraní**-speaking parishioners into small, self-supporting city-states built around mission settlements, similar to the Franciscan mission system in California during the same period.

Conexión Internet Students will find supporting Internet activities and links at **vhlcentral.com**.

Teaching Tip You may want to wrap up this section by playing the **Panorama cultural** video footage for this lesson.

El bienestar

el bienestar	*well-being*
la droga	*drug*
el/la drogadicto/a	*drug addict*
el masaje	*massage*
el/la teleadicto/a	*couch potato*
adelgazar	*to lose weight; to slim down*
aliviar el estrés	*to reduce stress*
aliviar la tensión	*to reduce tension*
apurarse, darse prisa	*to hurry; to rush*
aumentar de peso, engordar	*to gain weight*
disfrutar (de)	*to enjoy; to reap the benefits (of)*
estar a dieta	*to be on a diet*
(no) fumar	*(not) to smoke*
llevar una vida sana	*to lead a healthy lifestyle*
sufrir muchas presiones	*to be under a lot of pressure*
tratar de (+ inf.)	*to try (to do something)*
activo/a	*active*
débil	*weak*
en exceso	*in excess; too much*
flexible	*flexible*
fuerte	*strong*
sedentario/a	*sedentary; related to sitting*
tranquilo/a	*calm; quiet*

En el gimnasio

la cinta caminadora	*treadmill*
la clase de ejercicios aeróbicos	*aerobics class*
el/la entrenador(a)	*trainer*
el músculo	*muscle*
calentarse (e:ie)	*to warm up*
entrenarse	*to practice; to train*
estar en buena forma	*to be in good shape*
hacer ejercicio	*to exercise*
hacer ejercicios aeróbicos	*to do aerobics*
hacer ejercicios de estiramiento	*to do stretching exercises*
hacer gimnasia	*to work out*
levantar pesas	*to lift weights*
mantenerse en forma	*to stay in shape*
sudar	*to sweat*

La nutrición

la bebida alcohólica	*alcoholic beverage*
la cafeína	*caffeine*
la caloría	*calorie*
el colesterol	*cholesterol*
la grasa	*fat*
la merienda	*afternoon snack*
el mineral	*mineral*
la nutrición	*nutrition*
el/la nutricionista	*nutritionist*
la proteína	*protein*
la vitamina	*vitamin*
comer una dieta equilibrada	*to eat a balanced diet*
consumir alcohol	*to consume alcohol*
descafeinado/a	*decaffeinated*

Expresiones útiles	*See page 487.*

recursos

LM p. 89 — vhlcentral.com Lección 15

 Audio: Vocabulary

Plan de escritura

1 Ideas y organización

Begin by organizing your writing materials. If you prefer to write by hand, you may want to have a few spare pens and pencils on hand, as well as an eraser or correction fluid. If you prefer to use a word-processing program, make sure you know how to type Spanish accent marks, the **tilde**, and Spanish punctuation marks. Then make a list of the resources you can consult while writing. Finally, make a list of the basic ideas you want to cover. Beside each idea, jot down a few Spanish words and phrases you may want to use while writing.

2 Primer borrador

Write your first draft, using the resources and ideas you gathered in **Ideas y organización.**

3 Comentario

Exchange papers with a classmate and comment on each other's work, using these questions as a guide. Begin by mentioning what you like about your classmate's writing.

a. How can your classmate make his or her writing clearer, more logical, or more organized?

b. What suggestions do you have for making the writing more interesting or complete?

c. Do you see any spelling or grammatical errors?

4 Redacción

Revise your first draft, keeping in mind your classmate's comments. Also, incorporate any new information you may have. Before handing in the final version, review your work using these guidelines:

a. Make sure each verb agrees with its subject. Then check the gender and number of each article, noun, and adjective.

b. Check your spelling and punctuation.

c. Consult your **Anotaciones para mejorar la escritura** (see description below) to avoid repetition of previous errors.

5 Evaluación y progreso

You may want to share what you've written with a classmate, a small group, or the entire class. After your instructor has returned your paper, review the comments and corrections. On a separate sheet of paper, write the heading **Anotaciones para mejorar** (*Notes for improving*) **la escritura** and list your most common errors. Place this list and your corrected document in your writing portfolio (**Carpeta de trabajos**) and consult it from time to time to gauge your progress.

Spanish Terms for Direction Lines and Classroom Use

Below is a list of useful terms that you might hear your instructor say in class. It also includes Spanish terms that appear in the direction lines of your textbook.

En las instrucciones — *In direction lines*

Cambia/Cambien...	*Change...*
Camina/Caminen por la clase.	*Walk around the classroom.*
Ciertas o falsas	*True or false*
Cierto o falso	*True or false*
Circula/Circulen por la clase.	*Walk around the classroom.*
Completa las oraciones de una manera lógica.	*Complete the sentences logically.*
Con un(a) compañero/a...	*With a classmate...*
Contesta las preguntas.	*Answer the questions.*
Corrige las oraciones falsas.	*Correct the false statements.*
Cuenta/Cuenten...	*Tell...*
Di/Digan...	*Say...*
Discute/Discutan...	*Discuss...*
En grupos...	*In groups...*
En parejas...	*In pairs...*
Entrevista...	*Interview...*
Escúchala	*Listen to it*
Forma oraciones completas.	*Create/Make complete sentences.*
Háganse preguntas.	*Ask each other questions.*
Haz el papel de...	*Play the role of...*
Haz los cambios necesarios.	*Make the necessary changes.*
Indica/Indiquen si las oraciones...	*Indicate if the sentences...*
Intercambia/Intercambien...	*Exchange...*
Lee/Lean en voz alta.	*Read aloud.*
Pon/Pongan...	*Put...*
... que mejor completa...	*...that best completes...*
Reúnete...	*Get together...*
... se da/dan como ejemplo.	*...is/are given as a model.*
Toma nota...	*Take note...*
Tomen apuntes.	*Take notes.*
Túrnense...	*Take turns...*

Palabras útiles — *Useful words*

la adivinanza	*riddle*
el anuncio	*advertisement/ad*
los apuntes	*notes*
el borrador	*draft*
la canción	*song*
la concordancia	*agreement*
el contenido	*contents*
el cortometraje	*short film*
eficaz	*efficient*
la encuesta	*survey*
el equipo	*team*
el esquema	*outline*
el folleto	*brochure*
las frases	*statements*
la hoja de actividades	*activity sheet/handout*
la hoja de papel	*piece of paper*
la información errónea	*incorrect information*
el/la lector(a)	*reader*
la lectura	*reading*
las oraciones	*sentences*
la ortografía	*spelling*
el papel	*role*
el párrafo	*paragraph*
el paso	*step*
la(s) persona(s) descrita(s)	*the person (people) described*
la pista	*clue*
por ejemplo	*for example*
el propósito	*purpose*
los recursos	*resources*
el reportaje	*report*
los resultados	*results*
según	*according to*
siguiente	*following*
la sugerencia	*suggestion*
el sustantivo	*noun*
el tema	*topic*
último	*last*
el último recurso	*last resort*

Verbos útiles *Useful verbs*

adivinar	to guess
anotar	to jot down
añadir	to add
apoyar	to support
averiguar	to find out
cambiar	to change
combinar	to combine
compartir	to share
comprobar (o:ue)	to check
corregir (e:i)	to correct
crear	to create
devolver (o:ue)	to return
doblar	to fold
dramatizar	to act out
elegir (e:i)	to choose/select
emparejar	to match
entrevistar	to interview
escoger	to choose
identificar	to identify
incluir	to include
informar	to report
intentar	to try
intercambiar	to exchange
investigar	to research
marcar	to mark
preguntar	to ask
recordar (o:ue)	to remember
responder	to answer
revisar	to revise
seguir (e:i)	to follow
seleccionar	to select
subrayar	to underline
traducir	to translate
tratar de	to be about

Expresiones útiles *Useful expressions*

Ahora mismo.	Right away.
¿Cómo no?	But of course.
¿Cómo se dice _____ en español?	How do you say _____ in Spanish?
¿Cómo se escribe _____?	How do you spell _____?
¿Comprende(n)?	Do you understand?
Con gusto.	With pleasure.
Con permiso.	Excuse me.
De acuerdo.	Okay.
De nada.	You're welcome.
¿De veras?	Really?
¿En qué página estamos?	What page are we on?
¿En serio?	Seriously?
Enseguida.	Right away.
hoy día	nowadays
Más despacio, por favor.	Slower, please.
Muchas gracias.	Thanks a lot.
No entiendo.	I don't understand.
No hay de qué.	Don't mention it.
No importa.	No problem./It doesn't matter.
¡No me digas!	You don't say!
No sé.	I don't know.
¡Ojalá!	Hopefully!
Perdone.	Pardon me.
Por favor.	Please.
Por supuesto.	Of course.
¡Qué bien!	Great!
¡Qué gracioso!	How funny!
¡Qué pena!	What a shame/pity!
¿Qué significa _____?	What does _____ mean?
Repite, por favor.	Please repeat.
Tengo una pregunta.	I have a question.
¿Tiene(n) alguna pregunta?	Do you have any questions?
Vaya(n) a la página dos.	Go to page 2.

Glossary of Grammatical Terms

ADJECTIVE A word that modifies, or describes, a noun or pronoun.

muchos libros	un hombre **rico**
many books	*a rich man*
las mujeres **altas**	
the tall women	

Demonstrative adjective An adjective that specifies which noun a speaker is referring to.

esta fiesta	**ese** chico
this party	*that boy*
aquellas flores	
those flowers	

Possessive adjective An adjective that indicates ownership or possession.

mi mejor vestido	Éste es **mi** hermano.
my best dress	*This is my brother.*

Stressed possessive adjective A possessive adjective that emphasizes the owner or possessor.

Es un libro **mío**.
It's my book./It's a book of mine.

Es amiga **tuya**; yo no la conozco.
She's a friend of yours; I don't know her.

ADVERB A word that modifies, or describes, a verb, adjective, or other adverb.

Pancho escribe **rápidamente**.
Pancho writes quickly.

Este cuadro es **muy** bonito.
This picture is very pretty.

ARTICLE A word that points out a noun in either a specific or a non-specific way.

Definite article An article that points out a noun in a specific way.

el libro	**la** maleta
the book	*the suitcase*
los diccionarios	**las** palabras
the dictionaries	*the words*

Indefinite article An article that points out a noun in a general, non-specific way.

un lápiz	**una** computadora
a pencil	*a computer*
unos pájaros	**unas** escuelas
some birds	*some schools*

CLAUSE A group of words that contains both a conjugated verb and a subject, either expressed or implied.

Main (or Independent) clause A clause that can stand alone as a complete sentence.

Pienso ir a cenar pronto.
I plan to go to dinner soon.

Subordinate (or Dependent) clause A clause that does not express a complete thought and therefore cannot stand alone as a sentence.

Trabajo en la cafetería **porque necesito dinero para la escuela**.
I work in the cafeteria because I need money for school.

COMPARATIVE A construction used with an adjective or adverb to express a comparison between two people, places, or things.

Este programa es **más interesante que** el otro.
This program is more interesting than the other one.

Tomás no es **tan alto como** Alberto.
Tomás is not as tall as Alberto.

CONJUGATION A set of the forms of a verb for a specific tense or mood or the process by which these verb forms are presented.

Preterite conjugation of **cantar**:

cant**é**	cant**amos**
cant**aste**	cant**asteis**
cant**ó**	cant**aron**

CONJUNCTION A word used to connect words, clauses, or phrases.

Susana es de Cuba **y** Pedro es de España.
Susana is from Cuba and Pedro is from Spain.

No quiero estudiar **pero** tengo que hacerlo.
I don't want to study, but I have to.

CONTRACTION The joining of two words into one. The only contractions in Spanish are **al** and **del**.

Mi hermano fue **al** concierto ayer.
*My brother went **to the** concert yesterday.*

Saqué dinero **del** banco.
*I took money **from the** bank.*

DIRECT OBJECT A noun or pronoun that directly receives the action of the verb.

Tomás lee **el libro.** **La** pagó ayer.
*Tomás reads **the book.** She paid **it** yesterday.*

GENDER The grammatical categorizing of certain kinds of words, such as nouns and pronouns, as masculine, feminine, or neuter.

Masculine
articles el, un
pronouns él, lo, mío, éste, ése, aquél
adjective simpático

Feminine
articles la, una
pronouns ella, la, mía, ésta, ésa, aquélla
adjective simpática

IMPERSONAL EXPRESSION A third-person expression with no expressed or specific subject.

Es muy importante. Llueve mucho.
It's very important. It's raining hard.

Aquí **se habla** español.
*Spanish **is spoken** here.*

INDIRECT OBJECT A noun or pronoun that receives the action of the verb indirectly; the object, often a living being, to or for whom an action is performed.

Eduardo **le** dio un libro **a Linda.**
*Eduardo gave a book **to Linda.***

La profesora **me** puso una C en el examen.
*The professor gave **me** a C on the test.*

INFINITIVE The basic form of a verb. Infinitives in Spanish end in -ar, -er, or -ir.

hablar correr abrir
to speak to run to open

INTERROGATIVE An adjective or pronoun used to ask a question.

¿**Quién** habla? ¿**Cuántos** compraste?
***Who** is speaking? **How many** did you buy?*

¿**Qué** piensas hacer hoy?
***What** do you plan to do today?*

INVERSION Changing the word order of a sentence, often to form a question.

Statement: Elena pagó la cuenta del restaurante.

Inversion: ¿Pagó Elena la cuenta del restaurante?

MOOD A grammatical distinction of verbs that indicates whether the verb is intended to make a statement or command or to express a doubt, emotion, or condition contrary to fact.

Imperative mood Verb forms used to make commands.

Di la verdad. **Caminen** ustedes conmigo.
***Tell** the truth. **Walk** with me.*

¡**Comamos** ahora!
***Let's eat** now!*

Indicative mood Verb forms used to state facts, actions, and states considered to be real.

Sé que **tienes** el dinero.
***I know** that **you have** the money.*

Subjunctive mood Verb forms used principally in subordinate (dependent) clauses to express wishes, desires, emotions, doubts, and certain conditions, such as contrary-to-fact situations.

Prefieren que **hables** en español.
*They prefer that **you speak** in Spanish.*

Dudo que Luis **tenga** el dinero necesario.
*I doubt that Luis **has** the necessary money.*

NOUN A word that identifies people, animals, places, things, and ideas.

hombre gato
man *cat*

México casa
Mexico *house*

libertad libro
freedom *book*

NUMBER A grammatical term that refers to singular or plural. Nouns in Spanish and English have number. Other parts of a sentence, such as adjectives, articles, and verbs, can also have number.

Singular	Plural
una cosa	**unas** cosas
a thing	*some things*
el profesor	**los** profesores
the professor	*the professors*

NUMBERS Words that represent amounts.

Cardinal numbers Words that show specific amounts.

cinco minutos
five minutes

el año **dos mil veintitrés**
*the year **2023***

Ordinal numbers Words that indicate the order of a noun in a series.

el **cuarto** jugador	la **décima** hora
*the **fourth** player*	*the **tenth** hour*

PAST PARTICIPLE A past form of the verb used in compound tenses. The past participle may also be used as an adjective, but it must then agree in number and gender with the word it modifies.

Han **buscado** por todas partes.
*They have **searched** everywhere.*

Yo no había **estudiado** para el examen.
*I hadn't **studied** for the exam.*

Hay una **ventana abierta** en la sala.
*There is an **open window** in the living room.*

PERSON The form of the verb or pronoun that indicates the speaker, the one spoken to, or the one spoken about. In Spanish, as in English, there are three persons: first, second, and third.

Person	Singular	Plural
1st	**yo** *I*	**nosotros/as** *we*
2nd	**tú, Ud.** *you*	**vosotros/as, Uds.** *you*
3rd	**él, ella** *he, she*	**ellos, ellas** *they*

PREPOSITION A word or words that describe(s) the relationship, most often in time or space, between two other words.

Anita es **de** California.
*Anita is **from** California.*

La chaqueta está **en** el carro.
*The jacket is **in** the car.*

Marta se peinó **antes de** salir.
*Marta combed her hair **before** going out.*

PRESENT PARTICIPLE In English, a verb form that ends in *-ing*. In Spanish, the present participle ends in **-ndo**, and is often used with **estar** to form a progressive tense.

Mi hermana está **hablando** por teléfono ahora mismo.
*My sister is **talking** on the phone right now.*

PRONOUN A word that takes the place of a noun or nouns.

Demonstrative pronoun A pronoun that takes the place of a specific noun.

Quiero **ésta**.
*I want **this one**.*

¿Vas a comprar **ése**?
*Are you going to buy **that one**?*

Juan prefirió **aquéllos**.
*Juan preferred **those** (over there).*

Object pronoun A pronoun that functions as a direct or indirect object of the verb.

Te digo la verdad.
*I'm telling **you** the truth.*

Me lo trajo Juan.
*Juan brought **it** to **me**.*

Reflexive pronoun A pronoun that indicates that the action of a verb is performed by the subject on itself. These pronouns are often expressed in English with *-self: myself, yourself*, etc.

Yo **me** bañé antes de salir.
*I bathed **(myself)** before going out.*

Elena **se** acostó a las once y media.
*Elena **went to bed** at eleven-thirty.*

Relative pronoun A pronoun that connects a subordinate clause to a main clause.

El chico **que** nos escribió viene de visita mañana.
*The boy **who** wrote us is coming to visit tomorrow.*

Ya sé **lo que** tenemos que hacer.
*I already know **what** we have to do.*

Subject pronoun A pronoun that replaces the name or title of a person or thing, and acts as the subject of a verb.

Tú debes estudiar más.
***You** should study more.*

Él llegó primero.
***He** arrived first.*

SUBJECT A noun or pronoun that performs the action of a verb and is often implied by the verb.

María va al supermercado.
***María** goes to the supermarket.*

(Ellos) Trabajan mucho.
***They** work hard.*

Esos **libros** son muy caros.
*Those **books** are very expensive.*

SUPERLATIVE A word or construction used with an adjective or adverb to express the highest or lowest degree of a specific quality among three or more people, places, or things.

De todas mis clases, ésta es la **más interesante**.
*Of all my classes, this is the **most interesting**.*

Raúl es el **menos simpático** de los chicos.
*Raúl is the **least pleasant** of the boys.*

TENSE A set of verb forms that indicates the time of an action or state: past, present, or future.

Compound tense A two-word tense made up of an auxiliary verb and a present or past participle. In Spanish, there are two auxiliary verbs: **estar** and **haber**.

En este momento, **estoy estudiando**.
*At this time, **I am studying**.*

El paquete no **ha llegado** todavía.
*The package **has not arrived** yet.*

Simple tense A tense expressed by a single verb form.

María **estaba** enferma anoche.
*María **was** sick last night.*

Juana **hablará** con su mamá mañana.
*Juana **will speak** with her mom tomorrow.*

VERB A word that expresses actions or states-of-being.

Auxiliary verb A verb used with a present or past participle to form a compound tense. **Haber** is the most commonly used auxiliary verb in Spanish.

Los chicos **han** visto los elefantes.
*The children **have** seen the elephants.*

Espero que **hayas** comido.
*I hope you **have** eaten.*

Reflexive verb A verb that describes an action performed by the subject on itself and is always used with a reflexive pronoun.

Me compré un carro nuevo.
*I **bought myself** a new car.*

Pedro y Adela **se levantan** muy temprano.
*Pedro and Adela **get (themselves) up** very early.*

Spelling change verb A verb that undergoes a predictable change in spelling, in order to reflect its actual pronunciation in the various conjugations.

practicar	c→qu	practico	practiqué
dirigir	g→j	dirigí	dirijo
almorzar	z→c	almorzó	almorcé

Stem-changing verb A verb whose stem vowel undergoes one or more predictable changes in the various conjugations.

entender (e:ie)	entiendo
pedir (e:i)	piden
dormir (o:ue, u)	duermo, durmieron

Verb Conjugation Tables

The verb lists

The list of verbs below, and the model-verb tables that start on page A-11, show you how to conjugate every verb taught in **PANORAMA**. Each verb in the list is followed by a model verb conjugated according to the same pattern. The number in parentheses indicates where in the verb tables you can find the conjugated forms of the model verb. If you want to find out how to conjugate **divertirse**, for example, look up number 33, **sentir**, the model for verbs that follow the e:ie stem-change pattern.

How to use the verb tables

In the tables you will find the infinitive, present and past participles, and all the simple forms of each model verb. The formation of the compound tenses of any verb can be inferred from the table of compound tenses, pages A-11–12, either by combining the past participle of the verb with a conjugated form of **haber** or by combining the present participle with a conjugated form of **estar**.

abrazar (z:c) like cruzar (37)
abrir like vivir (3) *except* past participle is **abierto**
aburrir(se) like vivir (3)
acabar de like hablar (1)
acampar like hablar (1)
acompañar like hablar (1)
aconsejar like hablar (1)
acordarse (o:ue) like contar (24)
acostarse (o:ue) like contar (24)
adelgazar (z:c) like cruzar (37)
afeitarse like hablar (1)
ahorrar like hablar (1)
alegrarse like hablar (1)
aliviar like hablar (1)
almorzar (o:ue) like contar (24) *except* (z:c)
alquilar like hablar (1)
andar like hablar (1) *except* preterite stem is **anduv-**
anunciar like hablar (1)
apagar (g:gu) like llegar (41)
aplaudir like vivir (3)
apreciar like hablar (1)
aprender like comer (2)
apurarse like hablar (1)
arrancar (c:qu) like tocar (43)
arreglar like hablar (1)

asistir like vivir (3)
aumentar like hablar (1)
ayudar(se) like hablar (1)
bailar like hablar (1)
bajar(se) like hablar (1)
bañarse like hablar (1)
barrer like comer (2)
beber like comer (2)
besar(se) like hablar (1)
borrar like hablar (1)
brindar like hablar (1)
bucear like hablar (1)
buscar (c:qu) like tocar (43)
caber (4)
caer(se) (5)
calentarse (e:ie) like pensar (30)
calzar (z:c) like cruzar (37)
cambiar like hablar (1)
caminar like hablar (1)
cantar like hablar (1)
casarse like hablar (1)
cazar (z:c) like cruzar (37)
celebrar like hablar (1)
cenar like hablar (1)
cepillarse like hablar (1)
cerrar (e:ie) like pensar (30)
cobrar like hablar (1)
cocinar like hablar (1)
comenzar (e:ie) (z:c) like empezar (26)
comer (2)
compartir like vivir (3)

comprar like hablar (1)
comprender like comer (2)
comprometerse like comer (2)
comunicarse (c:qu) like tocar (43)
conducir (c:zc) (6)
confirmar like hablar (1)
conocer (c:zc) (35)
conseguir (e:i) (g:gu) like seguir (32)
conservar like hablar (1)
consumir like vivir (3)
contaminar like hablar (1)
contar (o:ue) (24)
contratar like hablar (1)
contestar like hablar (1)
conversar like hablar (1)
controlar like hablar (1)
correr like comer (2)
costar (o:ue) like contar (24)
creer (y) (36)
cruzar (z:c) (37)
cuidar like hablar (1)
cumplir like vivir (3)
dañar like hablar (1)
dar (7)
deber like comer (2)
decidir like vivir (3)
decir (e:i) (8)
declarar like hablar (1)
dejar like hablar (1)

depositar like hablar (1)
desarrollar like hablar (1)
desayunar like hablar (1)
descansar like hablar (1)
descargar like llegar (41)
describir like vivir (3) *except* past participle is descrito
descubrir like vivir (3) *except* past participle is descubierto
desear like hablar (1)
despedirse (e:i) like pedir (29)
despertarse (e:ie) like pensar (30)
destruir (y) (38)
dibujar like hablar (1)
dirigir (g:j) like vivir (3) *except* (g:j)
disfrutar like hablar (1)
divertirse (e:ie) like sentir (33)
divorciarse like hablar (1)
doblar like hablar (1)
doler (o:ue) like volver (34) *except* past participle is regular
dormir(se) (o:ue, u) (25)
ducharse like hablar (1)
dudar like hablar (1)
durar like hablar (1)
echar like hablar (1)
elegir (e:i) like pedir (29) *except* (g:j)

emitir like vivir (3)
empezar (e:ie) (z:c) (26)
enamorarse like hablar (1)
encantar like hablar (1)
encontrar(se) (o:ue) like contar (24)
enfermarse like hablar (1)
engordar like hablar (1)
enojarse like hablar (1)
enseñar like hablar (1)
ensuciar like hablar (1)
entender (e:ie) (27)
entrenarse like hablar (1)
entrevistar like hablar (1)
enviar (envío) (39)
escalar like hablar (1)
escanear like hablar (1)
escoger (g:j) like proteger (42)
escribir like vivir (3) *except* past participle is escrito
escuchar like hablar (1)
esculpir like vivir (3)
esperar like hablar (1)
esquiar (esquío) like enviar (39)
establecer (c:zc) like conocer (35)
estacionar like hablar (1)
estar (9)
estornudar like hablar (1)
estudiar like hablar (1)
evitar like hablar (1)
explicar (c:qu) like tocar (43)
faltar like hablar (1)
fascinar like hablar (1)
firmar like hablar (1)
fumar like hablar (1)
funcionar like hablar (1)
ganar like hablar (1)
gastar like hablar (1)
grabar like hablar (1)
graduarse (gradúo) (40)
guardar like hablar (1)
gustar like hablar (1)
haber (hay) (10)
hablar (1)
hacer (11)
importar like hablar (1)
imprimir like vivir (3)
indicar (c:qu) like tocar (43)
informar like hablar (1)
insistir like vivir (3)
interesar like hablar (1)

invertir (e:ie) like sentir (33)
invitar like hablar (1)
ir(se) (12)
jubilarse like hablar (1)
jugar (u:ue) (g:gu) (28)
lastimarse like hablar (1)
lavar(se) like hablar (1)
leer (y) like creer (36)
levantar(se) like hablar (1)
limpiar like hablar (1)
llamar(se) like hablar (1)
llegar (g:gu) (41)
llenar like hablar (1)
llevar(se) like hablar (1)
llover (o:ue) like volver (34) *except* past participle is regular
luchar like hablar (1)
mandar like hablar (1)
manejar like hablar (1)
mantener(se) (e:ie) like tener (20)
maquillarse like hablar (1)
mejorar like hablar (1)
merendar (e:ie) like pensar (30)
mirar like hablar (1)
molestar like hablar (1)
montar like hablar (1)
morir (o:ue) like dormir (25) *except* past participle is muerto
mostrar (o:ue) like contar (24)
mudarse like hablar (1)
nacer (c:zc) like conocer (35)
nadar like hablar (1)
navegar (g:gu) like llegar (41)
necesitar like hablar (1)
negar (e:ie) like pensar (30) *except* (g:gu)
nevar (e:ie) like pensar (30)
obedecer (c:zc) like conocer (35)
obtener (e:ie) like tener (20)
ocurrir like vivir (3)
odiar like hablar (1)
ofrecer (c:zc) like conocer (35)
oír (13)
olvidar like hablar (1)
pagar (g:gu) like llegar (41)
parar like hablar (1)

parecer (c:zc) like conocer (35)
pasar like hablar (1)
pasear like hablar (1)
patinar like hablar (1)
pedir (e:i) (29)
peinarse like hablar (1)
pensar (e:ie) (30)
perder (e:ie) like entender (27)
pescar (c:qu) like tocar (43)
pintar like hablar (1)
planchar like hablar (1)
poder (o:ue) (14)
poner(se) (15)
practicar (c:qu) like tocar (43)
preferir (e:ie) like sentir (33)
preguntar like hablar (1)
prender like comer (2)
preocuparse like hablar (1)
preparar like hablar (1)
presentar like hablar (1)
prestar like hablar (1)
probar(se) (o:ue) like contar (24)
prohibir like vivir (3)
proteger (g:j) (42)
publicar (c:qu) like tocar (43)
quedar(se) like hablar (1)
querer (e:ie) (16)
quitar(se) like hablar (1)
recetar like hablar (1)
recibir like vivir (3)
reciclar like hablar (1)
recoger (g:j) like proteger (42)
recomendar (e:ie) like pensar (30)
recordar (o:ue) like contar (24)
reducir (c:zc) like conducir (6)
regalar like hablar (1)
regatear like hablar (1)
regresar like hablar (1)
reír(se) (e:i) (31)
relajarse like hablar (1)
renunciar like hablar (1)
repetir (e:i) like pedir (29)
resolver (o:ue) like volver (34)
respirar like hablar (1)
revisar like hablar (1)

rogar (o:ue) like contar (24) *except* (g:gu)
romper(se) like comer (2) *except* past participle is roto
saber (17)
sacar (c:qu) like tocar (43)
sacudir like vivir (3)
salir (18)
saludar(se) like hablar (1)
secar(se) (c:qu) like tocar (43)
seguir (e:i) (32)
sentarse (e:ie) like pensar (30)
sentir(se) (e:ie) (33)
separarse like hablar (1)
ser (19)
servir (e:i) like pedir (29)
solicitar like hablar (1)
sonar (o:ue) like contar (24)
sonreír (e:i) like reír(se) (31)
sorprender like comer (2)
subir like vivir (3)
sudar like hablar (1)
sufrir like vivir (3)
sugerir (e:ie) like sentir (33)
suponer like poner (15)
temer like comer (2)
tener (e:ie) (20)
terminar like hablar (1)
tocar (c:qu) (43)
tomar like hablar (1)
torcerse (o:ue) like volver (34) *except* (c:z) and past participle is regular; e.g., yo tuerzo
toser like comer (2)
trabajar like hablar (1)
traducir (c:zc) like conducir (6)
traer (21)
transmitir like vivir (3)
tratar like hablar (1)
usar like hablar (1)
vender like comer (2)
venir (e:ie, i) (22)
ver (23)
vestirse (e:i) like pedir (29)
viajar like hablar (1)
visitar like hablar (1)
vivir (3)
volver (o:ue) (34)
votar like hablar (1)

Regular verbs: simple tenses

		INDICATIVE					SUBJUNCTIVE		IMPERATIVE
Infinitive		Present	Imperfect	Preterite	Future	Conditional	Present	Past	
1 hablar		hablo	hablaba	hablé	hablaré	hablaría	hable	hablara	
Participles:		hablas	hablabas	hablaste	hablarás	hablarías	hables	hablaras	habla tú (no hables)
hablando		habla	hablaba	habló	hablará	hablaría	hable	hablara	hable Ud.
hablado		hablamos	hablábamos	hablamos	hablaremos	hablaríamos	hablemos	habláramos	hablemos
		habláis	hablabais	hablasteis	hablaréis	hablaríais	habléis	hablarais	hablad (no habléis)
		hablan	hablaban	hablaron	hablarán	hablarían	hablen	hablaran	hablen Uds.
2 comer		como	comía	comí	comeré	comería	coma	comiera	
Participles:		comes	comías	comiste	comerás	comerías	comas	comieras	come tú (no comas)
comiendo		come	comía	comió	comerá	comería	coma	comiera	coma Ud.
comido		comemos	comíamos	comimos	comeremos	comeríamos	comamos	comiéramos	comamos
		coméis	comíais	comisteis	comeréis	comeríais	comáis	comierais	comed (no comáis)
		comen	comían	comieron	comerán	comerían	coman	comieran	coman Uds.
3 vivir		vivo	vivía	viví	viviré	viviría	viva	viviera	
Participles:		vives	vivías	viviste	vivirás	vivirías	vivas	vivieras	vive tú (no vivas)
viviendo		vive	vivía	vivió	vivirá	viviría	viva	viviera	viva Ud.
vivido		vivimos	vivíamos	vivimos	viviremos	viviríamos	vivamos	viviéramos	vivamos
		vivís	vivíais	vivisteis	viviréis	viviríais	viváis	vivierais	vivid (no viváis)
		viven	vivían	vivieron	vivirán	vivirían	vivan	vivieran	vivan Uds.

All verbs: compound tenses

PERFECT TENSES

INDICATIVE				SUBJUNCTIVE	
Present Perfect	Past Perfect	Future Perfect	Conditional Perfect	Present Perfect	Past Perfect
he	había	habré	habría	haya	hubiera
has	habías	habrás	habrías	hayas	hubieras
ha	había	habrá	habría	haya	hubiera
hemos hablado comido vivido	habíamos hablado comido vivido	habremos hablado comido vivido	habríamos hablado comido vivido	hayamos hablado comido vivido	hubiéramos hablado comido vivido
habéis	habíais	habréis	habríais	hayáis	hubierais
han	habían	habrán	habrían	hayan	hubieran

PROGRESSIVE TENSES

INDICATIVE

Present Progressive	Past Progressive	Future Progressive	Conditional Progressive		
estoy	estaba	estaré	estaría		
estás	estabas	estarás	estarías	hablando	
está	estaba	estará	estaría	comiendo	
estamos	estábamos	estaremos	estaríamos	viviendo	
estáis	estabais	estaréis	estaríais		
están	estaban	estarán	estarían		

SUBJUNCTIVE

Present Progressive	Past Progressive		
esté	estuviera		
estés	estuvieras	hablando	
esté	estuviera	comiendo	
estemos	estuviéramos	viviendo	
estéis	estuvierais		
estén	estuvieran		

Irregular verbs

Infinitive	INDICATIVE					SUBJUNCTIVE		IMPERATIVE
	Present	Imperfect	Preterite	Future	Conditional	Present	Past	
4 caber	**quepo**	cabía	**cupe**	**cabré**	**cabría**	**quepa**	**cupiera**	
	cabes	cabías	**cupiste**	**cabrás**	**cabrías**	**quepas**	**cupieras**	cabe tú (no **quepas**)
	cabe	cabía	**cupo**	**cabrá**	**cabría**	**quepa**	**cupiera**	**quepa** Ud.
Participles:	cabemos	cabíamos	**cupimos**	**cabremos**	**cabríamos**	**quepamos**	**cupiéramos**	**quepamos**
cabiendo	cabéis	cabíais	**cupisteis**	**cabréis**	**cabríais**	**quepáis**	**cupierais**	cabed (no **quepáis**)
cabido	caben	cabían	**cupieron**	**cabrán**	**cabrían**	**quepan**	**cupieran**	**quepan** Uds.
5 caer(se)	**caigo**	caía	caí	caeré	caería	**caiga**	**cayera**	
	caes	caías	**caíste**	caerás	caerías	**caigas**	**cayeras**	cae tú (no **caigas**)
	cae	caía	**cayó**	caerá	caería	**caiga**	**cayera**	**caiga** Ud.
Participles:	caemos	caíamos	**caímos**	caeremos	caeríamos	**caigamos**	**cayéramos**	**caigamos**
cayendo	caéis	caíais	**caísteis**	caeréis	caeríais	**caigáis**	**cayerais**	caed (no **caigáis**)
caído	caen	caían	**cayeron**	caerán	caerían	**caigan**	**cayeran**	**caigan** Uds.
6 conducir	**conduzco**	conducía	**conduje**	conduciré	conduciría	**conduzca**	**condujera**	
(c:zc)	conduces	conducías	**condujiste**	conducirás	conducirías	**conduzcas**	**condujeras**	conduce tú (no **conduzcas**)
	conduce	conducía	**condujo**	conducirá	conduciría	**conduzca**	**condujera**	**conduzca** Ud.
Participles:	conducimos	conducíamos	**condujimos**	conduciremos	conduciríamos	**conduzcamos**	**condujéramos**	**conduzcamos**
conduciendo	conducís	conducíais	**condujisteis**	conduciréis	conduciríais	**conduzcáis**	**condujerais**	conducid (no **conduzcáis**)
conducido	conducen	conducían	**condujeron**	conducirán	conducirían	**conduzcan**	**condujeran**	**conduzcan** Uds.

#	Infinitive / Participles	INDICATIVE Present	Imperfect	Preterite	Future	Conditional	SUBJUNCTIVE Present	Past	IMPERATIVE
7	**dar** — Participles: dando, dado	**doy** / das / da / damos / dais / dan	daba / dabas / daba / dábamos / dabais / daban	**di** / **diste** / **dio** / **dimos** / **disteis** / **dieron**	daré / darás / dará / daremos / daréis / darán	daría / darías / daría / daríamos / daríais / darían	**dé** / **des** / **dé** / **demos** / **deis** / **den**	**diera** / **dieras** / **diera** / **diéramos** / **dierais** / **dieran**	da tú (no **des**) / **dé** Ud. / **demos** / dad (no **deis**) / **den** Uds.
8	**decir (e:i)** — Participles: diciendo, dicho	**digo** / **dices** / **dice** / decimos / decís / **dicen**	decía / decías / decía / decíamos / decíais / decían	**dije** / **dijiste** / **dijo** / **dijimos** / **dijisteis** / **dijeron**	**diré** / **dirás** / **dirá** / **diremos** / **diréis** / **dirán**	**diría** / **dirías** / **diría** / **diríamos** / **diríais** / **dirían**	**diga** / **digas** / **diga** / **digamos** / **digáis** / **digan**	**dijera** / **dijeras** / **dijera** / **dijéramos** / **dijerais** / **dijeran**	**di** tú (no **digas**) / **diga** Ud. / **digamos** / decid (no **digáis**) / **digan** Uds.
9	**estar** — Participles: estando, estado	**estoy** / estás / está / estamos / estáis / están	estaba / estabas / estaba / estábamos / estabais / estaban	**estuve** / **estuviste** / **estuvo** / **estuvimos** / **estuvisteis** / **estuvieron**	estaré / estarás / estará / estaremos / estaréis / estarán	estaría / estarías / estaría / estaríamos / estaríais / estarían	esté / estés / esté / estemos / estéis / estén	estuviera / estuvieras / estuviera / estuviéramos / estuvierais / estuvieran	está tú (no estés) / esté Ud. / estemos / estad (no estéis) / estén Uds.
10	**haber** — Participles: habiendo, habido	**he** / **has** / **ha** / **hemos** / **habéis** / **han**	había / habías / había / habíamos / habíais / habían	**hube** / **hubiste** / **hubo** / **hubimos** / **hubisteis** / **hubieron**	**habré** / **habrás** / **habrá** / **habremos** / **habréis** / **habrán**	**habría** / **habrías** / **habría** / **habríamos** / **habríais** / **habrían**	**haya** / **hayas** / **haya** / **hayamos** / **hayáis** / **hayan**	**hubiera** / **hubieras** / **hubiera** / **hubiéramos** / **hubierais** / **hubieran**	
11	**hacer** — Participles: haciendo, hecho	**hago** / haces / hace / hacemos / hacéis / hacen	hacía / hacías / hacía / hacíamos / hacíais / hacían	**hice** / **hiciste** / **hizo** / **hicimos** / **hicisteis** / **hicieron**	**haré** / **harás** / **hará** / **haremos** / **haréis** / **harán**	**haría** / **harías** / **haría** / **haríamos** / **haríais** / **harían**	**haga** / **hagas** / **haga** / **hagamos** / **hagáis** / **hagan**	**hiciera** / **hicieras** / **hiciera** / **hiciéramos** / **hicierais** / **hicieran**	**haz** tú (no **hagas**) / **haga** Ud. / **hagamos** / haced (no **hagáis**) / **hagan** Uds.
12	**ir** — Participles: yendo, ido	**voy** / **vas** / **va** / **vamos** / **vais** / **van**	**iba** / **ibas** / **iba** / **íbamos** / **ibais** / **iban**	**fui** / **fuiste** / **fue** / **fuimos** / **fuisteis** / **fueron**	iré / irás / irá / iremos / iréis / irán	iría / irías / iría / iríamos / iríais / irían	**vaya** / **vayas** / **vaya** / **vayamos** / **vayáis** / **vayan**	**fuera** / **fueras** / **fuera** / **fuéramos** / **fuerais** / **fueran**	**ve** tú (no **vayas**) / **vaya** Ud. / **vamos** / id (no **vayáis**) / **vayan** Uds.
13	**oír (y)** — Participles: oyendo, oído	**oigo** / **oyes** / **oye** / **oímos** / **oís** / **oyen**	oía / oías / oía / oíamos / oíais / oían	**oí** / **oíste** / **oyó** / **oímos** / **oísteis** / **oyeron**	oiré / oirás / oirá / oiremos / oiréis / oirán	oiría / oirías / oiría / oiríamos / oiríais / oirían	**oiga** / **oigas** / **oiga** / **oigamos** / **oigáis** / **oigan**	**oyera** / **oyeras** / **oyera** / **oyéramos** / **oyerais** / **oyeran**	**oye** tú (no **oigas**) / **oiga** Ud. / **oigamos** / oíd (no **oigáis**) / **oigan** Uds.

#	Infinitive	INDICATIVE Present	Imperfect	Preterite	Future	Conditional	SUBJUNCTIVE Present	Past	IMPERATIVE
14	poder (o:ue) **Participles:** **pudiendo** podido	**puedo** **puedes** **puede** podemos podéis **pueden**	podía podías podía podíamos podíais podían	**pude** pudiste **pudo** pudimos pudisteis pudieron	**podré** **podrás** **podrá** **podremos** **podréis** **podrán**	**podría** **podrías** **podría** **podríamos** **podríais** **podrían**	**pueda** **puedas** **pueda** podamos podáis **puedan**	**pudiera** **pudieras** **pudiera** **pudiéramos** **pudierais** **pudieran**	**puede** tú (no **puedas**) **pueda** Ud. podamos poded (no **podáis**) **puedan** Uds.
15	poner **Participles:** poniendo **puesto**	**pongo** pones pone ponemos ponéis ponen	ponía ponías ponía poníamos poníais ponían	**puse** pusiste **puso** pusimos pusisteis pusieron	**pondré** **pondrás** **pondrá** **pondremos** **pondréis** **pondrán**	**pondría** **pondrías** **pondría** **pondríamos** **pondríais** **pondrían**	**ponga** **pongas** **ponga** **pongamos** **pongáis** **pongan**	**pusiera** **pusieras** **pusiera** **pusiéramos** **pusierais** **pusieran**	**pon** tú (no **pongas**) **ponga** Ud. **pongamos** poned (no **pongáis**) **pongan** Uds.
16	querer (e:ie) **Participles:** queriendo querido	**quiero** **quieres** **quiere** queremos queréis **quieren**	quería querías quería queríamos queríais querían	**quise** quisiste **quiso** quisimos quisisteis quisieron	**querré** **querrás** **querrá** **querremos** **querréis** **querrán**	**querría** **querrías** **querría** **querríamos** **querríais** **querrían**	**quiera** **quieras** **quiera** queramos queráis **quieran**	**quisiera** **quisieras** **quisiera** **quisiéramos** **quisierais** **quisieran**	**quiere** tú (no **quieras**) **quiera** Ud. queramos quered (no queráis) **quieran** Uds.
17	saber **Participles:** sabiendo sabido	**sé** sabes sabe sabemos sabéis saben	sabía sabías sabía sabíamos sabíais sabían	**supe** supiste **supo** supimos supisteis supieron	**sabré** **sabrás** **sabrá** **sabremos** **sabréis** **sabrán**	**sabría** **sabrías** **sabría** **sabríamos** **sabríais** **sabrían**	**sepa** **sepas** **sepa** **sepamos** **sepáis** **sepan**	**supiera** **supieras** **supiera** **supiéramos** **supierais** **supieran**	sabe tú (no **sepas**) **sepa** Ud. **sepamos** sabed (no **sepáis**) **sepan** Uds.
18	salir **Participles:** saliendo salido	**salgo** sales sale salimos salís salen	salía salías salía salíamos salíais salían	salí saliste salió salimos salisteis salieron	**saldré** **saldrás** **saldrá** **saldremos** **saldréis** **saldrán**	**saldría** **saldrías** **saldría** **saldríamos** **saldríais** **saldrían**	**salga** **salgas** **salga** **salgamos** **salgáis** **salgan**	saliera salieras saliera saliéramos salierais salieran	**sal** tú (no **salgas**) **salga** Ud. **salgamos** salid (no **salgáis**) **salgan** Uds.
19	ser **Participles:** siendo sido	**soy** **eres** **es** **somos** **sois** **son**	**era** **eras** **era** **éramos** **erais** **eran**	**fui** **fuiste** **fue** **fuimos** **fuisteis** **fueron**	seré serás será seremos seréis serán	sería serías sería seríamos seríais serían	**sea** **seas** **sea** **seamos** **seáis** **sean**	**fuera** **fueras** **fuera** **fuéramos** **fuerais** **fueran**	**sé** tú (no **seas**) sea Ud. **seamos** sed (no **seáis**) sean Uds.
20	tener (e:ie) **Participles:** teniendo tenido	**tengo** **tienes** **tiene** tenemos tenéis **tienen**	tenía tenías tenía teníamos teníais tenían	tuve tuviste tuvo tuvimos tuvisteis tuvieron	**tendré** **tendrás** **tendrá** **tendremos** **tendréis** **tendrán**	**tendría** **tendrías** **tendría** **tendríamos** **tendríais** **tendrían**	**tenga** **tengas** **tenga** **tengamos** **tengáis** **tengan**	**tuviera** **tuvieras** **tuviera** **tuviéramos** **tuvierais** **tuvieran**	**ten** tú (no **tengas**) **tenga** Ud. **tengamos** tened (no **tengáis**) **tengan** Uds.

21. traer
Participles: trayendo, traído

	INDICATIVE					SUBJUNCTIVE		IMPERATIVE
	Present	Imperfect	Preterite	Future	Conditional	Present	Past	
	traigo	traía	traje	traeré	traería	traiga	trajera	
	traes	traías	trajiste	traerás	traerías	traigas	trajeras	trae tú (no traigas)
	trae	traía	trajo	traerá	traería	traiga	trajera	traiga Ud.
	traemos	traíamos	trajimos	traeremos	traeríamos	traigamos	trajéramos	traigamos
	traéis	traíais	trajisteis	traeréis	traeríais	traigáis	trajerais	traed (no traigáis)
	traen	traían	trajeron	traerán	traerían	traigan	trajeran	traigan Uds.

22. venir (e:ie)
Participles: viniendo, venido

	INDICATIVE					SUBJUNCTIVE		IMPERATIVE
	Present	Imperfect	Preterite	Future	Conditional	Present	Past	
	vengo	venía	vine	vendré	vendría	venga	viniera	
	vienes	venías	viniste	vendrás	vendrías	vengas	vinieras	ven tú (no vengas)
	viene	venía	vino	vendrá	vendría	venga	viniera	venga Ud.
	venimos	veníamos	vinimos	vendremos	vendríamos	vengamos	viniéramos	vengamos
	venís	veníais	vinisteis	vendréis	vendríais	vengáis	vinierais	venid (no vengáis)
	vienen	venían	vinieron	vendrán	vendrían	vengan	vinieran	vengan Uds.

23. ver
Participles: viendo, visto

	INDICATIVE					SUBJUNCTIVE		IMPERATIVE
	Present	Imperfect	Preterite	Future	Conditional	Present	Past	
	veo	veía	vi	veré	vería	vea	viera	
	ves	veías	viste	verás	verías	veas	vieras	ve tú (no veas)
	ve	veía	vio	verá	vería	vea	viera	vea Ud.
	vemos	veíamos	vimos	veremos	veríamos	veamos	viéramos	veamos
	veis	veíais	visteis	veréis	veríais	veáis	vierais	ved (no veáis)
	ven	veían	vieron	verán	verían	vean	vieran	vean Uds.

Stem-changing verbs

24. contar (o:ue)
Participles: contando, contado

	INDICATIVE					SUBJUNCTIVE		IMPERATIVE
	Present	Imperfect	Preterite	Future	Conditional	Present	Past	
	cuento	contaba	conté	contaré	contaría	cuente	contara	
	cuentas	contabas	contaste	contarás	contarías	cuentes	contaras	cuenta tú (no cuentes)
	cuenta	contaba	contó	contará	contaría	cuente	contara	cuente Ud.
	contamos	contábamos	contamos	contaremos	contaríamos	contemos	contáramos	contemos
	contáis	contabais	contasteis	contaréis	contaríais	contéis	contarais	contad (no contéis)
	cuentan	contaban	contaron	contarán	contarían	cuenten	contaran	cuenten Uds.

25. dormir (o:ue)
Participles: durmiendo, dormido

	INDICATIVE					SUBJUNCTIVE		IMPERATIVE
	Present	Imperfect	Preterite	Future	Conditional	Present	Past	
	duermo	dormía	dormí	dormiré	dormiría	duerma	durmiera	
	duermes	dormías	dormiste	dormirás	dormirías	duermas	durmieras	duerme tú (no duermas)
	duerme	dormía	durmió	dormirá	dormiría	duerma	durmiera	duerma Ud.
	dormimos	dormíamos	dormimos	dormiremos	dormiríamos	durmamos	durmiéramos	durmamos
	dormís	dormíais	dormisteis	dormiréis	dormiríais	durmáis	durmierais	dormid (no durmáis)
	duermen	dormían	durmieron	dormirán	dormirían	duerman	durmieran	duerman Uds.

26. empezar (e:ie) (z:c)
Participles: empezando, empezado

	INDICATIVE					SUBJUNCTIVE		IMPERATIVE
	Present	Imperfect	Preterite	Future	Conditional	Present	Past	
	empiezo	empezaba	empecé	empezaré	empezaría	empiece	empezara	
	empiezas	empezabas	empezaste	empezarás	empezarías	empieces	empezaras	empieza tú (no empieces)
	empieza	empezaba	empezó	empezará	empezaría	empiece	empezara	empiece Ud.
	empezamos	empezábamos	empezamos	empezaremos	empezaríamos	empecemos	empezáramos	empecemos
	empezáis	empezabais	empezasteis	empezaréis	empezaríais	empecéis	empezarais	empezad (no empecéis)
	empiezan	empezaban	empezaron	empezarán	empezarían	empiecen	empezaran	empiecen Uds.

Infinitive	INDICATIVE					SUBJUNCTIVE		IMPERATIVE
	Present	Imperfect	Preterite	Future	Conditional	Present	Past	
27 entender (e:ie) Participles: entendiendo entendido	entiendo entiendes entiende entendemos entendéis entienden	entendía entendías entendía entendíamos entendíais entendían	entendí entendiste entendió entendimos entendisteis entendieron	entenderé entenderás entenderá entenderemos entenderéis entenderán	entendería entenderías entendería entenderíamos entenderíais entenderían	entienda entiendas entienda entendamos entendáis entiendan	entendiera entendieras entendiera entendiéramos entendierais entendieran	entiende tú (no entiendas) entienda Ud. entendamos entended (no entendáis) entiendan Uds.
28 jugar (u:ue) (g:gu) Participles: jugando jugado	juego juegas juega jugamos jugáis juegan	jugaba jugabas jugaba jugábamos jugabais jugaban	jugué jugaste jugó jugamos jugasteis jugaron	jugaré jugarás jugará jugaremos jugaréis jugarán	jugaría jugarías jugaría jugaríamos jugaríais jugarían	juegue juegues juegue juguemos juguéis jueguen	jugara jugaras jugara jugáramos jugarais jugaran	juega tú (no juegues) juegue Ud. juguemos jugad (no juguéis) jueguen Uds.
29 pedir (e:i) Participles: pidiendo pedido	pido pides pide pedimos pedís piden	pedía pedías pedía pedíamos pedíais pedían	pedí pediste pidió pedimos pedisteis pidieron	pediré pedirás pedirá pediremos pediréis pedirán	pediría pedirías pediría pediríamos pediríais pedirían	pida pidas pida pidamos pidáis pidan	pidiera pidieras pidiera pidiéramos pidierais pidieran	pide tú (no pidas) pida Ud. pidamos pedid (no pidáis) pidan Uds.
30 pensar (e:ie) Participles: pensando pensado	pienso piensas piensa pensamos pensáis piensan	pensaba pensabas pensaba pensábamos pensabais pensaban	pensé pensaste pensó pensamos pensasteis pensaron	pensaré pensarás pensará pensaremos pensaréis pensarán	pensaría pensarías pensaría pensaríamos pensaríais pensarían	piense pienses piense pensemos penséis piensen	pensara pensaras pensara pensáramos pensarais pensaran	piensa tú (no pienses) piense Ud. pensemos pensad (no penséis) piensen Uds.
31 reír(se) (e:i) Participles: riendo reído	río ríes ríe reímos reís ríen	reía reías reía reíamos reíais reían	reí reíste rió reímos reísteis rieron	reiré reirás reirá reiremos reiréis reirán	reiría reirías reiría reiríamos reiríais reirían	ría rías ría riamos riáis rían	riera rieras riera riéramos rierais rieran	ríe tú (no rías) ría Ud. riamos reíd (no riáis) rían Uds.
32 seguir (e:i) (gu:g) Participles: siguiendo seguido	sigo sigues sigue seguimos seguís siguen	seguía seguías seguía seguíamos seguíais seguían	seguí seguiste siguió seguimos seguisteis siguieron	seguiré seguirás seguirá seguiremos seguiréis seguirán	seguiría seguirías seguiría seguiríamos seguiríais seguirían	siga sigas siga sigamos sigáis sigan	siguiera siguieras siguiera siguiéramos siguierais siguieran	sigue tú (no sigas) siga Ud. sigamos seguid (no sigáis) sigan Uds.
33 sentir (e:ie) Participles: sintiendo sentido	siento sientes siente sentimos sentís sienten	sentía sentías sentía sentíamos sentíais sentían	sentí sentiste sintió sentimos sentisteis sintieron	sentiré sentirás sentirá sentiremos sentiréis sentirán	sentiría sentirías sentiría sentiríamos sentiríais sentirían	sienta sientas sienta sintamos sintáis sientan	sintiera sintieras sintiera sintiéramos sintierais sintieran	siente tú (no sientas) sienta Ud. sintamos sentid (no sintáis) sientan Uds.

34 — volver (o:ue)

Participles: volviendo, vuelto

	INDICATIVE					SUBJUNCTIVE		IMPERATIVE
	Present	Imperfect	Preterite	Future	Conditional	Present	Past	
	vuelvo	volvía	volví	volveré	volvería	vuelva	volviera	
	vuelves	volvías	volviste	volverás	volverías	vuelvas	volvieras	vuelve tú (no vuelvas)
	vuelve	volvía	volvió	volverá	volvería	vuelva	volviera	vuelva Ud.
	volvemos	volvíamos	volvimos	volveremos	volveríamos	volvamos	volviéramos	volvamos
	volvéis	volvíais	volvisteis	volveréis	volveríais	volváis	volvierais	volved (no volváis)
	vuelven	volvían	volvieron	volverán	volverían	vuelvan	volvieran	vuelvan Uds.

Verbs with spelling changes only

35 — conocer (c:zc)

Participles: conociendo, conocido

	INDICATIVE					SUBJUNCTIVE		IMPERATIVE
	Present	Imperfect	Preterite	Future	Conditional	Present	Past	
	conozco	conocía	conocí	conoceré	conocería	conozca	conociera	
	conoces	conocías	conociste	conocerás	conocerías	conozcas	conocieras	conoce tú (no conozcas)
	conoce	conocía	conoció	conocerá	conocería	conozca	conociera	conozca Ud.
	conocemos	conocíamos	conocimos	conoceremos	conoceríamos	conozcamos	conociéramos	conozcamos
	conocéis	conocíais	conocisteis	conoceréis	conoceríais	conozcáis	conocierais	conoced (no conozcáis)
	conocen	conocían	conocieron	conocerán	conocerían	conozcan	conocieran	conozcan Uds.

36 — creer (y)

Participles: creyendo, creído

	INDICATIVE					SUBJUNCTIVE		IMPERATIVE
	Present	Imperfect	Preterite	Future	Conditional	Present	Past	
	creo	creía	creí	creeré	creería	crea	creyera	
	crees	creías	creíste	creerás	creerías	creas	creyeras	cree tú (no creas)
	cree	creía	creyó	creerá	creería	crea	creyera	crea Ud.
	creemos	creíamos	creímos	creeremos	creeríamos	creamos	creyéramos	creamos
	creéis	creíais	creísteis	creeréis	creeríais	creáis	creyerais	creed (no creáis)
	creen	creían	creyeron	creerán	creerían	crean	creyeran	crean Uds.

37 — cruzar (z:c)

Participles: cruzando, cruzado

	INDICATIVE					SUBJUNCTIVE		IMPERATIVE
	Present	Imperfect	Preterite	Future	Conditional	Present	Past	
	cruzo	cruzaba	crucé	cruzaré	cruzaría	cruce	cruzara	
	cruzas	cruzabas	cruzaste	cruzarás	cruzarías	cruces	cruzaras	cruza tú (no cruces)
	cruza	cruzaba	cruzó	cruzará	cruzaría	cruce	cruzara	cruce Ud.
	cruzamos	cruzábamos	cruzamos	cruzaremos	cruzaríamos	crucemos	cruzáramos	crucemos
	cruzáis	cruzabais	cruzasteis	cruzaréis	cruzaríais	crucéis	cruzarais	cruzad (no crucéis)
	cruzan	cruzaban	cruzaron	cruzarán	cruzarían	crucen	cruzaran	crucen Uds.

38 — destruir (y)

Participles: destruyendo, destruido

	INDICATIVE					SUBJUNCTIVE		IMPERATIVE
	Present	Imperfect	Preterite	Future	Conditional	Present	Past	
	destruyo	destruía	destruí	destruiré	destruiría	destruya	destruyera	
	destruyes	destruías	destruiste	destruirás	destruirías	destruyas	destruyeras	destruye tú (no destruyas)
	destruye	destruía	destruyó	destruirá	destruiría	destruya	destruyera	destruya Ud.
	destruimos	destruíamos	destruimos	destruiremos	destruiríamos	destruyamos	destruyéramos	destruyamos
	destruís	destruíais	destruisteis	destruiréis	destruiríais	destruyáis	destruyerais	destruid (no destruyáis)
	destruyen	destruían	destruyeron	destruirán	destruirían	destruyan	destruyeran	destruyan Uds.

39 — enviar (envío)

Participles: enviando, enviado

	INDICATIVE					SUBJUNCTIVE		IMPERATIVE
	Present	Imperfect	Preterite	Future	Conditional	Present	Past	
	envío	enviaba	envié	enviaré	enviaría	envíe	enviara	
	envías	enviabas	enviaste	enviarás	enviarías	envíes	enviaras	envía tú (no envíes)
	envía	enviaba	envió	enviará	enviaría	envíe	enviara	envíe Ud.
	enviamos	enviábamos	enviamos	enviaremos	enviaríamos	enviemos	enviáramos	enviemos
	enviáis	enviabais	enviasteis	enviaréis	enviaríais	enviéis	enviarais	enviad (no enviéis)
	envían	enviaban	enviaron	enviarán	enviarían	envíen	enviaran	envíen Uds.

Infinitive	INDICATIVE					SUBJUNCTIVE		IMPERATIVE
	Present	Imperfect	Preterite	Future	Conditional	Present	Past	
40 graduarse (gradúo)	**gradúo**	graduaba	gradué	graduaré	graduaría	**gradúe**	graduara	
	gradúas	graduabas	graduaste	graduarás	graduarías	**gradúes**	graduaras	**gradúa** tú (no **gradúes**)
	gradúa	graduaba	graduó	graduará	graduaría	**gradúe**	graduara	**gradúe** Ud.
Participles:	graduamos	graduábamos	graduamos	graduaremos	graduaríamos	graduemos	graduáramos	graduemos
graduando	graduáis	graduabais	graduasteis	graduaréis	graduaríais	graduéis	graduarais	graduad (no graduéis)
graduado	**gradúan**	graduaban	graduaron	graduarán	graduarían	**gradúen**	graduaran	**gradúen** Uds.
41 llegar (g:gu)	llego	llegaba	**llegué**	llegaré	llegaría	**llegue**	llegara	
	llegas	llegabas	llegaste	llegarás	llegarías	**llegues**	llegaras	llega tú (no **llegues**)
	llega	llegaba	llegó	llegará	llegaría	**llegue**	llegara	**llegue** Ud.
Participles:	llegamos	llegábamos	llegamos	llegaremos	llegaríamos	**lleguemos**	llegáramos	**lleguemos**
llegando	llegáis	llegabais	llegasteis	llegaréis	llegaríais	**lleguéis**	llegarais	llegad (no **lleguéis**)
llegado	llegan	llegaban	llegaron	llegarán	llegarían	**lleguen**	llegaran	**lleguen** Uds.
42 proteger (g:j)	**protejo**	protegía	protegí	protegeré	protegería	**proteja**	protegiera	
	proteges	protegías	protegiste	protegerás	protegerías	**protejas**	protegieras	protege tú (no **protejas**)
	protege	protegía	protegió	protegerá	protegería	**proteja**	protegiera	**proteja** Ud.
Participles:	protegemos	protegíamos	protegimos	protegeremos	protegeríamos	**protejamos**	protegiéramos	**protejamos**
protegiendo	protegéis	protegíais	protegisteis	protegeréis	protegeríais	**protejáis**	protegierais	proteged (no **protejáis**)
protegido	protegen	protegían	protegieron	protegerán	protegerían	**protejan**	protegieran	**protejan** Uds.
43 tocar (c:qu)	toco	tocaba	**toqué**	tocaré	tocaría	**toque**	tocara	
	tocas	tocabas	tocaste	tocarás	tocarías	**toques**	tocaras	toca tú (no **toques**)
	toca	tocaba	tocó	tocará	tocaría	**toque**	tocara	**toque** Ud.
Participles:	tocamos	tocábamos	tocamos	tocaremos	tocaríamos	**toquemos**	tocáramos	**toquemos**
tocando	tocáis	tocabais	tocasteis	tocaréis	tocaríais	**toquéis**	tocarais	tocad (no **toquéis**)
tocado	tocan	tocaban	tocaron	tocarán	tocarían	**toquen**	tocaran	**toquen** Uds.

Guide to Vocabulary

Note on alphabetization

For purposes of alphabetization, **ch** and **ll** are not treated as separate letters, but **ñ** follows **n**. Therefore, in this glossary you will find that **año**, for example, appears after **anuncio**.

Abbreviations used in this glossary

adj.	adjective	*form.*	formal	*pl.*	plural
adv.	adverb	*indef.*	indefinite	*poss.*	possessive
art.	article	*interj.*	interjection	*prep.*	preposition
conj.	conjunction	*i.o.*	indirect object	*pron.*	pronoun
def.	definite	*m.*	masculine	*ref.*	reflexive
d.o.	direct object	*n.*	noun	*sing.*	singular
f.	feminine	*obj.*	object	*sub.*	subject
fam.	familiar	*p.p.*	past participle	*v.*	verb

Spanish-English

A

a *prep.* at; to 1
 ¿A qué hora...? At what time...? 1
 a bordo aboard 1
 a dieta on a diet 15
 a la derecha to the right 2
 a la izquierda to the left 2
 a la plancha grilled 8
 a la(s) + *time* at + *time* 1
 a menos que unless 13
 a menudo *adv.* often 10
 a nombre de in the name of 5
 a plazos in installments 14
 A sus órdenes. At your service. 11
 a tiempo *adv.* on time 10
 a veces *adv.* sometimes 10
 a ver let's see
¡Abajo! *adv.* Down! 15
abeja *f.* bee
abierto/a *adj.* open 5, 14
abogado/a *m., f.* lawyer
abrazar(se) *v.* to hug; to embrace (each other) 11
abrazo *m.* hug
abrigo *m.* coat 6
abril *m.* April 5
abrir *v.* to open 3
abuelo/a *m., f.* grandfather; grandmother 3
abuelos *pl.* grandparents 3
aburrido/a *adj.* bored; boring 5
aburrir *v.* to bore 7
aburrirse *v.* to get bored
acabar de (+ *inf.*) *v.* to have just done something 6
acampar *v.* to camp 5
accidente *m.* accident 10
acción *f.* action
 de acción action (genre)

aceite *m.* oil 8
aceptar: ¡Acepto casarme contigo! I'll marry you!
ácido/a *adj.* acid 13
acompañar *v.* to accompany 14
aconsejar *v.* to advise 12
acontecimiento *m.* event
acordarse (de) (o:ue) *v.* to remember 7
acostarse (o:ue) *v.* to go to bed 7
activo/a *adj.* active 15
actor *m.* actor
actriz *f.* actor
actualidades *f., pl.* news; current events
acuático/a *adj.* aquatic 4
adelgazar *v.* to lose weight; to slim down 15
además (de) *adv.* furthermore; besides 10
adicional *adj.* additional
adiós *m.* good-bye 1
adjetivo *m.* adjective
administración de empresas *f.* business administration 2
adolescencia *f.* adolescence 9
¿adónde? *adv.* where (to)? (destination) 2
aduana *f.* customs 5
aeróbico/a *adj.* aerobic 15
aeropuerto *m.* airport 5
afectado/a *adj.* affected 13
afeitarse *v.* to shave 7
aficionado/a *adj.* fan 4
afirmativo/a *adj.* affirmative
afuera *adv.* outside 5
afueras *f., pl.* suburbs; outskirts 12
agencia de viajes *f.* travel agency 5
agente de viajes *m., f.* travel agent 5
agosto *m.* August 5
agradable *adj.* pleasant 5

agua *f.* water 8
 agua mineral mineral water 8
aguantar *v.* to endure, to hold up 14
ahora *adv.* now 2
 ahora mismo right now 5
ahorrar *v.* to save (money) 14
ahorros *m.* savings 14
aire *m.* air 5
ajo *m.* garlic 8
al (*contraction of* **a** + **el**) 2
 al aire libre open-air 6
 al contado in cash 14
 (al) este (to the) east 14
 al fondo (de) at the end (of) 12
 al lado de beside 2
 (al) norte (to the) north 14
 (al) oeste (to the) west 14
 (al) sur (to the) south 14
alcoba *f.* bedroom 12
alcohol *m.* alcohol 15
alcohólico/a *adj.* alcoholic 15
alegrarse (de) *v.* to be happy 13
alegre *adj.* happy; joyful 5
alegría *f.* happiness 9
alemán, alemana *adj.* German 3
alérgico/a *adj.* allergic 10
alfombra *f.* carpet; rug 12
algo *pron.* something; anything 7
algodón *m.* cotton 6
alguien *pron.* someone; somebody; anyone 7
algún, alguno/a(s) *adj.* any; some 7
alimento *m.* food
 alimentación *f.* diet
aliviar *v.* to reduce 15
 aliviar el estrés/la tensión to reduce stress/tension 15
allá *adv.* over there 2
allí *adv.* there 2
 allí mismo right there 14
alma *f.* soul 9
almacén *m.* department store 6

almohada *f.* pillow 12
almorzar (o:ue) *v.* to have lunch 4
almuerzo *m.* lunch 4, 8
aló *interj.* hello (*on the telephone*) 11
alquilar *v.* to rent 12
alquiler *m.* rent (*payment*) 12
altar *m.* altar 9
altillo *m.* attic 12
alto/a *adj.* tall 3
aluminio *m.* aluminum 13
ama de casa *m., f.* housekeeper; caretaker 12
amable *adj.* nice; friendly 5
amarillo/a *adj.* yellow 6
amigo/a *m., f.* friend 3
amistad *f.* friendship 9
amor *m.* love 9
 amor a primera vista love at first sight 9
anaranjado/a *adj.* orange 6
ándale *interj.* come on 14
andar *v.* **en patineta** to skateboard 4
ángel *m.* angel 9
anillo *m.* ring
animal *m.* animal 13
aniversario (de bodas) *m.* (wedding) anniversary 9
anoche *adv.* last night 6
anteayer *adv.* the day before yesterday 6
antes *adv.* before 7
 antes (de) que *conj.* before 13
 antes de *prep.* before 7
antibiótico *m.* antibiotic 10
antipático/a *adj.* unpleasant 3
anunciar *v.* to announce; to advertise
anuncio *m.* advertisement
año *m.* year 5
 año pasado last year 6
apagar *v.* to turn off 11
aparato *m.* appliance
apartamento *m.* apartment 12
apellido *m.* last name 3
apenas *adv.* hardly; scarcely 10
aplaudir *v.* to applaud
apreciar *v.* to appreciate
aprender (a + inf.) *v.* to learn 3
apurarse *v.* to hurry; to rush 15
aquel, aquella *adj.* that; those (over there) 6
aquél, aquélla *pron.* that; those (over there) 6
aquello *neuter, pron.* that; that thing; that fact 6
aquellos/as *pl. adj.* those (over there) 6
aquéllos/as *pl. pron.* those (ones) (over there) 6
aquí *adv.* here 1
 Aquí está(n)... Here is/are... 5
 aquí mismo right here 11
árbol *m.* tree 13

archivo *m.* file 11
arete *m.* earing 6
Argentina *f.* Argentina 1
argentino/a *adj.* Argentine 3
armario *m.* closet 12
arqueología *f.* archaeology 2
arqueólogo/a *m., f.* archaeologist 2
arquitecto/a *m., f.* architect
arrancar *v.* to start (*a car*) 11
arreglar *v.* to fix; to arrange 11; to neaten; to straighten up 12
arreglarse *v.* to get ready 7; to fix oneself (*clothes, hair, etc. to go out*) 7
arriba: hasta arriba to the top 15
arroba *f.* @ symbol 11
arroz *m.* rice 8
arte *m.* art 2
artes *f., pl.* arts
artesanía *f.* craftsmanship; crafts
artículo *m.* article
artista *m., f.* artist 3
artístico/a *adj.* artistic
arveja *m.* pea 8
asado/a *adj.* roast 8
ascenso *m.* promotion
ascensor *m.* elevator 5
así *adv.* like this; so (*in such a way*) 10
asistir (a) *v.* to attend 3
aspiradora *f.* vacuum cleaner 12
aspirante *m., f.* candidate; applicant
aspirina *f.* aspirin 10
atún *m.* tuna 8
aumentar *v.* to grow; to get bigger 13
aumentar *v.* **de peso** to gain weight 15
aumento *m.* increase
 aumento de sueldo pay raise
aunque although
autobús *m.* bus 1
automático/a *adj.* automatic
auto(móvil) *m.* auto(mobile) 5
autopista *f.* highway 11
ave *f.* bird 13
avenida *f.* avenue
aventura *f.* adventure
 de aventura adventure (genre)
avergonzado/a *adj.* embarrassed 5
avión *m.* airplane 5
¡Ay! *interj.* Oh!
 ¡Ay, qué dolor! Oh, what pain!
ayer *adv.* yesterday 6
ayudar(se) *v.* to help (each other) 11, 12
azúcar *m.* sugar 8
azul *adj. m., f.* blue 6

B

bailar *v.* to dance 2
bailarín/bailarina *m., f.* dancer
baile *m.* dance
bajar(se) de *v.* to get off of/out of (a vehicle) 11
bajo/a *adj.* short (*in height*) 3
bajo control under control 7
balcón *m.* balcony 12
balde *m.* bucket 5
ballena *f.* whale 13
baloncesto *m.* basketball 4
banana *f.* banana 8
banco *m.* bank 14
banda *f.* band
bandera *f.* flag
bañarse *v.* to bathe; to take a bath 7
baño *m.* bathroom 7
barato/a *adj.* cheap 6
barco *m.* boat 5
barrer *v.* to sweep 12
 barrer el suelo *v.* to sweep the floor 12
barrio *m.* neighborhood 12
bastante *adv.* enough; rather 10; pretty 13
basura *f.* trash 12
baúl *m.* trunk 11
beber *v.* to drink 3
bebida *f.* drink 8
 bebida alcohólica *f.* alcoholic beverage 15
béisbol *m.* baseball 4
bellas artes *f., pl.* fine arts
belleza *f.* beauty 14
beneficio *m.* benefit
besar(se) *v.* to kiss (each other) 11
beso *m.* kiss 9
biblioteca *f.* library 2
bicicleta *f.* bicycle 4
bien *adj.* well 1
bienestar *m.* well-being 15
bienvenido(s)/a(s) *adj.* welcome 12
billete *m.* paper money; ticket
billón *m.* trillion
biología *f.* biology 2
bisabuelo/a *m., f.* great-grand-father/great-grandmother 3
bistec *m.* steak 8
bizcocho *m.* biscuit
blanco/a *adj.* white 6
blog *m.* blog 11
(blue)jeans *m., pl.* jeans 6
blusa *f.* blouse 6
boca *f.* mouth 10
boda *f.* wedding 9
boleto *m.* ticket 2
bolsa *f.* purse, bag 6
bombero/a *m., f.* firefighter
bonito/a *adj.* pretty 3
borrador *m.* eraser 2
borrar *v.* to erase 11

bosque *m.* forest 13
 bosque tropical tropical forest; rainforest 13
bota *f.* boot 6
botella *f.* bottle 9
 botella de vino bottle of wine 9
botones *m., f. sing.* bellhop 5
brazo *m.* arm 10
brindar *v.* to toast (*drink*) 9
bucear *v.* to scuba dive 4
bueno *adv.* well
buen, bueno/a *adj.* good 3, 6
 buena forma good shape (*physical*) 15
 Buena idea. Good idea.
 Buenas noches. Good evening; Good night. 1
 Buenas tardes. Good afternoon. 1
 buenísimo/a extremely good
 Bueno. Hello. (*on telephone*) 11
 Buenos días. Good morning. 1
bulevar *m.* boulevard
buscar *v.* to look for 2
buzón *m.* mailbox 14

C

caballero *m.* gentleman, sir 8
caballo *m.* horse 5
cabe: no cabe duda de there's no doubt 13
cabeza *f.* head 10
cada *adj. m., f.* each 6
caerse *v.* to fall (down) 10
café *m.* café 4; *adj. m., f.* brown 6; *m.* coffee 8
cafeína *f.* caffeine 14
cafetera *f.* coffee maker 12
cafetería *f.* cafeteria 2
caído/a *p.p.* fallen 14
caja *f.* cash register 6
cajero/a *m., f.* cashier 14
 cajero automático *m.* ATM 14
calavera de azúcar *f.* skull made out of sugar 9
calcetín (calcetines) *m.* sock(s) 6
calculadora *f.* calculator 2
caldo *m.* soup
calentamiento global *m.* global warming 13
calentarse (e:ie) *v.* to warm up 15
calidad *f.* quality 6
calle *f.* street 11
calor *m.* heat 4
caloría *f.* calorie 15
calzar *v.* to take size... shoes 6
cama *f.* bed 5
cámara digital *f.* digital camera 11
cámara de video *f.* video camera 11
camarero/a *m., f.* waiter/waitress 8

camarón *m.* shrimp 8
cambiar (de) *v.* to change 9
cambio: de cambio in change 2
cambio *m.* **climático** climate change 13
cambio *m.* **de moneda** currency exchange
caminar *v.* to walk 2
camino *m.* road
camión *m.* truck; bus
camisa *f.* shirt 6
camiseta *f.* t-shirt 6
campo *m.* countryside 5
canadiense *adj.* Canadian 3
canal *m.* (TV) channel 11
canción *f.* song
candidato/a *m., f.* candidate
canela *f.* cinnamon 10
cansado/a *adj.* tired 5
cantante *m., f.* singer
cantar *v.* to sing 2
capital *f.* capital city 1
capó *m.* hood 11
cara *f.* face 7
caramelo *m.* caramel 9
carne *f.* meat 8
 carne de res *f.* beef 8
carnicería *f.* butcher shop 14
caro/a *adj.* expensive 6
carpintero/a *m., f.* carpenter
carrera *f.* career
carretera *f.* highway 11
carro *m.* car; automobile 11
carta *f.* letter 4; (playing) card 5
cartel *m.* poster 12
cartera *f.* wallet 4, 6
cartero *m.* mail carrier 14
casa *f.* house; home 2
casado/a *adj.* married 9
casarse (con) *v.* to get married (to) 9
casi *adv.* almost 10
catorce *adj.* fourteen 1
cazar *v.* to hunt 13
cebolla *f.* onion 8
cederrón *m.* CD-ROM 11
celebrar *v.* to celebrate 9
cementerio *m.* cemetery 9
cena *f.* dinner 8
cenar *v.* to have dinner 2
centro *m.* downtown 4
 centro comercial shopping mall 6
cepillarse los dientes/el pelo *v.* to brush one's teeth/one's hair 7
cerámica *f.* pottery
cerca de *prep.* near 2
cerdo *m.* pork 8
cereales *m., pl.* cereal; grains 8
cero *m.* zero 1
cerrado/a *adj.* closed 5, 14
cerrar (e:ie) *v.* to close 4
cerveza *f.* beer 8
césped *m.* grass
ceviche *m.* marinated fish dish 8
 ceviche de camarón *m.* lemon-marinated shrimp 8

chaleco *m.* vest
champán *m.* champagne 9
champiñón *m.* mushroom 8
champú *m.* shampoo 7
chaqueta *f.* jacket 6
chau *fam. interj.* bye 1
cheque *m.* (bank) check 14
 cheque (de viajero) *m.* (traveler's) check 14
chévere *adj., fam.* terrific
chico/a *m., f.* boy/girl 1
chino/a *adj.* Chinese 3
chocar (con) *v.* to run into
chocolate *m.* chocolate 9
choque *m.* collision
chuleta *f.* chop (*food*) 8
 chuleta de cerdo *f.* pork chop 8
cibercafé *m.* cybercafé
ciclismo *m.* cycling 4
cielo *m.* sky 13
cien(to) one hundred 2
ciencia *f.* science 2
 ciencias ambientales environmental sciences 2
 de ciencia ficción *f.* science fiction (genre)
científico/a *m., f.* scientist
cierto *m.* certain 13
 es cierto it's certain 13
 no es cierto it's not certain 13
cima *f.* top, peak 15
cinco five 1
cincuenta fifty 2
cine *m.* movie theater 4
cinta *f.* (audio)tape
cinta caminadora *f.* treadmill 15
cinturón *m.* belt 6
circulación *f.* traffic 11
cita *f.* date; appointment 9
ciudad *f.* city 4
ciudadano/a *m., f.* citizen
Claro (que sí). *fam.* Of course.
clase *f.* class 2
 clase de ejercicios aeróbicos *f.* aerobics class 15
clásico/a *adj.* classical
cliente/a *m., f.* customer 6
clínica *f.* clinic 10
cobrar *v.* to cash (a check) 14
coche *m.* car; automobile 11
cocina *f.* kitchen; stove 9, 12
cocinar *v.* to cook 12
cocinero/a *m., f.* cook, chef
cofre *m.* hood 14
cola *f.* line 14
colesterol *m.* cholesterol 15
color *m.* color 6
comedia *f.* comedy; play
comedor *m.* dining room 12
comenzar (e:ie) *v.* to begin 4
comer *v.* to eat 3
comercial *adj.* commercial; business-related
comida *f.* food; meal 4, 8

como like; as 8
¿cómo? what?; how? 1
 ¿Cómo es...? What's... like? 3
 ¿Cómo está usted? *form.*
 How are you? 1
 ¿Cómo estás? *fam.* How are
 you? 1
 ¿Cómo les fue...? *pl.* How
 did ... go for you? 15
 ¿Cómo se llama usted?
 (form.) What's your name? 1
 ¿Cómo te llamas? *fam.*
 What's your name? 1
cómoda *f.* chest of drawers 12
cómodo/a *adj.* comfortable 5
compañero/a de clase *m., f.*
 classmate 2
compañero/a de cuarto *m., f.*
 roommate 2
compañía *f.* company; firm
compartir *v.* to share 3
completamente *adv.* completely 5
compositor(a) *m., f.* composer
comprar *v.* to buy 2
compras *f., pl.* purchases 5
 ir de compras go shopping 5
comprender *v.* to understand 3
comprobar *v.* to check
comprometerse (con) *v.* to get
 engaged (to) 9
computación *f.* computer science 2
computadora *f.* computer 1
computadora portátil *f.* portable
 computer; laptop 11
comunicación *f.* communication
comunicarse (con) *v.* to
 communicate (with)
comunidad *f.* community 1
con *prep.* with 2
 Con él/ella habla. Speaking./
 This is he/she. (*on telephone*) 11
 con frecuencia *adv.* frequently 10
 Con permiso. Pardon me;
 Excuse me. 1
 con tal (de) que provided
 (that) 13
concierto *m.* concert
concordar *v.* to agree
concurso *m.* game show; contest
conducir *v.* to drive 6, 11
conductor(a) *m., f.* driver 1
conexión *f.* **inalámbrica** wireless
 (connection) 11
confirmar *v.* to confirm 5
confirmar *v.* **una reservación** *f.*
 to confirm a reservation 5
confundido/a *adj.* confused 5
congelador *m.* freezer 12
congestionado/a *adj.* congested;
 stuffed-up 10
conmigo *pron.* with me 4, 9
conocer *v.* to know; to be
 acquainted with 6
conocido *adj.; p.p.* known
conseguir (e:i) *v.* to get; to obtain 4

consejero/a *m., f.* counselor;
 advisor
consejo *m.* advice
conservación *f.* conservation 13
conservar *v.* to conserve 13
construir *v.* to build
consultorio *m.* doctor's office 10
consumir *v.* to consume 15
contabilidad *f.* accounting 2
contador(a) *m., f.* accountant
contaminación *f.* pollution 13
 contaminación del aire/del
 agua air/water pollution 13
contaminado/a *adj.* polluted 13
contaminar *v.* to pollute 13
contar (o:ue) *v.* to count; to tell 4
contar (con) *v.* to count (on) 12
contento/a *adj.* happy; content 5
contestadora *f.* answering
 machine 11
contestar *v.* to answer 2
contigo *fam. pron.* with you 5, 9
contratar *v.* to hire
control *m.* control 7
 control remoto remote
 control 11
controlar *v.* to control 13
conversación *f.* conversation 1
conversar *v.* to converse, to chat 2
copa *f.* wineglass; goblet 12
corazón *m.* heart 10
corbata *f.* tie 6
corredor(a) *m., f.* **de bolsa**
 stockbroker
correo *m.* mail; post office 14
 correo electrónico *m.*
 e-mail 4
 correo de voz *m.* voice mail 11
correr *v.* to run 3
cortesía *f.* courtesy
cortinas *f., pl.* curtains 12
corto/a *adj.* short (*in length*) 6
cosa *f.* thing 1
Costa Rica *f.* Costa Rica 1
costar (o:ue) *f.* to cost 6
costarricense *adj.* Costa Rican 3
cráter *m.* crater 13
creer *v.* to believe 13
 creer (en) *v.* to believe (in) 3
 no creer (en) *v.* not to
 believe (in) 13
creído/a *adj., p.p.* believed 14
crema de afeitar *f.* shaving
 cream 5, 7
crimen *m.* crime; murder
cruzar *v.* to cross 14
cuaderno *m.* notebook 1
cuadra *f.* (city) block 14
¿cuál(es)? which?; which one(s)? 2
 ¿Cuál es la fecha de hoy?
 What is today's date? 5
cuadro *m.* picture 12
cuadros *m., pl.* plaid 6
cuando when 7; 13
¿cuándo? when? 2
¿cuánto(s)/a(s)? how much/how
 many? 1

¿Cuánto cuesta...? How
 much does... cost? 6
¿Cuántos años tienes? How
 old are you? 3
cuarenta forty 2
cuarto de baño *m.* bathroom 7
cuarto *m.* room 2; 7
cuarto/a *adj.* fourth 5
 menos cuarto quarter to (time)
 y cuarto quarter after (time) 1
cuatro four 1
cuatrocientos/as four hundred 2
Cuba *f.* Cuba 1
cubano/a *adj.* Cuban 3
cubiertos *m., pl.* silverware
cubierto/a *p.p.* covered
cubrir *v.* to cover
cuchara *f.* (table or large) spoon 12
cuchillo *m.* knife 12
cuello *m.* neck 10
cuenta *f.* bill 8; account 14
 cuenta corriente *f.* checking
 account 14
 cuenta de ahorros *f.* savings
 account 14
cuento *m.* short story
cuerpo *m.* body 10
cuidado *m.* care 3
cuidar *v.* to take care of 13
 ¡Cuídense! Take care! 14
cultura *f.* culture 2
cumpleaños *m., sing.* birthday 9
cumplir años *v.* to have a
 birthday 9
cuñado/a *m., f.* brother-in-law;
 sister-in-law 3
currículum *m.* résumé
curso *m.* course 2

D

danza *f.* dance
dañar *v.* to damage; to break
 down 10
dar *v.* to give 6, 9
 dar un consejo *v.* to give advice
 darse con *v.* to bump into; to
 run into (something) 10
 darse prisa *v.* to hurry; to rush
 15
de *prep.* of; from 1
 ¿De dónde eres? *fam.*
 Where are you from? 1
 ¿De dónde es usted? *form.*
 Where are you from? 1
 ¿De parte de quién? Who is
 speaking/calling? (*on telephone*)
 11
 ¿de quién...? whose...? (*sing.*) 1
 ¿de quiénes...? whose...? (*pl.*) 1
 de algodón (made) of cotton 6
 de aluminio (made) of
 aluminum 13
 de buen humor in a good
 mood 5

de compras shopping 5
de cuadros plaid 6
de excursión hiking 4
de hecho in fact
de ida y vuelta roundtrip 5
de la mañana in the morning; A.M. 1
de la noche in the evening; at night; P.M. 1
de la tarde in the afternoon; in the early evening; P.M. 1
de lana (made) of wool 6
de lunares polka-dotted 6
de mal humor in a bad mood 5
de mi vida of my life 15
de moda in fashion 6
De nada. You're welcome. 1
de niño/a as a child 10
de parte de on behalf of 11
de plástico (made) of plastic 13
de rayas striped 6
de repente suddenly 6
de seda (made) of silk 6
de vaqueros western (genre)
de vez en cuando from time to time 10
de vidrio (made) of glass 13
debajo de *prep.* below; under 2
deber (+ *inf.*) *v.* should; must; ought to 3
 Debe ser... It must be... 6
deber *m.* responsibility; obligation
debido a due to (the fact that)
débil *adj.* weak 15
decidido/a *adj.* decided 14
decidir (+ *inf.*) *v.* to decide 3
décimo/a *adj.* tenth 5
decir (e:i) *v.* (que) to say (that); to tell (that) 4, 9
 decir la respuesta to say the answer 4
 decir la verdad to tell the truth 4
 decir mentiras to tell lies 4
declarar *v.* to declare; to say
dedo *m.* finger 10
dedo del pie *m.* toe 10
deforestación *f.* deforestation 13
dejar *v.* to let 12; to quit; to leave behind
 dejar de (+ *inf.*) *v.* to stop (*doing something*) 13
 dejar una propina *v.* to leave a tip 9
del (*contraction of* de + el) of the; from the
delante de *prep.* in front of 2
delgado/a *adj.* thin; slender 3
delicioso/a *adj.* delicious 8
demás *adj.* the rest
demasiado *adj., adv.* too much 6
dentista *m., f.* dentist 10
dentro de (diez años) within (ten years); inside
dependiente/a *m., f.* clerk 6

deporte *m.* sport 4
deportista *m.* sports person
deportivo/a *adj.* sports-related 4
depositar *v.* to deposit 14
derecha *f.* right 2
derecho *adj.* straight (ahead) 14
 a la derecha de to the right of 2
derechos *m., pl.* rights
desarrollar *v.* to develop 13
desastre (natural) *m.* (natural) disaster
desayunar *v.* to have breakfast 2
desayuno *m.* breakfast 8
descafeinado/a *adj.* decaffeinated 15
descansar *v.* to rest 2
descargar *v.* to download 11
descompuesto/a *adj.* not working; out of order 11
describir *v.* to describe 3
descrito/a *p.p.* described 14
descubierto/a *p.p.* discovered 14
descubrir *v.* to discover 13
desde *prep.* from 6
desear *v.* to wish; to desire 2
desempleo *m.* unemployment
desierto *m.* desert 13
desigualdad *f.* inequality
desordenado/a *adj.* disorderly 5
despacio *adv.* slowly 10
despedida *f.* farewell; good-bye
despedir (e:i) *v.* to fire
despedirse (de) (e:i) *v.* to say goodbye (to) 7
despejado/a *adj.* clear (*weather*)
despertador *m.* alarm clock 7
despertarse (e:ie) *v.* to wake up 7
después *adv.* afterwards; then 7
 después de after 7
 después de que *conj.* after 13
destruir *v.* to destroy 13
detrás de *prep.* behind 2
día *m.* day 1
 día de fiesta holiday 9
diario *m.* diary 1; newspaper
 diario/a *adj.* daily 7
dibujar *v.* to draw 2
dibujo *m.* drawing
 dibujos animados *m., pl.* cartoons
diccionario *m.* dictionary 1
dicho/a *p.p.* said 14
diciembre *m.* December 5
dictadura *f.* dictatorship
diecinueve nineteen 1
dieciocho eighteen 1
dieciséis sixteen 1
diecisiete seventeen 1
diente *m.* tooth 7
dieta *f.* diet 15
 comer una dieta equilibrada to eat a balanced diet 15
diez ten 1
difícil *adj.* difficult; hard 3
Diga. Hello. (*on telephone*) 11
diligencia *f.* errand 14

dinero *m.* money 6
dirección *f.* address 14
 dirección electrónica *f.* e-mail address 11
director(a) *m., f.* director; (*musical*) conductor
dirigir *v.* to direct
disco compacto compact disc (CD) 11
discriminación *f.* discrimination
discurso *m.* speech
diseñador(a) *m., f.* designer
diseño *m.* design
disfraz *m.* costume
disfrutar (de) *v.* to enjoy; to reap the benefits (of) 15
disminuir *v.* to reduce
diversión *f.* fun activity; entertainment; recreation 4
divertido/a *adj.* fun 7
divertirse (e:ie) *v.* to have fun 9
divorciado/a *adj.* divorced 9
divorciarse (de) *v.* to get divorced (from) 9
divorcio *m.* divorce 9
doblar *v.* to turn 14
doble *adj.* double
doce twelve 1
doctor(a) *m., f.* doctor 3; 10
documental *m.* documentary
documentos de viaje *m., pl.* travel documents
doler (o:ue) *v.* to hurt 10
dolor *m.* ache; pain 10
 dolor de cabeza *m.* headache 10
doméstico/a *adj.* domestic 12
domingo *m.* Sunday 2
don *m.* Mr.; sir 1
doña *f.* Mrs.; ma'am 1
donde *prep.* where
 ¿Dónde está...? Where is...? 2
 ¿dónde? where? 1
dormir (o:ue) *v.* to sleep 4
dormirse (o:ue) *v.* to go to sleep; to fall asleep 7
dormitorio *m.* bedroom 12
dos two 1
 dos veces *f.* twice; two times 6
doscientos/as two hundred 2
drama *m.* drama; play
dramático/a *adj.* dramatic
dramaturgo/a *m., f.* playwright
droga *f.* drug 15
drogadicto/a *adj.* drug addict 15
ducha *f.* shower 7
ducharse *v.* to shower; to take a shower 7
duda *f.* doubt 13
dudar *v.* to doubt 13
 no dudar *v.* not to doubt 13
dueño/a *m., f.* owner; landlord 8
dulces *m., pl.* sweets; candy 9
durante *prep.* during 7
durar *v.* to last

E

e *conj.* (*used instead of* **y** *before words beginning with* **i** *and* **hi**) and **4**
echar *v.* to throw
 echar (una carta) al buzón *v.* to put (a letter) in the mailbox **14**; to mail **14**
ecología *f.* ecology **13**
ecologista *m., f.* ecologist **13**; *adj.* ecological **13**
economía *f.* economics **2**
ecoturismo *m.* ecotourism **13**
Ecuador *m.* Ecuador **1**
ecuatoriano/a *adj.* Ecuadorian **3**
edad *f.* age **9**
edificio *m.* building **12**
 edificio de apartamentos apartment building **12**
(en) efectivo *m.* cash **6**
ejercer *v.* to practice/exercise (a degree/profession)
ejercicio *m.* exercise **15**
 ejercicios aeróbicos aerobic exercises **15**
 ejercicios de estiramiento stretching exercises **15**
ejército *m.* army
el *m., sing., def. art.* the **1**
él *sub. pron.* he **1**; *adj. pron.* him
elecciones *f., pl.* election
electricista *m., f.* electrician
electrodoméstico *m.* electric appliance **12**
elegante *adj. m., f.* elegant **6**
elegir (e:i) *v.* to elect
ella *sub. pron.* she **1**; *obj. pron.* her
ellos/as *sub. pron.* they **1**; them **1**
embarazada *adj.* pregnant **10**
emergencia *f.* emergency **10**
emitir *v.* to broadcast
emocionante *adj. m., f.* exciting
empezar (e:ie) *v.* to begin **4**
empleado/a *m., f.* employee **5**
empleo *m.* job; employment
empresa *f.* company; firm
en *prep.* in; on; at **2**
 en casa at home **7**
 en caso (de) que in case (that) **13**
 en cuanto as soon as **13**
 en efectivo in cash **14**
 en exceso in excess; too much **15**
 en línea in-line **4**
 ¡En marcha! Let's get going! **15**
 en mi nombre in my name
 en punto on the dot; exactly; sharp (*time*) **1**
 en qué in what; how **2**
 ¿En qué puedo servirles? How can I help you? **5**
 en vivo live **7**
enamorado/a (de) *adj.* in love (with) **5**
enamorarse (de) *v.* to fall in love (with) **9**

encantado/a *adj.* delighted; pleased to meet you **1**
encantar *v.* to like very much; to love (*inanimate objects*) **7**
 ¡Me encantó! I loved it! **15**
encima de *prep.* on top of **2**
encontrar (o:ue) *v.* to find **4**
encontrar(se) (o:ue) *v.* to meet (each other); to run into (each other) **11**
 encontrarse con to meet up with **7**
encuesta *f.* poll; survey
energía *f.* energy **13**
 energía nuclear nuclear energy **13**
 energía solar solar energy **13**
enero *m.* January **5**
enfermarse *v.* to get sick **10**
enfermedad *f.* illness **10**
enfermero/a *m., f.* nurse **10**
enfermo/a *adj.* sick **10**
enfrente de *adv.* opposite; facing **14**
engordar *v.* to gain weight **15**
enojado/a *adj.* mad; angry **5**
enojarse (con) *v.* to get angry (with) **7**
ensalada *f.* salad **8**
ensayo *m.* essay **3**
enseguida *adv.* right away
enseñar *v.* to teach **2**
ensuciar *v.* to get (something) dirty **12**
entender (e:ie) *v.* to understand **4**
enterarse *v.* to find out
entonces *adv.* so, then **5, 7**
entrada *f.* entrance **12**; ticket
entre *prep.* between; among **2**
entregar *v.* to hand in **11**
entremeses *m., pl.* hors d'oeuvres; appetizers **8**
entrenador(a) *m., f.* trainer **15**
entrenarse *v.* to practice; to train **15**
entrevista *f.* interview
entrevistador(a) *m., f.* interviewer
entrevistar *v.* to interview
envase *m.* container **13**
enviar *v.* to send; to mail **14**
equilibrado/a *adj.* balanced **15**
equipado/a *adj.* equipped **15**
equipaje *m.* luggage **5**
equipo *m.* team **4**
equivocado/a *adj.* wrong **5**
eres *fam.* you are **1**
es he/she/it is **1**
 Es bueno que... It's good that... **12**
 Es de... He/She is from... **1**
 es extraño it's strange **13**
 es igual it's the same **5**
 Es importante que... It's important that... **12**
 es imposible it's impossible **13**
 es improbable it's improbable **13**
 Es malo que... It's bad that... **12**

 Es mejor que... It's better that... **12**
 Es necesario que... It's necessary that... **12**
 es obvio it's obvious **13**
 es ridículo it's ridiculous **13**
 es seguro it's sure **13**
 es terrible it's terrible **13**
 es triste it's sad **13**
 Es urgente que... It's urgent that... **12**
 Es la una. It's one o'clock. **1**
 es una lástima it's a shame **13**
 es verdad it's true **13**
esa(s) *f., adj.* that; those **6**
ésa(s) *f., pron.* that (one); those (ones) **6**
escalar *v.* to climb **4**
 escalar montañas *v.* to climb mountains **4**
escalera *f.* stairs; stairway **12**
escalón *m.* step **15**
escanear *v.* to scan **11**
escoger *v.* to choose **8**
escribir *v.* to write **3**
 escribir un mensaje electrónico to write an e-mail message **4**
 escribir una postal to write a postcard **4**
 escribir una carta to write a letter **4**
escrito/a *p.p.* written **14**
escritor(a) *m., f.* writer
escritorio *m.* desk **2**
escuchar *v.* to listen to
 escuchar la radio to listen (to) the radio **2**
 escuchar música to listen (to) music **2**
escuela *f.* school **1**
esculpir *v.* to sculpt
escultor(a) *m., f.* sculptor
escultura *f.* sculpture
ese *m., sing., adj.* that **6**
ése *m., sing., pron.* that one **6**
eso *neuter, pron.* that; that thing **6**
esos *m., pl., adj.* those **6**
ésos *m., pl., pron.* those (ones) **6**
España *f.* Spain **1**
español *m.* Spanish (*language*) **2**
español(a) *adj. m., f.* Spanish **3**
espárragos *m., pl.* asparagus **8**
especialidad: las especialidades del día today's specials **8**
especialización *f.* major **2**
espectacular *adj.* spectacular **15**
espectáculo *m.* show
espejo *m.* mirror **7**
esperar *v.* to hope; to wish **13**
 esperar (+ infin.) *v.* to wait (for); to hope **2**
esposo/a *m., f.* husband/wife; spouse **3**
esquí (acuático) *m.* (water) skiing **4**

esquiar *v.* to ski 4
esquina *m.* corner 14
está he/she/it is, you are
 Está (muy) despejado. It's (very) clear. (*weather*)
 Está lloviendo. It's raining. 5
 Está nevando. It's snowing. 5
 Está (muy) nublado. It's (very) cloudy. (*weather*) 5
 Está bien. That's fine. 11
esta(s) *f., adj.* this; these 6
 esta noche tonight 4
ésta(s) *f., pron.* this (one); these (ones) 6
 Ésta es... *f.* This is... (*introducing someone*) 1
establecer *v.* to establish
estación *f.* station; season 5
 estación de autobuses bus station 5
 estación del metro subway station 5
 estación de tren train station 5
estacionamiento *m.* parking lot 14
estacionar *v.* to park 11
estadio *m.* stadium 2
estado civil *m.* marital status 9
Estados Unidos *m., pl.* (EE.UU.; E.U.) United States 1
estadounidense *adj. m., f.* from the United States 3
estampado/a *adj.* print
estampilla *f.* stamp 14
estante *m.* bookcase; bookshelves 12
estar *v.* to be 2
 estar a (veinte kilómetros) de aquí to be (20 kilometers) from here 11
 estar a dieta to be on a diet 15
 estar aburrido/a to be bored 5
 estar afectado/a (por) to be affected (by) 13
 estar bajo control to be under control 7
 estar cansado/a to be tired 5
 estar contaminado/a to be polluted 13
 estar de acuerdo to agree
 Estoy de acuerdo. I agree.
 No estoy de acuerdo. I don't agree.
 estar de moda to be in fashion 6
 estar de vacaciones *f., pl.* to be on vacation 5
 estar en buena forma to be in good shape 15
 estar enfermo/a to be sick 10
 estar harto/a de... to be sick of...
 estar listo/a to be ready 15
 estar perdido/a to be lost 14

estar roto/a to be broken 10
estar seguro/a to be sure 5
estar torcido/a to be twisted; to be sprained 10
 No está nada mal. It's not bad at all. 5
estatua *f.* statue
este *m.* east 14
este *m., sing., adj.* this 6
éste *m., sing., pron.* this (one) 6
 Éste es... *m.* This is... (*introducing someone*) 1
estéreo *m.* stereo 11
estilo *m.* style
estiramiento *m.* stretching 15
esto *neuter pron.* this; this thing 6
estómago *m.* stomach 10
estornudar *v.* to sneeze 10
estos *m., pl., adj.* these 6
éstos *m., pl., pron.* these (ones) 6
estrella *f.* star 13
 estrella de cine *m., f.* movie star
estrés *m.* stress 15
estudiante *m., f.* student 1, 2
estudiantil *adj. m., f.* student 2
estudiar *v.* to study 2
estufa *f.* stove 12
estupendo/a *adj.* stupendous 5
etapa *f.* stage 9
evitar *v.* to avoid 13
examen *m.* test; exam 2
 examen médico physical exam 10
excelente *adj. m., f.* excellent 5
exceso *m.* excess; too much 15
excursión *f.* hike; tour; excursion 4
excursionista *m., f.* hiker
éxito *m.* success
experiencia *f.* experience
explicar *v.* to explain 2
explorar *v.* to explore
expresión *f.* expression
extinción *f.* extinction 13
extranjero/a *adj.* foreign
extrañar *v.* to miss
extraño/a *adj.* strange 13

F

fábrica *f.* factory 13
fabuloso/a *adj* fabulous 5
fácil *adj.* easy 3
falda *f.* skirt 6
faltar *v.* to lack; to need 7
familia *f.* family 3
famoso/a *adj.* famous
farmacia *f.* pharmacy 10
fascinar *v.* to fascinate 7
favorito/a *adj.* favorite 4
fax *m.* fax (machine) 11
febrero *m.* February 5
fecha *f.* date 5
feliz *adj.* happy 5

¡Felicidades! Congratulations! 9
¡Felicitaciones! Congratulations! 9
¡Feliz cumpleaños! Happy birthday! 9
fenomenal *adj.* great, phenomenal 5
feo/a *adj.* ugly 3
festival *m.* festival
fiebre *f.* fever 10
fiesta *f.* party 9
fijo/a *adj.* fixed, set 6
fin *m.* end 4
 fin de semana weekend 4
finalmente *adv.* finally 15
firmar *v.* to sign (*a document*) 14
física *f.* physics 2
flan (de caramelo) *m.* baked (caramel) custard 9
flexible *adj.* flexible 15
flor *f.* flower 13
folclórico/a *adj.* folk; folkloric
folleto *m.* brochure
fondo *m.* end 12
forma *f.* shape 15
formulario *m.* form 14
foto(grafía) *f.* photograph 1
francés, francesa *adj. m., f.* French 3
frecuentemente *adv.* frequently 10
frenos *m., pl.* brakes
frente (frío) *m.* (cold) front 5
fresco/a *adj.* cool 5
frijoles *m., pl.* beans 8
frío/a *adj.* cold 5
frito/a *adj.* fried 8
fruta *f.* fruit 8
frutería *f.* fruit store 14
frutilla *f.* strawberry 8
fuera *adv.* outside
fuerte *adj. m., f.* strong 15
fumar *v.* to smoke 15
 (no) fumar *v.* (not) to smoke 15
funcionar *v.* to work 11; to function
fútbol *m.* soccer 4
fútbol americano *m.* football 4
futuro/a *adj.* future
 en el futuro in the future

G

gafas (de sol) *f., pl.* (sun)glasses 6
gafas (oscuras) *f., pl.* (sun)glasses
galleta *f.* cookie 9
ganar *v.* to win 4; to earn (money)
ganga *f.* bargain 6
garaje *m.* garage; (mechanic's) repair shop 11; garage (*in a house*) 12
garganta *f.* throat 10
gasolina *f.* gasoline 11
gasolinera *f.* gas station 11
gastar *v.* to spend (*money*) 6
gato *m.* cat 13

gemelo/a *m., f.* twin 3
genial *adj.* great
gente *f.* people 3
geografía *f.* geography 2
gerente *m., f.* manager 8
gimnasio *m.* gymnasium 4
gobierno *m.* government 13
golf *m.* golf 4
gordo/a *adj.* fat 3
grabar *v.* to record 11
gracias *f., pl.* thank you; thanks 1
 Gracias por invitarme. Thanks for having me. 9
graduarse (de/en) *v.* to graduate (from/in) 9
gran, grande *adj.* big; large 3
grasa *f.* fat 15
gratis *adj. m., f.* free of charge 14
grave *adj.* grave; serious 10
gravísimo/a *adj.* extremely serious 13
grillo *m.* cricket
gripe *f.* flu 10
gris *adj. m., f.* gray 6
gritar *v.* to scream, to shout 7
grito *m.* scream 5
guantes *m., pl.* gloves 6
guapo/a *adj.* handsome; good-looking 3
guardar *v.* to save (on a computer) 11
guerra *f.* war
guía *m., f.* guide
gustar *v.* to be pleasing to; to like 2
 Me gustaría... I would like...
gusto *m.* pleasure 1
 El gusto es mío. The pleasure is mine. 1
 Gusto de verlo/la. *(form.)* It's nice to see you.
 Gusto de verte. *(fam.)* It's nice to see you.
 Mucho gusto. Pleased to meet you. 1
 ¡Qué gusto verlo/la! *(form.)* How nice to see you!
 ¡Qué gusto verte! *(fam.)* How nice to see you!

H

haber *(auxiliar) v.* to have (done something) 15
 Ha sido un placer. It's been a pleasure. 15
habitación *f.* room 5
 habitación doble double room 5
 habitación individual single room 5
hablar *v.* to talk; to speak 2
hacer *v.* to do; to make 4
 Hace buen tiempo. The weather is good. 5
 Hace (mucho) calor. It's (very) hot. *(weather)* 5

Hace fresco. It's cool. *(weather)* 5
Hace (mucho) frío. It's (very) cold. *(weather)* 5
Hace mal tiempo. The weather is bad. 5
Hace (mucho) sol. It's (very) sunny. *(weather)* 5
Hace (mucho) viento. It's (very) windy. *(weather)* 5
hacer cola to stand in line 14
hacer diligencias to run errands 14
hacer ejercicio to exercise 15
hacer ejercicios aeróbicos to do aerobics 15
hacer ejercicios de estiramiento to do stretching exercises 15
hacer el papel (de) to play the role (of)
hacer gimnasia to work out 15
hacer juego (con) to match (with) 6
hacer la cama to make the bed 12
hacer las maletas to pack (one's) suitcases 5
hacer quehaceres domésticos to do household chores 12
hacer (wind)surf to (wind)surf 5
hacer turismo to go sightseeing
hacer un viaje to take a trip 5
¿Me harías el honor de casarte conmigo? Would you do me the honor of marrying me?
hacia *prep.* toward 14
hambre *f.* hunger 3
hamburguesa *f.* hamburger 8
hasta *prep.* until 6; toward
 Hasta la vista. See you later. 1
 Hasta luego. See you later. 1
 Hasta mañana. See you tomorrow. 1
 hasta que until 13
 Hasta pronto. See you soon. 1
hay there is; there are 1
 Hay (mucha) contaminación. It's (very) smoggy.
 Hay (mucha) niebla. It's (very) foggy.
 Hay que It is necessary that 14
 No hay duda de There's no doubt 13
 No hay de qué. You're welcome. 1
hecho/a *p.p.* done 14
heladería *f.* ice cream shop 14
helado/a *adj.* iced 8
helado *m.* ice cream 9
hermanastro/a *m., f.* stepbrother/stepsister 3
hermano/a *m., f.* brother/sister 3
hermano/a mayor/menor *m., f.* older/younger brother/sister 3

hermanos *m., pl.* siblings (brothers and sisters) 3
hermoso/a *adj.* beautiful 6
hierba *f.* grass 13
hijastro/a *m., f.* stepson/stepdaughter 3
hijo/a *m., f.* son/daughter 3
 hijo/a único/a *m., f.* only child 3
 hijos *m., pl.* children 3
híjole *interj.* wow 6
historia *f.* history 2; story
hockey *m.* hockey 4
hola *interj.* hello; hi 1
hombre *m.* man 1
 hombre de negocios *m.* businessman
hora *f.* hour 1; the time
horario *m.* schedule 2
horno *m.* oven 12
 horno de microondas *m.* microwave oven 12
horror *m.* horror
 de horror horror (genre)
hospital *m.* hospital 10
hotel *m.* hotel 5
hoy *adv.* today 2
 hoy día *adv.* nowadays
 Hoy es... Today is... 2
hueco *m.* hole 4
huelga *f.* strike *(labor)*
hueso *m.* bone 10
huésped *m., f.* guest 5
huevo *m.* egg 8
humanidades *f., pl.* humanities 2
huracán *m.* hurricane

I

ida *f.* one way *(travel)*
idea *f.* idea 4
iglesia *f.* church 4
igualdad *f.* equality
igualmente *adv.* likewise 1
impermeable *m.* raincoat 6
importante *adj. m., f.* important 3
importar *v.* to be important to; to matter 7
imposible *adj. m., f.* impossible 13
impresora *f.* printer 11
imprimir *v.* to print 11
improbable *adj. m., f.* improbable 13
impuesto *m.* tax
incendio *m.* fire
increíble *adj. m., f.* incredible 5
indicar cómo llegar *v.* to give directions 14
individual *adj.* private *(room)* 5
infección *f.* infection 10
informar *v.* to inform
informe *m.* report; paper *(written work)*
ingeniero/a *m., f.* engineer 3

inglés *m.* English (*language*) 2
inglés, inglesa *adj.* English 3
inodoro *m.* toilet 7
insistir (en) *v.* to insist (on) 12
inspector(a) de aduanas *m., f.*
 customs inspector 5
inteligente *adj. m., f.* intelligent 3
intento *m.* attempt 11
intercambiar *v.* to exchange
interesante *adj. m., f.*
 interesting 3
interesar *v.* to be interesting to;
 to interest 7
internacional *adj. m., f.*
 international
Internet Internet 11
inundación *f.* flood
invertir (e:ie) *v.* to invest
invierno *m.* winter 5
invitado/a *m., f.* guest 9
 invitar *v.* to invite 9
inyección *f.* injection 10
ir *v.* to go 4
 ir a (+ inf.) to be going to do
 something 4
 ir de compras to go shopping 5
 **ir de excursión (a las
 montañas)** to go on a hike
 (in the mountains) 4
 ir de pesca to go fishing
 ir de vacaciones to go on
 vacation 5
 ir en autobús to go by bus 5
 ir en auto(móvil) to go by
 auto(mobile); to go by car 5
 ir en avión to go by plane 5
 ir en barco to go by boat 5
 ir en metro to go by subway 5
 ir en motocicleta to go by
 motorcycle 5
 ir en taxi to go by taxi 5
 ir en tren to go by train
irse *v.* to go away; to leave 7
italiano/a *adj.* Italian 3
izquierdo/a *adj.* left 2
 a la izquierda de to the left
 of 2

J

jabón *m.* soap 7
jamás *adv.* never; not ever 7
jamón *m.* ham 8
japonés, japonesa *adj.*
 Japanese 3
jardín *m.* garden; yard 12
jefe, jefa *m., f.* boss
jengibre *m.* ginger 10
joven *adj. m., f., sing.* (**jóvenes** *pl.*)
 young 3
 joven *m., f., sing.* (**jóvenes** *pl.*)
 youth; young person 1
joyería *f.* jewelry store 14
jubilarse *v.* to retire (*from work*) 9
juego *m.* game

jueves *m., sing.* Thursday 2
jugador(a) *m., f.* player 4
jugar (u:ue) *v.* to play 4
 jugar a las cartas *f., pl.* to
 play cards 5
jugo *m.* juice 8
 jugo de fruta *m.* fruit juice 8
julio *m.* July 5
jungla *f.* jungle 13
junio *m.* June 5
juntos/as *adj.* together 9
juventud *f.* youth 9

K

kilómetro *m.* kilometer 1

L

la *f., sing., def. art.* the 1
 la *f., sing., d.o. pron.* her, it,
 form. you 5
laboratorio *m.* laboratory 2
lago *m.* lake 13
lámpara *f.* lamp 12
lana *f.* wool 6
langosta *f.* lobster 8
lápiz *m.* pencil 1
largo/a *adj.* long 6
las *f., pl., def. art.* the 1
 las *f., pl., d.o. pron.* them; *form.*
 you 5
lástima *f.* shame 13
lastimarse *v.* to injure oneself 10
 lastimarse el pie to injure
 one's foot 10
lata *f.* (*tin*) can 13
lavabo *m.* sink 7
lavadora *f.* washing machine 12
lavandería *f.* laundromat 14
lavaplatos *m., sing.* dishwasher 12
lavar *v.* to wash 12
 lavar (el suelo, los platos) to
 wash (the floor, the dishes) 12
lavarse *v.* to wash oneself 7
 lavarse la cara to wash one's
 face 7
 lavarse las manos to wash
 one's hands 7
le *sing., i.o. pron.* to/for him, her,
 form. you 6
 Le presento a… *form.* I would
 like to introduce you to (name). 1
lección *f.* lesson 1
leche *f.* milk 8
lechuga *f.* lettuce 8
leer *v.* to read 3
 leer correo electrónico
 to read e-mail 4
 leer un periódico to read a
 newspaper 4
 leer una revista to read a
 magazine 4
leído/a *p.p.* read 14
lejos de *prep.* far from 2

lengua *f.* language 2
 lenguas extranjeras *f., pl.*
 foreign languages 2
lentes de contacto *m., pl.*
 contact lenses
 lentes (de sol) (sun)glasses
lento/a *adj.* slow 11
les *pl., i.o. pron.* to/for them, *form.*
 you 6
letrero *m.* sign 14
levantar *v.* to lift 15
 levantar pesas to lift
 weights 15
levantarse *v.* to get up 7
ley *f.* law 13
libertad *f.* liberty; freedom
libre *adj. m., f.* free 4
librería *f.* bookstore 2
libro *m.* book 2
licencia de conducir *f.* driver's
 license 11
limón *m.* lemon 8
limpiar *v.* to clean 12
 limpiar la casa *v.* to clean the
 house 12
limpio/a *adj.* clean 5
línea *f.* line 4
listo/a *adj.* ready; smart 5
literatura *f.* literature 2
llamar *v.* to call 11
 llamar por teléfono to call on
 the phone
llamarse *v.* to be called; to be
 named 7
llanta *f.* tire 11
llave *f.* key 5; wrench 11
llegada *f.* arrival 5
llegar *v.* to arrive 2
llenar *v.* to fill 11, 14
 llenar el tanque to fill the
 tank 11
 llenar (un formulario) to fill
 out (a form) 14
lleno/a *adj.* full 11
llevar *v.* to carry 2; *v.* to wear;
 to take 6
 llevar una vida sana to lead
 a healthy lifestyle 15
 llevarse bien/mal (con) to
 get along well/badly (with) 9
llorar *v.* to cry 15
llover (o:ue) *v.* to rain 5
 Llueve. It's raining. 5
lluvia *f.* rain
lo *m., sing. d.o. pron.* him, it, *form.*
 you 5
 ¡Lo he pasado de película!
 I've had a fantastic time!
 lo mejor the best (thing)
 lo que that which; what 12
 Lo siento. I'm sorry. 1
loco/a *adj.* crazy 6
locutor(a) *m., f.* (TV or radio)
 announcer
lodo *m.* mud
los *m., pl., def. art.* the 1

los *m. pl., d.o. pron.* them, *form.* you 5
luchar (contra/por) *v.* to fight; to struggle (against/for)
luego *adv.* then 7; *adv.* later 1
lugar *m.* place 2, 4
luna *f.* moon 13
lunares *m.* polka dots 6
lunes *m., sing.* Monday 2
luz *f.* light; electricity 12

M

madrastra *f.* stepmother 3
madre *f.* mother 3
madurez *f.* maturity; middle age 9
maestro/a *m., f.* teacher
magnífico/a *adj.* magnificent 5
maíz *m.* corn 8
mal, malo/a *adj.* bad 3
maleta *f.* suitcase 1
mamá *f.* mom 3
mandar *v.* to order 12; to send; to mail 14
manejar *v.* to drive 11
manera *f.* way
mano *f.* hand 1
manta *f.* blanket 12
mantener (e:ie) *v.* to maintain 15
　mantenerse en forma to stay in shape 15
mantequilla *f.* butter 8
manzana *f.* apple 8
mañana *f.* morning, a.m. 1; tomorrow 1
mapa *m.* map 2
maquillaje *m.* makeup 7
maquillarse *v.* to put on makeup 7
mar *m.* sea 5
maravilloso/a *adj.* marvelous 5
mareado/a *adj.* dizzy; nauseated 10
margarina *f.* margarine 8
mariscos *m., pl.* shellfish 8
marrón *adj. m., f.* brown 6
martes *m., sing.* Tuesday 2
marzo *m.* March 5
más *pron.* more 2
　más de (+ number) more than 8
　más tarde later (on) 7
　más... que more... than 8
masaje *m.* massage 15
matemáticas *f., pl.* mathematics 2
materia *f.* course 2
matrimonio *m.* marriage 9
máximo/a *adj.* maximum 11
mayo *m.* May 5
mayonesa *f.* mayonnaise 8
mayor *adj.* older 3
　el/la mayor *adj.* eldest 8; oldest
me *sing., d.o. pron.* me 5; *sing. i.o. pron.* to/for me 6
　Me duele mucho. It hurts me a lot. 10

Me gusta... I like... 2
No me gustan nada. I don't like them at all. 2
Me gustaría(n)... I would like...
　Me llamo... My name is... 1
Me muero por... I'm dying to (for)...
mecánico/a *m., f.* mechanic 11
mediano/a *adj.* medium
medianoche *f.* midnight 1
medias *f., pl.* pantyhose, stockings 6
medicamento *m.* medication 10
medicina *f.* medicine 10
médico/a *m., f.* doctor 3; *adj.* medical 10
medio/a *adj.* half 3
　medio ambiente *m.* environment 13
　medio/a hermano/a *m., f.* half-brother/half-sister 3
　mediodía *m.* noon 1
　medios de comunicación *m., pl.* means of communication; media
　y media thirty minutes past the hour (time) 1
mejor *adj.* better 8
　el/la mejor *m., f.* the best 8
mejorar *v.* to improve 13
melocotón *m.* peach 8
menor *adj.* younger 3
　el/la menor *m., f.* youngest 8
menos *adv.* less 10
　menos cuarto..., menos quince... quarter to... (time) 1
　menos de (+ number) fewer than 8
　menos... que less... than 8
mensaje *m.* **de texto** text message 11
mensaje electrónico *m.* e-mail message 4
mentira *f.* lie 4
menú *m.* menu 8
mercado *m.* market 6
　mercado al aire libre open-air market 6
merendar (e:ie) *v.* to snack 8; to have an afternoon snack
merienda *f.* afternoon snack 15
mes *m.* month 5
mesa *f.* table 2
mesita *f.* end table 12
　mesita de noche night stand 12
meterse en problemas *v.* to get into trouble 13
metro *m.* subway 5
mexicano/a *adj.* Mexican 3
México *m.* Mexico 1
mí *pron., obj. of prep.* me 8
mi(s) *poss. adj.* my 3
microonda *f.* microwave 12
　horno de microondas *m.* microwave oven 12

miedo *m.* fear 3
miel *f.* honey 10
mientras *adv.* while 10
miércoles *m., sing.* Wednesday 2
mil *m.* one thousand 2
　mil millones billion
milla *f.* mile 11
millón *m.* million 2
millones (de) *m.* millions (of)
mineral *m.* mineral 15
minuto *m.* minute 1
mío(s)/a(s) *poss.* my; (of) mine 11
mirar *v.* to look (at); to watch 2
　mirar (la) televisión to watch television 2
mismo/a *adj.* same 3
mochila *f.* backpack 2
moda *f.* fashion 6
módem *m.* modem
moderno/a *adj.* modern
molestar *v.* to bother; to annoy 7
monitor *m.* (computer) monitor 11
　monitor(a) *m., f.* trainer
mono *m.* monkey 13
montaña *f.* mountain 4
montar *v.* **a caballo** to ride a horse 5
montón: un montón de a lot of 4
monumento *m.* monument 4
morado/a *adj.* purple 6
moreno/a *adj.* brunet(te) 3
morir (o:ue) *v.* to die 8
mostrar (o:ue) *v.* to show 4
motocicleta *f.* motorcycle 5
motor *m.* motor
muchacho/a *m., f.* boy; girl 3
mucho/a *adj., adv.* a lot of; much 2; many 3
　(Muchas) gracias. Thank you (very much); Thanks (a lot). 1
　muchas veces *adv.* a lot; many times 10
　Muchísimas gracias. Thank you very, very much. 9
　Mucho gusto. Pleased to meet you. 1
muchísimo very much 2
mudarse *v.* to move (from one house to another) 12
muebles *m., pl.* furniture 12
muela *f.* tooth
muerte *f.* death 9
muerto/a *p.p.* died 14
mujer *f.* woman 1
　mujer de negocios *f.* business woman
　mujer policía *f.* female police officer
multa *f.* fine
mundial *adj. m., f.* worldwide
mundo *m.* world 8, 13
muro *m.* wall 15
músculo *m.* muscle 15
museo *m.* museum 4
música *f.* music 2
musical *adj. m., f.* musical

músico/a *m., f.* musician
muy *adv.* very 1
 Muy amable. That's very kind of you. 5
 (Muy) bien, gracias. (Very) well, thanks. 1

N

nacer *v.* to be born 9
nacimiento *m.* birth 9
nacional *adj. m., f.* national
nacionalidad *f.* nationality 1
nada nothing 1; not anything 7
 nada mal not bad at all 5
nadar *v.* to swim 4
nadie *pron.* no one, nobody, not anyone 7
naranja *f.* orange 8
nariz *f.* nose 10
natación *f.* swimming 4
natural *adj. m., f.* natural 13
naturaleza *f.* nature 13
navegador *m.* GPS GPS 11
navegar (en Internet) *v.* to surf (the Internet) 11
Navidad *f.* Christmas 9
necesario/a *adj.* necessary 12
necesitar (+ inf.) *v.* to need 2
negar (e:ie) *v.* to deny 13
 no negar (e:ie) *v.* not to deny 13
negocios *m., pl.* business; commerce
negro/a *adj.* black 6
nervioso/a *adj.* nervous 5
nevar (e:ie) *v.* to snow 5
 Nieva. It's snowing. 5
ni…ni neither… nor 7
niebla *f.* fog
nieto/a *m., f.* grandson/ granddaughter 3
nieve *f.* snow
ningún, ninguno/a(s) *adj.* no; none; not any 7
niñez *f.* childhood 9
niño/a *m., f.* child 3
no no; not 1
 ¿no? right? 1
 No cabe duda de… There is no doubt… 13
 No es para tanto. It's not a big deal. 12
 no es seguro it's not sure 13
 no es verdad it's not true 13
 No está nada mal. It's not bad at all. 5
 no estar de acuerdo to disagree
 No estoy seguro. I'm not sure.
 no hay there is not; there are not 1
 No hay de qué. You're welcome. 1
 No hay duda de… There is no doubt… 13

No hay problema. No problem. 7
¡No me diga(s)! You don't say!
No me gustan nada. I don't like them at all. 2
no muy bien not very well 1
No quiero. I don't want to. 4
No sé. I don't know.
No se preocupe. *(form.)* Don't worry. 7
No te preocupes. *(fam.)* Don't worry. 7
no tener razón to be wrong 3
noche *f.* night 1
nombre *m.* name 1
norte *m.* north 14
norteamericano/a *adj.* (North) American 3
nos *pl., d.o. pron.* us 5; *pl., i.o. pron.* to/for us 6
 Nos vemos. See you. 1
nosotros/as *sub. pron.* we 1; *ob. pron.* us
noticia *f.* news 11
noticias *f., pl.* news
noticiero *m.* newscast
novecientos/as nine hundred 2
noveno/a *adj.* ninth 5
noventa ninety 2
noviembre *m.* November 5
novio/a *m., f.* boyfriend/ girlfriend 3
nube *f.* cloud 13
nublado/a *adj.* cloudy 5
 Está (muy) nublado. It's very cloudy. 5
nuclear *adj. m. f.* nuclear 13
nuera *f.* daughter-in-law 3
nuestro(s)/a(s) *poss. adj.* our 3; (of ours) 11
nueve nine 1
nuevo/a *adj.* new 6
número *m.* number 1; (shoe) size 6
nunca *adj.* never; not ever 7
nutrición *f.* nutrition 15
nutricionista *m., f.* nutritionist 15

O

o or 7
o… o; either… or 7
obedecer *v.* to obey
obra *f.* work (*of art, literature, music, etc.*)
 obra maestra *f.* masterpiece
obtener *v.* to obtain; to get
obvio/a *adj.* obvious 13
océano *m.* ocean
ochenta eighty 2
ocho eight 1
ochocientos/as eight hundred 2
octavo/a *adj.* eighth 5
octubre *m.* October 5

ocupación *f.* occupation
ocupado/a *adj.* busy 5
ocurrir *v.* to occur; to happen
odiar *v.* to hate 9
oeste *m.* west 14
oficina *f.* office 12
oficio *m.* trade
ofrecer *v.* to offer 6
oído *m.* (sense of) hearing; inner ear 10
 oído/a *p.p.* heard 14
oír *v.* to hear 4
 Oiga/Oigan. *form., sing./pl.* Listen. (*in conversation*) 1
 Oye. *fam., sing.* Listen. (*in conversation*) 1
ojalá (que) *interj.* I hope (that); I wish (that) 13
ojo *m.* eye 10
olvidar *v.* to forget 10
once eleven 1
ópera *f.* opera
operación *f.* operation 10
ordenado/a *adj.* orderly 5
ordinal *adj.* ordinal (*number*)
oreja *f.* (outer) ear 10
organizarse *v.* to organize oneself 12
orquesta *f.* orchestra
ortografía *f.* spelling
ortográfico/a *adj.* spelling
os *fam., pl. d.o. pron.* you 5; *fam., pl. i.o. pron.* to/for you 6
otoño *m.* autumn 5
otro/a *adj.* other; another 6
 otra vez again

P

paciente *m., f.* patient 10
padrastro *m.* stepfather 3
padre *m.* father 3
 padres *m., pl.* parents 3
pagar *v.* to pay 6, 9
 pagar a plazos to pay in installments 14
 pagar al contado to pay in cash 14
 pagar en efectivo to pay in cash 14
 pagar la cuenta to pay the bill 9
página *f.* page 11
 página principal *f.* home page 11
país *m.* country 1
paisaje *m.* landscape 5
pájaro *m.* bird 13
palabra *f.* word 1
paleta helada *f.* popsicle 4
pálido/a *adj.* pale 14
pan *m.* bread 8
 pan tostado *m.* toasted bread 8
panadería *f.* bakery 14
pantalla *f.* screen 11
 pantalla táctil *f.* touch screen 11

porque *conj.* because 2
portátil *m.* portable 11
portero/a *m., f.* doorman/ doorwoman 1
porvenir *m.* future
 ¡Por el porvenir! Here's to the future!
posesivo/a *adj.* possessive 3
posible *adj.* possible 13
 es posible it's possible 13
 no es posible it's not possible 13
postal *f.* postcard 4
postre *m.* dessert 9
practicar *v.* to practice 2
 practicar deportes *m., pl.* to play sports 4
precio (fijo) *m.* (fixed; set) price 6
preferir (e:ie) *v.* to prefer 4
pregunta *f.* question
preguntar *v.* to ask (*a question*) 2
premio *m.* prize; award
prender *v.* to turn on 11
prensa *f.* press
preocupado/a (por) *adj.* worried (about) 5
preocuparse (por) *v.* to worry (about) 7
preparar *v.* to prepare 2
preposición *f.* preposition
presentación *f.* introduction
presentar *v.* to introduce; to present; to put on (*a performance*)
 Le presento a... I would like to introduce you to (name). (*form.*) 1
 Te presento a... I would like to introduce you to (name). (*fam.*) 1
presiones *f., pl.* pressures 15
prestado/a *adj.* borrowed
préstamo *m.* loan 14
prestar *v.* to lend; to loan 6
primavera *f.* spring 5
primer, primero/a *adj.* first 2, 5
primo/a *m., f.* cousin 3
principal *adj. m., f.* main 8
prisa *f.* haste 3
 darse prisa *v.* to hurry; to rush 15
probable *adj. m., f.* probable 13
 es probable it's probable 13
 no es probable it's not probable 13
probar (o:ue) *v.* to taste; to try 8
probarse (o:ue) *v.* to try on 7
problema *m.* problem 1
profesión *f.* profession 3
profesor(a) *m., f.* teacher 1, 2
programa *m.* 1
 programa de computación *m.* software 11
 programa de entrevistas *m.* talk show

programa de realidad *m.* reality show
programador(a) *m., f.* computer programmer 3
prohibir *v.* to prohibit 10; to forbid
pronombre *m.* pronoun
pronto *adv.* soon 10
propina *f.* tip 8
propio/a *adj.* own
proteger *v.* to protect 13
proteína *f.* protein 15
próximo/a *adj.* next 3
proyecto *m.* project 11
prueba *f.* test; quiz 2
psicología *f.* psychology 2
psicólogo/a *m., f.* psychologist
publicar *v.* to publish
público *m.* audience
pueblo *m.* town 4
puerta *f.* door 2
Puerto Rico *m.* Puerto Rico 1
puertorriqueño/a *adj.* Puerto Rican 3
pues *conj.* well
puesto *m.* position; job
puesto/a *p.p.* put 14
puro/a *adj.* pure 13

que *pron.* that; which; who 12
 ¿En qué...? In which...? 2
 ¡Qué...! How...!
 ¡Qué dolor! What pain!
 ¡Qué ropa más bonita! What pretty clothes! 6
 ¡Qué sorpresa! What a surprise!
 ¿qué? what? 1
 ¿Qué día es hoy? What day is it? 2
 ¿Qué hay de nuevo? What's new? 1
 ¿Qué hora es? What time is it? 1
 ¿Qué les parece? What do you (*pl.*) think?
 Qué onda? What's up? 14
 ¿Qué pasa? What's happening? What's going on? 1
 ¿Qué pasó? What happened? 11
 ¿Qué precio tiene? What is the price?
 ¿Qué tal...? How are you?; How is it going? 1; How is/are...? 2
 ¿Qué talla lleva/usa? What size do you wear? 6
 ¿Qué tiempo hace? How's the weather? 5
quedar *v.* to be left over; to fit (*clothing*) 7; to be left behind; to be located 14
quedarse *v.* to stay; to remain 7
quehaceres domésticos *m., pl.* household chores 12

quemado/a *adj.* burned (out) 11
quemar (un CD/DVD) *v.* to burn (a CD/DVD)
querer (e:ie) *v.* to want; to love 4
queso *m.* cheese 8
quien(es) *pron.* who; whom; that 12
 ¿quién(es)? who?; whom? 1
 ¿Quién es...? Who is...? 1
 ¿Quién habla? Who is speaking/calling? (*telephone*) 11
química *f.* chemistry 2
quince fifteen 1
 menos quince quarter to (time) 1
 y quince quarter after (time) 1
quinceañera *f.* young woman celebrating her fifteenth birthday 9
quinientos/as *adj.* five hundred 2
quinto/a *adj.* fifth 5
quisiera *v.* I would like
quitar el polvo *v.* to dust 12
quitar la mesa *v.* to clear the table 12
quitarse *v.* to take off 7
quizás *adv.* maybe 5

racismo *m.* racism
radio *f.* radio (*medium*) 2; *m.* radio (set) 2
radiografía *f.* X-ray 10
rápido/a *adv.* quickly 10
ratón *m.* mouse 11
ratos libres *m., pl.* spare (free) time 4
raya *f.* stripe 6
razón *f.* reason 3
rebaja *f.* sale 6
receta *f.* prescription 10
recetar *v.* to prescribe 10
recibir *v.* to receive 3
reciclaje *m.* recycling 13
reciclar *v.* to recycle 13
recién casado/a *m., f.* newly-wed 9
recoger *v.* to pick up 13
recomendar (e:ie) *v.* to recommend 8, 12
recordar (o:ue) *v.* to remember 4
recorrer *v.* to tour an area
recorrido *m.* tour 13
recuperar *v.* to recover 11
recurso *m.* resource 13
 recurso natural *m.* natural resource 13
red *f.* network; Web 11
reducir *v.* to reduce 13
refresco *m.* soft drink 8
refrigerador *m.* refrigerator 12
regalar *v.* to give (a gift) 9
regalo *m.* gift 6
regatear *v.* to bargain 6
región *f.* region; area 13
regresar *v.* to return 2

regular *adv.* so-so.; OK 1
reído *p.p.* laughed 14
reírse (e:i) *v.* to laugh 9
relaciones *f., pl.* relationships
relajarse *v.* to relax 9
reloj *m.* clock; watch 2
renovable *adj.* renewable 13
renunciar (a) *v.* to resign (from)
repetir (e:i) *v.* to repeat 4
reportaje *m.* report
reportero/a *m., f.* reporter; journalist
representante *m., f.* representative
reproductor de CD *m.* CD player 11
reproductor de DVD *m.* DVD player 11
reproductor de MP3 *m.* MP3 player 11
resfriado *m.* cold (*illness*) 10
residencia estudiantil *f.* dormitory 2
resolver (o:ue) *v.* to resolve; to solve 13
respirar *v.* to breathe 13
responsable *adj.* responsible 8
respuesta *f.* answer
restaurante *m.* restaurant 4
resuelto/a *p.p.* resolved 14
reunión *f.* meeting
revisar *v.* to check 11
 revisar el aceite *v.* to check the oil 11
revista *f.* magazine 4
rico/a *adj.* rich 6; *adj.* tasty; delicious 8
ridículo/a *adj.* ridiculous 13
río *m.* river 13
riquísimo/a *adj.* extremely delicious 8
rodilla *f.* knee 10
rogar (o:ue) *v.* to beg; to plead 12
rojo/a *adj.* red 6
romántico/a *adj.* romantic
romper *v.* to break 10
 romperse la pierna *v.* to break one's leg 10
romper (con) *v.* to break up (with) 9
ropa *f.* clothing; clothes 6
 ropa interior *f.* underwear 6
rosado/a *adj.* pink 6
roto/a *adj.* broken 10, 14
rubio/a *adj.* blond(e) 3
ruso/a *adj.* Russian 3
rutina *f.* routine 7
 rutina diaria *f.* daily routine 7

S

sábado *m.* Saturday 2
saber *v.* to know; to know how 6; to taste 8
 saber a to taste like 8

sabrosísimo/a *adj.* extremely delicious 8
sabroso/a *adj.* tasty; delicious 8
sacar *v.* to take out
 sacar buenas notas to get good grades 2
 sacar fotos to take photos 5
 sacar la basura to take out the trash 12
 sacar(se) un diente to have a tooth removed 10
sacudir *v.* to dust 12
 sacudir los muebles to dust the furniture 12
sal *f.* salt 8
sala *f.* living room 12; room
 sala de emergencia(s) emergency room 10
salario *m.* salary
salchicha *f.* sausage 8
salida *f.* departure; exit 5
salir *v.* to leave 4; to go out
 salir (con) to go out (with); to date 9
 salir de to leave from
 salir para to leave for (*a place*)
salmón *m.* salmon 8
salón de belleza *m.* beauty salon 14
salud *f.* health 10
saludable *adj.* healthy 10
saludar(se) *v.* to greet (each other) 11
saludo *m.* greeting 1
 saludos a... greetings to... 1
sandalia *f.* sandal 6
sandía *f.* watermelon
sándwich *m.* sandwich 8
sano/a *adj.* healthy 10
se *ref. pron.* himself, herself, itself, *form.* yourself, themselves, yourselves 7
se *impersonal* one 10
 Se nos dañó... The... broke down. 11
 Se hizo... He/she/it became...
 Se nos pinchó una llanta. We had a flat tire. 11
secadora *f.* clothes dryer 12
secarse *v.* to dry oneself 7
sección de (no) fumar *f.* (non) smoking section 8
secretario/a *m., f.* secretary
secuencia *f.* sequence
sed *f.* thirst 3
seda *f.* silk 6
sedentario/a *adj.* sedentary; related to sitting 15
seguir (e:i) *v.* to follow; to continue 4
según according to
segundo/a *adj.* second 5
seguro/a *adj.* sure; safe 5
seis six 1
seiscientos/as six hundred 2
sello *m.* stamp 14
selva *f.* jungle 13
semáforo *m.* traffic light 14
semana *f.* week 2

fin *m.* **de semana** weekend 4
 semana *f.* **pasada** last week 6
semestre *m.* semester 2
sendero *m.* trail; trailhead 13
sentarse (e:ie) *v.* to sit down 7
sentir(se) (e:ie) *v.* to feel 7; to be sorry; to regret 13
señor (Sr.); don *m.* Mr.; sir 1
señora (Sra.); doña *f.* Mrs.; ma'am 1
señorita (Srta.) *f.* Miss 1
separado/a *adj.* separated 9
separarse (de) *v.* to separate (from) 9
septiembre *m.* September 5
séptimo/a *adj.* seventh 5
ser *v.* to be 1
 ser aficionado/a (a) to be a fan (of) 4
 ser alérgico/a (a) to be allergic (to) 10
 ser gratis to be free of charge 14
serio/a *adj.* serious
servicio *m.* service 15
servilleta *f.* napkin 12
servir (e:i) *v.* to serve 8; to help 5
sesenta sixty 2
setecientos/as *adj.* seven hundred 2
setenta seventy 2
sexismo *m.* sexism
sexto/a *adj.* sixth 5
sí *adv.* yes 1
si *conj.* if 4
SIDA *m.* AIDS
sido *p.p.* been 15
siempre *adv.* always 7
siete seven 1
silla *f.* seat 2
sillón *m.* armchair 12
similar *adj. m., f.* similar
simpático/a *adj.* nice; likeable 3
sin *prep.* without 2, 13
 sin duda without a doubt
 sin embargo however
 sin que *conj.* without 13
sino but (rather) 7
síntoma *m.* symptom 10
sitio *m.* place 3
sitio *m.* **web;** website 11
situado/a *p.p.* located
sobre *m.* envelope 14; *prep.* on; over 2
 sobre todo above all 13
(sobre)población *f.* (over)population 13
sobrino/a *m., f.* nephew; niece 3
sociología *f.* sociology 2
sofá *m.* couch; sofa 12
sol *m.* sun 4; 5; 13
solar *adj. m., f.* solar 13
soldado *m., f.* soldier
soleado/a *adj.* sunny
solicitar *v.* to apply (*for a job*)
solicitud (de trabajo) *f.* (job) application
sólo *adv.* only 3
solo/a *adj.* alone

soltero/a *adj.* single 9
solución *f.* solution 13
sombrero *m.* hat 6
Son las dos. It's two o'clock. 1
sonar (o:ue) *v.* to ring 11
sonreído *p.p.* smiled 14
sonreír (e:i) *v.* to smile 9
sopa *f.* soup 8
sorprender *v.* to surprise 9
sorpresa *f.* surprise 9
sótano *m.* basement; cellar 12
soy I am 1
 Soy de... I'm from... 1
 Soy yo. That's me.
su(s) *poss. adj.* his; her; its; *form.* your; their 3
subir(se) a *v.* to get on/into (*a vehicle*) 11
sucio/a *adj.* dirty 5
sudar *v.* to sweat 15
suegro/a *m., f.* father-in-law; mother-in-law 3
sueldo *m.* salary
suelo *m.* floor 12
sueño *m.* sleep 3
suerte *f.* luck 3
suéter *m.* sweater 6
sufrir *v.* to suffer 10
 sufrir muchas presiones to be under a lot of pressure 15
 sufrir una enfermedad to suffer an illness 10
sugerir (e:ie) *v.* to suggest 12
supermercado *m.* supermarket 14
suponer *v.* to suppose 4
sur *m.* south 14
sustantivo *m.* noun
suyo(s)/a(s) *poss.* (of) his/her; (of) hers; (of) its; (of) *form.* your, (of) yours, (of) their 11

T

tabla de (wind)surf *f.* surf board/sailboard 3
tal vez *adv.* maybe 5
talentoso/a *adj.* talented
talla *f.* size 6
 talla grande *f.* large
taller *m.* **mecánico** garage; mechanic's repairshop 11
también *adv.* also; too 2; 7
tampoco *adv.* neither; not either 7
tan *adv.* so 5
 tan... como as... as 8
 tan pronto como *conj.* as soon as 13
tanque *m.* tank 11
tanto *adv.* so much
 tanto... como as much... as 8
 tantos/as... como as many... as 8
tarde *adv.* late 7; *f.* afternoon; evening; P.M. 1
tarea *f.* homework 2
tarjeta *f.* (post) card
tarjeta de crédito *f.* credit card 6

tarjeta postal *f.* postcard 4
taxi *m.* taxi 5
taza *f.* cup 12
te *sing., fam., d.o. pron.* you 5; *sing., fam., i.o. pron.* to/for you 6
 Te presento a... *fam.* I would like to introduce you to (name). 1
 ¿Te gustaría? Would you like to?
 ¿Te gusta(n)...? Do you like...? 2
té *m.* tea 8
 té helado *m.* iced tea 8
teatro *m.* theater
teclado *m.* keyboard 11
técnico/a *m., f.* technician
tejido *m.* weaving
teleadicto/a *m., f.* couch potato 15
(teléfono) celular *m.* (cell) phone 11
telenovela *f.* soap opera
teletrabajo *m.* telecommuting
televisión *f.* television 2; 11
televisión por cable *f.* cable television 11
televisor *m.* television set 11
temer *v.* to fear 13
temperatura *f.* temperature 10
temporada *f.* period of time 5
temprano *adv.* early 7
tenedor *m.* fork 12
tener *v.* to have 3
 tener... años to be... years old 3
 Tengo... años. I'm... years old. 3
 tener (mucho) calor to be (very) hot 3
 tener (mucho) cuidado to be (very) careful 3
 tener dolor to have a pain 10
 tener éxito to be successful
 tener fiebre to have a fever 10
 tener (mucho) frío to be (very) cold 3
 tener ganas de (+ inf.) to feel like (*doing something*) 3
 tener (mucha) hambre *f.* to be (very) hungry 3
 tener (mucho) miedo (de) to be (very) afraid (of); to be (very) scared (of) 3
 tener miedo (de) que to be afraid that
 tener planes *m., pl.* to have plans 4
 tener (mucha) prisa to be in a (big) hurry 3
 tener que (+ inf.) *v.* to have to (*do something*) 3
 tener razón *f.* to be right 3
 tener (mucha) sed *f.* to be (very) thirsty 3
 tener (mucho) sueño to be (very) sleepy 3
 tener (mucha) suerte to be (very) lucky 3

 tener tiempo to have time 4
 tener una cita to have a date; to have an appointment 9
tenis *m.* tennis 4
tensión *f.* tension 15
tercer, tercero/a *adj.* third 5
terco/a *adj.* stubborn 10
terminar *v.* to end; to finish 2
 terminar de (+ inf.) *v.* to finish (*doing something*) 4
terremoto *m.* earthquake
terrible *adj. m., f.* terrible 13
ti *prep., obj. of prep., fam.* you
tiempo *m.* time 4; weather 5
 tiempo libre free time
tienda *f.* shop; store 6
tierra *f.* land; soil 13
tinto/a *adj.* red (wine) 8
tío/a *m., f.* uncle; aunt 3
tíos *m., pl.* aunts and uncles 3
título *m.* title
tiza *f.* chalk 2
toalla *f.* towel 7
tobillo *m.* ankle 10
tocar *v.* to play (*a musical instrument*); to touch
todavía *adv.* yet; still 3, 5
todo *m.* everything 5
 en todo el mundo throughout the world 13
 Todo está bajo control. Everything is under control. 7
 todo derecho straight (ahead) 14
todo(s)/a(s) *adj.* all 4; whole
todos *m., pl.* all of us; *m., pl.* everybody; everyone
todos los días *adv.* every day 10
tomar *v.* to take; to drink 2
 tomar clases *f., pl.* to take classes 2
 tomar el sol to sunbathe 4
 tomar en cuenta to take into account
 tomar fotos *f., pl.* to take photos 5
 tomar la temperatura to take someone's temperature 10
 tomar una decisión to make a decision 15
tomate *m.* tomato 8
tonto/a *adj.* silly; foolish 3
torcerse (o:ue) (el tobillo) *v.* to sprain (one's ankle) 10
torcido/a *adj.* twisted; sprained 10
tormenta *f.* storm
tornado *m.* tornado
tortilla *f.* tortilla 8
 tortilla de maíz corn tortilla 8
tortuga (marina) *f.* (sea) turtle 13
tos *f., sing.* cough 10
toser *v.* to cough 10
tostado/a *adj.* toasted 8
tostadora *f.* toaster 12
trabajador(a) *adj.* hard-working 3
trabajar *v.* to work 2
trabajo *m.* job; work

traducir *v.* to translate 6
traer *v.* to bring 4
tráfico *m.* traffic 11
tragedia *f.* tragedy
traído/a *p.p.* brought 14
traje *m.* suit 6
 traje (de baño) *m.* (bathing) suit 6
trajinera *f.* type of barge 3
tranquilo/a *adj.* calm; quiet 15
 Tranquilo. Don't worry.; Be cool. 7
 Tranquilo/a, cariño. Relax, sweetie. 11
transmitir *v.* to broadcast
tratar de (+ *inf.*) *v.* to try (*to do something*) 15
trece thirteen 1
treinta thirty 1, 2
 y treinta thirty minutes past the hour (time) 1
tren *m.* train 5
tres three 1
trescientos/as *adj.* three hundred 2
trimestre *m.* trimester; quarter 2
triste *adj.* sad 5
tú *fam. sub. pron.* you 1
 Tú eres... You are... 1
tu(s) *fam. poss. adj.* your 3
turismo *m.* tourism 5
turista *m., f.* tourist 1
turístico/a *adj.* touristic
tuyo(s)/a(s) *fam. poss. pron.* your; (of) yours 11

U

Ud. *form. sing.* you 1
Uds. *form., pl.* you 1
último/a *adj.* last 7
 la última vez the last time 7
un, uno/a *indef. art.* a; one 1
 uno/a *m., f., sing. pron.* one 1
 a la una at one o'clock 1
 una vez once; one time 6
 una vez más one more time 9
único/a *adj.* only 3; unique 9
universidad *f.* university; college 2
unos/as *m., f., pl. indef. art.* some 1
 los unos a los otros each other 11
 unos/as *pron.* some 1
urgente *adj.* urgent 12
usar *v.* to wear; to use 6
usted (Ud.) *form. sing.* you 1
 ustedes (Uds.) *form., pl.* you 1
útil *adj.* useful
uva *f.* grape 8

V

vaca *f.* cow 13
vacaciones *f. pl.* vacation 5

valle *m.* valley 13
vamos let's go 4
vaquero *m.* cowboy
 de vaqueros *m., pl.* western (genre)
varios/as *adj. m. f., pl.* various; several 8
vaso *m.* glass 12
veces *f., pl.* times 6
vecino/a *m., f.* neighbor 12
veinte twenty 1
veinticinco twenty-five 1
veinticuatro twenty-four 1
veintidós twenty-two 1
veintinueve twenty-nine 1
veintiocho twenty-eight 1
veintiséis twenty-six 1
veintisiete twenty-seven 1
veintitrés twenty-three 1
veintiún, veintiuno/a twenty-one 1
vejez *f.* old age 9
velocidad *f.* speed 11
 velocidad máxima *f.* speed limit 11
vencer *v.* to expire 14
vendedor(a) *m., f.* salesperson 6
vender *v.* to sell 6
venir *v.* to come 3
ventana *f.* window 2
ver *v.* to see 4
 a ver *v.* let's see 2
 ver películas *f., pl.* to see movies 4
verano *m.* summer 5
verbo *m.* verb
verdad *f.* truth
 ¿verdad? right? 1
verde *adj., m. f.* green 6
verduras *pl., f.* vegetables 8
vestido *m.* dress 6
vestirse (e:i) *v.* to get dressed 7
vez *f.* time 6
viajar *v.* to travel 2
viaje *m.* trip 5
viajero/a *m., f.* traveler 5
vida *f.* life 9
video *m.* video 1, 11
videoconferencia *f.* videoconference
videojuego *m.* video game 4
vidrio *m.* glass 13
viejo/a *adj.* old 3
viento *m.* wind 5
viernes *m., sing.* Friday 2
vinagre *m.* vinegar 8
vino *m.* wine 8
 vino blanco *m.* white wine 8
 vino tinto *m.* red wine 8
violencia *f.* violence
visitar *v.* to visit 4
 visitar monumentos *m., pl.* to visit monuments 4
visto/a *p.p.* seen 14
vitamina *f.* vitamin 15

viudo/a *adj.* widower/widow 9
vivienda *f.* housing 12
vivir *v.* to live 3
vivo/a *adj.* bright; lively; living
volante *m.* steering wheel 11
volcán *m.* volcano 13
vóleibol *m.* volleyball 4
volver (o:ue) *v.* to return 4
volver a ver(te, lo, la) *v.* to see (you, him, her) again
vos *pron.* you
vosotros/as *form., pl.* you 1
votar *v.* to vote
vuelta *f.* return trip
vuelto/a *p.p.* returned 14
vuestro(s)/a(s) *poss. adj.* your 3; (of) yours *fam.* 11

W

walkman *m.* walkman

Y

y *conj.* and 1
 y cuarto quarter after (time) 1
 y media half-past (time) 1
 y quince quarter after (time) 1
 y treinta thirty (minutes past the hour) 1
 ¿Y tú? *fam.* And you? 1
 ¿Y usted? *form.* And you? 1
ya *adv.* already 6
yerno *m.* son-in-law 3
yo *sub. pron.* I 1
 Yo soy... I'm... 1
yogur *m.* yogurt 8

Z

zanahoria *f.* carrot 8
zapatería *f.* shoe store 14
zapatos de tenis *m., pl.* tennis shoes, sneakers 6

English-Spanish

A

a **un/a** *m., f., sing.; indef. art.* 1
@ (*symbol*) **arroba** *f.* 11
A.M. **mañana** *f.* 1
able: be able to **poder (o:ue)** *v.* 4
aboard **a bordo** 1
above all **sobre todo** 13
accident **accidente** *m.* 10
accompany **acompañar** *v.* 14
account **cuenta** *f.* 14
on account of **por** *prep.* 11
accountant **contador(a)** *m., f.*
accounting **contabilidad** *f.* 2
ache **dolor** *m.* 10
acquainted: be acquainted with
conocer *v.* 6
action (*genre*) **de acción** *f.*
active **activo/a** *adj.* 15
actor **actor** *m.,* **actriz** *f.*
addict (*drug*) **drogadicto/a**
adj. 15
additional **adicional** *adj.*
address **dirección** *f.* 14
adjective **adjetivo** *m.*
adolescence **adolescencia** *f.* 9
adventure (*genre*) **de aventura** *f.*
advertise **anunciar** *v.*
advertisement **anuncio** *m.*
advice **consejo** *m.* 6
give advice **dar consejos** 6
advise **aconsejar** *v.* 12
advisor **consejero/a** *m., f.*
aerobic **aeróbico/a** *adj.* 15
aerobics class **clase de
ejercicios aeróbicos** 15
to do aerobics **hacer ejercicios
aeróbicos** 15
affected **afectado/a** *adj.* 13
be affected (by) **estar** *v.*
afectado/a (por) 13
affirmative **afirmativo/a** *adj.*
afraid: be (very) afraid (of) **tener
(mucho) miedo (de)** 3
be afraid that **tener miedo
(de) que**
after **después de** *prep.* 7;
después de que *conj.* 13
afternoon **tarde** *f.* 1
afterward **después** *adv.* 7
again **otra vez**
age **edad** *f.* 9
agree **concordar** *v.*
agree **estar** *v.* **de acuerdo**
I agree. **Estoy de acuerdo.**
I don't agree. **No estoy de
acuerdo.**
agreement **acuerdo** *m.*
AIDS **SIDA** *m.*
air **aire** *m.* 13
air pollution **contaminación
del aire** 13
airplane **avión** *m.* 5
airport **aeropuerto** *m.* 5
alarm clock **despertador** *m.* 7
alcohol **alcohol** *m.* 15

to consume alcohol **consumir
alcohol** 15
alcoholic **alcohólico/a** *adj.* 15
all **todo(s)/a(s)** *adj.* 4
all of us **todos** 1
all over the world **en todo el
mundo**
allergic **alérgico/a** *adj.* 10
be allergic (to) **ser alérgico/a
(a)** 10
alleviate **aliviar** *v.*
almost **casi** *adv.* 10
alone **solo/a** *adj.*
along **por** *prep.* 11
already **ya** *adv.* 6
also **también** *adv.* 2; 7
altar **altar** *m.* 9
aluminum **aluminio** *m.* 13
(made) of aluminum **de
aluminio** 13
always **siempre** *adv.* 7
American (*North*)
norteamericano/a *adj.* 3
among **entre** *prep.* 2
amusement **diversión** *f.*
and **y** 1, **e** (*before words beginning
with i or hi*) 4
And you?**¿Y tú?** *fam.* 1;
¿Y usted? *form.* 1
angel **ángel** *m.* 9
angry **enojado/a** *adj.* 5
get angry (with) **enojarse** *v.*
(con) 7
animal **animal** *m.* 13
ankle **tobillo** *m.* 10
anniversary **aniversario** *m.* 9
(wedding) anniversary
aniversario *m.* **(de bodas)** 9
announce **anunciar** *v.*
announcer (*TV/radio*) **locutor(a)**
m., f.
annoy **molestar** *v.* 7
another **otro/a** *adj.* 6
answer **contestar** *v.* 2;
respuesta *f.*
answering machine **contestadora** *f.*
antibiotic **antibiótico** *m.* 10
any **algún, alguno/a(s)** *adj.* 7
anyone **alguien** *pron.* 7
anything **algo** *pron.* 7
apartment **apartamento** *m.* 12
apartment building **edificio de
apartamentos** 12
appear **parecer** *v.*
appetizers **entremeses** *m., pl.* 8
applaud **aplaudir** *v.*
apple **manzana** *f.* 8
appliance (*electric*)
electrodoméstico *m.* 12
applicant **aspirante** *m., f.*
application **solicitud** *f.*
job application **solicitud de
trabajo**
apply (*for a job*) **solicitar** *v.*
apply for a loan **pedir (e:ie)** *v.*
un préstamo 14
appointment **cita** *f.* 9
have an appointment **tener** *v.*
una cita 9
appreciate **apreciar** *v.*

April **abril** *m.* 5
aquatic **acuático/a** *adj.*
archaeologist **arqueólogo/a**
m., f.
archaeology **arqueología** *f.* 2
architect **arquitecto/a** *m., f.*
area **región** *f.* 13
Argentina **Argentina** *f.* 1
Argentine **argentino/a** *adj.* 3
arm **brazo** *m.* 10
armchair **sillón** *m.* 12
army **ejército** *m.*
around **por** *prep.* 11
around here **por aquí** 11
arrange **arreglar** *v.* 11
arrival **llegada** *f.* 5
arrive **llegar** *v.* 2
art **arte** *m.* 2
(fine) arts **bellas artes** *f., pl.*
article *m.* **artículo**
artist **artista** *m., f.* 3
artistic **artístico/a** *adj.*
arts **artes** *f., pl.*
as **como** 8
as a child **de niño/a** 10
as... as **tan... como** 8
as many... as **tantos/as...
como** 8
as much... as **tanto...
como** 8
as soon as **en cuanto** *conj.* 13;
tan pronto como *conj.* 13
ask (*a question*) **preguntar** *v.* 2
ask for **pedir (e:i)** *v.* 4
asparagus **espárragos** *m., pl.* 8
aspirin **aspirina** *f.* 10
at **a** *prep.* 1; **en** *prep.* 2
at + *time* **a la(s)** + *time* 1
at home **en casa** 7
at least **por lo menos** 10
at night **por la noche** 7
at the end (of) **al fondo (de)** 12
At what time...? **¿A qué
hora...?** 1
At your service. **A sus
órdenes.** 11
ATM **cajero automático** *m.* 14
attempt **intento** *m.* 11
attend **asistir (a)** *v.* 3
attic **altillo** *m.* 12
attract **atraer** *v.* 4
audience **público** *m.*
August **agosto** *m.* 5
aunt **tía** *f.* 3
aunts and uncles **tíos** *m., pl.* 3
automobile **automóvil** *m.* 5;
carro *m.*; **coche** *m.* 11
autumn **otoño** *m.* 5
avenue **avenida** *f.*
avoid **evitar** *v.* 13
award **premio** *m.*

B

backpack **mochila** *f.* 2
bad **mal, malo/a** *adj.* 3
It's bad that... **Es malo
que...** 12

It's not at all bad. **No está nada mal.** 5
bag **bolsa** *f.* 6
bakery **panadería** *f.* 14
balanced **equilibrado/a** *adj.* 15
 to eat a balanced diet **comer una dieta equilibrada** 15
balcony **balcón** *m.* 12
ball **pelota** *f.* 4
banana **banana** *f.* 8
band **banda** *f.*
bank **banco** *m.* 14
bargain **ganga** *f.* 6; **regatear** *v.* 6
baseball (*game*) **béisbol** *m.* 4
basement **sótano** *m.* 12
basketball (*game*) **baloncesto** *m.* 4
bathe **bañarse** *v.* 7
bathing suit **traje** *m.* **de baño** 6
bathroom **baño** *m.* 7; **cuarto de baño** *m.* 7
be **ser** *v.* 1; **estar** *v.* 2
 be... years old **tener... años** 3
 be sick of... **estar harto/a de...**
beach **playa** *f.* 5
beans **frijoles** *m., pl.* 8
beautiful **hermoso/a** *adj.* 6
beauty **belleza** *f.* 14
 beauty salon **peluquería** *f.* 14; **salón** *m.* **de belleza** 14
because **porque** *conj.* 2
 because of **por** *prep.* 11
become (+ *adj.*) **ponerse (+ adj.)** 7; **convertirse** *v.*
bed **cama** *f.* 5
 go to bed **acostarse (o:ue)** *v.* 7
bedroom **alcoba** *f.*; **dormitorio** *m.* 12; **recámara** *f.*
beef **carne de res** *f.* 8
been **sido** *p.p.* 15
beer **cerveza** *f.* 8
before **antes** *adv.* 7; **antes de** *prep.* 7; **antes (de) que** *conj.* 13
beg **rogar (o:ue)** *v.* 12
begin **comenzar (e:ie)** *v.* 4; **empezar (e:ie)** *v.* 4
behalf: on behalf of **de parte de** 11
behind **detrás de** *prep.* 2
believe (in) **creer** *v.* (**en**) 3; **creer** *v.* 13
 not to believe **no creer** 13
believed **creído/a** *p.p.* 14
bellhop **botones** *m., f. sing.* 5
below **debajo de** *prep.* 2
belt **cinturón** *m.* 6
benefit **beneficio** *m.*
beside **al lado de** *prep.* 2
besides **además (de)** *adv.* 10
best **mejor** *adj.*
 the best **el/la mejor** *m., f.* 8; **lo mejor** *neuter*
better **mejor** *adj.* 8
 It's better that... **Es mejor que...** 12
between **entre** *prep.* 2
beverage **bebida** *f.*

alcoholic beverage **bebida alcohólica** *f.* 15
bicycle **bicicleta** *f.* 4
big **gran, grande** *adj.* 3
bill **cuenta** *f.* 9
billion **mil millones**
biology **biología** *f.* 2
bird **ave** *f.* 13; **pájaro** *m.* 13
birth **nacimiento** *m.* 9
birthday **cumpleaños** *m., sing.* 9
 have a birthday **cumplir** *v.* **años** 9
black **negro/a** *adj.* 6
blackboard **pizarra** *f.* 2
blanket **manta** *f.* 12
block (city) **cuadra** *f.* 14
blog **blog** *m.* 11
blond(e) **rubio/a** *adj.* 3
blouse **blusa** *f.* 6
blue **azul** *adj. m., f.* 6
boarding house **pensión** *f.*
boat **barco** *m.* 5
body **cuerpo** *m.* 10
bone **hueso** *m.* 10
book **libro** *m.* 2
bookcase **estante** *m.* 12
bookshelves **estante** *m.* 12
bookstore **librería** *f.* 2
boot **bota** *f.* 6
bore **aburrir** *v.* 7
bored **aburrido/a** *adj.* 5
 be bored **estar** *v.* **aburrido/a** 5
 get bored **aburrirse** *v.*
boring **aburrido/a** *adj.* 5
born: be born **nacer** *v.* 9
borrow **pedir (e:ie)** *v.* **prestado** 14
borrowed **prestado/a** *adj.*
boss **jefe** *m.*, **jefa** *f.*
bother **molestar** *v.* 7
bottle **botella** *f.* 9
 bottle of wine **botella de vino** 9
bottom **fondo** *m.*
boulevard **bulevar** *m.*
boy **chico** *m.* 1; **muchacho** *m.* 3
boyfriend **novio** *m.* 3
brakes **frenos** *m., pl.*
bread **pan** *m.* 8
break **romper** *v.* 10
 break (one's leg) **romperse (la pierna)** 10
break down **dañar** *v.* 10
 The... broke down. **Se nos dañó el/la...** 11
 break up (with) **romper** *v.* **(con)** 9
breakfast **desayuno** *m.* 2, 8
 have breakfast **desayunar** *v.* 2
breathe **respirar** *v.* 13
bring **traer** *v.* 4
broadcast **transmitir** *v.*; **emitir** *v.*
brochure **folleto** *m.*
broken **roto/a** *adj.* 10, 14
 be broken **estar roto/a** 10
brother **hermano** *m.* 3

brother-in-law **cuñado** *m., f.* 3
brothers and sisters **hermanos** *m., pl.* 3
brought **traído/a** *p.p.* 14
brown **café** *adj.* 6; **marrón** *adj.* 6
brunet(te) **moreno/a** *adj.* 3
brush **cepillar** *v.* 7
 brush one's hair **cepillarse el pelo** 7
 brush one's teeth **cepillarse los dientes** 7
bucket **balde** *m.* 5
build **construir** *v.* 4
building **edificio** *m.* 12
bump into (*something accidentally*) **darse con** 10; (*someone*) **encontrarse** *v.* 11
burn (a CD/DVD) **quemar** *v.* **(un CD/DVD)**
burned (out) **quemado/a** *adj.* 11
bus **autobús** *m.* 1
 bus station **estación** *f.* **de autobuses** 5
business **negocios** *m. pl.*
 business administration **administración** *f.* **de empresas** 2
 business-related **comercial** *adj.*
businessperson **hombre** *m.* **/ mujer** *f.* **de negocios**
busy **ocupado/a** *adj.* 5
but **pero** *conj.* 2; (rather) **sino** *conj.* (in negative sentences) 7
butcher shop **carnicería** *f.* 14
butter **mantequilla** *f.* 8
buy **comprar** *v.* 2
by **por** *prep.* 11; **para** *prep.* 11
 by means of **por** *prep.* 11
 by phone **por teléfono** 11
 by plane **en avión** 5
 by way of **por** *prep.* 11
bye **chau** *interj. fam.* 1

C

cable television **televisión** *f.* **por cable** *m.* 11
café **café** *m.* 4
cafeteria **cafetería** *f.* 2
caffeine **cafeína** *f.* 15
cake **pastel** *m.* 9
 chocolate cake **pastel de chocolate** *m.* 9
calculator **calculadora** *f.* 2
call **llamar** *v.* 11
 be called **llamarse** *v.* 7
 call on the phone **llamar por teléfono**
calm **tranquilo/a** *adj.* 15
calorie **caloría** *f.* 15
camera **cámara** *f.* 11
camp **acampar** *v.* 5
can (tin) **lata** *f.* 13
can **poder (o:ue)** *v.* 4
 Could I ask you something? **¿Podría pedirte algo?**

Canadian **canadiense** *adj.* 3
candidate **aspirante** *m., f.*;
 candidate **candidato/a** *m., f.*
candy **dulces** *m., pl.* 9
capital city **capital** *f.* 1
car **coche** *m.* 11; **carro** *m.* 11;
 auto(móvil) *m.* 5
caramel **caramelo** *m.* 9
card **tarjeta** *f.*; *(playing)*
 carta *f.* 5
care **cuidado** *m.* 3
 Take care! **¡Cuídense!** *v.* 15
 take care of **cuidar** *v.* 13
career **carrera** *f.*
careful: be (very) careful **tener** *v.*
 (mucho) cuidado 3
caretaker **ama** *m., f.* **de casa** 12
carpenter **carpintero/a** *m., f.*
carpet **alfombra** *f.* 12
carrot **zanahoria** *f.* 8
carry **llevar** *v.* 2
cartoons **dibujos** *m, pl.*
 animados
case: in case (that) **en caso (de)**
 que 13
cash (a check) **cobrar** *v.* 14;
 cash **(en) efectivo** 6
 cash register **caja** *f.* 6
 pay in cash **pagar** *v.* **al contado**
 14; **pagar en efectivo** 14
cashier **cajero/a** *m., f.*
cat **gato** *m.* 13
CD **disco compacto** *m.* 11
CD player **reproductor de CD**
 m. 11
CD-ROM **cederrón** *m.* 11
celebrate **celebrar** *v.* 9
celebration **celebración** *f.*
 young woman's fifteenth
 birthday celebration
 quinceañera *f.* 9
cellar **sótano** *m.* 12
(cell) phone **(teléfono)**
 celular *m.* 11
cemetery **cementerio** *m.* 9
cereal **cereales** *m., pl.* 8
certain **cierto** *m.*; **seguro** *m.* 13
 it's (not) certain **(no) es**
 cierto/seguro 13
chalk **tiza** *f.* 2
champagne **champán** *m.* 9
change: in change **de cambio** 2
change **cambiar** *v.* **(de)** 9
channel *(TV)* **canal** *m.* 11
character *(fictional)* **personaje**
 m. 11
 (main) character *m.* **personaje**
 (principal)
chat **conversar** *v.* 2
chauffeur **conductor(a)** *m., f.* 1
cheap **barato/a** *adj.* 6
check **comprobar (o:ue)** *v.*;
 revisar *v.* 11; *(bank)* **cheque**
 m. 14
 check the oil **revisar el aceite** 11
checking account **cuenta** *f.*
 corriente 14
cheese **queso** *m.* 8
chef **cocinero/a** *m., f.*

chemistry **química** *f.* 2
chest of drawers **cómoda** *f.* 12
chicken **pollo** *m.* 8
child **niño/a** *m., f.* 3
childhood **niñez** *f.* 9
children **hijos** *m., pl.* 3
Chinese **chino/a** *adj.* 3
chocolate **chocolate** *m.* 9
 chocolate cake **pastel** *m.* **de**
 chocolate 9
cholesterol **colesterol** *m.* 15
choose **escoger** *v.* 8
chop *(food)* **chuleta** *f.* 8
Christmas **Navidad** *f.* 9
church **iglesia** *f.* 4
cinnamon **canela** *f.* 10
citizen **ciudadano/a** *adj.*
city **ciudad** *f.* 4
class **clase** *f.* 2
 take classes **tomar clases** 2
classical **clásico/a** *adj.*
classmate **compañero/a** *m., f.* **de**
 clase 2
clean **limpio/a** *adj.* 5;
 limpiar *v.* 12
 clean the house *v.* **limpiar la**
 casa 12
clear *(weather)* **despejado/a** *adj.*
 clear the table **quitar la**
 mesa 12
 It's (very) clear. *(weather)*
 Está (muy) despejado.
clerk **dependiente/a** *m., f.* 6
climate change **cambio climático**
 m. 13
climb **escalar** *v.* 4
 climb mountains **escalar**
 montañas 4
clinic **clínica** *f.* 10
clock **reloj** *m.* 2
close **cerrar (e:ie)** *v.* 4
closed **cerrado/a** *adj.* 5
closet **armario** *m.* 12
clothes **ropa** *f.* 6
 clothes dryer **secadora** *f.* 12
clothing **ropa** *f.* 6
cloud **nube** *f.* 13
cloudy **nublado/a** *adj.* 5
 It's (very) cloudy. **Está (muy)**
 nublado. 5
coat **abrigo** *m.* 6
coffee **café** *m.* 8
 coffee maker **cafetera** *f.* 12
cold **frío** *m.* 5;
 (illness) **resfriado** *m.* 10
 be *(feel)* (very) cold **tener**
 (mucho) frío 3
 It's (very) cold. *(weather)* **Hace**
 (mucho) frío. 5
college **universidad** *f.* 2
collision **choque** *m.*
color **color** *m.* 6
comb one's hair **peinarse** *v.* 7
come **venir** *v.* 3
come on **ándale** *interj.* 14
comedy **comedia** *f.*
comfortable **cómodo/a** *adj.* 5
commerce **negocios** *m., pl.*
commercial **comercial** *adj.*

communicate (with) **comunicarse**
 v. **(con)**
communication **comunicación** *f.*
 means of communication
 medios *m. pl.* **de**
 comunicación
community **comunidad** *f.* 1
company **compañía** *f.*;
 empresa *f.*
comparison **comparación** *f.*
completely **completamente** *adv.*
composer **compositor(a)** *m., f.*
computer **computadora** *f.* 1
 computer disc **disco** *m.*
 computer monitor **monitor**
 m. 11
 computer programmer
 programador(a) *m., f.* 3
 computer science **computación**
 f. 2
concert **concierto** *m.*
conductor *(musical)* **director(a)**
 m., f.
confirm **confirmar** *v.* 5
 confirm a reservation **confirmar**
 una reservación 5
confused **confundido/a** *adj.* 5
congested **congestionado/a**
 adj. 10
Congratulations! **¡Felicidades!**;
 ¡Felicitaciones! *f., pl.* 9
conservation **conservación** *f.* 13
conserve **conservar** *v.* 13
considering **para** *prep.* 11
consume **consumir** *v.* 15
container **envase** *m.* 13
contamination **contaminación** *f.*
content **contento/a** *adj.* 5
contest **concurso** *m.*
continue **seguir (e:i)** *v.* 4
control **control** *m.*; **controlar** *v.* 13
 be under control **estar bajo**
 control 7
conversation **conversación** *f.* 1
converse **conversar** *v.* 2
cook **cocinar** *v.* 12; **cocinero/a**
 m., f.
cookie **galleta** *f.* 9
cool **fresco/a** *adj.* 5
 Be cool. **Tranquilo.** 7
 It's cool. *(weather)* **Hace**
 fresco. 5
corn **maíz** *m.* 8
corner **esquina** *f.* 14
cost **costar (o:ue)** *v.* 6
Costa Rica **Costa Rica** *f.* 1
Costa Rican **costarricense** *adj.* 3
costume **disfraz** *m.*
cotton **algodón** *m.* 6
 (made of) cotton **de algodón** 6
couch **sofá** *m.* 12
couch potato **teleadicto/a**
 m., f. 15
cough **tos** *f.* 10; **toser** *v.* 10
counselor **consejero/a** *m., f.*
count (on) **contar (o:ue)** *v.*
 (con) 4, 12
country *(nation)* **país** *m.* 1
countryside **campo** *m.* 5

(married) couple **pareja** *f.* 9
course **curso** *m.* 2; **materia** *f.* 2
courtesy **cortesía** *f.*
cousin **primo/a** *m., f.* 3
cover **cubrir** *v.*
covered **cubierto/a** *p.p.*
cow **vaca** *f.* 13
crafts **artesanía** *f.*
craftsmanship **artesanía** *f.*
crater **cráter** *m.* 13
crazy **loco/a** *adj.* 6
create **crear** *v.*
credit **crédito** *m.* 6
 credit card **tarjeta** *f.* **de crédito** 6
crime **crimen** *m.*
cross **cruzar** *v.* 14
cry **llorar** *v.* 15
Cuba **Cuba** *f.* 1
Cuban **cubano/a** *adj.* 3
culture **cultura** *f.* 2
cup **taza** *f.* 12
currency exchange **cambio** *m.* **de moneda**
current events **actualidades** *f., pl.*
curtains **cortinas** *f., pl.* 12
custard (*baked*) **flan** *m.* 9
custom **costumbre** *f.* 1
customer **cliente/a** *m., f.* 6
customs **aduana** *f.* 5
 customs inspector **inspector(a)** *m., f.* **de aduanas** 5
cybercafé **cibercafé** *m.* 11
cycling **ciclismo** *m.* 4

D

dad **papá** *m.* 3
daily **diario/a** *adj.* 7
 daily routine **rutina** *f.* **diaria** 7
damage **dañar** *v.* 10
dance **bailar** *v.* 2; **danza** *f;* **baile** *m.*
dancer **bailarín/bailarina** *m., f.*
danger **peligro** *m.* 13
dangerous **peligroso/a** *adj.*
date (*appointment*) **cita** *f.* 9; (*calendar*) **fecha** *f.* 5; (*someone*) **salir** *v.* **con (alguien)** 9
 have a date **tener una cita** 9
daughter **hija** *f.* 3
daughter-in-law **nuera** *f.* 3
day **día** *m.* 1
 day before yesterday **anteayer** *adv.* 6
deal: It's not a big deal. **No es para tanto.** 12
death **muerte** *f.* 9
decaffeinated **descafeinado/a** *adj.* 15
December **diciembre** *m.* 5
decide **decidir** *v.* (**+ inf.**) 3
decided **decidido/a** *adj. p.p.* 14
declare **declarar** *v.*
deforestation **deforestación** *f.* 13

delicious **delicioso/a** *adj.* 8; **rico/a** *adj.* 8; **sabroso/a** *adj.* 8
delighted **encantado/a** *adj.* 1
dentist **dentista** *m., f.* 10
deny **negar (e:ie)** *v.* 13
 not to deny **no dudar** 13
department store **almacén** *m.* 6
departure **salida** *f.* 5
deposit **depositar** *v.* 14
describe **describir** *v.* 3
described **descrito/a** *p.p.* 14
desert **desierto** *m.* 13
design **diseño** *m.*
designer **diseñador(a)** *m., f.*
desire **desear** *v.* 2
desk **escritorio** *m.* 2
dessert **postre** *m.* 9
destroy **destruir** *v.* 13
develop **desarrollar** *v.* 13
diary **diario** *m.* 1
dictatorship **dictadura** *f.*
dictionary **diccionario** *m.* 1
die **morir (o:ue)** *v.* 8
died **muerto/a** *p.p.* 14
diet **dieta** *f.* 15; **alimentación**
 balanced diet **dieta equilibrada** 15
 be on a diet **estar a dieta** 15
difficult **difícil** *adj. m., f.* 3
digital camera **cámara** *f.* **digital** 11
dining room **comedor** *m.* 12
dinner **cena** *f.* 2, 8
 have dinner **cenar** *v.* 2
direct **dirigir** *v.*
director **director(a)** *m., f.*
dirty **ensuciar** *v.;* **sucio/a** *adj.* 5
 get (something) dirty **ensuciar** *v.* 12
disagree **no estar de acuerdo**
disaster **desastre** *m.*
discover **descubrir** *v.* 13
discovered **descubierto/a** *p.p.* 14
discrimination **discriminación** *f.*
dish **plato** *m.* 8, 12
 main dish *m.* **plato principal** 8
dishwasher **lavaplatos** *m., sing.* 12
disk **disco** *m.*
disorderly **desordenado/a** *adj.* 5
dive **bucear** *v.* 4
divorce **divorcio** *m.* 9
divorced **divorciado/a** *adj.* 9
 get divorced (from) **divorciarse** *v.* (**de**) 9
dizzy **mareado/a** *adj.* 10
do **hacer** *v.* 4
 do aerobics **hacer ejercicios aeróbicos** 15
 do household chores **hacer quehaceres domésticos** 12
 do stretching exercises **hacer ejercicios de estiramiento** 15
 (I) don't want to. **No quiero.** 4
doctor **doctor(a)** *m., f.* 3; 10; **médico/a** *m., f.* 3
documentary (*film*) **documental** *m.*
dog **perro** *m.* 13

domestic **doméstico/a** *adj.*
 domestic appliance **electrodoméstico** *m.*
done **hecho/a** *p.p.* 14
door **puerta** *f.* 2
doorman/doorwoman **portero/a** *m., f.* 1
dormitory **residencia** *f.* **estudiantil** 2
double **doble** *adj.* 5
 double room **habitación** *f.* **doble** 5
doubt **duda** *f.* 13; **dudar** *v.* 13
 not to doubt 13
 There is no doubt that... **No cabe duda de** 13; **No hay duda de** 13
Down with...! **¡Abajo el/la...!**
download **descargar** *v.* 11
downtown **centro** *m.* 4
drama **drama** *m.*
dramatic **dramático/a** *adj.*
draw **dibujar** *v.* 2
drawing **dibujo** *m.*
dress **vestido** *m.* 6
 get dressed **vestirse (e:i)** *v.* 7
drink **beber** *v.* 3; **bebida** *f.* 8; **tomar** *v.* 2
drive **conducir** *v.* 6; **manejar** *v.* 11
driver **conductor(a)** *m., f.* 1
drug **droga** *f.* 15
 drug addict **drogadicto/a** *adj.* 15
dry oneself **secarse** *v.* 7
during **durante** *prep.* 7; **por** *prep.* 11
dust **sacudir** *v.* 12; **quitar** *v.* **el polvo** 12
 dust the furniture **sacudir los muebles** 12
duster **plumero** *m.* 12
DVD player **reproductor** *m.* **de DVD** 11

E

each **cada** *adj.* 6
each other **los unos a los otros** 11
eagle **águila** *f.*
ear (outer) **oreja** *f.* 10
earing **arete** *m.* 6
early **temprano** *adv.* 7
earn **ganar** *v.*
earthquake **terremoto** *m.*
ease **aliviar** *v.*
east **este** *m.* 14
 to the east **al este** 14
easy **fácil** *adj. m., f.* 3
eat **comer** *v.* 3
ecological **ecologista** *adj. m., f.* 13
ecologist **ecologista** *m., f.* 13
ecology **ecología** *f.* 13
economics **economía** *f.* 2
ecotourism **ecoturismo** *m.* 13
Ecuador **Ecuador** *m.* 1
Ecuadorian **ecuatoriano/a** *adj.* 3
effective **eficaz** *adj. m., f.*
egg **huevo** *m.* 8

eight **ocho** 1
eight hundred **ochocientos/as** 2
eighteen **dieciocho** 1
eighth **octavo/a** 5
eighty **ochenta** 2
either... or **o... o** *conj.* 7
eldest **el/la mayor** 8
elect **elegir** *v.*
election **elecciones** *f. pl.*
electric appliance
 electrodoméstico *m.* 12
electrician **electricista** *m., f.*
electricity **luz** *f.* 12
elegant **elegante** *adj. m., f.* 6
elevator **ascensor** *m.* 5
eleven **once** 1
e-mail **correo** *m.* **electrónico** 4
e-mail address **dirrección** *f.*
 electrónica 11
 e-mail message **mensaje** *m.*
 electrónico 4
 read e-mail **leer** *v.* **el correo**
 electrónico 4
embarrassed **avergonzado/a**
 adj. 5 embrace (each other)
 abrazar(se) *v.* 11
emergency **emergencia** *f.* 10
 emergency room **sala** *f.* **de**
 emergencia 10
employee **empleado/a** *m., f.* 5
employment **empleo** *m.*
end **fin** *m.* 4; **terminar** *v.* 2
 end table **mesita** *f.* 12
endure **aguantar** *v.* 14
energy **energía** *f.* 13
engaged: get engaged (to)
 comprometerse *v.* **(con)** 9
engineer **ingeniero/a** *m., f.* 3
English (language) **inglés** *m.* 2;
 inglés, inglesa *adj.* 3
enjoy **disfrutar** *v.* **(de)** 15
enough **bastante** *adv.* 10
entertainment **diversión** *f.* 4
entrance **entrada** *f.* 12
envelope **sobre** *m.* 14
environment **medio ambiente**
 m. 13
environmental sciences **ciencias**
 ambientales 2
equality **igualdad** *f.*
equipped **equipado/a** *adj.* 15
erase **borrar** *v.* 11
eraser **borrador** *m.* 2
errand **diligencia** *f.* 14
essay **ensayo** *m.* 3
evening **tarde** *f.* 1
event **acontecimiento** *m.*
every day **todos los días** 10
everything **todo** *m.* 5
 Everything is under control.
 Todo está bajo control. 7
exactly **en punto** 1
exam **examen** *m.* 2
excellent **excelente** *adj.* 5
excess **exceso** *m.* 15
 in excess **en exceso** 15
exchange **intercambiar** *v.*
 in exchange for **por** 11
exciting **emocionante** *adj. m., f.*
excursion **excursión** *f.*

excuse **disculpar** *v.*
Excuse me. (*May I?*) **Con**
 permiso. 1; (*I beg your*
 pardon.) **Perdón.** 1
exercise **ejercicio** *m.* 15;
 hacer *v.* **ejercicio** 15;
 (a degree/profession) **ejercer** *v.*
exit **salida** *f.* 5
expensive **caro/a** *adj.* 6
experience **experiencia** *f.*
expire **vencer** *v.* 14
explain **explicar** *v.* 2
explore **explorar** *v.*
expression **expresión** *f.*
extinction **extinción** *f.* 13
extremely delicious **riquísimo/a**
 adj. 8
extremely serious **gravísimo**
 adj. 13
eye **ojo** *m.* 10

F

fabulous **fabuloso/a** *adj.* 5
face **cara** *f.* 7
facing **enfrente de** *prep.* 14
fact: in fact **de hecho**
factory **fábrica** *f.* 13
fall (down) **caerse** *v.* 10
 fall asleep **dormirse (o:ue)** *v.* 7
 fall in love (with) **enamorarse**
 v. **(de)** 9
fall (season) **otoño** *m.* 5
fallen **caído/a** *p.p.* 14
family **familia** *f.* 3
famous **famoso/a** *adj.*
fan **aficionado/a** *adj.* 4
 be a fan (of) **ser aficionado/a**
 (a) 4
far from **lejos de** *prep.* 2
farewell **despedida** *f.*
fascinate **fascinar** *v.* 7
fashion **moda** *f.* 6
 be in fashion **estar de moda** 6
fast **rápido/a** *adj.*
fat **gordo/a** *adj.* 3; **grasa** *f.* 15
father **padre** *m.* 3
father-in-law **suegro** *m.* 3
favorite **favorito/a** *adj.* 4
fax (machine) *fax* *m.* 11
fear **miedo** *m.* 3; **temer** *v.* 13
February **febrero** *m.* 5
feel **sentir(se) (e:ie)** *v.* 7
 feel like (*doing something*) **tener**
 ganas de (+ *inf.*) 3
festival **festival** *m.*
fever **fiebre** *f.* 10
 have a fever **tener** *v.* **fiebre** 10
few **pocos/as** *adj. pl.*
 fewer than **menos de**
 (+ *number*) 8
field: major field of study
 especialización *f.*
fifteen **quince** 1
 fifteen-year-old girl **quinceañera** *f.*

young woman celebrating her
 fifteenth birthday **quinceañera**
 f. 9
fifth **quinto/a** 5
fifty **cincuenta** 2
fight (for/against) **luchar** *v.* **(por/**
 contra)
figure (*number*) **cifra** *f.*
file **archivo** *m.* 11
fill **llenar** *v.* 11
 fill out (a form) **llenar (un**
 formulario) 14
 fill the tank **llenar el**
 tanque 11
finally **finalmente** *adv.* 15; **por**
 último 7; **por fin** 11
find **encontrar (o:ue)** *v.* 4
 find (each other) **encontrar(se)**
 find out **enterarse** *v.*
fine **multa** *f.*
 That's fine. **Está bien.** 11
(fine) arts **bellas artes** *f., pl.*
finger **dedo** *m.* 10
finish **terminar** *v.* 2
 finish (*doing something*)
 terminar *v.* **de (+ *inf.*)** 4
fire **incendio** *m.*; **despedir**
 (e:i) *v.*
firefighter **bombero/a** *m., f.*
firm **compañía** *f.*; **empresa** *f.*
first **primer, primero/a** 2, 5
fish (*food*) **pescado** *m.* 8;
 pescar *v.* 5; (*live*) **pez** *m., sing.*
 (peces *pl.*) 13
 fish market **pescadería** *f.* 14
fishing **pesca** *f.* 5
fit (*clothing*) **quedar** *v.* 7
five **cinco** 1
five hundred **quinientos/as** 2
fix (*put in working order*) **arreglar**
 v. 11; (*clothes, hair, etc. to*
 go out) **arreglarse** 7
fixed **fijo/a** *adj.* 6
flag **bandera** *f.*
flank steak **lomo** *m.* 8
flat tire: We had a flat tire. **Se nos**
 pinchó una llanta. 11
flexible **flexible** *adj.* 15
flood **inundación** *f.*
floor (*of a building*) **piso** *m.* 5;
 suelo *m.* 12
 ground floor **planta baja** *f.* 5
 top floor **planta** *f.* **alta**
flower **flor** *f.* 13
flu **gripe** *f.* 10
fog **niebla** *f.*
folk **folclórico/a** *adj.*
follow **seguir (e:i)** *v.* 4
food **comida** *f.* 4, 8
foolish **tonto/a** *adj.* 3
foot **pie** *m.* 10
football **fútbol** *m.* **americano** 4
for **para** *prep.* 11; **por** *prep.* 11
 for example **por ejemplo** 11
 for me **para mí** 8

forbid **prohibir** *v.*
foreign **extranjero/a** *adj.*
 foreign languages **lenguas** *f., pl.* **extranjeras** 2
forest **bosque** *m.* 13
forget **olvidar** *v.* 10
fork **tenedor** *m.* 12
form **formulario** *m.* 14
forty **cuarenta** *m.* 2
four **cuatro** 1
four hundred **cuatrocientos/as** 2
fourteen **catorce** 1
fourth **cuarto/a** *m., f.* 5
free **libre** *adj. m., f.* 4
 be free (of charge) **ser gratis** 14
 free time **tiempo libre**; spare (free) time **ratos libres** 4
freedom **libertad** *f.*
freezer **congelador** *m.* 12
French **francés, francesa** *adj.* 3
 French fries **papas** *f., pl.* **fritas** 8; **patatas** *f., pl.* **fritas** 8
frequently **frecuentemente** *adv.* 10; **con frecuencia** *adv.* 10
Friday **viernes** *m., sing.* 2
fried **frito/a** *adj.* 8
 fried potatoes **papas** *f., pl.* **fritas** 8; **patatas** *f., pl.* **fritas** 8
friend **amigo/a** *m., f.* 3
friendly **amable** *adj. m., f.* 5
friendship **amistad** *f.* 9
from **de** *prep.* 1; **desde** *prep.* 6
 from the United States **estadounidense** *m., f. adj.* 3
 from time to time **de vez en cuando** 10
 He/She/It is from... **Es de...**; I'm from... **Soy de...** 1
front: (cold) front **frente (frío)** *m.* 5
fruit **fruta** *f.* 8
 fruit juice **jugo** *m.* **de fruta** 8
 fruit store **frutería** *f.* 14
full **lleno/a** *adj.* 11
fun **divertido/a** *adj.* 7
 fun activity **diversión** *f.* 4
 have fun **divertirse (e:ie)** *v.* 9
function **funcionar** *v.*
furniture **muebles** *m., pl.* 12
furthermore **además (de)** *adv.* 10
future **futuro** *adj.*; **porvenir** *m.*
 Here's to the future! **¡Por el porvenir!**
 in the future **en el futuro**

G

gain weight **aumentar** *v.* **de peso** 15; **engordar** *v.* 15
game **juego** *m.*; (*match*) **partido** *m.* 4
 game show **concurso** *m.*
garage (*in a house*) **garaje** *m.* 12; **garaje** *m.* 11; **taller (mecánico)** 11

garden **jardín** *m.* 12
garlic **ajo** *m.* 8
gas station **gasolinera** *f.* 11
gasoline **gasolina** *f.* 11
gentleman **caballero** *m.* 8
geography **geografía** *f.* 2
German **alemán, alemana** *adj.* 3
get **conseguir (e:i)** *v.* 4; **obtener** *v.*
 get along well/badly (with) **llevarse bien/mal (con)** 9
 get bigger **aumentar** *v.* 13
 get bored **aburrirse** *v.*
 get good grades **sacar buenas notas** 2
 get into trouble **meterse en problemas** *v.* 13
 get off of (a vehicle) **bajar(se)** *v.* **de** 11
 get on/into (a vehicle) **subir(se)** *v.* **a** 11
 get out of (a vehicle) **bajar(se)** *v.* **de** 11
 get ready **arreglarse** *v.* 7
 get up **levantarse** *v.* 7
gift **regalo** *m.* 6
ginger **jengibre** *m.* 10
girl **chica** *f.* 1; **muchacha** *f.* 3
girlfriend **novia** *f.* 3
give **dar** *v.* 6, 9; (*as a gift*) **regalar** 9
 give directions **indicar cómo llegar** 14
glass (*drinking*) **vaso** *m.* 12; **vidrio** *m.* 13
 (made) of glass **de vidrio** 13
glasses **gafas** *f., pl.* 6
 sunglasses **gafas** *f., pl.* **de sol** 6
global warming **calentamiento global** *m.* 13
gloves **guantes** *m., pl.* 6
go **ir** *v.* 4
 go away **irse** 7
 go by boat **ir en barco** 5
 go by bus **ir en autobús** 5
 go by car **ir en auto(móvil)** 5
 go by motorcycle **ir en motocicleta** 5
 go by taxi **ir en taxi** 5
 go by the bank **pasar por el banco** 14
 go down **bajar(se)** *v.*
 go on a hike (in the mountains) **ir de excursión (a las montañas)** 4
 go out **salir** *v.* 9
 go out (with) **salir** *v.* **(con)** 9
 go up **subir** *v.*
 Let's go. **Vamos.** 4
goblet **copa** *f.* 12
going to: be going to (*do something*) **ir a (+ *inf.*)** 4
golf **golf** *m.* 4
good **buen, bueno/a** *adj.* 3, 6
 Good afternoon. **Buenas tardes.** 1

Good evening. **Buenas noches.** 1
 Good idea. **Buena idea.** 4
 Good morning. **Buenos días.** 1
 Good night. **Buenas noches.** 1
 It's good that... **Es bueno que...** 12
goodbye **adiós** *m.* 1
 say goodbye (to) **despedirse** *v.* **(de) (e:i)** 7
good-looking **guapo/a** *adj.* 3
government **gobierno** *m.* 13
GPS **navegador GPS** *m.* 11
graduate (from/in) **graduarse** *v.* **(de/en)** 9
grains **cereales** *m., pl.* 8
granddaughter **nieta** *f.* 3
grandfather **abuelo** *m.* 3
grandmother **abuela** *f.* 3
grandparents **abuelos** *m., pl.* 3
grandson **nieto** *m.* 3
grape **uva** *f.* 8
grass **hierba** *f.* 13
grave **grave** *adj.* 10
gray **gris** *adj. m., f.* 6
great **fenomenal** *adj. m., f.* 5; **genial** *adj.*
great-grandfather **bisabuelo** *m.* 3
great-grandmother **bisabuela** *f.* 3
green **verde** *adj. m., f.* 6
greet (each other) **saludar(se)** *v.* 11
greeting **saludo** *m.* 1
 Greetings to... **Saludos a...** 1
grilled **a la plancha** 8
ground floor **planta baja** *f.* 5
grow **aumentar** *v.* 13
guest (*at a house/hotel*) **huésped** *m., f.* 5 (*invited to a function*) **invitado/a** *m., f.* 9
guide **guía** *m., f.* 13
gymnasium **gimnasio** *m.* 4

H

hair **pelo** *m.* 7
hairdresser **peluquero/a** *m., f.*
half **medio/a** *adj.* 3
 half-brother **medio hermano** 3
 half-sister **media hermana** 3
 half-past... (*time*) **...y media** 1
hallway **pasillo** *m.* 12
ham **jamón** *m.* 8
hamburger **hamburguesa** *f.* 8
hand **mano** *f.* 1
hand in **entregar** *v.* 11
handsome **guapo/a** *adj.* 3
happen **ocurrir** *v.*
happiness **alegría** *v.* 9
Happy birthday! **¡Feliz cumpleaños!** 9
happy **alegre** *adj.* 5; **contento/a** *adj.* 5; **feliz** *adj. m., f.* 5
 be happy **alegrarse** *v.* **(de)** 13
hard **difícil** *adj. m., f.* 3

hard-working **trabajador(a)**
 adj. 3
hardly **apenas** *adv.* 10
haste **prisa** *f.* 3
hat **sombrero** *m.* 6
hate **odiar** *v.* 9
have **tener** *v.* 3
 have time **tener tiempo** 4
 have to (*do something*) **tener**
 que (+ *inf.*) 3; **deber** (+ *inf.*)
 have a tooth removed **sacar(se)**
 un diente 10
he **él** 1
head **cabeza** *f.* 10
headache **dolor** *m.* **de cabeza** 10
health **salud** *f.* 10
healthy **saludable** *adj. m., f.* 10;
 sano/a *adj.* 10
 lead a healthy lifestyle **llevar** *v.*
 una vida sana 15
hear **oír** *v.* 4
heard **oído/a** *p.p.* 14
hearing: sense of hearing **oído**
 m. 10
heart **corazón** *m.* 10
heat **calor** *m.* 5
Hello. **Hola.** 1; (*on the telephone*)
 Aló. 11; **Bueno.** 11; **Diga.** 11
help **ayudar** *v.* 12; **servir (e:i)**
 v. 5
 help each other **ayudarse** *v.* 11
her **su(s)** *poss. adj.* 3; (of) hers
 suyo(s)/a(s) *poss.* 11
 her **la** *f., sing., d.o. pron.* 5
 to/for her **le** *f., sing., i.o. pron.* 6
here **aquí** *adv.* 1
 Here is/are... **Aquí está(n)...** 5
Hi. **Hola.** 1
highway **autopista** *f.* 11;
 carretera *f.* 11
hike **excursión** *f.* 4
 go on a hike **hacer una**
 excursión 5; **ir de**
 excursión 4
hiker **excursionista** *m., f.*
hiking **de excursión** 4
him: to/for him **le** *m., sing., i.o.*
 pron. 6
hire **contratar** *v.*
his **su(s)** *poss. adj.* 3; (of) his
 suyo(s)/a(s) *poss. pron.* 11
 his **lo** *m., sing., d.o. pron.* 5
history **historia** *f.* 2
hobby **pasatiempo** *m.* 4
hockey **hockey** *m.* 4
hold up **aguantar** *v.* 14
hole **hueco** *m.* 4
holiday **día** *m.* **de fiesta** 9
home **casa** *f.* 2
 home page **página** *f.*
 principal 11
homework **tarea** *f.* 2
honey **miel** *f.* 10
hood **capó** *m.* 11; **cofre** *m.* 11
hope **esperar** *v.* (+ *inf.*) 2;
 esperar *v.* 13
 I hope (that) **ojalá (que)** 13

horror (genre) **de horror** *m.*
hors d'oeuvres **entremeses** *m.,*
 pl. 8
horse **caballo** *m.* 5
hospital **hospital** *m.* 10
hot: be (*feel*) (very) hot **tener**
 (mucho) calor 3
 It's (very) hot. **Hace (mucho)**
 calor. 5
hotel **hotel** *m.* 5
hour **hora** *f.* 1
house **casa** *f.* 2
household chores **quehaceres** *m.*
 pl. **domésticos** 12
housekeeper **ama** *m., f.* **de casa** 12
housing **vivienda** *f.* 12
How...! **¡Qué...!**
 how **¿cómo?** *adv.* 1
 How are you? **¿Qué tal?** 1
 How are you? **¿Cómo estás?**
 fam. 1
 How are you? **¿Cómo está**
 usted? *form.* 1
 How can I help you? **¿En qué**
 puedo servirles? 5
 How did it go for you...?
 ¿Cómo le/les fue...? 15
 How is it going? **¿Qué tal?** 1
 How is/are...? **¿Qué tal...?** 2
 How is the weather? **¿Qué**
 tiempo hace? 15
 How much/many?
 ¿Cuánto(s)/a(s)? 1
 How much does... cost?
 ¿Cuánto cuesta...? 6
 How old are you? **¿Cuántos**
 años tienes? *fam.* 3
however **sin embargo**
hug (each other) **abrazar(se)**
 v. 11
humanities **humanidades** *f., pl.* 2
hundred **cien, ciento** 2
hunger **hambre** *f.* 3
hungry: be (very) hungry **tener** *v.*
 (mucha) hambre 3
hunt **cazar** *v.* 13
hurricane **huracán** *m.*
hurry **apurarse** *v.* 15; **darse prisa**
 v. 15
 be in a (big) hurry **tener** *v.*
 (mucha) prisa 3
hurt **doler (o:ue)** *v.* 10
 It hurts me a lot... **Me duele**
 mucho... 10
husband **esposo** *m.* 3

I

I **yo** 1
 I am... **Yo soy...** 1
 I hope (that) **Ojalá (que)**
 interj. 13
 I wish (that) **Ojalá (que)**
 interj. 13
ice cream **helado** *m.* 9
 ice cream shop **heladería** *f.* 14

iced **helado/a** *adj.* 8
 iced tea **té** *m.* **helado** 8
idea **idea** *f.* 4
if **si** *conj.* 4
illness **enfermedad** *f.* 10
important **importante** *adj.* 3
 be important to **importar** *v.* 7
 It's important that... **Es**
 importante que... 12
impossible **imposible** *adj.* 13
 it's impossible **es imposible** 13
improbable **improbable** *adj.* 13
 it's improbable **es**
 improbable 13
improve **mejorar** *v.* 13
in **en** *prep.* 2; **por** *prep.* 11
 in the afternoon **de la tarde** 1;
 por la tarde 7
 in a bad mood **de mal humor** 5
 in the direction of **para** *prep.* 1
 in the early evening **de la tarde** 1
 in the evening **de la noche** 1;
 por la tarde 7
 in a good mood **de buen**
 humor 5
 in the morning **de la**
 mañana 1; **por la**
 mañana 7
 in love (with)
 enamorado/a (de) 5
 in search of **por** *prep.* 11
in front of **delante de** *prep.* 2
increase **aumento** *m.*
incredible **increíble** *adj.* 5
inequality **desigualdad** *f.*
infection **infección** *f.* 10
inform **informar** *v.*
injection **inyección** *f.* 10
 give an injection *v.* **poner una**
 inyección 10
injure (oneself) **lastimarse** 10
 injure (one's foot) **lastimarse** *v.*
 (el pie) 10
inner ear **oído** *m.* 10
inside **dentro** *adv.*
insist (on) **insistir** *v.* **(en)** 12
installments: pay in installments
 pagar *v.* **a plazos** 14
intelligent **inteligente** *adj.* 3
intend to **pensar** *v.* (+ *inf.*) 4
interest **interesar** *v.* 7
interesting **interesante** *adj.* 3
 be interesting to **interesar** *v.* 7
international **internacional**
 adj. m., f.
Internet **Internet** 11
interview **entrevista** *f.;*
 entrevistar *v.*
interviewer **entrevistador(a)**
 m., f.
introduction **presentación** *f.*
 I would like to introduce you to
 (name). **Le presento a...**
 form. 1; **Te presento a...**
 fam. 1
invest **invertir (e:ie)** *v.*
invite **invitar** *v.* 9

iron (clothes) **planchar** *v.* **la ropa** 12
it **lo/la** *sing., d.o., pron.* 5
Italian **italiano/a** *adj.* 3
its **su(s)** *poss. adj.* 3; **suyo(s)/a(s)** *poss. pron.* 11
It's me. **Soy yo.**
it's the same **es igual** 5

March **marzo** *m.* 5
margarine **margarina** *f.* 8
marinated fish **ceviche** *m.* 8
 lemon-marinated shrimp
 ceviche *m.* **de camarón** 8
marital status **estado** *m.* **civil** 9
market **mercado** *m.* 6
 open-air market **mercado al**
 aire libre 6
marriage **matrimonio** *m.* 9
married **casado/a** *adj.* 9
 get married (to) **casarse** *v.*
 (con) 9
 I'll marry you! **¡Acepto**
 casarme contigo!
marvelous **maravilloso/a** *adj.* 5
massage **masaje** *m.* 15
masterpiece **obra maestra** *f.*
match (*sports*) **partido** *m.* 4
match (with) **hacer** *v.*
 juego (con) 6
mathematics **matemáticas**
 f., pl. 2
matter **importar** *v.* 7
maturity **madurez** *f.* 9
maximum **máximo/a** *adj.* 11
May **mayo** *m.* 5
May I leave a message? **¿Puedo**
 dejar un recado? 11
maybe **tal vez** 5; **quizás** 5
mayonnaise **mayonesa** *f.* 8
me **me** *sing., d.o. pron.* 5
 to/for me **me** *sing., i.o. pron.* 6
meal **comida** *f.* 4, 8
means of communication **medios**
 m., pl. **de comunicación**
meat **carne** *f.* 8
mechanic **mecánico/a** *m., f.* 11
 mechanic's repair shop **taller**
 mecánico 11
media **medios** *m., pl.* **de**
 comunicación
medical **médico/a** *adj.* 10
medication **medicamento** *m.* 10
medicine **medicina** *f.* 10
medium **mediano/a** *adj.*
meet (each other) **encontrar(se)**
 v. 11; **conocerse(se)** *v.* 8
 meet up with **encontrarse con** 7
meeting **reunión** *f.*
menu **menú** *m.* 8
message **mensaje** *m.*
Mexican **mexicano/a** *adj.* 3
Mexico **México** *m.* 1
microwave **microonda** *f.* 12
 microwave oven **horno** *m.***de**
 microondas 12
middle age **madurez** *f.* 9
midnight **medianoche** *f.* 1
mile **milla** *f.* 11
milk **leche** *f.* 8
million **millón** *m.* 2
 million of **millón de** 2
mine **mío(s)/a(s)** *poss.* 11
mineral **mineral** *m.* 15
 mineral water **agua** *f.*
 mineral 8

minute **minuto** *m.* 1
mirror **espejo** *m.* 7
Miss **señorita (Srta.)** *f.* 1
miss **perder (e:ie)** *v.* 4;
 extrañar *v.*
mistaken **equivocado/a** *adj.*
modem **módem** *m.*
modern **moderno/a** *adj.*
mom **mamá** *f.* 3
Monday **lunes** *m., sing.* 2
money **dinero** *m.* 6
monitor **monitor** *m.* 11
monkey **mono** *m.* 13
month **mes** *m.* 5
monument **monumento** *m.* 4
moon **luna** *f.* 13
more **más** 2
 more... than **más... que** 8
 more than **más de (+**
 number) 8
morning **mañana** *f.* 1
mother **madre** *f.* 3
mother-in-law **suegra** *f.* 3
motor **motor** *m.*
motorcycle **motocicleta** *f.* 5
mountain **montaña** *f.* 4
mouse **ratón** *m.* 11
mouth **boca** *f.* 10
move (*from one house to another*)
 mudarse *v.* 12
movie **película** *f.* 4
 movie star **estrella** *f.*
 de cine
 movie theater **cine** *m.* 4
MP3 player **reproductor** *m.* **de**
 MP3 11
Mr. **señor (Sr.)**; **don** *m.* 1
Mrs. **señora (Sra.)**; **doña** *f.* 1
much **mucho/a** *adj.* 2, 3
 very much **muchísimo/a** *adj.* 2
mud **lodo** *m.*
murder **crimen** *m.*
muscle **músculo** *m.* 15
museum **museo** *m.* 4
mushroom **champiñón** *m.* 8
music **música** *f.* 2
musical **musical** *adj., m., f.*
musician **músico/a** *m., f.*
must **deber** *v.* (+ *inf.*) 3
 It must be... **Debe ser...** 6
my **mi(s)** *poss. adj.* 3; **mío(s)/a(s)**
 poss. pron. 11

N

name **nombre** *m.* 1
 be named **llamarse** *v.* 7
 in the name of **a nombre de** 5
 last name **apellido** *m.*
 My name is... **Me llamo...** 1
 name someone/something
 ponerle el nombre 9
napkin **servilleta** *f.* 12
national **nacional** *adj. m., f.*
nationality **nacionalidad** *f.* 1

natural **natural** *adj. m., f.* 13
natural disaster **desastre** *m.*
 natural
 natural resource **recurso** *m.*
 natural 13
nature **naturaleza** *f.* 13
nauseated **mareado/a** *adj.* 10
near **cerca de** *prep.* 2
neaten **arreglar** *v.* 12
necessary **necesario/a** *adj.* 12
 It is necessary that... **Hay**
 que... 12, 14
neck **cuello** *m.* 10
need **faltar** *v.* 7; **necesitar** *v.* (+
 inf.) 2
neighbor **vecino/a** *m., f.* 12
neighborhood **barrio** *m.* 12
neither **tampoco** *adv.* 7
neither... nor **ni... ni** *conj.* 7
nephew **sobrino** *m.* 3
nervous **nervioso/a** *adj.* 5
network **red** *f.* 11
never **nunca** *adj.* 7; **jamás** 7
new **nuevo/a** *adj.* 6
newlywed **recién casado/a**
 m., f. 9
news **noticias** *f., pl.*;
 actualidades *f., pl.*; **noticia**
 f. 11
newscast **noticiero** *m.*
newspaper **periódico** 4;
 diario *m.*
next **próximo/a** *adj.* 3
 next to **al lado de** *prep.* 2
nice **simpático/a** *adj.* 3; **amable**
 adj. m., f. 5
niece **sobrina** *f.* 3
night **noche** *f.* 1
 night stand **mesita** *f.* **de**
 noche 12
nine **nueve** 1
nine hundred **novecientos/as** 2
nineteen **diecinueve** 1
ninety **noventa** 2
ninth **noveno/a** 5
no **no** 1; **ningún, ninguno/a(s)**
 adj. 7
 no one **nadie** *pron.* 7
 No problem. **No hay**
 problema.
nobody **nadie** 7
none **ningún, ninguno/a(s)**
 adj. 7
noon **mediodía** *m.* 1
nor **ni** *conj.* 7
north **norte** *m.* 14
 to the north **al norte** 14
nose **nariz** *f.* 10
not **no** 1
 not any **ningún, ninguno/a(s)**
 adj. 7
 not anyone **nadie** *pron.* 7
 not anything **nada** *pron.* 7
 not bad at all **nada mal** 5
 not either **tampoco** *adv.* 7

not ever **nunca** *adv.* 7; **jamás** *adv.* 7
 not very well **no muy bien** 1
 not working **descompuesto/a** *adj.* 11
outside **afuera** *adv.* 5
notebook **cuaderno** *m.* 1
nothing **nada** 1; 7
noun **sustantivo** *m.*
November **noviembre** *m.* 5
now **ahora** *adv.* 2
nowadays **hoy día** *adv.*
nuclear **nuclear** *adj. m., f.* 13
 nuclear energy **energía nuclear** 13
number **número** *m.* 1
nurse **enfermero/a** *m., f.* 10
nutrition **nutrición** *f.* 15
nutritionist **nutricionista** *m., f.* 15

O

o'clock: It's... o'clock **Son las...** 1
 It's one o'clock. **Es la una.** 1
obey **obedecer** *v.*
obligation **deber** *m.*
obtain **conseguir (e:i)** *v.* 4; **obtener** *v.*
obvious **obvio/a** *adj.* 13
 it's obvious **es obvio** 13
occupation **ocupación** *f.*
occur **ocurrir** *v.*
October **octubre** *m.* 5
of **de** *prep.* 1
 Of course. **Claro que sí.; Por supuesto.**
offer **ofrecer (c:zc)** *v.* 6
office **oficina** *f.* 12
 doctor's office **consultorio** *m.* 10
often **a menudo** *adv.* 10
Oh! **¡Ay!**
oil **aceite** *m.* 8
OK **regular** *adj.* 1
 It's okay. **Está bien.**
old **viejo/a** *adj.* 3
old age **vejez** *f.* 9
older **mayor** *adj. m., f.* 3
 older brother, sister **hermano/a mayor** *m., f.* 3
oldest **el/la mayor** 8
on **en** *prep.* 2; **sobre** *prep.* 2
 on behalf of **por** *prep.* 11
 on the dot **en punto** 1
 on time **a tiempo** 10
 on top of **encima de** 2
once **una vez** 6
one **un, uno/a** *m., f., sing. pron.* 1
 one hundred **cien(to)** 2
 one million **un millón** *m.* 2
 one more time **una vez más** 9
 one thousand **mil** 2
 one time **una vez** 6

onion **cebolla** *f.* 8
only **sólo** *adv.* 3; **único/a** *adj.* 3
 only child **hijo/a único/a** *m., f.* 3
open **abierto/a** *adj.* 5, 14; **abrir** *v.* 3
open-air **al aire libre** 6
opera **ópera** *f.*
operation **operación** *f.* 10
opposite **enfrente de** *prep.* 14
or **o** *conj.* 7
orange **anaranjado/a** *adj.* 6; **naranja** *f.* 8
orchestra **orquesta** *f.*
order **mandar** 12; *(food)* **pedir (e:i)** *v.* 8
 in order to **para** *prep.* 11
orderly **ordenado/a** *adj.* 5
ordinal *(numbers)* **ordinal** *adj.*
organize oneself **organizarse** *v.* 12
other **otro/a** *adj.* 6
ought to **deber** *v.* **(+ *inf.*)** *adj.* 3
our **nuestro(s)/a(s)** *poss. adj.* 3; *poss. pron.* 11
out of order **descompuesto/a** *adj.* 11
outside **afuera** *adv.* 5
outskirts **afueras** *f., pl.* 12
oven **horno** *m.* 12
over **sobre** *prep.* 2
(over)population **(sobre)población** *f.* 13
over there **allá** *adv.* 2
own **propio/a** *adj.*
owner **dueño/a** *m., f.* 8

P

p.m. **tarde** *f.* 1
pack (one's suitcases) **hacer** *v.* **las maletas** 5
package **paquete** *m.* 14
page **página** *f.* 11
pain **dolor** *m.* 10
 have a pain **tener** *v.* **dolor** 10
paint **pintar** *v.*
painter **pintor(a)** *m., f.*
painting **pintura** *f.* 12
pair **par** *m.* 6
 pair of shoes **par** *m.* **de zapatos** 6
pale **pálido/a** *adj.* 14
pants **pantalones** *m., pl.* 6
pantyhose **medias** *f., pl.* 6
paper **papel** *m.* 2; *(report)* **informe** *m.*
Pardon me. *(May I?)* **Con permiso.** 1; *(Excuse me.)* Pardon me. **Perdón.** 1
parents **padres** *m., pl.* 3; **papás** *m., pl.* 3
park **estacionar** *v.* 11; **parque** *m.* 4
parking lot **estacionamiento** *m.* 14

partner *(one of a married couple)* **pareja** *f.* 9
party **fiesta** *f.* 9
passed **pasado/a** *p.p.*
passenger **pasajero/a** *m., f.* 1
passport **pasaporte** *m.* 5
past **pasado/a** *adj.* 6
pastime **pasatiempo** *m.* 4
pastry shop **pastelería** *f.* 14
patient **paciente** *m., f.* 10
patio **patio** *m.* 12
pay **pagar** *v.* 6
pay in cash **pagar** *v.* **al contado; pagar en efectivo** 14
pay in installments **pagar** *v.* **a plazos** 14
pay the bill **pagar la cuenta** 9
pea **arveja** *m.* 8
peace **paz** *f.*
peach **melocotón** *m.* 8
peak **cima** *f.* 15
pear **pera** *f.* 8
pen **pluma** *f.* 2
pencil **lápiz** *m.* 1
penicillin **penicilina** *f.* 10
people **gente** *f.* 3
pepper *(black)* **pimienta** *f.* 8
per **por** *prep.* 11
perfect **perfecto/a** *adj.* 5
period of time **temporada** *f.* 5
person **persona** *f.* 3
pharmacy **farmacia** *f.* 10
phenomenal **fenomenal** *adj.* 5
photograph **foto(grafía)** *f.* 1
physical (exam) **examen** *m.* **médico** 10
physician **doctor(a), médico/a** *m., f.* 3
physics **física** *f. sing.* 2
pick up **recoger** *v.* 13
picture **cuadro** *m.* 12; **pintura** *f.* 12
pie **pastel** *m.* 9
pill (tablet) **pastilla** *f.* 10
pillow **almohada** *f.* 12
pineapple **piña** *f.* 8
pink **rosado/a** *adj.* 6
place **lugar** *m.* 2, 4; **sitio** *m.* 3; **poner** *v.* 4
plaid **de cuadros** 6
plans **planes** *m., pl.* 4
 have plans **tener planes** 4
plant **planta** *f.* 13
plastic **plástico** *m.* 13
 (made) of plastic **de plástico** 13
plate **plato** *m.* 12
play **drama** *m.*; **comedia** *f.*; **jugar (u:ue)** *v.* 4; *(a musical instrument)* **tocar** *v.*; *(a role)* **hacer el papel de**; *(cards)* **jugar a (las cartas)** 5; *(sports)* **practicar deportes** 4
player **jugador(a)** *m., f.* 4
playwright **dramaturgo/a** *m., f.*
plead **rogar (o:ue)** *v.* 12
pleasant **agradable** *adj.* 5

please **por favor** 1
Pleased to meet you. **Mucho gusto.** 1; **Encantado/a.** *adj.* 1
pleasing: be pleasing to **gustar** *v.* 7
pleasure **gusto** *m.* 1; **placer** *m.* 15
 It's a pleasure to… **Gusto de** (+ *inf.*)
 It's been a pleasure. **Ha sido un placer.** 15
 The pleasure is mine. **El gusto es mío.** 1
poem **poema** *m.*
poet **poeta** *m., f.*
poetry **poesía** *f.*
police (force) **policía** *f.* 11
political **político/a** *adj.*
politician **político/a** *m., f.*
politics **política** *f.*
polka-dotted **de lunares** 6
poll **encuesta** *f.*
pollute **contaminar** *v.* 13
polluted **contaminado/a** *m., f.* 13
 be polluted **estar contaminado/a** 13
pollution **contaminación** *f.* 13
pool **piscina** *f.* 4
poor **pobre** *adj., m., f.* 6
 poor thing **pobrecito/a** *adj.* 3
popsicle **paleta helada** *f.* 4
population **población** *f.* 13
pork **cerdo** *m.* 8
 pork chop **chuleta** *f.* **de cerdo** 8
portable **portátil** *adj.* 11
 portable computer **computadora** *f.* **portátil** 11
position **puesto** *m.*
possessive **posesivo/a** *adj.* 3
possible **posible** *adj.* 13
 it's (not) possible **(no) es posible** 13
post office **correo** *m.* 14
postcard **postal** *f.* 4
poster **cartel** *m.* 12
potato **papa** *f.* 8; **patata** *f.* 8
pottery **cerámica** *f.*
practice **entrenarse** *v.* 15; **practicar** *v.* 2; (a degree/ profession) **ejercer** *v.*
prefer **preferir (e:ie)** *v.* 4
pregnant **embarazada** *adj. f.* 10
prepare **preparar** *v.* 2
preposition **preposición** *f.*
prescribe (*medicine*) **recetar** *v.* 10
prescription **receta** *f.* 10
present **regalo** *m.*; **presentar** *v.*
press **prensa** *f.*
pressure **presión** *f.*
 be under a lot of pressure **sufrir muchas presiones** 15
pretty **bonito/a** *adj.* 3; **bastante** *adv.* 13
price **precio** *m.* 6
 (fixed, set) price **precio** *m.* **fijo** 6
print **estampado/a** *adj.*; **imprimir** *v.* 11

printer **impresora** *f.* 11
private (*room*) **individual** *adj.*
prize **premio** *m.*
probable **probable** *adj.* 13
 it's (not) probable **(no) es probable** 13
problem **problema** *m.* 1
profession **profesión** *f.* 3
professor **profesor(a)** *m., f.*
program **programa** *m.* 1
programmer **programador(a)** *m., f.* 3
prohibit **prohibir** *v.* 10
project **proyecto** *m.* 11
promotion (*career*) **ascenso** *m.*
pronoun **pronombre** *m.*
protect **proteger** *v.* 13
protein **proteína** *f.* 15
provided (that) **con tal (de) que** *conj.* 13
psychologist **psicólogo/a** *m., f.*
psychology **psicología** *f.* 2
publish **publicar** *v.*
Puerto Rican **puertorriqueño/a** *adj.* 3
Puerto Rico **Puerto Rico** *m.* 1
pull a tooth **sacar una muela**
purchases **compras** *f., pl.* 5
pure **puro/a** *adj.* 13
purple **morado/a** *adj.* 6
purse **bolsa** *f.* 6
put **poner** *v.* 4; **puesto/a** *p.p.* 14
 put (a letter) in the mailbox **echar (una carta) al buzón** 14
 put on (*a performance*) **presentar** *v.*
 put on (*clothing*) **ponerse** *v.* 7
 put on makeup **maquillarse** *v.* 7

Q

quality **calidad** *f.* 6
quarter (*academic*) **trimestre** *m.* 2
 quarter after (*time*) **y cuarto** 1; **y quince** 1
 quarter to (*time*) **menos cuarto** 1; **menos quince** 1
question **pregunta** *f.* 2
quickly **rápido** *adv.* 10
quiet **tranquilo/a** *adj.* 15
quit **dejar** *v.*
quiz **prueba** *f.* 2

R

racism **racismo** *m.*
radio (*medium*) **radio** *f.* 2
 radio (set) **radio** *m.* 11
rain **llover (o:ue)** *v.* 5; **lluvia** *f.* 13
 It's raining. **Llueve.** 5; **Está lloviendo.** 5

raincoat **impermeable** *m.* 6
rainforest **bosque** *m.* **tropical** 13
raise (*salary*) **aumento** *m.* **de sueldo**
rather **bastante** *adv.* 10
reality show **programa** *m.* **de realidad**
read **leer** *v.* 3; **leído/a** *p.p.* 14
 read e-mail **leer correo electrónico** 4
 read a magazine **leer una revista** 4
 read a newspaper **leer un periódico** 4
ready **listo/a** *adj.* 5
 (Are you) ready? **¿(Están) listos?** 15
reap the benefits (of) *v.* **disfrutar** *v.* **(de)** 15
receive **recibir** *v.* 3
recommend **recomendar (e:ie)** *v.* 8; 12
record **grabar** *v.* 11
recover **recuperar** *v.* 11
recreation **diversión** *f.* 4
recycle **reciclar** *v.* 13
recycling **reciclaje** *m.* 13
red **rojo/a** *adj.* 6
red-haired **pelirrojo/a** *adj.* 3
reduce **reducir** *v.* 13; **disminuir** *v.*
 reduce stress/tension **aliviar el estrés/la tensión** 15
refrigerator **refrigerador** *m.* 12
region **región** *f.* 13
regret **sentir (e:ie)** *v.* 13
related to sitting **sedentario/a** *adj.* 15
relatives **parientes** *m., pl.* 3
relax **relajarse** *v.* 9
 Relax, sweetie. **Tranquilo/a, cariño.** 11
remain **quedarse** *v.* 7
remember **acordarse (o:ue)** *v.* **(de)** 7; **recordar (o:ue)** *v.* 4
remote control **control remoto** *m.* 11
renewable **renovable** *adj.* 13
rent **alquilar** *v.* 12; (payment) **alquiler** *m.* 12
repeat **repetir (e:i)** *v.* 4
report **informe** *m.*; **reportaje** *m.*
reporter **reportero/a** *m., f.*
representative **representante** *m., f.*
request **pedir (e:i)** *v.* 4
reservation **reservación** *f.* 5
resign (from) **renunciar (a)** *v.*
resolve **resolver (o:ue)** *v.* 13
resolved **resuelto/a** *p.p.* 14
resource **recurso** *m.* 13
responsibility **deber** *m.*; **responsabilidad** *f.*
responsible **responsable** *adj.* 8
rest **descansar** *v.* 2
restaurant **restaurante** *m.* 4
résumé **currículum** *m.*

retire (from work) **jubilarse** *v.* 9
return **regresar** *v.* 2; **volver (o:ue)** *v.* 4
returned **vuelto/a** *p.p.* 14
rice **arroz** *m.* 8
rich **rico/a** *adj.* 6
ride a bicycle **pasear** *v.* **en bicicleta** 4
ride a horse **montar** *v.* **a caballo** 5
ridiculous **ridículo/a** *adj.* 13
 it's ridiculous **es ridículo** 13
right **derecha** *f.* 2
 be right **tener razón** 3
 right? (*question tag*) **¿no?** 1; **¿verdad?** 1
 right away **enseguida** *adv.*
 right here **aquí mismo** 11
 right now **ahora mismo** 5
 right there **allí mismo** 14
 to the right of **a la derecha de** 2
rights **derechos** *m.*
ring **anillo** *m.*
ring (*a doorbell*) **sonar (o:ue)** *v.* 11
river **río** *m.* 13
road **camino** *m.*
roast **asado/a** *adj.* 8
roast chicken **pollo** *m.* **asado** 8
rollerblade **patinar en línea** *v.*
romantic **romántico/a** *adj.*
room **habitación** *f.* 5; **cuarto** *m.* 2; 7
 living room **sala** *f.* 12
roommate **compañero/a** *m., f.* **de cuarto** 2
roundtrip **de ida y vuelta** 5
 roundtrip ticket **pasaje** *m.* **de ida y vuelta** 5
routine **rutina** *f.* 7
rug **alfombra** *f.* 12
run **correr** *v.* 3
 run errands **hacer diligencias** 14
 run into (*have an accident*) **chocar (con)** *v.*; (*meet accidentally*) **encontrar(se) (o:ue)** *v.* 11; (*run into something*) **darse (con)** 10
 run into (each other) **encontrar(se) (o:ue)** *v.* 11
rush **apurarse, darse prisa** *v.* 15
Russian **ruso/a** *adj.* 3

S

sad **triste** *adj.* 5; 13
 it's sad **es triste** 13
safe **seguro/a** *adj.* 5
said **dicho/a** *p.p.* 14
sailboard **tabla de windsurf** *f.* 5
salad **ensalada** *f.* 8
salary **salario** *m.*; **sueldo** *m.*
sale **rebaja** *f.* 6

salesperson **vendedor(a)** *m., f.* 6
salmon **salmón** *m.* 8
salt **sal** *f.* 8
same **mismo/a** *adj.* 3
sandal **sandalia** *f.* 6
sandwich **sándwich** *m.* 8
Saturday **sábado** *m.* 2
sausage **salchicha** *f.* 8
save (*on a computer*) **guardar** *v.* 11; save (money) **ahorrar** *v.* 14
savings **ahorros** *m.* 14
 savings account **cuenta** *f.* **de ahorros** 14
say **decir** *v.* 4; **declarar** *v.*
say (that) **decir (que)** *v.* 4, 9
 say the answer **decir la respuesta** 4
scan **escanear** *v.* 11
scarcely **apenas** *adv.* 10
scared: be (very) scared (of) **tener (mucho) miedo (de)** 3
schedule **horario** *m.* 2
school **escuela** *f.* 1
science *f.* **ciencia** 2
 science fiction **ciencia ficción** *f.*
scientist **científico/a** *m., f.*
scream **grito** *m.* 5; **gritar** *v.* 7
screen **pantalla** *f.* 11
scuba dive **bucear** *v.* 4
sculpt **esculpir** *v.*
sculptor **escultor(a)** *m., f.*
sculpture **escultura** *f.*
sea **mar** *m.* 5
 (sea) turtle **tortuga (marina)** *f.* 13
season **estación** *f.* 5
seat **silla** *f.* 2
second **segundo/a** 5
secretary **secretario/a** *m., f.*
sedentary **sedentario/a** *adj.* 15
see **ver** *v.* 4
 see (you, him, her) again **volver a ver(te, lo, la)**
 see movies **ver películas** 4
 See you. **Nos vemos.** 1
 See you later. **Hasta la vista.** 1; **Hasta luego.** 1
 See you soon. **Hasta pronto.** 1
 See you tomorrow. **Hasta mañana.** 1
seem **parecer** *v.* 6
seen **visto/a** *p.p.* 14
sell **vender** *v.* 6
semester **semestre** *m.* 2
send **enviar; mandar** *v.* 14
separate (from) **separarse** *v.* **(de)** 9
separated **separado/a** *adj.* 9
September **septiembre** *m.* 5
sequence **secuencia** *f.*
serious **grave** *adj.* 10
serve **servir (e:i)** *v.* 8
service **servicio** *m.* 15
set (*fixed*) **fijo** *adj.* 6
 set the table **poner la mesa** 12
seven **siete** 1
seven hundred **setecientos/as** 2
seventeen **diecisiete** 1
seventh **séptimo/a** 5

seventy **setenta** 2
several **varios/as** *adj. pl.* 8
sexism **sexismo** *m.*
shame **lástima** *f.* 13
 it's a shame **es una lástima** 13
shampoo **champú** *m.* 7
shape **forma** *f.* 15
 be in good shape **estar en buena forma** 15
 stay in shape **mantenerse en forma** 15
share **compartir** *v.* 3
sharp (*time*) **en punto** 1
shave **afeitarse** *v.* 7
shaving cream **crema** *f.* **de afeitar** 5, 7
she **ella** 1
shellfish **mariscos** *m., pl.* 8
ship **barco** *m.*
shirt **camisa** *f.* 6
shoe **zapato** *m.* 6
 shoe size **número** *m.* 6
 shoe store **zapatería** *f.* 14
 tennis shoes **zapatos** *m., pl.* **de tenis** 6
shop **tienda** *f.* 6
shopping, to go **ir de compras** 5
 shopping mall **centro comercial** *m.* 6
short (*in height*) **bajo/a** *adj.* 3; (*in length*) **corto/a** *adj.* 6
short story **cuento** *m.*
shorts **pantalones cortos** *m., pl.* 6
should (*do something*) **deber** *v.* **(+ inf.)** 3
shout **gritar** *v.* 7
show **espectáculo** *m.*; **mostrar (o:ue)** *v.* 4
 game show **concurso** *m.*
shower **ducha** *f.* 7; **ducharse** *v.* 7
shrimp **camarón** *m.* 8
siblings **hermanos/as** *pl.* 3
sick **enfermo/a** *adj.* 10
 be sick **estar enfermo/a** 10
 get sick **enfermarse** *v.* 10
sign **firmar** *v.* 14; **letrero** *m.* 14
silk **seda** *f.* 6
 (made of) **de seda** 6
silly **tonto/a** *adj.* 3
since **desde** *prep.*
sing **cantar** *v.* 2
singer **cantante** *m., f.*
single **soltero/a** *adj.* 9
 single room **habitación** *f.* **individual** 5
sink **lavabo** *m.* 7
sir **señor (Sr.), don** *m.* 1; **caballero** *m.* 8
sister **hermana** *f.* 3
sister-in-law **cuñada** *f.* 3
sit down **sentarse (e:ie)** *v.* 7
six **seis** 1
six hundred **seiscientos/as** 2
sixteen **dieciséis** 1
sixth **sexto/a** 5
sixty **sesenta** 2
size **talla** *f.* 6
 shoe size *m.* **número** 6

(in-line) skate **patinar (en línea)** 4
skateboard **andar en patineta**
 v. 4
ski **esquiar** *v.* 4
skiing **esquí** *m.* 4
 water-skiing **esquí** *m.*
 acuático 4
skirt **falda** *f.* 6
skull made out of sugar **calavera**
 de azúcar *f.* 9
sky **cielo** *m.* 13
sleep **dormir (o:ue)** *v.* 4; **sueño**
 m. 3
 go to sleep **dormirse**
 (o:ue) *v.* 7
sleepy: be (very) sleepy **tener**
 (mucho) sueño 3
slender **delgado/a** *adj.* 3
slim down **adelgazar** *v.* 15
slippers **pantuflas** *f.* 7
slow **lento/a** *adj.* 11
slowly **despacio** *adv.* 10
small **pequeño/a** *adj.* 3
smart **listo/a** *adj.* 5
smile **sonreír (e:i)** *v.* 9
smiled **sonreído** *p.p.* 14
smoggy: It's (very) smoggy. **Hay**
 (mucha) contaminación. 4
smoke **fumar** *v.* 8; 15
 (not) to smoke **(no) fumar** 15
smoking section **sección** *f.* **de**
 fumar 8
 (non) smoking section *f.* **sección**
 de (no) fumar 8
snack **merendar** *v.* 8; 15;
 afternoon snack **merienda**
 f. 15
 have a snack **merendar** *v.*
sneakers **los zapatos de tenis** 6
sneeze **estornudar** *v.* 10
snow **nevar (e:ie)** *v.* 5; **nieve** *f.*
snowing: It's snowing. **Nieva.** 5;
 Está nevando. 5
so (*in such a way*) **así** *adv.* 10;
 tan *adv.* 5; **tan** *adv.* 5, 7
 so much **tanto** *adv.*
 so-so **regular** 1
 so that **para que** *conj.* 13
soap **jabón** *m.* 7
soap opera **telenovela** *f.*
soccer **fútbol** *m.* 4
sociology **sociología** *f.* 2
sock(s) **calcetín (calcetines)** *m.* 6
sofa **sofá** *m.* 12
soft drink **refresco** *m.* 8
software **programa** *m.* **de**
 computación 11
soil **tierra** *f.* 13
solar **solar** *adj., m., f.* 13
 solar energy **energía solar** 13
soldier **soldado** *m., f.*
solution **solución** *f.* 13
solve **resolver (o:ue)** *v.* 13
some **algún, alguno/a(s)** *adj.* 7;
 unos/as *pron./ m., f., pl; indef.*
 art. 1
somebody **alguien** *pron.* 7
someone **alguien** *pron.* 7
something **algo** *pron.* 7
sometimes **a veces** *adv.* 10

son **hijo** *m.* 3
song **canción** *f.*
son-in-law **yerno** *m.* 3
soon **pronto** *adv.* 10
 See you soon. **Hasta pronto.** 1
sorry: be sorry **sentir (e:ie)** *v.* 13
 I'm sorry. **Lo siento.** 1
soul **alma** *f.* 9
soup **caldo** *m.* **sopa** *f.*
south **sur** *m.* 14
 to the south **al sur** 14
Spain **España** *f.* 1
Spanish (*language*) **español** *m.* 2;
 español(a) *adj.* 3
spare (free) time **ratos libres** 4
speak **hablar** *v.* 2
 Speaking. (*on the telephone*)
 Con él/ella habla. 11
special: today's specials **las**
 especialidades del día 8
spectacular **espectacular** *adj. m.,*
 f. 15
speech **discurso** *m.*
speed **velocidad** *f.* 11
 speed limit **velocidad** *f.*
 máxima 11
spelling **ortografía** *f.,*
 ortográfico/a *adj.*
spend (*money*) **gastar** *v.* 6
spoon (*table or large*) **cuchara**
 f. 12
sport **deporte** *m.* 4
 sports-related **deportivo/a**
 adj. 4
spouse **esposo/a** *m., f.* 3
sprain (one's ankle) **torcerse**
 (o:ue) *v.* **(el tobillo)** 10
sprained **torcido/a** *adj.* 10
 be sprained **estar torcido/a** 10
spring **primavera** *f.* 5
(city or town) square **plaza** *f.* 4
stadium **estadio** *m.* 2
stage **etapa** *f.* 9
stairs **escalera** *f.* 12
stairway **escalera** *f.* 12
stamp **estampilla** *f.* 14; **sello**
 m. 14
stand in line **hacer** *v.* **cola** 14
star **estrella** *f.* 13
start (*a vehicle*) **arrancar** *v.* 11
station **estación** *f.* 5
statue **estatua** *f.*
status: marital status **estado** *m.*
 civil 9
stay **quedarse** *v.* 7
 stay in shape **mantenerse en**
 forma 15
steak **bistec** *m.* 8
steering wheel **volante** *m.* 11
step **escalón** *m.* 15
stepbrother **hermanastro** *m.* 3
stepdaughter **hijastra** *f.* 3
stepfather **padrastro** *m.* 3
stepmother **madrastra** *f.* 3
stepsister **hermanastra** *f.* 3
stepson **hijastro** *m.* 3
stereo **estéreo** *m.* 11
still **todavía** *adv.* 5

stockbroker **corredor(a)** *m., f.* **de**
 bolsa
stockings **medias** *f., pl.* 6
stomach **estómago** *m.* 10
stone **piedra** *f.* 13
stop **parar** *v.* 11
 stop (*doing something*) **dejar de**
 (+ *inf.*) 13
store **tienda** *f.* 6
storm **tormenta** *f.*
story **cuento** *m.*; **historia** *f.*
stove **cocina, estufa** *f.* 9, 12
straight **derecho** *adj.* 14
 straight (ahead) **derecho** 14
straighten up **arreglar** *v.* 12
strange **extraño/a** *adj.* 13
 it's strange **es extraño** 13
strawberry **frutilla** *f.* 8, **fresa**
street **calle** *f.* 11
stress **estrés** *m.* 15
stretching **estiramiento** *m.* 15
 do stretching exercises **hacer**
 ejercicios; *m. pl.* **de**
 estiramiento 15
strike (*labor*) **huelga** *f.*
stripe **raya** *f.* 6
 striped **de rayas** 6
stroll **pasear** *v.* 4
strong **fuerte** *adj. m. f.* 15
struggle (for/against) **luchar** *v.*
 (por/contra)
student **estudiante** *m., f.* 1; 2;
 estudiantil *adj.* 2
study **estudiar** *v.* 2
stuffed-up (*sinuses*)
 congestionado/a *adj.* 10
stupendous **estupendo/a** *adj.* 5
style **estilo** *m.*
suburbs **afueras** *f., pl.* 12
subway **metro** *m.* 5
 subway station **estación** *f.*
 del metro 5
success **éxito** *m.*
successful: be successful **tener**
 éxito
such as **tales como**
suddenly **de repente** *adv.* 6
suffer **sufrir** *v.* 10
 suffer an illness **sufrir una**
 enfermedad 10
sugar **azúcar** *m.* 8
suggest **sugerir (e:ie)** *v.* 12
suit **traje** *m.* 6
suitcase **maleta** *f.* 1
summer **verano** *m.* 5
sun **sol** *m.* 5; 13
sunbathe **tomar** *v.* **el sol** 4
Sunday **domingo** *m.* 2
(sun)glasses **gafas** *f., pl.*
 (oscuras/de sol) 6; **lentes** *m.*
 pl. **(de sol)** 6
sunny: It's (very) sunny. **Hace**
 (mucho) sol. 5
supermarket **supermercado**
 m. 14
suppose **suponer** *v.* 4

sure **seguro/a** *adj.* 5
 be sure **estar seguro/a** 5
surf (*the Internet*) **navegar** *v.* **(en Internet)** 11
surfboard **tabla de surf** *f.* 5
surprise **sorprender** *v.* 9; **sorpresa** *f.* 9
survey **encuesta** *f.*
sweat **sudar** *v.* 15
sweater **suéter** *m.* 6
sweep the floor **barrer el suelo** 12
sweets **dulces** *m., pl.* 9
swim **nadar** *v.* 4
swimming **natación** *f.* 4
 swimming pool **piscina** *f.* 4
symptom **síntoma** *m.* 10

T

table **mesa** *f.* 2
tablespoon **cuchara** *f.* 12
tablet (*pill*) **pastilla** *f.* 10
take **tomar** *v.* 2; **llevar** *v.* 6;
 take care of **cuidar** *v.* 13
 take someone's temperature **tomar** *v.* **la temperatura** 10
 take (*wear*) a shoe size **calzar** *v.* 6
 take a bath **bañarse** *v.* 7
 take a shower **ducharse** *v.* 7
 take off **quitarse** *v.* 7
 take out the trash *v.* **sacar la basura** 12
 take photos **tomar** *v.* **fotos** 5; **sacar** *v.* **fotos** 5
talented **talentoso/a** *adj.*
talk **hablar** *v.* 2
 talk show **programa** *m.* **de entrevistas**
tall **alto/a** *adj.* 3
tank **tanque** *m.* 11
taste **probar (o:ue)** *v.* 8; **saber** *v.* 8
 taste like **saber a** 8
tasty **rico/a** *adj.* 8; **sabroso/a** *adj.* 8
tax **impuesto** *m.*
taxi **taxi** *m.* 5
tea **té** *m.* 8
teach **enseñar** *v.* 2
teacher **profesor(a)** *m., f.* 1, 2; **maestro/a** *m., f.*
team **equipo** *m.* 4
technician **técnico/a** *m., f.*
telecommuting **teletrabajo** *m.*
telephone **teléfono** 11
 (cell) phone **(teléfono)** *m.* **celular** 11
television **televisión** *f.* 2; 11
 television set **televisor** *m.* 11
tell **contar** *v.* 4; **decir** *v.* 4
tell (that) **decir** *v.* **(que)** 4, 9
 tell lies **decir mentiras** 4
 tell the truth **decir la verdad** 4
temperature **temperatura** *f.* 10
ten **diez** 1
tennis **tenis** *m.* 4
 tennis shoes **zapatos** *m., pl.* **de tenis** 6
tension **tensión** *f.* 15
tent **tienda** *f.* **de campaña**

tenth **décimo/a** 5
terrible **terrible** *adj. m., f.* 13
 it's terrible **es terrible** 13
terrific **chévere** *adj.*
test **prueba** *f.* 2; **examen** *m.* 2
text message **mensaje** *m.* **de texto** 11
Thank you. **Gracias.** *f., pl.* 1
 Thank you (very much). **(Muchas) gracias.** 1
 Thank you very, very much. **Muchísimas gracias.** 9
 Thanks (a lot). **(Muchas) gracias.** 1
 Thanks for having me. **Gracias por invitarme.** 9
that **que, quien(es), lo que** *pron.* 12
 that (one) **ése, ésa, eso** *pron.* 6; **ese, esa,** *adj.* 6
 that (over there) **aquél, aquélla, aquello** *pron.* 6; **aquel, aquella** *adj.* 6
 that which **lo que** *conj.* 12
 that's me **soy yo**
 that's why **por eso** 11
the **el** *m.*, **la** *f. sing.*, **los** *m.*, **las** *f., pl.* 1
theater **teatro** *m.*
their **su(s)** *poss. adj.* 3; **suyo(s)/a(s)** *poss. pron.* 11
them **los/las** *pl., d.o. pron.* 5
 to/for them **les** *pl., i.o. pron.* 6
then (*afterward*) **después** *adv.* 7; (*as a result*) **entonces** *adv.* 5, 7; (*next*) **luego** *adv.* 7; **pues** *adv.* 15
there **allí** *adv.* 2
 There is/are… **Hay…** 1;
 There is/are not… **No hay…** 1
therefore **por eso** 11
these **éstos, éstas** *pron.* 6; **estos, estas** *adj.* 6
they **ellos** *m.*, **ellas** *f. pron.*
 They all told me to ask you to excuse them/forgive them. **Todos me dijeron que te pidiera disculpas de su parte.**
thin **delgado/a** *adj.* 3
thing **cosa** *f.* 1
think **pensar (e:ie)** *v.* 4; (*believe*) **creer** *v.*
 think about **pensar en** *v.* 4
third **tercero/a** 5
thirst **sed** *f.* 3
thirsty: be (very) thirsty **tener (mucha) sed** 3
thirteen **trece** 1
thirty **treinta** 1, 2; thirty (*minutes past the hour*) **y treinta; y media** 1
this **este, esta** *adj.*; **éste, ésta, esto** *pron.* 6
 This is… (*introduction*) **Éste/a es…** 1
 This is he/she. (*on telephone*) **Con él/ella habla.** 11
those **ésos, ésas** *pron.* 6; **esos, esas** *adj.* 6
those (over there) **aquéllos, aquéllas** *pron.* 6; **aquellos, aquellas** *adj.* 6

thousand **mil** *m.* 6
three **tres** 1
three hundred **trescientos/as** 2
throat **garganta** *f.* 10
through **por** *prep.* 11
throughout: throughout the world **en todo el mundo** 13
Thursday **jueves** *m., sing.* 2
thus (*in such a way*) **así** *adj.*
ticket **boleto** *m.* 2; **pasaje** *m.* 5
tie **corbata** *f.* 6
time **vez** *f.* 6; **tiempo** *m.* 4
 have a good/bad time **pasarlo bien/mal** 9
 I've had a fantastic time. **Lo he pasado de película.**
 What time is it? **¿Qué hora es?** 1
 (At) What time…? **¿A qué hora…?** 1
times **veces** *f., pl.* 6
 many times **muchas veces** 10
 two times **dos veces** 6
tip **propina** *f.* 9
tire **llanta** *f.* 11
tired **cansado/a** *adj.* 5
 be tired **estar cansado/a** 5
to **a** *prep.* 1
toast (*drink*) **brindar** *v.* 9
 toast **pan** *m.* **tostado**
toasted **tostado/a** *adj.* 8
 toasted bread **pan tostado** *m.* 8
toaster **tostadora** *f.* 12
today **hoy** *adv.* 2
 Today is… **Hoy es…** 2
toe **dedo** *m.* **del pie** 10
together **juntos/as** *adj.* 9
toilet **inodoro** *m.* 7
tomato **tomate** *m.* 8
tomorrow **mañana** *f.* 1
 See you tomorrow. **Hasta mañana.** 1
tonight **esta noche** *adv.* 4
too **también** *adv.* 2; 7
 too much **demasiado** *adv.* 6; **en exceso** 15
tooth **diente** *m.* 7
toothpaste **pasta** *f.* **de dientes** 7
top **cima** *f.* 15
 to the top **hasta arriba** 15
tornado **tornado** *m.*
tortilla **tortilla** *f.* 8
touch **tocar** *v.*
touch screen **pantalla táctil** *f.* 11
tour **excursión** *f.* 4; **recorrido** *m.* 13
tour an area **recorrer** *v.*
tourism **turismo** *m.* 5
tourist **turista** *m., f.* 1; **turístico/a** *adj.*
toward **hacia** *prep.* 14; **para** *prep.* 11
towel **toalla** *f.* 7
town **pueblo** *m.* 4
trade **oficio** *m.*
traffic **circulación** *f.* 11; **tráfico** *m.* 11
 traffic light **semáforo** *m.* 14
tragedy **tragedia** *f.*

trail **sendero** *m.* 13
 trailhead **sendero** *m.* 13
train **entrenarse** *v.* 15; **tren** *m.* 5
 train station **estación** *f.* **(de) tren** *m.* 5
trainer **entrenador(a)** *m., f.* 15
translate **traducir** *v.* 6
trash **basura** *f.* 12
travel **viajar** *v.* 2
 travel agent **agente** *m., f.* **de viajes** 5
traveler **viajero/a** *m., f.* 5
 (traveler's) check **cheque (de viajero)** 14
treadmill **cinta caminadora** *f.* 15
tree **árbol** *m.* 13
trillion **billón** *m.*
trimester **trimestre** *m.* 2
trip **viaje** *m.* 5
 take a trip **hacer un viaje** 5
tropical forest **bosque** *m.* **tropical** 13
true **verdad** *adj.* 13
 it's (not) true **(no) es verdad** 13
trunk **baúl** *m.* 11
truth **verdad** *f.*
try **intentar** *v.*; **probar (o:ue)** *v.* 8
 try (*to do something*) **tratar de (+ *inf.*)** 15
 try on **probarse (o:ue)** *v.* 7
t-shirt **camiseta** *f.* 6
Tuesday **martes** *m., sing.* 2
tuna **atún** *m.* 8
turkey **pavo** *m.* 8
turn **doblar** *v.* 14
 turn off (*electricity/appliance*) **apagar** *v.* 11
 turn on (*electricity/appliance*) **poner** *v.* 11; **prender** *v.* 11
twelve **doce** 1
twenty **veinte** 1
twenty-eight **veintiocho** 1
twenty-five **veinticinco** 1
twenty-four **veinticuatro** 1
twenty-nine **veintinueve** 1
twenty-one **veintiún, veintiuno/a** 1
twenty-seven **veintisiete** 1
twenty-six **veintiséis** 1
twenty-three **veintitrés** 1
twenty-two **veintidós** 1
twice **dos veces** 6
twin **gemelo/a** *m., f.* 3
twisted **torcido/a** *adj.* 10
 be twisted **estar torcido/a** 10
two **dos** 1
 two hundred **doscientos/as** 2
 two times **dos veces** 6

U

ugly **feo/a** *adj.* 3
uncle **tío** *m.* 3
under **bajo** *adv.* 7; **debajo de** *prep.* 2
understand **comprender** *v.* 3; **entender (e:ie)** *v.* 4

underwear **ropa interior** 6
unemployment **desempleo** *m.*
unique **único/a** *adj.* 9
United States **Estados Unidos (EE.UU.)** *m. pl.* 1
university **universidad** *f.* 2
unless **a menos que** *adv.* 13
unmarried **soltero/a** *adj.*
unpleasant **antipático/a** *adj.* 3
until **hasta** *prep.* 6; **hasta que** *conj.* 13
up **arriba** *adv.* 15
urgent **urgente** *adj.* 12
 It's urgent that... **Es urgente que...** 12
us **nos** *pl., d.o. pron.* 5
 to/for us **nos** *pl., i.o. pron.* 6
use **usar** *v.* 6
used for **para** *prep.* 11
useful **útil** *adj. m., f.*

V

vacation **vacaciones** *f., pl.* 5
 be on vacation **estar de vacaciones** 5
 go on vacation **ir de vacaciones** 5
vacuum **pasar** *v.* **la aspiradora** 12
 vacuum cleaner **aspiradora** *f.* 12
valley **valle** *m.* 13
various **varios/as** *adj. m., f. pl.* 8
vegetables **verduras** *pl., f.* 8
verb **verbo** *m.*
very **muy** *adv.* 1
 very much **muchísimo** *adv.* 2
 (Very) well, thank you. **(Muy) bien, gracias.** 1
video **video** *m.* 1, 11
 video camera **cámara** *f.* **de video** 11
videoconference **videoconferencia** *f.*
 video game **videojuego** *m.* 4
vinegar **vinagre** *m.* 8
violence **violencia** *f.*
visit **visitar** *v.* 4
 visit monuments **visitar monumentos** 4
vitamin **vitamina** *f.* 15
voice mail **correo de voz** *m.* 11
volcano **volcán** *m.* 13
volleyball **vóleibol** *m.* 4
vote **votar** *v.*

W

wait (for) **esperar** *v.* **(+ *inf.*)** 2
waiter/waitress **camarero/a** *m., f.* 8
wake up **despertarse (e:ie)** *v.* 7
walk **caminar** *v.* 2
 take a walk **pasear** *v.* 4;
 walk around **pasear por** 4

walkman *walkman* *m.*
wall **pared** *f.* 12; **muro** *m.* 15
wallet **cartera** *f.* 4, 6
want **querer (e:ie)** *v.* 4
war **guerra** *f.*
warm (oneself) up **calentarse (e:ie)** *v.* 15
wash **lavar** *v.* 12
 wash one's face/hands **lavarse la cara/las manos** 7
 wash (the floor, the dishes) **lavar (el suelo, los platos)** 12
 wash oneself **lavarse** *v.* 7
washing machine **lavadora** *f.* 12
wastebasket **papelera** *f.* 2
watch **mirar** *v.* 2; **reloj** *m.* 2
 watch television **mirar (la) televisión** 2
water **agua** *f.* 8
 water pollution **contaminación del agua** 13
 water-skiing **esquí** *m.* **acuático** 4
way **manera** *f.*
we **nosotros(as)** *m., f.* 1
weak **débil** *adj. m., f.* 15
wear **llevar** *v.* 6; **usar** *v.* 6
weather **tiempo** *m.*
 The weather is bad. **Hace mal tiempo.** 5
 The weather is good. **Hace buen tiempo.** 5
weaving **tejido** *m.*
Web **red** *f.* 11
website **sitio** *m.* **web** 11
wedding **boda** *f.* 9
Wednesday **miércoles** *m., sing.* 2
week **semana** *f.* 2
weekend **fin** *m.* **de semana** 4
weight **peso** *m.* 15
 lift weights **levantar** *v.* **pesas** *f., pl.* 15
welcome **bienvenido(s)/a(s)** *adj.* 12
well: (Very) well, thanks. **(Muy) bien, gracias.** 1
well-being **bienestar** *m.* 15
well organized **ordenado/a** *adj.*
west **oeste** *m.* 14
 to the west **al oeste** 14
western (*genre*) **de vaqueros**
whale **ballena** *f.* 13
what **lo que** *pron.* 12
what? **¿qué?** 1
 At what time...? **¿A qué hora...?** 1
 What a pleasure to...! **¡Qué gusto (+ *inf.*)...!**
 What day is it? **¿Qué día es hoy?** 2
 What do you guys think? **¿Qué les parece?** 9
What happened? **¿Qué pasó?** 11
 What is today's date? **¿Cuál es la fecha de hoy?** 5

What nice clothes! **¡Qué ropa más bonita!** 6

What size do you take? **¿Qué talla lleva (usa)?** 6

What time is it? **¿Qué hora es?** 1

What's going on? **¿Qué pasa?** 1

What's happening? **¿Qué pasa?** 1

What's... like? **¿Cómo es...?** 3

What's new? **¿Qué hay de nuevo?** 1

What's the weather like? **¿Qué tiempo hace?** 5

What's up? **¿Qué onda?** 14

What's wrong? **¿Qué pasó?** 11

What's your name? **¿Cómo se llama usted?** *form.* 1

What's your name? **¿Cómo te llamas (tú)?** *fam.* 1

when **cuando** *conj.* 7; 13

When? **¿Cuándo?** 2

where **donde**

where (to)? (*destination*) **¿adónde?** 2; (*location*) **¿dónde?** 1

Where are you from? **¿De dónde eres (tú)?** (*fam.*) 1; **¿De dónde es (usted)?** (*form.*) 1

Where is...? **¿Dónde está...?** 2

(to) where? **¿adónde?** 2

which **que** *pron.*, **lo que** *pron.* 12

which? **¿cuál?** 2; **¿qué?** 2

In which...? **¿En qué...?** 2

which one(s)? **¿cuál(es)?** 2

while **mientras** *adv.* 10

white **blanco/a** *adj.* 6

white wine **vino blanco** 8

who **que** *pron.* 12; **quien(es)** *pron.* 12

who? **¿quién(es)?** 1

Who is...? **¿Quién es...?** 1

Who is speaking/calling? (*on telephone*) **¿De parte de quién?** 11

Who is speaking? (*on telephone*) **¿Quién habla?** 11

whole **todo/a** *adj.*

whom **quien(es)** *pron.* 12

whose? **¿de quién(es)?** 1

why? **¿por qué?** 2

widower/widow **viudo/a** *adj.* 9

wife **esposa** *f.* 3

win **ganar** *v.* 4

wind **viento** *m.* 5

window **ventana** *f.* 2

windshield **parabrisas** *m., sing.* 11

windy: It's (very) windy. **Hace (mucho) viento.** 5

wine **vino** *m.* 8

red wine **vino tinto** 8

white wine **vino blanco** 8

wineglass **copa** *f.* 12

winter **invierno** *m.* 5

wireless (connection) **conexión inalámbrica** *f.* 11

wish **desear** *v.* 2; **esperar** *v.* 13

I wish (that) **ojalá (que)** 13

with **con** *prep.* 2

with me **conmigo** 4; 9

with you **contigo** *fam.* 5, 9

within (ten years) **dentro de (diez años)** *prep.*

without **sin** *prep.* 2; 13; 15; **sin que** *conj.* 13

woman **mujer** *f.* 1

wool **lana** *f.* 6

(made of) wool **de lana** 6

word **palabra** *f.* 1

work **trabajar** *v.* 2; **funcionar** *v.* 11; **trabajo** *m.*

work (*of art, literature, music, etc.*) **obra** *f.*

work out **hacer gimnasia** 15

world **mundo** *m.* 8, 13

worldwide **mundial** *adj. m., f.*

worried (about) **preocupado/a (por)** *adj.* 5

worry (about) **preocuparse** *v.* (**por**) 7

Don't worry. **No se preocupe.** *form.* 7; **Tranquilo.; No te preocupes.** *fam.* 7

worse **peor** *adj. m., f.* 8

worst **el/la peor** 8

Would you like to...? **¿Te gustaría...?** *fam.* 4

Would you do me the honor of marrying me? **¿Me harías el honor de casarte conmigo?**

wow **híjole** *interj.* 6

wrench **llave** *f.* 11

write **escribir** *v.* 3

write a letter/post card/e-mail message **escribir una carta/postal/mensaje electrónico** 4

writer **escritor(a)** *m., f*

written **escrito/a** *p.p.* 14

wrong **equivocado/a** *adj.* 5

be wrong **no tener razón** 3

You **tú** *fam.* **usted (Ud.)** *form. sing.* **vosotros/as** *m., f. fam.* **ustedes (Uds.)** *form.* 1; (to, for) you *fam. sing.* **te** *pl.* **os** 6; *form. sing.* **le** *pl.* **les** 6

you **te** *fam., sing.,* **lo/la** *form., sing.,* **os** *fam., pl.,* **los/las** *form., pl, d.o. pron.* 5

You don't say! **¡No me digas!** *fam.;* **¡No me diga!** *form.* 11

You are... **Tú eres...** 1

You're welcome. **De nada.** 1; **No hay de qué.** 1

young **joven** *adj., sing.* (**jóvenes** *pl.*) 3

young person **joven** *m., f., sing.* (**jóvenes** *pl.*) 1

young woman **señorita (Srta.)** *f.*

younger **menor** *adj. m., f.* 3

younger: younger brother, sister *m., f.* **hermano/a menor** 3

youngest **el/la menor** *m., f.* 8

your **su(s)** *poss. adj. form.* 3

your **tu(s)** *poss. adj. fam. sing.* 3

your **vuestro/a(s)** *poss. adj. form. pl.* 3

your(s) *form.* **suyo(s)/a(s)** *poss. pron. form.* 11

your(s) **tuyo(s)/a(s)** *poss. fam. sing.* 11

your(s) **vuestro(s)/a(s)** *poss. fam.* 11

youth *f.* **juventud** 9

Text Credits

31 © Joaquín Salvador Lavado (QUINO). *Toda Mafalda* – Ediciones de La Flor, 1993.

368–369 © Juan Matías Loiseau "Tute", *El celular*, reprinted by permission of the author.

474–475 © Denevi, Marco, *Cartas peligrosas y otros cuentos. Obras completas, Tomo 5*, Buenos Aires, Corregidor, 1999, págs. 192–193.

504–505 Gabriel García Márquez, "Un día de éstos", *Los funerales de la mamá grande* © Gabriel García Márquez, 1962.

Photo and Art Credits

All images © Vista Higher Learning unless otherwise noted.

Cover: Elogio del Horizonte by Eduardo Chillida. © 2011 Artists Rights Society (ARS), New York/VEGAP, Madrid. Photo credit: © Atlantide Phototravel/Corbis.

Front Matter (IAE): IAE-10 (tr, tmr) Carolina Zapata; IAE-11 (tl, tr) Anne Loubet; (tm, bl) José Blanco; (bm, br) Ali Burafi.

Front Matter (SE): iii (l) © Andresr/Shutterstock.com; xxviii (tl, tml, ml, tr, tmr, mr, ml, bl) Carolina Zapata; xxix (tl, tr, b) Carolina Zapata.

All Fotonovela photos taken by Carolina Zapata.

Lesson One: 1 (full pg) Paula Díez; 2 © John Henley/Corbis; 3 Martín Bernetti; 4 Martín Bernetti; 10 (l) Rachel Distler; (r) Ali Burafi; 11 (l) © Mark Mainz/Getty Images; (m) Paola Ríos-Schaaf; (r) © Hans Georg Roth/Corbis; 12 (l) Janet Dracksdorf; (r) © Tom Grill/Corbis; 16 (l) © José Girarte/iStockphoto; (r) © Blend Images/Alamy; 19 (m) Anne Loubet; (r) © Digital Vision/Getty Images; 28 (bl) © Digital Vision/Getty Images; 31 (ml) Ana Cabezas Martín; (mml) Martín Bernetti; (mmr) © Serban Enache/Dreamstime.com; (mr) Vanessa Bertozzi; (bl) © Corey Hochachka/Design Pics/Corbis; (br) Ramiro Isaza © Fotocolombia.com; 32 (t) © Robert Holmes/Corbis; (m) © Jon Arnold Images Ltd./Alamy; (b) © Andresr/Shutterstock.com; 33 (tl) © PhotoLink/Getty Images; (tr) © Tony Arruza/Corbis; (ml) © Shaul Schwarz/Sygma/Corbis; (br) Marta Mesa.

Lesson Two: 35 (full pg) Paula Díez; 38 Martín Bernetti; 44 (r) © Pablo Corral V/Corbis; 45 (t) © Murle/Dreamstime.com; (b) © Paul Almasy/Corbis; 53 © Stephen Coburn/Shutterstock.com; 55 (l) Paola Ríos-Schaaf; (r) © Image Source/Corbis; 63 (tl) © Rick Gómez/Corbis; (tr) © Hola Images/Workbook.com; 64 José Blanco; 65 (r) Pascal Pernix; 66 (tl) Sarah Kenney; (tr) José Blanco; (m) © Elke Stolzenberg/Corbis; (b) © Reuters/Corbis; 67 (tl) © Washington Post/Getty Images; (tmr) José Blanco; (ml) Diego Velázquez. *Las meninas*. 1656. Derechos reservados © Museo Nacional del Prado, Madrid. © Erich Lessing/Art Resource, NY; (bl) © Iconotec/Fotosearch; (mr) © Owen Franken/Corbis.

Lesson Three: 69 (full pg) © Ronnie Kaufman/Corbis; 71 Martín Bernetti; 72 (tl) Anne Loubet; (tr) © Blend Images/Alamy; (tml) Ana Cabezas Martín; (bml, br) Martín Bernetti; (bl) © Ariel Skelley/Corbis; 78 (tl) © AP Photo/David Cantor; (tr) © Rafael Pérez/Reuters/Corbis; (b) © Martial Trezzini/epa/Corbis; 79 (t) © Dani Cardona/Reuters/Corbis; (b) © Ballesteros/epa/Corbis; 82 (l) Martín Bernetti; (r) José Blanco; 84 © Andrés Rodríguez/Alamy; 89 (l) © Warren Morgan/Corbis; (r) Martín Bernetti; 90 Martín Bernetti; 98 (t, m, b) Martín Bernetti; 99 (t) Nora y Susana © Fotocolombia.com; (m) © Chuck Savage/Corbis; (b) Martín Bernetti; 100 © Tom & Dee Ann McCarthy/Corbis; 101 Martín Bernetti; 104 (tr, tl, b) Martín Bernetti; (ml) Iván Mejía; (mr) Lauren Krolick; 105 (tl, ml, bl) Martín Bernetti; (tr) © Oswaldo Guayasamín. *Madre y niño en azul*. 1986. Cortesía Fundación Guayasamín. Quito, Ecuador; (br) © Gerardo Mora.

Lesson Four: 107 (full pg) © Digital Vision/Getty Images; 109 © George Shelley/Corbis; 111 © Nora y Susana/fotocolombia.com; 116 (l) © Javier Soriano/AFP/Getty Images; (r) © AP Photo/Fernando Bustamante; 117 (t) © sportgraphic/Shutterstock.com; (b) © Aurora Photos/Alamy; 127 The Kobal Collection/Art Resource, NY; 131 Anne Loubet; 133 © Images.com/Corbis; 134 Martín Bernetti; 135 © AP Photo/Fernando Llano; 136 (tl) © Randy Miramontez/Shutterstock.com; (tr) Frida Kahlo. *Autorretrato con mono*. 1938. Oil on masonite, overall 16 x 12" (40.64 x 30.48 cms.) © 2012 Banco de México Diego Rivera Frida Kahlo Museums Trust, Mexico, D.F./Artists Rights Society (ARS), New York © Albright-Knox Art Gallery/CORBIS; (ml) Rubén Varela; (mr) Isabelle Alouane; (b) © Henry Romero/Reuters/Corbis; 137 (tl) © Radius Images/Alamy; (tr) © Bettmann/Corbis; (b) © David R. Frazier Photolibrary, Inc./Alamy.

Lesson Five: 139 (full pg) © Gavin Hellier/Getty Images; 150 © Gary Cook/Alamy; 151 (t) © AFP/Getty Images; (b) © Mark A. Johnson/Corbis; 155 © Ronnie Kaufman/Corbis; 168 Carlos Gaudier; 169 (tr, m ,b) Carlos Gaudier; 170 (tl) © Nanniqui/Dreamstime.com; (tr) José Blanco; (ml) Carlos Gaudier; (mr) © Capricornis Photographic Inc./Shutterstock.com; (b) © Dave G. Houser/Corbis; 171 (tl, bl) Carlos Gaudier; (tr) © Lawrence Manning/Corbis; (br) © StockTrek/Getty Images.

Lesson Six: 173 (full pg) © Asiapix Royalty-Free/Inmagine; 182 (l) © Jose Caballero Digital Press Photos/Newscom; (b) Janet Dracksdorf; 183 (t) © Carlos Álvarez/Getty Images; (bl) © Guiseppe Cacace/Stringer/Getty Images; (br) © Mark Mainz/Staff/Getty Images; 185 © Jack Hollingsworth/Corbis; 188 (tl, tm, tr, bl, bm, br) Pascal Pernix; 193 (tl, tr, ml, mr) Martín Bernetti; 194 (t, b) Paula Díez; 195 Paula Díez; 200 Paula Díez; 201 Paula Díez; 202 © Noam/fotolia; 206 (t, mtl, mtr, mb) Pascal Pernix; (b) © PhotoLink/Getty Images; 207 (tl) © Don Emmert/AFP/Getty Images; (tr, bl) Pascal Pernix; (br) The Kobal Collection/Art Resource, NY.

Lesson Seven: 209 (full pg) © Flying Colours Ltd/Getty Images; 218 © Stewart Cohen/Blend Images/Corbis; 219 (t) Ali Burafi; (b) Janet Dracksdorf; 221 (l, r) Martín Bernetti; 223 (l) Martín Bernetti; (r) © Ariel Skelley/Corbis; 226 José Blanco; 227 Martín Bernetti; 236-237 © DIDEM HIZAR/fotolia; 238 (t, mtr) Martín Bernetti; (mbl) © Richard Franck Smith/Sygma/Corbis; (mbr) © Charles & Josette Lenars/Corbis; (b) © Yann Arthus-Bertrand/Corbis; 239 (tr) © Mick Roessler/Corbis; (bl) © Jeremy Horner/Corbis; (br) © Marshall Bruce/iStockphoto.

About the Authors

José A. Blanco founded Vista Higher Learning in 1998. A native of Barranquilla, Colombia, Mr. Blanco holds a B.A. in Literature from the University of California, Santa Cruz, and an M.A. in Hispanic Studies from Brown University. He has worked as a writer, editor, and translator for Houghton Mifflin and D.C. Heath and Company and has taught Spanish at the secondary and university levels. Mr. Blanco is also the co-author of several other Vista Higher Learning programs: **Vistas, Aventuras,** and **¡Viva!** at the introductory level, **Ventanas, Facetas, Enfoques, Imagina,** and **Sueña** at the intermediate level, and **Revista** at the advanced conversation level.

Philip Redwine Donley received his M.A. in Hispanic Literature from the University of Texas at Austin in 1986 and his Ph.D. in Foreign Language Education from the University of Texas at Austin in 1997. Dr. Donley taught Spanish at Austin Community College, Southwestern University, and the University of Texas at Austin. He published articles and conducted workshops about language anxiety management, and the development of critical thinking skills, and was involved in research about teaching languages to the visually impaired. Dr. Donley was also the co-author of **Vistas** and **Aventuras,** two other introductory college Spanish textbook programs published by Vista Higher Learning.

About the Illustrators

Yayo, an internationally acclaimed illustrator, was born in Colombia. He has illustrated children's books, newspapers, and magazines, and has been exhibited around the world. He currently lives in Montreal, Canada.

Pere Virgili lives and works in Barcelona, Spain. His illustrations have appeared in textbooks, newspapers, and magazines throughout Spain and Europe.

Born in Caracas, Venezuela, **Hermann Mejía** studied illustration at the *Instituto de Diseño de Caracas*. Hermann currently lives and works in the United States.

Estados Unidos

Golfo de México

Bahía de Campeche

Golfo de California

Océano Pacífico

México

YUCATÁN

Belice

Guatemala

Honduras

El Salvador

ISTMO DE TEHUANTEPEC

Sierra Madre Oriental

Sierra Madre Occidental

BAJA CALIFORNIA

Río Grande

Río Bravo del Norte

R. Conchos

R. Colorado

R. Balsas

Cancún
Mérida
Campeche
Villahermosa
Veracruz
Jalapa
Oaxaca
México, D.F.
Puebla
Cuernavaca
Uruapan
Morelia
Acapulco
Tampico
San Luis Potosí
León
Guanajuato
Aguascalientes
Guadalajara
Puerto Vallarta
Zacatecas
Mazatlán
Ciudad Victoria
Saltillo
Monterrey
Nuevo Laredo
Reynosa
Matamoros
Chihuahua
Ciudad Juárez
Hermosillo
Nogales
La Paz
Mexicali
Tijuana

N
E
S
O

México

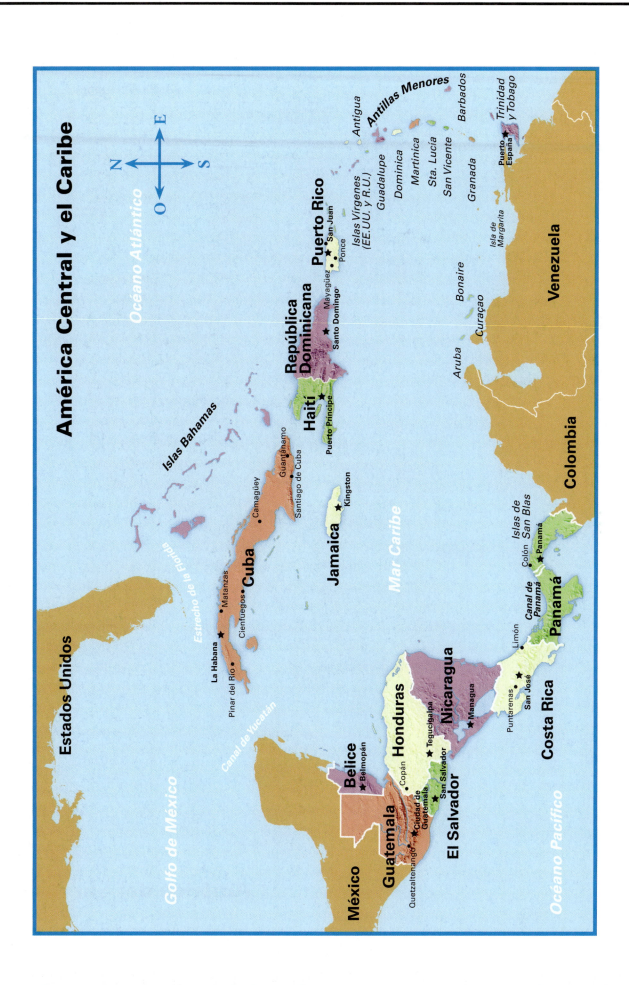

América Central y el Caribe

Estados Unidos

Golfo de México

México

Canal de Yucatán

Guatemala
Quetzaltenango • Ciudad de Guatemala ★
Copán •
Belice
★ Belmopán
El Salvador
San Salvador ★
Honduras
Tegucigalpa ★
Nicaragua
Managua ★
Costa Rica
Puntarenas •
San José ★
Limón •
Panamá
Canal de Panamá
Colón • Panamá ★
Islas de San Blas

Océano Pacífico

Mar Caribe

Jamaica
★ Kingston

Cuba
La Habana ★
Pinar del Río •
Cienfuegos • Matanzas •
Camagüey •
Santiago de Cuba •
Guantánamo •

Islas Bahamas

Estrecho de la Florida

Océano Atlántico

Haití
★ Puerto Príncipe

República Dominicana
Santo Domingo ★

Puerto Rico
Mayagüez • San Juan ★
Ponce •

Islas Vírgenes (EE.UU. y R.U.)

Antigua
Guadalupe
Dominica
Martinica
Sta. Lucía
San Vicente
Granada
Barbados

Antillas Menores

Bonaire
Aruba
Curaçao
Isla de Margarita

Trinidad y Tobago
Puerto España ★

Venezuela

Colombia

N
O E
S

Mar Caribe

Barranquilla • Maracaibo
Caracas ★
Puerto España
Trinidad y Tobago
Venezuela
Colombia
Medellín •
R. Orinoco
Guyana
Georgetown •
Paramaribo •
Cayena •
Bogotá ★
Cali •
Surinam
Guayana Francesa
Pasto •
Quito ★
Ecuador
Guayaquil
Iquitos •
Perú
R. Negro
R. Amazonas
Belém •
Manaus •
R. Madeira
Cordillera de los Andes
Recife •
Lima ★
Cuzco •
Lago Titicaca
Salvador •
Brasil
Brasilia ★
Arequipa •
La Paz ★
Bolivia
Arica •
Sucre ★
Iquique •
Belo Horizonte •
R. Paraguay
R. Paraná
Océano Pacífico
Antofagasta •
São Paulo •
Río de Janeiro •
Santos •
Paraguay
Salta •
Asunción ★
Chile
Porto Alegre •
R. Paraná
R. Uruguay
Córdoba •
Valparaíso •
Mendoza •
• Rosario
Santiago ★
Uruguay
Buenos Aires ★
Montevideo •
Concepción •
Argentina
Océano Atlántico
Cordillera de los Andes
• Bahía Blanca
Puerto Montt •
Estrecho de Magallanes
Islas Malvinas
Punta Arenas •
Tierra del Fuego

Islas Galápagos
Océano Pacífico
Isla Pinta
Isla Marchena
Isla Genovesa
Isla Isabela
Línea Ecuatorial
ECUADOR
Volcán Darwin
Isla Santiago (San Salvador)
Isla Fernandina
Puerto Ayora
Isla San Cristóbal
Isla Santa Cruz
Santo Tomás
Puerto Barquerizo Moreno
Isla Santa Maria
Isla Española

N
O — E
S

América del Sur